UNDERSTANDING HUMAN BEHAVIOR

8TH EDITION

Ronald P. Philipchalk
Western Washington University
Trinity Western University

James V. McConnell

HARCOURT BRACE COLLEGE PUBLISHERS

Fort Worth   Philadelphia   San Diego   New York   Orlando   Austin   San Antonio
Toronto   Montreal   London   Sydney   Tokyo

EDITOR IN CHIEF	Ted Buchholz
ACQUISITIONS EDITOR	Eve Howard
SENIOR DEVELOPMENTAL EDITOR	Meera Dash
SENIOR PROJECT EDITOR	Steve Welch
SENIOR PRODUCTION MANAGER	Tad Gaither
ART DIRECTOR	Peggy Young
PHOTO EDITOR	Elizabeth Banks

Cover and Chapter Opener illustrations: Gary Head/Rep. by Brooke and Company, Dallas, Tx.

Medical illustrations: Craig Zuckerman/Rep. by Gerald & Cullen Rapp, Inc.

Art program: Marco Ruiz, Dallas, Tx.

Address for Editorial Correspondence:
Harcourt Brace College Publishers
301 Commerce Street, Suite 3700
Fort Worth, TX 76102

Address for Orders:
Harcourt Brace, Inc.
6277 Sea Harbor Drive
Orlando, FL 32887
1-800-782-4479 or
1-800-433-0001 (in Florida)

(Copyright Acknowledgments begin on p. C-1, which constitutes a continuation of this copyright page.)

Printed in the United States of America

Library of Congress Catalog Card Number: 93–77648

ISBN: 0–15–500991–5

3 4 5 6 7 8 9 0 1 2   032   9 8 7 6 5 4 3 2 1

PREFACE

Psychology in the 1990s is an exciting field! It offers *insight* into human behavior, it is *relevant* to personal experience, and it is always embracing new information. My goal for the eighth edition of *Understanding Human Behavior* is to convey this excitement by helping students understand themselves and others.

Fortunately, I have an excellent base on which to build. Through seven successful editions, *Understanding Human Behavior* has proven to be insightful, relevant, and helpful. It has come to represent excellence in the teaching of psychology. More than a textbook, it is a fascinating picture of people trying to understand each other and understand themselves—as the title says, *"understanding human behavior."* I trust you will find the eighth edition to be the finest yet!

HIGHLIGHTS OF THE EIGHTH EDITION

The positive response to the seventh edition was most gratifying, and the eighth edition retains the unifying theme of different perspectives which together create a balanced or "holistic" view. It continues the emphasis on personal values. It maintains the relevance and excitement of psychology. Above all, the writing is student-oriented. The eighth edition continues a more "mainstream" treatment and organization of topics and terminology, more references that are recent and representative (approximately 50 percent more than in the sixth edition), a stronger cross-cultural perspective, and a contemporary focus.

Some of the chapter-by-chapter changes are as follows:

In *Chapter 1* James McConnell's voice continues to be heard in a new context. Much of the historical information and the idea of placing it in Chapter 1 came from Jim's notes. I have strengthened the discussion of the holistic perspective and created a diagram to illustrate the contribution of different views of the person. The role of *cultural* influences on human behavior is clearly identified as part of the social/behavioral viewpoint.

Chapter 2 is thoroughly revised and updated. I have condensed the discussion of the neuron and the brain and added material on the nervous system, the endocrine system, and genetic research. With these changes, Chapter 2 provides a more complete picture of biological psychology.

Chapters 3 through 6, sensation, perception, consciousness, and motivation have been updated with new research and new illustrations. At several points the discussion of cross-cultural variables has been strengthened—for example, through sections on "Sensations, Perceptions, and Culture," "Cultural Influences on Illusions," and "Achievement and Culture."

The discussion of sexual motivation in *Chapter 7* has been totally rewritten. The chapter includes not only issues of gender and sexual orientation, but also a discussion of sexual *behavior and values*. Topics such as masturbation, incest, sexually transmitted diseases, and date rape help to bring the matter of *values* and *choice* into focus.

The discussion of emotion, stress, and health in *Chapter 8* has been reorganized and updated.

Chapter 9 includes classical and operant conditioning as well as newer material on cognitive learning. (It also includes ideas from an article by James McConnell, published after his death.)

Chapter 10, memory, is reorganized and includes more information on mnemonics and more questions to stimulate student involvement.

In *Chapter 11* new research and additional discussion of cultural factors strengthens the contemporary relevance of cognition, language, and intelligence.

The development chapters retain their clear structure from the seventh edition. A new feature in *Chapter 12*, infancy and childhood, is a discussion of "parent-child relations." This leads into a consideration of "parenting style" and "recent changes in family structure." Revisions to *Chapter 13* include a greater emphasis on cultural factors in adolescence, adulthood, and aging.

In *Chapter 14*, personality theory and measurement, I have condensed and reorganized the discussion of Freud, and given expanded consideration to Horney and the trait theorists. New to this chapter are the discussions of Jungian "types," the Myers-Briggs Type Indicator, and a section on "Personality Theory and Culture."

Chapter 15 on abnormal psychology has been completely rewritten. It contains less emphasis on the DSM and its revisions and greater stress on descriptive symptomatology. Of special interest is a new section on "Cross-Cultural Considerations" for abnormal psychology.

The therapy discussion in *Chapter 16* is reorganized and updated with a new section on "Cultural Diversity."

The revisions to *Chapters 17 and 18* on social psychology include a new section on "Culture and Attributions" in Chapter 17, and in Chapter 18, a condensed discussion of the "Yale Model" of persuasion with an expanded consideration of the "Elaboration Likelihood Model."

Cross-cultural psychology, introduced in Chapter 1 as part of the holistic perspective, and strengthened *throughout* the eighth edition, receives special attention in an expanded *Chapter 19*. In this edition, I have decided to present cultural influence as a necessary part of the *holistic* perspective. This means that culture is always a potential factor and that cross-cultural comparisons seep into virtually every chapter. But because the study of cultural factors is an important approach in its own right, cross-cultural psychology receives special attention in Chapter 19. The discussion includes multiculturalism, patterns of acculturation, and problems in cross-cultural psychology. In addition, the chapter provides information about psychology and psychologists around the world and sets psychology in a "world context."

Finally, throughout the book you will find a new art program guided by values of accuracy, usefulness, and diversity. The biological illustrations are completely redeveloped to give students a stronger perspective on human features. Each visual aid functions as a resource as well as an effective illustration of the concepts in the text. New photographs and contemporary, stimulating charts, graphs, and tables entice students and facilitate mastery of the material.

THE PEDAGOGICAL STANDARD

Jim McConnell, through *Understanding Human Behavior*, his scientific articles, and his personal correspondence, taught me many things about writing for students. He invented and improved the pedagogical features of *Understanding Human Behavior* (UHB), edition after edition, in direct response to his students' needs. Continuing this tradition, I have given careful attention to making psychology accessible. I have kept the narrative style of writing, maintained and strengthened pedagogical features that have remained successful, and listened to students who responded to drafts of the manuscript. As a result, you will find important new technical terms defined in the margin of the page where they are first used. (UHB was the first textbook to use this "running glossary" format; its widespread use by other authors attests to its effectiveness.)

A chapter outline marks the start of each chapter. As we point out in our discussions on memory and cognition, organizing material in a meaningful way is an important part of efficient learning. The chapter outlines give students an overview of the chapter and a framework on which to hang new ideas.

Each chapter opens with a passage from popular literature. As novelist Jane Austen in *Northanger Abbey* says, somewhat sarcastically,

> "And what are you reading, Miss—?" "Oh! it is only a novel!" replies the young lady: while she lays down her book with affected indifference, or momentary shame.—"It is only Cecelia, or Camilla, or Belinda:" or, in short, only some work in which the most thorough knowledge of human nature, the happiest delineation of its varieties, the liveliest effusion of wit and humour are conveyed to the world in the best chosen language.

Literature reflects and explores human nature—but psychology is its *scientific* study. The literary chapter openers as well as the quotations you will see in the margins reinforce the theme that psychology studies questions of universal interest and is related to all of life.

The eighth edition retains the use of "thought questions" throughout each chapter. These questions do several things: They encourage students to reflect on the material they are reading, making it more memorable. They ask students to integrate new information with topics covered elsewhere in the book. And they invite students to apply new material to their own experiences.

A feature begun in the seventh edition and continued here is the "Answers for Thought" section at the end of each chapter. Many of the thought questions do not have a single objective answer, so the "Answers for Thought" provide additional food for thought. These suggestions are given so that students won't get "bogged down" or frustrated with a question not clear to them. (Students may also find some ideas here which they hadn't thought of on their own.)

Like earlier editions, the eighth has a clear summary in each chapter. Research indicates that many students rely heavily on these summaries. In order to simplify review, the summaries appear in point form with key terms set in bold type.

THE ANCILLARY PACKAGE

An expanded set of multimedia ancillary materials accompanies the eighth edition of *Understanding Human Behavior*. The package contains a wide range of materials in several different media that serve as enrichments for both the instructor and the student.

- **The Student Manual,** *Learning Psychology,* by Al Siebert of Portland State University and Tim Walter of the University of Tulsa, is available in printed and computerized formats. This manual will help students in two ways. First, Section I, "How to Succeed in College and Still Have Time for Your Friends," gives useful guidelines for studying and learning in all courses. Section II, "A Study Program for *Understanding Human Behavior,*" shows students how to succeed in their psychology course, improve their study habits, and acquire a solid understanding of psychology. Each chapter has
  - Predicting Exam Questions (short-answer questions)
  - Your Questions (space for students to create questions that they think will be asked in an exam)
  - Chapter Highlights (fill-in-the-blank exercises based on the text chapter summaries)
  - Testing the Tests (practice exams)
  - Psychology in Action (projects that show how to do psychology)
  - Questions and Issues for Critical Thinking

- Cultural Phrases and Terms (words and expressions that are defined by a society, culture, or broad social context)

■ **The Instructor's Manual,** prepared by Ron Philipchalk, facilitates coordination with the text and with other ancillaries. Each chapter has teaching objectives (which also appear in the Student Manual and are referenced from the Test Bank), ideas for lectures and demonstrations, cross-cultural material, and a section on additional media. The media sections suggest when to use software, films, videos, slides, and transparencies, most of which are offered in the package. The manual has an extensive video and videodisc instructor's guide, keyed to the eighth edition.

■ **The Instructor's Edition** provides the instructor with a full version of the student text with a condensed version of the instructor's manual bound into the front. Chapter-by-chapter suggestions facilitate use of the text book in the classroom.

■ **The Test Bank,** thoroughly revised this edition by Ron Philipchalk with the aid of Michael Vallante of Quinsigamond Community College, features at least 125 multiple-choice questions per chapter. The questions require comprehension, application, or analysis. Each item was revisited during the eighth edition to develop these cognitive skills and to differentiate levels of difficulty. Questions are grouped by learning objectives listed in the Instructor's Manual and the Student Manual. To encourage active use of the Student Manual, some questions in each chapter are taken from the manual and are so labeled.

■ **The computerized test bank** is available in IBM and Macintosh formats. The testing software, ExaMaster™, allows you to create tests using fewer keystrokes, with all steps defined in easy-to-follow screen prompts. ExaMaster offers three easy-to-use options for test creation:

1. EasyTest lets you create a test from a single screen, in just a few easy steps. You can select questions from the data base or let EasyTest randomly select the questions for you, given your parameters.

2. FullTest lets you use the whole range of options available:
   select questions as you preview them on the screen
   edit existing questions or add your own questions
   add or edit graphics in the MS-DOS version
   link related questions, instructions, and graphics
   have FullTest randomly select questions from a wider range of criteria
   create your own criteria on two open keys
   block specific questions from random selection
   print up to 99 different versions of the same test and answer sheet

3. RequesTest is there for you when you do not have access to a computer. When that happens, just call 1 (800) 447-9457. Software specialists will compile the questions according to your criteria and either mail or fax the test master to you within 48 hours!

Included with ExaMaster is ExamRecord, a gradebook program that allows you to record, curve, graph, and print out grades. ExamRecord takes raw scores and converts them into grades by criteria you set. You can set the curve you want, and see the distribution of the grades in a bar graph or a plotted graph.

If questions arise, the Software Support Hotline is available Monday through Friday, 9 AM–4 PM Central Time at 1 (800) 447-9457.

■ **The Whole Psychology Catalogue** is a manual with perforated pages designed to facilitate assignments and handouts in class. It contains page after page of innovative experiential exercises, questionnaires, lecture outlines, and visual aids.

- **Psychlearn,** an interactive software program for students, contains five experiments for IBM and Apple computers: Schedules of Reinforcement, Short-term Memory, Reaction Time, Self-consciousness Scale, and Social Dilemma. This full-color program comes with a guide containing instructional information and discussion questions for each lesson.

- **Brainstack,** an interactive software program for Macintosh users, provides students with a self-guided tour of the cerebral cortex, giving valuable information about brain-behavior relationships. Major topics include the motor and sensory cortex, visual and auditory cortex, memory, thinking, pattern recognition, facial identity, and the language system.

- **The Psychology Experimenter,** an interactive program for IBM users, performs psychological experiments and records and analyzes data. It also enables users to duplicate four classic memory and perception experiments and to modify experiments of their own design.

- **Supershrink II: Jennifer** is an interactive microcomputer simulation program for use on an IBM system. Users take the role of a counselor at a helpline clinic and conduct an interview with the client, Jennifer. This program is especially helpful to introductory psychology students learning concepts in psychopathology, personality, and assessment.

- **New overhead transparency acetates** enhance classroom lectures with a collection of more than 200 full-color acetates, including a set *specifically created for the eighth edition*. This new set allows the instructor to key classroom discussion directly to the book as well as to supplement the text with additional material.

- **The video library** includes video sources which are available as supplemental teaching aids. They are the Discovering Psychology Telecourse, the teaching video modules from the Discovering Psychology Telecourse, PBS' "The Brain" series teaching modules, PBS' "The Mind" series modules, PBS' "The Seasons of Life" series episodes, and an additional video featuring five broad areas of research. Availability is based on the Harcourt Brace video policy.

Two videodisc programs are offered with *Understanding Human Behavior*. Availability is based on the Harcourt Brace videodisc policy. To obtain more information on the videodisc policy, contact your publisher's representative.

Dynamic Concepts in Psychology is an innovative, versatile teaching device developed by John Mitterer of Brock University exclusively for Harcourt Brace College Publishers. Using state-of-the-art laser technology, this program makes thousands of concepts available to you and your students in four types of illustrations:

- Animated sequences, such as "The Inspectible Neuron," which bring structures and processes alive with color, motion, and sound.

- Film and video footage from a wide variety of sources.

- Demonstrations involving students in such classic research as Sperling's whole-report and partial-report memory studies.

- More than 2,000 still images, including 57 photographs, charts, graphs, and visual illusions from *Understanding Human Behavior*.

The program's fully integrated package includes *LectureMaker*, software available in IBM, Microsoft Windows, and Macintosh formats, giving you total freedom to design and customize presentations in conjunction with your lectures. It enables you to program and choreograph your lectures to facilitate learning and involvement from your students. With *LectureMaker*, you can use the material on the disc or import images from other videodiscs. Adhesive bar code labels facilitate access to images during lectures.

Dynamic Concepts in Psychology includes complete, user-friendly documentation. The faculty manual contains easy-to-follow instructions for using the videodisc and *LectureMaker*. The manual also includes descriptions of each visual frame, a book-to-videodisc index, which keys the material to *Understanding Human Behavior*, and an essay by the program's author to help you get the most out of this exciting new medium in teaching psychology.

Discovering Psychology Modules Videodisc provides video footage from the fifteen Discovering Psychology video modules in a user-friendly videodisc program. Clips of experiments are interwoven with interviews of prominent researchers. Extensive teaching suggestions with student activities and test items appear in the instructor's manual of *Understanding Human Behavior*.

ABOUT THE ARTIST

Gary Head, creator of the illustrations for the cover and chapter openers of *Understanding Human Behavior*, Eighth Edition, is a painter and a greeting-card designer in Kansas City. Head started taking private lessons in art at the age of 7, and by the age of 12 he was teaching art classes to adults. He has a degree in commercial art and illustration from East Texas State University.

Head's first love is painting. Working in *alkyds*—fast drying oils—he uses a rapid technique, which suits the spontaneity and simplicity of his style, his vital brush-work, and bold color choices. Head says, "*Understanding Human Behavior* gave me a conceptual challenge, which broadened my world and will affect my future work. Many people paint what is comfortable and familiar; here, I was pushed out of my familiar subjects—causing me to think how I was going to interpret the new subject matter and to do it in a positive way. One way is to show a lot by showing very little—to have viewers fill in the blanks with who they are. In this approach, an interesting visual can represent each concept. . . . Hopefully, the last painting is as good as or better than the first one."

ACKNOWLEDGMENTS

This book would not exist without the expert guidance of numerous professionals. At Harcourt Brace College Publishers, Publisher Ted Buchholz and Senior Acquisitions Editor Eve Howard encouraged me with their energy and enthusiasm for this project. Senior Developmental Editor Meera Dash refined every chapter with her meticulous scrutiny and expert suggestions. Senior Project Editor Steve Welch, Senior Production Manager Tad Gaither, and Art Director Peggy Young transformed the manuscript into the visually pleasing volume you are holding in your hands.

I am also indebted to the following instructors and researchers for their advice on the content, currency, and clarity of various chapter drafts for the eighth edition: Eric Cooley, Western Oregon State College; Don Cusumano, Community College of Forest Park; Florence Ginsburg, University of Rhode Island; Raymond Martinetti, Marywood College; Frank Mrykalo, Marywood College; Sharon Joy Ng, Yuba College; Michael Vallante, Quinsigamond Community College; and Walter Zimmerman, New Hampshire College.

In addition, reviewers of the seventh edition were also most helpful. *UHB* continues to reflect the input of: Jerry Annel, Illinois Valley Community College; John Bellefleur, Oakland Community College; Conrad Brombach, Christian Brothers College; Thomas Brothen, University of Minnesota; Tom Carskadon, Mississippi State University; Annabel Coldeway, Concordia College; Jane Davis, Christian

Brothers College; Roberta Eveslage, Johnson County Community College; Grace Galliano, Kennesaw State College; Ann Gilchrist, Ulster County Community College; Paul Koch, St. Ambrose University; Merlin Madsen, Ricks College; Deborah McDonald, New Mexico State University; Cheryl McFadden, York Technical College; Arthur Mueller, Community College of Baltimore; Pat Murphy, Spokane Community College; William Nish, Georgia College; Ann Rusk, Yuba College; and James Thomas, University of Nebraska.

Several specialists provided guidance—for both the seventh and eighth editions. For this guidance, and their encouragement, I thank John Berry, Queen's University; Douglas Bloomquist, Framingham State College; Richard Brislin, East-West Center—Institute of Culture and Communication; Gerard Connors, Research Institute on Alcoholism; Denise Cummins, University of Arizona; Leonard Hamilton, Rutgers, The State University; Elaine Hatfield, University of Hawaii; Alice Honig, Syracuse University; Walt Lonner, Western Washington University; Christopher Monte, Manhattanville College; David Payne, SUNY, Binghamton; Dalmas Taylor, Wayne State University; Wilse Webb, University of Florida; and Jeff Webster, Langara College.

Colleagues at Western Washington University and Trinity Western University, Dan Brinkman, Harold Faw, Brian Johnson, Ron Kleinknecht, Walt Lonner, Chuck McKnee, Craig Seaton, and Phillip Wiebe provided encouragement, and counsel, as well as access to their personal libraries. Thank you.

Finally, to my wife Gaydene, and my children, Joelle, Matt, Josh, and Amy, thank you for your patience, support, and understanding.

R.P.P.

BRIEF CONTENTS

DETAILED CONTENTS

CHAPTER
3

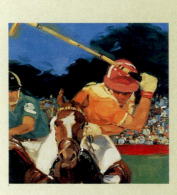

CHAPTER

4

CHAPTER 5

CHAPTER
6

CHAPTER 7

CHAPTER 8

CHAPTER 9

CHAPTER 10

CHAPTER 11

CHAPTER 12

CHAPTER 13

CHAPTER
14

CHAPTER
15

CHAPTER
16

CHAPTER 17

CHAPTER 18

CHAPTER
19

APPENDIX A

APPENDIX B

CHAPTER 1

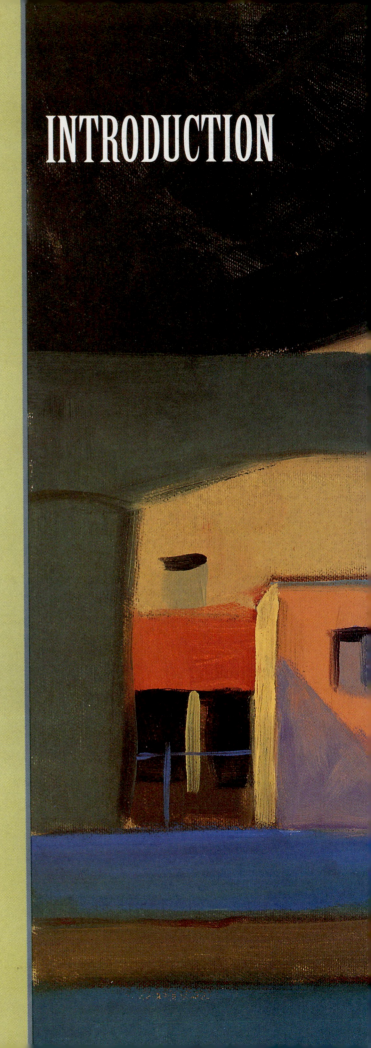

INTRODUCTION

Sherlock Holmes: " . . . You appeared to be surprised when I told you, on our first meeting, that you had come from Afghanistan."

Dr. Watson: "You were told, no doubt."

Holmes: "Nothing of the sort. I knew you came from Afghanistan. From long habit the train of thoughts ran so swiftly through my mind that I arrived at the conclusion without being conscious of the intermediate steps. There were such steps, however. The train of reasoning ran, 'Here is a gentleman of medical type, but with the air of a military man. Clearly an army doctor, then. He has just come from the tropics, for his face is dark, and that is not the natural tint of his skin, for his wrists are fair. He has undergone hardship and sickness, as his haggard face says clearly. His left arm has been injured. He holds it in a stiff and unnatural manner. Where in the tropics could an English army doctor have seen much hardship and got his arm wounded? Clearly in Afghanistan.' The whole train of thought did not occupy a second. I then remarked that you came from Afghanistan, and you were astonished."

Watson: "It's simple enough as you explain it. . . ."

SIR ARTHUR CONAN DOYLE
A STUDY IN SCARLET

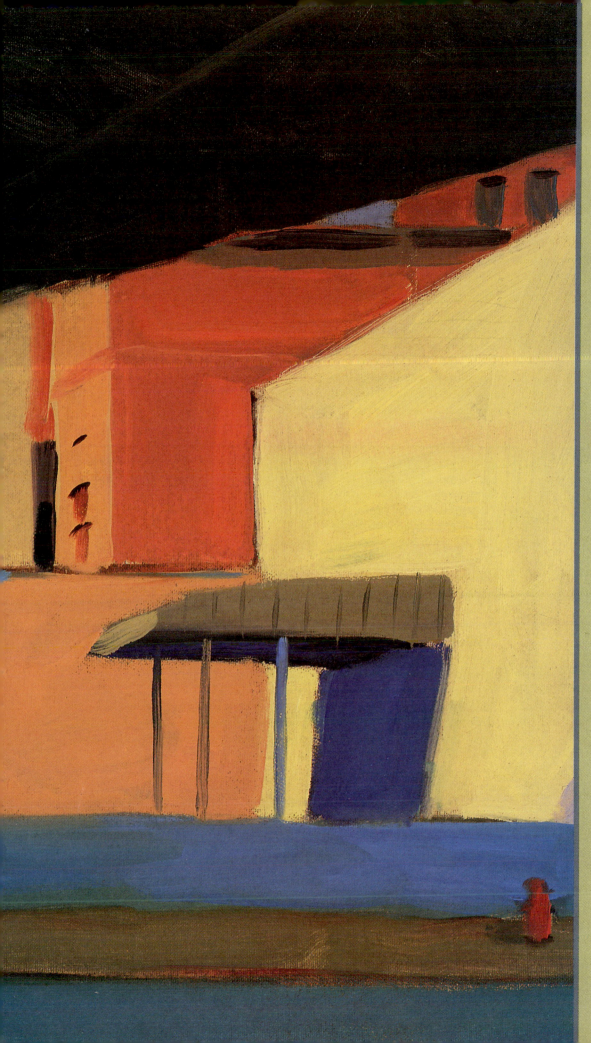

The solution may be simple after Sherlock Holmes has explained it, but human behavior is often a mystery—a *fascinating* mystery, begging to be solved. If you enjoy guessing what other people are really like, you probably will feel drawn to this mystery. And since psychology is the study of "what other people are really like," you may feel drawn to psychology. At any rate, you will surely find it interesting.

Like most sleuths, psychologists gather evidence and follow hunches. Their goal is not catching criminals, however. Their goal is *insight* into human behavior. Insight that would enable us to predict and possibly modify our own and others' actions. But as you will soon learn, modern psychologists have available to them two tools that not even the great Sherlock Holmes possessed.

1. The first tool is our collection of data and theories—the information we call *scientific psychology*. Because psychologists have studied human behavior in the laboratory and in real-life settings for more than a century, we simply know more *facts* about people than most detectives do. And we have many *theories* about human behavior that have stood the test of time. We frequently draw on these theoretical viewpoints to help us understand human behavior. We will be looking at these facts and theories throughout this book. To get a "feel" for some of these facts, you might try the quiz in Table 1.1.

The idea of psychology is to give us a totally different idea of the things we know best.

PAUL VALERY, 1943

TABLE 1.1

A BRIEF QUIZ COVERING A RANGE OF TOPICS IN PSYCHOLOGY.
For each question choose either "True" or "False." (The answers are given under the section "Answers for Thought" at the end of this chapter.)

1. Psychology developed in America and then spread to other parts of the world.
2. Even minor surgery to the brain (cutting or removing brain tissue) produces dramatic changes in personality or behavior.
3. The sensory system for pain is one of the simplest and most basic sensory systems in the human organism.
4. Reputable scientists never concern themselves with ESP and other parapsychological phenomena.
5. Marijuana use is the largest drug problem in America today.
6. Some people never dream.
7. Overweight people eat more than normal weight people even if the food is not very attractive.
8. Our personal feeling of being masculine or feminine is controlled by our hormones.
9. Research shows that, contrary to popular wisdom, smiling does not make you feel better.
10. Simple behaviors like reflexes and instinctive responses are unaffected by learning.
11. Some drugs can improve memory for an experience but only if they are given *before* the experience.
12. Although there is controversy over the use of I.Q. tests, psychologists agree on their definition of intelligence.
13. Newborn infants cannot remember sounds they heard before they were born.
14. Various measures of intelligence indicate that intelligence declines steadily after middle age.
15. Freud's theory of personality is the basis for all other theories of personality.
16. The psychological term for split personality is schizophrenia.
17. Therapy using electric shock is an outdated procedure rarely used today.
18. People's personalities affect their behavior more than do the roles they occupy.
19. In order to change people's negative behavior toward a group we must first change their attitudes to the group.
20. Students from other countries who come to North America to become psychologists are called cross-cultural psychologists.

ONE HUNDRED YEARS OF PSYCHOLOGY

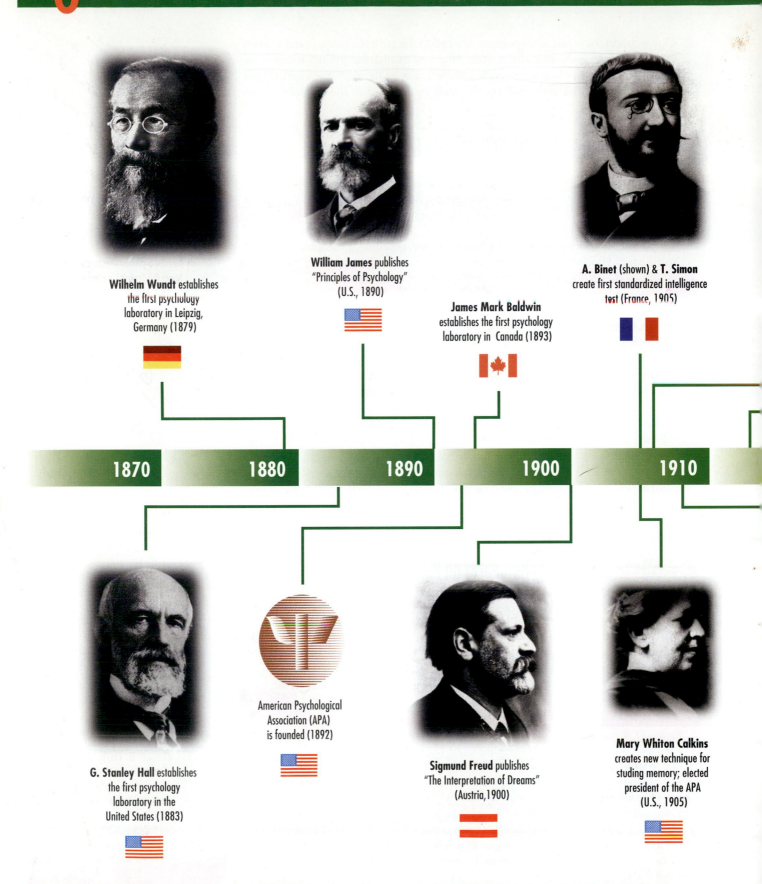

Wilhelm Wundt establishes the first psychology laboratory in Leipzig, Germany (1879)

William James publishes "Principles of Psychology" (U.S., 1890)

James Mark Baldwin establishes the first psychology laboratory in Canada (1893)

A. Binet (shown) & **T. Simon** create first standardized intelligence test (France, 1905)

1870   1880   1890   1900   1910

G. Stanley Hall establishes the first psychology laboratory in the United States (1883)

American Psychological Association (APA) is founded (1892)

Sigmund Freud publishes "The Interpretation of Dreams" (Austria, 1900)

Mary Whiton Calkins creates new technique for studing memory; elected president of the APA (U.S., 1905)

FIGURE 1.1

Some influential individuals and important "firsts" in the development of North American psychology. The country in which the person resided or the event occurred is indicated by the (1992) flag for that country. (We will have more to say about psychology in other parts of the world in Chapter 19.)

2. Our second tool is just as important. It's called the *scientific method*, and it gives us an extremely powerful way of collecting and evaluating the information we need to help us solve human mysteries. We will discuss the scientific method later in this chapter. But let's pick up the trail by looking at the "history of the mystery."

THE HISTORY OF PSYCHOLOGY

Traditionally, introductory psychology textbooks begin with a discussion of the *history of psychology*. Perhaps the reason for this tradition can be found in something Harvard professor George Santayana said years ago: Those who ignore history are doomed to repeat it.

To quote E. G. Boring, another Harvard professor, psychology has a long past, but a short history (Boring, 1950). What Boring meant is this: People surely have wondered about their thoughts, feelings, and actions since there first were people on earth. Literature, art, philosophy, and religion all help us understand ourselves. Thus, "psychology" has a *long past* because people were interested in understanding their own behavior—and that of others—for thousands of years before we decided to call such activities the study of *psychology*.

But the *academic discipline* we now call psychology has a formal history that goes back only a century or so. Departments of psychology began to appear in American colleges and universities in the late 1800s (Schultz & Schultz, 1992). Prior to that time, psychology had been taught in departments of philosophy (if it was taught at all). The first American laboratory for *demonstrating* psychological phenomena was established at Harvard about 1875 by William James. In Germany, however, Wilhelm Wundt opened the first laboratory for studying psychology in *scientific experiments* in 1879. And since psychology is usually defined as "the *scientific* study of thought and behavior," most people consider 1879 to be the birthday of modern psychology.

The young discipline grew quickly. Figure 1.1 lists several "first steps" taken by the new field of psychology.

Early Influences on Psychology

Historians often trace the origins of psychology back to ancient Greek philosophers. After all, Socrates and Plato had lots of interesting things to say about people and their relationship to the universe. Modern psychology, however, was more strongly influenced by social and cultural events in Europe in the middle of the 1800s than by the ancient Greeks.

The most significant influence on modern psychology was the development of experimental psychology by German scientists beginning around 1850. Wilhelm Wundt, for example, opened his laboratory of experimental psychology at the University of Leipzig in 1879. Many of the early American psychologists—such as James Angell and William James—studied in Germany with Wundt.

To Wundt, psychology was the study of the *contents of consciousness*. The way to discover what these contents were, Wundt said, was to perform *scientific research* on the conscious experience of *human subjects*. Although the use of human subjects in experiments is commonplace now, Wundt's belief that the human psyche could best be studied in an experimental laboratory was considered fairly radical a century ago. Wundt also proposed the development of a folk or *cultural* psychology to examine the way that *culture* influences mental development (Schneider, 1990; Wundt, 1900–1920).

More than 100 years later, some of Wundt's efforts have only begun to be appreciated. The modern emphasis on **cognitive psychology** surely is a direct result of Wundt's search for the elements of consciousness. So, of course, is the use of human

Cognitive psychology. The study of intellectual processes (such as attention, perception, reasoning, and problem solving), that we use to deal with the world. Sometimes more narrowly defined as the study of conscious thought processes.

Ivan Pavlov publishes research on a basic type of learning (Saint Petersburg, 1906)

John Walston publishes "Psychology as the Behaviorist Views It" (U.S., 1913)

Canadian Psychological Association is founded (1939)

Albert Bandura presents research that helps to begin the "cognitive revolution" (U.S., 1961)

| 1920 | 1930 | 1940 | 1950 | 1960 | 1970 |

Margaret Floy Washbum, the first woman to receive a Ph.D. in psychology, publishes "The Animal Mind" (U.S., 1908)

B.F. Skinner publishes "The Behavior of Organisms" (U.S., 1938)

Abraham Maslow promotes humanists perspective in psychology (U.S., 1954)

Kenneth B. Clark, who published influential research on the effects of segregation, becomes the first black president of APA (U.S., 1970)

beings as *scientific subjects* in controlled experiments. And in his proposal for folk or cultural psychology Wundt clearly anticipated the development of both social and cross-cultural psychology. We will have a great deal more to say about all of these topics in later chapters.

What important changes in "social thought" occurred during the 1800s that might have led Wundt to think that the human mind should be studied *experimentally* rather than *philosophically*?

As influential as Wundt's ideas were, by the 1900s other developments in European science began to affect the study of psychology in the United States. In St. Petersburg, Russia, Ivan Pavlov was studying a basic kind of learning in dogs. His work led to the development of both **psychobiology** and biological **psychiatry** in America, and also had a strong impact on American learning theorists. In Vienna, Austria, Sigmund Freud was creating a basis for modern theories of personality. Freud's visit to Clark University in 1909 first brought his ideas to the attention of many American psychologists, and probably marks the beginning of the **psychoanalytic** movement in North America. In Paris, France, Alfred Binet was pioneering research to measure the "mental capacities" of French school children. Binet and his colleague Theophile Simon developed the first real intelligence test. By 1917, the United States Army had created its own version of the Simon-Binet scale, which it gave to almost two million soldiers during World War I (Hothersall, 1990). The Stanford-Binet intelligence test, a derivative of the Simon-Binet scale, is still in use today.

The Changing Focus of Psychology

The work of Wundt, Pavlov, Freud, and Binet created a climate of enquiry and enthusiasm in psychology. But there was also uncertainty and controversy over what should be the major focus of attention in this rapidly evolving field.

THE *STRUCTURE* OF THE MIND: WUNDT AND TITCHENER

Wundt believed the major task of psychology was studying the *elements* of conscious experience. E. B. Titchener, a British psychologist who spent most of his career in the U.S., developed this viewpoint into a movement in psychology known as **structuralism** (Titchener, 1898).

Taking his cue from physics, Titchener assumed that *conscious experiences* were constructed of "mental atoms" just as a lump of coal is made up of carbon atoms. But how do you study consciousness? By looking for the "mental atoms" or other basic elements that make up consciousness, Titchener said. Then you find out how these "mental atoms" *combine* to form more complex structures. Eventually—if you learn enough—you should be able to *reduce* even the most complicated mental experience to the simple elements that make up consciousness.

But the structuralists faced a *procedural problem*. You can poke and prod a lump of coal in various ways to determine its inner structure, and you can *measure your results objectively*. But how do you measure consciousness, a subjective process that occurs *inside* people's minds? To solve the measurement problem, Wundt and Titchener developed a technique called **introspection.** That is, they trained observers to "look inside their minds" and "analyze their own mental experiences." They assumed that, by describing their *introspections*, their observers would be able to identify what the *atom* of the mind actually was (Wundt, 1908, 1912).

William James referred to the structuralists' desire to *reduce* the complexities of human consciousness to *mental atoms* as the **psychologist's fallacy.** The structuralists *assumed* these "atoms" existed, James said. They then *forced* their observers (all

Psychobiology. The study of the biological bases of behavior; also called biopsychology or physiological psychology (discussed in Chapter 2).

Psychiatry (sy-KY-a-tree). The branch of medicine that studies and treats people's mental disorders. Psychiatrists hold the M.D. degree. (Most psychologists have the Ph.D. degree.)

Psychoanalytic (sy-ko-annal-IT-ik). The movement begun by Freud, which emphasizes the need to deal with unconscious forces in understanding human motivation. Part of a larger *psychodynamic* movement which includes other ideas loosely connected to Freud's.

Structuralism. An early "school" of psychology started by Edward Bradford Titchener and Wilhelm Wundt (VILL-helm Voondt). The structuralists attempted to model psychology after chemistry, and thus hunted for the "atoms" or "elements" that composed the mind.

Introspection. The act of "inspecting" what's going on within your own mind. To introspect is to attempt to perceive and analyze your own stream-of-conscious experiences.

Psychologist's fallacy (FAL-ah-see). The assumption that complex experiences or phenomena are made up of ("caused by") combinations of simple elements. To prove this viewpoint correct, William James said, Wundt "rigged" his experiments so his observers reported *only* those experiences that Wundt wished them to report.

of whom were their students) to "discover" in their conscious experiences the "atoms" that the experimenters presumed were there (James, 1884, 1890). In its purest form, structuralism failed because it offered too limited and too **mentalistic** a view of human nature.

Like James, most modern psychologists reject structuralism's search for "mental atoms." As we will see throughout this book, however, the urge to explain human experience in terms of simple cognitive, neurological, or genetic "structures" is as strong today as it was in Wundt's time.

THE *FUNCTION* OF THE MIND: ANGELL AND JAMES

Two of Wundt's best-known students were James Angell and William James. By the 1890s, however, they viewed Wundt's approach as too theoretical, too impersonal, and (to be truthful) too European. They rejected Wundt's "atomism," but not his emphasis on studying the mind. Because Angell and James were particularly interested in the *individual* as he or she *functions* in the real world, they developed a **school of psychology** called **functionalism.**

Unlike Wundt, functionalists focused attention on mental *activities* rather than on mental *contents*. They were interested in the *usefulness* of mental processes in adapting to the environment. Functionalist psychologists considered mental processes to be activities leading to *practical* consequences, not elements in some kind of pattern.

Functionalism was an important and successful corrective to structuralism. By focussing on behavior as well as thought, functionalism was effective in restoring a more balanced approach to psychology. Indeed, functionalism no longer exists as a distinct approach because it has been so fully incorporated into the psychology of North America.

For all their grand dreams, however, the early functionalists had many problems trying to put their ideas into practice. For example, the functionalists believed in "free will." But they had a difficult time reconciling this belief with the usual *scientific* assumption that the actions of objects and organisms are *determined* by scientific principles and laws. And while the functionalists wanted to "help people improve their lot," they never came up with a very good *technology of personal change*. It took the **behaviorists** to accomplish that practical goal.

Functionalism (and Behaviorism) are *practical* approaches to psychology. Can you think of any reasons why these approaches were more likely to develop in America?

BEHAVIOR: WATSON AND SKINNER

In 1913, John B. Watson declared war on the functionalists by throwing out the concept of "mind" entirely. Why did Watson take such a radical step? For several reasons:

- First, Watson was not happy with such nebulous concepts as "consciousness" and "free will." Watson believed psychology should deal with concepts that were both substantial and measurable. "Mind" and "consciousness" didn't meet those criteria, but *behavior* surely did.

- Second, in the early 1900s, physics and chemistry were providing the American public with marvelous new devices, such as the telephone, the automobile, and the airplane. Watson wanted psychology to follow the lead of the physical sciences. To turn psychology into an *objective science*, however, he first had to discard such "mentalistic" tools as introspection (Watson, 1913).

- Third, Watson knew that the stated goal of physics and chemistry was the prediction and control of physical objects. Therefore, Watson said, the goal of

Mentalistic. Anything having to do with the mind. If you assume that the mind "runs" the body, you've taken a *mentalistic* approach to solving the mind-body problem

School of psychology. A group of psychologists with a similar view of the nature of psychology. The leaders of a school and their followers were sometimes, but not always, in the same geographic location.

Functionalism. An early school of psychology that developed in reaction to structuralism. American psychologists—particularly John Dewey, William James, and James R. Angell—were more interested in the *functions* and *contents* of the mind than in its *structures*. Functionalists proposed that psychology should study "what mind and behavior do."

Behaviorists. American psychologists, such as John B. Watson and B. F. Skinner, who believed that psychology could never become a science unless it dealt with *measurable* events (such as behaviors) rather than with unseen (and hence unmeasurable) events, such as thoughts and feelings.

behaviorism must be the *prediction and control of behavior* (Watson, 1919). In taking this stance, of course, Watson denied the functionalist view that people voluntarily determine their own actions. Rather than being *self-controllers*, Watson said, people are like simple machines. A stimulus input comes along, it strikes a button in people's brains, and out pops a response of some kind. And the response occurs because of the *input*, not because of any "mental state" inside the individual.

■ Fourth, Watson saw that it was often easier to change *external behaviors* than it was to change *inner mental processes*. Why bother with the mind, then, when actions are so much easier to deal with?

The mind is a strange machine which can combine the materials offered to it in the most astonishing ways.

BERTRAND RUSSELL, 1930

Wundt used *trained observers* in his experiments, but Watson used *subjects* instead. Furthermore, Watson often used animals in his studies, while Wundt (of course) couldn't. What changes in *social values* might help explain the difference between Wundt's approach and Watson's?

Forty years later, B. F. Skinner took Watson's ideas on behaviorism and made them work in real-world situations (McConnell, 1985). Skinner did so by demonstrating that organisms are particularly sensitive to the *consequences* of their actions. If a hungry pigeon gets a piece of corn when it pecks a button in a training box, this "positive feedback" encourages the pigeon to repeat the response that yielded the corn. If the feedback is negative instead of positive—or if there is no feedback at all—the pigeon will try some other response instead of continuing to peck at the button. In Skinner's view, it is *external feedback*, not *internal needs or desires*, that guides the behavior of organisms.

"Behavior is determined by its consequences," is one of Skinner's best-known sayings (Skinner, 1960). And with this slogan as his motto, Skinner developed one of the most impressive technologies of behavioral change the world has ever known. Indeed, many psychologists believe that two of the greatest influences on modern psychology are Freud's theory of psychoanalysis and Skinner's brand of behaviorism.

B. F. Skinner showed the power of consequences to control behavior. Animals (and humans) will learn complex behaviors in order to receive rewards for acceptable performance.

Do you think it's more important to *understand* why people think and act as they do, or to be able to help people *change* their thoughts and behaviors?

THE COGNITIVE REVOLUTION

The behaviorist movement gave American psychologists highly effective ways of "shaping" behavioral responses. However, *in its purest form* it always worked best with animals, with children, and with institutionalized individuals. With these populations, the "shaper" could exercise fairly effective *control* over most of the environmental inputs. And, as Skinner had pointed out early in his career, the greater control one gains over environmental *inputs*, the easier it is to control behavioral *outputs*.

Behavior modifiers. Those psychologists who focus primarily on changing behaviors—sometimes called *behavior therapists*. (Those psychologists who focus primarily on understanding and changing "thoughts and feelings" are usually called *psychotherapists*.) Most of the basic techniques used in behavior modification were developed by B. F. Skinner and his followers.

However, early **behavior modifiers** often ran into difficulties when they tried to apply Skinner's methods to other populations. Suppose, for example, you went to see a behavioral therapist in order to learn how to lose weight. If the therapist wanted to use Skinner's techniques *in their purest form*, the therapist would have to follow you around 24 hours a day, seven days a week, in order to prevent you from "snacking" and to offer you rewards when you stuck to your diet. (How else could the therapist gain *complete* control over your environment?) But you might resent such an intrusion into your life space, and so might the therapist! A far more effective approach—as behavioral therapists learned in the 1960s—would be to teach you "self-management skills," and to help you find *pride and self-satisfaction* in putting those skills to good use. "Self" and "pride" are *mentalistic concepts*, though, rather than *behavioral outputs*, and thus have no place in purely Skinnerian behaviorism.

Beginning in the 1960s, however, some of Skinner's followers began applying his techniques to "shaping" thoughts, perceptions, and feelings as well as to behaviors. This approach, called **cognitive behaviorism,** had several virtues. First, it proved to be a more effective type of therapy than "pure" behavior modification was. Second, it led to the development of **social learning theory,** or the belief that people learn to *change their own environments* in order to achieve their own personal goals. Finally, the rise of cognitive behaviorism helped make the study of mental activities an acceptable part of experimental psychology again.

Put more bluntly, Watson and Skinner had thrown "mind" out the window, but the cognitive behavior modifiers and the social learning theorists brought it right back in (McConnell, 1985). And by demonstrating the narrowness of the "pure" behavioral viewpoint, the cognitive behaviorists helped nudge many North American psychologists toward what is now called the **holistic** approach to understanding why people think, feel, and act as they do. Which means it's time for us to look at how all of these "influences," "focuses," and "revolutions" fit together to form contemporary psychology.

Cognitive behaviorism. The use of Skinnerian techniques to change thoughts and feelings in addition to changing behaviors.

Social learning theory. An approach by Albert Bandura and others that holds that, during your early years, your attitudes and behaviors are shaped almost entirely by your social and physical environment. However, as you mature, you learn ways of shaping your environment.

Holistic (ho-LISS-tick). From an old English word *hool,* meaning "whole." A holistic theory is one that assumes that "the whole is greater than the sum of its parts." Put another way, you are more than a collection of organs and cells, for you have properties (such as consciousness) that cannot be explained in terms of the actions of your parts.

PSYCHOLOGY TODAY

After its birth in the 19th century, psychology grew by leaps and bounds. Today there are literally hundreds of thousands of psychologists around the world, with professional psychological associations in almost every country (which we will discuss in Chapter 19). Psychology is no longer dominated by a small number of individuals or viewpoints. In fact, there are dozens of theories and mini-theories about why people think, act, and feel the way they do. Each approach, however, tends to emphasize one of three different views of human behavior.

Three Views of Human Behavior

Imagine your friend Amy is very depressed. No matter what you say, nothing seems to cheer her up. You find that Amy suffers these bouts every few months, and sometimes they last for weeks.

You want to help Amy, but what's wrong? When you talk to Amy's family and friends you get different answers. Her mother says that her father and her grandfather used to be just like Amy—it's in her genes. "Amy's depressed," she says, "because she inherited a depressive constitution." Amy's father, on the other hand, says that Amy is "feeling sorry for herself," and that she needs to get a more positive outlook on life. Amy's father believes that the source of Amy's problem is in her mind—in the way she *thinks.* But Amy's friends point out that things have not been going well for Amy. She broke up with her boyfriend last week, and she is not doing well in her studies. Amy's friends believe that Amy's major problem is in her environment and her relationships with other people.

If you asked a thousand psychologists to explain Amy's behavior, the answers you'd get would probably include one or more of the descriptive phrases mentioned above. These responses represent three major theoretical viewpoints on behavior within the behavioral sciences today. Let's look briefly at these three main ways of explaining human behavior.

THE BIOLOGICAL VIEWPOINT

Some psychologists emphasize the importance of biological factors in determining who you are and what you do. These scientists believe that everything you think and feel is controlled by electrical and chemical activity in your brain and the rest of your body. Thus, to these theorists, the body controls the mind, and not the other way around.

The area of psychology concerned with studying how bodily functions affect behavior is called *physiological* psychology. This old and highly respected field is now sometimes referred to by such newer names as *biological psychology, psychobiology, biopsychology,* or *neuropsychology* (TenHouten, 1991).

From the biological viewpoint, we would define Amy primarily in terms of her biological systems. And we would view her recurring bouts with depression as a natural consequence of chemical imbalances in her brain and endocrine system. From this perspective, we would probably recommend that the best way to help Amy would be through the use of drugs or possibly electrical stimulation of her brain.

Perhaps because biopsychologists tend to "do something physical" to the person and then note the behavioral changes, these scientists occasionally talk as if biology *causes* psychology. Not all biopsychologists use this biological answer to the **mind-body problem,** of course. But some of their theories do seem to imply that physical events in your nervous system are the major *cause* of all the subjective experiences in your mind. This is a viewpoint that *intra-psychic* psychologists object to strongly.

THE INTRA-PSYCHIC VIEWPOINT

Many psychologists would take an intra-psychic viewpoint toward Amy. Most psychologists believe that everything that goes wrong (or right) about someone's **psyche** or behavior cannot be explained in simple, biological terms. These scientists try to look (as best they can) at what goes on *inside the individual's mind,* rather than just looking at how a person's brain functions.

Intra-psychic psychologists are primarily interested in conscious and *unconscious mental processes.* Scientists study these inner processes in many ways. First, they observe what people actually do and say in a variety of settings. Second, they give people standardized tests of various kinds, and then compare their responses with those that other individuals make. Third, they listen very closely to statements that people make about their inner thoughts and feelings. The intra-psychic psychologists then try to explain the behaviors they've measured in terms of *mental processes*—such as perceptions, motives, values, attitudes, and memories.

The intra-psychic viewpoint includes a variety of more specific approaches to human thought and behavior. Psychodynamic theorists, like Sigmund Freud, emphasize *unconscious* mental processes. Cognitive psychologists, like Aaron Beck, focus on *conscious* thought patterns. Humanistic psychologists, like Abraham Maslow and Carl Rogers, emphasize the unique way each person perceives the world, and they stress the individual's potential for growth. Existential psychologists, like Rollo May and Victor Frankl, focus on the person's need for meaning and purpose in life. Figure 1.2 identifies these specific approaches and theorists associated with the three general viewpoints.

A psychologist taking an intra-psychic *cognitive* perspective might tend to agree with Amy's father. The psychologist might teach Amy to stop thinking about herself and her situation in negative ways. And the therapist would encourage Amy to set realistic positive goals.

From the biological viewpoint, the body exercises almost complete control over the mind. From the intra-psychic standpoint, however, the mind dominates most bodily activities. Both viewpoints can be very useful in helping you understand yourself (and others). But both viewpoints are—in and of themselves—incomplete.

THE SOCIAL/BEHAVIORAL VIEWPOINT

Everyone has both a mind and a body. But we are also *social beings* behaving in a particular **culture.** The people and events around Amy strongly influence her thoughts and behaviors, and she strongly influences the people she is around. Her environment affects her "mental state" as much as her biological makeup does.

Mind-body problem. Possibly the foremost problem in psychology (and philosophy). Namely, where and what is the mind, and how does it function? How does it affect the behavior of the body, and how does the body affect the behavior of the mind?

Psyche (SIGH-key). From the Greek word meaning "mind" or "soul." The term "intra-psychic" means inside the mind. *Webster's New Collegiate Dictionary* defines mind as "that element of complex of elements in an individual that feels, perceives, thinks, wills, and especially reasons." The same source also calls mind, "The conscious mental events and capabilities in an organism." Intra-psychic, then, has to do with your *inner* experiences.

Culture. The shared way of life of a group of people. The customs, ideas, and values which have developed to adapt to the environmental circumstances of the group. Sometimes referred to as the human-made part of the environment. We will generally discuss cultural influences as part of the environment (social/behavior approach).

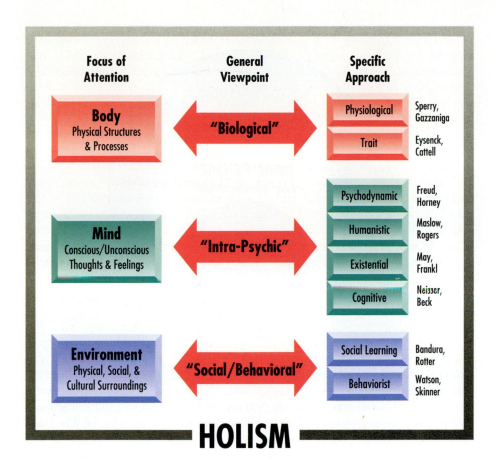

Focus of Attention	General Viewpoint	Specific Approach	
Body Physical Structures & Processes	◄ "Biological" ►	Physiological	Sperry, Gazzaniga
		Trait	Eysenck, Cattell
Mind Conscious/Unconscious Thoughts & Feelings	◄ "Intra-Psychic" ►	Psychodynamic	Freud, Horney
		Humanistic	Maslow, Rogers
		Existential	May, Frankl
		Cognitive	Neisser, Beck
Environment Physical, Social, & Cultural Surroundings	◄ "Social/Behavioral" ►	Social Learning	Bandura, Rotter
		Behaviorist	Watson, Skinner

HOLISM

FIGURE 1.2

Components of the holistic perspective showing three major viewpoints in psychology and several specific approaches derived from them. The names associated with specific approaches are individuals whom we will encounter in subsequent chapters.

Indeed, from the *social/behavioral viewpoint*, there is little about Amy's depression that couldn't be explained in terms of her physical, social, and cultural environment. We know, for example, that recently Amy has experienced several negative events in her social relationships. Also, Amy has probably observed that depressive behavior brought her grandfather extra attention and special treatment. And Amy's culture may have taught her (and you as her friend) that sadness is not normal—making Amy feel even worse about her "blues."

People often ignore the importance of the environment in shaping human thoughts and actions. Amy's mother was quick to blame heredity even though Amy's depression may not be inherited from but *modeled after* her grandfather. And Amy's father may reflect a couple of typically Western biases: the belief that we should always be happy, and the tendency to overemphasize personal characteristics in explaining other people's behavior. (We will discuss the second bias, called the "fundamental attribution error," in Chapter 17.)

As the poet John Donne indicated, you are not an island unto yourself. Rather, you grew up around other people who helped determine your ideas, your values, your joys, your disappointments, your speech, and your behaviors. However, because the biological and the intra-psychic viewpoints have dominated our thinking for so many centuries, it has taken us a long time to realize the importance of the social and physical environments we live in.

THE HOLISTIC APPROACH

Which of the three viewpoints, the biological, the intra-psychic, or the social/behavioral, gives you the greatest understanding of Amy and her problems—or for that matter, of yourself?

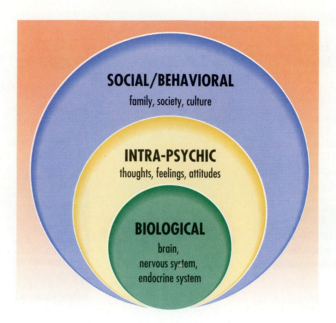

FIGURE 1.3

A "systems" view of the relationship between the biological, intra-psychic, and social/behavioral perspectives. Each system may be viewed as a subsystem of a larger system.

System. An organization of related parts. For example, the "nervous system" in the human body. A system has characteristics (called "emergent properties") which the individual parts of the system do not have. The conscious human "mind" can be thought of as an emergent property of our biological sub-systems.

Eclectic (eck-KLECK-tick). Selecting and combining what seems to be the best of various approaches or theories.

The answer is, *all three of them taken together*. Like Amy, you are an incredibly complex living system. There is a biological basis to your nature, a subjective mental quality, and an interactive social side. You cannot hope to understand yourself—or anyone else—unless you are willing to view human beings *holistically*. That is to say, you must learn to perceive people from the biological, intra-psychic, and social/behavioral perspectives. (Some people would even add a "transpersonal" dimension that includes religious and metaphysical phenomena [Leahey, 1992].)

SYSTEMS.   You might think of the biological, intra-psychic, and social/behavioral areas as **systems** within each other (see Figure 1.3). The biological viewpoint studies the hormones, nerves, and other tissues that make up your body system. From this "biological system" a "psychological system" emerges that is made up of your attitudes, feelings, and thoughts—the objects of study for the intra-psychic viewpoint. The psychological systems of different individuals combine to create larger systems called families, societies, and over time, cultures. The social/behavioral viewpoint treats this larger "social system."

This systems perspective on the different viewpoints stresses the fact that sub-systems combine to form larger systems with new properties. And a systems analysis emphasizes the *interrelationship* between each perspective.

ECLECTICISM.   Despite occasional arguments psychologists may have on the subject, very few of them hold rigidly to just one of the three viewpoints we have described—or follow one of the historical "schools" exclusively. Instead, modern psychologists are **eclectic.** This means they use whatever view seems most appropriate or useful in solving whatever human problem they happen to face at the moment. Different psychologists may emphasize the value of one viewpoint or another, but almost all psychological theories make reference to biological, intra-psychic, and environmental influences. In the study of psychological disorders, for example, there is increasing agreement on the value of a "bio-psycho-social" perspective (Kendler et al., 1992; McGlashan, 1986; Rose, 1984).

Modern psychology has learned from its past: structuralism, functionalism, behaviorism, and the cognitive revolution. And it has grown beyond the narrow confines of purely biological, intra-psychic, or social/behavioral perspectives. Because we are aware of this past, perhaps we can avoid its errors.

But despite the varied "influences," "schools," and "viewpoints" that created modern psychology, one thing remains unchanged: *the scientific method*. The scientific method continues to be the cornerstone of today's psychology just as it was when Wundt established psychology's first experimental laboratory in 1879. It is time for us to take a closer look at this important tool of the psychologist-detective.

You may derive thoughts from others; your way of thinking, the mould in which your thoughts are cast, must be your own.

CHARLES LAMB, 1823

The Scientific Method

One of the main purposes of any science is that of solving mysteries. Nature gives us a puzzle, human or otherwise. For some reason, due to our own peculiar nature as human beings, we are motivated to solve the puzzle. We could just use our "hunches," of course, and make wild guesses about the solution. But psychologists, like other scientists, prefer to adopt a logical process of some kind when trying to solve their mysteries.

Let's look at the logical process one scientist used to solve the mystery of "horse telepathy."

A CLEVER HORSE NAMED "HANS"

Around 1900, the newspapers of Berlin, Germany, were filled with exciting stories about a horse named Clever Hans. According to these reports, Hans could not only "read minds," but could also solve difficult mathematical problems. People by the thousands flocked to see Hans perform his amazing feats.

Hans was owned by a Mr. van Osten, who was so impressed by the horse's abilities that he built a large "answer board" for Hans to use (see photo). If you gave Mr. van Osten a question for Hans, the man would look directly at the horse and repeat the question. Hans would then lift his hoof and tap out the answer. If you asked, "What is 2+2?," Hans would tap the ground four times. But if your question was "Who is president of the United States?," Hans would point at the letters on the answer board that spelled out the correct response.

Most people concluded that Hans was a genuine telepath. But a few skeptics remained convinced that the animal was merely reacting to cues of some kind from the people who asked Hans questions. The controversy became so heated that, in 1904, several of the best-known scientists in Germany formed a commission to study the animal. After months of study, the commission issued its report. These distinguished scientists stated boldly that they could find no evidence Hans was

Mr. van Osten shows off Clever Hans and the "answer board" he built for Hans to use in giving his "answers" to questions from his audiences.

responding to external cues from his questioners. Hence, the commission said, Hans was a "special case," and perhaps really could read minds.

However, like most scientific commissions, this distinguished group recommended that "further research be done." So Professor Carl Stumpf, the psychologist on the commission, told one of his graduate students to look into the matter. This student, a young man named Oskar Pfungst, did just that.

DETECTIVE PFUNGST

Unlike Professor Stumpf, Oskar Pfungst simply didn't believe that Hans could "read minds." So, for many months, he observed Mr. van Osten very carefully as the owner talked to his horse. Then, in a controlled and systematic way, Pfungst began to change the conditions under which Hans worked.

Unlike Pfungst, most animal trainers are aware of the cues they give.

For example, Pfungst put blinders on Hans so the animal couldn't watch the people who were asking him questions. The horse's ability to respond correctly decreased significantly. This result strongly suggested that Hans was responding to some unintentional visual cue given him by the person asking the questions. And when Pfungst found ways to keep Hans from hearing the tiny noises that people made when asking him questions, Hans did even worse. Indeed, when Pfungst cut out both visual and auditory cues after someone asked the horse a question, Hans either refused to respond or gave the wrong answer.

To test the animal's ability to "think independently," Pfungst did something a little different. First, he asked Hans to add two numbers, such as 23+49. Hans immediately responded by tapping out 72. Then Pfungst asked a friend of his to select a number at random and whisper it in the horse's ear. Pfungst then did the same, and asked Hans to add the two numbers. If either Pfungst or his friend knew both numbers, Hans invariably got the correct answer. But if neither man was aware of what number the other had chosen, the horse usually failed the test.

These results indicated Clever Hans was indeed a clever horse, but he surely wasn't a mind-reader. Rather, the animal was superb at reading body-language cues that questioners almost always gave to him. These cues were so slight and so subtle, however, that most people were completely *unaware* they were giving "Hans signals."

For example, the moment most people finished asking Hans a question, they (unintentionally) inclined their heads forward a fraction of an inch. This was a signal to Hans to start tapping. When Hans had tapped out the correct response, the people leaned back just slightly. This cue told Hans to stop tapping. Other people, without realizing it, inhaled sharply when they asked a question, and then exhaled when Hans had reached the right number of taps. Similar cues helped the animal point his hoof to letters on the "answer board" that Mr. van Osten had constructed. Indeed, the horse was so sensitive to slight head movements that if anyone present raised an eyebrow or twitched a nostril while Hans was responding, he would stop instantly.

A final point: Once Pfungst became aware that Clever Hans was reacting to the body-language cues he was giving the horse, he deliberately tried to stop making these telltale twitches and snorts when he asked Hans questions. But no matter how hard Pfungst struggled to control his body language, Hans could almost always detect some sort of signal that told the animal when and how to respond. After months of study, Pfungst concluded Hans was a very bright horse indeed, even if the animal couldn't "read minds."

PEOPLE ARE A PUZZLE

The Clever Hans story taught psychologists that most of us continuously give cues in our body language that suggest how we feel and what we're thinking about. Usually, we're not aware that we're giving off these signals—but they're visible (or audible) to anyone who cares to notice.

The Pfungst research also shows just how critical scientific experiments are to understanding behavior. The commission of distinguished scientists that studied Clever Hans observed the horse carefully, asked questions, and gave the matter a lot of thought. Then they concluded that Hans could "read minds." However, they didn't do *adequately extensive scientific experiments* to test their conclusions. Pfungst observed the animal and Mr. van Osten too, because the scientific method always begins with careful observation. But he alone took the crucial next step. He guessed that environmental stimuli (or cues) could be affecting the horse's behavior, and then he altered these stimulus cues in a very systematic way. This creative use of *scientific experiments* led Pfungst to quite a different set of conclusions about Clever Hans than the commission had reached (Truzzi, 1981).

We'll come back to Clever Hans in a moment. First, however, we need to explain exactly what we mean by the scientific method.

STEPS IN THE SCIENTIFIC METHOD

The scientific method is based on the belief that most mysteries have measurable causes. If you think that events taking place in the world around you are affected primarily by supernatural powers acting in unpredictable ways, then the scientific method won't help you much. If, on the other hand, you believe that a mysterious event might have a natural cause, then you can look for it with the scientific method. To use the scientific method properly, you must follow several steps:

1. State the Problem. You have to recognize that a mystery of some kind exists. You make as many initial observations about the mysterious circumstances as you can. You try to make your observations as exact and complete as possible and you organize them in some meaningful way. As we saw, Pfungst observed Mr. van Osten very carefully for many months.

2. Form a Hypothesis. You use the results of your initial observations to come up with a tentative solution, or educated guess, about the *cause* of the mystery. Scientists often call this step "forming a **hypothesis.**" Pfungst's observations led him to suspect that Clever Hans was getting his answers from his questioners.

3. Test the Hypothesis. You draw up a plan for testing objectively whether or not your hypothesis about the problem was correct. This means constructing an "if . . . , then . . . ," statement to predict your future observations. For example, "*If Clever Hans could not see his questioners, then* he would not be able to answer their questions." The "if" conditions may occur naturally, or you may have to arrange them, perhaps even in a laboratory experiment.

4. Interpret the Data. Whether you merely observe things, or whether you undertake an experiment of some kind, you then look over the data you've gathered and try to decide whether your tentative solution to the problem was right or wrong. Psychologists use mathematical statistics to analyze their data. Statistics summarize and help psychologists determine if their results could have occurred by chance. If you observed what you predicted, and statistics indicate it was not a chance occurrence, you will begin to have faith in your hypothesis. You will probably want to refine your solution to the mystery by testing it again and again. This means making further predictions about future events. If your predictions continue to be accurate your trust in your explanation will increase. (Note that we say your hypothesis is *supported*—not proved.) If, however, you do not observe what you expected under the conditions specified, you will want to revise your hypothesis and make some more observations.

5. Draw Conclusions. Finally, when your explanation leads to reliable predictions you conclude that your explanation is valid. If you have been objective in your observations and careful in setting up the conditions so that someone else could do the same thing, then you are ready to compare your results with other relevant data and report them to the scientific community.

"With all I've learned about psychology recently, establishing who's naughty and who's nice is not as simple as it used to be."

Hypothesis (hi-PAWTH-es-is). A first guess about what is happening, or a tentative solution to a problem.

The whole of science is nothing more than the refinement of everyday thinking.

ALBERT EINSTEIN

The key concept in any definition of the scientific method is objectivity. And "being objective" means standing back and looking at the puzzle as unemotionally and impersonally as you can. True, your subjective, personal feelings are very useful in motivating you to want to solve problems. But your emotions can cloud your judgment if you don't know how to control them when necessary.

Pfungst was objective in his study of Clever Hans. His initial hypothesis was that the horse was responding to unconscious cues from Mr. van Osten and other questioners. Pfungst notes, for example, that van Osten never charged anyone for talking to Hans, and made not a penny out of the animal's fame. But Pfungst didn't allow his affection for either the man or the horse to get in the way of his pursuit of objective truth. Mr. van Osten, on the other hand, let his emotions blind him to what was really going on. He loved Hans and was convinced the horse could "read minds." Shortly after Pfungst proved otherwise, van Osten went into a deep depression. A few months later, he died, a bitter and very disappointed man (Rosenthal, 1965).

The scientific approach relies heavily on observing objectively. Research usually begins with **naturalistic observation,** observing an interesting phenomenon occurring spontaneously. Psychologists observe the phenomenon and collect background information, for example, in the form of a **case study.** The information observed may come from interviews, surveys, or questionnaires. Later, psychologists may attempt to reproduce the phenomenon in the laboratory where observation can take place under controlled conditions. These conditions often result in an *experiment*.

TESTING HYPOTHESES: THE EXPERIMENT

When detectives have enough clues they form a "hunch" or theory about the case. They may then "check out" their hunches in various ways. When psychologists have a hunch about their observations they typically perform an **experiment.** This means that they do something new or unusual to some organism or group. Then they sit back to see what *changes* occur.

VARIABLES.   When you "do something new or unusual" to an individual, you decide on the ways you are going to *vary* that person's environment. Since *you* make the choice, this *variable* in the experiment is "independent" of the subject's wishes. (We usually call people participating in an experiment *subjects*.) Psychologists call "what you do to a subject" the **independent variable** because it is under the experimenter's control.

When you act, people react. The subject's reaction is called the **dependent variable** because the response the subject makes obviously depends on what you've done to the individual.

But *why* do subjects react as they do? Psychologists aren't always sure. When we find that a certain act of ours almost always evokes the same response in someone else, however, we can often make guesses. These guesses or hypotheses are our ways of explaining what goes on inside the person that *connects* the act with the reaction. Put another way, we guess at what processes inside the person "intervene" between the independent and dependent variable. We call these inner processes **intervening variables.** However, we can't observe or measure these intervening variables *directly*; they are just our guesses about why the person acts as he or she does.

Suppose you show your friend Mary a kitten because you want to see how she will react to it. She smiles and pets the animal. "Aha!" you say. "She petted the beast because she loves cats." Showing Mary the kitten is the *independent variable*, because you could have shown her a snake. Smiling and petting are *dependent variables*, because her response depended on what you showed her. If you'd shown her a snake, she might have run away. "Love" is an *intervening variable*, because it's your explanation of why she responded as she did.

You can see kittens and petting behaviors. So independent and dependent variables are things that you can measure objectively. But you can't see "love" or "fear"

Naturalistic observation. Studying and learning about an individual or group of individuals by observing them in their normal or natural setting. The advantage is the realism of the setting; the disadvantage is the lack of control over the setting.

Case study. A form of psychological research in which one individual is studied in detail. Case studies are often used to explore psychological disorders. One of their main advantages is the detailed information which is obtained.

Experiment. An attempt to identify the cause of an effect by systematically manipulating certain conditions and observing the result.

Independent variable. The condition that the experimenter varies for the subjects.

Dependent variable. The behavior of the subject which the experimenter measures.

Intervening variable. The processes which the experimenter thinks might be causing the dependent variable to change when he manipulates the independent variable. The link between the independent and dependent variables.

or "mental telepathy." Someone else might explain Mary's behavior differently. Intervening variables are processes that you can't measure directly. Indeed, you can't even be sure they actually exist. You merely presume that they do, because intervening variables give you a way of *explaining* the relationship you have observed between the independent and the dependent variables.

COMPARING EXPLANATIONS.   Mr. van Osten had watched Clever Hans's performance many times, and he had an explanation for Clever Hans's behavior: Clever Hans could read minds. Pfungst watched the same performance, but offered a different intervening variable—one called "social cueing." Both "mind reading" and "social cueing" are suggested intervening variables because they each explain the relationship between the questions (the independent variable) and Clever Hans's responses (the dependent variable). Either explanation could be correct. How did Pfungst judge between the two? He created conditions in which the two competing explanations, or hypotheses, made different predictions. If Clever Hans could read minds, covering his eyes and ears shouldn't make a difference. But covering Clever Hans's eyes and ears would certainly affect his performance if he was responding to subtle cues in his environment.

This kind of comparison between different explanations is a key ingredient in scientific experimentation. For instance, let's assume you discovered a drug you thought would cure headaches. How would you decide between your hypothesis that the drug worked and the alternative hypothesis that the drug didn't work? You could just give the drug to 100 people with headaches and count how many of your subjects got better. Suppose 65 percent of them got immediate relief. Statistically, we could say that there was a strong *relationship* or high **correlation** between taking the drug and getting better. Wouldn't that prove that your drug was effective? Not really. For many scientific studies show that some people get better immediately even if you just give them a sugar pill. And many subjects recover even if you give them nothing at all. So, maybe your new drug is just another sugar pill. Simply *observing* that two things go together, or are correlated, *does not prove* that one causes the other.

Of course, observation *is* an important part of research. Psychologists frequently use observations from interviews, questionnaires, case histories, and natural settings to investigate their theories and explore new ideas. When they find two things together consistently, they may suspect that one *causes* the other. However, in order to *confirm* their suspicions, they must conduct an experiment. They need to *manipulate* an independent variable (such as an experimental drug) and show that it is the factor controlling the dependent variable (headache relief).

Correlation. A statistical measure of the strength of a relationship. Education and income are correlated, for example. Education and height are not. We must be careful not to assume that a correlation indicates a cause-effect relationship. Without additional data, we cannot assume that high education "causes" high income. High income may "cause" high education by creating more opportunities for education. Or both education and income may be "caused" by intellectual capacity, self discipline, hard work, or some other factor.

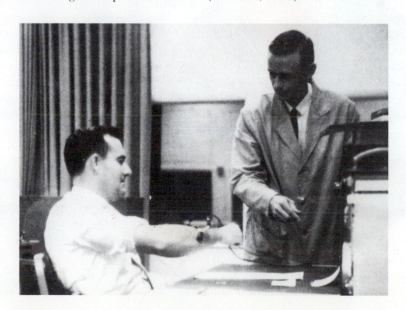

Experimental psychologists study the effects of particular stimuli on certain behaviors in humans and sometimes animals. They may look at how a method of teaching affects learning, or how a drug affects performance, or as in this photo, how far people will obey an authority figure who tells them to harm another person (see Chapter 18).

Experimental group. The group of research subjects which receives the conditions that the experimenter thinks might be causing a particular effect. The group given the "special" treatment.

Control groups. The group(s) used for comparison with the experimental group(s). Similar to the experimental group(s) in every way except that they are not given the "special" treatment.

EXPERIMENTAL AND CONTROL GROUPS.   So, to make sure your drug was really effective, you'd need to test some additional groups. You might give a sugar pill to one such group, and nothing at all to a second bunch of subjects. You could then *compare* the recovery rates shown by these two groups with the recovery rate shown by your original subjects.

In this study, the subjects you gave the "real" pill to would be called the **experimental group.** The two comparison groups are referred to as **control groups** because each comparison group you run actually "controls" for, and helps eliminate, another possible explanation of the results shown by the experimental group.

Now, suppose the experimental group subjects showed a significantly higher recovery rate than did the subjects in the two control groups. The fact that you compared their responses with those of the two control groups *strongly suggests* that your drug was effective in curing headaches. (For more information on different research methods, including correlation and causality, see Appendix A.)

Who Are Psychologists and What Do They Do?

In North America, psychologists may be either male or female and they may have any possible ethnic background. (We will discuss some characteristics of psychology and psychologists in other parts of the world in Chapter 19.) Although women and minority group members have made significant contributions to psychology, social pressures restricted their role in the past (Furumoto & Scarborough, 1986; Hershberger & D'Augelli, 1992). Fortunately, however, this is changing. Minority students can now take advantage of several programs encouraging them to pursue graduate degrees (although they are still seriously underrepresented among psychology faculty). And women now represent more than half of all graduates with doctoral degrees in psychology—prompting some observers to speak of "the feminization of psychology" (Goodheart & Markham, 1992; Howard et al., 1986; Quereshi, 1992). So, psychologists are men and women from many different backgrounds.

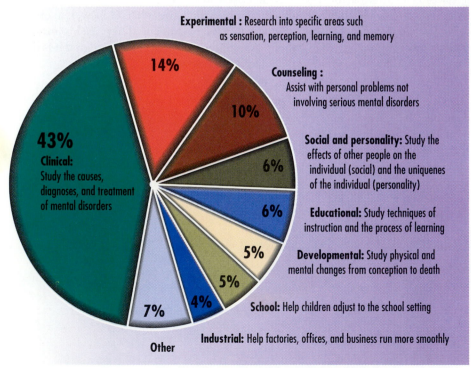

FIGURE 1.4

The approximate percentages of psychologists with different interests working in various settings in the United States. (Based on data from Pion et al., 1987.)

Clinical psychologists work with people who have various types of problems. They use a variety of methods to help these people. Clinical psychologists may work in clinics and hospitals, or they may be involved in private practice.

In addition, psychologists *do* many different things. Figure 1.4 illustrates some of the areas in which psychologists work. Often these areas overlap with each other. For example, an *experimental* psychologist might do research in *industrial* psychology, or a *clinical* psychologist might gather data for a research *experiment*. (This means that the percentage for each area is only a rough approximation.)

In addition to their diverse interests, psychologists work in a variety of settings. Clinical psychologists, for example, may practice in hospitals, mental health clinics, or their own private offices. Experimental psychologists conduct research in business and government laboratories as well as at universities.

Broadly speaking, some psychologists *generate* facts and theories; others *apply* this information in real-life settings. Gregory Kimble calls this dichotomy "psychology's two cultures." Experimental psychologists attach great value to increasing knowledge and to correct scientific methodology. Applied psychologists place greater emphasis on improving the human condition and on the social relevance of their work (Kimble, 1984). According to John Conway, which of psychology's "cultures" appeals to *you* will depend on your own personal characteristics, beliefs, and *values* (Conway, 1992; Zachar & Leong, 1992). So let's conclude this introduction with a consideration of the role of values in psychology.

Knowledge is one. Its division into subjects is a concession to human weakness.

SIR HALFORD JOHN MACKINDER, 1887

GOALS AND VALUES

In recent years psychologists and other scientists have become more aware that values play an important role in their work (Bergin, 1991; Kurtines et al., 1990; Morawski, 1992). The choice of which problem we study, the type of treatment we prescribe, and even the terms we use, reflect our viewpoints and our values. For example, whether we label certain sex acts as "sexual variations" or "sexual perversion" is a value judgment.

Books, even *text*books, inevitably contain the values and biases of their authors. Becoming aware of the authors' values and biases can help you as you read. One way to see these values and biases is to look at the goals that the authors had for their writing.

Goals

Of the many objectives for this textbook, two stand out:

1. That you learn something about the exciting field of psychology.
2. That you gain a clearer understanding of yourself and other people.

UNDERSTANDING PSYCHOLOGY

The first thing you will notice about psychology—one that we have already discussed—is that psychology is in a continuous state of development. In our brief look at psychology's history we saw a constantly shifting focus, from structuralism to the cognitive revolution. We continue to see the impact of new research and theorizing today in the hundreds of new books and articles on psychology that appear each month. (One consequence of this continued growth is the need to revise textbooks such as this one every few years.)

Science can only ascertain what is, but not what should be, and outside of its domain value judgments of all kinds remain necessary.

ALBERT EINSTEIN

The second thing to notice about psychology is that its *method* has not changed. Psychology continues to be the *scientific* study of thoughts, feelings, and actions—the "refinement of everyday knowledge." This is certainly psychology's strength and distinguishing feature.

Third, psychology is a young science. This means that there are important gaps in our knowledge which we are struggling to fill. Contemporary psychologists, for example, are focussing increased attention on the significance of gender and cultural differences in order to fill these gaps in our understanding. We will encounter these two topics several times throughout this book, especially in Chapters 7 and 19.

Psychology's youth also means that we are continuing to work out some of the *ethical* issues in the conduct of research. For example, what limitations should we place on the use of animals in psychological studies? And when are we justified in deceiving our human subjects? (We will discuss the ethics of deceiving research subjects in Chapter 18.)

How would you answer these two ethical questions in psychology?

The fourth thing that you will notice about psychology is its breadth. As you read this book, you may be struck by the variety of topics covered. Psychology is an extremely broad field. It ranges from neurobiological research in sophisticated laboratories, to philosophical speculation about the nature of the person. It includes elements of chemistry, biology, mathematics, computer science, anthropology, sociology, political science, philosophy, and religion. There is hardly an area of intellectual enquiry that is not in some way a part of psychology. This is exciting!

UNDERSTANDING YOURSELF

Learning about psychology doesn't consist of finding a set of magic keys that will unlock the "great secrets of your mind." Rather, understanding human behavior is chiefly a matter of discovering thousands of things that you've been thinking and feeling and responding to—but were never really aware of.

In the many small things that you will discover about yourself, two themes will emerge. The first theme is that you are complex. This means that your thoughts and actions have many causes—we say they are **multi-determined.** We have already seen that psychologists take different viewpoints on behavior. And we noted that the most complete viewpoint is a *holistic* one because it recognizes the many causes that contribute to your thinking and acting.

The second theme that you will notice is that people are similar to each other and yet different from each other. Biologically we are alike, we develop in similar ways, and we interact with our social context in similar ways. Yet we are not identical. For every statement that is true about people *generally*, there is a range of *individual differences* underneath. Each of us is unique.

Sometimes when you discover something new about yourself, you will feel that it is not very surprising—as Sherlock Holmes' companion says in our opening quote, "It's simple enough as you explain it. . . . " You may feel that you knew what was "discovered" all along. In fact psychologists have studied this phenomenon too! They call it the **hindsight bias.** The hindsight bias is the feeling you get, after you learn something new, that you knew it all along (Hawkins & Hastie, 1990). However, we believe that many of the things you will discover *are* somewhat surprising and unexpected (Furnham, 1992). How did you do on the quiz in Table 1.1?

Many fields of knowledge can offer you a *subjective* understanding of human behavior. Art, literature, and religion are good examples of subjective approaches that can give you important information about people. But because it uses the scientific method, psychology offers you two things that no other field can:

- First, a set of *objective* facts about how you think, feel, and behave.
- Second, theories and insights, based on objective facts, that attempt to explain in *objective terms why you think, feel, and act as you do.*

You will find that taking an unbiased, objective view of yourself (and others) is a skill that you have to "learn by doing." Also, not everyone appreciates—or even agrees with—the facts that psychologists have discovered about human nature. Sometimes people resist new knowledge, especially about themselves—like the student Dr. Philipchalk heard advising her friend, "Don't take psychology; they teach you about yourself and it takes all the fun away."

We believe there's a great deal of fun in understanding human behavior. But whether it's worth your time to learn how to be objective about people, only you can decide.

Values: The Authors' Viewpoints

We encourage you to reflect on your own values as you read the rest of this book. You will gain a more accurate view of psychology if you keep in mind the goals and values of your authors (and those of your instructor). Your authors would like you to learn about psychology and to learn about yourself. Another way of putting this is to say that your authors would like to "give psychology away" (Miller, 1969).

Your authors also have more specific biases and viewpoints. Both of them have experience in psychology's "two cultures." Dr. McConnell spent many years studying the biochemistry of memory in a scientific laboratory. Dr. Philipchalk's background is in the study of verbal learning, memory, and psycholinguistics. More recently, McConnell did research on autistic children. Philipchalk's recent research has been on psychological development in late adolescence, and the psychology of

Multi-determined. Having many causes, such as biological, intra-psychic, or environmental. Thus, for example, you cannot say that *the* cause of mental retardation is *brain damage* because the social environment in which the brain-damaged individual is brought up strongly affects the person, as does the person's present environment.

Hindsight bias. The feeling you get after you learn a new fact, that you knew it all along. Sometimes called the "I knew it all along" phenomenon.

Psychologists have developed ethical standards for their research. These standards include the humane use of animals. However, the question of humane, or any, use of animals in research is becoming more controversial.

religion. Both of them have consulted with government and private organizations. McConnell helped run a private psychological clinic; Philipchalk has counseled in a university counseling center. Their training and teaching experience also spans different cultural contexts: McConnell's in the United States, and Philipchalk's in both the United States and Canada. So, like most psychologists, they have their own set of biases or subjective viewpoints about people and psychology.

You may have noticed some of the authors' prejudices already (their bias toward the holistic approach, for example). But here are some others you should be aware of too:

1. The study of human behavior is one of the most fascinating, awe-inspiring, and important occupations imaginable. The authors hope that some of their enthusiasm for psychology rubs off on you by the time you finish the book. Indeed, enthusiasm is the greatest gift they can give you.

2. Learning should be both challenging *and* fun. One way of making the study of psychology enjoyable in this book is to focus on our own experiences. You will find that the authors frequently suggest how the material might apply to *you*. So you will find them referring to you, the reader, more often than in most other textbooks. You will also notice that each chapter begins with an excerpt from a book that you may have read. You may find that you can understand the characters in these books better after you have read the scientific material in the chapter itself.

3. Integration of ideas, and personal application are important. This is why at various points, the text includes "thought questions." The purpose of these questions is to push your mind beyond the facts on the printed page. However, if the answers don't come easily, you might look ahead to the end of the chapter where you will find some suggestions under the heading "Answers for Thought."

4. Facts are more important than opinions and unsubstantiated hunches. If you try to understand people before you have enough facts, you run the danger of seeing what you want to see—instead of seeing *objectively* what the people are like. You may have your own ideas about human behavior. But unless you have studied psychology before, chances are your present views are based more on your subjective impressions than on objective data. Thus, you may find that many of your feelings or hunches about yourself and others are challenged by the facts presented in

this textbook. The book does not ask that you give up your present views, merely that you try to examine them afresh in the light of what new scientific information it gives you.

5. Each person is unique and valuable, with unknown potential. Growth toward that potential is always possible. Through the wise and humane application of the *holistic approach*, we can come closer to achieving our personal goals in life and we can help others come closer to achieving their goals too.

As we go on to look at some of the areas psychologists study, you will learn many objective facts. We hope that you will also experience some of the excitement of unravelling the "mystery" that is human behavior.

SUMMARY

1. Psychology has a **long past,** but a **short history.** The first departments of psychology began to appear in American colleges only **100 years ago.**

2. The first real laboratory for studying psychology **experimentally** was founded by **Wilhelm Wundt** in Germany in 1879.

3. At the turn of the century, North American psychology was also influenced by **Pavlov's** research on learning, **Freud's** theory of **psychoanalysis,** and **Binet's** development of the **intelligence test.**

4. **Structuralism** was developed by Titchener based on Wundt's ideas. Wundt and Titchener asked trained observers to **introspect** their conscious experiences. They hoped thereby to determine the elements or **atoms of the mind.**

5. James Angell and William James, students of Wundt, rejected structuralism and promoted **functionalism** instead. Functionalism viewed behavior in terms of **active adaptation to the environment** and was a much more practical approach than was structuralism.

6. John B. Watson and other American **behaviorists** threw out the concept of **mind** entirely because, they said, mental activities can't be **measured objectively.**

7. B.F. Skinner added the concept of **feedback** to Watson's behaviorism and developed an impressive **technology** of personal change. Skinner's students brought "mind" back into respectability, however, by developing **cognitive behavior modification** and **social learning theory.**

8. By the 1960s, **cognitive psychology,** which had remained dominant in Europe, reasserted itself in American psychology. Behaviorists viewed humans as **responding passively to stimulus inputs.** Cognitive psychologists view the individual as capable of **interacting actively** with the environment and changing it to achieve their own goals.

9. The three major approaches in modern psychology are the **biological, intrapsychic,** and **social/behavioral viewpoints.**

10. **Biopsychologists,** or physiological psychologists, are primarily interested in the **interactions** between body processes and behavior.

11. **Intra-psychic psychologists** believe your mind has **voluntary control** over most bodily activities, and tend to focus on studying (and measuring) **mental activities.**

12. **Social/behavioral psychologists** see most human attitudes and behaviors as being controlled by (or learned from) the **external environment,** including physical, social, and cultural factors.

13. **Holistic** psychology is the belief that **behavior is multi-determined,** and hence each thought, feeling, and action is affected by biological, intra-psychic, and social/behavioral variables.

14. Psychology is different from other attempts to understand human behavior because it uses a logical step-by-step process for solving mysteries called the **scientific method.**

15. In using the scientific method you first must make careful observations and **state the problem.** Then you **form a hypothesis** or "best guess" about the solution to the problem. Next, you **test the hypothesis** by collecting and then **interpreting data** to see if your hypothesis leads to accurate predictions. And finally, you **draw conclusions** about your explanation on the basis of how well it predicted the results you obtained.

16. When psychologists test a hypothesis in an **experiment** they *vary* certain conditions and measure the effect of this variation on some reaction in the subject. We call the condition that we vary the **independent variable,** and the reaction that we measure the **dependent variable.**

17. An **intervening variable** is the name we give to an unobservable process that we guess is going on inside an individual, and is linking the independent variable to the dependent variable.

18. Observing that two events occur together, or are **correlated,** may suggest that one causes the other, but an experiment is necessary to confirm this suspicion.

19. An experiment always involves comparing one or more **experimental** conditions with one or more **control** conditions. We give the experimental conditions the treatment we want to test, and we compare their reactions to the reactions of the control conditions. The experimental and control conditions are identical in every way except that the control condition does not get the treatment we are testing.

20. Psychologists work in a wide variety of settings on many different problems. A simplification of this diversity divides psychology into "two cultures," **experimental** and **applied** psychology.

21. Science, including psychology, is affected by **values.** Knowing the biases and viewpoints of authors (and instructors) is an important part of becoming objective.

ANSWERS FOR THOUGHT

1. *Table 1.1: For each question, choose either true or false.*

   The correct answer for each of these questions is "false."

2. *What important changes in "social thought" occurred during the 1800s that might have led . . . ?*

   The increasing success of modern science with its faith in *empiricism* (observation of nature as the source of knowledge rather than authority or divine revelation) was a major force in the 19th century. Also, the theory of evolution had the effect of placing humans in the same category as animals and thus a possible object of scientific experimentation.

3. *Functionalism (and Behaviorism) are practical approaches to psychology. Can you think of . . . ?*

   The pioneer spirit through which America was settled was strongly utilitarian, practical, and functional. "Survival of the fittest" provided a basis for both American individualism, and in psychology, American functionalism.

4. *Wundt used trained observers in his experiments, but Watson used subjects instead. Furthermore, Watson . . . ?*

   By Watson's time scientific psychology had achieved greater respect and authority. The change in terminology reflects this increased status of the psychological researcher. Also, since Darwin's theory of evolution had placed man on a continuum with animals, the relative simplicity of dealing with animals made them a reasonable alternative to human subjects. In addition, Watson said, "I never wanted to use human subjects. I hated to serve as a subject. I didn't like the stuffy, artificial instructions given to subjects. I always was uncomfortable and acted unnaturally. With animals I was at home." (Watson, 1936, p. 276)

5. *Do you think it's more important to understand why people think and act as they do, or to be able to help people change their thoughts and behaviors?*

Both are important. The choice of which is more important is a matter of opinion based on personal biases and individual differences. People who choose "understanding" incline towards scientific values and the rewards of "knowledge for its own sake." People who choose "change" (regardless of understanding), incline towards humanistic values and the rewards of *practical* research. (See our discussion of psychology's "two cultures" later in Chapter 1.)

6. *How would you answer these two ethical questions in psychology?*

Psychologists are committed to the humane treatment of animal subjects. This means inflicting no unnecessary pain or discomfort. The definition of "unnecessary" is, however, open to interpretation. Human subjects are used in research with their "informed consent." This means the experimenter tells them as much as he or she can about the study and then asks for their voluntary participation. Deception is justified only if it is necessary and the potential gains justify the deception. All deception must be explained at the end of the study and every effort made to assure there are no lasting negative effects. Of course, the possibility of gains justifying deception in any particular study is open to different interpretations.

CHAPTER 2

BIOLOGICAL BASES OF BEHAVIOR

Boranova, her face expressionless, her voice toneless, said, "If the project fails, I will take full responsibility."

Kaliinin looked up and said, "Natalya, assigning blame will not help us. Right now, we have no choice. We must go ahead. Let us move on, miniaturize if we have to, and find some likely cell to enter."

"Any cell?" said Konev in a stifled fury, and addressing no one. "Any cell? What good would that do?"

"We might find something useful anywhere we go, Natalya," said Kaliinin.

When Konev made no response, Boranova said, "Is there any objection to that, Yuri?"

"Objection? Of course there's objection." He did not turn, but his very back seemed stiff with anger. "We have ten billion neurons* in the brain and someone is suggesting that we wander among them blindly and choose one at random. It would be easier to drive along Earth's roads in an automobile and randomly choose some human being on the wayside in the hope that he might be a long-lost relative. Much easier. The number of human beings on Earth is a little more than half the number of neurons in the brain."

"That is a false analogy," said Kaliinin, carefully turning her face toward Boranova. "We are not engaged in a blind search. We are looking for Pyotr Shapirov's thoughts. Once we detect them, we need only move in the direction in which the thoughts strengthen."

ISAAC ASIMOV
FANTASTIC VOYAGE II: DESTINATION BRAIN

*In recent years, scientists have estimated that there are more than 100 billion neurons in the brain.

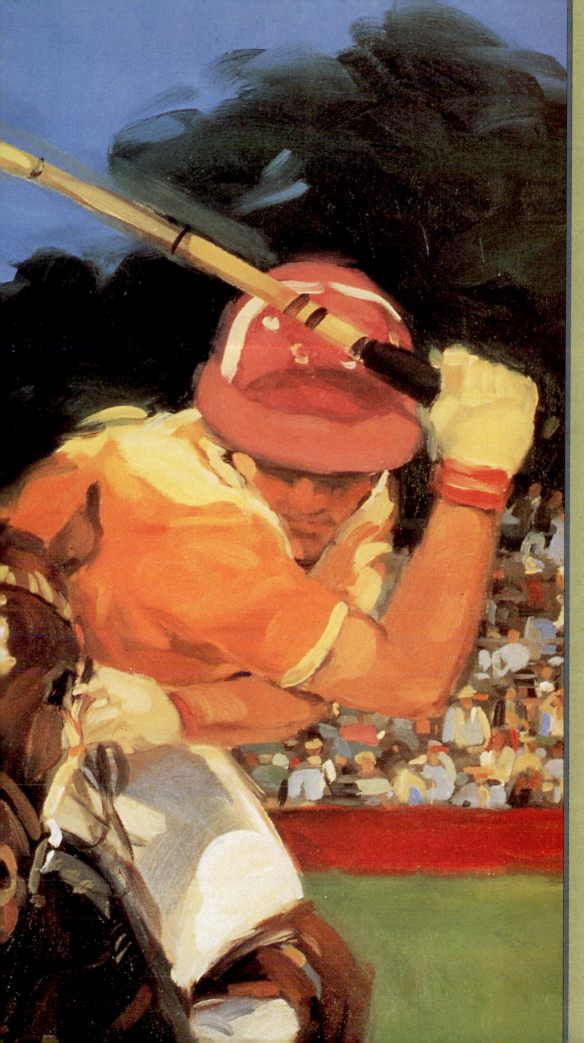

The biological component to our behavior is undeniable. In this emotional situation, the brains, endocrine systems, and nervous systems of this couple are extremely active.

Neuron (rhymes with "YOUR on"). A single nerve cell. Neurons range in size from microscopic to over 3 feet (1 meter) long.

Dendrites (DEN-drights). Tiny fibers at the front or "input" end of a neuron that are chemically excited by neurotransmitters released into the synapse.

Soma (SO-mah). The cell body of a neuron. Contains the cell nucleus (NEW-klee-us). The center or main part of a neuron that "processes" some types of inputs to the cell.

Axon (AX-on). The "tail" or "output" end of a neuron. Axonic end-fibers release neurotransmitters into the synaptic cleft which stimulate the next neuron in line.

Metabolism (mett-TAB-boh-lism). From a Greek word meaning "change." The sum total of biological processes inside the cell that (a) build up energy to be released, and (b) repair the cell and keep it functioning in a normal fashion.

Boranova, Kaliinin, and Konev are looking for Pyotr Shapirov's thoughts, which they believe are stored in the cells of his brain. Contemporary biological psychologists, or biopsychologists as they are sometimes called, also look for "thoughts" and their basis in the brain—as well as in related bodily systems. Because we are physical beings, this *biological approach* has added immensely to our understanding of human behavior.

Biopsychologists assume that *intra-psychic* experiences like thoughts have a physical basis. They believe that the mind is a *product* of the body and that the mind does not control the body. Biological psychologists do not deny that *non*-biological factors such as physical and social influences also affect us. Pyotr Shapirov, for example, is unconscious and dying because of factors in his *physical environment*. And *social* conflict between Boranova and her colleagues threatens the success of the scientists' expedition. "But," the biopsychologists say, "we are first and foremost *biological* creatures."

In this chapter we will examine biological structures that are basic to everything we think, feel, and do. We will begin with the basic unit of communication in the body, the **neuron.** Next, we will look at how neurons combine to form systems, including the most complex of all systems, the brain. And finally, we will conclude with a discussion of genetic influences on behavior.

You will see that from a biological perspective, you really are quite amazing. Scientists have discovered many intriguing things about our bodies. And the potential that biopsychology offers for curing and preventing disorders is exciting.

Let's begin our exploration of the biological basis of behavior in the same way that Boranova and her companions began their search, by looking at a single nerve cell.

THE NEURON

The major purpose of individual nerve cells, called neurons, is to communicate. Neurons pass information from one part of your body to another. Although neurons vary considerably among themselves in size and shape, they tend to have three main parts—the **dendrites,** the **soma** (cell body), and the **axon.** As you will see, all three parts of the neuron are necessary for transmitting "neural messages" through your body. Without these humble messengers you could not perform the simplest action or think a single thought.

Parts of the Neuron

The front end, or input side, of a neuron is a network of tiny fibers called dendrites. The dendrites project out from the cell body like the branches of a tree to make contact with surrounding nerve cells. The major activity of the dendrites is to receive information from other nerve cells. We will see how the dendrites accomplish this miracle in a moment.

The main part, or body, of the cell is called the soma. The soma seems to have two major functions. First, like the dendrites, it can receive inputs from other neurons. But second and just as important, the soma is the neuron's "housekeeper." Most of the complex chemical reactions involved in cellular **metabolism**—which keep the cell functioning in a healthy fashion—take place inside the soma.

The action end, or output system, of the neuron is called the axon. The axon stretches out from the soma like a branching telephone cable. At the end of each axonic branch or cable are tiny fibers which release chemicals that affect the dendrites and cell bodies of nearby neurons, or muscles and glands. As we will see in a moment, the axonic fibers come close to, but *do not touch*, the dendrites and cell bodies of the neurons, muscles, and glands that they affect. The axon is the *output area* of the neuron because it is the axonic fibers that actually pass messages along. (We might say the axon "acts on" other neurons, muscles, and glands.)

Types of Neurons

There are three different types of neurons in your nervous system. **Sensory neurons** convey information about smells, sights, and other sensory stimulation to your brain. **Motor neurons** transmit instructions from your brain to your muscles and glands. And **interneurons** simply convey information from one neuron to another in your brain and spinal cord. A large bundle of axons from many neurons is what we call a **nerve.**

Neurons come in a variety of shapes and sizes. Some neurons have complex axons, but no dendrites at all. Some have a highly complex dendritic structure but a relatively simple axon. Some have long axons and dendrites, and some have short axons and dendrites. Figure 2.1 illustrates some of these variations.

Scientists have discovered that neurons in the brain can change their shape by growing new branches on their dendrites and axons (Purves & Hadley, 1985; Greenough & Bailey, 1988). For example, rats kept in an "enriched" environment—one with other rats and "toys" to explore—develop more elaborate dendrite branching than rats kept alone in small cages (Camel et al., 1986; Black et al., 1989).

Motor neurons transmit instructions from the brain to muscles and glands, allowing us to move about.

Sensory neurons. Nerve cells that are involved in relaying information to your brain from your eyes, ears, and other sensory receptors.

Motor neurons. Nerve cells that are involved in relaying messages from your brain to your muscles and glands.

Interneurons. Nerve cells that convey impulses from one neuron to another in the brain and spinal cord. Most of the brain's neural activity is carried on by interneurons.

Nerve. A large bundle of axons from many neurons.

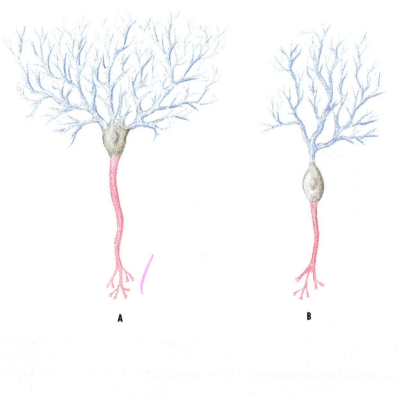

A   B

C

FIGURE 2.1

Some of the variations in neurons. The red portion indicates the axon; the blue indicates the dendrites. Some neurons have dendrites with many branches and can receive input from many other neurons (a). Some have an intermediate number of branches (b), and some have few (c).

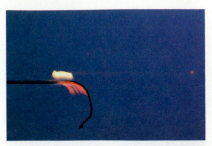

Like a fire burning along a fuse, the action potential travels along the neuron, reaching the end with as much "energy" as it began with.

Resting potential. The electrical energy stored up by a nerve cell ready to be discharged in a short burst.

Action potentials. Waves of electro-chemical energy that sweep down the axon of a neuron when the nerve cell releases its resting potential and hence "fires."

Refractory period (re-FRAK-tory). The brief time after a neuron fires. During this time the resting potential is re-established.

All-or-none process. Any process, like the firing of a gun, or the firing of a neuron, that happens either completely or not at all—there are no in-between levels. (You cannot "half fire" a gun.)

Synapse (SIN-aps). The region where two or more neurons come close to each other, but do not actually touch. If the axon of nerve cell A can stimulate the dendrites and cell body of B, we say the two neurons "make synapse."

Synaptic cleft (sin-APT-tick). A cleft is an opening or space made by splitting. A synaptic cleft is the fluid-filled space between an axonic end fiber on one cell and the dendrite or soma on a second neuron (although the synapse is not formed by a "split" of any kind).

Terminal buttons. At the end of axons, the slight enlargements that release chemicals (neurotransmitters) into the synaptic cleft.

In humans, elderly people who remain healthy and alert also show increased dendrite branching (Jacobs et al., 1993). One result of this greater contact with other neurons is to offset the effect of neurons lost through aging. In people who become senile, however, dendrite branching does not increase and may even decrease—for unknown reasons (Buell & Coleman, 1981; Jacobs & Scheibel, 1993).

Neural Firing

The major function of every neuron is to send information from one part of your body to another. Each nerve cell contains a certain amount of stored-up electrical energy—the **resting potential**—that it can discharge in short bursts. We call the bursts of energy **action potentials.** The action potential moves along the neuron by travelling from the dendrite at one end to the axon at the other.

As the action potential travels along a neuron, its energy does not decrease. You might think of the action potential as a fire burning along a string or fuse. The fire is just as intense at the end of the fuse as it was at the beginning. (Of course, the action potential does not destroy the neuron as it moves along it.) When a neuron has discharged an action potential, it takes a brief period of time—called a **refractory period**—to restore its resting potential and be ready to fire again.

Whenever an action potential passes along a neuron's axon, we say that the nerve cell has *fired,* because the action involved is much like the firing of a gun. For example, consider how a gun actually fires. There is a great deal of *potential* energy stored in the chemical gunpowder in a bullet. When you pull the trigger on a gun, you translate this *potential* chemical energy into the *active* energy of an explosion, and the bullet is propelled down the barrel of the gun. In similar fashion, when a neuron fires, it translates its resting potential into an action potential.

Let's carry the bullet analogy a step further. The neuron behaves in some ways as if it were a machine gun loaded with electro-chemical bullets. For example, a machine gun either fires, or it doesn't. The bullets travel at the same speed whether you fire one or a hundred in a row. In similar fashion, a neuron either fires, or doesn't fire—like the gun, in an **all-or-none process.** And all its action potentials are of the *same strength,* whether the neuron produces one action potential each second, or a hundred.

Also, if you press and release the trigger on a machine gun very quickly, you can fire the shells slowly, one by one. But if you hold the trigger down, you can fire off whole bursts of bullets in a second or two. In like manner, if you tap lightly on your arm, the receptor (input) nerve cells in your skin will fire at a very slow rate—a few times a second. If you press very hard on your arm, however, these same input neurons can fire hundreds or even thousands of times per second.

Every time you move a muscle—or think a thought, or experience an emotion—you do so in part because groups of nerve cells in your brain fire off messages to your muscles, glands, or other groups of neurons.

THE SYNAPSE

Now, let's consider three nerve cells that fire in an A-B-C sequence. As Figure 2.2 shows, the axonic end-fibers of A come close to (but do not actually touch) the dendrites and soma of cell B, and the axonic end-fibers of B come close to the dendrites and soma of cell B. The general area where two neurons come into near contact with each other is called the **synapse.** This synapse (or "area of contact") is so tiny you would have trouble seeing it even using a powerful microscope.

As we said, neurons A and B don't actually touch at their synapse. Instead, there is a tiny space between them called the **synaptic cleft.** When a neuron fires, the action potential causes the axonic fibers to release tiny drops of chemicals into the synaptic cleft. These chemicals come from little bulges called **terminal buttons** at

Synapses, neurons A and B

Synapses between
neurons B and C

A

B

C

Axon, neuron A

Cell body
or soma,
neuron B

FIGURE 2.2

Three neurons in sequence. In transmitting
the nerve impulse from neuron A to neuron C,
the axonic fibers of A make synapse with the
dendrites of cell body B, and the axonic fibers
of B make synapse with the dendrites of C.

the end of the axonic fibers. The chemicals move across the cleft and stimulate the
dendrites and soma of the next cell.

These stimulating chemicals are called neural transmitters or **neurotransmitters.**
The function of the neurotransmitters is to send, or transmit, information from one
cell to another. The more neurotransmitters that A's axonic end-fibers release into
the synaptic cleft between A and B, the more often cell B will be triggered into
firing.

If a neurotransmitter molecule from neuron A doesn't land on a receptor site—or
if the "pockets" are already filled by other molecules—the transmitter will rapidly
break down chemically and lose its effectiveness. And even if the transmitter molecule does find a receptor site on B, it still will break down quickly—so another transmitter molecule can take its place and cause B to fire once more. The broken pieces
of the transmitter will, in either case, mostly be taken up by A's axon, put together,
and used again.

Neurotransmitters. Chemical substances
released into the synaptic cleft by an axon
ending when an action potential reaches it.
These substances travel across the synapse
and act on the dendrite or cell body of
another cell.

EXCITATION AND INHIBITION

Our axons produce many different types of neurotransmitters with the potential to
excite nearby dendrites. Some of our axons, however, produce chemicals with the
opposite effect. These *inhibitory* molecules counteract the *excitatory* chemicals
released by other neurons. Inhibitory neurons *prevent* nearby cells from firing.

Consider the example in Figure 2.3. A releases its excitatory neurotransmitters
into the A-B synapse. But now neuron I releases its inhibitory molecules directly into
the A-I synapse too. Whether B fires at any moment in time depends on whether A
or I happens to release the most neurotransmitters. If more excitatory molecules are
present in the A-B synaptic cleft, B will fire. If more inhibitory molecules are present
in the A-I synaptic cleft, B is inhibited from firing.

Most neuron interactions in the central nervous system are of this A-I-B type.
That is, any given neuron B in your brain is likely to receive simultaneous inputs
from dozens of As and dozens of Is. Activity in the synaptic clefts resembles an election in which two candidates, "Fire," and "Don't Fire," are running for office.
Whether B fires at any given moment depends on the balance of excitatory and
inhibitory neurotransmitters it receives at that point in time.

In what way is the "chemical firing" in an *A-I-B* junction very different from the "electrical firing" within the neuron?

Scientists estimate that there are more than 100 billion neurons in your nervous
system (Williams & Herrup, 1988). An accurate count is impossible because of the

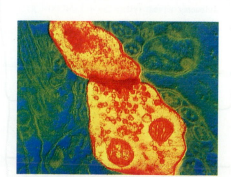

This photograph from an electron micrograph shows the
terminal buttons at the end of many axons forming
synapses around the cell body of a single neuron. These
terminal buttons release neurotransmitters that travel
across the synaptic cleft and act on the cell body.

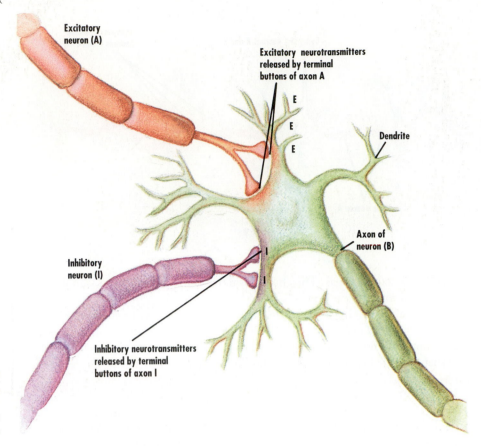

Excitatory neuron (A)

Excitatory neurotransmitters
released by terminal
buttons of axon A

E
E
E

Dendrite

Axon of
neuron (B)

Inhibitory
neuron (I)

I
I

Inhibitory neurotransmitters
released by terminal
buttons of axon I

FIGURE 2.3

Neuron B will fire or not fire depending on the balance of excitatory neurotransmitters (E) and inhibitory neurotransmitters (I) that neurons A and I produce in their synapses with B.

Central nervous system. The group of neurons that make up the brain and spinal cord.

Peripheral nervous system (per-IF-er-ul). The nerves connecting the central nervous system to the sense receptors as well as to the muscles and glands.

Somatic nervous system. The division of the peripheral nervous system that controls the voluntary muscles.

Autonomic nervous system (aw-toh-NOM-ick). *Autonomic* means "automatic" or "reflexive," "without volition." The autonomic nervous system takes care of most of your normal body functions (breathing, pumping of the blood, digestion, emotional reactions) that occur automatically—without your having to think about them.

Sympathetic nervous system. That half of the autonomic nervous system responsible for "turning on" or preparing your body for vigorous "fight or flight" activities.

Parasympathetic nervous system (PAIR-ah-sim-pah-THET-tick). That half of your autonomic nervous system that is "beyond" or opposed to the sympathetic system. The parasympathetic system "turns off" or slows down most activities "automatically" aroused by the sympathetic system.

vast number and because neurons are so small. The neurons in the outer layers of your brain, for example, are so incredibly tiny that 20,000 of them could fit on the head of a pin. Each neuron connects with other neurons—some to more than a thousand others! So in order to get a grasp of this vast complexity, we need to look at the way neurons are organized into *systems*.

CONTROL SYSTEMS

We could group together the billions of neurons in your body in several different ways. The largest and most obvious collection of neurons forms the structure we call your brain. Another large collection of neurons, (or more precisely, collection of *large neurons*), makes up your spinal cord. Your brain and spinal cord together form your **central nervous system.**

Outside of your *central* nervous system, in your **peripheral nervous system,** we can group your neurons in the most meaningful way by considering their *function*. Your peripheral nervous system is made up of your **somatic nervous system** and your **autonomic nervous system.** Your somatic system controls your *voluntary* muscles, like those which move your arm. Your autonomic system controls *involuntary* muscles in your kidneys, heart, and other internal organs. Figure 2.4 illustrates these divisions of your nervous system.

Autonomic Nervous System

Your autonomic nervous system has two major parts or divisions: (1) the **sympathetic nervous system** and (2) the **parasympathetic nervous system.** In general,

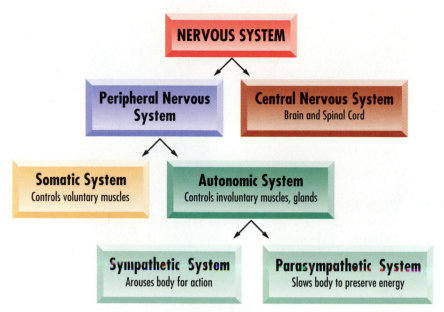

FIGURE 2.4
The divisions of the human nervous system.

activity in your sympathetic system tends to excite or *arouse* you. Activity in your parasympathetic system tends to *depress* many of your bodily functions.

SYMPATHETIC NERVOUS SYSTEM

Your sympathetic nervous system consists of a group of 22 neural centers lying on or close to your spinal cord (see Figure 2.5). From these 22 centers, axonic fibers run to all parts of your body—to the salivary glands in your mouth; to the irises in your eyes; to your heart, lungs, liver, and stomach; and to your intestines and your genitals. Your sympathetic nervous system also connects with your sweat glands, with your hair cells, and with the tiny blood vessels near the surface of your skin.

Whenever you encounter an emergency—something that enrages you, makes you suddenly afraid, creates strong desire, or calls for heavy labor on your part—your sympathetic nervous system swings into action by *speeding up* such bodily activities as heart rate, breathing, and sweating. It elevates your blood-sugar level and sets off various "fright reactions." Because it prepares you for action, sympathetic arousal is sometimes called the "fight or flight" reaction. Sympathetic arousal also controls orgasm and ejaculation, and *slows down* digestion and repair of bodily tissues. Put simply, activity in your sympathetic nervous system prepares you for fighting, for fleeing, and for sexual climax.

Why do people often get red in the face when they get angry?

PARASYMPATHETIC NERVOUS SYSTEM

Your parasympathetic nervous system connects to most (but not all) of the parts of your body that the sympathetic does (see Figure 2.5). In general, parasympathetic stimulation produces physical effects that are the opposite of those induced by sympathetic stimulation. Activity in your parasympathetic system decreases heart rate, slows down breathing, and promotes digestion and excretion. It also controls nipple erection in females and penis erection in males.

Generally speaking, activity in your parasympathetic nervous system *conserves* or builds up your body's resources. For this reason, many people refer to the parasympathetic nervous system as the *vegetative* nervous system (Brown & Wallace, 1980).

For the most part, the two divisions of your autonomic nervous system work together to achieve a *homeostatic balance*. There is one major difference between the

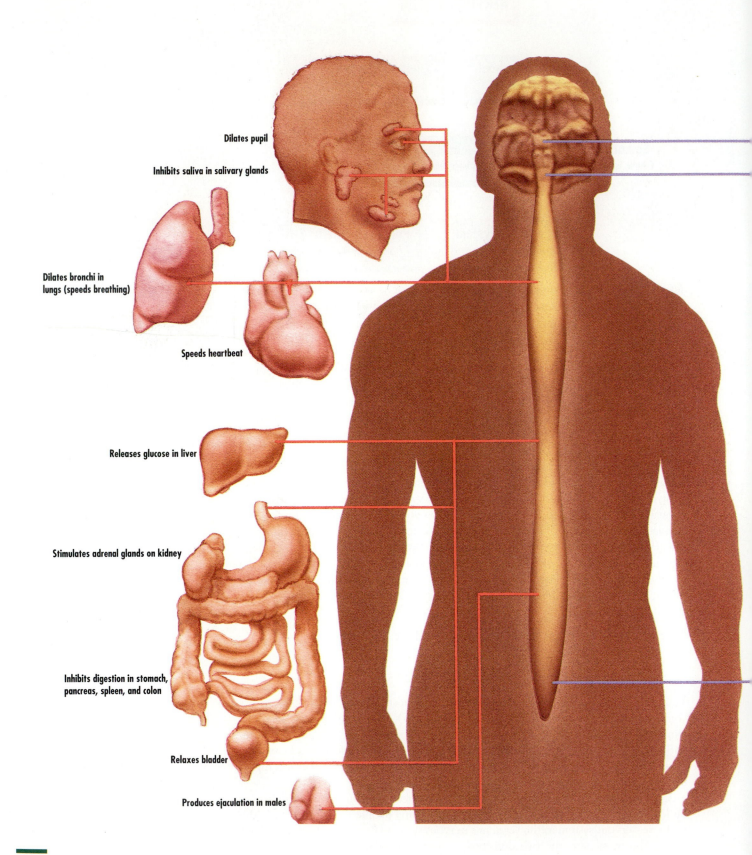

Dilates pupil

Inhibits saliva in salivary glands

Dilates bronchi in lungs (speeds breathing)

Speeds heartbeat

Releases glucose in liver

Stimulates adrenal glands on kidney

Inhibits digestion in stomach, pancreas, spleen, and colon

Relaxes bladder

Produces ejaculation in males

FIGURE 2.5

Schematic layout of the autonomic nervous system. The sympathetic division of the autonomic system prepares the body for action; the parasympathetic division slows down the body's activity to preserve energy.

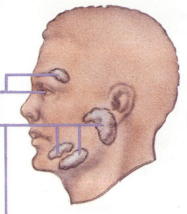

Constricts pupil, stimulates tears

Stimulates saliva in salivary glands

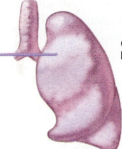

Constricts bronchi in lungs (slows breathing)

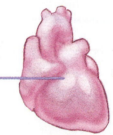

Slows heartbeat

Stimulates sex organs

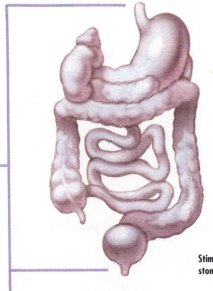

Stimulates digestion by liver, stomach, pancreas, spleen, and colon

Which division of the autonomic nervous system is probably most active as this woman skydives?

two, however: The sympathetic nervous system is connected to the adrenal glands in your endocrine system, while the parasympathetic system is not.

Endocrine System

Endocrine system (END-o-crin). A set of glands, distributed throughout the body, that releases hormones into the blood.

Hormones. Chemicals released by a gland and conveyed by the blood to another part of the body where they alter activity.

Although it is not a nervous system, your **endocrine system** is a control system that is closely related to your autonomic nervous system. Your endocrine system is really a set of glands. These glands exert their control by releasing chemicals, called **hormones,** into your blood. Your blood takes these hormones to other parts of your body where the hormones alter the activities going on there. Figure 2.6 illustrates the glands in your endocrine system.

Hormones alter activity by affecting your nervous system—just like neurotransmitters do. In fact, the same chemical may be used as both a hormone and a neurotransmitter. The difference is that travelling through your blood makes hormones take longer to get to the neurons they are to influence. Neurotransmitters simply travel across a synapse to influence the next neuron. The effect of hormones is more gradual and sometimes longer lasting than the effect of neurotransmitters. We can see the different type of action produced by hormones if we consider your adrenal glands.

You have two adrenal glands, one sitting atop each of your kidneys. Your adrenals produce hormones that influence sexual development and that control such bodily functions as urine production. But these glands also produce two "arousal" hormones—**epinephrin** and **nor-epinephrin.** (The older names for these hormones are adrenalin and nor-adrenalin.)

Epinephrin. (ep-in-EFF-rin, or ep-PIN-eff-rin). One of the two "arousal" hormones released by the adrenal glands. Also called adrenalin.

Nor-epinephrin (NOR-ep-in-NEFF-rin). The second of the two "arousal" hormones released by the adrenals. Injection of epinephrin or nor-epinephrin into the body causes a rise in blood pressure and pulse rate, an increase in the breathing rate, and a general speeding up of bodily functions. Also called nor-adrenalin.

When the adrenal glands release epinephrin and nor-epinephrin into your bloodstream, these hormones act to prepare your body to meet an emergency. Your blood pressure increases, your heart rate and breathing speed up, the pupils in your eyes widen, and your perspiration increases.

As you might guess from this description, the release of epinephrin and nor-epinephrin is under the control of your *sympathetic* nervous system, whose activities the hormones imitate or mimic. When you encounter an arousing situation, your sympathetic nervous system goes into action first, mobilizing your body's energy resources and also causing the secretion of the two "arousal" hormones. As you

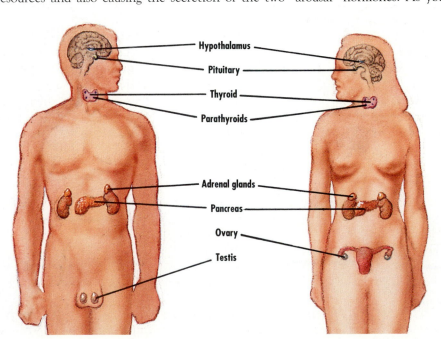

FIGURE 2.6

The major parts of the endocrine system. The hypothalamus (a part of the brain) controls the pituitary, which in turn regulates other glands in the endocrine system.

secrete epinephrin and nor-epinephrin, these hormones continue the arousal process by stimulating chemically the same neural centers that the *sympathetic nervous system* has stimulated electrically.

Why should you have two separate arousal systems? The answer seems to be this: Sympathetic arousal is quick—an "emergency alarm" that mobilizes your body almost instantly. But at times you need *sustained arousal*. It is more efficient for your body to maintain an aroused state by means of the adrenal hormones than by continuous activity in your sympathetic nervous system (Carlson & Hatfield, 1992).

Some other hormones in your body produce even more lasting effects. For example, your male or female physical characteristics are the result of the amount of the male sex hormone (testosterone) that was present when you were developing in your mother's womb. Testosterone at this time may even affect how your brain is organized and whether you are right- or left-handed (Geschwind & Galaburda, 1987).

The pituitary gland (located in your brain) is largely responsible for regulating your endocrine system. The pituitary is, in turn, controlled by a part of your brain called the hypothalamus. We will look at this and other parts of the brain next.

THE BRAIN

Your brain, weighing only about 3 pounds (or 1,350 grams), is the master organ of your body. During open heart surgery, a machine can take over many of the functions of your heart and kidneys. But even though a machine is cleaning and pumping your blood, you remain *you*. Which is to say that your thoughts, dreams, hopes, and general behavior patterns aren't much affected by mechanical substitutes for most of your bodily functions.

However, damage to even a few of your brain's 100 billion neurons may—under certain circumstances—cause you to lose consciousness for the rest of your life. More extensive damage might even lead to rather dramatic changes in your personality. Why? Because your brain is the seat of your self-awareness, the locus of your intelligence, your compassion, and your creativity. All of your mental activities—your thoughts, emotions, and feelings—and all of your bodily processes are affected by the functioning of your brain.

On the other hand, sometimes people can sustain massive damage to major portions of their brains and, if given proper therapy, still recover all the mental and physical abilities they had before the damage occurred. Still and all, from a psychological point of view, your brain is the *single most important part of your body*. Therefore, if you are to understand why you think and feel and act as you do, you must first have some notion of how this master organ operates. But before we look at the brain, let's briefly consider some of the tools scientists have to study the brain.

Windows on the Brain

The oldest method of studying the brain is to observe the functioning of a brain damaged by disease or accident. For example, at the University of Iowa, Antonio and Hanna Damasio are assembling records of hundreds of brain-damaged individuals. They study the damage an individual has suffered and then observe any changes in the person's psychological functioning over several months or years. By combining the results of hundreds of individuals, the Damasios are able to observe patterns of psychological change associated with specific types of damage (Palka, 1990).

In 1929, a German psychiatrist invented a machine to record broad patterns of *electrical activity* in the brain. This machine, called an **electro-encephalo-graph,** or

Brain, n. An apparatus with which we think that we think.

AMBROSE BIERCE, *The Devil's Dictionary*

Electro-encephalo-graph (ee-LEK-tro en-SEF-uh-low graf). An electronic machine that makes a graphic record of general electrical activity in the brain (brain waves).

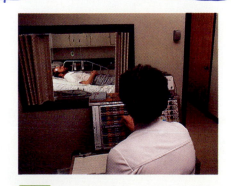

FIGURE 2.7

An electro-encephalo-graph (EEG) picks up patterns of electrical activity from electrodes on the scalp and displays them on a video monitor or prints them on a continuously moving piece of paper.

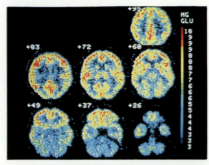

Position emission tomography (PET scan) images of the brain. Different colors indicate the amount of glucose absorbed and thus the level of activity in different regions. The arrangement of colors changes as the subject performs different tasks. By observing these changes, researchers can determine which parts of the brain are most involved in various tasks.

Positron emission tomograph (TOM-oh-graf). A technique for creating images of the brain that reveal areas of *activity*.

Computerized axial tomograph. A device that uses a computer to combine x-ray images and produce an image of the brain (or other internal structure).

Magnetic resonance imaging. A technique for creating an image of the inside of the body. The effects of radio waves on the body are interpreted by a computer to create an image.

EEG, translates electrical energy from the brain into visual patterns on a screen. A scientist who wanted to get an idea of how your brain was performing might place one or more small pieces of metal—called electrodes—on the outside of your head. These electrodes would be connected by wires to the EEG machine. The machine would display the patterns of electrical activity on a screen or print them on a continuously moving piece of paper. (See Figure 2.7.)

The EEG doesn't read the activity of *specific* brain cells, however. Rather, the EEG gives you the same sort of fuzzy, imprecise picture of what is going on inside the skull that you would get outside a huge football stadium if you tried to guess what was happening inside by listening to the roar of the crowd. Standing outside the stadium, you could tell whether the football game was exciting, and when an important play had been made. But you couldn't always tell which team had the ball, or what the score was—much less what individual members of the crowd were doing or experiencing.

Scientists can get a more precise indication of your brain's activity by using a newer tool called the **positron emission tomograph,** or PET scan. This device creates images of your brain that reveal which parts you are using at the time. When mildly radioactive sugar moves into your brain, it races to areas of activity (to provide energy). The area to which it goes depends on the type of mental activity you are involved in. Scientists monitor the location of the radioactive sugar on a video screen to discover the part of your brain involved in the mental activity.

Another way of determining the function of different areas of the brain is to use a small electric probe to stimulate different areas of a surgically exposed brain. We will have much more to say about this technique in a moment.

Scientists have used x-rays to study the interior of the body, including the brain, for years. Recently, however, they have combined the *computer* with x-ray techniques to produce the **computerized axial tomograph,** or CAT scan. This device feeds multiple x-ray pictures, from different angles, into a computer. The computer then combines these images into a "composite photograph" of the brain (or other body part).

One of the newest windows on the brain comes from **magnetic resonance imaging,** or MRI. MRI is a technique that uses radio waves and a strong magnetic field to create computer-generated images of any cross-section of your brain that scientists wish to study (see Figure 2.8). Although the equipment is expensive, the technique

FIGURE 2.8

A magnetic resonance image (MRI) photograph of the brain inside the skull.

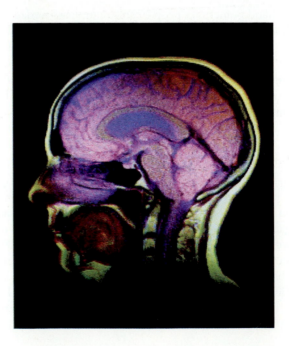

promises exciting advances in our knowledge of the brain's structure. For example, MRI indicates that obvious changes in brain structure accompany some forms of the severe mental disorder called **schizophrenia** (Degreef et al., 1992; Lieberman et al., 1992).

Brain Organization

Because of the extreme complexity of the brain and nervous system, we must think of the brain and its connections in terms of *systems*, and we use analogies or models to help us understand (Hebb, 1955; Melzack, 1989). For example, we might compare your body to a corporation that is organized into different levels of management. (The word corporation actually comes from the Latin word meaning body.)

LOWER MANAGEMENT: THE HINDBRAIN AND MIDBRAIN

The lowest level making "management" decisions is actually below your brain, in your spinal cord. For example, when you touch a hot stove, sensory-motor connections in your spinal cord withdraw your hand even *before* your higher levels of conscious awareness are notified.

The next level of management occurs at the top of your spinal cord. Your **medulla** and **pons** are two bulges just above the point where your spinal cord enters your brain (see Figure 2.9). The medulla controls your breathing, heart rate, and blood pressure, as well as your coughing and sneezing reflexes. Both the medulla and pons control head movements like chewing and swallowing. The medulla and pons also control *postural reflexes* which help you keep your balance as you move or stand. Finally, the

Schizophrenia (skitz-oh-FREN-ee-uh, or skitz-oh-FREEN-ee-uh). A serious psychological disorder (*not* split-personality). We will discuss this and other disorders in Chapter 15.

Medulla (med-DULL-uh). An enlargement of the brain stem involved in regulating vital bodily functions and certain reflexes. Also involved in conveying messages to higher brain centers.

Pons (PAHNZ). A bulb-like structure at the top of the brains stem involved in head movements and postural reflexes. Also involved in conveying messages to higher brain centers.

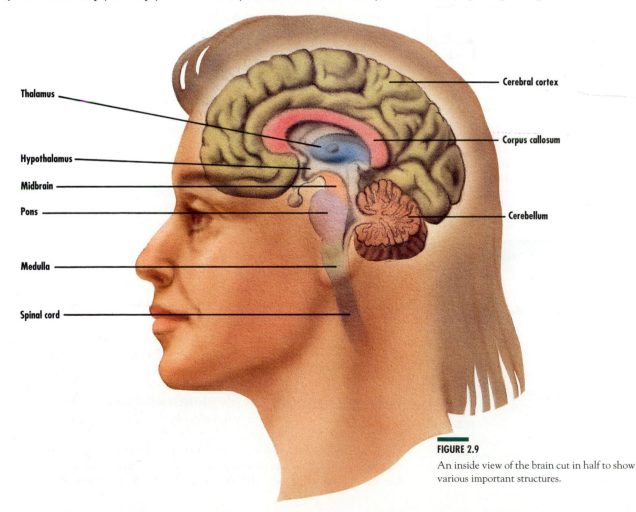

FIGURE 2.9

An inside view of the brain cut in half to show various important structures.

Cerebellum (sair-uh-BELL-um). The distinct ball-like structure behind the brainstem and below the cerebrum; involved in coordination and balance.

Midbrain. A small structure above the pons; plays a role in arousal, vision, and hearing.

medulla and pons relay incoming information to higher centers in your brain, and pass along responses from higher centers to muscles and glands.

Behind the medulla and pons is your **cerebellum.** Your cerebellum manages your muscular activities so that they are integrated smoothly. It also coordinates your sense of balance. The medulla, pons, and cerebellum, together form your *hindbrain*.

Your **midbrain** is a small structure just above the medulla and pons, and slightly in front of the cerebellum. It plays a limited roll in arousal, vision, and hearing. Damage to part of the midbrain leads to movement difficulties associated with Parkinson's disease.

We compare brain stem activities to a low level of management not because these activities are unimportant. Even a small amount of damage here can cause death. Brain stem control is "low level" because it governs basic functions, and does it without our conscious control.

In spite of the delegated authority of these lower centers, however, in emergency situations your "top management" may assume direct and voluntary control over almost any of your automatic responses. For the most part though, you are free to dream and scheme as you wish, leaving basic physical processes under the control of "lower management" in your spinal cord and the lower parts of your brain.

If you had to consciously think about keeping your heart pumping and your lungs breathing, what problems could you foresee?

UPPER MANAGEMENT: THE FOREBRAIN

Cortex (CORE-tex). The thin outer layer of the brain. The convoluted outer layer of the cerebrum. The millions of nerve cells (neurons) in your cortex influence most of what you think, feel, and do.

At the very top of your brain is a large collection of neurons that make up what is called the **cortex** of your brain. *Cortex* is a Latin word meaning the "bark" of a tree. The thin outer "bark," or skin of a mushroom is often darker and tougher than the tissue inside, and the cortex or thin outer layer of your brain likewise differs from the neurons inside.

Your cortex contains millions of very special neurons that seem to be intimately related to your moment-to-moment thoughts, or your "stream of consciousness." It is mostly in your cortex that conscious decisions are made about what your own "corporation" or body is going to do. The cortex is about 1/4 inch (0.6 centimeters) thick. This cortical "peel" covers the biggest part of your brain, which is called the **cerebrum** (from a Latin word for "brain").

Cerebrum (ser-REE-brum). The big, thick "cap" on the top of your brain. Human beings have bigger cerebrums than any other animal. The word "cerebral" (meaning "mental") comes from "cerebrum." Most of your important mental functions take place in your cerebrum. The outer layer of the cerebrum is the cortex.

Your cerebrum sits on top of your hind and midbrain much as the huge cap of a mushroom sits on top of its skinny stem. If you could look at your brain from the top, all you would see would be the cortical covering, or the cap of the cerebral mushroom (see Figure 2.10).

If you inspected the brains of lower animals, you would find that a human being has a better-developed cerebrum than a monkey, that a monkey has more cerebral tissue than a dog, a dog more than rat, a rat more than a pigeon, and a pigeon more than a goldfish. In general terms, the better developed an animal's cerebrum is, the more complex its behavior patterns are likely to be.

Human brains differ from the brains of lower animals mostly in the amount of cortex which they possess. If you looked at the brainstem of a sheep, you might not be able to distinguish it from the brainstem of a human being. But if you compared their cortexes you would have no trouble (Kolb & Wishaw, 1990). Human beings have a large area of cortex organized in a relatively small volume. This is accomplished by "crumpling" the cortex so that it looks like a range of mountains and valleys seen from the air.

Complex intellectual functions—such as writing song lyrics and performing scientific experiments—are controlled by your cerebrum and its cortex. Perhaps this fact explains why biology students are able to study the earthworm, but no one has

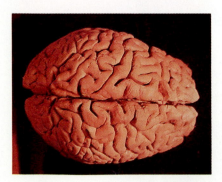

FIGURE 2.10

Top view of the human brain showing deep convolutions in the cortex and the deep fissure separating the two cerebral hemispheres.

ever noticed a worm taking notes on human behavior. It takes a very large corporate structure indeed to produce such complex outputs as songs, automobiles, or notes on your professors' lectures.

Your brain is the most important part of your body (psychologically), but what is the most important part of your brain?

Underneath the cerebrum, just above the brain stem, is a small structure called the **thalamus.** The thalamus is an intermediate "manager" for processing sensory information on its way to the cerebral cortex. Just ahead of the thalamus is the **hypothalamus.** The hypothalamus together with inner parts of the cerebrum (the **hippocampus** and the **amygdala**) make up the **limbic system.** The limbic system plays an important part in motivation and emotion (Joseph, 1992). In Chapter 10 we will discover that the hippocampus and amygdala are also important in memory.

But important as these other structures and systems are, it is the cerebrum and its outer layer the cortex which seem to control our most uniquely human capacities. So let's take a closer look at the cerebrum's two halves, how they are mapped, how they affect handedness, how they are connected, and finally, why they are sometimes *dis*connected.

The Cerebral Hemispheres

As we noted earlier, your cerebrum has "mountains" and "valleys" to it. The biggest "valley of the brain" is a deep groove that runs down the center from front to back, dividing your cerebrum in two parts called the **left cerebral hemisphere** and the **right cerebral hemisphere.** For the most part, the two hemispheres are physical mirror images of each other—just as the left half of your face is (more or less) a mirror image of your right half.

There are four main sections or **lobes** in *each* cerebral hemisphere (see Figure 2.11):

■ The **frontal lobe,** which lies just under the skull in the region of the forehead.

Thalamus (THAL-a-mus). A structure deep within the brain that conveys sensory information to the cerebrum and other parts of the brain.

Hypothalamus (HYPO-THAL-a-mus). A small structure deep within the brain that helps regulate the autonomic nervous system. Also part of the limbic system.

Hippocampus (hippo-CAMP-us). A small part of the inner layer of the cerebrum, that is important for memory. Also part of the limbic system.

Amygdala (am-MIG-dall-ah). A small part of the inner layer of the cerebrum, that is important for emotional arousal. Also part of the limbic system.

Limbic system (LIM-bic). An interconnected group of structures deep within the brain that together are important for emotional reactions.

Left cerebral hemisphere, right cerebral hemisphere (ser-REE-bral HEM-es-sphere). The two halves of the globe-shaped or spherical cerebrum, divided by a deep valley and connected through the corpus callosum.

Lobes. Rounded bumps that typically project out from the organs of the body. Each half of your cerebrum has four main lobes or projections.

Frontal lobe. The part of your cerebrum that lies just above your eyes at the front of the brain. Experiments suggest this part of your brain may be involved in decision-making, among many other things. The *motor cortex* is part of the frontal lobe.

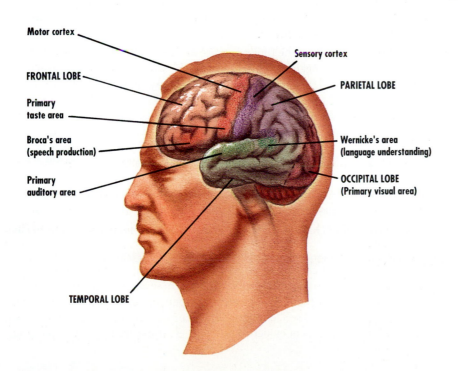

Motor cortex
FRONTAL LOBE
Primary taste area
Broca's area (speech production)
Primary auditory area
TEMPORAL LOBE

Sensory cortex
PARIETAL LOBE
Wernicke's area (language understanding)
OCCIPITAL LOBE (Primary visual area)

FIGURE 2.11

The left view of the brain showing the lobes on the cerebral hemisphere and several areas for different functions.

Parietal lobe (pair-EYE-uh-tal, or puh-RYE-uh-tal). Part of your cerebrum at the very top of your brain. Sensory input from your skin receptors and muscles comes to this part of your cerebrum.

Occipital lobe (ox-SIP-it-tal). The lower, rear part of your cerebrum just above the back of your neck contains the visual input area of your brain, among other things.

Temporal lobe (TEM-por-al). Part of your cerebrum that lies just above your ears, underneath your temples. It seems to be involved in hearing, in speech production, and in emotional behavior, among many other things.

- The **parietal lobe,** which lies under the top center of your skull.
- The **occipital lobe,** which lies at the back of your head, just above your neck.
- The **temporal lobe,** which lies under the skull just above each ear, in the general region of your temple.

As you will see, each of the four lobes of the cerebrum directs different psychological and physiological functions.

SENSORY, MOTOR, AND "SILENT" AREAS

If someone stuck a pin in your arm, you would experience pain. Surprisingly enough, though, if someone stuck a pin directly into your exposed cortex, you probably wouldn't consciously experience any discomfort at all.

With certain minor exceptions, there simply are no pain receptors in the brain. (There are pain receptors in the membrane covering the brain, however.) Because brain tissue is insensitive to pain, patients undergoing brain surgery are often conscious, so they can help the doctor locate whatever damaged section might need to be treated. During such surgery, the doctor may stimulate various parts of the patient's cortex electrically and ask what the patient feels the moment the current is turned on.

What would you experience if you were willing to let a scientist "map" your *entire cortex* with an electrical stimulator? The most dramatic results of all would surely come if the scientist touched the probe to your "motor cortex," which lies at the rear of the frontal lobe on each hemisphere (see Figure 2.11). Stimulation of the nerve cells in the motor cortex in your left hemisphere would cause the muscles on the right side of your body to twitch or jerk, even though you didn't consciously will these muscles to move. Stimulation of the motor cortex in your right hemisphere would, of course, make the muscles on the left side of your body move involuntarily. As confusing as it may seem to you at first, your *right* cerebral hemisphere mainly controls the *left* side of your body, and your *left* cerebral hemisphere mainly controls the *right* side of your body. Thus, the left half of your brain controls your right hand (and foot), and the right half of your brain controls your left hand (and foot).

Stimulation of other areas would also produce some interesting experiences. When the probe was applied to the *occipital lobe* at the back of your head, you would see brief flashes of light or "shooting stars." If the scientist stimulated parts of your *temporal lobe,* you would hear brief bursts of sounds. And if the probe were touched to parts of the *parietal lobe* at the top of your head, you might feel odd "prickly" sensations in your skin. Strangely enough, however, the scientist could apply the probe to large areas of all four lobes without your experiencing anything at all!

The researchers who first electrically mapped the brain concluded your cerebral cortex has three general types of areas:

1. Sensory input areas, where axons in nerve pathways carrying messages from your sense organs make synapse with dendrites of cortical neurons. We will discuss these areas in detail beginning with Chapter 3.

2. Motor output areas, which contains nerve cells whose axons reach out to make contact with the muscles and glands of your body.

3. "Silent" areas, which have no function that can be determined *directly* from electrical stimulation.

The early brain researchers were surprised to find that most of the surface area of the cortex is "silent" to an electrical probe. At first, these early scientists assumed the silent areas were where memories—or *associations* between sensory inputs and motor outputs—were located. These silent parts of the cortex were nicknamed the **association areas.** But many lines of evidence now suggest these are the *cortical processing*

Association areas. Those parts of your cortex which, when stimulated electrically, do not yield any sensory experiences. Although the full functions of these "silent areas" of your cortex are not fully understood, we assume that they are involved in cortical processing—that is, in evaluating incoming sensory information and in storing memories.

areas. It is in these regions that incoming sensory information is processed and evaluated, and where "command decisions" seem to be made.

But besides these basic differences within each hemisphere, there are important differences between each hemisphere.

HEMISPHERIC SPECIALIZATION

The major *physical* difference between the two halves of the brain is that the left hemisphere is usually slightly larger in the temporal lobe area just above the left ear. The major *psychological* difference is the fact that, in most people, the left hemisphere specializes in producing language and other coordinated muscular reactions. As you might guess, these physical and psychological differences are closely related.

Because in Western culture we place a high premium on language production and coordinated activities, we tend to call the left hemisphere the *dominant* half of the brain. If you are strongly right-handed, your left hemisphere is probably your "dominant" hemisphere. The term "dominant" may be a poor choice of words, however, for the *right* hemisphere surely "dominates" in other ways—for example, in the production of emotional and perceptual responses. And, in normal individuals, *both* hemispheres are involved in almost all activities.

A better name for the left half of your brain might be "motor control hemisphere," since this is the side of your brain that manages most of your body movements. When you write, your left hemisphere issues the orders that your right hand and fingers follow. And when you speak, it is this same "dominant" left side of your brain that makes your tongue, lips, and vocal cords move.

Your left hemisphere is better not merely at *producing* language, but also at *understanding* it than is your right hemisphere. (Figure 2.11 shows the primary location in the left hemisphere for both of these processes.) Indeed, your left hemisphere "processes" language *production* even if you are deaf, and use sign language (Damasio & Bellugi, 1986).

Your *right* hemisphere is called by many names—"minor" hemisphere, "perceptual" hemisphere, "emotional" hemisphere, or "monitoring" hemisphere. It understands language, but neither talks nor writes except under rather unusual circumstances. Your right hemisphere does seem to be better at understanding (and producing) art, music, and abstract mathematics than is your left hemisphere.

If you are left-handed, it may be that the right half of your cerebrum is the "talking hemisphere" and produces most of your spoken and written language. Usually, however, your left hemisphere specializes in language (though not other motor activities) whether you're right- or left-handed. However, in some left-handers, both hemispheres share the ability to speak and write, and neither of them is really "dominant." We don't really know why the pattern of hemispheric specialization is different in left-handed people.

"I claimed my left brain didn't know what my right brain was doing, but they didn't buy it."

Why does it seem logical that right-handers should be better at language, while left-handers are better at painting and abstract mathematics? And what reason could there be for the high frequency of right-handedness?

HEMISPHERIC INTERACTION

The two cerebral hemispheres of your brain are joined together by a bridge of very special tissue—much as the North American hemisphere is joined to the southern by a narrow bridge of land we call Central America. The tissue connecting the two hemispheres of your brain is called the **corpus callosum,** two Latin words meaning "thick or hardened body." The corpus callosum contains a large number of axonic fibers that act like telephone cables running from one side of your brain to the other.

Corpus callosum (KOR-pus kah-LOW-sum). The bridge of nervous tissue that connects the left and right hemispheres.

Your "talking" hemisphere and your "perceiving" hemisphere keep in touch with each other primarily through your corpus callosum (see Figure 2.9).

Sensory inputs that reach one of your hemispheres are almost automatically flashed to the other. Thus, if one of your hemispheres learns something, it usually shares the information with the other hemisphere almost immediately.

The situation is similar with your behavioral *outputs*. Suppose, for instance, your left hemisphere sends a message to the muscles in your right hand telling them to write the word "dog" with a pencil. Your dominant hemisphere would immediately let your right hemisphere know what it had commanded your hand to do.

Now, with these facts in mind, can you guess what would happen to you if your corpus callosum were cut, and the two hemispheres of your brain were suddenly *split apart*? This is precisely the question that psychologists Roger Sperry and R. E. Myers were trying to answer when, in the 1950s, they performed their first *split-brain operations* on cats. They ended up making one of the most exciting discoveries in modern psychology. In 1981 Sperry was awarded the Nobel Prize in medicine and physiology in large part because of his "split-brain" studies.

TWO MINDS IN THE SAME BODY.   The surgical technique used by Sperry and Myers involved opening up the cat's skull, then slicing the animal's corpus callosum. They also split part of the optic nerve that runs from the cat's eyes to its brain.

Normally, sensory input from *each eye* goes to *both* cerebral hemispheres along the **optic nerve.** When Sperry and Myers cut the corpus callosum and split part of the optic nerve, they left the cat's eyes as isolated from each other as were the two halves of its cerebrum. Now, whatever the animal's left eye saw was recorded only in the left hemisphere. And whatever the animal's right eye saw was recorded only in the cat's right hemisphere.

Once a cat had recovered from the surgery, Sperry and Myers gave the animal a variety of behavioral tests. First, they blindfolded its left eye and taught the cat to solve a visual problem using *just* its right eye (and, of course, just the right hemisphere of its brain). The cat learned this lesson very well.

Next, they covered the trained right eye with the blindfold and tested the cat on the same problem with its untrained left eye (and left hemisphere). The question was, would any information about the problem have "leaked" from the right half of the cat's brain to the left?

The answer was a resounding *no*. Using just its untrained left eye/left brain, the cat appeared to be entirely ignorant of what it had learned with its right eye/right brain. When Sperry and Myers subsequently trained *just* the left eye (on a different task), the right eye (and hemisphere) seemed unaware of what the left part of the brain had learned. Sperry and Myers concluded that the cat now had two "minds," either of which was capable of learning on its own—and of responding intelligently to changes in the world around it *on its own* (Myers & Sperry, 1958).

Subsequent experiments with rats and monkeys gave similar results. The animals recovered so nicely that, if you hadn't known about their operation, you might not have guessed there were two more-or-less independent "entities" inside each animal's body.

The split-brain surgery was seemingly safe and relatively easy to perform in animals. But what would the operation do to a human being, and why would anyone want to find out? To answer that question, we must look more closely at that odd and unfortunate condition known as epilepsy.

EPILEPSY.   Approximately 2.5 million people in the United States suffer from epilepsy (undoubtedly including some of the readers of this text) (McLin, 1992). Many epileptics are able to live fully functional lives (Seidenberg & Berent, 1992). For some, however, the condition can be life-threatening.

Just for a moment, try to imagine what it might be like if you were unfortunate enough to sustain the type of brain damage that caused you to suffer epileptic attacks.

Optic nerve (OP-tick). The visual input pathway from each eye to the brain. Half of the optic nerve from each eye runs to the left brain, half to the right brain. In order to make sure that input from the cat's left eye went only to its left hemisphere, and that input from the right eye went only to the right hemisphere, Sperry and Myers had to cut half of the optic nerve from each eye.

If damaged nerve cells were in the *input* or *processing* areas of your brain, you might never recognize that you suffered from epilepsy. Seizures in the input and processing areas of the brain typically lead to little more than momentary lapses in consciousness. This type of epileptic attack is called a **petit mal seizure**. If the injured neurons were in your *output* system, however, you might suffer from a full-blown *motor seizure*—a condition that is very hard to overlook.

If your epilepsy resulted from mild brain damage, or if the attack was caused by an overdose of some drug, your seizures would occur infrequently. But if your brain damage was severe, your attacks might happen several times a day—so frequently that you did not regain consciousness between seizures. This rare condition must be treated promptly, for it can lead to death.

The brain damage that causes most epileptic seizures usually has a specific focus or location on one side of the brain. But remember that the two hemispheres are more-or-less "mirror images." Almost every neuron in your *left* hemisphere has a nerve cell in your *right* hemisphere that is its "identical twin," or mirror image. Many of these nerve cells are tied together by axonic fibers that pass through the corpus callosum. Whenever a neuron in your dominant hemisphere fires, it may send a "command message" telling its mirror-image cell in the minor hemisphere to fire too. And whenever the mirror-image neuron fires, it sends a message back to the dominant hemisphere saying that it has fired.

When an epileptic seizure begins in the neurons of one hemisphere, the mirror-image neurons in the other hemisphere receive a "seizure message" via the corpus callosum. This "seizure message" causes the mirror-image neurons to fire very, very rapidly themselves. The cells may even start showing spike activity on their own as they "catch fire" from all the stimulation they are receiving from the other hemisphere. So the spike activity begins to build up simultaneously at the *same spot in both hemispheres*.

In addition, the mirror-image neurons may send seizure messages back to original site of the trouble. This return message from the undamaged hemisphere sets off even more spiking in the damaged area, which then sends even wilder messages back to the mirror-image cells, which causes them to fire even more rapidly.

Each time the seizure message flashes back and forth across the corpus callosum, a few more cells in each hemisphere get caught up in the spiking. Within a few seconds, the whole brain can become involved, and a **grand mal seizure** occurs. An epileptic seizure is a good example of what is called a *positive feedback loop*.

DISCONNECTING THE HEMISPHERES

When medical doctors learned of the Sperry-Myers split-brain operation, they reasoned that if they cut the corpus callosum and separated the two hemispheres of the brain, they could cut the positive feedback loop that typically causes an epileptic attack. And by "cutting the loop," they might prevent full-blown seizures from occurring in patients whose seizures couldn't be controlled by drugs or other medical treatment.

The doctors were right. They tried the operation on a middle-aged man whom we shall call John Doe. During the Korean War, John Doe had served in the armed forces. After parachuting behind the enemy lines, he had been captured and put in a concentration camp. While in the prison camp, he had been struck on the head several times with a rifle butt.

Shortly thereafter, John Doe's epileptic seizures began. By the time he was released from the concentration camp, his brain was in such bad physical shape that drugs couldn't help very much. His seizures increased in frequency and intensity until they were occurring a dozen or more times a day. Without the split-brain operation, John Doe would probably have died—or committed suicide, as had many other epileptic patients with similar problems.

Petit mal seizure (petty mahl). From the French words meaning "small evil," or "little badness." A person suffering a petit mal attack loses consciousness for a few seconds, but no motor seizure occurs. Often the person's eyes remain open during this loss of consciousness.

Grand mal seizure (grahn mahl). The most dramatic type of motor epilepsy. The person loses consciousness, collapses, and experiences muscle spasms (convulsions). (The French words *grand mal* mean "great sickness.")

But after the surgeons cut John Doe's corpus callosum, his seizures stopped almost completely—just as the surgeons had expected. Obviously, "cutting the positive feedback loop" had prevented the *grand mal* attacks from occurring.

However, when the doctors split John Doe's brain, they apparently cut his "mind" into two separate but similar personalities as well. Each of these "minds" seemed to exist more-or-less independently of the other, and each of them had its own unique claim on his body (Sperry, 1968). As far has his mental activities were concerned, John Doe had suddenly become Siamese twins.

JOHN-DOE-LEFT AND JOHN-DOE-RIGHT.   Immediately after the operation, John Doe was able to communicate in almost normal fashion. Some of his speech was slurred, as if he didn't have complete control over the muscles in his tongue. But his thinking seemed clear and logical, and he suffered no noticeable loss in intelligence.

But John Doe did have moments of confusion, and he was often unable to coordinate his body movements and his emotional reactions. Every now and then, he reported, the left half of his body did odd things, *as if it had a will of its own.*

John Doe was right-handed, so his "talking hemisphere" controlled his right hand and leg. Occasionally, when John was dressing, his right hand would zip up his pants (as it normally did) and John would start to go about his business. Moments later, however, his left hand (controlled by right hemisphere), would casually reach down and unzip his pants. His left hand did other odd things too, mostly in fairly emotional situations. These behaviors almost always embarrassed John Doe's dominant hemisphere, because he could offer no logical (verbal) explanation for why his left hand was behaving so peculiarly.

The doctors soon began to suspect that when John Doe answered their questions and reported his thoughts, it was *only* his left hemisphere that was doing the talking. Indeed, the left side of his brain seemed blissfully unaware of the perceptions and emotions that were occurring in his right hemisphere. And since his left hemisphere controlled speech output, the right hemisphere couldn't communicate by talking. So, it offered its comments behaviorally—by occasionally doing odd things that would disrupt the ongoing flow of behavior controlled by John Doe's left hemisphere.

The psychologists working with John Doe soon devised ways of communicating with either side of his brain without the other side's knowing what was going on. John-Doe-Left responded *verbally* to most questions the psychologists asked him, since this hemisphere possessed full language control. John-Doe-Right could not talk, but he could *point* to things (with the left hand) in response to questions that John-Doe-Left couldn't hear (Sperry, 1968).

As soon as John-Doe-Left responded out loud to a question that only it could hear, why would John-Doe-Right usually know what the question had been?

HEMISPHERIC INDEPENDENCE.   Several interesting experiments show the independence of the cerebral hemispheres in split-brain patients, and the specialized function of each hemisphere. In one study, Michael Gazzaniga presented a picture of a snow scene to a split-brain patient's right hemisphere while showing a different picture (a chicken's claw) to the left hemisphere (see Figure 2.12). Had Gazzaniga asked the patient to report *verbally* what he saw, the patient would have answered, "A chicken's claw." The patient also would have *denied* seeing anything else, for only the left hemisphere controlled speech and all it saw was the chicken's claw.

In fact, however, after showing the different pictures to the two hemispheres, Gazzaniga showed the patient drawings of various objects and asked him to select which of the objects "went with the scene." The patient's *right* hand (controlled by the *left* hemisphere) pointed to the drawing of the chicken, but the patient's *left* hand

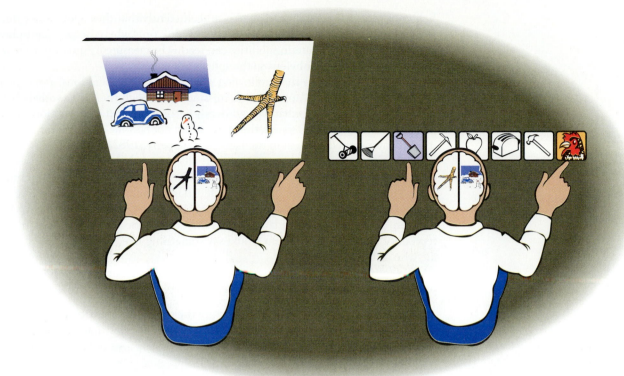

FIGURE 2.12

A patient who has had split-brain surgery is shown two large pictures simultaneously. The chicken's claw is seen by the talking left brain, which controls the right hand. The snowy scene is seen by the non-talking right brain, which controls the left hand. The patient is then shown a series of smaller pictures. Although only the left brain can say which small picture is related to the larger one projected earlier, both hands are capable of *picking out* the related pictures.

(controlled by the *right* hemisphere) pointed to the shovel. As Gazzaniga puts it, "After his response, I asked him why he did that; he looked up and without a moment's hesitation said from his left hemisphere, 'Oh, that's easy. The chicken claw goes with the chicken, and you need a shovel to clean out the chicken shed.'" Gazzaniga believes that, when asked to explain his left hand's "odd behavior," the patient's left hemisphere simply made up a logical story that would excuse the actions (Gazzaniga, 1985).

In another experiment, Sperry showed a male split-brain patient a complex design and then asked the man to reproduce the pattern by putting colored blocks together. When the patient used his left hand (right hemisphere), he completed the task rapidly. But when the man tried to match the design using his right hand (left hemisphere), he proceeded slowly, clumsily, and made many mistakes. And much to the surprise of both Sperry and the patient, the man's left hand often tried to "correct" the mistakes the right hand made (Sperry, 1982).

Oddly enough, there are no reports of cases in which the left hemisphere tries to correct any responses made by the right half of the brain. Indeed, the left hemisphere usually tends to *deny responsibility* for any of the right hemisphere's actions. And if it cannot deny responsibility, then the left hemisphere will *make up a story* explaining why the left half of the body behaved as it did.

The split-brain studies give us fascinating insights into the ways that the two hemispheres may function in individuals (like yourself) with intact brains. For one thing, it appears that the left hemisphere is quite capable of "dominating" the output from both hemispheres—although the right hemisphere may assert itself in certain situations. On the other hand, the right hemisphere is clearly better than the left at perceiving and manipulating visual patterns.

COOPERATION BETWEEN HEMISPHERES

If it seems highly unlikely to you that you have two minds locked away inside your skull, the reason is not hard to find. Although the split-brain research suggests that each of your hemispheres *specializes* in certain types of tasks, for the most part the two halves of your brain *cooperate* so quickly and efficiently that they operate as a "functional unit" rather than as two separate entities. It is only when the two hemispheres are isolated that their differing abilities can readily be measured. And even these differences are not always obvious to the split-brain patient.

Roger Sperry reports that, following their split-brain operations, none of his patients was aware that "anything was missing." Although their left (verbal) hemispheres had lost most of what we call depth perception, and could no longer hear music in full stereophonic sound, the patients did not become aware of this loss until it was demonstrated to them in the laboratory (Sperry, 1982).

More than this, the patients often verbally rejected those few responses that clearly came from their right hemispheres. When Sperry would show a picture of some kind to the right hemisphere, the left hand would identify the picture correctly—but the patient would frequently deny having seen anything at all. And just as often, when the patient's left hand would correct the right hand as it tried to reproduce a pattern, the patient would say something like, "Now, I know it wasn't me who did that!"

The split-brain research has taught us a great deal about human individuality, particularly as regards our "mental processes." Roger Sperry puts it this way:

> The more we learn, the more we recognize the unique complexity of any one individual intellect and the stronger the conclusion becomes that the individuality inherent in our brain networks makes that of fingerprints or facial features gross and simple by comparison (Sperry, 1982).

Sperry's comment reinforces a theme we mentioned in Chapter 1: You are unique. In this chapter we have been discussing *similarities* in the overall structure of our neurons, our nervous systems, and our brains. But underneath these similarities is a pattern for each individual that is like no other.

We will conclude this chapter by looking at another theme from Chapter 1: You are complex—which is to say, your behavior has many causes. One of the oldest issues in psychology, or in any speculation about human nature, is a question concerning two of those causes, "nature" and "nurture." How much of your behavior is the result of inherited characteristics (nature)? And how much is the result of your past experience (nurture)? Let's look at how psychologists try to answer this question.

If the human brain were so simple that we could understand it, we would be so simple that we couldn't.

EMERSON M. PUGH

Behavioral genetics. The study of inherited (genetic) influences on behavior.

Chromosomes (KROH-moh-sohms). From the Greek words *chromo*, meaning "colored," and *soma*, meaning "body." The genes of a cell are strung together like strands of colored beads. These "strands" are the chromosomes.

Genes. The segments of chromosomes that convey a particular characteristic.

FIGURE 2.13

The nucleus of each human cell contains 23 pairs of chromosomes. They have been lined up here in pairs to show they match.

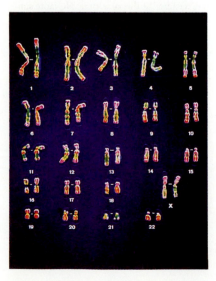

GENETICS

You probably realize that heredity had a lot to do with your physical characteristics like your height, your eye, hair and skin color, and your blood type. But what about your cheerful good nature, or your shyness, or your academic ability? Did you inherit your *psychological* qualities too?

Scientists in the subfield of psychology called **behavioral genetics** try to answer these questions by studying the effects of genes on behavior.

Genetic Development

You began life as a single cell. This egg cell, produced in your mother's reproductive organs, looked much like many other human cells. That is, the egg cell was a tiny round blob of material with a dark nucleus in its center. The nucleus contains what we might call the "managers" of the cell—its **chromosomes.**

Most of the cells in your body contain 23 *pairs* of chromosomes. If you looked at them through a microscope, each of these 46 chromosomes would seem to be a long strand of colored beads (see Figure 2.13). These 46 chromosomes contain smaller units called **genes.** Chromosomes (and genes) are composed chiefly of a substance

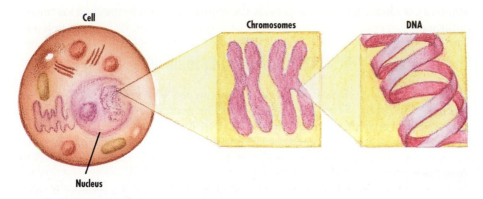

Cell   Chromosomes   DNA

Nucleus

FIGURE 2.14
The relationship of DNA, chromosomes, and the complete cell. The nucleus of each cell contains the chromosome "managers" that carry complex genetic information. This information is coded in spiral shaped molecules of DNA within the chromosomes.

DNA. An abbreviation for deoxyribonucleic acid. The molecules that make up genes.

called deoxyribonucleic acid, which is mercifully abbreviated **DNA** (see Figure 2.14).

Your cells reproduce by dividing. When a cell divides, its nucleus splits in two. Half the DNA in the original nucleus goes into one of the new cells, while the other half of the DNA goes into the other new cell. But before cell division takes place, the nucleus must *double* the amount of DNA present so each new cell will have its full complement of 46 chromosomes the moment the split occurs. Since the new cells have exactly the same DNA, the two cells are "genetically identical."

The only exception to this rule is the case of the sperm and unfertilized egg cells. When a sperm or an egg cell forms through division, the original 23 chromosome pairs split in half *without* doubling, so that the new cell contains exactly half the chromosomes it needs to survive and multiply. Thus, unless the sperm cell fertilizes the egg cell, providing the 46 chromosomes they need to survive, both new cells will soon die. But since the sperm and egg have *different* DNA, they unite to form a cell that is unlike any cell in either the mother's or father's body (Clark, 1985). This is why children are never identical to either parent.

But why are children from the same parents not identical to *each other* (except in the case of identical twins)? The reason that every child is unique is that each sperm and each egg cell is unique. When a sperm or egg cell forms, the original 46 chromosomes divide among the new cells in a *different way each time*. In other words, each new sperm or egg cell has a *different* set of 23 chromosomes. Thus, when a sperm and egg cell combine to form a **zygote,** an individual begins, with a set of chromosomes that has never existed before.

Occasionally, for unknown reasons, a zygote will divide, and two identical individuals will develop. These identical, or **monozygotic twins,** have exactly the same genetic makeup. Fraternal, or **dizygotic twins,** develop when two different sperm cells fertilize two separate egg cells. Fraternal twins are no more alike genetically than any other two children from the same parents.

So, children are never the same as each other (except for identical twins), because each sperm and each egg cell is unique. And children are different from their parents because the sperm and egg cell contribute different genes to the new individual. Children are also different from their parents because many traits are complex *blends* of several genetic characteristics inherited from both parents. Skin color, for example, appears to involve the interaction of four or five different genes. And many more genes may contribute to most psychological traits. Thus, a child may inherit some components of a particular trait from one parent and the rest of the components from the other parent. The result is a quality that neither parent had.

Why does it not make much sense to look for a gene for intelligence?

But despite all these variations, children are still more like their parents than they are like unrelated persons. The chromosomes each child receives are from the limited sample of only two individuals. It is this similarity and the even greater

Zygote (ZY-got). The fertilized egg. The first complete cell of a new individual.

Monozygotic twins (MON-o-zy-GOT-ic). Two genetically identical individuals formed when, for unknown reasons, a zygote divides.

Dizygotic twins (DY-zy-GOT-ic). Two individuals who develop from different zygotes that were fertilized at the same time. No more similar genetically than any other two siblings.

Identical twins develop if after the first division of a single fertilized egg, the two new cells separate. The separated cells will each grow into a complete individual.

similarity of identical twins that provide the main clues to understanding hereditary influences.

Researching Hereditary Influences

Now that you have these facts, perhaps you can see how psychologists begin to untangle the effects of heredity on behavior. The main clue is that people vary in their degree of relatedness, or genetic similarity, in a relatively systematic way. Figure 2.15 gives some examples of these variations. When we compare "relatedness" with similarity on some trait, we get an idea of how strongly the trait is connected to heredity.

For example, researchers sometimes look at families to see if a disorder is more common among people who are more closely related to a person with the disorder. Several researchers have done this for the serious psychological disturbance called schizophrenia. These researchers find that the more closely related a person is to someone who is schizophrenic, the more likely it is that that person will also develop schizophrenia. Figure 2.16 presents a summary of some of these results. First-degree relatives are many times more likely to develop the disorder than are unrelated persons (Gottesman & Shields, 1982; Gottesman, 1991).

These results show that schizophrenia runs in families. But they do not prove that schizophrenia is inherited. Families share environments as well as genes. Family studies provide clues which researchers then follow up in other ways.

One way researchers gather further evidence on the genetic basis of a characteristic is to compare identical twins and fraternal twins. Both types of twins usually develop in similar environments. Therefore, it seems reasonable to assume that if identical twins are more similar than fraternal twins on some trait, then heredity must be influencing the trait. (The comparison between identical and fraternal twins is an attempt to "control for," or equate, the influence of environment—as we discussed in Chapter 1.) In Figure 2.16, the difference between identical and fraternal twins is a further indication that heredity influences schizophrenia.

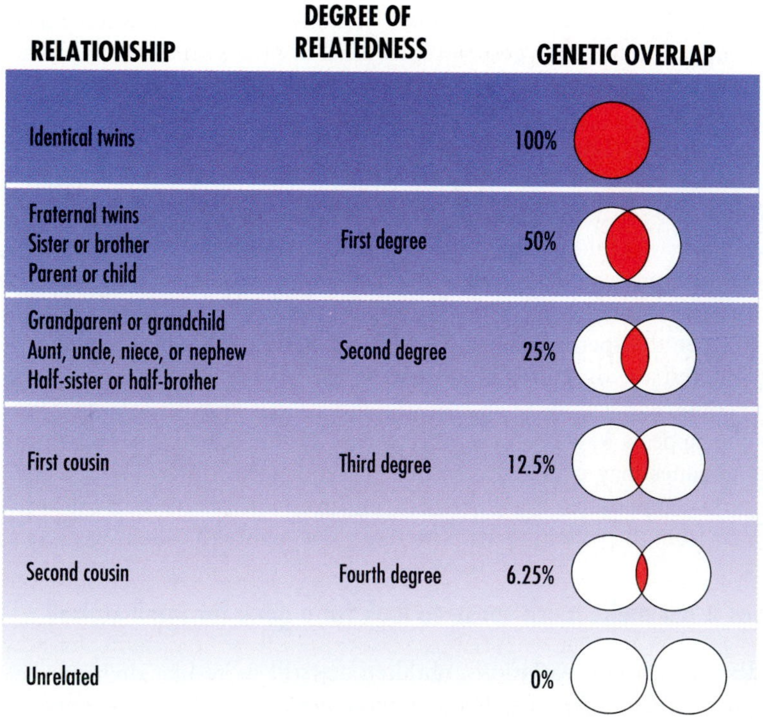

Deep in the cavern of the infant's breast
The father's nature lurks, and lives anew.

HORACE, *Odes* (23 B.C.)

RELATIONSHIP	DEGREE OF RELATEDNESS	GENETIC OVERLAP	
Identical twins		100%	
Fraternal twins Sister or brother Parent or child	First degree	50%	
Grandparent or grandchild Aunt, uncle, niece, or nephew Half-sister or half-brother	Second degree	25%	
First cousin	Third degree	12.5%	
Second cousin	Fourth degree	6.25%	
Unrelated		0%	

FIGURE 2.15

Genetic overlap in relatives with differing degrees of relatedness. As genetic overlap increases, inherited similarities also increase.

RELATIONSHIP TO SCHIZOPHRENIC	PERCENTAGE SCHIZOPHRENIC	DEGREE OF GENETIC RELATEDNESS
Identical twins	48	Identical
Fraternal twins	17	First degree
Siblings	19	"
Children	13	"
Grandchildren	5	Second degree
Nieces/nephews	4	"
Spouse	2	Unrelated
Unrelated people	1	"

FIGURE 2.16

Percentage of schizophrenics in different relationships to person with schizophrenia. (Based on Gottesman, 1991.)

Researchers also track down genetic influence by studying adopted children, in particular, children adopted at a very young age and who have no contact with their biological parents. The researchers compare the traits of these children with the traits of both their biological and their adoptive parents. Similarities between adopted children and their biological parents suggest hereditary factors. Similarities between adopted children and their adoptive parents suggest environmental factors.

Can you think of a way of combining the twin and adoption studies to get another clue to the influence of heredity?

When Steven Vandenberg and George Vogler compared adopted children to both their biological and their adoptive parents on intelligence, they found that adopted children resemble their adoptive parents almost as much as they resemble their biological parents (Vandenberg & Vogler, 1985). Apparently, intelligence is the result of both heredity and environment. This brings us back to the question we started with.

Nature or Nurture?

Actually, phrasing the question as "Nature or Nurture" is misleading. As Donald Hebb pointed out many years ago, it is like asking, "Which determines the area of a rectangle, the length or the width?" (Hebb, 1958). Of course, both are necessary. If either one was zero, the area would be zero, regardless of the other dimension. Similarly with behavior. Without heredity you would not come into being. And without an environment you could not exist.

When psychologists study families, twins, and adopted children, they are looking for *relative* influences in large numbers of people. In some cases we can identify specific chromosomal abnormalities that produce obvious physical and mental differences. But in most cases, the causes of behavior are so complex that we can only estimate relative contributions of heredity and environment. Even disorders with a clearly genetic basis, like **Down's syndrome** and **PKU,** respond dramatically to correct treatment and a supportive *environment*. And although schizophrenia is transmitted along genetic lines, as we have seen, it is never inherited directly. One identical twin may develop the disorder and the other twin remain free of it. So heredity and environment *interact* to produce the full range of human behavior—including your cheerful good nature, your shyness, and your academic ability—nature and nurture are *both* important (Smith, 1993).

Down's syndrome (SIN-drome). A relatively common form of birth defect in which the facial features of the person somewhat resemble Asian or Mongolian characteristics (hence previously called Mongolism). Also called Trisomy-21 (TRY-so-me) because the condition results when a third chromosome becomes attached to the 21st pair. (From the Greek words *tri*, meaning "three," and *soma*, meaning "body.") With proper support and treatment, the person may often lead a relatively normal life.

PKU (Phenylketonuria). A chromosomal disorder that results in reduced brain size, poor muscle coordination, and severe mental retardation. All of these problems may be avoided if the condition is diagnosed and treated early (i.e., from birth).

The Biology of Behavior

We began this chapter with explorer/scientists looking for thoughts in the cells of the human brain. We have examined the structure of those cells. We looked at the parts of the brain and nervous system. We considered how these biological characteristics are passed on from generation to generation. And although we have not discovered thoughts, we have learned something about the biology on which they depend.

We have also seen that these biological processes themselves depend on our environment. In the next two chapters we will see how our physical sense organs operate to keep us in contact with this environment. In later chapters we will discuss biological influences on our consciousness, memory, intelligence, and mental health. Some of the most exciting and promising research in psychology is being conducted on the *biological* bases of behavior. Clearly, the biological approach is an important part of a holistic understanding of human behavior.

SUMMARY

1. Most neurons have three main parts—the **dendrites,** the cell body or **soma,** and the **axon.** A **nerve** is a bundle of axons.

2. The three types of neurons, **sensory neurons, motor neurons,** and **interneurons,** all pass information from one part of the body to another.

3. Neural messages are really waves of electro-chemical energy called **action potentials.** After a nerve "fires" by releasing its action potential, it restores its electrical charge during a **refractory period,** and reaches its **resting potential** when it is ready to fire again.

4. When chemicals called **neurotransmitters stimulate** the dendrites sufficiently, an action potential sweeps down the axon like a bullet speeding down the barrel of a gun.

5. When the action potential reaches the end of the axon, it causes the axon to release **neurotransmitters** into the **synaptic cleft**—the fluid-filled space between the axon of one neuron and the dendrites and cell body of a second neuron.

6. Neurotransmitters released into the **synaptic cleft** excite the dendrites of the second neuron. It typically responds by **firing,** or generating an action potential of its own.

7. Neurons have **receptor sites** in their dendrites and cell bodies that are particularly sensitive to **neurotransmitters.**

8. Some neurons release chemicals which **inhibit neural firing.** If enough of these chemicals are released into a synapse, one neuron will not cause the next to fire.

9. Your brain and spinal cord together form your **central nervous system.** The balance of your nervous system is called your **peripheral nervous system.**

10. Your peripheral nervous system is made up of your **somatic nervous system,** which controls voluntary muscle movements, and your **autonomic nervous system,** which controls involuntary activities in your glands and organs.

11. Your autonomic nervous system is divided into your **sympathetic** and **parasympathetic nervous systems.** Activity in the sympathetic system prepares your body for "fight or flight." Activity in the parasympathetic system acts in the opposite direction to restore a state of relaxation.

12. Your **endocrine system** produces **hormones,** which travel in your blood to other areas of your body to alter the activities there. **Epinephrin** and **nor-epinephrin** are examples of hormones. These chemicals prepare your body for action just as the autonomic nervous system does.

13. Your **brain** contains approximately 100 billion nerve cells, weighs about 3 pounds (1,350 grams), and is the master organ of your body that coordinates or controls many of the functions of the other organs.

14. Reflexes and simple automatic activities like breathing are controlled by neural connections in your **spinal cord** and **brain stem.** Your brain stem is an enlargement of the spinal cord where the spinal cord enters the skull. The **medulla** and **pons** are two bulges in your brain stem.

15. The **cerebellum,** just behind the medulla and pons, controls the coordination of complex muscular activities. Above the brain stem is the **midbrain,** which plays a role in arousal, vision, and hearing.

16. The largest parts of your brain are the two **cerebral hemispheres** that sit atop the stem of your brain like the cap on a mushroom.

17. Underneath the cerebrum and above the brain stem are your **thalamus** and your **hypothalamus.** These structures together with the **hippocampus** and the **amygdala,** inner parts of the cerebrum, make up your **limbic system.**

18. The thin outer covering of the cerebral hemispheres is called the **cortex.** Many of the functions of the brain that relate to conscious decision-making are located in the cortex.

19. Your cortex is made up of the **frontal lobe,** the **parietal lobe,** the **occipital lobe,** and the **temporal lobe.**

20. The **major function** of your brain is to **process information** in order to produce **thoughts, feelings,** and **behaviors.**

21. The two hemispheres of your brain are connected by a bridge of tissue called the **corpus callosum.**

22. In right-handed people, the **left hemisphere** is specialized for speech, and controls coordinated movements of the body.

23. The **right hemisphere,** or perceptual/emotional hemisphere can understand most language, but does not usually speak. It seems more specialized to handle perceptual patterns and emotional expression than is the left hemisphere.

24. Damage to various parts of the brain can cause a condition known as **epilepsy.** If epileptic seizures become too frequent or severe, a surgeon may cut the corpus callosum. This **split-brain operation** may leave the patient with "two minds in the same body."

25. In split-brain patients, the right hemisphere can **communicate** with the outside world by moving the left hand. However, the left (speaking) hemisphere will often **deny** that responses initiated by the minor hemisphere actually occurred, or will **fabricate** excuses to explain the response.

26. In right-handed normal individuals, what we call the stream of conscious awareness seems to be mediated primarily by the **left hemisphere,** but it is strongly influenced by activities in many other cognitive and emotional systems, particularly those in the right hemisphere.

27. Scientists in **behavioral genetics** try to determine the influence of inherited characteristics on behavior. They study the mechanisms of heredity, **DNA, chromosomes,** and **genes.** And they study patterns of traits in different levels of **relatedness.**

ANSWERS FOR THOUGHT

1. *In what way is the "chemical firing" in an A-I-B junction very different from the "electrical firing" within the neuron?*

   "Electrical firing" within the *cell* is all-or-none. Within the *synapse* any level of excitatory and inhibitory chemical is possible. Since several neurons may junction at a particular synapse, and each may require a different amount of stimulation to fire, different levels of neurotransmitter may cause some neurons to fire and not others. Thus, chemical transmission at the synapse introduces an element of variability into neural transmission. (For computer buffs, this difference is similar to that between a digital and an analog computer.)

2. *Why do people often get red in the face when they get angry?*

   Anger, and other emotions, are associated with the action of the sympathetic nervous system. When you get angry your sympathetic nervous system prepares you to fight (or flee). Part of this preparation is an increase in heart rate and blood pressure, which could cause redness in the face.

3. *If you had to consciously think about keeping your heart pumping and your lungs breathing, what problems could you foresee?*

   Unless some other mechanism took control over your heart and lungs, when you went to sleep you would die.

4. *Your brain is the most important part of your body (psychologically), but what is the most important part of your brain?*

   Those abilities which we associate with being human, such as the ability to use complex language, abstract thought, and the ability for self-reflection, are all most closely associated with the outer layer of the cerebrum, called the cortex. Other areas, such as the brain stem, are necessary for life. But the convoluted cortex appears to be the most distinctive feature of the human brain, and thus arguably the most important.

5. *Why does it seem logical that right-handers should be better at language, while left-handers are better . . . ?*

   Biological factors produce superior development of one hemisphere over the other (Previc, 1991). For unknown reasons, the left hemisphere specializes in sequential activities (like language), and the right hemisphere specializes in spatial activities (like painting and abstract mathematics). Superior physical development of one hemisphere produces superior skills in the relevant areas. The more developed hemisphere also exercises greater control over the opposite side of the body, producing "handedness." Right-handers are probably more common because left hemisphere activities (like language), not right-handedness, are more important to human beings.

6. *As soon as John-Doe-Left responded out loud to a question that only it could hear, why would John-Doe-Right usually know what the question had been?*

   Because John-Doe-Right could still hear and understand language (although not speak it), he could hear and understand the answer. He could also think logically and come up with a reasonable guess as to what must have been asked.

7. *Why does it not make much sense to look for a gene for intelligence?*

   Virtually all behaviors and abilities are affected not by one but by *many* genes. Each gene may make different contributions in different people to the same overall ability. Furthermore, in the case of intelligence, there are probably *many different abilities* involved.

8. *Can you think of a way of combining the twin and adoption studies to get another clue to the influence of heredity?*

Identical twins reared together can be compared to identical twins separated at birth and reared apart (adopted). Greater similarity of twins reared together would be the result of their more similar *environment*. Similarities between twins reared apart would suggest *hereditary* factors.

CHAPTER 3

THE SENSES

When I had waited a long time, very patiently, without hearing him lie down, I resolved to open a little—a very, very little crevice in the lantern. So I opened it—you cannot imagine how stealthily, stealthily—until, at length a simple dim ray, like the thread of the spider, shot from out the crevice and fell full upon the vulture eye.

It was open—wide, wide open—and I grew furious as I gazed upon it. I saw it with perfect distinctness—all a dull blue, with a hideous veil over it that chilled the very marrow in my bones; but I could see nothing else of the old man's face or person: for I had directed the ray as if by instinct, precisely upon the damned spot.

And have I not told you that what you mistake for madness is but over acuteness of the senses?—now, I say, there came to my ears a low, dull, quick sound, such as a watch makes when enveloped in cotton. I knew that sound well, too. It was the beating of the old man's heart. It increased my fury, as the beating of a drum stimulates the soldier into courage.

But even yet I refrained and kept still. I scarcely breathed. I held the lantern motionless. I tried how steadily I could maintain the ray upon the eye. Meantime the hellish tattoo of the heart increased. It grew quicker and quicker, and louder and louder every instant. The old man's terror must have been extreme! It grew louder, I say, louder every moment!—do you mark me well? I have told you that I am nervous: so I am. And now at the dead hour of the night, amid the dreadful silence of that old house, so strange a noise as this excited me to uncontrollable terror. Yet, for some minutes longer I refrained and stood still. But the beating grew louder, louder! I thought the heart must burst. And now a new anxiety seized me—the sound would be heard by a neighbour! The old man's hour had come!

EDGAR ALLAN POE
"THE TELL-TALE HEART"

MAKING SENSE OF YOUR SENSES

According to popular opinion, there are but five senses—vision, hearing, taste, smell, and touch. But there is also "common sense," which is unfortunately rare; "non-sense," which is unfortunately common; and the "sixth sense," which some people claim warns them of impending disaster (and which may be just ordinary "horse sense").

In truth, there are *more* than five senses, no matter how you wish to define the word "senses." For example, in this chapter, you will discover that what most people call "touch" is not one sense, but several: (1) temperature, (2) pressure, (3) feedback from your muscles and joints, and even (4) the closely related sense of pain (which is not what it seems). To make matters even more complex, you will also find out that taste is both simpler and more complicated than you might have imagined, that you have a smell "signature," and that vision and hearing are both "vibratory" senses. And in case you have any doubts, some of these facts are guaranteed to be sensational!

In order to help you "make sense" of your senses, let's begin by taking an imaginary journey into the world of computer technology and robotics. That is, let's try to figure out what sorts of sensory information a *robot* would need in order to survive in outer space. For if you can understand what inputs a complex machine would need to survive "out there," perhaps you'll understand better what sorts of sensory experiences *you* require in order to survive on the planet Earth.

This life's five windows of the soul

WILLIAM BLAKE (1757–1827)

Project "Robot"

Let's assume that you are hired by the National Aeronautics and Space Administration (NASA) to help with "Project Robot." Your first assignment is to decide what kinds of sensory inputs the robot should have. If the robot is to survive, like you, it must be able to gather information from its environment as well as know what's going on inside its own "body."

There are two basic types of senses you might give your robot, "local" senses, and "distance" senses. Your skin senses, including taste, are *local* senses—that is, they give your brain information about the exact point on your body that is being stimulated. Olfaction, hearing, and vision are *distance* senses—that is, they typically tell your brain what is going on some distance away from the surface of your body.

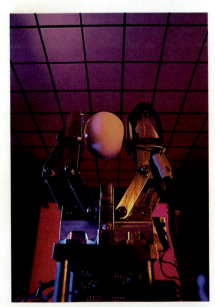

This robot reacts to sensory input much as people do.

Transduce (trans-DOOSE). To transduce is to change something from one form into another. Your eyes transduce light waves into neural energy, which is sent to your brain as a sensory input message.

Why are "distance" senses particularly important?

The major purpose of sensory inputs is to give you a coherent picture of both your internal and your external environments so you can achieve your goals in life—including that of surviving. If you don't get the proper inputs, or don't use them correctly, you won't be around for very long. Getting the proper inputs is not too difficult for most of us—we have but to open our eyes and ears and "take in the world." So how do you make sense out of these inputs? Well, that's one of the chief functions your brain serves—to tie together sight and sound and touch and smell and taste into one *coherent whole* (Bloom & Lazerson, 1988).

To "make sense" of an input may seem easy—after all, your brain performs this task routinely millions of times a day. But think about the *sensory process* for a moment. Suppose you are the murderer in Edgar Allan Poe's *The Tell-Tale Heart*. You see the "vulture's eye" because of light rays reflecting from the old man's face. Your *brain*, however, is not sensitive to light. Your eyes must *translate* or **transduce** those light rays into a pattern of neural messages. Then your eyes send those input messages to your brain. Your brain momentarily "stores" these neural signals while it checks its memory banks, and "recognizes" the pattern. Your brain then combines the *sight* of the eye with the "low, dull, quick sound" of the heart beat and somehow produces a coherent mental image—that of the despised old man.

Sensory psychology deals with each of the various types of inputs you can detect— sight, sound, smell, taste, and touch. Psychologists studying sensation examine the way you respond to these various types of stimulation. They look at three main areas: the physical stimulus, the biological sensory system, and your subjective reaction to the stimulus. You will see how these three areas interact when we look at thresholds in the next section.

On the other hand, psychologists studying *perception* are more interested in the way you interpret, integrate, and organize your sensations. Obviously sensation and perception are closely related. At times they even overlap. So, following our discussion of sensation in this chapter, we will focus on perception in Chapter 4.

Is there a difference between the way a measuring instrument, such as a scale for weight, "senses" a physical stimulus and the way you sense the same stimulus?

Thresholds: The Units of Sensation

One of the first questions asked by psychologists studying sensation was, "What are the basic units of sensation?" They wanted to know the lowest level of sensory stimulation that people could detect (the **absolute threshold**), and the smallest amount of increase which they could notice (the **difference threshold**).

Just how sensitive are you? Could you see a candle flame 30 miles away? hear a watch ticking 20 feet away? smell a drop of perfume in a three-room apartment? feel the wing of a bee falling on your cheek? For an average person, under optimal conditions, the answer to all of these questions is "yes" (Galanter, 1962).

Actually, the ability to detect stimuli presented near an absolute threshold varies from person to person and from time to time. Factors such as the type of stimulus, the state of your nervous system, and the costs of errors all make a difference. To overcome these problems, sensory psychologists studying **psychophysics** determine absolute thresholds by *averaging* the responses of many people at different times.

How much sugar would you have to add to a cup of coffee before the coffee would taste sweeter?

Besides knowing the *absolute* threshold for the different senses, psychophysicists also like to know the difference threshold. The difference threshold is the smallest amount a stimulus must *change* (increase or decrease) before you can detect that it has changed. For example, if you were carrying a 50-pound basket of apples, and a friend removed one which weighed 1/2 pound, you would not notice the difference in weight. But if your friend took 2 apples, the 1-pound difference would probably be just noticeable.

But what if you had only two apples in a bag, and your friend took one out? This time you would detect the reduction in weight quite easily. Why the difference? Because, as Ernst Weber discovered more than 100 years ago, the amount of change needed to produce a noticeable difference in a stimulus is a *proportion* of the original stimulus intensity.

Absolute threshold. The minimum amount of stimulus energy necessary for an observer to detect the stimulus.

Difference threshold. The minimum *difference* between two stimuli which can be detected. Also called a *just noticeable difference* or JND.

Psychophysics. The study of the relationship between a physical stimulus and the subjective (psychological) perception of it. One of the first topics in the new field of psychology in the 19th century.

Weber's law. The discovery by Ernst Weber, that the just noticeable difference (JND) is a constant proportion (K) of the original stimulus level (S). May be expressed as: K=JND/S.

Weber's discovery was more than an interesting fact about sensory stimuli. The significance of Weber's finding was that it showed there is *not* a direct correspondence between a physical stimulus and the experience of it. Equal-stepped increases in a stimulus do *not* produce equal-stepped increases in the sensory experience of the stimulus. (Adding an apple at a time to a basket causes a noticeable change when you have only few apples, but not when you have many.)

While **Weber's law** applies mainly to sensory stimuli in the mid-range, a similar principle seems to apply more generally in other situations. For example, imagine you are buying a tape recording by your favorite artist. The store you are in is selling it for $10. Before you buy it, you discover that another store 6 blocks away has the same tape for $5. Would you walk to the other store to save $5? What if you are ready to buy a stereo system for $1,000 in one store, and discover that another store has the same stereo for $995. Although you might walk to save $5 on the tape, it is less likely that you would walk to save $5 on the stereo system. The larger base price of the stereo makes $5 seem a very small difference.

In designing your robot then, you would have to decide for each type of stimulus, the minimum amount of stimulation to which it should respond. You would also have to decide how sensitive to stimulus *change* your robot should be. And you might want to consider whether or not sensitivity to change should be related to the original amount of stimulation.

What advantage can you see to tying stimulus-change sensitivity to stimulus intensity?

Adaptation and Habituation

The fact that you respond to slight changes in stimulation only when the basic level of stimulation is low, is probably a good thing. For example, if every small sound caught your attention when you were in a noisy crowd, you would probably find the stimulation overwhelming, or at least very distracting. By responding to small changes when stimulation is low, and large changes when stimulation is high, your nervous system is able to function more efficiently.

Your nervous system also increases its efficiency by ignoring *continuous* stimulation. It does this in two ways: first, by what we will call *receptor adaptation;* second, by what we will refer to as *central habituation*. Receptor adaptation occurs in the receptor neurons themselves, while central habituation occurs in your brain.

As an example of *receptor adaptation*, consider what happens when you first sink into a tub of water that is 20° F warmer than your skin. As you know, your temperature receptors will begin to fire vigorously. But as you remain lying in the tub, your skin itself warms up. After a short period of time, the temperature receptors in your skin will fire less vigorously because the temperature of your skin is now much closer to that of the water. Because your skin and your temperature receptors have adapted to the heat, the water will now seem much less hot to you (Schiffman, 1990).

As an example of *central habituation*, think of what happens when you move into a house beside a busy highway. At first, you notice the sounds of the traffic almost continuously. But after a few days, your brain will stop paying much attention to the continuous drone of the passing cars and trucks. Indeed, you may be surprised when a visiting friend asks how you can stand the noise. But in this case, it is your *brain* that has changed its ways of responding to a constant input, not the receptors in your *ears*.

In general, we use the term *adaptation* whenever your receptor cells themselves slow down or reduce their firing rates in response to a constant stimulus. We use the term *habituation*, however, to refer to your brain's tendency to ignore sensory inputs that seem of little interest or importance.

We learn to "tune out" background noises through a process called "central habituation."

When you have been soaking in a hot tub for a while, can you make the water feel warmer just by paying attention to it? When you have lived by a noisy highway for a while, can you hear the traffic just by paying attention to it? What do your answers to these two questions tell you about the differences between receptor adaptation and central habituation?

TOUCH—MORE THAN SKIN DEEP

Your skin is your main organ of touch, and it is *one of the most important sensory organs* your body has. It is by far the largest organ in your body: It weighs about 9 pounds (4 kg) on the average (your brain is but a third that weight), and covers about 3,000 square inches (1.9 m²). Your skin not only gives you sensory information, it gives your physical protection from the elements as well. Thus, when your boss at NASA assigns you the task of deciding what kind of "skin" the robot should have, you are rather pleased. You have been asked to design one of the most critical parts of the robot's body.

To start matters off, you ask yourself a very important question: "What purpose does the skin serve?" A little thought convinces you that your skin answers many needs. It keeps your vital organs "inside" where they belong, and keeps the outside world "outside" where it belongs. Your skin stretches as you gain weight and shrinks when you shed a few pounds. It also helps regulate your internal temperature, for it has several layers to it that help insulate you against the cold. And when you get too hot, your skin has sweat glands that release water which cools you by evaporation.

Most important, however, your skin is filled with *receptors* that let you know what the world around you is like. If you had no skin receptors, you wouldn't know when you had hurt yourself. You also wouldn't know when you were touching something, and whether what you touched was hard or soft, hot or cold. Imagine trying to type a term paper, or play a musical instrument, if your skin didn't give you *feedback* on what your fingers were doing. How long do you think you could survive without having *sensory knowledge* from your skin as to what your body was doing?

Just what kind of sensitivity do you have in your skin? If you like to experiment on yourself, find several small objects—items like a pencil, a glass, a rubber band, a ring, a key, a piece of cloth—and put them on a table near you. Now, close your eyes and feel each object. Begin by just pressing the palm of your hand down on the objects.

What can you tell about these small objects using what we call *passive touch*—that is, without fingering the objects? You can tell that they are hard or soft, large or small, that they have points, and sharp or rounded edges. All this you learn by detecting different patterns of *pressure*.

Now, close your eyes and have someone place first a wooden object and then a metal object in your hands. You can tell wood from metal in two ways: (1) The wood is softer than the metal; and (2) the wood will feel warm while the metal feels cold.

Your skin receptors give rise to two qualitatively different sensory experiences—*pressure* and *temperature*. It may come as a surprise to you that these two sensations (plus pain, which we will discuss in a moment) are the *only primary sensory qualities* your skin can tell you about. Most psychologists believe that all the information you get from your skin about the world around you is merely a *combination* of pressure sensations and temperature sensations—plus, occasionally, the experience of pain (Hensel, 1981). So let's consider the sensations of pressure, temperature, and pain.

The Pressure Receptors

When you touch an object gently (passively), you depress or deform your skin. Very sensitive nerve cells detect this deformation of your skin and fire off a message to your cortex. This input message moves down the axons of the receptor cells until it reaches your spinal cord, then moves up the cord to the stem of your brain. From your brain stem, the message flows through several "lower centers" and finally works its way up to your cortex. Your body may respond automatically and unconsciously to these inputs *before* they reach your cortex. But only when the sensory message arrives at your cortex do you realize *consciously* that your skin has encountered a foreign object of some sort.

Now, with the fingers of one hand, gently pinch the palm of your other hand. You will notice that the skin on your palm feels fairly thick. Next, gently pinch the skin on your forearm. The skin is much thinner there. But the major *biological* difference is that the skin on your forearm has hairs on it, while the skin on your palm does not. Some 95 percent of the skin on your body (whether you are male or female) is *hairy* skin. Only the palms of your hands, the soles of your feet, your lips and mouth, your eyeballs, some parts of your sex organs, and a few other scattered areas are covered with *hairless* skin.

HAIRLESS SKIN

Encapsulated nerve endings (en-CAP-sue-lated). Encapsulate means to enclose or to envelop. When you put on a cap, you encapsulate your head.

Corpuscles (KOR-pus-sulls). The Latin word corpus means "body." We get our English words "corpse" (a dead body), "corps" (the Marine Corps), and "corporation" (a body of people) from this same Latin term. A corpuscle is a "little body" or "little cell," particularly one that is isolated from others like it. The red blood cells, for instance, are called the "red corpuscles."

Hairless skin contains tiny receptor cells that are called **encapsulated nerve endings.** Some of these encapsulated nerve endings look much like small onions and are known as **corpuscles.** If you were to cut one open, you'd find that corpuscles have many layers to them, much like small onions (see Figure 3.1) (Van De Graaff & Fox, 1989).

HAIRY SKIN

Hairy skin has a few encapsulated nerve endings in it. It also has a unique type of touch-receptor neuron buried at the base of each hair. The fibers of these nerve cells wind around the bottom of each stalk of hair. Whenever the hair-stalk is pushed or pulled in any direction, it squeezes the nerve fibers so that they fire off a "pressure"

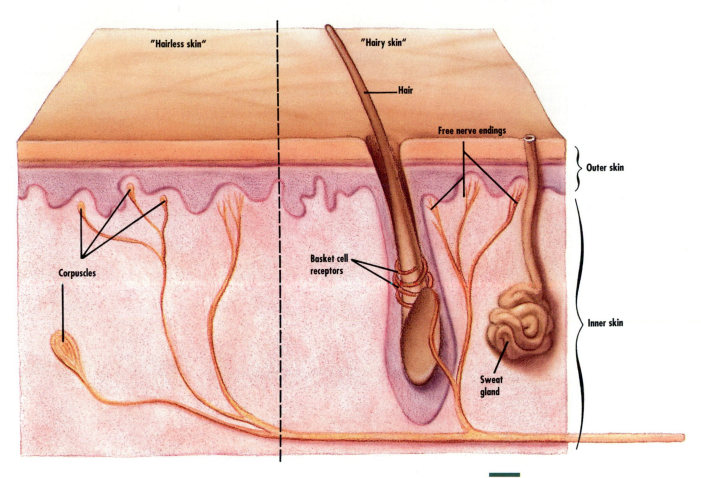

message to your brain. We call these hairy-skin receptors "basket cells" because they look like a wicker basket wrapped around the bottom of the hair stalk (Solomon & Davis, 1983). (It is the basket cell, not the hair itself, that is the "receptor," of course.)

FREE NERVE ENDINGS

Both hairy and hairless skin also contain receptor neurons called *free nerve endings*. "Free" in this case means the "input ends" of the receptor are not attached to any particular place (see Figure 3.1). The free nerve endings are very simple nerve cells whose fibers spread out freely like the branches of a vine just under the outer layers of your skin. Since the free nerve endings are found everywhere on the surface of your body, they are by far the most common sort of skin receptor that you have (Seeley et al., 1989).

Surprisingly, there does not appear to be a simple relationship between skin-receptor type and function. All three types of receptors—the encapsulated nerve endings (including the corpuscles), the basket cells, and the free nerve endings—yield a simple "pressure sensation" when they are stimulated. The free nerve endings are the primary source for the pain sensation, and some of the free nerve endings and basket cells are also sensitive to temperature.

DEEP RECEPTORS

You also have pressure receptors deep below your skin in your muscles, joints, and tendons. Pick up a pencil, close your eyes, and roll the pencil around in your hand. You can tell at once what size, shape, and weight the pencil has. It is not just your

FIGURE 3.1

A schematic diagram of the skin. Basket cell receptors are found only in hairy skin. Corpuscles are found primarily in hairless skin. Free nerve endings are found in hairy and hairless regions.

In zero gravity conditions, your proprioceptors don't give you the information you need to tell up from down.

Proprioceptor (proh-pree-oh-SEPT-tur). A type of pressure-sensitive nerve ending (corpuscle) located in the muscles, joints, and tendons, to provide feedback to the brain on muscle movements, muscle tension, and body position.

surface or skin receptors that give you this information. We could anesthetize all the nerves in the skin of your hand, and you would still be able to tell the size, shape, and weight of the pencil.

Whenever you contract a muscle in your hand, a tiny nerve cell, called a **proprioceptor,** buried in that muscle sends a feedback signal to your somatic cortex saying the muscle is in operation. The heavier an object is, the harder your muscle must work to lift the object and hold it steady. And the harder the muscle pulls or contracts, the more rapidly the tiny receptor neuron buried in the muscle fires—and the more intense feedback you get (Seeley et al., 1989).

COMPLEX PRESSURE SENSATIONS

Now, rub the palm of your hand over your clothes, the surface of the table, the cover of this book, the upholstery of a chair, or the top of a rug. Some objects feel smooth to your touch, others feel rough. How does your skin tell smooth from rough if it can experience just pressure and temperature?

The answer comes from this fact—when you move your hand across a surface, using what we call *active touch,* you stimulate many receptors at once. Generally speaking, large objects will stimulate a larger and more widely distributed group of sensory cells than will small objects. Thus, you can gain some notion of the *size* of an object by noting how many receptors, and *which* receptors, fire in response to the stimulation (Geldard & Sherrick, 1986). If the surface of an object is rough, some parts of your skin "vibrate" vigorously as you rub your palm across the object. Other parts of your skin vibrate little, if at all. Your brain perceives this pattern of incoming sensory information as "roughness" or "smoothness" (Lederman, 1983).

You can actually *improve* your perception of roughness using a simple technique. Rub your fingers over a smooth piece of ceramic pottery. Now place a piece of very thin paper, such as "onion skin," between your fingers and the pottery, and rub again. You will be able to detect more roughness *with* the paper than without. (If it didn't work, try a different surface, such as a car body.)

This "roughness enhancement" works by reducing friction between your fingers and the surface. When you move your fingers over a surface, the sideways (lateral) force on your skin interferes with the movements your skin must make to detect roughness (Royeen & Kannegieter, 1984).

So, let's presume you put pressure receptors in your robot's fingers, as well as its joints. You (or a computer in the robot's brain) could then tell if an object the robot touched was hard or soft, light or heavy, rough or smooth, simply by decoding the *pattern* of signals from the robot's pressure receptors. You could also put temperature detectors in the robot's fingers and learn whether the object was hot or cold.

But hot or cold in relation to what?

The Temperature Receptors

"Hot" and "cold" are relative terms that, in your body's case, are always related to whatever your skin temperature is. Anything you touch that is *colder* than your skin will seem *cool* to you because heat energy is moving out from your body. Anything you touch that is *hotter* than your skin will seem *warm* because heat energy is flowing into your body. The warmer or colder the object is in relation to your skin temperature, the more rapidly nearby free nerve endings will fire (Hensel, 1981, 1982).

In addition to this detection of *relative* temperature, you can also detect whether something is hot or cold in an *absolute* sense. You actually have specialized "heat receptors" and "cold receptors" (Berne & Levy, 1990). Heat receptors are free nerve endings that are sensitive to temperatures from 77° to 113° F (25–45° C). As 113° F is approached they become unresponsive. Cold receptors are most sensitive to temperatures from 50° to 68° F (10–20° C) (Hole, 1990). (Pain receptors are triggered above 113° F and below 50° F.)

Thus, you have receptors that are sensitive to temperature changes as well as receptors sensitive to warm and cold in an absolute sense.

Distribution of Receptors

If you were building a robot, you would surely want its *fingers* to be more sensitive to pressure and temperature than, say, the middle of its *back*. Robots (like people) would seldom be called upon to make fine discriminations about objects with the "skin" on their backs. So you would probably put *more* sensory receptors in the robot's fingers than on its back.

Generally speaking, those parts of your body that you use most to make sensory discriminations have the most pressure receptors, while those parts that you use least have fewer receptor neurons. Thus, there are more pressure receptors in your finger-tips, your lips, your eyeball, and on the tip of your tongue than elsewhere on your body (Geldard & Sherrick, 1986; Stevens, 1990).

The Somatic Cortex

The messages from receptors in your skin, muscles, and tendons, tell your brain four things:

1. The *location* of the experience—that is, what part of your body is detecting the sensations.
2. The *quality* of the experience—that is, pressure or temperature.
3. The *quantity* or strength of the experience—intense or weak pressure, slightly warm or very cold.
4. The *duration* of the stimulation—whether it is brief or continuing.

Let's see why all of this sensory information is important. Suppose you are walking along barefooted and you step on a tack. As you probably well know, you realize almost instantly what part of which foot has been punctured, how intense the wound is, and whether the tack is still in your foot or has fallen out. How do you become conscious of all this information so quickly?

Well, think for a moment about the NASA robot you are helping design. If you want the robot to *localize* its skin sensations, how would you hook the robot's skin receptors up to its brain? Probably you would want to put in a direct "telephone line" between each receptor and a *specific* part of the "brain." Each receptor would, in effect, have its own "telephone number." The robot could tell where the stimulation was coming from simply by checking to see which telephone line the message was coming over.

An old-fashioned telephone switchboard has a single connection for each incoming line. Message routes can be traced by following the individual lines. Your nervous system uses the same principle to connect sensory areas in your skin to specific input areas in your brain.

Parietal lobes (pair-EYE-uh-tull, or pah-RYE-uh-tull). That part of each cerebral hemisphere located at the very top of the brain. Sensory input from the skin receptors and the muscles comes to this part of your cerebrum.

Somatic cortex (so-MAT-ick KOR-tecks). The outer layer of the parietal lobe is called the parietal cortex. The front section of the parietal cortex receives sensory-input messages from the skin and muscle receptors. This front section is called the "somatic cortex."

Your nervous system is "constructed" in much the same way. Each receptor cell in your skin connects to a specific region in the *sensory input areas* in your **parietal lobes.** Thus, your brain can tell the location of any stimulation on your body by noting *where* the input message arrives in the parietal lobe (Berne & Levy, 1990).

You may recall from Chapter 2 that the parietal lobe in each of your cerebral hemispheres is located at the very top center of the brain. The front edge of the parietal lobe is immediately adjacent to the *motor output area* at the rear of the frontal lobe. The cortex at this front edge of the parietal lobe is often called the **somatic cortex.** "Soma" is the Greek word for "body," and it is to this part of your cortex that all of your body or *somatic receptors* send their sensory messages. Receptors in the left side of your body send their inputs primarily to the somatic cortex in the right half of your brain. The receptors in the right side of your body send their messages to your left somatic cortex (Kolb & Wishaw, 1990).

Now, since you just stepped on a tack, let's consider the experience of pain a little further.

Pain

Fifty years ago, most sensory psychologists believed there were four unique psychological experiences you could get from stimulating your skin—warmth, cold, pressure, and *pain*. Each of these four experiences was thought to be mediated by a specific type of receptor or nerve ending buried somewhere in your skin. But further study turned up some troubling facts:

First, there is the problem of what *receptors* signal pain. There are skin receptors concerned with temperature sensations, and other receptors reporting pressure. But no one ever found a nerve ending *solely concerned* with signalling pain.

Second, there is the problem of where in the brain painful inputs are processed. Investigations of the parietal lobe uncovered parts of the *somatic cortex* that, when stimulated electrically, give rise to the experience of pressure or temperature. But no one ever found a part of the parietal lobe whose stimulation produced *pain*. Nor has a "pain input center" been found anywhere else on the cortex (Wall, 1979). The role of the "higher brain centers" in the experience of pain is still a mystery (Kimble, 1992).

Every other type of sensation—vision, hearing, taste, smell, and touch—has both specific receptors and specific input areas in the cortex. What an enigma pain is, then, since it has *neither* special receptors nor cortical projection areas!

We are not completely ignorant about the path of pain, however. We are quite sure how painful inputs get from the "non-existent receptors" to the "invisible locus in the brain"! For scientists long ago proved that pain sensitivity is quite well represented in the *spinal cord* (Melzack, 1983).

FAST AND SLOW FIBERS

Your spinal cord carries messages from the basket cells and the encapsulated nerve endings in your skin to your brain by way of special cells. The axons of these cells have an *insulating sheath* wrapped around them. The speed with which the neural messages flow in these insulated axons is *faster* than in nerves that lack this insulation (Berne & Levy, 1990).

The free nerve endings, on the other hand, send their messages up your cord *slowly* by way of uninsulated axons. Neural messages travel about 30 times slower in your uninsulated "slow fibers" than in the insulated "fast fibers."

If you implant an electrode in the *fast fibers* of someone's spinal cord and stimulate these nerve cells directly, the person typically will report "pressure-like" feelings. If you stimulate the *slow fibers* instead, the person might report feeling either pressure or temperature changes. But if the current was intense enough, the person might also report feeling *pain* from slow-fiber stimulation. However, if you stimulate both fast and slow fibers simultaneously, the person will not feel pain no matter how intense the slow-fiber stimulation is. Apparently, slow-fiber activity turns pain *on*, but fast-fiber activity turns it *off!*

According to Ronald Melzack, the best guess as to why this "stimulation analgesia" occurs has to do with *channel capacity*. The lower brain centers (at the top of the spinal cord) can process only so many inputs per second. Fast-fiber activity overwhelms these centers, so they "turn the switch" and screen out slow-fiber activity—and hence pain (Melzack, 1983). You get the same sort of effect when you "scratch where it itches." The massive fast-fiber activity associated with scratching apparently overwhelms the mildly painful "itch input."

WHAT IS PAIN?

Because of the spinal cord data we've just discussed, some psychologists continue to classify pain as a sensory modality like warmth and pressure. Other scientists believe it is a *warning signal* that you experience whenever your senses are stressed or damaged. Pain specialists Arnold Holzman and Dennis Turk define pain as a "complex phenomenon that is the product of the interaction of [injurious] sensory stimulation, psychological factors . . . and socioenvironmental factors" (Holzman & Turk, 1986). Let's look at each of these factors briefly.

If the deadly Jararaca snake bit you, you would die an extremely painful death. By studying the Jararaca's venom (very carefully!), Brazilian researchers Mauricio Rocha e Silva and Wilson Beraldo discovered that the Jararaca's venom produced a substance called *bradykinin* in the victims' blood. Bradykinin caused the victims' pain.

Your body produces bradykinin whenever you are burned, infected, or injured in any way (McKean, 1986). So one source of pain is the chemical response of your body to harmful sensory stimulation. Your body probably produced bradykinin when you stepped on that tack.

But besides the actual injury, the mental expectation of pain can increase your pain. Horror movies take advantage of *psychological* factors in pain perception to make us almost "feel" the victim's pain. Screams of anguish, blood, and twisted and broken limbs lead us to *expect* pain. Similarly, you may have noticed that when a small child falls and is hurt, crying often begins only after investigation of the injury reveals blood. ("There's blood; therefore I must be hurt.") If you saw a large tack in your foot, with blood spurting out around it, your *experience* of pain would probably be greater than if the tack had not stayed in, and if there was no blood—even though the injury was the same.

Socioenvironmental factors also affect the experience of pain. A soldier injured in battle usually requires far less painkiller than a civilian who receives equally severe surgical "wounds." For the soldier the wound means status and relief from battle; for the civilian it means a serious disruption in an otherwise normal life (Beecher, 1959). If your friends reacted in shock at the tack in your foot, or if they overwhelmed you with expressions of sympathy, you would probably feel more pain than if they were unconcerned.

So the experience of pain is not a simple matter. Pain is a complex combination of *biological*, *intra-psychic*, and *social/behavioral* influences. The most successful treatments for pain take all of these factors into account (Keefe et al., 1992; Linssen & Spinhoven, 1992; Miró & Raich, 1992). We will have more to say about using these influences to cope with pain in Chapter 8.

The experience of pain may be greatly reduced if the painful activity helps to attain personal goals or if it is supported by social pressures.

Would you want your robot's "pain" response to be influenced by the same things that influence your reaction to an injury?

TASTE

Your skin is an important "input organ" in part because it protects you from things in the outside world that shouldn't get inside your body. But there are times when you *must* "input" certain items, such as food and water, if you are to survive. And much as it may surprise you, your skin helps you determine what to eat and drink, and what not to. For, as we will soon see, receptor cells in the skin that lines your tongue, mouth, and nose are responsible for reporting those sensory qualities we call "taste" and "smell."

Let's look first at what taste is all about. Pick your favorite food and imagine it in your mind's eye. Let's say you picked a steak—3 inches thick, wrapped in bacon, and cooked just the way you like it. Now, ask yourself what may seem a very stupid question: Why does the steak taste good to you?

Whatever reasons you come up with, chances are they're partly wrong. For even the best of steaks has almost no *taste* at all—at least if we restrict taste to the sensory qualities that come from receptors on your tongue. Steak *smells* good; it *looks* good; it has a fine *texture* to it as you chew it. And if it comes to your table sizzling hot, steak both *sounds* good and has just the right *temperature*.

But none of these sensory qualities has anything to do with the *taste* of steak. In fact, if we could block out all the other sensory qualities except those that come from your taste receptors, you'd find you could hardly tell the difference between the taste of steak and that of old shoe leather.

The Taste Receptors

Papillae (pap-PILL-eye, or pap-PILL-ee). The bumps on your tongue that contain the taste buds. (From the Latin word meaning "nipples.")

FIGURE 3.2a

Different areas of the tongue are extra sensitive to each of the four basic taste sensations, sweet, sour, salty, and bitter.

FIGURE 3.2b

Taste buds are located around the sides of papillae, which are bumps scattered over the tongue.

Your *taste buds* contain the hair cells which are your taste receptors. The taste buds are your body's "poor relations." Impoverished in almost every sense of the word, your taste buds are scattered in nooks and crannies all across the surface and sides of your tongue. Mostly, however, they are found clumped together in bumps on your tongue called **papillae** (see Figure 3.2). If you stick out your tongue and look at it, you will see the papillae very clearly.

Most of the papillae have grooves around their sides, like the moats or canals that circled old European castles. The taste buds line the sides of the papillae, like windows in the outer wall of a castle.

There are about 10,000 taste buds in your mouth, each made up of several receptor cells. Most of the buds are on your tongue, but there are also a few scattered else-

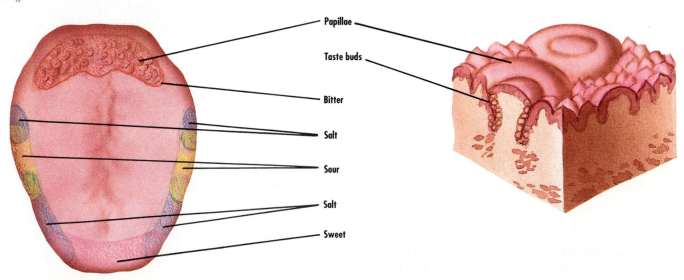

Papillae
Taste buds
Bitter
Salt
Sour
Salt
Sweet

where in your mouth. Each of the receptor cells in the taste bud has a hair at one end which pokes out into the "moat" around the papilla much as the hairs on the skin of your arm stick out into the air. When you eat or drink something, the liquids in your mouth fill up the moats around the papillae. Various molecules in the food stimulate the hair cells *chemically*. The cells then fire off sensory input messages to your brain, and you experience the sensation of taste (Hole, 1990).

Taste Qualities

There are only four basic taste qualities: *sweet, sour, bitter,* and *salty*—a paltry few primary qualities compared to the richness of the sensory experiences you get from vision, hearing, and smell. The noted psychologist E. B. Titchener once estimated that you can discriminate about 3,000 different tastes. However, all of them appear to be *mixtures* of the four basic taste qualities.

Research suggests there are four different taste receptors—one for each of the four primary taste qualities (see Figure 3.2). But our total experience of "taste" is made up of taste, smell, appearance, and texture. Food researchers suggest there may be 34 or more ways in which texture alone can vary (Schiffman, 1986)!

Taste Preferences

Newborn infants will usually drink milk shortly after birth, but will spit out sour or bitter substances (Blass & Teicher, 1980). However, by the time they are five months old, most children begin to show a slight preference for salty-tasting liquids (Beauchamp, 1987). The liking for sweet or slightly salty substances thus seems "built into your genes." But a fondness for beer (and other sour substances), or for "gin and tonic" (and other bitter tastes), and for exceptional hot or spicy foods (which trigger off the perception of pain) would seem to be a learned response (Shell, 1986). Even that sizzling steak we mentioned would be repulsive to someone whose cultural beliefs prohibited eating meat.

However, there is great variability in sensitivity to the taste of various substances, both in infants and adults. Some people are insensitive to the taste of certain foods—you must heavily saturate their tongues with these foods for these people to detect the substance at all. This *taste blindness*, which is far from rare, seems to be caused by some inherited deficiency in the chemical composition of the person's saliva. The taste-blind individual can sometimes detect the substance if you first dissolve the food in the saliva of a person with normal taste sensitivity.

Apparently the action of chewing and swallowing food wears down your taste receptors, and they must be replaced every four or five days. Older individuals often cannot regrow lost tissue as readily as younger individuals and therefore may have reduced numbers of receptors in their later years. Perhaps this fact explains why some older people add more seasoning to their food than most younger individuals prefer (Spitzer, 1988).

Taste is a necessary but not a particularly rich "sense." For the truth is, most of the flavor of food comes through your nose!

When you catch a cold, why does food suddenly lose its "taste"?

SMELL

Smell is a unique sense in at least two important ways. First, it is perhaps the most basic sense of all. The simplest organisms can detect molecules in the water around them by "smell" even when they are not sensitive to sights or sounds. Second, smell seems more directly related to emotion and motivation than are the other senses. Other sensory inputs pass through the thalamus and go directly to your cortex, as we discussed in Chapter 2. Smell sensations, however, mostly bypass the thalamus and go directly to those sub-centers of the brain that process *emotions*, not thoughts.

According to psychologist Trygg Engen, "*smell may be to emotion* what sight or hearing is to cognition. . . . When odor is involved it may well cause a feeling before it elicits a concern with the meaning of the odor" (Engen, 1982). Engen notes, for instance, that the first thing you typically notice about an odor is whether it's *pleasant* or *unpleasant*. Only after you have reacted to the odor *emotionally* do you usually (1) identify it, and (2) remember its name (Engen, 1987).

But naming an odor is not easy. There have been several attempts to classify smells in terms of "primary qualities," such as the "salty, sweet, sour, and bitter" qualities of taste. Different investigators have proposed from 6 to 32 different "basic odors." John Amoore, for example, suggested 7 primary odors: camphor, musky, floral, peppermint, ethereal, pungent, and putrid (Amoore, 1977). Today, most researchers agree that there is no simple system for classifying odors (Schiffman, 1990).

Many people report that a home or apartment they have lived in for a long time has a characteristic odor. Usually, these people report they can recognize the odor, but have trouble describing it in words. Why do you think they find this task difficult?

The Olfactory Membrane

Your nose has two cavities or open spaces inside it. The roof of each of these nasal cavities is lined with a thick covering called the **olfactory membrane,** which is really a type of skin. Covering the olfactory membrane is a thin layer of **mucus.** Embedded in the membrane itself are millions of receptor cells called *olfactory rods* (see Figure 3.3).

At the base end of each of the olfactory rods is an axon that runs directly to your brain. At the front end is a branched set of **cilia,** which act in much the same fashion as dendrites do. These cilia stick out of the olfactory membrane into the layer of mucus (Hole, 1990).

The stimuli that excite your olfactory rods are complex chemicals in *gaseous form* that are suspended in the air you breathe. As air passes over the olfactory membrane, some of the complex chemicals in the air are absorbed into the mucus. These gaseous molecules appear to lock onto specific receptor sites on the cilia. This "locking on" causes the olfactory rods to fire off an input message to your brain (Berne & Levy, 1990).

Smell: Gender and Aging

According to psychologists Avery Gilbert and Charles Wysocki, many people lack the ability to smell specific substances. In a recent survey, Gilbert and Wysocki found that 37 percent of American men and 30 percent of American women could not detect the odor associated with "sweaty armpits." Surprisingly enough, Americans seem worse at detecting this scent than do people almost anywhere else in the world. Gilbert and Wysocki also found that 25 percent of American women and 33 percent of American men couldn't detect a "musky" smell (Gilbert & Wysocki, 1987).

Judging from most recent research, your genes influence your ability to detect various odors. Recent experiments also suggest that the amount of sex hormones present in your body influences your olfactory thresholds. Researchers report a superiority for women not only in the detection of odors, but also in their identifi-

I have been here before,
But when or how I cannot tell:
I know the grass beyond the door,
The sweet keen smell . . .

DANTE GABRIEL ROSSETTI (1828–1882)

Olfactory membrane (oal-FACK-torr-ee). "Olfaction" (oal-FACK-shun) is the process of smelling. The olfactory membrane is a layer of tissue at the top of each nasal cavity that contains the receptors for smell. There are two olfactory membranes in your nose—one inside each nostril.

Mucus (MEW-kuss). The thick, slippery substance that covers (and protects) the olfactory membrane.

Cilia (SILL-ee-ah). From the Latin word meaning "eyelash." A hair-like structure attached to or projecting from many cells.

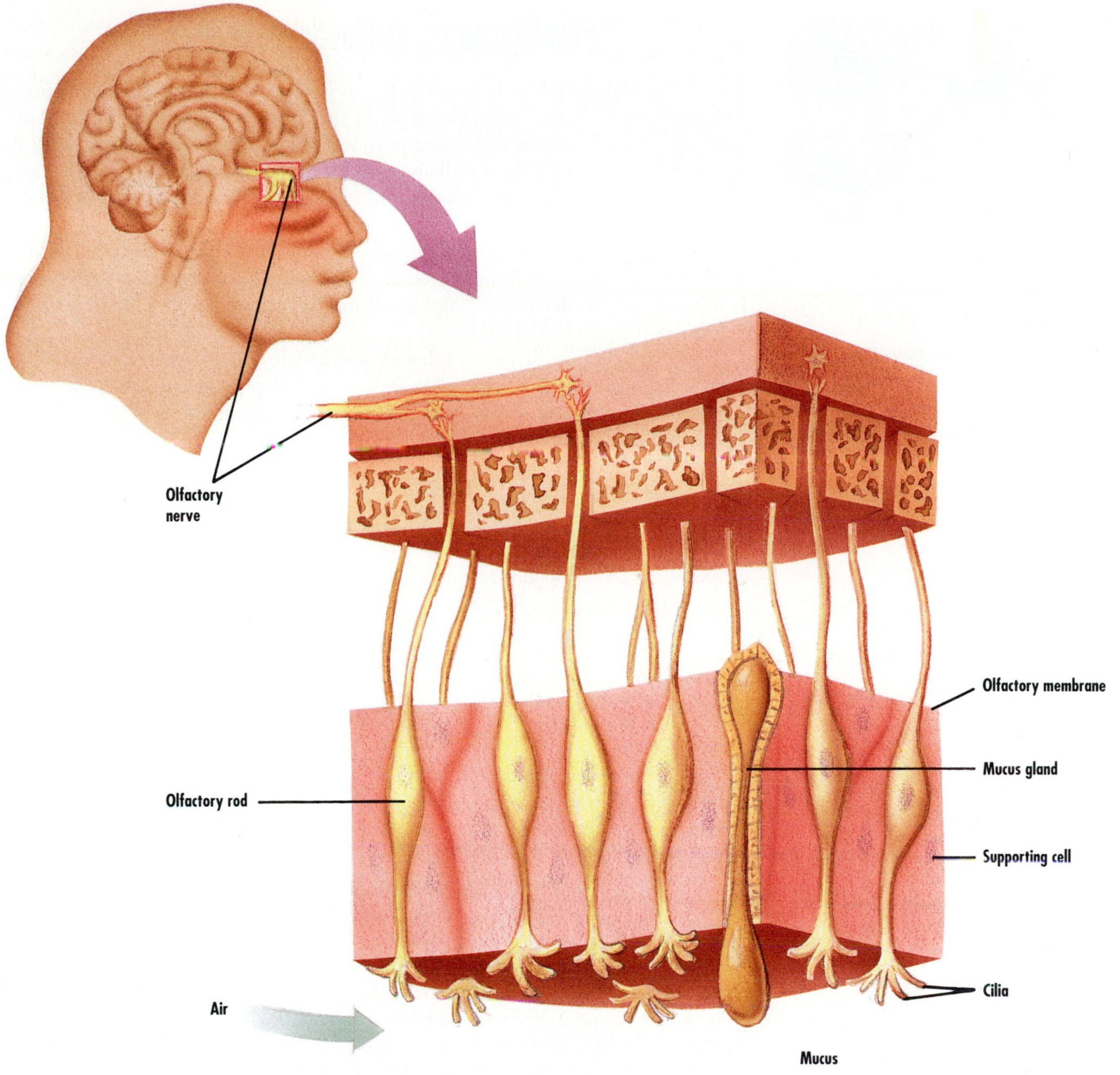

Olfactory nerve

Olfactory rod

Air

Olfactory membrane

Mucus gland

Supporting cell

Cilia

Mucus

FIGURE 3.3

Schematic representation of olfactory membrane, showing the olfactory rods and the cilia in the layer of mucus.

cation. For example, Cain (1982) found that not only were women better at identifying stereotypically "feminine" odors (baby powder, nail-polish remover), and foods, but they were also better at identifying stereotypically "masculine" odors such as cigar butts and machine oil.

According to Robert Henkin, a woman's olfactory sensitivity increases "up to 1,000 fold" in the middle of her menstrual cycle (cited in Niemark, 1986). However, Richard Doty and colleagues report that the odor identification superiority of females was also found between *prepubertal* girls and boys (Doty et al., 1984).

There is considerable evidence that, in some people, the sense of smell diminishes in old age (Murphy et al., 1991) (see Figure 3.4). According to a group of olfactory researchers in England, older people often find it more difficult to detect odors. More than this, however, the smells older people can still sense often lose their subjective (or emotional) characteristics. The British scientists suggest that this age-related loss may explain why some "senior citizens" don't always eat as balanced a diet as they did when younger.

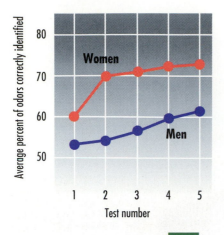

FIGURE 3.4

Outcome of an experiment by William Cain, who tested men and women on their ability to learn 80 odors. The ability of both women and men to come up with correct names improves over time. But, on the average, women correctly identified more items on the initial test and maintained this superiority in four later trials.

Pheromones (FAIR-oh-moans). A chemical released by one organism that serves to induce one or more behavioral responses in other organisms of the same species.

"I heard what you said. I'm processing it."

"Odor Signatures" and the Sweet Smell of Sex

Researcher Richard Porter believes that each person has a characteristic and unique "odor signature." In one study, Porter asked 28 adults to try to match the smell of T-shirts worn by 15 mothers with those worn by their children. The subjects were able to match mother and child at well above chance level. However, when Porter asked his subjects to try to match T-shirts worn by husbands and wives, the subjects had considerable difficulty doing so (Porter et al., 1986).

In a similar study, fathers, grandmothers, and aunts reliably discriminated the odors of close relatives from the odors of strangers (Porter et al., 1986). Porter believes that genes determine "odor signatures," which we learn to identify at a very young age (Porter et al., 1991).

It has long been known that both male and female animals secrete chemicals that attract the opposite sex. These chemicals are called **pheromones.** But what about humans? Do we secrete sex pheromones as do other mammals?

No one denies the strong influence that smell has on sexuality in the lower animals. And no one denies that humans have the necessary physiological mechanisms to transmit chemical signals. Still, the exact effects that odors have on human sexual behavior is an "open question" (Schiffman, 1990). Of course, the lack of experimental conclusions does not stop North Americans from spending millions of dollars each year to deodorize and re-odorize themselves.

HEARING

Imagine yourself seated a couple of feet above a very quiet pool in a forest. You take a stone and toss it in the center of the pond, and what happens? Wave after wave of ripples circle out from the center until they strike the edges of the pool. If you looked closely, you would see that when the waves passed over a reed growing in the water, the reed moved. The sound waves that stimulate the auditory receptors in your ear are not very different from the ripples that you create, and that move a reed, when you drop a rock in a pond.

This is because hearing is a *vibratory* sense. That is, the auditory receptors in your ears are sensitive to vibrations of the molecules in the air around you. These vibrations usually come in waves, which we call "sound waves." Thus, the stimulus for hearing is usually a vibratory wave of some kind.

Whenever any fairly rigid object is struck forcibly, it tends to vibrate. As this object vibrates back and forth, it makes "ripples" in the molecules of air around it. These "ripples" are really sound waves. That is, they are waves of energy that pass through the air just as the ripples pass across the surface of the water when you throw a stone in the pond. When these sound waves reach your ear, they set part of your eardrum to moving back and forth in rhythm with the vibrating object, just like the reed in the water. Other parts of your ear then translate the vibrations of the eardrum into patterns of neural energy that are sent to your brain so that you can "hear."

Why Two Ears?

Before we look at the parts of the ear, consider the fact that you have two ears—with a very important space between them. If you would like to demonstrate to yourself the importance of the "space between your ears," you might try a musical experiment. Find a *stereo* set with two movable speakers. Put the speakers as far apart in the room as you can. Now put on your favorite stereo record and sit between the two speakers with your eyes closed. You will hear music coming at you from all directions. But some sounds will seem to be on your left, while others seem to be on your right. Now, put the two speakers right next to each other and repeat the experiment. Chances are, the music will seem compressed, pushed together, cut down in size to a *point source*. In short, the stereo music will now sound monaural or "mono."

In a sense, your ears are similar to the microphones used to record music. To get a stereo effect, the record company must use at least two microphones that are some distance apart. When a band performs, each microphone "hears" a slightly different version of the music.

Suppose the lead guitarist in the band is on the left. The mike on the left would then "hear" the guitarist much more loudly than would the mike on the right. If the drummer is on the right, then the right microphone would pick up the sounds of the drum more loudly than would the mike on the left. By keeping the two channels *separate* during both recording and playback, you can maintain left-right relationships. That is, when you hear the record, the sounds made by the lead guitarist come primarily from the left speaker. The drummer's beat, however, will come to you mostly from the right speaker.

Your ears are just far enough apart so that you can readily detect left-right differences in sound sources. Sound waves travel at a speed of some 750 miles per hour at sea level. If a cricket 6 feet to the left of your head chirps loudly, the noise will reach your left ear a fraction of a second before it reaches your right ear. Since the insect is closer to your left ear than to your right, the noise will be louder when it reaches your left ear than when it finally gets around your head and reaches your right ear. Your brain *interprets* the intensity and time differences in the auditory stimulus at your left and right ears to mean that the cricket is to your left.

However, your brain can be fooled in such matters if you know how to go about it. Go back to your stereo set and put one speaker on the floor and the other as high up in the air as you can directly above the first. Sit with your head upright between the two speakers. When you play music now, it will seem strangely "mono," for each of your ears is the *same distance from both speakers*. Your ears can detect the location of sounds spread out in the *left-right* dimension rather well. But your ears do very poorly in locating sounds in the *up-down* dimension.

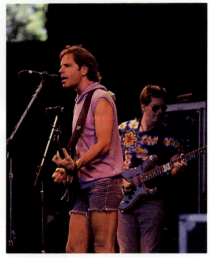

When a band performs, each microphone "hears" a slightly different version of the music.

Why does it help to cock your head to one side when trying to locate the source of a sound over your head?

Parts of the Ear

Your ear has three main divisions: (1) the outer ear, (2) the middle ear, and (3) the inner ear (see Figure 3.5).

1. The **outer ear** is that fleshy flap of skin and other tissue sticking out from either side of your head. Your outer ear "catches" sound waves and funnels them into a narrow tunnel called the **auditory canal.** At the inner end of this auditory canal is your *eardrum*, a thin membrane stretched tautly across the auditory canal like the skin on a drum. The eardrum separates your outer ear from your middle ear.

2. The **middle ear** is a hollow cavity in your skull that contains three little bones called the **hammer,** the **anvil,** and the **stirrup.** If you inspected these three little bones under a microscope, they would look much like the objects they are named after. One end of the hammer rests on the eardrum. When your eardrum moves, it pulls the hammer back and forth rhythmically (Berne & Levy, 1990).

   The hammer transmits this "wave" of sound energy to the anvil, making the anvil move back and forth. The anvil pulls the stirrup back and forth in similar fashion. The stirrup is connected to another membrane called the **oval window.**

Auditory (AW-ditt-tor-ee). From the Greek word meaning "to hear." Audition is the technical word for "hearing."

Outer ear. The fleshy outer part of the ear. Also called the auricle (AW-rick-cull), the pinna (PIN-nah), or the auditory meatus (me-ATE-us). The outer ear catches sound waves and reflects them into the auditory canal.

Auditory canal (AW-dit-tor-ee). The hollow tube running from the outer to the middle ear.

Middle ear. Contains the hammer, anvil, and stirrup. Lies between the eardrum and the oval window.

Hammer, anvil, and stirrup. Three small, connected bones in your middle ear that make sounds louder. (Also known by their Latin names, malleus, incus, and stapes.)

Oval window. The thin membrane lying between your middle and inner ears. The stirrup is connected to one side of the oval window. The basilar membrane (see below) is connected to the other.

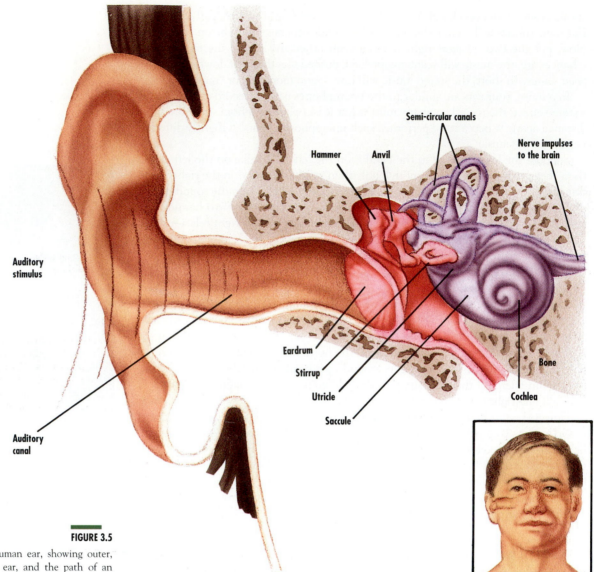

FIGURE 3.5

Structure of the human ear, showing outer, middle, and inner ear, and the path of an auditory stimulus.

Inner ear. A fluid-filled "worm hole" in your skull that contains both the motion detectors and your receptor neurons for hearing.

Cochlea (COCK-lee-ah). The snail-shaped portion of your inner ear that contains the basilar membrane.

Organ of Corti (KOR-tie). A highly complex structure lying on the basilar membrane that contains the sensory receptor cells for hearing.

Basilar membrane (BASS-ill-ar). A ribbon of tissue that supports the organ of Corti. One end of the basilar membrane connects to the oval window, the other to the round window.

As the stirrup moves, it forces part of the membrane on your oval window to wiggle back and forth in rhythm too.

The three little bones and the two membranes act as the *amplifiers* in your own biological stereo system. By the time the sound stimulus reaches your oval window, it is many times stronger than it was when it first struck your eardrum.

3. The oval window separates the middle ear from the **inner ear.** Your inner ear is a fluid-filled cavity that runs through your skull bone like a tunnel coiling through a mountain. This inner ear of yours has two main parts: (1) the **cochlea,** and (2) the motion detectors.

The cochlea gets its name from the Latin word for "snail shell," which is just what your cochlea looks like. Your auditory receptors are the 24,000 hair cells that are a part of the **organ of Corti** inside your cochlea. When a sound wave travels through the fluid in your cochlea it causes the hair cells to vibrate just like the reed did when you threw a rock in the pond. The organ of Corti (containing the hair cells) lies on the **basilar membrane,** which runs the length of the cochlea (see Figures 3.5 and 3.6).

Imagine uncoiling the basilar membrane into a flat strip. If you could follow the nerve messages from hair cells that were side by side, you would find that they

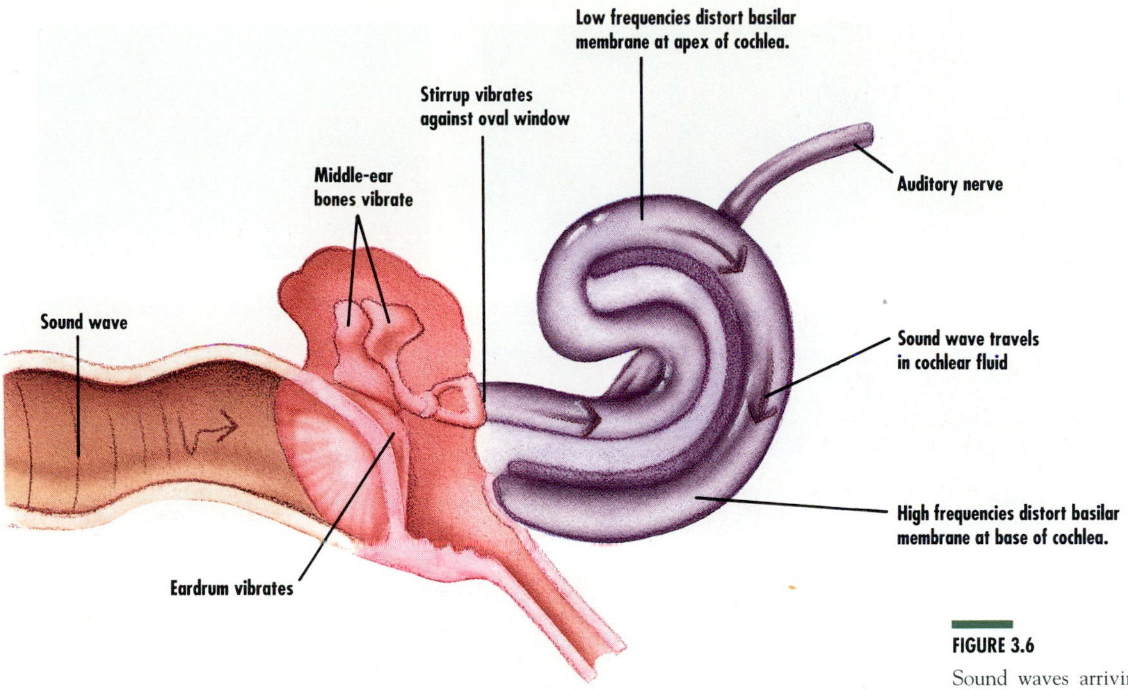

Low frequencies distort basilar membrane at apex of cochlea.

Stirrup vibrates against oval window

Middle-ear bones vibrate

Auditory nerve

Sound wave

Sound wave travels in cochlear fluid

High frequencies distort basilar membrane at base of cochlea.

Eardrum vibrates

FIGURE 3.6

Sound waves arriving through the auditory canal make the eardrum (tympanic membrane) vibrate. The three small bones in the inner ear amplify the sound and cause the oval window to vibrate. Sound waves travel through the cochlear fluid and cause the basilar membrane to distort or vibrate. The hair cells lying on the basilar membrane respond by sending an input message along the auditory nerve.

signalled points which were side by side on the auditory cortex in your brain (Carlson, 1991).

In addition to the mechanisms of hearing, buried away inside each of your ears are receptor organs that detect changes in motion. There are two basic types of motion that your body is sensitive to: (1) straight-line or linear movements, and (2) rotary or circular movements. The detectors in your ear that sense *changes in linear motion* are two small organs called the **saccule** and the **utricle.** Whenever your body starts or stops moving in a straight-line fashion, neural receptors in the saccule and the utricle fire off messages to your brain letting it know that linear movement has begun or is slowing down (see Figure 3.5).

Any *change in rotary motion* your body makes is detected by the **semicircular canals** in your ear. As shown in Figure 3.5, these three canals are positioned at right angles to each other inside your ear so they can detect changes in circular motion in any of the three dimensions of space.

Frequency and Amplitude

The waves of vibrating air molecules which strike your ear have two important physical aspects: **frequency** and **amplitude.** The physical *frequency* of a sound wave determines how *high* or *low* the tone sounds to your ear. In other words, the frequency sets the *pitch* of the tone. The *amplitude* of a sound determines how *loud* or *soft* the tone sounds to you. Amplitude sets loudness, or volume.

"Frequency" and "amplitude" are terms that describe the *physical* characteristics of an auditory stimulus. "Pitch" and "loudness," however, are terms that describe *psychological* attributes of the subjective experience of hearing.

FREQUENCY AND PITCH

When you pluck a string on a guitar the string creates sound waves that have *exactly the same frequency* as the number of vibrations that the string makes per second. You ear detects these sound waves, and your brain turns them into musical tones. The

Saccule (SACK-you'll). One of the two small organs in your inner ear that detects straight-line movements of your head (and hence of your body). The Greek word *sakkos* means "bag" or "sack." The saccule is thus a "little bag."

Utricle (YOU-trick-ull). From the Latin word meaning "little bag." The second of the small organs in your inner ear that detect linear motion.

Semicircular canals. Three fluid-filled cavities in the inner ear positioned at right angles to each other so that they can detect circular motion in any of the three dimensions of space.

Frequency. In auditory terms, the number of times a sound source vibrates each second. The frequency of a musical tone is measured in Hertz.

Amplitude (AM-ple-tood). From the Latin word meaning "muchness." We get our word "ample" from the same Latin source. Amplitude is the amount of sound present, or the strength of a musical tone. Literally, the "height" of a sound wave.

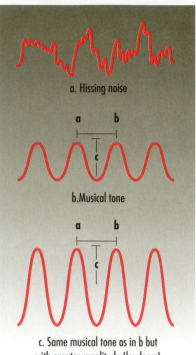

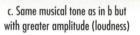

a. Hissing noise

b. Musical tone

c. Same musical tone as in b but
with greater amplitude (loudness)

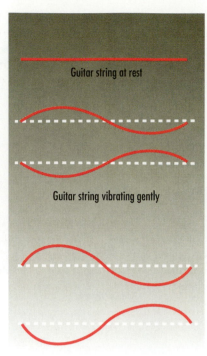

Guitar string at rest

Guitar string vibrating gently

Guitar string vibrating vigorously

FIGURE 3.7a

A sound wave "cycle" or "Hertz" is measured from peak to peak.

FIGURE 3.7b

A vibrating guitar string. The string produces the same frequency sound wave whether it vibrates gently or vigorously.

Hertz (hurts). The frequency of any wave, such as a sound wave. Used to be called "cycles per second," or cps. Named for the German scientist Heinrich Hertz, who made the first definitive studies of energy waves.

faster a particular string vibrates, the more "waves per second" it creates—and the *higher* the pitch of the tone will seem to be when you hear it.

If you plucked the "A" string on a guitar, it would vibrate 110 times per second. This number is called the *frequency* of the musical tone "A." In technical terms, we would say this tone has a frequency of 110 "cycles per second," or 110 **Hertz** (110 Hz). In general, the thinner and shorter a string is, the higher the frequency at which it vibrates—and the higher the pitch of the tone that it makes.

AMPLITUDE AND LOUDNESS

The loudness of a tone is determined primarily by the tone's *amplitude*, not by its frequency. If you happen to pluck the "A" string of the guitar very gently, it vibrates 110 times per second. But if you plucked the string as hard as you could, it would still vibrate at about 110 Hz. If it didn't, you wouldn't hear the note as being an "A."

But surely something different happens, for the more energetically you pluck a string, the louder the note sounds. The answer is that the string moves *farther up and down* during each vibration—but it still vibrates at about 110 times per second (see Figure 3.7, a and b). The sound waves are the same distance apart but they are "taller." In technical terms, the "taller the wave," the greater its *amplitude*. And the greater the amplitude that a sound wave has, the louder it will sound to you.

The Range of Hearing

Complex motor tasks such as gymnastics require complex feedback from the motion-change receptors in the inner ear and from proprioceptors in the muscles, joints, and tendons.

What kinds of musical tones can your ear hear?

Your range of hearing is, roughly speaking, from 20 Hz to about 20,000 Hz, but you are not equally sensitive to all frequencies within this range. Your hearing is *best* from about 400 to 4,000 Hz. Human conversation ranges between 200 and 800 Hz. The lowest tone a bass singer can produce is about 100 Hz, while the highest tone most sopranos can produce is about 1,000 Hz. Thus, your ear is "tuned" to listen to other people speak and sing (Moore, 1989).

There seems to be a general rule that holds across animal species: The smaller the cochlea, the higher the upper limit on the animal's range of hearing is likely to be. The dog can hear notes at least as high as 25,000 Hz, while the bat is sensitive to tones as high as 100,000 Hz. Elephants, on the other hand, probably have a hearing range that cuts off at about 7,000 Hz (Stebbins, 1983).

If you wanted to design a whistle that could be used for calling dogs but couldn't be heard by human beings, what frequency range would you want to investigate?

Deafness

What difference would it make to your life if you became deaf?

Hearing is the major channel for informal social communication. Our customs, social graces, and moral beliefs are still passed down from one generation to another primarily by word of mouth rather than in writing. And most of us (textbook writers included!) prefer the informal transmission of knowledge that comes from talking to the formality of the written word.

BONE DEAFNESS AND NERVE DEAFNESS

When people grow older, the three small bones in the middle ear often become brittle and thus do not work properly. Since the hammer, anvil, and stirrup serve to *amplify* the sound waves as they come into the ear, you could become deaf (or partially so) when these bones malfunction. This type of *bone deafness* can usually be corrected if you are fitted for a hearing aid, a device that acts like a miniature hi-fi set and "turns up the volume" electronically. Bone deafness can also occur because of disease or birth defects. The more severe types of bone deafness sometimes require surgery (Hole, 1990).

Many types of infection can attack the hair cells on the organ of Corti. If your receptor cells were permanently damaged for any reason, you would suffer from *nerve deafness*. If only a small section of your basilar membrane were affected, you would lose the ability to hear just high notes, or low notes, or perhaps notes in the middle of the auditory spectrum (see Figure 3.6). If the damage to your nerve cells was widespread, however, you might become totally deaf for *all frequencies*.

The major causes for nerve deafness are birth defects, disease, and exposure to extremely loud sounds. Even exposure to constant moderately loud noise can cause nerve deafness. The jet engines on modern airplanes create ear-splitting sounds, which is why people who work around jets wear protective earphones. The sound levels in many factories can cause damage too if the workers are exposed to the noise for too long a time.

In the past, nerve deafness could seldom be corrected either by surgery or by a hearing aid. In recent years, however, scientists have begun implanting tiny electrodes *directly into the ear*. These electrodes deliver short bursts of electricity to the auditory nerve. Normal speech is picked up by a small microphone and "translated" into pulses of electrical current by a pocket-sized computer. These devices bypass the damaged receptor cells on the basilar membrane by stimulating the auditory nerve itself.

According to psychologists Thomas Ayres and Paul Hughes, loud sounds can also cause a temporary decrease in *visual acuity*. Ayres and Hughes tested the ability of a group of students to discriminate visual stimuli while listening to a recording of a rock group called the Mahavishnu Orchestra. When the recording was playing at a normal level, the students' visual acuity was normal. However, when the recording was playing at about the loudness of a live concert, 80 percent of the students suffered a significant decrease in their visual acuity (Ayres & Hughes, 1986; Meer, 1985).

Many students turn up the volume of their car stereos to "live concert levels" while driving. According to Ayres' and Hughes' research, what effect might this have on their driving?

DEAFNESS AND PARANOIA

According to Philip Zimbardo, older individuals who slowly lose their hearing may be reluctant to admit their growing deafness. To do so, Zimbardo says, would be to admit that they are "growing old." Thus, many older people with hearing losses tend to blame their hearing problems on the behavior of others rather than on their own faulty ears. This "blaming behavior" often takes the form of a mild **paranoia,** in which the older person grows highly suspicious that other people are whispering about the person behind her or his back.

Zimbardo and two of his associates performed an interesting study on "experimental deafness." The psychologists began by hypnotizing some students in a discussion group and telling them that they would have severe difficulties hearing the other members of the group talk. (As you will see in Chapter 5, this sort of temporary hearing loss under hypnosis is completely reversible.) As predicted, most of the temporarily deaf students became convinced other members of their discussion groups were "talking ill of them," or were trying to do the subjects harm. They also became more hostile, confused, agitated, irritable, and less creative (Zimbardo et al., 1981).

Paranoia (pair-ah-NOI-ya). A severe type of mental disorder characterized by delusions of grandeur and suspicions that people are whispering or trying to control your behavior.

Deaf people can learn to rely on other sensory information to adapt to the world.

If you don't "speak up" around a person with hearing problems, how might your behaviors increase the deaf person's feelings of paranoia?

LANGUAGE LEARNING AND DEAFNESS

Learning to sing, dance, play the guitar, or drive a car—all these complex motor tasks require *feedback*. A girl who is born deaf, or partially deaf, has trouble learning to talk because she cannot hear what noises her voice is making. Without the auditory feedback from her vocal cords, the girl can never learn to shape her spoken words properly, because she simply does not know what her own voice sounds like.

Until scientists discovered how necessary some kind of feedback is in learning to talk, we often thought that partially deaf children were mentally retarded. Occasionally we mistakenly confined these children to homes for mentally handicapped people—although many of them were very intelligent. Fortunately, now that hearing tests for young children are much more common than they used to be, we are less likely to confuse partial deafness with mental retardation.

Suppose that a very bright but partially deaf child is mistakenly put in a home for mentally retarded persons. Would anyone be likely to try to train the child to read? Under some circumstances, could the child perhaps learn to read on his or her own?

VISION—MORE THAN MEETS THE EYE

Psychologically speaking, hearing is a far more complex sense than is touch, taste, or smell. But when it comes to "richness" of sensory experience, vision is perhaps more complicated than all the other sensory modalities put together. And because vision dominates so much of our lives, psychologists have studied it in greater detail than the other senses. As a result, we know more about how and why you see than we do about how you experience the rest of your sensory world.

Vision has often been called "the sense of wonder." To appreciate how your ability to see influences your thoughts and behaviors, however, you need to understand at least three things:

- What the visual stimulus (light) is like.
- How your eye converts light into a sensory input to send to your brain.
- How your brain interprets this incoming sensory information.

Once you have learned something about how the eye operates, perhaps you will understand why Robert Boynton claims, "the seemingly simple act of vision requires the most sophisticated biological instrumentation of any device in the entire world" (Boynton, 1980).

If you were designing a robot for NASA, where on the robot's body would you put its hearing and vision receptors? Why?

The Visual Stimulus

The stimulus for vision is *light*, which is a very small part of the **electro-magnetic spectrum.** The electromagnetic spectrum also includes x-rays and radio waves (see Figure 3.8). The smallest, most elementary unit of light is called the **photon,** which

Less vividly is the mind stirred by what finds entrance through the ears than what is brought before the trusty eyes.

HORACE (20 B.C.)

Electro-magnetic spectrum. The entire range of frequencies or wavelengths of electro-magnetic radiation ranging from gamma rays to the longest radio waves. Includes the visible spectrum.

Photon (FO-tohn). A tiny packet of energy that is the smallest unit of light. Under ideal circumstances, your eye is so incredibly sensitive that it can detect a single photon.

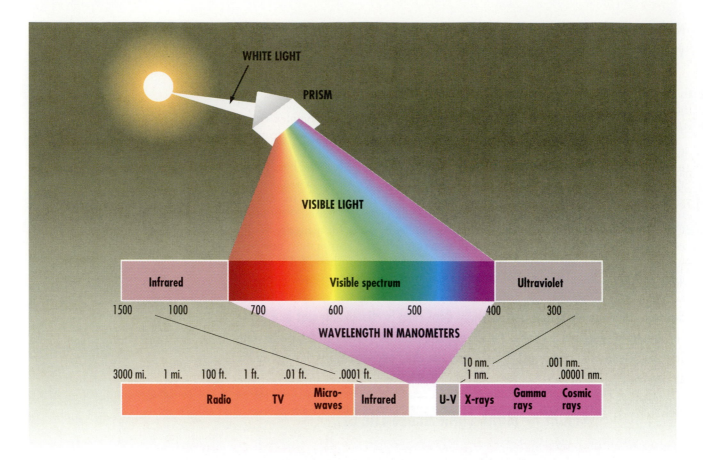

FIGURE 3.8

The location of the visible light spectrum on the total electro-magnetic spectrum.

gets its name from the Greek word meaning light. The flame from one match produces millions of photons. A flashlight produces a great many more photons than does a match. Thus, in general, the stronger the light source, the more photons it produces in a given unit of time (such as a second).

When you turn on a flashlight, photons stream out from the bulb at an incredible speed or velocity. To give you a better "feel" for this speed, consider the fact that the velocity of sound waves is about 0.21 miles per second (or 750 miles per hour). The speed of light, on the other hand, is about 186,000 miles per *second*.

Sound travels at slightly more than one-fifth mile a second. If you saw lightning hit the ground, and heard thunder about 5 seconds later, approximately how far away from you did the lightning bolt hit?

WAVELENGTHS OF LIGHT

The bulb of a flashlight produces photons in waves—much as the string on a guitar produces sound waves when the string vibrates, or the wind produces waves on the surface of the ocean. If you wanted to, you could take a boat out on the sea and actually measure the distance *between* one ocean wave and another. If you did so, you would find that the distance between the crests of the waves was remarkably consistent on any particular day.

Much the same sort of consistency holds for the wavelength of light and what color it appears to be. The "rainbow of colors" make up what is technically called the **visible spectrum.** The blue colors have very short wavelengths. The reds, at the other end of the spectrum, have much longer wavelengths. The colors between red

Visible spectrum (SPECK-trum). When you look at a rainbow in the sky, you see the array (spectrum) of visible colors that make up sunlight. For most purposes, "rainbow" and "visible spectrum" can be considered the same things.

and blue have wavelengths that fall between these two extremes. Thus, if you know what *wavelength* a visual input has, you will know what *color* it ordinarily will appear to be.

However, the distance between the crests of light waves is much, much smaller than the distance between any two ocean waves. The wavelength for red is so short that it takes about 38,000 "red waves" to make an inch. The wavelength for blue is much shorter—it takes about 70,000 "blue waves" to make an inch.

Scientists seldom measure the wavelength of light in fractions of an inch, because the figures are just too clumsy to use. Instead, scientists measure wavelengths in **nanometers.** There are *one billion* nanometers in each meter. The wavelengths for the visible spectrum run from about 400 nanometers (blue) through approximately 760 nanometers (red).

Nanometers (NAN-oh-meters). The Greek word for dwarf is "nanos." A nanometer is one-billionth of a meter, or about 1/40,000,000,000th of an inch.

AMPLITUDE OF VISUAL INPUTS

The physical *wavelength* of a light stimulus determines the color that it will appear to you, such as blue or red. But some blue lights are bright, while others are dim. The physical *intensity* of a light determines how bright it will seem. This physical intensity can be measured in terms of the height or *amplitude* or the wave.

If you measured the *length* between crests of ocean waves on a calm day, you might find that the wavelength was about 20 feet. The *height* of each wave, however, might be no more than 3 feet. During a storm, the wavelength might still be 20 feet, but the *height* of each ocean wave might now be 10 to 13 feet.

In similar fashion, a dim blue light might have a wavelength of 423 nanometers. If you "turned up the intensity" of this blue light until it was very bright, it would still have a *wavelength* of 423 nanometers—but the *amplitude* (height) of each wave would be many times greater. When you make a light brighter, you amplify the height of each light wave—just as when you turn up the volume on your stereo set you amplify the height of each sound wave the machine puts out.

The *physical wavelength* of a visual input determines its *psychological color*, or hue. And the *physical amplitude* of the light wave determines the *psychological brightness* of a visual stimulus.

Why does a psychologist interested in human behavior bother with such technical measures as wavelength and amplitude? For two reasons, really.

Light passing through a prism is broken up into an orderly progression of wave lengths, resulting in a "rainbow" of colors.

First, because visual inputs stimulate people to act and respond. The more precisely we can specify the stimulus that evokes a certain reaction, the better we can understand the behavior itself.

Second, because we are often interested in individual differences. If we show exactly the same visual stimulus to two people, and they report different psychological experiences, we know these reports are due to differences in the people and not to some variability in the physical stimulus itself. We will have more to say about this point when we discuss color vision disorders (or "color-blindness") later in this chapter.

How many "eyes" should your NASA robot have? Why?

The Eyes

If we stretch the facts a bit, we can say that your eye is like a color TV camera. (Your eye is far more complex and compact than a TV camera, but the similarities between the two may help you understand how your eye actually works.) Both your eye and the TV camera are "containers" that have a small hole at one end which admits light. The light then passes through a lens that focuses an image on a photo-sensitive surface. In both your eye and in the color TV camera, the "hole" can be opened to let in more light, or closed to keep light out. In both, the lens can be adjusted to bring near or far objects into focus.

In the case of the color television camera, the light coming through the lens falls on an electronic tube that contains several complex chemicals. These chemical are photo-sensitive—that is, they react chemically when struck by photons. The camera then produces several different images which, when properly combined on a TV set, reproduce the scene in vivid color.

STRUCTURE OF THE EYE

In the case of your eye, light first passes through the **cornea** and the **aqueous humor** (see Figure 3.9). The cornea is spherical in shape in order to bend the light waves entering the eye and begin the process of focusing. Once past the aqueous humor, light enters your inner eye through an opening called the *pupil*. The **iris** is the colored part of your eye which, by expanding and contracting around the pupil, controls the amount of light admitted inside your eye.

Just beyond the pupil is the *lens*. The main purpose of the lens in your eye, like the lens in a camera, is to allow you to focus clearly whether you are looking at something close or far away. As you change your point of focus from a near object to something several feet away, muscles inside your eye pull on the lens to change its shape and thus refocus the light. The lens projects the image through the **vitreous humor,** and focuses it onto the inner surface of your eyeball—just as the lens in a camera projects and focuses an image on the film in the back of the camera.

The inner surface of your eyeball is called the **retina,** from the Latin word meaning "net" or "network." Your retina is a network of millions of cells that, like the electronic tube in the TV camera, contains several photo-sensitive chemicals. In a sense, your eyeball is a hollow sphere whose shell has three layers.

- The outer layer, which contains the cornea, is called the **sclera.** The sclera is really the "skin" of your eyeball. Like most other skin tissue, the sclera contains *free nerve endings* that are sensitive to pressure, temperature, and pain (see Figure 3.9).

- The middle layer of the "shell" of your eye is a dark lining that is called the **choroid membrane,** or coat.

Cornea (CORN-ee-ah). From the Latin word meaning "horn-like." We get our words "horn" and "corn" (the kind of blister you get on your foot) from this same Latin source. The cornea is the tough, transparent tissue in front of the aqueous humor.

Aqueous humor (A-kwi-us). The watery substance between the iris and the cornea that keeps the front of your eyeball "inflated" to its proper size and provides nutrients to the cornea.

Iris (EYE-riss). The colored or pigmented area of the eye. When you say that someone has brown eyes, you really mean the person has brown irises. The Greek word for "rainbow" is iris.

Vitreous humor (VITT-tree-us). From the Latin word meaning "glass." The vitreous humor is a clear, glass-like substance in the center of the eyeball that keeps your eye in its proper rounded shape. Light must pass through the vitreous humor before it strikes your retina.

Retina (RETT-tin-ah). The photo-sensitive inner surface of your eye. Contains the visual receptor organs.

Sclera (SKLAIR-ah). The tough outer layer of the eyeball.

Choroid membrane (KOR-oid). The dark, middle layer of the eyeball that contains blood vessels and pigment cells.

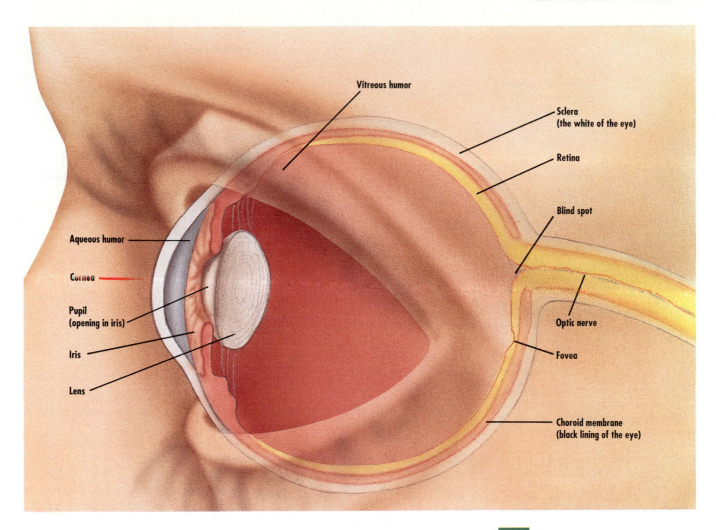

Vitreous humor

Sclera
(the white of the eye)

Retina

Blind spot

Aqueous humor

Cornea

Pupil
(opening in iris)

Iris

Lens

Optic nerve

Fovea

Choroid membrane
(black lining of the eye)

FIGURE 3.9

A diagram of the eye, showing the names of major structures.

■ The third layer is the *retina*, which is really the inner surface of your hollow eyeball.

THE RETINA

If you were called upon to design the eyes for a NASA robot, the odds are that you would never think of making the robot's retina like yours. To begin with, your retina has *10 distinct layers*. The inner layer of your retina contains the receptor cells that translate the physical energy of a light wave into the patterns of neural energy that your brain interprets as "seeing" (see Figure 3.10). These receptor cells are called the rods and cones. The tips of your rods and cones, which contain the photosensitive chemicals that react to light, are actually pointed *away* from the outside world. To strike your rods and cones, light must first pass through all nine other layers of your retina (Hole, 1990).

The receptor cells in your skin are a part of your *peripheral nervous system*. That is, they are nerve cells which lie outside your brain and spinal cord. The retina connects directly to the brain, however, and is considered by most authorities to be a part of the *central nervous system*.

The top layers of your retina contain a great many large neurons that are very similar in structure to those found in your cortex. These large neurons begin processing visual information right in the retina, before sending messages along to your visual cortex (in the occipital lobes at the back of your brain). Your retina is the *only receptor organ* in your body that processes input so extensively before sending it along to the cortex (Boynton, 1980).

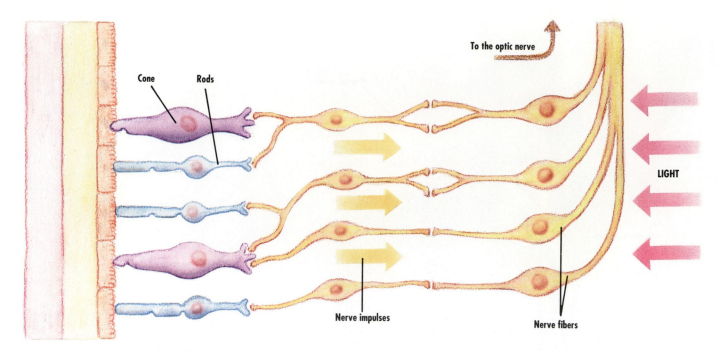

To the optic nerve
Cone Rods
LIGHT
Nerve impulses
Nerve fibers

FIGURE 3.10

The arrangement of synaptical connections in the human retina. Light, shown entering from the right, must travel through several layers to the rods and cones at the back of the eye. The rods and cones react to light and send nerve impulses back towards the front of the eye, to nerve fibers connecting with the optic nerve.

Rhodopsin (row-DOP-sin). The visual pigment in the rods that, when bleached by light, causes the rods to send a signal to the brain that a visual input has occurred.

RODS AND CONES. The receptor neurons for vision are the *rods* and *cones*. Their names are fairly descriptive of their shapes. In the human eye, the rods are slim, pencil-shaped nerve cells. The cones are thicker and have a cone-shaped tip at their "business" end (see Figure 3.11).

Both the rods and cones contain chemicals that are very sensitive to light. When a beam of light strikes a rod, it causes the *bleaching* or breakdown of a chemical called **rhodopsin**, or visual purple (the Greek word *rhod* means "rose-colored"). In ways that we still don't entirely understand, this bleaching action causes the rod to respond electrically. This visual input message passes up through the lower centers of your brain and eventually reaches the visual cortex on the occipital lobe (see Figure 3.12). At this point, you become "consciously aware" that you have actually seen something (Stryer, 1987).

FIGURE 3.11

Photograph of the retina greatly enlarged. The rods are the slim, horizontal cells on the left; the cones are the two fat cells squeezed in between the rods. Light enters the retina from the right; the back of the eye (choroid coat) is to the left in the photograph.

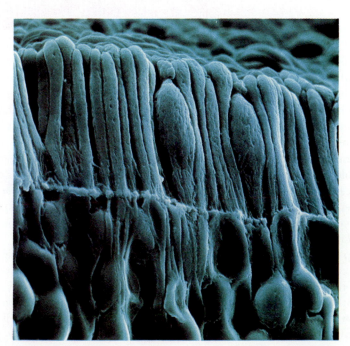

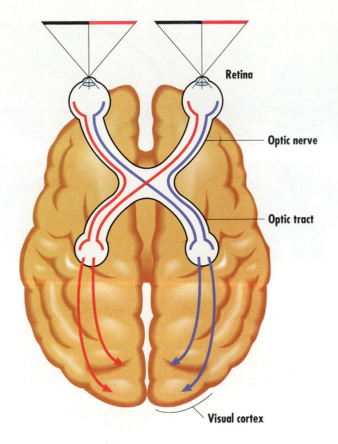

Retina

Optic nerve

Optic tract

Visual cortex

FIGURE 3.12

A cross section of the visual system. Any object (such as the gray part of the line) in the left half of your visual field will be focused on the right half of the retinas in both your left and right eyes. Inputs from the right half of both retinas are sent to the visual cortex in your right hemisphere. Inputs from the left half of both retinas go to the left visual cortex. In this drawing, your left brain perceives the red half of the line, while your right brain perceives the gray half of the line.

Your rods are *color-blind*. They "see" the world in blacks and whites no matter how colorful the world actually is. Your rods respond much like a "fast but grainy" black-and-white film you might use in a camera. That is, the rods need less light to operate than the cones do, but they give a less detailed picture of the world than the colorful view provided by your cones. For the most part, the rods are concentrated in the outer reaches or periphery of the retina. There are almost no rods in the central regions of the retina. All told, there are about 100 million rods in each of your eyes (Hole, 1990).

Your cones contain photo-sensitive chemicals which break down when struck by light waves. This chemical reaction triggers off an electrical response in your cones which passes along the optic nerve until it reaches the visual input area in your occipital lobes. Current research suggests there are three different types of cones. One type of cone is sensitive primarily to *red* light, a second is sensitive to *blue* light, and a third is sensitive to *green*. Each type of cone has its own unique photo-sensitive chemical (Berne & Levy, 1990).

There are a few cones in the periphery of the retina, but most of the cones are bunched together in the center of your retina near the fovea. There are some five to seven million cones in each of your eyes (Goldstein, 1989). Since your cones are located primarily in the center of your retina, this is the part of your eye that is most sensitive to color.

When you look at something straight on, the light waves coming from that object strike your fovea and stimulate the cones, giving you clear color vision. When the same object is at the outer edges (periphery) of your vision, the light waves from the object strike primarily the rods in the periphery of the retina. Since the rods are *color-blind*, you will see anything that appears at the edges of your visual world as lacking in color. However, you can see some color (very weakly) even in the periphery of your vision because there are a few cones scattered about in the periphery (Van De Graaff & Fox, 1989).

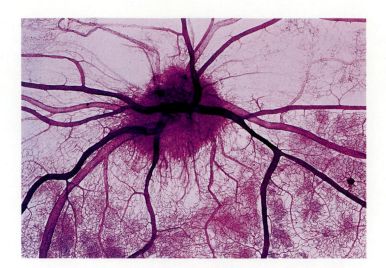

Enlarged photograph of the retina. The dark area is the point where nerve fibers and blood vessels converge, creating a blind spot.

Fovea (FOE-vee-ah). The tiny "pit" or depression right at the center of your retina that contains only cones, and where your vision is at its clearest and sharpest.

FOVEA AND BLIND SPOT.   There are two special parts of your retina that you should know about. The first is called the **fovea.** The second is your *blind spot.*

Fovea is the Latin word for "small pit." The fovea in your eye is a tiny pit in the center of your retina where your vision is at its sharpest. This is because the fovea contains only *cones.* Although the fovea is only about the size of a head of a pin, the fovea is crucial for such specialized tasks as reading or inspecting the fine detail of any object.

The top layers of your retina contain a few of the tiny blood vessels that serve the retina. Surprisingly enough, light must pass through these large neurons and the blood vessels before it can stimulate the rods and cones. Fortunately, these neurons and blood vessels are pushed aside at the point of the fovea. This fact helps explain why the fovea looks like a "pit," and why vision is clearest at this point.

It is probably hard for you to imagine that each of your eyes has a spot that is, for all practical purposes, *totally blind.* Thus, there actually is a "hole" in your visual field where you see nothing at all.

Why this hole in your visual field? Well, your eyeball is hollow like a balloon, and your retina is *inside* the eyeball. The axons from the large neurons must somehow get through the walls of the eyeball if they are to reach their destinations in your brain. These axons meet at a point near the fovea to form the *optic nerve,* which exits from your eye at the blind spot. There are no receptors at this point in your retina—only axonic fibers and blood vessels. So, the part of your visual world that falls on the *blind spot* is not recorded in your brain.

You are usually unaware of this "hole in your vision" because what one eye misses, the other usually picks up (see Figure 3.13). However, it is also true that your brain "cheats" just a bit. That is, your brain fills in the hole by making the empty spot in

FIGURE 3.13

Because there are no photoreceptors where the optic nerve leaves the eye, we have a blind spot in our vision. To demonstrate the blind spot, close your left eye, fix your right eye on the "+," and move the book slowly toward your face. At a viewing distance of about 14 inches the obnoxious person will disappear but the vertical lines will not.

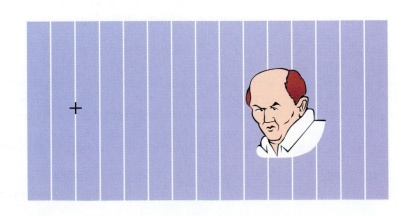

your visual world look like whatever surrounds it. You can prove this to yourself by following the instructions given in Figure 3.13. If you look at the picture from just right position, the man's face disappears. Notice too that the spot where the man's face should be is filled in by your brain with the lines that surround the man's picture.

Optical Defects

Many distortions of your visual world are caused by misinterpretations made by your brain. But quite a few distortions stem from physical problems with the eye itself. For example, the chances are one in four you either wear glasses or should wear them to help you overcome correctable visual difficulties. Many of these problems come from slight abnormalities in the shape of your eyeball.

NEARSIGHTEDNESS AND FARSIGHTEDNESS

If your eyeball is *too long*, the lens tends to focus the visual image a little *in front of* your retina rather than clearly on it. You then see *near* objects rather clearly, but distant objects would appear fuzzy and blurred to you. We call this condition *nearsightedness* (see Figure 3.14).

If your eyeball is *too short*, the lens tends to focus the visual image *behind* the retina rather that directly on it. Close objects are therefore indistinct to you, but *far* or distant objects are usually in clear focus. We call this condition *farsightedness*.

If you watch carefully in the next movie you attend, you may notice something like the following: A woman standing close to the camera is talking with a man some distance away. When the woman is speaking, the camera focuses on her face, which you see clearly—but the image of the distant man is blurred and fuzzy. This is approximately the way the nearsighted person sees the world.

Now, as the dialogue in the movie continues and the man begins to speak, the camera changes focus (but not position). Suddenly the woman's face, which is close to the camera, becomes blurred—but the distant image of the man sharpens and become distinct. This is approximately the way the farsighted person sees things in the world.

The lens in your eye operates much the same as does a camera lens, changing the focus from far to near as the occasion demands. As you grow older, however, your lenses become brittle, and you cannot focus back and forth between near and far objects as well as when you were young. This condition is called **old-sightedness,** or *presbyopia.* The typical solution to this problem is *bifocal glasses.* The upper part of the lens gives a clear picture of distant objects, while the lower half of the lens allows the person to see near objects clearly.

If your cornea is irregularly shaped, you could suffer from a common visual defect called **astigmatism.** Fortunately, you can usually overcome this problem by wearing the proper prescription glasses.

VISUAL ACUITY.   When you go to an eye doctor to be tested for glasses, or when you apply for a driver's license, you will be given one of several tests to determine how accurately your eyes *discriminate* small objects. Your ability to discriminate such things as the small print in a phone book is called your *visual acuity.*

One very common visual test is the Snellen chart, which presents letters of different sizes for you to read (see Figure 3.15). A person with normal vision can barely read the largest letter on this chart at a distance of 200 feet (60 meters), and can just make out the next largest letters standing 100 feet away.

If you took this test yourself, you probably would be asked to stand 20 feet away from the Snellen chart. If you could read the "normal" line of letters at this distance, we would say that you can "see at 20 feet what the normal person can see at 20 feet." Hence, you would have 20/20 vision.

If you stood 20 feet away from the chart and could only read what the normal person can easily see at 100 feet, your vision would be 20/100, which is fairly poor. But

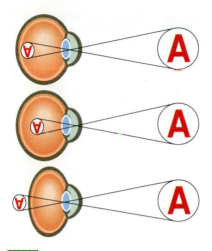

FIGURE 3.14

From bottom to top, a far-sighted, a near sighted, and a normal eye. Notice where the image focuses in each case.

Old-sightedness. A type of farsightedness associated with aging and caused by a hardening of the lens. Also called presbyopia (prez-bee-OH-pee-ah).

Astigmatism (as-STIG-mah-tism). A visual defect caused by imperfections in the shape of the cornea. Usually can be corrected with glasses.

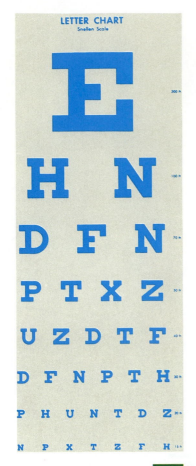

LETTER CHART
Snellen Scale

FIGURE 3.15

The Snellen chart. (The chart has been reduced, so don't worry if you have trouble seeing the letters at the normal distances!)

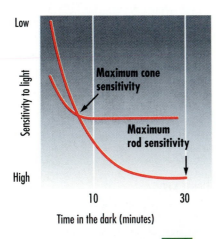

FIGURE 3.16

Dark adaptation as a function of time. The longer you spend in the dark (up to at least 30 minutes) the more accurate your visual detection becomes. The major dark adaptation occurs within the rods, which reach their full sensitivity to minimal light in about 30 minutes. The cones, which adapt less to darkness, reach maximum sensitivity in about 10 minutes.

if you could make out the very small letters on the bottom line when you were standing 20 feet away, you would be able to read letters that normal people can discriminate only when they are 10 feet away from the chart. In this case, you would have 20/10 or superior visual acuity.

VISUAL CONTRAST

Visual acuity alone is not enough for excellent vision. You also must be able to see *brightness* differences as well. *Visual contrast* is the difference in the levels of brightness between adjoining areas of your visual world. A black dot on a white background has a lot of contrast. A gray cat sitting on a fog-covered rock has little contrast.

According to Robert Sekuler and Patrick Mulvanny, some individuals seem innately to be able to perceive visual contrast better than others. Other people apparently lost the ability to detect subtle contrast effects because of disease or brain damage. At the moment, there is no "optical correction" that will improve your ability to see contrasts. However, it is known that people who can detect contrasts well when wearing ordinary glasses sometimes lose that ability when wearing soft contact lenses. Sekuler and Mulvanny believe that when you apply for a driver's license, you should be tested not merely for visual acuity but for visual contrast as well (Sekuler & Mulvanny, 1982).

Visual Sensitivity

Under normal circumstances—in daylight, for instance—your *visual acuity* depends primarily on your cones. But at night or in any dim illumination, when you are often more interested in *detecting* faint sources of light than in *discriminating* fine details, your rods come into play. Your rods are much more sensitive to light than are your cones. Indeed, under the best of conditions, your rods are capable of detecting a single photon of light (Stryer, 1987). Your cones, however, are better than your rods at seeing things in fine detail.

VISUAL ADAPTATION

When light strikes one of your rods or cones, the light causes the photosensitive chemicals in your receptors to *bleach*, or break down. Your eye replaces the "broken down" photo-sensitive molecules fairly rapidly. But, as you might guess, your eye can replace these "visual chemicals" more rapidly in the dark than in bright illumination. Thus, after you have "adapted" to the darkness for a while, your ability to detect faint light sources is much better than when you've been sitting in bright sunlight.

As Figure 3.16 suggests, your *cones* adapt more quickly in darkness than do your *rods*. Your cones become almost as sensitive as they are ever going to get in a matter of 10 minutes or so. Your rods continue to adapt for 30 minutes or more. Because they build up a larger "surplus" of photo-sensitive chemicals, your rods are a thousand times better at detecting weak visual inputs when fully dark-adapted than are your cones.

How long do you think an airplane pilot should be required to adapt to the dark before she or he is allowed to fly at night?

NIGHT-BLINDNESS

Some people do not see at all well at night. Usually this defect is caused by some disability of the rods. Night-blindness may have many causes, but a lack of Vitamin A is perhaps the most common one. Vitamin A is necessary for the build-up of rhodopsin in the rods.

In daylight, your eyes automatically focus the image of an object on your fovea, where your visual acuity is best in good illumination. But your fovea contains only cones, hence it is "blind" at night. So when you stare directly at an object in dim light, the object may "disappear" because you're trying to see it with your cones.

If you want to see something at night, stare at the object "out of the corner of your eye," so that the object's visual image will fall on the periphery of your retina. That way, you can look at the object with your rods, not your cones. And that way, you can actually see better in dim illumination.

Why do most objects look less colorful at twilight than at bright noon?

Color Vision

For the most part, there is a very close connection between the physical attributes of a stimulus and the psychological experiences the stimulus creates inside your head. That's why it is very important that you learn something about the physical aspects of various stimuli. As we will see, however, there are times when your eyes (and brain) respond to inputs in ways that cannot be explained in purely "physical" terms. This point becomes particularly important when we try to describe *color vision*.

HUE

When you speak of the color of something, you really are talking about that object's **hue.** The psychological experience of *color* is the *hue* caused by the wavelength of light from the stimulus object. Each wavelength of light in the rainbow (visible spectrum) produces a unique hue.

Most of the familiar colors appear on what psychologists call the *color circle*, which is made by joining the ends of the rainbow (see Figure 3.17). Arranged around the outer edge of this circle are all of the spectral colors that you can see, and each point on the circle has a unique hue and wavelength.

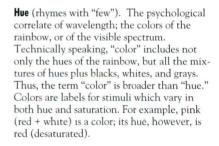

Hue (rhymes with "few"). The psychological correlate of wavelength; the colors of the rainbow, or of the visible spectrum. Technically speaking, "color" includes not only the hues of the rainbow, but all the mixtures of hues plus blacks, whites, and grays. Thus, the term "color" is broader than "hue." Colors are labels for stimuli which vary in both hue and saturation. For example, pink (red + white) is a color; its hue, however, is red (desaturated).

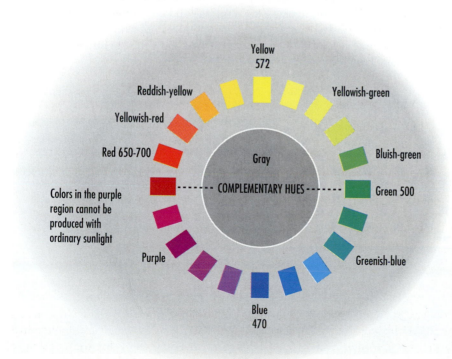

FIGURE 3.17

The color circle illustrates the facts of color and color light mixture. The color names and their corresponding wavelengths (in nanometers) are given along the outside of the circle. Complementary colors are those colors opposite each other in the circle (such as reddish-yellow and greenish-blue); they will result in gray when mixed. The mixing of any two other wavelengths gives us an intermediate color. By proper mixing of three wavelengths equidistant in the circle (such as blue, green, and reddish-yellow), we can produce all color sensations.

Any two colors that are *opposite* one another on the color circle are *complementary*. For reasons we still don't entirely understand, if you stare at a colored object for a minute or so, then close your eyes or look at white wall, you will see the image in "reverse color." Technically speaking, this "reverse color" is called a *negative afterimage*. Negative afterimages are always the complement of the color that you looked at. (See Figure 3.18.)

SATURATION

Hue alone is not enough to explain all the colorful visual experiences you have. For example, what is pink? Is isn't a mixture of any two hues, but rather is a pale or *diluted* red. The vividness or richness of a color is what we call **saturation.**

Saturated colors are rich-looking and strong. Desaturated colors are weak and diluted. For example, suppose you poured red coloring into a bowl filled with tap water. The water would become deep red—a highly saturated color. Now suppose you pour in a lot more tap water. What happens? The ruby red soon becomes a pale, *desaturated* pink.

The hues around the outer edge of the color circle were carefully picked to be the most saturated possible (see Figure 3.17). As you move inward toward the center of the circle, the colors become less and less saturated until you reach gray, which has no hue at all.

The *color solid* shown in Figure 3.19 is an "expansion" of the color circle into three-dimensional space. Notice, though, that the color solid is not a perfect globe. The light blue colors simply do not seem as saturated to most observers as do the dark blue colors. And the dark yellow colors do not seem as saturated as do the light yellows. There is no general agreement among scientists as to why light blue and dark yellows aren't as fully saturated as are dark blues and light yellows.

LIGHTNESS

As we mentioned, the color solid shown in Figure 3.19 is really a three-dimensional "color circle." The hue changes as you go around the figure, while saturation decreases as you move from the outer edge toward the center of the globe. But there is a third dimension to this figure, aside from hue and saturation. This third dimension is called *lightness*. The "north pole" of the solid is pure white. The "south pole" is pure black. Gray lies in the very center of the solid. The "lightness" of a visual stimulus, then, ranges from white to gray to black.

Saturation (sat-your-RAY-shun). The intensity or richness of a color. Pink is a weak (desaturated) red. The colors of the rainbow are about as saturated as any colors can be.

FIGURE 3.18

Stare at the center of this flag for about 30 seconds. Then look at a white wall or sheet of paper. You will see a negative afterimage in the colors complementary to those shown here.

FIGURE 3.19

The purple-blue to yellow color solid on the left is viewed from the green side. The yellow to purple-blue range on the right side is viewed from the red side.

By definition, black and white are completely desaturated colors. And like gray, black and white are "colors," but not "hues." We could say that white is a very light color, and black is a very dark color.

What is the difference between "lightness" and "brightness"?

COLOR MIXING

There are two types of color mixtures, **additive** and **subtractive.** If you mixed two or more paints to make a new color, you create a *subtractive* mixture. Paints create a subtractive mixture by blocking out or subtracting certain hues in the light they reflect. If you shine a white light on an object painted blue, the pigments in the blue paint will subtract, or block out, all the spectrum other than the hues in the blue area (that is, all the hues except blue and a little green). Thus, the object appears blue. Yellow paint blocks out (subtracts) all the hues in white light *except* those at the yellow end of the spectrum (that is, all but yellow and a little green and a little orange). If you mix blue and yellow paints, the blue pigments subtract out the yellows and the yellow pigments subtract out the blues. But both pigments will leave some of the greens unblocked. Thus, a subtractive mixture of blue and yellow paints often yields a green color (see Figure 3.20a).

You create an *additive* color mixture by combining colored *lights*. If you combine in an additive way, the same two colors we used in our subtractive example, the results will be quite different. If you shine a blue light and a yellow light on the same spot on a movie screen, the screen reflects back almost all of the light and thus "adds" the blue to the yellow light, giving white. Figure 3.20b shows additive color mixing. (Here, for example, red and green combine to give yellow, which when added to blue gives white.)

Additive color mixing. The mixing of colored lights. It is additive because as new colors are added, *additional* wavelengths of light are reflected back.

Subtractive color mixing. The mixing of pigments, such as in paints. This is subtractive because the pigments *block out* (subtract) certain wavelengths of light. As more pigments are combined, more wavelengths are blocked. What is reflected, and appears as color, is thus only what is *left over*.

Color Deficiencies

Suppose you wanted to determine whether other people saw the world in the same colorful way that you do. How would you go about finding out?

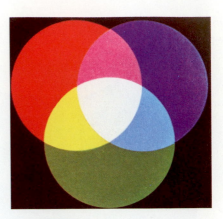

FIGURE 3.20a

The effect of combining pigments, such as in paints (*subtractive* color mixing).

FIGURE 3.20b

The effect of combining colored lights (*additive* color mixing).

You might just show a variety of objects—a rose, a lime, a blueberry, and a lemon—to a random sample of subjects and *ask* them what colors the objects were. But even if everyone in your sample announced that "the rose is red-colored," how would you know the subjects actually *saw* the rose as being the same color you did? Red, after all, is a *subjective experience*, not a physical dimension.

One way to bring some objectivity to your experiment might be to show your subjects a rose and then ask them to mix three colored lights until they just matched the redness of the rose. You could pick almost any three colored lights from the spectrum for your "mix colors," of course. But let's say you picked red, blue, and a green because you know you have a specific cone-receptor for each of these colors. You could then use these same three "mix colors" when you asked your subjects to match the greenness of a lime, the redness of a rose, and the blue of a berry.

COLOR WEAKNESS

If you tested enough people using an additive color mixture technique, you would soon find that a few of your subjects needed an abnormally large amount of red in order to reproduce the redness of a rose. These people would be *red-weak*. That is, they see the color red, but it appears much weaker to them than do green, blue, and

Does everyone see colors the same way? If you think so, try naming the colors of these flowers and comparing your answers with a friend's responses.

yellow. If you asked a red-weak individual to mix red and blue to match the purple of a plum, this person would mix in much more red than would a subject with normal red vision.

A few other subjects might need an unusually large amount of green to match a lime-colored light. These people would be *green-weak*. If you asked a person with normal color vision to mix green and blue to match a turquoise-colored light, the person might mix the two colors in equal proportions. A green-weak individual, however, might well need 80 percent green and 20 percent blue to get a "subjective match" for the turquoise-colored light. Most color-weak individuals have difficulties seeing either red or green, or have problems with both these hues.

PARTIAL COLOR-BLINDNESS

About 5 percent of the people in the world are almost totally insensitive to one or more hues on the color circle, although they can see most of the other hues perfectly well. The majority of these *color-deficient* people are men, for color deficiency is a sex-linked, inherited problem that seldom affects women.

The color-deficient person can reproduce all of the colors he or she can see by mixing just two basic hues. The main types of color deficiency involve a red deficiency or a green deficiency. Blue or yellow color deficiency is very rare. The rare individual who is blue-yellow deficient sees the world entirely in reds and greens (plus black and white).

A person suffering from either red or green deficiency sees the world almost entirely in terms of blues and yellows (plus black and white). Colors at the blue-green end of the spectrum appear blue, while colors at the red-yellow end of the spectrum appear yellow. Thus, to someone with either red or green deficiency, a bright red fire engine will look a dull yellow, and grass would appear to be a desaturated blue. Red-deficient individuals simply don't have properly functioning "red cones" in their retinas. Similarly, the cone that reports the sensory stimulus "green" is not functioning normally in green-deficient individuals.

Jeremy Nathans and his colleagues have shown that there are unique genes on the X-chromosome that "code" for the red, green, and blue cones in your retina. If you lack the "red gene," for example, no red cones appear in your retina and you are completely blind to the color red. Oddly enough, while just one gene determines red and one gene determines blue, some individuals have two (or more genes) that appear to code for green (cited in Schiffman, 1990). MIT geneticist David Botstein believes that, as humans evolve over time, these "extra" green genes may allow us to perceive one or more colors we currently are "blind" to (Botstein, 1986).

Suppose your NASA robot could perceive colors that you were blind to. What would it be like to try to understand the robot?

TOTAL COLOR-BLINDNESS

Only about one person in 40,000 is totally color-blind. A few of these totally color-blind individuals were born with normal vision, but lost the ability to see hues as a result of disease. Others became totally color-blind because their cones were poisoned by such pollutants as lead or carbon disulfide. Still others, such as an artist studied by Sacks and Wasserman, have suffered damage to parts of the visual cortex, leaving them totally color-blind (Sacks & Wasserman, 1987).

Most totally color-blind people, however, suffer from **albinism**—an inherited condition involving a lack of pigment throughout their bodies. Like albino rabbits and rats, these people have colorless hair, pink-white skin, and pinkish irises. Since the photosensitive chemicals in the cones are, in fact, *pigments*, albino people lack functional cones and *cannot see color at all*.

Albinism (AL-bin-ism). From the Latin word *albus*, meaning "white." Albinism is an inherited condition that involves a failure to produce colored pigments in the hair, skin, and elsewhere in the body.

FIGURE 3.21

These two illustrations are from a series of color-blindness tests. In the left plate, people with normal vision see a number 6, while those with red-green color-blindness do not. Those with normal vision see a number 12 in the right plate; red-green blind people may see one number or none. These reproductions of color-recognition tests cannot be used for actual testing. The examples are only representative of the total of 15 charts necessary for a complete color recognition examination (American Optical Corporation from their AO Pseudo-Isochromatic Color Tests.)

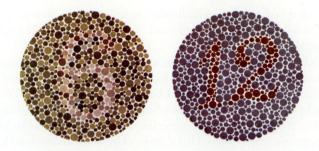

When albino people look directly at an object, it tends to "disappear" from their sight. Why?

TESTS FOR COLOR DEFICIENCIES

Odd as it may seem, many color-deficient individuals reach maturity without knowing they have a visual defect. For instance, Karl Dallenbach, a psychologist who spent his professional life studying sensory processes, learned of his red deficiency in an introductory psychology class.

During a lecture on vision, the professor wished to demonstrate an old color deficiency test called the Holmgren wools. The test consists of a large number of strands of colored wool that the subject is asked to sort into various piles according to their hues. Dallenbach happened to be tapped for the honor of being a subject. When asked to sort the reds into one pile, Dallenbach included all the wools with a greenish hue as well as those that were clearly red. When asked to sort all the greens, he included the reds.

At first the teacher thought that Dallenbach was playing a joke, but subsequent tests proved he was red-deficient. Like most color-deficient people, Dallenbach had learned to compensate for his handicap while growing up.

Despite this visual problem, however, Dallenbach went on to become a noted psychologist. But perhaps because of his red deficiency, Dallenbach specialized in the study of taste and smell—not color vision.

The Holmgren wools are but one (and perhaps the least accurate) of many different tests for color deficiencies. Most of the other tests contain hundreds of tiny dots of colors. These dots are so arranged that a person with normal vision sees letters, numbers, or geometric figures in the dots. A person with color deficiency, however, sees only a random jumble of dots or a different number than would the normal person. An example of this sort of color deficiency test is shown in Figure 3.21.

RESTRICTED SENSATION

Sights and sounds, smells, taste, and touch make the world a stimulating place indeed! But what if you lost your sensory abilities? What if you became not only blind and deaf, but you were given minimal touch, taste, and smell stimulation as well? If you lost your sensory abilities would you lose touch with your world?

This seemed to be what happened to subjects in a 1950s experiment on "sensory deprivation." Volunteer subjects reclined in a specially constructed chamber, cut off from all normal stimulation. They received constant, unvaried stimulation—"white noise" and unpatterned light through translucent goggles. Those subjects who remained for several days showed considerable intellectual impairment for several hours after the study. Many subjects reported visual hallucinations and other disturbed perceptions. All of the subjects found the experience stressful and even frightening (Bexton et al., 1954; Heron et al., 1956).

Subsequent research found much less dramatic effects (Suedfeld & Coren, 1989; Suedfeld & Kristeller, 1982). But if you've ever been bored you know the discomfort caused by lack of stimulation and the value of having a minimal level of sensory activation.

On the other hand, perhaps you have experienced the stress of *sensory overload*, when your senses were bombarded with stimulation. You felt like you just needed to get "a moment's peace and quiet." Recently, researchers have found that "sensory restriction" can be quite therapeutic (see Figure 3.22).

Peter Suedfeld and his colleagues report that "Restricted Environmental Stimulation Therapy," or **REST,** can help people lose weight, stop smoking, decrease their consumption of alcohol, and even improve their creativity and athletic performance (Suedfeld, 1980, 1990; Suedfeld & Baker-Brown, 1987; Suedfeld & Bruno, 1990; Suedfeld & Metcalfe, 1987).

In one study, for example, heavy-drinking students experienced 212 hours of the REST cure. After 90 minutes in the silence and darkness of REST, they heard short, factual, anti-alcohol messages. Compared to control conditions, the experimental

REST (Restricted Environmental Stimulation Therapy). Using sensory isolation to reduce stress and motivate people to change their attitudes and behaviors.

FIGURE 3.22

An example of a flotation tank used for REST. The subjects float in complete darkness and silence.

subjects decreased their alcohol consumption by more than half over the following 6 months (Cooper et al., 1988).

There are several possible reasons that REST works. First, it may increase the *attention* a subject pays to input received while in isolation. Second, it may increase the social *acceptability* of those inputs. Third, it may *motivate* people to make changes in their thoughts and behaviors. And fourth, it may induce an altered state of consciousness or "twilight state" in "RESTing" subjects (Suedfeld, 1990; Suedfeld & Metcalfe, 1987).

If your robot lost all its inputs, would it react any differently than you would? Why (or why not)?

SENSATION, PERCEPTION, AND CULTURE

People all over the world are born with the same sensory "equipment." Eyes, for example, always respond to the same wavelengths of light in the same way. But do we all *see* the same thing? For example, do we all "see" the same set of colors, red, green, blue, and yellow, as distinct categories?

It may surprise you to learn that not everyone divides the color spectrum in the same way that you do, or as we divided the circle in Figure 3.17. Robert MacLaury reports that Native North Americans of the Salish tradition use a single term for yellow and green (MacLaury, 1991). Paul Kay, Brent Berlin, and William Merrifield identify three additional language groups that name not only yellow and green, but also blue with a single term (Kay et al., 1991). These differences do not mean that our visual physiology is different, but that our cultural experience affects the way we organize our visual inputs—even so basic an input as variations in color (MacLaury, 1992).

The process of *organizing* sensory inputs and giving them *meaning* is the process of *perception*. But perception is the next stage in the processing of sensory information, so let's leave further discussion of cultural and other influences on perception for our next chapter.

SUMMARY

1. The **absolute threshold** is the smallest amount of sensory stimulation that can be detected. The **difference threshold** is the smallest noticeable increase in a stimulus. **Weber's law** says that the difference threshold increases as the comparison or base level of stimulation increases.

2. Receptor **adaptation** is a slowing down of the firing rate of your sensory receptors which occurs when the receptors are stimulated at a constant rate. Central **habituation** is a process that occurs in your brain when you no longer pay attention to a **constant stimulus input.**

3. Your skin is your window to a great part of the outside world. **Receptor cells** in your skin provide sensory inputs to your **somatic cortex (parietal lobe)** telling your cortex what your body is doing, what your skin is touching, and whether the outside world is warm or cold.

4. The **corpuscles** in the hairless regions of your skin detect pressure. The **basket cells** in the hairy regions, and the **free nerve endings** found in all skin, detect pressure, temperature, and pain.

5. The **deep receptors** in your muscles, joints, tendons, and bones tell your cortex the position and condition of various parts of your body.

6. Sensors in your skin can detect **absolute temperature** (hot or cold), as well as **differences in temperature** between your body and your surroundings.

7. The primary receptors for taste are the receptor cells in the **taste buds,** which are located in mushroom-shaped bumps called **papillae.** Most taste receptors lie on the surface of the tongue, but a few can be found elsewhere in the mouth.

8. The four basic taste qualities are **sweet, sour, bitter,** and **salty,** but most of the "taste" of food is really the smell of the food rather than its taste.

9. Smell is a **basic sense** more associated with **emotion** and **motivation** than with cognition.

10. The smell receptors are the **olfactory rods,** which lie on the **olfactory membrane** inside each of the two nostrils.

11. Chemical molecules in the air are absorbed into the **mucus** covering the olfactory membrane and excite the **cilia** of the olfactory rods. The rods respond by firing off a message to the brain.

12. Women are more sensitive to all types of sensory inputs in the middle of their **menstrual cycles,** when their **hormone level** is high, than at any other point in the cycle.

13. Smell and taste are both **mono** (one dimensional) senses in that they seldom help us locate objects in space very well. Hearing is a **stereo** sense. Your brain converts differences in what your two ears hear into an understanding of whether the source of the sound is to the left or right. While your ears discriminate **left-right differences** in sounds very well, they do not discriminate **up-down differences** at all well.

14. The middle ear contains three bones—the **hammer, anvil,** and **stirrup**—that amplify sound waves. The **eardrum** separating the outer from the middle ear is connected to the hammer. The stirrup is connected to the **oval window,** which separates the middle from the inner ear.

15. The inner ear is a snail-shaped space called the **cochlea.** The hair cells that are the true **auditory receptors** are part of the **organ of Corti.** The organ of Corti lies on the **basilar membrane,** which runs the length of the cochlea.

16. Buried away in your inner ear are your motion-change detectors—the **saccule,** the **utricle,** and the **semi-circular canals.** The saccule and utricle sense changes in straight-line or **linear motion.** The semi-circular canals respond to changes in circular or **rotary motion.**

17. Sound waves have both **frequency** and **amplitude.** The greater the frequency of a musical tone, the higher it generally sounds. The larger the amplitude of a sound, the louder it will usually seem to be.

18. **Bone deafness** is a hearing loss caused by improper functioning of the bones in your middle ear. **Nerve deafness** results from damage to the hair cell receptors.

19. Children **born deaf** have problems learning to speak because they cannot hear the sound of their own voice. People who become deaf later in life may develop **paranoia** because they fear other people are talking about them.

20. The stimulus input for vision is light, which is made up of waves of energy particles called **photons.**

21. The **frequency** of a light wave helps determine the color the light will appear to be. The **amplitude** (intensity) of the light wave generally determines how bright it will seem.

22. The **wavelengths** for the visible spectrum run from 400 **nanometers** (blue) through 760 nanometers (red).

23. Light enters your eye through the **cornea** and **aqueous humor,** then passes

through the **pupil,** the **lens,** and the **vitreous humor.** The light then strikes your **retina,** which is the **photosensitive** inner surface of the hollow eyeball.

24. The retina contains your **visual receptors**—the **rods** and **cones.** There are three types of cones, one sensitive to red, one to blue, and one to green. The rods contain **rhodopsin,** and are sensitive only to blacks, whites, and shades of gray.

25. In the center of your retina is a small pit called the **fovea** that contains only cones. Your vision is at its sharpest when the visual image falls on the fovea.

26. Near the fovea is the **blind spot,** which contains no visual receptors. The optic nerve, which runs from your retina to your brain, exits from the eyeball at the blindspot.

27. **Nearsighted** people typically see close objects more clearly than they do far objects. **Farsighted** people typically see distant objects more clearly than they do objects that are close to their eyes.

28. A person with normal **visual acuity** (keenness of vision) is said to have **20/20 vision.** This means that the person can see at a distance of 20 feet what the average person can see at a distance of 20 feet. However, the ability to perceive **visual contrast** is also important to good vision.

29. Your rods are more sensitive at night (or in dim illumination) than are your cones. If your rods malfunction, you may suffer from **night-blindness.**

30. Colors have **hue** (red, green, blue, yellow) and **saturation** or richness.

31. Black, white, and gray are completely **desaturated colors.** The black-white axis of the **color solid** runs from white to gray to black, and is called **lightness.**

32. If a person can see a color, but only when it is very intense, the person is said to be **color weak.** If a person cannot see a particular color no matter how intense it is, that person is said to be **color deficient.**

33. Men tend to be "color weak" and "color deficient" more frequently than women. The most common form of **color deficiency** is the failure to see reds and/or greens as people with normal color vision do.

34. **Albino** humans and animals lack the pigments necessary for normal color vision. They therefore see only with their rods and are **totally color-blind.** They are also totally blind in their foveas.

35. Although restricting sensory input for long periods of time may be stressful, short periods of **Restricted Environmental Stimulation Therapy (REST)** may help relieve problems and improve performance.

ANSWERS FOR THOUGHT

1. *Why are "distance" senses particularly important?*

   Distance stimuli (sound and sight) often provide information in time to permit a choice of whether to approach or avoid the stimulus source. Distance stimuli are also the main vehicles of communication.

2. *Is there a difference between the way a measuring instrument, such as a scale for weight, "senses" a physical . . . ?*

   Physical measuring instruments can often detect fainter stimuli and smaller differences in stimuli than a person can. More importantly, physical instruments are calibrated to indicate *equal* intervals between points on their scales. People notice small increments at low levels of stimulation, but only large increments at high levels.

3. *How much sugar would you have to add to a cup of coffee before the coffee would taste sweeter?*

It depends on how much sugar is in the coffee already. Weber's law of proportions says that for taste, increases must be approximately five times the base amount to be noticeable. This means that if you have five teaspoons of sugar in your coffee already, one more would be just noticeable. If you have more than five already, you probably wouldn't notice just one more.

4. *What advantage can you see to tying stimulus-change sensitivity to stimulus intensity?*

Responding to each slight change in every stimulus would not only be tiring and time-consuming, it would be impossible. Experience (and nature) teaches us that slight changes in intense stimuli rarely matter. Thus, it is no doubt a good thing that we are "wired" to be sensitive to small stimulus changes only in relatively weak stimuli.

5. *When you have been soaking in a hot tub for a while, can you make the water feel warmer just by . . . ?*

You cannot make the water feel warmer because your skin temperature sensors have adapted to the warm water and have stopped sending messages to your sensory cortex. You can notice the traffic noise because your *brain* had become habituated to the sound messages from your ears, but the sound messages were *still being sent to your brain.*

6. *Would you want your robot's "pain" response to be influenced by the same things that influence your reaction to an injury?*

You might want your robot to be more "objective." That is, you might not want its reaction to be affected by "emotions" or the social setting, but rather, by an objective assessment of the damage—like the reactions of *Star Trek's* Mr. Spock.

7. *When you catch a cold, why does food suddenly lose its "taste?"*

The experience of taste is a combination of several factors, including smell. A cold may block your nasal passages, preventing food aromas from reaching your olfactory membrane.

8. *Many people report that a home or apartment they have lived in for a long time has a characteristic odor . . . ?*

Smells appear to be "wired" directly to emotional responses. It is only after we have responded emotionally to a smell that we may respond cognitively. Often there is no reason to respond cognitively and so no verbal associations may become attached to the smell. If we were in the habit of labelling, or in some other way responding verbally to smells, we would probably be better at describing our memories for smells.

9. *Why does it help to cock your head to one side when trying to locate the source of a sound over your head?*

A sound directly over your head travels the same distance to each ear, preventing you from localizing it. By cocking your head, you vary the distance the sound has to travel to each ear. This provides additional information to your brain, which can then calculate the location.

10. *If you wanted to design a whistle that could be used for calling dogs but couldn't be heard by human beings . . . ?*

You would want to investigate the range above 20,000 Hz (the upper limit of human hearing), up to around 25,000 Hz, which approaches the upper limit of some dogs.

11. *Many students turn up the volume on their car stereos to "live concert levels" while driving . . . ?*

Their driving might be adversely affected because their visual acuity was decreased.

12. *If you don't "speak up" around a person with hearing problems, how might your behaviors increase the deaf person's feelings of paranoia?*

    The deaf person might feel that you are *purposely* speaking so that he or she wouldn't hear you. This might make the person suspicious of your other behaviors.

13. *Suppose that a very bright but partially deaf child is mistakenly put in a home for mentally retarded persons . . . ?*

    "Mentally retarded," like other labels, is very hard to overcome—even if the label is unjustified. Once the child was labelled, it is not likely that someone would try to teach the child to read. It is conceivable that the child could learn to read on his or her own, but highly unlikely.

14. *If you were designing a robot for NASA, where on the robot's body would you put its hearing and vision receptors? Why?*

    You would probably want to put hearing and vision receptors where they would have the best access to auditory and visual stimuli, without being too vulnerable to damage. You would probably mount the receptors high on the robot, in a relatively protected position.

15. *Sound travels at slightly more than one-fifth mile a second. If you saw lightning hit the ground . . . ?*

    In 5 seconds the sound of thunder would travel approximately 1 mile. Thus, the lightning bolt hit approximately 1 mile away—and you'd better take cover!

16. *How many "eyes" should your NASA robot have? Why?*

    If technically and economically feasible, the robot should have as many eyes as necessary to "see" the surrounding environment completely. If technology could accomplish this with one eye, an additional eye might be considered as a back-up in case of injury.

17. *How long do you think an airplane pilot should be required to adapt to the dark before she or he is allowed to fly at night?*

    Because of the important nature of their job, and the need to see well while performing it, airline pilots should be required to adapt to the dark for at least 30 minutes before flying at night (even though the amount of improvement near 30 minutes is small).

18. *Why do most objects look less colorful at twilight than at bright noon?*

    Cones, the receptors for color, are not as sensitive to light as rods. In low light cones do not function well, so we rely more on our rods. We can still see, but since our rods are not sensitive to color, our color vision suffers. Also, when we rely on our rods, we are using the periphery of our retina(s) where there are relatively few cones, and hence weak color vision.

19. *What is the difference between "lightness" and "brightness"?*

    "Brightness" refers to saturation of a color. "Lightness" is a separate dimension that goes from white through gray to black. Making a colored light brighter will make it less saturated, but not necessarily lighter. Washing the dirt out of your colored clothes should make them brighter, but not necessarily lighter (or whiter).

20. *Suppose your NASA robot could perceive colors that you were blind to. What would it be like to try to understand the robot?*

It would be like someone who was blind to red and green trying to understand you explaining red and green to him or her. The robot might try analogies and comparisons with colors you could see, but understanding would be very difficult.

21. *When albino people look directly at an object, it tends to "disappear" from their sight. Why?*

Looking directly at an object focuses its image on your fovea. The fovea has no rods but only cones. Since albino people have non-functional cones, they could not see an image focused on their fovea, that is, an object they looked directly at.

22. *If your robot lost all its inputs, would it react any differently than you would? Why (or why not)?*

Unless you had programmed your robot to do something when it received no inputs, it would probably just sit there, like your computer does when you are not entering data. Humans, however, seem to be "programmed" to require a certain average minimum level of stimulation. Our preferences vary from time to time and from person to person, but overall, if we had absolutely no contact with our environment we would probably experience a very "unrobot-like" *emotional* reaction.

CHAPTER 4

PERCEPTION

T hree years before I would have been ready to kill for what I had now. I had envied published writers, envied and adored them. I had imagined them to be demigods; invulnerable to pain, blessed with a constant supply of love and self-assurance. Now I was learning about the other side of the sun-house mirror of fame. It was as if I had entered a room which very few are allowed to enter and which everyone on the outside believes to be incredibly beautiful, opulent, and magical. Once inside, you discover it is a hall of mirrors and all you see are myriad distortions of self, self, self.

ERICA JONG
HOW TO SAVE YOUR OWN LIFE

PERCEPTION

Psychology is, in many ways, the scientific study of the obvious. Take the study of perception, for example. Psychologists consider perception to be the psychological process by which you *make sense* out of your sensory inputs. But don't sensations have an automatic "wired-in" meaning? Look at the photograph at the side of this page. Obviously, it's a photograph of a coin. But what *shape* is it, and how do you know it's a coin? Well, you say, it's round, and you know it's a coin because you recognize it from past experience. However, let's push matters a bit. How do you know the shape of the coin is round? Is the concept of roundness somehow *hard-wired* into your neural circuits? Or did you have to learn what roundness is all about?

Is an association between senses, such as sight and touch, innate or is it learned? For example, if you were born blind, and then received sight as an adult, would you be able to recognize objects just by looking at them, or would you have to touch them first?

These are the sorts of obvious questions that seldom concern people other than philosophers and behavioral scientists. And, as you have already learned, different theorists are likely to answer such questions in radically different ways. Let's begin this chapter by looking at four approaches to a major issue in understanding what perception is all about.

Nature Versus Nurture

One of the great battles in psychology is this: How much of what you experience is learned, and how much is innately determined by your genes? We call this the **nature-nurture problem,** and we will discuss it frequently in future chapters (as well as in this one). In the field of perception, the nature position is represented primarily by two theoretical schools—the Gestalt psychologists, and the Gibsonians. The nurture position is best represented by the *empirical* approach, and by what is now called the information processing viewpoint. Let's look briefly at these four positions.

THE GESTALT APPROACH

The **Gestalt** movement began in Germany around 1912. It was started by several psychologists who believed perception was determined by the interaction between (1) the physical properties of the external stimulus, and (2) various *innately determined* psychological principles or laws. For example, one of these innate principles, called the **Law of Pragnanz,** holds that we tend to perceive the simplest and most stable figure of all the possible alternatives.

What is the simplest shape you can think of? Probably, a circle. Therefore, according to the Law of Pragnanz, as you look at objects such as coins, you tend to perceive these objects in the simplest manner possible—in this case, a *round* coin. However, if we showed you a square coin, you'd see it as square, not round, because squares are also simple and stable forms, and the stimulus factors would be too strong for you to perceive it otherwise. According to the Gestalt position, it is always the interaction between external stimulus and internal psychological principles that determines what you actually perceive (Arnheim, 1986).

Nature-nurture problem. One of the major controversies in psychology is over the amount of behavior that is inherited ("nature") and the amount that is learned through experience ("nurture"). For a more complete account of this controversy, see Chapter 12.

Gestalt (guess-SHTALT). A German word that is difficult to translate. Literally, a Gestalt is a "good form" or "good figure." Also, the tendency to see things as "wholes" rather than as jumbled bits and pieces.

Law of Pragnanz (PRAEG-nants). A Gestalt law that states perceptions tend to take the simplest and most stable form possible.

If we showed you a picture of an oval, and asked you to draw what you had just been shown, you probably would make the oval rounder than it actually was. Why?

What is the shape of this coin?

THE GIBSONIAN APPROACH

The Gestalt view is that your mind *imposes* a kind of psychological order on the inputs you get from the outside world. Psychologist James J. Gibson took the opposite point of view. He held that perception is *direct* and *immediate*. Gibson believed sensory inputs *impose order on your mind* (Gibson, 1950, 1983).

According to the **Gibsonian Approach,** your brain is "hard-wired" to *see the world as it really is.* The coin *is* round, and the light rays coming from the coin are rich in sensory cues describing its roundness. The pattern of excitation the light rays make on your retina is round. Thus, how could you perceive the coin as anything other than circular in shape (Reed, 1988)?

Put more precisely, Gibson believed that we can explain almost all perceptual experiences in terms of information to be found in the stimulus itself. Therefore, we should study *stimuli,* not "internal processes." Gibson believed there is a one-to-one correspondence between sensory inputs and perceptual experiences, and that this correspondence is determined by the genes. Put more simply, as far as perception goes, Gibson didn't ask what goes on "inside your head," but rather asked, "what kind of stimulus world is your head inside of?"

Look at the photograph at the side of this page. Here's the same coin again, but now it's turned away from you in space. Do you still see it as round? Probably so, even though the "image" the coin casts on your retina is actually an ellipse. The Gestalt view would be that, since the circle is a "simpler form" than the ellipse, the Law of Pragnanz *forces* you to perceive the coin as round. Gibson, however, would say that sensory cues determine what you perceive, not some "innate tendency toward perceptual stability." For instance, notice that some of the edge is visible on the left side of the coin, but not on the right side. These *sensory inputs* would force you to perceive the coin as round, but turned away from you in space (Bickhard & Richie, 1983).

The Gibsonian Approach. Gibson believed we can account for almost all aspects of visual perception in terms of stimulus inputs, and that the nervous system is "hard-wired" to make use of these inputs to perceive the world "as it really is."

What is the shape of this coin?

According to both Gibson and the Gestalt psychologists, how would a newborn infant perceive the coin shown on an angle in the photograph?

THE EMPIRICAL APPROACH

Both Gibson and the Gestalt psychologists took the genetic (or naturist) viewpoint. And, as we will see, both approaches contributed greatly to our understanding of perceptual processes. However, the more traditional viewpoint puts greater emphasis on learning (nurture) than on nature.

According to the **empirical** position, two independent factors determine perception—*present sensations* and *mental images of past experiences.* Put another way, the empirical view is that "perception = sensory inputs + memories."

The empirical position holds that you were not born with the innate knowledge that the coin is round, nor with the ability to make use of the sensory stimuli coming from the coin. Rather, you *learned* through empirical observations that these types of inputs are typically associated with a class of round objects called coins. From the empirical viewpoint, you *acquired* the ability to see the world the way you see it—including the roundness of coins.

Empirical (em-PEER-ih-cal). To be empirical is to rely on observation and experimental data more than on theory.

THE INFORMATION PROCESSING APPROACH

According to the empirical viewpoint, sensations are pure experiences not influenced by learning. Thus, sensory inputs presumably arrive at your cortex unprocessed

A father said to his double-seeing son, "Son, you see two instead of one."
"How can that be?" the boy replied. "If I were, there would seem to be four moons up there in place of two."

IDRIES SHAN, *Caravan of Dreams*

Information processing. The scientific study of how informational inputs are received by the nervous system, processed, stored, and how they lead to various decisions and response outputs.

in any significant way by the lower centers in your brain. Once these inputs register on your consciousness, your mind checks through its memory files and *interprets* the inputs according to past experience. To the empiricists, perception is the process by which your mind adds meaning to sensations.

Much of perception does seem to consist of adding meaning to sensory inputs. But the *manner* in which your mind accomplishes this miracle is far more complex than most early empiricists dreamed. For instance, many neurons in your visual system seem sensitive to certain *critical features* of visual inputs. Dozens of studies suggest that some cells in your retina probably are more responsive to movement than to stationary objects. Other studies show that some neurons in your brain respond to vertical lines, but not to horizontal lines. Yet other nerve cells react to corners and sharp angles, but not to straight or curved lines. Thus, by the time a "circle" has registered on your consciousness, this input surely has been "analyzed" or "processed" in a variety of ways.

According to the **information processing** approach, stimulus inputs flow up to your brain in a series of steps or *stages*. For example, your rods and cones translate light rays coming from the coin into patterns of neural energy. The rods and cones then pass this information along to complex cells in your retina. These complex cells respond to critical features of the visual input, and send this "processed information" to the thalamus (and other lower brain centers). Neurons in the thalamus detect certain patterns of information coming from the retinal cells, and pass the information "upstream" to your visual cortex.

How do the cells in your brain process information? First, by searching for various specific features in sensory inputs. For example, when you look at a picture of a coin, the cells might ask the following sorts of questions: Does this input have corners? (No.) Does this input have rounded lines? (Yes.) The cortical neurons then check through your memory banks to see if you have experienced this type of input before. (You've seen a lot of circles.) Your cortex then tries to match the present input with an image stored in memory. Since the input matches the image of a coin, you "perceive" a coin!

There are several different types of information processing theories. However, they all assume that, at each "processing stage," your neurons *extract* some types of information from the input and pass it on. But your neurons also *simplify* the input by failing to pass on unimportant information. Indeed, one of the most important jobs the lower centers in your brain apparently have is that of filtering out trivial sensory information. For example, when you're at a noisy party, or listening to a rock group, you can still talk to a friend because your brain screens out the background noise.

Thus, you don't really see (or hear) what's there. Rather, information processing theories say, you typically perceive only certain *critical features* of the stimulus input. You then *construct* a perception of a stimulus such as a coin from these critical features. But it is your construction of the coin—not the coin itself—that you perceive.

Without looking at the photograph at the beginning of the chapter again, can you tell what date was on the coin? If you can't, did you simply "forget," or were you never consciously aware of what the date was?

THE FOUR VIEWPOINTS COMPARED

The Gestalt and Gibsonian positions emphasize the *innate* properties of perception. The empirical and information processing theories focus on those aspects of perception that are *learned*.

Gibson made the *stimulus* the most important part of perception. The empirical and the information processing views emphasize *internal processing*. The Gestalt theorists talked about the importance of both stimulus and internal processing.

Gibson and the empirical theorists believe that sensations arrive at the cortex relatively unprocessed and thus free of "higher" influence. The Gestalt position is that higher cortical processes shape perceptions, but the Gestalt psychologists are relatively silent on processing in the lower centers of the brain. The information processing viewpoint is that the input is highly processed by these lower centers, and that your cortex can influence what goes on in the lower centers in a variety of ways. For example, look at Figure 4.1. Did you read the words as "the cat"? Look again. The "H" and the "A" are identical; thus they must have identical "critical features." But you *perceived* them in different ways because your brain forced these letters to fit within the images of well-known words. The other viewpoints have problems explaining this type of perceptual error.

Gibson saw sensation and perception as being pretty much the same thing. The Gestalt and empirical theorists believe that sensation and memory are totally independent processes, but that both influence perception. However, the information processing theorists hold that sensation, perception, memory, and cognition are all part of the same global process by which you construct your own representation of external reality. We cannot separate the individual processes because each affects the other.

Each position begins with different assumptions about how we experience the world; each position approaches the study of perception differently. Nevertheless, we will see that each position has contributed to our understanding of the process of perception.

How could you prove to someone else that a coin you held in your hand really existed, independent of your own perception of it?

Perception: A Bottom-Up or Top-Down Process?

In a sense, the study of perception is the investigation of how you *come to know the world around you*. But there is a knotty problem buried in this seemingly simple definition—namely, can you ever really know what the external world is like? As psychologist David Presti points out, there are at least two well-known answers to this question (Presti, 1987):

Naive realists believe there is a "real world" that exists independent of your knowledge about it. From this viewpoint, you come to know that world *directly* because of the informational inputs you receive from your sensory receptors. Naive realists believe that perception is primarily a *bottom-up process* which is "driven" by sensory inputs. Gibson and the empirical theorists would probably fit best into this category.

Structural realists hold that you come to know about the external world *indirectly* because your brain *processes sensory* inputs before you are aware of them. As Ulric Neisser puts it, "The world of experience is produced by the man who experiences it. . . . There certainly is a real world of trees and people and cars . . . however, we have no direct, immediate access to the world nor to its properties. Whatever we know of reality has been mediated not only by the organs of sense, but by complex systems which interpret and reinterpret information" (Neisser, 1967).

Therefore, according to Neisser, you can never know what the external world is really like, for all you are aware of is your own "construction of reality." However, because you *survive* in this external world using your subjective constructs, it does seem likely that most of your perceptions are reasonably accurate. But you shouldn't be surprised if, from time to time, your perception of things turns out to be radically wrong.

From a structural realism viewpoint, perception is a *top-down process* that is "driven" primarily by your own cognitive constructs. The information processing theorists obviously fit best in this category as, perhaps, do most of the Gestalt theorists (Dodwell & Caelli, 1984).

TAE CAT

FIGURE 4.1

After you read the words, look at the middle letter in each word.

Take away the sensations of softness, moisture, redness, tartness, and you take away the cherry. Since it is not a being distinct from these sensations; a cherry, I say, is nothing but a congeries of sensible impressions or ideas perceived by various senses; which ideas are united into one thing.

GEORGE BERKELEY

As David Presti also points out, when we're talking about the perception of physical objects (such as coins and carrots), there's little difference between naive realism and structural realism. When it comes to the perception of *people*, however, the constructionist viewpoint has much to offer. As Presti puts it, "We form hypotheses about the behavior of individuals (ourselves and others) based on very little information and tend to hold our beliefs in the face of massive amounts of disconfirming evidence. . . . We are accountable for the nature of our social experience to an astounding degree" (Presti, 1987). In the quotation which opened this chapter, Erica Jong seems to take a constructionist view when she describes Isadora's illusory perceptions in "the sun-house mirror of fame." Her earlier expectations and the beliefs of others turn out to be quite different from her later experience. (We will have more to say about our perceptions of other people in Chapter 17.)

Each of the four major theoretical approaches to the study of perception has made its own contributions to our understanding of how you perceive the world. As we discuss perception, we will try to show what the strengths (and problems) associated with each of the theories seem to be.

VISUAL PERCEPTION

Your eyes are more than "the windows to your soul." Unless you are visually handicapped, your eyes are also the main sensory route by which you acquire information about the outside world. Thus, the bulk of perceptual research deals with vision—as does much of the material in this chapter. So let us begin by asking, "How do you perceive the world around you visually?"

Contours

The simplest form of visual information is the difference between light and darkness. A visual contour is a place where there is a sharp or sudden change in brightness—from light to dark, or vice versa. Figure 4.2 has two contours—one at the inner edge of the circle, and one at the outer edge. It is these two contours, actually, that give *shape* to the circle.

The two contours shown in Figure 4.2 are *objective*. That is, there is a *real* change in brightness between the darkness of the circle and the light color it is printed on. But now look at Figure 4.3. Do you see two triangles? Most people see a large white triangle (pointing up) superimposed on a triangle pointing down. If this is what you see, look at the center of the white triangle. Doesn't it somehow look *whiter* than the background outside the figure does? And don't you see a sharp contrast between the *imaginary lines* setting off the top triangle and the space outside the triangle? These are *subjective* contours, since they are generated by your brain, not by objective changes in brightness.

What causes subjective contours? One interesting answer was given by Stanley Coren and Lawrence Ward. Coren and Ward believe we have an innate tendency to perceive the world in meaningful but simple terms. You could perceive Figure 4.3 as a collection of (1) three black circles with pie-shaped wedges cut out of them, and (2) three V-shaped black lines. However, it is both simpler and more meaningful to see the drawing as a white triangle lying on top of three black circles, and thereby partially covering a second triangle as well (Coren & Ward, 1989).

FIGURE 4.2

The "contours" of this circle are the inner and outer edges.

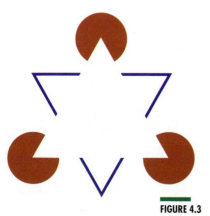

FIGURE 4.3

Do you see a solid white triangle that partially covers up a triangle with dark edges? Look again, and see if the solid white triangle is really there.

Figure 4.3 contains an important clue about depth perception. We will discuss it later, but can you guess what it is?

Shape

Look at Figure 4.4. What do you see? Most people see a solid black circle and a rather formless blob of black ink. Notice that the *contours* give shape to both figures.

Now, close your eyes and try to imagine both black figures. Chances are you have no problem with the circle. But what about the blob? Why is it so difficult to remember in detail?

There are many answers to this question. For one thing, you are quite familiar with circles, but you probably never have seen a blob just like this one before. For another, the blob is a much more complex figure than is the circle. In fact, Gestalt psychologists would predict that you will remember the blob as being *more circular* than it really is because circles are simpler and thus more stable perceptions than blobs are.

Consider another example. Most people see the drawing on the left of Figure 4.5(A) as a six-sided figure with three lines in the middle. But what about the drawing on the right (B)? Do you see it as a two-dimensional figure, or does it somehow project itself into three dimensions? Since the two drawings are really quite similar, why do you perceive A as two-dimensional, but B in three dimensions?

According to Gestalt principles, A is already a simple figure when viewed in two dimensions. Therefore, you see the figure in two dimensions. However, you *could* project it into three dimensions if you needed to do so. Figure B is more complex, so you tend to project the figure into three dimensions to simplify it. However, you *could* perceive it as a highly complex two-dimensional form if you needed to do so. Therefore, your perception of either figure is determined not only by innate principles of perception, but also by your own personal situation at the time that you look at the figures.

From this description, does the Gestalt position on perception seem to be "bottom-up" (determined by stimulus inputs) or "top-down" (determined by cognitive factors)?

Figure-Ground Relationships

According to the Gestalt position, you never perceive an object such as a circle "all by itself." Rather, you always see a circle as a shape *on a background*. The contours that define the circle as a "shape" also differentiate the circle from its surroundings.

In studying visual perception, the Gestalt theorists made many discoveries about *figure-ground relationships*. One such fact is that the figure almost always seems *brighter* and *closer* to you than does the background. Look again at Figure 4.3. Doesn't the (subjective) white triangle seem brighter than its surround? And doesn't it seem closer to you than the rest of the figure?

Another aspect of figure-ground relationships is this: The background seems to *continue behind the figure*. Look at Figure 4.6. Which is figure and which is background? Probably you see a cross on a background of concentric circles. Does the cross seem nearer to you than the circles? Why? If you stare at this figure long enough, you may get a "reversal" and see a cross with radial lines as the "figure." Why is it so hard to see the "radial cross" as *figure*? (Hint: Remember that the background always "continues behind the figure.")

AMBIGUOUS FIGURE-GROUND RELATIONSHIPS

Now look at Figure 4.7. What do you see? A white vase on a dark background? Or two dark profiles facing each other? Or do these two perspectives alternate?

FIGURE 4.4

Both the circle and the "blob" have contours.

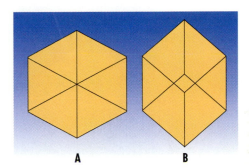

A   **B**

FIGURE 4.5

Most people see the figure on the left as two-dimensional and see the figure on the right in three dimensions. Why?

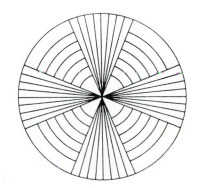

FIGURE 4.6

What is figure and what is ground in this drawing? Why?

FIGURE 4.7

What do you see first—two profile faces or a wine glass?

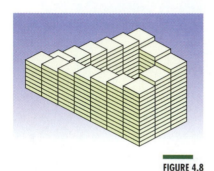

FIGURE 4.8

The magic stairs.

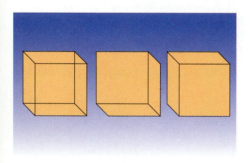

FIGURE 4.9

The Necker Cube. It can be seen as projecting up or down in three dimensions in the first cube. In the other two cubes, the perspective is stabilized.

Figure 4.7 is a very famous example of what the Gestalt psychologists called ambiguous figure-ground relationships. Many ambiguous figures involve *reversible perspectives*. Notice that when the wine glass (or vase) is figure, it seems closer. But when the faces become figure, the glass (or vase) retreats into the background and becomes *less important* psychologically. Generally speaking, you will also perceive the figure as having more *reality* or "thing-ness" than does the background (Hoffman, 1983).

Now, try to see both the vase and the faces as "figure" *at the same time*. Chances are, you'll find it impossible to do. Why? According to Gestalt theory, you always must perceive a figure on a background. Therefore, you can't see both as figure at the same time.

REVERSIBLE PERSPECTIVES

Look at the "impossible figure" in Figure 4.8. Do the stairs go up or down, or both ways? Is the platform on the right higher or lower than the platform on the left? What is there about the perspective of this figure that "fools" your eyes?

Now look at Figure 4.9, the famous Necker Cube. Does it project upward or downward? Actually, it projects *either way*. And, if you stare at it long enough, it will "reverse its perspective" from time to time. The *frequency* with which the cube changes perspective may depend in part on what sort of person you see yourself as being, however. Judith and Bruce Bergum showed the cube to 128 students and asked them how frequently the cube "changed directions." The Bergums report that students who had the highest reversal rates tended to perceive themselves as being more: (1) creative and original, (2) enthusiastic and optimistic, and (3) excitable and appreciative than did students with the *lowest* reversal rates (Bergum & Bergum, 1981).

Can you learn to make the cube reverse its perspective at a faster rate? Perhaps so. The Bergums note that architecture students tended to have much higher reversal rates on the cube than did business students. The Bergums believe the architecture students were probably rewarded by their teachers for being able to change perspectives rapidly. Students in business administration, the Bergums say, were probably expected to take a much more stable view of the world. The Bergums's results suggest that, with training, you can learn to make the cube reverse perspective almost as frequently or infrequently as you wish (Bergum & Bergum, 1981).

How else might the Bergums's findings be explained?

On the other hand, Benjamin Wallace reports that college students who were high on *hypnotizability* reported that the cube "changed directions" much more frequently than students who were low on hypnotizability (Wallace, 1986). As we will see in Chapter 5, hypnotizability appears to be related to early experiences. Perhaps the ability to reverse the Necker Cube reflects something more basic than being rewarded for being able to do it.

EFFECTS OF SURROUND

One of the major beliefs of the Gestalt position can be found in a phrase they made famous in psychology: "The whole is greater than the sum of its parts." In truth, the phrase really means that the whole is *different* from the sum of its parts, and that the whole *interacts* with its parts (Arnheim, 1986). For example, the background on which you perceive an object often strongly influences your perception of that object.

Look at Figure 4.10. Here is a gray circle displayed on a surround that is half white, half black. As you look at the circle, the gray seems uniform. But if you cover the border between the black and white sections with a pen, the gray semicircle on the white background will look much darker than the semicircle on the black surround. Why?

Figure 4.11 gives five examples of how the background influences the perception of the figure itself. One of the most striking examples of this effect, however, appears in Figure 4.12. Do you see a spiral moving in toward the center of the drawing? If you do, use your finger to trace out where the spiral actually goes.

How would you attempt to explain these illusions from the "information processing" viewpoint of perception? From the "empirical" approach? How do these explanations differ from those offered by the Gestalt psychologists?

Visual Grouping

As you look out at objects in space, your mind makes use of several Gestalt principles in tracing out the *relationships* among these objects.

FIGURE 4.10

The gray circle appears darker when viewed against a light background that when viewed against a dark background.

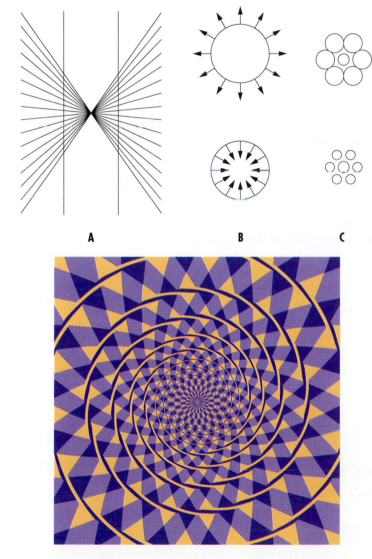

A   B   C

FIGURE 4.11

The context in which an object appears affects the way you perceive it. The two parallel straight lines in part A seem "bent" because of the backgrounds on which they appear. In part B the arrows make the top circle appear larger than the identical bottom circle. In part C the two center circles are the same size.

FIGURE 4.12

If you perceive one line that "spirals" in to the center, trace the line with your finger. The "spiral" is actually a set of circles. What in this illusion actually fools your eye?

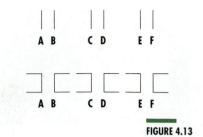

FIGURE 4.13

In part (1) we tend to see pairs of lines because of proximity. In part (2) the grouping changes, and we tend to see boxes because of closure.

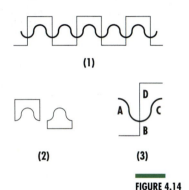

FIGURE 4.14

The Gestalt principle of continuity. In part (1) we tend to see two continuous lines. Parts (2) and (3) show that there are other ways of perceiving the same figure.

Proximity (procks-IM-it-tee). That which is close. Objects that are proximate (close to each other) tend to be perceived as units.

Closure. "To complete" or "to close." If you glance very quickly at a circle that has a tiny gap in it, you may very well see the circle as being closed, or complete.

Continuity. From the word "continue" or "continuous." Things that are connected together in time or space have continuity.

Similarity. Objects that are physically similar or like one another tend to be perceived as units or wholes.

FIGURE 4.15

How do you "group" these circles? Why do you group the circles in part (1) differently than you group those in part (2)?

PROXIMITY AND CLOSURE

One Gestalt principle is that you tend to *group things together* according to how close they are to each other. In part (1) of Figure 4.13, you probably see three "pairs" of lines. You will group A and B together because they are close to each other.

In part (2), however, things have changed. Now B and C seem to go together—to form a rectangle of some kind. Indeed, if you stare closely at the B-C rectangle, you will see rather faint but *imaginary* lines as your brain attempts to fill in or close up the open figure.

Part (1) of Figure 4.13 illustrates the Gestalt principle of **proximity,** or physical closeness. Part (2) illustrates the principle of **closure**—your brain's tendency to join broken lines together to make a closed figure of some kind.

CONTINUITY

A third perceptual principle is that of **continuity** and is illustrated in part (1) of Figure 4.14. In this illustration you will probably see a wavy line superimposed on a square-cornered line. If we now break up the pattern somewhat differently, as in part (2), you see not two lines but two closed figures joined together. Why do you think this is so? If you wish, you may even break the figure up into a different set of components, shown in part (3).

Once you have learned what the parts of the figure can be, you can perceive it many different ways. But, at the beginning, your eye tends to follow the wavy line because it is *continuous*.

SIMILARITY

A fourth principle of perceptual grouping is that of **similarity.** Part (1) of Figure 4.15 shows a series of 25 circles arranged in a square. If you fixate on this figure, you will notice that sometimes you "group" the circles together in bunches of 4s, or 9s, or 16s. And sometimes you see five horizontal rows of circles, sometimes five vertical columns. In such ambiguous situations, your brain apparently tests out various possibilities, attempting to see which fits the stimulus pattern best. But in Part (2) of Figure 4.15, you probably see a cross surrounded by four groups of empty circles. Why?

Simon Kemp has suggested that the perceptual principle of similarity is so strong that it even affects our memory. When he asked students to arrange historical events on a "timeline," he found they tended to bunch similar events together even when they didn't belong together (Kemp, 1987).

VISUAL DEPTH AND DISTANCE

So far, we have mostly discussed the viewing of two-dimensional objects. However, when you look at the world (beyond the printed page), it doesn't seem to be flat and two-dimensional. Rather, the world is *three-dimensional*. It has *depth* to it. This fact poses a problem to perceptual theorists, for the retinas in your eyes are, for all practical purposes, little more than flat "screens" on which the lenses in your eyes project two-dimensional images. How does your mind take these "flat" retinal images and *create* a third dimension—that of depth?

We are not entirely sure of the answer to this question. We do know, though, that true depth perception occurs only in people who have two eyes. And these two eyes must have slightly *different* views of the world for the third dimension to appear. It may also be the case (as we will see later in this chapter) that the *concept* of depth is innate. However, we are quite sure that some aspects of depth perception are *learned through experience*.

So, let's ask another of those supposedly obvious questions: What would your world be like if you had been born blind and only now opened your eyes? The answer to that question, as it happens, is anything but "obvious."

The Case of S.B.

Some years ago, British psychologist Richard L. Gregory reported the case of a man who had been blind from infancy, but whose vision was restored at age 52. This patient—whom Gregory calls S.B.—was an intelligent person whose vision had been normal at birth. At age 10 months, S.B. developed a severe infection of the eyes that left his corneas so badly scarred he couldn't see objects at all (Gregory, 1978).

Enough light leaked through his damaged corneas so that S.B. could just tell day from night. But he saw the world much as you would if someone cut a ping pong ball in two and placed the halves over your eyes. S.B.'s corneal scars were so bad, in fact, that for most of his life no doctor would operate on him. Nonetheless, S.B. led an enjoyable and very active life. He went places by himself, waving his white cane in front of him to let people know he was blind. He often went for rides on a bicycle, with a friend holding his shoulder and guiding him.

S.B. spent considerable time making wooden objects with rather simple tools. He had an open-faced watch so he could tell time by feeling the positions of the hands. He took care of animals and knew them all by touch, sound, and smell. And he always tried to imagine what things looked like. When he washed his brother's car, he would vividly try to picture what color and shape it really was. When S.B. visited the zoo, he would get his friends to describe the animals there in terms of how different they were from the dogs and cats in his home.

S.B.'S OPERATION

When S.B. was well past his 50th year, he prevailed upon a surgeon to attempt an operation in which his damaged corneas were removed and new ones were grafted on in their place. The operation was a great success but, as Gregory reports, S.B. was anything but happy with the results. When the doctor first removed the bandages, S.B. looked straight into the doctor's face—and saw nothing but a blur. He knew what he saw had to be the doctor's face, because he recognized the man's voice. But it was several days before he could begin to tell one person from another merely by *looking* at them. And he never became very good at identifying people visually.

Nonetheless, he progressed rapidly in some areas. Within a few days, S.B. could successfully navigate the halls of the hospital without running into things. He could tell time by looking at the face of a very large clock. And he dearly loved to get up early in the morning and sit at his window, watching the traffic rumble by on the street far below his hospital room.

But there were problems. S.B. rapidly learned the names of the colors red, black, and white. However, he had trouble identifying most other colors. He could judge *horizontal* distances fairly well when looking at objects whose size he was familiar with. But *heights* of any kind always confused him. One day the nurses found him crawling out the window of his fourth-floor hospital room, presumably because he

Like S.B., many blind people enjoy sports and other activities, sometimes aided by a guide. Note: BOLD stands for Blind Outdoor Leadership Development.

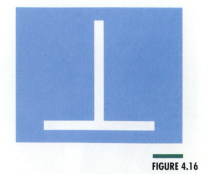

FIGURE 4.16

The figure appears taller than it is wide—but is it?

wanted to inspect more closely the automobile traffic in the street below. He looked at the ground 40 feet beneath him and thought it to be no more than 6 feet away.

Prior to the operation, S.B. had crossed even the busiest intersection alone without the faintest fear. He would plunge into traffic, waving his white stick in front of him. And somehow the river of cars and trucks would part for him, much as the waters of the Red Sea parted for Moses in Old Testament times. But after S.B. got his vision back, he was absolutely terrified of crossing a street. Gregory states it usually took two people holding his arms to force him across an intersection.

Often when S.B. saw a familiar object for the first time, he would be unable to identify it until he closed his eyes and felt it. Then he knew it by touch. And once he "had the picture in his mind," he could recognize it visually after he had looked at it a few times.

But objects he hadn't (or couldn't) run his hands over before regaining his sight always gave him problems. The moon, for instance, puzzled him greatly. The full moon he could make out, but the quarter moon he had expected to be wedge-shaped, rather like a large slice of pumpkin pie. And when S.B. looked at Figure 4.16, he saw the horizontal and the vertical lines as being the same length. How do they look to you?

S.B.'S DEPRESSION

Immediately after his operation, S.B. was very enthusiastic and happy. He loved bright colors (although he couldn't always give their right names), and he enjoyed being able to see the faces of people he knew. But then he began to get depressed. He complained bitterly about the ugliness in the world around him—houses with the paint coming off, buildings with dirty walls, people with blemishes on their faces. He would spend hours sitting in his local tavern watching people *in the mirror*. Somehow their reflections seemed more interesting to him than their real-life images.

Often S.B. would withdraw from human contact and spend most of the day sitting in darkness, claiming he could "see" better when there was no light.

There have been no more than half a dozen confirmed cases of people who have gained sight as adults. Depression and unhappiness are not unusual consequences of their getting back their vision.

We should note, however, that not all patients who recover sight late in life have the same problems—or the depression—that S.B. experienced. One woman who recovered her sight in 1980 had no problem at all seeing and naming colors the moment her bandages were removed. Nor did she become unhappy with her new-found sight. These facts suggest S.B.'s early illness may have damaged his rods and cones. Thus, many of the difficulties S.B. had in perceiving the world may have been due to retinal damage rather than to an inability to learn to see the world correctly so late in life.

Clues to Visual Distance

S.B. gained the ability to perceive *horizontal distance*. That is, he could tell how far away you were if he saw you walking down a hallway toward him. But he never could perceive *depth* very well. As we noted, depth is a three-dimensional property. People with *monocular* vision—that is, people who have just one functional eye—can also usually judge distance fairly well. However, like S.B., they typically don't perceive depth.

These facts suggest that *distance* cues are different from cues to *depth*. As James Gibson noted many years ago, distance cues are typically embedded in the visual stimuli themselves. However, your mind judges distance using more inputs than just those that come from the retina. It also takes into account the way your eyes move in their sockets, the sounds your ears report, the smells around you, your body posture, and all the memories it can dredge up (Reed, 1988).

A year after his operation, S.B. made this drawing of a typical London double-decker bus, complete with visual details such as the beer advertisement across the top. The front of the bus, however, which S.B. had never touched, is missing.

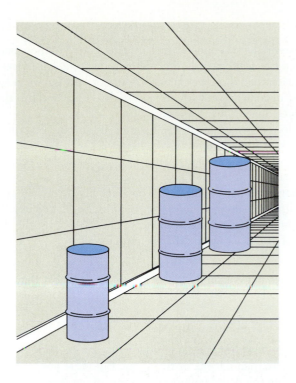

FIGURE 4.17

Although the three cylinders are actually the same size, they appear to be different. Why?

For example, an automobile passes you on the street. You know it is about 30 feet away because you remember what size cars ought to be, how long it takes you to walk 30 feet, and how the visual image of the car will change as you walk toward it.

The *apparent size* of an object gives you a good notion of how far away the object is. You tend to perceive small objects as being far away, and large objects as being closer. But you do this only if you know what the "real size" of the object is, and after taking into account the background the object appears on. There are other clues your brain uses, too, even though you are often unaware of what these clues are.

LINEAR PERSPECTIVE

Look at the photograph of the railroad tracks. Notice that all the lines seem to meet at a point right in the center of the scene. Figure 4.17 shows part of the same sort of illusion, but something new has been added. The three cylinders are actually the same size. But the cylinder on the far right appears more than twice as large as the cylinder on the far left. Can you use the lines on the drawing to explain why?

The apparent *convergence* of parallel lines as they approach the horizon is called **linear perspective**—one of the cues your brain uses to judge distance.

Linear perspective. "Linear" has to do with straight lines. "Perspective" means "viewpoint." Parallel lines (such as railroad tracks) appear to meet at the horizon. If you were drawing a realistic picture of railroad tracks, you would want to draw them so they "met" at the horizon in your picture.

According to the principles of linear perspective, parallel lines appear to meet at the horizon.

CONVERGENCE

Humans are essentially two-dimensional animals, bound to those parts of the surface of the earth our two feet can walk on. We judge *horizontal* distances rather well—if they are no greater than those we can walk or run or ride. But we judge heights rather poorly, at least in comparison with animals such as birds and fish that move readily through all three dimensions of space.

When you look at something in the distance, both your eyes point straight ahead. When you look at something up close, however, both of your eyes turn inward, toward your nose (see photograph). The amount of strain this **convergence** creates in your eye muscles is an index of how far away the object is.

To judge how *distant* an object is, you have merely to let your eyes converge and notice the strain on your eye muscles. But to judge *height*, you usually have to move your head up and down or crane your neck. For most of us, the neck muscles are poorer judges of distance than are the eye muscles.

Why are airplane pilots usually better at judging heights than are non-pilots?

AERIAL PERSPECTIVE AND TEXTURE

Anyone who has grown up in a smog-ridden city knows there often are days when you can't see more than a block or two away. But there are parts of the world still blessedly free from this aerial pollution. In some of our deserts, for instance, the air is often so clear that the visibility is practically unlimited. The city dweller who first visits these regions is sometimes shocked at how badly she or he actually judges distances in clean, fresh air. A mountain peak that appears to be no more than 5 or 10 miles away may actually be more than 50 miles down the road.

The more hazy and indistinct a remote object is, like the mountains in the photograph of the cactus, the farther away it appears to be. Psychologists refer to this "distance cue" as the atmospheric or **aerial perspective** of an object.

Texture is a distance cue very similar to aerial perspective. In real life, the texture of objects near to you is more detailed than the texture of distant objects. Over time, you learn to use texture as a cue. For example, in the photograph you can see fine details on the cactus, but not on the mountains.

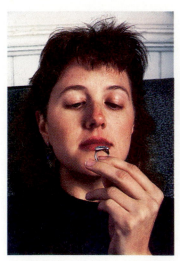

An example of convergence. When you focus on a near object, your eyes "converge" (turn toward each other).

Convergence (kon-VERGE-ence). Coming together or moving toward one another. Parallel lines converge at the horizon.

Aerial perspective (AIR-ee-ull). Literally, the "way you see an object through the air." Fuzzy objects seem distant; clear (distinct) objects seem close.

Distant objects appear less clear because of aerial perspective. Notice also that the texture of close objects is more distinct.

LIGHT AND SHADOW

Often we use the *lightness* of an object to give us some notion of its size or distance from us. For reasons we still don't understand, dark objects often appear to be smaller than light-colored objects. For example, look at the seven dots in Figure 4.18. Although it doesn't look like it at first glance, the distance between the dots is exactly the same as the size of the dots themselves.

Sometimes we make judgments about the visual world from what we *don't* see, instead of from what we do see. Look at Figure 4.19. Can you see the word "fly" spaced between the figures? Doesn't your eye actually *see* the forms of the letters as if they were really there? And after you recognize the word "fly," can you perceive the drawing as just a collection of odd-shaped black figures? Why not?

You also make use of shadows in judging whether you are looking at a mountain or at the hole left when somebody dug up the mountain and carted it away. When you look at the photograph of the crater, you automatically make an assumption about how the sunlight is falling on the landscape. If you make the wrong assumption, then your brain will show you a hill instead of a crater.

S.B. often mistook shadows for real objects. Why do you think this was the case?

INTERPOSITION

If one object seems to block another, you will usually perceive the "blocking" object as being closer to you than the object it masks. Look back at the photograph of the cactus. Notice how the cactus in the foreground blocks your view of some of the mountains. Your mind uses these *interposition* cues to perceive distance rather readily.

This photograph actually illustrates several of the distance cues we have already discussed. See if you can find examples of linear and aerial perspective, texture, light and shadow, and interposition. How do these cues give "apparent depth" (that is, distance) to the photograph?

REAL AND APPARENT MOTION

Motion can also be a cue to distance. Imagine you are riding in a car, looking out the window. You will see telephone poles flash by rapidly, but a cow in a distant meadow will move across your field of vision slowly. Objects (such as the cow) that seem to

FIGURE 4.18

How far apart do these dots look? The distance between the dots is actually the same as the diameter of each dot.

FIGURE 4.19

What do you see—a word or five odd-shaped objects?

FIGURE 4.20

If the lights go on and off in rapid sequence—with a slight pause between lights 4 and 5—you will perceive the gray rectangle as being in front of the row of lights.

move *slowly* as you are moving rapidly will seem *distant*. However, the telephone poles will seem *near* because they move *rapidly*. They also momentarily block out objects "behind them," such as the cow.

Apparent motion can also be a cue to distance. Look at Figure 4.20. Here you have eight light bulbs and a black rectangle. If you turned the bulbs on and off quickly in the order they are numbered, you might perceive just one bulb moving from left to right. (This sort of "apparent movement" is best illustrated by the flashing lights on theater marquees.) Now imagine that you turned on the first four light bulbs in Figure 4.20 in 1–2–3–4 order, then waited a second or two. Now you turn on 5–6–7–8 in sequence. The apparent movement of the lights might convince you the row of bulbs continued *behind* the black rectangle. Thus, you would perceive the rectangle as being closer to you than the lights (Ramachandran & Anstis, 1986).

Now, imagine you are standing in a dark hallway. Some distance from you is a large, white globe suspended in air. As you first look, the globe is dimly illuminated from within. But as you continue watching, the globe grows brighter and brighter. If you have no other cues as to distance, you will perceive two different effects. First, the globe will seem to get *larger*. And second, the globe will seem to *move closer*—even though it hasn't really moved at all. The change in brightness gives rise to apparent movement, for you tend to see bright objects as being nearer than dim objects.

Expectancy

FIGURE 4.21

Do you see an old woman or a young woman?

One of the principle laws of perception is this: *You see what you expect to see*. As you experience the world, you learn that objects typically grow brighter as they move closer to you. Thus, when you see an object growing brighter, you expect it to be moving closer to you. So you *perceive* it that way. Any clues you get from your environment that change your expectancies will also have a strong influence on your perceptual processes.

Keep that thought in mind as you look at Figure 4.21. As you can see, it is a drawing of an *old woman* with her chin buried in a fur coat. Look at it carefully and try to figure out what this old woman is thinking of.

The artist who drew the picture claims she is dreaming of her daughter. And if you inspect the drawing again, you will see the face of the old woman change into that of the daughter.

Several experimenters have shown this picture to groups of college students. If the students are told to expect a picture of an old woman, most of them discover the mother's face before finding the daughter's. But if the students are told they will see a drawing of a young woman, they tend to see the daughter's face easily but often have trouble "finding" the picture of the mother.

CONSTANCIES AND ILLUSIONS

Expectancy is closely related to another perceptual principle, that of *constancy*. A knowledge of both principles may help you understand some of the visual *illusions* that you experience daily.

Imagine yourself in the same situation S.B. faced, when he gained sight at the age of 52. Before your operation, you crossed streets safely. You knew people would stop for you—but you could also judge the flow of traffic reasonably well by listening to it. You knew what a truck sounded like when it was 200 feet away, and what it sounded like when it was but 20 feet away and still moving rapidly. Now, suddenly, you can *see*. When you *look* at that truck 200 feet away, it seems incredibly tiny, almost insignificant. Why? Because the truck's visual image on your retina is also incredibly small. As the truck moves rapidly toward you, the *size* of the image it casts on your retina grows by leaps and bounds. But would you see the truck as changing *position*? Why couldn't you perceive a stationary truck that was suddenly swelling up in *size* like a balloon?

The shop seemed to be full of all manner of curious things—but the oddest part of it was that, whenever she looked at any shelf, to make out exactly what it had on it, that particular shelf was always quite empty, though the others around it were still crowded as full as they could hold.

LEWIS CARROLL,
Through the Looking Glass

Size Constancy

Like most sighted people, you learned long ago that trucks don't change size. So you *interpret* changes in the *apparent size* of objects like trucks as evidence that they (or you) are moving. Put another way, there is a relationship between the perceived size of an object and its perceived distance. As long as you have some clue as to how far an object is from you, the object will appear to be the same "real size," whether it casts a large or small image on your retina. We call this relationship between size and distance the principle of **size constancy.**

Size constancy does break down under certain conditions. First, if you don't have any cues as to the object's distance, you will often make mistakes about its real size—unless, that is, the object is something familiar, such as a football or pencil. Then, *expectancy* (from past experience) will give you a clue as to the object's real size. Second, size constancy often fails when you look at objects from a great distance. If you view the objects below you from an airplane or the top of a tall building, they often look like toys rather than the real thing.

The principle of size constancy also provides a possible explanation for some illusions of size. For example, the moon often appears larger when it is near the horizon than when it is overhead. Since the moon is the same size and distance away in both cases, this is called the "moon illusion." According to a size constancy explanation, when the moon is near the horizon, we can tell that it is very far away by comparing it with other objects near the horizon. This enables us to use the principle of size constancy properly and judge that the moon is indeed large. However, when the moon is overhead, it does not seem so far away (having fewer cues, our estimate of distance is less accurate), and we conclude that the moon is therefore not as large as it really is.

Size constancy. The ability of your brain to perceive the size of an object as unchanging, even though the size of the image it projects onto your retina changes as the object moves either toward or away from you.

Shape Constancy

Look at the photograph of the coin, which is the same as one we showed you earlier in this chapter. Chances are, you *still* see it as a round coin turned away from you in space. As objects rotate in space, or as you move around the objects, the actual image they cast on your retina changes dramatically. The tendency to perceive objects as *maintaining their known shape* despite the image they project on the retina is known as **shape constancy.**

Generally speaking, shape constancy is good when you have cues as to whether you're viewing the object straight on, or whether it is tilted or slanted in space. As Gibson pointed out, there are many such cues, including light and shadow, texture, and linear and aerial perspective. Shape constancy breaks down in extreme conditions, however, or when you lack sufficient cues to guess the object's orientation in space (Gibson, 1950).

Adelbert Ames, an American psychologist who began his professional life as a painter, took advantage of *shape constancy* to produce a number of very amusing illusions that illustrate the Gestalt principles of perception. The best known of these illusions is Ames's "distorted room," shown in the photographs.

A coin viewed on edge. What is the shape of the coin? What is the shape of the image it projects to your eye?

Shape constancy. The tendency to perceive the shape of an object as invariant, or unchanging, even when the shape of the image the object casts on your retina changes considerably.

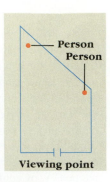

In the Ames room people appear to change sizes. In reality, the woman is much taller than the boy. As you can see from the diagram, the person on the left is almost twice as far from the viewer. This distance is not apparent to the viewer; hence, the illusion.

FIGURE 4.22

We perceive the opening door as being rectangular in shape despite the actual non-rectangular images.

When looked at head-on, the distorted room appears quite normal—until you see two people standing in the room. And then you know that something is very definitely wrong. The windows in the room look square. In fact, the windows are really trapezoids.

Look at Figure 4.22. At the left, the door is indeed a square. But as it opens, it casts a trapezoid-shaped image on your retina. But since you *know* that most doors are really squares, you *perceive* it as retaining its shape as it opens.

When you look at the Ames distorted room, your brain experiences a problem, for the doors and windows really are trapezoids, instead of being rectangles. In order to keep the windows *looking* like rectangles, your brain must produce *distance distortions* that make one of the people in the room look much larger than their smaller companions. Given the choice between preserving "good form" (the shape of the windows) or "size constancy" (the size of the people), your cortex typically votes in favor of good form.

The Mueller-Lyer Illusion

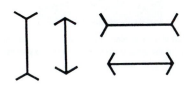

FIGURE 4.23

The Mueller-Lyer illusion: Are the lines equal?

Look at Figure 4.23, which shows two versions of the famous Mueller-Lyer illusion. Don't the two lines with the outward-pointing "V's" seem much longer than the two lines with the inward-pointing "V's"? Yet if you measure the lines in both these figures, you'll see they are exactly the same length.

Why does one line look longer than the other? Richard Gregory believes this illusion is based on your perception of corners (see Figure 4.24). If you are reading this book indoors, look at one of the corners of the room you're in. Notice that the angles the wall makes with the floor or the ceiling form lines much like those in the figures with the outward-pointing "V's." If you are sitting outdoors, look at the corner of a

FIGURE 4.24

The vertical line in the corner of the room is the same length as the vertical line that makes up the corner of the building. These two drawings make up a sort of "real-life" Mueller-Lyer illusion.

building. You will see that the angles made by the roof and the ground are similar to the same lines in the figures with the inward-pointing "V's." Gregory believes that the "V's," and our experience with the corners of buildings indoors and outdoors, fool us into thinking that one arrow figure is closer to us than the other—and is therefore bigger (Gregory, 1978).

It is rather simple to train a pigeon in a laboratory to peck at the shorter of two lines in order to get a bite of food. How might you use this procedure to test whether pigeons are as fooled by the Mueller-Lyer illusion as humans are?

Other Illusions

You seldom see an object *all by itself*. Instead, you almost always see an object in relationship to the other objects around it. In the Mueller-Lyer illusion, for example, the "V's" at the ends of the horizontal lines affect your perception of how long the lines are.

Now look at Figure 4.25. Is the hat taller than it is wide? If you think so, take out a ruler and measure the distances.

The apparent straightness of a line can easily be affected by whatever objects the line seems to penetrate. In Figure 4.26, the diagonal line crossing the two bars seems to be three disconnected lines. In fact, as you can determine by using a ruler, the line is absolutely straight. Oddly enough, the illusion disappears for most people if they turn the drawing around so that the line is straight up and down.

Cultural Influences on Illusions

You probably grew up in a world of straight lines, corners, and sharp angles. But suppose you had lived as a child in an environment where straight lines were taboo? How would you perceive these illusions?

The answer is: You probably wouldn't see some of them at all. The Zulus—a tribe in South Africa—live in what Richard Gregory calls a "circular culture." Their huts are round mounds with circular doors (see photograph). They plow their fields in curved lines, and even their toys and tools lack straight edges. When shown the Mueller-Lyer illusion, the typical Zulu native sees one line as being only very slightly longer than the other. Some illusions, such as the "top hat" drawing, affect the Zulu hardly at all (Gregory, 1978).

As the illusions we've just described suggest, perception is an exceptionally complex process. From the "information processing" point of view, visual inputs are processed at various stages as they work their way up to your brain from your eyes. However, once you have perceived something, your mind can send commands back to the lower brain centers. These "top-downward commands" affect the lower centers and your eyes and consequently what you perceive *next*.

FIGURE 4.25

The "top hat" illusion. Is the hat taller than it is wide? Check and see.

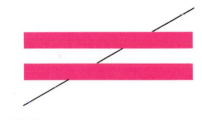

FIGURE 4.26

Is the diagonal line straight?

The "circular culture" of the Zulus.

COMPLEX PERCEPTUAL RESPONSES

Now that we have discussed simple eye-to-brain illusions, let's look at some complex perceptions that are created *after* your mind has made its initial response to a visual input.

Pupil Responses

One of the major purposes of your visual system is to gird you for *action*. When you walk out of a darkened movie theater, your pupils decrease in size rapidly to keep you from being blinded by the sudden increase in light. Your brain didn't have to *learn* how to make your pupils close under these conditions—the response is *innate*. And at dusk, when the sunlight dims, your pupils automatically open up or *dilate*. The wider your pupils open, the more light comes through and the better you can see and react to objects in your visual environment. Again, this response is determined by your genes, not by previous learning.

Your pupils also dilate when you look closely at some object, even though there is no change in illumination. The harder you stare at the object, the wider your pupils will open. *What* you choose to inspect closely, of course, is determined primarily by your past experience. So this type of pupil dilation is influenced by what you have learned about the world.

Psychologist Eckhard Hess made use of this information to test a hunch of his. Hess reasoned that people would stare more at something they were really interested in than at something they disliked. So he showed pictures of many different objects to the college students he used as subjects in his experiments.

Hess found that women typically had much larger pupil openings when he showed them pictures of babies or nude males than when he showed these women pictures of landscapes or nude females. Men, on the other hand, usually had wider pupils when shown pictures of nude females than when they were shown photographs of babies, landscapes, or nude males.

Hess's research suggests you can often discover a person's *real* interests simply by noting when the person becomes "wide-eyed" (Hess, 1965, 1975).

Is the tendency for women to become "wide-eyed" when looking at babies or nude males learned, innate, or both? How might you prove your answer is correct?

Visual Suppression

Under certain very special conditions, your mind can be forced to *choose* between two entirely different visual inputs.

Imagine a large black box with two eyeholes in one side. There is a wooden partition inside the box that divides it in half. Thus, when you look through the holes, your left eye sees a different scene than does your right eye. The apparatus is also arranged so that these different scenes are visible only for a brief fraction of a second. How would your mind handle this odd situation?

Generally speaking, you will make one of two responses when faced with conflicting, very brief visual inputs. Most of the time your nervous system simply suppresses or rejects one of the pictures and concentrates on the other. But on rare occasions, your cortex may *combine* the two inputs into one.

If we show a different scene to your left eye than to your right, which scene will you suppress? If your vision is clearer in one eye than in the other, you will almost always pick the scene that you see best. But if both your eyes are in good shape, you face a dilemma.

If your left eye is looking at a cup, while your right eye is looking at a teapot that is pouring liquid from its spout, your mind may actually *fuse* the two scenes together so that you see a pot pouring tea into a cup (see Figure 4.27). If one of your eyes sees a baby hanging in mid-air, while the other sees a woman holding out empty arms, your brain may superimpose one scene on the other so that you see the woman holding the child.

But suppose the two pictures are so different they can't be fused? Then you typically concentrate on whichever scene you find more interesting, and suppress the other scene almost completely. In many cases this suppression takes place so rapidly, you are not aware you are being shown two different objects or photographs (Bridgeman & Fisher, 1990; Volkmann, 1986).

In one study, psychologists Mark Gilson, Earl Brown, and Walter Daves tested both homosexual and heterosexual males in a visual suppression situation. The experimenters presented heterosexual stimuli to one of the subject's eyes, and presented homosexual stimuli to the other eye. Generally speaking, heterosexual males tended to suppress the homosexual stimuli, while homosexual males tended to suppress the heterosexual stimuli (Gilson et al., 1982).

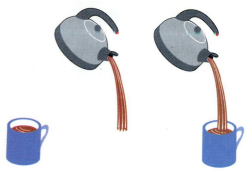

FIGURE 4.27

If your left eye is looking at a cup while your right eye is looking at a teapot pouring liquid, you may see the liquid going into the cup.

THE DEVELOPMENT OF PERCEPTION

You apparently are *born* with the tendency to suppress some types of threatening visual inputs. But *what* you find threatening is, of course, determined by your past experience and your outlook on life. These facts bring us back to the *nature-nurture problem* mentioned earlier in this chapter. There are some aspects of perception that appear so early after birth they can be considered *primarily* innate. And there are other parts of the perceptual process that emerge only when the infant has had a fair amount of "worldly experience." As we discuss this issue in detail, however, you should keep the following two points in mind: First, infants begin to learn about the world around them *even before the infants are born*. And second, all learning is based on innate responses the infants have available at birth (or even before). Perception, then—like all other parts of human experience—is truly multi-determined.

Innate Aspects of Perception

Al Yonas believes that many aspects of visual perception are controlled by the child's genetic blueprint. Yonas has shown that three-week-old infants will blink and recoil slightly from a black triangle moving toward them—even when no physical contact occurs. However, these same babies will be unresponsive when the triangle moves away from them. Yonas also notes that early visual development tends to be better in female infants, those who are above-average in size, and those born after their due dates. These facts are better explained in terms of genetic inheritance than in terms of early visual experience (Yonas, 1979).

FACE PERCEPTION IN INFANTS

Recent research suggests that, just an hour or so after birth, infants will mimic the facial expressions of adults (see Chapter 12 for details). This work indicates there is something rather special about the human face—at least from an infant's point of view (Meltzoff & Moore, 1977; Roder et al., 1992).

Look at Figure 4.28. One drawing is that of a face with the nose, eyes, and other features in their proper places. The other drawing has the same elements, but they are oddly scrambled. Now imagine a very young infant lying comfortably on her or his back looking up at these figures. What do you think the baby would spend more time looking at—the normal face, or the scrambled one?

Psychologist Robert L. Fantz photographed the eye movements of young babies using specially designed apparatus. The infants he measured spent much more time looking at the normal than at the scrambled face. This finding suggests children have innate response patterns which allow them to recognize what the human face looks like (Fantz, 1963).

Fantz also found that babies prefer looking at simple round objects rather than at two-dimensional drawings of the same objects. Fantz believes infants may have an *innate appreciation of depth*. He points out, however, that his experimental results may also mean that babies learn about faces and depths very early in their lives (Fantz et al., 1975).

According to psychologist Judith Langlois, infants pay more attention to pictures of *attractive* faces than to pictures of *plain* ones. Langlois and her associates (1987) showed pairs of women's faces to infants aged 6–8 months. Each pair of pictures contained one face that was rated "attractive" and one face that was rated "unattractive" by adult judges. Some 71 percent of the infants stared longer at the attractive than at the unattractive face. When younger infants (aged 2–3 months) were given a similar test, some 65 percent of them preferred the more attractive face. Langlois believes that "there may be universal stimulus dimensions of faces that infants, older children, and adults cross-culturally view as attractive." (Langlois & Roggman, 1990).

FIGURE 4.28

Infants tested in Fantz's apparatus looked at the simple face longer than they did at the design with randomly placed facial features.

Langlois notes that attractive faces "may be more curved and less angular, or more vertically symmetrical than unattractive faces." What would the Gestalt psychologists have to say about Langlois's remarks?

The "Margaret Thatcher Illusion"

The human face is an *emotionally powerful stimulus,* for we often judge how people are feeling by noting the expressions on their faces. However, we do a poor job of judging facial expressions if the face is turned upside down. Look at the normal and the slightly "doctored" photograph of former British Prime Minister Margaret Thatcher. The "doctoring," which was done by psychologist Peter Thompson, con-

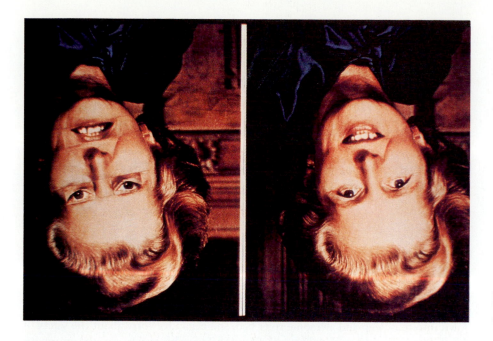

Look at the reconstructed photograph of Margaret Thatcher's face and try to imagine what it will look like when you turn the book upside down.

sists of cutting out both the eyes and the mouth from the original and pasting them back in upside down (Thompson, 1980). Since we rely heavily on the eyes and mouth when judging expressions, the doctoring is not obvious when the face is upside down.

What expression seems to appear on Thatcher's face? Now turn the page upside down and look at the face again.

Why do you think we do such a poor job of judging facial expressions when the face is upside down?

Visual Processing in Infants

Marshall M. Haith and his colleagues have made extensive studies of the ways in which infants learn to process visual inputs during the first weeks of life (see Figure 4.29). According to Haith, a four-week-old child is not mature enough to *process* such "complex visual stimulus patterns" as the human face. Therefore, very young infants gaze *away* from their mother's face about 80 percent of the time, and *fixate* on her face only about 20 percent of the time. Even when the 4-week-old child does gaze directly at the mother, the infant tends to fixate mostly at the *edge* of her face. Haith and his colleagues report that 4-week-old infants fixated on the *center* of the mother's face (her eyes, nose, mouth) but 22 percent of the time (Haith, 1980).

By 7 weeks of age, however, the normal infant has learned how to "process" faces. So the child gazes directly at the mother's face almost 90 percent of the time the child can see her. And when looking at her face, the infant fixates on the center of the face rather than the edges. Haith also reports 7-week-old infants looked at the mother's eyes almost twice as much as at her nose or mouth.

Haith believes newborn infants are innately attracted to *edges* or contours of objects in their visual world. By 7 weeks of age, however, the baby is sufficiently experienced so the child can begin to perceive the human face as a unified whole rather than as a collection of parts (Haith, 1980).

Haith notes that a 9-week-old infant is more likely to gaze at the mother's face when she is talking to the child than when she isn't. But Haith also points out the baby is more likely to gaze at the mother's *eyes* when she is talking than at the

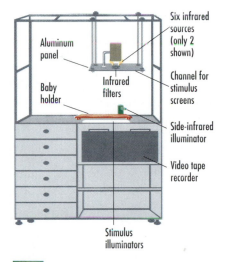

FIGURE 4.29

Drawing of Haith's apparatus. Infrared lights provide illumination for recording of image of the eye via infrared TV camera onto video tape. Stimulus illuminators light the stimulus screen above the baby holder so that a baby, lying in the holder, sees only the screen and the stimulus spray painted on it. A TV camera records through the screen.

The "visual cliff." Very few infants will crawl on the plexiglass over the "cliff" to reach their mothers.

Visual cliff. An apparatus constructed by Gibson and Walk that gives infants the illusion of great depth.

mother's *mouth*. Although Haith doesn't say so, it seems likely that the sound of the mother's voice speeds up the infant's visual development—perhaps by soothing the child's fears. The infant responds to the soothing sounds by gazing at the mother's eyes more often. The mother usually interprets increased "eye-gazing" as a sign the child is "paying attention." Thus, she talks to the child—and cradles the infant—more frequently. Whatever the case, it seems likely that visual perception in the human infant is as strongly influenced by auditory and skin-receptor inputs as it is by visual stimuli.

Haith's research seems to contradict Fantz's belief that infants are born with the ability to recognize the human face. How might you resolve this contradiction?

The Visual Cliff

Another intriguing bit of evidence concerning the innate properties of perception comes from a series of experiments pioneered by Eleanor Gibson. One day several years ago, Gibson was at a picnic on the rim of the Grand Canyon. Looking straight down into that deep and awesome river bed, she began to worry about the safety of the children around her. Would a very young child be able to perceive the enormous dropoff at the edge of the cliff? Or would the child go toddling right over the edge if no adult were around to restrain the child?

Gibson was really asking two very important questions about perception. First, are babies born with an *innate ability to perceive depth?* And second, do infants have a *built-in fear mechanism* that would make them retreat from sharp drop-offs, even without having been trained to do so?

Once Gibson had returned to her laboratory at Cornell University, she attempted to answer both these questions. And to do so, she designed an artificial **visual cliff** on which she could test infants safely (shown in the photograph).

Running down the middle of the apparatus was a raised plank of wood painted in a checkerboard pattern. To one side of the plank was a sharp dropoff. On the other side was a normal "floor" an inch or so below the center plank. The entire apparatus was covered with sturdy glass so the infant could see the cliff but could not fall off it.

When an infant was tested, the child was put on the center board and allowed to explore freely. Very few of the infants crawled off onto the "cliff" side, although most of them freely moved onto the "floor" side. Even when the child's mother stood at the side of the apparatus and attempted to coax the child to crawl out over the "cliff," most infants refused to do so. Instead, they began to cry loudly. If the mother stood on the "floor" side of the box, however, the infant would crawl toward her willingly (Gibson & Walk, 1960).

A variety of newborn animals—lambs, kittens, puppies, and rats—have been tested on the visual cliff, too. For the most part, these animals show an immediate perceptual awareness of the "dangers" of the cliff. Gibson concludes that many species have behavioral mechanisms built into their brains at birth that tend to protect them from the dangers of falling from high places (Gibson, 1981).

However, not all infants, nor all species, react to the visual cliff as did the babies in Gibson's first studies. Gibson and Rader point out there are great individual differences between infants in their response to the visual cliff. Some babies seem to be *visually oriented*. These infants recoil with fear from the sight of the cliff. Others tend to be *touch oriented*. These children apparently trust their skin senses more than their eyes, and crawl right out on the glass covering the cliff as long as it offers firm support. Thus, the issue of whether infants are born with an innate fear of heights is far from settled (Gibson & Rader, 1979; Gibson & Walker, 1984).

Developmental Handicaps of the Blind

Some innate visual tendencies are so subtle we tend to overlook them—except when we observe the development of the child who is born blind. In her book, *Insights from the Blind,* Selma Fraiberg says the blind youngster has two severe problems to overcome: (1) learning to recognize his or her parents from sounds alone, and (2) acquiring a healthy *self-concept* or perceptual "self-schema" (Fraiberg, 1977).

Fraiberg notes that normal 8-month-olds will reach out their arms the moment they hear their mother's voice—*anticipating* the sight of the parent even before she appears in the child's view. The blind baby does not show this reaching response until much, much later. The blind infant *hears* and *feels,* but cannot "integrate" these sensory experiences very well to form a unified schema of *mother.* Vision, then, is particularly important to a youngster, because sight allows the child to pull the other sensory modalities together in her or his mind (Fraiberg, 1977; Tröster & Brambring, 1992).

Blind children are frequently retarded in their speech development. They talk later and more poorly than do sighted children. Much of this speech retardation seems due to their slowness in recognizing the *permanence* of objects in the world around them. Blind children also have problems "imagining" things while young and do not identify readily with a doll or with a character in a story their mother reads to them. And, they often do not learn the correct use of "I" and "you" until they are 5 or 6 (Fraiberg, 1977).

Fraiberg concludes blind youngsters cannot picture themselves as objects that exist separate from their environments. And since they cannot *visualize* themselves as independent entities, they are slow to develop any real notion of "self." In brief, *seeing* yourself may be the easiest and most natural way of building up a perceptual schema of your own *self.*

But which aspects of vision are learned and which are innately determined? The issue is complex and may never be entirely solved. For instance, while children blind from birth are sometimes slow to develop social and verbal skills, they usually are able to move around in the world fairly readily. Indeed, according to Barbara Landau and her associates, children born blind perceive *physical space* (as distinct from visual space) about as well as sighted children do.

Landau and her group tested Kelli, a $2\frac{1}{2}$-year-old girl who was blind from birth, on a variety of tasks. When Kelli was allowed to explore a room on her own, she could thereafter take the shortest path from any spot to any other spot in the room. Landau and her colleagues believe Kelli could "perceive" the physical layout of the room even if she couldn't "see" the room visually (Landau et al., 1981).

Apparently, then, infants are born with an innate ability to *create three-dimensional space in their minds.* But even with this inborn tendency, they still need "worldly experience" if they are to learn to perceive "objects in space" (Carreiras & Codina, 1992).

How might auditory perception help a child like Kelli develop a perception of physical space?

Sensory-Based Perception: A Summary

As we mentioned at the beginning of this chapter, there are four main theories of perception: the Gibsonian, the Gestalt, the empirical, and the information processing approaches. Although there are major differences among them, all four theories attempt to describe how information about the outside world is "captured" by your sensory receptors, is "processed" by your nervous system, and then is "experienced" as reality in your stream of consciousness. Thus, while proponents of these four theories might disagree on many points, there is one belief they'd surely all have in common: Without *sensory inputs*, you wouldn't *perceive* anything.

But perhaps you have wondered if it is possible for you to acquire information by "channels" other than your sensory receptors? What about those people who claim they can "read other people's minds"? Or "communicate with supernatural spirits"? Or "foresee the future"? Obviously, if true, these sorts of experiences would involve *extrasensory perception*—that is, the acquisition of knowledge by means "beyond the normal sensory pathways."

The Latin word *para* means "beyond." The study of "extrasensory perception" and other phenomena that lie "beyond the normal bounds of scientific psychology" is called **parapsychology.** Let's look briefly at this fascinating field, both to see what it's like and because its study may yield important information about how people occasionally misinterpret "normal" perceptual processes.

Parapsychology. The scientific study of events that are "beyond" normal explanation.

Studies suggest that most people dream about the future fairly frequently. What kinds of "future events" would you be most likely to remember if you dreamed of them?

ESP AND PARAPSYCHOLOGY

Parapsychologists study many different types of unusual phenomena, most of which involve extrasensory perception (ESP) of one kind or another. Four of the best-known are mental telepathy, clairvoyance, precognition, and psychokinesis.

Mental telepathy is the technical term for "reading someone's thoughts."

Clairvoyance is the term we use to describe the perception of external objects or events without normal sensory stimulation. Comic book characters who can "see through walls" do so by using clairvoyance.

Precognition is the ability to perceive future events before they happen.

Psychokinesis is the power of "mind over matter." If you could influence the movement of physical objects simply by wishing them to move, or if you could "bend spoons" or other objects mentally, you would be using psychokinesis to do so.

Parapsychology also includes the investigation of such "supernatural" events as ghosts, reincarnation, communicating with the dead (or other non-physical beings), out-of-body experiences, and so forth. However, the four phenomena listed above are by far the most studied in the laboratory, so we will limit our discussion of ESP and parapsychology to these four.

Mental telepathy. The ability to communicate over distances without physical means—presumably via the mind.

Clairvoyance (clair-VOY-ants). From the French words meaning "clear-sighted." The ability to see things hidden from normal sight.

Precognition. The ability to see the future—literally "know before."

Psychokinesis (SIGH-ko-kin-EE-sis). The Greek work *kinesis* means "movement," or "to move." *Psyche* is the Greek word for "mind." Psychokinesis (PK) is the ability to move things mentally, by willing them to move, rather than by touching them physically.

Who Believes in ESP?

In 1978, psychologists Mary Monnet and Mahlon Wagner asked more than 1,100 college teachers if they believed in ESP. Overall, 16 percent thought ESP was an established fact, while 49 percent believed it probably was a real-life occurrence. About 24 percent of the teachers denied ESP existed, while the rest thought it "merely an unknown." Teachers in the humanities, arts, and education were the most enthusiastic supporters of ESP—about 75 percent believed in it. Only 5 percent of the psychologists thought ESP to be an established fact, and only 29 percent thought it was likely (cited in Edge et al., 1986).

The general public, however, is more likely to accept ESP as an "established fact" (Ross & Joshi, 1992). A 1978 Gallup poll found that more than half the U.S. population believed in ESP (in 1984 the figure was 48 percent for Canada). Psychologist

Thomas Gray points out that when more sensitive measures are used, the figure is closer to 80 percent (Gray, 1990).

How can we explain the discrepancy between what the general public believes and what psychologists will accept as factual? The answer probably lies in the *experimental method,* which we discussed in Chapter 1 (Crowe, 1990). If you (or one of your friends) has had what seemed to be a paranormal experience, chances are good that your belief in ESP will be fairly strong. But the *science of psychology* can accept "supernatural" explanations only when all *natural* explanations have been ruled out. As psychologist Richard B. Hoppe puts it, "The claim for some sort of nonsensory mental interaction with distant objects or persons is sufficiently extraordinary as to require very compelling evidence that the phenomenon even occurs and that evidence has not been produced by the parapsychologists" (Hoppe, 1988).

Demonstrating that an event can be explained in normal scientific terms often calls for a fair amount of ingenuity—and some knowledge of how people can exchange subtle cues without being aware they are doing so. So let us see why ESP experiments are so difficult to design, and how their results are sometimes misinterpreted.

ESP Experiments

Suppose you volunteered to participate in a parapsychological experiment. You might be shown a pack of ordinary bridge cards so that you could make sure that—like all other bridge decks—this one contained 52 cards divided into four suits. The experimenter would then shuffle the cards thoroughly and place the deck face down on the table between the two of you.

The experimenter might then pick up the cards one by one in such a manner that he or she could see the card, but you couldn't. Next, you would be asked to "read the experimenter's mind"—that is, to guess the *suit* of the card that the parapsychologist was looking at. Since there are four suits in the deck, you would have *one chance in four* of being right with any given card. If, the first time you tried this experiment, you guessed the suit correctly 13 times out of 52, you would have done no more than would be expected *by chance alone.*

Undaunted by your first experience, you try again. And this time you guess all 52 cards correctly! Surely this is evidence that mental telepathy occurred, isn't it?

The answer is—not yet. First, you must show that you had no *sensory cues* to help you out. Thousands of studies similar to this one have been performed in the past—and almost all of them are useless from a scientific point of view. Why? Because the experimenter did not control for the *exchange of subtle cues* such as those used by "Clever Hans" and described in Chapter 1. Indeed, the vast majority of studies in this area can be discounted because the experimenters failed to take into account the "Clever Hans" effect (Edge et al., 1986).

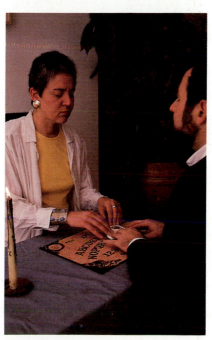

Unconscious "cheating" is very likely to happen with ESP parlor games like the Ouija board; scientists have tried to design "cheat-proof" experiments to test paranormal phenomena.

How many times would you have to guess the suit correctly before you might begin to suspect that something paranormal had occurred?

SCHMIDT'S PRECOGNITION STUDY

One of the problems with ESP studies is that the experimenter must make sure there is *no possible way* the information the subject is trying to "receive mentally" could be received by normal sensory pathways. A second problem is that the experimenters themselves may unconsciously "cheat" while recording the results of the study. Several years ago, physicist Helmut Schmidt reported a study on *precognition* that seemed to overcome these problems.

Schmidt built a *random generator*—a machine that would randomly turn on one of four colored lights. Beneath each light was a button that the subject could press. It was the subject's task to predict which light the machine would turn on.

Since the machine did not make its random selection until *after* the subject had pressed a button, there was no obvious way that either Schmidt or the subject could know which light would turn on—except through *precognition*. In his first experiment, Schmidt used three subjects, who made more than 60,000 guesses. The subjects' choices were correct far more often than chance would allow. In a second experiment, the subjects could guess either which light would turn on or which one wouldn't. Again they did far better than chance would predict. Schmidt has repeated these studies—usually with fair success—many times (Schmidt, 1976, 1981, 1985).

The Schmidt type of experiment controls for "unconscious whispering," but what other types of errors would you want to control for as well?

CRITICISMS OF SCHMIDT'S STUDIES

Do Schmidt's studies *prove* that precognition exists? No, not necessarily. A lengthy discussion of the pros and cons of Schmidt's work appears in the July 1980 issue of the *Zetetic Scholar*. Although some psychologists believe that Schmidt's research is fairly encouraging evidence, others are less convinced. As James Randi points out in the *Zetetic Scholar*, Schmidt's work has not as yet been properly observed by other scientists, nor has his work been replicated successfully by most other investigators. Randi also notes that in almost all of the famous ESP studies, subsequent investigations by skeptical scientists have either exposed a fatal defect or have uncovered evidence that the experimenter might have "fudged" the data. In a more recent survey, British scientist Susan Blackmore comes to the same conclusion, not only about Schmidt's research, but about ESP experiments in general (Blackmore, 1985).

Does ESP Exist?

Do all these objections mean that ESP is no more than a figment of people's imaginations? No, not at all. For the essence of science is that we must always keep an open mind. However, it does seem that extrasensory perception is at best a kinky, slippery, undependable thing that happens rarely, unpredictably, and for the most part, uncontrollably. It may be that ESP phenomena represent such "weak signals" that we can only observe them in special states of consciousness—like hypnosis, or dreaming (Child, 1985; Hyman & Honorton, 1986; Pekala et al., 1992).

Over the years a great many scientists have spent a fair amount of laboratory time trying to "prove" the existence of ESP and other paranormal phenomena (Rao & Palmer, 1987). For example, more than a decade ago, Susan Blackmore had an "out-of-body experience," which prompted her to spend 10 years studying ESP scientifically. Much to her dismay, she failed to produce any reliable proof at all. Speaking of ESP studies in general (including her own research), Blackmore concludes that the more controlled these studies have been, the less evidence for the existence of ESP they have provided (Blackmore, 1986). And after surveying the field, Richard Hoppe concludes that, "I know of no [paranormal] phenomenon that can be consistently produced under experimental conditions that rule out subject or experimenter fraud, statistical and procedural artifacts, or normal sensory functioning" (Hoppe, 1988).

If the scientific evidence doesn't generally support a belief in ESP, though, why do many people ignore the scientific facts and continue to place very strong faith in the paranormal? For many reasons:

Magician and skeptic James Randi demonstrates "spoon bending" using trickery. (With psychokinesis spoons are supposedly bent through the power of the mind.) For several years, Randi has offered $10,000 to anyone who can demonstrate parapsychological phenomena under controlled conditions—so far no one has succeeded.

1. ESP may, in fact, exist, but we do not as yet know how to reproduce it under laboratory conditions.

2. Many real-world events have, as yet, no reasonable, scientific explanation.

3. Most people tend to trust their own perceptions more than they do scientific evidence. And, as Susan Blackmore points out, "People who think they are intelligent, well-educated, and good observers believe that anything they cannot understand must be supernatural" (Blackmore, 1986).

4. Belief in the supernatural may, under certain circumstances, fulfill a very strong human need.

Let's look more closely at how perceptions of supernatural events come about, and why they are often highly rewarding.

What sorts of "scientific sources" mentioned in the news media are you most likely to trust?

BELIEF IN THE OCCULT

Barry Singer and Victor Benassi have spent many years studying **occult** beliefs among college students. In summarizing their work, they make three important points. First, their student subjects tended to believe whatever they saw in print or on TV—particularly if they thought the source of the information was "scientific" or "documentary." Second, when the students were asked to give examples of "scientific sources" and "documentaries," they listed *Reader's Digest,* the *National Enquirer,* and movies such as *Star Wars.* Third, as Singer and Benassi note, most newspapers, magazines, and TV programs report stories about paranormal events *without demanding scientific proof that the event occurred* (Singer & Benassi, 1981). Fourth, we might add that even when people hear something from a source they don't trust, as time passes they remember the information but often *forget where they heard it.* (We will return to this "sleeper effect" in Chapter 18.)

Occult. From a Latin word meaning "hidden" or "mysterious." Frequently having negative connotations of evil.

INTUITION VERSUS EXPERIMENTAL EVIDENCE

Singer and Benassi give another important reason that belief in ESP may be so strong. To begin with, they cite a number of scientific studies showing that people

Intuitive (inn-TOO-it-tive). Technically, the act of gaining direct knowledge without rational thought. Loosely speaking, to be intuitive is to act on your feelings or hunches without being able to defend your acts rationally.

tend to trust **intuitive** judgments rather than experimental evidence. Almost everyone has dreamed about something that eventually came true. But is this proof of *precognition?* No, because people have hundreds of similar dreams that don't come true. But we tend to forget those unfulfilled dreams and just remember the ones that "proved out." As Singer and Benassi put it, "A rare event is seen as one that seldom occurs, regardless of the number of opportunities for its occurrence. As a result of our natural tendency to misunderstand the probabilities involved in a match of dreams and reality," we are more likely to explain the dream as precognition than as mere chance (Singer & Benassi, 1981).

Thomas Gray claims that people continue to believe in ESP at least partly because they are unable (or unwilling) to evaluate properly the information they receive. They fail to make simple comparisons under controlled conditions, such as we discussed in Chapter 1 (Gray, 1990; Gray & Mill, 1990).

ESP AND MOTIVATION

Singer and Benassi point out that many people resist giving up their belief in ESP no matter how strong the experimental evidence is against it. In one study, Singer and Benassi had a magician perform various "psychic tricks" for introductory psychology students. Even when the students were told in advance that the performer was a magician—and even when they admitted that what they saw could easily have been "mere tricks," *more than half the students* insisted that the magician's "tricks" were proof that ESP exists!

Singer and Benassi state that belief in the paranormal tends to increase during wars and other disasters, but tends to decrease during good times. And, as Singer and Benassi note, belief in ESP seldom costs a person very much. Singer and Benassi conclude that accepting the supernatural gives people a feeling that they have greater control over their destinies than is actually the case (Singer & Benassi, 1981).

In a similar study, Peter Glick and Deborah Gottesman tested students' belief in astrology. The student subjects were given vague statements, such as "Though you are a friendly person, at times you are rather shy." As Glick and Gottesman point out, such statements can apply to almost everyone. Students who believed in astrology thought these statements were "highly accurate" descriptions of themselves, *particularly when told the statements were produced by astrologers.* And even some of the skeptics accepted the accuracy of the statements if they thought the descriptions were based on astrology. Glick and Gottesman conclude, "In contrast to skeptics, people who believe in astrology have a greater need for a simple system to understand themselves and to predict the behavior of others. However, all of us, including skeptics, appear to have tendencies that may lead us falsely to lend credence to astrology" (Glick & Gottesman, 1989).

Skepticism and Belief

But must we be skeptical or even cynical about everything we cannot demonstrate in the laboratory? Not necessarily. Psychology, as a science, limits itself to the study of observable cause-and-effect relationships. But as the famous early psychologist William James pointed out, this is not necessarily all there is to life. "Science, however, must be constantly reminded that her purposes are not the only purposes, and that the order of uniform causation which she has use for, and is therefore right in postulating, may be enveloped in a wider order, on which she has no claim at all" (James, 1890).

Some areas of human thought are simply beyond testability: the existence or nonexistence of God, the finality of death, or the reality of life after death. Even the existence of *mind* as a separate essence which can act on the body is an unproven *assumption.* (This position is known as **dualism,** and it contrasts with the position known as **monism.** Monists generally assume that what we call "mind," for the sake

Dualism. The philosophical position that as humans we are minds as well as bodies, and that our nonphysical minds can influence our physical bodies (and our bodies can influence our minds). This position was given its clearest modern presentation by the French philosopher René Descartes.

Monism. The philosophical position that we are nothing more than physical bodies. What we call our "mind" is purely the result of physical processes in our bodies (primarily our brains). The mind can exert no independent influence on the body. This position is adopted, at least as a working assumption, by virtually all neuropsychologists.

of convenience, is really nothing more than brain processes.) You must decide on these matters for reasons other than laboratory demonstration. The problem with ESP is that it is not scientifically verifiable. No reliable proof for it has been shown.

In fact, as psychologist Richard Gregory points out, if ESP were possible, scientific research itself would be jeopardized. Researchers' thoughts might influence their equipment or their subjects' thoughts. Experimenters might be able to tell which experimental condition a subject was in, even when they didn't want to know (to avoid biasing the results) (Gregory, 1988). The basis for *scientific psychology* would be extremely shaky.

All of this means it is very important to recognize when we are operating within a scientific framework and when we are not. Phenomena which are claimed to be in the scientific domain must be able to be reliably demonstrated. Apparently, ESP cannot.

Perception and Stress Reduction

Perception is the psychological process by which you give meaning to and thus make sense of your sensory inputs. But why do you bother to do so?

The best answer seems to be this: As you surely know from personal experience, uncertainty is stressful. Indeed, many psychologists believe that the need to reduce uncertainty is innately determined. Having a theory about why people act as they do reduces uncertainty. And the theory does so *whether the theory is accurate or not*. For, as Peter Glick found, you are strongly motivated to search for (and accept uncritically) evidence that confirms your theory, and you tend to screen out any inaccurate predictions the theory makes (Glick, 1987).

Put rather bluntly, you not only tend to perceive what you *expect* to perceive, but you also tend to perceive what you *want* to perceive. We will consider this topic of motivation further in Chapter 6, but first we must examine our total perceptual experience, or consciousness, and how it undergoes some amazing variations.

SUMMARY

1. Psychologists do not agree on how much of the perceptual process is determined innately and how much is learned. This is called the **nature-nurture** controversy.

2. There are four major theories of visual perception: the **Gestalt** approach, the **Gibsonian** viewpoint, the **empirical** position, and the **information processing** approach.

3. Gestalt psychologists believe that perception results from an **interaction** between external (stimulus) factors and internal (psychological) processes.

4. James Gibson believed perception is **innate** and **direct.** You **see the world as it actually is,** because visual stimuli are rich in sensory cues that tell your brain what the objects actually look like.

5. The empirical approach states that you **learn** to perceive through experience. Empirically, then **perception = sensory inputs + memories.**

6. The information processing approach holds that inputs are highly processed before they reach your cortex. Special nerve cells **detect critical features** of visual inputs and pass this patterned information along to your cortex. Lower brain centers also **screen out** trivial information. Perception, therefore, is an indivisible part of **cognition.**

7. For Gibson and the empirical approach, perception is **driven** by stimulus factors and thus is a **bottom-up process.** For the information processing approach, perception is **driven** by cognitive (psychological) factors and thus is a **top-down**

process. Gestalt theorists see perception as a **balance** between bottom-up and top-down factors.

8. The simplest type of visual information is **contours,** or a sudden change in lightness/darkness. Contours give **shape** to objects perceived visually.

9. The Gestalt **Law of Pragnanz** states you tend to perceive shapes or figures in the most **simple** and **stable** form possible.

10. **Figure-ground** relationships have a strong influence on perception. You tend to see **salient** objects as "figure" rather than as "background." The background always continues behind the figure.

11. **Ambiguous figures** show **perspective reversal.** The frequency with which the perspective reverses may be related to experience and personality factors.

12. You tend to group things together perceptually according to the Gestalt principles of **proximity, closure, continuity,** and **similarity.**

13. Humans who lose their sight in childhood but regain it as adults often have **severe problems adjusting.** They must **learn to recognize** visually objects that they had only touched or heard about. They do not perceive visual illusions in the same way that normally sighted humans do.

14. **Linear perspective, convergence, aerial perspective, texture, light and shadow, interposition,** and **real and apparent motion** give you clues which allow your brain to perceive visual distance.

15. **Expectancy** has a strong influence on perception. For the most part, **you see what you expect to see.** You also **fail to see** what you don't expect (or want) to see.

16. **Size constancy** and **shape constancy** are the tendencies to see objects as maintaining proper size and shape despite changes in the image they cast on the retina.

17. Your **pupil size** is primarily determined by visual reflexes that you had when you were born. However, your pupils open wider when you look at something interesting than when you look at something boring.

18. When your two eyes are shown different scenes, your mind may **suppress** one of the scenes, or it may **fuse** the two together to make a "Gestalt." You are more likely to suppress threatening scenes than pleasant ones.

19. Some aspects of visual perception occur so soon after birth they seem *primarily* **determined by your genes.** Three-week-old infants will recoil from objects moving toward them, 10-day-old infants mimic the facial expressions of adults around them, and babies prefer to look at pictures of human faces rather than mixed-up drawings of facial features.

20. Four-week-old infants tend to look away from their mothers' faces because they are **not mature enough** to process faces in a meaningful way. Seven-week-old babies are experienced enough to gaze directly at the mother's eyes and mouth. Infants also **prefer** looking at **attractive faces.**

21. Some (but not all) infants will avoid a **visual cliff.**

22. **Blind children** are slow to develop language and a **self-concept,** but do seem to have an innate appreciation of **physical space.**

23. **Parapsychology** is the scientific study of events that seem to have no "natural" explanation, such as **mental telepathy, clairvoyance, precognition,** and **psychokinesis.**

24. Although large numbers of people believe in **extrasensory perception** (ESP), laboratory studies do not offer much support for this belief.

25. Belief in the supernatural is based on **non-scientific support** and is not subject to scientific examination.

1. *Is an association between senses, such as sight and touch, . . . ?*

   If you saw for the first time as an adult, you probably would not be able to recognize many familiar objects without first feeling them. (We will discuss a case like this later in the chapter.) Apparently, learning plays an important role in many perceptions.

2. *If we showed you a picture of an oval . . . ?*

   As the Gestalt psychologists showed, we tend to perceive things in simple, stable forms. A circle is a simpler, more stable form than an oval (which can vary from nearly round to very elliptical).

3. *According to both Gibson and the Gestalt psychologists, . . . ?*

   Both would say the infant would perceive the coin as an ellipse—no learning was necessary.

4. *Without looking at the photograph at the beginning . . . ?*

   You were probably never consciously aware of the date. The date or other detailed inscription is not (usually) an important part of the perceptual stimulus necessary for identification. Once again, the most basic, *simple* features are the ones that you perceive and retain.

5. *How could you prove to someone else . . . ?*

   You could never prove it. Neither you nor the other person has knowledge of existence outside of your (fallible) perceptions. The best you could do would be to allow the other person to perceive it. The more senses the person was able to use, the more convinced the person would be.

6. *Figure 4.3 contains an important clue about depth perception. . . . ?*

   Objects that are closer overlap and partially hide objects that are farther away. (This clue is called "interposition.")

7. *From this description, does the Gestalt position on perception . . . ?*

   Both factors seem to be involved. Gestalt "laws" describe tendencies to respond in certain ways to *stimulus factors* (bottom-up). But we can sometimes times *choose* to perceive a figure in a different way (top-down).

8. *How else might the Bergums's findings be explained?*

   Perhaps people with a "creative, unstable view of the world" are more likely to choose architecture over business in the first place.

9. *How would you attempt to explain these illusions . . . ?*

   An information processing perspective would suggest the "source" of the illusion could be conflicting or incompatible information "extracted" at different stages of processing. An empirical position would suggest your past experiences may lead you to interpret parts of a stimulus in one way, and other parts in a different way, giving rise to conflicting perceptions, or illusions. Both points of view emphasize learning, or experience, over the kind of innate principles proposed by the Gestalt theorists.

10. *Why are airplane pilots usually better at judging heights than are non-pilots?*

    Pilots are generally better at judging heights probably because they frequently observe objects from great heights and then move down to the same level as the objects. This experience gives them a "feel" for the distance involved.

11. *S.B. often mistook shadows for real objects. Why do you think this was the case?*

    This mistake, like many of S.B.'s other problems, was probably a result of his lack of visual experience. In this case, the problem may have been caused by a failure to connect tactile (touch) information with visual information. It could also be the result of his reliance on simple shapes (outlines) to identify objects visually (rather than including complex information on color and texture). Or, it could have been his lack of experience with depth cues, such as light and shadow, which would have told him that shadows don't have the depth that objects do.

12. *It is rather simple to train a pigeon . . . ?*

If you trained a pigeon to peck at the shorter of two lines, when you showed it the Mueller-Lyer illusion it might be "fooled" into pecking at the line which appeared shorter. If it was *not* fooled, it would peck at both lines randomly— approximately an equal number of times.

13. *Is the tendency for women to become "wide-eyed". . . ?*

The tendency to become "wide-eyed" when looking at something which interests you is probably innate. However, your *experience* has a great influence over what interests you. You might examine the role of experience by testing people who had either no experience (blind people who first saw as adults, or adults in a culture where nudity was virtually unknown), or a lot of experience (people in occupations or cultures where nudity was common), with these stimuli. Differences between these groups would presumably be the result of experience.

14. *Langlois notes that attractive faces . . . ?*

Gestalt psychologists would say that attractive faces are more easily perceived in simple and stable forms. The tendency to perceive in this way is one of several inherited tendencies described by Gestalt laws.

15. *Why do you think we do such a poor job of judging facial expressions when the face is upside down?*

We have very little experience in judging upside-down faces. In contrast, the ability to judge rightside-up faces is learned very early, and may even be partially inherited.

16. *Haith's research seems to contradict Fantz's . . . ?*

Fantz's infants may have *learned* to recognize the human face before he tested them. The infants in Fantz's study may have been responding to visual *complexity* rather than human facial characteristics.

17. *How might auditory perception help a child like Kelli develop a perception of physical space?*

Blind children probably become more sensitive to auditory cues, such as the different quality of sounds reflected from various surfaces at different distances. Remember how different your voice sounds in an empty gymnasium than in a small closet?

18. *Studies suggest that most people dream about the future . . . ?*

You probably would notice and remember events and the associated dreams which were similar. In other words, the dreams which "came true," you would remember, the many which didn't, you would forget.

19. *How many times would you have to guess the suit correctly . . . ?*

You would want to be absolutely certain that no sensory cues were being used, and you would want to guess correctly at a much better rate than chance would predict. Remember that even by chance you could occasionally guess all 52 correctly. If you want to know how to reject a "chance" explanation, see the statistical appendix of this book.

20. *The Schmidt type of experiment controls for "unconscious whispering," . . . ?*

You might want to confirm that the machine was turning on the lights in a truly *random* order. Even a slight deviation could be picked up by the subject and used to increase his or her score. You might want a different experimenter, with a different machine, in a different location to run the experiment to eliminate influences you had not thought of.

21. *What sorts of "scientific sources" mentioned in the news media are you most likely to trust?*

We tend to trust sources which use statistics and other empirical evidence. We also tend to be persuaded by attractive sources. (We will discuss persuasion more in Chapter 18.)

C H A P T E R 5

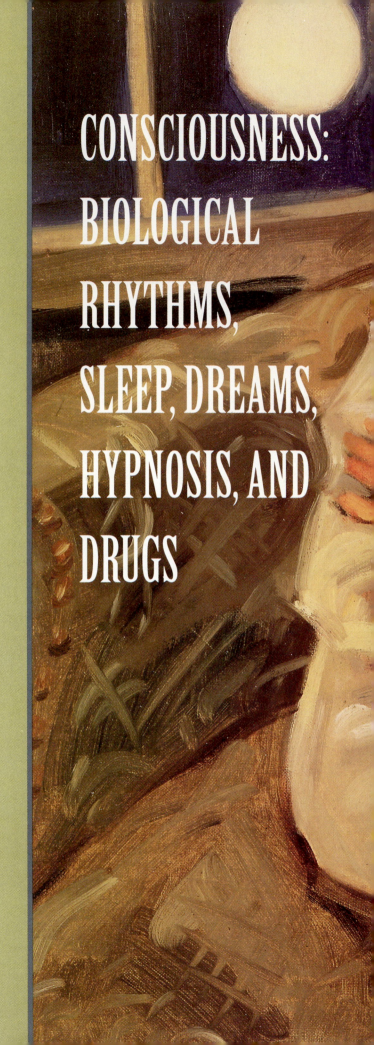

CONSCIOUSNESS: BIOLOGICAL RHYTHMS, SLEEP, DREAMS, HYPNOSIS, AND DRUGS

You are not the kind of guy who would be at a place like this at this time of the morning. But here you are, and you cannot say that the terrain is entirely unfamiliar, although the details are fuzzy. You are at a nightclub talking to a girl with a shaved head. The club is either Heartbreak or the Lizard Lounge. All might come clear if you could just slip into the bathroom and do a little more Bolivian Marching Powder. Then again, it might not. A small voice inside you insists that this epidemic lack of clarity is a result of too much of that already. The night has already turned on that imperceptible pivot where two A.M. changes to six A.M. You know this moment has come and gone, but you are not yet willing to concede that you have crossed the line beyond which all is gratuitous damage and the palsy of unraveled nerve endings. Somewhere back there you could have cut your losses, but you rode past that moment on a comet trail of white powder and now you are trying to hang on to the rush. Your brain at this moment is composed of brigades of tiny Bolivian soldiers. They are tired and muddy from their long march through the night. There are holes in their boots and they are hungry. They need to be fed. They need the Bolivian Marching Powder.

JAY McINERNEY
BRIGHT LIGHTS, BIG CITY

Consciousness. The act or process of being aware, particularly of one's surroundings, thoughts, and bodily condition. Also, being alert, understanding what is happening.

A n ancient Chinese philosopher mused,

> I, Chuang Chou, slept and dreamt I was a butterfly, flitting here and there. Then I awoke and knew I was Chuang Chou. Now, did Chuang Chou sleep and dream he was a butterfly? Or did the butterfly sleep and dream he was Chuang Chou?

Chuang Chou was reflecting on **consciousness** and its relationship to the physical world. In this chapter we too will look at consciousness and how it relates to our everyday experience. We will also consider how our experience of consciousness varies throughout the 24-hour day, and how consciousness can be altered through hypnosis, and drugs.

How do you know you are not dreaming right now?

Consciousness is a word worn smooth by a million tongues.

GEORGE MILLER (1987)

CONSCIOUSNESS

Every science has what are called *primitive terms*. That is, every science has ideas or concepts which are so elemental that they are exceptionally difficult to define. For example, "energy" and "matter" are two primitive terms in the field of physics. You must have a rough notion of what these words mean, but you should realize that great philosophical battles have been fought over their exact definitions. Psychology has its primitive terms too. One of these is *consciousness*.

What Is Consciousness?

When psychology began, about 140 years ago, one of its main goals was the analysis of consciousness. This proved to be so difficult that 65 years later most psychologists rejected the study of consciousness and turned to behavior. The focus on behavior became so narrow that one historian was prompted to observe that "psychology, having first bargained away its soul and then gone out of its mind seems now, as it faces an untimely end, to have lost all consciousness" (Burt, 1962).

We experience many different "states of consciousness" during a 24-hour period. Daydreaming is one very common "altered state."

Well, psychology has *regained* consciousness! The problems in definition, however, remain (Natsoulas, 1981, 1986–1987, 1991). When researcher Imants Baruss reviewed the literature on consciousness, he found 29 different definitions of the term (Baruss, 1987). But let's let the experts worry about subtle differences in meaning. We can appreciate some of the interesting findings in this area if we simply consider consciousness to be equivalent to our *awareness*—awareness of our behavior, awareness of our perceptions, awareness of our intentions—all of the things of which we, at any one time, are knowingly aware (Baars, 1988).

This means that consciousness is not actually a *thing* but a *process*—William James called it a "stream." And processes are much harder to measure—and to describe scientifically—than are things. You can describe a track shoe rather easily. Describing the *process of running*, however, is a more difficult task.

Altered States

If consciousness is our *awareness* of our behavior, thoughts, and surroundings, then an *alteration* in consciousness is any change in that awareness. Some altered states of awareness occur naturally. For instance, that blissful condition called *sleep*, and those sometimes unblissful experiences we call *nightmares*, are examples of natural altered states of awareness. But there are unnatural states, as well—unnatural in the sense that they are *artificially* brought about. The intoxication that you get from drugs such as alcohol is a good example of an artificially induced, altered state of consciousness. We will look at some more examples in a moment.

You have probably heard the terms "unconscious" or "subconscious." These terms refer to processes which are *outside* your present awareness. We will have more to say about processes outside of consciousness in Chapter 14.

Consciousness is a *subjective state* or "internal process." But it is controlled in large part by physical activities in our brains and bodies. Before we can discuss consciousness further, therefore, we must take a closer look at the biological rhythms that influence our states of awareness.

BIOLOGICAL RHYTHMS

One of the more common ways in which our consciousness *alters* is in the familiar experience of sleep. But sleep is just one part of a total biological and psychological cycle our bodies go through each day. We call these cycles **circadian rhythms,** because they repeat approximately once a day.

Your temperature, for instance, is usually lowest in the middle of the night. It begins to rise a few hours before you get up in the morning, and reaches the "normal" (98.6° F; 37°C) around 6:00 P.M. Then your temperature begins to drop, moving down toward its nighttime low, roughly 1.8° F lower by 3:00 A.M.

Your blood sugar level, pulse rate, and blood pressure also reach peaks around 5:00 or 6:00 P.M. Your sensory abilities—hearing, vision, taste, and smell—also are at their best in the late afternoon (Moore-Ede, Sulzman, & Fuller, 1982). However, your sensitivity to tooth pain is *lowest* at this time, so you might consider visiting the dentist then (Winfree, 1987).

Other biological cycles reach their high points at different times of day. For example, men have the greatest amount of male hormone present in their bodies at about 9 A.M. (Moore-Ede et al., 1982). Anesthesia "knocks you out" more easily in the early afternoon; the proper dose in the afternoon might be ineffective in the morning. In the wee hours of the night, allergic responses are triggered much more easily and are much more violent. And your liver removes alcohol from your blood much more quickly in the early evening than in the morning (Winfree, 1987).

Circadian rhythms (seer-KAY-dee-an). From the Latin words *circa*, meaning "about," and *dies*, meaning "day." A biological rhythm that is "about a day (24 hours) in length."

The most obvious circadian rhythm, however, is the sleep/waking cycle. Sleep is a good example of a biological rhythm that runs less than a day in length. As you will soon see, sleep is actually made up of a repeating sequence of events. Each individual sleep cycle runs about 90 minutes. Before we discuss sleep, though, there are several general points we should make about biological rhythms:

1. Most biological clocks run on a circadian rhythm of approximately 24 hours. (The human menstrual cycle, which runs about 28 days, is an example of a much longer biological rhythm.)

2. There is substantial individual variability among people as far as their biological rhythms are concerned. Your biological rhythms may peak at quite different times from those of the people around you. And, as you surely know, your own cycles may be disrupted under many different circumstances, such as sickness or a long trip on a jet airplane (Redfern, 1989).

3. Most of your biological clocks are controlled by various sub-centers in your brain. The overall pattern of activity in these sub-centers was probably determined by your genes and set before birth. Day-to-day *changes* in your activity cycles, however, are strongly influenced by inputs from your external environment and by conscious decisions (Webb, 1988).

Let's look at these points in more detail.

What problems are created when groups of people try to keep the same schedule—for example, in camps, or the military, or even in a family?

Biological Clocks

Biological clocks are typically set by external events. The most important of these is the daily cycle of light and darkness. If you live on the West Coast of North America, your clocks will normally operate on Pacific Time. If you fly to New York, you will likely experience several days of confusion as your body tries to reset all its clocks so that they operate on Eastern Time. When you fly back to the West Coast, you will undergo a similar sort of *jet lag*. In either case, however, once your biological clocks have stabilized, they will still run on a 24-hour cycle.

FREE-RUNNING TIME

Oddly enough, if we remove all environmental cues, so that your biological clocks can "run free," you won't set your own 24-hour cycle and follow it without fail. Rather, if you have no sensory inputs to tell you what time of day it really is, your sleeping/waking rhythm will soon settle down on a day-length of about 25 hours. This is what happened to 23-year-old Jacques Chabert when he undertook to live for six months in a cave in southern France (Jouvet et al., 1974). Unfortunately, no one really knows why your sleep/waking rhythm runs on a 25-hour rather than a 24-hour cycle in the absence of external cues (Winfree, 1987).

RESETTING

If you travel to different time zones, or change shifts on your job, you must reset your biological clock radically, and in a brief period of time. Scientists have developed several strategies in an effort to help you do this. These scientists might give you Melatonin, a drug which helps regulate circadian rhythms; they might systematically change the timing and content of your meals and your intake of caffeine; they might control your exposure to light; or they might prescribe certain outdoor activities (Redfern, 1989).

People who have to adjust their sleep patterns because of shift work or travel experience a disruption in their biological clocks.

You will adapt most easily to a new sleep/waking cycle if you change in the direction of your natural tendency towards a 25-hour cycle. For example, you would find it easiest to go from a day shift to an evening shift, to a graveyard shift, especially if during the period of transition, you move the time you begin sleep an hour later each day (Coleman, 1986).

How might biological rhythms contribute to the "home team advantage?"

Melatonin's Effects

Buried away inside your brain is a tiny sub-center called the **pineal gland.** More than 2,000 years ago, a Greek physician named Herophilus stated that the pineal gland was the "gatekeeper" which regulated the flow of thoughts through the mind. The noted French philosopher Rene Descartes called the pineal gland "the seat of the soul." In fact, recent studies show its main function seems to be that of producing *melatonin*, a hormone that acts on certain cells, called SCN cells, in the hypothalamus to control both the sleep/waking cycle and the body's responses to the annual cycle of the seasons (Reppert et al., 1988; Shafii & Shafii, 1990).

Pineal gland (pie-KNEE-al). A neural sub-center that secretes a hormone called melatonin (mell-ah-TONE-in) which helps regulate the day/night cycle as well as the annual "seasonal cycle."

MELATONIN AND THE SLEEP CYCLE.

Under normal circumstances, the level of melatonin builds up in your body during darkness, but decreases during the day. If you are a "morning person," your melatonin likely peaks around 2:00 A.M.—just when you probably feel most sleepy (Fellman, 1985). But if you received an injection of melatonin at *noon,* you would get very sleepy and show a significant slow-down in your reactions (Lieberman, 1985).

This daily build-up of melatonin occurs in most animals as well as in humans, and seems to be controlled by the onset and offset of visual stimulation from the external environment (Murray, 1989). If you blind an animal—or if you cut the neural pathways running from the optic nerve to the pineal gland—the melatonin cycle no longer matches the environmental light/dark cycle and the animal's sleep/wake cycle becomes free-running.

According to Steven Reppert and his colleagues, melatonin cycles begin before birth. In unborn rat pups, and even in humans, melatonin travels from the mother to the fetus and **entrains,** or *sets* their circadian rhythms on the same schedule (Reppert et al., 1988).

Entrain. A "train" is a collection of connected objects that move along the same track at the same speed. Two or more biological cycles that function on the same schedule are said to be "entrained."

Seasonal behaviors of many species, including the migratory habits of birds, are influenced by melatonin.

Why might it be important for a mother and her babies to be on similar biological schedules?

MELATONIN AND SAD

Recent research also suggests that melatonin may be involved in the onset of what is called **seasonal affective disorder,** or SAD.

As the length of day decreases in the fall, some people begin to overeat, oversleep, and become severely depressed. Come springtime—and the increase in daylight hours—their problems tend to disappear. (The symptoms of SAD also diminish significantly if the person goes south for the winter—that is, goes to a part of the world where the days are longer during the winter months.) Some, though not all, of the patients also go through an energetic "manic phase" during the summer months, when the days are particularly long (Eastman, 1990).

Research by Alfred J. Lewy and his colleagues suggests that almost all individuals afflicted with SAD may have abnormal daily melatonin rhythms. Lewy believes that daily treatment with bright light may "reset" the patients' abnormal melatonin cycles. Research by William Byerley and his colleagues suggests that repeated exposure to even five minutes of very bright light may relieve SAD symptoms, as well as help reset circadian rhythms (Byerley et al., 1989; Lewy et al., 1987; Sack et al., 1990).

We might note two SAD things: First, while SAD patients suffer from depression, there is as yet no reliable evidence that *all* depressive patients can be helped with "bright light" treatment. Some people suffer from "summer depression" when light is abundant (Wehr & Rosenthal, 1989). Second, there is no agreement among researchers as to what type of light is needed, how bright the light should be, or at what time of day (or night) the SAD patient should be exposed to the light (Avery et al., 1992a, 1992b; Murray, 1989; Shafii & Shafii, 1990).

What kind of melatonin cycle would you expect to find in people who suffer from insomnia?

DIMENSIONS OF SLEEP

Sleep is part of your daily activity cycle. And yet sleep is obviously an interruption in your normal stream of consciousness. Scientists are still uncertain as to what sleep actually is or what function it serves. In this section we will consider why we sleep, the stages we go through in sleep, how much sleep we need, what happens when we are deprived of sleep, and that most interesting phenomenon of sleep—our dreams. Finally, we will look at several disorders of sleep.

What Is Sleep?

In his book, *Sleep: The Gentle Tyrant,* and elsewhere, sleep expert Wilse Webb notes that there are two major theoretical explanations for sleep:

- The first is that sleep is an *adaptive response* that increases an organism's chances of surviving.
- The second theory is that sleep is a *restorative process* that allows the body (and perhaps the mind) to repair the day's damages (Webb, 1975, 1988).

Let's look briefly at both these theories.

Seasonal affective disorder, or **SAD.** In psychology, the word *affect* means "emotional" or "having to do with moods." People suffering from SAD typically become depressed during the dark winter months and may or may not become hyperactive (manic) during the long, bright days of summer.

Imagine yourself as a primitive being living thousands of years ago (or as an animal today). What sorts of behaviors would increase your chances of surviving? During the day, you'd have to be actively engaged in finding things to eat—and in protecting yourself from those animals that would like to dine on *you*. But what would you do at night? Without artificial light, you wouldn't be able to see either food or danger. If you went to sleep at night instead of remaining active, you could conserve your energy and avoid the terrors of the night. As Wilse Webb puts it, "Sleep, then, can be thought of as an instinctive response which is useful in 'keeping us out of harm's way'" (Webb, 1975). This is the "adaptive theory" of sleep.

On the other hand, if you ask people why they sleep, Wilse Webb says, most of them will respond, "To rest." According to the "restorative theory of sleep," you burn up energy during the day. Thus, you need to remain quiet for long hours each night to "recharge your batteries" (Webb, 1982).

It certainly is true that you often go to bed feeling tired and out of sorts, and wake up the next day feeling much better. It's also the case that, when you're weary, you *feel* the need for sleep—just as you feel the need for food when you're hungry. But does full sleep help your body recover more than would "deep rest," in which you stayed peacefully awake? The answer seems to be "no," for scientists have yet to discover any type of restorative process that functions *only* when you are unconscious in sleep (Webb, 1982).

There is no way to know which of the two approaches to explaining sleep is correct. Indeed, both theories have some validity to them. Because you are relatively immobile when you sleep, you do tend to stay out of harm's way. But it is also more likely you will get your daily "restorative rest" if you feel a need for sleep—and if you are unconscious while resting (Webb, 1975).

People spend about one-third of their lives in sleep. But less than 2 percent of all psychological research is on sleep and dreaming. How many reasons can you think of to explain why scientists have studied "awakeness" so much more than "sleep"?

Stages of Sleep

As Wilse Webb puts it, "Sleep is not simply a 'turning off' or 'going flat' or a 'nothingness' in which we lie awash. It is a very busy and active state of affairs" (Webb, 1975). In fact, there are at least six different stages of sleep, each marked by its own pattern of brain waves that can be measured with an EEG machine. If you are an average sleeper, your cycle will go something like this:

STAGE 0 SLEEP

When you first try to fall asleep, your muscles will relax, and your breathing will slow and become quite regular. Your brain waves slow down a bit. **Alpha waves** gradually replace **beta waves** (see Figure 5.1). This period is called Stage 0 sleep, or "pre-sleep." Stage 0 sleep is little more than a transition from being awake to being asleep. You spend from 0 to 3 percent of a night's sleep in Stage 0.

STAGE 1 SLEEP

For the next few minutes, as you relax more deeply, you will begin Stage 1 of the sleep cycle. Alpha waves disappear and your brain waves show irregular patterns. The disappearance of the alpha rhythm marks the real start of sleep. You spend from 1 to 10 percent of a night's sleep in Stage 1 sleep.

Sleep, that knits up the ravelled sleeve of care.

WILLIAM SHAKESPEARE

Alpha waves. Larger, slower (than beta) brain waves associated with the state of relaxation and falling asleep called Stage 0 sleep, or pre-sleep.

Beta waves. Small, fast brain waves associated with being awake and alert.

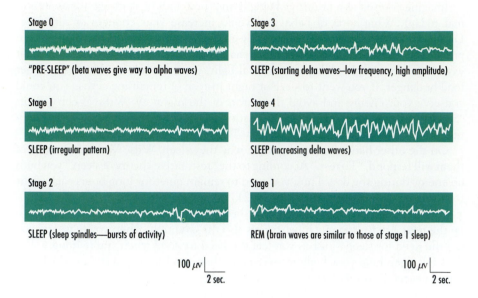

Stage 0

"PRE-SLEEP" (beta waves give way to alpha waves)

Stage 1

SLEEP (irregular pattern)

Stage 2

SLEEP (sleep spindles—bursts of activity)

Stage 3

SLEEP (starting delta waves—low frequency, high amplitude)

Stage 4

SLEEP (increasing delta waves)

Stage 1

REM (brain waves are similar to those of stage 1 sleep)

100 μV
2 sec.

100 μV
2 sec.

FIGURE 5.1

Sections of an EEG record showing the stages of sleep.

Sleep spindles. Bursts of brain waves with a frequency of 12–14 cycles per second that occur during Stage 2 sleep.

Delta waves. Large, slow brain waves with a frequency of less than 4 cycles per second.

REM. Rapid eye movement sleep that occurs toward the end of each 90-minute sleep cycle. It is during this period that most dreaming seems to occur.

STAGE 2 SLEEP

In Stage 2 sleep your brain shows **sleep spindles,** which are bursts of waves that occur about 13–16 times per second. You spend from 40 to 60 percent of a night's sleep in Stage 2.

STAGE 3 SLEEP

Stage 3 sleep is a brief transition period, during which your brain waves slow down even more and sleep spindles tend to disappear. The slow **delta waves** that characterize deep sleep also begin to appear. From 3 to 12 percent of sleep generally occurs at the Stage 3 level.

STAGE 4 SLEEP

About 40–60 minutes after you lose consciousness, you typically reach the deepest sleep of all. Your brain will show regular delta waves, and it will be very difficult for anyone to awaken you. This is Stage 4 sleep, and it is during this stage that sleep-talking, sleepwalking, nightmares, and (in young children) bed-wetting occur. From 5 to 25 percent of your night's sleep is at Stage 4.

STAGE 1—REM SLEEP

You may think you stay at the deep fourth stage all the rest of the night, but that turns out not to be the case. Instead, about 90 minutes after you fall into slumber, your activity cycle will increase slightly as you move back up through the sleep stages. The delta waves will disappear, to be replaced by the beta waves that signal an active or "awake" brain. Your eyes will begin to dart around under your closed eyelids as if you were looking at something occurring in front of you. This period of Rapid Eye Movements is called **REM** sleep. During the first sleep cycle, REM sleep usually lasts from 8 to 15 minutes. In subsequent cycles, REM sleep may last for 40 minutes or more. Overall, you spend from 15 to 35 percent of the night in REM sleep. (This and subsequent "Stage 1" periods differ from the first Stage 1 episode of the night since they typically involve REM and dreaming, while the first Stage 1 period doesn't.)

LATER CYCLES

The description we've just given is for the first sleep cycle, which usually lasts about 90 minutes. Occasionally (particularly if you are older), you may wake up briefly dur-

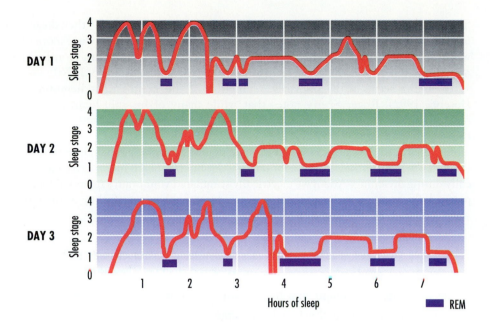

FIGURE 5.2

The sleep record of one subject tested for three nights by Wilse Webb at the University of Florida. The first night, the subject had some difficulty adjusting to sleeping in the laboratory. Note that the REM periods increase significantly in length in later sleep cycles of each night. During a good night's sleep, wakefulness gives way to deep sleep, then to the REM stage where most dreams occur. As the night wears on, dreams tend to lengthen.

ing the transition between Stage 4 and Stage 1—REM sleep. But if you don't awaken, your brain waves will slow again. If this was your first cycle of the night, you probably will slip down all the way to Stage 4 sleep once more. Later in the evening, you may go only as deep as Stage 2 or 3. Whatever the case, in the later stages of each subsequent cycle, your brain waves will speed up and you will go through another REM period (Webb, 1982).

If you are like most people, you will experience four to five complete sleep cycles per night, but both the quality and the intensity of the experiences change the longer you stay asleep (see Figure 5.2). Your first cycle usually yields the longest period of Stage 4 deep sleep, while your first Stage 1–REM period is typically the shortest. However, people have widely different sleep patterns, most of which lie within the "normal range" of 90-minute cycles (Webb, 1982).

REM Sleep

"Boy, are my eyes tired! I had REM sleep all night long."

Your eyes do not move constantly during REM sleep. Rather, as Webb notes, eye movements "tend to occur in 'bursts' of different 'densities' (eye movements per minute), with as much as five minutes between such bursts." However, there is much individual variation in such matters. Generally speaking, people who don't recall their dreams very well tend to have fewer eye movements per unit of time than do those who recall their dreams readily (Webb, 1982).

At the onset of Stage 1–REM sleep, males frequently experience an erection of the penis, and females frequently experience vaginal swelling and sometimes a hardening of their nipples. This sexual arousal typically occurs as the sleeper's brain "rises" from Stage 2 sleep and begins a Stage 1–REM sleep period. This physical arousal usually has very little connection with dream content.

Dreams, in one form or another, tend to occur throughout the sleep period. The way we know this is by waking people up at different points in the sleep cycle and asking them if they were dreaming. Generally speaking, most *organized* and *detailed* dreams occur during REM sleep. However, the connection between dreaming and REM sleep depends on how you define dreaming.

After looking over several experiments in which subjects were awakened at various times, Webb concludes that, "If one required the dream to be a clearly present, visual, storylike event, then almost all such 'dreams' occurred with REM awakenings." However, Webb says, "If one accepted the presence of any mental content—

'thinking about something' or a brief or vague recall of 'something' . . ." then *dreaming* occurs during all stages of sleep. Webb states that REM dreams produce more of what we tend to think of as dreams—visual, hallucinatory-type events. Non-REM awakenings produce more "thought-like" and realistic material (Webb, 1975).

Dreaming seems to be primarily a function of the brain's right hemisphere (Joseph, 1992). Roger Sperry notes that while many of his split-brain patients reported having vivid dreams prior to the surgery, they reported no dreams at all after the operation (Sperry, 1968). However, patients in other laboratories have given different reports, so the question is still in some doubt (Antrobus, 1987; Greenberg & Farah, 1986). Nevertheless, the right half of your brain is much more active electrically during dreaming. And if we electrically stimulated your brain's temporal lobes, particularly on the *right* hemisphere, you would probably report feeling a "dreamy state" (Halgren et al., 1978; Kolb & Wishaw, 1990).

Why might you have trouble consciously remembering your dreams unless you say the dream out loud as soon as you awaken? And when you first awaken in the morning, why might you have difficulty "talking sensibly and getting your act together" for a short period of time?

Voluntary muscles. Those muscles that are under your conscious control, such as the muscles that move your arms and legs. As opposed to involuntary muscles, such as those that make your heart beat.

During non-REM sleep the muscles of your body are relaxed but still capable of moving. However, as you slip into REM sleep, most of the **voluntary muscles** in your body become *paralyzed*—a process called *muscular inhibition*. Although your brain is very active, and often sends messages to your muscles telling them to move, they simply don't respond. However, sometimes the brain's tremendous activity "spills over" and your arms and legs may occasionally "twitch" in an irregular and unusual fashion (Kolb & Wishaw, 1990).

No one knows why this muscular inhibition takes place during REM sleep, but many scientists speculate that it serves to keep you from acting out your dreams. Adrian Morrison studied the effect of brain lesions on REM sleep in cats. In one experiment, he destroyed a very small amount of tissue in one of the lower brain centers of his animals. While awake, the cats behaved normally. When an REM period occurred during their sleep, though, the animals raised their heads, moved about, and struck out at imaginary objects. Morrison believes that the lower brain center he destroyed *actively inhibits* the acting out of dream behavior in normal animals (Morrison, 1983).

How would the two different theories of sleep account for muscular inhibition?

During most stages of sleep, your parasympathetic nervous system maintains a relaxed, "vegetative" state. However, Virend Somers and his colleagues report that during REM sleep the sympathetic nervous system—which helps the body prepare for emergencies—jumps into action. The heart speeds up, the blood pressure climbs, and stress hormones prepare the body to run or fight. The researchers say that even at 4 in the morning when you think your body should be fast asleep and quiet, everything is pounding away. They speculate that this internal turmoil may even trigger heart attacks in vulnerable individuals (Somers et al., 1993).

Amount of Sleep

How much you sleep—and when and how deeply you sleep—are determined as much by psychological and social factors as by biological "needs."

In many countries, afternoon naps, or siestas, are common for adults as well as children.

AGE DIFFERENCES

Generally speaking, the younger you are, the more you sleep and the deeper your sleep is likely to be. As a newborn, you probably slept about 16 hours each day/night cycle. This sleep was scattered in six or more bursts of a few hours each throughout the night and day. Gradually you moved from an almost random pattern of sleeping and waking, into a rhythm of regular naps, and then into a single daily sleep. As you age, you may move back again to a nap pattern (Webb, 1988).

By adolescence and early adulthood, the amount you sleep drops to about 8 hours. Wilse Webb found that University of Florida students averaged about 7 hours and 40 minutes of sleep at night. In addition, they napped about 25 minutes per day. During the two-week period the students were studied, 84 percent of them took at least one nap and about 42 percent napped daily or almost every day. There was considerable variation, however. Some students averaged but 6 hours per day; others got as much as 10 hours of sleep per 24-hour period. And almost all the students slept more on weekends than during the week (Webb, 1982).

Older people tend to sleep less deeply than do infants or young adults. By 40 or 50 years of age, people wake up more frequently during the night. And by age 60, almost everyone naps on a regular basis.

These data, however, are for people in the United States and Canada who live in more-or-less normal circumstances. People in institutions, individuals who work at night, and persons who are sick or experiencing other unusual situations will often show quite different sleep patterns no matter what their age (Benca et al., 1992). In other countries, a nap or "siesta" is part of the daily routine for people of all ages.

"MORNING" AND "EVENING PERSONS"

As you probably know, some people are "morning persons," and some people are "evening persons" (Adan, 1990, 1991, 1992; Horne & Östberg, 1976). (Evening persons sometimes find morning persons incredible if not intolerable.)

T. Akerstedt and J.E. Froberg asked Swedish soldiers questions designed to find out whether the men were more active during the day or night. Some of the men preferred daytime activities and were early risers (morning persons group). Others said they typically did better at night and hence were late risers (evening persons group).

Although we can often avoid sleep when we want to, our bodies will eventually force us to drift off into slumber.

Thalamus (THAL-ah-muss). One of the most important subcenters in the brain. The thalamus acts as a "relay station" that processes sensory inputs from the eyes, ears, and other receptor organs and then passes the inputs on to the cortex.

The rest of the soldiers (intermediate group) had no clear-cut preference (Akerstedt & Froberg, 1976; Torsvall et al., 1985).

Over a period of several months, Akerstedt and Froberg found adrenalin levels for "morning persons" were higher than for "evening persons," indicating they were probably more active overall. As you might expect, adrenalin levels were higher early in the day for "morning persons," but higher at night for "evening persons." The "intermediate group" was in between the two extremes. These results support findings by Hans Caminada and Frans De Bruijn that morning and evening persons experience different levels of "energetic arousal" at different times of the day (Caminada & De Bruijn, 1992).

TOTAL SLEEP DEPRIVATION

You can go for many days without sleep—if circumstances demand that you stay awake. But eventually your body will force you to drift off into slumber. Missing one night's sleep causes little change in your behavior. However, if you stay awake for more than 48 hours, you will probably begin to show an increased irritability and impulsiveness. Your decision-making processes will be affected, and you will react more slowly and make poorer intellectual judgments than you would when rested.

If you deprive yourself of sleep for 100 hours or more, you will very likely show considerable stress. You may experience "moments of confusion," lose your train of thought, become momentarily irritated, feel "spacey," or become quite apathetic. You may "misperceive" what is going on around you, become inattentive, and show bursts of anger. A few people—perhaps 5–10 percent of those tested in several studies—show panic behaviors or symptoms of some type of mental disorder. The surprising thing is, however, that most individuals can tolerate long periods of total sleep deprivation with so *little* change in performance.

When you sleep after being severely deprived, your cycles may change to include much more Stage 4 (deep) sleep than usual—and a good deal less REM sleep than usual. However, you are unlikely to sleep for more than 11–16 hours even after you've been kept awake for 10 days straight (Moore-Ede et al., 1982).

At one time, the record for *normal* sleep deprivation was held by 17-year-old Randy Gardner. He stayed awake for 11 days and nights (264 hours) so that he would be listed in the *Guinness Book of World Records*. During the final night of sleep deprivation he beat sleep researcher William Dement at a hundred straight games on a baseball machine in a penny arcade—which suggests that his motor coordination was not seriously affected (Gulevich et al., 1966).

Until recently, scientists assumed that no one had ever died of lack of sleep. However, in 1986 Italian and American researchers reported the case of a 53-year-old man who died of exhaustion because he could no longer sleep. During his younger years, the man's sleep patterns had been more or less normal. However, at age 52, the man abruptly began to lose the ability to fall asleep. Within a few months, he was getting less than one hour of sleep a night. He sank deeper and deeper into a stupor, was unable to perform even the simplest of tasks, did not respond to sleep medication, and soon died. An autopsy showed a dramatic loss of nerve cells in the man's **thalamus**—a very important sub-center that channels inputs from the sense organs to the cortex (Lugaresi & Medori, 1986).

REM SLEEP DEPRIVATION

Several researchers have deprived human subjects of REM sleep by waking the subjects up each time REM sleep occurred. These subjects were allowed all the Stage 2, 3, and 4 sleep they needed. But whenever the subjects cycled up to Stage 1—REM, they were awakened. A few experimenters reported their subjects soon became cross, anxious, and showed some signs of mental disturbance. However, most recent studies show little or no evidence of these kinds of symptoms. What is true, though, is that when REM-deprived subjects are allowed to sleep normally, they show what is called a **rebound effect.** That is, they show a great increase in Stage 1—REM sleep, and a marked decrease in Stage 4 "deep sleep," for a night or two thereafter (Webb, 1982).

Wilse Webb calls sleep a "gentle tyrant," and this tyrant struggles to assert its rights. As Webb puts it, "Sleep cannot be ignored or lost without worry or care. Sleep is a fundamental, built-in way of behavior. It is not something we can choose to do or choose not to do . . . " except for short periods of time (Webb, 1975).

Dreams

We've always known that sleeping people dream, but we didn't know much about the frequency of dreaming until the early 1950s. Prior to that time, scientists could do little more than record what people remembered about their dreams. However, some people insisted they never dreamt at all; other individuals were confident that they dreamed the whole night long.

In 1953 Nathaniel Kleitman and Eugene Aserinsky discovered the connection between REM sleep and dreaming by waking up their subjects at various times during the sleep cycle. We now know that everyone dreams *several times a night*, during each sleep cycle.

If Kleitman and Aserinsky woke up their subjects during "deep sleep" (Stages 3 and 4), the subjects seldom reported they were dreaming. However, if the subjects were awakened during Stage 1–REM sleep, they frequently stated they had been dreaming and could almost always describe what they had just dreamed (Aserinsky & Kleitman, 1953).

According to Kleitman (and most other authorities), you usually have several dreams within each REM period. Each dream probably runs from a few seconds to several minutes in length. And since REM periods at the beginning of your sleep tend to be the shortest, you probably dream less in the early evening than later on (Kleitman, 1987).

DREAM CONTENT

If you are like most people, your first dreams of the night will tend to be rather dull and trivial—mostly having to do with things you have done during the day (Battaglia & Cavallero, 1987). In later REM periods, however, your dreams will probably become more unusual, vivid, colorful, easier to remember, and sometimes more anxiety-provoking. During any one REM period, you are likely to experience a *sequence of related dreams*, or to run through the *same dream two or three times*. Mostly, though, you will dream about things that are of some interest or importance to you (Corsi-Cabrera & Becker, 1986; Lortie-Lussier et al., 1992; Rinfret et al., 1992; see Table 5.1).

There is little or no agreement among the experts as to the *significance* of what people dream. As we will see in a later chapter, Sigmund Freud thought that dreams revealed a person's fears and anxieties. And there is some evidence that people who have dreams that recur almost nightly for long periods of time may suffer from stress and anxiety (Bower, 1986). In contrast, some modern-day sleep researchers believe that during sleep the brain performs a kind of "neural housecleaning," like a computer checking its circuits while it is "off-line." Dreams, they say, are simply your conscious attempt to impose meaning on this meaningless neural activity.

From a holistic point of view, both may be correct. Dreams may be produced by random neural activity; but the "sense" you make out of your dream—the meaning you bring to it—is unique. And it may even tell us something significant about you (Miller, 1989).

Rebound effect. When your body is deprived of something it needs for a period of time (such as sleep), it tends to overindulge briefly when whatever the body needed is again available.

What did I dream? I do not know.
The Fragments fly like chaff.
Yet strange my mind was tickled so;
I cannot help but laugh.

CHILDREN'S NURSERY RHYME
AUTHOR UNKNOWN

TABLE 5.1

Percentage of College Students Who Have Experienced Common Dream Themes (FROM GRIFFITH, ET AL., 1958)

HAVE YOU EVER DREAMED OF . . . ?	%
1. being attacked or pursued	82.8
2. falling	77.2
3. trying again and again to do something	71.2
4. school, teachers, studying	71.2
5. being frozen with fright	58.0
6. sexual experiences	66.4
7. eating delicious food	61.6
8. falling with fear	67.6
9. arriving too late (e.g., missing the train)	63.6
10. fire	40.8
11. swimming	52.0
12. dead people as though alive	46.0
13. being locked up	56.4
14. loved person as dead	57.2
15. snakes	48.8
16. being on verge of falling	46.8
17. finding money	56.0
18. failing an examination	38.8
19. flying or soaring through air	33.6
20. being smothered, unable to breathe	44.4
21. falling without fear	33.2
22. wild, violent beasts	30.0
23. being inappropriately dressed	46.0
24. seeing self as dead	33.2
25. being nude	42.8
26. killing someone	25.6
27. being tied, unable to move	30.4
28. having superior knowledge or mental ability	25.6
29. lunatics or insane people	25.6
30. your teeth falling out	20.8
31. creatures, part animal, part human	14.8
32. being buried alive	14.8
33. seeing self in mirror	12.4
34. being hanged by the neck	2.8

LUCID DREAMING

Most people state they have little conscious control over what happens in their dreams. In recent years, however, psychologists have developed ways of helping people maintain "conscious awareness" that they are dreaming even while the dream is taking place (Galvin, 1982).

The act of maintaining some low level of consciousness during REM periods is often called *lucid dreaming*. Canadian researcher Jayne Gackenbach says, "It is as if the dreamer were making an interactive movie, creating a fantasy and watching it unfold at the same time" (Gackenbach, 1989). According to Stephen LaBerge, lucid dreaming is most likely to occur during the last dream cycles of the night. LaBerge states that, during a lucid dream, you are aware that your "experiences" were dreams rather than reality, and you can remember the dream quite well after you have wakened.

"Dreaming lucidly of doing something is more like doing it than imagining it," according to La Berge. During sexual lucid dreams, for example, you undergo physiological changes that are remarkably similar to those that occur during actual sexual activity, LaBerge claims. Sometimes you can even evaluate what is happening during the dream, and take an active role in resolving the conflict that occurs in a lucid dream (Gackenbach et al., 1985; LaBerge, 1986; LaBerge & Rheingold, 1990).

How might the differing abilities of the two hemispheres help explain lucid dreaming—that is, the fact that one part of your mind can be dreaming while another is aware that a dream is taking place?

UNPLEASANT DREAMS

If you could control the content of your dreams, you'd probably make them pleasant experiences. However, the most vivid (and disturbing) type of dream you are likely to have is one that you seldom have much influence over—the *night terror*. Let's look at night terrors and nightmares in some detail.

STAGE 4 NIGHT TERROR Imagine yourself comfortably sleeping in your bed, unaware of everything around you. Then you slowly regain enough consciousness to realize that you are suffocating, that some heavy weight is lying on your chest and crushing your lungs. Realizing that your breathing has almost stopped, and that you are dying for air, you become terrified and scream. At once, you seem to awaken and perceive there is this *thing* hovering over you, crushing the very life out of your lungs. Despite a strange feeling of paralysis, you start to resist. Your pulse begins to race, your breathing becomes rapid, and you push futilely at the *thing* that is choking you to death. Your legs tremble, then begin to thrash about under the covers. You sweep the bedclothes aside, stumble to your feet, and mumbling loudly to yourself, you flee into the darkness.

Then, all at once, you find yourself in your living room. The lights come on, the thing instantly retreats to the shadows of your mind, and you are awake. You are safe now, but you are intensely wrought up and disturbed. You shake your head, wondering what has happened to you. You can remember that you were fleeing from the *thing* which was crushing you. But you have forgotten your scream and talking in your sleep.

The thing dream is a classic example of a night terror. According to Anthony Kales, night terrors occur to but one person in several hundred. However, if someone else in your family has a history of night terrors, you are 10 times more likely to experience night terrors than would ordinarily be the case (Guilleminault, 1989; Kales & Kales, 1984).

Unlike most other dreams, the night terror begins during Stage 4 (deep) sleep and not during an REM period (see Figure 5.2). According to Charles Carlson and David White, night terrors are a "nighttime disorder of arousal" that are often stress-related. Night terrors can also be triggered by highly emotional environmental events, and by anti-depressant drugs (Carlson & White, 1982).

Night terrors are more frequent in children than in adults. They are almost always associated with sleepwalking, sleeptalking, and other types of sleep disorders (Kohen et al., 1992).

Night terrors can be dangerous. Sleep researcher Ernest Hartmann reports the case history of a man who experienced a night terror while sleeping in his car by the side of a major highway. The man "sleep-drove" his car onto the highway and crashed into another automobile, killing three people. Hartmann admits this is an extreme case, but believes that night terrors are always a *potentially* dangerous experience for those few people who experience them (and for others who are around when the attack occurs) (Hartmann, 1983).

Psychotherapy, behavior therapy, self-hypnosis, and the use of tranquilizing drugs can be effective in reducing both the number and the severity of night terror attacks (Kales & Kales, 1984; Kohen et al., 1992; Kryger et al., 1989).

ANXIETY REM NIGHTMARE Much more common than the night terror is the anxiety nightmare, which occurs late in the sleep cycle at the end of a very long REM period. If you have an anxiety nightmare, your body will seldom be aroused to a panic state. In fact, there may be little change in your body's biological responses during the nightmare. It is, therefore, the psychological content of the dream itself that leads to the anxiety attack.

These stressful nighttime experiences may be related to extremely stressful daytime happenings (Belicki, 1992). Although most people have a nightmare less often than once a year, Richard Ross and his colleagues report that almost 60 percent of Vietnam combat veterans reported one a month for some time after returning from the war (Ross et al., 1989).

According to Ernest Hartmann, anxiety nightmares are most frequent when your psychological need for REM sleep is greatest. Hartmann notes that various illnesses and high fevers often reduce the amount of REM sleep you experience. So do sleeping pills. Thus, anxiety nightmares often occur when you are recovering from sickness, or just after you have stopped taking sleeping pills (Hartman, 1978).

A common anxiety nightmare is that of "running through molasses"—trying to escape something terrible, but not being able to move. What happens to your muscles during REM sleep that might help explain the commonness of this type of anxiety nightmare?

Sleep Disorders

There are a number of different types of *sleep disorders*. These include such things as involuntarily falling asleep, the inability to get to sleep in the first place, the inability to stay asleep for very long, disruption of normal breathing during sleep, and walking and talking while asleep. Let's look at these problems in some detail.

NARCOLEPSY

Suppose you were sitting in a chair after lunch, listening to a friend tell a very funny joke. At the "punch line," of course, you laughed loudly. And just as you did so, you fell asleep involuntarily and stayed asleep for several minutes. How would you explain this odd behavior?

The best explanation would be that you had just experienced an attack of **narcolepsy,** or a "sleep attack." This rare condition seems to affect 2–5 people per 1,000 (Herbert, 1983).

Narcolepsy can strike at any time, but according to Swedish psychiatrist Olle Hambert, it is usually associated with *pleasurable events*. The person with this problem can often "ward off" the attacks in dangerous situations—but not always. The attacks typically occur one or more times per day, and sometimes are so severe that the individual cannot drive and may have problems getting (and keeping) a normal job (Hambert, 1984).

Many scientists believe that narcolepsy is a hereditary disorder (Parkes & Lock, 1989). Relatives of narcoleptics are 60 times more likely to have the disorder themselves. Researchers have even successfully bred dogs with narcolepsy (Carlson, 1991). However, French researchers Jacques Montplaisir and Gaetan Poirier are not convinced. They point out that narcolepsy can affect one identical twin, but not the other (Montplaisir & Poirier, 1987).

Narcolepsy is *not* a form of epilepsy, since the EEG record shows the normal Stage 1–REM sleep pattern during an attack. Nor are there any known personality traits that are associated with narcolepsy. However, drugs that tend to suppress REM sleep are sometimes of considerable help to narcoleptic patients (Hambert, 1984; Carlson, 1991).

Narcolepsy (NARK-oh-LEP-see). An attack of very suddenly falling asleep. From the Greek words *narke*, meaning "sleep" or "unconscious," and *lepsis*, meaning "seizure." (The word "narcotic" comes from the same Greek source.)

INSOMNIA

People who suffer from narcolepsy have trouble staying awake. Individuals who experience **insomnia** have the opposite problem. William Dement, who founded the Sleep Disorders Center at Stanford in California, says that almost everyone occasionally has problems getting to sleep. However, Dement estimates that more than 30 million Americans suffer from a *chronic* inability to initiate or to maintain sleep.

According to Wilse Webb, *insomnia* is "a summary term for all real and imagined failures of the sleep process." The word "imagined" is important for, as Webb notes, some people who claim to be insomniacs in fact show normal sleep when tested in the laboratory (Webb, 1975).

As you might suspect, insomnia is more common among older persons than young adults. According to William Dement, the average healthy older person either wakes up or comes close to doing so about 153 times during a normal 7-hour sleep period. The typical 25-year-old, however, experiences only 10 arousals during the same period of sleep (Dement, 1982, 1986).

There are now numerous sleep clinics around the country that deal with insomnia and related sleep disorders with varying degrees of success (Chambers, 1992; Chambers & Alexander, 1991). If you suffer from insomnia, the Sleep Disorders Center at Stanford states that sleeping pills are not a long-term solution to the insomnia problem. The Center also recommends that you set up a *regular schedule* for going to bed and for getting up (Lacks & Morin, 1992; Nino & Keenan, 1988).

People suffering from insomnia may toss and turn for long periods of time without being able to sleep.

Insomnia (in-SOM-knee-ah). From Latin and Greek words meaning "sleeplessness." An inability to fall asleep—the most common type of sleep disorder.

Since sleep is a "gentle tyrant," you eventually get what sleep you really need. Why does this fact suggest that the psychological discomfort of insomnia is more important than the physical effects?

SLEEPWALKING

Until the 1960s, sleepwalking was considered either a personality disorder of some kind or an "acting out of dreams." More recent research suggests there is little connection between personality problems and sleepwalking. It does seem to "run in families," however, and is associated with other deep-sleep disturbances, such as night terrors, sleep-talking, and (to some extent) bed-wetting (Chase & Weitzman, 1983).

Sleepwalking almost always occurs during Stage 4 deep sleep, and almost never during Stage 1–REM sleep. Children—particularly those between 9 and 12 years of age—tend to sleepwalk more than do adults. And the problem seems to be more common than originally was thought to be the case. In one survey, almost 20 percent of the people questioned could recall one or more sleepwalking episodes (Chase & Weitzman, 1983).

SLEEP-TALKING

Although there are many old beliefs that people who talk in their sleep tend to "tell secrets," the truth is quite different. Some 90 percent of sleep talk occurs during dream-free sleep and is marked by rather unemotional and "situation-bound" discussions. The 10 percent or so of sleep talk that occurs during dream sleep is more emotional and usually relates to the dream in progress (Kales & Kales, 1984).

Generally speaking, most sleep talk occurs during Stage 0 or dreamless Stage 1 sleep. Thus the "talker" is really more awake than asleep—which explains why the person can respond to questions. There is no indication that sleep-talking is related to any personality traits or disorders and, at worst, it usually is little more than a minor social problem. However, sleep talk can be a symptom of other difficulties, thus it usually is included in the list of "sleep disorders."

SLEEP APNEA

Apnea (AP-nee-uh). A sleep disorder in which individuals stop breathing in their sleep.

One of the most common sleep disorders is sleep **apnea,** or the tendency to stop breathing during sleep. Many people stop breathing for short periods of time during their sleep—especially people who snore—but they begin to breathe again before it wakes them up (Carlson, 1991). If you had sleep apnea, you would wake up several times each night *gasping* for air. When you stopped breathing during sleep, the build-up of carbon dioxide in your blood would stimulate receptors in your brain to wake you up. During the day you might experience sleepiness, and headaches caused by a build-up of carbon dioxide, lack of oxygen, and loss of sleep.

Some researchers believe that sleep apnea is to blame when an older person "dies of natural causes" while asleep (Kales et al., 1982), or even when an infant dies of sudden infant death syndrome (SIDS), "crib death."

The most common cause for sleep apnea is a blockage of the airway. It may be treated in several ways, including relaxation training, changing your sleeping position (not sleeping on your back), placing a pillow behind your neck to tilt your head back during sleep, losing weight, using tongue-restraining devices or special air-pressure masks, and in severe cases, surgery.

Sleep and dreams are altered states of consciousness that most of us experience every evening. Now that we have talked about them at some length, suppose we look at some other types of altered awareness and then try to determine what *causes* your conscious awareness to shift from one state to another.

What relationship do you see between sleep apnea and a possible component of "night terrors"?

HYPNOSIS

Hypnosis is surely one of the most interesting and controversial examples of an altered state of consciousness. It is controversial because not even the major researchers of hypnosis agree that it is an "altered state." We will return to this issue later. First, let's look at how hypnosis was discovered, and then consider some of the interesting facts about hypnosis.

"Mesmerism" and "Deep Sleep"

Humors. From the Latin word meaning "fluids" or "moisture." According to early Greek medical men, the body secreted four different humors: black bile, yellow bile, blood, and phlegm. See Chapter 14.

One of the most famous eccentrics in all of medical history was a man named Anton Mesmer. Born in 1734 in a tiny Austrian village, Mesmer took degrees in theology and medicine at the University of Vienna. At the time that Mesmer began his medical practice, the prevailing view toward mental disorders was that they were due to an imbalance of certain chemicals called **humors** (see Chapter 14). Mesmer rejected the humoral theory in favor of the even more "humorous" notion that the mind was strongly affected by magnetic radiation from outer space (Bloch, 1980).

Mesmer lived at a time when magnetism and electricity were newly discovered physical forces. At that time, people believed that the stars and planets radiated "magnetic fluids." Little wonder, then, that Mesmer thought that magnets could focus these "celestial fluids" on a sick person's body and thus restore the person to health.

In the 1780s Mesmer opened a healing salon in Paris. The salon had in its center a huge tub containing "magnetized water," with twisted, oddly shaped rods sticking out from all sides. Mesmer made his patients sit around the tub, holding hands in a closed circle so the rods could touch the injured parts of their bodies. The rods supposedly directed the "magnetic fluids" toward the wound and thus promoted healing.

To help things along, Mesmer dressed in a long purple robe and walked around the tub, touching his patients with a wand. He frequently urged them to yield themselves up to the magnetic fluids that surrounded them, saying they would be cured if only they could focus on the heavenly powers within their sick bodies. Some of the patients apparently went into trance-like states. They would sit or stand as if frozen in place, apparently unseeing and unhearing. Mesmer had, in fact, discovered *hypnosis*. He called hypnosis "Mesmerism," but Mesmer made no real scientific study of what this unusual state was like or what really induced it.

Until fairly recently, most scientists considered "Mesmerism," or hypnosis, more of a parlor trick than a legitimate psychological phenomenon. However, a few dauntless physicians and psychologists over the years did try to study hypnosis objectively.

James Braid, a Scottish physician, gave *hypnosis* its present name in 1842. He took the term from the Greek word for "sleep." After attending a session held by a wandering Mesmerist, Braid became convinced that magnetic fluids had nothing to do with the effect. Rather, Braid felt, it was an abnormal or *intense form of sleep* that the hypnotist induced by somehow affecting certain centers in the subject's brain.

Hypnotizability

One sometimes frustrating aspect of hypnosis is that not everyone can be hypnotized. This is one reason that Freud renounced hypnosis as a useless therapeutic tool (Parisi, 1987). Stage hypnotists have developed techniques for selecting very quickly the most hypnotizable volunteers from their audiences. Serious hypnosis researchers, such as Ernest Hilgard, use standardized tests, such as the Stanford Hypnotic Susceptibility Scale (Hilgard, 1965). Your "hypnotizability" score is the degree to which you are responsive to standardized suggestions. It is important to remember that the "power" of hypnosis rests in this ability, not in the hypnotist.

Your hypnotizability is a relatively stable characteristic. If you are high on this trait today, you will probably be high on it in 25 years; if you are low today, you will

In the 18th century, Anton Mesmer convinced people that magnetic forces could heal their illnesses. Modern hypnotists rely on the ability of the subject's own mind to follow their suggestions.

probably be low in 25 years (Piccione et al., 1987). One reason may be that your hypnotizability probably reflects early experiences with fantasy, imagination, and punishment.

FANTASY

Several years ago, Theodore X. Barber developed a "Suggestibility Scale" that he uses in his hypnosis research. The major questions on the scale have to do with your ability to imagine yourself in a variety of unusual situations. One of the primary traits that the scale seems to measure is the ease with which you can create mental fantasies (Barber, 1969).

Barber's research suggests there is a high correlation between the ability to "fantasize" and the ability to be hypnotized. As Barber notes, however, the fact that you are "suggestible" or are "addicted to fantasy" doesn't mean you can't live a happy and productive life. Psychologists Steven Lynn and Judith Rhue note that while people with rich fantasy lives do make good hypnotic subjects, many individuals who are not "fantasy prone" also fall into hypnotic trances rather readily (Lynn & Rhue, 1988).

What is the relationship between being able to "fantasize" and being able to "dissociate yourself" from the aches and pains of reality?

IMAGINATION AND PUNISHMENT

Data gathered by Ernest Hilgard, Josephine Hilgard, and their associates at Stanford tend to support Barber's views on the close connection between suggestibility and fantasy. The Hilgards' research suggests that the response you make to a hypnotist is partially determined by the type of upbringing you had. For example, Josephine Hilgard and Samuel LeBaron report that, if your parents were inclined to punish you severely and frequently when you were young, chances are that you will be able to "go under" in a hypnotic trance rather easily (Hilgard & LeBaron, 1984). And Lynn and Rhue note that the fantasizers they studied "recollected being physically abused and punished to a greater degree than other subjects did and reported experiencing greater loneliness and isolation as children" (Lynn & Rhue, 1988).

Ernest Hilgard gives three reasons there is a correlation between a punitive upbringing and suggestibility. First, continual punishment can *condition* you to respond to authority automatically and without questioning what you are told to do. Second, you may learn to escape parental wrath by retreating into your own imagination. And third, you may find you can prevent punishment by learning to play various social roles (Hilgard, 1986). We will have more to say about this last point in a moment.

Hypnotic Feats

One of the reasons hypnosis continues to attract attention is the many interesting claims which have been made for it. Let's consider a few of these claims.

AGE REGRESSION

The early behaviorists were particularly impressed with the rapid access that hypnosis seemed to give to a person's early-life memories. For instance, while in a deep trance, subjects apparently could "relive" certain events of childhood. When told to "go back" to her fifth birthday, for instance, a young woman might begin to talk in a very childish voice. She would then recount in detail who was at her birthday party, what presents she got, what her parents said and did, and even what she dreamed later that night (Barber, 1970).

A few hypnotic subjects went much farther. When pressed to do so, some of them reported detailed conversations they thought had occurred between their mothers and fathers while they themselves were still being carried in the womb. Other subjects recounted events that happened to them centuries before, when they were seemingly *living in a different body*. The "memory feats" these people performed under **hypnotic age regression** seemed fabulous indeed to those early psychologists who had not yet discovered the connection between hypnosis and fantasy.

Michael Nash, in reviewing 60 years of hypnotic age-regression studies, concludes that "the mental and physiological activity of hypnotically age-regressed subjects is not regressed." If you were in an "age-regressed state," you might speak and act like a 6-year-old. But careful observation would probably show that you were performing mental tasks that most adults wrongly believe 6-year-olds can perform, but that real children of 6 years cannot (Nash, 1987).

Hypnotic age regression. To regress to an earlier age under hypnosis. To return to an earlier time when a hypnotist tells you to do so. Many psychologists believe that when you regress hypnotically, you are just "role-playing" because you wish to please the hypnotist.

MEMORY IMPROVEMENT

Many police agencies now routinely make use of hypnosis in criminal investigations. In particular, the police hypnotize witnesses to help them recall details of events that seem lost to ordinary memory. Martin Reiser of the Los Angeles Police Department claims that in 77 percent of the cases where hypnosis was used, "Important information was elicited from witnesses and victims that was not available by routine interrogation" (cited in Dellinger, 1978).

However, most psychologists now take rather a dim view of the use of hypnosis by the police (Mingay, 1987; Pinizzotto, 1989). Ernest Hilgard states, "It is well-known that hypnotists may implant memories, so that the hypnotized person accepts them as his [or her] own" (Hilgard, 1986). And Martin Orne, past president of the International Society of Hypnosis, notes that what people remember under hypnosis is often *completely inaccurate* (cited in Turkington, 1982).

To summarize, the major reasons that evidence obtained under hypnosis is not admitted in most courtrooms are the following:

1. While hypnotized, witnesses often report "as fact" events that simply did not occur (Dellinger, 1978; Labelle et al., 1990).

2. Once a witness reports (under hypnosis) a false memory of "the facts," the witness's *confidence* in the "truth" of the report often increases dramatically (Sheehan, 1988; Turkington, 1982).

3. The more confident a witness is, the more likely it is that jurors will believe the witness (Wells & Lindsay, 1983).

As we will see in Chapter 10, Elizabeth Loftus has shown that the questions you ask someone about an event can actually transform the person's memories. What problems does Loftus's research raise about the use of hypnotism by various police agencies to "recover forgotten memories"?

PAIN REDUCTION

In several studies, Ernest Hilgard has shown that, while under hypnosis, a subject may both experience pain and simultaneously not feel it.

In one of his experiments, Hilgard asked 20 volunteers to hold their arms in ice water for 45 seconds (see photograph). The water was painfully cold—as the subjects reported only too willingly if they were not hypnotized. Hilgard then "suggested" that they try consciously to control their experience of pain. Most of them were able to do so and now reported much less pain than before.

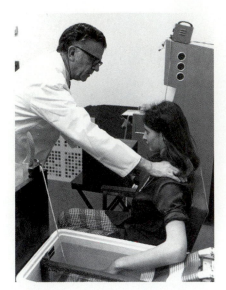

Ernest Hilgard measures the pain response of a hypnotized subject when the subject's hand is submerged in ice-cold water.

Next, Hilgard hypnotized the subjects and suggested they would feel *no pain at all* from the ice water. While their arms were in the water, Hilgard asked them if they experienced pain. The subjects told him, "Some, but not much." Then Hilgard asked them to move a finger on the hand *not* in the water if the subjects *really* felt the pain at some "unconscious level." Most of the subjects immediately did so. Hilgard believes that *consciously* the subjects were suppressing the pain. But at some deeper level, Hilgard says, they apparently knew the pain was really there (Hilgard, 1978, 1992).

Hilgard believes hypnosis is an *altered state of consciousness* in which your consciousness can "split." One part of you acts in a hypnotized fashion and experiences no pain if the hypnotist tells you not to. But another part of your mind—which can communicate by gestures during the trance—remains unhypnotized and perceives the discomfort your conscious mind is repressing. Hilgard calls this part of the mind the subject's "hidden observer" (Hilgard, 1986, 1992).

Two Views of Hypnosis

In the 18th century Anton Mesmer said hypnosis was the result of "magnetic fluids." The phenomenon was called "Mesmerism." In the 19th century James Braid believed Mesmerism was a deep sleep. He called it "hypnosis." At the end of the 20th century, students of hypnosis still do not agree on exactly what hypnosis is. As Frank McGuigan says, "It seems clear that hypnosis is not just a state of concentration. Nor is it a state of relaxation," and "the only consensus seems to be that if there *is* a unique state of hypnosis, it is not sleep" (McGuigan, 1987). Then what *is* hypnosis?

Today, there are two main views of hypnosis:

- The first is that hypnosis is a unique *altered state of consciousness*.

- The second view is that hypnosis is a normal state of consciousness, and that hypnotic subjects are simply playing the role expected of them.

AN ALTERED STATE OF CONSCIOUSNESS

Hypnosis researchers such as Ernest Hilgard and Kenneth Bowers believe hypnosis is an altered state of consciousness in which your conscious mind becomes dissociated or split off from your surroundings (Bowers, 1992; Hilgard, 1992).

Dissociation is not as unusual as it may sound. Driving down the highway, you begin to feel bored. The road is familiar; the scenery monotonous. Your mind begins to wander. You think how nice it would be at the beach, lying in the sun, no cares. You can almost hear the surf and feel the breeze. You are totally absorbed in the scene. Meanwhile, you have driven several miles without being consciously aware of your surroundings. You say your "mind wandered," or you were "daydreaming." Psychologists call it "highway hypnosis," a kind of dissociation much like they study in the lab.

If you are a long-distance runner or other athlete you may have used dissociation to shut out the pain of fatigue or injury. You might concentrate on the competition or even on completely unrelated thoughts. After the race, or the game, you are suddenly aware of how much you hurt. But as long as you are concentrating on the competition, your mind is dissociated from your body and you are unaware of pain.

Ernest Hilgard believes that hypnotized subjects are simply showing an intensification of the process of dissociation, and that hypnosis thus involves a change in consciousness with distinct mental processes. Kenneth Bowers points out that certain phenomena are unique to hypnosis. And he believes that a special state of consciousness is required to explain them (Bowers, 1989).

PLAYING A ROLE

Social psychological theorists, such as Theodore X. Barber, disagree with Hilgard's definition of hypnosis as an "altered state of consciousness" (Lynn et al., 1990). They believe Hilgard's subjects may be unconsciously "faking" the presence of a hidden observer, just as people unconsciously "fake" any experience they think the hypnotist may want them to have.

In fact, Barber seriously doubts whether "hypnosis" actually exists! According to Barber, hypnotism is actually made up of equal parts of (1) "role playing" and (2) learning how to control the way in which you *perceive* your sensory inputs (Barber, 1978). Over the past 20 years, Barber has conducted a series of studies in which he has taught people *conscious strategies* for reducing the intensity of pain. Some of these strategies are more effective than others, but the best of them seem to reduce pain at least as much as does a hypnotic trance. Barber concludes that, since hypnosis is no better as an **analgesic** than is "mental discipline," perhaps we should discard "hypnosis" entirely as a psychological concept (Barber, 1978).

Not all psychologists agree with Barber, and the matter is far from settled (Fromm, 1992; Sarbin, 1992; Waxman et al., 1985). On the one hand, the hypnotist–subject relationship is a social one with all of the influences that are potentially involved in such a relationship. On the other hand, we do experience different states of consciousness; and hypnosis has the appearance and subjective feeling of a different state. Hypnosis researcher John Kihlstrom suggests that we view hypnosis as both an altered state of consciousness *and* a product of social influence (Kihlstrom, 1985, 1987a, 1987b).

As we turn our attention to the effects of drugs on our consciousness, we will see that social influence is important there as well.

Do you think that Barber's view of hypnosis could apply to some drug experiences? That is, could people's expectations about a drug cause them to experience an altered state of consciousness, even if the drug didn't have this effect?

Analgesic (an-al-GEE-sick). From the Greek words meaning "no pain." Technically speaking, any drug that reduces pain without causing a loss of consciousness.

DRUGS

A drug is any chemical which changes cellular activity somewhere in your body. Drugs are a direct chemical method of speeding up or slowing down neural transmission—a quick if sometimes deadly way that people all over the world have chosen for a great many centuries. When we look at the effects of drugs on human behavior in just a moment, we will find there is a chemical compound that can affect your brain, and your consciousness, in almost any way you wish—but usually *at a cost of some kind.*

The drugs we will discuss in this chapter have their main effects on neural transmission. Often drugs alter the speed at which your nerve cells release synaptic transmitters or the speed at which other nerve cells respond to these transmitters. Some drugs mimic your body's natural neural transmitters. Other drugs block the activity of natural transmitters. In each case the drug affects you psychologically because it acts on your *nervous system*.

Psychologists generally assume that everything you feel or experience is mirrored in some way by the functioning of your body—particularly by the way in which your nervous system reacts. For example, when some change occurs in the speed at which your brain takes in and processes information, there is usually some corresponding

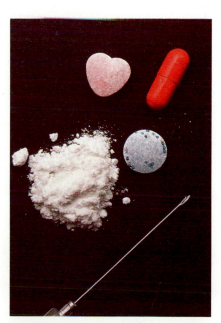

Illegal drugs are a growing concern for law enforcement authorities.

CATEGORY	DRUG NAMES	COMMON NAMES	DESIRED EFFECTS	UNDESIRABLE EFFECTS
Analgesics (Narcotics)	acetylsalicylic acid	aspirin, ASA	pain relief,	retards blood-clotting
	codeine		pain relief, relaxation	lethargy, drowsiness
	heroin	smack, horse, junk, black tar	relaxation, anxiety reduction, euphoria	lethargy, drowsiness; impaired coordination & mental functioning; constipation, nausea; decreased respiration, blood pressure, & pulse rate; constricted pupils (high doses produce coma, shock & respiratory arrest)
	fentanyl	Sublimaze	pain relief	
	meperidine	demerol	pain relief	
	opium	poppy	relaxation, anxiety reduction, euphoria	
	morphine	Miss Emma	pain relief, relaxation	
	*AMF *PMF *MPPP	China white, synthetic heroin new heroin	potent substitute for heroin— same effects	drooling, paralysis, tremors, & brain damage (MPPP causes irreversible Parkinson's disease when contaminated with MPTP)
Stimulants	caffeine	coffee, colas, tea, chocolate	alertness, energy	increased talkativeness, restlessness, agitation, anxiety, confusion, paranoia, aggressiveness, confusion, tremors, blurred vision; reduced appetite; increased blood pressure, heart rate; sweating; insomnia (high doses produce delirium, panic, & hallucinations)
	nicotine	tobacco	alertness, energy	
	amphetamines	speed, uppers, ice, bennies		
	cocaine	coke, snow, lady, blow, Bernice	alertness, energy, excitement, elation	
	freebase cocaine	crack		

TABLE 5.2

Psychoactive Drugs and Their Effects

Psychoactive drugs. Drugs that alter consciousness or awareness.

change (1) in the way that you think and feel about yourself, and (2) in how pleasant or unpleasant you perceive the world around you to be.

The actual effects a particular drug will have on a particular person are often complex and hard to predict. Thus, a drug that affects you one way might affect another person in quite a different manner. And a drug that has a mild effect on you at one time of day may be much more potent at some other point in your daily activity cycle. For example, anesthetics are more potent in the early afternoon than in the morning (Winfree, 1987). Also, the *environment* in which you take a drug—and your own *past experience* with and *personal expectations* about a drug—can strongly influence the actual effect the drug has on your thoughts, feelings, and behaviors. We'll talk about these environmental effects at the end of the chapter.

Because this chapter deals with consciousness, we are interested in **psychoactive drugs.** Psychoactive drugs are chemicals that alter conscious awareness, perception, or behavior. Thus, we are not concerned here with drugs such as anti-biotics which have no known effect on behavior or mental processes. Furthermore, we will confine our discussion to what is called "recreational" drug use (or abuse). This means we will

CATEGORY	DRUG NAMES	COMMON NAMES	DESIRED EFFECTS	UNDESIRABLE EFFECTS
Depressants	alcohol	beer, wine, coolers, liquor	relaxation, reduced anxiety & inhibitions, euphoria	lethargy, drowsiness; impaired coordination & mental functioning; mood swings, dejection; decreased respiration, blood pressure & pulse (high doses produce death)
	barbiturates	downers, barbs, yellow jackets		
	methaqualone	quaaludes, ludes, sopors		
	tranquilizers	Valium, Librium Xanax, Serax		
Psychedelics	cannabis	marijuana, pot, grass, weed; hashish, hash	relaxation, altered perception & awareness, mild euphoria	dry mouth, bloodshot eyes, poor coordination & mental ability, lethargy, anxiety
	LSD	acid, blotter acid	altered perceptions, increased sensory awareness, euphoria, hallucinations, insight	anxiety, panic, paranoia, confused thinking, impaired judgment, emotional swings, flashbacks, nausea; dilated pupils, increased blood pressure (high doses of PCP may cause brain hemorrhage, heart & lung failure, & death)
	phencyclidine	PCP, THC, peace pill, angel dust		
	mescaline	mesc, buttons, peyote		
	psilocybin	magic mushrooms		
	*MDA	love	lower anxiety, desire for interpersonal contact, increased tactile sense	grinding of teeth as well as other effects similar to other amphetamine-like drugs
	*MDMA	ecstasy, Adam, XTC	mild euphoria, improved interpersonal relations & self-esteem	

look primarily at non-therapeutic or non-medical use of drugs. We will discuss *therapeutic* drug use in Chapter 16.

The question of recreational drug use versus drug *abuse* is a controversial one which involves moral, ethical, and cultural considerations. These decisions you must make for yourself. However, an awareness of some of the facts about "recreational" drugs will help you make decisions which are better informed.

Table 5.2 presents a list of common psychoactive drugs and their effects. We will look at some of these under the headings of *analgesics, stimulants, depressants,* and *psychedelics* (including *designer drugs*).

*So-called "designer drugs." These lab-produced drugs are "analogs" of other drugs in their category. (SEE BECK & MORGAN, 1986; CLALLAHAN & APPEL, 1988; CLIMKO ET AL., 1986–87; GERLER & MOORHEAD, 1988.)

Why do people use drugs that affect their consciousness?

Analgesics

Analgesics are pain-reducing drugs which do not cause a loss of consciousness. Aspirin, opium, morphine, and heroin are all analgesic drugs. In addition to their pain-relieving qualities, the desired effects on consciousness are generally relaxation, a reduction in anxiety, and sometimes a light-headed feeling of euphoria. (Several undesirable effects are also noted in Table 5.2.)

ASPIRIN

Aspirin is perhaps the most common analgesic, or pain-killing, drug we know. Along with caffeine, aspirin is one of the few drugs that almost everyone reading this book will have tried at least once. Aspirin occurs naturally in the bark of the willow tree and was first synthesized in 1860. Some 50 million aspirin tablets are consumed each day in the United States. As useful a painkiller as aspirin is, though, it is also a deadly poison (when ingested in very large amounts) that must be treated with respect. Aspirin follows only barbiturates, alcohol, and carbon monoxide in the number of poisoning deaths attributed to it each year (Dusek & Girdano, 1987).

OPIUM

Opiate (OH-pee-ate or OH-pee-at). Any of the narcotic drugs that come from the opium poppy. Almost all opiates are habit-forming.

Aspirin is a mild painkiller. In case of severe pain, a more potent medicine—such as an **opiate**—is needed. Opiates are derived from opium, a drug used for centuries as an analgesic in the Near and Far East. When the seed pods of the opium poppy are slashed, a sticky resin oozes out. This resin is collected by hand, heated and rolled into balls, and then smoked in tiny pipes as opium.

MORPHINE

Morphine (MORE-feen). A product of opium. Morphine is a dream- or sleep-inducing drug and, like all opiates, is a powerful painkiller.

In 1806, **morphine** was first synthesized from opium. Since morphine can be injected directly into the body in controlled amounts, and since it lacks some of the side effects of opium, morphine rapidly gained wide use in medical circles.

No one really knows why the opiates reduce or kill the experience of pain. It seems likely, however, that these drugs stimulate inhibitory neurons which then "turn off" the synapses in your brain which are involved in processing the painful inputs (Carlson, 1988).

Morphine has one terrible side effect: it is very *addictive*. The exact biological mechanism underlying addiction is still not fully understood. However, there is considerable evidence suggesting that natural painkillers *produced by the body itself* may be involved. These naturally occurring analgesics have many names, including *enkephalin* and *beta-endorphin*, and are collectively referred to as **endorphins.**

Endorphin (en-DORF-in). A type of natural painkiller found in the body. The word *endorphin* is a contraction of the term *endogenous morphine*. Both the endorphins and the enkephalins are opioid peptides.

When an enkephalin—or an endorphin—is injected into the body, it appears to reduce pain at least as much as does morphine. However, the effects these **opioid peptides** have on both physical and mental processes are complex and—as we will see at the end of this chapter—perhaps a little surprising.

Opioid peptides (OH-pee-oid PEP-tides). Peptides are rather small molecules of a fairly specific type. The endorphins and the enkephalins are all peptides that resemble opiates such as morphine. Thus, the endorphins and the enkephalins are included in a class of molecules called opioid peptides.

If, for medical reasons, you were to take morphine, it would (1) block neural transmission in your pain centers, and (2) stimulate certain nerve centers involved in experiencing pleasure. But according to Solomon Snyder, morphine also inhibits the production of endorphins. So, when you take morphine for any length of time, your body *stops* manufacturing its natural painkillers almost entirely (Snyder, 1987).

If you use morphine daily for a month or so, you are likely to become *addicted* to the drug. Then, if you don't get your "daily fix," you feel miserable, you ache all over, you are depressed, and you may even experience convulsions. Why? Because, when you stop taking morphine, your body needs several weeks before it can replenish its supply of natural painkillers. During this period of time, your body has no defense against pain. Thus, even the slightest cut or bruise will be *excruciatingly* unpleasant. (The word *excruciating* is from the Latin word meaning "to nail to a cross.") Little wonder, then, that so few morphine addicts voluntarily withdraw from using the drug.

HEROIN

Late in the 1800s, scientists hunting for a non-addictive opiate (to replace morphine) stumbled upon **heroin,** which is also made from opium. Heroin is several times more powerful than morphine as a painkiller. It gets it name from hero, because this drug was supposed to be a "heroic" solution to the "morphine problem." So, in the early 1900s, morphine addicts were given heroin instead. Unfortunately, heroin soon proved to be even more addictive and dangerous than morphine. Because of its addictive qualities, heroin is seldom used as an analgesic in the United States today—except by the million or so drug addicts who take it as regularly as their funds allow them to.

Heroin. An opiate derived from morphine. Very addictive, or habit-forming.

Stimulants

Stimulants are drugs that typically facilitate or increase synaptic transmission, making you physically and mentally more active. They do this by affecting nerve cells in your *autonomic nervous system*, which controls such involuntary activities as breathing, heart rate, and so forth. Stimulants affect consciousness by increasing alertness and promoting a feeling of energy. The increased feeling of alertness may extend to feelings of excitement and even elation. (Less desirable effects are presented in Table 5.2.)

CAFFEINE AND NICOTINE

Caffeine and nicotine are two widely used substances considered general cellular stimulants. When you drink coffee, the caffeine acts to increase your body's production of glucose (for energy). When your body absorbs nicotine, the nicotine activates the acetylcholine receptors in your muscles, preparing you for activity (Kolb & Wishaw, 1990). Both chemicals are toxic in large doses. The amount of nicotine in a single cigarette could kill you if it was extracted and injected (Carlson, 1991).

AMPHETAMINES

Less common—and considerably more dangerous—is a class of drugs called **amphetamines,** or pep pills. Amphetamine is often found under the brand name Benzedrine. Two other similar, but more powerful, drugs are Dexedrine and Methedrine.

Amphetamines (am-FETT-ah-meens). A class of stimulants, or "uppers," any of which may also be called "speed."

Caffeine increases the rate at which neurons fire, thus speeding up all types of motor activities.

Methedrine has been popularized under the street name "ice." Since they all increase neural activity, any or all of these "uppers" are sometimes called "speed."

Both the amphetamines and cocaine act on nerves in the central nervous system (brain and spinal cord) to increase firing across the synapses. Like any other drugs, "uppers" can be dangerous. For example, continued use of amphetamine (or any other type of "speed") can produce symptoms that are much the same as a severe mental disorder called **paranoid schizophrenia** (Dusek & Girdano, 1987).

COCAINE

Cocaine is a moderately strong drug made from the leaves of the coca plant. Although cocaine is legally classified as a narcotic in Canada and the United States, pharmacologically it is a central nervous system *stimulant*.

Cocaine, or "coke," is notorious for the rush of pleasure or **euphoria** it gives almost immediately after a person takes it (usually by sniffing). In some cases, users go on a "spree," much like an alcoholic's "binge." Like the user in *Bright Lights, Big City* whom we met at the beginning of this chapter, they try to avoid the "crash" which follows heavy use by taking more of the "Bolivian Marching Powder" (so-named because of its origins in Bolivia or Peru).

Frequent use of cocaine can lead to a variety of problems, including severe damage to the nose and throat as well as psychiatric disturbances (Mendoza & Miller, 1992; Mendoza et al., 1992). Repeated consumption of cocaine can lead to seizures and death (Maisto et al., 1991; Wallace 1991).

Widespread use of cocaine is a recent phenomenon, although problems caused by cocaine abuse are not new (Siegel, 1982, 1992). According to drug researcher Oakley Ray, "It has been known for many years that prolonged high doses of either cocaine or amphetamine produce the same toxic syndrome: enhanced sense of physical and mental capacity, loss of appetite, grinding of teeth . . . repetitious behavior, and paranoia" (Ray, 1983).

For the most part, cocaine users inhale or "snort" the drug in powder form. However, by 1986 the number of users who smoke a processed type of cocaine known as **crack** had increased dramatically. In 1977, less than 1 percent of the people who sought emergency hospital assistance for cocaine abuse had smoked the drug. By 1986, however, this figure had increased to 14 percent (Kozel & Adams, 1986), and to over 44 percent by 1988 in New York (Maisto et al., 1991).

Paranoid schizophrenia (PAIR-uh-noid skits-zoh-FREE-knee-uh). The major symptoms of this serious mental disorder are illogical thought patterns and changeable delusions. Delusions of persecution ("they're controlling my mind by radio waves") are most common.

Euphoria (you-FOR-ee-ah). From the Greek word meaning "good feeling," hence a rush of pleasure.

Crack. Small, smokable pellets of "free base" cocaine, which when heated often produce an audible "crack" sound. Also called "rock" or "base" cocaine prior to 1986. Extremely addictive.

Cocaine is produced from the leaves of the coca plant in illegal "factories" such as this one in Bolivia.

Drug researchers Stephen Maisto, Mark Galizio, and Gerard Connors summarize the impact of crack cocaine in these words:

> Since the introduction of crack cocaine to America's streets in 1986, the drug scene has changed tremendously. Cocaine was a glamour drug in the 1970s and early 1980s, more associated with movie stars and Hollywood than youth gangs and ghettos. But the introduction of inexpensive and highly addictive crack has changed the image and demographics of cocaine. Crack has become one of the major problems of inner city America. . . . one of the deadliest and most dangerous of drugs today (Maisto et al., 1991).

Depressants

The depressants, or *sedative-hypnotics,* are drugs that reduce anxiety at low doses, produce sedation at medium doses, and result in anesthesia or **coma** at high doses. Depressants act on the central nervous system, although the exact mechanism of their effect is not known (Kolb & Wishaw, 1990). Desirable effects on consciousness are relaxation, reduced inhibitions and anxiety, and sometimes euphoria. (Undesirable effects are presented in Table 5.2.)

Coma (KOH-mah). A deep sleep or state of unconsciousness usually brought on by illness or brain damage.

ALCOHOL

The social and financial costs of alcohol in the United States are, to coin a phrase, fairly sobering. In November 1987, the U.S. Health and Human Services Department held a conference on alcohol. At the conference, Thomas Burke, the agency's chief of staff, reported that alcoholism and alcohol abuse cost $117 billion annually. Direct medical costs account for roughly $15 billion of that total. Burke expected the figure to rise to $136 billion by 1990, and to $150 billion by 1995.

Alcohol is partially or wholly responsible for some 100,000 deaths each year, and it is involved in some half of the automobile accidents on American highways. More than half the people in the United States who commit murders each year have measurable amounts of alcohol in their blood at the time of the crime (and many of their victims do as well). At least 25 percent of the admissions to American mental hospitals involve alcohol abuse.

Alcohol affects the brain in many ways, but two effects seem most important. First, alcohol kills nerve cells—but in a highly selective fashion. Charles Golden and his associates report that alcohol tends to destroy brain tissue *primarily in the dominant hemisphere.* The behavioral changes associated with chronic drunkenness tend to support Golden's findings. For example, the slurred speech, the inability to think logically and to plan effectively, and the emotional outbursts shown by many alcoholics all suggest that alcohol disrupts the dominance normally shown by the left hemisphere. Indeed, Golden and his colleagues believe these symptoms result from the right hemisphere's attempts to take over the functions lost through destruction of tissue in the left hemisphere (Golden et al., 1981).

Second, alcohol appears to affect the same inhibitory synapses in the brain that are blocked by cocaine and morphine. Consumed in larger amounts, however, alcohol disrupts motor coordination—presumably by making it difficult for the person to inhibit many types of muscle movements (Snyder, 1987).

Alan Marlatt and his associates note that, at low doses, alcohol is perceived as a stimulant. However, at higher doses, it acts as a depressant. A heavy drinker may consume alcohol for its stimulating effects, but then fall into a depression that triggers further consumption. Little wonder, Marlatt and his colleagues say, that alcohol is such an addictive substance (Mooney et al., 1987). The use of alcohol in the United States has increased slightly but steadily over the past 40 years (USDHHS, 1987).

Barbiturates (bar-BITT-your-rates). Neural inhibitors that come from barbituric acid, often used as sleeping pills. Not to be confused with narcotics, most of which come from opium or alcohol. Narcotics are more effective as painkillers than are barbiturates, but both types of drug are habit-forming.

Hallucinogens (hal-LEW-sin-oh-jens). Drugs that affect sensory input neurons, or processing neurons, and hence "trick" you into seeing or hearing or feeling things that really aren't there.

Cannabis (KAN-ah-biss). The common hemp plant, from which come such drugs as marijuana (also spelled marihuana) and hashish. In the Western world, the most widespread species is cannabis sativa (SAT-ee-vah), which grows wild in most of the continental United States.

THC. An abbreviation for tetra-hydro-cannabinol (TET-trah HIGH-dro kan-NAB-ih-nol). Marijuana contains many chemicals, of which THC seems the main one that induces a "high." The "street drugs" sold as THC are usually some other substance, since THC loses it powers when exposed to air.

Chemotherapy (KEY-moh-THER-a-pee). Treatment that involves giving a person drugs or other chemicals to improve health.

BARBITURATES AND TRANQUILIZERS

The strongest depressants in general use are the **barbiturates** or "downers." Barbiturates are sometimes called "sleeping pills" because they depress neural activity so much they often put a person to sleep.

"Downers" have physical and psychological side effects that range from mildly unpleasant to downright deadly. Wisely used, these drugs can be of considerable medical help. When abused, these chemicals can lead to depression and other severe types of mental disorders. According to many reports, "downers" are the drug used most frequently for suicide. They are particularly likely to be abused by women (Ray, 1983; Dusek & Girdano, 1987).

The tranquilizers are both more specific in their effects and usually less powerful than the barbiturates. Tranquilizers affect the nervous system in several different ways. However, many of them act by exciting those neurons which *inhibit* other nerve cells from firing (Maisto et al., 1991).

Psychedelics

Psychedelics are drugs taken for their more dramatic effects on consciousness. Frequently, they produce distortions in perception and sometimes hallucinations. Some psychedelics also produce relaxation, mild euphoria, or other mood changes.

Hallucinogens cause little physical damage to the body. Their danger comes from their effects on mental processes and behavior. One of the most frequent problems associated with use of these drugs is that the user loses control of his or her flow of thoughts and emotions. This sort of experience is often called a "bad trip." (Other undesirable effects of psychedelics are noted in Table 5.2).

No one really knows why the psychedelics, or hallucinogens, affect people as they do. But according to Edward Domino, psychedelic drugs seem to influence neural processing in two important ways. First, they decrease the brain's ability to screen out many types of sensory inputs. And second, the drugs seem to disrupt the brain's attempts to *integrate complex stimuli* (Domino, 1981; Dusek & Girdano, 1987). And like all drugs, the effect of psychedelics depends heavily on the user's experience with the drug as well as the social environment in which the drug is taken (Carlin et al., 1972; Maisto et al., 1991).

MARIJUANA

Marijuana is a product of the hemp or **cannabis** plant, a weed found in abundance in many parts of the world. The active ingredient in marijuana is a chemical that goes by the complex name of delta-9-trans-tetrahydrocannabinol—which we can gladly abbreviate as **THC.** THC is also the active ingredient in hashish, which is a resin secreted by the cannabis plant. The concentration of THC is much higher in hashish than in marijuana.

As Solomon Snyder points out in his book *Uses of Marijuana,* cannabis has a long and interesting history. A century ago cannabis was almost as commonly used for medicinal purposes as aspirin is today and could be purchased without a prescription in any drug store (Snyder, 1972). Cannabis became illegal in the United States in 1937, but scientific evidence suggests that it still might be useful as a medicine. It seems particularly effective against diseases caused by tension and high blood pressure, menstrual bleeding, and glaucoma (a build-up of pressure within the eyeball). But its most important use may be that of helping relieve the nausea that cancer patients often experience when given **chemotherapy** (Ray, 1983; Dusek & Girdano, 1987).

"Recreational" marijuana use increased dramatically in the 1960s and 1970s. Since 1979 there has been a steady decline. However, marijuana is still the most frequently used illicit drug in the United States (Maisto et al., 1991).

Very little is known about how cannabis affects the central nervous system, for it is chemically very different from the opiates, from all other known hallucinogens, and from cocaine. In small doses cannabis produces a general feeling of relaxation, well-being, as well as a variety of perceptual and sensory distortions. Mild impairment in thinking and motor ability also occurs. In larger amounts, particularly associated with hashish, it can produce hallucinations similar to those brought about by a small dose of **LSD** or **mescaline.** In very large doses it can induce vomiting, chills, and fever—as well as the "bad trip" loss of control associated with other hallucinogens (Ray, 1983; Jacobs & Fehr, 1987). Other negative effects are noted in Table 5.2.

Can you think of any reason that "medicinal use" of marijuana might produce a different effect from "non-medicinal use"?

Marijuana cultivated today is many times more potent than the marijuana used in the 1960s.

LSD. Synthetic hallucinogen first synthesized in Switzerland. Also called "acid."

Mescaline (MESS-kah-lin).   An hallucinogen found in the peyote (pay-YO-tee) cactus.

LSD

LSD (lysergic acid diethylamide) is an artificial, or synthetic, chemical not found in nature. It was first made in a Swiss laboratory in 1938. However, its rather profound effects on human behavior were not appreciated until five years later. In 1943 Albert Hofmann—the Swiss scientist who had first synthesized LSD—accidentally licked some of the drug off his fingers. About half an hour later, knowing that something unusual was happening to him, Hofmann decided to stop work and bicycle home from the lab. Wobbling and weaving all the way, he finally made it. But by the time he reached his house, everything he saw looked so terrifying Hofmann was sure he had gone mad (Ray, 1983).

Because LSD caused people who took it to experience some of the symptoms associated with schizophrenia, Hofmann believed the drug might be useful in brain research. Therefore, he suggested it be given to people with mental disorders. LSD was first tried with patients in a Swiss mental hospital. And, as is often the case when *any* new therapy is first tried, a few of these patients did seem to get better. Whether this improvement was due to the drug or to the special attention the patients got was never proven, however. Research in subsequent years has failed to demonstrate any therapeutic value to LSD (Maisto et al., 1991).

PCP

PCP (phencyclidine) or "angel dust," rivals LSD and mescaline as the most abused hallucinogen in the United States. Discovered in 1956 by Victor Maddox and Graham Chen, PCP was used for a time as an anesthetic for both humans and animals. However, it was banned for human use after tests showed that in large doses it produced convulsions, uncontrollable rage, coma, and death.

One of the greatest dangers of PCP seems to be the unpredictability of its effects. Sometimes it causes euphoria, sometimes fear, sometimes rage, sometimes severe depression, and sometimes a complete loss of contact with reality. Consequently, street use of PCP has declined somewhat.

Oddly enough though, while street use of PCP has decreased, medical use has increased. Recent studies suggest that, when given to heart attack victims, PCP can protect against brain damage during the recovery period.

PCP. Common name for phencyclidine (fenn-SIGH-kli-deen). Also called "angel dust."

MESCALINE AND PSILOCYBIN

Mescaline is a chemical found in buttons on the peyote cactus. It can also be produced in synthetic form in a laboratory. The hallucinogenic effects of mescaline have been known for centuries to Native Americans, some of whom continue to eat peyote buttons as part of their religious ceremonies.

Psilocybin (SILL-oh-SIGH-bin). An hallucinogenic drug that comes from a wild mushroom.

Less well known is a drug called **psilocybin,** found in a mushroom that grows wild in certain parts of the world. Psilocybin also produces hallucinations and also has been used in religious ceremonies.

DESIGNER DRUGS

Designer drugs, or "microchip drugs," are synthetic substances which closely resemble other drugs in structure and effects. Originally, these drugs were "designed" to take advantage of laws which did not specifically prohibit their manufacture and use. In 1986 laws were passed to make it possible to immediately classify a "designed" drug as illegal. However, unscrupulous "kitchen" chemists continue to modify drugs to change their molecular structure while retaining their psychoactive effects.

Since designer drugs are derivatives, or "analogs," of other drugs, their effects are similar to the imitated drug. In fact, often the effect of a designer drug is greater than the effect of the imitated drug (Jacobs & Fehr, 1987; Gerler & Moorhead, 1988).

There are three groups of drugs generally considered to be designer drugs (although many more may be on the way). These groups are the meperidine analogs (MPPP), the fentanyl analogs (AMF, PMF), and the amphetamine analogs (MDA, MDMA) (see Table 5.2). MPPP, AMF, and PMF produce effects like heroin. They are very potent heroin substitutes. MDA and MDMA resemble not only the amphetamines, but also mescaline. Consequently, these drugs act as both stimulants and psychedelics (Callahan & Appel, 1988; Beck & Morgan, 1986; Climko et al., 1986–87). Both MDA and MDMA were first synthesized in the early 1900s, long before the advent of designer drugs. Thus, strictly speaking, they are not true designer drugs.

Designer drugs can be extremely dangerous because of the lack of control in their production. For example, if a chemist applies too much heat or acid in the production of MPPP, a certain amount of MPTP will also be produced. MPTP produces severe and irreversible Parkinson's disease. Hundreds of cases of Parkinson's disease produced by MPTP have been reported in areas as widely distributed as California, Maryland, and British Columbia (Jacobs & Fehr, 1987).

Drugs and Mental Processes

For the most part, we take drugs because certain chemical compounds make us feel better than we do without the drugs—or because we *believe* the drugs will make us feel better. And beliefs often can have just as strong an influence on the drug experience as does the biochemistry of the drug itself (Bailey et al., 1992; Fromme & Dunn, 1992).

For example, Alan Marlatt and Damaris Rohsenow suggest that most of the social effects of alcohol may be due to people's expectations about the drug. In a study described by Marlatt and Rohsenow, subjects who drank tonic water but thought it was alcohol showed most of the classic symptoms of intoxication, while subjects who drank alcohol but thought it was tonic water failed to get "high." More specifically, men who thought they had consumed alcohol became less anxious in social situations. The men also became more aggressive and sexually aroused. Women who consumed tonic water thinking it was alcohol became more anxious in social situations. The women *reported* they became sexually aroused, but physically they actually became less so (Marlatt & Rohsenow, 1981).

The social setting has a strong influence on how you react to *all* drugs, including alcohol. Canadian researchers Patricia Pliner and Howard Cappell found that solitary drinkers describe the effects of drinking primarily in terms of physical symptoms—they feel dizzy or numb. Drinkers in social situations (who have consumed the same amount of alcohol) tend to say they feel more "outgoing" or "friendly." The setting in which alcohol is consumed and the drinker's expectations may be even more influential in determining the drinker's social and emotional reactions than

The effect of alcohol depends partly on the social context. These people probably find that alcohol lowers their inhibitions and makes them more socially outgoing.

are the physical effects of the alcohol itself (Adeso, 1985; Kalin, 1972; Pliner & Cappell, 1974).

Psychiatrist Norman Zinberg came to similar conclusions regarding the effects of expectations and social settings on drug abuse. Some of Zinberg's subjects were able to control their use of drugs; other subjects could not. Zinberg concludes that the *social setting* and the *social skills* of the user are "a major, if not the primary, element in determining degree of control" (Zinberg, 1984). Put more simply, people who learn to control their use of intoxicants are significantly less likely to have drug-related problems than are people who have never learned self-control.

Some people believe alcoholism is a "disease," and that even one drink will set off a strong physical reaction in an alcoholic. Why does the research cast some doubt on this belief?

CONSCIOUSNESS AND THE ENDORPHINS

Almost all descriptions of that altered state of consciousness we call "getting high" have two important aspects to them: (1) The person feels no pain; and (2) the person feels detached from his or her body and from ordinary reality. Oddly enough, these experiences may well be like those brought about by great shock, and the release of massive amounts of the endorphins inside the brain.

Researcher Janet Hopson suggests that the onset of intense shock may lead a tiny region in the center of the brain to create an abnormal amount of one or more of the endorphins. The sudden release of all these "natural opiates" apparently puts the organism in a *trance state* similar to that occasionally achieved by Eastern mystics, and perhaps related to the transcendence of a "near-death experience." This altered state of consciousness is also akin to the euphoria caused by some drugs, the "runner's high," and even the pleasure of a good laugh or a good cry (Hopson, 1990).

It is tempting to speculate that *almost all altered states of consciousness* are associated with the release of natural opiates within the brain. Sometimes you secrete endorphins because of the drugs you have taken. But just as often, you secrete these chemicals because of your *expectations* about how the drugs will affect you. Thus, some of the effects of alcohol, the opiates, marijuana, and cocaine are due to biochemical changes these drugs cause at various synapses. But other effects of these drugs are caused by the types of neural transmitters and inhibitors your brain secretes in response to what you *think* the drugs ought to be doing to you.

There are many experiences of altered consciousness which we have not discussed here. These include daydreaming, meditation, near-death experiences, and religious mystical phenomena. If we had the time to explore these experiences, we would see that each of them involves the same factors we have been discussing—a combination of biochemical changes, mental expectations, and social/environmental influences.

To restate an important point we made earlier, your mental processes have as much influence on the behavior of your neurons as the behavior of your neurons has on what you think and feel. Which is to say, "your mind influences your body as much as your body influences your mind."

Try to keep this "in mind" as we consider what *motivates* our behavior.

SUMMARY

1. **Consciousness** is a **primitive term** that is defined as your ordinary state of **awareness.**

2. Certain experiences—such as falling asleep, dreaming, and taking various drugs—can lead to unusual or **altered states of consciousness.**

3. Your body has certain **biological rhythms,** such as daily fluctuations in temperature, that follow predictable patterns. These **circadian rhythms** suggest there are **biological clocks** in the body that control many physical processes, including sleep and waking.

4. **Circadian rhythms** are typically determined at (or before) birth, but can be **reset** by inputs from the environment.

5. **Melatonin,** a hormone produced by the **pineal gland,** affects both the sleep/waking cycle and the body's responses to the annual cycle of seasons.

6. Sleep is both an **adaptive response** that helped early humans survive, and an innate **restorative process** that allows the body and mind to rejuvenate themselves.

7. The stages of sleep run from **Stage 0** (pre-sleep) to **Stage 4** (deep sleep). Following Stage 4, you typically go into **Stage 3,** then **Stage 2,** and from there into **Stage 1–REM sleep** during which you will have one or more dreams.

8. Each **sleep cycle** is about 90 minutes long, including an REM period that runs from 8 to 15 minutes (first cycle of the night) to more than 40 minutes (final sleep cycle of the night). Stage 4 (deep) sleep predominates during the first and second sleep cycles of the night. Stage 2 sleep, Stage 1–REM periods, and **dreaming** increase during later cycles.

9. Stage 1–REM sleep usually develops out of Stage 2 sleep. During REM, most of the **voluntary muscles** in your body are paralyzed—except for those that control eye movements.

10. **Dreaming** seems to be primarily a function of the right hemisphere.

11. **Infants** sleep about 16 hours per 24. **Young adults** sleep about 8 hours, but **older people** sleep slightly less. Both infants and elderly individuals nap more than do young adults.

12. If **deprived of sleep** for 100 hours or more, you will typically feel stress and some mental confusion. When you do go to sleep again, you will usually sleep 11–16 hours at most and normal amounts thereafter.

13. People deprived of REM sleep usually show a **rebound effect** when allowed to sleep normally.

14. You **dream** several dreams during each REM period. REM dreams are noted for their completeness and their fantastic quality. Dreams that occur during Stages 2, 3, or 4 are at best **brief and fragmentary,** and are "reality-oriented."

15. Some people have **lucid dreams** in which they can control the content and outcome of their dreaming.

16. There are two main types of nightmares: **anxiety nightmares** and **night terrors.** Anxiety nightmares develop out of Stage 1–REM sleep, while night terrors develop out of Stage 4 sleep and occasionally are followed by sleepwalking.

17. Sleep disorders include **narcolepsy** (involuntary "attacks" of sleep), **sleep apnea, insomnia, sleepwalking,** and **sleep-talking.**

18. **Hypnotism** was made famous in the late 1700s by Anton Mesmer, who thought he could "cure" his patients by putting them in a **trance state.**

19. T. X. Barber has shown that people with rich **fantasy lives** often make good hypnotic subjects.

20. Ernest and Josephine Hilgard believe that people with **punitive parents** often resort to fantasy as a way of **dissociating** themselves psychologically from parental wrath.

21. Under hypnosis, you may perform **unusual feats** of mind and body—but nothing that you couldn't do anyhow if **highly motivated.** The primary motivation for performing these feats seems to be a strong desire to **please the hypnotist.**

22. Subjects undergoing **hypnotic age regression** often act as if they had access to **past lives** or forgotten memories. Most of these experiences can be explained as a type of **role playing** engaged in to please the hypnotist.

23. Under hypnosis, **witnesses** to a crime often report events that simply did not occur.

24. Hilgard believes that, under hypnosis, the mind "dissociates" and that painful inputs not experienced by the conscious mind are felt by a **hidden observer.**

25. Barber believes that hypnosis is not an **altered state of consciousness,** and that Hilgard's data can better be explained in terms of **role playing.**

26. **Drugs** can affect many neural processes by mimicing or blocking neural transmitters, or by causing either an increase or decrease in the speed of **neural transmission** at specific synapses.

27. The **opiates** inhibit sensory inputs and thus reduce the intensity of painful stimulation. However, the opiates also have a strong effect on **moods.**

28. Your brain produces a variety of natural pain killers called **endorphins,** which are known chemically as **opioid peptides.**

29. **Morphine** inhibits the production of the natural pain killers. **Withdrawal** from morphine addiction is painful because your body has no **opioid peptides** to inhibit the perception of pain.

30. Use of **cocaine,** especially **crack,** by young people has increased dramatically in recent years, while use of **marijuana** and other **hallucinogens** has decreased. Use of **alcohol** has increased slightly.

31. Drugs that affect **cortical processing** can also alter the experience of pain, change moods, and cause you to **hallucinate** or misinterpret your sensory inputs.

32. **PCP** is a **hallucinogen** with unpredictable effects.

33. **Marijuana** affects motor coordination, perception and thinking. In large amounts it can produce hallucinations. It is sometimes used to treat glaucoma and the nausea associated with chemotherapy.

34. **Alcohol** is the most widely abused drug in the United States and is a major health and social problem.

35. The effects of all drugs are strongly influenced by **psycho-social factors,** including expectations.

36. The brain reacts to shock and stress by secreting opioid peptides. In large amounts, these natural pain killers can bring about a **trance state** or **euphoria.**

37. Your **mental processes** have as much influence on the behavior of your neurons as the behavior of your neurons has on what you think and feel.

ANSWERS FOR THOUGHT

1. *How do you know you are not dreaming right now?*

   Some evidence: Subjectively, we "feel" awake. Other people support our perception of wakefulness. People and objects behave in more consistent fashion than in dreams. When we dream we are not usually aware of another type of consciousness ("wakefulness"); when we are awake we are aware that dreaming exists.

2. *What problems are created when groups of people try to keep the same schedule . . . ?*

   Conflicts might arise when "morning persons" and "evening persons" want to do different things, especially in the morning or evening when their activity levels are very different.

3. *How might biological rhythms contribute to the "home team advantage"?*

   If a visiting team travels from a different time zone, they may have to play when their bodies are used to being relatively inactive or even when they are used to sleeping.

4. *Why might it be important for a mother and her babies to be on similar biological schedules?*

   Babies need the most attention when they are active, so it is helpful for mothers to be active at the same time.

5. *What kind of melatonin cycle would you expect to find in people who suffer from insomnia?*

   Insomnia *might* be related to a failure to build up melatonin. Melatonin might fail to build up if the individual is exposed to bright light. Thus, we might expect to find more insomnia as the days got longer, and among people who spend a lot of time in bright light, and perhaps even have to sleep when it is light.

6. *People spend . . . explain why scientists have studied "awakeness" so much more than "sleep?"*

   Wakefulness is more obvious than sleep. When we are awake we are more active, we affect other people more, we can reflect on ourselves, we can compare our experiences more easily. When we are asleep we are inactive, and unresponsive, giving the appearance that nothing of significance is going on. Sleep is difficult to study, and easy to ignore.

7. *Why might you have trouble consciously remembering your dreams unless you . . . period of time?*

   Both of these experiences would probably be the result of your nonverbal (usually right) hemisphere being active and your verbal (usually left) hemisphere being relatively inactive during dreams and shortly after waking. Speech and the ability to articulate memories are primarily a function of the verbal hemisphere.

8. *How would the two different theories of sleep account for muscular inhibition?*

   As an "adaptive response," muscular inhibition would prevent us from attracting the attention of our enemies or hurting ourselves while we slept. As a "restorative process," muscular inhibition would prevent muscles from expending further energy, and would allow the process of restoration to proceed uninterrupted.

9. *How might the differing abilities of the two hemispheres help explain lucid dreaming . . . ?*

   Lucid dreaming might be your verbal hemisphere observing and interpreting the dream activity in the nonverbal hemisphere.

10. *A common anxiety nightmare is that of "running through molasses." . . . What happens to your muscles . . . ?*

During REM sleep, your muscles are paralyzed. This muscular inhibition might help explain the common nightmare of being unable to move.

11. *Since . . . you eventually get what sleep you really need . . . more important than the physical effects?*

Your body will force you to get the sleep you need. So the possibility of physical damage from loss of sleep is slight. However, without adequate sleep you may feel tired, listless, irritable, and unhappy. These psychological effects can cause other problems, such as disrupted relationships with other people. These problems may be more important than any physical consequences of sleep loss.

12. *What relationship do you see between sleep apnea and a possible component of "night terrors"?*

Many "night terrors" involve a panic associated with being unable to breathe (perhaps because a monster is squeezing the life out of you). Perhaps the combination of deep Stage 4 sleep and the experience of sleep apnea *produces* some night terrors.

13. *What is the relationship between being able to "fantasize" and being able to "dissociate yourself" . . . ?*

Both processes involve using mental processes to escape from the full impact of your current surroundings. Fantasy is a complete escape to a world of your choosing; dissociation is an escape from unpleasant components of the present situation.

14. *As. . . . What problems does Loftus's research raise about the use of hypnotism by various police . . . ?*

It is very difficult, if not impossible, for the police to avoid suggesting memories to a person they are questioning under hypnosis. Hypnotic subjects are usually so cooperative that, under hypnosis, the suggested memory may be even more likely to be accepted as real.

15. *Do you think that Barber's view of hypnosis could apply to some drug experiences?*

Drug experiences are highly influenced by the user's expectations and the social setting in which the drug is taken. This is one reason for the variation in drug "trips." Research with alcohol indicates that expectation and social influences may cause people to experience changes in mood and sociability even when they are taking a placebo.

16. *Why do people use drugs that affect their consciousness?*

Some possible reasons: escape from unpleasant memories, emotions, or surroundings; experimentation and searching for new experiences; social pressure to conform; ignorance of possible harmful consequences.

17. *Can you think of any reason that "medicinal use" of marijuana might produce a different effect from "non-medicinal use"?*

The medicinal user's therapeutic expectations (such as relief from nausea), are very different from the non-medicinal user's expectations (getting "high"). These effects would be exaggerated by the corresponding social setting.

18. *Some people believe alcoholism is a "disease," and that even one drink will set off a strong physical . . . ?*

Research indicates that psychological and social factors are very important in predicting the effects of alcohol and other drugs. Patterns of drug use may be controlled by the social setting and personal skills of the person as much as by the physical effects of the drug.

CHAPTER 6

INTRODUCTION TO MOTIVATION

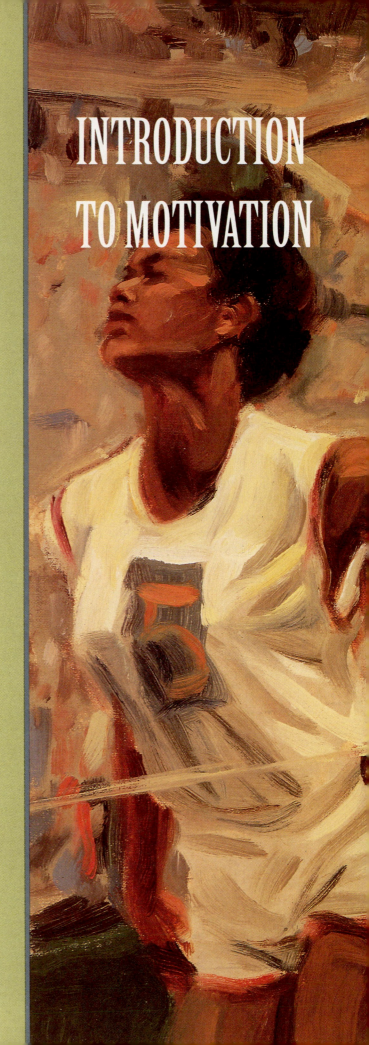

Fair-haired hippopotamus!—that was how he looked to himself. He saw a big round face, a wide, flourishing red mouth, stump teeth. And the hat, too; and the cigar, too. I should have done hard labor all my life, he reflected. Hard honest labor that tires you out and makes you sleep. I'd have worked off my energy and felt better. Instead, I had to distinguish myself—yet.

He had put forth plenty of effort, but that was not the same as working hard, was it? And if as a young man he had got off to a bad start it was due to this very same face. Early in the nineteen-thirties, because of his striking looks, he had been very briefly considered star material, and he had gone to Hollywood. There for seven years, stubbornly, he had tried to become a screen artist. Long before that time his ambition or delusion had ended, but through pride and perhaps also through laziness he had remained in California. At last he turned to other things, but those seven years of persistence and defeat had unfitted him somehow for trades and businesses, and then it was too late to go into one of the professions. He had been slow to mature, and he had lost ground, and so he hadn't been able to get rid of his energy and he was convinced that this energy itself had done him the greatest harm.

SAUL BELLOW
SEIZE THE DAY

MOTIVATION: FACT AND THEORY

There is occasions and causes why and wherefore in all things.

SHAKESPEARE

Have you ever felt like the character from *Seize the Day*? Have you been concerned about your weight, or the goals you have achieved, or the choices you have made? In this chapter we will discuss body weight, the motivation to achieve, and the concept of choice, as we consider the study of motivation.

David Edwards notes, *motivation* isn't really an "area" in psychology. It's a series of questions we ask as we try to explain why people act as they do (Edwards, 1972). Different psychologists tend to ask different sorts of questions. Therefore, there are about as many definitions of *motivation* as there are behavioral scientists.

Almost all scientists agree, however, that humans have *needs*, and that the study of needs makes up a large part of what we call "motivation." So, suppose we begin this chapter by asking four important questions about needs:

First, what kinds of needs do you have? Obviously, you have a biological requirement for things such as food and water. But can we explain everything you do in terms of your attempt to satisfy these basic physical requirements? Or do you have intra-psychic and social needs that are (in their way) as strong as your need for food and water? If so, what are these psychological and social needs? Do they vary much from person to person, or do all people develop the same social and psychological motives at the same stage in life? (In a sense, this is "the mind-body" problem revisited. Those psychologists who take a biological viewpoint tend to emphasize bodily needs. Those theorists who emphasize the mind through "mental" and "social" activities often hold that these psychological needs are as "basic" as physical needs.)

Second, where do your motivations *come from*? Your genetic blueprint determines your basic physical needs. But what causes social and intra-psychic motives? Are they also determined (even in part) by your genetic blueprint? Or are they entirely imposed on you by your culture and your past experiences? (In brief, how much of your motivation is *innate*, and how much is *learned*? This is, of course, the "nature-nurture" debate extended to the field of motivation.)

Motivation "moves" us to accomplish feats despite great odds.

Third, what are the various *mechanisms* by which you satisfy your needs? Are all your behaviors aimed at reducing stress and pain? Or does the promise of pleasure motivate you most of the time? That is, do you eat to reduce your hunger pangs, or because food tastes so good? Or are your eating behaviors—and their associated feelings—primarily controlled by such environmental inputs as cultural values and social expectations? (Put briefly, are motivated behaviors determined by such single factors as stress and arousal? Or are motivated acts multi-determined?)

Fourth, what is the relationship between motivation and *conation*, or "the act of willing." Does your mind do anything more than yield to your body's itches and urges (the behavioral viewpoint)? Or can you voluntarily *choose* among a variety of behaviors in any given situation (the conative viewpoint)? (Put more simply, can we explain your motives entirely in terms of blind biological drives, or is motivation a matter of your consciously selecting among various behaviors available to you at a given time?)

These are some thorny questions you must try to answer when you try to explain *why* people do what they do. Although there are other questions, and consequently many definitions of motivation, we will consider **motivation** to be *an internal state that guides our behavior and gives it direction.*

Motivation and Self-Movement

The word motivation comes from the Latin term meaning "to move." Ancient scholars were fascinated that some objects in the world are self-movers, while other objects remain stationary unless acted upon by an outside force. The ancients assumed that a *spirit* inside the object—a "little person" of some kind—initiated motion by pushing or impelling the object into action. Whenever the "spirit was moved," so was the object or body that the spirit inhabited (Petri, 1986).

It was not until about the 16th century that Western scientists gained enough knowledge of physics to explain the "behaviors" of such *inanimate* objects as rocks and rivers in purely *mechanical* terms. That is, it was not until a few hundred years ago that we managed to get the **animus** out of inanimate objects. And once scientists had made this giant intellectual step, they began to wonder if they could also understand the actions of *living* organisms in physical or non-spiritual terms. Many of our theories of motivation are thus based on the belief that human activities are just as mechanical as are the movements of bedbugs and bacteria. The best-known of these mechanistic approaches are *drive theory* and *arousal theory*.

Opposed to these biological viewpoints are a variety of psychological and social theories which stress the importance of intra-psychic and environmental influences on behavior. But these approaches are limited, too, in that most of them neglect the importance of biological needs.

Fortunately, there is one holistic theory which more or less encompasses the biological, the social, and the intra-psychic approaches to motivation. Although it too is far from being complete, let's talk about that approach first, and then explain drive theory and arousal theory. Finally, we will attempt to show the real complexities of motivation by discussing one very human problem in some detail—why some people overeat, while others deliberately undereat.

Maslow's Theory of "Self-Actualization"

According to Abraham Maslow, human needs can be placed on a hierarchy, or ladder. This hierarchy runs from the simplest biological motives up to the most complex of intra-psychic and social desires (Maslow, 1971).

If you are fortunate, you will finally reach the top rung of Maslow's hierarchy and become *self-actualizing*. Self-actualizing means reaching your own greatest potential, doing the things you do best in your own unique way, and then helping those around

Motivation. Motivation is an internal state that guides our behavior and gives it direction. It may be more broadly defined as a series of questions that you ask about *why* people think, feel, and behave as they do.

Animus. The Latin word meaning "spirit."

FIGURE 6.1

Maslow's hierarchy of needs.

you achieve these goals too. But you can only begin working on this final stage of human development by first solving the problems associated with the four lower levels (Maslow, 1970).

Maslow says there are five primary levels on the ladder of human motivation, as shown in Figure 6.1.

1. *Biological needs*. Maslow assumes you start life at the lowest level. You must satisfy your physical wants before you can take care of any psychological or social needs you may have. You cannot take the next step up the motivational ladder unless, and until, you meet your primary biological needs.

2. *Safety needs*. Once an infant's basic needs are satisfied, the child is ready to explore the physical environment. But as we will show in later chapters, young children typically don't explore unless they feel secure. A predictable world is, generally speaking, a much safer environment than one which is unpredictable. Thus, one reason that you "move about" in your environment is to reduce your uncertainty about what the world has to offer. With this knowledge, you can choose sensibly among the various physical inputs you need to sustain life. And once you know what to expect from the world, you can move on to the next rung of the motivational ladder.

3. *Belongingness* and *love needs*. Once you have gained control over your physical environment, you can then turn your attention to social inputs. As the poet John Donne once said, "No man is an island, complete to itself." Donne knew quite well that, to be a *human* being, you must have other people around you. Thus, according to Maslow, you have an innate need for affection and love that only other people can satisfy. You must *affiliate* with others, and identify yourself with one or more like-minded individuals. When you identify with someone else, you learn to perceive part of the world as that person presumably does.

4. *Esteem needs*. One reason you need other people is to help you set your life's goals. Under the right conditions, the groups you affiliate with can offer you *models* of what your future behavior might (or should) be. Groups also offer you external *feedback* on how close you are coming to achieving your targets in life. And the better you get at reaching your goals, the more esteem you likely will have for yourself (and the more esteem you will probably get from others). According to Maslow, "esteem needs" are just as important for human life as are food and water (Maslow, 1971).

5. *Need for self-actualization*. Until you have achieved self-esteem, you probably will not feel secure enough to become a "fully actualizing person." Unless you have confidence in yourself, Maslow says, you will not dare to express yourself in your unique way, make your special contribution to society, and thus achieve your true inborn potential.

And once you have become self-actualizing, Maslow says, you will find you have a strong urge to help others get where you are. And to do that you will need to

One of the basic needs that all people have, according to Maslow, is the sense of approval and belonging.

teach others the lessons you learned as you worked your way up the four lower levels of the motivational hierarchy (Maslow, 1971).

How far up the ladder would a frequently abused child be likely to climb? Or a student whose teachers gave the student nothing but criticism?

Like all theories in psychology, Maslow's *hierarchical* approach to human motivation has been criticized. Because Maslow based his theory on the study of highly successful people in the Western world, his viewpoint is most applicable to middle- and upper-class individuals whose values are derived from Western European cultures. Thus his theory may not apply to other cultures, nor even to all segments of Western society.

Maslow also presumed that *all* humans move up through five clearly definable steps as they mature. Whether there are actually five rungs to the motivational ladder, or 15, or 150, is something that Maslow never really proved. Furthermore, he assumed that you must somehow "conquer" the problems associated with each lower rung before you could move on to a higher one. This assumption is, at best, highly debatable.

Other than the case histories Maslow offers, there simply is no *experimental* evidence proving that Maslow's approach is correct. Indeed, it is difficult to imagine how one might put many of Maslow's notions to a critical test.

Despite these criticisms, Maslow's approach has many strengths. To begin with, it is one of the few theories that emphasizes the importance of *individual choice* in determining behavior. That is, Maslow views the human organism as capable of choosing between alternative courses of action. True, your biological state and your social environment influence many things you do. But given these limitations, you still are able (in Maslow's view) to exercise choice in most situations.

Second, Maslow's hierarchy is by far the best known of the *holistic* approaches to the study of motivation. That is, Maslow's theory is one of the few which gives roughly equal value to biological, intra-psychic, and social/behavioral influences on behavior. Drive theory—which we will discuss in a moment—does a good job of explaining how organisms react in situations of extreme deprivation. Arousal theory incorporates the best aspects of drive theory and adds a number of its own strengths. However, neither of these narrow theoretical viewpoints can begin to explain the enormous complexities of even the simplest of human activities, such as eating.

We will first take a look at drive and arousal theory. Then we will discuss a highly specific problem—that of obesity—and show how drive and arousal theory simply cannot explain why we eat as we do. ("Obesity" is from a Latin word meaning "to eat up.") Next, we will consider how we might use our knowledge of eating to help meet our own weight goals. Then, we will talk about a type of self-induced starvation. Finally, we will look at another line of motivational research to see some of the "mental manipulations" we go through in explaining our behavior (including eating) to ourselves and others.

To live is to choose.

PAUL TOURNIER

Drive Theory

For the past century, many psychologists have attempted to imitate the "hard" sciences by reducing the complexities of human motivation to fairly uncomplicated *biological* equations. Rather than assuming people (or animals) are capable of self-determined actions, these psychologists theorized that organisms are *driven* or pushed into motion much the way an automobile engine is cranked into activity when you turn the ignition key.

At its simplest, the biological approach to motivation is often called *drive theory*. Psychologist Clark Hull, one of the first great drive theorists, assumed *biological* needs are the ones that rule your life. Biological pain arouses or *drives* you to movement. *Reducing* your drives gives you biological pleasure and "rewards" those movements that led to the drive reduction. Hull made the concepts of drive and drive reduction the cornerstones of his theory of learning.

You do have motives other than biological pain and pleasure, of course. But drive theorists such as Hull assume that you *learned* these needs by associating them with the major physical needs that "drive" you along life's highway.

HOMEOSTASIS

Homeostasis (home-ee-oh-STAY-sis). The tendency to move toward a need-free or drive-free condition. Any action by an organism to reduce drives is called a "homeostatic behavior."

The key concept in understanding drive theory is that of **homeostasis.** The term itself comes from a Greek work meaning "homestate" or "normal condition." To a drive theorist, your body is like an automobile engine. To keep a car's engine in a state of fine tune—its "normal condition"—you need to take constant care of it. For example, you must give the engine oil, water, fuel, and lubrication. And you must protect it from damage. To keep your body in "fine tune"—or *homeostasis*—you must also give it the things it needs to function properly. These needs include food, water, air, a given range of temperatures, and protection from germs and accidents (Stellar & Stellar, 1985).

Whenever the engine in your car departs from its normal condition, red lights blink on the dashboard telling you what is wrong. Perhaps you need to add oil, or buy some fuel. Whatever the case, those lights will continue to flash until you satisfy the engine's needs. In similar fashion, whenever your body runs low on food or water, warning signals go off inside you, telling you something is wrong. That is, you experience hunger or thirst. And you go on being hungry or thirsty until you satisfy your body's need and return your body to its usual *homeostatic* condition. "Homeostasis," then, simply means the innate biological urge you have to keep your bodily processes in a balanced or need-free state.

What similarities do you see between the concept of homeostasis and the Gestalt Law of Pragnanz discussed in Chapter 4?

PRIMARY NEEDS AND DRIVES

Most drive theorists refer to those things you absolutely must have to survive as *primary needs*. These basic needs include such things as air, food, water, and a proper temperature. Whenever you run short of one of these things, built-in mechanisms in your body detect that need. As the need increases, the firing rates in various neural centers in your brain start to increase. This increased neural activity creates a *primary drive* inside you that *arouses* you to action. When your arousal is great enough, you are *driven* to seek out whatever you need. Thus, a need, which is *physiological*, produces a drive, which is *psychological*.

Generally speaking, the longer you are deprived of something you need, the faster your nerve cells will fire. And the more *aroused* your nervous system becomes, the greater the primary drive you will experience. And the stronger the drive becomes, the more "motivated" you are to reduce that drive.

For example, you have a "primary need" for food. The longer you go without food, the greater your primary drive (hunger) becomes, and the more aroused or driven you are to find something to eat. If you go hungry long enough, your aroused movements will probably bring you into a position to satisfy your need. Once you do so, the "hunger centers" in your brain stop firing. At this point, your drive level decreases, your arousal (motivation) disappears, and your normal homeostatic balance is reinstated. Figure 6.2 shows a diagram of drive theory, using food deprivation as an example.

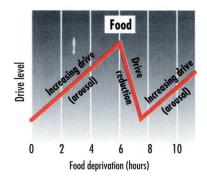

FIGURE 6.2

A simple diagram of drive theory, using food deprivation as an example. As time passes, the drive for food increases. When food is consumed, the drive decreases and a state of homeostasis is temporarily restored.

INTRA-PSYCHIC AND SOCIAL NEEDS

You need to take in food to maintain your normal homeostatic "good biological health." But *what* you eat depends in large part on what drive theorists call learned or *secondary needs*. Other psychologists refer to these as "intra-psychic needs" and "social needs" (Stellar & Stellar, 1985).

You came into the world with primary (biological) needs. But you *learn* secondary needs, presumably through some association with the satisfaction of a primary need. For example, suppose you get hungry for a pizza. According to drive theory, this *specific hunger* is an acquired, secondary drive. At some time in the past when you were hungry, you ate pizza. This behavior reduced your hunger drive, rewarding you for consuming the pizza. As a consequence, when you get hungry in the future, you are more likely to want pizza than some food you've never eaten before.

What position do drive theorists appear to be taking in solving the mind-body problem?

CRITICISMS OF DRIVE THEORY

Many objections have been raised to the simple form of drive theory we have just outlined. Three of the major objections are as follows:

Rather than a general drive to eat, we often seem to experience hunger for a specific food.

1. Not all psychologists agree with drive theorists that intra-psychic needs are *learned*. For instance, most young animals (including children) seem to have an innate desire to explore their environment. The genetic blueprint apparently specifies this "exploratory drive," but it is difficult to think of "exploration" as a *biological* need. Indeed, although we have some notion of the physical mechanisms that underlie the hunger drive, we simply don't know what parts of the brain control "exploration." Thus, to many psychologists, it seems more appropriate to consider exploration an innately determined *intra-psychic* drive (Lichtenberg, 1989).

2. In similar fashion, not all psychologists believe social needs are merely acquired by association with the reduction of some biological drive. For example, most newborn animals seem to have an innate urge to identify with a "mother figure." And as we will see in later chapters, most female animals readily develop an intense "social bond" with their infants immediately after birth. Thus, the genetic blueprints seem to specify many mother-infant behaviors. However, we don't know what biological mechanisms underlie these instinctual needs. And it is difficult to think of these highly motivated social behaviors in terms of "homeostasis." *Homeostasis* always involves some *physical need*, but mother-infant behaviors involve *informational* or *social* inputs, not *physical* quantities such as food and water (Toates, 1985).

3. Drive theory equates an *increase* in neural excitation with an *increase* in motivation. Yet sometimes a *decrease* in excitation can cause an *increase* in psychological arousal. For example, boredom might lead you to seek additional stimulation.

As we will see, the scientists who raised these objections often were "driven" to create competing motivational theories of their own.

Arousal Theory

In the late 1950s, Elizabeth Duffy (and others) made a telling criticism of classical drive theory. Duffy had spent many years studying the exploratory drive in animals. Her work convinced her that arousal is not always caused by a lack of such things as food, air, or water, for you have *informational needs* that are as innate and as highly

Arousal Theory. A one-level, biologically oriented theory in which motivation comes from some departure from a norm or optimum point of neural excitation. Any increase or decrease in neural firing moves the organism away from this optimum point and hence is arousing.

Set point. Your body has a "set point" for internal temperature—98.6° F (37° C). If your temperature rises above this point, you sweat. If your temperature falls below this point, you shiver or seek warmth. Your body tends to have a set point for weight, too. That is, your body tends to "defend" or maintain a given weight in a homeostatic manner.

motivating as are your life-sustaining or *energy needs.* However, classical drive theory almost totally ignores informational inputs (Petri, 1986).

This objection led Duffy and other scientists to create a new approach to motivation called **arousal theory.** We can summarize this position as follows:

1. Homeostasis isn't really a point of *zero* neural excitation, but rather is a point of *optimum* stimulation. The optimum point is the level at which you function best *at any given moment.*

2. This optimum point—often called the **set point**—may change from time to time, depending on your biological condition.

3. There are *opposing processes* associated with each set point. Some of these processes are excitatory, and come into play when you move *below* your optimum set point. The other processes are inhibitory, and start to function when you move *above* your optimum set point. Working together, these *opponent processes* help you maintain your homeostatic set point.

4. You have set points for *informational needs* as well as for physical needs.

BOREDOM AND HOMEOSTASIS

The concept of *boredom* was always a difficult one for the drive theorists to handle. For example, consider the hunger drive. Technically speaking, any balanced diet should satisfy all of our biological needs for food. Therefore, from a drive theory point of view, you might well be expected to eat the same menu at every meal. But eating *exactly the same foods* at every meal gets boring, so you tend to vary what you consume. Yet, according to classical drive theory, you should eat primarily those foods you've eaten most often in the past. And it's difficult for a drive theorist to explain why you should ever eat something entirely new to you, when old (and satisfying) foods are available.

The conclusion Duffy drew from these points is as follows: You do not have a single "homeostatic level" that is set at birth and never varies thereafter. Rather, you have a different "set point" for each type of need, whether that need is related to energy inputs or informational inputs. Furthermore, each "set point" changes according to your past experience and present conditions. You are motivated to maintain this optimum level, Duffy says, whenever your inputs *increase* too much or *decrease* too much, for a movement in either direction will take you away from your optimum level of performance.

Some people occasionally "pig out" on rich foods, then starve themselves for days afterward. Why would it be easier for Duffy to explain this type of behavior than it would for a drive theorist to do so?

OPTIMUM AROUSAL

According to Duffy, the optimum level of stimulation that you need *varies from moment to moment.* There is a good reason this is so. If your sensory inputs become too constant, your receptors "turn off" and leave you with little or no stimulation at all. And if your inputs vary too much, your environment becomes too unpredictable.

Thus, you need a certain amount of *stability* in the world around you—just as the homeostatic model would predict. However, you also need a certain amount of *variability* in stimulation. According to Duffy, your "set point of optimum arousal" will fluctuate from moment to moment in response to the level of inputs that you receive from your environment. But this optimum point will always lie somewhere between complete stability and complete variability. Figure 6.3 illustrates how we might diagram arousal theory.

Unlike drive theory, arousal theory can explain why people choose to eat foods they are not accustomed to, for example, sushi, which is often made with raw fish.

High stimulation

Need reduction

Increasing arousal (motivation)

Decreased arousal

Optimum arousal level (varies from moment to moment)

Increasing arousal (motivation)

Decreased arousal

Stimulation inputs

Low stimulation

FIGURE 6.3

A simple diagram of arousal theory. Arousal increases as stimulation rises too high or falls too low.

In Chapter 5, we noted that certain drugs such as LSD lead to a stressful experience called "loss of personal control." How might this unpleasant situation be related to a need to predict and control your inputs?

PROBLEMS WITH AROUSAL THEORY

Arousal theory was a noticeable improvement over drive theory in that Duffy could explain a number of motivational situations that early drive theorists had difficulties with. But the arousal position still is a homeostatic theory that tends to reduce motivation to what seem to be purely physical processes.

There is an appealing simplicity to homeostatic models such as those proposed by Duffy and by the drive theorists. These models attempt to explain all human behavior in terms of an innate urge to "return to a pre-set level of normal functioning." Unfortunately, as Robert Bolles and Rob Neiss point out, the experimental data just don't give much support to simple homeostatic theories.

Neiss calls arousal "an excessively broad physiological construct artificially severed from its psychological context." He claims that the concept of arousal cannot distinguish between the physiological states associated with anger, fear, or even sexuality. And he points out that a high level of arousal, which might interfere with performance, is physiologically no different from the level of arousal associated with being "psyched up," which *helps* performance. Bolles notes, both drive theory and the arousal position tend to ignore intra-psychic and social factors (Bolles, 1975). Neiss suggests a holistic approach which would investigate what he calls "complex psychobiological states" (Neiss, 1988, 1990).

To show why psychologists such as Bolles and Neiss prefer a broader, more *holistic* view of motivation, suppose we look in considerable detail at an important North American problem, that of people who overeat.

OBESITY: A HOLISTIC APPROACH

Dietitians estimate that 10–25 percent of the American public are **overweight.** The exact number of *obese* individuals varies, depending not only on how you define "fatness," but also according to what part of the country you're speaking of. For instance, in a nationwide study of several thousand children and young adults by William Dietz and Steven Gortmaker, the "obesity rate" for the northeast is about 23 percent. For the midwest, the rate is about 19 percent. It drops to 15 percent for the south, and to 14 percent for the western states. Generally speaking, young people who live in urban areas are more than twice as likely to be overweight as are young people who

Overweight. Scientists have worked out an "ideal weight" for people, depending (mostly) on their age and height. Anyone who tips the scales at 10 percent more than this "ideal" is usually considered to be "slightly overweight," and anyone more than 25 percent above this "ideal" is usually considered to be "noticeably overweight." The definition of "overweight," however, varies considerably from one expert to another.

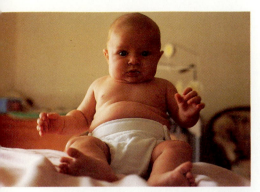

Many factors influence our actual body size as well as our ideas of "ideal" body size.

Calories (KAL-or-rees). The Latin word *calor* means "heat." The caloric (kal-LOR-ick) content of anything is the amount of heat it will generate when burned. Your body "burns" food when it converts what you eat into energy to keep you alive. Rich, sweet, fatty foods have lots of calories (that is, a high caloric content). Water has no calories at all. Fat burns; water doesn't.

live in rural areas. There are strong racial differences, too. White youngsters are 2.5 times as likely to be obese are are black children (Dietz & Gortmaker, 1984).

Presuming that your own weight is normal, however, why should you worry about such things as the national obesity rate? First, because fatness could happen to you someday, and probably has already happened to several of your friends or relatives. Second, because fat people are a very discriminated-against minority.

Overweight people face many problems. If you are overweight, you have difficulty buying attractive clothes. You may also find it hard to get out of many chairs, and to squeeze into some small cars. Gina Kolata reports that 6-year-old children, when shown drawings of an obese child, described the youngster as "lazy," "dirty," "stupid," and "ugly." Kolata also notes that, in a recent survey of employers, 16 percent said they would not hire an obese woman *under any circumstances* (Kolata, 1986).

Why do you think the attitude toward obese people is such a socially acceptable form of prejudice?

Unfair? Of course it is. So is our society's discrimination against people with dark skin or slanted eyes. Of course, most of us realize you had little to say about your skin color—but fatness is primarily a *voluntary choice*, isn't it?

No, in a very strange way, you are not entirely responsible for how much you weigh. There is a strong genetic component in fatness, and you are no more to blame for inheriting "fat genes" than for inheriting a certain skin color. For instance, Albert Stunkard and several of his associates found that adopted children showed the obesity pattern of their biological parents and siblings, not of their adoptive parents (Stunkard et al., 1986; Price et al., 1987; Sorensen et al., 1989). They also found that identical twins *reared apart* were more than twice as similar in "body-mass" as non-identical twins even when the non-identical twins were *reared together* (Stunkard et al., 1990).

In one very interesting study, Claude Bouchard and his associates had young men who were identical twins overeat by 1,000 **calories** a day. After 100 days, Bouchard measured their weight gain, the composition of the new weight (muscle or fat), and the distribution of the added pounds (where on their bodies it was added). He found big differences in the amount gained (from 9 to 29 pounds), and in the composition and distribution of the added weight. But the differences between *pairs* of twins were much greater than the differences between twins in the *same pair*. Bouchard concludes that there is a strong genetic component in fatness (Bouchard, et al., 1990).

The psychological and social influences on fatness or thinness are also extremely important. So if you happen to be snacking on something delicious, perhaps you'll want to put the food aside while we look at various biological, intra-psychic, and social/behavioral influences on gluttony.

Biological Influences on Obesity

Motivated behaviors are often related *sequences* of responses. To understand behavioral sequences, you must answer the following questions:

1. Why does a given behavioral sequence begin? That is, what inputs prompt the thought or get the action going (and keep going)?

2. Why does the behavior go in a particular direction once it begins?

3. Why does the thought or behavior eventually end? That is, once a behavioral sequence has begun, what brings it to a stop (Reeve, 1992)?

Eating is a motivated behavior—but so are overeating and undereating. Therefore, to understand why you eat as you do, we must answer three critical questions about your eating habits: Why do you start eating, why do you prefer pizza and ice cream to fried worms and boiled monkey brains, and why do you eventually stop eating?

As we will see, drive theory and arousal theory offer partial answers to these questions. But they have little to say about why you select the foods you choose to consume, much less why you eat when you're not really hungry.

From a motivational point of view, fat people might be overweight for at least four reasons: (1) They eat too frequently; (2) once started, they don't know when to quit; (3) they prefer rich, fat-laden foods; and (4) they don't burn up enough energy through exercise and physical labor. Why might different forms of therapy be needed, depending on what combination of these four behaviors the person engaged in?

BLOOD-SUGAR LEVEL

When you eat a dish of ice cream for dessert, how does your body make use of this fuel? To begin with, your digestive system breaks the food into tiny molecules, most of which contain sugar. These molecules enter your blood stream, flow through your body, and pass sugar on to any cell that might be "hungry." A few hours after you have eaten a large meal, your blood contains a great many sugar molecules. However, if you starved yourself for 24 hours or so, your blood would contain relatively few of these energy particles.

Here is our first clue as to what the *hunger drive* is all about. To maintain its homeostatic balance, your body needs a certain level of sugar in its blood. And when this level drops below a certain point, you experience hunger "pangs" and you are aroused to seek out food. Therefore, if we could somehow control the molecules floating around in your bloodstream, might we not be able to control your sensation of hunger directly?

From a purely biological point of view, the answer is a probable yes. However, to understand how blood sugar affects your behaviors, we first must look at the relationship between sugar and a chemical called **insulin.** Under normal conditions, your body secretes *insulin*, which stimulates your body to digest sugar. If we let a hungry rat eat all that it wants, then take a blood sample from the animal a little later, we would find a lot of sugar molecules in the rat's blood. If we now inject the animal with insulin, its blood-sugar level drops—and to our surprise the rat will soon begin to eat again (even though it had just consumed a very large meal) (Stellar & Stellar 1985).

According to psychologist Judith Rodin, it's not the amount of sugar in your blood that matters. Rather, it's the amount of insulin *in relationship to* the amount of sugar. And it's not even the gross amount of sugar that counts—it's what *kind* of sugar is present in your body. Rodin injected 20 normal-weight men and women with varying amounts of either insulin or *glucose* (the type of sugar found in many prepared foods and baked goods). When given insulin, the subjects became hungrier, liked sweet tastes more, and also *consumed more food*. Injections of sugar water had no effect on the subjects' appetites or cravings for sweets. Rodin also reports that while *glucose* causes a massive increase in insulin in the body, *fructose* (the type of sugar found in fruits and honey) causes only a moderate increase in insulin levels and often brings about a *decrease* in appetite (Rodin, 1984, 1991).

Somewhere in your body, then, there must be a "sugar detector" that lets your cortex know how many glucose molecules are floating around in your bloodstream. Recent research suggests that this "detector" is located in a central part of your brain called the hypothalamus.

Insulin. A hormone secreted by the pancreas, which is a small organ near the stomach. Insulin makes it easier for the cells in your body to take in sugar molecules. People whose bodies do not secrete enough insulin may suffer from a disease called diabetes. Diabetics have to control the amount of sugar they eat, and may have to take daily injections of insulin.

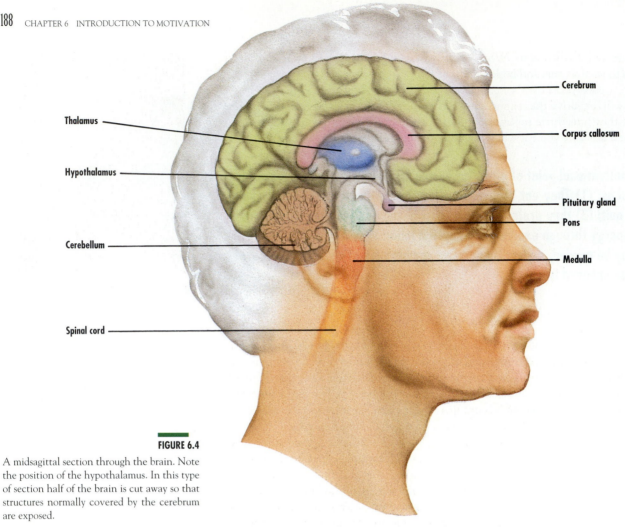

FIGURE 6.4

A midsagittal section through the brain. Note the position of the hypothalamus. In this type of section half of the brain is cut away so that structures normally covered by the cerebrum are exposed.

THE HYPOTHALAMIC "FEEDING CENTER"

As we saw in Chapter 2, your hypothalamus is a small structure located deep in your brain just above your brain stem (see Figure 6.4). One small part of your hypothalamus contains neurons that are particularly sensitive to the amount of sugar in your blood. When the blood-sugar level drops too low, the cells in this region of your hypothalamus begin to fire more rapidly—and you typically begin to feel hungry (Carlson & Hatfield, 1992).

If we put a metal electrode into this part of a rat's brain and stimulate the cells electrically, the rat will begin to eat at once—even if it has just had a big meal. If we stimulate this hypothalamic *feeding center* continuously, the rat will eat and eat and eat—until it becomes so obese that it can barely move around. If we continue the electrical stimulation even when food is not present in the rat's cage, the animal will often gnaw on anything handy, including air. If we destroy this "feeding center" in the rat's hypothalamus, the animal often refuses to eat at all. Some of the animals will die of starvation unless we force-feed them (Stellar & Stellar, 1985).

Does this one "feeding center" in the hypothalamus control all aspects of eating behavior? Certainly not. To begin with, even the "dumb rat" knows better than to overeat continuously, no matter what we do to it. If we give rats continual hypothalamic stimulation, the animals will become very, very fat. But eventually they will reach a cut-off point beyond which they will not go. Their weights will stabilize at this "set point" and we cannot induce them to become much fatter. (You may be pleased to know that, when we stop prodding the rat's brain with electrical stimulation, the animal will typically go on a "crash diet" and return to its normal body weight.)

As we noted in Chapter 5, your body produces a number of natural painkillers called *endorphins,* and endorphin secretion increases dramatically when you experience stress. However, stress also induces eating behaviors in laboratory animals. John Morley and Allen Levine report they got well-fed rats to eat immediately after a meal by administering mild stress to the animals. However, if they gave the animals naloxone (which blocks the release of the endorphins), the stressed rats *gnawed* at the food, or *licked* it, but typically did not ingest it. Morley and Levine believe that "bingeing" in humans may be mediated by endorphins released in stressful situations (Morley & Levine, 1980).

Surgical removal of a small part of the "satiation center" in the hypothalamus causes a rat to overeat.

Morley and Levine report that naloxone reduces eating, but not other stress-related "oral behaviors." Many surveys show that people tend to smoke more cigarettes (and consume more alcohol) in stressful situations than when they are not under stress. What connection do you see between these two sets of facts?

Drive theory can explain rather readily why you start to eat. As the sugar content in the blood reaching your brain *decreases,* insulin production *decreases,* and electrical activity in your hypothalamic "feeding center" *increases.* Your cortex translates this *increased neural activity* into the psychological experience of "hunger pangs." And you go looking for a decent meal, just as drive theory would predict. But why do you *stop* eating once you've begun? Why don't you munch away for hours and hours?

Because, you say, as soon as you start eating, the sugar content in your blood goes up dramatically, the production of insulin increases, and your "feeding center" turns off. That explanation would surely fit drive theory, but it happens not to be so. Eating behavior doesn't have a simple explanation, even at a biological level.

If you ate some pizza right now, it would take several hours for the food to be digested and assimilated into your bloodstream. It takes only 10–20 minutes for you to eat the pizza, though. Therefore, you actually *stop eating* long before that pizza can greatly affect your blood-sugar level. In fact, if you're a quick eater, your "feeding center" may still be signaling "eat! eat! eat!" at the top of its neural voice at the very moment when you push yourself away from the table, so stuffed with food that you can't imagine ever being hungry again (Stellar & Stellar, 1985).

So, a lowered blood-sugar level (or increased insulin level) can turn on your hunger. But what biological mechanism turns it off?

THE HYPOTHALAMIC "SATIATION CENTER"

As arousal theory points out, homeostasis is more a balance between opposing processes, rather than being a point of zero excitation. Thus, for every biological function that pushes you in one direction, there presumably is another function that pulls you back toward an optimum level of existence.

So if there is a "feeding center" in your hypothalamus that causes you to start eating, wouldn't you guess there might also be a center that, when stimulated, causes you to stop eating? It is called the **satiation center,** and it is also located in your hypothalamus, close to your "feeding center."

Suppose we implant an electrode in a rat's hypothalamic "satiation center." Then, just as the hungry animal starts to eat, we pass a weak electrical current through this "satiation center." The animal will suddenly refuse its meal. And if we continue the stimulation for a long enough time, the animal will come close to starving itself to death.

On the other hand, if we surgically remove the rat's "satiation center," the animal will go on an eating jag. Soon it will become as obese as the rats whose "feeding

Satiation center (say-she-A-shun). Our word "satisfied" comes from the Latin words *satis,* meaning "enough," and *facere,* meaning "to do" or "to make." Satiation is the condition of being completely satisfied. The "satiation center" is that part of the hypothalamus which, when stimulated electrically, causes a hungry animal to stop eating—that is, to behave as if it were already satisfied.

centers" were electrically stimulated. But as you might already have surmised, eventually the animal will reach its "obesity set point" and will taper off its wild consumption of food (Stellar & Stellar, 1985).

Under normal conditions, your "satiation center" functions *symmetrically* with the "feeding center." When your blood-sugar level goes up, the neurons in your "feeding center" *decrease* their response rate, and the nerve cells in your "satiation center" *increase* their firing rate. When your blood-sugar level falls, your "feeding center" turns on and your "satiation center" turns off.

Furthermore, your "satiation center" seems sensitive to inputs from your digestive system as well as to your blood-sugar level. R. D. Myers and M. L. McCaleb report that receptor cells in the stomach are connected directly to the "satiation center." When Myers and McCaleb injected food into the stomach of rats, these receptors sent messages to the hypothalamus that caused neurons in the "satiation center" to increase their firing rate (Myers & McCaleb, 1980). The Myers and McCaleb research is important because it may tell us why you stop eating before your blood-sugar level rises—the mere presence of food in your stomach may decrease your hunger pangs by causing your "satiation center" to start responding.

Additionally, the stomach apparently secretes chemicals that circulate to the brain and affect the satiation center. James Gibbs and his colleagues have found that the gut releases these chemicals whenever an animal ingests most types of food. When Gibbs and his associates injected rats with these chemicals before giving them *bland* food, the animals ate little or nothing at all (Kulkosky & Gibbs, 1982). (Oddly enough, the chemicals had no effect on the consumption of *sweet* foods. We will return to this point in a moment.)

So now we know why you start eating and stop eating, don't we? No, we've learned only part of the answer. What do you think would happen if we surgically removed *both* the "feeding center" and the "satiation center" from a rat's hypothalamus? Would the animal starve, or would it become obese?

The answer is, some animals will starve, but many will continue to eat pretty much as they did before the operation. So there must be systems in the brain other than the "feeding" and "satiation" centers that strongly influence eating behaviors (Stellar & Stellar, 1985). One mechanism for turning off eating behavior is what we might call the **swallow counter.**

Swallow counter. A mechanism in the brain that keeps track of swallowing so that eating may be stopped without waiting for blood-sugar levels to rise.

THE "SWALLOW COUNTER"

A young rat eats almost continuously. As it grows up, however, it soon learns to associate the intensity of its hunger pangs with the amount of food that it ought to eat. If we deprive the rat of food for a couple of hours, it eats a small amount. But when it has gone without eating for 12 hours, it will consume a great deal more food (Stellar & Stellar, 1985). The question is, how does the rat *know* how much food it actually needs?

Research indicates that some part of the animal's brain actually *counts* the number of swallows the animal makes as it eats. When the rat has had enough to satisfy its *present* state of hunger, it stops eating. And it stops *before* there is much of a change in its blood-sugar level, or in the firing rates in its "feeding" and "satiation" centers. So *learning* plays as much of a role in turning the hunger drive on and off as do the centers in the hypothalamus.

YOUR STOMACH KNOWS

Even the swallow counter doesn't give us the whole answer to the puzzling question, "Why do you stop eating?" For example, experiments by Eliot Stellar and his associates suggest that people are able to control their food inputs even if they can't count what they're swallowing.

As your usual time for eating approaches, your stomach becomes active and you begin to feel hungry. When the time for eating passes, even if you haven't eaten, your stomach will calm down until the next scheduled mealtime.

Stellar and his colleagues asked students to swallow a tiny plastic tube that pumped liquid food directly into their stomachs when the students pressed a lever. The students could not see, smell, taste, chew, or swallow the food. But they somehow learned to control the amount they consumed just as readily as if they were drinking it from a glass. Perhaps the most interesting result of these experiments was the students were completely unable to explain to Professor Stellar how they managed this feat (Stellar & Stellar, 1985)!

Stellar's experiments suggest that your stomach "knows" things about your eating habits that your "feeding" and "satiation" centers are only dimly aware of. For example, when you've packed your stomach with a huge meal (or with liquid), the muscles in your stomach are stretched out, or distended. The feedback nerve cells in your stomach would surely let your brain know how inflated your stomach was. Then your cortex could inhibit, or block out, the input messages from your "feeding center" even before your blood-sugar level changed.

It is possible that Stellar's results could be explained by appealing to the research just cited by Myers and McCaleb, and by James Gibbs and his colleagues. That is, perhaps the liquid food merely stimulated the stomach receptors that are connected to the "satiation center." Or perhaps the liquid food caused chemicals to be released in the gut that "turned on" the satiation center. However, research by Walter Cannon suggests that yet another mechanism may be involved.

Long before the "feeding center" was discovered, physiologist Walter Cannon performed a very important experiment on hunger. He got a student volunteer to swallow a balloon attached to a long hose. Once the balloon was inside the man's stomach, Cannon pumped air through the hose and inflated the balloon until it pushed firmly against the walls of the subject's stomach. (Fortunately, the man suffered little or no pain from this procedure.) Now, whenever the man's stomach contracted, it pinched the balloon and forced air up the tube. By measuring the air pressure in the tube, Cannon got a rough reading of when the man's stomach muscles churned about.

Cannon found that stomach contractions began an hour or so before the man would normally have eaten a meal. As lunch time approached, for instance, the man's stomach began to contract more and more vigorously and the man reported an increased interest in food. An hour or so after the man's usual lunch time, the stomach contractions almost stopped—*despite the fact that the man hadn't eaten a thing.* The man's subjective experience of hunger also decreased (Cannon & Washburn, 1912).

If you eat lunch every day at 12 noon, your "feeding center" and other parts of your brain begin to *anticipate* when they will have to go to work. An hour or so before noon, your brain starts sending neural signals to the muscles in your stomach, telling them to "wake up" and get ready to start performing. The muscles contract in response to these signals, and your stomach "growls."

Other parts of your brain notice the growling (and the input signals coming from your "feeding center") and decide you're probably hungry. The closer the clock gets to noon, the more vigorously your stomach muscles respond.

Oddly enough, if you get past the lunch hour without eating, your stomach will often calm down, just as it does after you have eaten. Then your hunger pangs will decrease, only to rise again as supper time approaches.

Why do both your hunger "pangs" and your stomach contractions tend to decrease after lunch even though you didn't eat anything?

Conditioned. When an organism is trained to give a particular response to a specific stimulus, we say that it has been conditioned to respond to that stimulus. As we will see in Chapter 9, there are different types of conditioning. Psychologists often use the words "learning" and "conditioning" as if they were the same.

The hunger pangs that come from stomach contractions are **conditioned.** But almost any conditioned habit can be unlearned if you go about it the right way. If you stop eating *entirely,* your subjective experience of hunger will rise to a maximum in 3–5 days, as the centers in your brain and the muscles in your stomach continue to anticipate meal after missed meal. By the end of 5 days of *complete* starvation, however, your body will have learned that food simply isn't going to be coming along as it once did. Your stomach contractions will *habituate,* and your subjective experience of hunger will drop to a low ebb. However, if you go on a diet and "eat just a little" at each regular meal time, your "habitual" stomach contractions will take a very long time to change, and you may experience biting, gnawing hunger for weeks on end.

The fact that people on a complete fast soon lose the subjective experience of hunger suggests that hunger is, to some extent, a "habit." Thus, if you want to lose weight, it might help if you eat on a highly irregular schedule before going on a diet. Once you break the "hunger habit," dieting might well be less stressful and hence less painful (psychologically speaking).

METABOLISM, SET POINT, AND OBESITY

Joel Gurin, editor of *American Health* magazine and author of several books on dieting, believes "fat people" are born that way. Gurin argues that people who tend to be overweight have a higher "weight set point" than do thin people, and that they inherit this "high set point," and so cannot readily change it. Gurin says, "Two people can have virtually identical diets and exercise habits—eat the same number of calories and the same amount of fat, log the same number of hours jogging or watching TV—and one may still be much fatter than the other. The difference is in the genes." As if that wasn't enough, Gurin points out what many overweight people have long suspected, that some research shows that lean people, as a group, actually tend to eat *more* than fat people (Gurin, 1989).

Metabolic rates. Metabolism is the sum of internal processes that provide the energy to keep your body going. People with high metabolic rates are usually more active and thinner than people with low metabolic rates.

Then why do fat people remain overweight? Because of their **metabolic rates.** Overweight individuals have much lower metabolic rates than do thin people. So fat people "burn up" food at a much slower pace than do thin people. That's why fat people can eat the same amount as thinner individuals, yet the fat people remain fat while the thin individuals remain thin. The fat person's body simply uses food *more efficiently* than does the thin person's body (Bennett & Gurin, 1982; Gurin, 1989).

How do you lose weight, then? According to Gurin, besides changing intra-psychic and social influences (which we will consider in a moment), you must increase your metabolic rate. The most effective way to do that, he claims, is to exercise more and eat a low-fat diet (Gurin, 1989). The gains may be slow. Apparently, lasting changes in metabolic rates are obtained only with intense exercise over long periods of time (Kolata, 1987). But there is also hope that if you do this long enough, you will also lower your "metabolic set point," making it easier to *maintain* your weight loss (LeBow, 1981; Dintiman et al., 1989).

Many overweight people have a low metabolic rate, which means their bodies need very little food to operate. Extra food is stored as fat.

SUGAR, NICOTINE, AND FAT

Almost all of us have known a person who gave up smoking—and who immediately gained several pounds. In the past, psychologists frequently interpreted this weight gain in terms of "eating as a substitute oral activity for smoking." More recently, however, scientists have discovered a series of complex biochemical relationships between nicotine and eating.

First, a group of Swiss researchers report that smoking 24 cigarettes a day increases the energy expenditure of the human body by 10 percent. Giving up cigarettes typically leads to a weight gain of more than 20 pounds, the Swiss scientists say. These researchers believe that nicotine causes the release of noradrenalin, which leads to an increase in physical arousal of the nervous system as we saw in Chapter 2. (Nicotine withdrawal also leads to a marked increase in the weight of rats [Grunberg & Bowen, 1985].)

Second, smoking seems to decrease the need for sweets. According to psychologist Neil Grunberg and his associates, both animals and humans given nicotine tend to choose fewer sweet foods than do subjects not given nicotine. Furthermore, humans who give up smoking tend to be less anxious and hostile—and twice as successful at staying off tobacco—when given a high- rather than a low-carbohydrate diet (Grunberg et al., 1985).

Carbohydrates may also help in another way: Carbohydrates as well as proteins are helpful substitutes for fat. The fat you eat is converted into body fat much more readily than the carbohydrates and proteins you eat. This means that a tablespoon of butter (100 calories) is much more likely to go to your hips than 2 slices of whole-wheat bread (also about 100 calories) (Gurin, 1989).

Thus, your "metabolic set point," and consequently what you weigh, depends in part on what drugs you are taking, the amount of fat you eat, and what exercise you get—as well as on how *much* you eat. You might try to keep these points about the *biology* of weight control in mind as we look at intra-psychic influences on eating and obesity.

Intra-Psychic Influences on Obesity

Consciously or unconsciously, many parents train their children to be overeaters. Sometimes the parents are overweight themselves and, without realizing it, *overfeed* their children in order to make the children like themselves. Other parents may believe that "fatness" and good health are pretty much the same thing. If the usual reward the parents offer the child for good behavior is an extra helping of pie or cake, the child will soon come to associate rich foods with the act of winning parental approval. Food then takes on the *symbolic meaning of love* and acceptance. Later, as an adolescent or young adult, the person may feel a yearning to "raid the refrigerator" whenever she or he feels rejected or disappointed by life (LeBow, 1981).

Data to support this view come from a series of studies by psychoanalyst Hilde Bruch, who found that many overweight people felt unwanted, inadequate, and insecure as children. According to Bruch, these subjects began overeating not only to gain attention from their parents, but also because eating too much made them feel big and important to themselves (Bruch, 1973; Lehman & Rodin, 1989).

In the late 1960s and early 1970s, Stanley Schachter suggested that weight differences might be related to individual differences in perceptual sensitivity. Some people are more sensitive to food and other *external* stimuli around them than other people are. Under the barrage of food advertising in contemporary North America, and the ready availability of high calorie foods, this sensitivity becomes vulnerability—and these "externals" overeat. "Internals," on the other hand, eat when their bodies tell them to—that is, when their stomachs contract and their "feeding centers" are active.

In one set of studies, Schachter showed that externals, who also tend to be overweight, ate "by the clock" rather than eating when their stomachs were contracting. In another study, Schachter showed that externals tend to be "plate cleaners" who eat everything set before them whether they need it or not. Internals, however, paid attention to their stomachs and ate only what they needed, even if this meant "leaving a little something on the plate" (Schachter, 1971).

The *taste* of food also affects externals more than internals. When offered food of average or above-average taste, externals eat a great deal more than internals eat. When offered food of below-average or miserable taste, however, externals eat a great deal *less* than internals do. Externals are also less likely to perform physical labor for food, or to suffer mild amounts of pain to get to eat, than are internals (Schachter, 1971, 1982).

Judith Rodin, one of Schachter's former students, found evidence that we may *inherit* our differences in sensitivity or "responsivity" to external stimuli. Rodin reports that infants show differences in their responsiveness to taste and visual stimuli, even when the infants are less than one day old. Later, when these children enter school, the more responsive children at birth are also more likely to be *overweight* than their less responsive peers (Rodin, 1984). Schachter and Rodin's work suggests that perceptual differences, which are probably present at birth, predispose some people to be overweight—especially in a culture where food and related stimuli are so prevalent.

Joel Gurin suggests that sensitivity differences may also be *acquired*, ironically, as a result of trying to *lose* excess weight. Gurin says that frequent dieting may *increase* our responsiveness to external cues by making us less sensitive to true hunger pangs. As a result we become more likely to lose control of our eating (Gurin, 1989).

When we see people who are extremely overweight, we might assume their problem is that they are greedy, or psychologically immature, (if they don't have a medical difficulty of some kind). That is, we attribute their obesity to some sort of "character defect." But if Schachter, Rodin, and Gurin are right, we do the overweight individual an injustice by presuming the problem is a controllable "weakness." To make this assumption, we have neglected the strong effects that individual differences in perceptual sensitivity have on our eating habits.

We may also be ignoring powerful factors in the overweight person's social environment. Let's look briefly at how our family and culture can influence what and how we eat.

As we noted, James Gibbs and his colleagues found that chemicals released by the gut inhibit the ingestion of bland food, but not of sweet foods. What possible relationship do you see between this fact and Schachter's finding that "externals" will work hard to get rich foods but not bland or bad-tasting foods?

Social/Behavioral Influences on Obesity

The culture you live in plays a great part in controlling what you eat and when you eat it. In some places where food is or has been scarce, "eating regularly and frequently" is not only a habit, but a status symbol of sorts. In other societies, being fat is a sign of wealth.

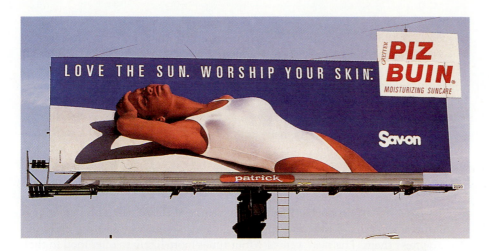

Different cultures may have very different views of "ideal" body size and shape.

For example, the reigning beauty in New York City in the 1890s was Lillian Russell, who weighed 186 pounds. And until recently, in parts of Africa, young girls went into "fattening houses" when they reached puberty so they could gain weight prior to getting married. Anthropologist Claire Cassidy reports that, when she was doing field research in Central America, she began (to her dismay) to gain weight. But, she says, "the fatter I got, the more they admired me. 'Finally,' one woman told me, 'you're starting to look healthy. And furthermore, you are starting to look marriageable'" (cited in Kolata, 1986).

The social class you belong to is also an important factor in determining your weight. People from different social classes have quite different types of eating (and exercise) habits (Plimpton & Regimbal, 1992). Men and women who belong to the wealthiest or "upper class" tend to be thinner, and healthier, and to live longer than do men and women of the so-called "lower class."

Ronald Brone and Celia Fisher believe that *family patterns of interaction* play a major role in the development of obesity, as well as another eating problem we will look at in a moment—anorexia. Obese and anorexic children (mis)use their eating in an attempt to gain some control of their lives in an overprotective and controlling family environment (Brone & Fisher, 1988).

Many of our social needs are pressed upon us by the people around us. Thus, we may overeat because individuals we love may be *rewarded* in various ways when we are fat. Richard Stuart worked for many months with married women who were complete failures at losing weight. Stuart eventually began to suspect that the women's husbands were partially responsible for keeping their wives overweight. To test his hypothesis, Stuart asked these couples to make tape recordings of their dinner-table conversations.

Stuart found that, although all the women were on diets and their husbands knew it, the husbands were 12 times more likely to *criticize* their wives' eating behaviors than to praise them. The men were also four times more likely to offer food to their wives than the wives were to offer food to the husbands (Stuart & Jacobson, 1987). These "food pushing" husbands fell roughly into four groups:

1. Some husbands enjoyed demonstrating their masculine power by coaxing or forcing their wives to become fat. If the wife was overweight, the husband sometimes found this a useful fact to bring up in family arguments. The man could win almost any battle by calling the woman "a fat slob." Stuart believes the husbands realized (perhaps unconsciously) that if the wife lost weight, the husband would lose more arguments.

2. Other husbands viewed dinner time as the main social event of the day. When the wives refused to eat very much, the husbands saw this as a rejection of themselves and the rest of the family group.

3. Some men had lost any sexual interest in their wives. They seemed to want to keep their wives fat as an excuse for their "playing around" with other women. Stuart's data also indicate that the husband lost sexual interest first, and then began rewarding the woman for overeating, rather than losing interest after the wife was already fat.

4. Other husbands apparently feared their wives might be unfaithful to them if the women were too attractive. These men encouraged their wives to overeat in an attempt to make them unattractive—and therefore faithful.

Do you think even a superb therapist could help these women change their eating behaviors unless the husbands were somehow motivated to solve their own psychological problems?

To summarize, obesity is a *multi-determined* problem controlled by a combination of genetic, metabolic, psychological, and environmental events.

WEIGHT CHANGE

Perhaps you are not happy with your weight. You would love to be just a few (or even several) pounds lighter or heavier. Let's look at some factors which you should take into account when designing a weight-change program. After this, we will consider whether or not you gain by losing.

How to Gain or Lose Weight

You eat not just because you've been without food for a while, but also because (1) your blood-sugar level has fallen, (2) your stomach is contracting, (3) your "feeding center" has increased its neural activity, (4) your "satiation center" has decreased its neural activity, (5) your "swallow counter" has been silent for a while, (6) your regular dinner time is approaching, (7) you smell food in the air and hear other people talking about "what's for lunch," and (8) because food and eating have a variety of symbolic values for you. Obviously, then, if you want to gain or lose weight, your dietary program must take into account not just the amount and type of calories you consume, and how you burn them up, but your *motives* and *habits*, and your *perceptions* and *emotions*, as well as the behavior of the people around you.

If you wish to embark on a well-rounded weight-loss or weight-gain program, the first thing you should do is to have a medical check-up. That way you can make sure you are not that one North American in 20 who is under- or overweight because you have a physical problem of some kind. If you want to gain or lose more than 10–20 pounds, you probably should do so under medical guidance. Your physician may wish to prescribe drugs to help increase or decrease your appetite, and may also send you to see a registered dietician.

However, diets and pills are only the first step in a long journey. The real problem usually lies in learning enough about yourself to recognize what internal and external *stimulus inputs* affect your eating behavior. You must somehow *measure* these inputs, and their consequences, and then change the way you react to these inputs.

If you wish to gain or lose weight, you might consider using *cognitive behavior modification* to help you. A variety of studies show this approach yields the best long-term results as far as controlling your weight is concerned (LeBow, 1981; Stuart & Jacobson, 1987). Cognitive behavior modification is a *tool* to help you change long-standing habits—in this case, habits related to eating and exercise. For it is only through a permanent change in these patterns of behavior that you will be able to keep from regaining the weight you lose (or losing the weight you gain) (Simon, 1989). Weight loss through cognitive behavior modification involves:

1. Taking a **baseline** of present food intake so that you know clearly what you have to change (probably reducing calories, and especially reducing fats).

2. Establishing goals, both ultimate goals and intermediate goals along the way.

3. Exercising to increase your metabolism and eventually lower your weight set point.

4. Keeping precise records of food-related activities, in order to identify those that need to be changed.

5. Establishing personal and social rewards for progress.

We will discuss cognitive behavior modification more in Chapter 9, but as a way of summarizing what you have learned about weight control, consider the following question:

Can you design a weight-control program that takes advantage of biological, intra-psychic, and social influences in order to succeed where "fad diets" fail?

To Lose or Not to Lose

But is thinness all it's supposed to be? Perhaps not. In a recent 16-year-long study of 17,000 Harvard alumni, those men who had gained less than 15 pounds since graduation had a 30 percent *higher* death rate than those men who had gained 25 pounds

"Are you eating properly and getting plenty of exercise?"

Baseline. The record of behavior *before* any change is attempted. The starting point.

or more. The researchers point out, however, that the "skinny group" included many more cigarette smokers and that men in this group tended to exercise less (Labich, 1986).

Then what about dieting? Some research suggests it may actually be *counter-pro-ductive*. Whenever you diet, your metabolism slows down, and so (typically) does your activity level. Thus, you actually *need* less food when dieting than when eating normally (Dintiman et al., 1989). Furthermore, recent studies suggest that the more frequently you diet, the more efficiently your body metabolizes food, and the more slowly you lose weight (Kolata, 1986). Therefore, the more times you try to diet, the harder it becomes to achieve your weight-loss goals. And, finally, if all this isn't enough, when you diet without exercising, you lose fat *and* lean muscle. If you put the weight on again without exercising, it is mostly fat (Sizer & Whitney, 1988).

And what about those charts of "ideal weight"? Should we slavishly adhere to them? Joel Gurin points out that people who are less than 20 percent over the accepted medical standard are at relatively little risk from their weight. Apparently, extra weight is more dangerous when we gain it on the abdomen (as men usually do) than when we gain it on our hips (as women usually do) (Gurin, 1989). Weight control expert Kelly Brownell suggests our goal should be "leanness not lightness." The real threat to our health, if we are overweight, is from fat. The real goal of our diet and exercise program should be to reduce body fat. If we are exercising as well as dieting, as most experts recommend, we will lose fat but *gain* muscle. And we might not actually lose *weight* at all. However, since muscle takes up less room than fat, and improves our overall appearance, we will still be pleased with the results. Brownell suggests we gauge our improvement with a tape measure rather than a scale (Brownell, 1989).

Finally, we need to keep weight loss in perspective. We have seen how our friends, family, and culture can exert tremendous pressure on us to reach some "ideal" weight—one which actually changes from culture to culture and even within the same culture from time to time. Most experts agree these pressures are a major factor in the eating disorders we will consider next.

EATING DISORDERS

So far, we've talked mostly about the problems associated with being overweight. However, there are also a number of eating disorders that are related to being too thin—or to attempts to maintain a low weight through rather unusual eating behaviors.

The two major types of eating disorders associated with abnormal concern for thinness are **anorexia** (or anorexia nervosa) and **bulimia** (or bulimia nervosa). *Anorexia* involves self-induced starvation, even to the point of death. *Bulimia* is also known as the "binge-purge" syndrome.

Statistically speaking, not everyone is equally likely to develop anorexia or bulimia. In North America, you are most likely to develop one of these disorders if you are a white upper-class woman. Both anorexia and bulimia are about ten times as likely to affect women as men, and both disorders are found primarily among young upper-middle-class and upper-class whites (Bell & Kirkpatrick 1986; Mahowald, 1992).

According to Margaret Balentine and her colleagues, young black females and members of other minority groups seem to have a more realistic perception of their body weight than white females do. As a result, they are not so overly preoccupied with thinness and at risk for eating disorders (Balentine et al., 1991; Wadden et al., 1990).

Anorexia (an-or-REX-ee-ah). From the Greek words meaning no appetite. A psychological disorder that involves self-starvation in order to achieve certain unusual or "disordered" personal goals.

Bulimia (boo-LEE-me-ah). From the Greek words meaning "great hunger." A psychological disorder that involves massive overeating, usually followed by an attempt to purge the body of the food.

Andres Pumariega points out, however, that Hispanic females who showed greater adaptation to North American culture, also showed increasingly disordered attitudes towards eating (Pumariega, 1986). And several researchers suggest that eating disorders may be increasing among Hispanics and young black females, especially in the middle and professional classes (Balentine et al., 1991; Pumariega et al., 1984; Silber, 1984, 1986).

Anorexia

Hilde Bruch was one of the first psychiatrists to take an interest in anorexia. She states there are two types, *primary* (or true) anorexia, and *atypical* anorexia. Primary anorexia is a pathological fear of "being fat." The disorder is found primarily in young women in their teens. A woman suffering from this condition usually has a skeleton-like appearance. She also denies that she is abnormal in any way, but strives actively to maintain all her abnormal behavior patterns.

Atypical anorexia, Bruch says, differs from primary anorexia in just one important way. The woman knows her behaviors are abnormal, but feels helpless about changing them (Bruch, 1973).

THREE SYMPTOMS OF ANOREXIA

The chart in this section lists some symptoms associated with anorexia. According to Bruch, there are three main symptoms that define primary anorexia. First, the anorexic woman has a false perception of her body image. Thus, even though the woman weighs but 80 pounds, she may perceive herself as "grossly fat." So she starves herself and frequently engages in abnormal amounts of exercise. If she doesn't receive help, the woman may well starve herself to death in a desperate attempt to "avoid obesity."

The second symptom is a disturbance in the manner in which the woman "processes" bodily sensations. Bruch believes many overweight individuals confuse arousal with hunger. Therefore, she says, they eat when they are frightened or stressed in any way. The anorexic woman, on the other hand, does just the opposite: She confuses hunger with stress. When her body gives her "hunger signals," she *interprets* them as signs of stress or fear. Therefore, she denies that she feels hungry, insisting she is merely "anxious" or even "depressed" instead.

The third symptom is that of abnormally low self-esteem. Bruch says the anorexic woman typically perceives herself as "enslaved by others, exploited by family and friends, and thus incapable of living a life of her own." Therefore, she isolates herself from "the exploiting others" whenever she can. And her refusal to eat, Bruch believes, is really a "struggle to attain self-respect." By not eating, she attempts to show others (and herself) that she can maintain some *control* over her life (Bruch, 1978).

THE ANOREXIC'S FAMILY

According to Bruch, the family plays an important role in bringing about the anorexic disorder. Almost all anorexic women are from the upper class, or from the top levels of the middle class. Bruch states that few parents of anorexic women are sensitive to the problems their daughters experience. The parents tend to carry an "idealized image" of the young woman in their minds which is quite different from reality. Bruch claims that treatment of anorexia is seldom successful unless the parents participate actively, and unless they are willing to change the way in which they perceive and relate to their daughter (Bruch, 1978; Mahowald, 1992).

Psychiatrist Arnold Andersen takes a more *holistic* view of anorexia than does Bruch. He believes that both anorexia and bulimia are caused by an *interaction* among sociocultural, psychological, familial, and biological factors that *predispose*

Anorexia is found primarily in middle-upper-class women and upper class women. Singer Karen Carpenter, shown here with her brother Richard Carpenter, died of a heart ailment brought on by anorexia.

SOME SYMPTOMS ASSOCIATED WITH ANOREXIA
(Found primarily in upper– and upper–middle–class women)

Substantial weight loss (20% or more)
Anxiety about being fat
Distorted body image (overestimates body size)*
Denial of hunger*
Distorted, implacable attitude toward eating
Amenorrhea (cessation of menses)
Low self-esteem*
May practice self-induced vomiting or purging
May exercise relentlessly
May have unusual food habits and rituals
May show preoccupation or obsession with food
May be depressed, unable to concentrate, withdrawn

---

*A symptom of primary anorexia defined by Bruch.

the individual toward a given eating disorder. Treatment, according to Andersen, must involve not merely family therapy, but intra-psychic counseling and behavioral retraining as well (Andersen, 1985; Harris et al., 1991; Wadden et al., 1990).

THE MALE ANOREXIC

In her 1983 book *The Slender Balance,* Susan Squire states that about 10 percent of anorexic patients are males. Male anorexics differ from female anorexics in several ways. For one thing, the males frequently are homosexuals, while the females are chiefly heterosexual. The women tend to be overachievers; the males, underachievers. The women often develop "work rituals" and are almost obsessive about being "orderly." The men usually are hard workers, but their attempts at getting things done are often ineffectual and haphazard. And the families of male anorexics typically are more "emotionally disturbed" than are the families of female patients, Squire says (Squire, 1983).

Squire believes that male anorexics are much more difficult to treat than are women patients. However, the "success rate" for therapy with either male or female anorexics is fairly low (Herzog & Keller, 1988).

How can you "eat your cake" and not have it too?

Bulimia

Bulimia is an eating disorder characterized by "binges" of caloric intake followed by desperate attempts to get rid of the food consumed. The three most common ways of ridding the body of the food are self-induced vomiting, "purging" (using laxatives), and post-binge starvation.

Anorexia and bulimia are similar in some ways, different in others. Like the anorexic patient, the bulimic individual tends to fear "fatness" and to prize "thinness." And both types of disorders are found primarily in upper-middle-class and upper-class individuals. However, the bulimic individual seldom denies reality to the extent that anorexics do. Indeed, the "binge-purge" person often feels guilty about his or her behaviors and hides them from family and friends as much as possible. In addition, most bulimic individuals engage in "binge-purge" activities only on occasion, but most anorexics starve themselves continuously (Striegel-Moore et al., 1986). (Anorexics who binge occasionally may be classified "anorexia nervosa: bulimic type" (Walsh, 1992).)

Anorexics are usually extremely thin. Most people who suffer from bulimia, however, are of normal weight. A few are even overweight.

Bulimia is much more common than is anorexia. According to psychologists Janet Polivy and Peter Herman, recent surveys of college populations have found a high incidence (13–67 percent) of self-reported binge eating in "normal," nonclinical samples (Polivy & Herman, 1985). Binging becomes bulimia when it occurs at least twice a week for at least 3 months, when body shape and weight unduly influence self-evaluation, and when strict dieting, fasting, exercise, or purging are used (Walsh, 1992).

Bulimics almost always "binge" on rich, sweet foods. How might this fact be related to James Gibbs' finding that chemicals released by the gut inhibit the consumption of bland foods, but not the consumption of sweet-tasting foods?

There are almost as many viewpoints toward what causes bulimia—and how best to treat the problem—as there are professionals working to solve the mysteries of this odd disorder. For example, in a recent book, psychiatrists Harrison Pope Jr. and

Bulimics feel compelled to eat totally unreasonable quantities of food.

James Hudson report that two-thirds of the bulimic patients they treat also suffer from depression. Some patients "binge" in order to fight feelings of depression, Pope and Hudson say. However, others "pig out" and then feel depressed because of their failure to exercise self-control.

Consider a conversation Pope and Hudson had with a 21-year-old bulimic woman named Susan: "It would start to build in the late morning. By noon, I'd know I had to binge. I would go out . . . and buy a gallon . . . of maple-walnut ice cream and a couple of packages of fudge brownie mix—enough to make 72 brownies. . . . I'd stop the car, buy a dozen doughnuts. . . . On the way home I invariably finished all 12 doughnuts. . . . I'd hastily mix up the brownie mix and get the brownies in the oven . . . then, while they were cooking, I'd hit the ice cream. Sometimes I'd finish the whole gallon even before the brownies were done, and I'd take the brownies out of the oven while they were still baking. Seventy-two brownies later, the depression would begin to hit" (Pope & Hudson, 1984).

Janet Polivy and Peter Herman believe that *prior dieting* causes most "binge attacks." First, the bulimic individual tries to lose weight by going on a diet. But since the individual *lacks internal self-control,* the person fails. Considering himself or herself a complete failure, the person then just gives up and "pigs out." Therapy for bulimics that involves any form of dieting typically will fail, Polivy and Herman say, for dieting merely triggers another "failure/binge" attack. They believe that treatment should focus on training bulimics in self-awareness and self-control (Polivy & Herman, 1985).

Maria Root, Patricia Fallon, and William Friedrich take rather a different view of bulimia. They see the disorder as resulting primarily from the *socialization* that often occurs in three specific types of North American families: the "perfect" family, the "overprotective" family, and the "chaotic" family. Root, Fallon, and Friedrich take a *holistic* approach to treatment, one that includes the use of drugs, group therapy, intra-psychic treatment, and behavior therapy. Their treatment involves both the patient and his or her entire family (Root et al., 1986).

Finally, psychiatrists Harrison Pope and James Hudson view bulimia almost entirely from a biological point of view. They claim that most bulimic patients suffer from depression, and are best treated with anti-depressant drugs (Pope & Hudson, 1984). As we will see in Chapter 16, however, the use of these drugs typically *causes* as many problems as it *cures.*

Compulsive runners, who are most often middle-aged men, have been shown to share many personality traits with anorexic women.

Compulsive Eating and Compulsive Running

Alayne Yates, Kevin Leehey, and Catherine Shisslak compare "compulsive runners" to "compulsive eaters" (bulimics) and "compulsive non-eaters" (anorexics). These behavioral scientists define *compulsive runners* as "those who are consumed by running, who run in spite of illness, and who suffer depression when they cannot run." The typical compulsive runner is an upper-middle-class or upper-class male. Like anorexic women, these men tend to be "introverted, compliant, self-effacing, and unable to express anger." Most compulsive runners are high achievers, just as anorexic women tend to be. And, like anorexic women, most of these men have "an unstable self-concept," according to Yates, Leehey, and Shisslak. The men perceive themselves as "out of shape" even when they are "dangerously overtrained," just as anorexic women perceive themselves as "grossly fat" even when they are mere skeletons. There are differences, however. The men tend to focus on controlling "physical strength," while the women tend to focus on slimness. And the disorder hits women during adolescence, while it primarily appears in men during middle age (Yates et al., 1983; McDonald & Thompson, 1992).

Yates, Leehey, and Shisslak believe that the self-destructive behaviors associated with anorexia and compulsive running become *self-rewarding* because they lead to the release of endorphins, the body's "natural painkillers." According to these researchers, anorexic women often have elevated *endorphin* levels. These women also often report that starvation gives them a euphoric feeling similar to "runner's high." Thus, both anorexia and compulsive running may be learned reactions to social or personal stress that are maintained by the release of biological reinforcers— endorphins (Leehey et al., 1984).

Symptom Choice in Eating Disorders

There is almost no life-sustaining behavior that isn't considered abnormal if you engage it in too frequently—or too infrequently. Sleep, sex, and eating all offer evidence supporting this statement. The question then becomes, if you depart from the norm, why do you deviate in one direction and not the other?

Generally speaking, disordered behaviors are as multi-determined as are "ordered" activities. Some people overeat in response to stress, while others undereat when faced with the same problems (Grunberg & Straub, 1992). The *choice* between undereating and overeating, however, is clearly affected by biological, intra-psychic, and social factors. Unfortunately, "symptom choice" is a problem we can only speculate about at the moment, for scientists have gathered little valid data in this area.

We will understand "symptom choice" a little more clearly if we first examine a very different kind of motive—the motive to accomplish, to excel, to *achieve*.

ACHIEVEMENT MOTIVATION

Imagine you volunteer for a psychology experiment and it turns out to be a simple "ring-toss" game. The experimenter gives you several rings to toss over a peg which stands upright on the floor. The experimenter tells you that you can stand as close to the peg or as far back as you like. You take the rings, stand far enough back to make it interesting, and begin to toss. Several rings go onto the peg, and several rings miss.

It may surprise you to find out that the experimenter was probably studying **achievement motivation.** Researcher David McClelland believes that individuals as well as whole societies differ in their motivation to compete and succeed, that is, to

Achievement motivation. The desire to compete, to excel, to master a task. It has been studied in individuals, groups, or even whole cultures.

achieve (McClelland, 1961). McClelland uses the ring-toss game to study the way different people seek achievement satisfaction. When you stand "far enough back to make it interesting," you reveal a significant need for achievement—too close and there's no satisfaction in success, too far back and success is almost impossible.

Achievement and Culture

Achievement motivation is an example of a motive that has very strong intra-psychic and social components. McClelland believes that you learn achievement motivation primarily from your family and culture.

This raises an important consideration for comparing achievement in different cultures. For one thing, different cultures associate achievement with different goals. Most North Americans, for example, place a high value on *individual* achievement. But Japanese and ethnic Hawaiians emphasize affiliation and *group* success (DeVos, 1968; Gallimore, 1974). Filipinos and Indians strive for *social approval* over personal performance (Church & Katigbak, 1992; Triandis, 1972). And some cultures (and some ethnic groups within a multi-cultural society) simply value achievement more than other cultures and groups do. As a result of these differences, many North Americans misinterpret a lack of personal assertiveness and self-promotion as laziness and negligence when they meet individuals from other backgrounds.

Where there is a desire for North American–style achievement, McClelland has demonstrated that appropriate behavior can be taught. In one project, McClelland and his associates trained businessmen in Hyderabad, India, to think, talk, and act like people who are high in achievement motivation. In the two years following training, McClelland found that compared to an untrained group, the trained group started more new businesses, invested more money in their businesses, and hired more than twice as many new employees (McClelland & Winter, 1971).

Not surprisingly, business, government, and education leaders in the Western world have shown considerable interest in motivating achievement (Maehr, 1987; Singh, 1989; Wehrung-Schaffner & Sapona, 1990). In fact, according to Raymond Katzell and his associates, work motivation is a topic of much current interest in the area of **industrial-organizational psychology** (Katzell & Austin, 1992; Katzell & Thompson, 1990).

But achievement is not as simple as it might seem at first.

Industrial-organizational psychology. Psychologists in this field study behavior in the world of business. Their goal is to enhance the effectiveness of human performance through improving areas such as personnel selection, job training, motivation, feedback, and incentives.

Attribution and Locus of Control

Imagine once again that you are in the ring-toss experiment. This time you decide to stand way back—say, 15 feet from the target. You throw and it's a ringer! What are you thinking? "Boy, am I good. Hand-eye coordination always was a strong point with me." You feel pretty good about yourself. But what if you miss, and you continue to miss the next 20 shots in a row? What do you say? "Bad luck. The situation is against me. No one could be expected to hit from back here."

These two situations illustrate a frequent response to success and failure. When we succeed, we like to attribute the cause of the success to our own internal abilities. When we fail, we like to attribute the failure to external conditions (Weiner, 1980).

Sometimes, however, we do just the opposite. When we succeed we say it was "good fortune," or a "lucky break—couldn't happen again in a million years." If we fail we might say, "I knew I couldn't do it. This just proves what I knew all along, I have no talent for this sort of thing." As you can easily see, if this pattern of attribution becomes a habit, our self-esteem suffers and we may even become depressed.

The two types of attribution—for success and failure—which we have been discussing are represented in the opposing corners of Figure 6.5. Actually we have been considering extremes. Most often, people are fairly consistent in their attribution of

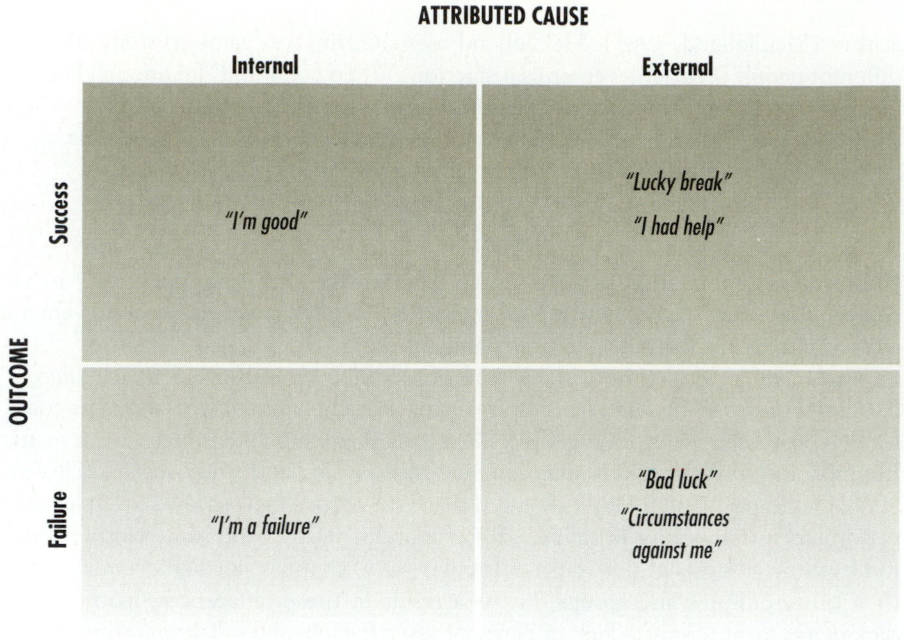

ATTRIBUTED CAUSE

FIGURE 6.5

Some cognitive reponses as a result of different outcomes and attributed causes.

Locus of control. A belief about the primary source of control for your behavior—either internal (within yourself) or external (in your physical and social environment).

Cognitive motivation. The study of cognitive motivation emphasizes the thinking, judging, and deciding, which leads to action.

causes to either internal or external influences. "Internalizers" tend to attribute *either* success *or* failure to their own abilities. They believe they have control over what happens to them; we say they have an "internal **locus of control.**" "Externalizers" attribute *both* successes *and* failures to their environment. They tend to believe they have no control over what happens to them; we say they have an "external locus of control" (Rotter, 1972, 1982). These possibilities are represented in the vertical columns of Figure 6.5. We will have more to say about locus of control in Chapter 8.

How could the attributions you make about your weight gain or loss affect your attitudes towards changing your weight and even your "symptom choice?"

Cognitive Motivation

In order to understand your achievement motivation we need to know something about your cultural background (Duda & Allison, 1989), and we also need to examine your "cognitions," or thoughts, including attribution processes and locus of control. These thoughts represent your **cognitive motivation.** When we study intra-psychic and social factors in cognitive motivation, we are not assuming that biological influences do not exist. The study of cognitive motivation *assumes* that you are physically aroused and active and that your cognitions are directing or "steering" your behavior. In the case of achievement, the roots of the motive may lie in the innate need to master the environment in order to survive (Spence, 1985). However, the study of cognitive motivation emphasizes your *thoughts* about your situation, your *thoughts* about your behavior, and your *intentions* and *choices* (Mook, 1987; Heckhausen & Beckmann, 1990).

THE CONCEPT OF CHOICE

There is a great deal more to the field of motivation than just those behaviors, thoughts, and emotions involved in eating or achieving. The field of motivation also includes thirst, aggression, sexuality, parenting, stress, love, the desire to be with

Motivation can be viewed as primarily a *choice* between alternatives.

others, and thousands of other motives. We will discuss sexual motivation in Chapter 7, stress and emotionality in Chapter 8, and the influence of motivation on learning in Chapter 9, love and parenting in Chapters 12 and 13, and social motives in Chapters 17 and 18. However, now that we've looked at two examples of motives, perhaps you can understand several things about *all types of motivation* better than when you started the chapter. For example, probably you can now see why a simple question such as, "Why do some people overeat?" is so difficult to answer. Even when we attempt to study the simplest of human behaviors, there are biological, intra-psychic, and social influences that we must always take into account.

Several theorists prefer to describe motivation as a *choice* among options that biological, psychological, and environmental factors present to us. Scott Ridley calls it a "self-determining process" involving *intentions* (Ridley, 1991). Robert Bolles thinks of motivation as a "response selector mechanism." Bolles notes that you are always active, always doing something, even if that "something" is just daydreaming or watching television. Thus, you are always *aroused* (behaviorally speaking) both to your external world and to your internal thoughts and needs (Bolles, 1975). According to Bolles, you "behave" when you (1) respond to external stimulation, or (2) commit yourself to some course of action. In extreme situations, your physical needs will probably govern your responses. But in most circumstances, you will *select* the one thing you want to do "right now" from a long list of possible actions. And the factors that most influence (but do not totally determine) what you select are your past experiences and your present social environment (Bolles, 1978, 1979).

What "moves" you? According to Bolles, *you move yourself*. True, many of your actions are fairly predictable—but only if we know a great deal about who you are, what you have experienced in the past, and what your present environment is like.

Life's business being just the terrible choice.

ROBERT BROWNING

The study of motivation, then, boils down to knowing as much as we can about you and your own set of personal choices.

To repeat our opening point from David Edwards, motivation is a set of questions we ask in order to determine why you do what you do. As you must realize by now, those questions are so numerous and so complex that you may never answer them to your complete satisfaction. However, the study of human behavior remains a delightful and rewarding journey for most people. And a journey of a thousand miles begins with the *motivation* to take the first step.

SUMMARY

1. **Motivation** is an internal state or condition that guides our behavior and gives it direction. It may be seen as a series of questions about *why* people do what they do.

2. Many "why" questions involve human **needs**—what kinds of needs do you have, are these needs **learned** or **innate,** what are the **mechanisms** by which you satisfy your needs, and do you exercise any voluntary **choice** over your behavior patterns?

3. Motivation implies **movement.** Ancient scholars differentiated between objects that were **animate** or "self-movers" and those that were not.

4. According to Maslow, human needs can be placed on a **hierarchy** with five levels: **biological, safety, belongingness, esteem,** and **self-actualization** needs.

5. **Drive theory** focuses primarily on biological needs. Clark Hull assumed that associated with each physical need was a **primary drive.** Whenever your body lacks something needed for life, the appropriate drive increases, causing you pain and thus motivating you to satisfy that need and return your body to **homeostasis.**

6. Hull assumed that **secondary needs** or social needs were learned by being associated with the pleasures that accompany primary **drive reduction.**

7. Criticisms of drive theory include the fact that you have **information** needs as well as **energy needs,** and the fact that some social behaviors seem innately determined rather than being learned.

8. **Arousal theory** was developed by Elizabeth Duffy to counter the criticisms of Hull's drive theory. Duffy assumed that homeostasis is a point of **optimum arousal,** and that a decrease in sensory inputs can be as arousing as an increase in biological drives. The optimum homeostatic **set point** changes from moment to moment.

9. At a biological level, the **hunger drive** is affected by **blood-sugar level** and *insulin level.* When you go without food, your **hypothalamic feeding center** detects a decrease in blood sugar molecules and corresponding increase in **insulin** level and motivates you to eat.

10. Your **hypothalamus** also contains your **satiation center** which, when stimulated, causes you to stop eating. Hunger pangs are also affected by your **swallow counter,** by your knowledge of how much you have already eaten, by **conditioned stomach contractions,** and by your **metabolic rate.** Chemicals released by the gut decrease consumption of bland foods but not **sweet-tasting foods.**

11. **Intra-psychic influences** on obesity include the fact that some parents train their children to be fat, thus giving overeating a **symbolic value.**

12. **Social/behavioral influences** on obesity include the fact that in some cultures fatness suggests wealth, and that some **social classes** place more of a premium on thinness than do others. Your desired weight is also influenced by the people around you. For example, **insecure husbands** may reward their wives for remaining fat.

13. A successful **weight-loss program** will consider biological, intra-psychic, and social influences on eating behavior. **Cognitive behavior modification** has been shown to be a very effective tool for losing weight.

14. **Cognitive behavior modification** is a method for changing behavior. It relies on the use of principles of learning and takes account of the thought processes which are involved in the behavior.

15. The most common **eating disorders** are anorexia (self-starvation) and **bulimia** (the "binge-purge" syndrome). Both disorders affect primarily upper- and upper-middle-class women who have **a distorted self-image** and low **self-esteem.**

16. Men with similar social backgrounds and psychological problems as female anorexics often engage in **compulsive running.**

17. The study of **cognitive motivation** is the study of the thought processes involved in considering, evaluating and deciding upon an action.

18. **Achievement motivation** is an example of a motive strongly influenced by **cognitive** factors such as **attribution** processes, and **locus of control** orientation.

19. According to Robert Bolles, for the most part, humans are not *driven* to behave, but appear to be able to **choose** which behavior patterns are most satisfying to them.

ANSWERS FOR THOUGHT

1. *How far up the ladder would a frequently abused child be likely to climb? Or a student whose teachers . . . ?*

   These people would be limited in their growth because they would be forced to spend extra time and energy trying to satisfy safety and esteem needs instead of moving to higher needs.

2. *What similarities do you see between the concept of homeostasis and the Gestalt Law of Pragnanz discussed in Chapter 4?*

   Both suggest there is a pressure to move towards stability.

3. *What position do drive theorists appear to be taking in solving the mind-body problem?*

   Drive theorists appear to take a "monist" position on the mind-body problem. They assume that all behaviors, including those which might be called mental, arise from the reduction of biological drives. The mind depends on the body; the body controls the mind.

4. *Some people occasionally "pig out" on rich foods, then starve themselves for days afterward. Why would . . . ?*

   Neither "pigging out" nor self-starvation are explained by a simple homeostatic need for food (where the homeostatic set-point does not change). Duffy's theory predicts that an optimum level of satisfaction, such as how much food you want, is affected by your past experiences and your surrounding conditions. Both "pigging out" and self-starvation could be the result of these intra-psychic and social/behavioral factors.

5. *In Chapter 5, we noted that certain drugs such as LSD lead to a stressful experience called . . . ?*

   If we have a basic need to predict and control our inputs, then anything which disrupts our ability to predict and control would be very unpleasant.

6. *Why do you think the attitude toward obese people is such a socially acceptable form of prejudice?*

   It is a common notion that obesity is the fault of the obese person—that if the obese person tried hard enough, he or she could be thin. And since contemprary Western society has made thinness an ideal, obese people are seen to be *intentionally* violating the standard of thinness. Therefore, (the reasoning goes), they have brought the negative attitudes of other on themselves.

7. *From a motivational point of view, fat people might be overweight for at least four reasons: (1) They . . . ?*

The most effective therapy is one which is focussed directly on the source of the problem. Since people are overweight for different reasons, the therapy which is most effective will be different for different people. Focussing on sources of obesity which are not a problem for a person may be a discouraging waste of effort.

8. *Morley and Levine report that naloxone reduces eating, but not other stress-related "oral behaviors." Many . . . ?*

Stress apparently leads to oral behavior, including food consumption. If the link with food is blocked, either by naloxone, the knowledge that one is not hungry, the unavailability of food, or some other factor, then other non-food oral behaviors will predominate. (We might also expect people to chew gum under stress.)

9. *Why do both your hunger "pangs" and your stomach contractions tend to decrease after lunch even though you didn't eat anything?*

These physiological symptoms of hunger tend to become associated with the time of day when you usually eat. They increase as the time approaches, and decrease as it passes—even if you haven't eaten. They are *conditioned* responses. (We will discuss conditioning in Chapter 9.)

10. *As we noted, James Gibbs and his colleagues found that chemicals released by the gut inhibit . . . ?*

Apparently, the mechanism studied by Gibbs is working in the externals, shutting down their hunger for most foods. But since this mechanism doesn't affect their desire for sweet foods, other factors, such as past experience, and the attractiveness of the foods, continue to motivate them to eat.

11. *Do you think even a superb therapist could help these women change their eating behaviors unless . . . ?*

If the women's relationships with their husbands are important to the women, and if the husbands continue to encourage overeating, then a successful program of weight loss *must* deal with the husbands as a major cause of the problem. In fact, if weight loss is somehow achieved *without* treating the husbands, the husbands' problems may even intensify, causing them to exert new pressure on their wives and their relationships.

12. *Can you design a weight-control program that takes advantage of biological, intra-psychic, and . . . ?*

The most successful diet programs, such as "Weight Watchers," use all three factors. For example, they not only provide explicit information on food intake, but they also encourage a positive attitude towards weight loss, and they use social factors such as group meetings to reinforce their program.

13. *How can you "eat your cake" and not have it too?*

Bulimics, and some anorexics, are so disturbed by the amount they have eaten that they will try to "get rid of" what they have eaten before it digests. They frequently use self-induced vomiting, and occasionally, heavy doses of laxatives.

14. *Bulimics almost always "binge" on rich, sweet foods. How might this fact be related to . . . ?*

Once the bulimic's physical needs for food are satisfied, the chemical inhibitor from the gut makes bland foods unappealing. Therefore, if eating is to continue, sweet foods must be found.

15. *How could the attributions you make about your weight gain or loss affect your attitudes towards . . . ?*

If you attribute your weight to inherited physiological factors (beyond your control), you are less likely to try to change, than if you attribute your weight to intra-psychic or social factors (controllable). And you are more likely to choose a "symptom" for which you perceive an acceptable cause (probably one over which you have no control).

CHAPTER 7

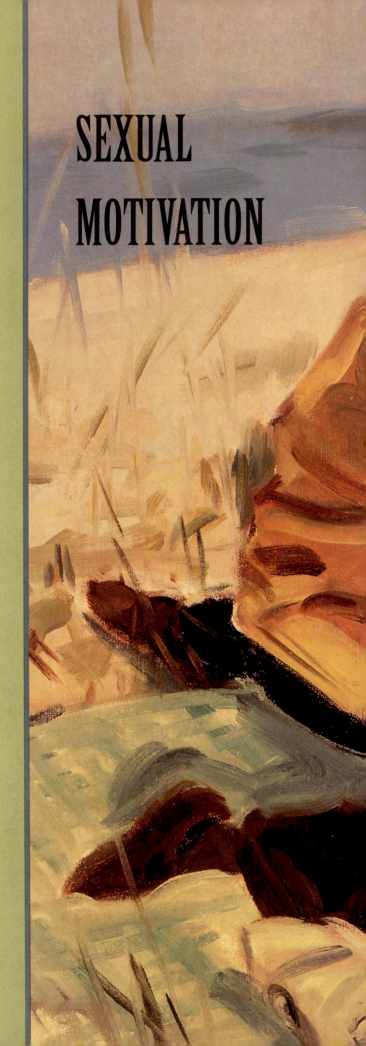

SEXUAL MOTIVATION

But Robert thought women were different. And he expressed, better than any woman with whom I'd talked, why women and men may be reacting differently to the threat of AIDS, why women may be so much more serious about it.

"Women have an innate sense of their physical being," he said. "They menstruate. They have these serious things going on in their bodies that men don't. We have this thing between our legs that doesn't change—it doesn't put us through any cycles; we don't have to have contact with our bodies. But women have to deal with their bodies all the time. Birth control generally falls to the women. And it's going to be women who put the brakes on, especially since it seems that it's the women who are being infected by the men, more than vice versa.

"I have a friend who has the best attitude about sex: He just says, 'Listen, I don't want it to fall off. You've only got one—it doesn't grow back. And I'm gonna know the girl before we have sex.' And he stands by it. It comes down to just being responsible for yourself."

DAVID SEELEY
TOO COOL TO GET MARRIED

SEXUAL MOTIVATION

R obert, in *Too Cool to Get Married*, believes that biological differences between men and women cause women to *think* about sex differently. In addition, the *behavior* of other people, especially men, contributes to womens' *attitudes* to sexual behavior. Thus, Robert sees sexual motivation and sexual behavior as a result of biological, intra-psychic, and social/behavioral factors.

In this chapter we will examine how these factors account for sexual motivation across a broad range of male/female differences. This is a complex topic which we can examine in only a limited fashion in a single chapter. In the first part of the chapter we will look at the questions, "How are males and females different?" and "How do they get that way?" In the second part of the chapter we will turn our attention to some sexual *behaviors*. This will lead us to look at sexual *values* and the process of choice. But before we do either of these, we need to consider how we learn about sex.

Learning about Sex

Sex has always posed something of a problem for the psychologist. It would seem that sexual needs should be explainable in the same terms as are hunger, thirst, and the other biological needs. However, there is a crucial difference: Food, air, and water are necessary for the survival of the *individual*; sex is not. (Although it is necessary for the survival of the human race.) And unlike hunger and other motives sex involves at least two different sets of behavior patterns, *male* and *female*. Men and women breathe the same way, drink the same way, eat the same way. But their sexual behaviors are typically very different, and so presumably their sexual motivations are different, too. Thus, because sex involves unique behavior with unique motivation, psychologists have problems with sex.

In Chapter 6 we said that the study of human motivation is really an attempt to answer questions about *why* people do what they do. And we noted that the answers to these questions must tell us why people *begin* a certain activity, why the behavior

Men and women satisfy most of their needs in the same way—for example, they eat the same foods. Sexually, however, most men and women exhibit two different behavior patterns.

goes the *direction* is does, why it *continues* for a period of time, and why it eventually stops.

When it comes to sex, however, psychologists have difficulty with these questions. Most people assume that sexual behavior *begins* because of some innately determined "sex drive." And there are some data suggesting a connection between hormone levels and sexual activities. However, hormones don't determine how we *feel* about being male or female (our gender). Hormones don't control the *directions* in which sexual desires take us (our sexual orientation). And hormones have little to do with the *patterns* of behavior we consider to be masculine or feminine (our gender-roles). Nor can we appeal to hormones for an explanation of why some people are *inhibited* in their sexual activities, or why a particular sex act may be *prohibited* in some societies but allowed in others (Tavris & Wade, 1984).

One reason for our ignorance is the difficulty many people have in being objective about human sexuality. But suppose we try to put our preconceptions aside, and look at two things: what we know about sexual motivation and behaviors, and why our knowledge of these subjects has been so difficult to gain.

Early Research

Early research on sexuality began with physicians who believed that many of the "abnormal" sexual behaviors reported by their patients were not as unusual as the patients thought. Two of the most significant 19th-century investigators were Havelock Ellis in England and Sigmund Freud in Austria.

Ellis believed that his patients' sexual "deviations" (such as masturbation) were usually harmless, and he urged his patients, as well as society, to accept a broader range of sexual expression. Freud was convinced that sex was the *primary* motivator of human behavior. He believed that childhood sexuality shaped the personality and influenced the behavior of virtually *every* adult.

Ellis and Freud published their views and information about their patients' sex lives in the last decade of the 19th century and the first few decades of the 20th century. Their work helped to make sexuality a more acceptable topic of conversation and research (Byer & Shainberg, 1991; Hyde, 1990).

WATSON'S STUDIES

The most controversial early research was conducted by John B. Watson (who also started the behaviorist tradition in psychology). In 1929 Watson wrote that sex "is admittedly the most important subject in life. . . . And yet our scientific information is so meager. Even the few facts that we have must be looked upon as more or less bootlegged stuff" (Watson, 1929). By "bootlegged stuff" Watson meant the information that physicians like Ellis and Freud had collected from their patients.

In 1917 Watson tackled the issue directly by constructing a set of instruments to measure the physical responses of a woman during sexual intercourse. Watson's wife refused to participate in such a project. Watson, however, apparently talked his laboratory assistant, Rosalie Rayner, into serving as a subject.

With Rayner's help, Watson gathered what were probably the first reliable data on the female sexual response. Watson's wife eventually discovered why her husband was spending so much time in the laboratory. She not only sued him for divorce, she also confiscated the scientific records (McConnell, 1985; Kelley & Byrne, 1992).

Watson's academic career was over. He had to resign his professorship at Johns Hopkins University, and most of his friends and colleagues deserted him. The Baltimore newspapers reported the divorce in lurid detail, and the judge presiding at the trial gave Watson a severe tongue-lashing—calling him, among other things, an expert in *mis*behavior.

After the divorce, Watson married Rayner. But he still could not find a job at any other college or university. In desperation, Watson took a position with a large advertising agency and stayed there the rest of his professional life. In 1929 he concluded, "The study of sex is still fraught with danger. It can be openly studied only by individuals who are not connected with universities" (Watson, 1929). Although he continued to write books and scientific papers, he considered himself a ruined man and soon slipped into the solace of alcohol (McConnell, 1985). Watson died at the age of 80 in 1958.

KINSEY'S INTERVIEWS

Watson's influence on the scientific study of human sexuality was profound, but largely indirect. One of Watson's students, Karl Lashley, got a noted biologist interested in studying human sexual responses—a man named Alfred Kinsey (Magoun, 1981).

In 1948 Kinsey and his associates published a monumental volume called *Sexual Behavior in the Human Male*. *Sexual Behavior in the Human Female* followed in 1953. These were the first surveys of sexual behavior based on adequately large segments of the public. Using a standardized set of questions, the Kinsey group got many thousands of men and women to describe their sexual feelings and behaviors.

What they said surprised and shocked many Americans. For example, 3 out of 10 men reported that they had experienced orgasm with another male; 4 out of 10 husbands had been unfaithful to their wives; and 6 out of 10 women had tried masturbation (Kinsey et al., 1948, 1953).

As many critics noted, however, there were methodological problems with Kinsey's surveys. Since Kinsey depended on volunteers, his sample may have been biased. That is, perhaps the sexuality of those people who *wouldn't* talk to Kinsey was quite different from the sexuality of those who *did*. And perhaps those who talked to Kinsey embellished their accounts to make them more interesting.

The public response to Kinsey's efforts was decidedly a mixed bag. Shortly after Kinsey published the study on women, New York Congressman Louis B. Heller had this to say about Kinsey: "He is hurling the insult of the century against our mothers, wives, daughters and sisters, under the pretext of making a great contribution to scientific research" (Gould, 1982). In 1954 a special House committee accused the Rockefeller Foundation of "directly supporting subversion" and of promoting com-

Sexual motivation is difficult to study because people may be reluctant to talk about it and because they may distort their reports in order to create a favorable impression.

munism because the Foundation gave money to the Kinsey Institute. Citing these facts, Harvard biologist Stephen Jay Gould notes that, "Kinsey never did find an alternate source of support (after the Congressional attack); he died two years later, overworked, angry, and distressed that so many years of further data might never see publication . . . " (Gould, 1982).

MASTERS AND JOHNSON'S RESEARCH

Freud used a clinical case study approach to study sex; Ellis and Kinsey used surveys to gather their data. But in each case the researchers merely asked subjects to *talk* about their sex lives while they recorded memories and attitudes. When Watson measured what people actually *did,* society was shocked. It was not until the 1950s that researchers again ventured to measure sexual *behavior.*

In 1954 William Masters and Virginia Johnson, a physician and a behavioral scientist, made recordings of female prostitutes' bodily reactions while the women experienced various types of sexual arousal (chiefly masturbation). Later, they studied the biological changes that accompany sexual excitement in males, as well.

When Masters tried to present his early data to a gathering of American physicians, the majority of them urged him to give up his research. Many of the best-known medical journals would not publish his findings, and political pressure prevented him from getting government support for his work. The first public discussion of Masters and Johnson's work was delayed until 1962, when the researchers presented their findings at a meeting of the American Psychological Association (Masters & Johnson, 1966; Masters et al., 1992).

Almost all the early research on human sexuality focused on intra-psychic or social variables, that is, personal feelings and thoughts, and public attitudes. Those few scientists who attempted to look at the *biology* of human sexuality paid the price for so doing.

More recently, however, a greater openness has prevailed. Scientists and society alike recognize that in order to deal with sexual problems and ethical issues, or even to appreciate and enjoy normal sexuality, we need a *holistic* understanding of sex. Let's look at some of the biological, intra-psychic, and social-behavioral facts we have learned about what makes us different sexually.

SOURCES OF SEXUALITY

In our opening quotation from *Too Cool to Get Married,* Robert points out some differences between men and women that he thinks are important. Well, we all know that men and women are different, but *how* different? Where do these differences come from, and what is their effect? Do they originate in our *biology?* Do we *think* about ourselves and the world differently? Or are we different merely because *society* tells us we have to be?

Biological Factors in Sexuality

Let's start at the beginning and see why men develop differently from women. And while we are discussing biology, let's look at that most interesting physical phenomenon, the sexual response cycle.

SEXUAL DEVELOPMENT

As we saw in Chapter 2, the sperm cell and the egg cell each contain 23 chromosomes. These chromosomes contain the genes and DNA that "program" our development. But the chromosomes of the sperm cell have one important difference from the chromosomes of the egg. The 23rd chromosome in the sperm can be either the large X type or the smaller Y type. The 23rd chromosome of the egg cell is *always* a large X type.

If an X-type sperm is the first to enter the egg cell, the fertilized egg will have an XX 23rd chromosome pair—and the child will be a genetic female. If a Y-type sperm fertilizes the egg, the 23rd chromosome pair will be of the XY variety and the child will be a genetic male.

Occasionally a female is born with only one X chromosome (XO), and males are sometimes born with an extra X (XXY), or an extra Y (XYY) pattern. What differences would you expect in the sex-related characteristics of these individuals?

But combining different genes on the 23rd chromosome pair (or "sex chromosomes") is only the beginning of your **sexual differentiation.** As you developed, chromosomes triggered the production of *hormones,* some of which had a direct effect on your sexual development. These "sex hormones" were produced by your adrenal glands and your **gonads**—the testes in males, and the ovaries in females. From shortly after conception onward, your adrenals and your gonads worked together to provide your body with the chemicals it needed to develop into, and to remain, a sexually mature adult.

Genetic males produce more **testosterone** and other **androgens.** Genetic females produce more **estrogen** and **progesterone.** Whether you are a woman or a man, however, your adrenals and your gonads produce *both* male and female hormones. It is the *relative amount* of these two types of hormones that is important for sexual differentiation.

If female sex hormones predominate during your prenatal growth, you will develop female **primary sex characteristics**—a vagina, uterus, clitoris, and ovaries. If male sex hormones predominate, you will develop male primary sex characteristics—a penis and testes.

Approximately 11 or 12 years later, at **puberty,** your chromosomes will again "turn up" their stimulation of sex and growth hormones, and change you from a child into an adult. Young men will grow facial hair and develop deeper voices. Young women will develop breasts and broader hips. In addition to these **secondary sex characteristics,** both men and women will develop pubic and underarm hair and both will grow rapidly.

To summarize, you were genetically programmed at conception to develop either a male or a female physical form. As this program unfolded, sex hormones in your body stimulated first the growth of *primary* sex characteristics (prenatally), and then *secondary* sex characteristics (at puberty).

But sex hormones affect more than physical sexual development. Sex hormones also play a role in sexual *arousal.*

SEXUAL AROUSAL

Following Masters and Johnson (1966), most researchers describe the process of sexual arousal in four stages—excitement, plateau, orgasm, and resolution. These stages are similar in men and women. Figure 7.1 shows the course of arousal passing through these four stages.

The first sign of physical arousal is vaginal lubrication in women and penis erection in men. Arousal also brings "vasocongestion," an increased flow of blood to the **genitals** and female breasts. As arousal continues, there is a buildup of energy in the

---

This is a boy, sir. Not a girl. If you're baffled by the difference it might be as well to approach both with caution.

JOE ORTON

Sexual differentiation. The process of developing sex-related differences.

Gonads (GO-nads). The primary sex glands—the ovaries in the female and the testes in the male.

Testosterone (tess-TOSS-ter-own). The most important of the androgens, or male hormones. Found in small quantities in females, as well as males.

Androgens (ANN-dro-jens). Male hormones. From the Greek words meaning "producer of males." There are several male hormones; collectively these are known as androgens.

Estrogen (ESS-tro-jens). Estrogens are the hormones that generate or bring about estrus, the period in a female's reproductive cycle when she is fertile and hence capable of becoming pregnant.

Progesterone (pro-JEST-ter-own). A female hormone produced in the ovaries and placenta.

Primary sex characteristics. The actual organs involved in sexual reproduction. Ovaries, vagina, uterus, and clitoris in females; penis and testes in males.

Puberty (PEW-burr-tee). The onset of sexual maturity, when the person becomes physically capable of sexual reproduction.

Secondary sex characteristics. Physical differences related to sex, but not essential for reproduction. In females, breast development, broadening of the hips, and the growth of pubic hair; in males, widening of the shoulders, lowering of the voice, and growth of pubic and facial hair.

Genitals (JEN-it-tulls). The external sex organs; also called *genitalia* (jen-it-TAIL-ee-uh). From the Latin word meaning "to beget, to reproduce, to generate children."

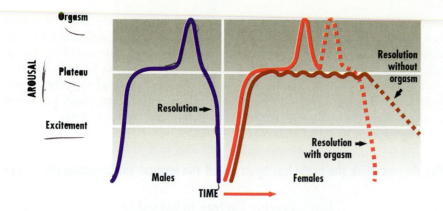

FIGURE 7.1

The male and female cycle of sexual response. The phases—excitement, plateau, orgasm, and resolution—are defined by physiological changes (From Masters & Johnson, 1966).

nerves and muscles throughout the body. This buildup, called "myotonia," may reach a climax with orgasm and then dissipate rapidly. Or it may dissipate slowly without orgasm.

HORMONES. In nonhuman species, hormones play a direct role in sexual arousal. In humans however, the effect is not so clear. Deprived of testosterone (through castration or drugs) men experience a lessening of sexual desire (Berlin & Meinecke, 1981; Money et al., 1976). Some women report a reduction in sexual behavior after their ovaries have been removed (Zussman et al., 1981). On the other hand, women show greater sexual interest when their estrogen level is highest (Adams et al., 1978; Udry & Morris, 1968). And both men and women who lose interest in sex after surgery, report an increase in activity when the depleted hormones are replaced (Michael, 1980; Sherwin, 1988). But these effects are often slow and inconsistent. It may take a week or two before a change in hormone level affects behavior, and then the influence is often slight (Segraves, 1988).

THE NERVOUS SYSTEM. The nervous system controls sexual arousal much more directly. Erection and vaginal lubrication begin with stimulation by the parasympathetic branch of the autonomic nervous system. Orgasm is a reflex mediated by neural activity in the spinal cord and the pleasure centers in the limbic system—parts of the central nervous system. And the sympathetic division of the autonomic system controls ejaculation.

Neural firing in the spinal cord associated with orgasm leads to a massive arousal of the autonomic nervous system, similar to that which occurs during great fear or anger. According to some researchers, the electrical activity that occurs in the pleasure centers during orgasm is as intense as what the whole brain experiences during an epileptic seizure (Gallagher, 1986).

THE BRAIN. The right hemisphere also seems to be involved in the production of human orgasm. According to Alan Cohen and his associates, there is a large increase in electrical activity in the "non-dominant" brain hemisphere, from several minutes before orgasm until the moment it occurs—although whether this is cause or effect is unclear (Cohen et al., 1985).

Other areas of the brain contribute to sexual behavior. These areas include the hypothalamus, and both the frontal and temporal lobes of the cerebral cortex (Blumer, 1970; Malsbury & Pfaff, 1974). However, we do not know the precise roles of these areas in human sexual behavior (Kolb & Wishaw, 1990).

To summarize, sexual arousal is a complex "act." The central and autonomic nervous systems play key roles; hormones occupy subordinate parts; and the entire body forms the supporting cast.

But arousal is primarily a physical *response* set in motion by other factors. Psychological and social influences "set the stage." For example, arousal may begin with a romantic setting, or thoughts about sex with an attractive partner. Sexual imagery, fantasy, and dreams can produce physical arousal to the point of orgasm even without direct physical stimulation (Wells, 1986; Levine, 1988). And touching, massaging, and caressing, as well as erotic pictures and tape recordings arouse both men and women (Heiman, 1977; Lazarus, 1988; Schmidt & Sigusch, 1970).

So before we assign all the "credit" to our biology, we need to consider psychological and social factors. We also need to consider these other influences because sexuality is much more than the sexual response cycle, or having a male or female body.

Why do you think the brain has been called the largest sex organ in the body?

Intra-Psychic Factors in Sexuality

Men and women look different—at least without their clothes on. Men have penises, women have vaginas; women have breasts, men don't. But are men and women identical otherwise?—like "Barbie" and "Ken" dolls, the same material poured into different molds? Or could having a different body *shape* make you *think* differently? One theorist who thought so was Sigmund Freud.

PENIS ENVY, CASTRATION COMPLEX, AND LIBIDO

Freud said that "Anatomy is destiny." He meant that your course for life was set by your physical structure, the chief component of which is your biological sex (Freud, 1924/1961). For instance, according to Freud, little girls feel cheated because they have no penis ("penis envy"); little boys are afraid of losing theirs ("castration complex"). Although these ideas are not widely accepted today, Freud believed that penis envy and castration complex were powerful forces in forming girls' and boys' personalities. It was the difference between penis envy and castration complex that led Freud to the unpopular idea that women have a less developed superego (conscience) than men.

Freud also believed that sexual motivation was the major force in human behavior. Freud called this force **libido.** Freud saw sexual motivation everywhere. Even *personality* develops as libido finds expression through various **erogenous zones** in the young child's body. This means, for example, that an infant sucks his or her thumb in order to receive *oral sexual pleasure*. And frustration, satisfaction, or overindulgence of this sexual outlet shapes the child's developing personality. We will return to Freud's theory later, but it is important to note that this highly influential viewpoint makes *sex* the foundation of motivation and psychological development.

SELF-ACTUALIZATION

Abraham Maslow also believed that sex was an important motive. People who are growing and realizing their full potential—self-actualizing people—experience love and belonging. Between self-actualizing individuals sex may be a mystical or even a playful experience.

> It is quite characteristic of self-actualizing people that they can enjoy themselves in love and in sex. Sex very frequently becomes a kind of game in which laughter is quite as common as panting. It is not the welfare of the species, or the task of reproduction, or the future development of mankind that attracts people to each other. The sex life of healthy people, in spite of the fact that it frequently reaches great peaks of ecstasy, is nevertheless also easily compared to the games of children and puppies. It is cheerful, humorous, and playful. (Maslow, 1954/1970)

Sexual behavior held a high value for humanistic psychologists like Abraham Maslow and Carl Rogers. They also recognized that impersonal sex or sexual intercourse with someone who is not loved is undesirable (Maslow, 1954/1970).

Libido (li-BEE-doh). Freud's term for sexual energy. May be thought of as "life force." It includes sensuality and pleasure-seeking, as well as genital procreation.

Erogenous zones (air-AW-jen-us). Areas on the body that produce sexual pleasure when stimulated. According to Freud the main focus of sexual pleasure is the mouth in newborns until around 18 months, the anus from 18 months until 3 or 4 years old, and the genitals in 4- to 6-year-olds. After a latency period, puberty begins the genital stage, an integration of earlier stages with primary pleasure derived from genital stimulation.

Humanistic psychologists recognized the value of sexual behavior for healthy psychological development. They did not, however, emphasize psychological *differences* between the sexes.

But the question of psychological differences between men and women is unavoidable in the 1990s. And to answer a question we raised earlier, physical differences certainly *do* lead us to think differently about ourselves. The psychological difference will become more clear as we consider the difference between *sex* and *gender*.

SEX AND GENDER

Many people use the terms sex and gender interchangeably. Psychologists who study male and female differences, however, use the word "sex" to refer to a person's *biological* "maleness" or "femaleness." They use the word *gender* to refer to the *non*-biological aspects of sex—the social definition of masculinity and femininity.

Your **gender identity** is your personal sense of being male or female. It includes your thoughts and feelings about masculinity and femininity, as these concepts are defined by your culture. Your gender identity forms such a central part of your self-concept, and is so resistant to change, that you might have assumed that you were born with it. Try imagining yourself as the other sex.

What would it be like to be unsure of your gender, or even your physical sex?

You were probably born clearly male or female. But your personal sense of masculinity or femininity was not pre-packaged—your *culture gave it to you*, bit by bit. For unknown reasons, some individuals do not develop a clear sense of gender identity. They experience **gender dysphoria,** the desire to be a member of the opposite sex. *Transsexualism* is an extreme form of sexual dysphoria. Transsexuals may undergo surgery and take hormones in order to reshape their bodies to be consistent with their psychological feelings of gender.

Most people, however, develop a clear idea of their masculinity or femininity that is consistent with their physical sex. The evidence seems to suggest that our gender identity is an intra-psychic, or psychological, development that is primarily the result of being consistently treated in a way which our culture considers appropriate for males or females. It also seems that the first few years of life are particularly important. But how does this development take place? What processes either *inside* the individual or *outside*, in the culture, are responsible?

To answer these questions we will consider two theories of gender development. The first, identification theory, is the unique theory of Sigmund Freud. The second, gender schema theory, is a recent outgrowth of other theories.

IDENTIFICATION THEORY.   Like so many of Freud's ideas, the concept of **identification** has become so widely known that we scarcely recognize its source.

According to Freud, we see ourselves as either masculine or feminine because at an early age we began to *identify* with our parent of the same sex—boys with fathers, and girls with mothers. Freud said that the sexual attraction that a 3–6-year-old child feels for the parent of the opposite sex leads to a crisis of anxiety (heightened by castration anxiety and penis envy). The child resolves the crisis by age 5 or 6 through identification with the parent of the same sex. In identifying with his father, the boy takes on masculine values, behaviors, and standards; in identifying with her mother, the girl takes on feminine values, behaviors, and standards. By identifying with the same-sexed parent, the young child psychologically possesses the opposite-sexed parent in a sexual relationship. The main motive for identification is sexual, but the result is a clear *gender* identity. The girl now *thinks of herself* as a female; the boy now *thinks of himself* as a male.

Two main criticisms have been made of this position. First, children appear to have a fairly clear idea of gender identity much earlier than Freud said—probably

Gender identity. The personal feeling of being masculine or feminine (as opposed to sexual identity—the awareness of one's physical sex).

Gender dysphoria (dis-FOR-ee-uh). Discontent with one's biological sex and the desire to have the body of the opposite sex and be regarded as a member of the opposite sex. Transsexualism is an extreme form of gender dysphoria.

Identification. The process of attributing to oneself the characteristics or traits of someone else, such as a parent or other significant person in one's life.

"She wants so much to identify with her kindergarten teacher, who is a wonderful, patient person—but he's 6 feet 2 and he has a moustache."

before 3 years of age (Maccoby, 1990). Second, *sexual* motivation is probably not necessary for identification to take place (White, 1963).

It seems reasonable to conclude that from a very early age, children may identify with any powerful yet warm individual, and so learn a sense of being male or female. But this sounds less like Freud, and more like one of several theories which have emphasized *learning* as the basis of gender development. Let's look at one of those next.

GENDER SCHEMA THEORY.   The most recent and influential view of how gender identity develops is **gender schema theory.** Gender schema theory includes elements of learning from social learning theory and a focus on cognition, or thinking, from cognitive developmental theory (Kohlberg, 1966).

According to Sandra Bem, as we process information from our environment, we organize it around various *schemata* or categories. One of these schemata, which we *learn* from our environment, is gender (Bem, 1981, 1983). From a very early age, our culture teaches us that gender differences are significant. As a result, we look for gender differences whenever we encounter new information—particularly information affecting our self-concept. As our gender schema develops from our experience, it soon begins to influence our experience—both of ourselves and the world around us (de la Haye & Askevis, 1988).

For example, our culture seems to teach us that masculine means strong and aggressive, and that feminine means sensitive and helpful. As we acquire experiences consistent with these schemata, we strengthen the schemata, and we develop a clearer idea of what masculinity or femininity means *for us*.

So gender identity is an intra-psychic, or psychological, development which seems to occur primarily as a result of social and environmental influences. We *think* about ourselves differently because we have come to see ourselves as either male or female. However, when it comes to defining exactly what it means to be male or female in a particular society, *social* influences once again come into play.

Social/Behavioral Factors in Sexuality

A society cannot control which genes and hormones are present in your body. Nor can a society determine whether you feel psychologically male or female. But society does define what it *means* to be male or female. It does so by specifying which sexual *roles*, *behaviors*, and *values* are "acceptable" within that culture (Sonderegger, 1984).

Society not only sets sexual standards, it enforces them as well—in at least two ways. First, society surrounds you with *models*—that is, with people (such as your parents, peers, and media personalities) who have adopted its standards. And second, society rewards you when you imitate these models, and punishes you when you don't (Etaugh & Liss, 1992). Much of the socialization process by which you incorporate society's values involves learning **gender-role stereotypes.**

Suppose you are a heterosexual male, hence strongly attracted to females. If men and women dressed and acted alike, how would you know whom to pursue sexually?

In her chapter in the *Handbook of Developmental Psychology*, Dee Shepherd-Look defines gender-role or sex-role stereotypes as "widely shared and pervasive concepts that prescribe how each sex ought to perform." According to Shepherd-Look, "There is considerable agreement both within and between cultures as to the appropriate sex-role behaviors for males and females." Most societies expect a man to be "competent, independent, assertive, aggressive, dominant, and competitive in social

Gender Schema Theory. A currently influential view of how we come to see ourselves as masculine or feminine. It includes elements of both learning and cognitive descriptions of behavior.

Gender-role stereotypes. A stereotype is a "cognitive model" that loosely represents all of a certain class or type. A gender-role stereotype is thus a "cognitive prototype" that describes expected dress and behavior of males or females within a given culture.

and sexual relations." Most societies expect a woman, on the other hand, to be "passive, affiliative, affectionate, nurturant, intuitive, and supportive, particularly in her familiar role as wife and mother" (Shepherd-Look, 1982). These broad stereotypes are found in North Americans (Deaux & Lewis, 1984; Ruble, 1983), and in a variety of non–North American cultures including Spanish, Oriental, and Indian groups (Mendonsa, 1981; Mukhopadhyay & Higgins, 1988; Schultze et al., 1991; Segall, 1988; Springer & Gable, 1981).

FORMING GENDER-ROLE STEREOTYPES

Shepherd-Look cites more than a hundred studies suggesting that the environment controls gender-role differentiation, starting at birth (Shepherd-Look, 1982). For example, Jeffrey Rubin and his associates interviewed parents within 24 hours after their infants were born. They asked the parents to rate their new child on a number of scales. Both mothers and fathers of *daughters* described their infants as "softer, finer featured, weaker, smaller, prettier, more inattentive, more awkward, and more delicate" than did parents whose infant was a son. Parents described *sons* as "firmer, larger featured, more coordinated, alert, stronger, and hardier" than daughters. Despite these parental *perceptions*, however, Rubin and his colleagues note that there were no *measurable* physical or behavioral differences between the male and female infants (Rubin et al., 1974).

In a similar study, Jerrie Ann Will and her colleagues asked a number of women to play with a 6-month-old child while the investigators watched. The women were all mothers who had small children (of both sexes) of their own. Half the time, the infant wore blue pants and the mothers were told the child's name was "Adam." The other half of the time, the child was called "Beth" and wore a pink dress. The mothers who played with "Adam" almost uniformly offered the child a masculine toy (such as a train). The mothers who played with "Beth" typically offered the child a doll. The women also smiled at "Beth" more than at "Adam." Will and her associates note that the mothers seemed entirely unaware that they were engaging in gender-role stereotyping (Will et al., 1976).

More recently, Marilyn Stern and Katherine Karraker reviewed these 2 studies along with 21 other similar ones. They found that when other information was unclear or absent, gender labels frequently influenced adults' perceptions of infant behavior, adults' *expectations* of infants' future actions, and adults' *behavior* towards the infants. They also found that children respond even more strongly than adults to the gender-labels of other children (Stern & Karraker, 1989).

In a related study, psychologist Nancy Weitzman and her colleagues observed both traditional and "feminist" mothers telling stories and talking to their young children. No matter what their orientation, mothers of sons asked them more questions, particularly those beginning with the word "what." They also used more numbers and more action verbs than when talking to daughters. The researchers conclude that "Mothers, regardless of their attitudes toward women's rights and roles, appear to stimulate verbally their sons more than their daughters on a number of language variables." And in doing so, the mothers may be "subtly and unknowingly steering girls and boys in different directions with regard to intellectual mastery and self-confidence" (Fagot et al., 1992; Weitzman et al., 1985).

What benefits do you gain from having ready-made social responses for the males and females you meet?

CHILDHOOD STEREOTYPING.   Children learn by age 2 that there are some toys that boys play with, and others that girls play with. By that age, they self-select games that are stereotypically "correct" for their gender (Shepherd-Look, 1982).

As to the qualities of mind peculiar to each sex, I agree with you that sprightliness is in favor of females and profundity of males. Their education, their pursuits would create such a quality even tho' nature has not implanted it.

ELIZA SOUTHGATE

According to Will's observations, a woman will play more boisterously with a baby if she is told it is a boy, more gently if told it is a girl.

During childhood, boys are more likely to avoid sex-inappropriate activities and toys than are girls. Apparently, parents strongly influence boys' choices. Several investigators have found that parents are not concerned when their daughters engage in "inappropriate" activities. However, both parents tend to react negatively and punitively when their sons make choices the parents consider inappropriate. In other words, "tomboy" girls are more acceptable than "momma's boy" boys.

By the time children reach puberty, society has "shaped" them into *perceiving their own sexuality* in a socially approved manner (Shepherd-Look, 1982).

ARE THE STEREOTYPES VALID? Stereotypes can be a useful way of understanding similar people. But very few people fit a stereotype exactly. So stereotypes can cause misunderstanding and become tools of prejudice (as you will see in Chapter 17). Unfortunately, this has often been the case with gender stereotypes.

In the past, researchers have looked for evidence to support gender stereotypes in literally thousands of studies. Many of these studies have found male/female differences, but most recent studies have found that when they take social and cultural factors into account, the differences disappear. This research has helped modify inaccurate and harmful gender stereotypes.

There are, however, some gender differences that have stood up to repeated testing, and that cannot be attributed entirely to social influences. We can summarize these as follows:

1. Males are more aggressive and dominant (Lips, 1988; Maccoby & Jacklin, 1974; Nyquist & Spence, 1986).

2. Females have greater verbal ability (Feingold, 1992; Halpern, 1986, 1989; Lips, 1988; Maccoby & Jacklin, 1974).

3. Males have greater mathematical and visual-spatial ability (Friedman, 1989; Linn & Petersen, 1986; Lips, 1988; Maccoby & Jacklin, 1974).

It is very important to note that in each case these are general trends and the differences are small. In the case of aggression, some research indicates that females may simply use less noticeable *indirect* means to vent an equal level of aggression (Björkqvist et al., 1992; Björkqvist & Niemelä, 1992). No psychological or behavioral differences exist between *all* men and *all* women. In fact, the average differences *between* the sexes is always less than the range of differences *within* each sex.

Of course, *any* differences between people can be either exaggerated or ignored by society. It is not the differences but the personal and social *evaluation* of differences which produces prejudice. If we accepted people equally, regardless of their differences, even *valuing* their differences, prejudice would be eliminated. Another approach to reducing prejudice between the sexes is to reduce the differences by encouraging *androgyny*.

How might culture amplify male/female differences, for example in verbal and mathematical ability?

ANDROGYNY

Have you ever wished that you didn't have to "act like a lady" or "be a man"? If you feel uncomfortable with gender-role expectations like these, you may be interested in the psychological concept of **androgyny.**

Androgyny means being able to choose from the whole range of human behaviors those that best suit your own personality and the immediate situation, without being limited to behaviors traditionally associated with your gender (Bem, 1975; Cook, 1985; Kaplan & Sedney, 1980). Androgyny does not mean you are bisexual, want to abolish all gender-roles, or are an activist for economic equality. Androgynous people believe that men should be free to express traditionally femi-

Androgyny (an-DRAW-jen-ee). The concept that men and women should not be restricted in their behavior by society's sex-role expectations. Both sexes should be free to express behaviors traditionally associated with the other sex. (The concept of androgyny does not specify that the behaviors be desirable. For example, men should be free to be "bitchy" as well as empathetic.)

nine qualities (like warmth and sensitivity), and women should be allowed to take on traditionally masculine behaviors (like initiating sexual activity).

Despite the apparent advantages of expressing both male and female characteristics, however, androgyny should not be taken as a new standard to which we all aspire. Androgyny does not necessarily lead to better adjustment (Bassoff & Glass, 1982; Lee & Scheurer, 1983; Rotheram & Weiner, 1983). Rather, androgyny should be seen as one more legitimate option for gender-roles offered by contemporary (North American) society.

A CROSS-CULTURAL LOOK AT GENDER

Gender-role differences exist in all cultures. The extent of these differences is so great that researchers refer to a broad "gender asymmetry" (Mukhopadhyay & Higgins, 1988). Cross-cultural studies of gender differences frequently discuss "male dominance" or "female subordination," because, on the whole, gender-role differences favor men.

The reasons for gender asymmetry are complex. Many studies have examined the role *biological differences* play in gender asymmetry. These studies have assumed that a "universal fact" like asymmetry, must have a "universal cause," so they have looked for "universal determinants," such as biological causes for aggressiveness, strength, and parenting behaviors.

Biological differences do seem to be related to many cases of gender asymmetry, but not in a simple way. Cultures often amplify differences based on biology. For example, men and women may be taught that "men's work" requires more strength than "women's work," even when the difference is slight or nonexistent. Biological differences may be crucial in defining roles in one culture, and be almost insignificant in another. For example, in many cultures women do not hunt, presumably because they are restricted by their strength or their reproductive functions. However, women in the Agta culture of the Philippines hunt regularly, even when they are pregnant. The women take hunting trips of the same distance and duration as the men, and they kill the same range of animals (Estioko-Griffin, 1985; Goodman et al., 1985). Thus, the assumption that men are always the hunters and providers is a "false universal."

Sexual behavior also contains "false universals." In North America it is widely assumed that men are naturally more interested in sex, experience orgasm more

Gender role differences exist in all cultures, but they usually favor men.

reliably, and if sex is going to happen, a man has to start it. On the Polynesian island of Mangaia, however, women are sexually active at a very young age, they are expected to initiate sex, and all women learn to be orgasmic (Marshall, 1971).

This type of cross-cultural comparison provides further evidence that gender-roles and sexual behavior are not as firmly rooted in biology as we might assume. Psychological and sociocultural factors exert strong influences on biological predispositions (Mukhopadhyay & Higgins, 1988).

To summarize, males and females are different *biologically*. As a result men and women come to think of themselves as *masculine* or *feminine* (their *gender*). But the *definition* of masculinity and femininity comes from society. This definition includes ideas about how men and women should think, feel, and act (their gender-roles).

SEXUAL BEHAVIOR AND VALUES

At the beginning of this chapter we said that we were going to consider a broad range of behavior related to male/female differences. We have looked at some ways in which we are different, and we have discussed some of the factors that produce these differences. Now it is time to look directly at explicitly sexual behaviors. We will conclude this section by returning to the important motivational question of choice, which ultimately depends on *values*.

Sexual Behaviors

What "turns you on"? Are you aroused by the opposite sex? the same sex? both? neither? Is it the actual person that arouses you? Or do you find an image, a fantasy, or even a piece of clothing equally stimulating?

And what about other people? Why do some individuals *force* sexual behavior on unwilling partners?

These questions refer to some of the explicitly sexual behaviors we will look at. As you can see, they are all behaviors where sexual arousal is an important component.

SEXUAL ORIENTATION

If you find members of the opposite sex more arousing sexually than members of your own sex, your **sexual orientation** is **heterosexual**. If you are equally sexually attracted to members of your own sex, you are **bisexual**. If you are *primarily* attracted to members of your own sex, you are **homosexual**. (If you show little or no interest in sexual activity you might be considered **asexual**.)

It is difficult to define heter-, homo-, and bisexuality precisely, or to determine their prevalence exactly, for several reasons:

1. People may be reluctant to admit their true feelings because the social prejudices against homosexuality (and bisexuality) have not entirely disappeared.

2. Many people report having had some homosexual experience but consider themselves heterosexual and live a heterosexual lifestyle.

3. People vary along a continuum of sexual orientations depending on the type of attraction they feel. At one end are those whose sexual feelings are exclusively heterosexual; at the other end are those whose feelings are exclusively homosexual. In between are all combinations of the two, including those who live out their *bi*sexual feelings (see Figure 7.2).

Sexual orientation. The *orienting reflex* is the automatic response of turning toward a new or interesting stimulus. "Sexual orientation" is the term used to describe which sex you are most likely to "orient to," or be romantically interested in.

Heterosexual. Feeling attracted to members of the opposite sex more than to members of the same sex.

Bisexual. Feeling approximately equal sexual attraction to men and women.

Homosexual. Being sexually attracted to members of your own sex more than to members of the opposite sex.

Asexual. Feeling little or no sexual attraction.

0	1	2	3	4	5	6
Exclusively heterosexual	**Predominantly heterosexual:** only incidentally homosexual	**Predominantly heterosexual:** more than incidentally homosexual	**Equally heterosexual and homosexual**	**Predominantly homosexual:** more than incidentally heterosexual	**Predominantly homosexual:** only incidentally heterosexual	**Exclusively homosexual**

FIGURE 7.2

Visual representation of the heterosexual-homosexual rating scale used by Kinsey to describe a sexual orientation continuum (Based on Kinsey et al., 1948).

In Kinsey's original samples 4 percent of the men and 2 to 3 percent of the women were mostly or exclusively homosexual on a lifelong basis (Kinsey et al., 1948, 1953). More recent data from the Kinsey Institute places the figure at 3.3 percent of the American adult male population who have had homosexual contact "occasionally" or "fairly often" after age 20 (Fay et al., 1989). But given the likelihood of concealment and the difficulty of finding an exact definition, researcher Janet Shibley Hyde may be closer to the truth when she concludes that ". . . about 80 percent of men and 90 percent of women are exclusively heterosexual. About 2 percent of men and 1 percent of women are exclusively homosexual. And the remaining group have had varying amounts of both heterosexual and homosexual experience" (Hyde, 1990).

Like other complex human responses, sexual orientation is the product of many factors. Some researchers believe that different hormone balances both before birth and in adulthood produce different sexual orientations (Dörner, 1976, 1988; Ellis & Ames, 1987; Meyer-Bahlburg, 1977, 1979). Until fairly recently, most scientists assumed that hormonal bias determined whether a person turned out to be heterosexual, homosexual, or bisexual. However, as Robert Rubin and his colleagues suggest, this doesn't seem to be the case. With certain minor exceptions, the hormonal patterns of homosexual males is the same as that of heterosexual males. And no one has yet reported reliable hormonal differences between homosexual and heterosexual females. Furthermore, injecting homosexual males with testosterone *increases their sexual activities* rather than changing their sexual *orientation* (Rubin et al., 1981).

Jane Stewart cautions against the "all-too-easy assumption that sex differences in behavior and sexual differentiation itself are determined solely by . . . gonadal hormones" (Stewart, 1988). Ruth Doell and Helen Longino believe that too much

I'm a practicing heterosexual . . . but bisexuality immediately doubles your chances for a date on Saturday night.

WOODY ALLEN

Like other complex human behaviors, sexual orientation is the product of many factors.

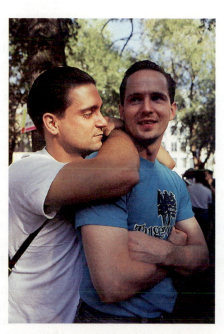

emphasis has been placed on the study of fetal hormones, especially fetal hormones in animals. Doell and Longino argue that sexual behavior in humans is a product of "each individual's unique integration of her or his physiological, developmental, and environmental/social history" (Doell & Longino, 1988). The evidence for a biological basis of sexual orientation is not very strong. Although no one would rule out the possibility of biological factors, other causes are at least as important (Hoult, 1984; Friedman, 1988; Lips, 1988; Money, 1987; Risman & Schwartz, 1988).

Non-biological influences on sexual orientation, however, are not at all clear. Researchers have studied early family experiences from both intra-psychic and social/behavioral approaches with inconclusive results. In the case of homosexuality, there are a variety of conditions that researchers have investigated—for example, an extremely negative first heterosexual encounter, or a family with a domineering mother and an ineffectual father (Greenspoon & Lamal, 1987; Al-Issa, 1987). But many people with similar experiences *do not* become homosexual, and many homosexuals do not have these experiences. It seems most likely that sexual orientation is multi-determined—that biological, intra-psychic, and social factors *all* play a role—and quite possibly different roles in different people.

The combination of factors is similar to the influences on body weight that we discussed in Chapter 6. Just as we are biologically set to be a certain weight, perhaps we are biologically inclined to a particular sexual orientation. And just as numerous intra-psychic and social/behavioral influences affect our body composition, so intra-psychic and social influences affect our choice of sexual object. Each of these factors may have different degrees of influence in different people at different times.

How is your understanding of homosexuality affected by your knowledge of its causes?

MASTURBATION

Masturbation refers to stimulation of one's own genitals in order to create sexual pleasure. The sexual pleasure comes from rubbing, stroking, fondling, squeezing, or otherwise stimulating the genitals. Masturbation frequently, but not always, leads to orgasm.

Masturbation begins at an early age. Infants of both sexes enjoy self-stimulation and may use masturbation to soothe and comfort themselves (Kestenberg, 1979). This type of sexual activity was one reason Freud believed that sexual pleasure motivated behavior throughout life. Infants can even experience orgasm, although before puberty boys do not ejaculate semen (Kinsey et al., 1948, 1953).

Parents usually discourage sexual self-stimulation in their children. In some cultures, however, parents fondle their infants' genitals to soothe and quiet them (Hyde, 1990).

Adolescents engage in masturbation with the greatest frequency. By age 15 more than 80 percent of boys have masturbated to orgasm (Kinsey et al., 1948). The figure for girls is much lower (around 20 percent) but rises steadily to over 60 percent in young adulthood (Arafat & Cotton, 1974; Hite, 1977; Hunt, 1975; Miller & Lief, 1976).

In 1987 Joan Atwood and John Gagnon asked 1,177 college students about their masturbation behavior. They found that more than 75 percent of the males and 30 percent of the females masturbate during their freshman year of college. In their senior year more than 80 percent of the males and 40 percent of the females masturbate (Atwood & Gagnon, 1987). Although there is a great deal of variability, males masturbate more frequently than females. A rough estimate would be about once a week for males, and twice a month for females. Comparison of Kinsey's data with more recent information suggests that female masturbation is increasing in frequency (Atwood & Gagnon, 1987; DeMartino, 1979; Sorenson, 1973).

Masturbation does not necessarily cease with marriage, although single adults masturbate more frequently than married adults (Huey et al., 1981; Hunt, 1975; Levin & Levin, 1975; DeMartino, 1979). The incidence and frequency of masturbation declines after age 30 among males, but continues to increase among females (Hunt, 1975; Kinsey et al., 1953).

In the past, physicians, religious leaders, and parents blamed masturbation for a variety of mental and physical problems, from weight loss to insanity, and even death. Today's experts consider these fears to be unfounded. Some sex therapists encourage masturbation as a way of discovering one's personal patterns of arousal (Byer & Shainberg, 1991). Masturbation can bring a relief from sexual tension when one's sexual partner is unavailable. Within a sexual relationship such as marriage, however, excessive masturbation can interfere with one's interest (or ability) in intercourse, thus possibly weakening the sexual relationship.

Many people do not masturbate because it produces anxiety, conflict, or guilt. About these individuals, Masters, Johnson, and Kolodny say,

> People who choose not to masturbate—whether or not they've tried it, whether or not their choice is based on religious conviction, personal preference, or some other consideration—have every right to their decision without being made to feel guilty or strange by self-proclaimed experts in sexual health.
>
> (Masters et al., 1992)

Decisions about masturbation are a personal matter. Fortunately, this attitude is also developing among those who have traditionally opposed this practice (Dobson, 1989).

FANTASIES AND DREAMS

Sexual fantasies are an important aspect of human sexuality (Chick & Gold, 1987–88). Sexual fantasies are mental images of people, settings, and actions that one finds sexually exciting—a sexy daydream. Fantasies are not the same as plans; we do not intend to carry them out.

Adolescents are particularly likely to fantasize about sex. These fantasies help them to come to terms with their own sexuality. Fantasies can also increase feelings of sexual arousal and heighten physical responsiveness (McCauley & Swann, 1980; Smith & Over, 1990). They are a common component of arousal in masturbation as well as in sexual intercourse. For example, Morton Hunt found that 80 percent of women and 75 percent of men fantasized about intercourse with a loved partner when they masturbated (Hunt, 1975). And many other researchers report that sexual fantasies are very common during intercourse (Davidson & Hoffman, 1986; Friday, 1973; Hariton & Singer, 1974).

Fantasies are generally a controlled and safe method of exploration, rehearsal, and excitement. They may lead to problems, however, if they recur over and over again despite being unwanted, or if they cause inner turmoil, guilt, and conflict. In these cases of distressing intrusive fantasies, professional counseling can be helpful.

Sometimes the exciting sexual images that arouse us occur in our dreams. According to Kinsey, 83 percent of males and 37 percent of females experience dreams that are so sexually arousing they lead to orgasm. The greatest frequency of these **nocturnal orgasms** is in late adolescence for males and in the forties for females (Kinsey et al., 1948, 1953).

Nocturnal orgasms, or wet dreams, are a common and natural experience. They are generally considered the body's way of releasing pent-up sexual tension.

Nocturnal orgasms (nawk-TURN-ul). Orgasms in both males and females that occur during sleep, usually associated with sexual dreams. In males, nocturnal orgasms also include ejaculations called "nocturnal emissions." Thus the experience is sometimes called a "wet dream."

SEXUAL ASSAULT

Sex is a pleasurable and fulfilling experience when it occurs by mutual consent in a loving relationship. But sex can also be a destructive instrument of violence, subjugation, and humiliation when it is forced upon an unwilling participant.

As the problem of date rape grows, many people are trying to become more aware of the possibilities and responsibilities of new relationships.

Rape. From the Latin word "rapio" meaning to seize, snatch, carry away. Sexual assault with penile penetration of the vagina without the victim's full consent, usually under the threat or use of force to overcome the victim's earnest resistance.

We commonly use the word **rape** to refer to the situation where a man, perhaps a stranger, uses violent force to have sexual intercourse with a woman despite her clear protests. And we may imagine that the rapist is driven by an uncontrolled sex drive. But rape occurs *whenever* sexual intercourse takes place without full consent. And rape usually has more to do with power and control than sexual release (Fonow et al., 1992). Two of the most common types of this severe form of sexual assault are "acquaintance" or "date rape," and "incest."

DATE RAPE.   Date rape is a growing problem on college and university campuses (Miller, 1988). Beverley Miller and Jon Marshall found that 27 percent of the women in their study reported date rape (Miller & Marshall, 1987). In addition, most researchers believe that many date rapes are not reported.

Sexual relationships involve much more than pleasure. For example, when you relate to someone sexually, you expose yourself to that person physically, and usually, emotionally. This gives the other person a certain amount of power over you. Being sexually desirable gives you power over the other person. So power, and the related ideas of control and dominance, are also components of sexual relationships (Barry, 1986). (Sadists find their power arousing.)

Sometimes the power element is minor (we speak of someone granting "sexual favors"). Sometimes it is part of a larger "power struggle" in a relationship. And sometimes, as in the case of rape, it overwhelms the relationship. Rape is then an attempt to subjugate and humiliate another person. It is more an act of violence than of passion.

In her research on rape Charlene Muehlenhard described 11 different dating scenarios to 545 male and female undergraduates. She asked them to rate how much they thought the woman wanted sex ("sex-willingness"), and how justified the man would be in having sex with her if she didn't want it ("rape-justifiability"). The students rated "sex-willingness" and "rape-justifiability" highest when the female initiated the date, when the couple went to the male's apartment, and when the male paid the dating expenses. In general, the men rated the rapes as more "justifiable" than the women did. Muehlenhard also found that students with more traditional attitudes towards women rated the rapes as more "justifiable." Her results, and the results of other research, suggest that certain dating behaviors may be misinterpreted to indicate that rape is acceptable (Bostwick & DeLucia, 1992; DeSouza et al., 1992; Muehlenhard, 1988; Norris & Cubbins, 1992).

Several studies have found traditional attitudes towards women to be a factor in date rape, and research is continuing on this dimension (Fischer, 1986a, 1986b; Weis et al., 1992). Perhaps traditional attitudes of power and dominance associated with the male role are factors in date rape. However, there are other influences. Variables that appear to be "risk factors" include heavy alcohol or drug use; the man's initiating the date, paying all the expenses, and driving; miscommunication about sex; "parking"; and men's acceptance of traditional sex roles, interpersonal violence, adversarial attitudes about relationships, and rape myths such as the belief that women enjoy rape (Muehlenhard & Linton, 1987). Avoiding these risk factors will reduce the likelihood of date rape.

In a broader context, Baruch Fischhoff and his colleagues have developed a list of rape prevention strategies to reduce the likelihood of rape generally (Fischhoff, 1992; Fischhoff et al., 1987). These strategies include steps that society can take, such as increasing the perceived chances of punishment for rape, and steps that an individual can take. Table 7.1 lists some steps that an individual can take.

INCEST.   Incest refers to sexual interactions between close relatives. Approximately 15 percent of females and 10 percent of males have been involved in an incestuous relationship (Finkelhor, 1980). The most common types of incest are between brothers and sisters and between first cousins (Renshaw, 1983; Stark, 1984). This type of incest is often limited to a few isolated experiences that occur by

DISCOURAGE ASSAULT

1. Reduce visibility of women to potential assailant
   Avoid dangerous neighborhoods
   Do not hang around bus terminals
2. Reduce accessibility of women to potential assailant
   Do not hitchhike
   Move to a place with a doorman
3. Increase perceived ability to cope with assailant if assault were to take place
   When approached by a stranger, make direct eye contact
   When entering a house, let dog in first to scare person
4. Increase perceived chances of outside intervention if assault were to take place
   Do not drive alone
   Fake presence of others
5. Increase perceived chances of punishment if assault were to take place
   Wear identifying armband to designate membership in rape prevention group
   Report known rapists/press charges
6. Reduce potential assailant's propensity to rape
   Don't wear tight or revealing clothes
7. Manage yourself in ways that increase ability to implement prevention measures successfully
   Get educated about high-risk situations
   Notice other people's behavior
8. Contribute to societal action
   Be involved in political action
   Encourage setting up or participate in rape crisis center

PREPARE FOR REACTING TO AN ASSAULT

1. Increase ability to cope with assailant in the event of an assault
   Own a dog
   Learn self-defense
2. Increase chances of outside intervention in the event of an assault
   Install burglar alarm system
   Carry noisemaker

DEFEND YOURSELF DURING AN ASSAULT

1. Manage yourself in ways that maximize your ability to implement self-defense measures successfully
   Try not to faint or pass out
   Assess attacker's personality
2. Reduce/minimize assailant's propensity to rape
   Do crude, unfeminine things
   Make him see you as human
3. Increase perceived ability to cope with assailant
   Make it known you have a weapon
   Clear verbal resistance
4. Increase perceived chances of outside intervention
   Fake arrival of others
5. Increase actual chances of outside intervention
   Yell "fire"
   Summon nearest male
6. Increase perceived chances of punishment
   State you will press charges against attacker
7. Establish distance or barrier between self and assailant
   Get out of house
   Run away
8. Physically impede or incapacitate assailant
   Incapacitate him with drugs or alcohol

TABLE 7.1

Possible strategies for reducing the risk of rape.
(ADAPTED FROM FISCHHOFF, 1992; FISCHHOFF, FURBY, AND MORGAN, 1987)

1. Having a stepfather. (This more than doubles a girl's chances of victimization and is the single most important predictor. In some studies the rate is more than *five* times higher for girls with stepfathers (Finkelhor, 1979; Foster, 1988).)

2. Having a mother who is punitive or highly negative about sexual matters. (This is the next most important predictor.)

3. Living separately from the mother.

4. Not having a good relationship with the mother.

5. Having a mother who did not complete high school.

6. Having a father who does not express physical affection.

7. Having less than three close friends in childhood.

8. Having a family income under $10,000.

FIGURE 7.3

Eight conditions that predict the likelihood of a young girl being sexually abused by her father (or step-father) (Based on Finkelhor, 1984).

mutual consent. The long-term effect of these encounters, especially those that occur before age 10, appears to be minimal (Greenwald & Leitenberg, 1989).

The most destructive form of incestuous relationship is a father-daughter (including stepfather-stepdaughter) one that extends over several years (Byer & Shainberg, 1991). It is also the form of incest most often reported to authorities (Weinberg, 1955; Masters et al., 1992).

Father-daughter incest typically begins when the child is from 8 to 10 years old and continues through adolescence. It may begin as early as infancy. The father uses his authority to coerce the child, often so subtly that the child may believe the behavior is normal (Phillips, 1981). The oldest daughter is the most frequent victim. Some fathers abuse more than one child at a time or begin again with a younger one when the older one is no longer available.

From his research on incest and family violence David Finkelhor developed a list of eight conditions to predict the likelihood of a young girl being sexually abused. These eight conditions are presented in Figure 7.3.

When Finkelhor asked 796 college students about childhood victimization, his 8 risk factors predicted well. When none of the factors were present, students reported virtually no childhood victimization. When 5 or more factors were present, 2 out of 3 students reported sexual abuse (Finkelhor, 1984).

Childhood victimization involves the abuse of power in a relationship that should be characterized by love and trust. It is particularly destructive because it occurs at a time when the victim is just developing, physically, emotionally, and socially. Many victims of childhood sex abuse develop adjustment problems in adulthood, frequently in their sexual relationships (Ainyette, 1989; Bracey, 1983; Everstine & Everstine, 1989). Increasingly, therapy and support groups are available for these sufferers.

Motivation for sexual assault is complex. It has important intra-psychic and social components, including anger, hostility, and personal inadequacy, in the perpetrator, as well as social pressures, expectations, and lack of support in the environment. To repeat a point made earlier, the motivation for this apparently sexual behavior goes far beyond mere sexual gratification.

SEXUAL BEHAVIOR AND CULTURE

As you travel around the world, you will find tremendous variety in the sexual behaviors that you observe. We have already noted some specific examples. The only generalization that seems safe to make is that all societies regulate sexual behavior in some way. The exact rules vary, however. For instance, virtually all societies condemn forced sexual relations. And incest is a nearly universal taboo. But the *definition* of incest—who's a close relative and who's not—varies.

We need to interpret accounts of sexual behavior in other cultures cautiously. Most cultures consider sexual behavior to be a personal and private area. It is hard enough to study sex in one's own culture. It is even more difficult to get accurate data from other cultures where investigators are considered outsiders and are viewed with suspicion.

Within North American society, several survey studies have compared black and white subgroups. Blacks tend to hold more liberal views about extramarital and pre-marital sex and to engage in premarital sex more frequently and at a younger age (Furstenberg et al., 1987; Glenn & Weaver, 1979; Weinberg & Williams, 1988). They also talk more openly and freely about sex and report fewer sexual problems (Weinberg & Williams, 1988).

Blacks and whites are also very similar (Belcastro, 1985; Robinson & Calhoun, 1983; Tanfer & Cubbins, 1992). They hold similar attitudes towards homosexuality. And the sexual behavior of blacks and whites has been affected in the same way by social changes (Glenn & Weaver, 1979; Wyatt et al., 1988). In fact, sex, social class, and religion are often more accurate than race as predictors of differences in sexuality between blacks and whites. In other words, knowing an individual's sex, social class, and religion will tell you more about his or her sexual attitudes and behavior than knowing whether he or she is black or white (Tanfer & Cubbins, 1992; Wyatt, 1989).

Some research has found that Hispanic students report more conservative atti-tudes and less frequent sexual activity than Anglo-American students. They are also less informed about sex (Baldwin et al., 1992; Padilla & O'Grady, 1987). But once again these differences are small and other factors need to be considered as well.

No matter what your ethnic origin, it is tempting to look at this kind of data and assume your position is best, that is, to make a *value judgment*. Value judgments are inevitable, but they need a better basis than simply whether or not they agree with your own particular group. Since values are such an important part of sexual behav-ior, let's conclude this section by looking at "sexual values."

Sexual Values and Choice

In Chapter 6 we said that motivation can be viewed as a "response selector mecha-nism," that is, as a process of *choice* (Bolles, 1975; Ridley, 1991). When it comes to sexual behavior many people are troubled by choices: What's right? What's wrong? These people are looking for *values* on which to base their choices. Values are stan-dards or guides which give direction to all of life (Raths et al., 1978).

We can either passively absorb our values from our culture—family, friends, church, the media—or we can actively question and choose from among the various possibilities. In this section we will consider some information which can help us to choose our values in the area of sexuality.

VALUES: A SHIFTING LANDSCAPE

It is no secret that attitudes about acceptable sexual behavior have changed dramat-ically in the last 100 years of Western culture. The shift from sexual repression in the Victorian era to sexual liberation in the last half of the 20th century has been called a *sexual revolution*.

In general terms, the revolution brought a greater openness and freedom to sex (Bauman & Wilson, 1976; Gallup, 1985). More specifically, there has been a marked increase in non-marital sex (pre-marital, extra-marital, or simply non-marital cohabitation) (Pratt, 1990; Tanfer & Schoorl, 1992). And there has been a move-ment towards greater equality between the sexes, for example in recognizing women's sexuality. (We can see the effects of both of these trends in the weakening of the so-called "double standard," which said that non-marital sex was fine for men but not for women. Today it's much more accepted for both.)

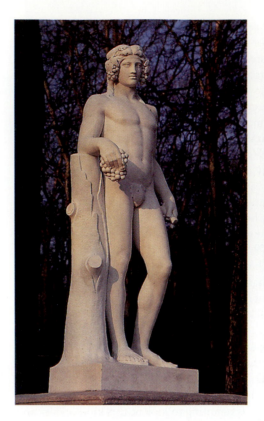 

The degree of sexual explicitness encountered in Western culture has changed significantly during the last 100 years.

When it comes to choosing our values, however, we need to be careful not to assume that because something is acceptable for other people—even for many other people—it is necessarily the best for us. Freedom from Victorian repression and from the denial of women's sexuality was a welcome relief. But in the rush to greater sexual expression, we may have created a new ideology and a new oppression.

For many people in Western culture the new ideal has become a high level of sexual competence and *performance*. Unfortunately, this new "freedom" does not allow for the freedom to say no. Instead of feeling guilty when we experience sex, as a Victorian man or woman might have, we are made to feel guilty when we *don't* experience sex—or enough sex, or the "best" sex (Greer, 1984; Hettlinger, 1974).

In the last 10 years, however, there has been a partial return to more conservative values. One evidence of this movement is the greater interest in "safer sex" (Masters et al., 1992).

SAFER SEX: RESPONSIBILITY AND FREEDOM

Existential psychotherapist Viktor Frankl suggests that just as there is a statue of liberty on the east coast of the United States, there should be a "statue of responsibility" on the west coast. Responsibility must balance freedom.

When we have sex with another person there are potential consequences for which we are responsible. First, in heterosexual intercourse, there is the possibility that fertilization will take place and a new human being will begin to develop. Second, there is the possibility of contracting or spreading disease.

In order to enjoy the *freedom* of sex without pregnancy, both you and your partner are *responsible* to see that you take adequate birth control measures. If you don't, and pregnancy occurs (either intentionally or unintentionally), you are *responsible* to decide between abortion, adoption, or a long-term commitment to providing for the needs of your child.

The *freedom* to enjoy sexual contact also includes the *responsibility* to protect yourself and your partner from sexually transmitted diseases (STDs). There are more than a dozen diseases that are spread primarily through sexual contact. Some produce mild discomfort and are mainly a nuisance; some are life threatening. Some are curable; some are not.

Two of the most serious STDs are hepatitis B and AIDS. Both hepatitis B (not to be confused with hepatitis A, C, or D) and AIDS, are incurable, and potentially fatal.

Hepatitis B is a viral infection of the liver. Most newly infected people experience flu-like symptoms: fever, fatigue, jaundice (yellowish skin), abdominal pain, and vomiting. The symptoms can be treated and usually subside in a few weeks, although the individual continues to carry the disease for the rest of his or her life. Occasionally, the initial inflammation of the liver can be so severe that death results. On the other hand, some individuals (approximately 500,000 in the United States) carry and transmit the disease without showing *any* symptoms. Hepatitis B sufferers, with or without the usual symptoms, have a greatly increased chance of developing cirrhosis of the liver and liver cancer. Despite the fact that there is a vaccine against hepatitis B, there are approximately 200,000 new cases of the disease in the United States each year.

AIDS is caused by the HIV (human immunodeficiency virus), which breaks down the body's ability to fight other diseases. After infection, the virus may progress very slowly or remain dormant for several years. It takes 2–3 months or even longer before HIV infection progresses to the stage where it can be detected in a blood test. And symptoms may not develop for years, although the infected person can still infect others. HIV infections lead to AIDS in an average of 5 years. Death follows the onslaught of AIDS symptoms usually in a matter of 1 to 2 years (Bachetti & Moss, 1989; Cohen et al., 1990).

While there is no single pattern of AIDS symptoms, some signs are common. These include progressive, unexplained weight loss, persistent fever, swollen lymph nodes, and slightly raised reddish-purple coin-sized spots on the skin. At this stage the body's disease defense system has been broken down and the individual may develop any of a series of other "opportunistic" infections. It is these infections, such as pneumonia and tuberculosis, that eventually lead to death.

FIGURE 7.4

Annual rates per 100,000 population for AIDS cases reported in the United States during 1992 (Centers for Disease Control and Prevention. HIV/AIDS Surveillance Report, February 1993).

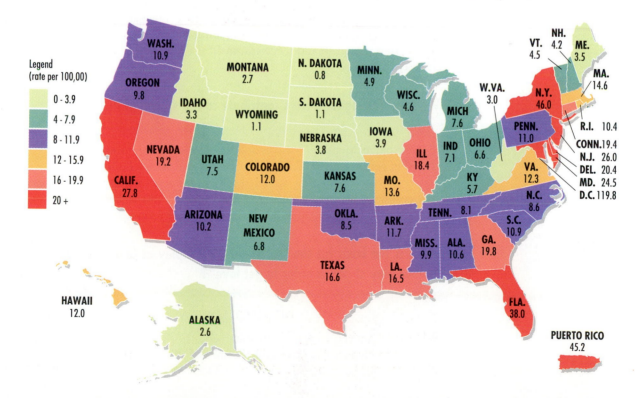

HIV infection produces psychological impairment in about 10 percent of cases (Egan, 1992; Egan & Goodwin, 1992). This figure rises to 30 to 65 percent when full-blown AIDS symptoms develop (Liskin & Blackburn, 1986; Gabuza & Hirsch, 1987). Possible symptoms include disturbances in concentration, learning, memory, speech, motivation, and emotional control.

According to the U.S. Centers for Disease Control, there had been 253,448 cases of AIDS reported by the end of December 1992 (Doll, 1993). This figure is just the tip of the iceberg, however, since AIDS is only the final stage of the HIV infection. In the United States, more than 1.5 million people are thought to have the HIV infection and therefore are expected to develop AIDS (Coolfront Report, 1986; Centers for Disease Control, 1989). In other parts of the world the rate of infection is more than 10 times higher (Carballo et al., 1989; Tierney, 1990).

Look around at the people on your campus. How many do you think are infected with HIV/AIDS? How would you know?

Both HIV/AIDS and hepatitis B are spread by the exchange of body fluids. The spread occurs primarily through intimate sexual contact (homosexual *and* hetero-sexual) and through sharing intravenous needles. More rarely, these diseases spread through the transfusion of contaminated blood, and in the womb from an infected mother to her unborn child. It is also possible for a nursing mother to infect her child through her breast milk (Levy, 1989).

The fear of AIDS has made more people aware of the dangers of all STDs and of their responsibility to take steps to avoid these infections. Condoms, the most pop-ular precaution, greatly reduce the risk of most infections (and pregnancy). However, since condoms are less than 90 percent effective, sex with a condom can only be considered "saf*er* sex" (Hatcher et al., 1990; Masters et al., 1992; Miller et al., 1988). The only *safe* sex occurs in a mutually faithful relationship with an unin-fected person.

Unwanted pregnancies and sexually transmitted diseases are potential conse-quences of irresponsible sex. Responsible sexuality means frank and honest commu-nication with your partner *before* it's too late. If pregnancy is not desirable, what method of birth control will you use? And if either of you has ever been sexually active, that person should receive a medical examination for sexually transmitted diseases.

What *non*-biological factors contribute to the spread of AIDS?

A sexual relationship involves another person, and the responsibility we take for the other person is an important part of our sexual values. Perhaps the return to more conservative standards that we noted earlier represents a recognition of *responsibility* that corresponds with our increased sexual *freedom*. As Robert says in our opening quotation, "It comes down to being responsible for yourself."

What is the basis for the statement: "Men play at love in order to get sex; women play at sex in order to get love"?

INTIMACY, LOVE, AND SEX

Whether or not you agree with the statement, the "Thought Question" you have just seen clearly implies that love and sex are not the same thing. Most people would agree.

Sometimes, however, we tend to confuse the two. We may talk about "making love" when we mean having sexual intercourse. Many movies and television shows reinforce this conclusion by delivering a "love equals sex" message.

Do love and sex go together? Or is it O.K. to have one without the other? When is sex appropriate in a relationship? What kind of relationship? These are questions of sexual values. They deal with the role of relationships in determining sexual behavior.

In deciding on your values it may help if you reflect on your view of the purpose of sex. After we have considered the purpose of sex, we will look at some views of the relationship we call "love."

THE PURPOSE OF SEX.   From a biological and evolutionary perspective, the purpose of sex is procreation. We have sex in order to have children. According to this perspective, birth control, masturbation, oral-genital stimulation, and anal intercourse are not acceptable. This **procreational attitude** also implies that sex should occur only between a man and a woman who are prepared to provide for the needs of the children they produce. Many religions also emphasize this *procreational attitude* toward sex. From the religious viewpoint the procreational attitude means that sex should occur only within the context of marriage. Consequently, people with a religious perspective tend to adopt more conservative values regarding sexual behavior, although there is great variability between groups and between individuals (Falbo & Shepperd, 1986; Reed & Meyers, 1991). If you adopt a procreational attitude toward sex, your main concern in a sexual relationship will be the commitment of both people to maintain that relationship.

For some people the purpose of sex is pleasure. These people have a **recreational attitude** toward sex. The recreational attitude toward sex developed out of the sexual revolution of the 1960s and 1970s. At that time birth control technology separated procreation from sexuality. If you adopt a strongly recreational attitude toward sex your main concern is pleasure, and you will have little concern for factors in your relationship which do not affect your pleasure.

Today, more and more people are adopting a **relational attitude** toward sex. (Sherwin & Corbett, 1985). This means that the *type of relationship* determines whether or not sexual acts are permitted. Children and pleasure may be secondary concerns, but the primary consideration is the relationship: Has it progressed to the point where sex is appropriate? For some people, marriage is the only relationship appropriate for sex. For others a more limited commitment is satisfactory. But for most people relational sex means that the partners must *love* each other.

LOVE.   We use the word "love" in many ways, from the strong bond we feel toward someone we would die for, to the attraction we feel for pizza. In describing sexual relationships, many psychologists refer to *passionate love* and *companionate love* (Hatfield & Walster, 1985).

Passionate love is the intense whirlwind of emotions and sexual desire we feel for someone in the initial stages of a romantic relationship (Hatfield & Rapson, 1987). The expressions "falling in love" or "head over heels in love" refer to this type of intense emotional experience. Some people call this feeling "infatuation," preferring to reserve the term "love" or "true love" for a more mature relationship. During the passionate stage sexual attraction may be very strong. However, the ability to consider long-term consequences of sexual behavior is limited by intense emotions and irrational thinking (Hatfield & Walster, 1985).

The emotional "high" from passionate love usually lasts from 6 to 30 months before it inevitably dissipates. Some individuals find this stage so addictive that they look for another "fix" as soon as one wears off, moving from relationship to relationship. If a relationship lasts beyond this stage it invariably changes.

In committed partners **companionate love** develops as passionate love cools. Companionate love is the strong affection we feel for those with whom our lives are

Sometimes the procreational potential of sex is not recognized by those who adopt a recreational attitude toward sexual behavior.

Procreational attitude. As applied to sex, the view that the purpose of sex is reproduction (procreation).

Recreational attitude. As applied to sex, the view that the purpose of sex is recreation, pleasure, and enjoyment.

Relational attitude. As applied to sex, the view that sex affects relationships, and that the characteristics of the relationship should determine the role of sex.

Passionate love. The highly emotional and erotic first stage of strong attraction between two people in a romantic relationship.

Companionate love. The strong affection between people whose lives are deeply intertwined. May include periods of passionate love but does not depend on this type of intense emotion.

deeply intertwined (Hatfield & Walster, 1985). Lovers at this stage are also best friends who enjoy each other out of bed as well as in bed. They accept the fact that their partner is not perfect and that their feelings for him or her will vary. But companionate lovers are committed to riding out the variations.

In choosing your sexual values you may find it helpful to consider the *purpose* of sexual behavior—procreation? recreation? or relationships? And if you believe *love* to be important, you might want to consider some of the ways love changes, and then decide which elements are important for you. Will your sexual behavior be tied to the intense emotions of passionate love, or the intimacy and commitment of companionate love?

People who choose to follow their religion or culture may have these choices prescribed for them. In many cultures recreational sex is unheard of, sex is for procreation only, and love, if it occurs at all, *follows* a pre-arranged marriage. In North America, most religions recognize some recreational value of sex, but only within the bounds of love *and* marriage.

Finally, whatever you decide, you would do well to make sure that your partner feels the same way.

SEXUAL VALUES: A SUMMARY

We have noted three factors that you might want to consider in choosing your sexual values:

1. Are you being unduly influenced by arbitrary cultural standards?

2. Are you prepared to accept responsibility for the consequences of your sexual behavior?

3. What is the purpose of sex? And what is the relationship of sex to love?

If we do not actively consider these and related issues, chances are that we will simply passively absorb the standards displayed around us, especially those presented in the mass media. The mass media, however, are designed to entertain, not educate. Consequently, violence, coercive sex, and sexually stimulating topics are presented in disproportionate amounts in order to capture and hold our attention (Radecki, 1990; Yang & Linz, 1990). When we expose ourselves to this unbalanced view repeatedly, we tend to see sexual and other forms of violence as much more common and acceptable than they really are (Linz et al., 1992). And we may become preoccupied with our sexual pleasure and ignore our corresponding responsibility.

Values are important. They not only guide specific behaviors, they give overall direction to our lives. Values deserve our active attention and thoughtful consideration.

A HOLISTIC VIEW OF SEXUAL MOTIVATION

Human sexuality is obviously a complex experience that is multi-determined. And we still have much to learn. William Masters puts it this way: "The science of sexuality is in its infancy, and there's no one orientation to it—not medicine only, not behavioral science only, but also theology, social work, politics, on and on. No matter what your background, there's always some postgraduate work to do" (quoted in Gallagher, 1986).

What we do know is this: The androgens, estrogens, and progesterone shape our bodies, bias our brains, and energize our behaviors. But *overriding* these biological motivations are the neural commands that come from the higher centers of our brains. And these neural commands are primarily learned or the product of voluntary choice.

Society influences your choice in such matters by providing you with models of "appropriate" behaviors. Some of these models are arbitrary, and may vary markedly from one culture to another. Other models, though, may be based on "genetic reality," for males typically are larger and stronger than females. On the other hand, females can bear and nurse children, while males cannot. These facts subtly shape, *but do not entirely determine*, our sexual attitudes and behaviors.

Ultimately, however, sexual motivation comes down to a matter of values and choice. We must choose how we will respond to the biological, psychological, and social influences on our sexuality. It is the *interaction* between these factors that helps make sex the fascinating topic that it is—and probably always will be.

1. Sexual needs have a **biological basis,** but differ from hunger and thirst in that they are necessary for the survival of the species, but not the individual. Many aspects of sexual motivation cannot be explained biologically.

2. **Havelock Ellis** and **Sigmund Freud** published information about the reported sexual lives of their patients and helped to make sexuality a more acceptable topic of conversation and research.

3. **John B. Watson** studied the female sexual response, but lost his professorship because of his research.

4. **Alfred Kinsey** published the first **scientific survey** of sexual behavior in 1948. The first published studies of actual **human sexual behavior** were done by Masters and Johnson.

5. You began life as a single **egg cell** that contained 23 **chromosomes.** At the moment of **fertilization,** one of your father's sperms penetrated the egg and added 23 chromosomes of its own.

6. If an **X sperm** unites with the egg, the 23rd chromosome will be **XX,** and the child will be a genetic female. If a **Y sperm** unites with the egg, the 23rd chromosome will be **XY,** and the child will be a genetic male.

7. The **sex hormones** are secreted by the **adrenal glands** and by the **gonads,** the **testes** in males and the **ovaries** in females.

8. The male hormones are called **androgens,** the best-known of which is **testosterone.** The female hormones are the **estrogens** and **progesterone.**

9. Both male and female hormones are found in both sexes. It is the relative amount of these hormones during development that determines **primary** and **secondary sex** characteristics.

10. Sexual arousal follows a similar cycle in men and women, going from **excitement** to **plateau** to **orgasm** to **resolution.**

11. **Hormones** play an indirect role in sexual arousal in humans. The **autonomic nervous system, spinal reflexes,** and **higher brain centers** all play more direct roles in human sexual arousal and orgasm.

12. Freud believed that **physical sexual characteristics** had a direct influence on our **psychological development.**

13. Humanistic psychologists believe that sexuality can be an important part of a **self-actualizing** person's development.

14. Psychologists use the word **sex** to refer to a person's **biological** maleness or femaleness; they use the word **gender** to refer to the **nonbiological** aspects of sex. Gender refers to the **social** definition of what is "masculine" and what is "feminine."

15. **Identification theory** and **gender schema theory** are two views of how we develop our **gender identity.**

16. **Gender-role stereotypes** are widely shared concepts that prescribe how each sex ought to behave.

17. **Stereotyping** begins at birth and affects the way people **perceive** males and females—and the way they perceive themselves.

18. An **androgynous** person is someone who feels free to express emotions and behaviors regardless of whether or not they are traditionally considered appropriate for the person's gender.

19. The three main types of sexual orientation are **heterosexual, bisexual,** and **homosexual.** Orientation is influenced by biological, intra-psychic, and cultural factors.

20. Sexual self-stimulation, or **masturbation,** is no longer considered harmful as it once was. It is more common among males than females.

21. **Sexual fantasies** and **dreams** can be sexually arousing to the point of orgasm. Fantasies are frequent accompaniments to masturbation and sexual intercourse.

22. Date rape and incest are two examples of **coercive sex.** Coercive sex is usually more an act of power (including elements of anger, hostility, and violence), than it is an act of passion.

23. **Date rape** is a growing problem on college and university campuses. It is often related to personal and social factors in the situation more than to an uncontrolled sexual urge.

24. Although not the most common, the most often reported and damaging form of **incest** is father-daughter (and stepfather-stepdaughter) incest. Several situational factors have been identified which seem to predict the likelihood of a young girl being sexually abused.

25. Sexual motivation involves **choices** based on **values.**

26. Sexual values should be based on individual **choice, responsibility,** and decisions about the **purpose of sex** and the role of **love.**

27. Sexual motivation is **multi-determined.** A **holistic** view incorporates biological, intra-psychic, and social factors. An important element in all motivation is the role of choice.

ANSWERS FOR THOUGHT

1. *Occasionally a female is born with only one X chromosome (XO), and males are sometimes born with . . . ?*

   In general these unusual patterns lead to deficiencies (XO) or excesses (XXY, XYY) in sex-related traits. XO females (Turner's syndrome) are sterile and do not develop secondary sex characteristics (unless they take estrogen pills). XXY males (Klinefelter's syndrome) usually have small penises and testes, high-pitched voices, and little facial hair. They may develop breasts in puberty and they are generally sterile. XYY males are taller than average. They are usually sexually active with many partners.

2. *Why do you think the brain has been called the largest sex organ in the body?*

   This statement refers to the power of the mind to stimulate sexual arousal. Sexual images, fantasies, and dreams can arouse the body even to the point of orgasm—without direct physical stimulation.

3. *What would it be like to be unsure of your gender, or even your physical sex?*

   People who suffer *gender dysphoria* feel that they were born with the body of the wrong sex. If the feelings are strong enough they may undergo surgery and take hormones in order to change their physical characteristics to agree with their feelings of gender. On the other hand, some people are born with ambiguous sex organs as the result of pre-natal hormone imbalances. In most cases these "inter-sexes" (or pseudohermaphrodites) develop normal feelings of gender identity providing they are assigned a gender before age 3 and then are reared consistently according to the assigned gender.

4. *Suppose you are a heterosexual male, hence strongly attracted to females. If men and women dressed . . . ?*

   The task would certainly be more difficult. Other cues, such as physical size, shape, voice pitch, and even smell, would become more important.

5. *What benefits do you gain from having ready-made social responses for the males and females you meet?*

   Ready-made responses reduce uncomfortable uncertainty in social relationships. Having a set of basic responses frees us to think about more complex interactions.

6. *How might culture amplify male/female differences, for example in verbal and mathematical ability?*

   Teachers often have a bias which leads them to respond differently to boys and girls (Shepardson & Pizzini, 1992). Teachers also overestimate male/female differences and subtly steer children in different directions (Klauer, 1992). By the time students reach college they know that society *expects* men to become scientists and women to become nurses and teachers (Hennin-Stout & Conoley, 1992; Lips, 1992; Fox & Firebaugh, 1992). In this way society encourages stereotypical behavior and discourages non-stereotypical behavior. As attitudes towards sexual equality have changed in the last few years, male/female differences in verbal and mathematical ability have declined (Feingold, 1992).

7. *How is your understanding of homosexuality affected by your knowledge of its causes?*

   As we saw in our discussion of obesity, people are inclined to be less tolerant of minority group members if they believe the group members chose to belong to the minority group. Similarly, people may be less understanding and accepting of homosexual individuals if they believe that they are homosexual by choice.

8. *Look around at the people on your campus. How many do you think are infected with AIDS? How would you know?*

   It is estimated that 1 in 500 college or university students are infected with the AIDS virus (Caron et al., 1992; Leary, 1989). You would not know a person was infected by looking at him or her. In fact, the person might not even know!

9. *What non-biological factors contribute to the spread of AIDS?*

   Some non-biological factors that contribute to the spread of AIDS: ignorance about how AIDS is spread (believing only homosexuals or drug users get AIDS), condom failure (through ignorance about how to install one properly or through a flawed condom), embarassment over asking one's partner if he or she has been tested for AIDS, fear of getting tested for AIDS, false beliefs ("It can't happen to me"), implicit personality theories or assumptions about being able to tell "the kind of person" who would have AIDS.

10. *What is the basis for the statement: "Men play at love in order to get sex; women play at sex in order to get love"?*

    This statement reflects the so-called "double standard" which says that it's fine for men to have non-marital sex but not for women. Although both may enjoy sex, women may be more concerned with love than men are because love implies a commitment to care for her during pregnancy and for their offspring after birth. Men are less aware of the long-term consequences of sex because they are not forced upon men as directly. This statement and the double standard are also products of a male-dominated society.

CHAPTER 8

EMOTIONS, STRESS, AND HEALTH

Our lips are deliciously soft and responsive. Their touch sensations are represented by a large part of the brain, and what a boon that is to kissing.

When I was in high school in the early sixties, nice girls didn't go all the way. But man, could we kiss! We kissed for hours in the busted-up front seat of a borrowed Chevy; we kissed extravagantly beside a turtlearium in the park, we kissed wildly, almost painfully, with tough soul-searching rigor, we kissed as if kissing could save us from ourselves.

DIANE ACKERMAN
"A NATURAL HISTORY OF THE SENSES"

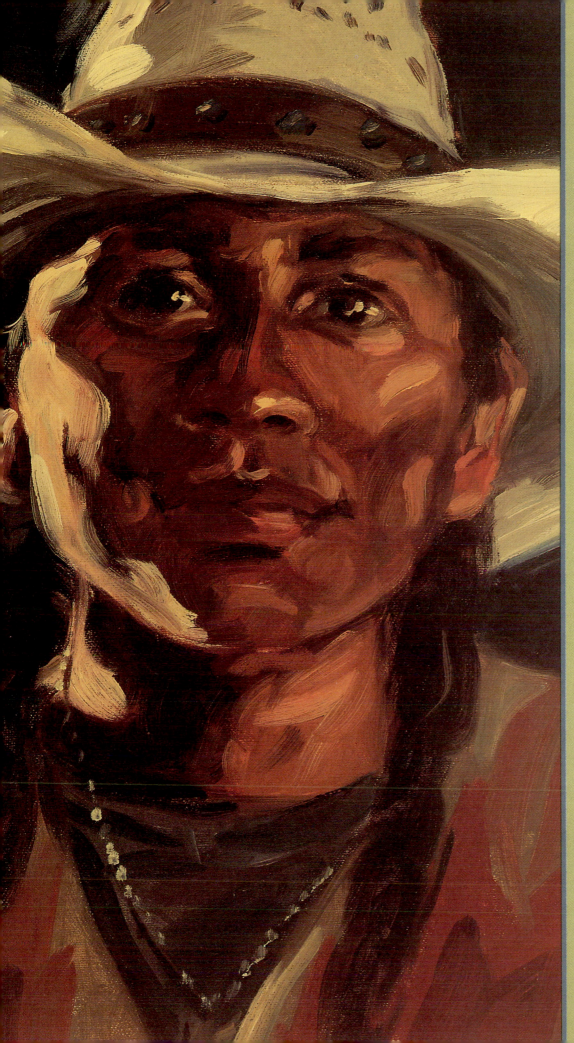

EMOTIONS

Emotions. Mood, affect, or strong feeling. A combination of physiological changes, mental responses, and expressive behaviors.

Kissing "extravagantly," "wildly," "almost painfully," is certainly an emotional experience! And according to the founder of stress research, Hans Selye, a passionate kiss can produce the same physical stress reaction as the lash of a whip!

In this chapter we will look at emotions and at stress. Selye defined stress as "the body's nonspecific response to *any* demand placed on it" (Selye, 1978). Emotions, however, are not as easy to define (Haaland, 1992; Lazarus, 1991). The word "emotion" comes from the same Latin source as the word "motivation" and it means "to move." We can think of **emotions** as "movements" in feelings and thoughts accompanied by physiological changes and frequently expressive behaviors.

More specifically, emotions are made up of the following five elements:

- Physical arousal or depression.
- Feelings—usually those of pleasure or displeasure.
- Cognitive awareness and appraisal of the experience.
- Emotionally expressive behaviors.
- Environmental inputs and consequences.

Various theorists tend to emphasize one or more of these five elements. For simplicity, we can divide views of emotionality into three categories. These are the familiar biological, intra-psychic, and social/behavioral perspectives.

In the first part of this chapter, we will look at your emotions from the each of these viewpoints. We will pay particular attention to such stressful emotional reactions as fear, anger, rage, and aggression. Then we will define emotions from a holistic point of view. Finally, we will discuss the study of health, and the way stress affects health.

Which of the "elements of emotionality" does each of these theoretical perspectives seem to stress?

Emotions produce intense physical responses, which can be very stressful.

THE BIOLOGY OF EMOTION

Those psychologists who view emotionality as primarily a biological event tend to perceive emotional reactions as being your body's way of preparing to respond to some kind of physical or psychological challenge. Perhaps you are in danger; then you must prepare yourself either to fight (in anger or rage) or to get out of the threatening situation because you are afraid. Or perhaps you are hungry and discover some food; then you must calm yourself down so that you can consume and digest your meal in comfort. In either case, your biological reactions are likely to be *reflexive* and hence *beyond your voluntary control*.

Put in simple terms, biological theorists tend to view emotions as "instinctual survival mechanisms," "animal instincts," or "primitive passions" that civilized humans must constantly strive to control. Because of this viewpoint, many biological theorists believe that "emotional problems" can only be cured by means of *physical* treatment, such as pills and surgery. We'll return to *physical treatments* of "emotional problems" in a moment. First let's look more closely at what goes on in your body when you experience an emotion.

Adrenalin and the ANS

In Chapter 2 we discussed two major "control systems" that mediate emotional responses. These are the *endocrine system* and the *autonomic nervous system* (ANS). When you feel an emotion, such as rage, the sympathetic division of your ANS swings into action. It slows down your digestion, and speeds up your heart rate, breathing, and sweating; it increases your blood-sugar level. In short, the sympathetic system prepares you for fighting or fleeing.

The sympathetic nervous system also stimulates the *adrenal glands* in your endocrine system. The adrenal glands then release adrenalin and noradrenalin into your bloodstream. These hormones *sustain* the physical arousal that your sympathetic nervous system began.

The Limbic System

In addition to the ANS and the adrenal glands in your endocrine system, your *limbic system* also plays a key role in emotional arousal. The Latin word *limbus* means "border." The limbic system is so named because it makes up the "border" or inner surface of both your cerebral hemispheres. There are identical limbic systems in both your hemispheres. But since they are usually in close touch with each other (via the corpus callosal bridge), we can consider the two systems as one unit.

Your limbic system has several parts or structures to it (see Figure 8.1). One of these structures is the **amygdala,** which is buried deep within the temporal lobe on each side of your head. The amygdala is a nut-shaped group of neurons that gets its name from the Latin word for "almond." Since the amygdala in each of your temporal lobes has a decided influence on how violent you are, and on your sex life, it is well worth studying.

CORTEX VERSUS LIMBIC SYSTEM

Under normal circumstances, your cortex maintains control over the "primitive, emotional reactions" that activity in your limbic system sets off. But what happens when you lose cortical control of the limbic system? In cats and other lower animals, the answer is clear. If we remove the animal's cortex surgically while leaving the limbic system intact, this "de-cortex-ed" (or **decorticate**) animal gets along surprisingly well, considering that it has been deprived of more than 10 percent of its brain. There seems to be no basic change in the animal's personality—friendly cats remain

Amygdala (a-MIG-dah-lah). An almond-shaped nerve center in your temporal lobes that is part of your limbic system. Removal of the amygdala makes a monkey rather unemotional and easygoing, but has other effects as well.

Decorticate (de-CORT-ih-kate). An animal or human whose cortex has been removed, usually through surgery.

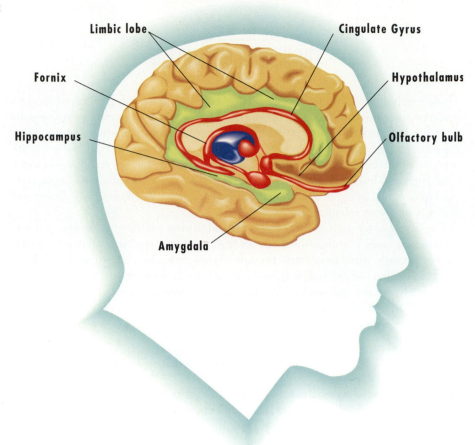

FIGURE 8.1

The limbic system is a related set of nerve centers in your brain that influences your emotional behavior. The structures labeled in this diagram are generally considered to be part of the limbic system. Although it can't be seen in this cross-section, the hippocampus and amygdala extend into the temporal lobes in each hemisphere of the brain.

Aggressive behavior in monkeys has been shown to increase when parts of the limbic system—especially the amygdala—are stimulated.

friendly, and aggressive felines remain aggressive. However, even very slight pain or frustration is enough to set these animals into an explosive, violent rage (Isaacson, 1974).

Next, what do you think would happen if we "reversed" the kind of operation just described? That is, what if we removed parts of the limbic system in animals but left most of the cortex intact? Heinrich Kluever and Paul Bucy were probably the first scientists to perform this operation. Their experimental animals were rhesus monkeys, a species of primate noted for its vile temper and its readiness to aggress. Kluever and Bucy removed the temporal lobes from *both* hemispheres in their animals—thus taking out the amygdalas and other parts of the limbic system. After the monkeys had recovered, their personalities appeared to have changed rather profoundly. They were gentle and placid in almost all circumstances, even when attacked by another animal (Kluever & Bucy, 1937). Later studies by other scientists confirmed the Kluever and Bucy experiment by showing that removal of the amygdala in several species of wild animals makes them relatively tame (Isaacson, 1974).

STIMULATING THE AMYGDALA

Given the results of the Kluever-Bucy study, what do you think would happen if you could somehow stimulate the amygdala in a normal cat? The answer is not particularly surprising. If you insert a long, thin needle electrode into a cat's amygdala and turn on the current, the animal flies into a rage. Its hair stands on end, its back arches, it spits and screams, and it will usually attack anything nearby (including the experimenter) (Isaacson, 1974).

BRAIN DAMAGE AND VIOLENCE IN HUMANS

Most humans can tolerate a fair amount of stress without becoming violent. Others of us, however, seem to fly off the handle at the slightest provocation. Could it be that extremely bad-tempered individuals might suffer from some subtle damage to their amygdalas?

Vernon Mark and Frank Ervin, two scientists who worked together in Boston for many years, believe that senseless human violence is almost always associated with some form of brain damage. Mark and Ervin studied many patients who were hospitalized because they had killed or maimed others in "fits of rage." Some of these patients also had epileptic-type seizures, and EEG recordings often suggested the presence of scar tissue in their amygdalas.

When drugs and psychotherapy failed to reduce the number of violent attacks these patients had, Mark and Ervin decided to remove the damaged amygdalas surgically. Some of the patients showed a dramatic improvement following the operation. Unfortunately, many of the patients either were unchanged in their behaviors, or even became worse (Mark & Ervin, 1970).

If the "amygdal operation" were perfected, do you think that all violent criminals should have their amygdalas removed, whether they wished the surgery or not?

PSYCHOSURGERY

Physicians call operations such as the removal of the amygdala, "psychosurgery." The purpose of the surgery is to "cure" patients of inappropriate emotions or behaviors that seemingly cannot be "cured" by pills or psychotherapy.

But before we routinely chop up people's brains in order to "make them behave," we should take note of the following dangers:

1. Mark and Ervin have been able to demonstrate clear-cut brain damage in but a small fraction of the patients they have studied. There is no doubt that people with damaged amygdalas often are violent. However, there is little or no reliable evidence that most people who are violent have damaged amygdalas.

2. The surgery did not improve all of Mark and Ervin's patients.

3. Not all scientists have been successful in their attempts to repeat the Mark and Ervin research (Valenstein, 1980).

Despite the evidence showing that psychosurgery is not a particularly effective way to change behavior, the technique continues to be used on some patients. The people in favor of psychosurgery are primarily those scientists and medical doctors who believe the brain controls the mind, who feel that most emotions must be *controlled* if civilization is to survive, and who have little faith that people can *learn self-control*. We will return to this point later.

What kind of experiment might you perform to determine if it were the removal of the amygdala that decreased the patient's violent episodes, or merely the fact that the patient had an operation of some kind?

Biological Theories

The complex interplay between autonomic arousal on the one hand, and emotional behaviors and feelings on the other, has long fascinated theorists. It may surprise you to see the way theorists have tried to separate these different elements.

THE JAMES-LANGE THEORY

In 1884, psychologist William James proposed one of the earliest theories of emotion. According to James, your body always takes the lead in emotional situations.

Your feelings, James said, are mental responses to the changes that have *already occurred* in your autonomic nervous system, muscles, and glands.

Let's see what James was really saying. Suppose you are driving down the expressway on a lovely summer day when another driver suddenly (and stupidly) cuts right in front of you. Chances are, you will immediately experience a classic "rage reaction." That is, your heart will start pounding, your face will flush, and you will breathe more rapidly. You may express your opinion of the other driver in a loud tone of voice, and you may make various gestures at the person.

Now, you might think that you first became angry and then experienced autonomic arousal. But that is not the case, James said. Rather, your body reacted *automatically* to the situation, and *then* you experienced the "subjective" qualities associated with anger or rage. According to James, your physical responses precede and thus *cause* your emotional "feelings."

In 1885, the noted Danish scientist Karl Lange independently proposed much the same sort of explanation of emotional behavior. For that reason, this viewpoint is often called the **James-Lange theory of emotions.**

Suppose you encounter a snake unexpectedly and you run away. According to James, do you run because you're afraid, or do you become afraid because you ran?

James-Lange theory of emotions. A theory proposed by William James and Karl Lange (LAHNG-gah) that presumes emotional "feelings" are caused by and follow bodily responses, not vice versa.

According to the James-Lange theory, if you met this snake unexpectedly, you would first react physically and then identify your response as fear.

THE CANNON-BARD THEORY

The James-Lange approach led to a lot of highly "emotional" debate and, happily, a lot of useful research as well. For example, in 1927 physiologist Walter Cannon pointed out three objections to the James-Lange theory: First, James-Lange assume your feelings are dependent upon activity in your sympathetic nervous system. However, people who (through accident or disease) have lost use of their sympathetic systems still feel emotions and show emotional behaviors. Second, the physical changes associated with emotion generally occur *after* the "feelings and behaviors" have started, not *before* they take place. And third, the *same* physical changes occur in very *different* emotional states, and in non-emotional states as well (Cannon, 1927).

Cannon held that two different parts of the brain, the *thalamus* and the *hypothalamus*, processed emotional inputs *simultaneously*. According to Cannon, the thalamus controls emotional *feelings*, while the hypothalamus controls *bodily responses*. Thus, Cannon said, you would experience conscious "fear" of a snake even if your body were totally paralyzed and you *couldn't* run. Why? Because different centers in your brain mediate "fear" and "running" (Cannon, 1929).

Philip Bard advanced almost the same viewpoint in 1927. For that reason, this explanation of emotionality is often called the **Cannon-Bard theory.**

As it turned out, however, critics levelled the same sort of arguments against the Cannon-Bard theory that Cannon leveled against James and Lange. Karl Lashley noted people with a damaged thalamus still experience emotional feelings, and people with a damaged hypothalamus still show emotional responses (Beach et al., 1960). Other scientists showed that both the *limbic system* and the cerebral hemispheres were involved in mediating emotional feelings and behaviors.

Cannon-Bard theory of emotions. Cannon and Bard believed that "feelings" and "bodily responses" occurred in parallel in emotional situations. The "feelings" supposedly were mediated by the thalamus, while emotional responses were presumably mediated by the hypothalamus.

How do you know to run from a snake until you have perceived the snake and been aroused by this perception? And since arousal is a part of both rage and fear, if you merely realized that you were "aroused," how would you know whether to run from the snake or attack it?

No one disputes the fact that bodily reactions do play an important role in *creating* and *sustaining* emotions. However, our feelings are so frightfully complex that we simply can't reduce them to mere hormonal and neural activity. To gain a more complete understanding of emotionality, we must look at intra-psychic and social variables as well.

INTRA-PSYCHIC ASPECTS OF EMOTION

In 1962 Stanley Schacter and Jerome Singer reported an interesting study which demonstrated that emotions are not just physical arousal. The researchers first gave participants an injection of adrenalin and then led them to a waiting room to fill out a questionnaire. They told one group of participants that the injection would raise their heart rate and make them feel aroused. They did not tell the other participants what to expect from the drug. In the waiting room the participants found an accomplice of the experimenters who began to act in either a happy, carefree manner, or an angry, disturbed manner. Participants who had not been told what to expect from the drug used the behavior of the accomplice to interpret their arousal. These participants reported feeling either happy or angry depending on how the accomplice had acted. Subjects who knew what to expect from the drug already had an explanation for their arousal. The actions of the accomplice did not affect them.

Male subjects who met an attractive young woman on this suspension bridge were more likely to call her later than those who met her on level ground. Apparently, the subjects interpreted their arousal as attraction.

Schachter and Singer conclude that emotions are the result of two factors: bodily arousal and cognitive appraisal. You experience an emotion when your body is aroused *and* you have a cognitive label for the experience (Schachter, 1971; Schachter & Singer, 1962).

Several more recent studies illustrate the influence of a cognitive label on our experience of arousal. For instance, Donald Dutton and Arthur Aron found that arousal caused by danger can be misinterpreted as sexual attraction. These experimenters had an attractive female accomplice interview male hikers in one of two conditions: on solid ground, or on a swaying footbridge high above a rocky canyon. The men who met the woman on the swaying bridge were much more likely to call her later for a date than those who met her on solid ground. Apparently, the men attributed their physical arousal to sexual attraction for the woman rather than to fear (Dutton & Aron, 1974, 1989).

Some people report that they are most easily aroused sexually when they are hungry, or immediately after a frightening experience or a violent argument. Why might this often be the case?

Intra-Psychic Theories

Actually, the discussion about the role of cognition in emotion goes back long before Schachter's research. Almost 100 years ago William James, Wilhelm Wundt, and Carl Stumpf debated this issue (Reisenzein & Schönpflug, 1992).

Today there are several newer theories that follow Schachter in recognizing the importance of intra-psychic processes. Each theory contributes to our understanding by giving different emphasis to either unconscious, intuitive, and feeling responses on the one hand, or conscious, rational, cognitive responses on the other. Let's look at five of these intra-psychic views of emotion.

In presenting these theories, we have given them labels to help distinguish them from each other. Although each one recognizes the importance of intra-psychic processes, they differ in the emphasis they assign to the various elements. Some believe that the cognitive *appraisal* or labeling of an emotion comes *after* the emotional feeling. Some believe that the cognitive appraisal is an integral component of the emotion itself. We will approach the theories in a sequence which moves from an unconscious, intuitive, "feeling" emphasis to a conscious, rational, "cognitive" emphasis.

FREUD'S "ENERGY" THEORY

Sigmund Freud is undoubtedly the best known of the psychologists who view emotions as "inner passions." Freud believed you were born with the capacity to feel two types of sensations—pleasure and unpleasure (or pain). These powerful sensory drives exist in the unconscious portions of your mind, Freud said. The "emotions" you are aware of as an adult—love and hate, anger and disgust—actually *differentiated* out of the primitive sensory drives through experience. That is, as you matured, you associated certain types of situations with pleasure, and other situations with unpleasure. For example, you learned to love your mother because she gave you pleasure by feeding you and caring for you. But your love for your mother exists in the combination of your conscious associations with your unconscious feelings.

Freud's view of the emotions has often been called an *energy theory*. He believed your body continuously creates "psychic energy," much as a dynamo continually produces electrical power. Freud called this psychic energy libido. According to Freud, *libido* is the motivating force that "powers" all your thoughts, feelings, and behaviors. *Expending* libidinal energy is associated with sensory pleasure. *Repressing* libidinal energy almost always leads to unpleasant tension, anxiety, and other negative emotional states.

Whenever you suppress an unpleasant thought or emotion, Freud said, you *block the release of libidinal energy*. Psychic tension builds up in your unconscious mind in much the same way physical pressure builds up in an overheated steam boiler. Some of the repressed energy will "leak out" in a variety of ways—through unusual dreams, fantasies, "slips of the tongue," and feelings of anxiety. However, according to Freud, the best way to discharge the pent-up tension is through **catharsis,** which involves the open expression of your feelings.

Because Freud's theory is so rich and detailed, we will postpone a fuller discussion of his views until later. We should note, though, that one emotion frequently repressed is that of *anger*. From a Freudian point of view, releasing pent-up anger, particularly through aggressive acts, should always reduce stress through catharsis.

Do you feel less emotional after you have acted out your emotions?

ARNOLD'S "INTUITIVE" THEORY

In 1960, Magna Arnold revived the James-Lange approach noting the importance of *perception* (Arnold, 1960). Arnold recognizes the role of cognitions, but she gives *feelings* the primary emphasis.

According to Arnold, you perceive a situation and then immediately you *unconsciously* and *intuitively* "feel" the situation is good or bad. You tend to approach situations that make you feel good, while avoiding or fleeing from situations that make you feel bad. The intuitive "feeling" response occurs *before* you have a chance to appraise the situation consciously, or make decisions about how you will act. According to Arnold, arousal, cognitive appraisal, and all other behavioral reactions *follow* your intuitive emotional evaluations rather than precede them.

Once you have both "felt" and "responded behaviorally" to a situation, Arnold says, then you may well appraise the situation from a cognitive point of view. And, at that time, you may well make *conscious decisions* about the situation (and your own response to it). But according to Arnold, cognitions *follow* emotions rather than setting them off (Arnold, 1981).

Arnold is highly critical of approaches which place cognitions before feelings, or which lump intuitive feelings together with cognitive appraisals. To begin with, she says, there is a great difference between "conscious appraisals" and "unconscious feelings." And you only have to inspect your own inner experiences to realize this is the case. Cognitive appraisals are *deliberate value judgments*. Arnold says. Emotions, however, are *intuitive* and *unconscious*. To confuse emotions with cognitions is to blur the distinction between "thoughts" and "feelings." We have but to introspect our own emotions to know how wrong the cognitive approach is, she claims (Arnold, 1981).

ZAJONC'S "FEELING" THEORY

In basic agreement with Arnold's position is Robert Zajonc (Zajonc rhymes with "science"), who also believes that you first react to a situation emotionally, and then subsequently evaluate the experience in cognitive terms (Zajonc, 1980).

Zajonc admits that cognitions play a role in emotional reactions. His point is that feelings are *more* important. It often takes a long time to figure out what we think; we generally know immediately what we feel. When we meet a stranger, for example, we may feel an instant liking or disliking for the person—long before we could assess the person's characteristics.

Zajonc suggests that the greater importance of feeling than thinking is the result of our evolutionary history. He speculates that in the past, thinking was less critical

Catharsis (cah-THAR-sis). An act designed to "purge the system of its wastes or poisons." Freud believed that expressing your feelings was "cathartic" because it released pent-up energy.

I was angry with my friend:
I told my wrath, my wrath did end.
I was angry with my foe:
I told it not, my wrath did grow.

WILLIAM BLAKE

to survival than was feeling. Confronted with danger, an *immediate* response is necessary. He says, "Affective reactions can occur without extensive perceptual and cognitive encoding, are made with greater confidence than cognitive judgments, and can be made sooner" (Zajonc, 1980).

PLUTCHIK'S "EVOLUTIONARY" THEORY

Robert Plutchik also looks for the adaptive role of emotional responses which he believes evolution has programmed into us. He notes, however, that evolution is "ultraconservative," meaning that adaptive responses may outlive their usefulness by millions of years. For example, lashing out in anger, while once useful, may not be an appropriate adaptive response in today's society.

Plutchik places more emphasis on conscious cognitive processes than does Zajonc. He believes emotions are *conscious interpretations* of what happens to you when you become emotionally aroused.

According to Plutchik, when you go through an emotional experience, you *evaluate* it. Then you construct a "cognitive appraisal" of what has happened to you. This appraisal includes your interpretation of your physical arousal, your unconscious feelings, your behavioral responses, and your conscious thoughts while the experience was occurring. It is the *total combination* of all these events that we rightfully call an "emotion" (Plutchik, 1980).

LAZARUS'S "COGNITIVE" THEORY

According to Richard Lazarus, "An emotion is not definable solely by behavior, subjective reports, *or* physiological changes; its identification requires all three components, since each one can be generated by conditions that do not necessarily *elicit*

Cognitive theories of emotion point out that you can experience arousal just by exercising. Therefore, emotion must be more than just physical arousal.

emotion." Thus, much like Plutchik, he says emotions are composed of a *mix* of "action impulses and bodily expressions," various types of cognitive activities, inner feelings, and physical responses such as arousal or depression (Lazarus, 1984, 1991).

Lazarus was led to this point of view by the following facts:

1. You can experience "arousal" just by exercising. So, emotion is *more* than just changes in your bodily processes.

2. You can experience "feelings" that aren't really emotions. The "cold rage" you might feel following an injection of epinephrin is one example. Another example would be sensory pleasure or pain. Lazarus believes these are "sensations" and not "emotions." He says, you don't really know what you're feeling until you apply a *cognitive label* to your inner experience. Thus, the true value of the inner experience lies in the label, not the "feeling."

3. You can learn to behave in a stereotyped manner that will make others presume you're experiencing an emotion when you're really just faking it. Actors and other performers do this all the time.

According to Lazarus, it is only when you *consciously participate* in an experience that has three elements—physical arousal, subjective feelings and evaluations, and expressive behaviors—that you experience "emotion." It is your *awareness* of the simultaneous occurrence of all three components that lets you evaluate the experience as "emotional" (Lazarus, 1982, 1991).

When you stop to "appraise" your emotions, do you become more aroused or less aroused?

The mind is its own place, and in itself
Can make a Heav'n of Hell, an Hell of Heav'n.

JOHN MILTON, *Paradise Lost*

SOCIAL/BEHAVIORAL ASPECTS OF EMOTION

Behaviors, thoughts, and feelings don't occur in a vacuum. Everything you think, feel, and do occurs within some social context. Therefore, we cannot describe emotions without taking environmental inputs and consequences into consideration. In fact, almost all theories of emotion make some mention of environmental inputs and behavioral outputs. You may recall that in Schachter and Singer's experiment the subjects used a cognitive label to identify their bodily arousal as a particular emotion. But the subjects derived the cognitive label from their *social context*—provided by the happy or angry accomplice. It is the *relative emphasis* placed on biological, intrapsychic, and social/behavioral influences that allows us to put the theory in one of the three major categories.

Social Theories: Communication of Emotion

One of the most obvious *social* aspects of emotion is its power to communicate. When you're happy, your friends know it—and when you're angry, they stay clear! Although you may not always "wear your feelings on your face," face it, your expression is one of the surest signs of how you feel. In fact, Darwin believed that facial expressions form a "universal language" (Darwin, 1872).

Several studies by Paul Ekman and his associates support this idea. In one study, Ekman and Friesen showed photographs expressing different emotions to members of a pre-literate culture in New Guinea (the Fore culture) (see photographs). Ekman chose the Fore tribespeople because they had virtually no contact with Western culture and thus no chance to learn Western habits of emotional expression. Would they recognize happiness, sadness, anger, fear, surprise, and disgust in a Western face?

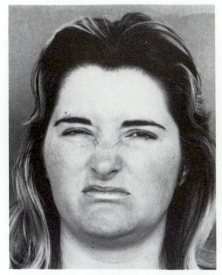
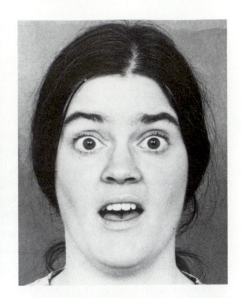
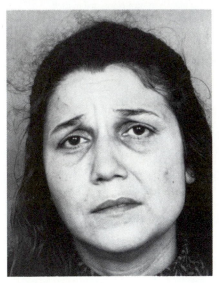
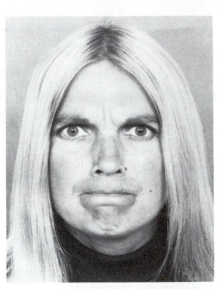
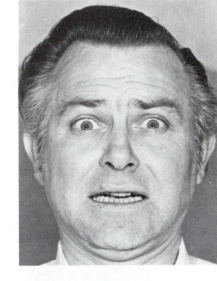

An example of the type of photograph Ekman and his associates showed to Fore Tribesmen in New Guinea. Can you identify the emotions expressed? (See "Answers for Thought" for the answers.)

The answer is "yes," although they had some difficulty distinguishing fear from surprise. Ekman and Friesen also found that American college students had no difficulty in identifying emotions in photographs of the faces of the Fore (Ekman & Friesen, 1971). Research with other cultures indicates a widespread recognition of happiness, sadness, anger, fear, surprise, and disgust (Ekman, 1972; Ekman & Friesen, 1986; Ekman et al., 1969; Izard, 1971; Matsumoto, 1992).

Other factors affect individual judgments, but the main effect is still the same. For example, David Matsumoto found that Americans were more accurate than Japanese in recognizing anger, disgust, fear, and sadness (Matsumoto, 1992). Harald Wallbott found that female faces conveyed fear and sadness best, while males faces conveyed anger best (Wallbott, 1988). James Russell found that expressions that included a raised and tightened lip conveyed either contempt, disgust, or sadness, depending on the context. And several studies report that subjects recognize happiness more reliably than fear (Matsumoto, 1992; Matsumoto & Ekman, 1989). But in each of these studies the same group of emotions was observed. Faces around the world speak a common basic language (Ekman, 1992a).

DISPLAY RULES

Of course, on some occasions we hide our emotions or display an emotion we don't really feel. Each year the new Miss America is expected to look surprised and then break into tears when her name is announced. Her disappointed rivals are expected to smile, and not break into tears—although they may feel very much like crying. We call cultural expectations such as these **display rules.**

As a result of different *display rules* in different cultures, we may get the impression that people from another culture are less emotional, or more emotional, than we are. An interesting experiment by Ekman and his associates sheds some light on this problem. Unknown to their subjects, Ekman and his associates filmed the facial expressions of Japanese and American subjects while they watched an emotion-arousing movie in private. Japanese and Americans showed the same type and amount of emotional facial expression. Later, however, when the Japanese subjects talked with a Japanese interviewer, they hid their feelings about the movie, and presented a happy face. When the American subjects talked with their American interviewer, they expressed their emotions about the movie. So, while emotional expression may be a "universal language," culture often distorts the communication (Ekman, 1972, 1982; Friesen, 1972; Matsumoto, 1990).

Display Rules. The cultural expectations which determine when it is acceptable to show various emotions.

TELLING LIES

Sometimes people intentionally disguise their emotional expression. The truth, however, often leaks out. In his book, *Telling Lies*, Paul Ekman identifies several expressive "clues" to a "false face."

1. The lower brain centers probably control true, spontaneous expressions. False expressions involve the cerebral cortex more. Because of the assymetry of the cortex (as we saw in Chapter 2), a false expression tends to be unbalanced and crooked.

2. Because they are *intentional* rather than *spontaneous*, false expressions are often incorrectly *timed*. Ekman observes, for example, that expressions of long duration, say five seconds or more, are probably false.

3. Ekman's detailed analysis reveals that false expressions involve different facial muscles than true expressions. For example, in a false smile, a slight furrowing of the muscle behind the eyebrows reveals true feelings of sadness.

4. Ekman observes that a false expression might be interrupted from time to time by fleeting "micro-expressions" which reveal true feelings (Ekman, 1985).

Many of these clues are subtle, and painstaking research has been necessary to document them. They are, however, important parts of the emotional "message" we send and receive continuously.

FACIAL FEEDBACK

Common sense tells us that our facial expression is a "mirror" which reflects our inner feelings—that facial expression follows inner experience. However, there is also a certain amount of folk wisdom which says "put on a happy face," "whistle a happy tune," and somehow you'll feel better. Perhaps feedback from our facial expressions can actually influence our emotions.

Israel Waynbaum first suggested a physiological basis for this idea in 1907. Robert Zajonc, whose "feeling" theory of emotions we met earlier, has recently revived and updated the theory. Zajonc suggests that movement of the facial muscles affects cooling of the blood flowing to the brain. Changes in the temperature of blood flowing to different parts of the brain may in turn affect the production of different neurotransmitters in those parts of the brain, thus influencing emotions (Zajonc, 1985; Zajonc et al., 1989).

Whether facial feedback occurs through changes in blood temperature or not, there seems little doubt that feedback occurs. In their book, *Psychology of Emotion,* John Carlson and Elaine Hatfield report that twenty or more studies have demonstrated that changes in facial expression affects emotional experience (Carlson & Hatfield, 1992; Ekman, 1992b; Larsen et al., 1992). Future research may show that our facial expressions merely intensify our emotions, or that our faces can actually generate our emotions. In any case, "keep smiling."

EMOTION: A HOLISTIC APPROACH

Our discussion leads us back to the questions we raised at the beginning of the chapter: What are emotions? Are they physical arousals, subjective feelings, cognitive appraisals, social responses, or a mix of all these factors?

More than a century ago, Charles Darwin decided that emotions served several noble purposes: First, they motivated the animal to approach pleasure and avoid pain—behaviors that clearly have survival value. Second, emotions *communicate*

Thoughts stir emotions and emotions energize thoughts—both of these processes are valuable in many situations.

one animal's feelings to other animals. If you were a lion and you roared in anger, other animals survived by running away. If you were a junior wolf and you bared your neck to the senior wolf, you didn't get bitten as often. Social psychologists such as James Averill (1982), and Robert Zajonc (1984) have built their theories of emotion on Darwin's early insights about the adaptive and *communicative* value of emotional expression.

Those scientists with a biological bent also owe a debt to Darwin. In *Principles of Psychology*, William James quotes Darwin extensively, and Freud's thoughts on the importance of instincts and unconscious motivation surely stem in part from Darwin's theory.

It is only the cognitive theorists who, putting the mind "above" the body and thoughts "above" feelings, sometimes appear to downgrade the importance of emotions (Lazarus, 1982). Emotions, however, add meaningfulness to your thoughts and actions. To paraphrase Oscar Wilde, if all you did was *think*, you'd "know the price of everything and the value of nothing." And while it is true that your cognitions can *guide* your emotions, it is equally true that your emotions *energize* your cognitions. Even Darwin recognized that you need both thoughts and feelings in order to survive.

So emotions are bodily states, subjective feelings, cognitive appraisals, and social/behavioral responses. And a complete theory of emotions must take *all* of these factors into account (Cacioppo et al., 1992; Pittman & Heller, 1987).

But sometimes emotions seem to get out of control. When we are under extreme stress we may feel overwhelmed by our thoughts and feelings. We will look at stress—and how to manage it—in a moment, but first let's consider why stress interests psychologists.

Seeing's believing, but feeling's the truth.

THOMAS FULLER, M.D., 1732

HEALTH PSYCHOLOGY

Stress is one of many *psychological* conditions related to *physical* illness. Most of us don't need to be reminded that psychological and physical responses go together. Remember those sweaty palms when you wrote that big exam? Or the way you feel during a good horror movie?

Some psychological conditions can actually lead to physical illness. By studying these conditions, psychologists hope to alleviate and prevent a great deal of physical suffering. Psychologists who apply their knowledge of psychology to the understanding of physical health and illness are part of the rapidly growing field of **health psychology** (Rodin & Salovey, 1989).

There are many ways in which psychologists can contribute to health. Consider the following:

Health Psychology. A rapidly growing branch of psychology which attempts to apply psychological knowledge to prevent and treat physical illness and to promote positive health.

1. Approximately 93 percent of patients do not fully follow the treatment procedures they are prescribed. Why?

2. Under conditions of stress, some people become ill, and some people do not. Why?

3. Some people ignore illness until it is too late, and some people seek help when there is nothing wrong. Why?

4. Some people adjust to illness and cope with treatment procedures well; some do not. Why?

These are some of the issues which health psychologists are studying.

The field of health psychology has grown dramatically in recent years. Health psychology became a division of the American Psychological Association in 1978; by 1990 it had approximately 3,000 members (Taylor, 1990). But the need is even

If I had my way I'd make health catching instead of disease.

ROBERT GREEN INGERSOLL

greater. Roughly $400 billion a year is spent on health care in the United States each year. The growing AIDS epidemic and an aging population will push these costs further (Schneider & Guralnik, 1990).

Many of the illnesses which bolster these costs are *preventable*, not by the use of some miracle drug, but by a *change in behavior*. For example, the American Heart Association (AHA) points out that 25 percent of all cancer deaths and approximately 350,000 premature deaths from heart attack could be avoided each year by changing one behavior: smoking. The AHA also says that dramatic reductions in coronary heart disease, degenerative arthritis, gastrointestinal cancer, diabetes, stroke, and heart attack could be accomplished through weight and exercise modifications in middle-aged men (cited in Taylor, 1990). And countless injuries and deaths in motor vehicle accidents could be prevented with the simple behavior of "buckling up" (Geller, 1989, 1990, 1991). Similar arguments could be made for the prevention of other controllable problems.

What kind of sexual motivation problems, discussed in Chapter 6, might be of interest to health psychologists?

Then why don't people change their behavior to improve their safety and their health? Kenneth Wallston points out that in order for people to change their health-related behaviors they must do three things: (1) they must value health as an outcome, (2) they must believe that certain actions *do* affect health, and (3) they must feel capable of carrying out the necessary behaviors (Wallston, 1992). This means they must feel *in control* of their health-related behaviors. Wallston and his colleagues have developed several scales to measure feelings of control over health-related behaviors (Wallston & Wallston, 1981; Wallston, 1989, 1992). We will have much more to say about control later.

So the challenge and potential for health psychology are great—the field is "healthy and growing." Let's see what health psychology can tell us about one psychological threat to health that we all experience: *stress*.

STRESS

By now, it won't come as much of a surprise to you to learn that there are several dozen definitions of what *stress* is, hundreds of theories as to what causes it, and perhaps thousands of beliefs as to how best to cope with it. Some of these approaches focus on the biological aspects of stress, some on the intra-psychic factors involved, some on the effects of the environment, and a precious few approach the problem of stress from a multidimensional viewpoint.

Roughly speaking, however, most scientists tend to view stress as a situation which challenges you *beyond your ability to adapt* (Krantz, 1986). The challenge itself may be *physical* (a virus, for instance), *psychological* (feelings of guilt, frustration, or conflict), *social* (war), or some combination of these factors (the death of a loved one). According to Richard Lazarus and Susan Folkman, "Psychological stress is a particular relationship between the person and the environment that is appraised by the person as taxing or exceeding his or her resources and endangering his or her well-being" (Lazarus & Folkman, 1984).

Generally speaking, the *biological responses* your body makes to stressful situations have been studied with greater frequency than have the intra-psychic or social responses. Perhaps this is because there is more research money available for medical research than for psychological experimentation (a situation most psychologists find distinctly dis-stressing).

Let's begin, therefore, by looking at how your body reacts when you are *stressed*.

Stress: The Biological Response

Given the frequency with which we discuss stress today, it may surprise you to learn that the concept was first linked to emotionality little more than 40 years ago.

Canadian scientist Hans Selye was the first to outline in detail the physical responses your body makes to stressful situations. Selye said your reaction to stress almost always follows the same adaptive pattern. He called this pattern the **general adaptation syndrome,** or GAS (Selye, 1976).

According to Selye, the GAS has three main stages or parts.

STAGE 1: ALARM REACTION

Suppose you suffer from a severe physical or emotional trauma. Your body will immediately respond with what Selye calls the alarm reaction, which is the first stage of the General Adaptation Syndrome (see Figure 8.2). During this stage, your body and mind are in a state of shock. Your temperature and blood pressure drop, your tissues swell with fluid, and your muscles lose their tone. You don't think clearly, and your ability to file things away in long-term memory may be disrupted.

STAGE 2: RESISTANCE

The second part of the GAS is the stage of resistance, or counter-shock. During this stage, your body begins to repair the damage it has suffered, and your mind begins to function more clearly. The pituitary gland in your brain releases a complex hormone known as **ACTH.** The ACTH acts on your adrenal glands, causing them to release their own hormones. These adrenal hormones counteract the shock in several ways, chiefly by raising your temperature and blood pressure.

However, you pay a price for resisting the shock, for your body uses up its available supply of ACTH and adrenal hormones at a rapid pace. If the stress continues, your adrenal glands will swell as they strive to produce enough hormones to neutralize the stress.

STAGE 3: EXHAUSTION

During the first two GAS stages, your sympathetic nervous system is intensely aroused. However, if the emergency continues for too long, an overwhelming counter-reaction may occur in which your parasympathetic system takes over. You may fall into the third state, the stage of exhaustion. During this stage, you go into shock again because your body is depleted of ACTH and adrenal hormones. Further exposure to stress at this time can lead to depression, insanity, or even death.

Selye believed that excessive stress causes many "diseases of adaptation"—high blood pressure, arthritis, and some types of ulcers (Selye, 1981–1983). We will have more to say about this point in a moment.

Almost everyone agrees Selye made the concept of stress a respectable part of science. However, further research studies suggest that Selye's theory, while correct in many aspects, needs updating (Cooper, 1983). Selye tended to focus almost entirely on reactions to biological stressors, but a great many of life's demands are *psychological* or *social*. And furthermore, a particular stressor does not affect each person in the same fashion. The effect of a stressor depends on how the person appraises or evaluates the total situation.

General Adaptation Syndrome (GAS). Selye's attempt to describe the characteristic way in which the body responds to stress, particularly that caused by disease or physical trauma. (Selye (SELL-ye) takes a biological view of emotionality.)

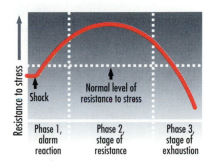

FIGURE 8.2

Selye's "General Adaptation Syndrome" (GAS). In the initial reaction to stress, the body enters a state of shock and resistance to the stressor falls below normal. Resistance rises as the body mobilizes its resources. If the stress persists long enough, resistance begins to fall and eventually a state of exhaustion is reached.

ACTH. Adrenocorticotrophic (add-DREEN-oh-CORT-tih-coh-TROF-fick) hormone, usually abbreviated as ACTH. A hormone released by cells in the pituitary gland in the brain. ACTH stimulates cells in the "cortex" or head of the adrenal glands to release "arousal" hormones. *Trophic* comes from a Greek word meaning "to nourish." Thus ACTH is a hormone that "nourishes" or stimulates cells in the adrenal cortex.

Some people thrive under pressure and others burn out. The difference may be their "psychological appraisal" of the situation.

Why would Selye say that a passionate kiss and the lash of a whip can produce the same stress reaction?

Stress: The Psychological Appraisal

Why do some people thrive under pressure, giving their best only when the stakes are high? And why do other people wilt and burnout under similar circumstances? The difference is in how they *appraise* the situation. One person considers the situation "stimulating," and "challenging," while another person views the same circumstances as "trying," or "catastrophic."

In more psychological terms, we might say that we feel stress when we believe that (1) the situation is threatening to goals that we value, and (2) that we will be unable to meet, or cope with the demands or dangers (Lazarus & Folkman, 1984; Lazarus et al., 1985). For example, Janet Spence and Ann Robbins found that "workaholics" experienced more stress and reported more health problems than "work enthusiasts," even though both types of individual were equally involved in their work. The circumstances were the same, but the workaholics felt overwhelmed by their responsibilities and all they expected themselves to do. They *appraised* the situation and their ability to cope differently (Spence & Robbins, 1992).

This research, and a great deal more like it, illustrates the importance of the cognitive appraisal "I can cope; I am in control." The positive effect of feeling in control is one of the most thoroughly documented findings in health psychology. Individuals who feel in control experience less stress, have greater resistance to disease, adjust to illness better, and recover more quickly (Rodin & Salovey, 1989; Taylor, 1990). Let's look at what happens when we feel we have lost control and then we will consider two types of control.

LEARNED HELPLESSNESS

Laboratory research by Martin Seligman and his associates demonstrates the damage that follows feeling helpless to control your situation. Seligman and his associates first put dogs in a chamber and gave them a mild *unavoidable shock*. The dogs (as you might suspect) were fairly upset at first—they jumped about randomly, barked, and whined. Eventually, however, the dogs settled down and "coped" with the inescapable pain as best they could.

Then, the researchers put the dogs in a "shuttle box," where, by jumping over a small barrier, the dogs could escape the shock. However, none of them did. Even though they could see safety on the other side of the barrier, *the animals refused to escape*. They simply sat there, apparently "depressed," and endured the shock for trial after trial (Maier et al., 1969).

Seligman then tried a number of "tricks" to get these animals to jump. For instance, he put food on the other side of the barrier. The dogs ignored the food. He tried coaxing them over by calling to them. But the dogs sat passively, just accepting their "bad luck." Finally, Seligman tied ropes around their necks and pulled them over the barrier by brute force. He reports it sometimes took more than 30 "pulling sessions" before the dogs learned they could avoid the shock by voluntarily jumping the barrier.

Seligman believes the dogs had *learned to be helpless*. Since there was nothing they could do to escape the shock on the first trials, the animals simply "gave up" and "closed their minds" to thoughts of improving their lot (Seligman, 1975).

Learned helplessness. The feeling one gets as a result of continued failure, that ones efforts to succeed make no difference.

Seligman's theory of **learned helplessness** holds that when people (or animals) experience outcomes that are independent of their actions, they come to expect that their efforts to "gain control" will be futile. They become depressed and simply "suffer the stress" rather than trying to reduce it. And they frequently become prime candidates for stress-related diseases (Seligman, 1976).

Not everyone who faces unavoidable stress responds with "learned helplessness." How might the concepts of internal and external attribution (from Chapter 6) be used to explain this fact?

There is a fair amount of evidence that gives general support to Seligman's position. For example, Rona Harrell and Felice Strauss note that many visually handicapped individuals have *learned* to act in a helpless fashion. Teaching these individuals to be more assertive, Harrell and Strauss say, "can increase their effectiveness in communicating with others and [help them] feel more in control of their lives" (Harrell & Strauss, 1986).

In similar fashion, Judith Voelkl notes that "activity personnel" at many nursing homes tend to *do too much* for elderly patients. In this way they encourage them to adopt a "learned helplessness" way of coping with their world. Voelkl suggests that teaching elderly individuals to "maintain control" over what happens to them is the best way to help them remain active and continue to lead productive lives (Voelkl, 1986).

Several lines of research suggest that people who perceive the world as being either *unpredictable* or *uncontrollable* are likely to adopt a passive method of coping with stress (Overmier, 1986). For this reason, psychologist William Mikulas urges psychotherapists to encourage all their clients to *develop self-control skills*. Learning such skills protects clients from stress and depression (Mikulas, 1986).

LOCUS OF CONTROL

Roughly 20 years ago, Julian Rotter noticed that some people believe they are **autonomous.** That is, they seem convinced they are masters of their own fates and take responsibility for what happens to them. They see their own *locus of personal control* as being inside themselves. And they believe that whatever rewarding inputs they get from their environments are due to their own actions. Julian Rotter calls these people *internals*.

On the other hand, many people believe they are helpless pawns of fate, controlled by outside forces over which they have little if any influence. These individuals feel their locus of personal control is external rather than internal, and that all rewards and punishments they receive are due to chance rather than to their own actions. Rotter calls these people *externals*.

According to Rotter, externals usually believe an impersonal God or "fate" controls whatever happens to them. When faced with an external threat of some kind, externals either block off the stressful inputs, ignore them, or become depressed. Internals, on the other hand, don't believe in fate or "luck." They feel "getting ahead in the world" is primarily a matter of what you do, not what accidents befall you. When faced with a threat, internals tend to face the matter directly, or to remove themselves to temporary safety (Rotter, 1971).

If you saw a tornado heading your way, would you be more likely to (1) stand still and pray for deliverance, or (2) seek shelter as best you could (and perhaps then pray)?

In fact, as many theorists have noted, both internals and externals have found a way to gain some *apparent* control over their inputs. Internalizers do so by noting the consequences of their acts, and changing their outputs accordingly. Externals gain "the illusion of control" by such acts as reading horoscopes, using magic, or appealing to such supernatural concepts as "ghosts" and "gremlins" to explain what happens to them.

Autonomous (aw-TON-oh-muss). From the Greek word meaning "independent," or "self-directed." If you make your own decisions, you are autonomous. If you obey other people's orders, you are not.

To summarize, stress results when we feel we are losing control—that is, when our *cognitive appraisal* determines that we cannot protect a valued goal. And stress produces a predictable biological sequence of responses. But can we predict which situations we will find stressful and what the long-term consequences will be? Can we also predict who of us will feel stress and who will not feel stress in a particular situation?

Predicting Stress Reactions

Research predicting the effects of stress has focussed on two major tasks: (1) developing scales to measure stress and its physical consequences, and (2) identifying personality "types" that are vulnerable to stress.

STRESS SCALES

In the mid-1960s Thomas Holmes and Richard Rahe compiled a list of "major life events" that are likely to produce stress. Major life events are such things as losing your job, moving from one place to another, getting married (or divorced), becoming a parent, or losing a family member to death. Holmes and Rahe then developed a "checklist" that assigned "stress scores" to each type of "event." They found a significant correlation between *major events* in people's lives and their *physical condition* in the following year or two. People with high stress scores were much more likely to become ill (Holmes & Rahe, 1967).

Subsequent research suggests that the "major events" that Holmes and Rahe described do not tell the whole story. There is tremendous variability in how various situations affect different people. People appraise situations differently (as we have seen) and then they react to those appraisals differently by using different methods of coping. For example, women tend to be stressed by quite a different set of "major events" than do men (Baruch et al., 1987). And the situations described as "most traumatic" by Holmes and Rahe are not particularly relevant for the very young or the very old (Lazarus, 1981). And finally, Richard Lazarus suggests that many people can handle life's "major events," but have problems adjusting to the "little hassles" that bedevil each of us daily (see Table 8.1) (Lazarus, 1981; Lazarus et al., 1985; Williams et al., 1992).

In response to these criticisms, stress researchers have developed a variety of more specialized scales (including a "Computer Technology Hassles Scale" to measure the frustration caused by computers (Hudiburg, 1989)!). Table 8.2 illustrates items from an *Undergraduate Stress Questionnaire*.

One promising refinement of the Holmes and Rahe approach is the "Life Experiences Survey" (LES) developed by Irwin Sarason and his colleagues. The LES has two special features. First, it measures recency of life events and whether or not

TABLE 8.1

The 10 most frequent hassles identified by a sample of 100 middle-aged adults. (Based on Kanner et al., 1981. Used by permission.)

HASSLE	PERCENT CHOOSING
1. Concerns about weight	52.4
2. Health of a family member	48.1
3. Rising prices of common goods	43.7
4. Home maintenance	42.8
5. Too many things to do	38.6
6. Misplacing or losing things	38.1
7. Yard work and home maintenance	38.1
8. Property, investment, or taxes	37.6
9. Crime	37.1
10. Physical appearance	35.9

STRESSOR	RANKED SEVERITY
Death (family member or friend)	1
Had a lot of tests	2
Found out a boy/girlfriend cheated on you	3
You have a hard upcoming week	4
Lost something (especially a wallet)	5
Death of a pet	6
Did worse than expected on a test	7
Had projects, research papers due	8
Dependent on other people	9
Having roommate conflicts	10
Lack of money	11
Dealt with incompetence at a university office	12
Coping with addictions	13
Thought about unfinished work	14
No sleep	15
Fought with boy/girlfriend	16
Performed poorly at a task	17
Can't finish everything that you needed to do	18
Trying to decide on major	19
Parents controlling with money	20
Noise disturbed you while trying to study	21
Someone borrowed something without permission	22
Erratic schedule	23
Job requirements changed	24
Felt some peer pressure	25
You have a hangover	26
Used a fake ID	27

TABLE 8.2

A selection of stressors, in order of rated severity, from the *Undergraduate Stress Questionnaire*. The more stressors (regardless of overall rated severity) that a student reported experiencing, the more likely that the student would also report negative mood and physical symptoms of illness. For example, 63 percent of the students checking nine or more items reported a high level of physical symptoms; only 32 percent of those checking eight or less items reported a high level of physical symptoms. (Based on data from Crandall et al. 1992 and personal communication. Used by permission.)

changes in life events are increasing or decreasing. Second, it measures the *personal significance* of each event (Sarason et al., 1978). This is important because two people may perceive the same event in entirely different ways. For instance, for one person losing a job is personally and financially devastating; for another person it means freedom to pursue new ambitions and dreams (Turner & Avison, 1992).

Stress scales have come a long way since Holmes and Rahe's pioneering work. But research with improved scales confirms Holmes and Rahe's original conclusion: Negative events take a physical and psychological toll.

But stress affects people differently. Can we predict who it will affect the most?

STRESS "TYPES"

In 1974, Meyer Friedman and Ray Rosenman suggested that people could be divided into two types: "Type A" individuals are competitive, aggressive, and impatient; "Type B" individuals are mellow, relaxed, and patient. Friedman and Rosenman claimed that Type A individuals are "at risk" for a variety of stress-related illnesses, especially heart attacks (Friedman & Rosenman, 1974).

Since Friedman and Rosenman's original work, a number of investigators have identified more clearly the Type A characteristics that lead to stress and heart attacks (Siegman & Dembroski, 1989; Westra & Kuiper, 1992; Williams, 1989). It appears that Type A individuals develop a *belief system* that creates, or at least contributes to, their own problems (Williams et al., 1992; Yuen & Kuiper, 1992). These irrational beliefs include "the conviction that self-worth is contingent upon personal accomplishments, the related fear of being judged worthless, a need to seek revenge, a belief that resources are in scarce supply, and finally, the associated fear that one will not acquire one's share of desirable commodities" (Westra & Kuiper, 1992, p. 8).

Stop your anger! Turn off your wrath. Don't fret and worry—it only leads to harm.

PSALM 37:8 *(Living Bible)*

Patti Lou Watkins and her colleagues have developed a "Type A Cognitive Questionnaire" to measure these beliefs. It includes items such as, "My accomplishments are signs that I'm worthy of approval and esteem," "It's OK to use other people as stepping stones to get what you want," and "If someone screwed me over, I think it's only right to do the same to him" (Watkins et al., 1987). Watkins and her associates found that people who agree with these statements have difficulties. They tend not only to experience greater stress, but also to *create* social problems and stress for themselves. And they lack social support in coping with their stress (Watkins et al., 1989; Watkins et al., 1992). All of these factors dispose Type A individuals to a higher incidence of heart disease and other stress-related illnesses.

Psychologists have learned a great deal about stress: the biological basis, the psychological appraisal, and predicting the effects of situations and personality types. However, most of the research on stress and personality types has focussed on Type A—the coronary-prone individual. Berton Kaplan proposes that we begin to study "the Type B story"—those individuals who face the world without experiencing stress and related illnesses. With that in mind, let's conclude our discussion of stress with some practical suggestions on responding to stress.

COPING WITH STRESS

Coping (KO-ping). From Latin and Greek words meaning "to strike." To cope with something is to fight against it successfully.

During your lifetime you have met many challenges, experienced many stressful situations, and worked your way through many emotional events. That is to say, you have *learned to adjust* to the problems that you face in life. Psychologists often speak of "learning to adjust" as **coping** with the world. Coping is not always easy, and it is often very time-consuming. Still, there are certain things you can do to help ensure success.

LEARN TO RELAX

It almost always helps to learn how to relax. In her recent review of the health psychology field, Shelley Taylor identified relaxation as a "broad principle of behavior" that "cuts across specific diseases and issues of health and illness." "Relaxation training," she says, is "a psychological intervention that requires little training and expense," and "can be applied in a wealth of settings" (Taylor, 1990).

To learn relaxation, practice paying attention to individual muscles in your body so that you can recognize levels of tension in each. You might begin by getting in a comfortable position and then tensing and relaxing each muscle or muscle group, one by one throughout your body. This will give you the "feel" of relaxation. Relaxation training is sometimes combined with training in meditation or yoga as a technique for coping with stress.

John Hoffman and his colleagues found that subjects who had learned to relax showed significantly less sympathetic arousal when stressed than did subjects who hadn't been taught this technique (Hoffman et al., 1982). Put more bluntly, it may help your *psychological* health if you find ways to reduce your *physical* tension (Engel, 1992).

TRY BIOFEEDBACK

Biofeedback. The amplification of one or more bodily processes so that the individual can observe them and learn to bring them under conscious control.

One very direct way to reduce physical tension is to employ **biofeedback.** Biofeedback training uses electronic equipment to *feed back* to your attention *biological* processes of which you may be only dimly aware. Biofeedback apparatus is like a mirror enabling you to "see" things about your physiology that you couldn't see before. For example, apparatus might be arranged to display your blood pressure on a screen. You must then learn *mental strategies* to control the blood pressure yourself; the apparatus only helps you to become aware of it. A mental strategy for reducing blood pressure might include imagining yourself reclining in a quiet, peaceful setting.

David Olton and Aaron Noonberg report considerable success in training hypertensive patients to gain voluntary control over their heart rate, blood pressure, and muscle tension (Olton & Noonberg, 1980). Neal Miller and his associates used biofeedback to help paralyzed patients increase their blood pressure so that they could remain in a sitting position without blacking out (Miller & Brucker, 1979). The secret of success lies in finding some way of giving patients new types of feedback about their bodily processes so that the patients can then learn to control their physical responses.

Patients who must learn to live with pain because physicians are unable to find its cause, often benefit from learning to relax with biofeedback (Linssen & Spinhoven, 1992). If you suffer tension or migraine headaches, or if simply want to learn to relax more thoroughly, you might consider biofeedback training.

In what way is biofeedback training similar to the relaxation training we discussed above?

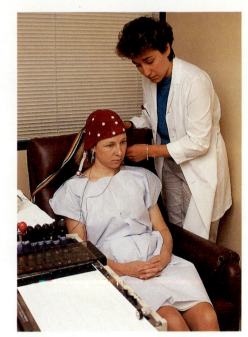

This woman, using biofeedback, can reduce the pain of a migraine headache by learning to lower the temperature of her forehead.

WORK OUT

Research shows that exercise, especially aerobic exercise, which gives your heart and lungs a workout, is effective in reducing stress and improving feelings of well-being (Emery & Blumenthal, 1990; McAuley et al., 1991). For example, Richard Norris and his colleagues compared adolescents in a high-intensity aerobic exercise program with those in other exercise programs and with a no-exercise control group. After 10 weeks the adolescents in the high-intensity aerobic program were considerably lower than the others in stress, anxiety, depression, and hostility (Norris et al., 1992).

Other research has found that high blood pressure (a symptom of stress) occurs much less frequently among men and women who are physically fit (Blair et al., 1984). Larry Tucker and his associates call physical fitness a "buffer against stress." They tested 4,628 people and found that physically unfit individuals perceived significantly more stress in their lives than did physically fit individuals (Tucker, 1986).

In addition to preparing you for stress, or providing a "buffer against stress," exercise may reduce the after-effects of stress. Kenneth Cooper points out that people who participate in an aerobic exercise at the end of a stressful day, report that the exercise seems to dissipate the tension and help them relax—perhaps because it helps remove the accumulated adrenal secretions (Cooper, 1982).

Closely related to relaxation and exercise, is the experience of laughter. After exercising you relax more fully; the same is also true after laughing (Robinson, 1983). Have you ever noticed how relaxed you feel after a good laugh? People who have a sense of humor and laugh easily are less upset by stressful life events (Martin & Lefcourt, 1983; Nezu et al., 1988). As we saw earlier, even smiling may have a direct positive physiological effect on mood (Zajonc et al., 1989). So remember, "Greet the world with a smile," because "One who laughs, lives to laugh *longer*."

START SMALL

You can often build up a "tolerance" for stress by learning how to handle mildly threatening events first. Canadian psychologist Donald Meichenbaum suggests that you begin by keeping track of your thoughts and behaviors in order to identify circumstances that produce stress. Next, practice rational mental responses to imagined stressful situations. When a stressful situation does occur you can then respond with "I can handle the situation; take one step at a time," instead of "This is the end of the world; I'll never get through this. I can't handle it." First in your mental practice, and then in your actual experiences, you begin with mildly stressful events and then "move up" to more challenging situations in a step-by-step fashion. Michenbaum

A cheerful heart does good like medicine

PROVERBS 17:22 *(Living Bible)*

"In order to keep pace with modern life, we will have a one-hour program each day to help create stress."

God grant me the serenity to accept the things I cannot change, the courage to change the things I can, and the wisdom to know the difference.

REINHOLD NIEBUHR

Eustress (YOU-stress). From the Greek word *eu*, meaning "good." (Euphoria is "good feelings.") Eustress is the amount of stress you need in order to operate at an optimum level of performance.

Some kinds of stress can have positive effects on many people.

reports this sort of "stress inoculation training" is particularly effective if combined with relaxation training (Harins, 1992; Meichenbaum, 1985).

GET HELP

It often "helps to have help." There appears to be one "anti-stressor" that helps in almost all situations—having a strong system of social support. Researchers report that social support is a helpful factor in coping with bereavement, mental stress, suicide potential, depression, anxiety, and job stress (Buunk & Janssen, 1987; D'Attilio et al., 1992; Edens et al., 1992; Nakano, 1991; Pescosolido, 1992; Sherkat & Reed, 1992).

Your friends and family can provide you with an objective view of your problems, and they can also give you encouraging feedback as you make progress in learning how better to handle stress. Under some circumstances, however, the best help you can get might well be that offered by a professional counselor.

ACCEPT YOUR LIMITATIONS

Earlier we emphasized the value of feelings of control. At times, though, we face things we *cannot* control: aging, incurable illness, death. What then?

Paul Wong calls control a double-edged sword. Believing that we have more control than we really do is maladaptive (Wong, 1992). Lynda Powell points out that the ideal of feeling in control needs to be tempered with realism. Not everything is controllable—at least not to the extent we would like. At times we may need to "control" our own wishes and aspirations in the face of things we cannot change. Sometimes one needs to "switch from trying to bring the environment in line with one's wishes to bringing oneself in line with the environment" (Powell, 1992, p. 123).

Berton Kaplan found that many Type B individuals had learned a balance between personal control and "trust." This balance, he says, is reflected in the Hebrew prayer book: "Pray as if everything depends on God, act as if everything depends on you" (Kaplan, 1992, p. 7). Some things we can and should control. But some things rest in the hands of God, fate, or simply "circumstances *beyond* our control."

Eustress

Hans Selye died in October 1982. Shortly before his death, however, he talked at length about **eustress,** or "good" stress. According to Selye, we shouldn't try to avoid all stress. Rather, we should recognize what our typical response to stress is, and then try to adjust our lifestyles to take advantage of that response.

Selye believed some of us are "turtles"—that is, we prefer peace, quiet, and a tranquil environment. Others of us are "racehorses," who thrive on a vigorous, fast-paced way of life. The optimum amount of stress we may require to function best is what Selye called *eustress* and it varies from individual to individual (Selye, 1978).

Society depends on emotions and stress, for cultures are kept going by motivated people who are willing to learn how to cope with each other, and with their own individual needs and personalities. Thus, *emotionality is necessary for life*. The problem comes in discovering ways to make your emotions helpful to you rather than harmful. Needless to say, the more you know about your feelings, the better off you will be. And that means not only discovering what your emotions are, but learning effective ways of handling them as well. Then you can lead a happier, healthier life.

SUMMARY

1. **Emotion** comes from the same Latin word as does **motivation.** Emotions are "movements" in feelings and thoughts accompanied by physiological changes and frequently expressive behaviors.

2. Biological theorists view emotions primarily in terms of **physical reactions,** such as arousal and depression, or as psychological responses to biological reactions.

3. Major control of the emotions lies in the **autonomic nervous system,** the **endocrine system,** and the **limbic system.**

4. The limbic system contains the **amygdala.** Damage to the amygdala can lead to episodes of uncontrollable rage, but there is little evidence that *all* emotional problems are caused by brain damage.

5. The **James-Lange theory of emotions** states that you are "afraid because you run, not that you run because you are afraid."

6. According to the **Cannon-Bard theory of emotions,** your **thalamus** controls "feelings," while your **hypothalamus** controls bodily responses.

7. Intra-psychic theorists see emotions either as **subjective feelings** or as **cognitive appraisals** of complex experiences.

8. Schachter believes that your **appraisal** of the situation you are in is as important a determinant of your emotions as is your physiological state of arousal.

9. Freud believed the two innate emotions, **pleasure** and **unpleasure,** were correlated with discharging or suppressing **libidinal energy.** Releasing repressed libidinal energy leads to **catharsis.**

10. Magda Arnold believes that emotions are **unconscious** and **intuitive** perceptions of the goodness or badness of a situation.

11. Robert Zajonc also considers emotions to be **immediate feeling reactions** to a situation. Cognitive evaluation may follow later, but it is *not necessary* for the **feeling.**

12. Plutchik states that emotions are **cognitive appraisals** that are **conscious evaluations** of feelings and physical reactions.

13. According to Lazarus, you have an emotion when you **consciously participate** in an experience that includes **physical arousal, subjective feelings, cognitive evaluations,** and **expressive behaviors.**

14. Social/behavioral theorists think of emotions in terms of **expressive reactions** that **communicate.**

15. Emotions perform the **social** function of **communication.** Seven **universal** expressions of emotion have been identified. We may modify the expression of our emotions to conform to certain **display rules** or even to **lie.**

16. Emotions **energize** thoughts and behaviors, while cognitions **guide** emotional responses. But emotions also **communicate** a biological and psychological state of arousal. So from a **holistic** point of view, emotions are **physical arousals, subjective feelings, cognitive appraisals,** *and* **social responses.**

17. Research in **health psychology** attempts to improve physical health through a better understanding of psychological factors in health and illness.

18. **Stress** is a situation that challenges you beyond what you think you can handle.

19. In his **General Adaptation Syndrome** theory, Hans Selye says your body goes through three rather distinct stages when stressed: the **alarm reaction,** the **stage of resistance,** and the **stage of exhaustion.**

20. Seligman's **theory of learned helplessness** holds that when you cannot control what happens to you, you may give up, become depressed, or suffer stress-related diseases.

21. Julian Rotter believes people respond to psychological pressures in different ways, depending in part on their own personal **locus of control. Internals** believe they are **autonomous,** while **externals** believe their reinforcers are controlled by fate.

22. Since their first introduction, **stress scales** have been refined so that they can give an indication of **life events** that are likely to lead to stress-related illness.

23. Individuals with a **Type A** personality and certain **beliefs** seem to increase their stress and vulnerability to illness, especially heart disease.

24. There are many ways of coping with stress. These include **relaxation, biofeedback, exercise, mental preparation, outside help,** and **acceptance** of the "unchangeable."

25. All motivation is based on stress of some kind. Selye calls the amount of stress you need to function properly **eustress,** or good stress.

ANSWERS FOR THOUGHT

1. *Which of the "elements of emotionality" does each of these theoretical perspectives seem to stress?*

   The "biological perspective" stresses the first, "physical arousal or depression." The "intra-psychic perspective" stresses the next two, "feelings," and "cognitions." And the "social/behavioral perspective" stresses the last two, "expressive behaviors," and "environmental inputs and consequences."

2. *If the "amygdal operation" were perfected, do you think that all violent criminals should have their amygdalas . . . ?*

   This is a personal value decision. (Some thoughts to consider: What are the side-effects? How would this reflect upon and influence the concept of responsibility in the rest of society? Is this different from cutting off the hands of a thief (or other physical mutilation related to a crime?) How far would you go in using biological control for other behaviors? What if the operation were reversible?)

3. *What kind of experiment might you perform to determine if it were the removal of the amygdala . . . ?*

   You might compare patients who have had their amygdalas removed (experimental group), with those who are given a "fake" operation or an operation of some other kind, thinking they were having their amygdalas removed (control group).

4. *Suppose you encounter a snake unexpectedly and you run away. According to James, do you run because . . . ?*

   According to James, you run first, and only later do you experience the actual "feelings" of fear.

5. *How do you know to run from a snake until you have perceived the snake and been aroused by this . . . ?*

   You would probably run from the snake before your body had time to become physically aroused. James and Lange would say this response was automatic and preceded "feelings" of fear. Cannon and Bard would say the feelings of fear and the running occurred simultaneously and independently. More contemporary cognitive theorists would emphasize the role of your conscious evaluation of the situation in producing the experience of "fear."

6. *Some people report that they are most easily aroused sexually when they are hungry, or immediately . . . ?*

The physical arousal associated with different emotions may be indistinguishable. When you are aroused for one reason, such as fear, you might falsely label your arousal as sexual if there are cognitive reasons (such as the presence of sexual stimuli) for doing so (Dutton & Aron, 1974).

7. *Do you feel less emotional after you have acted out your emotions?*

   Critics of the catharsis view of emotion point out that people who act out their emotions, such as fans at a sports event, are often *more* violent afterward. Many psychologists are skeptical of the catharsis concept.

8. *When you stop to "appraise" your emotions, do you become more aroused or less aroused?*

   When you become aware of your physical arousal, your subjective feelings, and the way you are expressing those feelings, you may very well become *more* aroused. This is one reason "giving vent" to an emotion often does not reduce it.

9. *Fore photographs*

   The photographs that were shown to the Fore are expressing happiness, disgust, and surprise (top row), and sadness, anger, and fear (bottom row). The expressions posed by the Fore man show happiness, sadness, anger, and disgust.

10. *What kind of sexual motivation problems, discussed in Chapter 6, might be of interest to health psychologists?*

    The population widely ignores scientific information that would enable people to avoid sexually transmitted diseases and unwanted pregnancies. Health psychologists would like to know *why* so that they could help people avoid unnecessary suffering.

11. *Why would Selye say that a passionate kiss and the lash of a whip can produce the same stress reaction?*

    Selye was primarily interested in the *biological* response to stress. At the biological level, the autonomic arousal, hormone reaction, and other physical responses are the same, regardless of the source. They may vary in degree but not in kind. For example, depending on how passionate the kiss or severe the whipping, one may produce more arousal than the other, but the systems involved are the same.

12. *Not everyone who faces unavoidable stress responds with "learned helplessness." How might the concept . . . ?*

    If the stress is attributed to an internal factor, and therefore something which the person could learn to control, the person might not give up, but instead respond with increased effort. The person also might not give up if the stress is attributed to an unusual external factor which is unlikely to occur again.

13. *If you saw a tornado heading your way, would you be more likely to (1) stand still and pray for deliverance . . . ?*

    "Externalizers" would tend to rely on outside forces, such as God or fate, to protect them. "Internalizers" would do what they could to control their circumstances.

14. *In what way is biofeedback training similar to the relaxation training we discussed above?*

    In the relaxation method we discussed, you first tense each muscle or muscle group and then relax it. Tensing and relaxing muscles makes you aware of them and how tension and relaxation feel. The feeling of tension and relaxation is *biological information* which is *fed back* to your brain—biofeedback. You then use this information—the feelings you get—to control the state of tension in your muscles.

C H A P T E R 9

LEARNING

Raskolnikov got up and walked into the other room where the strong box, the bed, and the chest of drawers had been; the room seemed to him very tiny without furniture in it. The paper was the same; the paper in the corner showed where the case of ikons had stood. He looked at it and went to the window. The elder workman looked at him askance.

"What do you want?" he asked suddenly.

Instead of answering, Raskolnikov went into the passage and pulled the bell. The same bell, the same cracked note. He rang it a second and a third time; he listened and remembered. The hideous and agonisingly fearful sensation he had felt then began to come back more and more vividly. He shuddered at every ring and it gave him more and more satisfaction.

FYODOR DOSTOYEVSKY
CRIME AND PUNISHMENT

Habit is stronger than reason.

GEORGE SANTAYANA

A planarian worm "squinches" when a light flashes.

A rat finds its way through a maze.

A child takes her first steps.

A nuclear physicist solves a complicated equation.

Michael Jordan flies through the air and executes a reverse slam.

What do all of these have in common? They are all examples of *learned* behavior. The first fact to learn about learning is that it doesn't have to be complex. In fact, some very complex behaviors, like the migration behaviors of fish or birds are instinctual and not learned. Learning is any relatively permanent change in behavior brought about as a result of experience.

We constantly change and adapt to our environment. If we did not we would not survive, either as individuals, or as a species. Sometimes this change is intentional and conscious; sometimes it is not. In either case it is called learning. Learning is a basic fact of human and animal existence. Because we can change we have hope— hope that whatever problems we have: alcoholism, shyness, irrational fears, ignorance—we can learn to overcome them.

Besides the facts you have learned for tests and exams, you have learned skills such as writing, or throwing a ball, swimming, or playing a piano. You have learned to speak and to read. And you have learned many different associations, some of them unique to you—such as the association between various sounds and the feelings they arouse in you. For Raskolnikov, in *Crime and Punishment,* the sound of the bell ringing brought back "hideous and agonisingly fearful" sensations associated with his crime.

You may have noticed that already in our discussion we have used several words referring to learning—"change in behavior," "adapt," "experience," and "association." Learning is indeed a broad topic. Psychologists use several different descriptions to explain the wide variety of human and animal learning that they study.

In considering learning, we will look first at a basic type of associative learning called *classical conditioning.* Next, we will consider learning which occurs as a result of consequences—*instrumental conditioning.* Finally, we will consider the role of thought in learning as we discuss *cognitive learning.*

CLASSICAL CONDITIONING

In *Crime and Punishment,* the ringing of the bell produced "hideous and agonisingly fearful" sensations in Raskolnikov, but not in the elder workman. For Raskolnikov, the bell was connected with the emotions surrounding his crime through *association.* Dostoyevsky and other writers as far back as Aristotle have recognized this kind of simple association as an important form of learning.

Twitmyer's Experiment

Sometime about the beginning of this century, a young man named E.B. Twitmyer began work on his doctoral dissertation in psychology at the University of Pennsylvania. Twitmyer explored *innate reflexes*—those automatic behavior patterns that are wired into your brain circuits by your genetic blueprint. And most particularly, he studied the **patellar reflex,** or knee-jerk.

Twitmyer rigged up a small hammer that would strike the subject's patellar tendon when he let the hammer fall. He didn't tell his subjects when he was about to

Patellar reflex (pat-TELL-are). The patella is the knee bone. If you strike your leg just below this bone, the lower part of your leg will jerk. This "knee-jerk," or patellar reflex, is an automatic response over which you have little volitional control.

stimulate their reflexes: He just dropped the hammer and measured how far their legs jerked. But his subjects complained the hammer blow often caught them by surprise. Couldn't he ring a bell as a warning? Twitmyer agreed, and began sounding a signal to announce the hammer drop.

One day when Twitmyer was working with a subject whose knee had been hit hundreds of times, he accidentally sounded the warning signal without dropping the hammer. As promptly as clockwork, the subject's knee jerked although his tendon hadn't been stimulated. Twitmyer had discovered the **conditioned response** (CR).

Twitmyer realized he was on to something important. He dropped his original research plans in order to investigate his discovery. Twitmyer found some of the conditions under which this type of learning occurred and he reported his findings at the 1904 meeting of the American Psychological Association. He published his research in a scientific journal the next year (Twitmyer, 1905).

Although the conditioned response is now one of the "basic facts" on which experimental psychology rests, Twitmyer's report provoked little more than a yawn in the United States (Dallenbach, 1959). Discouraged by the frosty reception his ideas received, Twitmyer dropped his laboratory research and went on to other matters.

Meanwhile, half a world away, the soon-to-be-famous Russian scientist Ivan Pavlov was performing similar studies in his Leningrad laboratory. Whether Twitmyer or Pavlov was the first to "discover" the conditioned reflex is a matter of some dispute, although it does seem Twitmyer was the first to publish his findings (Windholz, 1986). Whatever the case, it was Pavlov who ended up making most of the important early discoveries in this area.

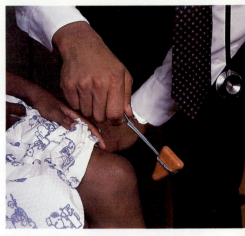

Tapping the patellar tendon with a hammer elicits the "knee-jerk" reflex.

Conditioned response. Any reaction set off by a conditioned stimulus (CS).

Pavlov's Conditioning Studies

Ivan Pavlov, who lived from 1849 to 1936, is perhaps Russia's most famous scientist. After taking his medical degree in 1883, Pavlov traveled in Europe, studying with various other scientists. In 1890, he founded the Institute of Experimental Medicine in Leningrad, which he directed the rest of his life.

Pavlov's early interests were in the biological processes of digestion, and he chose dogs for his experimental animals. Because of the pioneering nature of his work, Pavlov received the Nobel Prize in 1904—the first Russian to be so honored (Wertheimer, 1987).

PSYCHIC STIMULATIONS

Since digestion begins in the mouth, where saliva starts breaking up food particles chemically, Pavlov began his work by studying the salivary glands. He developed a way of diverting and accurately measuring the saliva. Then when he gave the dog food he could count the number of drops of saliva the dog produced.

Dogs salivate without training: Salivation is a *reflex* just as the knee jerk is a reflex. Salivation, like all reflexes, is an innate *response* elicited by a specific *stimulus*, in this case food in the mouth.

Pavlov wanted to determine the neural pathways that connected the stimulus receptors in the dog's mouth with its salivary glands. But his research was often interrupted by peculiar responses the animal would make. After an animal had gotten accustomed to being fed in its harness, it would often begin to salivate *before* it got the food. In fact, an experienced dog would usually start salivating if one of Pavlov's assistants merely rattled the food dishes in the sink or walked toward the dog carrying a plate.

Pavlov called these "unusual reactions" *psychic stimulations*. These odd reactions infuriated him because they "got in the way" of his planned research. He did his best to ignore them because he wasn't interested in anything "psychological." However, the psychic stimulations refused to go away. And so, around 1901, Pavlov began to study them systematically, hoping to get rid of these "annoyances." He told his friends this work surely wouldn't take more than a year or two to complete. In fact, Pavlov spent the final 34 years of his life determining the properties of these annoying "psychic stimulations" (Goldenson, 1970).

UNCONDITIONED STIMULUS AND RESPONSE

If you blow food powder into a dog's mouth, the animal will salivate reflexively. This response is determined by the dog's genetic blueprint. Because the association between food powder in the mouth and salivation is not dependent on past learning, Pavlov called the food powder an **unconditioned stimulus** (UCS) and the salivation an **unconditioned response** (UCR).

Unconditioned stimulus. You are born with certain innate responses, such as the patellar reflex. These reflexes are set off (elicited) by innately determined (unconditioned or unlearned) stimuli. The blow to your patellar tendon is an unconditioned stimulus that elicits the unconditioned response we call the knee jerk. The term "unconditioned" is used to describe these stimuli because their ability to elicit the response is *not* the result of learning.

Unconditioned response. Any innately determined response pattern or reflex that is set off by a UCS. The knee jerk is a UCR.

How would you go about teaching a dog to salivate when you gave it food if it didn't do so instinctively?

CONDITIONED STIMULUS AND RESPONSE

Pavlov soon made an important discovery: If he sounded a musical tone just before he blew food into the animal's mouth, the dog soon salivated almost as much to the tone alone as it did to the tone plus the food powder. Apparently, the animal learned to "associate" the stimulus of the tone with the stimulus of the food. And thus, each time the tone sounded, it salivated to the tone just as it did to the food.

We might say the dog *anticipated* or *expected* the food, although Pavlov would not have used these terms. Because he wanted to avoid all language he considered non-scientific, Pavlov described the association in terms of new "connections in the brain" between stimuli (Ss) and responses (Rs). (We will have more to say about mentalistic descriptions like *anticipate* and *expect* later.)

The neural connection between the unconditioned UCS_{food} and the unconditioned $UCR_{salivation}$ is innately determined. Therefore, it is an unlearned, or reflexive, S-R connection that we might diagram as follows:

$$UCS_{food} \xrightarrow{\text{(innate S–R connection)}} UCR_{salivation}$$

However, when the previously neutral S_{tone} is presented just prior to the unconditioned UCS_{food}, a new "connection" is built up in the animal's brain that links the S_{tone} with the $UCR_{salivation}$.

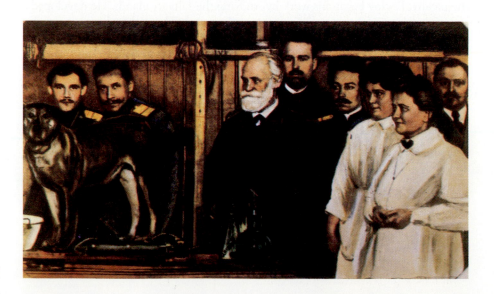

Ivan Pavlov (with white beard) and his students with a dog in the training apparatus.

Pavlov called the tone a **conditioned stimulus** (CS) because its power to call forth the salivation response is the result of pairing it with the food powder. We can diagram the situation as follows:

$$S_{tone} \xrightarrow{\text{(S–S association)}} UCS_{food} \xrightarrow{\text{(innate S–R connection)}} UCR_{salivation}$$

Once the dog has learned the connection between the tone and food, we can present the tone alone—without giving the food—and the dog will salivate.

This sort of *conditioning* occurs in people as well. The smell of bacon frying in the morning is enough to set your mouth to watering, but only because you have *learned to associate* the smell of the meat with how it tastes. Once you have learned to associate the aroma of bacon with its taste, the mere smell of it cooking will set off your salivary glands, even if you don't eat any of the bacon.

Is the odor of bacon more likely to cause you to salivate when you're hungry or when you've just finished a large meal?

But what can we call the salivary response when the tone along triggers it? Surely it is no longer an *unconditioned* response since there is no innate connection in the brain between a "neutral" tone and salivation. Pavlov named this learned reaction to the neutral stimulus a conditioned response (CR).

Conditioning is the term Pavlov used to describe the process by which the previously neutral stimulus (CS) gains the power to *elicit* the conditioned response (CR) (Pavlov, 1927). The CS gains the power because of the new neural connections that occur in the animal's brain linking the tone (CS) with the salivation (CR).

Once the conditioning process has taken place, we can diagram the situation as follows:

$$CS_{tone} \xrightarrow{\text{(learned S–R connection)}} CR_{partial\ salivation}$$

When psychologists use the term *conditioning*, they refer to some situation in which a previously neutral stimulus gains the power to elicit a response in a reflexive or mechanical fashion. So when we say that you have been "conditioned" to do something, we mean that you have learned to respond rather automatically to a particular stimulus. Conditioning occurs because of the association that develops when the CS and the UCS occur together repeatedly. From Pavlov's point of view, this pairing allows the CS to become "connected" (or bonded) to the UCR. When Pavlov spoke of conditioning, he almost always referred to S–R bonds. Modern researchers of classical conditioning, such as Robert Rescorla, speak of conditioning as the learning of *relations* among events in the environment (Rescorla, 1988a, 1988b). And, these researchers are much more likely to refer to the "cognitive" (or thought) processes involved (Martin & Levey, 1989).

The type of training studied by Pavlov is called by many names: classical conditioning, reflex conditioning, Pavlovian conditioning, respondent conditioning, and stimulus–response (S–R) learning.

FACTORS AFFECTING CONDITIONING

During the many years that Pavlov studied the conditioning process, he discovered several interesting facts about this type of learning:

1. The more frequently the CS and the UCS are paired, the stronger the S–R bond becomes. The left part of Figure 9.1 illustrates this stage of learning, called **acquisition.** The more often a tone is associated with food powder, the more drops of saliva the tone will elicit (up to a theoretical limit). And the more frequently the CS and the UCS are paired, strengthening the S–R bond, the better the animal will remember the learning later on.

Conditioned stimulus. The CS is the "neutral" stimulus which, through frequent pairings with an unconditioned stimulus, acquires the ability to elicit a new response—the CR. This CR is very similar to the UCR. In Pavlov's studies, for example, the CR was also salivation—but usually a few drops less than the UCR to the UCS.

Acquisition (ak-kwi-ZISH-un). The process of "acquiring" or developing a learned response, or habit.

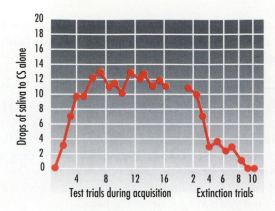

FIGURE 9.1

This chart shows the acquisition and extinction of a salivation response (CR) in a dog conditioned to a tone (CS).

Extinguished. To "extinguish" a response is to reduce the frequency (or intensity) of a learned response, either by withdrawing the reward that was used during training or by presenting the CS many times without the UCS. In fact, it is the "bond" or "connection" between the CS and the CR that is extinguished.

Spontaneous recovery. A return to a previous condition without practice or assistance. When a response which has undergone extinction returns without practice, spontaneous recovery has occurred.

Generalized. When a response occurs to a stimulus which was not the stimulus originally associated with the response, the response has *generalized* to the different stimulus. The more similar the second stimulus is to the original stimulus, the stronger the response, or the more likely it is to occur.

Discriminate. Reacting differently to fairly similar stimuli. If you can tell the difference between two things, you know how to discriminate between them.

2. Conditioning typically is fastest when the CS occurs *immediately* before the UCS. For example, the optimum interval for conditioned salivation in the dog is about half a second between the onset of the tone and the insertion of food powder in the dog's mouth. If the tone occurs more than a few seconds *before* the food, or occurs *after* the food, little or no learning usually occurs. However, the optimum interval does vary from animal to animal, from species to species, and from situation to situation.

3. Conditioned responses are *unlearned* just as easily as they are learned. Suppose you train a dog to salivate. That is, you set up a CS–CR connection in the animal between a tone and salivation. Now you present the dog with the tone *without* giving it the food. You would find that the animal salivates less and less on each trial. Finally, the response is **extinguished** completely (see Figure 9.1). Put another way, the S–R bond is broken.

4. An "extinguished response" is not completely forgotten. Suppose you condition a dog, then extinguish the response. Then you pair the CS and the UCS for a second round of training trials. The dog will now relearn the conditioned response much more quickly than it did the first time around. Apparently the original conditioning has left a "trace" of some kind that makes relearning easier.

5. Similarly, suppose you *extinguish* a dog's conditioned salivation response and then let the animal sit in its cage for two weeks. Now you bring the dog back to the lab, hook it up in its harness, and again sound the tone. What will happen? The dog will have *forgotten the extinction* and it will again salivate. Psychologists call this **spontaneous recovery** of a previously extinguished S–R bond.

6. The mere passage of time can act as a conditioning stimulus. When Pavlov fed his animals regularly each half-hour, they began to salivate a minute or so before the next feeding was due, even though there was no external stimuli such as dish rattles to give them cues that it was almost time to eat.

7. Pavlov found that when a dog had learned to salivate to a particular tone, it would also salivate to similar-sounding tones. He said the response **generalized** from one stimulus to other similar stimuli. As the tone got less like the original one, the dog salivated less and less.

8. If food always followed a particular tone but not similar-sounding tones, the dog would gradually stop salivating to the similar tones and salivate only to the tone which reliably preceded food. In this way, the dog had learned to **discriminate** between the tones.

Conditioned Emotional Responses

Once Pavlov had shown the way, a number of other psychologists began experimenting with conditioning procedures using humans rather than animals. John B.

Watson saw Pavlov's work as a fine example of the rigorous laboratory research necessary to establish psychology as a scientific discipline. He used classical conditioning to study how emotional responses (such as fear) might get established in children.

In one of his most famous experiments, Watson and his second wife (Rosalie Rayner) conditioned a boy named Albert to fear a white rat. At the beginning of the study, Albert was unafraid of the rat and played with it freely. While Albert was doing so one day, Watson deliberately frightened the child by sounding a terrifying noise behind him. Albert was startled and began to cry. After this, he avoided the rat and cried if it came close to him (Watson & Rayner, 1920). (This sort of experimentation is now forbidden by the American Psychological Association Code of Ethics.)

In Pavlovian terms, Watson and Rayner had set up a bond or connection between the sight of the rat (CS) and an arousal response (CR) in Albert's autonomic nervous system. Once this S–R bond was fixed, showing Albert almost any furry object elicited the fear response. Fears often *generalize* to stimuli similar to the CS. The burnt child dreads not only fire, but often comes to fear stoves, pots and pans, ovens, pictures of flames, and even stories about the great Chicago fire.

Many emotional responses, including the debilitating fears we call **phobias,** are probably established by classical conditioning (Davey, 1992; Lovibond, 1988). Once established, conditioned emotional responses can be set off by stimuli of which we are not consciously aware. It is even possible that emotional responses may be established without our awareness, although the research is not as conclusive on this point (Huertas-Rodriguez, 1985; Ohman, 1988).

Phobia (FOE-bee-uh). From the Greek word for "fear." A phobia is a strong and often unusual fear of something. A fear is considered a phobia when it interferes with normal activities.

Counter Conditioning

If Pavlov's classical conditioning procedures produced fear, maybe they could extinguish it. Furthermore, maybe learning a new pleasant association to the feared stimulus would speed up the process. In 1924, a student of Watson's named Mary Cover Jones tried this "counter conditioning."

To appreciate how counter conditioning works, imagine that at some time in the future, your own 2-year-old son accidentally learned to fear small furry animals. You might try to cure the boy the way Mary Cover Jones did, by attempting to attach a strongly positive response to the fear-arousing stimulus.

The sight of a white rat would presumably upset your son, but the sight of food when he was hungry would surely make him happy and eager to eat. If you could somehow "bond" the "rat" stimulus to the "positive" eating response, you could "decondition" the child by making him like the rat rather than fear it.

You might begin the counter conditioning procedure by bringing a white rat into the room with your son while you were feeding him. At first, you would want to keep the animal so far away that your son could barely see it out of the corner of his eye. Since the animal wouldn't be close enough to bother him, he probably would keep right on eating. (If it upset him you would remove the rat and begin with a less threatening object such as a stuffed animal or a picture of an animal). Then, step by step, you might bring the rat closer.

Since your son could not cry and eat at the same time, the CS–CR fear response would gradually *extinguish*. And while the strength of the fear reaction was decreasing, the strength of the CS–CR "pleasure of eating" bond would increase. Eventually, your son would be *conditioned* to give a new response to the animal that was *counter* to his previous reaction. When Mary Cover Jones followed this procedure (actually using a white rabbit instead of a rat), she found that children soon learned to play with animals that had previously terrified them (Jones, 1924).

The important point about counter conditioning is this: The technique almost always involves *breaking* an inappropriate S-R bond by attaching the *old* "S" to a *new* and more appropriate "R."

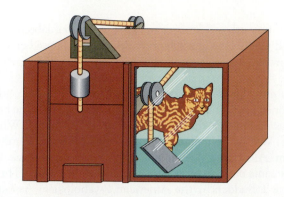

FIGURE 9.2

Puzzle box used by Thorndike. In this version, the cat can escape from the box and get food outside by pressing the treadle inside the box. A cord-and-pulley system unlocks the door.

For most people, the sight of a big, hairy spider is a stimulus that evokes a very strong avoidance reaction. How might you try to "treat this fear" by counter conditioning?

INSTRUMENTAL CONDITIONING

Our discussion of classical conditioning dealt largely with a Russian scientist's study of dogs. It is perhaps appropriate then that we begin our look at instrumental conditioning with an American scientist's study of cats.

E.L. Thorndike

At about the same time as Pavlov was studying one type of learning in dogs, Edward Thorndike was studying a very different kind of learning in cats. He called this type of learning "trial and error," but it could also be called "instrumental." As we will see, it is closely related to the type of learning B.F. Skinner called "operant conditioning."

Thorndike's early work involved putting cats inside a "puzzle box" (see Figure 9.2). If the cat could figure out how to unlatch the door to the box, it escaped and received a bit of food as a reward. At first the cat typically showed a great deal of what Thorndike called "random behavior." It sat and scratched or licked itself, it mewed and paced the box, or it bit at the bars and tried to squeeze between them. Eventually, the cat would accidentally press a pedal that was connected to the door. The door would fly open, and the animal would rush out and receive food.

In the following trials, the cat spent more and more time near the pedal and got out of the box sooner and sooner. Eventually the cat learned what it must do. The moment it was placed in the box, it pressed the pedal, escaped, and claimed its reward (Thorndike, 1898).

When Thorndike plotted on a graph the amount of time it took the cat to exit from the box on each trial, he came up with something that we now call a "learning curve" (see Figure 9.3). Similar experiments on monkeys, chickens, and even humans yielded the same shaped curves. This finding confirmed Thorndike's original theory that animals and humans solve such simple tasks in much the same manner.

Thorndike believed that animals learn to escape from puzzle boxes by **trial and error.** That is, they perform various behaviors in a blindly mechanical way until some action is effective in getting them out of the box. Ineffective actions, such as sitting and scratching, bring the animal little satisfaction. So these responses rapidly drop out of the animal's behavioral **repertory.** But those actions that gain the ani-

Children do not generally fear rabbits, unless one or more unpleasant experiences have "taught" them to feel fearful. Teaching children to overcome such learned fears has been done successfully using counter-conditioning techniques.

Trial and error. To learn by making mistakes until you discover the correct solution to a problem—usually without having someone to teach or guide you.

Repertory (REP-purr-torr-ee). A storehouse or collection. Your own behavioral repertory is whatever skills, talents, or response patterns you possess.

mal's release and lead to food are very satisfying, so these responses become strongly connected to the stimuli in the puzzle box. The "satisfying" responses thus are much more likely to occur whenever the animal is next put in the box.

How would you go about solving a "puzzle box" using "logic" or "trial and error"?

The results of his puzzle box experiments led Thorndike to formulate two basic *laws of learning*: (1) the **law of exercise,** and (2) the **law of effect.** In part, the law of exercise states that the S–R connections you make get stronger when they are repeated—in short, that practice makes perfect. The law of effect holds that S–R bonds are also modified by the "effects" of what you do. These effects may either be "satisfying" or "punishing." Thorndike defined satisfiers as situations you willingly approach or do nothing to avoid, and punishers as situations you typically avoid or do nothing to approach.

If the response you make to a stimulus somehow gives you pleasure or satisfaction, the connection (or association) between the S and the R will be appropriately strengthened. This is the first half of the law of effect, and it holds today just as it did when Thorndike first announced it.

The second half of the law has to do with the effects of punishment on learning. Early in his career, Thorndike stated that "punishers" weakened or broke S–R bonds (Thorndike, 1898). But he changed his mind on this point later, when laboratory research showed that punishment *suppresses* responses temporarily rather than breaking S–R connections (Thorndike, 1935).

B.F. Skinner

B.F. Skinner, who died in August 1990 at age 86, was arguably the most influential psychologist of the 20th century. He coined the term "operant" behavior to refer to behavior which *operated* on the environment (as opposed to the behavior in classical conditioning, which was merely an involuntary response to the environment— hence **respondent conditioning**). If behavior led to a change in the environment (e.g., escape or reward), subsequent behavior would change. This change in behavior he called **operant conditioning.** The type of situation he studied is similar to that studied by Thorndike, although Skinner rejected all "mentalistic" sounding terms such as "pleasure" or "satisfaction." Generally speaking, both men studied what is sometimes called **instrumental conditioning.** Instrumental conditioning is the learning of behavior as the result of its being *instrumental* in bringing about some desired consequence. Let's consider why operant (or instrumental) conditioning is recognized as such a powerful method for teaching new behavior patterns to both animals and people.

Operant Techniques

Suppose that, as a final examination in one of your psychology classes, your instructor gives you a common, ordinary pigeon. The instructor then says that if you want to get an "A" in the course, you must teach the pigeon to bowl!

After you recover from your surprise, you take stock of the situation. The apparatus you can use is a large box with a wire screen over the top of it (see Figure 9.4). Inside the box is a small bowling alley with a tiny ball at one end and pigeon-sized bowling pins at the other. In one corner of the box is a metal cup into which you can drop food pellets from the outside. Just above the food cup is a bell. Fortunately, the pigeon has already been trained to run to the food cup to get pellets whenever you ring the bell.

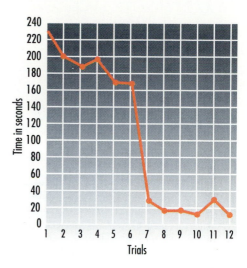

FIGURE 9.3

The seventh trial shows a remarkable improvement in the time it took one of Thorndike's cats to open a puzzle box.

Law of exercise. The first of Thorndike's two laws describing how stimulus–response (S–R) bonds are formed. The more frequently an S–R bond is "exercised," the stronger the bond becomes.

Law of effect. Thorndike's second law, which states that (1) satisfiers tend to strengthen S–R connections; (2) punishment tends to weaken S–R bonds. The first part of the law–describing the *effect* that reward has on learning—is generally accepted as being correct. However, we now know that punishment doesn't "extinguish" learning—it merely suppresses the learned response or causes the organism to avoid the learning situation.

Respondent conditioning. Also called "classical conditioning," or "Pavlovian conditioning." So named because the organism always *responds* with the CR when the CS is presented.

Operant conditioning (OPP-per-rant). Skinner's technique for "shaping" responses by rewarding successive approximations to a goal. The term *operant* is used because the behavior *operates* on the environment.

Instrumental conditioning. Another term for the type of learning studied by Skinner (and Thorndike). The behavior is learned because it is *instrumental*, or plays a role, in obtaining a reward.

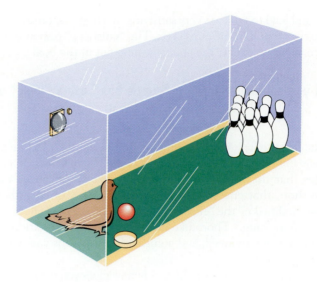

FIGURE 9.4

A "pigeon bowling alley": experimental apparatus used to teach pigeons to "bowl." When the pigeon makes an appropriate response, it receives a food pellet in the food dish.

Your instructor tells you that if you can teach the pigeon to bowl in a matter of two hours or less, you pass the exam and get your "A" reward. Keeping in mind all of the practical knowledge on learning you have acquired so far in this book, how would you go about educating your pigeon in order to satisfy your instructor, yourself, and, of course, the bird?

According to Skinner, whenever you wish to change an organism's behavior, you always begin by defining precisely what it is you want to accomplish. For instance, to get your "A" you must train the pigeon to bowl. But what do we mean by "bowling"? Do we have some objective, clear-cut, agreed-upon way of measuring the response pattern we call "bowling"? If so, then we know when to terminate the training, and we know when you've passed the exam.

TERMINAL RESPONSE OR GOAL

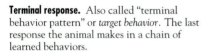

Terminal response. Also called "terminal behavior pattern" or *target behavior*. The last response the animal makes in a chain of learned behaviors.

Bowling is obviously a complex sequence of responses that ends when the pigeon has hit the ball down the alley toward the pins. Therefore, your goal must be that of getting the bird to hit the ball in the proper direction.

Skinner called the final step in any chain of behaviors the **terminal response.** When the organism has performed this final act, the chain of responses is terminated—usually by a reward or punishment of some kind. Thus, when the pigeon finally "bowls," you will ring the bell and give the bird a pellet of food. And when the pigeon "bowls" regularly, you will terminate the training and receive your "A."

It is most important, however, that the terminal response be *measurable*. As you will soon see, pigeons can be trained to bowl in two hours or less if you go about it in the right way.

College catalogs often state that the goal of higher education is to turn students into "creative individuals" who are "good citizens" and "productive members of modern-day society." What might B.F. Skinner say about such terminal responses?

BASELINE

Baseline behaviors. The behavior patterns of an organism before training begins. According to behavioral therapists, you must always build upon the client's strengths (the good or "appropriate" responses) and select out of these "baseline behaviors" those actions that can be shaped toward the terminal response. Entering behaviors also include problematic or inappropriate actions, but these should be ignored (or at least not rewarded) in the hope that they will thereby be extinguished.

Once you have a well-defined goal to work toward, you are ready to tackle the second stage in Skinner's analysis of behavioral change—that of determining what the organism is doing before you begin to train it. Skinner referred to these "prior responses" as the organism's **baseline behaviors.**

To determine the baseline behaviors, you measure what the organism is already doing and plot its responses on a graph or record of some kind. Skinner called this "taking a baseline." Like the terminal response, the baseline behaviors must be stated in objective, measurable terms. Clever animal trainers (or people educators) always take advantage of the response patterns the organism brings to the training situation. You always build new learning on old, according to Skinner.

If an instructor wanted to increase oral responses to her questions in a class which was not very responsive, how should she react to a student's incorrect answer?

SUCCESSIVE APPROXIMATIONS

When you are sure of (1) the organism's baseline behaviors, and (2) the terminal behavior you hope to achieve, you are ready to move from (1) to (2). Skinner would suggest you do so in a step-by-step fashion called **reinforcing successive approximations to a goal.**

Neither people nor pigeons typically change their behaviors in large jumps. We *can* do so occasionally, but most of the time we change slowly, bit by bit. And we usually need to be coaxed and encouraged whenever we must acquire a new way of doing things. That is, we typically need to be rewarded, or **reinforced,** for each tiny step we make toward the goal. (We will have more to say about the importance of reward in a moment.)

The technique of reinforcing successive approximations to a goal is one of the cornerstones of the Skinnerian system. But mastery of the step-by-step technique calls for a rather penetrating insight on your own part. Namely, you must realize that even the faintest, feeblest movement toward the goal is a step in the right direction, hence something you must vigorously reward. Most people unfamiliar with Skinner's techniques seem unable or unwilling to analyze behavior in these terms. So, they give reinforcements grudgingly and infrequently. This fact may explain why most people would not be able to train a pigeon to bowl in two hours or less.

Shaping

The Skinnerian technique of (1) setting a goal, (2) taking a baseline, and then (3) reinforcing successive approximations to the goal is often called behavioral **shaping.** Why? Because, just as a potter takes clay and shapes it into a new form (such as a vase), so operant conditioning involves taking old behavior patterns and "shaping" them into new response sequences.

What "old" responses does the average pigeon already make (without training) that are part of the terminal response we call "bowling"?

If we apply what Skinner called behavioral analysis to the problem of getting a pigeon to perform, we can perhaps see how shaping actually works.

DEFINING THE GOAL

The terminal behavior your instructor has set is that of "bowling." But how shall we define it? Humans usually pick up the bowling ball in their hands and roll it down the alley. But the pigeon has wings instead of arms, and feathers are poor substitutes for fingers when it comes to lifting a heavy ball.

Reinforcing successive approximations to a goal. Rewarding any incremental (in-kree-MENT-tal) response that will lead the organism toward the terminal response. That is, reinforcing any slight behavioral change (increment) that represents a step in the right direction.

Reinforced. Concrete with steel rods inside it is called *reinforced* concrete, because the steel strengthens the concrete. Positive feedback strengthens, or reinforces, an S–R bond by making it more likely the response will occur again the next time the stimulus input appears.

Shaping. To control and gradually change a response by reinforcing successive approximations to a goal.

But could we teach an armless man to bowl? Couldn't the man kick the ball down the alley, or even butt it with his head? Do you really care how he manages it, so long as the ball zings down the alley and hits the pins?

One of the purposes of getting you to "take a baseline" of the pigeon's normal response patterns is this: it forces you to see what the bird *already* does that you can make use of during training. If you watch pigeons for a while, you will notice that they use their beaks much as we use our hands. So if you can train the bird to hit the ball with its beak (so the ball rolls down the alley and hits the pins), you surely have taught the animal to "bowl" within the stated definition of the problem. And you surely will get your reward.

REWARDING THE "FIRST STEP"

Once you have determined the goal and measured the baseline behaviors, what's your next step in the bowling lesson? Actually, as Skinner would point out, the next step is up to the bird. As it wanders around the box excitedly, at one time or another it will accidentally move toward the bowling ball. If you have the insight to recognize this simple movement as being a "step in the right direction"—and if you ring the bell at once and reward the animal with food—you will have no difficulty in training the bird. But if you insist the bird doesn't deserve a reward until it scores a strike, it may take you years to pass the exam, if you ever do.

Presuming you do sound the bell the first time the bird moves tentatively in the general direction of the ball, how does the pigeon respond? By running to the food cup to claim its reward. After eating the food, it will pause for a while near the food cup. But when pausing doesn't ring the bell, it will usually begin its random trial-and-error movements around the box again. Once more, as soon as it heads toward the ball, you sound the bell. And again the bird runs to the food cup and eats.

After doing this several times, the pigeon will learn the connection between doing something and getting a reward. This will mean that you can go much faster with your training. Each time you sound the bell, the pigeon will dash to the food cup, then return at once to where it was the instant the bell rang. Now, on each successive trial, you merely wait until the animal accidentally moves one step nearer to the ball before you ring the bell. In a matter of minutes, the bird will be hovering over the bowling ball.

STEP BY STEP

Once the bird is standing over the ball, you must find a way of getting the animal's beak down to floor level. Again, you go back to the natural responses the animal makes. As pigeons move, their heads bob up and down. Sometimes, then, the bird's beak is closer to the ball than at other times. An experienced animal trainer will soon perceive the bird's downward head movements as "good responses," and begin to reward them.

After several such reinforcements, the pigeon begins to return from the food cup holding its head a little lower than before. If you demand that the bird depress its head an additional inch or so on each subsequent trial, you can get it to touch the floor with its beak in a matter of minutes (see Figure 9.5).

FIGURE 9.5

Whenever the pigeon's head bobs below the normal level that it keeps its beak at, you ring the bell and reward the pigeon. Then, step by step, you reward it for moving its head lower and lower. Finally, the bird's beak will be on the floor, where the ball is.

Normal level

Do you think that at any time during training, the pigeon gains a cognitive awareness that it is "learning to bowl"? If you could somehow "explain" to the animal what you were doing, might this "cognitive understanding" speed up learning? Why?

THE GOAL

By now the pigeon's beak is close to the floor, and the bird is moving about near the ball. Within a few moments, its beak will touch the ball "accidentally." Skilled animal trainer that you are, you ring the bell joyously, knowing victory is near.

When the bird returns from claiming its reward, it typically takes a second swat at the ball. You reward it again. Soon the pigeon is scooting back and forth from food cup to ball, whacking the ball each time it comes close to it.

Now it is up to you to shape the bird's "whacking responses" so the animal knocks the ball straight down the alley instead of merely hitting it at random. Such "shaping" should take only a few minutes, for at first you reinforce only those hits that aim the ball in the general direction of the pins. Then you selectively reward those hits that are closer and closer *approximations* to your stated goal. The pigeon soon learns it will be fed only when it strikes the ball so it rolls straight down the alley and hits the pins.

An experienced pigeon handler can usually shape a hungry pigeon to bowl in less than an hour. (Good scores take a little longer!)

Variations in Response Consequences

There are several fairly subtle points about operant conditioning that are sometimes overlooked. Most of these are related to variations in the *consequences* of responding:

1. Inputs may be either *pleasant* (satisfying) or *unpleasant* (dissatisfying), and they may be either *presented* or *removed*, when an organism responds. If the stimulus input *increases* the rate of responding, we call it a *reinforcer*. If the stimulus input *decreases* the rate of responding, we call it a *punisher*. As we will see, both reinforcers and punishers may be either positive or negative.

   When a *pleasant* input is *presented* following a response, we call the input a **positive reinforcement.** A food pellet is a positive reinforcement to a food-deprived pigeon. Positive reinforcement *increases* the rate of responding. Animal trainers use positive reinforcement almost exclusively.

   When an *unpleasant* input is *withdrawn* following a response, the organism experiences **negative reinforcement.** A dog that jumps over a barrier to escape an electric shock is acting under negative reinforcement. The negative reinforcement will strengthen the behavior of jumping over the barrier. (If the dog jumps before the electric shock is administered, we call the situation "avoidance" learning. If the dog receives the shock before jumping, we call the situation "escape" learning. Both conditions are examples of negative reinforcement.) Negative reinforcement (like positive reinforcement) is used to *increase* the frequency of a response. (In Chapter 8 we saw that unavoidable negative input may produce a condition of "learned helplessness.")

   When a *negative* input is *presented* following a response, we call the input a punishment—or **positive punishment,** to distinguish it from negative punishment. A brief electric current delivered through the floor of a rat's cage whenever it presses a lever is a positive punishment. Positive punishment is used to *decrease* the rate of responding.

   When a *positive* input is *withdrawn* following a response, the organism experiences **negative punishment.** Sending a child to a room where attractive toys or friends are not available is giving the child negative punishment. Negative

Positive reinforcement. The *onset* or appearance of a positive stimulus input—one which "satisfies" an organism in some way. Positive reinforcement strengthens or increases the behavior it follows.

Negative reinforcement. The *termination* of a stimulus situation which the organism would ordinarily avoid. Both positive and negative reinforcement increase or strengthen the behavior they follow.

Positive punishment. The *onset* of a painful or unpleasant stimulus following a particular behavior. Punishment suppresses behaviors temporarily, or teaches an organism to avoid an unpleasant situation.

Negative punishment. (Sometimes called "response cost" or "time out.") The removal of a pleasant stimulus, or withdrawal of the organism from a pleasant environment. Negative punishment reduces the behavior it follows.

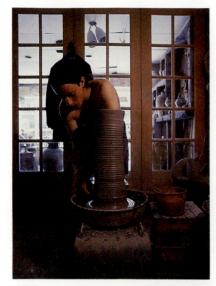

Complex human behaviors may be seen as simple responses chained together and performed in order to receive some reward. Rewards need not follow every response, however. In addition, rewards may be "rewarding" only because they have been associated with other more basic rewards.

punishment (like positive punishment) is used to *decrease* the frequency of certain (undesirable) behaviors. Prison is usually a negative as well as a positive punishment because it removes pleasant stimuli and presents unpleasant ones.

So both positive and negative reinforcers *increase* response rates. And both positive and negative punishers *decrease* response rates (Flora & Pavlik, 1990; McConnell, 1990).

2. Punishment, especially positive punishment, does not always have the effect that is expected. Punishment *disrupts* behavioral sequences. It may occasionally *suppress* certain responses, but it usually does so only temporarily. Punishment seldom "wipes out" inappropriate behaviors. And punishment usually results in negative attitudes towards the punisher. Thus, those teachers who punish you unless you perform correctly often teach you little more than to avoid them (and all academic settings).

If punishment must be used, here are some ways to make it more effective: (1) Try ignoring the problem first (extinction), or using positive reinforcement to train an incompatible response. (2) Use the minimum punishment necessary to suppress the behavior. (3) Apply punishment as close in time to the undesired behavior as possible. (4) Preserve the person's self-respect; don't punish in front of other people. (5) Be consistent; don't punish a behavior one day and ignore it the next, or threaten and then back down.

Because of some of the negative effects of punishment, both positive and negative reinforcement are usually more effective in training new behaviors. The relationship between positive and negative reinforcement, and positive and negative punishment, is presented in Figure 9.6.

Notice that in teaching the pigeon to bowl, *no punishment* was necessary to get the animal to perform. The pigeon obviously *can* learn. If it fails to do so, the fault presumably lies with the teacher (or with the learning environment) and not with the student.

3. You control the *timing* of the reinforcement, but the pigeon's behavior determines whether it receives the reward you make available. The pigeon freely **emits** the behavior. It is not **elicited** involuntarily the way the UCR$_{salivation}$ was in Pavlov's experiments. If the reinforcement is truly "rewarding," then the animal will respond. But if the animal has not been deprived of the "reward" (e.g., if it is not hungry for food)—or if you expect too much work for what you give the bird in return—it will not respond. (Surprisingly, pigeons appear to enjoy this type of training, and once they have learned the task, will "bowl" again and again with but a minimal amount of encouragement.)

Emit. To "emit" is to produce voluntarily. If a rat is trained to press a lever only when a light is turned on, the rat is said to "emit" the response *in the presence of* the light stimulus. The light doesn't *elicit* the bar-press response reflexively—that is, automatically. The light merely serves as a "discriminative" stimulus that lets the rat know that if it now emits a response, that response will be rewarded.

Elicited. To elicit is to pull out, to evoke, to stimulate into action. In Pavlovian conditioning, stimuli *elicit* responses—reflexively, or automatically.

FIGURE 9.6

The relationship between positive and negative reinforcement, and positive and negative punishment. Stimulus inputs may be either positive or negative, and they may be either presented or removed. The "plus" and "minus" signs indicate the effect of each condition on responding: reinforcers *increase* responding (+); punishers *decrease* responding (−).

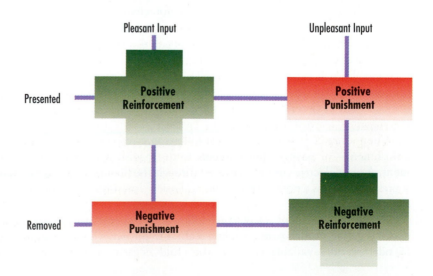

4. "Bowling" is obviously a very complicated set of responses which the animal has to learn in a *particular order or sequence*. You got the bird to learn one simple part at a time, never demanding too much. You encouraged each "right" move the pigeon made, and you ignored (or certainly didn't punish) the bird's mistakes. By doing so, you **chained** the sequence of responses together, from the pigeon's first, approaching step to its last whack at the ball. However, the experienced pigeon will perform its bowling routine so smoothly and efficiently that it is not easy to see the various *individual responses* that have been chained together during training.

Chained. Linked together. Behaviorists believe complex human behavior patterns are mostly long chains of related responses that must be learned one at a time.

If you can train a pigeon to bowl without using punishment, would it be possible to teach a child how to read and write without criticizing or spanking the child when she or he made a mistake? Why aren't more children taught this way?

5. Stimuli such as food that satisfy a biological need of the organism are called **primary reinforcers**. Any other stimulus that is *associated* with a primary reinforcer will gradually become a **secondary reinforcer**. A secondary reinforcer is any stimulus that has *become* reinforcing because of its association with a primary reinforcer.

   Money is a secondary reinforcer. Money itself does not satisfy any biological need, but because of its close association with primary reinforcers (it can purchase food, water, sex, etc.), money has developed (secondary) reinforcing properties of its own.

   Skinner believed that most of our behavior was controlled by secondary reinforcers. Attention, approval, and affection are all reinforcing because they have been linked so often with having our basic needs met.

Primary reinforcer. Any stimulus that satisfies an innate need of the organism, for example, food, water, air, sex. The organism does not need to learn that these stimuli are reinforcing.

Secondary reinforcer. Any stimulus that has acquired reinforcing value as a result of having been paired with a primary reinforcer. Secondary reinforcers are learned.

6. According to Skinner, at the beginning of training you should reward each move the bird makes toward the goal. However, once the pigeon has mastered a given response in the chain, you may begin slowly fading out the reward by reinforcing the response intermittently. You never fade out the reward completely. However, you can shift to a much less frequent "schedule of reinforcement" (Ferster & Skinner, 1957).

Continuous reinforcement is necessary at first, both to keep the animal motivated and to give it immediate feedback on its performance. However, once the pigeon is responding correctly, you may begin reinforcing the correct response every second time, then every third or fourth time, then perhaps every tenth time. If you fade out the reward very gradually, you can get a pigeon to repeat a simple response (such as pecking a button) several thousand times for each reinforcement.

During the fading process, the exact *scheduling* of the reward is crucial. If you reinforce *exactly* every tenth response, the bird will soon learn to anticipate which response will gain it food. Skinner called this **fixed-ratio** reinforcement, because the *ratio* between the number of responses required and the rewards given is fixed and never varies. If we make a **cumulative record** of the animal's responses, we would find it responds at a rapid and steady rate on a fixed-ratio schedule (see Figure 9.7).

We can get the pigeon to respond at a more or less constant rate by tricking it a bit—that is, by rewarding it on a **variable ratio** rather than at a fixed ratio. Instead of reinforcing *exactly* the tenth response, we vary the schedule so that sometimes the third response yields food, sometimes the seventh, sometimes the eleventh, sometimes the twentieth—or any response in between. A hundred responses will yield about ten rewards, but the bird will never know when the next reward is coming. When trained on variable-ratio schedules, pigeons respond at a very rapid steady pace.

Continuous reinforcement. Without stopping. If you reward a rat for *every* bar press, it is on a schedule of "continuous reinforcement."

Fixed-ratio reinforcement. If you reward a rat for *exactly* each third bar-press it makes, the ratio between responses (bar presses) and reward is fixed. Jobs which directly tie payment to production ("piece work") pay on a fixed-ratio schedule.

Cumulative record. From the word *accumulate*, meaning "to acquire." A cumulative record is an increasing graph or record of all the responses an animal makes in a certain time period. The record also shows the time between responses, and each reinforcement the animal receives.

Variable-ratio reinforcement. A schedule of reinforcement where reward is based on the number of responses made, but the number of responses necessary *varies* around some average.

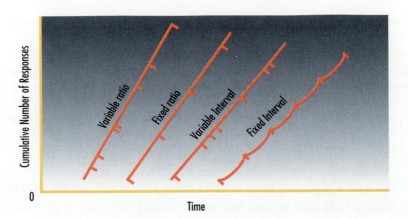

FIGURE 9.7

Cumulative record of response rates for four schedules of reinforcement. Steeper slopes indicate faster rates of response. The downward "blip" indicates a reinforcement was received.

Fixed-interval reinforcement. Rewarding the first response an organism makes after a certain time interval which does not change—say, every 60 seconds.

Variable-interval reinforcement. Rewarding the first response an organism makes after a time interval which *varies* around some average.

We could also reward the pigeon using *interval reinforcement*. For example, we could reward the first correct response the bird made after each **fixed interval** of time—say every 60 seconds. When a reinforcement is made available after a fixed period of time, animals will respond rapidly as the time period ends and reward becomes available. They then pause and respond slowly as the interval begins again, accelerating as the interval passes.

We might also *vary* the time period between available reinforcements. On this **variable interval** schedule animals will respond at a very steady rate (see Figure 9.7).

Rewarding an organism just "part of the time" when it makes a correct response is called *partial reinforcement*. In most real-life settings, you get rewards on a partial reinforcement schedule. For example, at work, instead of getting a few pennies each time you do something right, you receive a paycheck at the end of the week (or month). And in school, you don't get praise each time you read a sentence or two in a textbook. Instead, you receive encouraging feedback (let's hope!) when you have read several chapters and take (and do well on) an examination.

What type of schedule do the slot machines in Las Vegas pay off on? What type of response rate does this schedule produce?

Operant Versus Respondent Conditioning

Skinner called the type of learning he studied "operant conditioning." Sometimes it is called "instrumental conditioning," because the behavior is *instrumental* in bringing about a desired consequence (reward). Skinner chose the term *operant* because he believed the organism must learn to *operate* on its environment in order to obtain rewards.

Skinner referred to Pavlovian, or classical, conditioning as "respondent conditioning," because Pavlov taught his animals to respond in a specific way to a specific stimulus (Skinner, 1950).

ELICITED VERSUS EMITTED RESPONSES

There are many differences between operant and respondent conditioning. An obvious difference is that Pavlovian (respondent) learning is always tied to a unique and specific stimulus, while operant conditioning is not. Food powder blown into a dog's mouth elicits the salivary response. Pairing the bell with the food gives the bell the power to elicit the same sort of salivation, whether the dog likes it or not. The important point is that neither dogs nor humans go around salivating unless they are stimulated to do so by a highly specific sensory input. Respondent conditioning thus involves setting up involuntary, elicited responses to specific stimuli.

On the other hand, pigeons (and people) perform all kinds of actions that don't seem to be "elicited" or pulled out of the organism automatically. Rather, said Skinner, we typically emit, or produce, a wide variety of behaviors rather freely. Those activities that are reinforced, we tend to repeat. Those behaviors that aren't reinforced tend to drop out of our behavioral repertoire.

STIMULUS–RESPONSE CONNECTIONS

Respondent conditioning involves attaching a new stimulus to an already established response. Thus, the important association in Pavlovian conditioning is that between the CS and the UCS. Once this connection is made, the connection between the CS and the CR follows rather automatically.

Operant conditioning, however, involves attaching a new response to already present stimulus inputs. Thus the important association is between the response itself and the feedback the response generates (e.g., reward).

Pavlov didn't train his animals to respond in a new way. He merely taught them to give the same old salivation response to a new stimulus (the bell). Skinner, however, almost always shaped organisms to respond in ways they never had before. But the only new *stimuli* Skinner added to the picture were those associated with reinforcement.

VOLUNTARY VERSUS INVOLUNTARY MUSCLES

Respondent conditioning typically involves those involuntary muscle groups controlled by the autonomic nervous system and the lower brain centers. Most emotional learning—such as developing a fear or phobia—is a type of Pavlovian conditioning. The fear response is already present in the organism's repertoire. All the respondent conditioning does is to attach the involuntary fear reaction to a novel stimulus.

Operant conditioning typically involves *voluntary muscle groups* controlled by the cortex and higher brain centers. Motor skills, such as typing or playing football, are usually the result of operant conditioning. Put another way, acquiring a motor skill involves learning a new way of responding to stimuli that were already present in your environment.

The subtle differences between operant and respondent conditioning are probably of greater interest to learning theorists than to anyone else. Much real-life learning involves *both types of conditioning*. And both kinds of conditioning are built on the innate response tendencies with which most organisms are born (Rescorla, 1987). Later we will see that these innate response tendencies also impose some limitations on conditioning.

Suppose you trained a dog to press a bar to get food using operant techniques. Do you think that, at some time during the training, the animal might learn involuntarily to salivate at the sight of the bar?

Learning and Behaviorism

Up to this point we have discussed learning as changes in *behavior*—the behavior of dogs, cats, pigeons, and humans. In the past, the study of learning was virtually identical with the movement in psychology called **behaviorism.**

When psychology was just beginning to get established in North America as an independent discipline at the beginning of this century, many of its leaders felt that a new approach was necessary. They argued that for psychology to advance and gain scientific respectability it must be established on *scientific* principles. And what

Behaviorism. An approach to psychology that emphasizes the study of *behavior* and tends to ignore intra-psychic processes. Behaviorism began under the influence of John Watson, around 1913, and dominated psychology until the 1960s.

better way to gain scientific respectability than to imitate a quantitative science such as physics? Thus, they argued, the only suitable subject for psychological study was observable, measurable behavior. These ideas crystalized into a movement called behaviorism when John B. Watson published an article in 1913 called "Psychology as the Behaviorist Views It" (Watson, 1913).

The work of Pavlov was quickly embraced by the behaviorists. Pavlov, like a good behaviorist, carefully avoided all references to supposed mental events. He spoke only of external, observable responses.

However, more than anyone else, B.F. Skinner was responsible for the powerful influence which behaviorism ultimately achieved. Throughout his long and productive career, Skinner studied only one thing, the "behaving organism," not the "thinking" or "feeling" or "deciding" organism, but the *behaving* organism (Skinner, 1987). Because of his narrow and unwavering study of behavior, Skinner's approach became known as "radical behaviorism."

In 1973 Skinner published a best-selling book, called *Beyond Freedom and Dignity*, in which he applied his analysis of behavior and his determinist assumptions to the problems facing the world. His arguments may be condensed as follows:

1. All behavior is controlled by the environment.
2. Our subjective feeling of freedom is simply an illusion brought about by gaps in our understanding of the environmental factors which control us.
3. All the major problems facing humankind are problems in behavior.
4. Therefore, the greatest need of humankind is for a technology of behavior to control behavior and thus solve our problems. (The complete control brought about by this technology of behavior would *not* mean a reduction in freedom since we are already completely controlled by our environment, and personal freedom is an illusion.)

Whether you agree with Skinner or not, he must be credited for the consistent and logical application of his basic assumptions, and his vision in seeing their far-reaching effects. His place of prominence in psychology is secure and his contributions to the study of learning will probably never be surpassed (Massaro, 1990).

However, as we will see, not all psychologists studying learning were as radical as Skinner in their adoption of behaviorist ideals.

COGNITIVE LEARNING

In recent years there has been a growing appreciation of the non-observable "mental events," or *cognitions*, which affect learning. This appreciation has grown into a movement known as **cognitive behaviorism.** Although a recent movement, cognitive behaviorism has its roots in some very early studies of learning.

Cognitive Maps

One early learning psychologist, E.C. Tolman, dared to suggest that not all learning, even in rats, was simply a matter of attaching a response to a stimulus. He speculated, for example, that in exploring a maze, rats develop a "cognitive map," which they then use to find their way. His ideas directly opposed those of his contemporary E.L. Thorndike. (Remember, Thorndike saw all learning as simply S–R associations.) The resulting controversy led Tolman to develop several ingenious experiments.

In most of Tolman's experiments, the rats learned very complicated **mazes.** Typically, the animals explored the apparatus at their leisure, but did *not* find food

Habit second nature? Habit is ten times nature.

DUKE OF WELLINGTON

Cognitive behaviorism. The use of Skinnerian techniques to modify or change inner processes (thoughts, feelings) as well as behavioral outputs.

Mazes. A network of pathways and blind alleys between a starting point and a goal, used chiefly to study problem solving in animals and humans. The first maze for laboratory animals was built by psychologist W.S. Small in 1900 and was similar to a famous maze made of hedges at Hampton Court Palace in England that has delighted millions of visitors.

When you are trying to remember directions, what do you do—form a mental picture of the route (cognitive map) or memorize the instructions (S–R associations)?

at the end of the maze. Usually it took them a very long time to get from the start to the end of the maze. Thorndike, of course, would say that the animals learned little or nothing about the maze during these explorations since their efforts weren't rewarded. Tolman, however, claimed the rats had "created a cognitive map" of the maze while poking around inside the apparatus. And he soon found a way to prove his point.

After a rat had been given several unrewarded "exploration" trials, Tolman suddenly introduced a food reward at the end of the maze. On the very next trial, the rat typically ran through the apparatus making very few mistakes, and ate the food at the end. This behavior suggested—to Tolman, at least—that the rat had *learned the spatial relationships in the maze without being rewarded*. The food merely motivated it to perform at a rapid pace.

In another series of studies, Tolman used a type of apparatus in which the animal could reach the food reward by a great many pathways. However, one pathway was typically much shorter than the rest and was preferred by the animals. When that pathway was blocked, however, most of the rats would instantly shift to the next most efficient route—even if they had never used that path before. This sort of behavior posed a real problem for Thorndike and his "S–R connectionism." For how could the animals use a new pathway when they had never formed the specific S–R bonds associated with running that particular pathway?

To make matters worse—at least from Thorndike's point of view—if at any time the experimenter moved the reward from one part of the maze to another, the rats responded immediately and appropriately. That is, the rats behaved as if they understood a great deal about the *spatial relationships* involved in getting quickly from one part of the maze to another. From Tolman's point of view, the animals acted as if they had somehow acquired a "cognitive map" of the maze (Tolman, 1938).

When you give a person directions to get somewhere, do you assume they will follow a "stimulus–response" strategy, or do you assume they will use a cognitive map? Which method are you using as you "picture" the route yourself in order to give the directions?

Insight

Another early psychologist who took a more "cognitive" approach to learning was Wolfgang Koehler. In 1913 he travelled to the Canary Islands to study chimps and chickens. While he was there, World War I broke out and he was unable to leave. Koehler took the opportunity to perform several interesting experiments.

Koehler's most famous study involved a particularly bright chimpanzee named Sultan. First, Koehler taught Sultan to reach through the bars of his cage with a stick and rake in a banana. After Sultan had mastered this trick, Koehler set the animal the much more difficult task of *putting two sticks together* to get the food. He moved the banana farther away from Sultan's cage and gave the chimp two bamboo poles. If the two poles were fitted together they would be just long enough to gather in the reward.

At first Sultan was confused. He tried to pull the fruit in with one stick and then with the other, but neither would reach. Although this approach didn't get the banana, Sultan repeated the behavior again and again. Then the chimp abandoned the banana and (perhaps in frustration) retreated into his cage to play with the sticks. So, Koehler decided the animal had failed the test. Koehler went home, leaving an assistant to observe Sultan.

Not long after Koehler left, Sultan happened to hold one stick in each hand so that their ends pointed toward each other. Gently, he pushed the tip of the smaller one into the hollow of the larger. *They fitted.* Even as he joined the two sticks together, Sultan was up and running toward the bars of his cage. Reaching through with the double stick, he touched the banana and started to draw it toward him.

At this point fate played Sultan a nasty trick for which Koehler was most grateful. The two sticks came apart! Annoyed at this turn of events, Sultan gathered the sticks back into the cage, pushed them *firmly* together, tested them briefly, and then "rescued" the banana.

These actions proved, at least to Koehler's satisfaction, that Sultan actually *understood* that joining the poles together was an effective way of lengthening his arm. Koehler used the term **insight** to refer to this very rapid perception of relationships that sometimes occurs in animals and humans. He believed that insight

Insight. The very rapid—almost immediate—learning that takes place when you "see" the solution to a problem. Insight is sometimes called the "aha" phenomenon. Cartoonists often use a light bulb to illustrate insight.

Observation of chimpanzees shows that they are able to perceive relationships, reorganize their perceptual world, and then take the necessary steps to obtain a goal—a process Koehler called *insight* in his work with the chimpanzee named Sultan.

involved a sudden restructuring or reorganization of the organism's perceptual world into a new pattern, for which he used the German word **Gestalt** (Koehler, 1929).

Although strict behaviorists like Pavlov and Thorndike attacked the research of Koehler and Tolman, it stood as a reminder that internal events like thoughts, feelings, and intentions have a role to play in a complete psychology of learning.

Today, cognitive events are recognized as an important part of most learning situations. For example, we noted that your mouth might water at the smell of bacon cooking, but you were certainly aware of the connection. That is, you had *thoughts* about it—thoughts of expectation and anticipation. In fact, you could probably produce much the same response by merely *thinking about* the smell of bacon cooking. Modern psychologists are turning more and more attention to the role played by thought in learning. Let's consider some examples.

Self-Directed Behavior

Have you ever wondered if you could apply any of the knowledge that psychologists have gained about learning to your own behavior? Of course you can, but for years the primary use of learning principles has been to change someone *else's* behavior: parents training children, teachers training students, therapists training clients, and so on. However, with the recognition of the importance of thought processes in learning has come a movement to teach people to use their behavior and their thought processes to reach their own goals.

In this approach, sometimes called **self-directed behavior modification** or self-directed behavior therapy (Watson, 1988), you are both therapist and client. Self-directed behavior modification has been used to help people change habits such as smoking, overeating, drinking, public-speaking anxiety, and many others. You must analyze your problem behavior in terms of the learning concepts we have already discussed (e.g., baseline behavior, terminal response, shaping). You then use rewards to *shape* your *baseline behavior* step-by-step towards your *goal*.

What is different from your shaping of the pigeon's behavior is that you will use cognitive processes as well. You might practice thought processes that are consistent with your goal ("I am a confident speaker"). You would stop any interfering thoughts ("I am nervous in front of groups") and substitute helpful ones. You might form an image of yourself succeeding at your goal and go over and over it. You might also imagine the reward you have arranged for yourself.

The approach of self-directed behavior modification recognizes that behavior is not emitted by an empty organism. We can harness our thoughts (cognitions) and make them a powerful ally in our effort to change our behavior.

Observational Learning

Have you ever taught someone a skill such as throwing a ball? It is unlikely that you simply "shaped" the person's existing arm movements by rewarding closer and closer approximations to a throw, although some of this would be involved. It is even less likely that you classically conditioned an existing reflex. Almost certainly you demonstrated by throwing a ball yourself. This is the way we have learned much of our behavior, from speaking a language (or languages) to playing tennis or driving a car. When we want to learn or to improve a particular behavior we often look for a good *model* and then imitate the model.

Unfortunately, the models that affect us do not always model good behavior. In a famous experiment, Bandura and his colleagues showed that children will learn aggressive, violent behavior through watching a violent model. Children who watched a model display aggressive behavior (hitting and kicking a toy "Bobo doll"), later became much more violent when they were frustrated than did children who

Gestalt (guess-STAHLT). A German word that means "good form" or "good figure." Also means the tendency to see things as "wholes" rather than as jumbled bits and pieces.

Self-directed behavior modification. The application of cognitive behavior modification to oneself.

No living person has sunk so low so not to be imitated by somebody.

WILLIAM JAMES

"How come I never hear you say 'please' and 'thank-you'."

HERMAN copyright 1977
Jim Unger. Reprinted with
permission of Universal Press
Syndicate. All rights reserved.

had not watched the violent model. A televised model was just as effective, and a cartoon model was only slightly less influential (Bandura et al., 1963).

This type of learning is called *observational learning*, *modelling*, or *imitation*. It is the type of learning most thoroughly studied by Albert Bandura. Bandura admits that we do learn by direct reinforcement, as Skinner said. But as he points out, "Learning would be exceedingly laborious, not to mention hazardous, if people had to rely solely on the effects of their own actions to inform them what to do" (Bandura, 1977b). However, as Bandura has shown, models can teach bad as well as good behavior.

Because Bandura says observational learning takes place "in the mind," his approach must be considered *cognitive behaviorism*.

What effect do you think watching television shows like "Teenage Mutant Ninja Turtles" might have on children?

BEHAVIORISM TODAY

As we noted above, the study of learning has closely paralleled the development called "behaviorism." When behaviorism was narrowly defined, the study of learning was narrowly defined. As behaviorism matured and mellowed, the study of learning broadened to include cognitive events.

The "radical behaviorism" of B.F. Skinner has given way to the "moderate behaviorism" of Albert Bandura. Bandura is "moderate" not only in admitting cognitive processes, but also in viewing the person-environment interaction as a complementary one. That is, the person is influenced by the environment, but the person also *chooses* and shapes the environment (which in turn shapes the person, who . . .). This **reciprocal determinism** admits an element of freedom which Skinner's complete environmental determinism denies.

Reciprocal determinism. Determinism is the idea that people are not free to choose their actions, but are controlled by forces, such as their inherited instincts, or their environment. *Reciprocal* determinism is the idea that people can *choose* the forces which control them. Thus the relationship between control and choice is a reciprocal, or "back-and-forth" one.

Constraints on Learning

Many early behaviorists exhibited an unbounded optimism about the potential of learning to shape and change both animals and humans. Watson boasted not only that he could take a healthy dog, make it "neurotic," and then "cure it," but also that, given

> a dozen healthy infants, well-formed, and my own specified world to bring them up in and I'll guarantee to take any one of them at random and train him to become any type of specialist I might select—doctor, lawyer, artist, merchant-chief and, yes, even beggar-man and thief, regardless of his talents, penchants, tendencies, abilities, vocations, and race of his ancestors (Watson, 1924).

Today, psychologists are more cautious in their claims. For example, they recognize there are certain *biological limitations* to learning.

BIOLOGICAL PREDISPOSITIONS

Perhaps you have seen some of the amazing tricks that animals can be trained to do. Maybe you have assumed that by using the right training techniques, such as those studied by Skinner, an animal could be taught to do just about anything. This was the assumption of Keller and Marian Breland, two animal trainers who have used operant procedures to train thousands of animals for movies, TV shows, and circuses.

However, after many years of experience, the Brelands changed their minds. They have become convinced that animals have certain biological predispositions which limit the way their behavior can be shaped.

Animals can most easily be trained using responses that draw on their natural behaviors. If they are taught responses contrary to their natural predispositions, the learned behavior will gradually "drift" toward the original natural behavior. For example, the Brelands trained a pig to pick up large tokens and drop them into a piggy bank. However, it wasn't long before the animal began to slip back toward its natural behavior—dropping the coins, rooting (poking) at them with its snout, tossing them in the air, and rooting at them again—all natural food-seeking behaviors for pigs in the wild. The Brelands had learned that biological predispositions may have to take precedence over operant principles (Breland & Breland, 1961).

CONDITIONED TASTE AVERSION

Another situation which teaches us the limitations of general conditioning principles is **conditioned taste aversion.** You may have had the experience of getting sick after eating a particular food. You may have developed a strong dislike for the food, even if you know it didn't cause you to become sick. The fact that you avoid the food even when you know it wasn't responsible suggests that a very basic form of conditioning has taken place. However, your experience violates one important finding in conditioning studies. The time delay between eating the food and getting sick is far too long for any normal conditioning. And it is not simply your "higher mental processes" which bridge this time gap. Rats, without your advanced cognitive abilities, respond the same way. Several hours after tasting poisoned food, they become ill. If they have eaten a small amount (which they usually do), they will survive. After this single experience and the long delay between their response and the consequences, they will avoid similar-tasting foods. Of course, rats have a "natural" reason (their own survival) for rapid learning under these circumstances. But the principles we have discovered in classical conditioning cannot account for this learning from a single trial, particularly with such a long delay between eating and sickness.

Today, researchers are much more balanced in their approach to learning than they were at the beginning of the century. They have a greater awareness of (1) the several "kinds" of learning which may take place, (2) the influence of cognitive processes on learning, and (3) the effect of differences between species and between different learning situations (Cloninger & Gilligan, 1987; Rescorla, 1988a, 1988b).

Learning Versus Disease

Skinner and other behaviorists believed that symptomatic behaviors associated with so-called "mental disorders" are actually learned. Thus, therapy should consist of helping people learn new and healthier habits. Many psychotherapists, of course, take the opposite view. They see "mental illness" as being just that—an illness or disorder of the mind, not a disorder of learned behavioral outputs. Therefore, treatment should consist of techniques designed to "uncover the patient's underlying psychological problem." Once the patient has insight, the symptomatic behaviors would disappear more or less automatically.

The cognitive behaviorists stand somewhere between these two extremes. They agree with Skinner that the ultimate focus in most types of therapy must be on learning new behavior patterns. But the cognitive behaviorists believe that teaching people how to control their own thoughts and feelings is often a very effective way of helping them learn to control their behavioral outputs (Kendall & Hollon, 1981).

We will discuss these issues at greater length in later chapters. But to give you an example of a therapeutic application of learning principles—and a better

Conditioned taste aversion. The tendency to avoid food with a particular taste as the result of associating an unpleasant experience, such as getting sick, with eating the food. Conditioned taste aversion appears to be a natural mechanism of survival which is difficult to explain using ideas from Pavlovian conditioning. (There is too long a time delay between tasting the food [CS] and getting sick [UCR].)

understanding of the disease versus learned behavior controversy—let's close this chapter by considering the case of alcoholism.

ALCOHOLISM: TWO SCHOOLS OF THOUGHT

Millions of North Americans consume alcohol on a regular basis. But only a small percentage of these people are "problem drinkers." How can we explain the behavior of this relatively small group of individuals? Why can approximately 95 percent of the population voluntarily control their alcohol intake, while the other 5 percent can't?

There are two main schools of thought today as to what alcoholism is and how to treat it. One school views alcoholism as a *disease*. The other school perceives problem drinking as a *failure to learn self-control techniques*.

How would the term you used—"alcoholism" versus "problem drinking"— bias your beliefs, both as to the causes and the cures of the disorder?

Complete abstinence is easier than perfect moderation.

ST. AUGUSTINE

THE DISEASE MODEL   E.M. Jellinek first proposed the "disease model" of alcoholism. According to Jellinek, alcoholism is a medical disorder that has a biological basis. Because of defective genes (or perhaps a combination of genetic and developmental problems), the alcoholic cannot control her or his drinking the way "normal" people can. The alcoholic becomes dependent on alcohol, and comes to crave it the way a heroin addict "craves a fix." Since this is a chemical dependency, Jellinek implies, the only solution to the dependency must be total withdrawal from drinking (Jellinek, 1952).

People who adopt the disease model believe alcoholism is a "progressive disorder." Therefore, there can be no "cure" for the problem. However, the course of the illness can be arrested if the alcoholic gives up drinking entirely. Thus, the goal of treatment must be abstinence, or complete sobriety (Miller & Francis, 1989), for, theoretically speaking, even one drink will reinstitute both the craving and the progressive physical deterioration. To help alcoholics achieve sobriety, disease-model therapists often use confrontation (and even punishment) to *condition* patients to avoid alcohol—much as Watson used a loud noise to condition Little Albert.

In Chapter 5, we reported on data (the "think-drink" effect) showing that people who consumed alcohol but thought they were drinking tonic water showed no effects of alcohol. But people who drank tonic water believing it was alcohol did report effects. How are these data an attack on the disease model?

Temperate temperance is best; intemperate temperance injures the cause of temperance.

MARK TWAIN

THE BEHAVIORAL MODEL   In 1962, British physician D.L. Davies published a report that seemed to challenge Jellinek's disease model of alcoholism. Davies studied a group of 93 alcoholics for almost ten years after they had received "abstinence training" in a hospital setting. Some of the patients achieved and maintained sobriety. Most had fallen into alcoholic drinking patterns again. However, without any training or treatment to help them do so, several of the patients had become "normal, social drinkers" (Davies, 1962).

On the basis of this admittedly small sample of subjects, Davies (and other researchers like him) concluded that the major difficulty most alcoholics have is this: They never learned the type of "self-control" most people develop early in life. The researchers then set out to find ways to *teach* alcoholics the cognitive and behavioral skills they lacked. As it happened, the researchers not only discovered new and more effective therapeutic techniques for working with alcoholic patients, they also found substantial evidence that the disease model is an inadequate explanation of why many people have alcohol-related problems (Fingarette, 1988, 1990; Miller & Hester, 1980; Robertson, 1989).

Rather than forcing alcoholics to achieve *total abstinence,* the cognitive-behavioral approach attempts to help them become "non-problem" drinkers. From this viewpoint, if the person no longer has any alcohol-related difficulties, then the alcoholism has been "cured" for all practical purposes (Miller & Hester, 1986).

Psychologist Alan Marlatt and most other cognitive behaviorists see the "alcoholism problem" as one of teaching people self-management skills. Marlatt says most people who take the disease-model perspective refuse to accept "controlled drinking" as a worthy therapeutic goal. From their standpoint, turning an alcoholic into a social drinker is no more a "cure" than turning a murderer into a mugger (Marlatt, 1983, 1984). The disease-model position is that alcoholism *cannot be cured.* Disease-model researchers contend that patients who learn to moderate their intake are still alcoholics even though most of them no longer have any significant alcohol-related problems (McCrady, 1985; Pendery et al., 1982).

How shall we decide which view is right?

Which would you think is a better outcome, complete abstinence or controlled drinking? Why?

Alcoholics Anonymous and its related groups—like Alateen, shown here—believe in the disease model of alcoholism.

A HOLISTIC APPROACH

As we have said many times before, behavior is multidetermined. Thus, any attempt to change behavior must address all the factors that influence those response outputs, including biological predispositions.

Pairing pain with the sight, smell, and taste of alcohol (**aversion training**), or confronting an alcoholic with his or her problem, may well lead to a *suppression* of drinking, as Pavlov and Watson would have predicted. But the data suggest this suppression is often fairly temporary (Marlatt, 1983, 1984). Rewarding alcoholics for learning new responses that compete with the "urge to drink" (counter conditioning) does help. And teaching alcoholics the cognitive skills involved in self-control is also important (Marlatt, 1983, 1984). You can't always have some external agency (such as Fred Skinner) standing over the alcoholic to administer positive reinforcement at just the right time.

Aversion training. Pairing punishment with an undesirable response with the hope that the pain associated with the punishment will generalize to the response and thus prevent its recurrence.

Finally, any type of therapy goes better if you help the person solve a wide range of social and personal problems in addition to changing symptomatic behaviors. For example, Mansell Pattison notes that even those patients who give up alcohol entirely still tend to function poorly in society unless given training specific to solving their social problems (Pattison, 1987).

Holistic treatment programs recognize that alcoholism is multidetermined. These programs may be called "biobehavioral" (Laberg et al., 1989), "biopsychosocial" (Daley, 1989; Wallace, 1989), or simply "multimodal" (Brown et al., 1988). Their common feature is that they all attempt to deal with the several factors which contribute to the problem (Levy, 1992).

To summarize, each of the various approaches to learning tells us something important about how organisms acquire (and change) their behavior. Indeed, one approach often complements another. For instance, Robert Rescorla suggests using *Pavlovian* techniques to help analyze what happens during *operant* conditioning (Rescorla, 1987). However, no one theory gives us the complete story even in the simplest of learning situations. Thus, we cannot expect *therapy* or *educational practices* based on just one type of learning to work well in all situations and with all types of patients—alcoholic or otherwise.

We will discuss these matters again in several later chapters. However, there is one important aspect of learning we've not yet touched upon—that of *memory*. So, it is to this important topic that we now turn our attention.

How could you use the various theories of learning to construct a holistic approach to education?

SUMMARY

1. The American psychologist E.B. Twitmyer was probably the first to publish research on the **conditioned reflex,** but Ivan Pavlov developed most of the conditioning techniques and terminology still in use.

2. Conditioning involves pairing a **neutral stimulus** (the CS) with an **unconditioned stimulus** (the UCS). The UCS already has the power to elicit the **unconditioned response** (the UCR). If the CS is associated with the UCS enough times, it takes on the power to evoke a reaction similar to the UCR. This "similar" reaction is called the **conditioned response** (the CR).

3. **Pavlov** paired a bell (CS) with food powder blown into a dog's mouth (the UCS). The food naturally evoked salivation (the UCR). Once the bell had been paired with the food for several trials, sounding the bell without food caused the dog to salivate (the CR).

4. Psychologists often use the term **conditioning** to mean **learning.**

5. According to Pavlov, all learning or conditioning is built on—or is an adaption of—**innately determined stimulus–response connections,** the UCS–UCR bond.

6. Conditioning is sometimes referred to as strengthening S–R, or **stimulus–response bonds.** The stronger the bond, the more likely it is the conditioned stimulus will elicit the desired conditioned response.

7. The more frequently the CS and the UCS are paired, the stronger the **S–R bond** becomes.

8. Conditioning typically proceeds fastest when the CS is presented immediately **before** the UCS. The exception to this rule is a **conditioned taste aversion.** If you become ill several hours after eating some particular food, you may avoid that food in the future.

9. Conditioned responses are unlearned just as easily as they are learned. Unlearning proceeds fastest when the CS is presented several times without being followed by the UCS. Once the S–R bond is broken, the response is said to be **extinguished.**

10. An extinguished response is not totally forgotten. If the CS is again paired with the UCS, **relearning** usually takes fewer trials than did the original learning. Furthermore, extinguished responses often show **spontaneous recovery** after some time has passed.

11. If an animal is trained to respond to an orange light, this response may **generalize** to other similar stimuli, such as a red or yellow light. However, with the proper training, the animal can usually learn to **discriminate** among similar stimuli and give different responses to each.

12. Watson and Rayner conditioned a boy called Little Albert to fear a rat by pairing the sight of the rat with a frightening noise. Mary Cover Jones reduced this sort of **conditioned emotional response** by pairing the sight of the animal with food, using a technique called **counter conditioning.**

13. Many psychologists believe that most human **phobic reactions** are conditioned in the same manner that Watson and Rayner created a fear response in Little Albert.

14. E.L. Thorndike assumed that humans learn in much the same way that animals do. His studies with cats in a **puzzle box** led him to believe most new behaviors come about by **trial and error learning.**

15. Thorndike stated learning is influenced by two laws:
    (1) The **law of exercise** states that the more frequently an animal repeats an **S–R bond,** the stronger it becomes.
    (2) The **law of effect** states that stimulus–response (S–R) bonds are strengthened if the effect of the response is **satisfying.** Early in his career, Thorndike believed punishment "broke" S–R bonds, but later he stated punishment only **suppresses** responses temporarily.

16. B.F. Skinner studied **operant conditioning**—a method of training organisms that differs from **Pavlovian,** or **respondent conditioning.** Operant technology is far more effective in the classroom (and elsewhere) than either Pavlovian or Gestalt techniques.

17. Skinner believed animals **emit** responses freely and that the environment **rewards** or **reinforces** some of those responses but ignores or punishes others.

18. Training an organism by operant (Skinnerian) techniques consists of several steps:
    (1) The **terminal response** or goal of the training must be stated in measurable terms.
    (2) The **baseline behaviors** (what the organism is doing before intervention begins) must be measured precisely.
    (3) Those baseline behaviors that seem directed toward the terminal response are **rewarded,** a technique called **reinforcing successive approximations to a goal,** or **shaping** a new response.

19. **Positive reinforcement** is the presentation of a pleasant stimulus after a response; **negative reinforcement** is the removal of an unpleasant stimulus after a response. Both **positive** and **negative reinforcement** *increase* the probability that an organism will emit the same response the next time it is free to do so.

20. **Positive punishment** is the presentation of an unpleasant stimulus after a response; **negative punishment** is the removal of a pleasant stimulus after a response. Both **positive** and **negative punishment** *decrease* the probability that an organism will emit the same response the next time it is free to do so. Punishment has several undesirable consequences and is less preferable than reinforcement for training.

21. **Fixed ratio, variable ratio, fixed interval,** and **variable interval** schedules are all different kinds of **intermittent schedules** of reinforcement.

22. Pavlovian, or respondent, conditioning typically involves those **involuntary muscles** controlled by the **autonomic nervous system,** while operant conditioning typically involves those **voluntary muscles** controlled by the **cortex** and **higher brain centers.**

23. According to Tolman, animals do not learn a maze by acquiring hundreds of S–R connections. Rather, they make a **cognitive map** of the maze, which guides their behavior. Tolman believed that reward affected **performance,** but not **learning.**

24. Thorndike and Pavlov believed all learning is mechanical, or **reflexive. Gestalt psychologists,** such as Wolfgang Koehler, assume animals are capable of solving problems mentally (through **insight**) rather than just through mechanical trial and error.

25. Many behavioral psychologists have adapted Skinner's methods to the shaping of thoughts and feelings, an approach called **cognitive behaviorism.** Cognitive behaviorists recognize that a great deal of learning is **self-directed** and also that it can occur through **observation.** They have also discovered certain *exceptions* to a simple approach to learning.

26. The two major explanations of alcoholism are the **disease model** and the **learned behavior model.** Disease-model theorists believe the goal of treatment should be **abstinence.** Learning theorists believe that **controlled drinking,** which involves **skills training,** is a more achievable goal.

27. Alcoholism is probably best treated by a mix of **aversion training** (or social confrontation) during the early stages of therapy and **skills training** to maintain initial gains.

ANSWERS FOR THOUGHT

1. *How would you go about teaching a dog to salivate when you gave it food if it didn't do so instinctively?*

   You would have to find a stimulus which *did* elicit salivation in the dog. You would then pair this stimulus with food. The dog would learn to associate food with the saliva-producing stimulus and eventually salivate to food.

2. *Is the odor of bacon more likely to cause you to salivate . . . ?*

   The odor of bacon is a conditioned stimulus because it has been associated with bacon in the mouth. Since bacon in the mouth would not elicit as much salivation when you are not hungry, neither would the smell.

3. *For most people, the sight of a big, hairy spider . . . ?*

   You might associate spider stimuli with pleasant, relaxing stimuli (such as reclining in your favorite chair with good music and a snack). You should begin with relatively mild stimuli (pictures, spider webs, small spiders), and very gradually move up to stronger stimuli. If you become fearful you should remove the stimulus, relax, and begin again.

4. *How would you go about solving a "puzzle box" using "logic" or "trial and error"?*

   You would probably use a combination of both. You might begin with trial and error, but if you were unsuccessful, you would probably try logic.

5. *College catalogs often state that the goal of higher education . . . ?*

   These terminal responses, stated in this way, are very difficult to measure. Skinner would want the goals defined in *measurable* terms. This would probably mean breaking down each term, such as "good citizen," into clearly identifiable components, such as "does not break the law," "supports charities," "votes," and so on.

6. *If an instructor wanted to increase oral responses to her questions . . . ?*

   She should be careful not to punish the student in any way—especially she should not embarrass the student. She should try to find something positive in what the student said so that she could give positive reinforcement. For example, she might thank the student for responding.

7. *What "old" responses does the average pigeon already make . . . ?*

   Pigeons frequently "bob" their heads up and down and peck at things on the ground. These behaviors can be used to help bring the pigeon's head into contact with the ball.

8. *Do you think that at any time during training, the pigeon gains a cognitive awareness . . . ?*

   It is unlikely that pigeons have the ability to grasp what we mean by the concept "learning to bowl." If a pigeon had the ability to grasp our explanation, learning would progress much faster because the intermediate steps in shaping could be omitted.

9. *If you can train a pigeon to bowl without using punishment, would it be possible to teach a child . . . ?*

Children can be taught without punishment. Punishment is used primarily because it *seems* more efficient, and because we are in the *habit* of using it.

10. *What type of schedule do the slot machines in Las Vegas pay off on? What type of response . . . ?*

Slot machines pay off on a variable ratio schedule. A variable ratio schedule produces a rapid rate of responding. Because it is a *ratio* schedule, the more responses that are made (coins or tokens paid in), the more likely a reinforcement (payoff). Because it is a *variable* schedule, the time or the number of responses since the last payoff doesn't matter—it's always possible that the next one could bring a big payoff.

11. *Suppose you trained a dog to press a bar to get food using operant techniques. Do you think . . . ?*

The bar could become a conditioned stimulus the same way that the tone did in Pavlov's experiment. The dog would then salivate at the sight of the bar.

12. *When you give a person directions to get somewhere, do you assume they will follow . . . ?*

If they don't have a map to show someone, most people given directions in the form of stimulus–response instructions—"turn right at the second traffic light." However, they may be picturing the route in their mind as a map before transforming the instructions into stimulus–response directions.

13. *What effect do you think watching television shows like "Teenage Mutant Ninja Turtles" might have on children?*

According to Bandura's research, children will tend to model behavior they see on television—even the behavior of cartoon characters. The "heroes in a half-shell" tend to be quite violent. Their fans can be expected to learn that violence is an acceptable solution to a problem.

14. *How would the term you used—"alcoholism" versus "problem drinking"—bias your beliefs, both as to the causes and the cures of the disorder?*

"Alcoholism" suggests a *disease* with a physical cause and cure. "Problem drinking" implies an *acquired habit* which could be changed through learning.

15. *In Chapter 5 we reported on data (the "think-drink" effect) showing . . . ?*

The disease model implies that the response to alcohol is physical and automatic. These data suggest that *psychological factors* play an important role in determining the effect alcohol has. Research by Scott Geller also suggests that alcohol consumption is effected more by environmental and social determinants than by a need for a certain amount of alcohol (Geller, 1990, 1991).

16. *Which would you think is a better outcome, complete abstinence or controlled drinking? Why?*

The ability to exercise control over one's behavior is a desirable goal with positive psychological consequences. Thus, being able to control one's drinking behavior would be preferable to forced limitations. Of course, personal control might include the decision to abstain for economic, health, social, or religious reasons.

17. *How could you use the various theories of learning to construct a holistic approach to education?*

You would want to take advantage of innate abilities, set clearly defined step-by-step goals, use positive reinforcement to shape behavior towards the goals (avoiding punishment), and provide models of effective learning. You would also provide instructions for the use of cognitive processes (such as mental imagery and verbal reasoning).

CHAPTER 10

MEMORY

All I remember is the feel of the leather seats, the texture of the map upon my knee, its frayed edges, its worn seams, and how one day, looking at the clock, I thought to myself, "This moment now, at twenty past eleven, this must never be lost," I shut my eyes to make the experience more lasting. When I opened my eyes we were by a bend in the road, and a peasant girl in a black shawl waved to us; I can see her now, her dusty skirt, her gleaming, friendly smile, and in a second we had passed the bend and could see her no more. Already she belonged to the past, she was only a memory.

I wanted to go back again, to recapture the moment that had gone, and then it came to me that if we did it would not be the same, even the sun would be changed in the sky, casting another shadow, and the peasant girl would trudge past us along the road in a different way, not waving this time, perhaps not seeing us. There was something chilling in the thought, something a little melancholy, and looking at the clock I saw that five more minutes had gone by. Soon we would have reached our time limit, and must return to the hotel.

"If only there could be an invention," I said impulsively, "that bottled up a memory, like scent. And it never faded, and it never got stale. And then, when one wanted it, the bottle could be uncorked, and it would be like living the moment all over again." I looked up at him, to see what he would say. He did not turn to me, he went on watching the road ahead.

"What particular moments in your young life do you wish uncorked?" he said. I could not tell from his voice whether he was teasing me or not. "I'm not sure," I began, and then blundered on, rather foolishly, not thinking of my words, "I'd like to keep this moment and never forget it."

DAPHNE DU MAURIER
REBECCA

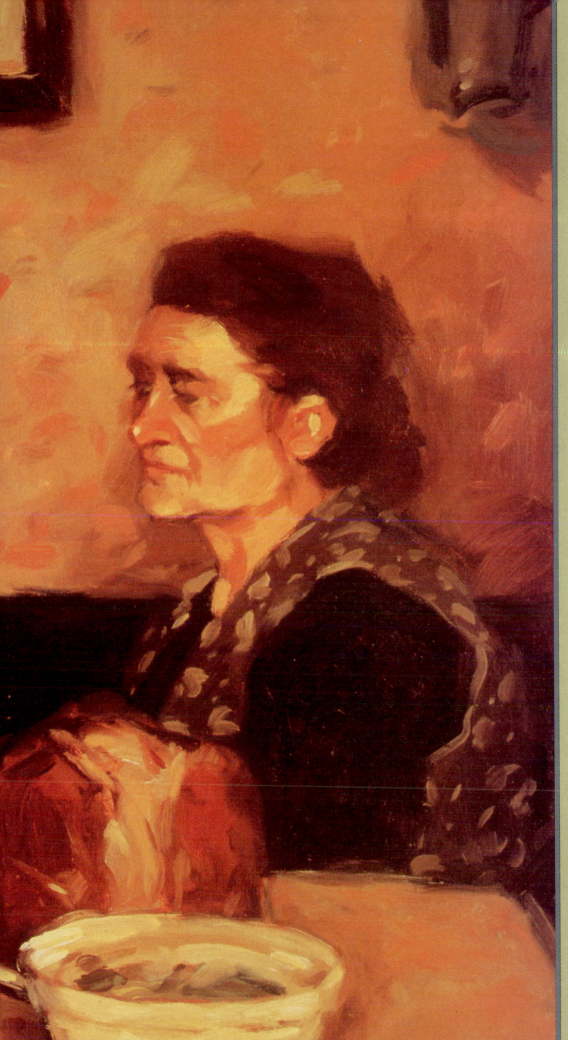

YOUR MEMORY

Have you ever wished, like Rebecca, that you could keep a moment and not forget it? Bottled up like a scent? Like Rebecca, we often think of memory as a simple recorder of sights, sounds, and smells—perhaps this is why cameras and recorders are so popular. But memory is much more than a snapshot or a recording you play back.

Consider the simple question, "What time is it?" When someone asks you for the time, how do you respond? Probably you look at your watch, or at a clock, and you give the answer almost automatically. As simple as this process may seem, however, we know very little about how your brain handles inputs such as this one. And we know even less about how your mind responds so appropriately—and so quickly. However, we are reasonably certain about some aspects of this cognitive process.

To answer any question, you must make use of your **memory.** If someone asks you the time, you must first recognize that someone has spoken to you. Next, you must check your memory banks to make sure you recognize the words and phrases the person has used. Then you must realize that you have been *asked a question* to which you might respond.

But while your brain is "checking all these things out," it must have some way of *remembering* what the original question was. If you had no way of holding the question in some kind of "temporary storage," you might end up knowing you'd been asked a question without being able to recall what it was. However, you must remember several other things as well as what the question was. For example, you can't tell someone "what time it is" unless you can recall what a clock or watch is, and how to tell time. Nor can you respond to such questions correctly unless you can remember how to reproduce the words you must use in your answer. Memory, then, is a much more complicated process than it might seem at first glance.

As in the study of all other areas of psychology, there are certain *major problems* that memory researchers are trying to solve. In this chapter we will look at several basic issues. For once you understand what some of the basic issues are, you will be in a better position to answer the question of how *you* answer such questions as, "What time is it?"

If we could answer the following questions fully, we'd know a great deal more about your memory than we presently do:

1. How many types of memory—or memory systems—do you have?
2. What is forgetting, and what causes it?
3. What do memory disorders tell us about memory?
4. What physical changes occur in your brain during memory storage?
5. Can you improve your memory?

As you will see, we can't answer any of these questions as fully as we might wish. However, discovering what we *do* know will surely give you greater respect for your own memory. And it will give you some ideas of how to improve your ability to remember things.

MEMORY SYSTEMS

In point of fact, you don't have just one "memory system," you have several different systems. Psychologists don't agree on how many systems there are, or how each functions. And, as you might suspect, there are many different theories that attempt to

Memory. From the Latin and Greek words meaning "to be mindful," or "to remember." Your memory is your store of past experiences, thus the seat of your ability to recreate or reproduce past perceptions, emotions, thoughts, and actions.

Unless we remember we cannot understand.

EDWARD M. FORSTER

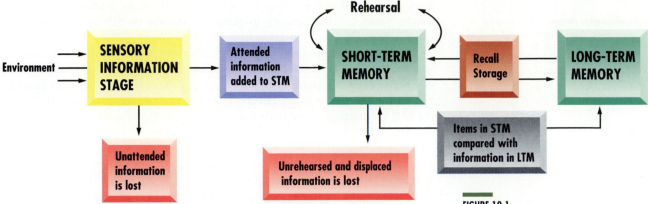

FIGURE 10.1

The stages of memory. Information enters the sensory information stage, and if it is attended to it enters short-term memory. Rehearsal keeps information in short-term memory and helps transfer it to long-term memory as well.

explain how memory works. But we might as well begin our investigation of memory by looking at the **information processing approach,** which has driven research for the last three decades. We'll discuss other theoretical approaches later on.

Information Processing Approach

The information processing approach assumes you are not a mere recorder of data, but that you actively transform and *process* stimulus inputs, much like a high-speed computer. This approach proposes that there are certain memory structures for storing information, and certain memory processes for transferring information from one structure to another. Information *processing* occurs at three different levels:

1. First, sensory inputs from the environment are translated, or **transduced,** into patterns of neural energy by the *sensory receptors*. The incoming information is held briefly in *sensory registers*, one for each sensory modality. Initial processing occurs at this level, and consists primarily of feature detection and pattern recognition. This is the *sensory information stage* of input processing.

2. Second, information which catches your attention is then **encoded** as it moves to the next stage, which is called *short-term memory* (STM) (see Figure 10.1). At this point, you categorize the input after comparing it with information filed away in long-term memory storage.

3. And third, if the input is important, you are likely to rehearse it and transfer it to *long-term memory* (LTM).

The three-stage, information-processing model has guided most memory research since the 1960s. Since this model is so dominant, let's look at it more closely.

How might being a "processor of information" affect your view of learning?

Sensory Information Stage

What time is it?

When the image of those words first strikes the retinas in your eyes, your rods and cones respond by sending a characteristic *pattern of nerve impulses* along your optic nerve to the visual centers of your brain.

Suppose that we flashed the words "What time is it?" on a screen for exactly one-tenth of a second. How long would your rods and cones continue to respond after the words had disappeared? The answer is—it depends. If you had been sitting in absolute darkness for several minutes, the words *"What time is it"* would hang suspended in your visual field for quite some time. However, if you were sitting in a lighted room, the next thing you looked at would erase the phrase "What time is it?"

Information processing approach. A major perspective in memory research that attempts to understand the "flow" of information. Assumes there is a set of "structures" for storing information, and a set of "processes" for transferring information from one structure to another.

Transduced (trans-DOOST). Changed from one form into another. A lamp transduces electrical energy into light and heat. Sensory receptors transduce stimulus energy into neural energy.

Encoded. Converted into a form that can be entered into memory.

Sensory information storage. The first stage of memory storage. Your sensory receptors hold a more-or-less exact copy of an input for a fraction of a second before that copy fades or is "erased" by the next input.

Iconic memory (eye-KON-ick). The word "icon" (EYE-kon) comes from a Greek word meaning "a visual representation or image." Iconic memory is a visual form of Sensory Information Storage.

Echoic memory (eh-KOH-ick).   An auditory form of sensory information storage.

FIGURE 10.2

The type of stimulus pattern used in the Sperling experiment.

from your visual system. Your memory *begins*, then, in your receptors, in what psychologists call the **sensory information storage** or SIS stage of information processing.

Under normal conditions, as you look from one object to another in your visual world, your visual system holds on to each stimulus pattern for but a fraction of a second before yet another visual input replaces the previous pattern. According to psychologists Peter Lindsay and Donald Norman, this storage time typically lasts from 0.1 to 0.5 seconds under normal viewing conditions (Lindsay & Norman, 1977). (As we noted, though, the storage lasts longer if no new stimulus "erases" the input.)

You can measure your own Sensory Information Storage time by using a technique Lindsay and Norman describe. Extend your index finger on one hand, and then wave your finger back and forth in front of your eyes while you stare straight ahead. You'll notice that a "shadowy image" trails behind your finger. Studies suggest this image lasts for about 0.25 second. Swinging a flashlight around in a circle in the dark gives the same sort of "trailing visual image."

George Sperling, one of the first psychologists to work in this area, refers to visual SIS as **iconic memory.** For the amount of information stored in visual SIS is much like that in an *icon*, which is a "detailed image" of a person or event (Sperling, 1963). In similar fashion, auditory SIS is sometimes called **echoic memory,** because it seems to be an "exact echo" of an auditory input. However, by the time this sensory information reaches your cortex—and you become aware of what you are looking at—much of the rich detail is lost.

Imagine that you are sitting in a dark room staring at a blank movie screen. Behind you, a slide projector clicks briefly, and the stimulus pattern shown in Figure 10.2 flashes onto the screen. The pattern appears for just 1/20th of a second (50 milliseconds), then disappears.

Your task in this experiment is to report all the letters you remember seeing after the brief exposure time. You do the best you can, but trial after trial you can't recall more than 3 or 4 of the 9 letters (less than 50 percent). Does this result mean that your SIS system *recorded* only 3 or 4 of the letters? Not at all, as Sperling demonstrated more than 30 years ago.

Sperling suspected that his subjects actually saw all 9 letters, but *forgot* most of them during the time it took them to *report* what they had seen. So he changed the experimental procedure slightly. Immediately *after* presenting the stimulus pattern visually, he gave the subject an *auditory signal*—a high-, medium-, or low-pitched tone. This signal told the subject *which letters to report*. For instance, the high-pitched tone might signal the subject to recall the top row, the medium-pitched tone might be the signal for the middle row, and the low-pitched tone might signal the bottom row.

Again, suppose you were a subject in this type of study. After you see the stimulus pattern, you hear a tone indicating which row you are to report. Now you find that you have no trouble recalling any single row of items. Since the auditory signal occurred a fraction of a second *after* you had seen the 9 stimulus letters, you didn't know which of the 9 letters to pay attention to when they were flashed on the screen. But you were able to remember *any* row of the 9 letters you were signaled to report. So you obviously *saw* them all and recorded them briefly in visual SIS. However, you would achieve this accuracy *only* if the auditory signal occurred within 100 milliseconds after the letters had disappeared from the screen. If the signal didn't come on until 500 milliseconds (1/2 second) afterwards, your performance would drop dramatically (see Figure 10.3).

Sperling's research showed three important things: First, your SIS *records* inputs in much greater detail than we previously suspected. Second, we normally *forget* (or "erase") items stored in SIS, within half a second. Thus, the reason subjects in previous studies couldn't report more than 3 or 4 of the letters is this: During the time it took them to *report* the first 3 or 4 letters, they had actually forgotten the rest of

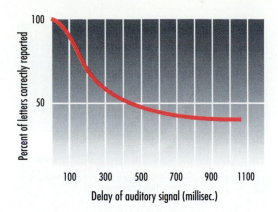

FIGURE 10.3
The effect on Sperling's subjects of delaying their responses. When Sperling signalled them with a tone which row to recall and asked for an immediate response, they could recall any row of the stimulus letters. When the subjects' reports were delayed for half a second (500 milliseconds), they could identify only half the letters.

the 9. Last but not least, Sperling's studies suggested that the eye sends a *visual* copy of the input to the brain. When Sperling delayed the auditory signal for more than one-half second, his subjects often made mistakes. But these were *visual* mistakes. That is, the subjects reported seeing a "P" rather than an "F." These letters are visually similar. However, the subjects seldom reported seeing an "X" when the letter actually was an "F" (Sperling, 1960, 1963). The importance of this point will become clearer in a moment.

Do you believe your brain actually makes an "exact video tape recording" of everything you see, and that this "exact tape" is filed in your memory forever? What does Sperling's research suggest is the case?

Short-term Memory

Your eye apparently sends a very detailed representation of each visual input up to your brain. The lower centers in your brain then *extract the critical features* of the inputs and relay this information to your cortex. At this point, you become conscious of the input. Then you attempt to *categorize* the input and make certain cognitive decisions about it (Lindsay & Norman, 1977).

However, you must have some means of *storing* the input for a few seconds while you "think" about it. So your brain *codes* the input and tucks it away in "temporary hold" while you continue to "process," or think about it (Baddeley, 1992).

How do the errors Sperling's subjects made support the belief that the lower centers extract critical features rather than sending the entire input to the cortex?

DEFINING SHORT-TERM MEMORY

Now, let's suppose you're a subject in yet another memory experiment. The experimenter shows you a card. Printed on the card are three large letters: C F M. You look at the letters for a few seconds, then the experimenter removes the stimulus card. Some 20 seconds later, the experimenter asks you what the letters were. You respond correctly. The fact that you can remember the letters for more than half a second shows that you aren't using SIS in this case. Could it be that you're using "permanent" storage instead? Let's continue the study and see.

Next, the experimenter asks you to repeat the task with different letters. But this time, you have to perform a difficult cognitive task during the 20-second delay: You must "count backwards by threes," starting at some arbitrary number such as 487. That means you must say, "487, 484, 481, 478 . . ." until told to do otherwise. After

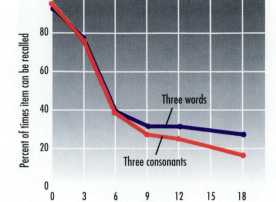

FIGURE 10.4

When Murdock made his subjects "count backwards" after exposing them to three consonants (or three words), the subjects couldn't rehearse and thus tended to forget.

Short-term memory. A temporary information storage between the sensory information stage and long-term memory. Short-term memory has a limited capacity of about seven items. Items in short-term memory are frequently represented in an acoustical format.

you have counted backwards for 20 seconds, the experimenter stops you and asks you what the three stimulus letters were. Now, how do you think you'd fare?

When Bennett Murdock performed this study in 1961 (following the lead of Brown (1958) and Peterson & Peterson (1959)), he got the sort of results shown in Figure 10.4. If you count backwards for just three seconds, you probably will recall only two of the three stimulus letters. If you count backwards for more than six seconds, you're lucky to remember one of the three letters. And, as Murdock showed, you'd perform at about the same level if you were given three words to remember instead of three letters (Murdock, 1961).

Since you forgot so much so rapidly, it's obvious you're not using "permanent" storage to recall the letters. However, since you remember the letters for more than half a second, you can't be using SIS either. Psychologists use the term **short-term memory** (STM) to refer to this type of "temporary hold" during information processing. (Some of the forgetting in Murdock's study was caused by interference from previous trials. We will have more to say about different kinds of interference in a moment.)

A number of studies suggest that items filed in short-term memory remain available for recall no more than about 30 seconds before "vanishing forever" (Lindsay & Norman, 1977).

REHEARSAL

Why could you remember the three stimulus letters so well when you didn't have to "count backwards by threes"? If you've ever had to look up a phone number in a directory, you probably know the answer. What happens when you look up the number? Probably you silently repeat the number to yourself several times so you won't forget it during the length of time it takes you to close the directory, pick up the phone, and start dialing.

Psychologists use the term *rehearsal* to refer to the act of "silently saying things over and over again." When you rehearse an item, you actually keep putting it back into temporary storage again and again. By rehearsing the item in short-term memory several times, you can keep it available for a period of several minutes (see Figure 10.1).

Most people must "rehearse" a telephone number continuously until they dial it. What does this fact tell you about the length of time an item typically remains in short-term memory?

ACOUSTICAL CODING

In describing George Sperling's research on visual SIS, we said the type of mistakes his subjects made was important. As it turns out, subjects in short-term memory experiments make quite different sorts of errors than the mistakes Sperling's subjects made. And this fact has given us a clue to how the brain actually stores items in STM.

When Sperling's subjects made mistakes, they often confused an "F" with a "P" or an "E." The fact that these letters all *look alike* suggests that *visual* SIS coding is *visual*. However, subjects in a short-term memory study will typically confuse an "F" with an "X," but seldom with an "E" or a "P." What's going on here?

If you say "F" and "X" aloud, you'll hear the answer. For the initial sound you make when you say each letter is the same. But "F" doesn't *sound* at all like "E" or "P." Thus, you must be *translating* these visual inputs into *sounds* prior to tucking them away in short-term memory. We call this process **acoustical coding.** Technically speaking, *acoustical coding* refers to the tendency to "translate" certain visual inputs into something related to the sound or production of words when you put them in temporary memory storage.

Not all short-term memory is made up of "auditory translations," however. Suppose we ask you to watch a young woman playing an accordion. Then we ask you to look away and describe what you saw. You will probably recall *visual images*. And you might try to reproduce them by moving your own hands the same way the woman had. That sort of short-term memory is obviously visual and muscular, not acoustical coding.

LIMITED CAPACITY

Your short-term memory ordinarily cannot store more than about seven items simultaneously (Miller, 1956). At the moment that your brain inserts an item into short-term memory, that item is strong and clear and easy to recall, if you do so immediately. But shortly thereafter, your brain tucks away a second item, and then a third item, and a fourth. Although only a few seconds have passed, you will now have much more trouble recalling what the first item was.

By the time your brain has pressed five or six new items down on top of the first, that original item has lost most of its strength and has faded away. The new items appear to *interfere with* or erase the earlier items—just as each new visual pattern you look at wipes clean the stimulus you were looking at just a moment before (see Figure 10.5).

While you are holding an item in short-term memory, you can recall it more or less at will. And you can keep the item around for several minutes by "rehearsing" it. However, once the item drops out of this "temporary storage," it is likely to be gone forever, unless some more or less permanent record of the stimulus input has been made in *long-term memory* (Peterson, 1966).

Acoustical coding (ah-KOO-stick-cal). Converting to sound. Research suggests you "code" language inputs by converting them to sounds before you store them in short-term memory.

FIGURE 10.5

Short-term memory has a limited storage of approximately seven items. Adding a new item (shown here as a boat) may bump an old one (chair) out of short-term storage.

If you "rehearse" an item for a long enough period of time, you might well not forget it at all. What does that fact tell you about how items get shifted from short- to long-term memory?

Long-term Memory

Try to remember the last long trip that you took. Can you recall *right at this instant* the exact date and hour that the trip began and ended? Chances are that you can't. But if you take the time to think about the details—and perhaps write them down as you go—you'll find you can *reproduce* a surprising amount of detail about that trip, even though it may have occurred months or years ago. However, if you inspect those memories carefully as they pop back into consciousness, you'll find they are *qualitatively* different from the immediate memory you have of a face you've just seen.

In fact, your recollection of things that happened long ago usually is hazy and incomplete at first. More than 100 years ago, Hermann Ebbinghaus, one of the earliest and greatest investigators of human memory, offered one reason for this haziness. Ebbinghaus suggested that you typically don't *remember* complex events. Rather, you recall a few "high points" and then *reconstruct* the experience piece by little piece (Ebbinghaus, 1885/1964).

Your SIS system briefly stores a more-or-less exact copy of the original sensory input. Your short-term memory is rather like an "instant replay" on television—a few seconds of highlight action that you can recall with considerable clarity for a brief period of time thereafter. But it is a processed copy of the input, rather than all the rich sensory detail, that you can replay at will until the input fades away into obscurity. Your **long-term memory** (LTM) seems to be much more complex. It stores many different aspects of your experiences. First, rather than merely recording total inputs as they are received, LTM abstracts certain critical features. It then files these meaningful features in appropriate memory stores. When you draw on your long-term memory, it then *reconstructs* the event from the associations and auditory representations it has in its files.

TWO MEMORY CODES

Alan Paivio suggests that we have two different memory storage areas and corresponding memory codes in our LTM. According to Paivio's **dual-coding** view, information is stored in a *verbal* code and an *imaginal* code (Paivio, 1971, 1990). We store abstract information, such as concepts of "truth" or "justice," in the verbal system. We store concrete material, which can be represented by images, in the imaginal or imagery system *as well as in the verbal system*. Paivio came to this conclusion after he and his colleagues found in numerous studies that concrete imagery-producing material is remembered much better than abstract material (Paivio, 1971, 1990; Paivio et al., 1968; Philipchalk, 1972). Subjects remember concrete nouns, like "table," better than abstract nouns like "honor." Presumably, having stored an item in two memory codes increases the chances of remembering it.

What do you know about the two hemispheres of the brain that seems to support Paivio's idea of two different ways of storing information?

Many **mnemonic strategies,** or memory improvement techniques, rely on the fact that adding images to information being stored improves later recall. Memory expert Harry Lorayne suggests that you make the images unusual and link them together in a meaningful but unusual way (Lorayne, 1990).

Long-term memory. Your store of permanent memories. Inputs important enough to survive your short-term memory are transferred to long-term storage. Salient (critical) features of an input are stored according to various categories.

Dual-coding. Storing information in two forms. Paivio's research indicates that we may have separate memory codes for verbal and imaginal (imagery) items.

Mnemonic strategies (knee-MON-ick or nem-MON-ick). Mnemonic strategies are methods for improving memory. Mnemonics use imagery, and rhymes, to link new information with material that is already well-learned. A popular treatment of mnemonics is given by Harry Lorayne in his book *Super Memory, Super Student: How to Raise your Grades in 30 Days* (Lorayne, 1990).

For instance, if you wanted to remember the American states in alphabetical order you might begin by forming an image that reminds you of Alabama, such as "album." For Alaska you think of the flaming dessert "baked Alaska." Now you might imagine a gigantic album serving baked Alaska to other albums. For Arizona, you could imagine an "air zone" and link this to Alaska by picturing a gigantic piece of baked Alaska floating in the air over a safety zone (Lorayne & Lucas, 1974).

Imagery always improves memorability. At the end of the chapter we will apply this principle to the material we have discussed in this chapter. We will also have more to say about other mnemonic devices at that time.

Can you think of a simple way to use "pictures in your mind" to help you remember the material in this chapter?

ITEM STORAGE AND RETRIEVAL

Your long-term memory is practically limitless—rather like a huge library with billions of books stashed away on the shelves. You add thousands of new volumes to that library every day of your life (for example, an average of 10 new words per day for the first 18 years of your life), but you never seem to run out of shelf space for new arrivals! But how in the world do you retrieve the correct item when you're searching your memory "stacks" for it?

Long-term memory is like a huge library with new books added every day. Recall depends on proper categorization during storage.

The answer seems to lie in how you catalogue or *categorize* your experiences in the first place. We will discuss memory categories in just a moment. But first, we might note an odd thing: It may take you some time to resurrect an item stored in your long-term memory; however, you often know *immediately* that you *don't* have an item stored in LTM. For example, what was George Washington's phone number? Ah ha! you say, he lived before phones were invented, so he didn't have a phone number. But what is the *present* president's phone number? Chances are, you know at once that you *don't* know what it is, even though you also know the president *does* have a phone number.

Now, how many windows are there in the rooms where you live? Probably you can figure out the answer to this question by *visualizing* the rooms (imaginal code) and then mentally *counting* the windows (verbal code). But why did it take you so much longer to answer something you *did* know than it took to answer a question when you *knew you didn't know*?

When you try to retrieve an item from long-term memory, you apparently check through your "mental file cards" to see where the item is located in LTM. However, if at any time you come across a "blank file card" (or one that says, "This item does not exist"), then your search stops and you say, "I don't know." We're not really sure how you know what information exists in your brain—and what doesn't. But it does seem clear that most people use the same sort of scheme for "constructing mental file cards."

What is the first word in the first sentence on this page? Chances are, you don't know. But you also know immediately that you could have known. Since you did know the answer at one point in time, why can't you remember what the word was?

MEMORY CATEGORIES

You tend to tuck items away in permanent storage not as a single complete stimulus, but in terms of several rather specific attributes or categories (McClelland & Rumelhart, 1986; Metcalfe, 1990). We can best illustrate these categories by asking you to consider how you might go about filing the word "chair" in long-term memory.

1. *Identity.* First you would try to remember the word itself, "chair." But, as you will see, you rapidly split up this category in a variety of ways.

2. *Class.* A chair is a piece of furniture. Thus, you would file this item not merely as a word unto itself, but as part of a class ("furniture") which would include such other items as "table," "couch," "bed," and "lamp."

3. *Attributes.* A chair is soft or hard, large or small, metal or wood, upholstered or plain. You may enjoy chairs, or hate them. Your memory of a chair, then, includes some notion of the various physical and psychological attributes that a chair has.

4. *Context.* You expect to see a chair in a living room, not inside a bathtub. But you may also remember a specific chair in an unusual context, such as an electric chair in a prison, or your mother's chair in her bedroom.

5. *Function.* You associate the word "chair" with certain verbs denoting its function, such as "sit," or "recline."

6. *Sensory Associations.* The word "chair" will be paired with the *sight* of typical chairs, with the smell of leather and wood, the *feeling* your skin has when you sit on a chair, and perhaps with a squeaking *sound* that old chairs make when you lean back too far in them.

7. *Clangs and Visual Patterns.* You not only file the *concept* of a chair away in your memory, but also certain salient features of the word itself, such as its *sight and*

sound. Thus, you will store "chair" according to its **clangs,** or "sound-alike" words (bare, pear). You will also file it according to the visual pattern the letters c-h-a-i-r make, the initial letter of the word, the number of syllables in the word, and so forth.

8. *Reproductive Information.* Your long-term memory also includes information on the muscle movements needed to say the word "chair," to *write* it, to *draw* a picture of a chair, and so forth.

These eight "memory categories" are by no means the only ones having to do with *item storage* in long-term memory. But they are important ones frequently studied by psychologists.

Clangs. A technical term meaning words that sound alike, such as worm, squirm, term, firm, germ.

How might "acoustical coding" of items in short-term memory make it easier to store the items in long-term memory according to "clangs" and "reproductive information?"

IT'S ON THE TIP OF MY TONGUE

Have you ever tried to retrieve a name from memory, and been quite confident that you knew the word you were looking for? Yet somehow you couldn't reproduce the item when first you tried? Chances are that you also knew the sound and the shape of the word, its meaning, and the letter it starts with. And if someone told you the name, you recognized it immediately as the word you'd been searching your memory banks for (Brown, 1991; Brown & McNeill, 1966).

This "tip-of-the-tongue phenomenon" is a good illustration that memories are filed according to attributes or categories. You knew some of the word's attributes, but you simply couldn't find the right "file card" in your long-term memory. (See Figure 10.6).

If you momentarily forget a name, why might thinking of names that start with the same letter help you retrieve the name?

FIGURE 10.6

In the "tip-of-the-tongue" phenomenon, you may search your memory for words with the same first letter and number of syllables as the word you are looking for.

ELABORATION AND DEPTH OF PROCESSING

As you file an item such as "chair" in memory, you are developing or *elaborating* upon the original information. Each category that the word fits, provides another possible way of retrieving the word at a later time. Also, other information which was present at the time you learned the word "chair" might help to recall the word you are looking for (Tulving, 1978). For example, if you have trouble remembering the word later, you might recall that it belonged to the class "furniture," or that you saw the word in a list of household items. This might then remind you that the word was "chair." The more thoroughly you process new information, or relate it to previous experience, the more likely you are to be able to recall it later.

In fact, Fergus Craik and Robert Lockhart suggest that it is not rehearsal which is responsible for information moving from short-term to long-term memory, but how much we process the information. For example, as you walk down a busy street, your sensory apparatus is bombarded with stimuli—some you pay attention to, but most you ignore. If you pass someone who looks like an old friend of yours, a complex series of thoughts might arise, which involve a large amount of associated information. The **depth of processing** for this new information (the face) is much greater than for the many other faces you pass. And you are more likely to remember this fact later (Craik & Lockhart, 1972).

Thus, if you want to remember new information, you should try to process it as deeply, or in as many ways as possible. For example, think about how it relates to

Depth of processing. The number and complexity of the ways which you relate new information to information already in long-term memory.

other information you already have, ask questions about it, or restate it in different ways (Craik & Tulving, 1975; King, 1992).

We will return to the matter of improving memory later. But first we must look a little more carefully at why we forget and what can go wrong with memory.

How do "Thought Questions" help your memory?

FORGETTING

Sigmund Freud once said that you learn about the normal by studying the abnormal. In the field of memory research, that certainly is the case. For we have discovered a great deal about *memory* by studying *forgetting*. And we have learned an amazing amount about *item storage* in normal people by investigating the difficulties that brain-damaged people have in *retrieving* even the simplest of items from long-term storage.

Let's look at the most common types of "disremembering" in some detail.

Neural Decay

Neural decay is perhaps the simplest type of forgetting. Neural decay refers to a breakdown in the physical process that is maintaining an item in memory.

The SIS system in your receptors provides you with sharply etched neural impressions of the world around you. This pattern of neural firing is quickly destroyed in one of two ways—either the receptor neurons adapt to the input (and hence the neural pattern *decays*), or the next visual input "erases" the first input.

Once an input reaches your brain, it may be put into short-term memory. But your short-term memory is very limited. As new items enter this "temporary hold," they displace older items, and the processes maintaining the older items fade. Thus you forget the older items.

In long-term memory the picture is more complicated. For many years people assumed that memories faded like etching in the sand, simply the result of the passage of time—a process of neural decay. Today we're not so sure. If neural decay does occur in long-term memory, it is less important than other factors that cause forgetting. One of the most important is interference.

Interference

One of the major causes of forgetting is interference between memories. New memories interfere with old ones; old memories interfere with new ones. And new inputs can actually distort or *transform* old memories.

RETROACTIVE AND PROACTIVE INTERFERENCE

Imagine you are a subject in a memory study. The experimenter shows you a list of words (list A) and then asks you to remember as many as you can. After you have studied the list, the experimenter shows you another list (list B) and asks you to learn this list. The experimenter then asks you to recall the words from list B. If the words on the lists are similar, when you are tested on list B you might recall some of the words from list A instead. We would say that your memory for list A interfered with your recall of list B. This type of interference we call **proactive interference** because earlier items *act ahead* to interfere with later items.

Proactive interference. The tendency of previously learned material to get in the way of recall for new material.

Now imagine that after you had studied list A and list B, the experimenter asks you to recall list A. This time you might mistakenly recall some items from list B instead of list A. We would say that your memory for list B interfered with your recall of list A. This type of interference we call **retroactive interference** because later items *act backwards* to interfere with earlier items. As you might expect, both retroactive and proactive interference are greater when the items in memory are more similar.

Retroactive interference. The tendency of newly learned material to get in the way of recall for material learned earlier.

How can you use the information on interference to make your studying more efficient?

SERIAL POSITION EFFECT

The serial position effect is an example of how learning one thing can interfere with storing and recalling other items. Let's again imagine that you are a subject in a memory study. The experimenter shows you a list of 20 words, one at a time, and asks that you remember as many of the words as you can. Since you see each word for only one second, you surely won't recall all 20 later on. But which ones will you remember?

When Bennett Murdock ran a similar study in 1962, he got the results shown in Figure 10.7. As you can see, Murdock's subjects tended to recall items at the beginning and end of the list much better than words in the middle. Apparently, items at either end of the list *interfere* with your ability to recall the words in the middle. Items at the beginning of the list suffer from retroactive (but not proactive) interference. Items at the end of the list suffer from proactive (but not retroactive) interference. Only items in the middle of the list suffer from both proactive and retroactive interference. In short, the *position* of the item in the series affects the total amount of interference and consequently how readily you can remember it later on.

The serial position effect is actually a combination of two other effects: primacy and recency. The *recency effect* is the tendency to recall best (or be most influenced by) what's just happened to you. The *primacy effect* is the tendency to recall best (or be most strongly influenced by) the *first* item in a series.

MEMORY DISTORTIONS

In an elegant series of studies, Elizabeth Loftus has shown that what you learn today may actually distort your memory of what happened to you yesterday (Loftus, 1984, 1991; Loftus & Hoffman, 1989). In one experiment, Loftus showed films of auto

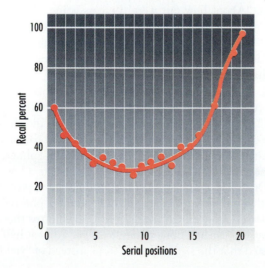

FIGURE 10.7

Murdock's subjects tended to remember the first and last items in a 20-item list better than items in the middle, a result called the "serial position effect."

FIGURE 10.8

Elizabeth Loftus found that when subjects who saw the second photograph (with a yield sign) were later asked what the car did at the *stop sign*, almost half of them insisted there indeed had been a stop sign (as in the first photograph) when in fact they had seen only a yield sign (as in the second photograph). The question distorted their memory.

The true art of memory is the art of attention.

SAMUEL JOHNSON

accidents to people, and then asked them questions about what they had seen. If she asked her subjects, "About how fast were the cars going when they smashed into each other?", her subjects gave much higher estimates of speed than did subjects when she asked, "About how fast were the cars going when they collided?" Apparently, the use of the word "smashed" somehow changed the subjects' memories of what they had seen!

A week later, Loftus asked these same subjects if they had seen any broken glass in the films. In fact, there was *no* broken glass. But more of the subjects exposed to the word *smashed* "remembered" seeing broken glass than did those exposed to the word *collided*. Once again, the question Loftus used to pull the memory out of long-term storage seemingly *changed the memory itself* (Loftus & Palmer, 1974).

In another experiment, Loftus showed half her subjects a series of photographs involving a car. One photograph showed the automobile approaching a yield sign. She showed the other half of the subjects the same series of photographs, except now the car was approaching a stop sign (see Figure 10.8). Loftus then asked the "yield sign" subjects what the car had done *at the stop sign*. Almost half of these subjects subsequently insisted that the sign had said "stop" instead of "yield" (Loftus, 1979).

According to Loftus, "No matter how well meaning or how well trained observers are, there are ways to make people see, hear, and even smell things that never were. Every time we recall an event we must reconstruct the memory, and so each time it is changed" (quoted in Rodgers, 1982).

In brief, items filed in your memory banks can be radically altered by new inputs, even though you are unaware that the change has taken place. Appropriately, Loftus calls this the **"misinformation effect"** (Loftus, 1991; Loftus & Hoffman, 1989).

Misinformation effect. Memory distortion as the result of unknowingly incorporating new misleading information into the recall of an event.

How might the way that a lawyer phrases a question affect the answer a witness might give when testifying in court?

The misinformation effect occurs when misleading information is *intentionally* introduced. But memory distortions can occur spontaneously—for example, when we "recall" the first three digits of one friend's phone number together with the last four digits of another friend's number (Reinitz et al., 1992). And memory distortions can be very subtle, as when we misremember facts to fit our *cultural expectations*. Richard Harris and his colleagues found that both Mexican and American students misremembered stories from each other's cultures. The students *distorted* the stories in memory to be more consistent with what they would expect in their own culture (Harris et al., 1992).

Rejection and Repression

In Chapter 4, we stated that the lower centers in your brain *reject* inputs that are meaningless or unimportant to you. Although you are usually unaware of it, this "screening out" of trivial items goes on constantly and is a very necessary part of the forgetting process. (Can you recall exactly what the skin on your back felt like 20 minutes ago? How often do you need to recall such items?)

In addition, if a given stimulus input is threatening or disturbing, the emotional centers in your brain may *repress* the stimulus and hence make it very difficult for you to remember later on. This type of *motivated forgetting* may be the reason you forget a dental appointment or a term paper deadline (Guenther, 1988).

Cataloguing, Filing, and Retrieval Errors

You "hold" items in short-term memory temporarily while you decide how important they are. You usually transfer *meaningful* items to long-term memory. This transfer involves cataloging the item in terms of categories and previous experiences. Your brain also seems to make a "mental index card" for *each category* under which that experience will be filed. You use these index categories when you try to *retrieve* an item from your memory storage banks. Mostly, this system works well. However, these "mental index cards" occasionally get catalogued in the wrong way, mis-filed, or even totally lost.

Cataloging errors seem to occur most frequently when you have to learn too many things at once. For example, if you are introduced to a dozen unfamiliar people at a party, you may well make some mistakes as you try to attach the right names to the proper faces. If you met one new person a day for a dozen days, you would have a better chance of getting the "file cards" filled out correctly.

This is the principle of massed versus distributed practice. It means that you will learn a large volume of new material more effectively if you study it for a few minutes every night rather than studying it for the whole night before the exam.

Your memory also *mis-files* things occasionally, and thus you will have trouble locating it in your memory banks. The more similar two items are, the more likely it is that one of them will be filed in the place supposedly reserved for the other.

Retrieval errors occur when we cannot recall an item at one time, but we can recall it at a later time. The item may be correctly filed, but we are unable to retrieve it. The tip-of-the-tongue phenomenon is an example. Retrieval errors may occur because the information that we are using to search for an item does not match the information that was emphasized when we stored the item (Tulving & Thomson, 1973).

For example, say you learn the French word for garden, "jardin." While you are learning it you concentrate on how to pronounce it since it is not pronounced in French as it would be in English. Later, when your instructor asks you for the French word that *means* garden you have difficulty, because the *sound* of the word and not its *meaning* was emphasized during storage. However, when your instructor asks you for a list of words that begin with a soft "j" sound, "jardin" comes to mind easily (Morris et al., 1977).

This means that the best form of studying will be one which practices the same type of task that will be given on a test. If the test will be factual, study facts; if the test will require problem-solving, practice solving problems (Adams et al., 1988).

Can you think of a way to reduce cataloging, filing, and retrieval errors? Hint: How does a librarian decide where to file a book?

MEMORY DISORDERS

There are many types of memory disorders. Among the most common of these are the *amnesias* and the *aphasias*. We will discuss these problems in a moment. However, our coverage of the memory disorders will make more sense if we first look at rather a different type of "memory model" than the information processing approach we've been describing so far.

Anderson's ACT Model

The "information processing model" of memory has many strengths. However, it does rather a poor job of explaining some types of memory disorders. For that reason, John R. Anderson proposed what he calls the **ACT**—or Adaptive Control of Thought model (Anderson, 1976).

"WHAT" VERSUS "HOW TO"

As we noted earlier, the information processing approach assumes there are three different memory systems: sensory information storage, short-term memory, and long-term memory. Anderson, however, assumes that there is but one "giant storehouse" for memories. This "unitary storehouse" has two major divisions. One division stores factual information, which Anderson calls *declarative* knowledge. The other division stores the skills, rules, and strategies that your mind uses to "make sense" out of the factual information in your memory. Anderson calls this type of memory *procedural* knowledge.

PROCEDURAL VERSUS DECLARATIVE KNOWLEDGE

If we look at the game of baseball, perhaps Anderson's views will become a bit more clear. You know what a baseball and a bat look like, and may even know that there are several types of gloves used in the game. That's "factual information," thus these items are a part of your "declarative knowledge" even if you've never touched a ball

ACT. Anderson's "Adaptive Control of Thought" model of memory. Anderson assumes there is a single, unified memory storage unit that has two major parts or divisions: "declarative knowledge" and "procedural knowledge."

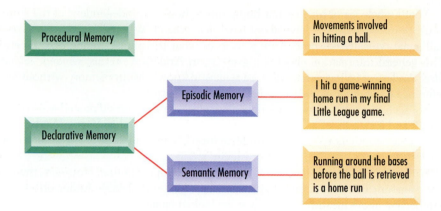

Procedural Memory	Movements involved in hitting a ball.
Declarative Memory	Episodic Memory — I hit a game-winning home run in my final Little League game.
	Semantic Memory — Running around the bases before the ball is retrieved is a home run

FIGURE 10.9
Anderson's view of the divisions of memory.

or bat in your life. **Declarative knowledge,** therefore, is your storehouse of information about objects and items, the "whats" of daily existence. We use the term "declarative" to describe this type of memory because it consists of things you can declare, that is, describe in words.

However, the *muscular movements* you use in throwing a ball or hitting it with a bat are motor skills you had to learn. Skills, both muscular and cognitive, are a type of "procedural knowledge." So **procedural knowledge** is your storehouse of the "how-tos" of getting along in the world (Anderson, 1985).

Declarative knowledge. Anderson's term for that part of memory which stores factual information, most of which can be readily described in words.

Why is it easier to describe a baseball bat (in words) than it is to describe how to hit a home run using a baseball bat? And what does your answer to that question tell you about the difference between "declarative knowledge" and "procedural knowledge?"

Procedural knowledge. Anderson's term for that part of memory which stores motor skills, strategies for manipulating facts, and knowledge of various rules for manipulating objects or events.

EPISODIC AND SEMANTIC KNOWLEDGE

Anderson also believes that declarative knowledge is divided into two types: The first he calls **episodic knowledge.** The second he calls **semantic knowledge** (see Figure 10.9) (Anderson, 1985; Tulving, 1972).

Let's assume that when you were younger, you once hit a home run in the bottom of the ninth inning and won a baseball game for your team. You'd probably remember this *episode* rather clearly (and perhaps with some pride). This unique event in your life is an example of what Anderson means by "episodic knowledge"—something you participated in or experienced first hand, at a particular time and place.

Episodic knowledge (epp-ih-SOD-ick). Anderson's term for memory of things you have done and episodes you have experienced. Perhaps, when you were younger, you won a spelling contest. Your memory of this specific event is a part of episodic memory.

Semantic knowledge (see-MAN-tick). Anderson's term for abstract knowledge, such as how to spell certain words. Abstract knowledge is said to be "independent of the circumstances in which it was learned."

The "experiential memory" of having hit a home run is independent of factual memories about how the game is played.

Your knowledge of hitting that home run is, however, independent of the store-house of information you have about *baseball in general*. When did you learn a base-ball game typically has nine innings in it, or what the phrase "home run" means? This general information about the game is, in Anderson's terms, *semantic knowl-edge*. Anderson believes that we store semantic knowledge in memory without any reference to when or where we acquired the information.

So, according to Anderson, we have memories of procedures ("procedural knowl-edge") and memories of facts ("declarative knowledge"). And our factual knowledge is divided into memory for general information ("semantic knowledge") and mem-ory for specific events ("episodic knowledge").

Anderson's ACT model of memory may seem complex at first. However, there is a fair amount of evidence to support his views (Tulving, 1985). Anderson's terms will become more meaningful to you as we look at *amnesia*.

Amnesia

Memory is the process by which you store information in your brain. *Amnesia*, the failure to recall information, results when the information is physically erased from your memory banks, blocked off from easy access, or prevented from being stored in the first place. Amnesia has both *biological* and *psychological* causes.

There are two main types of amnesia caused by physical damage to the brain: *ret-rograde* and *anterograde* amnesia. These types of memory loss are far more common than is *psychological amnesia*.

PSYCHOLOGICAL AMNESIA

Psychological amnesia, caused by an emotional shock, is really a form of repression. Witnessing a terrible automobile accident can cause you to "block off" all your mem-ories of that fateful day. The items are still in your long-term storage banks, however, and you could probably retrieve them if you tried hard enough to do so (or under-went some types of psychotherapy).

True psychological amnesia is fairly rare, at least compared to memory loss caused by disease, accident, and old age. Indeed, some psychologists believe psychological amnesia occurs much more frequently on TV soap operas than it does in real life.

RETROGRADE AMNESIA

Memory storage does not occur instantaneously. Rather, it takes up to 30 minutes for your long-term memory to file an item away. Any physical or psychological trauma that occurs to you during this half-hour-long **consolidation period** can prevent the item from being recorded in your memory banks. We call this type of forgetting **ret-rograde amnesia,** because a shock to your nervous system now can erase the mem-ory of something that happened several minutes earlier. For example, people who survive a blow to the head in car accidents often can recall everything that happened immediately *after* the crash. However, they frequently can't remember anything that happened in the period just *prior* to the accident. Because these memories were still being "consolidated" at the time of the crash, they got "erased" by the blow to the head (Squire, 1986).

Retrograde amnesia doesn't usually affect memories already in long-term storage since they are already "consolidated."

What do the data on retrograde amnesia suggest about the nature of memory storage?

Consolidation period. The period of time (20 to 30 minutes) it takes your brain to file an input or experience away in long-term memory. Any trauma that disrupts your nervous system during the consolidation process will probably prevent that input from being put in perma-nent storage.

Retrograde amnesia (RETT-tro-grade am-KNEE-see-ah). "Amnesia" comes from the Greek word meaning forgetfulness. When you are hit on the head, you are likely to forget most of the things that had happened to you for 20 to 30 minutes prior to the blow—but you may remember things that happened immediately after the trauma. The amnesia is "graded" because you will very likely forget *everything* that happened immediately before the trauma, *most of* what happened 5 minutes before, and *some* of what happened 20 min-utes before. The term *retro* means "after the fact."

Anterograde amnesia may affect a person's ability to keep score and even remember where the ball was hit but not the person's ability to play the game.

ANTEROGRADE AMNESIA

Severe brain damage and the diseases associated with old age can cause a type of forgetting, called **anterograde amnesia.** If you suffered from anterograde amnesia, you could retrieve old items with ease, but you no longer would be able to file certain types of new items in long-term storage.

Psychologist Daniel Schacter describes what it is like to play golf with a patient suffering from anterograde amnesia. This 58-year-old man had been a good golfer most of his life before suffering from **Alzheimer's disease.** Once the anterograde amnesia associated with Alzheimer's set in, however, his game become "horrendous."

There were some things the man could do perfectly. For example, he used golf jargon correctly, he teed up properly, he hit the ball well, and his selection of golf clubs was "virtually flawless." However, he couldn't keep score because a minute or two after playing a hole he forgot how many strokes he had taken. Unless he could walk straight from the tee to his ball, he usually lost track of where the ball had gone. When asked what brand of golf ball he used, he simply couldn't recall. However, as Schacter notes, when the man had to pick out his ball from several examples, he was always correct.

According to Schacter, most of the patient's problems can be explained in terms of anterograde amnesia—that is, an inability to file new items away in long-term memory (Schacter, 1983).

Did Schacter's patient seem to be forgetting "procedural" or "declarative" knowledge?

FORGETTING "WHAT" BUT NOT "HOW TO"

Larry Squire has studied amnesia for many years. According to Squire, both retrograde and anterograde amnesia typically involve the loss of "declarative" rather than "procedural" knowledge.

In one study, Squire and Neal Cohen tested brain-damaged patients who suffered from anterograde amnesia. These patients typically couldn't remember at noon what they had eaten for breakfast, nor did they recall from one day to the next who Squire

Anterograde amnesia (AN-terr-oh-grade). Memory disorder usually caused by trauma or brain damage involving inability to transfer items from short-term to long-term memory. You can recall things prior to the trauma quite well, but not what happened to you an hour ago.

Alzheimer's disease (ALTS-high-mer's). A disorder associated with old age, which usually involves an inability to file new items away in long-term memory. We will discuss this disorder more fully in Chapter 13.

and Cohen were. When Squire and Cohen tried to train these patients to remember *specific words*, the patients did poorly. They could recall the words after brief intervals, but this knowledge was pretty well "wiped out" by the next day. However, when the experimenters tried to teach the patients how to read words printed backwards, an odd thing occurred. The patients showed *marked improvement* in the skill from one day to another, but they couldn't remember *specific words* from one day to another—nor could the patients recall anything about prior training sessions (Cohen & Squire, 1980). Put briefly, the patients could acquire new *skills*, but not new *facts*.

Squire believes "deep" brain structures mediate the procedural ("how to") memory system, so strokes or disease usually don't affect it. However, cortical and other "higher" centers in the brain mediate the declarative ("what") memory system, and thus accidents and illness are more likely to disrupt it. Both systems, of course, may store the same information, although in slightly different form (Mishkin & Appenzeller, 1987; Squire, 1986, 1987).

Squire found further evidence of separate memory systems when he asked anterograde amnesia patients to complete a list of "word stems." First he gave patients a list to learn which included words like "defend," "carnal," and "burped." Then, an hour or so later, he asked the patients to reproduce the words on the list. The patients couldn't do it. Indeed, the patients insisted that they couldn't recall being asked to learn the list! Next, however, he gave the patients a list of "word stems" to complete—such as "car——," "bur——," and "def——." The patients were much more likely to say "carnal," "burped," and "defend" than "carpet," "burned," and "define" (Schacter & Graf, 1986; Squire, 1986; Warrington & Weiskrantz, 1970).

Peter Graf, George Mandler, and Patricia Haden demonstrated a similar effect with college students. They had the students go through a list of words as rapidly as they could. They told the students to ignore the meaning of the words, but asked them to compare the *vowels* in each word with the vowels of words in a different list. Later, when they asked the students to *recall* the words on the comparison list, they were unable to do so. However, when the experimenters gave the students "word stems" to complete, they were much more likely to use words from the list than chance would allow (Graf et al., 1982).

It seems that even when we don't *intentionally* try to remember something, our memories are at work filing information away. This incidental, or **implicit, memory** has several characteristics that distinguish it from intentional, or **explicit, memory**. In contrast to explicit memory, implicit memory is unconscious; it is largely unaffected by amnesia, age, drugs (such as alcohol), interference, or the length of the retention interval. Larry Squire and Daniel Schacter believe that different memory systems store explicit, declarative knowledge and implicit, procedural knowledge (Schacter, 1992; Squire, 1986).

Implicit memory. Memory for information that was not learned intentionally. Possibly a separate system associated with procedural memory.

Explicit memory. Memory for information that was learned intentionally. Possibly a separate system associated with declarative memory.

What type of memory is involved in the ability to ride a bicycle? Does this example support a link between procedural and implicit memory?

Aphasia

Aphasia (uh-FAZE-ya). An impairment in the ability to use or remember language.

We can define **aphasia** as impairment in the ability to use or remember language. In right-handed individuals, aphasia typically results from damage to the left hemisphere of the brain. The exact type of language impairment the person suffers from depends on what part of the left hemisphere is affected.

Some aphasic patients can understand the spoken names of American cities and can locate them on a map, but may totally fail to understand names of common body parts. Other patients can understand nouns but not pronouns. And one brain-damaged patient, called "M.D." by Rita Sloan Berndt and her associates at the University of Maryland, had great difficulties naming fruits and vegetables. When the researchers showed M.D. a picture of a pyramid (or just about any other object), he immediately responded with the name. But if they showed him a photograph of a carrot or a peach, M.D. was "dumbfounded," and simply couldn't produce the name. When they provided him with a list of names of fruits and vegetables, however, he could correctly match the names with the corresponding picture. It was as if the name were the key to his knowledge of fruits and vegetables. Apparently, M.D. could not find the key for himself. Although the data is from only one patient, it clearly suggests that items in the mental "encyclopedia" are organized along specific categories in the same brain area (Hart et al., 1985).

Aphasic patients are better at naming things they can *see* than things they *smell* or words they *hear*. They are also better at remembering objects they can touch and feel (ball, spoon) than objects they experience at a distance (cloud, moon). They can occasionally write words they cannot say, and they sometimes can speak words that they cannot write. There are several types of aphasia. Many of them seem related to the memory categories we described earlier.

Based on his study of aphasic patients, Harold Goodglass assumes you probably go through three distinct stages when you are shown an item (such as a picture of a chair) and asked to retrieve the item's name from long-term storage:

1. First, you recognize the item and search through your memory banks for its "file card."

2. Second, you hunt for the *auditory representation* (or acoustical coding) of the item's name.

3. Third, you attempt to discover the set of *motor commands* that will permit you either to speak or write the name.

As support for his views, Goodglass offers the following evidence:

1. Some aphasic patients cannot recognize a word at all. For example, if shown a picture of a chair, they will respond, "Something you sit on," or "I've got one in my living room." These patients apparently suffer from a breakdown in *stage one* of the retrieval process. That is, they simply cannot find the right "file card" and often do not recognize the word when you say it aloud for them.

The different types of memory disorders that people suffer lead us to believe that the simple process of naming an object involves several distinct processes. Different memory problems result from the failure of these different processes.

2. Other aphasic patients will say "stool" or "sofa" for "chair." This fact suggests they can get close to the right "file" card, but must settle for the *class* of the item rather than for the item itself. This, too, is a breakdown in *stage one* of the retrieval process.

3. Some patients seem to recognize the word, but say "tssair" for "chair." This mistake suggests they suffer from a breakdown in the *second stage* of item retrieval. They can retrieve the item itself, and they can get close to the *sound* of the word. Indeed, they can often repeat the word when told what it is. But they cannot generally find the correct "acoustical coding" on their own.

4. Still other aphasic patients recognize the stimulus word, can tell you what other words it sounds like, and indicate in a variety of ways they know the meaning of the word and most of its attributes. For example, they may say, "Flair . . . no, swair . . . fair." These individuals simply cannot write the word or say it aloud. Goodglass believes that these patients suffer from a breakdown in the *third stage* of retrieval. They can find the "file card" and its "acoustical coding," but they have lost access to the "motor commands" that would allow them to reproduce the word as language.

Judging from evidence Goodglass presents, these three different stages of item retrieval are *mediated by different parts of the temporal lobe*. The way your brain manages to work through all three stages so rapidly when you're asked to name an item, is really quite remarkable (Goodglass, 1980).

By studying memory disorders, we have learned a great deal about how our memory works. A different approach to understanding memory is to look directly at its physical basis in the brain.

THE PHYSICAL BASIS OF MEMORY

Engram (ENN-gram). A memory trace. The physical change that presumably occurs in the brain each time you store some item away in long-term memory.

Logic suggests there must be a *physical change* of some kind in your brain associated with storing that item away in your permanent memory banks. We call that physical representation of a memory an **engram** (Deutsch, 1983).

We assume there must be a different engram for each tiny bit of information you have ever learned. Your brain, therefore, should be jampacked with billions of engrams. But we have no real proof for these assumptions. No one has ever been able to put a finger on an engram or view one under a microscope. About all we can say is this: On the basis of the laboratory data gathered so far, different sorts of engrams appear to be stored in different parts of your brain (Thompson, 1986).

The "search for the engram," as it is sometimes called, has occupied the attention of thousands of scientists for the past century or so. When scientists first discovered the amazing amount or electrical activity that occurs in the brain they speculated that the engram might be an electrical loop or circuit of some kind. As long as the electricity flowed in its proper pathway through the brain, the engram was maintained. Early computers were built on this memory model. The problem was, if you shut off the electricity even for an instant, the computer lost its memories and had to be completely "reprogrammed" when it was turned on again.

Years ago, Ralph Gerard and his colleagues tried to test this viewpoint using animal brains rather than computers. That is, Gerard and his colleagues tried to "turn off" all the electrical activity in an animal's brain to see if this act would erase the animal's memories. But how to accomplish this "turning off the juice"? As it happens, they found a way. When bears, hamsters, and other beasts go into the deep sleep associated with hibernation, their brain temperatures drop considerably and most electrical activity ceases. So Gerard and his group trained a hamster, then put it to sleep and cooled its brain down until they could no longer detect any electrical responses at all. Later they warmed the animal up again and checked to see what it would remember. The answer was, it could recall *almost everything*. The electrical current hypothesis had failed, and scientists had to look elsewhere for the engram (Gerard, 1953).

Synaptic Switches

Computers store information in a variety of ways. One memory device used in computers is a simple *switch*, which can be left in either an open or closed position. When a message passes through the computer, the switches can route the information from one point to another—much the way the switches in a railroad yard can route a train from one track to another. If you ask a computer a simple question such as "what is 2+2?", the computer routes your question through a series of switches until it reaches the final destination "4." Switches are not very complicated mechanisms. But given enough of them, the computer can store almost any information, no matter how complicated.

Most scientists believe that the *synapses* in your brain function in much the same way the switches in a computer do. When someone asks you a question such as "What is your name?", the question must cross over a number or synaptic switching points before you can answer it. If you could rearrange the functioning of these synaptic connections—opening some neural switches and closing others—you could send the message to any part of your brain that held the right answer.

As John David Sinclair points out, however, there are important differences between the synapses in your brain and the switches in a computer. To begin with, synapses can be partly open and partly closed. Thus, memory storage in the brain is infinitely more complex than is memory storage in computers. Second, the "chips" in a computer do little more than store information. However, the 100 trillion synapses in your brain both *store* and *process* information. According to Sinclair, this fact means that your brain can *store* less data than can a large computer—but your brain can *process* complex sensory inputs much faster than can a computer because processing *occurs throughout the brain*, not just in a "central processing unit" (Sinclair, 1983).

We know how computers store memories. Unfortunately, we still have no good idea of what the engram is. Which is to say, we still don't know how you *physically* file away data in your long-term memory. Most neuroscientists believe that memory storage involves some functional change at the synapse. But there is not much agreement (or solid data) about how you go about shifting the switches in your brain. However, it does seem that when you learn, one or two things must happen. Either your brain grows new nerve cells, which seems unlikely, or the neurons already present in your brain grow *new dendrites* (or parts of dendrites). These dendrites then make new synapses with the axons of other neurons during some stage of learning or memory storage (Rosenzweig, 1984; Greenough et al., 1987).

The question then becomes, what *causes* dendritic growth at the synapse? No one knows for sure. However, many scientists believe some sort of *chemical change* has to occur at the synapse whenever you learn something (Kuroda, 1989; Rose, 1989).

The Biochemistry of Memory

Perhaps the first person to speculate in public that chemicals might be involved in memory storage was Ward Halstead. In 1950, Halstead advanced the theory that ribonucleic acid (RNA) and protein molecules might be the *engrams* that scientists had sought for so many years (Katz & Halstead, 1950).

At about the same time, Swedish biologist Holger Hyden said much the same thing. Hyden and his colleagues taught various tricks to rats, then looked at the chemical composition of the animals' brains. Hyden and his group theorized that the brain of a trained rat should be *chemically different* from the brain of an untrained rat, and their research tended to support this belief. They found noticeable changes in the amounts of RNA in the brains of trained animals, as compared with the brains of untrained rats (Hyden & Egyhazi, 1962).

Subsequent experiments in laboratories in both North America and elsewhere have generally confirmed the view that an organism's brain chemistry is *subtly altered* by whatever experiences the organism has. More important, it now appears that different types of psychological experiences can give rise to quite different sorts of chemical changes.

Whenever an *action potential* sweeps down the axon of a neuron, the cell responds by suddenly increasing its production of RNA and many other chemical molecules. The more vigorously a neuron fires, the more RNA it produces. And the more RNA a nerve cell produces, the more protein it typically manufactures as well. In short, nerve cells are not only generators of electrical activity, they are very efficient chemical factories too (McConnell, 1968).

CHEMICAL "ERASERS"

You are not consciously aware of all of the chemical changes taking place in your brain as they occur, of course. But if the changes didn't come about, you probably wouldn't be "aware" of anything at all! For example, what do you think might happen if, while you were studying for an exam, someone injected into your brain a substance that *destroyed* RNA? How might that injection affect your ability to learn?

This question was first asked by E. Roy John. In the mid-1950s, John taught a cat a rather difficult task involving visual perception. Once the cat had learned the task, John injected RNA-destroying **ribonuclease** into the animal's visual cortex. After the ribonuclease injection, the cat performed as if it had never been trained at all. Later, John and William Corning demonstrated the same sort of memory loss in simpler animals (Corning & John, 1961).

Memory loss in older people is the exception rather than the rule, as we will see in Chapter 13. However, some elderly individuals do suffer the type or anterograde amnesia we discussed earlier. That is, they are much better at recalling events that happened years ago than they are at learning new things. Psychiatrist Ewen Cameron spent many years trying to help older patients in several hospitals in Canada and the United States. His studies were, for a time, aimed at discovering whether or not the body chemistry of his patients was measurably different from that of other individuals who were just as old, but who did not suffer this type of memory loss.

In one of his experiments, Cameron and his colleagues found that elderly patients with anterograde amnesia had more *ribonuclease* in their bloodstreams than did other oldsters. Cameron guessed this enzyme might be destroying brain RNA as fast as the amnesic person's neurons could manufacture it. And if RNA helped the brain store away long-term memories, then too much ribonuclease would *wipe out the engrams* before they could become permanent. If so, Cameron thought he might be able to help his patients by *lowering* the amount of ribonuclease in their bodies.

Cameron tried two different types of chemical therapy. First, he injected his patients with large amounts of yeast RNA, hoping the ribonuclease would attack this foreign RNA rather than the RNA produced by the patient's brains. While this approach seemed to help *some* patients recover *part* of their memory functions, the yeast RNA was often impure and caused many patients to come down with fevers. Hoping to avoid the fevers, Cameron gave his subjects a drug intended to increase the *production of brain RNA*. Again, he was fairly successful, but only with people whose memories had not deteriorated too much. And once the patient was taken off the drug, the person's memory often began to deteriorate again (Cameron, 1967).

Ribonuclease. (RYE-bo-NEW-klee-aze). A protein that breaks up or destroys RNA. Ribonuclease is found in most living cells.

A few older people suffer memory deficits, but most retain good memories throughout their lives.

In 1982, Michael Warren reported that "elderly" mice who were good at problem solving had more RNA in their brains than did equally old mice who had difficulties with the same tasks (Warren et al., 1982). Mark Rosenzweig and his colleagues found that keeping the mice in "exciting environments" increased their brain RNA levels, while confining the mice to "sensory isolation chambers" decreased the amount of RNA in their brains (Rosenzweig, 1984). Both Warren and Rosenzweig suggest that older humans who maintain an active life in stimulating circumstances need not fear a decline in their mental abilities.

Recent research has identified several other chemicals which play a role in memory loss in the elderly. Some of these substances appear to be related to specific disorders such as Alzheimer's or Parkinson's disease, and other substances appear to be related to a more general senility (Allain et al., 1989).

MEMORY CONSOLIDATION

As we noted earlier, your long-term memories take time to form or consolidate. Anything that disrupts normal brain function during this consolidation period will interfere with your ability to remember. A number of chemicals, including some antibiotics, will disrupt memory consolidation in animals, if the drugs are given either before or immediately after training trials (Deutsch, 1983; McGaugh, 1990).

The other side of the memory coin is perhaps a bit more intriguing, however. For it is also true that anything that speeds up your brain activity during the consolidation period will make it *easier* for you to form engrams.

We usually think of strychnine as a poison. In fact, it is a neural excitant. In large doses, it causes convulsions and eventual death. In very small doses, however, strychnine increases neural firing rates, much as does the caffeine found in coffee or cola drinks. (At least one athlete at the 1992 Olympics was suspended for using strychnine.)

If you inject a rat with a tiny amount of strychnine just *before* you train it on a simple task, the rat typically will learn the problem faster. One explanation for this effect is that strychnine makes the animal more active and alert to its environment, hence it learns faster. However, you can cause a similar "memory facilitation" by giving the strychnine a few minutes *after* you train the animal. Now, when you retest the rat on the same problem a day or so later, the animal injected with strychnine will remember the task much better than does a rat injected with salt water.

How can a post-training injection speed up learning? It can't, for the rat given the strychnine takes just as long to learn the task as does the animal injected with salt water. What the drug apparently does is to make the animal's brain more active during the *consolidation period* following training. And the more active the animal's brain is following the experience, the more of the experience it remembers later on. However, the strychnine must be given within 30 minutes or so after the training, or the "facilitation effect" does not take place. A rat injected two hours after training remembers no better than does an uninjected animal (McGaugh, 1973). Memory consolidation is also improved through mild electrical stimulation of the brain following learning (Kesner, 1982; McGaugh & Gold, 1976).

Recent research indicates that one part of the brain which is particularly important in the "facilitation effect" is the amygdala. (As you may recall from Chapter 8, the amygdala is part of the limbic system and plays an important role in emotionality.) Drugs which stimulate the amygdala tend to assist the consolidation of memories. Naturally, the brain has its own built-in ways of activating the amygdala, and thus assuring that certain memories will be stored (McGaugh, 1990, 1992).

What does the amygdala's involvement in emotion and memory consolidation suggest about the kind of events we are most likely to remember?

CHEMICAL CORRELATES

The most controversial evidence that the engram may be a chemical molecule comes from the so-called "memory transfer" experiments conducted by James McConnell and his colleagues. McConnell discovered that common flatworms (planaria) learned a simple association more quickly if they were first injected with RNA extracted from other worms that had learned the same association—or even if they were first *fed* these "trained" worms. These researchers seemed to have transferred an engram from one animal to another (McConnell et al., 1961; Loomis & Napoli, 1975).

The "memory transfer" research led to the hypothesis that memories were "coded" in complex chemicals called *macromolecules*, much like inherited characteristics are coded in genes. Subsequent research, however, has failed to support this idea. For one thing, in transfer studies it is very difficult to show that you are really transferring *specific* memories and not just giving the animal molecules that excite its brain activity as do caffeine and strychnine (Hartry et al., 1964; Luttges et al., 1966). Recent research has also shown that memory involves changes in many more neurotransmitters than researchers first thought (Allain et al., 1989).

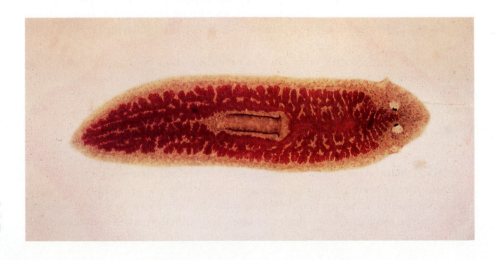

The freshwater planarian has a true brain, a simple nervous system, and a food tube in the middle of its body instead of a mouth. It can regenerate any missing part of its body.

Modern studies of the biochemistry of memory focus on "correlates" or corresponding processes in brain chemistry and memory function. In other words, researchers are trying to identify which chemical changes go with different memory functions and disorders. And rather than look for one, or a few "macromolecules," which encode memories, they are looking at many chemicals which act under different circumstances to "label" or identify a nerve pathway which has undergone a change (Chapouthier, 1989).

For example, on the basis of their review of recent research, French researcher Hervé Allain and his colleagues identify 14 different "memory enhancing molecules." Many of these appear to be helpful for specific memory problems, such as those in Alzheimer patients, Korsakoff patients, elderly depressed subjects, or even young healthy subjects (Allain et al., 1989).

If we can ever devise safe drugs that would speed up learning, we could improve memory (we might even make college a more effective and less boring experience). Then students who "dropped chemicals" might get a higher education, rather than merely "get high."

However, since we don't have "miracle memory drugs" yet, let's return to the psychological side of memory, and conclude with a look at how we can apply what we have discovered so far.

MEMORY FOR MEMORY: A PRACTICAL APPLICATION

Earlier we listed "eight conclusions" about memory research. These eight can be condensed into four basic principles for improving memory: *attention, organization, association,* and *rehearsal.* Let's see how we could use each of these to help us remember what we have covered in this chapter so far.

Attention

The first step in improving your memory is to increase your interest and focus your attention. Not much information "sticks" if you don't pay attention to it.

Begin by selecting a study environment which does not contain too many distractions *for you* (people differ on what they find distracting). Then, try to read *actively*. Question the author (or anticipate the questions your instructor will ask), perhaps even debate with the author. And think about how the material you are learning applies to your own experience. For example, in studying this chapter, you might think about how *you* use different memory systems, what caused *you* to forget what you studied, what it would be like for *you* to have a memory disorder, and how *you* would look for the "engram."

Memory is the diary that we all carry around with us.

OSCAR WILDE

Organization

You might think of your memory as a huge library. If you don't "catalog" the items in a systematic way, you are unlikely to be able to "withdraw" them when you need to.

Many people find that a simple hierarchy, or division into "levels," is a helpful way of organizing new material. In learning the material in this chapter, for example, you might find it helpful to organize the information in terms of first and second level headings. This hierarchy is given for you as an "outline" at the beginning of the chapter.

Association

We have already mentioned the value of associating new information with your own experience, to increase your interest and attention. But association is also a very important part of many mnemonic strategies, or *special techniques* for improving memory.

Although they are sometimes called "memory tricks," there is nothing sneaky or underhanded about mnemonic devices. The ancient Greeks and Romans devised mnemonics; ancient orators used mnemonics to remember their long speeches.

The most common features of the many different mnemonics are their use of imagery, and their use of rhymes, to link new information with material that is already well-learned. Some mnemonics impose meaning on essentially meaningless material. For instance, music students often use the first letters of the words in the sentence, "Every good boy does fine" as a mnemonic to help them remember the notes of the music scale (EGBDF). To remember numbers, some people have memorized a technique of transforming the numbers into letters of the alphabet which they then form into words. In this way several numbers become a single item or **chunk** in memory.

One of the easiest mnemonics to use is the **method of loci,** developed by the ancient Greeks. About 500 B.C., the Greek poet Simonedes was asked to give a recitation at a large banquet. He was called out after the recitation. While he was out, the floor of the banquet hall collapsed, killing all the guests. Because Simonedes had associated the guests' faces with the places they were sitting, he was able to identify the disfigured bodies for their relatives. From this experience, Simonedes developed the "method of loci," or "method of *places.*"

To use this method, form an image of each thing you want to remember. Then imagine a very familiar setting, such as your home, and place the images around your house. When you want to recall the items, imagine yourself walking through the house, and seeing the images you placed there.

Chunk. A single item in memory composed of two or more pieces of information. A word is a chunk composed of letters. Combining information into chunks is a way of increasing the amount of information which can be held in STM. Seven words in STM contain many more than seven pieces of information.

Method of loci (LO-sye). ("method of *places*") A mnemonic technique developed about 500 B.C., by the Greek poet Simonedes. To use this mnemonic device, you create an image of each item you want to remember, and imagine placing the images along a familiar route or path. To recall the items, imagine yourself walking along the route, and seeing the images you placed there.

The "method of loci" is a common mnemonic device. To use this technique, imagine a familiar setting and "place" images of the items you want to remember in various places in the setting. To recall the items, imagine yourself walking around the setting and "seeing" the items that you placed there.

Let's try this system on the outline for this chapter. Each paragraph includes the second-level headings for one major heading. Here we go. Relax and imagine:

You just *remembered* to go home and you walk up the steps into *your* house ("YOUR MEMORY").

Your house has several rooms ("MEMORY SYSTEMS"), and you begin to walk through them. You start in the kitchen, where you *process* food ("Information Processing Approach"), move to the living room where you receive a *sensory* barrage of *information* from the TV and stereo ("Sensory Information Stage"), and then to the bathroom where you spend only a *short time* ("short-term memory"). Finally, you go into the bedroom where you spend a *lot of time* ("long-term memory").

You don't want to *forget* your house ("FORGETTING"), but as you leave, you look back and see your house *fading* into the distance ("Neural Decay"). Pretty soon it's lost from sight as trees and buildings *interfere* ("Interference"). This makes you feel *rejected* and *depressed* ("Rejection and Repression"). Suddenly you realize you have made an *error,* and you are lost ("Cataloging, Filing, and Retrieval Errors").

You return to your house to find it in *disorder* ("MEMORY DISORDERS"); it is being attacked by a man named *Anderson* with a big *axe* ("Anderson's ACT Model"). He suddenly *sneezes* ("Amnesia"), but that doesn't *phase you* ("Aphasia").

You decide to get *physical* ("THE PHYSICAL BASIS OF MEMORY"). You hit him with a *switch* ("Synaptic Switches") and you throw some *chemicals* at him ("The Biochemistry of Memory").

Seem ridiculous? Perhaps. But it works. In adapting the method of loci for your own use, or in creating other mnemonic aids, remember, try to use rhyme, familiar associations, vivid and unusual imagery, and try to imagine the images interacting (Kroll et al., 1986; Riefer & Rouder, 1992). The method of loci is easy because it is based on something you already know well—your own house or other familiar setting. Other mnemonics may require a greater investment in time, but the results are unforgettable!

Rehearsal

Although rehearsing is a time-honored method of learning, there are a few things you can do to help "make practice perfect."

For one thing, as we saw earlier, distributed practice is more effective than massed practice. Short periods of study spread over several weeks or months are much more useful than a single long period of study. You can also make your practice more effective by varying the ways in which you review. For example, one time you might review thinking of how you could inter-relate the information ("Is the biochemistry of short-term and long-term memory different?"). Another time you might review thinking of how you could relate the material to your own experience ("Which stage of memory failed when I forgot that person's name?").

And don't be afraid of *overlearning.* Research shows that practicing something even *after* you are able to recall it satisfactorily, leads to better performance later.

By conscientiously applying each of these principles, *attention, organization, association,* and *rehearsal,* you can put psychology to work for you. You can improve your memory, and make your studying more efficient. You will find these same ideas developed more fully in the many books which are available on improving memory (e.g., Baddeley, 1982; Cermak, 1978; Hersey, 1989; Lorayne, 1990).

In our opening literary selection, Rebecca says she would like an invention that would permit her to keep a moment bottled up, to preserve it forever. While our memories do not work like this, memory is probably still our most precious ability. Without it we could not learn, we would not know our past, and we wouldn't even know who we are. By studying and using our memories more efficiently we can live a richer, fuller, more satisfying life.

The memory represents to us not what we choose, but what it pleases.

MONTAIGNE

SUMMARY

1. The major problems that memory researchers study include: How many **memory systems** are there? What is **forgetting?** What do **disorders** tell us about memory? What is the **physical basis** of memory storage? And how can we **improve memory?**

2. According to the **information processing approach,** when sensory inputs arrive at your receptor organs, they are held for up to half a second in **sensory information storage** (SIS)—an exact copy of the stimulus itself. Visual SIS is sometimes called **iconic** memory, while auditory SIS is sometimes called **echoic** memory.

3. **Short-term memory** (STM) usually lasts for up to 30 seconds. You can increase the time an item is in STM by using **rehearsal.**

4. **Language inputs** are often translated into sounds while in STM, a process called **acoustical coding.**

5. Usually you can store no more than **six or seven items** in STM.

6. Important inputs move from short-term memory into **long-term memory,** (LTM) which is the permanent "memory bank" of your brain.

7. Recall from LTM involves remembering significant facts and then **reconstructing** a "memory" by filling in plausible details.

8. Paivio believes that we store words and images in different **memory codes.**

9. Long-term memories seem to be filed by **categories,** for more rapid **retrieval.**

10. The **tip-of-the-tongue phenomenon** illustrates the ability to retrieve certain category information which is insufficient to recall the complete item.

11. As you relate new information to more and more of the information already in storage, you are increasing the **depth of processing** of the new information. This increases the likelihood of being able to recall the information later.

12. There are many types of **forgetting:**
    a. Inputs to sensory information storage and short-term memory either **decay** rapidly, or are "wiped out" by the next input.
    b. Items in your long-term memory **interfere** with each other, thus are continually forgotten. Old items interfere with new items through **proactive interference,** and new items interfere with old items through **retroactive interference.** Both of these cause you to remember items at the start of a list (**primacy effect**) and at the end of a list (**recency effect**) better than items in the middle (**serial position effect**).
    c. Items in your long-term memory **interact** with each other, thus old items can be distorted or changed by new inputs.
    d. Some inputs are **rejected** by the lower centers of your brain because they are meaningless or unimportant, while other inputs are deliberately (if unconsciously) **repressed.**
    e. Your long-term memory also suffers from **cataloging, filing,** and **retrieval** errors.

13. **Amnesia** is a type of memory loss caused by brain damage or emotional trauma. Amnesia typically involves forgetting "what" you have experienced (**declarative knowledge**), but not "how to" do things (**procedural knowledge**).

14. According to Anderson's **ACT** model, there are two types of declarative knowledge: **episodic knowledge** (memory of specific events) and **semantic knowledge** (general information).

15. It takes about 30 minutes for your brain to **consolidate** an item in long-term memory. Interruption of the consolidation process leads to a type of forgetting called **retrograde amnesia.**

16. Brain damage can also cause **anterograde amnesia,** in which new items are no longer translated from short-term to long-term memory.

17. **Aphasia** is an impairment in the ability to use or remember language.

18. According to Goodglass, retrieving the name of an item from long-term storage involves three steps:

    a. You must **recognize** the item and search your memory banks for the item's "file" or identity card.

    b. You hunt for the **auditory representation** of the item's name.

    c. You try to discover the set of **motor commands** that will permit you to say or write the name.

19. The physical representation of a memory is called an **engram.** No one knows what the engram really is, but remembering does seem correlated with rearranging the **synapses** and **neurotransmitters** in your brain.

20. Recent studies of the **biochemistry of memory** suggest that many different molecular changes occur in your neurons whenever you learn something. Modern research is trying to identify the chemical changes which are associated with different memory functions and disorders.

21. Four principles are particularly important for improving memory. They are **attention, organization, association,** and **rehearsal.**

ANSWERS FOR THOUGHT

1. *How might being a "processor of information" affect your view of learning?*

   Being a processor of information means that you are not a mere recorder or sponge that soaks up facts. If you accept this viewpoint, you will *actively involve* yourself in the process of learning and retaining information. You will adapt facts to your situation and you will seek personal applications for new information. We strongly encourage you to do this throughout the chapter (and in all your learning). For example, as we present information on memory, ask yourself, "How can I use this to improve my memory and study habits?" (The "Thought Questions" will help you do this.)

2. *Do you believe your brain actually makes an "exact video tape recording" of everything you see . . . ?*

   Sperling's research suggests that the "video tape recording" fades very rapidly, and that material which you don't pay attention to is lost almost immediately. His research also indicates that the amount of information which you can pay attention to is very limited.

3. *How do the errors Sperling's subjects made support the belief that the lower centers extract . . . ?*

   The fact that subjects made errors in simple visual features (reporting "P" rather than "F") suggests that they were extracting only basic critical features (rather than other information, such as the sound of the letters, or their place in the alphabet).

4. *Most people must "rehearse" a telephone number continuously until they dial it. What does this fact . . . ?*

   Apparently, without rehearsal short-term memory would not retain the number long enough for us to use it. So we rehearse the number until we've dialed it (or until something else distracts us).

5. *If you "rehearse" an item for a long enough period of time, you might well not forget it at all. What does . . . ?*

The fact that rehearsal leads to retention suggests that items are moved from short-term memory to long-term memory simply as a result of rehearsal. As we will see in a moment, an alternative view suggests that during rehearsal you may be relating the item to other information in memory and this "deeper processing" may be the cause for remembering the item rather than moving it from one system to another.

6. *What do you know about the two hemispheres of the brain which seems to support Paivio's idea of two . . . ?*

In most people the left hemisphere is specialized for processing language in orderly, step-by-step (sequential) fashion. The right hemisphere is specialized for processing non-verbal material (including images) in parallel fashion. ("Parallel" means more than one feature at a time.) Paivio has found that the difference in memory for language versus memory for pictures is closely analogous to the difference in abilities of the verbal and non-verbal cerebral hemispheres.

7. *Can you think of a simple way to use "pictures in your mind" to help you remember the material in this chapter?*

You might form "pictures in your mind" of the "pictures on the page." In other words, you might use the *illustrations* in the chapter to "remind" you of the concepts that were discussed. For example, Figure 10.5 (the tabletop with too many items) can remind you of the limited capacity of STM. A more elaborate use of imagery will be presented at the end of the chapter.

8. *What is the first word in the first sentence on this page? Chances are, you don't know. But you also . . . ?*

Presumably, words pass through SIS and remain in STM only long enough for you to extract their meaning or *semantic content*. The semantic content is stored in long-term memory. As you continued to read sentences on this page, new words came into STM and old words were bumped out. Thus, the only thing that is retained for very long is the *meaning* of the items, which is stored in LTM.

9. *How might "acoustical coding" of items in short-term memory make it easier to store the items . . . ?*

Very little transformation is necessary to relate a word to its "clangs" or its "reproductive information" because the acoustical coding in STM is already in a closely related form. Echoing or rehearsing a word in STM readily evokes similar sounding words and the muscle movements necessary to say the word.

10. *If you momentarily forget a name, why might thinking of names that start with the same letter help you retrieve the name?*

Usually you are able to recognize the name once you think of it. Thinking of names that start with the same letter is a good way of reducing the number of possibilities and zeroing in on the correct name.

11. *How do "Thought Questions" help your memory?*

"Thought Questions" require you to relate the material being presented to other material in the text or to your own experience. In this way they force you to *elaborate* upon the new material and to use greater *depth of processing*.

12. *How can you use the information on interference to make your studying more efficient?*

In your studying, avoid studying *similar* materials close together. For example, separate your study of French and Spanish by a time period filled with other activities (or studying something different). And remember, interference comes from material you learned *previous* to what you are studying (proactive) as well as from material you learn later (retroactive).

13. *How might the way that a lawyer phrases a question affect the answer a witness might give when testifying in court?*

   If a lawyer uses words which imply or assume a certain scenario, a witness might reconstruct memories using available information from LTM and fill in lost information consistent with the lawyer's implications.

14. *Can you think of a way to reduce cataloging, filing, and retrieval errors?*

   Librarians follow a well-organized system of categories and subcategories based on the Library of Congress or the Dewey Decimal system. In memory, *organization* provides a "mental scaffold" or framework around which to arrange information. (This is one reason that we give an outline at the beginning of each chapter.) You can reduce cataloging, filing, and retrieval errors if you *organize* your study materials in a meaningful and systematic way.

15. *Why is it easier to describe a baseball bat (in words) than it is to describe how to hit a home run . . . ?*

   Objects, such as a baseball bat, are readily described with a few words (a noun and a few adjectives), and this information is apparently readily available from LTM. Actions, however, are difficult to put into words, and are apparently stored as images and motor movements. Occasionally words accompany actions ("keep your eye on the ball," "follow through") but this is the exception. Generally, declarative knowledge is verbal; procedural knowledge is imaginal and motor. Furthermore, procedural knowledge seems to be "absorbed" unconsciously or *implicitly*, whereas declarative knowledge is learned consciously and *explicitly*.

16. *What do the data on retrograde amnesia suggest about the nature of memory storage?*

   The data suggest that memory storage must involve *physical* processes because *physical* shock to the nervous system can cause memory failure.

17. *Did Schacter's patient seem to be forgetting "procedural" or "declarative" knowledge?*

   The man seems to have suffered a loss of ability to store and use factual information—declarative knowledge. The fact that he retained his procedural knowledge (how to golf) supports the distinction between these two types of knowledge and suggests that they involve different portions of the brain.

18. *What type of memory is involved in the ability to ride a bicycle? Does this example . . . ?*

   Your ability to ride a bike is a skill stored in *procedural memory*. This memory also shows traits of implicit memories. It is largely unconscious, unaffected by amnesia, age, or the length of time since you learned to ride. The example of bike riding supports the idea that implicit memories are handled by the procedural memory system.

19. *What does the amygdala's involvement in emotion and memory consolidation suggest about the kind of events we are most likely to remember?*

   Emotional events are remembered better because emotional events stimulate the amygdala which is probably then better prepared to assist in consolidating the memories being processed at the time.

CHAPTER 11

COGNITION, LANGUAGE, AND INTELLIGENCE

Ayla looked with concentration at the slash marks, holding out the fingers of her hand. Then she brightened. "I am as many years as this!" she said, showing him her hand with all the fingers extended. "But, how long before I can have a baby?" she asked, far more interested in reproduction than in reckoning.

Creb was thunderstruck. How had the girl been able to grasp the idea so quickly? She hadn't even asked what the slash marks had to do with fingers or what either had to do with years. It had taken many repetitions before Goob had understood. Creb made three more slash marks and put three fingers over them. With only one hand, it had been especially difficult for him when he was learning. Ayla looked at her other hand and immediately held up three fingers, folding down her thumb and forefinger.

"When I am this many?" she asked, holding out her eight fingers again. Creb nodded affirmatively. Her next action caught him completely by surprise; it was concept he had spent years mastering himself. She put down the first hand and held up only the three fingers.

"I will be old enough to have a baby in this many years," she gestured with assurance, positive of her deduction. The old magician was rocked to his core. It was unthinkable that a child, a girl child at that, could reason her way to that conclusion so easily.

JEAN M. AUEL
THE CLAN OF THE CAVE BEAR

How did Ayla develop the concept of counting years? Why did she solve the problem of subtraction so quickly? And were her intellectual abilities superior to Goob's? In the understanding of human behavior, one of the most challenging puzzles is the exploration of these kinds of questions—the study of human intellectual, or *cognitive*, abilities. It is these abilities which seem to be responsible for many of our highest attainments as a species. In this chapter we will look at some of these intellectual abilities—the ability to form concepts, solve problems, and communicate with language. We will consider attempts to model human thought with computers. And since "the ability to *use* intellectual processes to meet the demands of day to day living" is a general definition of *intelligence*, we will discuss the concept of intelligence and the attempts which have been made to measure it.

COGNITION

Cognition. All of the mental or intellectual processes we use to deal with the environment.

St. Thomas Aquinas (1225–1274), was probably the first to use the term "cognition." He divided the understanding of human behavior into two areas: the cognitive and the affective. Affect, he said, refers to our bodily *feelings* and *emotions*; **cognition,** to our intellectual *knowledge* or *understanding* of the world.

Today, cognitive psychology is an extremely active and broad perspective on human behavior. It is part of a larger "cognitive science" movement, which includes anthropology, computer science, linguistics, neuroscience, and philosophy (Bernsen, 1991; Hunt, 1989). Cognitive psychologists study the *intellectual processes* we use to deal with the world. This includes the obvious ones like "reasoning" and "problem solving." But it also includes more "basic" processes such as "attention" and "perception." In the words of Ulric Neisser, the "founder" of cognitive psychology, "Cognitive psychology refers to all processes by which the sensory input is transformed, reduced, elaborated, stored, recovered, and used" (Neisser, 1967). A moment's reflection will convince you that cognitive psychology touches upon almost every area of psychology.

Most cognitive psychologists tend to view the human being as a processor of information, something like a computer. They study the many ways in which we obtain, transform, and use information from our environment. This means they work in areas such as perception, association, memory, thinking, and language. But their perspective is to see these experiences as "transformations of information."

Information processing approach. A view of the individual as a processor of information. Cognitive processes are examined as stages in the transformation of input from the sensory apparatus to the cortex and back to the output, or response stage.

You may recognize this approach from earlier chapters. In Chapter 4, we saw that the **information processing approach** examines the way neurons *process sensory information* in stages, from the sense organs to the cerebral cortex. In Chapter 10, we noted that the information processing approach to memory proposes three stages in the *flow of information* from input to storage. In this chapter we will look at three more processes which have caught the attention of cognitive psychologists—forming concepts, solving problems, and using language. We will conclude the chapter with a discussion of intelligence testing, in which we will examine attempts to apply our knowledge of cognition.

Concepts

Concept. A set of ideas or objects grouped together on the basis of some characteristic or dimension which they have in common; a category.

Let's begin our discussion of cognition by looking at the "building blocks" of thought—concepts. A **concept** is a set of objects or ideas grouped together on the basis of some dimension which they have in common. We often use the word "category" to refer to things organized in this way. Eleanor Rosch says, "Categorization

occurs . . . to reduce the limitless variation . . . to manageable proportions" (Rosch, 1977).

First we will look at some different types of concepts, next we will consider how we form concepts, and then we will look at some problems with "fuzzy" concepts.

NATURAL VERSUS ARTIFICIAL CONCEPTS

Rosch believes there are two major types of cognitive concepts: natural and artificial. "Natural concepts" are those that occur in real-world situations, and which are immediately understandable to most people. Examples of natural concepts are such things as "big or small," "hard or soft," "red or green," "male or female," and even "normal or abnormal."

What we call concepts are usually "artificial concepts." Artificial concepts are contrived or synthetic groupings. Usually they are made up by human beings (particularly by academics!). Dividing college departments into the physical sciences, natural sciences, social sciences, and the humanities is one example of an artificial classification scheme. Classifying students by such titles as freshman, sophomore, junior, senior, and graduate is another artificial set of concepts (Mervis & Rosch, 1981). You sort objects into either natural or artificial concepts, Rosch says, according to various *attributes* you perceive the objects as having (Rosch, 1973).

SUPERORDINATE, BASIC, AND SUBORDINATE CONCEPTS

How are a dog and a cat alike? They are both animals. But how are a collie and a cocker spaniel alike? They are both dogs. Animal is a more *general* concept than dog.

Natural concepts fall into *three levels of generality:*

1. *Superordinate* concepts—such as "animal"—tend to be extremely broad. For example, you are an animal, and so is an earthworm. What attributes do you share with an earthworm?

2. *Basic concepts*—such as "dog"—tend to be of moderate generality. They are neither very specific nor very general.

3. *Subordinate concepts*—such as "collie"—are highly specific (see Figure 11.1).

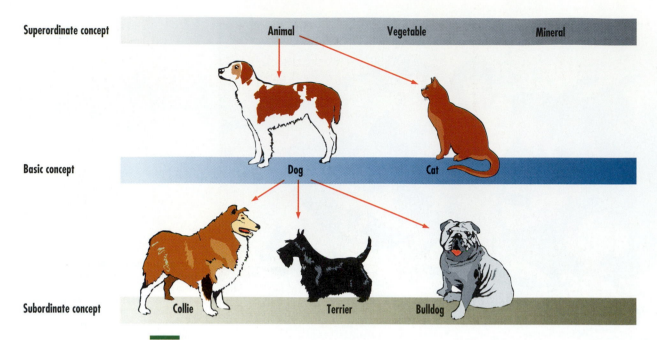

Superordinate concept — Animal · Vegetable · Mineral

Basic concept — Dog · Cat

Subordinate concept — Collie · Terrier · Bulldog

FIGURE 11.1

In cognition, three levels of natural concepts are superordinate, basic, and subordinate.

Generally speaking, basic concepts are easy to create and easy to think about. Very young children tend to be quite good at handling basic level concepts, but have problems dealing with superordinate concepts. For example, look at Figure 11.2. When Eleanor Rosch asked 3-year-olds to select two items that were alike, they had no difficulty at all with Set (1). A "cat is a cat" is a basic level concept. But the 3-year-olds missed the correct answer in Set (2) about half the time. By the time they were 5, however, the children almost always got perfect scores when given tests such as this one (Rosch et al., 1976). Thus, concept development usually begins at the level of basic concepts and moves outward to both superordinate and subordinate categories (MacLaury, 1991; Rosch, 1978).

When you think of the basic concept "bird," what example first comes to mind?

FORMING CONCEPTS

Over the years, there has been a fair amount of psychological research on "concept formation." You will see an example of the sorts of concepts usually studied in these experiments in Figure 11.3. Follow the instructions to see if you can form the correct concept.

To form this concept, or any other concept, you must decide what is relevant and what isn't relevant. But how do you decide what's relevant and what's not?

ATTRIBUTES. As we mentioned, using cognitive concepts lets you put objects, or events, into convenient groupings. One way you may do this is by looking for attributes that each member of the concept shares with other members. For example, a birthday cake, a bowl of soup, and an apple all share at least one common attribute: they are edible. Therefore, these objects fall within the natural concept "food." A tennis shoe and a tuxedo wouldn't fit within this concept. Shoes and suits would fit within the "clothing" concept, though, while soup and apples wouldn't.

Most concepts are complex. An object must often possess several attributes to fit within a certain concept—and perhaps *not* possess certain other attributes. Using attributes allows you to group objects together (into concepts) by including some objects while excluding others.

Set (1)

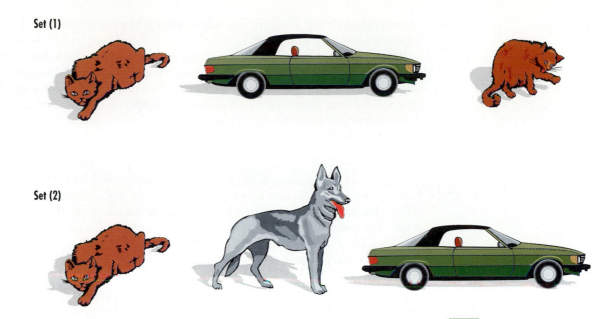

Set (2)

FIGURE 11.2

Pictures similar to those used by Rosch et al. (1976).

According to this "Classical" view of concept formation, which may be traced back to Aristotle, *attributes* determine which concept an object belongs to. Checking attributes allows you to impose an organized, if somewhat artificial, structure on your environment.

PROTOTYPES. Eleanor Rosch has criticized most of the work on concept formation because it involves artificial rather than natural concepts (Rosch, 1973). If you tried to figure out what the critical attribute in Figure 11.3 was, for instance, you probably came to the conclusion that it was "eyebrows." Any face with rounded eyebrows fit within the concept. Any face with peaked eyebrows didn't fit. But how often in real life do you see faces like these, or "peaked" eyebrows?

Now, think of the basic concept "bird." How did you form this concept? And how do you know what animals to include in it, and which to exclude? You *could* make up a list of defining features, or attributes, such as "it flies," "lays eggs," and "has feathers." Then, when you had to put an animal into this concept or in some other concept, you could check to see how many of the defining attributes the animal possessed. When you tried to solve the puzzle in Figure 11.3, you had to use the *defining features* approach. But that's because the puzzle was structured that way.

According to Rosch, that's not the way the human mind usually functions. Instead, she says, you tend to create a **prototype** (often unconsciously), for each basic concept and compare any new possibility to the prototype. You create a prototype by selecting the concept member which has the most attributes in common with other concept members, and the fewest attributes in common with other concepts. Most people in the United States tend to use either the robin or the sparrow as a prototype of a "bird." Now, suppose you have never seen a canary. If someone showed you a canary, you wouldn't ask, "Does it fly?" or "Does it lay eggs?" Rather, you'd

Prototype. A single member of a category or concept which comes to stand for the concept as a whole.

FIGURE 11.3

An attribute discovery task. Before you begin, place a piece of paper so that it hides the correct answers below the figures. Looking only at the figures say "yes" if you think that the figure is an example of the concept, and "no" if you think that it is not. Only one attribute is relevant in this task. After judging each pair, move the paper along to see the answer. Continue until you think you know what the concept is, and then check the text to see whether you are correct.

1	2	3	4	5	6	7	8

| Yes | Yes | No | No | No | Yes | No | Yes |

immediately say it *was* a bird because it is very much like your prototype—a robin or a sparrow (Mervis & Rosch, 1981).

Rosch has shown that concept formation is quick and easy if you have a ready-made prototype available. You can readily sort colored objects into concepts such as "blue," "green," "red," and "yellow" because these are natural concepts for which you already have clear-cut prototypes. It is much more difficult to sort colored objects if the concepts you must use are "aquamarine," "magenta," "turquoise," and "chartreuse" (Rosch, 1977).

"FUZZY" CONCEPTS

Forming and using concepts is often difficult because not all concepts have well-defined boundaries. Is a penguin a bird? You know the answer to that question, of course. But compare a penguin with that prototype of a bird, a robin. The two animals are quite dissimilar, yet both are birds.

Natural concepts (such as "bird") often have fuzzy or indistinct boundaries. For instance, both "wolf" and "dog" are basic concepts. But if you mated the two, which basic concept would the offspring belong to? Artificial concepts, on the other hand, have fairly clear-cut boundaries. After all, they were artificially structured so the boundaries would be as clear as possible.

The "fuzzy boundary" problem becomes worse if you tend to use prototypes rather than defining features. For example, "chair" is a basic concept. What does your prototype of a chair look like? Does it have arms and legs? A seat and a back? Now think of a large canvas bag filled with beans. Does it *look* like your prototype of a chair? Probably not. And yet, if you examine your *attributes* and *rules* you will probably have no trouble fitting the object into the concept "chair." In this case, attributes work better than a prototype.

Neither the prototype approach nor the defining features approach can account for all of the research findings. It appears that human beings are remarkably flexible in the strategies they use to apply concepts, sometimes using one method, and sometimes using another (Best, 1992; MacLaury, 1991).

If you told your household robot to bring you a "chair," and the machine brought you the head of the psychology department, what would that tell you about the robot's prototype of a "chair"?

FUZZY CONCEPTS IN PSYCHOLOGY

Psychologists often try to assign people to concepts or categories. For example, when they describe people in terms of their "personality traits," they are attempting to group individuals according to the attributes (or "traits") they display (Cantor, 1990). According to British psychologist Sarah Hampson, many of the problems trait theorists have in grouping people stem from their use of personality categories, or concepts, that have rather fuzzy boundaries (Hampson, 1985).

The same sort of problem arises when you attempt to diagnose mental patients according to some diagnostic scheme. For instance, Nancy Cantor and Nancy Genero found that clinical psychiatrists could readily differentiate manic and depressive patients. However, the psychiatrists often included manic patients in the schizophrenic category, and often included schizophrenic patients in the manic category. Cantor and Genero conclude that conceptual boundary between mania and depression is fairly clear, but the boundary between schizophrenia and mania is fairly fuzzy. They suggest that psychiatric diagnoses would become more accurate if the *conceptual boundaries* between the categories used were more clearly defined (Cantor & Genero, 1986; Fink, 1991; Murray et al., 1992).

Now that we've discussed how you form concepts and put objects into them, let's see how you *use* concepts to solve problems.

Problem Solving

To many researchers, conscious and deliberate *problem solving* is one of the most important areas of study in cognitive psychology. To give you a feel for the types of research that psychologists perform when investigating problem solving, let's examine a "prototypical" study by Gestalt psychologist Norman Maier.

MAIER'S RESEARCH

Imagine that you volunteered to be a subject in a psychology experiment. The researcher asks you to put on a bathing suit, then escorts you into an almost empty room. Two ropes are hanging from the ceiling. In one corner of the room there is a pair of pliers. Otherwise, the room is bare. Your job is to tie the two ropes together. There are many ways you might approach this problem. Let's imagine that you take a fairly organized, goal-directed approach (Newell & Simon, 1972). Here are some steps you might go thorough in trying to solve this problem.

1. *Specify the Goal.* To begin with, the experimenter has made things easy for you by specifying the goal. For the first two steps in most types of problem solving are (1) realizing that a problem exists, and (2) defining what goal you are trying to achieve. If you don't know there's a problem, of course, you won't do much of anything. And if you don't know what goal you're trying to reach, you won't know when you have solved the problem. Generally speaking, the more specific you can be in describing the goal, the more likely it is you will reach it.

    Your goal in the experiment, of course, is to tie the two ropes together. Since that's a fairly specific goal, you should know when you've achieved it.

2. *Determine the Original State.* The next step in problem solving is to find out where you're starting from. Some psychologists call this "determining the original state." Other researchers—as you saw in Chapter 9—call it "taking a baseline."

    What is your "original state" in the rope experiment? Well, you start with two ropes hanging from the ceiling, a pair of pliers, and your own body. That's it.

3. *Identify the Rules.* In most problem situations, there are rules that determine what you can do and can't do. In the rope experiment, you're told right away what the rules are. First, you can't pull the ropes from the ceiling or change them in any way. Second, you can't use anything not presently in the room. Third, you can't take off your bathing suit and use it. (A fourth rule is usually unstated, but almost always exists. Namely, you can't behave in an abnormal way, such as assaulting the experimenter, setting the place on fire, and so forth.)

4. *Try Possible Solutions.* Once you know the goal and the rules, you can try out some possible solutions. You go over to one of the ropes, take hold of it, and walk toward the second rope. You pull on the first rope as hard as you can (to stretch it a bit, perhaps). Then you extend your free arm as far as it will go. Unfortunately, you can't quite reach the second rope. So you drop the first rope, take hold of the second rope, stretch it out, and try to grab the first rope with your free hand. But that, of course, won't work either. Now, what do you do?

5. *Conceptualize the Problem.* Actually, you didn't really know what the problem was until you tried to tie the ropes together and found they wouldn't reach. At this point, you have to stop and think. Which is to say, you have to conceptualize the problem. "Conceptualizing" means to "construct an internal representation" of the problem. This "internal representation" may be a set of mental images of the elements or concepts involved in the problem. Once you conceptualize the

problem using mental images, you can manipulate the various elements of the problem *cognitively* rather than *physically* (Kosslyn, 1983, 1985).

When Maier tested University of Michigan students on the problem, he found they tended (at first) to conceptualize the problem in fairly standard ways (Maier, 1931). Some students decided "their arms were too short." Their first trial solution was to "extend their arms" using the pair of pliers. They would pull one rope over as far as they could, then reach out for the other rope holding the pliers in their free hand. Unfortunately, using the pliers to "extend their arms" didn't work.

Other students conceptualized the difficulty as being, "The rope is too short." These students would "extend the rope" by grasping it with the pliers. Then they'd try to reach the other rope with their free hand. Again, no luck. (Before Maier learned to dress the students in bathing suits and tell them, "Don't take off your clothes," some of the students used their belts or shirts to "extend the rope.")

Still other subjects decided the problem was that "the rope won't come to me." They would stretch out one rope as far as it would go, then beckon to the other rope as if they could "will" it to swing toward them. These students sometimes solved the problem. Can you guess how they did so?

RECONCEPTUALIZING THE PROBLEM

Once you have conceptualized a problem in a certain way, you may find it difficult to see the problem in a different light. Psychologists call this **fixation.**

Gestalt psychologist K. Duncker, working in the 1930s, was the first psychologist to study a kind of fixation he called **functional fixedness.** Like other Gestalt psychologists, he was interested in basic patterns of perception. He found that perceptions of a problem (and perception of the *functions* of items in the problem) may become *fixed* or limited, so they interfere with the solution. Duncker's best known example of functional fixedness is the "candle-mounting" problem (Duncker, 1945).

How would you mount a candle on a bulletin board using only the candle, some thumb tacks, and a box of matches?

Abraham Luchins also made an extensive study of fixation in problem solving. To try one of his problems, find Table 11.1 and work through the problems before you read any farther.

As you probably noticed, the best solution to problem 1 is first to fill up jar B. That gives you 130 gallons. Then you dip jar A into B and remove 24 gallons. That

Fixation. The tendency to remain set or limited in a particular approach to a problem.

Functional fixedness. The tendency to remain set in the way we see things may be used.

TABLE 11.1

Imagine that you have three jars, A, B, and C. In each of seven problems the capacity of the three jars is listed. You must use the three jars in order to obtain the amount of liquid specified to the "Goal" column. You may obtain the goal amount by adding or subtracting the quantities listed in A, B, and C. (The answers can be found in the discussion of the experiment.)

PROBLEM	A	B	C	GOAL
1	24	130	3	100
2	9	44	7	21
3	21	58	4	29
4	12	160	25	98
5	19	75	5	46
6	23	49	3	20
7	18	48	4	22

leaves 106 gallons. Now you dip jar C into B twice and remove 6 more gallons. That operation leaves you with 100 gallons in B, which is your goal. The best way to solve problems 2 through 5 is in much the same fashion. Check your answers and see if that's the way you solved the first five problems.

If you did solve 1–5, how about 6? In fact, you can solve 6 and 7 exactly the same way. However, that's a very round-about way. Look at the last two problems again and see if you can't find an easier method.

When Luchins asked students to solve 1–5 *first*, they did so. Then they almost always used the round-about method to solve problems 6 and 7 as well. However, when he gave students just problems 6 and 7 (without exposing them to 1-5 first), the subjects almost always came up with the "easy" solution first. The success the first group of students had solving problems 1–5 tended to "fix" a certain procedure in their minds. Because of this "fixation," the students continued to use the round-about solution even when better solutions existed (Luchins, 1942).

How does "functional fixedness" relate to the perceptual principle that "you see what you expect to see"?

As you may have guessed by now, the solution to Maier's rope problem is to break your "mental set" about pliers. That is, you must see that pliers are not only tools—they also can be placed in a basic cognitive concept called "pendulum weights." If you tie the pliers to the end of one rope, you can set it swinging back and forth. Then you can pull the other rope out far enough to catch the swinging rope when it comes close to you.

Many of Norman Maier's students failed to solve the problem because they couldn't "conceptualize" the pair of pliers as a pendulum weight. So Maier gave them some clues. First, he brought a type of pendulum into the room and set it in motion. This clue helped a few of the subjects. But most still conceptualized the problem in terms of "my arm is too short" or "the rope is too short." Then Maier gave them a more important clue. He started talking to the subject, to get the person's attention. Next Maier slowly walked toward the student. As he walked, he deliberately brushed into one of the ropes, so it caught against his body. When Maier walked past the rope, it slid over his shoulder and swung back and forth a couple of times. Shortly thereafter, almost all of the students solved the problem!

Maier then asked the subjects what gave them the clue to solving the problem. Oddly enough, almost all the students said, "The pendulum." Very few of them were conscious of having seen the rope swing back and forth. However, if Maier just showed them the pendulum but *didn't* brush into the rope, few of the students found the solution (Maier, 1931).

How does Maier's experiment support the belief that factors that influence cognition are not entirely conscious?

CREATIVE PROBLEM SOLVING

Creativity of one sort or another is often called for in problem-solving situations. For instance, to solve the Maier rope problem, you have to discover a "creative" or "unusual" use for a pair of pliers.

As you might suspect, there is no single (or even creative) view of creativity that all psychologists will agree to (Solso, 1991). A common view is that creative thinking is the discovery of new solutions to problems, new techniques and devices, or new artistic expressions (Goldenson, 1970). Israeli psychologists Jonathan Smilansky and Naftali Halberstadt disagree. They believe that creativity is the mark

When we use objects in ways they were not designed for, we overcome a perceptual habit of "functional fixedness."

Imagination is more important than knowledge.

ALBERT EINSTEIN

Divergent thinking. Generating inventive solutions to a problem. The solutions are not right or wrong in the usual sense, but are novel and original. Often contrasted with *convergent* thinking in which a problem leads to a single factual answer.

of people who invent *new* problems, not a property of individuals who "merely find new solutions to old problems" (Smilansky & Halberstadt, 1986). Other investigators define creativity as a type of **divergent thinking** associated with the "intuitive" right hemisphere of the brain (Guilford, 1984; Lewis & Houtz, 1986). According to Frank Farley, creative individuals are "thrill-seekers" who enjoy breaking the rules (Farley, 1986; Morehouse et al., 1990).

Most experts agree, however, that creativity is an ability we all have to some degree and that positive reinforcement fosters it, while criticism and punishment inhibit it (Dormen & Edidin, 1989; Skinner, 1954, 1987). Martin Greer and Elaine Levine report that college students became more creative when they were trained to use fantasy, or when they found the creative task intrinsically rewarding (Greer & Levine, 1991). Thus, like so many other behaviors, creative problem solving is multidetermined. It has biological, intra-psychic, and social/behavioral roots (Katz, 1986; Simonton, 1992).

What do you think would happen if a "creative" individual came up with a new idea? Would people be happy to hear about it? Why or why not?

RECENT RESEARCH ON PROBLEM SOLVING

Recent research on problem solving has focused on three main topics: (1) personality factors associated with problem solving; (2) problem solving in real-life (or social) situations; and (3) *metacognition*, or "ways of thinking about thinking." Let's look briefly at each of these three topics.

PERSONALITY FACTORS ASSOCIATED WITH PROBLEM SOLVING. There is not all that much agreement about what personality traits lead to good performance in problem solving situations. However, psychologists Penny Armstrong and Ernest McDaniel found that subjects who perceive themselves as "competent learners" tended to make fewer mistakes when solving problems than did subjects who didn't give themselves high competence ratings (Armstrong & McDaniel, 1986).

There is some evidence that females and males differ in their problem-solving abilities. For example, Monique Lortie-Lussier and her colleagues studied 118 8- and 9-year-old children with English, French, or Italian cultural backgrounds. Many of the girls had more "interpersonal skills" than did the boys, but the boys tended to show higher "resourcefulness and problem solving abilities" (Lortie-Lussier et al., 1986). However, females may resort to problem solving in social situations more readily than in "academic situations." Caryl Rusbult and her colleagues found that women were more likely to use problem-solving skills to improve close relationships, while "traditional males" tended to "exit" relationships rather than trying to resolve the problems and thus make the relationships better (Rusbult et al., 1986).

What have you learned about the socialization of men and women in our culture that could explain the findings described above?

PROBLEM SOLVING IN SOCIAL SITUATIONS.   Several investigators have reported that teaching "social problem-solving skills" is an effective way of bringing about change in many real-life situations. For example, Robert Hierholzer and Robert Liberman found that chronically mentally ill patients benefitted from learning how to set and achieve both short and long-term goals (Hierholzer & Liberman, 1986). Richard Perlmutter and James Jones found that helping families who experience "psychiatric emergencies" learn problem-solving skills was a particularly effective method of treatment (Perlmutter & Jones, 1985). Carolyn Mills and Tim Walter report a marked reduction in anti-social behavior among youths who were taught "job-appropriate behaviors" and skills in handling personal and school-related problems (Mills & Walter, 1979). Even complex social problems often yield to appropriate problem-solving skills.

METACOGNITION. Teaching people problem-solving skills often helps improve their performance. However, many psychologists and educators believe that teaching people to monitor their mental activities, and to evaluate their own performance as they work through a problem, yields even better results (King, 1991). The term **metacognition** is often used to refer to the mental processes by which we "deliberately and consciously take charge of [our] own cognitive functioning" (Pinard, 1992). Metacognitive training encourages individuals to think about their own thought processes while they are solving problems (Bjorklund, 1989).

Psychologists Scott Paris, David Saarnio, and David Cross report that when they gave third- and fifth-grade students metacognitive training, "the students increased their awareness about reading and their [own] use of reading comprehension strategies." In most situations, these students also learned to read faster than did children given traditional training (Paris et al., 1986).

Another emphasis in problem-solving research—one that is not so recent—is the study of "artificial intelligence."

Metacognition. Literally, "beyond normal thought"; becoming aware of, and thinking about, your own thoughts *while you are thinking them.*

Artificial Intelligence

More than 40 years ago, scientists interested in cognitive processes asked themselves a very sticky question: Can we program a computer so that it *thinks* like a human being? The scientists plunged into the problem headfirst. They assumed that, since the human brain "processes" information in much the same way that computers do, it should be simple to get computers to solve problems in the same "logical" way that people do.

As philosopher John Haugeland points out, however, it soon became apparent that rules of logic don't work very well in poorly defined situations. And most real-world problems are, unfortunately, very poorly defined. As it turned out, the frustration the computer scientists experienced led them to look more creatively at how human beings actually reason (Haugeland, 1985).

In 1978 Herbert A. Simon received a Nobel Prize in economics for his research and theorizing on human thought processes. Simon takes the "information processing approach" in his study of cognition. According to Simon, people tend to use two main strategies as they search for solutions to various problems: **algorithms** and **heuristics.**

Algorithms are exact rules you must follow to achieve some goal. It's usually a simple task to teach a computer to use an algorithm because computers can readily follow precise instructions. Heuristics are rather loosely defined rules along with the knowledge of when to use them. The more knowledge you have about a situation, the more precise the heuristics can become. Simon believes that the ability of human beings to cope with real-world situations depends primarily on the use of heuristics, not algorithms. And since we typically have but a limited amount of knowledge about the real world, it's difficult to teach either human beings or computers which heuristics to use—and how to employ them (Simon, 1981).

Algorithms. Precise, step-by-step procedures for solving a particular problem. A *recipe* is an algorithm for preparing a particular food.

Heuristics. Problem-solving techniques that involve making use of what you find to change the direction of your efforts. Often these techniques are short-cuts and may become "rules of thumb."

HEURISTICS VERSUS ALGORITHMS

As we noted, we can program computers to use algorithms rather easily. For instance, a computer programmed to play chess can search through millions of possible chess

Human chess players often use heuristics to help them win. Computers, in contrast, rely on algorithms.

moves, following a simple formula that tells it how to evaluate each possibility. The computer then decides on a move based on the evaluation it has made.

But when experts look at a chess board, they tend to perceive patterns rather than think about exact search strategies. Instead of evaluating *all* the possibilities, the expert will remember, from past experience, what *sort* of move works best in the present situation (a heuristic approach). Ulric Neisser puts it this way: "Capablanca, the former world [chess] champion, was once asked by an admirer how many moves he typically examined in a difficult position. He said, 'One, but it is the right one.'" Neisser goes on to say that "Master players see the whole board at a glance; they see patterns and configurations that suggest moves to them. The more they play, the better they get. . . . The computer doesn't do what the human player does: It doesn't recognize patterns, it doesn't get any better with experience, it doesn't learn" (quoted in Goleman, 1983).

Human beings using heuristics may not realize they are following any kind of rule. They might describe their behavior as going by "intuition," or by "the seat of their pants." However, chances are that in the same situation, they would do the same thing. And if they repeat a successful heuristic often enough it may become a conscious "rule-of-thumb." Even a "rule-of-thumb" is still a heuristic, however, since there are no exact guidelines and no *logical* justification for when to apply the heuristics; there is only a general pattern.

Unfortunately, no one has yet developed high-level, general heuristic techniques for computers. And the major reason for this inability to teach computers how to "think" in this way is that we still don't really know how human beings recognize patterns in real-world situations.

COMPUTERS AND "EXPERT SYSTEMS"

Several years ago, artificial intelligence (AI) specialists tried to program a computer to diagnose various types of illnesses by asking patients for their symptoms. In its simplest form, this sort of "medical diagnostics" is really an exercise in concept formation. So, the AI researchers told themselves, diagnostics should involve little more than (1) identification of "defining attributes," and (2) rules for combining these attributes. Therefore, the AI experts created various highly logical algorithms that would make the computer ask the patient various types of questions. The computer would then try to combine the answers into a precise description of the patient's illness.

This algorithmic approach has succeeded fairly well with a few well-defined illnesses. However, computers do rather poorly with complex medical problems. And they fail miserably when trying to diagnose mental disorders (Trotter, 1986).

By 1980, the AI specialists started looking at medical diagnostics in rather a different light. Rather than building logical algorithms, they tried to mimic the decision-making skills of human experts. We now call this the search for *expert systems*, or computer programs that give expert-level advice.

For example, Robert Glaser and his associates studied how highly experienced physicians made medical diagnoses just from inspecting x-rays of patients. They tried to discover what kinds of "critical features" the skilled physicians looked for in the x-rays, and how they put these features together to make a diagnosis. Glaser and his group then compared the approach used by experienced physicians with that employed by young doctors who were just learning how to read an x-ray.

Glaser suggests that skilled and beginning doctors use quite different decision-making strategies. An expert looks at an x-ray and immediately perceives features that a beginner either overlooks or finds only after a lengthy search. The young doctor may have all the facts she or he needs to arrive at a correct diagnosis. But the beginner uses an *algorithm*—a "logical search." The expert has learned to use *heuristics*. That is, the expert uses "rules-of-thumb" plus facts. The rules—or heuristics—

tell the experienced doctor which features (or facts) are important, and which aren't. And the doctors learn these heuristics through experience.

According to Robert Glaser, knowledge equals facts plus rules. "As individuals acquire knowledge, they also should be empowered to think and reason," Glaser says. If and when we gain enough knowledge about the ways in which human beings acquire and use knowledge, then perhaps we will know enough to teach a robot to "think and reason" too (Glaser, 1984).

Today, computer chess programs can beat human players, even those who have "played a million games." Theoretically, you should be able to build the experience of "playing a million games" into the computer's program. Why do you think this has turned out to be so difficult to do?

LANGUAGE

As you read and comprehend this sentence you are involved in one of the most complicated cognitive processes we know of—the communication of thoughts and feelings through vocal sounds and written symbols. We are using language to communicate.

According to Robert Solso, "It is now generally agreed that the study of language occupies a central position in contemporary psychology and plays a specifically important role in cognitive psychology" (Solso, 1988). George Miller adds, "No general theory of psychology will be adequate if it does not take account of language" (Miller, 1990). Let's look in some detail at how we develop language ability, and then consider the important relationship between language and thought.

Language Development

Language acquisition is often said to be one of the most spectacular of human accomplishments. This makes it of special interest to cognitive psychologists. As Steven Pinker put it: "Language acquisition is the jewel of the crown of cognition. It is what everyone wants to explain. . . . In a sense, language acquisition defines what it is to be an intelligent human being" (quoted in Kolata, 1987).

Think of what you have already accomplished: By the time you were 6 years old, you had a vocabulary of about 14,000 words; by the time you graduated from high school your vocabulary approximated 80,000 words. To acquire this large a vocabulary, you averaged more than ten new words each day from the time you started speaking (Carey, 1978; Miller & Gildea, 1987).

Learning to use language, and to use it properly, when you were a youngster changed your world profoundly. Having a language available is an important aid to learning new concepts (Rice, 1989). According to Neil Salkind and Sueann Ambron, having a verbal label to attach to an experience makes that experience easier to remember and deal with. "In fact," they say, "one reason most of us fail to remember much of what happened to us in our earliest years may be that we had not learned to use such verbal labels. We had nothing to file away in our memories as a coded symbol of the experience" (Salkind & Ambron, 1987).

Can you think of other reasons you might have difficulties recalling early experiences?

Ambron and Salkind believe that the stages children go through while progressing from baby talk to adult communication are roughly identical regardless of native tongue, socioeconomic class, or ethnic background. Children everywhere talk about the same things while going through these developmental stages, Salkind and Ambron say. "They all speak of objects and situations, make demands, use mostly nouns and verbs, and talk to themselves a great deal but never about themselves or their relationship with others" (Salkind & Ambron, 1987).

According to language researchers, language acquisition has four aspects to it:

1. Knowledge of how to produce **phonemes,** which are the basic sounds of speech.

2. Learning **semantics,** or the meaning of words.

3. Mastery of **syntax,** or the rules by which words can be combined into sentences.

4. Discovering the **pragmatics** of language, or the appropriate social use of speech.

Let's look at each of these four aspects of language acquisition in more detail.

PHONEMES

Phonemes. The basic unit of spoken language; the smallest part of speech, such as "da" or "ba," without regard to meaning. (The smallest unit with meaning is called a *morpheme*.)

Semantics. The study of the meanings of words.

Syntax. The orderly structure of language; the rules that govern the combination of words into phrases and sentences.

Pragmatics. The study of the way something (in this case language) is used in everyday affairs.

Obviously, an infant can't talk if it doesn't make sounds. Since phonemes are the basic sounds that make up human speech, the developmental problem then becomes, how does an infant acquire the ability to produce phonemes? Do infants naturally (and spontaneously) produce all the phonemes they will need in order to speak any human language? Or are they born with a readiness to imitate the sounds their parents (and others) say to them?

If you have been around infants very much, you probably have observed them happily chattering to themselves in a language made up of repetitive syllables, such as "da da da" and "ba ba ba." We call this type of early speech babbling. Babbling occurs in all normal children between 3 and 7 months of age (see Figure 11.4) (Bower, 1986a).

Babbling frequently occurs early in the morning, when children first wake up and before they begin their daily "social life" with their parents and other adults. Normal patterns of babbling occur in Down's syndrome children, but do not occur in deaf children (Smith & Oller, 1981). Deaf children may babble briefly, but then stop producing the sorts of sounds that children with normal hearing do. This fact suggests that infants need to hear the sounds they are producing in order to continue producing them. Therefore, the absence of babbling may be a sign that the child needs special attention (Oller et al., 1985).

Several studies suggest that infants everywhere in the world make the same sounds when babbling (Olney & Scholnick, 1976; Saito et al., 1981). And until recently, scientists believed that children produced the entire range of human

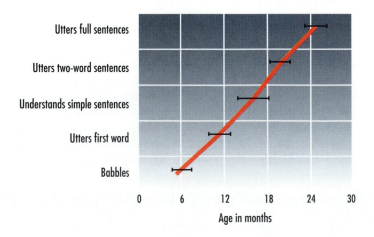

FIGURE 11.4

The range and average age for several landmarks of verbal behavior.

sounds in their babbling. Recent studies, however, show that many speech sounds are almost never heard in babbling. The most common sounds (worldwide) are those involving consonants such as *n, m, d, t,* or *b* combined with vowels such as *e* or *a.* Consonants such as *l, r, f,* and *v,* and combinations such as *st* are quite rare. According to Rebecca Eilers and Kimbrough Oller, the sounds produced during babbling are also those the child favors a few months later, when the child begins to speak in words (Eilers & Oller, 1985).

In summary, current thinking holds that the early acquisition of phoneme production has three distinct aspects to it. First, most children babble innately, but do not produce all the sounds of speech in their babble. Second, parents selectively reinforce some sounds which then come to predominate. Third, children innately imitate phonemes not produced in their babbles, and parents reward the children for doing so. Eventually, the child can produce all the sounds found in its "native language."

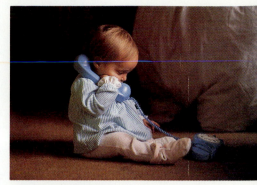

Babbling is a signal that a baby is developing normally.

Is speech in human beings innately determined, or acquired through learning?

SEMANTICS

Words represent objects and actions. Thus, words have meanings that infants must learn as they progress from babbling to true communicative speech. The problem children face as they learn semantics is that most words have more than one meaning. "Drink," for instance, is both a noun and a verb. "I drink the milk," and "Give me a drink," are examples of how the same word can mean either an action or an object. Furthermore, words such as "sea" and "see," and "dear" and "deer," sound alike but have quite different meanings.

At about a year of age, infants begin uttering **holophrastic,** or one-word sentences. The child may actually say single words earlier, but doesn't appear to grasp the meaning of words (and to use them to communicate) until he or she is about 1 year old. At this stage, a single-word sentence may have several meanings. For example, "Cup" may mean "I see the cup," or "Get me my cup," or even "This cup is just like the one I use at home."

Holophrastic. The expression of a complex idea in a single word or phrase.

Most infants begin using two-word sentences at about 18 months. At first, these sentences are of the agent-plus-action ("Mama drink") or action-plus-object type ("Drink milk"). At this age, children also use negative statements, such as "No milk." They also use the so-called *Wh*-questions, such as "Where milk?" or "When drink?"

Some two-word sentences are called **telegraphic speech** because the youngster includes important words (such as nouns and verbs) but omits other parts of speech. Thus, rather than saying, "Mommy, I want to be picked up now," the child may say, "Mommy up."

Telegraphic speech. A simplified form of speech which eliminates all unnecessary words— much like a telegraph message for which the customer pays by the word.

By the time they are 2, most children can speak in complete and fairly complex sentences, such as "Where is my milk?" and "I drank my milk." At this age, too, youngsters typically learn to change the meaning of words or sentences by changing the inflection they use. For example, "I drink milk?" might be a question asking if it's all right to drink milk rather than water. But "I drink milk!" might be the child's way of telling the mother the child has already consumed the milk.

Generally speaking, the meaning children assign to words tends to change from the overly general to the specific. Thus, at an early age, a little girl might use the word "Daddy" to refer to any adult male. Later, "Daddy" might refer just to males who look like her father. Finally, she learns to use "Daddy" only when referring to her father, and "man" when referring to other adult males.

By the age of 4, most children can use simple "relationship" words, such as moreless, young-old, and weak-strong. Relationships such as before-after give youngsters difficulty, however. If you say to a 4-year-old "I drank the milk after I played in the park," the child will probably think you consumed the liquid before you went to the park. Until they are 8 or 9, most children seem to think that whatever is mentioned in the first part of a sentence must have occurred before whatever is mentioned in the second part. And until they are 9, most youngsters have difficulties with "come" versus "go," and "bring" versus "take."

At any point in a child's development, the meaning the child assigns to words tells a lot about how far the youngster's cognitive development has progressed. These "meanings" also give some clues as to the child's notions about the rules by which words can be combined into sentences.

SYNTAX

Where do children learn about syntax—the "grammar" or "rules" that govern language? These rules are often frightfully complex—so much so that even people who never make a mistake in English can't always tell you what "laws" they are following. And most parents don't teach syntax to their children; they just provide models and then correct the youngster's mistakes. Therefore, the first questions we have to answer in our study of syntax are the following:

1. Are there innate language structures that are coded in the genes, or is syntax entirely learned?
2. Presuming some aspects of syntax must be acquired through experience, do children learn "syntactic rules" which they then apply to all language? Or do they learn the order of words by rote, one at a time?

We will discuss the evidence for and against the existence of "innate language structures" in a moment. First, let's look at "rote versus rule" learning.

REASONING BY RULE OR BY ANALOGY? David Rumelhart and James McClelland suggest that the "rules of syntax" are far too complex for most children to learn. Children just beginning to speak cannot grasp such concepts as "noun," "verb," "prefix," and "root," according to Rumelhart and McClelland. Instead, these experimenters say, young people learn a few words by rote. The children then increase their vocabularies by making analogies—that is, by reasoning that "this word sounds like that word." As evidence that this sort of "rule-less learning" is technically possible, Rumelhart and McClelland have created a computer software program that "learns" English without knowledge of syntactic rules. Rumelhart and McClelland claim that the computer makes many of the same verbal mistakes that children make (Rumelhart & McClelland, 1986, 1987).

Steven Pinker takes the opposite point of view. He notes that the rules versus analogies debate is a classical issue that keeps popping up in studies of philosophy and psychology whenever people try to understand what it is that underlies cognitive behavior and regulates thought. Pinker believes that children learn rules or procedures which they then test out in their speech. Feedback from adults helps the children determine which rules "work," and which ones don't (Pinker, 1984; Pinker & Prince, 1987).

In fact, the data suggest that both positions may be right—in part. For example, several studies show that children start out by forming irregular past tenses correctly. That is, they say "brought" and "went" when first learning to speak. Then they discover the "past tense rule" for regular verbs and overgeneralized this rule: They begin to say "bringed" and "goed." Finally, the youngsters learn that the "past tense rule" works only with regular verbs. At this point, they return to saying "brought" and "went." These studies suggest that children learn syntax both by rule and by analogy (Gropen et al., 1991; Pinker, 1991).

"What's the big surprise? All the latest theories of linguistics say we're born with the innate capacity for generating sentences."

If you isolated two infants at birth, would the children learn to speak spontaneously? If they did speak spontaneously, what language would they "invent"? Would different pairs of children dream up different languages? If so, would these invented languages have similar grammars?

NATURE VERSUS NURTURE IN LANGUAGE LEARNING   Is there an innately determined "universal language" structure underlying all types of human speech? Or is syntax entirely learned?

Behaviorists such as B.F. Skinner have long insisted that children don't directly learn syntax at all (unless specifically taught it). Rather, they learn proper speech from imitation and "selective reinforcement." Skinner does admit that genes carry the code for the physical potential to produce speech. He puts it this way: "The human species took a crucial step forward when its vocal musculature came under operant control in the production of speech sounds. Indeed, it is possible that all distinctive achievements of the species can be traced to that one genetic change." But, according to Skinner, we inherit the ability to *learn*, not some "innate knowledge" of what syntax is all about. Thus, Skinner comes down strongly on the side of "nurture" (Skinner, 1987).

On the other hand, **linguists** such as Noam Chomsky have long taken the "naturist" position in this argument. Some 20 years ago, Chomsky stated that there is a universal **deep structure,** or grammar, underlying all human languages. Chomsky believes that languages are far too complex for children to learn in the short time it takes them to do so, unless the children are born with some innate knowledge of the "rules" or syntax that govern speech in all human societies (Chomsky, 1986; Crain, 1991).

By the deep structure of language, Chomsky means "the innate tendency to process information in linguistic form." To understand what Chomsky is talking about, consider the behaviors involved in walking. You had to learn to walk, didn't you? And you probably learned very quickly. But could you have acquired those motor skills so readily if the "deep structure" of walking weren't somehow imbedded in your genes? In similar fashion, could you have learned to talk if the neurons in your brain weren't genetically biased to produce spoken language as readily as they produce running and walking (D'Agostino, 1986)?

Myrna Gopnik presents evidence which seems to support Chomsky's position. She studied dysphasia (the inability to acquire language normally) in a large family spanning three generations. Her findings suggest that a single gene was responsible for this family's language difficulties (Gopnik, 1990).

Who is correct, Skinner or Chomsky? The answer seems to be, "both of them." Skinner looks at how we acquire verbal behaviors through learning. He explains quite well how parents use selective reinforcement to "shape" the sounds children produce when babbling. But parents cannot possibly reinforce all possible word combinations. Chomsky's strength lies in his discussion of how we develop complex rules to regulate the ways we combine words (grammar).

Steven Pinker's research seems to support both ideas. His studies suggest that learning words and learning to apply the rules of grammar are two separate processes springing from different parts of the brain (Gropen et al., 1991; Pinker 1991).

PRAGMATICS

Languages are necessary because people living together need to communicate with each other. Communication involves more than phonemes, semantics, and syntax, however. It involves practical, or pragmatic, rules about when to speak and when not to speak, what is acceptable talk and what isn't. Put another way, children must learn

And I would fain have any one name to me that tongue, that any one can learn or speak as he should do, by the rules of grammar. Languages were made not by rules or art, but by accident and the common use of the people.

JOHN LOCKE (1693)

Linguists (LIN-gwists). Scientists who study the structure and development of language, as well as the relationship between languages.

Deep structure. The universal inherited predisposition to process language into meaningful patterns of relationship.

To go through the grammar of one language is of great use for the mastery of every other grammar; because there obtains, through all languages, a certain analogy to each other in their grammatical construction.

SYDNEY SMITH (1809)

not only how to communicate their needs, but also to predict what the social consequences of saying something will be.

Newborns cry to express their needs. As they acquire language, they find more complex ways to communicate. As Margaret Matlin notes, a 7-month-old child who wants a ball will reach out for the ball and make a fuss. By about 9 months of age, the youngster will attempt to use adults to help gain what the child wants. That is, the child will alternately look at the adult and at the ball while fussing. By now, the child has learned there is a connection between making the right kind of sounds and getting the ball (Matlin, 1989). Linguists often call this type of verbal behavior intentional communication, since the child announces his or her intentions in order to get assistance from someone else.

Society, however, puts constraints on what the child can say, and on how and when the child must say things. As Michael McTear points out, all cultures have polite forms of social discourse. Often these polite forms of speech are a part of social rituals, such as saying "please" when you want something, and "thank you" when you get it. These rituals often include body language (Lohaus, 1992). In some societies, children must bow their heads and gaze at the floor when talking to adults in order to show respect. Other cultures teach children to stand up straight and look directly into the adults' eyes while talking. Children must also learn to "take turns" when speaking, and how to correct their own verbal mistakes (McTear, 1985).

Several studies indicate that men use language differently from women. What kind of differences would you expect? Why?

Animal Language and the Brain

As we mentioned in Chapter 2, the left hemisphere of the brain, which is primarily responsible for speech in most right-handed people, is physically a little larger than the right hemisphere. This size difference between the hemispheres exists to a much lesser extent in the higher primates, such as chimpanzees, and not at all in lower animals. Furthermore, the vocalizations made by monkeys and chimpanzees seem to be primarily under the control of centers in the limbic system rather than under the control of the cortex (as is the case in human beings). Destruction of the "cortical speech center" in human beings typically leaves them speechless. Destruction of similar areas of the monkey cortex does not affect the animal's vocalizations at all (Segalowitz, 1983).

It would appear, then, that human brains are uniquely suited for language learning. However, many scientists have been successful in teaching chimpanzees to communicate either in "sign language" or by pressing keys on a computer console.

For example, psychologists Sue Savage-Rumbaugh and Duane Rumbaugh have trained chimps to use an artificial language called Yerkish. To help the animals learn, the Rumbaughs present word-symbols on an overhead projector. The chimps respond by pressing illuminated buttons on a computer console. If the chimps use the word-symbols correctly, they are rewarded. Several chimpanzees have been able to learn 100 or more symbols, and use them as correctly as might a 2-year-old child (Savage-Rumbaugh et al., 1980). Scientists working with the Rumbaughs have also used the same equipment to teach three severely retarded women who were essentially nonverbal to communicate using word-symbols (Yarbrough, 1986).

Other psychologists have taught apes to use American Sign Language, and have claimed that their animals could "create sentences" and "use language in a symbolic way." There is a continuing controversy in the scientific literature about this research, however. A detailed analysis of "ape language" often suggests that the trainers are cueing the animal's responses in various subtle ways much as did the man

If you are writing to your friend, when you want to know what words to write, grammar will tell you; but whether you should write to your friend or should not write, grammar will not tell you.

EPICTETUS (c. A.D. 100)

Chimpanzees can learn many different "signs" to represent actions and objects in their environment.

who owned the famous "talking horse," Clever Hans (Premack, 1986; Terrace, 1980).

Can apes speak? The answer depends on how you define "speak." Some apes can surely communicate by "signing," or by pressing buttons on a computer console. But no one has yet proven that ape language has "grammar." Nor is there concrete evidence that apes can manipulate symbols with, say, the sophistication and creativity of even a fairly young child (Best, 1992; Morris, 1979; Reynolds & Flagg, 1983).

Similar conclusions can be drawn from the research on dolphins. Louis Herman has taught dolphins to respond to hand signals as well as to computer-generated sounds. However, at least so far, the dolphins seem to have no greater ability to use language than chimpanzees. And in the wild, their "communication" apparently consists of a signal giving their identity and possibly their emotional state, but nothing more (Chollar, 1989). Despite the size of the dolphin's brain (larger than the human brain, and about 4 times larger than the chimpanzee brain), it does not seem to have the specialized areas for language that are the basis for complex verbal abilities in humans.

One point seems clear, as James and Carol Gould note, human beings talk spontaneously, and do so worldwide in their natural environment. Other animals do not. "You cannot keep a normal, healthy child from learning to talk. . . . Chimpanzees, by contrast, can be [coaxed] into mastering some sort of linguistic communications skills, but they really could not care less about language: The drive just is not there" (Gould & Gould, 1981).

Put more simply, our genes program us to learn to talk, and we have a nervous system complex enough to support speech production. No other animal can make that statement!

Language and Thought

If you want a friend to talk about what she is thinking, you might say, "A penny for your thoughts." Talking is a familiar method of expressing what we think. Freud believed that "slips" in our speech revealed even *unconscious* thoughts. But is the relationship between thinking and talking only in one direction? We know our thoughts affect what we say, but is it also possible that our language affects our thoughts? Let's look at this question in two parts: "Do we need language in order to think?" and "Does language influence what we think?"

IS LANGUAGE NECESSARY?

In his influential "behaviorist" approach to psychology, John Watson equated thinking with language, and language with talking. He could then study "thought" through analysis of verbal utterances. Even silent thought became potentially measurable "sub-vocal movements of the throat and larynx" (Watson, 1924).

Today, we sometimes use the expression, "I'm just thinking out loud," to indicate the close relationship between what we are saying and what we are thinking. We may even talk to ourselves as we work through a difficult problem. It seems intuitively clear that a kind of "self-talk" is an important part of our thinking. But is it necessary?

If language, and especially talking, were necessary for thought, people without the ability to use language, or the ability to speak, would not be able to think—as we normally think. Two lines of research indicate this is not so.

In 1947, researcher Edward Smith reported the daring step of having his body temporarily paralyzed by the drug curare. Since the drug paralyzed even the muscles he needed to breathe, Smith had to be artificially respirated during the experiment. After the effects of the drug wore off, Smith reported that even though he had not been able to speak, he had been able to think in words as clearly as ever (Smith et al., 1947). So speech is not necessary, but what about words?

Language is the blood of the soul into which thoughts run and out of which they grow.

OLIVER WENDELL HOLMES

Researcher Hans Furth has examined several individuals who were born deaf and could not speak any language, including sign language. He found that their thinking and intelligence was essentially normal. Their lack of language had limited their development somewhat, but there was no doubt about their ability to think (Furth, 1966).

Language does not appear to be necessary for thought. Actually, when you think about it, we often think without words—using visual, auditory, and other images. So, although language plays an important role in much of our thinking, it is not absolutely necessary.

DOES LANGUAGE INFLUENCE THOUGHT?

Obviously we use language to influence and persuade other people. They in turn influence our thinking by what they say. But does our own language influence what we *think* and even what we *perceive?* For example, the ancient Hebrews had a word for God which could not be pronounced. Because of their deep fear and reverence for God, they did not want to limit their concept of God. If we used different words, or spoke a different language, would we experience the world differently?

Linguistic relativity hypothesis. The idea that our thinking is limited by the words we know.

This idea, known as the **linguistic relativity hypothesis,** is most clearly associated with Benjamin Whorf. Whorf claimed that the language we speak affects the way we think and even the way we experience the world. For example, if a language possesses words for certain concepts, the speakers of that language are much more likely to think in terms of those concepts than are speakers of a language without names for the concepts. Whorf observed that Eskimos have several different words for different kinds of snow. He suggested that this caused them to *see* snow differently, with finer distinctions than someone from the tropics would make (Whorf, 1956). Critics argue that even someone from the tropics can discriminate between different kinds of snow. They simply need to learn the labels.

If thought corrupts language, language can also corrupt thought.

GEORGE ORWELL

The linguistic relativity hypothesis has some interesting implications for the relationship between different groups. For example, some Native North American languages do not make clear distinctions between past, present, and future (Solso, 1988). Speakers of these languages may find it difficult to understand the English-speaking person's concern with time. In his review of "Black English," Ronald Butters points out that many American blacks speak a version of English with its

Eskimos have several different words to refer to different types of snow. According to Benjamin Whorf, this means that Eskimos perceive snow differently than someone who does not have the vocabulary for these distinctions.

own sounds, words, and syntax (Spears, 1989). Does this distinct dialect lead to a different pattern of thought, or perception of the world? Some research says "yes" (Bernstein, 1970). Other research says "no" (Labov, 1970).

It seems safe to conclude that language influences thought to some degree. The extent of the influence remains an exciting topic for further research (Bourne et al., 1986).

Do the words we use to refer to certain positions, such as chairman, fireman, paperboy, restrict our thinking about who could occupy those positions?

INTELLIGENCE

Few topics in the study of *cognition* generate such *affect* (to use St. Thomas Aquinas's terms) as the study of intelligence. For one thing, there is no generally agreed-upon definition of intelligence (Aquinas called it "the ability to combine and separate"). This is one reason researcher Robert Sternberg went out and asked people in supermarkets, commuter trains, and other natural settings to give their definitions of intelligence (Sternberg, 1982). He wanted to see if there were consistent defining features of the concept "intelligence." We will look at Sternberg's conclusions in a moment.

Another reason the topic of intelligence sometimes generates more heat than light, is that in the values of contemporary Western culture, intelligence apparently ranks near the top, along with thinness and wealth—characteristics of which you can presumably never have too much. And when people come along and claim, as they occasionally do, that certain racial groups are born more intelligent than other racial groups, the heat of controversy bursts into a destructive flame.

Part of the problem in understanding intelligence is that it is a **hypothetical construct,** which means that it cannot be observed directly. So let's begin our consideration of intelligence with a look at attempts to measure it.

How would you go about designing a measure of intelligence? What does this tell you about your own definition of intelligence?

Intelligence Tests

In 1904 the French government asked psychologist Alfred Binet and physician Theophile Simon to devise a test that would allow teachers to identify "retarded" children who might not benefit from schooling. Since "measuring heads" hadn't worked, Binet and Simon decided that seeing how well the students performed ordinary tasks might give some indication of how bright the students were.

To begin, Binet and Simon pulled together a large number of rather simple problems that seemed to require different mental skills. Then they tried out the test problems on a large number of school children of different ages. This technique allowed Binet and Simon to select "appropriate" test items for each age group. They found, for example, that the average 7-year-old could correctly make a pencil copy of the figure of a diamond, but most 5-year-olds could not (see Figure 11.5).

If a boy of 9 got the same score on the test as did the *average* 7-year-old, Binet and Simon presumed that the boy's mental development was retarded by 2 years. The boy would thus have a chronological age of 9 but a "mental age" of 7. If an

We should take care not to make the intellect our god; it has, of course, powerful muscles, but no personality.
ALBERT EINSTEIN

Hypothetical construct. Any concept devised to tie together a variety of observations.

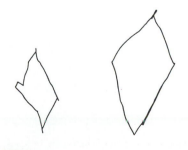

FIGURE 11.5

Drawing of a diamond by a 5-year-old (left) and a 7-year-old (right).

8-year-old girl did as well on the test as the average 11-year-old, then she had a mental age of 11, although her chronological age was but 8.

Later, psychologists in Germany and in the United States put the relationship between chronological age and mental age into an equation:

$$(\text{Mental age/Chronological age}) \times 100 = \text{Intelligence Quotient, or IQ}$$

A girl with a mental age of 6 and a chronological age of 6 would have an IQ of

$$6/6 \times 100 = 1 \times 100 = 100 = \text{IQ}$$

By *definition*, she would be of average intelligence. A boy with a mental age of 7 and a chronological age of 9 would have an IQ of

$$7/9 \times 100 = .777 \times 100 = 78 = \text{IQ}$$

A girl with a mental age of 11 and a chronological age of 8 would have an IQ of

$$11/8 \times 100 = 1.375 \times 100 = 138 = \text{IQ}$$

The Binet-Simon test did so well at predicting the academic performance of school children that intelligence testing became a standard part of educational psychology. However, as psychologists have grown more sophisticated at measuring intelligence, they have almost completely abandoned the use of the "intelligence quotient" itself. Instead, most psychologists now convert intelligence test scores into "standard scores" or "percentiles," for these measures give a more accurate and reliable measure of intellectual performance (Tyler, 1973).

From the start of his research, Binet worried about the *misuse* of his test. Binet didn't believe that intelligence could be captured by any single number, nor did he think intelligence was primarily inherited. He was afraid that teachers would "rank" their students according to some simple (and incorrect) scheme, and then respond to the rankings, not to the students. So Binet refused to rank all the students he tested (Gould, 1981).

American psychologists tended to ignore Binet's warnings. For example, the noted Stanford psychologist Lewis Terman made up his own version of the French scale early this century. He called his device the Stanford-Binet intelligence test. It yielded a single number, which Terman called the IQ. Other psychologists soon followed Terman's lead, and now there are hundreds of intelligence tests available. When used properly, by people who understand both the strengths and weaknesses

Mensa is an international organization open to anyone whose IQ falls within the top 2 percent of the general population.

of intelligence tests, these measures of individual differences can be of considerable value. Unfortunately, however, these tests have been abused almost as often as they have been properly used—substantiating Binet's worst fears.

The issue of "test abuse" will become more clear if we first consider the matter of different "types of intelligence."

Types of Intelligence

The results of many psychological studies suggest that intelligence is not a single trait. Rather it is made up of a great many related talents or abilities. Psychologists don't entirely agree what these related talents are, but they often mention such things as the ability to memorize words and numbers, to learn motor tasks, to solve verbal and numerical problems, to evaluate complex situations, to be creative, and to perceive spatial relationships. Indeed, in 1959, J.P. Guilford listed 120 "factors of intelligence," each one representing a different intellectual ability (Guilford, 1959, 1967).

GENERAL AND SPECIFIC INTELLIGENCE

To Charles Spearman, the noted British psychologist, there are but two types of intelligence. Many years ago, Spearman noted that, if you took 10 different intelligence tests, you would usually wind up with 10 different scores. True, the scores probably would be *related* to each other. But which one gave your *real* IQ? And why so many different scores?

Spearman decided each test item actually measured two factors. One he called *general* intelligence, or the "g factor." But each item also measured one or more *specific* types of mental ability, which he called "s factors." Thus, different tests yield different scores because each test tends to emphasize "s" or "g" to a different degree. However, the *mix* of "s" and "g" factors for each test could still fit a bell-shaped curve. That is, a few people had a low total of "s" and "g," a few people had a high total "s" plus "g," and most people were between these extremes (Goldenson, 1970; Spearman, 1904).

FLUID AND CRYSTALLIZED INTELLIGENCE

Raymond Cattell agrees that there are two "intellectual factors," but disagrees with Spearman on what they are. Cattell says you have *"fluid"* intelligence and *"crystallized"* intelligence. You inherit your "fluid" intelligence. "Fluid" intelligence involves such talents as the ability to think and reason. "Crystallized" intelligence involves *learned* skills such as being able to add and subtract, or use a large vocabulary.

According to Cattell, your "fluid" intelligence sets limits on your "crystallized" abilities. If you aren't innately bright, all the training in the world won't help you get through school. On the other hand, if you have a high "fluid" intelligence, and you grow up in a deprived and unstimulating environment, you won't acquire many skills—and you won't get a high score on most intelligence tests. From Cattell's point of view, if everyone grew up in the best of all possible environments, everyone's "crystallized" intelligence would be fully developed, and "fluid" intelligence would be the major determinant of IQ (Cattell, 1982).

Do you think "street smarts" are the same thing as "book smarts"?

ANALYTIC, CREATIVE, AND CONTEXTUAL INTELLIGENCE

Robert Sternberg disagrees with both Cattell and Spearman. Sternberg thinks there are *three* different kinds of intelligence.

Intelligence is what intelligence tests measure.

EDWIN G. BORING

"Street smarts" may be more important to success in some occupations than are the more traditionally recognized forms of intelligence.

Describing his early experiences, Sternberg says, "I really stunk on IQ tests. I was just terrible" (quoted in Trotter, 1986). Despite his poor test performance as a child, Sternberg somehow managed to obtain a Ph.D. from Stanford and become a professor at Yale. And perhaps *because* of his early difficulties, Sternberg has spent many years studying what intelligence is, and how best to measure it (Sternberg, 1982, 1984).

By the 1980s, Sternberg had come up with a triarchic, or three-factor, theory (Sternberg, 1986). He claims there are three entirely different sorts of intelligence:

1. *Analytical,* or *componential* intelligence. People with this kind of intelligence tend to do beautifully on test scores that require them to *analyze* a problem into its component parts.

2. *Creative,* or *experiential* intelligence. People with this kind of intelligence often have mediocre test scores, but can combine different experiences to come up with new insights. They not only solve unusual problems quickly, but usually train themselves to handle familiar problems by rote memory in order to free their minds for creative efforts.

3. *Contextual* intelligence, or "street smarts." People with this kind of intelligence learn quickly how to "beat the game" in any context, but usually don't have the highest scores on standardized tests, nor are they necessarily creative. Sternberg defines contextual intelligence as "all the extremely important things they never teach you in school."

Sternberg believes we should have three different *kinds* of intelligence tests, for the ones we now use tend to measure only analytic, or componential intelligence. Sternberg believes that standard IQ tests are fairly good for predicting how people will do in school, but he thinks they are much less important when it comes to job performance (cited in McKean, 1985).

Sternberg thinks that intelligence is primarily learned, not innate. Therefore, *all* children would do well on intelligence tests if the youngsters were reared in the best possible environment. But what constitutes "the best of all possible environments"? We can't as yet answer that question. But research does suggest that the early environment can have a significant effect on a child's intelligence test scores (Bjorklund, 1989).

In which of Sternberg's three "types" of intelligence would you expect school teachers (and other academics) to be highest? Why?

IQ and Experience

Children whose early experience is one of deprivation, often show remarkable improvements in their IQs if they are later given the proper intellectual stimulation. One of the first psychologists to make this point was Harold Skeels. In the 1930s, Skeels shocked many of his colleagues by reporting he had been able to *increase* the IQ's of apparently retarded children by putting them in an unusual environment.

Skeels took several children out of a dreary orphanage and gave them to a group of retarded women to rear. The first children he studied were two little girls, whose IQs rose from below 50 to near normal. Skeels believed the girls got higher scores because the retarded women gave them massive stimulation and attention, which children at the orphanage didn't receive. Over a period of several years, Skeels and his colleagues repeated their study and later followed up the children when they were between 25 and 35 years old. The contrast in intellectual ability and social success between the adults who had been in Skeels' experimental group and those who had remained in the orphanage was striking. Skeels was thus the first psychologists to suggest that an enriched environment can have a dramatic effect on IQ (Skeels & Dye, 1939; Skeels, 1966).

COERCIVE DISCIPLINE

In 1981, sociologist Zena Blau reported a study which suggested that *coercive discipline* might also be a factor in restricting intelligence. Blau measured the IQ of more than a thousand children in Chicago. Half of the youngsters were black, and the other half were white. Blau reports that black and white children who had *similar home environments* tended to have highly similar intelligence test scores. Blau notes, however, that IQs were lowest among children (black or white) whose mothers used punitive and "coercive discipline" on their children. And IQs were highest among children (white or black) whose mothers tended to reward their children for learning self-control rather than punishing them for misbehaving (Blau, 1981).

Results supporting Blau's position come from a study by psychologists Thomas Power and Lynn Chapieski. These researchers observed 16 mothers and their 14-month-old infants in their home environments for several weeks. Some of the mothers used physical discipline, such as slapping the child on the wrist, while other mothers didn't. Power and Chapieski report that infants whose mothers physically punished them *continued to misbehave*, while infants whose mothers used verbal discipline (or none at all) tended to learn appropriate behaviors rather readily. Furthermore, when the researchers tested the infants 7 months later, the physically punished youngsters did more poorly on problem-solving tasks than did the infants whose mothers never slapped their children (Power & Chapieski, 1986).

Suppose you grew up in an environment that rewarded you for answering questions quickly rather than for answering correctly—and for defending your answers vigorously, whether right or wrong. How would your early experiences affect your performance in school and on intelligence tests?

LEARNING COGNITIVE SKILLS

As Robert Sternberg notes, most intelligence tests place rather heavy emphasis on *analytical reasoning*—the ability to work your way through a complicated mental task step-by-step. But where does this ability come from?

Some people assume that reasoning is an inherited ability. Few psychologists doubt that genes determine *some* aspects of intelligence. (According to David Bjorklund, the current estimate is that 50 percent of the difference in IQ scores among people is the result of inheritance (Bjorklund, 1989).) But are people poor reasoners because of their genes? Or is some aspect of that trait learned?

Earlier we noted that teaching cognitive skills such as goal-setting and self-monitoring (metacognition), can improve problem solving ability. Research by Benjamin Bloom and Lois Broder suggests that at least some of the difference between high and low scores on IQ tests may be caused by a lack of appropriate cognitive learning experiences.

Bloom and Broder studied how college students with either low or high IQs react to mental challenges. They gave these subjects various problems to work on and asked the students to "talk out loud" as they proceeded. High IQ subjects tended to read the instructions carefully, then diligently eliminated all the incorrect answers. The low IQ students often skipped over the instructions, and lacked the patience to isolate the correct answers when faced with questions that required formal reasoning. The low scorers didn't seem to carry on an "internal conversation" with themselves, nor did they proceed through a step-by-step sequence of deductions. If the low IQ students couldn't see the answer immediately, they usually guessed.

Bloom and Broder were convinced that the low-scoring students had never acquired the proper cognitive skills. So they developed a training program aimed at helping these young people "learn how to reason." First, they made the low scorers read the instructions aloud. Many of the students showed immediate improvement, because they were forced to pay attention to what was required of them. Next the experimenters asked the students to solve various problems aloud. After Bloom and Broder had discussed the student's solution with the student, the experimenters read the correct solution aloud. Then they asked the student to explain what had gone wrong if the student had been incorrect. The students had many difficulties at first, and the instructors had to show tremendous patience. But once the students *learned* what was required to do well on the tests, they began to perform much better. Although Bloom and Broder did not retest the students' IQs after this training, the psychologists report most of their subjects got much higher grades in college thereafter (Bloom, 1982, 1985).

In terms of "street smarts," which is better: being "right," or being "quick and aggressive"?

Each year elementary and secondary students take 127 million tests of mental abilities. Unfortunately the way these tests are used often *magnifies* apparent differences in intelligence. Many schools use IQ tests to place students in "fast track" or "slow track" programs. However, it is usually just the "fact-track" students who receive training in cognitive skills, such as critical-thinking and problem-solving strategies. This means that on future IQ tests, such as those which screen job or college applicants, "slow-track" students are at an even *greater* disadvantage (Madaus, 1990; Tobias, 1989).

Reliability and Validity of Intelligence Tests

When a psychologist makes up a measurement scale of any kind, the psychologist has to prove two things to other scientists before they will accept the scale and use it themselves. First, the creator of the test must show that it is *reliable*. Second, the psychologist must provide evidence that the test is also *valid*.

At its simplest, the term "reliable" merely means that a test will yield the same results no matter how frequently you give it. A reliable test is free from chance effects which might vary from time to time (Walsh, 1989).

At its simplest, the term "validity" means that the test measures what it says that it does. However, Leona Tyler also notes that modern psychologists take a more complex view of the term. To Tyler, you cannot judge the validity of a test unless you know all of the current research showing just what a test does and does not measure. Determining the validity of a psychological scale, therefore, is both a complicated and continual undertaking (Tyler, 1973; Walsh, 1989).

With these simplified definitions in mind, let's examine both the reliability and the validity of intelligence tests.

ARE INTELLIGENCE TESTS RELIABLE?

If IQs were absolutely fixed at birth, psychologists would probably have little trouble making up highly reliable tests. However, intelligence tests actually measure your *present level of functioning,* not the underlying factor that Cattell calls "fluid intelligence." Thus, your IQ is always affected by your genes, your past experience, and your *present* situation.

If you are unmotivated when you take a test, or if you are worried about something or have a toothache, you probably will do more poorly than if you were "up" for the exam. In similar fashion, if you grew up in a deprived environment, or if you never learned to reason, your test scores won't be as high as they otherwise might have been.

Intelligence tests are much more reliable than are many other psychological scales. And when given under the best of circumstances, chance effects are reduced to a minimum.

As we noted, however, no two intelligence tests will yield identical scores. That's one of the reasons intelligence test results are now often quoted in percentiles. And even if you take the same test several times, your IQ may vary considerably depending on how you feel and what you have learned since the last time you took the test. Thus, your IQ score is not a fixed quantity.

ARE INTELLIGENCE TESTS VALID?

The term *validity* has several different meanings, and can be measured in several different ways. For our purposes, however, we can assume an intelligence test is valid if it successfully predicts how you will do in situations where you presumably need intelligence in order to succeed.

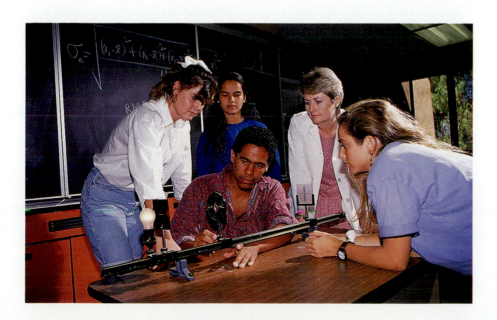

Because IQ test scores are correlated with school performance, they are often used to direct children into "fast track" and "slow track" programs.

Test builders usually offer their own carefully limited definition of what they think intelligence is, and then show that their particular instrument is valid within those limits. For instance, Binet and Simon assumed that intelligence was whatever mental properties were needed to succeed in French schools. Children who scored high on their tests generally got good grades and were rated by their teachers as being intelligent. Students who scored lower on the Binet-Simon test got lower school grades and were rated "less intelligent" by their teachers. Binet and Simon then used the correlations among test scores, teacher ratings, and grades to validate their intelligence test. And within the limits of their definition, Binet and Simon were correct.

The first indication that intelligence tests can be valid, therefore, is the fact that IQs have a high correlation with academic grades. A second indication is that IQs often predict how well people will do in various occupational levels. That is, if you have an IQ of 80, you probably will do better in an unskilled or semi-skilled job than you would trying to become a nuclear physicist. IQs can also predict which individuals are most likely to succeed *within* a given occupation. One way this might occur is through higher intellectual ability leading to better job knowledge, which in turn leads to better job performance (Barrett & Depinet, 1991; Hunter, 1983, 1986).

IQ scores can be a fairly valid indicator of performance in school and on the job (provided that the testees aren't given the kind of "special training" that Bloom and Broder used). A problem arises, however, when we use IQs to make judgments in situations where we know they don't yield valid predictions—in situations where IQ has practically nothing to do with performance.

In May 1990, the National Commission on Testing and Public Policy released a report called "From Gatekeeper to Gateway: Transforming Testing in America." The report recommends limitations on the way IQ tests can be used. It notes that too often schools and employers use tests to screen out promising students and competent employees, that scores can be influenced by irrelevant facts such as noise, and that most tests have cultural biases (Madaus, 1990). Let's consider this question in more detail.

IQ Tests and Bias

In the early days of intelligence testing, Paul Broca and Sir Frances Galton proposed that the size of your brain determined the amount of your intelligence. A century or so ago, Broca performed some very inexact measurements on brain size and incorrectly concluded that men were brighter than women and that whites were smarter than blacks.

Most modern psychologists reject Broca's notions about the superior mental abilities of males and whites. However, a few scientists do still cling to a belief in genetically determined racial differences. For example, in 1969, Arthur Jensen published an article in the *Harvard Educational Review* entitled "How Much Can We Boost IQ and Scholastic Achievement?" In this paper, and in many books and articles he has published subsequently, Jensen writes that blacks are genetically different from whites as far as intelligence goes. Jensen's writings have, to say the least, created a storm of controversy. Let's look at the evidence that Jensen cites, then at the counter-claims.

Jensen begins by quoting a national survey of 81 different studies of black-white IQs. According to this survey, blacks tend to average about 15 IQ points lower than do whites on standardized intelligence tests. Blacks also score somewhat below other disadvantaged minority groups, such as Hispanics. Jensen also claims that blacks from "upper-status" homes tend to obtain significantly lower test scores than do whites reared in similar circumstances. Jensen then attributes these differences to genes rather than to environmental influences, although he offers little in the way of reliable evidence to support his views on the genetic superiority of whites (Jensen, 1969, 1979).

1. (A) "handkerchief head" is
   (a) a cool cat
   (b) a porter
   (c) an uncle Tom
   (d) a hoddi
   (e) a preacher

2. Which word is most out of place here?
   (a) splib
   (b) blood
   (c) gray
   (d) spook
   (e) black

3. A "gas head" is a person who has a:
   (a) fast-moving car
   (b) stable of "lace"
   (c) "process"
   (d) habit of stealing cars
   (e) long jail record for arson

4. "Bo Diddley" is a:
   (a) game for children
   (b) down-home cheap wine
   (c) down-home singer
   (d) new dance
   (e) Moejoe call

5. If a man is called a "blood," then he is a:
   (a) fighter
   (b) Mexican-American
   (c) Negro
   (d) hungry hemophile
   (e) Redman or Indian

TABLE 11.2
THE CHITLING TEST[1]
[1]This IQ test was designed by Adrian Dove, a sociologist who is familiar with black ghetto culture. It probably seems as unfair to white middle-class culture as the tests designed by them appear to other culture groups. The answer to all the questions is (c). (Copyright © 1968 by Newsweek, Inc.)

However, as Robert Guthrie points out in his book, "Even the Rat Was White," the psychologists who constructed most of the widely used intelligence tests were almost all middle-class, white males. (For a different type of test see Table 11.2.) Most of them shared Jensen's view that intelligence is primarily an inherited trait. Thus, if blacks did poorly on standard intelligence tests, the test-makers *presumed* this difference was due to bad genes and not to bad environments. Guthrie also notes that, until recently, psychologists studying blacks tended to focus on *differences* between the races, not similarities (Guthrie, 1976).

In his book, "The Intelligence Men: Makers of the IQ Controversy," Raymond Fancher states that the study of intelligence is "unusual among scientific problems for the degree to which it interacts with the extra-scientific and sometimes even non-rational concerns of its investigators" (Fancher, 1985). With Fancher's words in mind, suppose we try to put aside our own cultural biases and look at the data on racial differences in IQs—and what factors presumably cause these differences.

How would it affect government policies and financial expenditures if it could be proved that IQ differences among racial subgroups were due to cultural rather than genetic factors?

THE PROFILE OF AMERICAN YOUTH SURVEY

In 1986, Darrell Bock and Elsie Moore published a report entitled "Advantage and Disadvantage: The Profile of American Youth Survey." The study, which was supported by both the U.S. Department of Labor and the Department of Defense, was an attempt to assess the cognitive development and vocational aptitudes of 12,000 Americans between the ages of 15 and 23.

The American Youth Survey data tend, at first glance, to support Jensen's views. On standardized intelligence tests, Hispanic young people tended to score below whites, and blacks tended to score (on the average) below Hispanics. However, Bock and Moore show rather conclusively that these differences are *not* due either to genetic endowment or to linguistic ability. Rather, Bock and Moore say:

> A more satisfactory explanation [for overall group performance differences on the tests] is simply that the communities represented. . . . maintain, for historical reasons, different norms, standards, and expectations concerning performance within the family, in school, and in other institutions that shape children's behavior. Young people adapt to these norms and apply their talents and energies accordingly (Bock & Moore, 1986).

Put more simply, the data from this survey suggest that young people take on the values of the culture they grow up in. If their subculture rewards them for learning "street smarts" rather than "analytical skills," the young people will do well in their own subcultures, but do poorly in school—and on standard intelligence tests that emphasize only one of the three types of thinking Sternberg has described (Church & Katigbak, 1988, 1992).

We can see further evidence for this position in a comparison of white children in the United States with their age-mates in Japan.

Academic psychologists (among others) sometimes use the term "disadvantaged" when referring to lower-class children (either black or white). What kind of cultural bias does the use of this term suggest?

CROSS-CULTURAL STUDIES OF INTELLIGENCE

Several recent studies have shown that Japanese children tend to score about 11 points *higher* on intelligence tests than do white American children of similar ages and socioeconomic status. Harold Stevenson, Hiroshi Azuma, and Kenji Hakuta describe some of the cultural differences that may lead to this cross-cultural difference in IQ scores.

First of all, Japanese children spend more hours per day in school than is the case in the United States and go to school more days of the year. Furthermore, they typically spend several hours a week outside of school in special "cram courses" designed to help them pass the nationwide exam that determines which children can enter college (and which can't). Students who don't pass the exam have problems getting good jobs and are usually considered "failures." As a result, the students' level of motivation to succeed in school may be much higher in Japan than in the United States.

Second, in Japan the husband traditionally has worked while the wife's main job has been that of making sure the children do well in school. If her children didn't pass the exam, their mother was considered a failure.

Third, in the United States, there are many more one-parent homes, and more families where both parents have jobs. Thus, in America, the parents typically spend less time per week tutoring their children in "school skills" than is the case in Japan.

Fourth, in Japan the use of coercive or physical discipline is much lower than in the United States. And, as we have already noted, children who are rewarded for improvement tend to have higher cognitive skills than do children who are physically punished for their mistakes (Power & Chapieski, 1986). Given these data, perhaps we shouldn't wonder that Japanese school children have higher IQs (d'Ailly, 1992; Stevenson et al., 1986).

Similar cultural factors are probably behind the tremendous academic success of recent immigrants from Asia (Geary et al., 1992). Although Asian-Americans make up only 2.4 percent of the American population, they constitute 17.1 percent of the undergraduates at Harvard, 18 percent at MIT, 27.3 percent at the University of

In addition to spending more time in school, most Japanese teenagers attend *juku,* or "cram school." These *juku* students wear headbands to indicate the level of study they have achieved.

California at Berkeley, and 35.1 percent at the University of California at Irvine (Butterfield, 1990). Psychologists Stanley Sue and Sumie Okazaki suggest that Asians are *forced* into education because of heavier restrictions on their upward mobility in non-educational areas (Sue & Okazaki, 1990, 1991).

However, scientist Susumu Tonegawa believes Asian-Americans have a cultural *disadvantage*. Tonegawa, who won the 1987 Nobel Prize in medicine for his pioneering studies on immunology, was born and raised in Japan. He did his graduate work and most of his award-winning research in the United States. In an interview in *Science,* Tonegawa states that he would not have won the Nobel Prize had he stayed in Japan, because creativity is punished rather than rewarded in most segments of Japanese society. Japanese education focuses almost entirely on "rote learning and memorization," Tonegawa claims (Marx, 1987).

In their "profile of American youth," Bock and Moore state that each society has its own values, as does each sub-culture within any given society. In middle- and upper-class America, and even more so in Japan and other Asian cultures, the emphasis in child rearing and in school is on rote memorization and the acquisition of "analytical skills," coupled with a strong motivation towards academic success. Grades and intelligence test scores are, therefore, a direct measure of our cultural biases, not of some "biologically determined trait" that we might call general intelligence. Blacks, Hispanics, and lower-class whites will continue to do poorly on intelligence tests, Bock and Moore imply, until we do one of two things: First, we could change our "culturally biased definition" of what "intelligence" is, and then alter the educational process itself to reflect the new definition. Or second, we could find some way to incorporate *the same set of cultural values and child-rearing practices* into all segments of society. To achieve either change, Bock and Moore say, would take "decades" (Bock & Moore, 1986).

How would following Bock and Moore's two suggestions reduce criticisms of IQ tests?

Like most of our abilities, intellectual capacity appears to be the result of both inherited abilities and environmental opportunities; IQ tests are just our best attempt to measure one aspect of this capacity. We will have more to say about the interaction between nature and nurture as we turn our attention next to development in infancy and early childhood.

SUMMARY

1. **Cognitive psychology** is an approach to the study of human behavior which emphasizes intellectual **processing of information** in order to deal with the world.

2. There are two types of cognitive concepts: **natural** and **artificial.**

3. There are three levels of concepts: **superordinate, basic,** and **subordinate.** Basic concepts are the easiest to deal with cognitively.

4. One way the mind puts objects in concepts or categories is by using **attributes** of the objects.

5. Humans often create **prototypes** of basic concepts to speed concept formation, although this sometimes leads to **fuzzy concepts.**

6. **Problem solving** typically begins with **goal setting** and a description of the **original state** or **baseline.** It continues with **identifying the rules, trying possible solutions,** and **conceptualizing the problem.**

7. Finding solutions to problems may be inhibited by **functional fixedness,** a kind of **fixation.** Breaking the fixation involves **reconceptualizing** the problem.

8. **Creative thinking** is difficult to define, but it is an ability we all have which is encouraged by reward and inhibited by criticism and punishment.

9. Recent research on problem solving has focused on **personality factors** associated with problem solving, **real-life** problem solving, and **metacognition,** or "thinking about thinking."

10. The study of **artificial intelligence** is a search for ways to program computers to **reason** (process inputs) as human beings do.

11. Computers typically must use **algorithms** or exact formulas to solve problems. Humans tend to use **heuristics,** or "rules of thumb."

12. Studies suggest a child may learn **10 new words a day** and by age 6 may have acquired a vocabulary of **14,000 words.**

13. **Language acquisition** refers to learning both **words** and **rules** for using language correctly. Included in language acquisition are learning of **phonemes, semantics, syntax,** and **pragmatics.**

14. Children worldwide between 3 and 7 months of age **babble** by uttering repetitive **phonemes** such as "da da da" but do not reproduce all the sounds in most languages. Parents **selectively reinforce** some babbled sounds, and urge infants to imitate those phonemes not produced during babbling.

15. At about 1 year of age, children produce **holophrastic,** or one-word, sentences, and produce two-word sentences at about the 18th month. Many of the sentences are **telegraphic speech** that contains just the important words. Most children produce complex sentences by age 2.

16. Some **linguists** believe humans have an innate tendency to process information in linguistic form, which they call the **deep structure of language.** Behaviorists, however, believe language production is entirely learned.

17. Chimpanzees have been taught to "speak" 100 or more words and phrases, and dolphins have learned to comprehend many different signs. Whether these "languages" have **grammar** and whether they can communicate in **symbols** is still a matter of debate.

18. Although language is often involved in thought, it does not appear to be necessary *for* thought. And although **language influences thinking,** there is not much evidence that it seriously *restricts* thinking.

19. The first true intelligence scale was the **Binet-Simon** test, which measured **mental age.**

20. **Intelligence Quotient,** or IQ, is often defined as mental age divided by **chronological age** times 100. Most modern intelligence tests measure IQ using **standard scores** or **percentiles** rather than mental age.

21. Charles Spearman listed two types of intelligence, a **general** or "g" factor, and several **special** or "s" factors.

22. Raymond Cattell claims there are two intellectual factors, **fluid intelligence,** which is inherited, and **crystallized intelligence,** which involves learned skills.

23. According to Robert Sternberg's **triarchic theory,** there are three types of intelligence: **analytical,** or componential; **creative,** or experiential; and **contextual** intelligence, or "street smarts."

24. Children brought up in deprived or **disadvantaged circumstances** generally have lower IQ scores than do children brought up in **stimulating environments.** Making the child's environment more stimulating can often help increase the child's **IQ.**

26. Research suggests that children whose mothers use **coercive discipline** tend to have lower IQs than do children whose mothers train them to exercise **self-control.**

27. Individuals who have failed to learn the **analytical skills** required to do well in school can often raise their test scores by learning **step-by-step reasoning.**

28. Intelligence tests are fairly **reliable,** but tend to be **valid** only when used to predict school performance or job performance where **analytical reasoning** is considered the "mark of intelligence."

29. There are **performance** differences among cultural groups in the United States, but research suggests these differences are due to **cultural norms,** not to genetic differences among racial groups.

30. Because of the strong emphasis on school performance and rote memory in Japan, Japanese children tend to have **higher IQs** than do American children. However, Japanese children may well be **less creative** than are youngsters in the United States.

---

1. *When you think of the basic concept "bird," what example first comes to mind?*

   Most people in North America think of a robin or sparrow when they think of the concept bird. If other birds have been more common in your experience (perhaps you breed pigeons), you might have a different response. In other cultures another bird, such as the eagle, might form the prototype (Hage & Miller, 1976).

2. *If you told your household robot to bring you a "chair," and the machine brought you the head . . . ?*

   The robot's prototype of "chair" is either very fuzzy, including everything that is called a chair, or its prototype is limited to the concept of occupational positions.

3. *How would you mount a candle on a bulletin board using only the candle, some thumb tacks, and a box of matches?*

   You need to break your fixation of match boxes functioning only as containers, and consider that it contains rigid right-angles which could be used as a shelf. Insert the thumb tacks through the bottom of the box into the bulletin board, and stand the candle on one of the horizontal sides of the box.

4. *How does "functional fixedness" relate to the perceptual principle that "you see what you expect to see?"*

   Like the perceptual principle, functional fixedness limits our present experience as the result of our past learning. Past experience gives us expectations for certain similar situations; past experience tells us the (usual) functions of certain objects.

5. *How does Maier's experiment support the belief that factors that influence cognition are not entirely conscious?*

   Some subjects were guided to the solution by watching the rope move as it draped over the experimenter's shoulder, but they apparently *were not aware* of the influence of this experience.

6. *What do you think would happen if a "creative" individual came up with a new idea? Would people be happy to hear about it? Why or why not?*

   New ideas are not always received well. Some factors which might influence this situation are the creativity and flexibility of the audience, and the reputation and social esteem of the person with the new idea.

7. *What have you learned about the socialization of men and women in our culture that could explain the findings described above?*

ANSWERS FOR THOUGHT

Very often men are not expected (nor taught) to be as socially competent as women. The ideal for men is often a "no-nonsense, direct approach." For women, a greater emphasis is placed on getting along with other people and being cooperative.

8. *Today, computer chess programs can beat human players, even those who have . . . ?*

When a human being "plays a million games," he or she tries out various heuristics based on past experience, present circumstances, and general patterns on the board. The human being then discards the ineffective heuristics. Successful heuristics may be described to a large extent by logical rules of chess (and thus learned by computers). But heuristics may also include intuitions about an opponent's personal characteristics, the environment, and the social setting which would be virtually impossible to program into a computer.

9. *Can you think of other reasons you might have difficulties recalling early experiences?*

One other reason is that your brain continues to develop after you are born (connections between the hippocampus and the cortex, for example), and it may not have been sufficiently developed at the time of these early experiences to encode them properly.

10. *Is speech in human beings innately determined, or acquired through learning?*

The tendency towards oral expression appears to be innate; the shaping of this behavior into language is the result of learning. The development of language takes place during a time of life when human beings are apparently especially "sensitive" to this type of learning.

11. *If you isolated two infants at birth, would the children learn to speak spontaneously? If they did . . . ?*

The two infants would probably learn to communicate in various ways, including orally. Their "language" would probably be a very crude form of "grunts" and gestures. At this basic level languages between different pairs would probably be quite similar. Skinner would say their "grammar" would depend on their experience and so could be quite different. Chomsky would say their "grammar" developed from an inherited structure and so would be similar.

12. *Several studies indicate that men use language differently from women. What kind of differences would you expect? Why?*

In conversations, (in America, Britain, and France) men have been found to take control more often, to interrupt more, and to be more direct and assertive in their language. Women tend to be more attentive, personal, emotional, and concerned with collaboration and mutual understanding (for numerous studies supporting these generalizations see Pillon et al., 1992). Similar differences emerge in their writing, where men are less emotional, and focus on themselves and their own point of view. Women are more likely to discuss their relationship with other people, and to acknowledge the legitimacy of opposing points of view (Peterson, 1991; Rubin & Greene, 1992; Shuman, 1992). While these tendencies have been observed for some time, there is evidence that the differences are decreasing, possibly as a result of changing sex-role stereotypes (Pearson & Lee, 1992; Pillon, Degauquier & Duquesne, 1992; Rubin & Greene, 1992). This trend suggests that gender differences in the use of language are learned.

13. *Do the words we use to refer to certain positions, such as chairman, fireman, and paperboy, restrict . . . ?*

Terms which include gender-specific components reveal basic assumptions which our culture makes (or has made in the past) about these positions. When we use these terms they tend to restrict our thinking about the people who could fill them. Could a *woman* be a fire*man*? Could a *man* be a paper*boy*?

14. *How would you go about designing a measure of intelligence? What does this tell you about your own definition of intelligence?*

You might pick out people that you consider intelligent, and see what's different about them. You might make up some kind of test that you think intelligent people, but not unintelligent people, could pass. Your ideas of intelligence would be shown in the kind of person you selected, or in the kind of test you designed.

15. *Do you think "street smarts" are the same thing as "book smarts"?*

"Street smarts" and "book smarts" certainly appear different. However, if you believe intelligence is a single basic characteristic, such as "the ability to learn," you may see little difference. Both may be expressions of the same underlying trait; different only because of different experiences.

16. *In which of Sternberg's three "types" of intelligence would you expect school teachers (and other academics) to be highest? Why?*

School teachers and other academics would need to be high in Sternberg's first type, "analytical or componential intelligence." They need these abilities to understand academic studies, to score well on academic tests, and to pass academic entrance exams. They *may* also be high on the other two "types," but they wouldn't need to be.

17. *Suppose you grew up in an environment that rewarded you for answering questions quickly rather than . . . ?*

This kind of early experience would not be rewarded in school or on intelligence tests. The individual with this background would have to learn a new way of responding—in a more careful, analytical way—if he or she is to succeed in an academic setting or do well on intelligence tests.

18. *In terms of "street smarts," which is better: being "right," or being "quick and aggressive?"*

Being right is probably less important than being quick and aggressive in "street smarts."

19. *How would it affect government policies and financial expenditures if it could be proved that IQ differences . . . ?*

Governments would be under greater pressure to equalize environmental factors if these could be shown to be the sole cause of differences among racial subgroups.

20. *Academic psychologists (among others) sometimes use the term "disadvantaged" when referring to . . . ?*

It suggests that they consider their own standards of intelligence and education to be superior to those of the lower-class children.

21. *How would following Bock and Moore's two suggestions reduce criticisms of IQ tests?*

First, if we changed our "culturally biased definition" of intelligence, we would recognize that IQ tests measure only a limited part of overall intellectual ability. IQ tests do fairly well at predicting academic performance (their original purpose); for this they deserve little criticism. Second, if we could "incorporate the same set of cultural values into all segments of society," systematic difference in IQ scores would cease to exist. Hence, IQ tests would no longer be criticized for being biased. (Note that the "bias" is actually in the broader culture which limits the opportunities of certain economic and racial groups. When IQ tests are used to predict academic performance, they do so accurately and fairly. To say the tests are biased is to "shoot the messenger of bad news." The bias is in the culture that produces the differences, not in the test that reveals them.)

CHAPTER 12

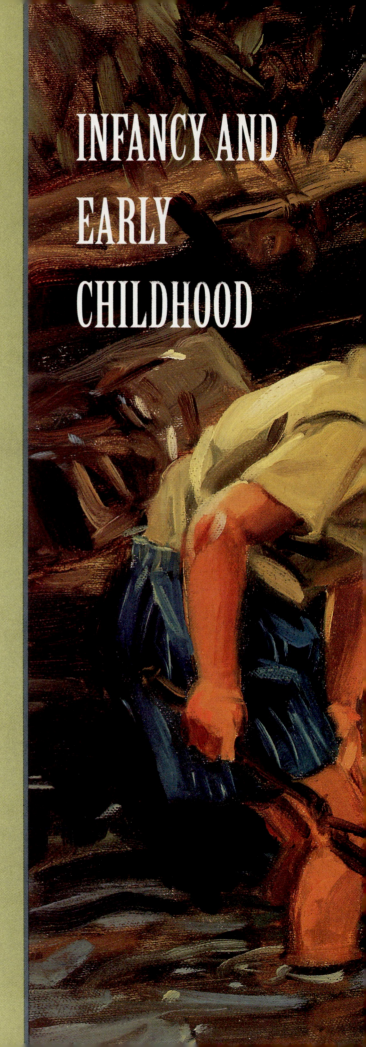

INFANCY AND EARLY CHILDHOOD

Whether I shall turn out to be the hero of my own life, or whether that station will be held by anybody else, these pages must show. To begin my life with the beginning of my life, I record that I was born (as I have been informed and believe) on a Friday, at twelve o'clock at night. It was remarked that the clock began to strike, and I began to cry, simultaneously.

In consideration of the day and hour of my birth, it was declared by the nurse, and by some sage women in the neighborhood who had taken a lively interest in me several months before there was any possibility of our becoming personally acquainted, first, that I was destined to be unlucky in life; and secondly, that I was privileged to see ghosts and spirits; both of these gifts inevitably attaching, as they believed, to all unlucky infants of either gender, born towards the small hours on a Friday night.

I need say nothing here on the first head, because nothing can show better than my history whether that prediction was verified or falsified by the result. On the second branch of that question, I will only remark, that unless I ran through that part of my inheritance while I was still a baby, I have not come into it yet. But I do not at all complain of having been kept out of this property; and if anybody else should be in the present enjoyment of it, he is heartily welcome to keep it.

CHARLES DICKENS
DAVID COPPERFIELD

In the previous 11 chapters, we have been pulling you apart. We have discussed the biological and psychological *sub-systems* that make up your body and mind. These sub-systems included your neurons and the various parts of your brain, your sensory inputs and perceptions, your cognitions, and your motives and memories. Now we will begin to put you back together. In the next four chapters, we will combine these bits and pieces to form a bigger picture of what you are like and how you got to be that way.

In this chapter and the next, we will look at human development across the life span. The "life span" approach to human development traces the maturation of a "typical" individual from birth through middle age to old age and death. According to child psychologist Margarita Azmitia, "The term *life span perspective* . . . entails both the holistic delineation of age periods (e.g., integrating biological, physical, social, and cognitive development during infancy) and the delineation of connections between age periods (e.g., how achievements during infancy influence the preschooler's development)" (Azmitia, 1987). Life span theorists look at the "whole person" as she or he passes through various stages, or "life crises."

In this chapter we will focus primarily on infancy and early childhood. In Chapter 13, we will look at the years from adolescence through adulthood to old age. And in Chapters 14 and 15, we will put all this material together in quite a different manner as we look at *personality*—what it is, how it develops, how psychologists try to measure it, and what can go wrong with it.

But before we can cover any of these topics we must first discuss three important theoretical issues. As we will see, psychologists studying human development often organize their research efforts (and their theories) around these three issues.

DEVELOPMENTAL ISSUES

The three theoretical issues that run through the literature on developmental psychology all have to do with change. They are:

- The matter of the *amount* of change that takes place.
- The question of whether changes are *gradual* or *abrupt*.
- The issue of whether *nature or nurture* controls change.

Let's begin by looking at each of these three major issues briefly.

Changes: Small or Large?

Give me the children until they are seven and anyone may have them afterwards.

ST. FRANCIS XAVIER

Are you still growing? During late adolescence, or early adulthood, most young people stop growing physically. They may add a few pounds during their middle years, and lose weight during the final period of life, but their physical growth tends to stop a few years after puberty. But does *psychological* development follow this same pattern?

Sigmund Freud thought it did. As you will see in Chapter 14, he believed your personality was "set" by the time you were 6 or 7 years old. Thereafter, you might *regress*, but you surely didn't *progress* very much. As you can see, Freud took the view that, at least after early childhood, developmental change was slight.

Most modern-day psychologists disagree with Freud. Indeed, the entire thrust of the "life-span development" viewpoint is to demonstrate that, psychologically speaking, you never stop growing.

According to Jerome Kagan, the main exception to the rule of growth and change, has to do with temperament. Kagan notes that the temperamental trait "that seems to be the strongest, best-preserved throughout life and most likely to be genetic has to do with infants who, on the one hand, are wary, timid, vigilant, shy and fearful or, on the other hand, are outgoing, bold and sociable." According to Kagan, "These qualities can be seen toward the end of the first year and are obvious in children two to three years of age" (Kagan, 1987). Some researchers believe that differences in temperment may even be observed before birth (Eaton & Saudino, 1992). However, Kagan also notes that at least 40 percent of the timid children he has studied became less inhibited as they grew older. Thus, he says, it is the *interaction* between genetic tendency and environment that determines even such traits as sociability, arousal, and timidity (Kagan, 1986, 1989).

In this chapter, we will present some findings that seem to support the growth and change position—and some data that seem to contradict that position. We then will discuss the matter more fully in Chapter 13.

Give us the child for eight years, and it will be a Bolshevist forever.
NIKOLAI LENIN

Research findings aside, would you like to *think* that you will continue to change?

Changes: Gradual or Abrupt?

Physical growth often occurs in spurts. You may have stayed about the same height for a period of time, and then grown several inches during a single year. Both Sigmund Freud and Jean Piaget believed that the human personality followed this same physical pattern. That is, they said that the mind goes through several *stages* of growth. Each stage is marked by a period of fairly sudden change followed by a period of consolidation. Put simply, stage theorists believe development occurs much as promotions do in the military—suddenly you are no longer a corporal but a sergeant, with new duties and new responsibilities.

As we will see, there is still considerable debate as to whether psychological development occurs in stages, or whether it occurs fairly smoothly and continuously.

Although infants may inherit traits of temperament, even identical twins tend to exhibit different traits as they develop.

Have you ever been told you were "just going through a phase"? How did this make you feel? Is this a gradual or an abrupt-change position?

Changes: Nature or Nurture?

There is probably no issue more hotly debated in developmental psychology than the question of what is learned and what is innately determined. "Like father; like son," we say—but *why?*

The issue really boils down to determining how nature and nurture interact (Bjorklund, 1989; Scarr, 1992). Even the "gifts" with which David Copperfield was presumably endowed at birth (as he says in the quotation which began this chapter), were identified by his *culture* and proclaimed through the nurse and some "sage women." Thus, we cannot really discuss the nature-nurture controversy in a sensible manner unless we know the social environment the child grows up in, and what sorts of *values* that society places on children and childhood.

Do you think parents should be allowed to sell their children as slaves, or even to murder their children, if the parents so desired? If you answer "no," why not? What does your answer to this question tell you about your own perceptions of what childhood should be?

Issues and Culture

We have identified three "developmental issues" because questions raised by these issues have guided much of the research on development. It is important to note, however, that the cultural context is also an important influence on the direction of research. As psychologist Frank Kessel puts it, in recent years "developmental psychology shows signs of becoming increasingly aware of its social, cultural, and broadly historical contexts or dimensions" (quoted in Bronfenbrenner et al., 1986). Put more bluntly, developmental psychologists are beginning to realize that the society in which *they* live determines—in part—not only their theories, but also the experimental facts they discover in their laboratory studies (Lawrence & Adler, 1992).

William Kessen surely had the same idea in mind when he wrote that "Both the child and child psychology are 'cultural inventions'" (Kessen, 1983). What Kessen means, of course, is that our notions of what childhood *should be* help determine the sorts of developmental theories we adopt.

And our notions of what childhood *should be* have changed dramatically over the years (Boas, 1990). Robert Trotter notes, "Incredible as it may seem to today's doting parents, infants have not always been seen as bundles of joy. Throughout most of human history, in fact, they were treated as mewling, puking bundles of trouble, easier to be rid of than to rear. Infanticide, the murder of babies, appears to have been a common practice in many ancient societies and was not even outlawed in Rome until A.D. 374" (Trotter, 1987). And even when children were allowed to live, they were not always kept by their parents. Until 300 years ago, many children in western Europe were routinely sold into slavery. And as recently as 150 years ago in England, middle-class parents often "farmed out" their infants—that is, gave them to servants to rear—until the children were old enough to be sent away to school or put to work. Quite obviously, then, the study of human development in Europe 300 years ago would have yielded quite different "facts and theories" from today.

Cultural expectations of what childhood should be vary greatly around the world.

It is equally true, of course, that certain *fairly constant* aspects of the developmental process have helped determine what our culture is like. Fetuses still spend about nine months in the womb before they are born, and they don't start walking or talking until a year or so after birth. These "facts" haven't changed over the course of human history.

However, it will surely help you understand the developmental process better if you realize one thing: Most of the important theoretical battles we will discuss in this and later chapters involve *social values* as much as experimental "facts."

Now that we have introduced these three major issues in developmental psychology, let's turn our attention to three main areas of change: physical, cognitive, and social development.

PHYSICAL DEVELOPMENT

As you move through life, you develop and change physically, mentally, and socially. At certain periods in your life one or two of these areas of development become more important than the other(s). Let's begin with the most important type of development which took place during your early life—your physical growth. We will look first at genetic origins, then prenatal and neonatal development, and finally, developmental possibilities and limitations.

Genetic Development

As we noted in Chapter 2, you began life as a single cell. All of your physical development was programmed into the genes on 46 chromosomes in this cell. Twenty-three of these chromosomes came from your mother, and were present in the egg cell before it was fertilized. The other 23 chromosomes were contributed at fertilization by your father's sperm cell.

Besides carrying many different traits from your ancestors, the chromosomes contributed by the sperm and egg cells differ in one very important respect: The 23rd chromosome of the sperm cell can be either the large X type or the smaller Y type. The 23rd chromosome of the egg cell is *always* a large X type.

If an X-type sperm is the first to enter the egg cell, the fertilized egg will of course have an XX 23rd chromosome pair, and the child will be female. If a Y-type sperm fertilizes the egg, the 23rd chromosome pair will be of the XY variety and the child will be a male (see Figure 12.1).

TURNER'S SYNDROME

Because the human reproductive system is so complicated, it occasionally breaks down. Sometimes the 23rd chromosome pair does not divide properly and the child ends up with but a single 23rd chromosome—always an X type—or with one or more additional X or Y chromosomes.

In what is called **Turner's syndrome,** the child's cells contain just a single X chromosome. Individuals who experience this chromosomal problem have female genitalia but lack ovaries. If given injections of female hormones at puberty, they develop the normal behavioral and physical characteristics of an adult female. Turner's syndrome occurs in about 1 in 3,000 live female births (Santrock, 1990).

There are rare cases where an infant is genetically an XX female, but is born with male genitalia because one of the X chromosomes contains a tiny fragment of the Y chromosome that "codes" for the male sex organs. This "XX male" condition occurs about once in each 20,000 births (Edwards, 1988).

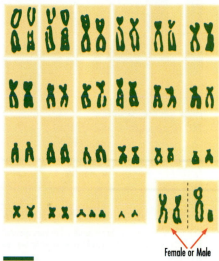

Female or Male

FIGURE 12.1

Human beings have 23 pairs of chromosomes. The 23rd pair is either XX or XY and determines the person's sex. If the 21st pair has an extra member, the person will suffer from trisomy 21, or Down's syndrome (as shown in the photograph near the end of this chapter).

Turner's syndrome (SIN-drome).   A collection of symptoms (a "syndrome") associated with a woman's having a single X 23rd chromosome, rather than the normal XX 23rd chromosome. The woman will be sterile, have some learning difficulties, and in some cases have webbing of the neck or fingers.

Kleinfelter's syndrome (rhymes with "MINE-belter"). A set of related physical characteristics (small penis and testes, high-pitched voice, and little facial hair) found in males who have an extra X chromosome.

XYY Male. A male with an extra Y chromosome; associated with excess amounts of testosterone, which may lead to earlier puberty, greater height, and a tendency towards impulsive behavior.

Chicago serial killer Richard Speck's lawyers pleaded for leniency in his murder conviction because he was an XYY male.

KLINEFELTER'S SYNDROME

A child with an XXY 23rd chromosome will be physically a male, with penis and testicles, but may have many feminine characteristics. This condition, known as **Klinefelter's syndrome,** occurs in about one child out of every 900.

Sex chromosome abnormalities (SCAs) do not always produce great difficulties (Miller, 1986). Indeed, as Daniel Berch and Bruce Bender put it, "The developmental difficulties associated with abnormal sex chromosomes are not always as devastating as once thought. . . . It is likely that many SCA children will lead normal, productive lives if they are reared by sensitive, realistic parents in a supportive environment" (Berch & Bender, 1987).

"XYY" MALES

About 1 boy in 1,000 has two Y chromosomes and one X. The **XYY male** is typically taller than average, and most XYY males reach sexual puberty a year or more before the normal XY male does. About half of the XYY males suffer from moderate to severe acne—a much higher percentage than among normal men. Promiscuous sexual practices and patterns of homosexual behavior are much more frequent in XYY males than in XY males. And, for reasons we still don't understand, the XYY condition appears primarily in white males.

Research reported in the 1960s and 1970s suggested that an abnormally large number of XYY males turn up in hospital wards reserved for the criminally insane. Some scientists at first believed the extra Y chromosome *caused* the criminal behavior to occur. However, current thinking takes a different view. The extra *male* chromosome causes the boy's adrenal glands to secrete abnormal amounts of testosterone during his development. This excess testosterone seems responsible both for the early onset of puberty and for the acne (Plomin et al., 1980). However, excess amounts of testosterone also typically lead to an increase in *impulsive behaviors*.

Most XYY males who get into trouble with the law appear to come from lower-class families in which the parents apparently lacked the social skills needed to teach such an impulsive child how to control himself. XYY males born to middle- or upper-class families seldom show this lack of self-discipline, and thus seldom end up in prisons or mental hospitals. Thus, the XYY male is at risk only if he is born to parents who fail to give him adequate training in self-control during his early years. It is the *interaction* between genes and social environment that causes the problem, not the genes alone.

Some XYY males accused of crimes have asked to be pardoned, claiming their genetic disability "made them do it." If you were on the jury, what would your thinking be?

TRISOMY-21

Occasionally the 21st chromosome pair does not divide properly, and the child is born with three 21st chromosomes rather than the normal pair. This **trisomy-21** condition leads to a type of mental, physical, and behavioral deficiency called Down's syndrome. In the past, the mental retardation often associated with trisomy-21 was blamed on the genetic abnormality. However, recent research suggests that a Down's syndrome child need not experience severe psychological problems, provided the child receives special treatment starting at birth. We will discuss this matter more fully at the end of this chapter.

Trisomy-21 (TRY-so-me). From the Greek words *tri*, meaning "three," and *soma*, meaning "body." The modern term for mongolism, or Down's syndrome. A relatively common form of birth defect in which the facial features of the person somewhat resemble Asian or Mongolian characteristics.

Many other disorders also have a genetic basis and can be predicted from genetic testing. What is your attitude towards testing? When should it take place? What is the purpose of testing?

Prenatal Development

At the moment of conception, you were no more than a single fertilized egg cell locked away in your mother's body. But within 24 hours after your conception, that original egg cell had grown large enough to divide into two "daughter" cells. (We use the term "daughter" to mean one of two new cells derived from the original cell—even if the child will develop into a son.) In the next 24 hours the daughter cells will divide again, creating four cells. Within a third 24-hour period, all four of these cells will divide once more.

While this cell division goes on, the group of cells travels slowly down a tiny tube to the mother's womb. About 6 days after fertilization, the rapidly forming human being attaches itself to the wall of the womb (Hole, 1990). At this point in your own life, you were about 0.5 millimeters (0.02 inches) in size (Clark, 1985).

CELLULAR DIFFERENTIATION

Some 2 weeks after your life started, a remarkable change occurred in the tiny cluster of cells that made up your rapidly forming body. Up until this point, all of your cells were pretty much identical—because the commands from the chromosomes were identical. But 13 to 14 days after fertilization, some of the chromosomes began giving out slightly different sets of "command" instructions. As a result, these cells began to produce slightly different proteins (and other materials). As these new proteins and other molecules appeared, they forced the cells to *differentiate*—that is, to take on different shapes, sizes, and functions.

By the 14th or 15th day of your life, you were made up of three clearly different groups of cells. One of these groups developed into what we call the **ectoderm,** a technical term that means "outer skin." Eventually these cells became your skin, your sense organs, and your nervous system. Another group of cells, on instructions from their chromosomes, developed into what we term the **mesoderm,** or "middle skin." These cells eventually became your muscles, bone, and blood. A third group of cells received instructions to become **endoderm,** or "inner skin." These cells turned into your digestive system.

When this differentiation into the three "derms" occurred, 2 weeks after conception, you were a hollow ball about 2.5 millimeters (0.1 inch) in size, and technically you were then an **embryo.** Approximately 6 weeks later—some 2 months after conception—the three types of cells arranged themselves into a recognizable human form, and you could then be called a **fetus** (Hole, 1990).

THE PLACENTA

Developing cells, like developing children, are unusually sensitive to the environments they find themselves in. Fortunately, as you grew within your mother's womb, a part of her womb called the **placenta** protected you from dangerous chemicals that might be in her body. This placenta acted as a barrier, blocking out most of the substances in your mother's blood that might have harmed you.

Illness can cause the pregnant woman's body to secrete somewhat different chemicals than usual. If these chemicals (or the germs that cause them) infiltrate the placenta, they can upset the normal development of the fetus. If a woman has German measles during the 3rd month of her pregnancy, for instance, the child is often born badly retarded. The AIDS virus can also pass through the placenta, infecting the child before birth.

Various drugs also pass through the placenta and affect the fetus. For example, if the mother is addicted to morphine or cocaine during pregnancy, the infant will be born with an addiction. Smoking may also be harmful. Smoking increases the level of carbon monoxide in the mother's blood, leading to oxygen deprivation and possible damage in the fetus (Mactutus & Fechter, 1984). Mothers who smoke heavily

Ectoderm (ECK-toh-durm). *Ekto* is the Greek word meaning "outer." *Derma* is the Greek word for "skin." A dermatologist (durr-mah-TOLL-oh-jist) is a medical doctor who specializes in treating skin diseases.

Mesoderm (MEE-so-derm). The "middle skin." The Greek word *mesos* means "in the center."

Endoderm (EN-doh-durm). The "inner skin." The Greek word *endon* means "inside" or "within."

Embryo (EM-bree-oh). An unborn child from the time of conception to the second or third month of development, when the child takes on more distinct human form and is thereafter called a fetus. From the Greek word meaning "to swell within."

Fetus (FEE-tuss). An unborn child after its second or third month in the womb, when it begins to take on more distinct human characteristics. Prior to this time, the child is referred to as an embryo.

Placenta (plah-SENT-ah). The organ inside a woman's womb that links the child's blood system with the mother's. Many drugs, such as cocaine, alcohol, and thalidomide, can cross the placental barrier and affect the fetus. Some harmful chemicals, however, are screened out by the placenta before they can affect the fetus or embryo directly.

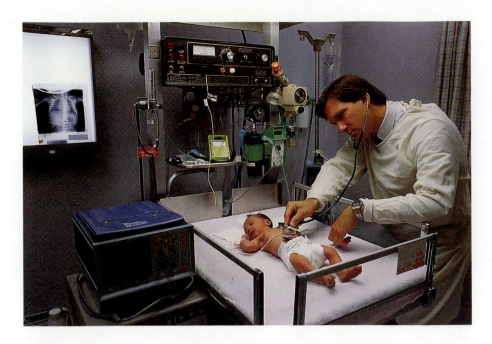

Like certain other diseases and substances, the AIDS virus can cross the placenta and infect or otherwise harm the infant before birth.

Fetal alcohol syndrome, or FAS. A developmental disorder associated with consumption of alcohol by the mother during pregnancy. The child is born smaller than normal; often has malformations of the eyes, ears, and mouth; and may suffer from mental retardation and other physical and psychological abnormalities.

are more likely to miscarry or give birth to underweight or premature babies. A woman who smokes during pregnancy has a 27 percent higher chance of her infant dying immediately before, during, or after birth (Matarazzo, 1984).

Alcohol can also affect the fetus by damaging developing muscles and restricting oxygen supply through the umbilical cord (Altura et al., 1982). The result can be widespread damage, including low birth weight, facial and body abnormalities, poor sucking responses, brain-wave abnormalities, sleep disturbances, short attention span, restlessness, irritability, hyperactivity, learning disabilities, and motor problems.

Most alcohol-affected children do not experience all of these problems (only about 1 in 10 do). However, a cluster of these symptoms appears in children of drinking mothers often enough to prompt researchers to give the problem a name—**fetal alcohol syndrome** (FAS). FAS affects more than 40,000 American babies each year (about 1 in 750 newborns) (Papalia & Olds, 1990). FAS is now the third largest cause of birth defects in the U.S. and the major cause of mental retardation (Abel & Sokol, 1987; Peterson & Lowe, 1992; Warren & Bast, 1988).

Some researchers caution against the simple conclusion that a certain (large) amount of alcohol triggers a *syndrome* or specific cluster of symptoms (Maurer & Maurer, 1988). The danger in this approach, they say, is that it relegates the problem to a small number of alcoholic mothers. They argue that alcohol consumption should be viewed as an unhealthful habit with a general tendency to induce a wide variety of birth defects. No safe level or pattern of drinking has been identified, including a single binge, frequent small amounts, or rare indulgences. Both the U.S. Surgeon General and the March of Dimes Birth Defects Foundation warn pregnant women to avoid alcohol entirely.

EFFECTS OF PHYSICAL DEPRIVATION

Your genetic blueprint specified in rather general terms what you would be like and how you would grow. Orders from the chromosomes in each cell, always bring the genetic blueprint to life. But environmental circumstances can either speed up or retard physical growth and development.

If a pregnant woman experiences starvation, her body protects the fetus by giving it almost all the resources the woman's body has available to it. Still, the child may be born much smaller than usual. If food-deprived children receive enough to eat immediately after birth, however, they usually catch up to the size their genetic blueprints had set for their normal development.

For example, consider a study on Korean children reported by Myron Winick and his associates. During the Korean conflict in the 1950s, many very young children in that Asian country were separated from their parents and were placed in orphanages. Most of these youngsters suffered from severe malnutrition before they entered the institutions. After the hostilities ended, some of these children returned to their war-shattered homes. But many others were placed in adoptive homes in the United States. After several years of good care in the United States, *all* of these children were taller and stronger than the average child who remained in Korea (Winick et al., 1975).

It would seem that your genes *set limits* for your physical development. But it is the environment you were reared in that determines *where within these limits* your actual growth will fall.

Neonatal Development

As an infant, as soon as your muscles, sense organs, and nerves formed completely, you began to use them. But much of your nervous system did not develop fully until you were a year or two old. Virtually all neurons were *present* at birth, but new connections continued to form between them. Some parts of your nervous system, such as your corpus callosum, continued to mature for many years.

Children develop at different speeds, in part because of their environments, but also because they follow different genetic schedules. For example, most children begin to walk between 12 and 18 months of age. No matter how much coaxing and practice the parents may give their 6-month-old child, the youngster will not walk significantly sooner than if the parents had simply let the child alone. However, encouraging children to practice such basic skills as walking increases parent-child interaction and so may have a number of positive side-effects.

How might early encouragement affect a child's later social behavior?

CULTURAL DIFFERENCES

In many cultures, infants often spend the first year or so of their lives bound to a board or bundled tightly inside a bag carried on their mothers' backs. Their mothers release these children from their restraints for only an hour or two each day, so the children have little chance to practice motor skills. Yet their muscular development is not retarded. They creep, crawl, and walk at about the same ages as do children who are not restrained (Chisholm, 1983).

The practice of "bundling" infants is more common in the Orient than it is in Africa and the Western world. The reason for this difference may lie in part in subtle genetic differences among the races of the world. According to a report by Daniel Freedman and Marilyn DeBoer, children in Europe, Africa, and America tend to be much more active and irritable than are Asian infants. White and black youngsters will usually struggle when confined, but Asian and Native American infants accept restraint rather passively. Asian children typically continue to be much less active physically during their developmental years than are white or black children. Freedman and DeBoer believe these behavioral differences are caused by genetic factors, for Asian children born and reared in the United States respond like infants in China and Japan, not as white and black American infants do (Freedman & DeBoer, 1979).

Support for the Freedman and DeBoer position comes from a study by James Chisholm, who compared Navajo and "Anglo" infants who were "bundled" by their

In cultures where children are bundled they have much less opportunity to practice motor skills. Yet they creep, crawl, and walk at about the same age as children who have not been restricted.

mothers. Both groups of mothers began weaning when the child's protests to the bundling board became excessive. Chisholm reports that the average age of weaning for the "Anglo" children was 5.9 months, while it was 10.3 months for the Navajo infants. Chisholm believes this difference in weaning times reflects a genetic difference in irritability between white and Native American infants (Chisholm, 1983).

What other explanations for Chisholm's results can you think of?

CRITICAL PERIODS

Many psychologists believe that the best time for a child to learn a given skill is when the child's body is just mature enough to allow mastery of the behavior in question. This viewpoint is often called the **critical-period hypothesis**—the belief that an organism must have certain experiences at a particular time in its developmental sequence if it is to reach its most mature state.

There are many studies from the animal literature supporting the critical-period hypothesis. For instance, Nobel Prize winner Konrad Lorenz discovered many years ago that birds, such as ducks and geese, will follow the first moving object they see after they hatch. Usually the first thing they see is their mother, of course, who was sitting on the eggs. However, Lorenz hatched goose eggs in an incubator, and then let the goslings see him immediately after hatching instead of seeing another goose. The freshly hatched geese followed him just the way they ordinarily would have followed their real mother.

After the goslings had waddled along behind Lorenz for a few hours, they acted as if they thought they were humans, not geese. When Lorenz returned the goslings to their real mother, they ignored her. Whenever Lorenz appeared, however, they became very excited and flocked to him for protection and affection (see photograph). It was as if the *visual image* of the first moving object they saw had become so strongly "imprinted" on their minds that, forever after, this object was "mother" (Lorenz, 1957).

Imprinting ability reaches its peak 16 to 24 hours after the baby goose hatches. During this period, the baby bird has an innate tendency to follow anything that moves. And once the goose has been imprinted, this very special form of learning

Critical-period hypothesis. The belief that there is a best time for a child to experience certain things or learn certain skills. If the experience does not come at the right time it may be largely or completely ineffective.

Imprinting. To imprint is to make a permanent impression on something. In psychological terms, imprinting refers to the very rapid and long-lasting learning that occurs during the first day or so of a young animal's life, when it attaches itself emotionally to the first moving object that it sees or hears.

Konrad Lorenz is shown followed by his grayleg goslings.

has long-lasting consequences. For example, when the birds Lorenz imprinted on himself grew up and became sexually mature, they showed no romantic interest in other geese. Instead, they attempted to court and mate with humans.

Imprinting takes place in many (but not all) types of birds, and it also seems to occur in mammals such as sheep and seals. As we will see in a moment, however, there is still considerable argument as to whether anything like imprinting occurs in humans (Wachs & Gruen, 1982).

Possibilities and Limitations

Are there "critical periods" in human development? As it turns out, we cannot answer this question satisfactorily without knowing what things newborn infants *can* and *can't* do—what's possible and what is not. A century ago, many scientists believed that a neonate had few if any innate abilities. For example, almost 100 years ago, William James stated that the newborn's sensory world was a "blooming, buzzing confusion." Taking a very strong "nurturist" position, James saw the neonate's mind as a "blank piece of paper." It was only when *experience* wrote on this piece of paper that the child's mind began to form and develop (James, 1890).

The notion that infants are almost totally helpless at birth continued to dominate the field until the 1970s. Even a decade or so ago, many pediatricians assumed that infants were "functionally blind" until they were several months of age.

In recent years, however, the pendulum of scientific opinion has begun to swing back toward a "naturist" position. For instance, we now know that almost from birth, an infant can not only see and hear with great precision, but can also sort out stimuli, remember, and predict future inputs. Neonates apparently can recognize their own names by 2 weeks of age, and they can distinguish among colors by the time they are 3 months old. They seem to develop depth perception by the 4th month of life. There is even some evidence that fetuses can acquire simple associations while still in the womb.

PRENATAL LEARNING

In an article in *Science*, Gina Kolata describes a number of experimental studies which suggest that both animal and human fetuses can be *conditioned* to respond to specific stimuli before birth (Kolata, 1984). For example, William Smotherman and his colleagues studied prenatal conditioning in rats. Smotherman injected a pleasant substance (apple juice) directly into the amniotic fluid surrounding one group of fetal rats. Later, he also injected an unpleasant substance (lithium chloride) into the fluid of the same rats. When these experimental rats were born, they refused to suck on nipples that were coated with apple juice. Control fetuses who received *just* lithium chloride or *just* apple juice while still in the womb did not avoid the nipples coated with apple juice (Smotherman, 1982). Smotherman and S.R. Robinson successfully repeated this experiment using mint flavoring rather than apple juice (Smotherman & Robinson, 1985). Smotherman believes the experimental animals *associated* the mint or the apple juice with the unpleasant properties of the lithium chloride. They then developed a "conditioned taste aversion" to the apple juice (see Chapter 9 for a discussion of "conditioned taste aversion").

Several studies have shown that near term fetuses can hear and respond to sounds from outside the womb (Lecanuet et al., 1991, 1992; Shaw & Paul, 1990). Anthony DeCasper performed several experiments showing that neonates preferred the sound of their mother's voice shortly after birth to the sound of women's voices they had not previously heard. They also preferred the sound of their mother's heart beat to the sound of male voices, including the sound of their father's voice (DeCasper & Prescott, 1984).

In a related experiment, DeCasper and Melanie Spence asked pregnant women to "talk" to their fetuses daily. During the last 6 weeks of their pregnancy, the women read aloud from *The Cat in the Hat* (a children's book) twice a day. Then, shortly after the infants were born, DeCasper and Spence tested them. The infants preferred hearing their mothers read aloud from *The Cat in the Hat* to hearing them read from another children's book.

In a second study, DeCasper and Spence had pregnant women repeat a phrase aloud, several times a day, during the last weeks of their pregnancy. After birth, the infants preferred the spoken phrase to other similar phrases. DeCasper concludes that prenatal auditory experience is sufficient to influence postnatal auditory preferences (DeCasper & Spence, 1986).

How much information fetuses can acquire before birth, we don't yet know. However, the fact that they can learn *anything* while still in the womb may help explain many of the early behaviors infants typically show.

In the Smotherman conditioning experiment involving apple juice and lithium chloride, what was the CS and what was the UCS?

NEONATAL LEARNING

Infants seem to come prepared for the massive learning tasks ahead. Only moments out of the womb, their eyes are alert, and they turn their heads in the direction of any voice they hear. They prefer female voices to male, but apparently search their visual world to locate the source of *any* human voice. They move their arms and legs in synchrony to human speech, but not to random noise, or many other sounds (such as tapping). Furthermore, they respond to any *human language*, but not to *artificial sounds* and broken-up speech patterns (Kuhl & Meltzoff, 1984).

By the time they are a day or so old, infants can learn conditioned responses to stimuli in any sensory modality (Lipsitt, 1990), and they can discriminate between two sounds in order to receive a taste of sugar water (Lipsitt, 1982). At this same age, they can remember an odor and respond to it more than 2 weeks later (Davis & Porter, 1991). Tiffany Field and her colleagues found that, only 45 hours after birth, newborns could integrate sights, sounds, smells, and touch into a meaningful perceptual pattern or *schema* that allowed them to discriminate their mother from a woman they had never seen before (Field et al., 1985).

EXPRESSIVE IMITATION

According to Andrew Meltzoff, an infant can imitate some facial expressions *1 hour after birth*. But because such newborn children are difficult to work with, Meltzoff and his colleagues have performed most of their research on 2-week-old babies. In an elegant series of studies begun in 1977, Meltzoff has shown that 2-week-old infants will stick out their tongues or open their mouths fully the first time they see these expressive facial expressions in the adults around them (see photograph) (Meltzoff, 1981).

Meltzoff's experiments seem particularly well controlled. The adults whose expressions the babies imitated were all strangers to the infants. Meltzoff filmed the infants' responses then showed them to judges who did not know what expression the baby was supposed to be imitating. Furthermore, Meltzoff did not tell the children's parents what he was up to. (In one early study when the experimenters told the parents, the mothers trained the infants to stick out their tongues before bringing them to the lab. One mother said, "I didn't want my baby to fail his first test.")

Meltzoff has also shown that 2-week-old infants can remember facial expressions for brief periods of time. In one study, he stuck pacifiers in the babies' mouths and

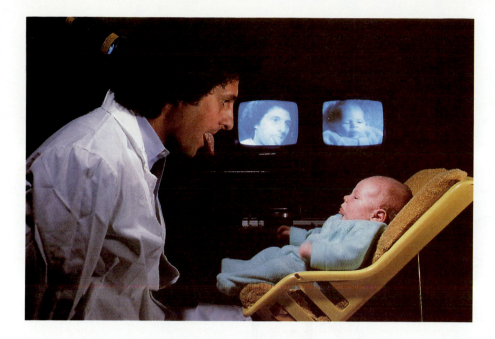

In Meltzoff's research two- to three-week-old infants clearly imitated an adult experimenter.

then exposed them to adults who either opened their mouths or stuck out their tongues. A few minutes later, when he removed the pacifier, the infants still gave the proper imitative response (Meltzoff & Moore, 1983).

In a similar set of studies, Tiffany Field and her colleagues found that 36-hour-old infants can imitate such facial expressions as happiness, sadness, and surprise (Field et al., 1986). However, psychologist Marsha Kaitz and her colleagues are not so sure. They studied 26 newborn infants who were held by a woman who modeled various facial expressions, such as sadness and happiness. Two observers rated the newborns' reactions. The infants did open their mouths, stick out their tongues, and pout their lips in response to the model's facial expressions. However, Kaitz says, these reactions were merely "innate motor responses" triggered by the facial expressions. Kaitz and her associates contend that "voluntary imitation of emotional expressions is not within a newborn's repertoire" (Kaitz et al., 1988).

NATURE OR NURTURE?

If newborns can do so much immediately after birth, doesn't that prove that most *mental development* is determined by *physical growth*? And if that is the case, isn't most of what we call "personality" shaped primarily by the genes, not the environment?

Probably the *interactionist* position taken by James and Carol Gould is the one best supported by present data. The Goulds believe that genes *sensitize* newly born organisms to certain aspects of their environments. But both the environment, and training techniques, determine what the infants actually learn (see Figure 12.2). Simple animals, such as birds and bees, inherit rather rigid "learning programs," the Goulds say. These programs specify rather precisely what the animals can (and can't) learn from their environments, and when in the developmental sequence this learning should take place (Gould & Gould, 1981).

The restrictions on *human* learning are much more subtle. We come into the world with the ability (and the desire) to learn almost anything. However, we do best when our environment "shapes" us following the laws of learning outlined in Chapter 9. Thus, at all levels, *nature and nurture interact*. But according to James Gould, the *relative importance* of "nature" and "nurture" varies widely in different species (Gould, 1986; Plomin, 1990). So, it appears that nurture interacts with

With a good heredity, nature deals you a fine hand at cards; and with a good environment, you learn to play the hand well.

WALTER C. ALVAREZ, M.D.

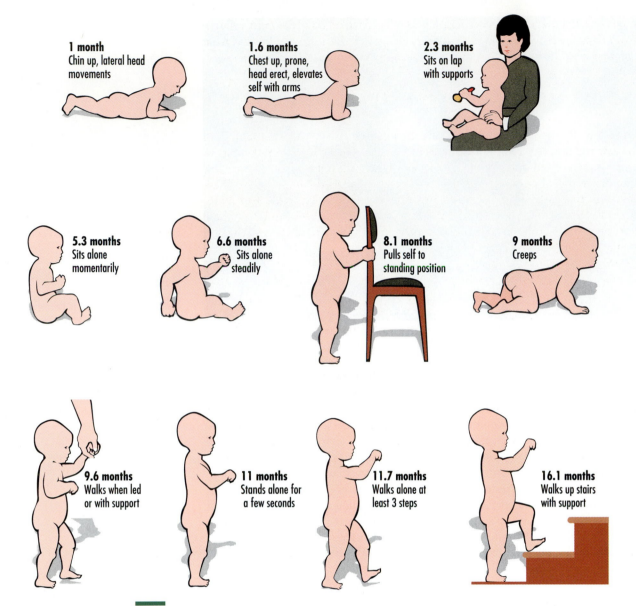

1 month
Chin up, lateral head movements

1.6 months
Chest up, prone, head erect, elevates self with arms

2.3 months
Sits on lap with supports

5.3 months
Sits alone momentarily

6.6 months
Sits alone steadily

8.1 months
Pulls self to standing position

9 months
Creeps

9.6 months
Walks when led or with support

11 months
Stands alone for a few seconds

11.7 months
Walks alone at least 3 steps

16.1 months
Walks up stairs with support

FIGURE 12.2

Typical pattern of motor development in an infant. Environmental opportunity and inherited readiness combine to produce new abilities at each stage.

nature; nurture determines the level of development which is achieved within the possibilities and limitations which nature sets.

Given the past history of the nature-nurture controversy, it's likely this issue will never be entirely settled. But as long as scientists continue to argue about what is innate and what is acquired, the more we will learn about the factors that influence human growth and development.

COGNITIVE DEVELOPMENT

As we noted in Chapter 11, cognition refers to intellectual processes, and *cognitive psychology* is the study of the intellectual processes we use to deal with the world. We have already discussed many cognitive processes, both in Chapter 11 and in earlier chapters. However, the *development* of cognitive abilities deserves special consideration.

For more than 40 years, the study of cognitive development has been virtually synonymous with the work of Swiss psychologist Jean Piaget. When Piaget died in

September 1980, Harvard psychologist Jerome Kagan called him "the most influential developmental theorist of this century, if not of all time." Let's look at what Piaget had to say about cognitive *structures*, cognitive *functions*, and *stages* of cognitive development.

Cognitive Structures and Functions

Piaget was really an information processing theorist before such a label existed. That is, he saw the mind as a kind of computer that used sensory inputs to develop an internal representation of the outside world. Piaget believed you were born with innately determined notions of what to expect from the world around you. These innate cognitive structures allow you to process sensory inputs (and therefore represent reality) in a crude sort of way. At birth, however, you begin to adapt these inborn mental structures as you construct your own **schemata** for processing and responding to reality. The history of a child's cognitive development is that of creating ever more complex schemata.

Schemata develop in complexity as the infant adapts to the world by processing information in one of two ways. The child may either try to incorporate inputs into already existing schemata, a process Piaget calls assimilation. Or, if the inputs simply will not fit the child's present view of reality, the child may be forced to change, add to, or reorganize existing schemata. Piaget refers to this process as accommodation (Piaget, 1976, 1977).

ASSIMILATION

The process of cognitive **assimilation** works in much the same way as the biological process of digestion. According to Piaget, when you "encode" an input in order to store it in your mind, you break the input down just as your stomach breaks food down into tiny particles. You then incorporate the "encoded" input into already existing mental structures, just as the cells assimilate food particles into already existing cellular structures. Cognitive assimilation thus involves changing sensory inputs to make them part of your mind.

For instance, a newborn girl tends to suck any small object that enters her mouth. She soon builds up a mental schema related to "suckability" and assimilates all small objects into this category whether they really fit there or not. Therefore, when she encounters any new small object, she often pops the object in her mouth at once. As long as she is able to assimilate her experiences into existing schemata, equilibrium is maintained (Piaget, 1977).

ACCOMMODATION

Sometimes a given input simply will not fit within the schemata a child already has available. For instance, little Mary finds a small red pepper and pops that into her mouth. Very rapidly, Mary discovers she must create a new schema, that of "not suckable!" Any new experience which contradicts her already-existing mental structures will cause Mary to experience disequilibrium. This will lead to the process of **accommodation**—that is, the alteration of her schemata to make them fit reality—and the restoration of equilibrium.

To restate matters, assimilation is the mental function that allows you to change *inputs* so that they fit your present schemata or other mental structures. Accommodation is the mental function that allows you to change your *schemata* so that they match the reality represented by your present inputs. The innate tendency to equilibrium drives both of these "functions of the mind." Assimilation and accommodation guide your cognitive development from birth to death (Piaget, 1977).

Little Mikey calls all adult males—including the letter carrier—"Daddy." Which cognitive process is Mikey using?

Schemata. Plural of "schema." Schemata are mental structures that represent reality in some abstract manner. Similar to "perceptual schemata" that allow you to recognize and respond to sensory inputs.

Assimilation. The process of adaptation by which inputs are altered to fit into present schemata or mental structures.

Accommodation. The process of adaptation by which mental schemata are created, changed, or added to in order to match them to reality.

Infants who suck on every new object may be classifying items according to a mental "suckability" schema.

Stages of Development

According to Piaget, there are four major stages of cognitive development: (1) the sensory-motor period, (2) the pre-operational stage, (3) the stage of concrete operations, and (4) the stage of formal operations. Each of us goes from one stage upward to the next stage at slightly different ages. But the *average age* at which children attain each maturational level is about the same in all cultures (Piaget, 1977).

SENSORY-MOTOR STAGE

The first of Piaget's four stages, the sensory-motor period, begins at birth and usually ends when the infant is about 24 months old. It is during this time that infants build up their initial schemata, most of which involve the objects and people around them.

For the first month or so of life, infants "know the world" solely in terms of the innate reflexes that serve to keep them alive. But, within a month or two, infants begin to form crude "action schemata" that let them explore and respond to their world.

Through the processes of assimilation and accommodation, these initial action schemata develop and become organized into more complex mental structures. The infant begins to associate sensory inputs with muscular movements. For example, the child gazes at his or her hands while grasping for a toy, and thus connects visual inputs with motor responses and sensory feedback. Eventually the child can reach for the toy without looking at his or her hands (Piaget, 1977).

Do the data cited earlier in this chapter on what newborns can and can't do support Piaget's position, or not?

OBJECT PERMANENCE   According to Piaget, during the first months of life, infants do not realize that an object can exist outside of their own perception of the object. Six-month-old children will typically follow an object with their eyes as the object moves across their field of vision. But if the object disappears, they show no disappointment, Piaget said, nor do they appear to anticipate the object's reappearance. Playing "peek-a-boo" with a child this young is often frustrating because the infant seems not to know what the game is about. When the child reaches 8 months of age (on the average), however, the infant will usually reach for an object hidden from view, provided that the infant has seen the object being hidden.

By the time children are 18 months of age or so, they will search for something they haven't seen hidden. According to Piaget, this is an indication that they have acquired the concept of **object permanence.** Piaget believed this concept is the beginning of *symbolic thought,* for the child maintains a mental symbol of the object even when the object is out of sight.

When youngsters gain the ability to represent objects symbolically, Piaget said, they pass from the sensory-motor period into the pre-operational period of development (Piaget, 1977).

What else does the child acquire during the first 2 years of life that allows the child to represent objects internally using easy-to-manipulate cognitive symbols?

OBJECT PERMANENCE RECONSIDERED   Several researchers have questioned the inability of young children to grasp object permanence. They find that you must test the infants in different ways than Piaget did in order to observe it.

Object permanence. According to Piaget, a very young infant does not realize that an object has an existence independent of the child's own perceptions of the object. Once the infant is capable of symbolic thought, the child builds up complex schemata involving the object and then realizes the permanence of the object.

For example, psychologists Hildy Ross and Susan Lollis played a variety of "turn-taking" games (such as "peek-a-boo") with 9-month-old infants. After four "rounds," the experimenter would sit quietly and refuse to take her turn. "When the adults failed to participate, the infants showed considerable independent understanding of the games they played," Ross and Lollis report. That is, they made sounds and other signals urging the adults to take their turn. When the game involved playing with a toy, the infants gave clear evidence they understood the *permanence* of the toy, and who should play with it at a specific time during the game. Thus, Ross and Lollis say, object permanence (and several other cognitive skills) seem to emerge in infants *much sooner* than Piaget assumed was the case (Ross & Lollis, 1987). Other researchers report similar results, using different methods with even younger children (Baillargeon, 1987; Butterword, 1983).

Whether or not Piaget was correct about the precise *time* at which infants gain the concept of *object permanence* is, perhaps, not all that important to our understanding of his theory of child development. And it surely remains true that at a very early age, children do not seem to be able to think in symbols, while at a later age they can.

PRE-OPERATIONAL STAGE

During the sensory-motor period, the infant responds to its environment directly and rather automatically. But as the child acquires *sophisticated language*, the youngster passes to the second, or pre-operational stage of development, which runs from about age 2 to 7. Language gives the child the ability to deal with many aspects of the world in symbols, by talking and thinking about objects rather than having to manipulate them directly. Piaget believed that language also allows the child to *remember past events* and hence to *anticipate* their happening again (Piaget, 1976).

EGOCENTRISM IN CHILDREN   According to Piaget, during all the early developmental periods—and sometimes even much later in life—the child makes use of **egocentric reasoning.** But this type of thinking is particularly noticeable during the pre-operational period. By "egocentric," Piaget didn't mean "selfish." Rather, he meant that children cannot readily differentiate themselves from their environments. For instance, Piaget had 3-year-old children close their eyes and then asked them, "Can you see me?" The children replied, "No." He then asked. "Can I see you?" Again the children replied, "No." Five-year-olds answered both questions correctly. Piaget concluded that the 3-year-olds simply were not mature enough to realize that other people have different points of view than they do.

Whether or not young children are *actually* egocentric, however, depends not only on how you define the term, but also on how you question them (Cox, 1985). Some research in this area suggests that egocentrism is not the "hallmark" of infancy that Piaget assumed it was.

For example, when John Flavell and his colleagues repeated Piaget's experiments, they got quite different results. Flavell had 3-year-olds close their eyes and put their hands over their eyes. Then he asked, "Can I see you?" The children said "No," just as Piaget's subjects had. However, when Flavell asked, "Can I see your arms?" the children replied, "Yes." They also agreed that Flavell could see an object placed in front of them, but could not see their backs. Flavell and his associates conclude that "adults take 'you' to mean their whole body while young children take it to mean primarily their face region." Flavell concludes that had Piaget asked different questions, he might have changed his mind about "egocentrism" in children (Flavell et al., 1980).

TRANSFORMATIONS AND CONSERVATION   Piaget believed that the pre-operational stage is also marked by perception-bound thinking. That is, the child realizes that objects have permanence, but struggles with the fact that objects can undergo transformations without being destroyed or physically changed. By "transformations," Piaget meant the fact that some aspects of an object may change,

Egocentric reasoning. According to Piaget, young children cannot differentiate themselves from the external world. Thus, they see the world from a self-centered viewpoint.

A Piagetian experiment: When asked to place the man where the policeman cannot see him, the child at the egocentric stage would place him where *she* cannot see him. The child who has passed the egocentric stage would correctly place the man where the policeman could not see him, *regardless* of whether or not she could see him.

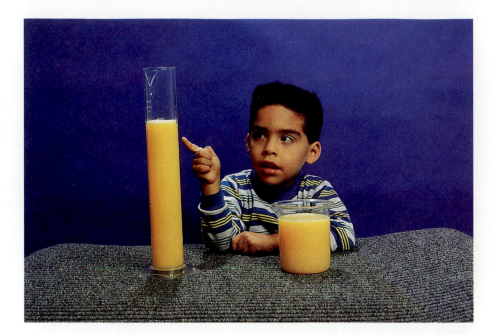

FIGURE 12.3

A child in the pre-operational stage is unable to *conserve* volume, and so does not realize that there is as much liquid in the low, wide container as there is the taller narrow container, even if he watches the water being poured from one to the other.

Conserve. In Piaget's terms, to "conserve" something is to realize that an object is not necessarily transformed when it changes in some way. To Piaget, the mental process involved in transforming inputs was always reversible. But a child must be fairly mature to realize that this is the case.

but the object itself remains intact. For instance, if you turn a sock inside out, then back again, the child is surprised to see that the sock remains the same. When the youngster's perception of the sock changed, the child assumed the sock had changed too.

Because the child doesn't realize that *transformations are reversible*, Piaget claimed, the youngster cannot **conserve** physical properties such as quantity and length. For instance, if you fill two identical, tall, thin glasses with water, the child will agree both glasses have the same amount of water in them. But suppose you empty the water from one glass into a wide container (see Figure 12.3). The water level is, of course, lower in the wide container than in the tall, thin glass. You "know" the fat glass holds the same *quantity* of water as does the thin glass because you can "conserve quantity" in your mind. But when Piaget tested 4-year-olds on this problem, they responded that the tall glass now had more liquid in it because the water level in that glass was higher. Piaget assumed the children didn't realize that the process of pouring didn't *alter* the quantity of liquid in any way. And, when he poured the water back into the tall, thin glass, he reported the children were surprised that the water level rose. Piaget concluded that the youngsters couldn't yet grasp the fact that transformations are reversible (Piaget, 1977). As we will see, however, Piaget's results may depend more on *how you test* children than on their cognitive development.

Piaget's research suggested that children do not seem to be able to deal with abstractions—such as love and hate, up and down, large and small—until they are 4 or 5 years of age. In Piaget's terms, children this age can think—that is, they can use language to generate expectancies—but they cannot *reason*. Reasoning, to Piaget, is the mental manipulation of abstract symbols, the process of "knowing why."

The pre-operational stage is a transition period. As the child acquires more complex language and mental structures, the young person moves into the stage of concrete operations.

Piaget seems never to have used the shaping techniques (described in Chapter 9) to teach a child to conserve quantity. How might you go about using these techniques to see if children could be taught conservation of quantity at an early age?

CONCRETE OPERATIONAL STAGE

By the time children reach the age of 6 or 7 years, they typically enter into what Piaget called the stage of concrete operations. Now young persons can conserve quantity, Piaget said, because they can perform this transformation mentally. But children this age usually cannot conserve weight until the 9th or 10th year. If you place two identical rubber balls in front of a young boy, he will assure you they weigh the same. But if you now cut one ball in pieces, he may say the cut-up pieces don't weigh the same as does the intact ball. According to Piaget, the boy's answer suggests he actually *perceives* weight in quite a different way than do older children. However, once the boy learns to conserve weight, he finally realizes that the whole is equal to the sum of its parts.

The concept of *number* is another acquisition the child usually makes during the stage of concrete operations. Suppose you lay out 10 pennies in two rows on a table, and show them to a girl still at the pre-operational stage:

The girl will see at once that the two rows are identical and that they both contain the same number of pennies. But suppose you widen the spaces between the pennies in the bottom row:

A pre-operational girl may say the second row has more pennies, despite the fact that she can count the coins in each row with no difficulty. Piaget emphasizes that *counting* is not the same thing as the *concept of number,* a schema the child usually attains only during the stage of concrete operations. (As we will see shortly, however, more recent research suggests that the answer the child gives may be more dependent upon the questions you ask than Piaget apparently realized.)

According to Piaget, during the stage of concrete operations the child begins to visualize a *complex sequence of operations.* A 5-year-old boy can walk to school without getting lost—that is, he can perform a series of complex operations in order to reach a goal. But the boy usually must be 6 before he gains the ability to draw a map showing the route he takes from home to school. And it is only at this point he realizes that anyone else could follow the map as well. However, he cannot describe the *abstract principles* involved in map making (or anything else) until he reaches the stage of *formal* operations (Piaget, 1976).

If you ask a pre-operational girl, "Which row has more pennies?" how do you know she understands you mean "more pennies" and not "more space"?

FORMAL OPERATIONAL STAGE

The last of Piaget's four periods of intellectual development is called the stage of formal operations. It begins about age 12 and continues through the rest of the person's life. Some people may never really reach this stage, Piaget said, and those that do may not go very far into it. Whatever the case, children usually don't reach the last stage until at least age 12.

Prior to the 12th year of life, Piaget said, the child is limited to thinking in concrete terms. Only in the final stage can the young person think in completely abstract terms. At this level of development, people can solve problems in their minds by isolating the important variables and manipulating them mentally. Now, at last, the individual is able to draw meaningful conclusions from purely abstract or hypothetical data. For example, if you ask a child "What would happen if people were not punished for breaking the law?" the child might say, "A policeman would get you," or "Then I could take Jenny's bike." The adolescent could go beyond these concrete responses and consider more abstract possibilities, such as the anarchy or breakdown of society which would result from this "what if" situation.

Adolescents entering the formal operational stage also become more capable of taking another person's perspective. They begin to think about how the world might look through someone else's eyes. And they begin to wonder (or even become preoccupied with) how they look to other people.

What could it mean for a democratic society if many of its citizens fail to function at a formal operational level of thought?

It is during the stage of formal operations that the structures of the mind become complex enough to allow the individual to create a personal "theory of knowledge." This theory involves all types of knowledge—"how," "what," and most important, "why."

In a sense, Piaget's *stage theory* is an attempt to explain "why" children develop as they do. Now that we have briefly described it, let's see how others have reacted to his theory.

Piaget: An Evaluation

As you might suspect, any theory as influential as Piaget's is bound to draw criticism. For example, the children Piaget spent a lifetime observing were for the most part white, middle-class youngsters reared in normal European homes. His 4-stage theory appears to hold to some extent for such children. There is less evidence that it holds in other cultures, however (Dasen, 1977; Mwamwenda & Mwamwenda, 1991; Mwamwenda, 1992).

Some controversy over Piaget's theory is based on his use of *developmental stages*. As popular as this approach is among some theorists, the data give limited support to the notion that development is a matter of "moving up a clearly-defined ladder" (Flavell, 1985; Levin, 1986). Cognitive development may be more a matter of gradual learning than cognitive "jumps." For example, children who watch their parents make pottery can correctly answer questions about the conservation of clay at a much earlier age than Piaget predicted (Bransford et al., 1986).

Psychologist Jean Berko Gleason makes an interesting observation about conservation: "Young children shown a liquid poured from a short, fat container into a tall, thin container . . . have been known, in the laboratory, to assert that the amount of liquid has increased; yet, in their real lives, preschoolers who want more juice at snack time are not known to pour their existing juice into taller glasses in order to accomplish this end" (Gleason, 1987).

Piaget made certain assumptions about cognitive development in children, and then performed demonstrations that tended to support his prior beliefs. Had Piaget performed "controlled experiments" rather than simply observing children in cleverly constructed situations, he might have come to different conclusions.

Piaget knew about most of these criticisms, but he was convinced his basic assumptions were correct. Therefore, he saw little need to test them experimentally. This is not to say that Piaget felt his theories were above improvement. He frequently revised his own ideas (Block, 1982). And it is in this spirit that his former students continued to develop his work. Juan Pascual-Leone, for example, has added a view of "mental processing capacity" which explains some of the unexpected results Piaget's critics found (Pascual-Leone & Smith, 1969; Pascual-Leone, 1976, 1984).

Some current research on cognitive development is moving away from Piaget's search for general principles of cognitive growth. There is an increasing focus on specific cognitive areas or "domains" rather than on broad general stages. In other words, some researchers believe that different cognitive abilities (e.g., processing speed, different types of memory) may develop at different rates depending on the *content* of the domain (Wellman & Gelman, 1992). For example, children who are chess experts may have better memories than adults who are novices for chess board positions, even though the adults' memories are better in other domains (Chi, 1978).

Piaget's theories, however, continue to influence both education and psychology (Smith, 1991a). Their impact has been enormous, not only in focussing attention on early development, but also in stimulating the further study of cognitive abilities at all levels (Overton, 1990; Smith, 1991b).

SOCIAL DEVELOPMENT

Most early research on social development focused on parent-child interactions and how "good mothering" affected the child's social development. Slowly, over the years, psychologists came to realize three important things: First, mothers and infants constitute *social systems*. That is, the infant influences the mother as much as the mother affects her child. Second, peers play a very important role in social development. And third, the father also often plays a crucial role in helping the child develop socially. We will look at the roles of peers and fathers in a moment—after we have considered mother-child interaction and the development of attachment.

Parent-Child Attachment

The earliest form of emotional and social development is the attachment which forms between a child and an adult caregiver—usually the mother (Hartup, 1989; Vaughn et al., 1989). From this "secure base," to use Mary Ainsworth's term, the child grows and explores the world (Ainsworth, 1973; Ainsworth et al., 1978).

Daniel Stern describes how mother and child form a **social dyad** almost immediately after the infant's birth. Stern films the reactions of mothers to their newborn children, and then slows the movies down to analyze the pictures one frame at a time. By making this sort of "slow-motion analysis," Stern is able to spot subtle mother-infant interactions that otherwise might be missed.

Stern reports that both the mother and her infant appear to have an "inborn mutual readiness" to respond to each other. This "readiness" apparently is a genetically determined *social behavior* in both the mother and the child. But it is also a pattern of interactions that society strongly reinforces once the behaviors occur (Stern, 1983).

Robert Emde believes that the infant triggers off maternal and paternal behaviors in the parents as much as parents set off innate responses in the child. He sums up the matter in this way: "For years, theories described how mothers shaped babies, but

Social dyad (DIE-add). A mutually interacting group composed of just two members.

A mother and her child form an interacting system or "social dyad."

we are now beginning to appreciate how much babies shape mothers." And how they shape their fathers, too, as Emde also points out (Emde, 1983; Klinnert et al., 1986).

The question then becomes, what are the crucial variables that determine parental-child patterns of interactions? Some of these variables are biochemical, and are determined by the genes. Other factors are psychological, and are influenced by past experience and the social and cultural environment.

HORMONAL INFLUENCES ON ATTACHMENT

Psychologist Berry Brazelton has for many years studied the ways that parents and infants react to each other. Brazelton states that a mother's emotional attachment to her infant does not appear "instantaneously, by magic" in the hospital delivery room. Rather, he says, this emotionality begins early in pregnancy and develops fairly slowly. It shows itself initially in the *feelings and dreams* that many woman experience during pregnancy.

Brazelton notes that most women experience considerable anxiety about themselves and their yet-to-be-born child during pregnancy. These fears are part of the normal attachment process, Brazelton says, and probably reach their peak a few days before labor begins. The anxiety and nervousness are needed in order to break old habit patterns and prepare the woman to take on the new role of mothering. These fears also provide the woman with the heightened arousal and energy she will need in order to care for her infant.

Brazelton believes that the attachment process has two aspects to it. The first is an *increased interest in infants*. Research suggests this part of the process develops rapidly, is controlled primarily by hormones, and is usually found only in pregnant females (Rosenblatt, 1983). The second part of parental attachment involves a need for *continued contact with infants*. This need seems to be psychological rather than biological in origin, develops rather slowly, is strongly influenced by reinforcement, and can be seen in males as well as females (Brazelton, 1987; Brazelton & Als, 1979).

IMPRINTING IN HUMANS BEINGS?

Once Konrad Lorenz had demonstrated imprinting with birds, scientists began hunting for similar effects in humans. Among the first researchers to report success were Marshall Klaus and John Kennell.

In their 1976 book, *Maternal-Infant Bonding,* Klaus and Kennell state there is a *critical period* in the first hour or so of life during which an infant can *bond* with its mother. This bonding takes place only if the mother and child are in close physical contact during the "sensitive period," according to Klaus and Kennell. Supposedly, the "bonding" increases the mother's love for her child and makes her more attentive to the infant's needs. Indeed, Klaus and Kennell cite several studies suggesting that the mother is likely to neglect or abuse the child if the "bonding" fails to occur (Kennell & Klaus, 1979).

Some scientists remain skeptical, however. Psychologist Michael Lamb has reviewed many of the experiments purporting to show that "bonding" occurs. Lamb believes most of the "bonding" studies have such serious flaws that they offer little support for the position taken by Klaus and Kennell. "Taken together," Lamb says, "the studies . . . show no clear evidence for any lasting effect of early physical contact between mother and infant on subsequent maternal behavior. The most that can be said is that it may sometimes have modest short-term effects on some mothers in some circumstances" (Lamb, 1982).

Lamb notes that there are no known *ill effects* from early mother-infant contacts. But he fears that those mothers who were not allowed to hold their children immediately after birth may feel they are somehow "inadequate parents." That simply isn't so, Lamb says, and offers as proof the fact that most *adoptive mothers* are at least as loving as are "bonded" mothers (Lamb & Brown, 1982).

According to Brazelton, intimacy between mother and baby develops during the nine months of pregnancy; he believes the moments of "bonding" just after birth are not as crucial as some other researchers contend.

However, as John Santrock notes, the weakness of the bonding research should not be used to interfere with early mother-infant contact. He says, "the practice of bonding may set in motion a climate for improved mother-infant interaction after the mother and infant leave the hospital" (Santrock, 1990). Thus, the role of early contact is unclear and the question of whether any form of imprinting occurs in human infants has not as yet been decided.

LONG-TERM SEPARATION

A human infant cared for by a mother with consistent behavior patterns rapidly builds up an emotional *attachment* to its mother. The child learns that much of what is pleasant and satisfying comes through the actions of the mother. Psychologists call this an anaclitic relationship, the phrase coming from the Greek word meaning "to lean on."

John Bowlby has studied infant-mother attachments for a great many years. According to Bowlby, disturbing the anaclitic relationship can be dangerous. If it is the mother who *always* feeds the child, the infant soon builds up a *perceptual schema* that incorporates both "food" and "mother." When food appears, the child expects the mother to be there too, because the youngster is not yet mature enough to discriminate food from mother. If the infant is suddenly separated from the mother during the first months of life, Bowlby says, the child may have considerable difficulty adjusting to changes in the environment (Bowlby, 1973; 1989).

Evidence supporting Bowlby's beliefs comes from research by R.A. Spitz. He studied the reactions of infants 6 to 12 months old who, for various reasons, had been separated from their mothers and put into institutions or foster homes. In their new environments, these infants received at best impersonal care. Almost as soon as the infants were institutionalized, they began showing signs of disturbance. They became quite upset when anyone approached them. They lost weight, became passive and inactive, and they had trouble sleeping. Spitz calls this condition **anaclitic depression.**

The first sign of anaclitic depression is a behavior Spitz describes as "a search for the mother." Some babies quietly weep big tears; others cry violently. None of them can be quieted down by any type of intervention, although at the initial stage of the depression they still cling tightly to any adult who picks them up. If the mother does not return in 3 to 4 weeks, the infant's behavior changes. The child withdraws, lies quietly in the crib, will not play if offered a toy, and does not even look up if someone enters the room. The baby becomes dejected and passive, refuses food, and becomes more susceptible than usual to colds and other ailments.

Spitz believes that anaclitic depression might well account for some types of mental retardation, since the children he studied seemed to show considerable physical and intellectual impairment during and immediately after their periods of depression (Spitz, 1945).

SHORT-TERM SEPARATION

Bowlby's ideas about attachment also have important implications for short-term separation, as more and more mothers choose to work outside the home. What is the effect of leaving an infant in a day-care center several days a week?

In the 1970s, most of the research on this question found that day-care did not affect the infant's attachment to the mother (Belsky & Steinberg, 1978; Farran & Ramey, 1977). However, most of the day-care centers studied were university facilities of very high quality. More recently, in a study of more typical day-care centers, Jay Belsky found that even twenty hours per week in a day-care center significantly interfered with infants' attachment to their mothers (Belsky, 1986). Other researchers have drawn similar conclusions (Barglow et al., 1987).

These results have been questioned, and further study is under way. It does seem safe to conclude, however, that the quality of day-care makes a difference.

Anaclitic depression (ann-ah-KLITT-ick). Depression as the result of separation from a person in a strong relationship of dependency and trust.

The best day-care centers have a well-trained teacher for each small group of children. Teachers interact frequently with each child on his or her own level.

High-quality day-care seems to be an acceptable alternative to constant parent-care (Howes et al., 1992).

And what distinguishes a high-quality day-care center? Such factors as less staff turnover, smaller groups of children for each teacher, well-trained teachers, and involved child-teacher interactions all seem to be important components of the best day-care centers (Phillips et al., 1987).

Short-term separation may also occur when parents are travelling, or absent for other reasons. On their return, the reactions of their children often surprise them. Rather than hugs and a warm welcome, children left for a few days may greet their parents with the "cold shoulder." This reaction, which soon passes, appears to be a childish false bravado, saying "I can get along without you."

So the effects of separation vary, depending on the length of separation and the quality of the alternative care. John Bowlby believes that early attachment establishes a pattern for relationships *throughout* life (Bowlby, 1973, 1989). Childhood attachment may even predict the later adjustment to marriage (Quinton et al., 1984; Senchak & Leonard, 1992).

Peer Relationships

Although adults are the most important people to the newborn child, it is not long before other children come into the picture. By 6 months, an infant will smile and reach toward another infant, and by one year more complex social interactions develop (Furman & Buhrmester, 1992).

Good peer relationships seem to develop from good parent-child relationships. Deborah Vandell and Margaret Owen found that 6-month-old infants who developed a secure attachment to their mothers were more likely to interact with their peers than infants whose attachment to their mothers was not as secure (Vandell & Owen, 1988). Other researchers have observed that foster children are more often disliked and rejected than their home-reared peers (McIntyre & Lounsbury, 1988).

Peers perform an important role as a child reaches out beyond the home. Peers are a practice ground for future social interactions. And as children grow, peers provide a source of information about their abilities and how they compare with other children. According to Henry Grunebaum and Leonard Solomon, children who develop good peer relationships are more likely to develop a good sense of self-esteem (Grunebaum & Solomon, 1987).

Apparently, good parental relationships lead to good peer interactions, which in turn promote healthy personality development (Budman, 1987; Dunn & McGuire, 1992). Michael Lamb cautions, however, that some of these relationships may be the result of the fact that good parental relationships, peer interactions, and personality development, all tend to go together in stable families (Lamb et al., 1984).

FRIENDS

Although peer interactions and even preferences for certain peers begin in the first year, it is not until 3 or 4 years that a child's interactions develop into friendships. As a child grows, friendships become more and more important. And by the time a child is 7, the time spent with friends and peers is approximately equal to the time spent with adults.

Young children are attracted to a child who has an interesting toy or game. A friendship will follow if the children communicate and manage conflicts successfully. Older children prefer a child who has desirable skills, is physically attractive, and is of the same sex and race. Even a child's name may have an effect on peer acceptance and friendship, with contemporary names like Scott or Jennifer having a more positive effect than more "old-fashioned" names (Dworetzky, 1990).

Failure to gain peer acceptance and make friends can be a devastating experience for a child. In addition to daily rejection, disliked children may face additional social problems as they enter adolescence—problems leading to delinquency, criminal behavior, and mental illness (Chance, 1989).

Several psychologists are trying to develop ways to help these children. Michael Guralnick and Joseph Groom found that providing successful models of peer interaction helped mildly developmentally handicapped children improve their peer interactions (Guralnick & Groom, 1987). Other researchers have found it is also important to train the rejecting peers to give the rejected child another chance (Fantuzzo & Jurecic, 1988; Bierman & Miller, 1987; Schneider, 1992).

PLAY

Play allows the child to interact with peers and practice social roles (Musser & Graziano, 1991). Play also helps children learn about aggression, and how to control their own aggressive urges (Hartup, 1983). Play lets children explore their physical and social environments, and thus helps children learn to perceive the world more accurately (Rubin et al., 1983). Little wonder, then, that Otto Weinberger says, "Play isn't everything—it's the only thing!" (Weinberger, 1979).

There are several types of play, and most children go from one type to another in much the same fashion as they presumably "move upward" in Piaget's developmental stages. The first type of play that infants engage in is rightly called "pre-social." That is, 6-month-old infants play with dolls dangling from their cribs, with bells and rattles and balls and teddy bears, and they play with their own hands and feet. Only later do they discover the marvelous possibilities for play that other people offer (Harlow, 1973).

As children pass from pre-operational to the concrete operational stage of intellectual development, their play becomes more complex and *social*. Other people begin to become animate partners rather than mere objects to be manipulated (Smith, 1984).

Social play seems to be of three major types: (1) free play, (2) formal play, and (3) creative play. Of the three, physical free play with other children is perhaps the easiest for the child, and hence often the first to appear. As Anthony Pellegrini points out, this sort of "rough-housing" is also the most disturbing to the middle-class

Formalized play allows children to learn how to interact according to rules.

parent, who is often afraid the child will either hurt others or be hurt by them. Yet this type of activity may help children learn to tolerate minor frustrations and how to control their tempers (Pellegrini, 1987).

As the child becomes more verbal, rough-and-tumble play drops off sharply, and *formalized play* begins. The mock fights of 4-year-old boys develop rapidly into games of tag and "cops and robbers" in which the youngsters must follow formal rules. These rules, of course, constitute what Piaget would call "schemata."

In Piaget's terms, *creative play* is primarily a matter of assimilation—of pretending that things might happen that haven't yet happened. Piaget believes that creative play is the child's way of learning to manipulate symbols rather than objects. He calls it the "high point" of all types of play. He also calls it "a child's work" (Piaget, 1965).

Play serves to stimulate the physical, emotional, social, and intellectual development of the child. And its hallmark is *pleasure*. Children who laugh while they are fighting seldom hurt one another. Adults who grin as they play computer games seldom smash their video monitors. Play is therefore a vital part of peer interaction and social development which will become even more crucial as we move into the pressures of the 21st century.

Which type of play is probably meant in the saying, "All work and no play makes Jack a dull boy"?

The Father's Role in Social Development

The noted anthropologist Margaret Mead once said that "fathers are a biological necessity but a social accident." However, data gathered by developmental psychologists tend not to support Dr. Mead's viewpoint (Robinson & Barret, 1986).

Even early attachment is not dependent upon the association of mothers with feeding, as both Freud and learning theorists once thought. Research by Harry Harlow and his colleagues with rhesus monkeys, suggests that warmth, rhythmic rocking, and especially physical contact, are more important factors in establishing early attachment (Harlow et al., 1971). Fathers needn't feel at a disadvantage!

Michael Lamb agrees that fathers contribute significantly to an infant's emotional growth, although the father's contributions are often quite different from the mother's. While the father is just as capable of taking care of an infant as the mother is, one of the father's chief roles (at least in North America) seems to be that of *play-mate* to the child (Lamb, 1981).

Lamb reports several studies suggesting that men are just as likely to nurture and stimulate their children as are the mothers. In fact, there is some evidence that fathers are more likely to hold their infants and to look at them than are mothers. Furthermore, fathers are just as likely to interpret correctly the cues the infants give as are mothers. However, in most real-life settings, men are less likely to feed infants and change their diapers than are women. This difference in parental behaviors seems due to cultural roles, however, and not to innate differences in male-female "instincts" (Pleck et al., 1985–1986).

Berry Brazelton and his colleagues found that fathers *talked* to their infants less than did the mothers. However, the men were much more likely to *touch* or *hug* the child than were the women. The fathers primarily engaged in rough-and-tumble play with their children, while the mothers were more likely to play conventional games, such as peek-a-boo. Brazelton notes that "When several weeks old, an infant displays an entirely different attitude—more wide-eyed, playful, and bright-faced—toward its father than toward its mother." One explanation for this, Brazelton says, is that the fathers apparently *expect* more playful responses from their children. And the children then respond to the father's expectations (Brazelton, 1986).

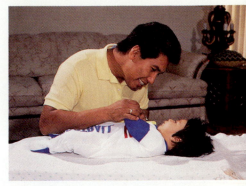

In contemporary Western culture, fathers are taking a more nurturant role than they did in the past.

Given the fact that a father's influence on his child is more strongly emotional than intellectual, what would be the result of the father's absence during the child's early years? Would boys react differently to paternal deprivation than would girls?

FATHER-SON DEPRIVATION

Several studies reported in the 1950s suggested that boys reared without fathers become less aggressive, more dependent, and have more "feminine" interests and behavior patterns than boys from two-parent families. However, Sandra Scarr states that most of these experiments are of questionable value. In the 1950s and 1960s, Scarr says, "Families without fathers at home were studied extensively for their bad effects on the son's masculinity and were thought to result in poor mathematical skills and poor psychosocial development. The implicit, or sometimes explicit, assumption of the investigators of the period was that families without a masculine presence were doomed to inadequacy as rearing environments for children" (Scarr, 1985). Scarr questions the value of these studies.

Paul Adams, Judith Milner, and Nancy Schrepf report that boys who grow up without a "male identity figure" present are neither more nor less "masculine" than boys reared in intact families (Adams et al., 1984). For example, in a classic study, Elizabeth Herzog and Cecilia Sudia found that boys who grow up in fatherless homes turn out to be just as normal and well adjusted as boys reared in intact families. The only exception to this finding is that fatherless boys show a slight increase in delinquency and in school disciplinary problems. However, this same increase occurs in both boys *and* girls reared by a single parent of *either* sex (Herzog & Sudia, 1968).

FATHER-DAUGHTER DEPRIVATION

Research by Mavis Hetherington suggests that young girls may need their fathers if they are to learn the social "dating skills" that our culture views as normal. Hetherington began by observing the activities of three types of girls: (1) those whose mothers had gotten divorces when the girls were very young, (2) those whose fathers had died when the girls were very young, and (3) those who had grown up in intact family situations. None of the girls had brothers. Although few of these young women had noticeable behavior problems, and all were doing reasonably well in school, there were marked differences in the way these adolescent girls *reacted to the males* in their environments.

According to Hetherington, girls reared by divorced mothers sought more attention and praise from males than did girls in the other two groups. They were also more likely to hang around places where young males could be found—gymnasiums, carpentry and machine shops, and the stag lines at school dances. In marked contrast, girls with widowed mothers tended to avoid males as much as possible. These fatherless girls stayed away from typically male gathering places, and many of them remained in the ladies' room the entire evening during dances and other social events. These differences apparently were not due to popularity, for both groups of girls received equal numbers of invitations to dance when they were actually present in the dance hall.

All three groups of girls appeared to have similar and quite normal relationships with other women. However, girls reared by divorced mothers dated earlier and more frequently than did the others, and were more likely to have engaged in sexual intercourse (Lopez, 1987). By contrast, girls with widowed mothers tended to start dating much later than normal and seemed to be sexually inhibited (Hetherington et al., 1975). Data collected on the same girls 10 years later tended to confirm the original findings (Hetherington et al., 1985).

Hetherington concludes that girls apparently need the presence of an adult male during their formative years in order to learn appropriate responses to men when the girls reach puberty (Hetherington, 1981).

Parent-Child Relations

In the movie *Parenthood*, Steve Martin plays a father who, because of his own troubled childhood, tries to be the "perfect parent." The movie explores the effect of different parenting styles and different family structures. Let's conclude this chapter with a look at what psychologists have learned in these two areas.

PARENTING STYLE

Classifying parenting styles is not easy. However, psychologists studying parent-child relations often talk about four general types of parenting—indulgent, authoritative, authoritarian, and neglectful (Lamborn et al., 1991). *Indulgent* parents are heavily involved with their children, but they allow the children freedom to make their own choices. *Authoritative* parents are strict, but they explain the reasons for their actions, and they allow their children to question the rules. *Authoritarian* parents require strict, unquestioning obedience. Authoritarian parents are not heavily involved with their children. *Neglectful* parents are not involved with their children, and they do not enforce strict discipline.

Children with the highest self-esteem, self-confidence, and social competence come from families with either indulgent or authoritative parenting (Baumrind, 1991; Lamborn et al., 1991; Maccoby & Martin, 1983). These styles seem to teach the child that he or she is important (Moritz & Motta, 1992).

As we mentioned earlier, however, it is important to remember that the family is a "system." Children influence parents as well as parents influence children. For instance, parents are able to give *socially competent* children more freedom. Thus the parents appear more indulgent, although the children may be socially competent for other reasons. And children who respond to explanations for rules are encouraging their parents to discipline this way. Thus the children *reinforce* the parents for adopting an authoritative style.

Because we cannot experimentally subject children to different parenting styles we are limited to observations. And since these observations are *correlations*, we cannot infer cause and effect.

Perhaps this is not very helpful for parents looking for guidance. Should they be like Steve Martin's character, indulgent, super-sensitive, involved—taking their children to ball games, museums, movies? Or does it matter? For these parents, Sandra Scarr offers some encouragement:

> Good enough, ordinary parents probably have the same effects on their children's development as culturally defined super-parents (Rowe, in press). This comforting idea gives parents a lot more freedom to care for their children in ways they find comfortable for them, and it gives them more freedom from guilt when they deviate (within the normal range) from culturally prescribed norms about parenting.
>
> (Scarr, 1992. p 15)

Can you think of some "culturally prescribed norms" that might be different if you were a parent in another country?

RECENT CHANGES IN FAMILY STRUCTURE

What is your "prototype" of a family? Many people in North America assume a "normal" family means a married couple (man and woman), including an employed father, a housewife mother, and two or more school-age children. While this pattern may have been common in the 1950s, it describes only 7 percent of American households today (Otto, 1988).

Many factors have contributed to the family structure of the 90s. In the past 40 years there have been steady increases in the number of births outside of marriage, the number of marriages ending in divorce, the number of single-parent and step families, and the number of dual-earner marriages.

Along with these changes there has been a steady decline in children's well-being. Academic achievement has dropped, and delinquency of all types has risen (Forehand, 1992; Uhlenberg & Eggebeen, 1986).

We must be careful, however, in blaming these negative effects on a particular family structure. As David Demo points out, "Children's well-being depends much more on enduring parental support and satisfying family relationships than it does on a particular family structure" (Demo, 1992). For example, single-parent families almost always suffer economic hardship. And fathers absent from these families usually fail to maintain adequate interaction with, and social support of their children. Bonnie Barber and Jacquelynne Eccles suggest that, "negative outcomes attributed to divorce may, in fact, be due to economic struggle or parent conflict." They add, "Although it may be true that two parents can do a better job of raising children than one parent, it does not follow that all children are better off if their parents stay together" (Barber & Eccles, 1992).

"Typical" family structures have undergone tremendous changes in the last 40 years. We do not know the full effect of these shifts on the development of the child, just as we do not know the relative contribution of heredity or individual differences.

It does seem, however, that regardless of heredity, cognitive ability, parenting style, or family structure, children have certain basic psychological and social needs. If they are given consistent love and support from one or more adults who are willing to spend time developing a close relationship, they will likely succeed *in spite of* apparent disadvantages. We can demonstrate this point rather dramatically by returning to the subject of chromosomal abnormalities, and by discussing more fully the developmental disorder called *Down's syndrome*.

A Special Social Environment

Most authorities agree that Down's syndrome is the most common chromosomal defect affecting a child's development (Patterson, 1987). This disorder was once

Thyroid (THIGH-roid). A large endocrine gland lying at the base of the neck that produces growth hormones.

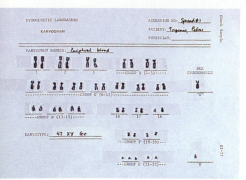

FIGURE 12.4

Trisomy-21. Note the three chromosomes instead of the usual two on the 21st pair.

Children with Down's syndrome are capable of learning more skills than was once thought. Chris Burke, an actor with Down's syndrome, has shown his considerable talents on network television.

called "mongolism," because the child has an Oriental-looking skin fold at the inner corners of the eyes. The young person also typically has a small head; a flat nose; a protruding and thick tongue; a defective heart, eyes, and ears; and a defective **thyroid** gland. An extra 21st chromosome causes this disorder (see Figure 12.4).

According to a study by the National Academy of Sciences, Down's syndrome occurs in one birth in 600. However, the age of the mother is a crucial variable. Among 25-year-old mothers, the incidence is 1 in 2,000 births. Among 40-year-old mothers, however, the incidence is 1 in 100 births. When the mother is 45 or older, the rate rises to 1 in 40. While some pediatricians believe the problem is due to "aging eggs," other specialists disagree. For example, some experts believe that mothers under 35 may conceive as many Down's syndrome fetuses as do older mothers. However, because they are younger, these women's bodies are more capable of spontaneously aborting defective fetuses than are the bodies of older women (Yulsman, 1985).

About 3 percent of the time, Down's syndrome is inherited and may be due to defective genes on the father's as well as the mother's part. In most cases, however, a "genetic accident" causes the disorder. For some reason, the 21st pair of chromosomes does not separate properly during cell division, and the extra chromosome is carried over in either the egg or the sperm. In the great majority of these "genetic accidents" cases, some 75–80 percent of the time, the defect is carried in the egg, not the sperm (Tyndall, 1986).

The mortality rate for Down's syndrome children is very high early in life—especially for females—with 40–55 percent of them dying in their first year. These children seem to have defective immune systems, since they are particularly sensitive to viral diseases such as the flu. If their medical problems are handled properly, however, individuals with Down's syndrome often live until middle age (Patterson, 1987).

Until fairly recently, most developmental psychologists assumed all Down's syndrome children were doomed to be mentally handicapped because of their defective chromosomes. And it is true that when given "ordinary" training as infants, these children typically have a limited intellectual potential. However, the cause of the "retardation" is both biological and environmental.

We now know that appropriate medical intervention can greatly relieve the biological component. As neurologist Mary Coleman puts it, "Some of the retardation that is associated with Down's syndrome can actually be traced to a thyroid deficiency, which is easily corrected." Most of the children also suffer from middle- and inner-ear problems, which can be solved by minor surgery. "In the past," Coleman says, "people assumed that these children couldn't speak because they were dumb. But in fact, one major reason they were slow to speak was that they couldn't hear properly" (Pines, 1982).

Once the medical problems have been taken care of, the key to development is how much verbal stimulation and encouragement the children receive in their environment. Coleman recommends a program called *infant-stim*, which requires the parents of Down's syndrome children to spend several hours daily talking to and teaching the children. The parents avoid using punishment and they give the children as much positive reinforcement as possible. Children treated with infant-stim usually show a remarkable jump in IQ within a few months. "The older literature on these children says that they plateau at five," Coleman says. "More recently, after the first infant-stim programs, people began to say that they plateau at seven. Then they said these children plateau at twelve. I'm still waiting for them to plateau!"

Coleman states that Down's syndrome children "can never become normal. Because of their hearing problems, they will never speak quite clearly. On the average, they have lower IQs than other children and, in some cases, they have certain brain deficits that prevent them from making much progress. But most of them can improve far beyond what used to be expected of them" (quoted in Pines, 1982).

The more athletic style of play in which fathers often engage may give the child experience with different kinds of muscular and neural stimulation.

Ronald Strauss and his colleagues agree that a *coordinated* series of interventions is most effective. They suggest this involves giving the child cognitive, behavioral, vocational, speech, medical and surgical help (Strauss et al., 1989).

In the past, because we presumed that Down's syndrome was caused entirely by a chromosomal defect, we often considered these children to be hopelessly retarded. Now that we see both the problem and the youngsters in a different perspective, we can be more optimistic. As we noted earlier, your position on both the mind-body and the nature-nurture controversies determines not only *how you perceive people*, but *how you treat them* as well.

In the early 1980s, physicians began using "cosmetic surgery" to help Down's syndrome children. The surgery involves removing the extra skin from the corners of the eyes, reshaping the nose, and trimming excess tissue from the child's tongue. Immediately after the surgery, the child often shows a dramatic rise in cognitive development. How could cosmetic surgery influence cognitive growth?

In some ways we have only scratched the surface in our discussion of early development. Each of the sub-areas of psychology which we have discussed in other chapters, has its own special interest in infancy and early childhood. We have already considered some of these topics, such as the development of language (Chapter 11); others, such as the development of personality, we will consider later (Chapter 14). Still other areas of study become more significant as the individual develops into adolescence and adulthood. It is to these areas that we now turn.

SUMMARY

1. There are three main *theoretical* issues in the **life-span** approach to development—the matter of the **amount of change** which takes place, the question of whether changes are **gradual or abrupt,** and the **nature-nurture** controversy.

2. Very few psychological traits seem to be **continuous** over long periods of time. An exception seems to be **temperament,** which may be genetically determined.

3. You began life as a single **egg cell** that contained 23 **chromosomes.** At the moment of **fertilization,** one of your father's sperms penetrated the egg and added 23 chromosomes of its own. These chromosomes contain the **genes** that govern the functioning of each cell.

4. If an **X sperm** unites with the egg, the 23rd chromosome will be **XX,** and the child will be born a female. If a **Y sperm** unites with the egg, the 23rd chromosome will be **XY,** and the child will be born a male.

5. Sometimes the chromosomes of the mother and father contain **genetic defects.** If the child's cells contain but a single X chromosome, the child will suffer from **Turner's syndrome.** A child with an **XXY 23rd chromosome** becomes an infertile male and is said to suffer from **Klinefelter's syndrome.** A child with an **XYY 23rd chromosome** becomes a normal-appearing male but may have difficulty learning **impulse control.**

6. If the child's cells have three **21st chromosomes** rather than two, the child will suffer from **Down's syndrome,** or **trisomy-21.**

7. Two weeks after fertilization, the cells begin to **differentiate** or take on different roles. The three main types of cells are **ectoderm, mesoderm,** and **endoderm.**

8. During pregnancy, the fetus is protected from the mother's body by an organ called the **placenta.**

9. Various **germs** and **drugs** can pass through the placenta and affect the developing fetus.

10. If the mother is starved during pregnancy, the child may be born smaller than usual. If the infant is given ample food, however, it will usually "catch up" to the size its **genetic blueprint** originally specified.

11. While training cannot appreciably speed up **motor development,** encouraging the child to be active often has positive side effects such as encouraging the child's social development.

12. Baby geese (and the young of other animals) often **imprint** on the first moving object they see or can follow. Whether imprinting or **affectionate bonding** actually occurs in humans is not yet decided.

13. There is some evidence that **fetuses** can learn **simple associations** while still in the womb. And only moments after birth, infants apparently can **imitate** (or at least respond to) facial gestures, **search** visually for the source of human voices, and **move their limbs in synchrony** with the human voice. By two weeks, babies **recognize** their mother and form perceptual **schemata.**

14. Not only can newborns do a great deal immediately after birth, they may even be able to **learn** *before* they are born.

15. It appears that **nurture interacts with nature** by determining the level of development which is achieved within the possibilities and limitations set by nature.

16. **Jean Piaget** was one of the most respected figures in child psychology. According to Piaget, you were born with certain structures of the mind, or **schemata,** for processing and responding to reality. Mental development proceeds as a child develops more and more complex schemata.

17. The two **mental functions** that guide cognitive adaptation are **assimilation** and **accommodation.**

18. Assimilation involves **changing inputs** to fit the child's present mental structures. Accommodation involves **changing mental structures** (or making new ones) to make them match present inputs.

19. According to Piaget, all children pass through four **developmental stages,** each of which grows out of, and is more complex than, the preceding one.

20. During the **sensory-motor period** (birth to 2 years), the infant learns to integrate various sense impressions into complex **schemata.**

21. During the **pre-operational stage,** the child learns to speak and to deal with the world in **symbolic terms,** by talking about abjects rather than by having to manipulate them directly. But the child's reasoning may be **egocentric,** and the child does not realize that objects can be **transformed** without being changed.

22. During the **stage of concrete operations,** children learn to visualize a whole series of operations in their minds and to differentiate themselves from the outer world. They also discover that the process of transformation is **reversible.**

23. During the **stage of formal operations,** the young person gains the ability to think in purely **abstract terms.**

24. Piaget believes children pass through these stages at their own individual speeds, but that the stages cannot be **reversed.**

25. Criticisms of Piaget include such problems as whether his theory applies to **children in all cultures,** whether children are really **egocentric,** whether **developmental stages** actually exist, and whether **stage reversals** occur.

26. A major criticism of Piaget is that he performed **demonstrations** rather than tightly controlled **experiments.**

27. Mother and newborn child form a **social dyad.** Evidence suggests that both mother and child have an **inborn mutual readiness** to respond to each other. Infants also **shape** parental responses as much as parents shape the child's reactions.

28. During pregnancy, a change in **hormones** may cause an increased interest in infants. In addition, women (and men) develop a **psychological** need for continued contact with infants.

29. Maternal contact also allows the infant to build up **perceptual expectations** about its world. When its expectancies are grossly violated, the infant falls into an **anaclitic depression** and may suffer physical and psychological impairment if not returned to its mother.

30. Children placed in high quality day-care centers show little negative effect of this **short-term separation.** High-quality day-care centers have frequent teacher-child interactions, well-trained teachers, and small numbers of children for each teacher.

31. Peers, friends, and play are important sources of learning for **social relationships.** Good peer relationships are associated with good **parent-child attachment,** and high **self-esteem.**

32. When given the opportunity, human fathers seem as interested in and as responsive to their infants as are mothers. Fathers tend to engage in rough-housing and **physical contact** with their children more than do mothers.

33. Mothers tend to **talk** to their children more than do fathers, but **touch** and play with the children less.

34. Early studies suggested that boys who grow up without fathers often show very "feminine" behavior patterns, but later experiments contradict the early findings. The only consistent result is that fatherless boys show a slightly greater tendency to **delinquency.**

35. Girls who grow up **without fathers** may either be strongly attracted to adult males or tend to avoid them, depending in part on whether the girls' mothers were divorced or widowed.

36. Parent-child relations exist in a variety of forms as a result of different **parenting styles** and different **family structures.** Parent-child relations affect children's development, although the exact effects are not easy to specify.

37. Beyond parenting style and family structure, the most important need that children have is for a stable **loving relationship** with an adult (or adults) who provide consistent, involved support.

38. **Down's syndrome** children suffer from a variety of physical problems. However, the **mental retardation** often associated with this developmental disorder can be overcome to a great extent if the child is given medical attention and **intensive stimulation** during its early years.

ANSWERS FOR THOUGHT

1. *Research findings aside, would you like to think that you will continue to change?*

   Most people would like to think they continue to change, probably because they would like to overcome their faults and retain their good qualities. Of course, this does not always happen. People often change much less than they think (as we will see in the next chapters). Stability is affected not only by inherited traits and dispositions, but also by our tendency to choose environments where we feel comfortable. This reinforces our existing characteristics and creates a self-perpetuating cycle (Bandura's "reciprocal determinism").

2. *Have you ever been told you were "just going through a phase"? How did this make you feel? Is this . . . ?*

   You probably didn't appreciate being told you were just "going through a phase" because it suggests your feelings are temporary and should not be taken seriously. This view seems to assume an abrupt change position—that you will suddenly "snap out of it" and move on to another "phase" or stage.

3. *Do you think parents should be allowed to sell their children as slaves, or even to murder their children, if the . . . ?*

   Most people in 20th-century Western society believe that children are *persons* and not mere chattels or possessions. As a result children possess certain basic rights regardless of their parents' wishes. These basic rights would certainly prevent them from being murdered or sold into slavery by their parents. This view reflects a perception of childhood as *continuous* with the rest of life. Life is valuable at all ages and not just in adulthood.

4. *Some XYY males accused of crimes have asked to be pardoned, claiming their genetic disability . . . ?*

You might want to consider more generally how you see the relationship between responsibility and punishment. If you believe punishment should be based on the crime *regardless* of predisposing factors, you would ignore this plea for leniency. If you believe possibly relevant factors such as socioeconomic background, childhood training, and physical and psychological traits should be taken into account, you would probably want to learn more about the relationship between the XYY pattern and criminal behavior.

5. *Many other disorders also have a genetic basis and can be predicted from genetic testing. What is your . . . ?*

Most people in the U.S. are in favor of genetic testing for defective genes (Singer, 1991). Testing of prospective mates can predict defects in their children. Testing of a fetus can predict defects before birth. Predicting defects raises many moral issues regarding what to do with the knowledge. Should a couple with defective genes be prevented from having children? Should a fetus with defective genes be aborted? Ultimately, it is hoped that we will be able to correct genetic defects. But in the meantime, the response to genetic information remains an often difficult personal decision.

6. *How might early encouragement affect a child's later social behavior?*

If encouragement is carefully matched to the child's level, challenging the child to move ahead but not pushing too quickly, it can be effective. For example, one of the best predictors of adult prosocial behavior (helping others in need) is the amount of early teaching and modeling of this behavior that children have seen from their parents as they were growing up. In short, the proper early encouragement can be effective.

7. *What other explanations for Chisholm's results can you think of?*

Perhaps the Navajo mothers were less responsive to their children's protests. The children may have been responding similarly in the two groups, but the mothers may have been socialized by their culture to respond differently to the infants. It may have taken less protesting for the Anglo mothers to consider it "excessive" and begin weaning.

8. *In the Smotherman conditioning experiment involving apple juice and lithium chloride, what was . . . ?*

The unconditioned stimulus (UCS) was the lithium chloride since it produces an unconditioned response (UCR) of withdrawal and avoidance *without* any learning. The conditioned stimulus (CS) was the apple juice (or mint flavoring in the second study) because as a result of pairing the lithium chloride with the apple juice (UCS with CS), the apple juice came to produce the avoidance response (CR) which it did not produce initially.

9. *Little Mikey calls all adults males—including the letter carrier—"Daddy." Which cognitive process is Mikey using?*

Mikey's mental schema for "Daddy" is very broad, apparently defined by two features: adult, and male. Any adult male is *assimilated* into this schema. His mother would probably like to teach him that most adult males do not fit this schema. This will lead to *accommodation* as Mikey sets up a new schema for "Daddy"—a sub-category of the old one which he might re-label "man."

10. *Do the data cited earlier (in this chapter) on what newborns can and can't do support Piaget's position, or not?*

The research cited earlier in the chapter (in the section on neonatal learning) indicates that newborns can perceive their environment and begin to form perceptual schemas. This is consistent with Piaget's position.

11. *What else does the child acquire during the first 2 years of life that allows the child to represent . . . ?*

    During the first 2 years of life children begin to acquire language. This enables them to represent and manipulate objects as internal cognitive symbols.

12. *Piaget seems never to have used the shaping techniques (described in Chapter 9) to teach a child to conserve . . . ?*

    Shaping involves small successive approximations to the goal. Beginning with equal amounts of liquid in two identical containers, you could pour the liquid from one container into a container which was only slightly narrower. If the child said the amount of liquid was still the same (perhaps with your coaxing), you would reward the child. In very gradual steps, you would pour the liquid into narrower and narrower containers, each time rewarding the child for saying the liquid had not changed in volume.

13. *If you ask a pre-operational girl, "Which row has more pennies?" how do you know she understands . . . ?*

    You might check by showing her the original row and a comparison row which had wider spacing between pennies but had *one less penny* than the original row. If she still said the "spaced row" had more pennies you would conclude she is responding to quantity of space rather than quantity of pennies.

14. *What could it mean for a democratic society if many of its citizens fail to function at a formal operational level of thought?*

    Citizens who function at concrete operational or pre-operational levels do not consider the long-range consequences of government policies, and so tend to vote for immediate, concrete gains. Since they also have trouble seeing themselves through the eyes of others, they are insensitive to the views of outside interest groups and different countries. This could lead to intolerance, unjust laws, and international conflict.

15. *Which type of play is probably meant in the saying, "All work and no play makes Jack a dull boy"?*

    Although all types of play are beneficial, creative social play probably provides the greatest number of benefits which are not usually gained from work.

16. *Given the fact that a father's influence on his child is more strongly emotional than intellectual, what would . . . ?*

    Boys (and girls) usually have frequent opportunities to observe male models— men fulfilling accepted social roles—on television, in school, and other social settings. Their learning would probably not suffer at this general social level. Boys, however, usually have male friends among their peers. For girls close male relationships may be non-existent. As a result, girls might suffer more from their lack of experience in learning appropriate responses to males.

17. *Can you think of some "culturally prescribed norms" that might be different if you were a parent in another country?*

    Many non-Western countries do not value autonomy and personal independence as much as North Americans do. Asian and African cultures, for example, often place a greater emphasis on emotional closeness and *inter*dependence. They stress a greater concern for social harmony and loyalty to the family and other social groups (Bond, 1988; Cheek & Melchoir, 1990; Triandis et al., 1988). These groups might not be impressed with the possible results of indulgent and authoritative parenting.

18. *In the early 1980s, physicians began using "cosmetic surgery" to help Down's syndrome children. The surgery . . . ?*

It would improve the child's ability to speak clearly and so could encourage social interaction. It could improve the child's self-esteem. And it could improve the way other people respond to the child. All of these could have positive effects on motivation and the opportunity for cognitive development. (The effect of this type of surgery varies, and its value has been questioned (Katz & Kravetz, 1989).)

CHAPTER 13

ADOLESCENCE, ADULTHOOD, AND AGING

She rang off, put the telephone back on the table, and leaned back in her chair.

Now, there was nothing to be done. She discovered that she was very tired, but it was a gentle tiredness, assuaged and comforted by her surroundings, as though her house were a kindly person, and she was being embraced by loving arms. In the warm and firelit room and the deep familiar armchair, she found herself surprised by, filled by, the sort of reasonless happiness she had not experienced for years. *It is because I am alive. I am sixty-four, and I have suffered, if those idiot doctors are to be believed, a heart attack. Whatever. I have survived it, and I shall put it behind me, and not talk nor think about it, ever again. Because I am alive. I can feel, touch, see, hear, smell; look after myself; discharge myself from the hospital; find a taxi, and get myself home. There are snowdrops coming out in the garden, and spring is on the way. I shall see it. Watch the yearly miracle, and feel the sun grow warmer as the weeks slip by. And because I am alive, I shall watch it all happen and be part of that miracle.*

She remembered the story of dear Maurice Chevalier. *How does it feel to be seventy?* they had asked him. *Not too bad,* he had replied. *When you consider the alternative.*

But for Penelope Keeling it felt a thousand times better than just not too bad. Living, now, had become not simple existence that one took for granted, but a bonus, a gift, with every day that lay ahead an experience to be savoured. *Time did not last forever. I shall not waste a single moment,* she promised herself. She had never felt so strong, so optimistic. As though she was young once more, starting out, and something marvellous was just about to happen.

ROSAMUNDE PILCHER
THE SHELL SEEKERS

Probably the most familiar metaphor for human development is the seasons of the year. In the terms of this metaphor, we have been discussing only spring-time—infancy and early childhood. The *life span* perspective requires that we move on to look at summer, autumn and winter, for like the seasons, we cannot avoid change.

In this chapter we will consider changes in three familiar areas: physical, cognitive, and social. And once again, we will encounter the "three developmental issues." Keep in mind the following questions as we consider growth and change after childhood: How much do we change as we move through life? Do the changes we observe come in abrupt stages, or are they smooth and gradual? How much change is the result of inevitable biological processes (nature), and how much is the result of social and other environmental influences (nurture)?

PHYSICAL DEVELOPMENT

Like a clock that never stops ticking, biological processes push us through life with relentless determination. In our first few years, physical changes are obvious and dramatic—and our parents await them with anticipation. In adulthood they are more subtle but equally uncompromising—and we try to accept them graciously. Sometimes, like Penelope in the quotation which opened this chapter, a physical "change" turns our world upside down. Let's begin our discussion of physical development by looking at a time when the rate of physical change rivals that of infancy—the period of adolescence.

Adolescence

Puberty (POO-bur-tee). The period of sexual development and rapid physical growth triggered by an increase in sex hormones, from as early as 9 years to as late as 14 years of age.

Adolescence begins with the onset of **puberty,** and extends to the achievement of adulthood. In some non-industrialized societies, puberty signals the beginning of adulthood; adolescence does not exist. As soon as puberty indicates that individuals are capable of sexual reproduction, they assume adult status and roles. Even in Europe and North America in the 19th century, the interlude between childhood and adulthood was very brief or non-existent, and adolescence as we know it, did not exist. Twentieth-century Western culture, however, withholds adult status for several years *after puberty*, creating the period we call adolescence.

Probably the main reason contemporary Western culture delays adult status is because of the type of preparation that a young person must go through. Our society considers many years of training and experience necessary before we become adults. The length of time this takes varies, and so the transition into adulthood is not clearly defined. It may mean the age when we can vote, or consume alcohol, when we complete our formal education, when we leave home, when we achieve financial independence, or when we reach some other milestone. So while adolescence has a clear beginning in biology, its ending is social, and at the whim of changing culture (Feldman & Rosenthal, 1991).

The end of adolescence may be unclear; its beginning is not. Adolescence starts with a growth spurt and the development of primary and secondary sex characteristics.

SEXUAL DEVELOPMENT

As we discussed in Chapter 7, primary sex characteristics are the actual sex organs—the ovaries, vagina, uterus, and clitoris in females, and the penis and testes in males. At the onset of puberty (about age 11 in girls and 13 in boys), these organs begin the

In some cultures, ceremonies celebrate puberty and indicate that the individual is ready to assume adult roles.

development that will make them capable of performing their reproductive function. Over a period of about 2 years, *sex hormones*, produced by the ovaries in females and the testes in males, cause a series of physical changes. Some of these changes lead eventually to ovulation and menstruation in females, and in males, to the production of sperm.

The first menstrual period, called **menarche,** usually occurs before age 13, although it may be another year before the cycle includes ovulation. This is earlier than in previous generations, and earlier than in many less developed parts of the world. (Researchers believe the change is probably the result of improved nutrition.) Boys become capable of ejaculation at about age 14, but they may be 15 before they produce a normal amount of sperm (Chilman, 1983; Tanner, 1970, 1978, 1990).

Hormones are also responsible for the development of secondary sex characteristics at this time. Females experience breast development, broadening of the hips, and the growth of pubic hair. In males, the shoulders broaden, the voice lowers, and pubic and facial hair appears. As these physical differences develop, both males and females begin to experience increased sexual interest and sexual desire.

Menarche (men-AR-kee). The first menstrual period of a girl in puberty.

GROWTH SPURT

At the beginning of puberty, both males and females begin to grow more rapidly. Although growth takes place in all dimensions, the most obvious is height. The *rate* of growth in height increases until it reaches a peak at about 12 years in girls and 14 years in boys (see Figure 13.1). At his time a boy may be growing at a rate he has not experienced since he was 2 years old (Tanner, 1990). During the peak year of growth, a boy may grow 4 or 5 inches, a girl 3 or 4, making additional gains in the 2 or 3 years before and after this peak.

Before puberty, girls and boys of a particular body size are similar in strength. Since girls reach puberty sooner than boys, there is a period from about 12 1/2 years to 13 1/2 years when girls are stronger than boys of the same age. However, boys soon catch up and surpass girls in strength, relative heart and lung size, and several other characteristics (which might be adaptively related to the need to hunt, fight, and forage for food) (Tanner, 1990).

Along with dramatic gains in height, adolescents make significant gains in weight. During the early period of rapid growth, they gain very little fat. And the percentage of body fat may actually decrease. However, as their growth slows down,

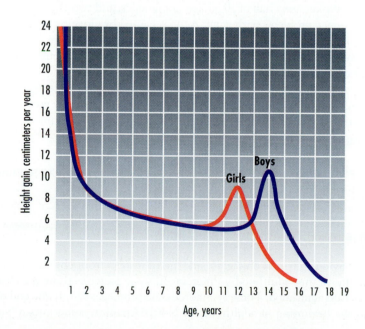

FIGURE 13.1

Typical changes in growth rates for height in males and females. (From Tanner & others, 1966).

Brain asymmetry (aye-SIM-eh-tree). The fact that the two cerebral hemispheres are not identical. The left hemisphere, which is usually dominant for language abilities, is slightly larger than the right hemisphere.

In early adolescence girls often experience a growth spurt before boys.

the rate at which their bodies convert calories into energy also decreases, and they frequently begin to accumulate fat.

The hormones which produce the growth spurt, as well as primary and secondary sex changes, are also active in other areas. Many researchers believe hormones are largely responsible for the male-female differences in cognitive abilities which emerge at this time. Hormones may affect cognitive abilities by influencing neural processing, or controlling **brain asymmetry,** or acting in some other way. Of course, social factors always play a role in sex differences, but in this case, biological differences appear to be at least as important (Lloyd, 1986; Newcombe & Dubas, 1992).

"STORM AND STRESS"

All of these changes can produce great emotional upheaval, prompting many people to label adolescence a time of "storm and stress" (Buchanan et al., 1992). The adolescent girl's first menstrual period can be a positive sign of maturity, of becoming a woman (Brooks-Gunn & Ruble, 1983; Grief & Ulman, 1982; Ruble & Brooks-Gunn, 1982). Or it may be a negative sign of lost childhood, a "hassle," "something you have to put up with" (Boxer & Peterson, 1986; Brooks-Gunn & Ruble, 1984). For adolescent boys, uncontrolled erection and the first ejaculation (usually in a "wet dream") may cause surprise and worry.

Other adjustment problems may be associated with the fact that puberty does not begin at the same age for everyone. Early-maturing girls may feel self-conscious, and unhappy with their body-image. They are often less popular with other girls, and they tend to perform more poorly in school. However, by late adolescence they are more popular, more self-directed cognitively, socially, and emotionally, than their later-maturing peers. Late-maturing girls do not seem to experience the same stress, although they may be concerned about the delay.

For boys, early maturity seems to be a blessing. Early-maturing boys, being bigger and stronger, have an advantage in athletics. They tend to be given adult privileges earlier. And they usually feel more secure and confident. Late-maturing boys, in contrast, often have difficulties with athletics, are more likely to be treated as children, and frequently have difficulty establishing relationships with girls. Several studies have found that personality differences between early- and late-maturers persist long into adulthood (Clausen, 1975; Livson & Peskin, 1980).

Changes in appearance, particularly facial appearance, may also cause stress at this time. Approximately half of all adolescent females, and two-thirds of adolescent males, experience problems with acne. Acne is caused by clogging of the sebaceous (oil-producing) glands, which become more active in adolescence. There is some evidence that acne may be made worse by stress, and relieved through stress-reduction methods such as relaxation training (Wood, 1987).

Less expected than acne at this time is the discovery that facial features may grow at an irregular and uneven rate. For example, the nose or ears may grow faster than the rest of the face. One ear may grow faster than the other. At a time when attractiveness is crucial, these events can be traumatic.

Is adolescence a time of "storm and stress" partly because of expectations that it will be?

Adulthood

Although obvious physical changes mark the transition from childhood to adolescence, the move into adulthood is different. In some societies there are clear "rites of passage" into adulthood. These ceremonies and privileges signify the end of childhood and the beginning of adulthood. In North America, sometimes a "sweet 16

Late adolescence to young adulthood is the time of peak athletic performance.

party" or getting a driver's license becomes a significant transitional event. But usually adult status is still incomplete. However, by the early 20s other milestones have been reached (the right to vote, perform military service, consume alcohol), and the rapid physical changes of adolescence are pretty well over. It is now appropriate to consider the individual a "young adult" rather than an adolescent.

PHYSICAL CHANGES

In young adulthood, physical strength and stamina continue to increase up to about age 30. During this time, all physical systems are generally functioning at their peak. Young adulthood is the time of peak performance for professional athletes (even earlier in some sports) and others in physically demanding occupations (e.g., firefighters).

By this time, most people have come to accept their adult physical form. And their health is usually not a concern. This means that they can focus their attention on other areas of change, such as career and family. However, biological processes never remain static, and it is not long before the signs of aging begin to emerge.

In the 20s, our first gray hairs often appear, and our hair begins to thin. The decrease in our basal metabolism, which began in adolescence, frequently results in an accumulation of 14 or 15 pounds of fat by the time we reach 40. Skin wrinkles begin to appear on our face in our late 20s, and fat deposits cause our face to begin to sag. Unless we maintain regular exercise, our muscles lose their tone, and other parts of our body begin to sag. Lack of exercise, poor diet, and unhealthful habits such as smoking also accelerate the inevitable loss of efficiency in all our organ systems.

Under normal conditions, many changes that begin in young adulthood are usually not noticeable until middle adulthood or even later. Because of what is called "organ reserve," bodily systems are capable of handling more than they normally have to. This extra ability erodes with age, meaning that we become less capable of dealing with prolonged exertion or extra stress. As we continue to age, extra exertion, stress, and disease become greater enemies because the reserve we once had is no longer available. Still, for most people, the reserve is great enough to carry them through the years of young and middle adulthood. Some people diminish these

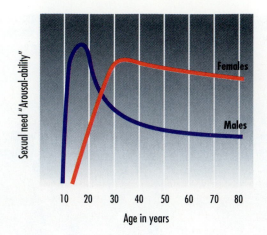

FIGURE 13.2

Most psychologists believe that sexual arousability reaches a peak in males at about age 18 and thereafter declines, while arousability peaks in females at about age 35 and remains fairly constant thereafter.

reserves faster through an unhealthy lifestyle, others adopt a lifestyle that slows the depletion, but the depletion is inevitable.

How does the rate of physical aging reflect the interaction of nature and nurture?

SEXUALITY

There is not much agreement among the experts on how aging affects sexuality, much less *why* these changes occur. Figure 13.2 shows the generally accepted view of sexual arousability. From this point of view, males tend to reach their peak about age 18, then show a sharp drop that continues the rest of their lives. Arousability in women, however, tends to peak about age 35 or so and stays relatively high thereafter.

The truth of the matter is that there simply aren't enough studies, made in enough situations, to tell us all we need to know about sexuality in later years. It is true that hormone levels reach a peak in the male at about age 18 and fall thereafter. But it is just as true that a healthy 90-year-old male typically has a high enough hormone level to perform the sex act several times a week (Soules & Bremner, 1982; Starr, 1987).

Most research suggests that sexual arousability at any age past puberty is as greatly affected by intra-psychic and social factors as by hormone levels (von Sydow, 1992a, 1992b). Our society has certain expectations about sex among older individuals, and those expectations are primarily negative. Older individuals probably need more psychological (and perhaps more physical) stimulation to maintain a high level of sexual performance. But then, this need for increased stimulation among older people may also be true of areas other than sex (Rowe & Kahn, 1987).

Almost all researchers in this area have come to the same conclusion: People who, in their later years, continue to have an active sex life typically look younger, have more energy, and show a greater zest for living than do people who shun sexuality.

Sexual arousal is determined by many factors, including mental attitudes and social expectations, for adults of all ages.

COGNITIVE DEVELOPMENT

In Chapter 12 we ended our consideration of cognitive development with Piaget's stage of formal operations, begun in early adolescence. So, let's begin our discussion of cognitive development in adolescence and adulthood, with a look at *postformal* thought. After this we will consider changes in information processing, intelligence, and moral reasoning.

Postformal Thought

According to Piaget, the development of formal operational thought means that the adolescent is capable of thinking in abstract and hypothetical terms. This type of thinking may begin about age 11, but it does not become fully developed until late adolescence (Piaget, 1972). Some adolescents apparently do not use formal operational thought, and as you may recall, Piaget's critics have pointed out that his conclusions may not apply to other cultures (Neimark, 1982).

Despite these qualifications, several researchers suggest that new abilities emerge following adolescence. Piaget himself recognized that adult thought could involve a more advanced style of thinking, although he felt that this was only an elaboration of the basic stage of formal operations.

Gisela Labouvie-Vief suggests that young adult thought represents a significant change. She believes that the practical considerations of our complex society limit and even transform the idealistic logic of youth. Young adult thought becomes more concrete and pragmatic, something Labouvie-Vief says is a sign of *maturity* (Labouvie-Vief, 1982, 1986).

Jan Sinnott argues that *relativistic* thinking might be more advanced than formal operations. Relativistic thought recognizes that the distinction between classes of objects or events is not absolute, but relative, and dependent on context (Sinnott, 1981). As we will see, this type of thought appears to be necessary for the more "advanced" levels of moral decision-making.

Other researchers suggest that postformal thought is able to accept contradictions, and to integrate these into a more inclusive system (Kramer, 1983). None of these proposals has gained acceptance as a distinct "stage." John Rybash and his colleagues sum up the current view of postformal thought when they say, "Postformal cognitive development should be regarded as a set of *styles* of thinking that emerge during adulthood . . . , not as a true structural stage of thought" (Rybash et al., 1986).

So cognitive abilities continue to develop during adulthood. And the argument persists as to whether this development occurs as a gradual change or an abrupt stage. Not all cognitive change in adulthood may be in the direction of increasing potential, however. Let's consider some cognitive abilities which are sometimes thought to decline with age.

Information Processing

There are two areas of cognitive processing which some researchers believe are affected by age: One is response time; the other is memory.

RESPONSE TIMES

It would not surprise most people to learn that response times increase with age. Researchers observe this slowing down in all sensory modalities and all methods of response (Kimmel, 1990). However, there are some interesting exceptions to this generalization. Researcher Timothy Salthouse found that older typists were not slower than younger typists, despite their slower reaction times. The older typists had developed a strategy of looking farther ahead in the material in order to give themselves more time. They used another cognitive ability to compensate for their slower responses (Salthouse, 1984, 1987).

Some researchers suggest that slower response times on mental tasks are a result of older people taking a different position on a "speed/accuracy trade-off." Older people seem to have a greater preference for accuracy than younger people do. This

Older people may be able to keep their reaction times fast by regular participation in activities where timing is crucial.

means that older people are willing to sacrifice some speed for increased accuracy. If accuracy concerned young people *more*, or older people *less*, the difference between them in response times would probably decline (Kimmel, 1990).

Practice may also affect response rates by lowering reaction time. Robert Dustman and his colleagues found that the reaction times of 60- to 79-year-old subjects decreased after they played video games for 1 hour, 3 times a week for 11 weeks. Control subjects who watched movies for approximately the same amount of time, or who did not participate in a structured program, showed no change in reaction times (Dustman et al., 1992). Following a similar study, Jane Clark concludes, "The present research indicates that declines in response times in the elderly can be reversed" (quoted in McCarthy, 1987).

Despite the reasons for slower performance, or the mental strategies and practice they might use to compensate, it seems that as people get older they *do* tend to process information more slowly (Birren et al., 1963; Nettelbeck & Rabbitt, 1992). And slower processing of information may be one reason we often suspect that memory suffers with age.

MEMORY

The results of memory studies do not show the steady decline with age that many people have expected. For one thing, sensory memory and short-term memory do not appear to suffer with aging (see Chapter 10 to "refresh your memory" for these terms). In addition, evidence for "everyday" memory loss is not very conclusive.

One reason for this uncertainty is that it is difficult to eliminate "outside influences" on tests of memory. For example, in comparison with younger people, older people may not consider the same events to be important, and so may not be as *motivated* to remember them. This may be one reason Janice Howes and Albert Katz found a decline in memory for public events among the elderly, but no decline in memory for autobiographical happenings (Howes & Katz, 1992). Perhaps the elderly didn't consider the public events worth remembering.

On the other hand, their greater experience might enable older persons to select *less material* to remember, allowing them to continue to function socially without revealing any memory loss. In fact, their greater experience and accumulated knowledge leads many older people to be recognized *experts* in particular areas. And they may surpass young adults with less experience.

Hilary Horn Ratner notes that another problem in drawing conclusions about memory in older people is that most memory studies have involved unfair comparisons. In almost every case, researchers compared a *random sample* of older individuals with a *non-random sample* of college students. She and her colleagues, therefore, compared three groups: (1) college students; (2) young subjects *who weren't in college*; (3) older subjects who also weren't in college.

The subjects in all three groups had similar verbal abilities at the start of the experiment. In the main part of the study, the experimenters required the subjects to learn four short prose passages. They then asked the subjects to repeat what they had learned. Ratner and her colleagues found that both the younger and older out-of-school groups had similar recall, while the college students were superior to both the other groups. The researchers conclude that "Without the demands to memorize that education requires, the old and perhaps any out-of-school group may lose the ability to remember as effectively as possible" (Ratner et al., 1987).

Psychologists sometimes assume that older individuals cannot remember either the recent or the distant past with as much accuracy as can younger individuals. However, Regula Herzog reports this is not the case. She and her associates found that subjects 70 and older were as accurate in their recall as were subjects 60 and younger. When differences in accuracy did exist, Herzog says, the older subjects tended to remember better than did younger ones (Herzog & Dielman, 1985; Rodgers & Herzog, 1987).

So it is not at all clear that there is a significant memory loss with aging. Perhaps the major "memory problem" that elderly people have is the set of cultural expectations we have about memory loss in old age (McFarland et al., 1992; Ryan, 1992). As Samuel Johnson observed more than 200 years ago, "If a young or middle-aged man, when leaving a company, does not recollect where he laid his hat, it is nothing. But if the same inattention is discovered in an old man, people will shrug their shoulders and say, 'His memory is going.'"

When elderly people seem to recall their distant past with clarity, why can we not conclude that their memory for these events is very good?

Intelligence

In Chapter 11 we noted that intelligence is not a single ability. We also discovered that there is no agreement on just how many abilities intelligence involves, or on just how to measure these abilities. This uncertainty means that as definitions and measures of intelligence have changed, so have the findings on intelligence differences through the life span.

The first studies of adult intelligence at different ages used standardized IQ tests to measure mental ability in a large sample of adults at various ages. These studies used a **cross-sectional** method, which means they tested a "cross-section," or sample of various ages, from the population at one time. The researchers found that the older the people were that they tested, the lower their IQ scores. The researchers concluded that intelligence drops steadily, and fairly rapidly, from age 20 on.

As more and more researchers became interested in studying adulthood and aging, several investigators undertook **longitudinal** studies of intelligence. This meant that they measured IQ scores of the *same* people at *different periods* in their lives. The results surprised many people, and for a while, they were not widely accepted (Woodruff-Pak, 1988). IQ scores did not decline with age!

Cattell's theory of *fluid* and *crystallized* intelligence can explain this IQ stability in the following way: Fluid intelligence (the ability to take in information and deal with it quickly) declines with biological capacity, while crystallized intelligence (accumulated knowledge and experience), increases with age. The result is an *overall* IQ score which is stable through most of adult life (Cattell, 1971; Horn & Cattell, 1967; Horn, 1982).

More recent research indicates that even tested abilities which apparently decline with age do so only because of disuse. Often these abilities can be restored to earlier levels, or even beyond, by appropriate training (Schaie & Willis, 1986; Willis & Schaie, 1986). These findings have generated a great deal of optimism about intelligence in old age. They have also helped to re-open the question of just what is intelligence.

Several researchers have questioned the appropriateness of measuring intelligence with tests originally designed for children (Kramer, 1986; Woodruff, 1983). They argue that IQ tests are valid as a measure of school-related intellectual abilities, but not as a measure of abilities appropriate to the rest of life. Robert Sternberg's triarchic theory of intelligence is an example of a recent approach to intelligence which recognizes that intelligence is more than what most IQ tests measure. He believes that adults continue to profit intellectually from their experience. As familiar behaviors become automated, adults free their minds for more novel and creative work, and they become *experts*. Adults also learn more successful methods of adaptation to a variety of environments or *contexts* (Berg & Sternberg, 1985; Sternberg, 1985, 1986). And the later years of life may be a time of exceptional creativity and achievement (Simonton, 1988, 1990, 1991). IQ tests do not measure these elements.

Cross-sectional method. A research method which looks at individuals of different ages tested once, at the same point in time.

Longitudinal method (long-i-TOO-din-ul). A research method which measures the changes in an individual, or group of individuals, over a period of time—usually several years.

The meaning of intelligence or wisdom may be different at different times in life. It may also be different in different cultures.

The purpose of learning is growth, and our minds, unlike our bodies, can continue growing as we continue to live.

MORTIMER ADLER

Researcher Vivian Clayton argues that intelligence is not an appropriate word to describe adult mental capacities, especially in later adulthood. She says that as we age we develop the ability to understand human nature, to grasp principles of paradox, contradiction, and change, and to understand the meaning of life, the universe, and God (Clayton, 1982; Clayton & Birren, 1980). These abilities have been recognized in most cultures for centuries as the "crown of old age." We often call them *wisdom* or *maturity* (Erikson, 1982; Kiefer, 1988).

How does intelligence change with age? That depends on how you define intelligence, and on how you measure it. Intelligence measured by traditional IQ tests, appears to be relatively stable across the life-span. Intelligence defined broadly to include "maturity" and "wisdom" probably increases with age.

Moral Reasoning

Moral behavior is behavior which is judged to be acceptable by generally acknowledged standards of right and wrong. Moral behavior, like any other behavior, is multi-determined. In recent years, however, most research has focussed on the mental, or *cognitive*, processes involved in moral decision making.

KOHLBERG'S LEVELS OF MORAL DEVELOPMENT

Some twenty years ago, Lawrence Kohlberg created a theory of moral growth that he based on Piaget's stages of cognitive development. Kohlberg believes children move progressively through various levels of moral development. He says that moral reasoning is merely one example of the general ability to think and reason. Therefore, *cognitive* development guides (and limits) a child's *moral* development (Kohlberg, 1976).

According to Kohlberg, there are three levels of moral development, each of which contains two stages (see Table 13.1). "One way of understanding the three levels," Kohlberg says, "is to think of them as three different types of relationships between the *self* and *society's rules and expectations.*"

If you are at Level I, you are *pre-conventional*. You believe that rules and social expectations are external to you and are imposed on you "by God and society."

If you are at Level II, you are *conventional*. By now you have "internalized" society's rules, especially those imposed by authority figures.

LEVEL AND STAGE	REASONS FOR DOING RIGHT
LEVEL I—PRE-CONVENTIONAL	
Stage 1—Authoritarian morality	Avoidance of punishment, and the superior power of authorities.
Stage 2—Individualism, Instrumental Purpose, and Exchange	To serve one's own needs or interests in a world where you have to recognize that other people have their interests, too.
LEVEL II—CONVENTIONAL	
Stage 3—Mutual Interpersonal Expectations, Relationships, and Interpersonal Conformity	The need to be a good person in your own eyes and those of others. Your caring for others. Desire to maintain rules and authority that support stereotypical good behavior.
Stage 4—Social System and Conscience	To keep the institution going as a whole, to avoid the breakdown in the system "if everyone did it," or the imperative of conscience to meet one's defined obligations. (Easily confused with Stage 3 belief in rules and authority.)
LEVEL III—POST-CONVENTIONAL, or PRINCIPLES	
Stage 5—Social Contract or Utility and Individual Rights	A sense of obligation to law because of one's social contract to make and abide by laws for the welfare of all and for the protection of all people's rights. A feeling of contractual commitment, freely entered upon, to family, friendship, trust, and work obligations. Concern that laws and duties be based on rational calculation of overall utility, "the greatest good for the greatest number."
Stage 6—Universal Ethical Principles	The belief as a rational person in the validity of universal moral principles, and a sense of personal commitment to them.

TABLE 13.1

The Six Stages Divided Into Three Levels of Moral Development

If you are at Level III, you are *post-conventional*. You realize that society's rules are arbitrary, and you define your values in terms of your own self-chosen principles.

Like almost all stage theorists, Kohlberg believes that movement through the six stages is always "upward, gradual, and without significant regressions" (Snarey et al., 1985a).

In order to determine at what stage (or level) a given person might be, Kohlberg uses "doll play" with young children and stories about moral dilemmas with older individuals. Here is one of Kohlberg's dilemmas:

In Europe, a woman was near death from cancer. There was one drug that the doctors thought might save her. It was a form of radium that a druggist in the same town had recently discovered. The drug was expensive to make, but the druggist was charging ten times what the drug cost him to make. He paid $200 for the radium and charged $2,000 for a small dose of the drug. The sick woman's husband, Heinz, went to everyone he knew to borrow the money, but he could only get together $1,000, which is half of what it cost. He told the druggist that his wife was dying and asked him to sell it cheaper or let him pay later. But the druggist said, "No, I discovered the drug, and I am going to make money from it." So Heinz got desperate and broke into the man's store to steal the drug for his wife. Should the husband have done that?

What do you think? Actually, your *reasons* for your answer are more important than which position you take. Each answer may be justified by a reason at any level of development.

For example, a pre-conventional child might answer, "He *shouldn't* do it because he'll be punished," or, "He *should* do it because it he lets his wife die he would get into trouble." Either answer reveals the same level of development. A young person at the conventional level might respond, "He *shouldn't* do it because if people are allowed to take the law into their own hands, the social order would soon break down," or, "He *should* do it because society expects a husband to help his wife whatever the consequences." And a person at the post-conventional level might say, "He *shouldn't* do it because he would have to face his own self-condemnation in knowing he had not lived up to his conscience and standards of honesty," or, "He *should* do it because saving a life is a higher principle than disobeying a law."

Kohlberg differentiates between *moral reasoning* and *moral behavior*. He believes that "to act in a morally high way requires a high stage of moral reasoning. . . . One can, however, reason in terms of such principles and not live up to them" (Kohlberg, 1976).

Kohlberg does not tie his stage to specific ages. The development of post-conventional morality must wait for the cognitive development of Piaget's stage of formal operations in adolescence. However, being capable of formal operational thought does not guarantee that an individual will reach the level of post-conventional morality. In fact, many people never reach this level.

Kohlberg and his associates have tested children and adults in several countries, including the United States, Israel, and Turkey. Kohlberg reports that individuals in all these cultures appear to achieve the same levels of moral development (as measured by his tests) at about the same ages. These results convince Kohlberg that his stages are as "natural and universal" as the stages of cognitive development described by Piaget (Moon, 1986; Nisan & Kohlberg, 1982; Snarey et al., 1985a).

CRITICISMS OF KOHLBERG'S THEORY

Kohlberg's description of moral development is subject to all the criticisms of Piaget's stage theory mentioned in the last chapter, and to a few that are unique to Kohlberg's work.

First, the "moral dilemmas" he uses may not be representative of the types of moral dilemmas that children, adolescents, college students, and older individuals routinely face in their daily lives (Yussen, 1977).

Second, Kohlberg bases his conclusions on *his* interpretations of his subject's responses, and this may bias his conclusions.

Third, Kohlberg derives his theory from his own interpretation of Western (democratic) morality, and thus it may not apply to cultures where people do not perceive individual autonomy as the highest moral goal (Flavell, 1985). Furthermore, his levels may not even be an adequate description of moral development within many sub-cultures in the United States (Stack, 1986).

Fourth, Kohlberg's approach focuses on rational, cognitive concepts, and tends to ignore emotional, *empathic* responses which might also be related to moral growth (Vitz, 1990). Martin Hoffman's research indicates that moral behavior develops *gradually* from concrete experiences of empathy, rather than in *steps* tied to cognitive stages, as Kohlberg says (Hoffman, 1984, 1987). Alida Westman and Lisa Lewandowski found that *empathy with humankind* was a better predictor of students' attitudes toward the Persian Gulf war than was level of moral development (Westman & Lewandowski, 1991).

Perhaps the strongest objection to Kohlberg's theory, however, comes from those psychologists who point out that his approach is strongly "male-biased" (Mwamwenda, 1991). Kohlberg sees *autonomy* as the peak of moral development, and *objectivity* as being at a higher level than *subjectivity*—just as Piaget did. However, as Carole Gilligan points out, our society socializes men to place a high value on *independence*, while it teaches women to value *interdependence, caring,* and *sharing.* If Kohlberg is right, then women will almost always score somewhat lower on his tests than men do (Bloom, 1986; Gilligan, 1983, 1986). Beverly Gelman puts the objection this way: What right has Kohlberg to say that "objectivity" is morally superior to "subjectivity" (Gelman, 1985)?

This raises an important point: Kohlberg's theory should be seen as *descriptive* not *proscriptive.* In other words, he has described what he observed in his particular sample, and not necessarily what *should* occur. To move from a description of observed changes, to the conclusion that these changes are developments or *improvements,* involves an unproven assumption that moral decision making always changes for the better as we get older.

As you might imagine, the issues raised by Kohlberg's theory are far from settled. It does seem clear, however, that the cognitive basis for moral judgments changes over a person's life span.

When someone speaks of obeying "good laws" and disobeying "bad laws," at what level of morality would Kohlberg say they are operating?

SOCIAL DEVELOPMENT

Our interaction with other people, and their influence on us, are important parts of our growth throughout our life span. The influence that our peers have on us is perhaps most obvious in adolescence. So let's begin our discussion of social development by considering a theory in which social development in adolescence plays a key role.

Erikson's Psychosocial Theory of Development

Erik Erikson was a follower of Freud. He accepted many of Freud's ideas on the biological determinants of personality, but he proposed an important shift in emphasis. First, he moved away from Freud's stress on *unconscious* influences from the past, to emphasize conscious factors in the present, and anticipation of the future. Second, Erikson placed a strong emphasis on *sociocultural* determinants of development. He believed it is the conflict between instincts and cultural demands that shapes our development.

Cultural demands, according to Erikson, change throughout life. But within each culture, they occur in a consistent order, and at fairly predictable times. The conflict between continuous biological development, and cultural demands occurring at predictable times, results in distinct *stages* of development (Erikson, 1950, 1978).

According to Erikson, your ego, or conscious self, passes through eight developmental stages on the way to complete maturity. Each of these stages is characterized by its own type of *crisis,* or conflict. Erikson saw these crises as being eight great tests of the ego's character.

Typically there are two *opposing tendencies* operating at the time of each crisis. The crisis at each stage is resolved when the *relative balance* between the two tendencies is settled. Out of these crises grow the "ego strengths" or "virtues" that people need in order to mature and survive in a healthy fashion (see Table 13.2).

Life is a constant becoming: all stages lead to the beginning of others.

GEORGE BERNARD SHAW

STAGE	AGE	PSYCHOSOCIAL TASK	RELATED "VIRTUE"
1	0–1	*Trust versus mistrust* Basic needs must be met reliably	*Hope*
2	2–3	*Autonomy versus shame and doubt* Learning independence and self-confidence	*Will*
3	3–6	*Initiative versus guilt* Initiating activities and learning self-control	*Purpose*
4	6–12	*Competence versus inferiority* Developing physical, cognitive, and social skills	*Competence*
5	12–19	*Identity versus role confusion* Trying out roles and forming an integrated identity	*Fidelity*
6	20–40	*Intimacy versus isolation* Forming close, lasting relationships and making career commitments	*Love*
7	40–65	*Generativity versus stagnation* Contributing to the world through family, and creative, productive work	*Care*
8	65 on	*Integrity versus despair* Thinking back on life with either satisfaction or disappointment	*Wisdom*

THE SENSORY STAGE

Erikson called the first developmental stage the "sensory stage." To Erikson, the crisis at the sensory stage is that of learning a basic *trust or mistrust* of other people. As Erikson puts it, "A basic sense of trust means both that the child has learned to rely on his (or her) caregivers to be there when they are needed, and to consider himself trustworthy" (quoted in Hall, 1983). If the mother (or someone else) meets the infant's needs consistently, the child learns to depend on others in later life.

Erikson adds, "Out of the conflict between trust and mistrust, the infant develops hope, which is the earliest form of what gradually becomes faith in adults." The infant gains the "ego strength" of hope, however, only if the mother is consistent in satisfying the infant's needs. If she is inconsistent, the tendency to mistrust becomes dominant. But the infant cannot be trusting in all cases. "Just imagine," Erikson says, "what somebody would be like who had no mistrust at all" (quoted in Hall, 1983). Thus, it is the *balance* between the opposing tendencies that actually determines personality.

MUSCULAR DEVELOPMENT

The second of Erikson's stages is that of *muscular development*. During toilet training children learn to control their bladder and sphincter muscles and they begin to assert their individuality. The two opposing tendencies are *autonomy* and *shame and doubt*. If children learn to control their bodily functions, they become self-directed and autonomous and develop the ego strength of *will*, or volition. If the opposing tendency prevails, the young person may develop a sense of shame, or what Erikson calls "rage turned against the self." If this happens, the child may fear losing self-control and may suffer a loss of self-esteem.

LOCOMOTOR CONTROL

Erikson's stage of *locomotor control* is the third stage of development. The opposing tendencies at this age are *initiative* versus *guilt*. Children now turn from total dependency on the parents to *identification* with one or both parents. Urged by their instincts to possess the opposite sex parent (at least in fantasy), children face the crisis of inner desires versus society's demands. If their inner controls become too strict and strong, the children may experience excessive guilt. However, if they resolve these difficulties by identifying with the same-sex parent, the youngsters gain the *ego strength* of *purpose*—the sense that they can control their own lives. (We will discuss the process of identification more fully when we discuss Freud in Chapter 14.)

LATENCY

Erikson called the fourth developmental stage that of *latency*. During these (typically) school years, the opposing tendencies are *competence* versus *failure* or, as Erikson put it, "industry versus inferiority." Children who do well in school and other activities learn that they can succeed. Therefore, they become industrious and gain the *ego strength* of *competence*. If the children do poorly, they experience failure and may develop a sense of inferiority.

PUBERTY

At *puberty* sexual interest returns and we must make the adjustment to sexual drives and roles. Puberty awakens an awareness that in a few years society will expect us to assume adult roles. The interaction of biological maturity and society's expectations forces us to begin a search for occupational roles and ideological beliefs and values that we feel comfortable with. Erikson calls this a search for *identity*, and its opposite, *role confusion*.

The development of our identity is a life-long process. However, it reaches a critical stage in adolescence. At this time we look back at what we have been, consider our strengths and weaknesses, and look forward to where they will lead us. We try to project an acceptable identity, and then take steps to develop in that direction.

We may try on several different identities, shopping for one that fits. Sometimes we try to copy the identity of people we admire—musicians, movie stars, or sports heros. If the identity society seems to expect of us is too difficult, we may give up and develop a *negative identity*—in effect saying, "If I can't be what I'm supposed to be, then I'll be what I'm *not* supposed to be." The drive to develop an identity is so strong that even this negative identity may be less stressful than the confusion of no identity.

How would Erikson explain the fact that most members of extreme religious cults are young people?

Through extensive interviews with adolescents, James Marcia has shown that the development of a personal identity may involve four different "identity statuses." In the first, which Marcia calls the "foreclosed" status, adolescents have a rigid, unexamined identity, usually derived from their parents. They hold beliefs and make occupational plans the way their parents expect them to, because they have never seriously considered doing otherwise. In the final identity status, called "achieved," adolescents have questioned and examined their beliefs and goals, and come to a point of commitment. The goals and beliefs may even be the same as they were in the "foreclosed" status; the important point is that the adolescent has critically evaluated them.

Adolescent rebellion is sometimes an effort to assert an independent identity.

In addition to "foreclosed" and "achieved," there are two other positions, called "diffused," and "moratorium." In the "diffused" status, adolescents have not made an identity commitment, but neither are they concerned about it. They drift without worrying. In some ways this is the least mature position because questioning and commitment are both absent. In the "moratorium" status, concern over identity has reached an "identity crisis," but the adolescent has not been able to make a commitment to an identity. This is an uncomfortable state of questioning and searching (Marcia, 1966, 1980; Philipchalk & Sifft, 1985; Prager, 1986).

Adolescents are very different in the way they experience these four statuses. Some may experience them hardly at all, some may stay for a long time in one or the other, and some may go back and forth between them (Stephen et al., 1992; Waterman, 1982).

According to Erikson, achieving a satisfactory identity allows us to make a commitment and remain true to it, without fear of "losing ourselves." We develop the virtue of faithfulness, or *fidelity*, fidelity to our goals, and our beliefs, fidelity to who we are. Without a strong identity we cannot truly commit ourselves to a goal, a cause, or even another person. The search for identity is thus an important step towards young adulthood when commitment is a necessary foundation for intimacy and love.

Drug and alcohol abuse, delinquency, and suicide all increase during adolescence. Can you think of some biological, intra-psychic, and social reasons?

YOUNG ADULTHOOD

Erikson postulated three stages of maturation in adulthood. The first of these stages, which occurs in young adulthood, presents us with the crisis of *intimacy* versus *isolation*. According to Erikson, "Real Intimacy includes the capacity to commit yourself to relationships that may demand sacrifice and compromise. The *ego strength* of young adulthood is *love*—a mutual, mature devotion" (quoted in Hall, 1983).

Erikson sees a great difference between "Intimacy" with a capital I and "intimacy," by which he means sexual activity. He put it this way: "Some people today may fool themselves in their so-called recreational sexuality and actually feel quite isolated because they lack mutuality—real intimacy. In extreme cases, you could have a highly active sex life and yet feel a terrible sense of isolation because you're never there as a person; you're never perceiving your partner as a person" (quoted in Hall, 1983).

Mature intimacy involves sacrifice and commitment in a relationship of equality. Many marriages lack intimacy because young adults get married searching for the identity they failed to establish in adolescence. In the past this was particularly true for women, who tried to find their identity through their husbands.

ADULTHOOD

One of Erikson's greatest contributions to personality theory has been his descriptions of what happens to people during their middle years. He sees the opposing tendencies here as being *generativity* and *stagnation*.

Generativity is composed of three related activities—procreativity, productivity, and creativity. Procreativity is an instinctual wish to have children. But procreativity can be redirected into productivity and creativity.

Productivity is an innate desire to "take care of things. The Hindus call it the maintenance of the world" (quoted in Hall, 1983). In part, this drive is a desire to make society better for one's children, or to clean up and preserve the natural environment for future generations.

Creativity involves learning to accept the new rather than rigidly trying to maintain things as they were in the past. But creativity is also linked to procreativity because it often involves childlike activities. Erikson says, "Einstein used the word

Erikson says adults have a need to contribute to society.

'wonder' to describe his experience as a child, and he was considered childlike by many people. And I think he claimed that he was able to formulate the theory of relativity because he kept asking the questions that children ask" (quoted in Hall, 1983).

The ego strength the person gains at this stage is *care*. Care is "a widening commitment to *take care of* the persons, the products and the ideas one has learned to *care for*" (Erikson, 1982). A person shows a lack of care by being self-centered, and rejecting groups of people who are "different."

MATURITY

Erikson's final stage is that of *maturity*. The opposing tendencies at this age are *integrity* and *despair*. Erikson defines integrity as "a sense of coherence and wholeness." He says further that "What is demanded [at this stage of life] could be simply called Integrality, a readiness to keep things together. The [ego] strength that grows out of resolving this final conflict is that of 'wisdom'" (quoted in Hall, 1983).

In a sense, Erikson has extended the tendency for generativity to this age as well. However, as he notes, "Old people can no longer procreate, but they can be productive, and they can be creative." Even if they no longer must take care of their own children, they can "care for" other children. "I'm convinced that old people and children need one another and that there's an affinity between old age and childhood that, in fact, rounds out the life cycle. You know, old people often seem childlike, and it's important that we be permitted to revive some qualities that we had as children" (quoted in Hall, 1983).

If older people remain active, and if they still relate directly to society, they can *integrate* all of life's experiences and thus bring integrity to their egos. However, if they fail to solve most of their earlier crises, they may succumb to feelings of despair at the futility of existence. Integration is in many ways the final stage of a lifelong formation of identity. At the end, we should be able to look back and see that the life we have lived has been the best, the only, and inevitable route to the person we have become.

Erikson's views of development, especially in adulthood, have been very influential. We will evaluate them after we have considered another well-known stage theory of development.

Levinson's Stages of Adult Development

Psychiatrist Daniel Levinson has taken the "stage view" of adult development a step further than Erikson, and proposed 11 stages of development from late adolescence to old age. Levinson also differs from Erikson in two other ways: First, he ties each stage more closely to a specific age (with a range of two years above and below the average); and second, he believes stages of conflict regularly intersperse periods of calm (see Figure 13.3).

Like most theorists, Levinson sees late adolescence as a time to break away from adolescence and make choices for adulthood. The mid-20s are a period to establish values of love, occupation, and lifestyle; a time to begin career and family. The late 20s and early 30s bring a phase of transition, a time to reassess our earlier choices. It may be a period of stress when we make radical changes in our marriage, our job, or our living location. This is followed by a term of settling down to develop our family and career.

Age 40 often brings another transition, which for many is traumatic—the so-called "mid-life crisis." At this time, we must put unfulfilled dreams of youth into perspective. We must come to grips with the realization that we are not the unqualified success we had aspired to be, and that our time is running out. We may explore neglected areas of our life in an attempt to find new meaning. By about age 45, most

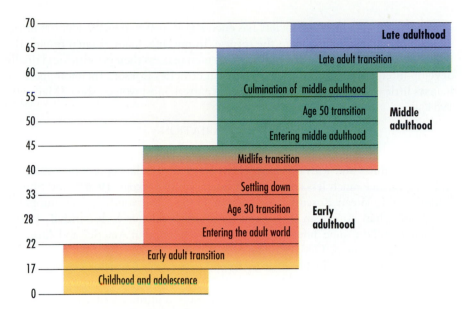

70	**Late adulthood**
65	Late adult transition
60	Culmination of middle adulthood
55	
50	Age 50 transition **Middle**
	Entering middle adulthood **adulthood**
45	
40	Midlife transition
33	Settling down
28	Age 30 transition **Early**
	Entering the adult world **adulthood**
22	
17	Early adult transition
0	Childhood and adolescence

FIGURE 13.3

Developmental periods in early and middle adulthood. (Adapted from Levinson, 1986.)

of us settle down into the next period of calm. We pursue new, more attainable goals with vigor.

Age 50 brings another transition in which we again reevaluate goals and lifestyle. If we did not experience a crisis at age 40 we are more likely to now. Another period of calm follows, a culmination of middle adulthood. This is often a time of great fulfillment, when we reap the rewards of more realistic goals which we set in our earlier periods of transition.

The end of another decade brings another phase of transition. At age 60 we begin a reappraisal of our life. We review our achievements with mixed feelings of pride and despair. The late adulthood term from age 65 to 80 is a time for us to make peace with ourself and others. It is a time to take a broader, more philosophical view of life, a time of wisdom. The final transition follows in the period from 80 to death. It is a time for us to let go and prepare for death.

Levinson developed his theory from extensive interviews with middle-aged American men (Levinson, 1978). Priscilla Roberts and Peter Newton found evidence of the same periods in American women (Roberts & Newton, 1987). And Levinson reports that preliminary studies in other cultures have found evidence for alternating periods of transition and stability, with one transition occuring around age 30 and another slightly after age 40 (Levinson, 1986).

Sages, Ages, and Stages

Do we go through predictable stages of development, as Erikson and Levinson say? Many people believe we do. Stage theories have a certain appeal: They are simple and easy to apply, they lead to fairly clear predictions, and they are optimistic in proposing lifelong growth and development. Different stages or phases of adult development have been suggested by Charlotte Buhler, Roger Gould, Robert Havighurst, Carl Jung, and others (Buhler, 1968; Gould, 1972; Havighurst, 1972; Jung, 1933/1971).

Many other people are not so sure. They point out that stage theories often reflect the biases of the researchers and their samples.

GENDER DIFFERENCES

David Matteson notes that Erikson's choice of *identity* as the central theme of adolescence has a "male bias" to it. "From my reading of the life span literature,"

Identity struggles may be greater in cultures that require long periods of preparation for rapidly changing adult roles.

Matteson says, "I believe our society has encouraged men to develop identity at the expense of intimacy and women the reverse. In mid-life, many women resume the task of developing mature identity, and many men reassess their priorities and finally develop interpersonal sensitivities." Matteson criticizes Erikson, therefore, because he pays little attention to the developmental pattern most women show (Matteson, 1984).

CULTURAL VARIATION

Adolescent identity struggles are probably not the same in all cultures. They occur at different times and with different intensity. A. K. Sikdar reports that youth in India experience much less crisis than Western youth (Sikdar, 1974). And Shirley Feldman and Doreen Rosenthal report that Hong Kong youth expect autonomy much later than American or Australian youth (Feldman & Rosenthal, 1991). Feldman found the same differences in Asian youth living in America and Australia (Feldman & Quatman, 1988; Feldman & Rosenthal, 1990).

These differences, which persist in second generation Chinese-Americans and Chinese-Australians, are possibly the result of different emphases on individualism versus social-connectedness in Eastern and Western cultures. Eastern (Asian) cultures may provide a smoother transition to adulthood by placing less emphasis on autonomy and individualism. Western cultures on the other hand, stress autonomy, and personal identity—the need to *break away* from the group as soon as possible. In this emphasis Western cultures may "set the stage" for the adolescent struggles described by stage theories.

Social Clock. The socially correct time for the occurrence of certain significant social tasks, such as getting married, having children, retiring from work, etc.

So the developmental patterns "discovered" by Erikson, Levinson, and others, may not apply to as many people as their proponents would like to believe. The timing of social tasks, the **social clock,** is different for different cultures, and even for different periods in the same culture. For example, the socially acceptable age to marry and the age to have children have both increased significantly in the past 20 years in North America. And as we have seen, different cultures expect autonomy to different degrees and at different ages.

GRADUAL CHANGE

Some critics of stage theories suggest that we should focus on gradual and steady change throughout the life span. They point out, for example, that relatively few people experience a "mid-life crisis" (Rossi, 1980; Farrell & Rosenberg, 1981). Paul Costa and Robert McCrae found that those people who suffered a crisis at mid-life also tended to experience crises across the whole adult life span. In short, they were generally more neurotic people (Costa & McCrae, 1978, 1980). Similarly, Daniel Offer and his colleagues found that most adolescents do not experience a time of crisis. They found that adolescent crisis is more a reflection of individual personality than a cultural universal (Offer et al., 1981; Offer & Schonert-Reichl, 1992; Galambos, 1992). These studies suggest that adolescent and adult development is gradual and varies greatly from person to person.

What effect would talk of a "mid-life crisis" have on someone approaching this age?

Other research shows that not only do we not change in abrupt stages, but also we actually change very little (Krosnick & Alwin, 1989). After reviewing numerous studies of personality change, Diana Woodruff-Pak concludes, "Personality inventory measures which assess self-conceptions and professional observations of personality over long periods of time suggest stability more than change" (Woodruff-Pak, 1988). Leonard Baird found the same stability in a 24-year study of religious ideas (Baird, 1990).

The apparent stability of personality over the life span actually contradicts some frequent stereotypes of older people. For example, many people assume that as we grow older, our ideas become more rigid and unchangeable. And it is true, at least at the present time, that older people *do* tend to be more rigid than younger people. However, *longitudinal* studies find that as we grow older, our thinking does *not* become more rigid. Research indicates that people who are older and more rigid now, were also more rigid when they were young (Schaie et al., 1973; Schaie & Labouvie-Vief, 1974).

Why would someone born in the 1920s or '30s be more rigid in their thinking than someone born in the 1960s or '70s?

THEME APPROACH

A different approach to the study of adult development is to follow certain major themes through the life span. Freud suggested that after we reach adolescence, the major areas of healthy development are meaningful production (work) and satisfying interpersonal relationships (love) (Freud, 1935/1960). (You may recognize these as Erikson's concepts of "generativity" and "intimacy.") The way we deal with these basic aspects *throughout* our lives may be more important than apparent crises and stages.

Researchers Steven Baum and Robert Stewart asked subjects from 17 to 96 years of age about their meaning and purpose in life. They found that the amount of purpose and the sources of meaning did not vary with age or sex. Older men and women had just as much purpose and meaning in life as younger men and women. And consistent with Freud's perspective, work and love were the most often mentioned meaningful themes. Crises were not absent. Subjects reported that divorces, accidents, illnesses, and deaths were all significant events. Consistently, however, subjects at all ages considered themes of work and love to be the most important (Baum & Stewart, 1990).

It seems that stage theories pinpoint some significant issues that we must deal with at various junctures in our lives. Stage theories also make us aware of the important interaction between biological and social forces in our growth. However, it also seems that the idea of universal stages may be an oversimplification of our development throughout life.

AGING

Psychologists have studied children for more than a century, but their interest in older people is fairly new. Thus, we know a great deal more about how infants grow and develop than we do about how people at the opposite end of the life span meet life's challenges. The scientific study of aging is still in its infancy.

The relatively new study of old age is called **gerontology.** Gerontologists study physical, psychological, and social changes associated with the later period of life. One result of their work is to dispel some of the myths and false stereotypes associated with older people. In this way they help to reduce **ageism,** or discrimination on the basis of age.

Gerontology (jair-on-TALL-ah-jee). The study of the physical, psychological, and social changes associated with old age and aging.

Ageism. Discrimination against people because of their age.

Biological Processes in Aging

At the beginning of this chapter we discussed some of the physical changes associated with aging. These processes become more noticeable in old age. Facial skin wrinkles and sags; scalp hair thins and turns gray. Height decreases from 1 to 2

Maintaining exercise and other healthful habits from youth is one of the best ways of assuring vitality and health in old age.

If wrinkles must be written upon our brows, let them not be written upon the heart. The spirit should never grow old.

JAMES A. GARFIELD

inches, due to weakening muscles and bone deterioration in the spine. Weight often increases up to middle age, and then drops slowly in later adulthood and old age. The vocal cords stiffen and the voice becomes higher-pitched. Sensory acuity decreases, and all organ systems lose their reserve (Berger, 1988; Potter & Perry, 1989; Schulz & Ewen, 1988).

Many of the effects of biological aging are cosmetic. Some, such as deficits in hearing and vision, can be corrected. Most of the biological changes of aging have little effect on our vigor, daily functioning, or health. Older people who maintain healthy habits from their youth tend to be as physiologically fit as are younger individuals (Rowe & Kahn, 1987). In fact, maintaining a high level of regular activity is one of the best ways of maintaining health and increasing life expectancy (Buchner et al., 1992; Wagner et al., 1992; Woodruff-Pak, 1988).

The most significant effect of aging is that the depletion of our organ reserve means we become more susceptible to disease. And it is usually disease, not old age, which ultimately leads to death.

We don't know the cause for physical change and breakdown. Some people believe that the body simply wears out, like a machine (Pearl, 1924). Others suggest that the "wear and tear" on DNA results in the inability to replace damaged cells in many organs (Harrison, 1985). Several theories blame the negative effects of certain chemicals called *free radicals,* produced in normal metabolism (Carlson & Forbes, 1992; Saul et al., 1987). Some theories assume that deficiencies in the immune system cause aging (Ebersole & Hess, 1985; Potter & Perry, 1989). And one intriguing line of research suggests that certain body cells may be capable of only a fixed number of divisions (about 50), after which they die (Hayflick, 1965, 1970).

Not surprisingly, each of these theories (and many others) has spawned attempts to avoid aging. Americans spend more than two billion dollars each year on anti-aging remedies (Meister, 1984). None of them, however, has proven effective. The search for the fountain of youth continually comes up dry.

What is your response to imagining your own physical changes in old age? Why do you think you feel that way?

STRESS AND HEALTH

Some older individuals are obviously in poorer health than when they were young. But long-term studies of hundreds of subjects in California suggest that many of the physical problems of mature individuals can be seen as poor responses to psychological stress. Dorothy Eichorn and her colleagues report there is a significant relationship between mental health early in life and physical health during maturity. Those subjects who showed emotional stability and controlled responses to stress as adolescents had far better health at age 50 than did those subjects who had poor stress reactions when young (Eichorn et al., 1981).

Judith Rodin believes that the relationship between health and a sense of personal control grows stronger in old age. According to Rodin, "Studies show that there are detrimental effects on the health of older people when their control of their activities is restricted." Individuals who "lose control" of their world experience increased stress, and their immune systems become less responsive. Unfortunately, she notes, most nursing home operators prefer to take control away from their clients. Rodin recommends that nursing home operators and others should encourage those older patients to maintain as much control over their lives as possible (Rodin, 1986).

Some research suggests that many college students believe you should talk "baby talk" to elderly persons. Why do you think this is? And what effect do you think it would have?

THE AGING BRAIN

The human body tends to shrink slightly as it ages, and so apparently does the brain. M.J. de Leon and his colleagues report that the brain of a healthy 70-year-old is slightly smaller than that of a healthy 25-year-old. But it is not the number of neurons, but rather the amount of fluid in the brain that decreases. Sugar metabolism, which is a measure of activity in the brain, is the same in the 70-year-old as in the 25-year-old. Thus, there is no medical support for the belief that older individuals must become infantile or senile because their brains either "shrivel up" or "stop functioning properly" (de Leon et al., 1987).

The belief that "you lose brain cells every day of your life" apparently got its start in 1958, when a noted scientist estimated that "humans lose 100,000 neurons a day after age 30." This belief is nonsense, according to Marian Diamond. She has studied the brains of both animals and humans for many years in her laboratory. Diamond reports that, "In the absence of disease, our studies provide no reason to believe that normal aging in humans produces brain-cell loss until, perhaps, extreme old age" (Diamond, 1978; Diamond et al., 1979).

DEMENTIA AND ALZHEIMER'S DISEASE

Dementia is a general term for a marked deterioration of mental functioning in old age. ("Senility" is a more familiar, but somewhat pejorative term.) Dementia occurs in less than 10 percent of the population from age 65 to 80. After 80 years of age the rate rises to almost 20 percent, and then begins to drop slightly (Kay & Bergman, 1982; Kolb & Wishaw, 1990).

There are several different causes for dementia. A reversible form of dementia may be brought on suddenly by overmedication, lack of emotional stimulation, or abrupt changes in living conditions. More severe and lasting dementia may be caused by diseases, the most serious of which is **Alzheimer's disease.**

Although researchers can make an accurate diagnosis only by an autopsy, they estimate that two-thirds of the people suffering from dementia have Alzheimer's disease (Katzman, 1984; Kolb & Wishaw, 1990). In the later phases of the illness, Alzheimer's patients require constant care. As a result, the United States government spends more than half of its Medicare payments on the treatment of patients with Alzheimer's disease (Mortimer & Schuman, 1981).

Alzheimer's disease is not limited to old age. Victims can be in their 50s or even their 40s. Some researchers believe very mild symptoms may begin as much as 20 years before diagnosis (La Rue et al., 1985). The disease begins very slowly with mild losses of memory and verbal ability. Patients are aware of their difficulties, and usually make attempts to compensate by writing notes, and making excuses. As deterioration progresses, patients cannot recall even familiar items such as their address, the names of family members, or even their spouse (Mendez et al., 1992). Personality and emotional changes follow (Teri & Wagner, 1992). Eventually, they lose all ability to speak, control bodily functions, or even walk (Dhooper, 1992). Death, it seems, is a merciful conclusion.

Alzheimer's is particularly tragic for several reasons: First, it seems to strike at the core of the individual—what we prize most about ourselves—our mind, our personality. Second, the victim is aware of having the disease, and its inevitable progression. Third, it takes, on average, from 5 to 7 years for total deterioration and death; some individuals have survived for more than 14 years after diagnosis. Fourth, it is incurable. Alzheimer's is one of the cruelest diseases of all—killing its victims twice. First it slowly kills the mind; then it gradually destroys the body.

Medical researchers disagree both on what causes Alzheimer's disease and how best to treat it. At first they thought it was the result of "hardening of the arteries," but they have now discarded that theory. More recently, scientists suspected that a chromosomal defect related to Down's syndrome might cause Alzheimer's. However, further research has not supported this viewpoint (St. George-Hyslop et al., 1987).

Alzheimer's disease (ALLZ-hime-ers). A disorder of mid- to late adulthood which begins with mild memory loss and progresses, over a period of years, to include emotional and personality disturbance, physical deterioration, and eventually, death.

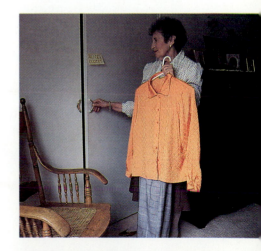

In the early stage of Alzheimer's disease, reminders may serve to compensate for failing memory.

Several researchers have identified neurological changes in the brain that are associated with Alzheimer's disease (Hyman, 1989; Pearlson et al., 1992; Risse et al., 1990). But at this point they cannot say whether these changes *produce* the disease or are the *result* of the disease. There appears to be little reason to change the conclusion pronounced by leading researcher Caleb Finch, who said, "At this point in time, we don't even know what we don't know about Alzheimer's disease" (Finch, 1985).

Psychological Reactions to Aging

Menopause. The permanent cessation of menstruation.

Our bodies age gradually, almost imperceptibly. The transition from young adulthood to middle and later adulthood, and then old age is usually gentle, with no universally accepted physical milestones. The only exception, is the period of **menopause** in women, which occurs in the late 40s or early 50s. However, even this clear sign of aging is more often welcomed than feared because it means that sexual activity is no longer accompanied by the fear of pregnancy, and that the monthly "hassle" is over (Luria & Meade, 1984).

Because physical changes are so subtle, and develop so slowly, some people ignore them for years. And then, suddenly, they reach a minor crisis. Author Jim Fixx describes his experience of pulling a muscle in his mid-30s:

> What was striking was the way I felt about the damage. My body had betrayed me, and I was angry. I still thought of myself—secretly, at least—as an athlete. Someone who all his life had played tennis, touch football and Saturday-afternoon softball shouldn't be thus laid low.

Fixx's reaction was to begin a program of regular exercise. He went on to become a marathon runner and an advocate of running as an antidote to the effects of aging (Fixx, 1977). Many other people have found that exercise and a generally healthful life-style leads to increasing productivity with age—even old age (Horn, 1989).

For others, each birthday is a nail in their coffin. They begin in their early 20s to watch for a gray hair, an added pound, or a new wrinkle. They dread the "oh" birthdays—"the big 3-0," "the big 4-0," "the big 5-0,". . . . With such a focus on aging, especially at the end of each decade, perhaps it's not surprising that Levinson found these to be difficult periods of transition.

If we counted our age by a number system that was not based on 10, would we still be prone to "crises" every 10 years?

As they approach later adulthood, most people struggle to accept the increasing limitations of age. Instead of trying to re-capture lost youth, they are more philosophical, as comedian Bill Cosby tries to be:

> What is the *point* of all this? That mothers should be impersonating their daughters? That all of us should be one big happy teenage generation? Can you imagine a more frightening horror film than one in which all the adults in America turned into teenagers?
>
>   This is a wonderful country, but the people in it are quite insane about reversing the aging process. They are trying to wake up every morning heading for yesterday. Where will it all end? Since there seems to be a stampede back to the womb, it will all end with one fetus trying to call out to another, "I'm less developed than *you!*" (Cosby, 1988).

Aging is not disease, because it is not contrary to nature.
                    ARISTOTLE

As the signs of aging become undeniable, and middle age moves into old age, there are several views on the psychological pathway we should take (Atchley, 1992; Fry, 1992). One prominent view is disengagement, and withdrawal; another is involvement, and continued activity.

DISENGAGEMENT THEORY

For several years, researchers Elaine Cumming and William Henry studied the social involvement of a large number of older adults in Kansas City. They noticed that there was a tendency for these people to become more reflective and socially withdrawn with age. At the same time, they found that society gradually released them from social roles. They suggested that this process protects us from possible failure and rejection, and it allows society to replace us with younger, more capable persons. Cumming's and Henry's **disengagement theory** suggests that life satisfaction is highest when we disengage ourselves from society at the same time as society is withdrawing from us. Thus, *disengagement* is desirable and mutually beneficial. (Cumming & Henry, 1961; Maddox, 1974).

Disengagement theory. The view that the greatest satisfaction in late adulthood is obtained by withdrawing from societal involvement at the same time as society is drawing away from the individual.

ACTIVITY THEORY

In direct contrast to engagement theory, **activity theory** states that in old age our satisfaction with life is directly related to our level of social activity (Lemon et al., 1972; Sill, 1980). Activity theorists see disengagement by society as an unfortunate consequence of our culture's *ageism*. When society forces us to withdraw, we are happier, activity theorists say, if we can find new forms of engagement. The loss of a spouse might generate greater contact with friends. Disengagement from work could lead to involvement in social and community activities. If we do not find new forms of engagement, according to activity theory, we risk isolation, loneliness, and despair (Berger, 1988; Woodruff-Pak, 1988).

Neither disengagement theory nor activity theory predicts every case—individuals vary. Some people withdraw from social participation and are happy; some in this situation are unhappy. Some people are actively socially engaged and highly satisfied; some are active and unsatisfied (Schulz & Ewen, 1988; Woodruff-Pak, 1988). Apparently, individual differences in personality are just as important as activity level in predicting the best strategy for old age (Neugarten, 1977).

Activity theory. The view that the greatest satisfaction in late adulthood is obtained by continued activity and involvement in society, including compensating for any forced withdrawal by finding new involvements.

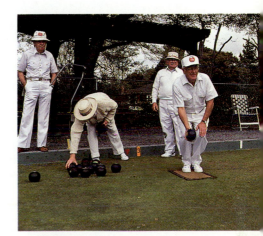

Activity theory says we are happiest if we find new activities when forced retirement and other disengagements occur.

DEATH AND DYING

Death seems to be the taboo topic of 20th-century Western conversation. In the 19th century, sex was a prohibited subject and death was acceptable; today the reverse seems to be true. As Diana Woodruff-Pak says, "Until recently researchers and writers on this topic have described death as the 'new pornography'" (Woodruff-Pak, 1988). Herman Feifel calls it "*terra incognita* and an off-limits enterprise," at least until the mid-20th century (Feifel, 1990).

When psychiatrist Elizabeth Kübler-Ross began to study death she found the resistance almost insurmountable. She wanted to talk to dying patients about their experiences, but she found many physicians were unwilling to admit they had patients who were dying. Others thought it was cruel and sadistic to talk with terminally ill patients about their own death. She reports that in the first year of her research, it took an average of ten hours to search for each patient and get permission from a physician (Kübler-Ross, 1970). However, thanks to Kübler-Ross's persistence, the shroud of secrecy surrounding death has begun to lift.

The Dying Process

Kübler-Ross's discussions with dying patients convinced her that we go through five stages in the process of dying. Our first reaction to a terminal illness is usually denial.

We say, "There must be some mistake; no, it can't be me." Denial is a healthful reaction to shocking news. It provides a short-term buffer while we muster our defenses to cope with the undeniable reality.

We cannot maintain denial for long, in most cases. And we soon react with *anger*—anger at family, nurses, doctors, God, or fate. The central feeling now is, "Why me?" We feel resentment and envy towards those who are healthy. And we may become very difficult to deal with.

The third stage is often very brief and may not be noticed by those around us. Our anger softens and we try to *bargain* for additional time. We try to convince fate, God, the staff, or the illness, that we will "behave" if only we could live longer. We might set the goal of living to a certain significant date—we will accept death *if only* we could live to see. . . .

When we are faced with the relentless progress of time and disease we are likely to sink into *depression*. This depression results from guilt or shame at losses in the past, as well as from "preparatory grief" for the coming separation. It is, however, a necessary step towards final *acceptance*.

We feel acceptance when we have experienced and overcome our denial, anger, depression, and more extreme fear or anxiety about death. This is the final stage of relative calm. One of Kübler-Ross's patients described it as "the final rest before the long journey" (Kübler-Ross, 1969).

Most research does not support the simple progression through stages we have just outlined. It seems more common that the terminally ill experience all of these reactions at various times and in various orders (Kastenbaum, 1986). Moreover, elderly people with painful debilitating illnesses seem much less likely to experience anger or denial than the middle-aged cancer patients Kübler-Ross studied. The elderly are also less likely to bargain and more likely to accept the inevitable (Retsinas, 1988).

Our reaction to death is very personal. According to the cross-cultural research of Richard Kalish and David Reynolds, and the cross-sex study of Judith Stillion, our sex, our culture, and other individual differences, make our approaches to death very different (Kalish & Reynolds, 1981; Stillion, 1985).

The real gain from Kübler-Ross's pioneering work has been to draw attention to the dying process, and to sensitize health workers to approach rather than avoid the terminally ill. The greatest danger is that we will "sanitize" the process of dying by placing the terminally ill in neat categories, and once again distancing ourselves from them—"Oh don't worry about her, she's just going through the anger stage."

Preparing for Death

Probably everyone faces death with at least some anxiety. Young children fear separation from their parents. Adolescents may fear disfigurement by terminal illness or fatal accident. Young adults usually fear the interruption of their plans, and the ability of survivors to cope. Older adults fear a long and lonely death. And all of us probably experience all of these feelings from time to time.

Healthy children will not fear life if their elders have integrity enough not to fear death.

ERIK ERIKSON

Nevertheless, part of successful aging is coming to grips with our own mortality. Researcher Vern Bengtson and his colleagues found that people showed less fear of death as they moved from middle age to old age. This was true of African-Americans, Mexican-Americans, and Anglo-Americans, of both sexes, and at all socioeconomic levels. Age was the only variable that made a consistent difference (Bengtson et al., 1977).

Men generally show less fear of death than women do (Buzzanga et al., 1989; Davis et al., 1992; Templer, 1991). And several studies have found that individuals with strong religious beliefs also have less fear of death (Jeffers et al., 1961; Orbach & Florian, 1992; Osarchuk & Tatz, 1973).

An important part of preparing for death is adequate time. Many people fear a sudden unexpected death because they would not have time to make final preparations and say good-bye. Beyond this, as life draws to a close, many people enjoy frequent periods of "life review" (Butler, 1974; Webster & Cappeliez, 1993). This enables them to put their life into perspective, to find its meaning and purpose, and to see death as a natural conclusion (Magee, 1988).

While most of us would like adequate time to prepare for death, we would also like to avoid a long terminal illness which might bring pain, isolation, and loneliness. We also fear a long illness which leads to the extensive use of medical procedures to sustain what becomes an almost inhuman existence. This has led many people to embrace **passive euthanasia** through a **living will.** Before they are near death, they draw up a legal document specifying a limit to the medical care they want to receive if they become ill (Ely et al., 1992; Watts, 1992). This authorizes medical personnel and family to withhold treatment which would prolong life in an unacceptable form (unlike *active euthanasia*, which involves performing an act which kills, such as a lethal injection).

Most people would like to spend their last days with dignity in an atmosphere of warmth and acceptance. They would rather die a few days sooner than live hooked up to numerous tubes and wires in an impersonal setting. One solution is the hospice.

A hospice is a setting where the terminally ill can receive self-controlled pain-killing medication without artificial life-support systems. In addition, an atmosphere of warmth and support, is assured. Sometimes the patient's home can become the hospice; sometimes it is a separate section in a hospital. Medical personnel visit often to provide medication and comfort. Patients wear their own clothes, and move about freely, socializing with each other and the staff. A close friend or family member stays with the patient most of the time, and assists in care of the patient. When death comes, the staff continue to support and help the family (More, 1987).

The hospice movement began in Britain, and has spread to Canada and the United States. However, there are many areas where hospice care is not available. Hospice work is very demanding, and it is sometimes hard to find staff. In addition, it is often difficult to determine when an illness is terminal and the patient a candidate for a hospice.

If you had a very serious illness, would you go to a hospice, or would you try one more operation that might give you a little more time?

DEVELOPMENTAL ISSUES IN REVIEW

How much do we change as we move through life? Physically we change a lot: from a helpless newborn, to a robust adult, and then, if we live long enough, to a frail elderly person. Cognitively, the picture is somewhat different. Some of our abilities deteriorate slightly (performance on speed-related tasks), while others increase to compensate (knowledge based on experience). The result is that, barring disease, overall cognitive performance changes little throughout the adult years. The research on social development is not definitive. Erikson, Levinson, and others report significant change from adolescence to old age. Other researchers find that adult development is remarkable for its consistency through the life span.

Do the changes come in abrupt stages or are they smooth and gradual? With the exception of puberty and menopause, and excluding serious accidents or disease, physical development is slow and steady. Even before we reach our full stature in late adolescence, our basal metabolic rate has begun to drop, and fat is usually accumulating. Similarly, small changes in cognitive ability develop imperceptibly. Stage

Passive euthanasia. Voluntarily ending a life deemed to be not worth living, by withholding excessive medical treatment. (As opposed to *active euthanasia* in which specific action is taken to end the life—once again, one which is deemed not worth living.)

Living will. A legal document made out before a person becomes terminally ill, in which he or she specifies at what point in a terminal illness he or she would want medical treatment discontinued.

The hospice provides a "homey" atmosphere of caring and support. Medical attention focuses on pain relief.

theories give a plausible account of abrupt changes caused by the interaction of social demands and the aging process. However, these theories may be accurate for only a limited number of people.

And finally, how much change is the result of inevitable biological processes (nature), and how much is the result of social and other environmental influences (nurture)? Unfortunately, we cannot answer this question very precisely. We develop physically, cognitively, and socially as the result of a complex interaction of inherited and environmental influences. Stage theories tend to emphasize the importance of the environment, especially the social environment, in our growth. And non-stage theories emphasize the stability brought on by biologically programmed development. Both views, however, recognize that growth depends on nature plus nurture (or more exactly, nature *times* nurture).

Many of the apparent contradictions between the theories we have been looking at can be reconciled by taking into account personality differences in the researcher's subjects. For example, some types of people may go through stages of development and other types may not. It is, thus, to the topic of personality and individual differences that we now must turn our attention.

SUMMARY

1. The period of **adolescence** is usually considered to extend from the onset of **puberty** to the achievement of independent adult status.

2. Adolescence is a period of very rapid physical development. The development of **primary** and **secondary sex characteristics,** and the rapid **growth spurt** produce changes that can be difficult to cope with.

3. Adulthood is a period of physical stability. Although biological systems are slowly declining, for most people their **reserve** is sufficient to allow them to "coast" into old age. A **healthful lifestyle** will assure greater vitality in older age.

4. During adulthood, **cognitive abilities** continue to develop and change. Some decreases in the **speed** of information processing may be the result of lack of practice or the use of different cognitive strategies. Changes in **memory** appear to be slight. Greater experience often results in greater **expertise.** Overall **intelligence** is relatively stable into old age.

5. Lawrence Kohlberg has identified three levels of **moral development** which he says are dependent upon increasing **cognitive** ability. His critics say that his theory does not apply to everyone.

6. Erik Erikson believes that we go through **eight stages** in our development from birth to old age. Each stage produces a **crisis** or conflict between the person and society. Dominant characteristics of our personality are formed as we resolve each crisis.

7. A major theme of Erikson's theory is the development of personal **identity.** Identity formation is particularly important in adolescence, where an **identity crisis** may occur.

8. Daniel Levinson believes we pass through **11 stages of growth,** with periods of crisis interspersed between years of calm.

9. Critics of stage theories point out that **gender** and **culture** affect development through the life span in ways that stage theories often ignore. Some critics also suggest that **change is gradual** and that adulthood may be characterized more by **stability** than change.

10. Many characteristics of some elderly people were **also true of them when they were young.** Mentally rigid elderly people were also mentally rigid when they were young. Older adults who go through **crises** in their development also went through crises when they were young. Older people who **respond poorly to**

stress, also responded poorly to stress when they were young. **Healthy and active** older people were usually healthy and active when they were younger.

11. An alternative to the stage approach is to look at major **themes,** such as **love** and **work,** *throughout* the life span.

12. Although only a small percentage of the elderly suffer **dementia,** the majority of those who do develop the serious progressive disorder known as **Alzheimer's disease.**

13. People's **psychological reactions to aging,** and theories of how best to age, are different. **Disengagement theory** claims that the greatest satisfaction is brought about by separating ourselves from society as society is withdrawing from us. In contrast **activity theory** says we are happier if we remain active and involved at the end of life. Forced withdrawal should lead to efforts to find new sources of involvement.

14. Elizabeth Kübler-Ross has done a great deal to open up the study of the process of dying. She has proposed a theory of **five stages** in the dying process. She says the terminally ill person goes through **denial, anger, bargaining, depression,** and **acceptance.**

15. Not everyone agrees with Kübler-Ross. Many people experience these emotions in **different orders and combinations.**

16. Most people would like to die a painless death, with adequate time to make preparations and say good-bye. Part of the process of preparing for death is a **life review.** Periods of life review begin before old age, but may increase as the person gets closer to the end.

17. In order to avoid "heroic efforts" of medical science to extend their life past a meaningful point, some people have written a **living will.** This indicates at what point they would like to have medical efforts discontinued, resulting in **passive euthanasia.**

18. Another attempt to restore dignity to the process of dying is the **hospice** movement. People who are terminally ill may decide to forgo additional medical treatment in a traditional hospital setting, and accept only pain-relieving medication either at home or in a separate facility. Hospice staff are trained to provide support and care to the dying person and his or her family.

ANSWERS FOR THOUGHT

1. *Is adolescence a time of "storm and stress" partly because of expectations that it will be?*

   Gallup polls and other research indicates that only a small minority of adolescents say they do not get along with their parents at all. (The worst period seems to be in the mid-teens.) The great majority of adolescents say they get along with their parents "fairly well" or "very well." Adolescents and parents usually agree on major issues. But adolescents tend to overestimate the differences between themselves and their parents. The "rebellious adolescent" may be an exaggerated stereotype—a product of cultural expectations—with only a kernel of truth.

2. *How does the rate of physical aging reflect the interaction of nature and nurture?*

   Many of the inevitable changes brought on by nature can be delayed or their impact softened by nurture. For example, positive mental attitudes and a healthful life-style prolong youthful vigor and appearance, and can help to keep options open for greater activity throughout life.

3. *When elderly people seem to recall their distant past with clarity, why can we not conclude that their memory for these events is very good?*

   We usually have no way of checking the accuracy of recall for these distant events. The memories may have undergone gradual distortion over the years, (details lost and replaced according to expectations) and yet, perhaps because they were recalled frequently, they seem as vivid as ever.

4. *When someone speaks of obeying "good laws" and disobeying "bad laws," at what level of morality would Kohlberg say they are operating?*

Kohlberg would say this person is operating at a postconventional level of morality. The person recognizes that society's standards are arbitrary and the person is defining values in terms of his or her own self-chosen principles.

5. *How would Erikson explain the fact that most members of extreme religious cults are young people?*

Sometimes young people have difficulty finding or discovering their identity, and extreme religious cults offer a ready-made solution. Cults often define what is appropriate dress and behavior, and they provide an accepting social context and a world-view which gives these activities meaning and purpose.

6. *Drug and alcohol abuse, delinquency, and suicide all increase during adolescence. Can you think of some biological, intra-psychic, and social reasons?*

Each behavior is multi-determined and we do not know all the causes, but here are some possibilities. *Biological factors:* rapid change of body shape and size, stress of early or late puberty, hormonal influence on moods and sexual desire. *Intra-psychic factors:* low level of moral development, or moral development tied to a delinquent group, identity crisis and role confusion (unsure of religious and political beliefs, or occupational goals), "negative identity," greater tendency to take risks. *Social factors:* family breakdown and consequent lack of support, lack of acceptance by society, confused by rapid changes in the world, inheriting a "messed-up" world.

7. *What effect would talk of a "mid-life crisis" have on someone approaching this age?*

It could cause the person to be more sensitive to feelings they might have at this time, it could lead to an expectation of difficulty, and it could help to bring on a crisis.

8. *Why would someone born in the 1920s or '30s be more rigid in their thinking than someone born in the 1960s or '70s?*

Most people born in the 1920s or '30s did not have the variety of options which are available to young people today. They also faced a world which was not changing as rapidly. And they were less aware of happenings outside of their immediate context (before the advent of television and communication satellites). These things meant that they were not forced to consider different options and perspectives. They did not need to be as flexible.

9. *What is your response to imagining your own physical changes in old age? Why do you think you feel that way?*

Your response to imagining yourself in old age is affected by the attitudes you see in the culture around you as well as by your own experience with older people. Because of their negative stereotype of old age, many people find it difficult or unpleasant to imagine their physical aging. As a result they avoid thinking of the subject.

10. *Some research suggests that many college students believe you should talk "baby talk" to elderly persons. Why . . . ?*

This may be because the young people have a stereotype of old age which includes mental deterioration at this time. It may also be related to the fact that some elderly people suffer hearing loss, and a common reaction to deafness is to raise one's voice and speak a very simplified form of language. Speaking to an elderly person this way could be frustrating and humiliating to him or her. This behavior also reinforces the younger person's stereotype of old age.

11. *If we counted our age by a number system that was not based on 10, would we still be prone to "crises" every 10 years?*

    If we counted age on a number system based on, say 6 (the digit on the left changed every 6 years, and the symbols from 7 to 9 were not used) crises might come every 6 years (or every 12 if 6 was too frequent). Crises are probably at least partly an artifact of our number system.

12. *If you had a very serious illness, would you go to a hospice, or would you try one more operation which might give you a little more time?*

    This is a personal decision which would be affected by many things. Some factors might be the amount of hope you held for the operation, your experience in hospitals (versus hospices), your philosophy of life (especially your attitude to death), and the response of your loved ones.

CHAPTER 14

PERSONALITY THEORY AND MEASUREMENT

Would it not be strange, in a city of seven million people, if one man were never mistaken for another . . . if with seven million pair of feet wandering through the canyons and corridors of the city, one pair of feet never by chance strayed into the wrong footsteps? Strange, indeed.

ERNEST LEHMAN
NORTH BY NORTHWEST

There is an invisible garment woven around us from our earliest years; it is made of the way we eat, the way we walk, the way we greet people, woven of tastes and colors and perfumes which our senses spin in childhood.

JEAN GIRADOUX

Personality. From the Greek word *persona*, which means "mask." The unique pattern of psychological and physical processes which control your behavior and thought and make you distinctly *you*.

I n Chapters 12 and 13, we described how you grow in physical, emotional, social, and cognitive areas of your life. But you are more than the sum of these parts. That's one of the reasons that describing your own growth as a *person* is a far more difficult task than is merely detailing how your "mind" or "body" develops. Psychologists often use the term *personality theory* to describe their attempts to discover how you become a whole or fully functioning person.

There is no single definition of the term **personality** that will do justice to all of the theories and research found within this important psychological area. This lack of agreement has the advantage of allowing individual personality theorists the freedom to investigate personality from their unique perspectives. In this way they shed new light on areas which other theories ignore (Wakefield, 1989). For our purposes, however, we will consider your personality to be the pattern of psychological and physical processes which controls your characteristic behavior and thought (Allport, 1961). Generally speaking, personality is everything about you that is uniquely typical of you—that which distinguishes you from everyone else "in a city of seven million people."

Different theorists have, of course, emphasized different aspects of personality. We will look at several theories which can be grouped in four categories: psychodynamic theories, humanistic theories, social learning theories, and trait theories. After this we will consider some attempts to measure personality through personality tests.

PSYCHODYNAMIC THEORIES

Those who go beneath the surface do so at their peril.

OSCAR WILDE

Personality psychologists study people's individual differences—the characteristics that make each person unique.

Psychodynamic personality theorists view the personality as an ever-changing interaction of complex psychological processes. And they tend to emphasize *unconscious* influences in personality. Psychodynamic theorists base their views mostly on clinical observations of troubled individuals. Sigmund Freud proposed the first and most influential psychodynamic theory of personality almost 100 years ago.

Sigmund Freud

Freud was born in 1856 in what is now the Czech Republic, but he lived most of his life in Vienna, Austria. After taking his degree in medicine in 1881, economic pressures forced Freud to set up practice as a *neurologist* specializing in disorders of the human nervous system. But Freud was more *holistic* in his approach than other specialists of his day. Freud believed that many of his patients' *physical* problems had a *psychological* basis.

One reason for this belief was Freud's experience with **hysteria** sufferers. These patients had physical problems without a known biological cause. For example, a patient might lose all feeling in one hand. But the pattern of numbness did not correspond with the distribution of nerves in the hand. Freud believed the problem was psychological, and therefore the cure must be psychological too.

Freud's beliefs were confirmed when he talked with these patients about their past. Many of them reported unpleasant experiences associated with the onset of their symptoms. And, particularly exciting for Freud, when he gave these patients a chance to express their anger, humiliation, and disgust about these experiences, their symptoms began to vanish!

Listening to what his patients said about their lives taught Freud many lessons. Besides unpleasant memories, most of the people he treated seemed to be **repressing** immoral or antisocial wishes and impulses. Often the patients would convert these repressed feelings into physical symptoms of some kind.

Freud's theory of personality grew out the observations he made on his patients (as well as his own painstaking self-analysis). At first he used hypnosis to get his patients to talk about their past. Later, he abandoned hypnosis and relied on **free association** and dream analysis. Since he saw patients almost until his death in 1939, he continued to rework his psychoanalytic theory of personality throughout his lifetime.

THE "STRUCTURE" OF PERSONALITY

In the final form of his theory, Freud divided the mind into three parts, the *id,* the *ego,* and the *superego* (Freud, 1923/1961). These were not physical structures in the brain, but psychological *forces* in the personality.

THE ID "Originally, to be sure, everything was id." By this phrase, Freud meant that the **id** is the most primitive portion of the personality. It exists at birth, and contains all of the basic *life instincts*—basic needs like hunger, thirst, and the need for sex. Freud called the life instincts **eros,** and he said they were fueled by a form of energy called **libido.** Eros is the organizing, creative instinct that strives to keep the organism alive and to reproduce the species. Eros is love and pleasure.

The id also contains a *death instinct* called **thanatos.** Thanatos is the disruptive, disorganizing instinct that strives to destroy the integrity of the personality and to move the organism down "its own path to death" (Freud, 1920/1955). Thanatos produces self-hatred, aggression, and misery. Thanatos and eros motivate all human behavior throughout life.

According to Freud, the id lives by the **pleasure principle.** That is, it cries out for *immediate* satisfaction—no matter what. But because the id behaves *as if reality did not exist,* its desires can be satisfied in symbolic or imaginary form. For example, the infant can gratify its need for food by sucking on its thumb or by dreaming about eating (Freud, 1933/1964).

In adults, dreams often disguise the id's disturbing sexual and aggressive impulses.

> The desire of pleasure—the libido, as we put it—chooses its objects without inhibition, and by preference, indeed, the forbidden ones: not only other men's wives, but above all incestuous objects . . . a man's mother and sister, a woman's father and brother. . . . Hatred, too, rages without restraint. Wishes for revenge and death . . . are nothing unusual (Freud, 1916/1963).

Hysteria. A physical symptom of a psychological disturbance. For example, hysterical paralyses is an inability to move certain parts of the body without a neurological cause for the problem.

Repressing. The act of willfully, but unconsciously, forgetting something.

Free association. Freud's psychoanalytic method of encouraging the patient to say whatever comes to mind without fear of criticism. The analyst looks for meaningful associations between thoughts and for pauses and abrupt changes in direction which might signal blocking of emotional material.

Id (rhymes with "kid"). The primitive, instinctual, childish, unconscious portion of the personality that obeys the pleasure principle.

Eros (AIR-ros). The Greek god of love. For Freud, the life force, or life instinct.

Libido (lib-BEE-doh). Freud's term for the psychic energy which drives the personality.

Thanatos (THAN-ah-toes). The Greek god of death. For Freud, the death instinct.

Pleasure principle. Freud's notion that the id (or the unconscious) is driven by the innate desire to satisfy its needs (or reduce its innate drives) immediately. Reducing the drive gives pleasure; an increase in a drive gives displeasure. According to Freud, "The id lives by the pleasure principle."

"All I want from them is a simple majority opinion on things."

Ego. From the Latin word for "I." That part of the personality which mediates between the id, the superego, and reality. Some parts of the ego are conscious, but the ego also extends into the preconscious and the unconscious.

Reality principle. The basis on which the ego operates as it tries to find real-world objects to satisfy the id's demands, as much as possible, in socially acceptable ways. In doing so, the ego obeys the reality principle.

Superego. That part of your personality which "splits off from your ego," and which contains both your own and society's "rules of conduct." The superego has two parts: the stern "conscience," which you acquired from your parents (mostly during the latency period and the genital stage), and the "self-ideal," which you acquired mostly from other people during puberty.

Conscience. Our internal ideas of what we *shouldn't* think, do, or say—the things for which we have been punished and now punish ourselves by feeling guilty. According to Freud, part of the superego.

Ego-ideal. Our internal ideas of what we *should* think, do, or say. Those things for which we have received approval, and to which we aspire. According to Freud, part of the superego.

Everyone is a moon, and has a dark side which he never shows to anybody.

MARK TWAIN

Dreams are *compromise structures* that provide a limited amount of satisfaction to the id while still maintaining the adult's ethical standards. "In all of us," Freud said, "even in good men, there is a lawless wild-beast nature which peers out in sleep" (Freud, 1900/1953).

The id "knows no judgments of value: no good and evil, no morality. . . . It has no organization, produces no collective will, but only a striving to bring about the satisfaction of the instinctual needs subject to the observance of the pleasure principle" (Freud, 1933/1964).

THE EGO   Left to its greedy self, the id would soon destroy itself *and* the individual. However, Freud said, at a very early age, the **ego** begins to differentiate out of the id. The development of the ego is brought about by the person's need to control the id and to respond appropriately to demands from the external environment.

While the id follows the pleasure principle, the ego obeys the **reality principle.** This means that the ego differentiates between fantasy and reality and scans the environment for "real" gratification. The ego decides whether a given instinctual demand must be satisfied immediately (and how), whether satisfaction can be postponed, or whether the instinct should be repressed. The ego represents common sense. "We might say that the ego stands for reason and good sense while the id stands for the untamed passions" (Freud, 1933/1964).

The ego tries to satisfy the childish demands of the id in a realistic way. In doing so, however, it must also deal with the demands of society represented by a third mental agency, the superego.

THE SUPEREGO   The *id* drives the infant to cry helplessly until it is fed. The *ego* guides the toddler to find food. But the young child soon learns that the cookie jar is "out of bounds" because mommy and daddy don't approve. The part of personality that comes to represent the "approval" of mommy and daddy (and the rest of society) is the **superego.** Our superego contains all our ideas of what we *shouldn't* do (our **conscience**) as well as all our ideas of what we *should* do (our **ego-ideal**).

In a general way, the id is the biological component of personality, the ego is the psychological component, and the superego is the social component. These three components interact continuously. Consider a hungry child in a candy store: The id says, "Grab the candy and eat it." The superego says, "Stealing is wrong. Besides, a piece of fruit is better for you." The ego says, "Wait. Go get some money and buy the candy."

The ego's task, Freud said, is to mediate not only between the id's urgings and reality's requirements, but to do so in a manner that satisfies the superego's strictures. Little wonder that Freud remarked, for the ego "Life is not easy!" (Freud, 1923/1961).

LEVELS OF CONSCIOUSNESS

One of Freud's major contributions to our understanding of personality was his insight into unconscious motivation. Freud likened the mind to an iceberg in which the small part above water represents our conscious experience while the much larger mass underwater represents *unconscious* influence.

Conscious thoughts occupy our present awareness. *Unconscious* thoughts are beyond our reach. Only through careful (psycho)analysis of conscious thoughts, actions, and dreams can we gain insight into the mysteries of unconscious processes.

In addition, Freud said, thoughts which were conscious in the past, and could be recalled again, exist in a *preconscious* state. This includes distant memories as well as objects in your present environment which you are not paying attention to at the moment. Long before Freud's analysis of consciousness, German psychologists had likened consciousness to a cluttered stage in a darkened theater. A narrowly focused spotlight sweeps across the stage, illuminating now this, now that. As you sit in the theater, you see a continuous flow of images flash into focus, then disappear into

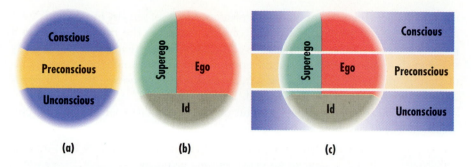

FIGURE 14.1

(a) Freud's "levels of consciousness."

(b) Freud's "structures of the mind."

(c) "Levels of consciousness" occupied by the "structures of the mind"—the id, ego, and superego.

darkness. The narrow beam of the spotlight is your momentary consciousness—what you are thinking about now. The rest of the stage is *potentially* visible to you, if and when the spotlight shines on it. It is *preconscious* (Freud, 1912/1958).

In 1933, Freud combined his ideas of consciousness and mental structure in a drawing similar to that shown in Figures 14.1a, 14.1b, and 14.1c. Freud saw the ego as lying mostly in the conscious and preconscious regions of the mind, but also extending deep into the unconscious. The superego lies mostly in the preconscious and the unconscious. The id, of course, resides entirely in the unconscious. However, Freud had a warning about interpreting this sort of diagram too literally:

> We cannot do justice to the characteristics of the mind by linear outlines like those in a drawing or in a primitive painting, but rather by areas of color melting into one another as they are presented by modern artists. After making the separation we must allow what we have separated to merge together once again (Freud, 1933/1964).

In Freudian theory, it is the *dynamic interaction* of these various elements—id, ego, superego; conscious, preconscious, unconscious—that determines what your personality is like.

CHILDHOOD SEXUALITY

As we mentioned earlier, Freud developed his theory of personality in part because, during free association, his patients frequently talked about having "unacceptable desires." What were these desires like? To Freud's amazement, many of them turned out to be sexual. Even more surprising was the fact that most of the repressed urges could be traced back to early childhood. This discovery led Freud to focus much of his therapy on exploring childhood memories.

Many patients reported that their fathers had attempted to abuse them sexually when the patients were quite young. At first, Freud assumed his patients were telling the truth. He soon abandoned this position, however, since he could not bring himself to believe that all fathers attempt to seduce their offspring. Rather, he decided, the patients were reporting as fact the *sexual fantasies* they had while still very young.

What effect might Freud's ideas have on the reporting of childhood sexual abuse?

The notion that children have sexual fantasies soon led Freud to make several important changes in his theoretical position. First, he concluded that the sexual instinct was one of the strongest forces shaping human nature. Second, he decided that most of his patients' problems resulted from the conflict they experienced between their early sexual desires and society's rules against expressing sexual feelings. And third, Freud came to the conclusion that, from birth on, infants actively sought sexual stimulation (Freud, 1905/1953).

By "sexual stimulation," however, Freud did not mean the genitally oriented sexuality of adults. Rather, he meant sensual pleasure. Sucking on the mother's breast not only reduces hunger, but becomes a pleasant source of sensory inputs. This "sexual" pleasure soon generalizes to other objects, including the infant's thumb or a pacifier. It also generalizes to other parts of the body. Soon the infant begins actively searching both his or her body and the environment for new sources of sensory stimulation. From Freud's point of view, adult sexuality has its roots in the child's constant striving for *sensual* pleasure (Freud, 1901/1960).

These "radical-for-their-times" insights on infant sexuality soon led Freud to create his **theory of psychosexual development.**

PSYCHOSEXUAL DEVELOPMENT

Freud's description of the psychosexual stages a child passes through is a narrative account of how the "expression of libido" changes over time. Freud believed that, in each of the major stages, the libido was "organized" or expressed in a characteristic manner through stimulation of a specific **erogenous zone** of the body.

If one's needs are met satisfactorily at each stage, the focus of libidinal energy shifts to the next erogenous zone—always in the same order. If, however, one's needs are either frustrated or overindulged at a particular stage, a certain amount of libidinal energy remains focussed on the related erogenous zone. This hinders full development, and the person is said to be *fixated* at that stage. **Fixation** in psychosexual development produces related personality characteristics in adulthood.

ORAL PERIOD   In the first year of life, Freud said, libido is organized around the pleasurable activities of the mouth (see Table 14.1).

During the first part of the oral stage, the infant releases libido primarily through self-stimulation, or **autoerotic** activities. After a few months, however, autoeroticism decreases as the infant begins to seek an external love object. For most infants, as we noted, the first external love object is the breast. The intense sensual pleasure the child derives from sucking on the mother's breast then becomes the "model" for sexual orgasm in the adult. As Freud put it, "No one who has seen a baby sinking back satiated from the breast and falling asleep with flushed cheeks and a blissful smile can escape the reflection that this picture persists as a prototype of the expression of sexual satisfaction in later life" (Freud, 1905/1953).

Theory of psychosexual development. Freud's belief that all children must pass through similar periods in the development of their personalities. Each stage has its own crisis, and during each stage the child discharges libidinal energy in a different manner.

Erogenous zones (air-RODGE-en-us). Those parts of the body which, when stimulated, provide sexually pleasurable feelings.

Fixation. Freud's term for the failure in development that occurs when the needs of a particular stage are frustrated or over-indulged. The result of a certain amount of libidinal energy remaining attached or "fixed" to the related erogenous zone.

Autoerotic (AW-toh-air-ROT-tick). Self-stimulation of the erogenous zones, such as in masturbation.

TABLE 14.1

The Psychosexual Stages

PSYCHOSEXUAL STAGE	LIBIDINAL ZONE	CHIEF DEVELOPMENTAL ISSUE	LIBIDINAL OBJECT
1. *Oral* (birth to 1 year)	Mouth, skin, thumb	Passive incorporation of all good through mouth; autoerotic sensuality	Mother's breast; own body
2. *Anal* (2 to 3 years)	Anus, bowels	Active seeking for tension reduction; self mastery; passive submission	Own body
3. *Phallic* (3 to 5 years)	Genitals, skin	Oedipus and Electra complexes; possession of mother; identification with same-sexed parent; ambivalence of love relationships	Mother for boy; father for girl
4. *Latency* (6 to 8 years)	None	Repression of pregenital forms of libido; learning culturally appropriate shame and disgust	Repressed previous objects
5. *Genital* (adolescence onward)	Genital primacy	Reproduction; sexual intimacy	Heterosexual partner

Based on Freud, 1905 and 1916.

Oral *fixation* in infancy produces a tendency to "oral" activities in adulthood. These may range from physical stimulation (kissing, smoking, chewing gum) to verbal activities (making "biting" remarks, willing to "swallow" any story), and even motivational traits (need to acquire possessions or "consume" knowledge).

ANAL PERIOD During the first year of life, Freud said, children tend to be fairly passive. However, at some point between the first and second year, they begin to strive for self-mastery. Toilet training typically begins around 18 months of age, and the libido becomes organized around the anus. Children soon learn to associate the retention and expulsion of feces not only with pleasure, but also with the mother's love and approval. According to Freud, gaining voluntary control over the sphincter muscle serves as the prototype not only for self-mastery, but also for mastering the social and physical environment in later life (Freud, 1905/1953).

Anal fixation from overly strict toilet training leads to obsessive neatness, stinginess, and cruelty. Anal fixation from enthusiastic and indulgent toilet training, where the parents praise the child for bowel movements, leads to adult productivity and creativity (not to mention a fascination with "bathroom humor").

PHALLIC PERIOD Freud believed that, beginning about the start of the fourth year of life, the libido becomes organized around genital stimulation. At about this age, and extending into the fifth year, youngsters discover that manipulation of their genitalia can provide intense sensory pleasure. And because they have not yet developed a sense of shame, the children also develop an intense interest in the genitalia of others. It is at this age, Freud said, that the **Oedipus complex** arises in males and the **Electra complex** develops in females (Freud, 1908/1959).

In boys, the Oedipus complex begins when mothers punish them for the nearly universal practice of masturbation. This punishment often involves threats that the mother (or perhaps the father) will *remove* the offending organ if the boy doesn't stop "playing with himself." But masturbation itself, Freud said, makes the boy love his mother more intensely because he somehow associates the intense pleasures of genital self-stimulation with the mother. However, the boy soon notes two things:

> First, his mother often pays a great deal of attention to the boy's father. The boy becomes jealous of and wants to get rid of the father in order to have the mother all to himself. But the boy also suspects the father is aware of this jealousy, and that parental threats of castration are therefore only too real.
>
> Second, because the boy has by now learned that little girls lack a penis, he decides that they have already been castrated for loving the mother too much. This insight serves to intensify his fears of losing the "valuable possession" that has brought him so much pleasure.

Overwhelmed by anxieties concerning castration, the boy *represses* all libidinal expression and begins to **identify** with his father. Indeed, Freud said, "In boys . . . the complex is not simply repressed, it is literally smashed to pieces by the shock of threatened castration" (Freud, 1925).

The boy resolves the Oedipus complex by taking three important steps:

1. He gives up his first love object, his mother.

2. He *identifies* with the father by taking on the father's values and views.

3. He develops a superego (conscience and ego-ideal) that incorporates his parents' sense of morality.

During the phallic period, the Electra complex in girls occurs because girls discover that they "lack a penis." Freud said they tend to blame their mother for the loss of "this important part of their bodies" (Freud, 1908/1959). The girl then abandons her first love object (the mother) and turns to the father. She knows the father has a penis, and hopes to get one for herself from him. Since this is not possible, she begins to yearn for a "symbolic penis substitute," a son (Freud, 1925).

During the Oedipus conflict, boys are strongly attracted to their mothers and girls are strongly attracted to their fathers.

Oedipus complex (ED-ih-pus or EED-ih-pus). Oedipus was a young man from Greek mythology who inadvertently killed his father and married his mother. Freud believed that, during the phallic stage, all young boys develop an intense incestuous desire for their mothers and a strong hatred for their fathers. Eventually the boy gives up his Oedipal love for the mother and takes on the standards of his father, thus creating his superego.

Electra complex (ee-LECK-trah). Electra was a Greek woman whose mother killed her father. Electra then talked her brother into murdering their mother. Freud believed that all young girls (during the phallic stage) develop an intense incestuous desire for their fathers and a strong hatred for their mothers. The Electra complex *dissipates* over time as the girl creates her superego in part by taking on the mother's values and standards.

Identify. To identify with someone is to take on the characteristics of that person. More than mere imitation; almost seeing yourself as the other person.

The only tyrant I accept in this world is the still voice within.

MAHATMA GANDHI

Freud believed that the Electra complex *dissipates* in girls because they come to *identify with the mother*. They take on her values and feminine behaviors, Freud said, in order to appeal to the father. Over time, the girls' "penis envy" typically fades, and because they now identify with the mother, they slowly cease to hate her for depriving them of a penis in the first place.

Freud believed that, because the Electra complex *dissipates* rather than being fully resolved, women do not develop as strong a superego as do men. In other words, males develop a *higher level of morality* than females (Freud, 1933/1964). Little wonder that Freud's theory has been criticized for its male bias!

Resolving the Oedipus and Electra complexes brings about the end of the phallic period and the start of the latency period (Freud, 1925).

LATENCY PERIOD From about age 6 until puberty, children experience a period of *sexual latency*. They suppress and sublimate libido by re-directing this sexual energy into learning the cultural tools of "reading, writing, and arithmetic." Children typically avoid the opposite sex at this time, although suppressed sexuality may surface in masturbation, sexual curiosity, and sexually oriented jokes. This relatively brief period ends with the onset of puberty (Freud, 1905/1953).

One of the reasons Freud developed the notion of the "latency period" is that the children he observed seemed to give up self-stimulation at about age 6. What other reasons can you think of for the decrease in observed sexual activity at this age?

GENITAL PERIOD Puberty signals the final stage of development. Sexual energy is re-focussed on the genital area, but autoeroticism is given up and an external love object is desired. At this stage, Freud said, libidinal energy is organized around the "discharge of sexual products." He noted, however, that this sort of activity brought intense sensory pleasure to the individual as well as leading to the procreation of the species.

During the genital period, which lasts for the rest of life, the personality bears the fruit of earlier developmental stages. The genital period is an eruption and synthesis of earlier stages. This is why Freud said personality was basically formed by age 6, the end of the phallic period (Freud, 1905/1953).

Freud alluded to a later stage of adult maturity, but he never really developed the concept (Feist, 1990). Probably the main reason for his relative neglect of adulthood was his belief that personality was formed in childhood. With Wordsworth he affirmed, "The child is father of the man."

Anna Freud

Anna was Freud's sixth child, born in 1895. Eventually she became her father's most trusted companion and a famous psychoanalyst in her own right. In the end, "Freud bequeathed to her his place as leader of the psychoanalytic movement" (Monte, 1991). Anna Freud made many contributions to psychoanalytic theory, chief among them (1) her development of techniques for analyzing children, and (2) her descriptions of the psychological mechanisms the ego uses to defend itself.

Sigmund Freud believed that the mechanisms the ego used to defend itself were "trivial things" that got in the way of analysis. Anna Freud, however, recognized how important they could be. In her classic monograph, *The Ego and the Mechanisms of Defense*, she made a lengthy list of the ego defenses that her father had mentioned in his writings. She then added several of her own. The best known of these defense mechanisms are as follows:

REPRESSION   is the blocking off from conscious awareness of any desire or memory the ego finds threatening. It is perhaps the most common of the defense mechanisms. A man may *repress* his sexual urges so that he is no longer aware of them because he is afraid they will get out of control.

DENIAL   is the cutting off from consciousness of external threats to the ego. (Repression is the shutting off of internal threats.) A woman may *deny* that she is in danger of losing her job.

PROJECTION   is attributing your own forbidden desires to someone else. If you hate someone, but cannot tolerate this hatred, you may *project* your dislike onto the other person by assuming that he or she hates you.

DISPLACEMENT   is the redirection of unacceptable urges onto a substitute. If you become angry at your boss, but fear expressing your anger openly, you may *displace* your anger onto the cat, and kick it instead of your boss.

TURNING-AGAINST-SELF   is the redirection of forbidden urges onto yourself. Now, instead of kicking the cat, you *turn against yourself* and develop feelings of inferiority, guilt, and depression as a reaction to the anger you have towards your boss.

REACTION FORMATION   is turning unacceptable feelings into their opposite. A girl who hates her mother but also sees herself as a faithful and loving daughter may *react* by smothering her mother with (apparent) love instead.

INTROJECTION   is making the characteristics of someone you admire or love part of your own personality. An adolescent who adopts the tastes and mannerisms of a movie star is *introjecting* these characteristics.

IDENTIFICATION-WITH-AN-AGGRESSOR   is making the characteristics of someone you hate or fear part of your own personality. Hostages sometimes show *identification-with-an-aggressor* in trying to protect their captors.

REGRESSION   is returning to an earlier and more childish form of behavior. Under stress, a recovered alcoholic may begin drinking again.

SUBLIMATION   is changing forbidden impulses into behaviors that are socially acceptable. A man with strong aggressive urges may join the military forces or become a policeman.

These are some of the major ego defense mechanisms listed by Anna Freud. However, as Christopher Monte notes, "It should be pointed out that other psychoanalysts have added endlessly to this list, so that the total number of possible ego defenses is considerably larger" than those mentioned by Anna Freud (Monte, 1991).

Almost all of the defense mechanisms available to the ego have four characteristics in common:

1. They are ways of trying to reduce stress and anxiety.
2. They involve the denial or distortion of reality.
3. They operate at an unconscious level.
4. They operate mechanically and involuntarily (which is why Anna Freud called them *mechanisms*).

The defense mechanisms are really indirect or "defensive" ways of coping with stress and anxiety. By encouraging their patients to bring their unconscious problems to the fore, and thus deal with them at a conscious level, psychoanalysts attempt to get their patients to use a more direct method of coping with their developmental difficulties.

Carl Jung

Born in Switzerland in 1875, Carl Gustav Jung came from a family of devout church-men and physicians. His father was a minister, and his mother a minister's daughter. As a medical student at the University of Zurich, he dabbled in biology, philosophy, archeology, mythology, and mysticism. Later, he used ideas from many different cultures in developing his theory.

Jung was impressed with Freud's early work. After a brief correspondence, in 1907, Freud invited Jung to visit him in Vienna. Soon after, Freud "anointed" Jung as his chosen successor. By 1912, however, Jung had developed his own psychodynamic theory, and broke with Freud. The two remained bitter enemies the rest of their lives.

Jung rejected Freud's emphasis on sexuality and unconscious negative influences as the major determiners of personality. Instead, Jung emphasized our ability to set positive and purposeful goals for ourselves, and our capacity for lifelong growth.

THE PERSONALITY

Personal unconscious. Jung's term for the part of the mind, or psyche, containing repressed or forgotten material.

Collective unconscious. Jung's term for the part of the psyche which all humans share and which we inherit from our ancestral past. Contains the archetypes.

Archetypes. Jung's idea that because of our common human ancestry, we are all born with certain predispositions or patterns (archetypes) from which we develop similar symbols and themes. These archetypal ideas have an important influence on the development of our personality.

Anima (ANN-ih-mah). A Jungian archetype. The "feminine" side of a man's nature.

Animus (ANN-ih-muss). Another Jungian archetype. The "masculine" side of a woman's nature.

Like Freud, Jung had his own "structural theory" of the psyche, or mind. Unlike Freud, however, Jung believed the ego was entirely conscious. And because of his feelings about the relative unimportance of sexuality and the drive for pleasure, his theory contained no id. But probably the most controversial part of Jung's theory was his belief that in addition to a **personal unconscious,** our personalities contain a **collective unconscious.**

The collective unconscious is a part of our mind that we share with all other human beings, past and present. As a result of experiencing the same things in different generations and in different cultures, human beings have an unconscious awareness of common themes and symbols. Jung called these shared themes and symbols **archetypes.**

Archetypes are *predispositions* to respond to certain real-world events in specific ways. For example, in times of social crisis, humans tend to seek out (and follow) great leaders. We do so, Jung said, because each of us contains a "hero archetype" that predisposes us to react to social stress by becoming emotionally attached to charismatic leaders (Jung, 1936/1953).

Jung saw many "opposing tendencies" in the personality. For example, each person has an unconscious archetype of the opposite sex which struggles to offset the person's *conscious* sex-related tendencies and bring balance to the personality. Buried inside the collective unconscious of each man are feminine attitudes and intuitions. These result from ages of experience with mothers and other women, and they form the **anima** archetype. This feminine side of each man determines his relationships with the women he meets in life. Buried inside each woman, Jung said, is an **animus** archetype, which constitutes the masculine side of her nature.

According to Jung, there is a certain danger to the animus and anima, for they *oppose* our normal feelings of sexual identity. And they might, under certain circumstances, gain primary control over our personalities. However, unless we recognize, and deal with, these "opposites" inside us, we are not likely to become "whole individuals" (Jung, 1917/1966).

Jung also said we have archetypes for birth, death, God, the trickster, the child, the wise old man, and others. The *shadow* is our archetype of the dark, sinister, inferior parts of ourselves—and the universe. The *persona* is our archetypal idea of proper social relations. It is a social mask we wear in order to function adequately in our relationships with other people.

Healthy development occurs when we recognize the polarities within us and accept our unique diversity. The result is the development of a new "center" of personality, the archetype called *self*.

PSYCHOLOGICAL TYPES

Jung's most widely accepted ideas (which were actually precursors to modern trait theories), have to do with *introversion* and *extraversion*. Jung said we are born with two innate *attitudes*, one of which leads us to look inward, the other of which leads us to look outward. Jung described them in this manner:

> The first attitude [introversion] is normally characterized by a hesitant, reflective, retiring nature that keeps itself to itself, shrinks from objects, is slightly on the defensive and prefers to hide behind mistrustful scrutiny. The second [extraversion] is normally characterized by an outgoing, candid, and accommodating nature that adapts easily to a given situation, quickly forms attachments, and . . . will often venture forth with careless confidence into unknown situations (Jung, 1917/1966).

Jung believed you are born with both these tendencies, but that one usually comes to predominate. You are usually conscious of which attitude is dominant but, according to Jung, you may not realize that the other attitude often expresses itself unconsciously through your dreams and fantasies.

In addition to our basic attitudes, Jung said we relate to the world through four different *functions*: sensing, thinking, feeling, and intuiting. Sensing is experiencing the world through our physical senses, without interpreting or evaluating it. Thinking is naming and interpreting experience. Feeling is evaluating experience for its emotional worth to us. Intuiting is relating directly to the world without physical sensation and without reason or interpretation (Progoff, 1953).

Imagine that you encounter a stranger of the opposite sex. First, you detect an object in your environment (sensing). Then you realize that the object is a stranger who is a member of the opposite sex (thinking). Next, you feel attracted toward the person (feeling). And finally, you believe that you could relate to this person in a lasting relationship (intuition) (Hergenhahn, 1984).

Ideally, we utilize all four functions and two attitudes equally in dealing with experience. In practice, however, one function and one attitude usually become dominant. This leads to eight different "types" of individuals, as shown in Table 14.2. Remember that the non-dominant attitude and functions still exert an influence, so these "pure" types are hypothetical examples only. Each person is a unique combination of attitudes and functions in various stages of development.

The "Myers-Briggs Type Indicator" is a popular personality test based on Jung's view of personality "types." We will discuss this test at the end of the chapter.

As we mentioned, Jung broke with Freud in 1912. Freud's other major disciple, Alfred Adler, made the break a year or so earlier.

Jung's popularity probably reached a high point in America during the 1960s. Can you guess why?

People remain what they are, even when their faces fall to pieces.

BERTOLT BRECHT

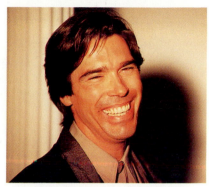

Jung believed we tend to be either introverted or extraverted. Extraverts are outgoing and confident; introverts are hesitant and retiring.

FUNCTION	ATTITUDE	
	EXTRAVERT	INTROVERT
Thinking	Repressed feelings; objective; cold; dogmatic; goal oriented.	Repressed feelings; inhibited; impractical; intellectual.
Feeling	Repressed thinking; emotional; respects social norms and harmony.	Repressed thinking; quiet; appear unfeeling to others.
Sensing	Pleasure-seeking; jolly; social; very realistic; repressed intuition.	Passive; detached; artistic; irrational; repressed intuition.
Intuiting	Changeable; creative; guided by hunches; repressed sensation.	Creative; eccentric; guided within; repressed sensation.

TABLE 14.2

Some personality characteristics associated with eight combinations of Jung's two "attitudes," or orientations toward the word, and his four "functions," or ways of experiencing the world.

Alfred Adler

Alfred Adler was born and educated in Vienna. Although he lived for 67 years, sickness and death haunted him all of his life. A rather sickly child, Alfred Adler often was angry because his older brother was athletic, while he wasn't. When he was 3, his younger brother died in the bed next to Adler's. And when he was just 4, he had such a bad case of pneumonia that the doctor gave him up for dead. Much of Adler's theorizing on human nature can be seen as an attempt to *overcome* his fear of death and feelings of *physical inferiority*.

As a young adult, Adler often recalled the times when, as a boy, he had to walk to school daily past a cemetery. Remembering the situation later, he was convinced that all the other children were brave enough to ignore the graveyard. But Adler felt fear and horror each time he came near the place. Deciding that he was *less courageous* than his peers, he determined he would have to train himself to overcome his fears. He did so, as he remembered things, by deliberately running back and forth over the graves until he had mastered his fears. When Adler was 35, however, he discovered to his amazement that there actually *had not been a cemetery* near his school. He had somehow made up the memory, perhaps as a way of explaining his early feelings of *inferiority*, his fear of death, and his angry determination to overcome that fear (Adler, 1959).

Adler joined Freud's group a few years after taking his medical degree. But as fascinated as Adler was by Freud's ideas, he broke away from "the master" in 1911 and formed his own group, the Society for Individual Psychology. Adler emphasized the importance of the social environment, and rejected Freud's theory of sexual drives. He thought that people could shape their own destinies, and that they could build a superior society by satisfying their basic need to transcend their personal problems (Ansbacher & Ansbacher, 1973).

FEELINGS OF INFERIORITY

Some children are, Adler said, unhealthy when young. Others are born smaller than average. But even large, healthy children learn very early in life that adults can do things that youngsters cannot. This knowledge creates in all of us *feelings of inferiority* that motivate us to succeed. Children who are neglected, pampered, or abused, or who have a physical deformity, may develop stronger feelings of inadequacy called an "inferiority complex."

Our inferiority feelings also create in us a drive for *compensation*, the urge to overcome our failures in one part of life by excelling in another. Early in his career, Adler practiced medicine in a neighborhood close to a large amusement park. Some of the artists and acrobats were Adler's patients. Adler noticed that many of them had developed extraordinary physical abilities as a reaction to weakness and illness in childhood. In the same way, the small, weak boy may try to succeed in his school studies or become a great musician in order to *compensate* for his physical weakness (Adler, 1931).

To Adler, life is a conscious struggle to move from what he called a "felt minus" to a "felt plus." By this, Adler meant you have an innate urge to rise above your own inferiorities *as you feel or perceive them,* and to become superior to what you were in the past. Adler called this "striving for superiority."

BIRTH ORDER

Adler believed that your birth order—the position in the family into which you were born—affects your personality. Adler studied four positions, the firstborn, the second-born, the youngest, and the only child. Adler pointed out that the firstborn receives all the attention of new parents, until he or she is "dethroned" by the birth of the second child. The second-born does not suffer this experience. For the second-born, the firstborn is a model to follow and try to catch. The youngest child receives the attention of parents and older siblings, who often spoil the child and don't allow the child to become independent. "Only" children are like firstborn children who are not dethroned until much later—perhaps in school when they discover that they are no longer the center of adult attention. Without siblings, "only" children have greater difficulty learning a feeling for others, or "social interest."

The social forces unique to each position in the birth order, produce characteristic patterns of personality. Adler believed that by studying your birth order, your dreams, and your first memories, he could understand the origins of your particular "style of life."

Adler said the first-born child is like a "king dethroned." When a sibling is born, the first-born no longer receives all the attention.

STYLE OF LIFE

Adler was an optimist. He believed that you have buried in your genes a basic need to cooperate with others and to work toward building a better society. But you need guidance from others in order to express this need. For it is only through training and experience that you develop your *style of life*—your own unique way of expressing yourself (Ansbacher & Ansbacher, 1956).

Adler believed that the style of life is the self-consistent, goal-oriented core of personality. At first, Adler thought this style was set in childhood. Later, he decided that you continue to mature even as an adult. Thus, Adler was one of the first theorists to emphasize *life span development*.

Adler's belief in the importance of *social factors* in determining personality was, for a time, unique in psychoanalytic circles and helped give rise to what we now call "social psychology." And by assuring people that they were basically humane, open-minded, and in control of their own destinies, Adler encouraged the development of "humanistic psychology."

Indeed, as humanist Abraham Maslow stated shortly before his (Maslow's) death, "Alfred Adler becomes more and more correct year by year. As the facts come in, they give stronger and stronger support to his image of man."

To have a life style is to have an identity.

ALFRED ADLER

Freud called his theory psychoanalysis. Jung named his approach analytical psychology. Adler referred to his viewpoint as individual psychology. What do these three terms tell you about the theories themselves?

Karen Horney

Like Alfred Adler's childhood, Karen Horney's (HORN-eye) early experiences had an enormous impact on her view of personality. She was born to a tyrannical sea captain 18 years older than his wife. Although loved by her mother, Horney felt alienated from her father and brother whose love she was unable to win. As a young adult she rebelled against her father's teachings.

Initially attracted to Freudian theory, Horney gradually rejected many of Freud's ideas and added some of her own. She could not accept the obvious male bias in Freud's theory—based on his assumption that "anatomy is destiny." Consequently she reworked some of Freud's ideas, such as his description of the Oedipus conflict, giving them a more balanced *cultural* context. She also disagreed with Freud that psychological disturbances are the result of a struggle with forbidden id drives. She came to view personality, and personality disturbances, as driven by **basic anxiety.**

Perhaps reflecting her own background, Horney said we experience basic anxiety as a result of feeling isolated and helpless in a hostile world. This leads us to be alienated from our *real* selves and try to be what we think we *should* be in order to gain the security we crave.

Basic anxiety. The negative feelings which originate in childhood as a result of parental domination, indifference, erratic behavior, disparaging attitudes, injustice, and so on.

Karen Horney adapted to Freud's views to remove the male bias and emphasize cultural and interpersonal forces.

For the normal person the "real self" is not very different from what the person would like to be, the person's "*ideal* self." But for the disturbed (neurotic) person the "real" and the "ideal" are very different. The neurotic not only believes his or her "real self" is worthless, but also imagines an unrealistically high "ideal self." The neurotic's ideal self is an unrealistic dream of "shoulds." Horney called this the "tyranny of the should." In effect, the neurotic says to himself or herself:

> Forget about the disgraceful creature you actually are: this is how you should be; and to be this idealized self is all that matters. You should be able to endure everything, to understand everything, to like everybody, to be always productive—to mention only a few of these inner dictates. Since they are inexorable, I call them "the tyranny of the should" (Horney, 1950).

As a result of this unrealistic view of ourselves, we develop certain neurotic needs. These lead to unbalanced trends in our *mode of interacting* with other people. For example, we might move *toward* others and become overly submissive and dependent on them; we might move *away* from others and become indifferent and withdrawn; or we might move *against* others and try to compete with or control them. When we are emotionally healthy we show a balance in these three modes of interacting, using each one in its appropriate situation (Horney, 1945).

Karen Horney's reworking of Freud's "male bias," her emphasis on cultural and family influences, and her insight into neurotic struggles are valuable contributions to psychodynamic theory. As Christopher Monte says, ". . . it would be difficult to find another personality theorist with whom to compare her lucid and brilliant descriptions of neurotic misery and compulsive overstriving for imaginary and defensive self-excellence" (Monte, 1991).

Freud and Psychodynamic Theories: An Evaluation

Gary Leak and Steven Christopher give this evaluation of Sigmund Freud: "There can be little doubt that Freudian psychoanalysis is the 'first force' in 20th-century psychology. Psychoanalysis as a personality theory is the most comprehensive one available, detailing the structure, dynamics, and development of personality to a degree unsurpassed by its competitors" (Leak & Christopher, 1982).

One reason for this influence is the fact that Freud paid attention to the *unconscious* aspects of human behavior. Prior to Freud's time, psychologists either studied overt behavior patterns or used introspection to study *conscious* activities. But neither introspection nor the study of conditioned responses yielded the insights into personality development that Freud gave the world because he looked at the hidden aspects of the mind.

When it comes to experimental evidence, psychoanalysis has not fared so well. Freud's account of "what happens when" during childhood is simply not supported by most recent developmental research. And because he was a stage theorist, his description of psychosexual development is subject to many of the criticisms raised against Piaget and Kohlberg. Freud cared little for these criticisms, however. Convinced of the wisdom of his insights into the structure and dynamics of the human personality, he felt no need for experimental validation of his theoretical views.

The major criticism that can be made of Freudian theory, therefore, is this one: Like most other "narrative accounts" in science, psychoanalysis tends to "explain almost everything, but predicts almost nothing." For that reason, perhaps, Freud's views have appealed more to humanists—to artists and writers, to philosophers and natural historians—than to data-oriented experimental scientists. In his assessment, Thomas Parisi concludes, "I have not tried to argue that Freud was 'right' or that his theory is 'true.' If forced to choose—right or wrong—one must of course admit that Freud was wrong on many counts. But he was richly wrong" (Parisi, 1987).

What can we learn from psychodynamic theories of personality? Probably the most important insight which the psychodynamic viewpoint gives us is the knowledge of our ignorance. Our thoughts and behaviors may be influenced by irrational, primitive, and childish impulses that are largely beyond our awareness.

Since the time of Freud, and even during his lifetime, Freud's followers have continued to develop the psychodynamic approach. Many of them place less emphasis on control by the id and more emphasis on rational choice by the ego than Freud did. For example, Erikson's theory, which we saw in the last chapter, is primarily a theory of ego development. And most psychodynamic approaches, following Adler and Horney's lead, now include a greater role for social influence.

For some theorists of personality, these changes were not enough. They championed radically different approaches which emphasized our ability to change and grow, either by controlling our environment, or by striving towards personal goals.

We will look at some of these ideas by first discussing two humanistic psychologists, Abraham Maslow and Carl Rogers. Then we will consider the various behavioral approaches, including social learning theory. As you will see, all these theorists tend to emphasize *conscious ego control, personal growth and psychological health,* and/or the influence of the social environment.

HUMANISTIC THEORIES OF PERSONALITY

Freud believed that our destinies lay in our genetic blueprints, and that the interaction between our social environments and our genes determines the structures of our personalities. This rather rigid view of the human personality is rejected by a group of theorists who call themselves **humanistic psychologists.** They believe that you help shape your own destiny.

Like many medical doctors, Freud tended to define "health" as the lack of pathology. The humanistic psychologists disagree. As Abraham Maslow put it, "Health is not simply the absence of disease or even the opposite of it. Any theory of [personality] that is worthy of attention must deal with the highest capacities of the healthy and strong man as well as with the defensive maneuvers of crippled spirits" (Maslow, 1970).

To humanistic psychologists, being healthy means being yourself.

Humanistic psychologists. Psychologists who are devoted to human welfare, who have a strong interest in or love for individuals (as opposed to loving nations, organizations, or abstract ideals). Humanistic psychologists, unlike Freud, tend to believe in the basic goodness of humankind.

Abraham Maslow

Abraham Maslow was something of a "stranger in a strange land." In an interview late in his life, he stated that, as a child, "I was isolated and unhappy. I grew up in libraries and among books, without friends" (quoted in Hall, 1968).

Neither of Maslow's parents were educated. He described his mother as "a pretty woman—but not a nice one." She was cruel and showed him little affection. He described his father as "a nice man," and as a "vigorous man, who loved whiskey and women and fighting" (quoted in Wilson, 1972). However, early in his life, his parents lost interest in caring for their children. From that time on, one of Maslow's uncles reared him.

THE SEARCH FOR PERFECTION

During his early life, Maslow felt insecure and even "inferior" to his professors. He saw them as being "angels," while he was a poor sinner. And he apparently projected onto his teachers those psychological perfections he feared he lacked. This early idealism apparently was destroyed, however, when one day he found himself standing at a urinal next to one of his professors: "It stunned me so that it took hours, even

TABLE 14.3

Abraham Maslow's Characteristics of Self-Actualizing People

They have more efficient perceptions of reality and are more comfortable with it. They accept themselves and their own natures almost without thinking about it.

Their behavior is marked by simplicity and naturalness and by lack of artificiality or straining for effect.

They focus on problems outside themselves; they are concerned with basic issues and eternal questions.

They like privacy and tend to be detached.

They have relative independence of their physical and social environments; they rely on their own development and continued growth.

They do not take blessings for granted, but appreciate again and again the basic pleasures of life.

They experience limitless horizons and the intensification of any unself-conscious experience often of a mystical type.

They have a deep feeling of kinship with others.

They develop deep ties with a few other self-actualizing individuals.

They are democratic in a deep sense; although not indiscriminate, they are not really aware of differences.

They are strongly ethical, with definite moral standards, though their attitudes are conventional; they relate to ends rather than means.

Their humor is real and related to philosophy, not hostility; they are spontaneous less often than others, and tend to be more serious and thoughtful.

They are original and inventive, less constricted and fresher than others.

While they tend toward the conventional and exist well within the culture, they live by the laws of their own characters rather than those of society.

They experience imperfections and have ordinary feelings, like others.

Source: Condensed from "Self-Actualizing People: A Study of Psychological Health," in *Motivation and Personality,* 2nd ed., by Abraham H. Maslow, Copyright © 1954 by Harper & Row, Publishers, Inc.: Copyright © 1970 by Abraham H. Maslow. By permission of the publishers.

Self-actualizers. Maslow's term for people who are reaching their full potential; people who are becoming all that they are capable of becoming; self-fullfilling people.

They can do all because they think they can.

VIRGIL

weeks, for me to assimilate the fact that a professor was a human being and constructed with the plumbing that everybody else had" (quoted in Wilson, 1972).

Maslow apparently overcame this early shock rather well. But as he continued his career, he deliberately sought out the "top people," the **"self-actualizers,"** both in the academic world and in the realms of arts and politics. But, wisely, he now realized that they were "nearly perfect," and thus not quite "angels."

Some of these individuals were his personal friends. Others—such as Lincoln, Einstein, Eleanor Roosevelt, and Beethoven—he studied through books, papers, and letters. Maslow assumed these individuals had achieved a high degree of self-fulfillment or they wouldn't have been so prominent and have demonstrated so much leadership. By determining the similarities among the members of this noted group, he arrived at the characteristics of a truly "self-actualizing" person. A list of these characteristics appears in Table 14.3.

B-VALUES

In Chapter 6 we noted that Maslow developed a "hierarchy of needs" to describe motivation. As we grow, our needs change from basic (physical) needs, to social and love needs, and finally to the need for full development that Maslow called self-actualization. Late in his life, Maslow concluded that self-actualization was more complex than he originally had thought:

It may turn out to be useful to add to the definition of the self-actualizing person, not only (a) that he be sufficiently free of illness, (b) that he be sufficiently gratified in his basic needs, and (c) that he be positively using his capacities, but also (d) that he be motivated by some values which he strives for or gropes for and to which he is loyal (Maslow, 1971).

Self-actualizing people, Maslow said, are motivated by the need to grow. That is, they develop "Being-needs" or "B-values." Among the fifteen B-values Maslow listed are truth, goodness, beauty, uniqueness, perfection, simplicity, and playfulness.

MASLOW: A SUMMARY

According to Maslow, the two major theories that shaped modern psychology are Freudian psychoanalysis and behaviorism. He believed that *humanistic psychology* took the best of both schools of thought and added something extra:

If I had to condense [my theory] into a single sentence, I would have said that in addition to what the psychologists of the time had to say about human nature, man also [has] a higher nature. . . . And if I could have had a second sentence, I would have stressed the profoundly holistic nature of human nature in contradiction to the analytic . . . approach of the behaviorists and of Freudian psychoanalysis (Maslow, 1970).

We will have more to say about Maslow's contribution after we look at another major humanistic psychologist, Carl Rogers.

Carl Rogers

Carl Rogers was born in 1902 in Chicago to parents he described as being "highly practical, 'down to earth' individuals." They were also, perhaps unfortunately, "rather anti-intellectual, with some of the contempt of the practical person toward the long-haired egghead" (Rogers, 1967).

Rogers remembered both of his parents as being "extremely loving and 'masters' of the art of subtle control" (Monte, 1991). They were quite stringent in the way they reared their six children. Rogers' mother, who was extremely religious, managed to convey to the youngsters the belief that they were in some way "elect," or "superior." She also taught them that there were certain things they were not to do: "Such was the unity of our family that it was understood by all that we did not dance, play cards, attend movies, smoke, drink, or show any sexual interest" (Rogers, 1967).

Much of Rogers's professional life can be seen as an attempt to help people overcome external control (no matter how subtle) and become themselves (Atwood & Tomkins, 1976).

Rogers began his collegiate training at the Union Theological Seminary in New York, hoping to become a minister. However, he soon broke not only with organized religion, but also with his family. He married his childhood sweetheart and enrolled at Columbia University to study clinical psychology.

At that time, Columbia was something of a hotbed of behaviorism. However, while still in training, Rogers undertook an internship at the Institute for Child Guidance, where the staff was primarily Freudian in its orientation. Eventually he rejected both viewpoints and developed his own approach.

CLIENT-CENTERED THERAPY

We will discuss Rogers's approach to therapy more fully in the next chapter. However, some of his early experiences as a therapist helped shape his theory of personality.

For example, when (as a beginning therapist) he tried to apply Freudian techniques, he found they often "simply did not work." Nor did "trying to give the patient insight by direct questioning" seem particularly helpful. Indeed, it appeared that the *less direct* Rogers became, and the less he tried to manipulate the therapeutic situation, the more likely it was that his patients improved. Rogers soon concluded that "it is the *client* who knows what hurts, what directions to go, what problems are crucial, what experiences have been deeply buried." Rogers decided that traditional types of treatment were *therapist-centered*. His type of therapy was, instead, to be *client-centered*. And he wanted his clients to *experience* their feelings rather than merely talk about them (Rogers, 1961).

Shortly after obtaining his doctoral degree in clinical psychology, Rogers took a job as head of the counseling center at the University of Chicago. Later he taught at Ohio State and at the University of Wisconsin. On retirement, he moved to California, where he continued to write for many years. He died in 1987. Prior to his death, however, he was considered the "reigning king" of the humanistic psychologists.

THE PHENOMENAL WORLD

Rogers believed you were born with no self-concept, and no self. But Rogers held that you did have an innate urge to become a fully functioning and actualized person.

At birth, all you had was a confusing set of sensory impressions, biological processes, and motor activities. Rogers put it this way: "Every individual exists in a continually changing world of experience of which he is the center." Rogers called this the **phenomenal world,** which is *reality as you experience it* (Rogers, 1959).

During your early childhood, Rogers said, you slowly learned to differentiate your "self" from other parts of your phenomenal world. As you did so, you learned to see yourself as "I" or "me." Eventually, you came to realize you are an "independent self" capable of acting on your own (Rogers, 1951).

Phenomenal world. Rogers' term for the sum total of all your experiences (sensory inputs, processings, outputs).

SELF-STRUCTURE

According to Rogers, you developed your self-concept through your interactions with others, by *evaluating* the way that others treated you. In particular, you evaluated positive and negative feedback from your parents and incorporated that feedback into your *self-structure*.

As an infant, why would you do something your parents perceive as "bad"? Because, Rogers says, it is part of you, part of your self-structure, part of the way *you* perceive reality. When your parents punish you for this act, however, you face a difficult problem. You want to maintain your parents' love, so you must change the behavior itself. But you may also be tempted to change your *perception* of the behavior too. That is, you may decide that the part of you that initiated the punished

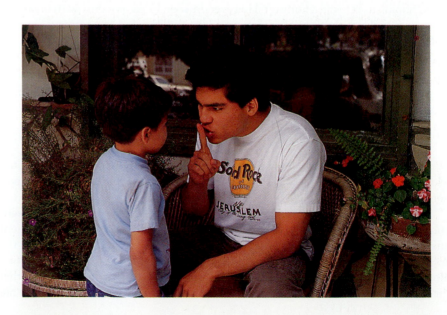

Rogers says we learn to deny aspects of our self when parents or others won't accept these parts of our personality.

behavior *isn't really you*. And so you may reject part of your self-structure by blocking it off from consciousness.

Rogers explained the situation this way: "The accurate symbolization would be: 'I perceive my parents as experiencing this behavior as unsatisfying to them.' The *distorted* symbolization, distorted to preserve the threatened concept of self, is: 'I perceive this behavior as unsatisfying.'" He calls this, "experiencing reality secondhand" (Rogers, 1951).

Put in simpler terms, Rogers said that, in order to maintain your parents' love, you may become someone you aren't. What you really want to be is still part of your self, but it is now part of your unconscious mind. According to Rogers, client-centered therapy allows the person to bring this repressed material to consciousness. Once clients have done this, they can reject "external influences" and get on with the task of "becoming what they really are."

What similarities—and differences—do you see between Rogers's explanation of the development of the "self-structure" and Freud's description of how the superego is formed?

UNCONDITIONAL POSITIVE REGARD

A key concept in Rogerian client-centered therapy is **unconditional positive regard.** By this term, Rogers meant that the therapist must accept the patient as she or he is, as being a *genuine person* with his or her own set of values and goals.

Rogers believed that parents should give their children the same "unconditional positive regard." To accomplish this goal, he said, the parents should do three important things:

1. Learn to accept the child's own feelings and goals.
2. Learn to accept their own feelings about what the child does without trying to force their values on the child.
3. Find ways to let the child know they accept the child as a person.

Children whose parents treat them with "unconditional positive regard" eventually learn to treat *themselves* in the same fashion. Put more simply, Rogers said that before you can accept yourself, you must first see that others respect you for what you are.

When you can accept yourself completely, you become what Rogers calls a *fully functioning individual*. Self-acceptance does not mean merely giving a superficial approval to what you are consciously. It involves a process of discovery, of uncovering parts of your self-structure which you have repressed in order to gain the approval of others. As a fully functioning person, you are open to all experience, and you do not suppress knowledge of anything that is a real part of you. You are aware of both your faults and your virtues, but you have a high positive regard for yourself. And most of all, you maintain happy and humane relationships with others (Rogers, 1951).

In what ways does Rogers's theory of emotional and cognitive development in the child appear to be a reaction to the way his own parents reared him?

Humanistic Psychology: An Evaluation

Neither Rogers nor Maslow offered a full-fledged theory of personality development, as did both Freud and Erikson. We discussed the pros and cons of Maslow's hierarchy of needs in Chapter 6. His explanation of motivational development appeals to

Unconditional positive regard. The act of giving non-judgmental feedback to a person, of accepting the person as he or she actually is.

many people because of its simplicity and because of its emphasis on personal choice. However, there is little in the way of experimental data to support his views. And his hierarchy of needs is subject to all the criticisms raised against Piaget's and Freud's "stage theories."

The major strengths of the humanistic approach appear to be twofold: (1) It emphasizes health rather than sickness; and (2) it holds that people actively participate in shaping their personalities. The major weaknesses seem to be a de-emphasis on behavior and objective measurement, and a failure to explain in *precise terms* how personality forms.

At the same time that Maslow and Rogers were developing the holistic approach they called "humanistic psychology," Stanford psychologist Albert Bandura was beginning to "shape" B.F. Skinner's notions on operant conditioning into what is now called social learning theory (Bandura, 1986a). We discussed the early history of social learning theory in Chapter 9, and we will describe Bandura's ideas further in Chapter 18. At this point, let's look briefly at what social learning theory is, and how it differs from psychoanalysis and humanistic psychology.

SOCIAL LEARNING THEORY

In a sense, social learning theory is an interesting mixture of Piaget, Adler, and Skinner. Like Piaget, social learning theorists, such as Albert Bandura and Julian Rotter, tend to emphasize cognitions rather than observable behaviors. Like Adler, social learning theorists believe that your interactions with your environment determine much of what you become. And like Skinner, social learning theorists believe learning is the key to understanding personality.

However, social learning theorists differ from earlier theorists in many ways. For example, Piaget believed that "mental structures" were determined primarily by the genes, but the social learning theorists see cognitive processes as being "shaped" the same way that Skinner says behavior is "shaped." Skinner says you learn because your actions are *directly* rewarded or punished. The social learning theorists agree that consequences are important, but add that *thoughts* intervene between your perception of a stimulus and your decision to respond (Rotter, 1982). Albert Bandura also adds something unique—the concept of learning by imitation, or *observational learning*.

Albert Bandura

Albert Bandura is a native of Canada. He received his undergraduate training at the University of British Columbia and his graduate training at the University of Iowa. Since 1953, he has spent most of his career at Stanford University.

Unlike many other personality theorists, Bandura bases his views on careful laboratory research. Probably his best-known studies have been on the topic of **observational learning.**

Observational Learning. Acquiring a new behavior by watching someone else perform the behavior, and then imitating or modeling that person's performance.

OBSERVATIONAL LEARNING

Skinner believes that you learned to act as you do because certain of your responses were *directly reinforced.* The social learning theorists agree that direct reinforcement does work, particularly with children. But they say that you also learn by observing the consequences of other people's actions. We met an example of this in Chapter 9. Children who watched a model hit and kick a toy "Bobo doll," later became much more violent when they were frustrated, than did children who had not watched the violent model (Bandura et al., 1963).

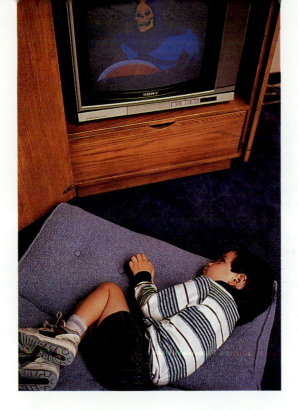

Bandura's research indicates that children learn to perform violent acts by watching violent models.

We learn to imitate those behaviors that yield rewards, and avoid those actions that bring unpleasant results. Since learning by observation takes place "in your mind," it is far too *cognitive* a concept to fit readily within the "pure" behavioral theory of B.F. Skinner (Bussey & Bandura, 1984).

According to Bandura, first you observe someone else attaining a particular goal, then you *rehearse* the behaviors involved in achieving that goal. The "motor rehearsal" helps you create a more accurate *cognitive representation* of the skill. And the more accurate this "cognitive representation" becomes, the better you can reproduce the observed behavior in real life (Carroll & Bandura, 1985).

TWO STAGES OF PERSONALITY DEVELOPMENT

According to Bandura, personality development tends to occur in two broad stages. When you were very young, your parents and the rest of your social environment shaped your behaviors the way that Skinner shaped pigeons to perform behavioral tricks. That is the first, or "passive," stage of development. The second, or "interactive," stage grows out of the first. As you behaved, you were also creating *cognitive structures* in your mind much as Piaget claimed was the case. These cognitions do at least two things for you: First, they allow you to observe and evaluate the actions of others, and to change your own behaviors consciously; and second, your cognitions allow you to *reshape your own environment*.

As your external world changes, you respond to it differently. Thus, to the social learning theorist, the person-environment interaction is a continuous process of *complementary shaping*. Bandura refers to this process as **reciprocal determinism** (Bandura, 1984).

People are not simply reactors to external influences. They select, organize, and transform the stimuli that impinge upon them.

ALBERT BANDURA (1977)

SELF-EFFICACY

Adler believed that such motives as the inferiority complex and the need to cooperate with others drive development. Both Maslow and Rogers thought that you had an innate drive to become a fully functioning person. However, according to Bandura, the need for a feeling of "self-efficacy" determines much of development.

By "self-efficacy," Bandura means your own perception of how well you can cope with the situations you face in life (Bandura, 1986b). People with high perceived

Reciprocal determinism. Bandura's belief that psychological processes are a joint function of behavioral, cognitive, and environmental influences. According to Bandura, the environment influences your cognitions and thus your behavior, but you can also choose to change your environment and thus change your cognitions and behavior. You influence your environment and your environment influences you.

self-efficacy in any situation, Bandura says, tend to be more highly motivated to succeed. Their desire to "meet their own standards" causes them to *monitor* their performance carefully in any given situation.

SELF-EVALUATION AND PERSONAL AGENCY

Why do you monitor your actions? According to Bandura, you do so because of your need to *maintain control*. But it is not only your own internal processes that you must influence (self-control); you strive to find ways to shape your environment, as well. This "desire to establish personal control over things" is what Bandura refers to as the sense of *personal agency* (Bandura & Cervone, 1983).

In a sense, what Bandura has done is to translate Skinner's notions on shaping the behavior of others into a scheme for *self-shaping* in various social situations. But this self-shaping involves changing your own *cognitions* as well as changing your *behavioral outputs*.

Because social learning theory grew out of experimental psychology, Bandura has tested his theory in the laboratory more than most other personality theorists have. As we noted, Bandura believes that high perceived self-efficacy goes along with high motivation. In one study, Bandura and his colleagues measured "perceived self-efficacy to withstand pain" in subjects, and then taught the subjects cognitive methods of pain control. Bandura and his associates report that the higher the subject's perceived self-efficacy, the more pain the subject could actually withstand (Bandura & O'Leary, 1987).

Because many of Bandura's concepts (and terms) come from social psychology, we will encounter him again in Chapter 18.

Social Learning Theory: An Evaluation

There are many strengths to social learning theory. To begin with, it is more holistic in its approach to describing personality development than some other approaches. And because it sprang from behavioral learning theory, social learning theory is also more firmly grounded on empirical evidence. Unlike Skinner, however, Bandura accepts the importance of "conscious thought" and "cognitive representations of the outer world" as important determinants of human behavior. And also unlike Skinner, Bandura describes methods of "shaping" these cognitive processes.

On the negative side, Bandura's approach places far more emphasis on *social* than on *biological* influences in personality development. Thus, it is not quite the "full-fledged" holistic theory that perhaps some day it will become. And, as yet, Bandura has not given us the sort of detailed picture of how personal growth occurs throughout the life span that can be found in either Freud or Erikson. (Other social learning theories, such as Julian Rotter's, have similar strengths and weaknesses as Bandura's.)

TRAIT THEORIES

In recent years, one of the most popular approaches among psychologists to the study of personality has been the trait approach (Wiggins & Pincus, 1992). As psychologist Arnold Buss puts it, "If there is to be a specialty called personality, its unique and therefore defining characteristic is traits" (Buss, 1989).

Most trait theorists believe that your basic **traits,** or dispositions, are strongly influenced by biological characteristics, such as your general activity level (Eaves et al., 1989). And since we inherit our basic biology, some of the most fascinating data

Traits. According to *Webster's Ninth New Collegiate Dictionary*, a trait is "a distinguishing quality (as of personal character); an inherited characteristic."

on psychological traits comes from the study of people with identical biology—identical twins—who have been reared in non-identical circumstances.

Twin Studies: Evidence for Inherited Traits?

In 1979, University of Minnesota psychologist Thomas Bouchard, Jr., began a long-term study of twins reared apart from each other since very early in life. So far, Bouchard and his group have discovered 77 sets of twins and 4 sets of triplets who were separated at birth. The Minnesota group has also studied several hundred sets of twins reared together. The group's main research focus is discovering what aspects of the personality are determined primarily by genetic factors (Bouchard, 1983: McGue et al., 1984).

One member of the Minnesota group is psychologist David Lykken. He notes that many of the twins reared apart are surprisingly similar in terms of their personality traits. For instance, consider a set of identical twins named Jerry Levey and Mark Newman who were separated at birth and put up for adoption. When the men finally met, they were about 30 years old. Aside from a difference in weight, they looked identical. They had the same sort of mustache and sideburns, and they wore the same type of glasses. Both were captains of volunteer fire-fighting groups. Both men drank only Budweiser, and held the beer bottle in the same rather odd way when drinking. Both were bachelors, compulsive flirts, and both were loudly good-humored. At their first meeting, both men found that their tendency to make "the same remarks at the same time and use the same gestures" was "spooky" (quoted in Rosen, 1987).

Lykken describes another set of twins studied by the Minnesota group as follows:

Identical twins Mark Newman and Jerry Levey were separated at birth and reunited at the age of 32. They found that they are both firefighters and have many other things in common.

> Despite growing up in opposite socioeconomic circumstances, [Daphne and Barbara] both were penny-pinchers. And both were stingy not just with their money but also with their opinions. . . . Both had suffered miscarriages during their first marriage but went on to have three healthy children. The women shared a fear of heights. Shortly after meeting for the first time, they began finishing each other's sentences and answering questions in unison (cited in Rosen, 1987).

David Lykken points out that, despite the amazing similarities in the temperaments of some identical twins reared apart, other twins are fairly dissimilar. "Genes do not fashion IQ or personality, they make proteins. And those proteins are many biochemical steps removed from the complex traits and abilities we see in a person. . . . Subsequent experience can sometimes overcome nature" (quoted in Rosen, 1987). Lykken's research indicates that even in twins reared together, very little of their similarity is the result of similar environments (Tellegen & Lykken, 1988). Lykken believes that traits are *inherited*, but learning can "reshape" these basic tendencies. As we will see, not all psychologists agree with him.

One theorist who does support Lykken's views is British psychologist Hans Eysenck, whose *typological theory* we will examine next.

How unusual is it that two individuals would have some "amazing" similarities?

Eysenck's Biological Typography

Hans Eysenck's first job after taking his doctorate in experimental psychology was at a British mental hospital. When Eysenck suggested performing a study to see if the treatment the patients were given was *actually effective*, his superiors threatened to fire him. This experience obviously "soured" him against the practice of psychotherapy, and since that time he has seldom passed up a chance to criticize psychoanalysts and other therapists.

For example, in his book *Psychology Is about People*, Eysenck writes that

> Most people of course, whatever they may say, do not in fact want a scientific account of human nature and personality at all. . . . They much prefer the great story-teller, S. Freud, or the brilliant myth-creator, C.G. Jung, to those who, like Cattell or Guilford, expect them to learn matrix algebra, study physiological details of the nervous system, and actually carry out experiments rather than rely on interesting anecdotes, sex-ridden case histories, and ingenious speculation. (Eysenck, 1972)

We will discuss Cattell later in this chapter. For the moment, we might note that, despite Eysenck's protests against psychoanalysis, Jung's ideas on *introversion* and *extraversion* strongly influenced him.

Would you be willing to spend years studying matrix algebra and neurophysiology in order to understand people fully?

EYSENCK'S NEW VERSION OF GALEN'S FOUR TEMPERAMENTS

In one of his earliest studies, Eysenck asked psychiatrists to evaluate the personal histories and "mental functioning" of 700 hospitalized patients. He then performed a **factor analysis** on the data. From this statistical analysis, Eysenck determined that most of the patients could be placed on two **bi-polar scales.** Each of these scales represented, really, a *cluster of related traits* (Eysenck, 1947).

Almost 2,000 years ago a Greek physician named Galen suggested that there were four basic types of personality, based on four different "humors," or fluids, in the body. Galen called these personality types *sanguine, phlegmatic, choleric,* and *melancholic.* When Eysenck combined his two basic personality scales, he found that he had a "less humorous" version of a classic theory.

The first of Eysenck's two personality scales runs from "normal" at one end to "neurotic" at the other. Those patients who scored at the "normal" end of the scale seemed to have fairly well-organized personalities, stayed out of trouble, and had good muscle tone. Those patients who scored at the "neurotic" end of the scale, however, seemed to have disorganized personalities, had problems adjusting, and had poor muscle tone.

The second of Eysenck's personality scales runs from introversion to extroversion. Jung used these same terms, of course. But Eysenck rejected Jung's descriptions and has tried to tie his concept of "introversion-extroversion" to *patterns of neural functioning.*

Eysenck believes that you were born with certain *innate neural tendencies* that place you somewhere on both the "neurotic-normal" and the "extroversion-introversion" scales. These two tendencies *interact* with each other to produce the four classic "temperaments" that Galen described so many centuries ago (see Figure 14.2) (Eysenck, 1957).

NEUROTICISM AND INTROVERSION-EXTRAVERSION

According to Eysenck, introverts are people who have a *higher level of cortical arousal* and *strong excitatory processes* in their nervous systems. Thus, introverts *acquire* new habits rather rapidly. But introverts also have rather weak inhibitory neural processes. Therefore, introverts tend to *unlearn* (or give up) old habits rather reluctantly. Put more simply, introverts learn things easily. But once they do acquire a

Factor analysis. A statistical procedure of examining the relationship (correlation) between a large number of different variables in order to determine the smallest subset of variables which have a significant effect.

Bi-polar scales. A scale with opposite characteristics at each end. Presumably these characteristics are different ends of the same continuum, for example, hot and cold, or high and low.

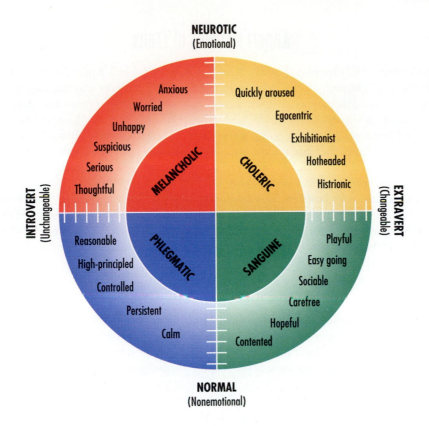

NEUROTIC
(Emotional)

Anxious
Worried
Unhappy
Suspicious
Serious
Thoughtful

Quickly aroused
Egocentric
Exhibitionist
Hotheaded
Histrionic

MELANCHOLIC

CHOLERIC

INTROVERT
(Unchangeable)

EXTRAVERT
(Changeable)

Reasonable
High-principled
Controlled
Persistent
Calm

PHLEGMATIC

SANGUINE

Playful
Easy going
Sociable
Carefree
Hopeful
Contented

NORMAL
(Nonemotional)

FIGURE 14.2
When Eysenck's two bi-polar scales (introversion-extraversion and neuroticism-normal) are shown intersecting, the four segments they create are closely related to Galen's four temperaments (choloric, sanguine, phlegmatic, and melancholic).

new habit, it tends to "stick forever" because the introvert's nervous system doesn't generate enough inhibition for extinction to occur. For that reason, Eysenck says, introverts tend to adopt rather "passive" and "unchanging" lifestyles.

Extraverts are just the opposite, Eysenck says. Extraverts have a *lower level of cortical arousal* and *weak excitatory neural processes*. So extraverts require *more stimulation* to be aroused cortically and they are *poor* at learning new tasks. Furthermore, they have strong inhibitory neural processes. Indeed, extraverts build up inhibition so quickly that they soon "give up" whatever new habits they do manage to acquire. Therefore, Eysenck says, extraverts tend to adopt rather "active" and "changeable" lifestyles because they need more stimulation and they lack the ability to *acquire* and *stick* to consistent behavior patterns (Eysenck, 1957; Eaves et al., 1989).

Eysenck has also added a third scale to the original two (Eysenck, 1952). This "third dimension" is *psychoticism*, which Eysenck says runs in one direction from average, through criminal, psychopathic, alcoholic, and drug addictive behavior generally, to schizoid and finally entirely psychotic states. In the other direction the scale goes from conformist to empathic, and then to altruistic behavior (Eysenck, 1992; Eysenck & Eysenck, 1985). The psychoticism dimension has not been thoroughly integrated with the other two dimensions, however. Nor has it been related in as effective manner to patterns of neural functioning, as were the other two scales (Briggs, 1987).

More important than the number of scales or dimensions, however, is the idea that we may inherit basic personality traits through *innate neural tendencies*. Several other researchers report evidence to support a neural basis for basic dimensions of personality (Buss, 1990; Stelmack, 1990; Zuckerman, 1990, 1992).

What kind of therapy does Eysenck's personality theory suggest should be used to treat "mental illness"?

Allport's Theory of Traits

According to Christopher Monte, "Gordon Allport created American personality psychology" (Monte, 1991). Born in Indiana in 1897, Allport was the youngest of four brothers. His parents, Allport wrote, believed in "plain Protestant piety and hard work" (Allport, 1967). As a child, Allport had few friends. "I never fitted the general boy assembly. I was quick with words, poor with games." Indeed, when he was about 10, another boy said of him, "Aw, that guy swallowed a dictionary." To compensate, Allport said, he "contrived to be the 'star' for a small cluster of friends" (Allport, 1967).

One of his older brothers, Floyd Allport, took his Ph.D. at Harvard and became a noted social psychologist. Floyd Allport then encouraged his younger brother to enroll at Harvard too. Gordon Allport found the first semester as an undergraduate a difficult time, but persevered, did exceptionally well, and went on to take his doctorate in psychology at Harvard too.

ALLPORT AND FREUD

Shortly after finishing his undergraduate work, Gordon Allport wrote to Sigmund Freud. Allport was going to be in Vienna, and he thought that Freud would be most happy to meet him. Freud agreed to receive this brash young American. The visit proved to have a lasting impact on Allport's subsequent career as a personality theorist.

Allport writes that, when they met, Freud sat in "expectant silence," waiting for Allport to say something. In desperation, Allport described the behavior of a boy he had seen on the bus en route to Freud's. The boy had "a conspicuous dirt phobia," which Allport believed could be traced to the boy's mother, who was "so dominant and purposive looking that I thought the cause and effect apparent." Freud, however, saw things differently. When Allport finished the story, "Freud fixed his kindly therapeutic eyes upon me and said, 'And was that little boy you?'" (Allport, 1968).

Allport was unnerved. Thinking about it later, he said,

> I realized that he was accustomed to neurotic defenses and that my manifest motivation (a sort of rude curiosity and youthful ambition) escaped him. . . . This experience taught me that depth psychology, for all its merits, may plunge too deep, and that psychologists would do well to give full recognition to manifest motives before probing the unconscious. (Allport, 1968)

Allport continued to believe that unconscious forces were important shapers of personality, and that the past helps determine the present. However, he insisted that quite often the best way to find out what people were like was simply to ask them to talk about themselves.

CARDINAL, CENTRAL, AND SECONDARY TRAITS

Gordon Allport believed that the very concept of traits was buried deep within the structure of language. Early in his career, he and H.S. Odbert made a list of 18,000 English words, each of which was actually a *trait description* (Allport & Odbert, 1936). You cannot even *think* of another person, Allport claimed, without generating a whole list of "trait words" that you associate with that individual. Little wonder, then, that "traits" are such an important part of personality theories.

In Allport's theory, there are three types of traits: *cardinal*, *central*, and *secondary*.

1. Cardinal traits are those aspects of personality that so dominate the way a person acts that you cannot fail to notice them. Allport named many of these traits after well-known figures, such as "Christ-like" and "Napoleonic." Few people have cardinal traits, Allport said.

2. Central traits "are those usually mentioned in careful letters of recommendation, in rating scales where the rater stars the outstanding characteristics of the individual, or in brief verbal descriptions of a person" (Allport, 1937).

3. Secondary traits are less important in determining behavior than are cardinal or central traits. Secondary traits are fairly weak tendencies to respond to certain specific situations in fairly specific ways. Put more simply, perhaps, we might say that secondary traits are the "little things" that make you the unique person that you are—your tastes and preferences.

Allport believed that traits resulted from learning imposed on biological tendencies. However, he said, once you acquire a trait (or a motive), it may take on a life of its own. That is, the conditions that *maintain* a motive (or a trait) may not be the same that caused you to acquire the motive in the first place. Allport called this the **functional autonomy** of motives.

Cattell's Factor Analytic Approach

Raymond Cattell reduced the 18,000 traits that Allport and Odbert had listed to a mere 16. Cattell did this by using *factor analysis*, which we have already described, and by making certain assumptions about human behavior.

Cattell's first assumption was that there are just a few "common factors" underlying all the traits other scientists had described. And his research soon suggested that many of the traits clustered together. From observing people, and from looking at the results of tests he gave his subjects, Cattell identified about 35 of these "trait clusters." To Cattell, though, these were mere "surface" expressions of more fundamental personality patterns. Cattell thus called these 35 clusters of related behaviors *surface traits* (Cattell, 1950).

Once he had identified this limited number of "trait clusters," Cattell tried to *factor out* the basic relationships among the surface traits. He ended up with a list of 16 factors that he called *source traits*. To Cattell, these 16 source traits are the dimensions by which everyone's personality structure can be measured.

All 16 of Cattell's source traits are *bi-polar*. That is, each trait has two extremes, such as "warm-cold," "bright-dull," and "relaxed-tense" (see Table 14.4). Cattell then devised a test, the "16 Personality Factor Inventory" (16PF), which he believed would measure each person's location on all 16 of the source-trait scales. Cattell

Functional autonomy (aw-TAHN-oh-me). Allport's notion that the motive that impels you to *learn* a habit may not be the same motive that *maintains* the habit. For example, you may begin a rigorous exercise program because the doctor tells you to do so, but continue to exercise because you then lose weight and feel better, or simply because exercising is now "a habit" that has an "autonomy" all its own.

Personality is that which permits a prediction of what a person will do in a given situation.

RAYMOND B. CATTELL

TABLE 14.4
The Sixteen Factors of Personality

1. Schizothymia (aloof, cold) vs. Cyclothymia (warm, sociable)
2. Dull (low intellectual capacity) vs. Bright (intelligent)
3. Low Ego Strength (emotional, unstable) vs. High Ego Strength (mature, calm)
4. Submissiveness (mild) vs. Dominance (aggressive)
5. Desurgency (glum, silent) vs. Surgency (enthusiastic, talkative)
6. Low Superego Strength (casual, undependable) vs. High Superego Strength (conscientious, persistent)
7. Threctia (timid, shy) vs. Parmia (adventurous, thick-skinned)
8. Harria (tough, realistic) vs. Premsia (sensitive, effeminate)
9. Inner Relaxation (trustful, adaptable) vs. Protension (suspecting, jealous)
10. Praxernia (conventional, practical) vs. Autia (Bohemian, unconcerned)
11. Naivete (simple, awkward) vs. Shrewdness (sophisticated, polished)
12. Confidence (unshakable) vs. Timidity (insecure, anxious)
13. Conservatism (accepting) vs. Radicalism (experimenting, critical)
14. Group Dependence (imitative) vs. Self-Sufficiency (resourceful)
15. Low Integration (lax, unsure) vs. Self-Sentiment Control (controlled, exact)
16. Low Ergic Tension (phlegmatic, composed) vs. High Ergic Tension (tense, excitable)

Source: Reprinted from *Personality Theories: A Comparative Analysis* by S. R. Maddi. Copyright © 1973 by Dorsey Press. Reprinted by permission of Brooks/Cole Publishing Company, Pacific Grove, CA 93950.

believed that your scores on this test described your "source traits" in objective, measurable terms. But to paint a complete picture of your personality, he needed additional information (Cattell, 1957).

Cattell took his data about human behavior from three sources: (1) from records of people's lives, and from reports by friends and relatives; (2) from asking people what they thought they were like; and (3) from scores on objective tests such as his "16 PF" test. Only by analyzing all three types of data, Cattell said, could you give a complete description of an individual's personality and hence predict what the person would do in the future (Cattell, 1965).

Trait Theory: An Evaluation

Despite the elegance and apparent precision of their mathematical underpinnings, trait theories suffer from several difficulties. First, they tend to assume that the *structure* of your personality determines your thoughts and behaviors almost entirely. However, research shows that people are often more responsive to present environmental inputs than most trait theorists assume is the case (Mischel, 1977).

Second, trait theories tend to rely rather heavily on self-reports. But as we will see in future chapters, there is often a great difference between what you say your response will be in a given situation and how you *actually behave* when you face that situation in real life. Thus, test scores and interviews often do a poor job of predicting future responses.

Third, although trait theorists admit that traits are partially learned and partially hereditary, they generally give no indication of how traits develop during the early years of life.

Last, but surely not least, trait theorists give quite different lists of "basic traits"—from Eysenck's 3 to Cattell's 16. Several lines of research point to a "big five" cluster of basic traits. For example, psychologist Warren Norman reduced the Allport and Odbert list of 18,000 traits to some 20 trait scales. Then Norman had trained judges rate other people on the 20 scales, and factor-analyzed the results. He found five "underlying factors" that could account for the results (see Table 14.5) (Norman, 1961, 1963). Other researchers have produced similar sets of five "basic" traits (Costa & McCrae, 1992; Briggs, 1992). Parallel basic traits have also been

TABLE 14.5

Some Trait Dimensions And Their Components

TRAIT DIMENSION	DESCRIPTIVE COMPONENTS[1]
I. Extraversion or Surgency	Talkative—Silent Frank, Open—Secretive Adventurous—Cautious Sociable—Reclusive
II. Agreeableness	Good-Natured—Irritable Not Jealous—Jealous Mild, Gentle—Headstrong Cooperative—Negativistic
III. Conscientiousness	Fussy, Tidy—Careless Responsible—Undependable Scrupulous—Unscrupulous Persevering—Quitting, Fickle
IV. Emotional Stability	Poised—Nervous, Tense Calm—Anxious Composed—Excitable Not Hypochondriacal—Hypochondriacal
V. Culture	Artistically Sensitive—Artistically Insensitive Intellectual—Unreflective, Narrow Polished, Refined—Crude, Boorish Imaginative—Simple, Direct

Adapted from Norman (1963).
[1]Adjectives describing the two ends of the scales that comprise the dimension.

found in non-American Western and non-Western cultures (Church & Katigbak, 1989; De Raad, 1992; Paunonen et al., 1992).

Given the problems associated with trait theory, why do we bother with it? For one thing, some trait theorists do recognize the dual effects of traits and environment, and they are working to integrate the two (Buss, 1989; Carson, 1989). In addition, some theorists argue that we could overcome deficiencies in trait theory by adding other points of view. Cognitive psychologist Nancy Cantor, for example, suggests that if we added a cognitive perspective to trait theory, we would have a better understanding of how traits are acted out (Cantor, 1990).

And finally, trait theories provide a convenient summary of individual differences. And since we can hardly hope to discuss individual differences meaningfully without having measuring instruments available, most present-day attempts to measure human performance or personality are based on some form of trait theory.

PERSONALITY THEORY AND CULTURE

In this chapter we have considered the most influential theories of personality in Western psychology. But each of these theories was developed by individuals working in a particular culture at a particular time. Consequently, they are all open to the criticism that they may not apply to people from other cultures and other times.

For example, Freud based his theory on his experience with a relatively small sample of disturbed patients. These individuals were predominantly white middle- and upper-middle-class neurotics living in Vienna in the Victorian era. We have already noted that his theory has a male bias; it may very well have a Viennese, a Victorian, or other biases as well.

Jung's theory has a somewhat broader base. Jung studied the art and religion of cultures all around the world and related his findings to the reports of his patients and the records of other disturbed individuals. It was the common themes in these diverse sources that led Jung to his ideas of "archetypes" and the "collective unconscious."

But Erik Erikson, whose theory we saw in the last chapter, probably did the most for our understanding of cultural effects on personality. While Freud concerned himself with the influence of parents on the child's emerging personality, Erikson stressed the "sociocultural" setting in which the child's ego is molded. Erikson conducted in-depth studies of people in other cultures and other times, including Mahatma Gandhi, Martin Luther, and two Native American groups (the Sioux of South Dakota and the Yurok of Northern California).

It was his experience with the Sioux and the Yurok that confirmed Erikson's ideas on the central role of identity in personality. He noticed symptoms in these groups that orthodox Freudian theory could not explain. The symptoms seemed to revolve around a sense of uprootedness from a cultural tradition and they resulted in a lack of a clear self-image or *identity*.

Erikson noticed similar feelings of confusion in veterans returning home after World War II, in many young people during adolescence, and in his own past. In each case the individuals struggled with *identity*—with who they were, and how they related to the culture around them. Thus, as we saw in the last chapter, sociocultural influences and identity became central themes in Erikson's theory of personality development.

More recently, trait researchers have begun investigating the universality of personality traits which were first identified in North American subjects. For example, Sampo Paunonen and Douglas Jackson and their colleagues in Poland and Germany found evidence for the same "big five basic traits" among subjects in Canada,

Finland, Poland, and Germany (Paunonen et al., 1992). Boele De Raad found similar traits among Dutch subjects (De Raad, 1992). And Timothy Church and Marcia Katigbak report support from their work with bilingual Filipino college students. Whether they use English or Tagalog for their descriptions of personality, the Filipinos structure their descriptions using the same "big five basic traits" that North American subjects use (Church & Katigbak, 1988, 1989).

A *holistic* theory of personality, one which will apply to individuals everywhere, still seems a long way off. But the cross-cultural efforts of Jung, Erikson, and recent trait researchers are significant steps in that direction.

RECENT AND FUTURE TRENDS

If you look back over the personality theories we have discussed (including some ideas from earlier chapters) certain "developmental trends" become apparent.

1. A decreased interest in genetically programmed "developmental stages," and a growing belief that the pattern of personality development is shaped by a continuous interplay between you and your social environment.

2. A movement away from Freud's and Skinner's view of the organism as a "passive reactor" toward the humanistic and social learning position that you are an "active participant" in the shaping of your own personality.

3. A trend away from Freud's emphasis on emotions, and an increasing emphasis on cognitive processes.

4. A shift from Freud's emphasis on unconscious processes toward a belief that conscious processes are the important elements in personality.

5. A movement away from Freud's belief that the personality structure was fixed at age 5 or 6 toward the belief that you continue to grow and mature all your life.

6. A growing effort towards accurate measurement of personality traits, and investigation of the ways in which traits interact with environment.

7. A movement away from elaborate "grand" theories such as those of Freud and Jung, to "mini-theories" that explore one aspect of personality in depth (e.g., Bandura's concept of "self-efficacy").

8. A greater awareness of the need to explore beyond the boundaries of a single culture and examine the impact of culture itself.

Someday, perhaps, we will have a master theory that tells us everything about the human personality that we want to know—one that is *holistic* enough to give us deep understanding of ourselves as well as the power to shape our personal development. But both understanding and shaping imply that we can somehow measure what it is we are trying to comprehend and change. So it is to the measurement of human personality that we now turn our attention.

PERSONALITY MEASUREMENT

At the beginning of this chapter we said that personality is what makes you different from other people—unique. So let's conclude our discussion of personality with a look at how psychologists measure *individual differences* in performance and personality.

Objective Versus Subjective Tests

Although intelligence tests have received most of the publicity in recent years, there are many other types of psychological scales that attempt to measure traits or some other aspect of human performance or personality. Some of these tests are *objective*, in that they yield numbers which describe how much of a given trait you possess. The person giving the test can then compare your results with those of a large number of people, to see where you fall in a "normal" distribution. Others tests are *subjective*, in that an expert must "analyze" your responses and then give a subjective evaluation of what the responses mean. (In the academic world, a multiple-choice test is usually "objective," while an essay exam is usually "subjective.")

Both objective and subjective tests have been used for years in the study of human personality. Let's look at both kinds, then discuss the problems and benefits associated with using them. Keep in mind that good tests are both **reliable** and **valid** (as we discussed in Chapter 11).

SUBJECTIVE TESTS—"PROJECTING" YOUR PERSONALITY

Suppose that you wanted to devise a means of getting at the *unconscious* aspects of a person's mind. You could hardly ask the person about such matters directly, using a pen-and-paper test, because *by definition* the person isn't aware of unconscious processes.

But what if you presented the subject with a variety of unstructured or ambiguous situations? Wouldn't you expect people to *project* themselves into the task given them? After all, the "first law of perception" is that you *perceive what you expect to perceive*. Therefore, shouldn't people perceive ambiguous stimuli according to their unconscious needs and desires? If they did, then you could easily interpret their responses to these **projective tests** as reflecting unconscious processes. This is the idea behind "projective tests."

Projective tests are among the most widely used subjective scales. So let's look briefly at several of them.

WORD ASSOCIATION TEST   The first projective instrument was the word association test devised by Sir Francis Galton more than 100 years ago. Carl Jung subsequently revised it in the early 1900s. The test consists of a list of stimulus words that the tester presents to you one at a time. Some of the words are "emotionally charged"—words like "sex" and "death." Others are presumably "emotionally neutral"—words like "table" and "window." The tester asks you to respond to each word with the first thing that comes to mind.

Both Galton and Jung assumed that if you reacted to a word like "sex" by blocking (refusing to answer)—or if you started sweating, or fainted, or gave a wildly inappropriate reaction such as "firecrackers" or "death"—then you might have sexual problems. Sometimes the tester will use a **polygraph,** or "lie detector," to check your physical reactions as you respond to the words.

APPERCEPTION TESTS   The first **apperception test,** the *Thematic Apperception Test* (TAT), consists of a set of twenty stimulus pictures that depict rather vague but potentially emotional situations (Murray, 1943). The *Apperceptive Personality Test* (APT), is a more recent version with eight pictures showing more modern figures and greater cultural diversity (Holmstrom, 1992; Karp et al., 1989, 1992).

With both tests you respond by making up a story telling (1) what led up to the situation shown in the picture, (2) what the people are thinking and feeling and doing right then, and (3) what will happen to them in the future. (For the APT you would also answer some multiple-choice questions.) Each story you produce is scored and interpreted individually. The psychologist giving the test usually assumes you

Reliable. A test is reliable if it gives the same result time after time. That is, it is not affected by irrelevant factors (such as the weather).

Valid. A test is valid if it measures what it is supposed to measure. Height is not a valid measure of intelligence.

Projective tests. Vague stimuli that a psychologist might ask you to describe or talk about, in the hope that you will somehow structure the stimuli in the same way that your personality is structured.

Polygraph. Literally, "many graphs." A machine that records many physiological measurements, such as heart rate, blood pressure, and skin conductance. A polygraph record indicates a person's level of physical arousal. When used as a "lie detector," the operator *assumes* that arousal in response to certain stimuli indicates guilt. This is a questionable assumption.

Apperception Test. A test containing stimuli that are vague with the idea that you will *interpret* the stimuli in a personal and unique way. Frequently the stimuli are pictures that you are asked to "tell stories about," presumably because you will perceive the pictures in terms of your own personality.

will express your deep-seated needs and personality problems by *projecting* them onto the hero or the heroine in the story.

INKBLOT TESTS   By far the most famous of the projective instruments is the inkblot test, first devised in the 1920s by Swiss psychiatrist Hermann Rorschach. The **Rorschach test** is a series of ten inkblots that you look at one at a time. You report what you see in each inkblot, much as you might look at clouds passing overhead and tell someone what "faces" and other things you saw in the clouds. The psychologist then interprets your responses according to one of several scoring methods (Exner, 1986, 1990).

It is sometimes said that Rorschach interpretations tell us more about the person doing the "interpreting" than they do about the person who took the test. Why might this sometimes be the case?

USEFULNESS OF PROJECTIVE TESTS   The bulk of scientific research suggests that most projective tests are neither very reliable nor particularly valid as presently used. After reviewing nearly 10,000 studies on projective instruments, Richard Lanyon and Leonard Goodstein state that, as for the Rorschach, "the empirical basis for interpreting this test remains thin" and, "although the volume of literature on the TAT is large . . . its status as a proven, clinically useful instrument is still in doubt" (Lanyon & Goldstein, 1982). Testing experts Kevin Murphy and Charles Davidshofer conclude their discussion of projective tests by noting that "their importance and widespread use in personality measurement cannot be justified on the basis of current research data" (Murphy & Davidshofer, 1988).

Despite the fact that the scientific evidence argues against the validity and reliability of projective tests, they still are in widespread use. We will return to this point in a moment.

OBJECTIVE TESTS

Objective tests have several purposes. One is to measure present skills and knowledge. *Achievement tests*, for example, measure how much you have learned about a given topic. Teachers routinely give achievement tests to see how much their students have learned. The tests do not indicate either why you learned as much as you did, nor how much you *could have learned* under different circumstances. Achievement tests simply measure your present level of performance (Walsh, 1989).

Some objective tests attempt to predict future performance. These *aptitude tests* try to determine whether you possess enough of a certain ability to succeed in some job or other situation. Some aptitude tests are fairly simple measures of such skills as mechanical or clerical aptitude. Other tests, such as those given to prospective airline pilots, measure a broader range of potentials. Scores on these simple scales tend to predict future performance fairly well.

Personality tests, or **personality inventories,** attempt to measure the enduring characteristics that make you unique. They assess your important traits and dispositions and yield a numerical score and often a personality "profile" or graph. One example is Cattell's 16PF, which we discussed earlier. Another is the Myers-Briggs Type Indicator (**MBTI**).

THE MBTI   The MBTI is one of the most widely used measures of normal personality. It is an inventory of 166 items designed to identify the "personality types" described by Carl Jung. Subjects choose one of two answers for each question. On the basis of their answers, subjects can be assigned to one of Jung's eight personality "types" (see Table 14.2) (or the additional types developed by the test authors). Table 14.6 gives some sample questions and the Jungian "attitudes" and "functions" they represent.

Rorschach test. A famous test devised by Hermann Rorschach in which you are asked to say what you see in ambiguous blobs (originally created by placing a "blot" of ink on a piece of paper and then folding the paper over to make the pattern of ink symmetrical).

A sample Rorschack ink blot. A psychologist would be interested in such things as what you saw, where you saw them, what colors were used, and how unusual your perceptions were.

"RORSCHACH! WHAT'S TO BECOME OF YOU?"

Personality inventories. Long questionnaires that assess several traits at once.

MBTI. An objective personality test designed to identify the (normal) personality "types" discussed by Jung.

"Are you
(A) easy to get to know, or
(B) hard to get to know?"

(*Extraverts* tend to choose (A); *introverts* choose (B).)

"Do you usually
(A) value sentiment more than logic, or
(B) value logic more than sentiment?"

(Alternative (A) represents a *feeling* preference; (B) represents a *thinking* preference.)

"When you start a big project that is due in a week, do you
(A) take time to list the separate things to be done and the order of doing them, or
(B) plunge in?"

(Choosing (A) shows a *thinking* tendency; choosing (B) shows an *intuiting* tendency.)

TABLE 14.6

Sample items from one form of the Myers-Briggs Type Indicator (MBTI) and the tendencies that they reflect. Subjects are instructed to indicate which answer comes closer to telling how they usually feel or act. Answers are not "right" or "wrong," but rather indicate tendencies characteristic of different personality types. (From the *Myers-Briggs Type Indicator–Form* G by C. Briggs and Isabel Briggs Myers. Copyright 1977 by Peter B. Myers and Katherine D. Myers. Used by permission of Consulting Psychologists Press, Inc.)

The MBTI appears to have good reliability and validity. Most people recognize themselves in the way they are classified. And several studies have found that "types" are predictive of other behaviors (Carlson, 1980; Fling et al., 1981). In one study, for example, students who were "intuitive" preferred jobs as musicians and psychologists; "thinkers" preferred public accounting; "feelers" leaned toward service occupations; and "sensers" gravitated to banking (Stricker & Ross, 1962).

Perhaps these results are not too surprising, however, since it is fairly easy to see the purpose of each question. Subjects may simply respond the way they think they *should* to create a good impression, for example, or to appear consistent with their other behaviors. The same criticism can be made of another popular test of personality, the MMPI-2.

THE MMPI-2   The second edition of the Minnesota Multiphasic Personality Inventory, or **MMPI-2,** is the most widely used device for detecting individuals who might have personality problems (or mental disorders). The MMPI-2, which became available in 1990, is a revision of the earlier MMPI (Butcher & Pope, 1992). A new version of the MMPI for pre-college adolescents is called the MMPI-A.

The MMPI-2 consists of some 567 short statements that were **standardized** on large numbers of people with different occupations, ethnic backgrounds, and educational levels. Some of the sample were mental patients, some were presumably normal. Many of the statements concern psychiatric problems or unusual thought patterns. Some examples are, (1) "There is something wrong with my mind," (2) "I am sure I am being talked about," or (3) "I often feel as if things are not real."

When you take the MMPI-2, you respond to each statement either by agreeing or disagreeing with it. Your answers are then sorted into scores on several scales (Butcher, 1989; Butcher et al., 1989).

As you might expect, mental patients react to many of the statements in ways quite different from non-mental patients. And depressed or suicidal patients give responses different from patients diagnosed as being schizophrenic or paranoid. Figure 14.3 shows one individual's scores on the "clinical" scales presented as a "profile." (There are other ways of analyzing the items to give further insight into different "content" areas, but the clinical profile is the most commonly used summary (Butcher et al., 1990).)

If an otherwise normal individual takes the test and receives an abnormally high score on the "Depression" scale, the psychologist interpreting the test might well worry that the person could become depressed if put under great psychological stress or pressure. By looking at the pattern or *profile* of a subject's scores on the different

MMPI-2. An objective personality test that yields scores on many different scales. By looking at the *profile* of your test scores, a trained interpreter can often determine those areas in which you are "normal" (that is, like most other people) and those areas in which you might be somewhat abnormal, or might experience problems.

Standardized. Obtaining norms for comparison with some reference group. (If the person taking a test is different from the reference group, for example, from a different culture, the test may not be valid for that person.)

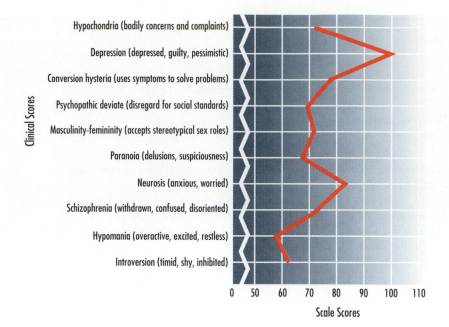

FIGURE 14.3

An example of a profile on the "clinical scales" from the Minnesota Multiphasic Personality Inventory -2 (MMPI-2). Approximately two-thirds of the people taking the MMPI-2 score between 40 and 60 on each of these scales. This particular individual shows a pattern typical of patients hospitalized for depression.

MMPI-2 scales, a psychologist might also be able to predict which areas of the subject's personality needed strengthening.

This approach to the study of personality—judging people in terms of their objective responses—gives the MMPI-2 a very high reliability. Several steps have been taken to assure the MMPI-2 is also valid. First, items used in the test were selected by experienced clinicians and have undergone careful scrutiny, testing, and revision before being included in MMPI-2. Second, items were chosen which were answered differently by individuals who had already been diagnosed as either normal or abnormal by other criteria. And third, test results from the MMPI-2 continue to support diagnoses based on other clinical instruments.

As with other personality tests, however, if you are a sophisticated test-taker you can fake a good impression on the MMPI-2 by giving socially desirable responses. (Don't forget to admit to minor imperfections which are true of nearly everyone.)

Psychological Testing in Review

By now, a certain trend may be obvious to you: Psychologists have devised a large number of instruments for measuring personality traits, intelligence, aptitudes, achievement, and unconscious processes. Too often, however, both the scientific reliability and the validity of these measures are suspect. Yet most of these instruments are presently in widespread use. Why?

The answer seems to lie in the difference between "academic respectability" and "practical experience." Most scientifically oriented psychologists do argue against the usefulness of these sorts of tests (Piotrowski & Keller, 1984a, 1984b). However, the vast majority of *clinical psychologists* continue to employ the tests in everyday practice (Piotrowsky, 1984; Piotrowsky et al., 1985). And, of course, school personnel continue to use intelligence and aptitude tests on a daily basis.

Why then the difference between the beliefs of "scientific" and "practicing" psychologists? In part, because of practical limitations. School administrators often must decide the fates of hundreds of students during a given school year. Intelligence and aptitude tests may not be perfect, but they are the only instruments administrators typically have available to them. And, as we noted, the tests are valid for predicting academic and job-related performance unless the testees receive special training.

In addition, practicing psychologists tend to place greater faith in their own clinical experience than they do in experimental evidence. And in fact, clinical assessment based on interviews, case histories, and reports from other clinicians, *as well as* psychological tests, may be sufficiently reliable and valid (Matarazzo, 1990). However, this remains to be demonstrated (Faust & Ziskin, 1988).

Finally, real-world constraints for practicing psychologists are different from those that hold in academic circles. Research-oriented scientists can take years making up their minds about the reliability and validity of a given psychological test— and their daily lives aren't much affected by the decisions they ultimately make. Clinical and counseling psychologists, however, must decide each day how best to treat or advise a number of clients. Over the years, these practicing psychologists build up strong viewpoints about what works for them and their patients. And since the test-builders have not yet devised instruments that are more valid and reliable than the ones presently in use, the old ones continue to serve an urgent professional need.

We could make the same sort of comments about personality theories. They aren't perfect, but they're the best we've got. And until something better comes along, the need to explain behavior and prescribe treatment where necessary, will impel us to continue to use them.

With these thoughts in mind, let's look more closely at how psychologists describe abnormal thoughts, feelings, and behaviors. We will look at how they treat them in Chapter 16.

SUMMARY

1. The study of **personality** is concerned with identifying the psychological and physical processes which characterize your unique pattern of behavior and thought.

2. **Psychodynamic theories** follow Freud in viewing personality as a complex interaction of psychological processes, many of which are unconscious and have their roots in early childhood.

3. Freud's theory grew out of his observation that patients often improved after they gave vent to **repressed emotions** and gained insight into their **unconscious** motives.

4. Freud suggested that the mind was made up of three parts, the **id,** the **ego,** and the **superego.**

5. The **id** exists at birth and contains the basic instincts: **eros,** the life instinct, and **thanatos,** the death instinct. All psychic energy derives from the id in the form of **libido.** The id is entirely unconscious. It operates selfishly by the **pleasure principle.**

6. The **ego** splits off from the id in order to protect the organism by finding realistic ways of satisfying the id's demands for immediate gratification of its needs. The ego operates on the **reality principle.**

7. The **superego** is created as the Oedipal/Electral complex ends and the child **identifies** with the parent of the same sex.

8. The superego contains both the **conscience** and the **ego-ideal.** The conscience represents the "should nots" and the ego-ideal represents the "shoulds" that we adopt from our parents and society.

9. The id is entirely **unconscious;** both the ego and superego are partly **conscious,** partly unconscious, and partly **preconscious.**

10. As the individual grows from infancy to adulthood, the focus of **libidinal energy** shifts from one **erogenous zone** to another through five stages of **psychosexual**

development. If the needs of any stage are not met satisfactorily, a certain amount of libidinal energy remains **fixated** at that stage and the developing personality is affected.

11. During the **oral stage** of development, libido is expressed through the mouth, while during the **anal stage,** libido is released through the anus. At the **phallic stage,** the libido becomes organized around genital stimulation. Libido is repressed during the **latency period,** but reasserts itself in heterosexual activities during the **genital stage.** The genital period last for the rest of life.

12. Freud believed boys give up their early attachment to the mother in different ways than do girls. The boy experiences the **Oedipus complex,** in which he fears the father will castrate him. He resolves the complex by taking on the father's values. The girl experiences the **Electra complex,** in which she slowly takes on the mother's values in order to appeal to the father.

13. Anna Freud used psychoanalytic therapy with children and studied the **defense mechanisms** used by the ego. These mechanisms include **repression, denial, projection, displacement, turning-against-self, reaction formation, introjection, identification-with-an-aggressor, regression, sublimination,** and several others.

14. Jung divided the unconscious into two regions: the **personal unconscious,** which contains past memories and plans for the future, and the **collective unconscious,** which contains universal **archetypes,** or racial tendencies to respond in the same way to certain experiences.

15. Jung believed everyone is born with two innate, opposing attitudes: **introversion,** which leads us to look inward, and **extraversion,** which leads us to look outward.

16. Jung also suggested we relate to the world through four possible **functions: thinking, feeling, sensing,** and **intuiting.** One attitude and one function usually dominate, but the others are always present.

17. The combination of a dominant attitude and a dominant function creates a **personality type.** Jung said there were eight possible types.

18. Alfred Adler broke with Freud before Jung did, and formed the **Society for Individual Psychology.** He emphasized **social values** and **striving for superiority** rather than infantile sexuality.

19. Adler believed children feel **inferior** when they discover adults have superior strength. They **compensate** by trying to become superior to what they were in the past.

20. Adler believed that your position in the family—your **birth order**—affected the way your personality developed.

21. Adler said each person develops a **style of life** which is the self-consistent, goal-oriented core of personality and which continues to change over the entire life span.

22. Karen Horney removed Freud's male bias from her version of psychodynamic theory. She said we are driven by **basic anxiety** and may become alienated from ourselves, and develop unrealistic views of ourselves.

23. According to Horney, if we have an unrealistic view of our **"real"** and **"ideal"** selves, we may feel worthless and dream of what we *should* do, leading to a "tyranny of the should." This may also lead us to overemphasize one of three different **modes of interacting.**

24. The **humanistic psychologists** emphasize health rather than pathology, active rather than passive participation in your own development, and the need to **be yourself** rather than being what others wish you to be.

25. Abraham Maslow created his theory by studying the "most perfect" people he could find. He called these people **self-actualizing individuals.** Self-actualizing people continue to grow by developing **Being-needs** or **B-values** such as the need for truth, goodness, beauty, and perfection.

26. Carl Rogers believed you exist in a **phenomenal world** that is reality as you experience it. Early development involves learning to differentiate your **self** from other parts of the phenomenal world.

27. Rogers urged parents to give their children **unconditional positive regard** by accepting the children as they are rather than trying to force the children to become what the parents want.

28. **Social learning theorists** such as Albert Bandura believe behavior is learned through **cognitive processes.** Personality development is thus the study of how people use **social models** and **observational learning** to **construct reality** in their minds.

29. According to Bandura, people have a need to establish control over themselves and their environments, which Bandura refers to as a sense of **personal agency.**

30. Bandura believes that **perceived self-efficacy** motivates people to monitor their own cognitions and behaviors as they attempt to change themselves and their environments, an interactive process Bandura calls **reciprocal determinism.**

31. Studies of **twins reared apart** suggest that some aspects of traits may be inherited.

32. Hans Eysenck believes human personality can be measured using three scales: **neuroticism, introversion-extroversion,** and **psychoticism.** By combining the first two scales, Eysenck develop a personality typology that was similar to the classic theory of body humors proposed by Galen.

33. Allport believed there were three main types of traits, **cardinal, central,** and **secondary.** Cardinal traits are "ruling passions." They are rare. Central traits are a person's "outstanding characteristics." Secondary traits are less important and consistent aspects of personality.

34. Raymond Cattell believes there are but two types of traits, **surface** and **source** traits. Using **factor analysis,** Cattell determined there are 16 source traits, which determine some 35 surface traits. Warren Norman and others have reduced Cattell's list of traits to 5 "basic traits."

35. Personality theory has **continued to develop** since Freud's first proposals. All types of personality theories have contributed to our ability to understand and predict human experience, but no theory is complete in itself.

36. **Projective tests,** such as the **Rorschach,** the **word association test,** and the picture **apperceptive tests,** contain ambiguous stimuli that you are supposed to "structure" in terms of your own personality. Both the **validity** and the **reliability** of these tests is questionable in most circumstances.

37. **Objective personality tests,** such as Cattell's **16PF,** the **MBTI,** and the **MMPI-2,** tend to be more reliable measures of personality, with greater validity.

38. **Practicing psychologists** continue to use personality tests because they believe the tests are helpful—and because there simply aren't better instruments available.

ANSWERS FOR THOUGHT

1. *What effect might Freud's ideas have on the reporting of childhood sexual abuse?*

   According to Freud's theory *fantasized* abuse is common. People who accept this part of Freud's theory might not believe that reported incidents of abuse actually occurred.

2. *One of the reasons Freud developed the notion of the "latency period" is that the children he observed . . . ?*

   Some reasons sexual activity might decrease are, (1) because of the socialization that takes place in school, (2) because of greater social pressure against self-stimulation, (3) because of the development of other interests, and (4) because the child's curiosity has been satisfied.

3. *Jung's popularity probably reached a high point in America during the 1960s. Can you guess why?*

   Jung's interest in mysticism made him popular with people who were tired of materialism and were looking for a more "spiritual" dimension to life—a common quest in the '60s.

4. *Freud called his theory psychoanalysis. Jung named his approach analytical psychology. Adler . . . ?*

   Freud and Jung were "psychological sleuths," *analyzing* the personality in depth through common features of the unconscious mind. Adler emphasized the uniqueness of the person as he or she developed in an *individual* way. Jung and Adler chose different names to distinguish their theories from Freud's.

5. *What similarities—and differences—do you see between Rogers's explanation of the development . . . ?*

   Both show the individual taking on the values of society as interpreted by the parents, in order to control (and limit) natural inclinations. For Freud this was good and necessary; for Rogers it was not (the person is naturally good and doesn't need to be restricted). Rogers did not see the sexual motivation for this process that Freud did.

6. *In what ways does Rogers's theory of emotional and cognitive development in the child appear . . . ?*

   As an adult, Rogers chose different values from his parents and decided that his parents had been unnecessarily restrictive. From his adult perspective, Rogers felt that as a child he had been made to deny natural parts of his personality.

7. *How unusual is it that two individuals would have some "amazing" similarities?*

   When you consider the countless habits and preferences we have, perhaps it isn't too surprising if some things happen to be similar. Maybe we should ask, "In how many ways were the twins *different?*"

8. *Would you be willing to spend years studying matrix algebra and neurophysiology in order to understand people fully?*

   This is a personal choice. All psychologists must study *some* physiology and math (especially statistics).

9. *What kind of therapy does Eysenck's personality theory suggest should be used to treat "mental illness"?*

   One criticism of many trait theories is that they *don't* suggest how traits might be changed.

10. *It is sometimes said that Rorschach interpretations tell us more about the person doing the "interpreting" . . . ?*

There are no universally accepted guidelines for interpreting most projective tests. Therefore, *interpretation* may involve as much projection as the initial responses to the test.

CHAPTER 15

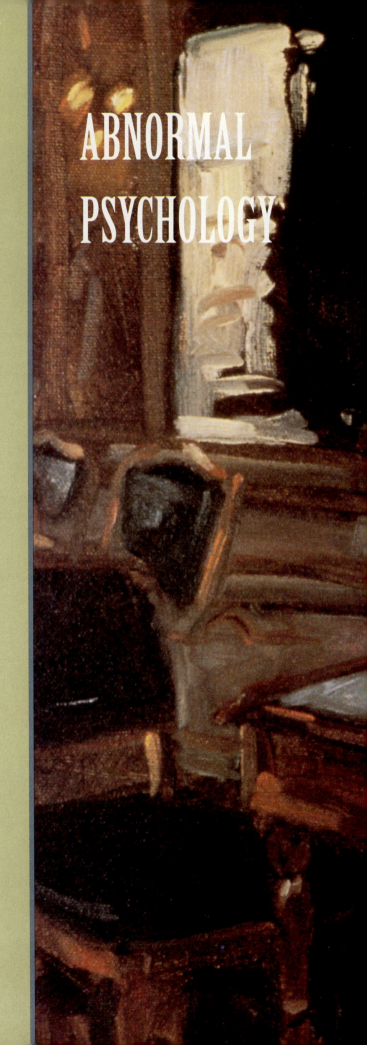

ABNORMAL PSYCHOLOGY

S pence said, his voice shaking, "I think—I'm afraid I think I might be having a nervous breakdown. I'm so very, very afraid."

"No," said his wife, "—you're the sanest person I know. All surface and no cracks, fissures, potholes."

Spence turned to her. His eyes were filling with tears.

"Don't joke. Have pity."

She made no reply; seemed about to drift away; then slipped an arm around his waist and nudged her head against his shoulder in a gesture of camaraderie. Whether mocking, or altogether genuine, Spence could not have said.

"It's just that I'm so afraid."

"Yes, you've said."

"—of losing my mind. Going mad."

She stood for a moment, peering out toward the street. The elderly gentleman standing at the curb glanced back but could not have seen them, or anyone, behind the lacy bedroom curtains. He was well dressed, and carried an umbrella. An umbrella? Perhaps it was a cane.

Spence said, "I seem to be seeing, more and more, these people—people I don't think are truly there."

"He's there."

"I think they're dead. Dead people."

His wife drew back and cast him a sidelong glance, smiling mysteriously. "It does seem to have upset you," she said.

"Since I know they're not there—"

"He's there."

"—so I must be losing my mind. A kind of schizophrenia, waking dreams, hallucinations—"

Spence was speaking excitedly, and did not know exactly what he was saying. His wife drew away from him in alarm, or distaste.

JOYCE CAROL OATES
"THE OTHERS"

DEFINING DISORDERS

Spence is afraid—afraid he is "having a nervous breakdown," "losing his mind," "going mad." His wife says he is the "sanest person" she knows. But Spence has been seeing people that he thinks he recognizes from his past and this is impossible since the people from his past are dead. Is Spence *abnormal?* Does he have a "mental illness"?

In this chapter we will consider how we decide if someone is "normal" or "abnormal." And we will see what it means to say a person is *"mentally ill."*

We will also look at symptoms or "signs" of abnormality. Spence refers to hallucinations and waking dreams which he thinks indicates "a kind of schizophrenia." His speech is rambling and agitated. We will discuss these kinds of symptoms and see how psychologists use symptoms and other information to *classify* abnormality.

You have surely met one or more abnormal people in your life. What about these individuals suggested to you that they might not be "entirely right"? And what does your answer to that question tell you about your own "theory of abnormality"?

Normal or Abnormal?

"Crazy," "mixed-up," "mental"—sometimes we use these and related terms with little thought for their meaning. Psychologists use similar terms—mental disorder, mental illness, behavior disorder—but psychologists struggle with how to define these labels exactly. (The legal profession uses the word **insane** in reference to individuals with certain psychologically based problems.)

How do we decide if someone has a mental disorder? This basic question has not proven as easy to answer as you might imagine. Psychologists and other mental health professionals take many different approaches to "mental abnormality." Some people suggest that mental conditions are disorders if they are *statistically rare* (Eysenck, 1986; Taylor, 1971). Others propose that mental disorders are "the absence of mental health," or "failure to live up to one's potential" (Shoben, 1957). Some feel that mental disorder is purely a value concept or that we should define mental disorders as "whatever professional therapists treat" (Kendell, 1986; Sedgwick, 1982). And a few skeptics argue that mental "disorders" are *not even disorders*—at least in the sense that a broken leg is a disorder—since no biological damage has been found for most of them. "Mental disorders," they say, are merely labels used to explain *socially disapproved behaviors* (Sarbin, 1969; Szasz, 1974).

In 1992, psychologist Jerome Wakefield reviewed these and other views of mental disorders and proposed an all-encompassing definition. For our purposes, we can summarize the relevant parts of his arguments in the following statement:

> A condition is a mental disorder if . . . the condition causes some harm or deprivation of benefit to the person as judged by the standards of the person's culture . . . and the condition results from the inability of some mental mechanism to perform its natural function . . .
>
> (Wakefield, 1992a, p. 385).

In other words, people suffer mental disorders when their culture recognizes that their mental condition is causing them harm (Wakefield, 1992a, 1992b). This interpretation seems to avoid many of the problems in other definitions. Two important implications of this position stand out:

Insane. The legal term for a "mental disorder" which renders you not responsible for your actions. In courts in the United States, you must be *judged* "insane" either by the judge or a jury of your peers.

"I can remember when paranoia was unusual."

1. Every unusual mental condition is not a mental disorder.
2. Mental disorders are socially and culturally defined.

Let's consider each of these points in turn.

UNUSUAL IS NOT ABNORMAL

Can there be "good" deviances? Of course there can be. If someone said you were "much brighter than average," would you be insulted? No, you probably would be pleased (or even flattered). Yet the person has said, really, that you are intellectually deviant. Physical beauty, creative talent, and even excellent health are other examples of what most people would consider to be "good" deviancies. (This is why a purely statistical definition of disorders is inadequate.)

Mental disorders, on the other hand, are maladaptive or harmful. They may also be unusual, but they are definitely undesirable. Spence's experience, for example, frightened and upset him. His behavior is also beginning to distress his wife. Spence's behavior is clearly maladaptive and therefore abnormal.

We might also note that there is nothing in our definition to indicate that mental disorders must involve unique or bizarre behavior. Disorders are often exaggerations of *normal* processes (Eysenck, 1992). Take Spence's experience for example. It is not unusual for someone to remind us of a person we have known, even a person who has died, and for us to find the experience somewhat unsettling. For Spence, however, the experience occurred frequently, and completely unnerved him. His response was an *exaggeration* of normal behavior.

So, unusual behavior is not necessarily disordered (some unusual behavior is good); and disordered behavior is not necessarily unique (some disordered behavior is an exaggerated normal reaction). Mental disorders are *disorders* because they are maladaptive—they cause harm—to the individual's sense of well-being, for example, and to the person's relationships with other people.

SOCIALLY AND CULTURALLY DEFINED

All definitions of "abnormal" must assume some concept of what is "healthy" or "normal" for a given person in a given culture (Gaines, 1992a). If you decide to seek psychological help, you might well tell the therapist, "I am unhappy," or "I have trouble concentrating," or "I don't have any friends." These statements of your problem imply a *comparison* to some standard (or norm) of how happy you *should* be, how much you *should* concentrate, or how many friends you *should* have. And the therapist, in evaluating your difficulties, must always realize that some people are happier than others are, concentrate more easily than others do, and have more friends than perhaps you have (or want to have). So the therapist must deal not only with your own "norms," but also with the "norms" of the culture you live in. Furthermore, the therapist must also have some way of *measuring* how far you depart both from your own and from societal definitions of normality (Krupinski, 1992).

Asian cultures, for example, emphasize emotional restraint and social interdependence. They also place greater stigmatization on mental disorders than American culture does. This could mean that Chinese- or Japanese-Americans are less likely to come to the attention of mental health professionals. It might also mean that when they do come to the professionals' attention, the Chinese- or Japanese-Americans might hide the extent of their disturbance (Narikiyo & Kameoka, 1992; Raskin et al., 1992). In this type of situation a mental health professional must adjust his or her view of abnormality to fit the cultural norms.

In other parts of the world, sexual problems and eating disorders are not the concern they are in Western industrial societies (Gremillion, 1992; Kendell, 1991). When they occur, sexual and eating problems may have an entirely different

Mother Theresa, who has devoted her life to helping the "poorest of the poor," is certainly unusual. Is she abnormal?

Mental health problems do not affect three or four out of every five persons but one out of one.

WILLIAM MENNINGER

Does this scene match your image of fishing? Some behaviors that are very unusual in one culture may be quite acceptable in another.

meaning in these cultures. Professionals need to understand the cultural context in order to avoid either *underestimating* or *overestimating* levels of disturbance (Lopez & Hernandez, 1986).

Richard Brislin summarizes the influence of culture in this area when he says, "As part of their socialization, people learn to express psychological disturbances in ways that are acceptable within their culture, in ways that will be understood, and in ways that will evoke sympathy from others" (Brislin, 1993, pp. 345–346). Mental disorders are *culturally* defined. (We will have more to say about cultural influences on abnormality later.)

How might the personality theory you believed in affect your judgment about who was mentally disordered and who wasn't? How would it affect your opinion of what was wrong with the person?

Classifying Abnormality

When you get a "runny nose" and sore throat, you say you have a cold; when you get a fever, an upset stomach, and you ache all over, you have the flu; and if you get a fever and you have small spots all over your skin, you probably have the chicken pox. "A cold," "the flu," and "chicken pox" are labels for groups of symptoms. Having a label helps you to communicate with other people about your problem, it helps you decide what kind of treatment is appropriate, and it helps you to know how your problem is likely to progress and how long it will last. And having labels for similar problems grouped together in meaningful ways helps medical researchers direct their efforts more effectively.

Mental health professionals expect similar gains from the systematic classification of mental disorders. An accurate classification system should facilitate communication, specify treatment, predict the course of disorders, and direct research efforts. With these potential benefits in mind, let's consider efforts to classify mental abnormality.

DSM AND ICD

Over the years, psychologists and psychiatrists have worked out a variety of diagnostic schemes to classify people according to their problems. Of these, the two best known and most widely used are surely the *Diagnostic and Statistical Manual of Mental Disorders* (DSM), and the *International Classification of Disease and Related Health Problems* (ICD). The DSM was first published by the American Psychiatric Association in 1952; a draft of the fourth revision, DSM-IV, appeared in 1993 (American Psychiatric Association, 1993). The World Health Organization publishes the ICD. The latest version, ICD-10, was officially introduced in eight languages in 1993 although an incomplete version was available in 1990 (World Health Organization, 1990). The DSM is the most widely used system in North America. The ICD is more commonly used in the rest of the world.

Both systems are elaborate attempts to group disorders in a meaningful way. The developers assumed that different symptoms, or combinations of symptoms, signified different *underlying disorders*, with different treatments preferred, and different prospects for recovery. This approach is analogous to the way physicians view physical diseases; it is known as the **medical model** of disease.

In the medical model, or "medical analogy," disorders are "mental illnesses." A "sick" *patient* comes to a *doctor* (usually a psychiatrist) for *diagnosis* and *treatment*. Because this approach is "medical" does not necessarily mean that the therapist assumes a biological cause for the problem, although the therapist may. The essential features of the medical model are first, the doctor-patient relationship, and second, the assumption that "symptoms" are merely expressions of a deeper problem (which the doctor, as an expert, is competent to deal with).

BEHAVIORAL AND NEUROLOGICAL ASSESSMENT

Some critics of the medical model (and the basis for the DSM and the ICD) argue that mental disorders are *not* analogous to physical diseases (Millon, 1991). They suggest that symptoms are not necessarily signs of an underlying "illness," but in some cases may actually be all there is to the problem (Szasz, 1974). They may even take the position, "The symptom *is* the disease."

For these critics, it makes more sense to identify and treat obvious difficulties. So, rather than label and classify disorders, they *assess behaviors*—cognitive-verbal behaviors, emotional-physiological behaviors, as well as overt motor behaviors (Galassi & Perot, 1992). They focus on "disturbed behavior" or "problems in living" and avoid medical-sounding labels.

Clinical neuropsychologists, on the other hand, prefer to focus on *disturbed brain processes*. They use physiological measures—EEGs, brain scans, genetic tracking—as well as psychological tests, to identify problems in *brain* functioning (Meier, 1992; Puente, 1992). And they group disorders according to the neurological deficits they discover.

Since they believe that mental disorders have a neurological basis, clinical neuropsychologists argue that having a ready label for a group of symptoms *before* we know their neurological cause may be counter-productive. Different symptoms can represent the *same* neurological problem; similar symptoms can represent *different* neurological problems. Grouping disorders together by behavior or some other superficial factor is premature and "short-circuits" research into the biological cause (Carson, 1991).

Both the neurological and behavioral assessment approaches, however, are limited. Behavioral assessment is not really a "classification system," and so it does little to simplify the confusing array of disturbed behaviors. Neurological analysis has not progressed to the point where we can identify physical components in very many disorders. And even when we do, these components may be *results* rather than *causes* of disturbed functioning.

In the "medical model" of mental disorders, the "patient" comes to see a "doctor," who observes "symptoms," then "diagnosis" the "illness," and "prescribes" a "treatment." The patient is relatively passive; the doctor is the authority.

Medical model. The belief—in psychiatry and psychology—that mental disorders are caused by some "underlying" or "deep-seated" psychological problem, just as influenza is caused by an infectious virus. The "patient" comes in a submissive role, to the expert "doctor," who is expected to "diagnose" the problem, "prescribe" treatment, and "cure" the "patient."

Order and simplification are the first steps toward the mastery of a subject—the actual enemy is the unknown.

THOMAS MANN

Clinical neuropsychologists. Psychologists who study the physical basis of psychological problems by exploring abnormalities in the structure and function of the brain and nervous system.

DESCRIBING DISORDERS

In the course of their development, both the DSM and the ICD have changed. They now focus more on objectively measured symptoms (behavioral assessment) and they incorporate the most recent developments in neuropsychology. With all their limitations, DSM-IV and ICD-10 are probably the best, and certainly the most widely used, systems we have for classifying abnormality.

Let's look at some of the mental disorders included in the DSM's major categories of disorders. We will examine characteristic symptoms, and we will consider what we know about underlying causes.

Anxiety Disorders

Anxiety disorders are a group of relatively common psychological problems which used to be known collectively as **neuroses.** The main psychological feature of anxiety disorders is the unhappiness, the tension, and excessive **anxiety** felt by their sufferers. Except for their symptomatic behavior (which we will discuss in a moment) individuals with anxiety disorders usually respond appropriately to their surroundings, both cognitively and emotionally. They are aware that something is wrong, but they are generally able to cope without hospitalization. Their main characteristic is what we might call "personal distress." The two most common types of anxiety disorders are "generalized anxiety disorder" and "phobic disorder" (Blazer et al., 1991; Eaton et al., 1991). Let's look at these as well as the less common "panic," "obsessive-compulsive," and "posttraumatic stress" disorders.

GENERALIZED ANXIETY DISORDER

Generalized anxiety disorder is a chronic (ongoing) high level of anxiety that is not tied to any specific threat. An individual might describe such a condition in this way:

> I am frightened, but I don't know what I fear. I keep expecting something bad to happen. . . . I have thought I could tie it to definite things, but this isn't true. It varies, and is unpredictable. I can't tell when it will come on. If I could just put my finger on what it is . . . (Laughlin, 1967, p. 107).

Generalized anxiety sufferers worry constantly about past mistakes and future problems. Generalized anxiety produces a mild emergency reaction in the body: sweating, racing heart, upset stomach, clammy hands, and lightheadedness.

PANIC DISORDER

Panic disorders involve recurrent episodes of unbearably intense anxiety called "panic attacks." In an attack, physical symptoms, such as a pounding heart, dizziness, and trembling, accompany feelings of dread or terror and thoughts of impending disaster—death or "going crazy" (Norton et al., 1992). These attacks seem to "come out of nowhere," with no obvious cause. When they subside they leave the victim wondering when the next one will occur.

If you suffered a panic disorder you might describe your experience in this way:

> My heart was beating so hard and fast it would jump out and hit my hand. I felt like I couldn't stand up—that my legs wouldn't support me. My hands got icy and my feet stung. There were horrible shooting pains in my forehead. My head felt tight, like someone had pulled the skin down too tight and I wanted to pull it away. . . .

Neuroses (new-ROW-sees). Also called "psychoneuroses" or "anxiety neuroses." An older term for mild forms of mental disorder that usually do not keep the individual from living a reasonably successful life.

Anxiety. Mental stress or uneasiness of mind. Anxiety is like fear but without a specific object.

Anxiety disorders (neuroses) are characterized by great personal distress.

I couldn't breathe, I was short of breath. I literally got out of breath and panted like I had run up and down the stairs. I felt like I had run an eight-mile race. I couldn't do anything. I felt all in; weak, no strength. I can't even dial a telephone. . . .

It was just like I was petrified with fear. If I were to meet a lion face to face, I couldn't be more scared. Everything got black, and I felt I would faint; but I didn't. I thought I won't be able to hold on. . . .

These things are terrible. I can go along real calmly for awhile. Then, without any warning, this happens. I just blow my top (Laughlin, 1967, p. 92).

Most of us feel "panicky" at times. Only about one percent of the population, however, experiences severe, recurring attacks, or constant fear of attacks, and is diagnosed with panic disorder (Bourdon et al., 1992).

Because panic attacks seem to come "out of the blue," without warning, some sufferers remain at home for fear of having an attack in public. This creates a condition called "agoraphobia," or fear of open places (literally "fear of the marketplace"). Although psychologists traditionally viewed this condition as a phobia, there is mounting evidence that it is more akin to panic disorder (Turner et al., 1986).

Their fear of panicking often confines agoraphobics to their homes. Agoraphobics find it difficult or impossible to hold jobs or engage in ordinary social activities. Most agoraphobics are women. Panic attacks leading to agoraphobia usually begin in late adolescence or early adulthood (Barlow & Waddell, 1985).

PHOBIC DISORDERS

Phobias are the most common type of anxiety disorder, afflicting approximately 12 percent of the population (Bourdon et al., 1992). In a phobic disorder, the focus of anxiety is very specific. A phobia is an intense fear of an object or situation where the fear is out of proportion to any real danger. A fear becomes a phobia when it interferes with everyday activities. The phobic suffers not only in his or her intense reaction to the phobic object, but also in being preoccupied with fears that he or she might encounter the feared object. Consider Anna's fear of cats:

Anna was terrified that if she left her house, a cat would spring on her and attack her. Her fear of cats was of thirty years' status, having begun at age four when she remembered watching in horror as her father drowned a kitten. In spite of saying that she believed that it was unlikely that her father actually did such a thing, she was haunted by the fear. At the sight of a cat, she would panic and sometimes be completely overwhelmed with terror. She could think of nothing else but her fear of cats. She interpreted any unexpected movement, shadow, or noise as a cat. (Rosenhan & Seligman, 1989, p. 197)

Phobias come in a wide variety. Figure 15.1 presents the most frequently reported phobias in a recent survey. More unusual phobias include fear of flowers, fear of the number 13, and fear of snow.

Can you think of some reasons that some phobias are more common than others?

OBSESSIVE COMPULSIVE DISORDER

Obsessions are irrational thoughts that break through to conscious awareness in a constantly recurring pattern. The most frequent subjects for obsessions are themes of dirt or contamination, religion, sex, and aggression (Turner et al., 1992).

Compulsions are irresistible urges to repeat some ritualistic behavior or set of activities. If prevented from acting out his or her compulsions, the person may experience considerable anxiety. Common compulsions include rituals to bring good luck,

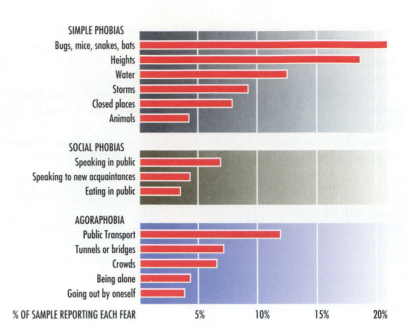

FIGURE 15.1

The most common fears reported in a large survey. Fears become phobias when they interfere with normal activities, that is, when the individual begins planning his or her life around the fear. In this study only about 40 percent of the subjects reporting each fear would qualify as having a phobia. (Data adapted from Eaton et al., 1991.)

Billionaire Howard Hughes exhibited many of the signs of obsessive compulsive disorder.

continual checking to see that doors are locked and windows closed, and constant checking to see that faucets are turned off. One of the most common types of compulsions is the "need for cleanliness."

> One of the richest men of his times, Howard Hughes was obsessed with the possibility of being contaminated by germs. He made his close employees carry out elaborate hand-washing rituals and wear white cotton gloves, sometimes several pairs, when handling documents he would later touch. He once wrote a three-page memo instructing assistants on exactly how to open cans of fruit for him. Newspapers had to be brought to him in stacks of three so that he could slide out the middle, and presumably least contaminated copy, grasping it with Kleenex. He ordered his employees to put masking tape around the doors and windows of his cars and houses so that he could escape contamination by dust. He would spend several hours cleaning a single telephone. Planning and carrying out these elaborate rituals came to occupy much of Hughes' daily life (Adapted from Barlett & Steele, 1979, Barton, 1982, and Fowler, 1986).

Usually sufferers attempt to ignore their obsessions and they generally realize their compulsive behavior is excessive, senseless, and unpleasurable. But they are captives of their own anxieties, and unless they receive help they are unable to escape.

In most cases obsessions and compulsions are found together, although they do occur alone (Zetin & Kramer, 1992). Obsessive compulsive disorders occur in approximately 2–4 percent of the population (Karno & Golding, 1991).

POSTTRAUMATIC STRESS DISORDER

Unlike other anxiety disorders, posttraumatic stress disorder (PTSD) is clearly connected to a traumatic event or series of events that happened to the person. Traumatic events include such things as grim accidents, rape and other violent assaults, natural disasters, or the horrors of concentration camps or war (Murray, 1992).

PTSD typically involves uncontrollable episodes of reliving the trauma in terrifying nightmares and painful daytime thoughts. Sleeplessness, guilt, depression, and general irritability are also common. Symptoms may begin immediately after the traumatic experience or appear gradually over a period of several months. In some cases, symptoms do not emerge until years later.

PTSD seems particularly likely if the victim cannot justify the trauma that he or she has experienced. Vietnam veterans, for example, often felt rejected for their participation in an unpopular war. And wounded Vietnam veterans suffer PTSD at a rate many times greater than other groups. PTSD occurs in the general population at a rate of about 1 percent; in Vietnam veterans who were not wounded, at a rate of about 3.5 percent; and in veterans wounded in Vietnam, at a rate of 20 percent (Helzer & Robins, 1987). Military personnel who served in Germany or elsewhere in the world during the period of the Vietnam conflict do not show the same reaction, even if they too suffered traumatic experiences while in the military. Thus, it may be the combination of trauma-induced stress *plus* the lack of sufficient justification for their suffering that accounts for the problems many Vietnam veterans have experienced (Escobar, 1987).

Highly traumatized veterans of World War I often suffered from what was called "shell shock"—fearful avoidance of loud noises or other stressful situations. Vietnam veterans often reacted to their trauma with anger and aggression. How did American veterans of the Gulf war react? What changes in society might account for the different reactions to war-related trauma?

ORIGINS OF ANXIETY DISORDERS

Why do people develop anxiety disorders? There are many possible reasons because, to repeat a familiar theme, behavior is *multi-determined*. This is no less true of *abnormal* than of normal behavior. Let's consider some different theoretical views on what causes anxiety disorders.

PSYCHOANALYTIC PERSPECTIVE   The earliest explanations for the anxiety disorders came from the psychoanalytic perspective of Sigmund Freud. Psychoanalysts look for early experiences and repressed emotions that might cause adult disturbances. Anxiety, they say, results from the fear that the sufferer might lose control of repressed feelings. Some symptoms, such as a phobic reaction, may serve to *externalize* and *disguise* the fear in a more acceptable form. Obsessive-compulsive symptoms seem to be an unconscious effort to gain control over one's life and to avoid thoughts or situations that produce anxiety. Perhaps admitting to a compulsion is more acceptable than admitting that one is afraid that one's sexual urges might gain the upper hand.

LEARNING PERSPECTIVE   Learning theorists offer several explanations for anxiety disorders. Phobias, for example, may be established by *classical conditioning* (as we saw in Chapter 9). Phobias may continue because of *instrumental conditioning:* Other people *reward* the phobic with extra attention or allow the phobic to avoid an unpleasant situation (as in a school phobia). A child may also learn a phobia through *modeling*—by watching a parent who displays an intense fear of spiders, for example (Bandura, 1986).

In general, learning theorists assume that the symptoms of anxiety disorders are responses which the individual has learned for the rewards they bring. Obsessive-compulsive behaviors, for example, divert attention from more difficult matters such as personal relationships and career choices. Thus, *negative reinforcement* maintains the obsessive-compulsive symptoms.

BIOLOGICAL AND TRAIT PERSPECTIVES   Some theorists look for *inherited* or *acquired biological predispositions* that lead to anxiety disorders and other problems.

There is evidence, for example, that anxiety disorders tend to run in families. On measures of anxiety proneness, parents are more like their natural children than their adopted children, and identical twins are more similar than fraternal twins (Torgersen, 1983; Turner et al., 1991). In a study of more than two thousand twins, Kenneth Kendler and his colleagues found that genetic factors were a strong influence on phobias (Kendler et al., 1992). Perhaps some people inherit a highly reactive autonomic nervous system that predisposes them to "anxious" reactions (Eysenck, 1975).

Other researchers have linked anxiety disorders to specific brain irregularities. Panic disorders, for example, may derive from abnormalities in the right temporal lobe (George & Ballenger, 1992; Reiman et al., 1984). And unusual brain-wave patterns as well as abnormal levels of certain neurotransmitters have been noted in obsessive-compulsive patients (Barr et al., 1992; Turner et al., 1985; Zetin & Kramer, 1992).

There are several possible reasons that trauma produces PTSD in some people and not others. Researcher Matthew Friedman reports evidence that distinct changes in the sympathetic and neuroendocrine systems accompany PTSD (Friedman, 1988). Other investigators find that PTSD is linked with intra-psychic variables such as hypnotizability, the use of imagery, and the type of defenses employed under stress (Makler et al., 1990; Spiegel & Hunt, 1988). And finally, Naomi Breslau and Glenn Davis point out that researchers must consider the social environment when dealing with PTSD or any reaction to stress (Breslau & Davis, 1987).

The combination of traumatic experiences while in the military and a sense of rejection for having fought in an unpopular war may account for the problems that Vietnam veterans often experience.

A *holistic* view of anxiety disorders recognizes that each of these perspectives has something to contribute. Biological differences and early experience may lead some people to perceive and respond to the world in a way that predisposes them to anxiety disorders (Mineka & Sutton, 1992). Family and other social agents may further shape individual reactions to stressful environmental conditions.

Moreover, different cultural conditions may create stressful situations (e.g., racism) or insulate against anxiety producing situations (e.g., extended family support systems). In addition, cultural factors may lead to the expression of different symptoms in anxious individuals. For example, Angela Neal and Samuel Turner report that phobias are more common among African Americans and that unlike Caucasians, African Americans with panic disorders often experience "isolated sleep paralysis" (Neal & Turner, 1991). (Isolated sleep paralysis occurs in the transition between waking and sleeping. The person feels paralyzed and may experience hallucinations or feelings of impending danger. When the paralysis ends, the individual is overwhelmed with panic.)

It is safe to conclude that physiology, emotions, thoughts, learning, and the sociocultural environment, all contribute, in varying degrees, to anxiety disorders.

Somatoform Disorders

Somatoform disorders are physical complaints *without* an organic basis. They are not the same as psychosomatic illnesses, which are actual physical problems caused in part by psychological factors (e.g., stress-induced ulcers).

In Chapter 14 we described some of Freud's patients who had lost all sensitivity in some part of their body. Freud believed that these individuals had "converted" their psychological fears and anxieties into physical symptoms. Many of the patients with "glove anesthesias" (loss of feeling in the hand), for example, apparently feared having to touch some dreaded object. As a neurologist, Freud knew that the pattern of nerve distribution in the hand made a physiological explanation of this disorder impossible. Their problem was *psychological*. Freud's patients were classic examples of people suffering from a type of somatoform disorder called a conversion disorder.

A more contemporary example of this problem is illustrated by the hero in the rock opera *Tommy*. When Tommy sees his mother's lover kill his father, Tommy becomes deaf, blind, and mute.

In other cases of somatoform disorder the patient may experience pain that has no relation to medical problems. Or an individual may so fear having a particular disease that the patient goes to one doctor after another in an attempt to get someone to confirm the patient's fears. This latter type of somatoform disorder is called **hypochondriasis.** The essential features of these and other somatoform disorders are recurrent and multiple complaints about illnesses or body dysfunctions that apparently are not due to any physical disorder. Unlike individuals with anxiety disorders, these patients do not appear to be overly anxious or emotionally distraught—although they are usually preoccupied with their physical complaints.

Psychoanalysts view somatoform disorders as a physical symptom of unconscious psychological distress. Behavioral theorists believe symptoms are learned responses to the environment. They may lead to escape from unpleasant situations (negative reinforcement) or increased attention (positive reinforcement). There is at present no evidence for a biological basis to somatoform disorders.

Dissociative Disorders

Dissociative disorders are related to the somatoform disorders in that both appear to be ways of dealing with anxiety without revealing the anxious feelings. The essential feature of the dissociative disorders is a *dissociation* or *separation* of certain memories from consciousness so that they cannot be recalled (or can be recalled only

The diseases of the mind are more destructive than those of the body.

— MARCUS TULLIUS CICERO (106–43 B.C.)

Hypochondriasis (high-poh-kon-DRY-a-sis). A hypochondriac (high-poh-KON-dree-ack) is someone with a morbid concern about his or her health, often with the belief that he or she is sick.

under special conditions). The dissociated memories may cover a period of a few minutes or several years. Dissociative responses seem designed to permit the individual to avoid or escape anxiety associated with traumatic events. (This is apparently the reason that dissociative responses are sometimes found with post-traumatic stress disorders.)

AMNESIA AND FUGUE

Dissociative amnesia is the inability to recall important personal information, usually after some stressful episode (such as witnessing the violent death of a loved one). No brain damage is involved. Memory loss may be partial (for specific events) or complete. Complete memory loss might cover the person's entire life and include the inability to recognize relatives and friends. The victim's memory for new events is normal, and the victim is able to speak, read, and perform old skills. Recovery usually follows after a few hours, but sometimes requires as much as several years.

Dissociative fugue. Memory loss as the result of psychological stress where the loss includes assuming a new identity.

If a person experiences complete dissociative memory loss and moves to a new location and assumes a new identity, the person is said to suffer from **dissociative fugue.** After recovery the person does not remember what took place during the fugue state. With both dissociative amnesia and complete fugue, recovery is usually complete and without recurrence.

IDENTITY DISORDER (MULTIPLE PERSONALITY)

At first thought to be extremely rare, multiple personality disorders (MPDs) have been reported in increasing numbers in recent years, and may still be under-reported (Dunn, 1992; Kluft, 1987). In MPD, more than one self exists within the same individual. In fact, several dozen personalities may exist in one person at the same time, many of them unaware of the others.

Imagine you are a therapist interviewing a new client. Susan is a quiet, depressed, and insecure young woman, devoted to her husband and two children. Lately she has been having headaches and memory lapses. She recently tried to commit suicide. In the course of your conversation, you ask her how she is feeling now. She closes her eyes for a few seconds, and when she opens them you see a different person. She sits up straight, squares her shoulders, and speaks with confidence. She is vivacious and talkative. She calls herself "Sherry." Sherry tells you that she has no husband or children but she does "enjoy men," and she winks at you. Sherry knows Susan and she despises her. Sherry claims that Susan always left her (Sherry) to handle her father's sexual abuse. When you ask to speak to Susan again you discover that Susan has no knowledge of Sherry or of your conversation with her. Susan is troubled by several events that she can't explain. For example, she sometimes finds empty whiskey bottles in her car and wakes up with a headache although she says she doesn't drink. Her friends tell her she has made sexual advances to men at work. Susan is shocked and has no memory for these episodes. In subsequent sessions Sherry introduces you to several other personalities, none of whom are known to Susan.

This example is based on clinical cases reported by therapists David Fink and Kathleen Anne Lyon (Fink, 1992; Lyon, 1992). In the actual cases, the patients had gone through several months of treatment by different therapists before their "alter" personalities appeared in therapy.

MPD is a controversial diagnosis. On the one hand, virtually all MPD sufferers are the victims of severe trauma—usually childhood sexual abuse (Coons et al., 1988; Putnam et al., 1986). And we know that dissociation is a frequent reaction to severe stress (Bremner et al., 1992; Young, 1992). We also know that MPD sufferers are better at tasks such as hypnosis that require dissociation. Thus, it seems reasonable to assume that *some* individuals "split off" a new personality to deal with the stressful situation, just as Susan created Sherry to handle her father's abuse. (Note: Not all abused individuals develop MPD.)

On the other hand, skeptics argue that MPD may be simply a convenient excuse for behavior the client would like to disown—particularly criminal behavior. Alternatively, the client may simply "play the role" that the client believes the *therapist expects*. The skeptics point out that MPD diagnoses are much more common than they used to be. And they suggest that this is because many more people—clinicians and patients—are aware of this "option." Using hypnosis, some therapists may unintentionally "create" personalities by asking to speak to additional selves in their clients. Clients may then unconsciously go along with this suggestion (Merskey, 1992; Ross, 1992).

Some researchers hope to resolve this issue *physiologically*. They are looking for differences in physical processes between different personalities in the same individual, or between MPD patients and normals who are role-playing MPD. They have found some differences (Miller, 1989; Putnam, 1991; Putnam et al., 1990). So far, however, these have not proved to be very reliable, and the question remains open.

What similarities do you see between patients with "multiple personalities" and the "hidden observers" Hilgard reported finding in his hypnotized patients?

Mood Disorders

Mood disorders are disturbances in emotionality. We all feel happy at times and sad at other times. But people suffering from what we call the mood disorders seem stuck at one end of the emotionality scale or the other. That is, they usually are very "up" or very "down," although sometimes they "flip-flop" from one extreme to the other. The intensity of a mood disorder may vary from mild to severe. Individuals with severe cases sometimes suffer from delusions and hallucinations as well as from their inappropriate emotions. Patients with mood disorders are often unable to function from day to day and may require hospitalization.

Mental health professionals usually refer to two major types of mood disorders: bipolar disorders, and depressive disorders. Bipolar disorders involve both "highs" and "lows" of emotion. Depressive disorders involve only the "lows."

Depressive disorders are 10 to 20 times more common than bipolar disorders. In fact, clinical depression is the most common mental disorder—so common that it has been called "the common cold of mental illness."

DEPRESSIVE DISORDERS

We all feel sad from time to time, sometimes without really knowing why. Some people seem to have a regular pattern of "valleys"—they are "down" every few weeks or months. But for a few people these "valleys" are "bottomless pits." They appear completely overwhelmed by the sadness and futility of life. They become passive, may refuse to move from their beds, and sometimes have to be force-fed to be kept alive. Particularly in younger individuals, there is always the danger of suicide. These people experience "major depression."

Depressive disorders can be triggered by the loss of a job, a loved one, or by some other traumatic event. For example:

Mr. J. was a fifty-one-year-old industrial engineer who, since the death of his wife five years earlier, had been suffering from continuing episodes of depression marked by extreme social withdrawal and occasional thoughts of suicide. . . . He began to drink, sometimes heavily. . . . He lost all capacity for joy—his friends could not recall when they had last seen him smile. . . . When friends invited him for dinner, this previously witty, urbane man could barely manage to engage in

The hopelessness and gloom of major depression are evident in this man's posture.

small talk. . . . His work record deteriorated markedly. Appointments were missed and projects haphazardly started and then left unfinished (From Davison & Neale, 1990, p. 221).

In contrast to Mr. J., many people experience severe depression without any obvious "triggering event." Others endure more moderate episodes which may evolve into a relatively permanent condition known as "dysthymic disorder."

For most of us, sadness lifts after a time and does not become severe. But for the individual who suffers a depressive disorder, life seems to come to a halt.

BI-POLAR MOOD DISORDER

Depressive disorders are *unipolar* because the disturbed emotion is at one extreme. In contrast, *bi-polar* mood disorders also contain periods of emotional "high," or *mania*. Mania is inappropriate elation, excitation, or aggression. The mood is "disordered" because it doesn't seem to be a response to any real-world event.

A person experiencing a manic attack typically becomes hyperactive, and cannot sleep. The person may shout and scream, or talk so rapidly and so loudly that other people may not be able to understand him or her. The person may express grandiose ideas and become physically aggressive to those who get in the way. Mr. M. illustrates many of these symptoms:

On February the twelfth Mr. M. let his wife know that he was bursting with energy and ideas, that his job as a mail carrier was unfulfilling, and that he was just wasting his talent. That night he slept little, spending most of his time at a desk, writing furiously. The next morning he left for work at the usual time but returned home at eleven a.m., his car filled to overflowing with aquaria and other equipment for tropical fish. He had quit his job and then withdrawn all the money from the family's savings account. The money had been spent on tropical fish equipment. Mr. M. reported that the previous night he had worked out a way to modify existing equipment so that fish "won't die anymore. We'll be millionaires." After unloading the paraphernalia, Mr. M. set off to canvass the neighborhood for possible buyers, going door to door and talking to anyone who would listen.

The following bit of conversation from the period after Mr. M. entered treatment indicates his incorrigible optimism and provocativeness.

Therapist: Well, you seem happy today.
Client: Happy! Happy! You certainly are a master of understatement, you rogue! (Shouting, literally jumping out of his seat.) Why I'm ecstatic. I'm leaving for the West Coast today, on my daughter's bicycle. Only 3,100 miles. That's nothing, you know. I could probably walk, but I want to get there by next week. And along the way I plan to contact a lot of people about investing in my fish equipment. I'll get to know more people that way—you know, Doc, "know" in the biblical sense (leering at the therapist seductively). Oh, God, how good it feels. It's almost like a nonstop orgasm   (From Davison & Neale, 1987, p. 222).

Individuals diagnosed with a bi-polar disorder suffer mood swings from one "pole" to the other. They are manic some of the time, normal some of the time, and depressed some of the time—with no consistent pattern from person to person. As with depressive disorders, bi-polar mood disorder can occur in a milder recurring form (called "cyclothymic disorder").

There is considerable controversy among experts about the manic phase of bi-polar disorder. Some researchers believe it is possible for individuals to suffer from a "manic psychosis" that never develops into a depressive condition. Other theorists contend that all patients who experience manic episodes will eventually become depressive.

ORIGINS OF MOOD DISORDERS

There is little agreement among experts as to the cause of the mood disorders. Investigators are searching for clues in biological mechanisms, in unique thought processes, and in environmental conditions.

BIOLOGICAL FACTORS   In the mid-1980s, several research groups reported results suggesting there may be a genetic factor of some kind that "codes" for depression (Biron et al., 1987; Egeland et al., 1987; Fieve et al., 1984; Price et al., 1987). It is important to note, however, that in almost all of these studies, only about 60 percent of the depressed patients showed the "genetic marker" associated with depression. Therefore, we cannot say that all types of depression are "inherited." It is also true that the genetic abnormalities showed up in some normal individuals who had never experienced depression. Thus, the tendency to become depressed may be inherited by some people. But even in these individuals, it must be "triggered" by other factors such as past experiences or present circumstances. These same "triggering" experiences may also bring about depressions in individuals who don't carry any known genetic tendency toward depression.

Other biological research has centered on the possibility that depression involves a biochemical imbalance in the brain. On the one hand, certain drugs are often effective treatments for severe depression. On the other hand, some drugs produce symptoms of depression. These mood altering drugs seem to affect either the production or the effectiveness of three neurotransmitters: norepinephrine, serotonin, and dopamine (Hirschfeld & Goodwin, 1988; Meltzer, 1990). Thus, it seems likely that depression has a biological component. Exactly how these neurotransmitters produce their effects on mood, however, is not clear.

In terms of *electrical* activity in the brain, Richard Davidson and his colleagues report that EEG measures reveal different brain-wave patterns in depressed and nondepressed subjects (Davidson, 1992; Davidson et al., 1987). Even more intriguing, similar differences exist between recovered depressives and individuals who have never experienced depression (Henriques & Davidson, 1990). Thus, unusual brainwave patterns may not be just a sign of being depressed but perhaps an indicator of a history of depression or a tendency to depression.

But what produces different patterns of brain activity or different levels of neurotransmitters if they are not inherited? The answer may lie in distinctive reactions to environmental events.

COGNITIVE AND BEHAVIORAL THEORIES OF DEPRESSION   From his research on "learned helplessness" with dogs (discussed in Chapter 8), Martin Seligman proposes that human depression may be a learned response to stressful events. When we are continually hit with problems that appear insurmountable, we may eventually give up and become depressed.

Jay Weiss has demonstrated that animals in a "helpless" condition generate more of the neurotransmitters that produce depression than animals that can control their environmental stressors (Weiss et al., 1976). Thus, a *helpless situation* leads to a *neurological response*, which in turn produces a *depressive reaction*.

In his later work, Seligman adds a cognitive component to his learned helplessness theory. He notes that while depressed people tend to have experienced more negative events than nondepressed people, some nondepressed people also experience many negative events. He suggests that the difference is in how we *think* about these events, and what we blame them on.

Our failures are most likely to depress us if we attribute their cause to our own weakness or to unchangeable conditions in our environment. If we can attribute failure to temporary conditions, such as fatigue or bad luck, our disappointment is less likely to cause depression (Abramson et al., 1989; Alloy, 1992; Metalsky et al., 1987). So while environmental events produce depression, *the way we interpret* those events also affects our mood.

Psychiatrist Aaron Beck agrees. Beck found that his depressed patients had a "depressing" way of interpreting the world. They held consistently negative views of themselves and their surroundings, as well as pessimistic views of the future. And they maintained these views by exaggerating bad experiences and overlooking or minimizing good happenings. Beck believes that a vicious circle of self-defeating thought produces depression and then maintains it (Beck, 1976; Beck & Burns, 1978; Sacco & Beck, 1985).

Ironically, depressed people may actually have a *more realistic* view of themselves and the future than nondepressed individuals—a phenomenon known as "depressive realism" (Alloy & Abramson, 1988). Most of us, however, would rather live with our "optimistic *unrealism*." A little optimism goes a long way!

How could you relate Seligman's view of depression to the fact that two times more women than men suffer from depression?

ENVIRONMENTAL FACTORS   We have already noted that environmental stress may be a factor in producing depression. Stress may lead to neurochemical reactions that directly create depressive symptoms (Healy & Williams, 1988; Wehr et al., 1987). But reactions to stress seem to depend on *cognitive interpretations* of events.

In addition, sometimes depression-prone people seem to *create* their own environmental stress. They may lack the social skills necessary to obtain friends and other social rewards (Blechman et al., 1986; Lewinsohn, 1974). As a result they feel inadequate and become depressed. And, as you probably know, depressed people are depressing! Consequently, other people tend to avoid them. This, of course, confirms their feelings of inadequacy and deepens their depression (Klerman & Weissman, 1986; Segrin, 1990, 1992; Segrin & Dillard, 1992).

Depression has many possible causes, and almost certainly these causes interact with each other (Caplan & Ahmed, 1992). Which is to say, depressive behavior is multi-determined.

In our discussion of the origins of mood disorders we have centered on depressive disorders because this is the focus of most current research and theory. The less frequent bipolar disorders have received much less attention.

Some evidence suggests that there is a genetic predisposition to bi-polar disorders (Bertelsen, 1979). Biological factors are also implicated since bi-polar disorder is often effectively treated with drugs (especially a drug called lithium carbonate). From an intra-psychic perspective, some theorists believe that depression is the primary symptom and that mania is a desperate attempt to ward of impending depression. In addition, there is evidence that stressful life events may bring on bipolar disorder (Ambelas, 1987).

SUICIDE AND DEPRESSION

Depression can be fatal. In the United States, about 13 people per 100,000 take their lives each year (Tolchin, 1989). Most of these people are deeply depressed (NIMH, 1984).

The rate of suicide is highest among the elderly, with the peak period being from age 75–84 (*Morbidity & Mortality Weekly Report*, 1987). In recent years, however, the rate of suicide among young people in America has more than tripled from what it was 30 years ago. Suicide is now the second most frequent cause of death, after accidents, among high school and college students (U.S. Department of Health and Human Services, 1987).

Statistics reveal disturbing increases in suicide rates among adolescents and even young children. However, white males between the ages of 20 and 24 seem most affected—their suicide rate is now five times as great as it was three decades ago. Among both males and females, white Americans are more likely to commit suicide than are African-Americans (U.S. Bureau of the Census, 1989). And while young women threaten or even attempt suicide more than men do, men are much more likely to complete the act. However, the proportion of completed suicides among women has also increased in recent years (Roy, 1986).

Since the genetic make-up of young Americans surely hasn't changed much in the past 30 years, the increase in the rate of suicides supports the belief that the cause of depression cannot be entirely biological.

What reasons can you think of to explain the dramatic rise in suicide rates?

Schizophrenic Disorders

Schizophrenia is certainly one of the most puzzling and profound of the psychological disorders. It is found in every culture and historic period. Descriptions of people who apparently suffered from schizophrenia can be found in the Bible. The modern-day conception of schizophrenia, however, dates from 1911, when the noted Swiss psychiatrist Eugene Bleuler first described the disorder in detail and gave it its present name.

The term schizophrenia comes from the Latin words that mean "splitting of the mind." The use of this term is unfortunate, for the "multiple" or "split personality," as we saw earlier, is a more rare type of disorder which has nothing to do with schizophrenia. As we will see, "shattered mind" is a better description than "split mind."

An older name for schizophrenia is dementia praecox, from the Latin words meaning "youthful insanity." And schizophrenia is primarily a disorder of the young. About 1 percent of the general population has schizophrenia—although estimates for college students are moderately higher. Men are at greatest risk from age 18 to 25. Women are at greatest risk from age 25 to 45. Recent data indicate that men are somewhat more likely to develop schizophrenia than women (Iacono & Beiser, 1992a, 1992b).

O, let me not be mad, not mad, sweet heaven! . . . I would not be mad!

SHAKESPEARE (KING LEAR)

The "rule of thirds" for schizophrenia says that of all the people who suffer schizophrenia, roughly one-third will get better after treatment with little danger of relapse, one-third will improve, but need additional treatment from time to time, and one-third will need to be hospitalized the rest of their lives.

SYMPTOMS OF SCHIZOPHRENIA

Schizophrenia usually begins with deterioration of social and mental functioning—withdrawal from social interaction, neglect of duties and hygiene, exhibition of strange thoughts and emotions. (This is called the *prodromal phase*.) These changes are usually slow, and people who notice them might say "she's just out of sorts" or "he's not quite himself." Gradually, and sometimes suddenly, markedly disturbed behaviors emerge—delusions, hallucinations, odd speech, unusual emotional reactions, or abnormal motor behavior. (This is called the *active phase*.) Behavior at this stage is clearly abnormal and usually brings the person into some kind of treatment where the patient is given drugs to relieve the most serious symptoms. As the active phase subsides, the person continues to show disturbed social and mental functioning, especially neglect of duties and lack of emotions. (This is called the *residual phase*.) Most schizophrenics move between the active and residual phases for the rest of their lives. Complete *remission*, or release from symptoms, is rare (Vitkus, 1988).

Before we consider attempts to subtype schizophrenia, let's look at some general characteristics common to most cases. The following example, from a person we'll call Karen, illustrates many of these characteristics:

The artistic productions of schizophrenics reflect their disturbed perceptions of the world.

No, I never was crazy, a little nervous. Look at my teeth. I came here to have my teeth fixed. We are going to have a strawberry party now. Yesterday I heard voices. They said, "I ran to the drugstore and I am going home tomorrow." I heard J.B. Scott's voice and it came from up here in the air. We've got 39 banks on

Delusions. A fixed, false belief maintained in the face of virtually undeniable proof to the contrary.

Hallucinations (hal-ou-sin-AY-shuns). Sensory perceptions without sensory input or from distorted input, for example, "seeing things," or "hearing voices."

Market Street. We've got lots of property. Say, take me home and I'll give you three laundry bags. I'm 29 and a half, 29 and a half. Now I want you to get me 10 apples—10 of your most beautiful apples and two dozen lemons. Now listen, if I get you some pineapple will you preserve it? (Zax & Stricker, 1963).

The central feature of schizophrenic disorders is disturbed, irrational thinking. Karen's speech clearly shows this chaotic and disjointed association of ideas. Karen also exhibits **delusions,** another common feature of schizophrenic thought. Karen says she has "39 banks" and "lots of property." Delusions are false beliefs that are held even though they clearly have no basis in reality. *Delusions of grandeur* are beliefs that one is a famous figure like the President, Christ, or Satan.

Karen also shows another common feature of schizophrenia, **hallucinations.** Hallucinations are sensory perceptions based on distorted or nonexistent sensory input. The most frequent form of hallucination is auditory—hearing voices. Karen says she heard J.B. Scott's voice from up in the air. Hallucinatory voices are often insulting and argumentative. They may occasionally order the person to do bizarre or dangerous things.

Schizophrenics often show inappropriate emotional responses. They may cry at a humorous cartoon or laugh at a tragic event. They may giggle for no apparent reason. Or they may show little emotional reaction at all—a response called "flattened emotion."

In addition to these disturbances of *thought, perception,* and *emotion,* schizophrenics also exhibit *behavioral* abnormalities. Schizophrenics frequently withdraw from social contacts and break off work or school activities. They neglect personal hygiene. Sometimes they walk in an unusual way, or sit and rock back and forth constantly, or even refuse to move.

None of these features is always present. For a diagnosis of schizophrenia to be made, however, either delusions, hallucinations, or disturbed thinking must appear.

SUBTYPES OF SCHIZOPHRENIA

There is considerable argument in psychological circles as to whether schizophrenia really exists as a *single* mental illness, or whether we simply call people "schizophrenics" because we don't know what else to call them. The fact that so many people are diagnosed as schizophrenic suggests that this category may be too loose and too large to be meaningfully applied to the complex living systems we call human beings.

In an effort to refine their diagnoses, and to prescribe treatment and predict the course of the disorder, researchers have made several efforts to classify subtypes of schizophrenia. Table 15.1 shows the traditional classification into catatonic, disorganized, paranoid, undifferentiated, and residual types of schizophrenia, with some related symptoms of each type.

Critics of this system doubt its value. For one thing, it is often difficult to assign an individual to a subtype. Symptoms come in a bewildering array of combinations making the "undifferentiated" category a popular and meaningless catch-all for leftovers. Even when assignment is clear, the critics say, it is of little value. Knowing the traditional subtype for a particular case of schizophrenia is not very helpful in explaining its cause or in predicting the individual's response to treatment.

Nancy Andreason and others have proposed an alternative classification for "types" of schizophrenia based on "positive" and "negative symptoms" (Andreason & Olsen, 1982; Lewine et al., 1983). A symptom is positive if it is shown by schizophrenics but not by other people. A symptom is negative if it is *not* shown by schizophrenics but *is* shown by other people. Table 15.2 lists typical positive and negative symptoms.

Andreason believes that these two subtypes will be predictive of consistent differences in the disorder's cause, progress, and recovery rate. For example, people with

Catatonic schizophrenics show severe disturbances in motor behavior. They may pose in rigid and unusual positions, perhaps for hours. They are often mute and totally unresponsive. They may occasionally show brief periods of agitated and excited, but purposeless behavior.

Disorganized schizophrenics show strange, incoherent, and often silly behavior. Unlike the catatonic they will respond to other people. But their thoughts are disorganized and their emotions are inappropriate or even absent. They may cry at a joke or laugh at sad news. Their speech (and writing) rambles incoherently from topic to topic.

Paranoid schizophrenics are preoccupied with delusions or frequent auditory hallucinations concerning a single idea—usually that they are some great person, or that they are being persecuted. Except when they are acting on these ideas, paranoid schizophrenics may appear to be fairly normal.

Undifferentiated schizophrenics show clear signs of serious disturbance from more than one of the other categories, or which don't clearly fit in the other categories. Many patients show a variety of symptoms which change from time to time. These patients are not easily placed in one of the other categories and so are considered undifferentiated schizophrenics.

Residual schizophrenics show some of the general signs of schizophrenia, such as illogical thinking, lack of emotions, social withdrawal, and disorganized daily functioning. However, they have not had a time when the more bizarre and delusional behavior of the other types was active, or else they have recovered from most of the effects of their schizophrenia.

positive symptoms are expected to have a better chance of recovery since their symptoms are less crippling and less resistant to change.

Robin Murray and his colleagues propose that schizophrenia is best divided into *three* subtypes based on *when the disorder first appears*. *Congenital* schizophrenia is present at birth, although not necessarily recognizable. Genetic defects or maternal illness during pregnancy are probably the main cause of the congenital type. Abnormalities appear early in life. *Adult-onset* schizophrenia appears in adulthood, frequently young adulthood. Murray believes this subtype develops from the same genetic weaknesses as the mood disorders. *Late-onset* schizophrenia usually appears after age 60. Unlike the other two subtypes which are more common in men, late-onset schizophrenia is more common in women. Again, brain abnormalities may be involved, but these are more likely the result of injury or illness rather than heredity (Castle & Murray, 1993; Murray et al., 1992).

Like Andreason, Murray believes his classification system will prove more useful than the traditional one. Only time, and research, will tell.

ORIGINS OF SCHIZOPHRENIA

The search for causes of schizophrenia has focused on two areas: biological origins, and social or other environmental influences. Let's consider these two possibilities.

BIOLOGICAL FACTORS IN SCHIZOPHRENIA   The thought that some genetic or biochemical malfunction in the brain causes schizophrenia is particularly

POSITIVE SYMPTOMS	NEGATIVE SYMPTOMS
Incoherent and irrational thinking; delusions; hallucinations; bizarre or disorganized behavior; inappropriate emotional responses	Impoverished, ungrammatical speech; flattened emotional responsiveness; social withdrawal; apathy; impaired attention

RELATIONSHIP TO SCHIZOPHRENIC	PERCENTAGE SCHIZOPHRENIC	DEGREE OF GENETIC RELATEDNESS
Identical twins	48	Identical
Fraternal twins	17	First degree
Siblings	19	"
Children	13	"
Grandchildren	5	Second degree
Nieces/nephews	4	"
Spouse	2	Unrelated
Unrelated people	1	"

TABLE 15.3

Percentage of schizophrenics in different relationships to person with schizophrenia.

(Based on Gottesman, 1991.)

appealing to those scientists who believe that the "brain controls the mind," and not vice versa. Many types of data do support the notion that there is some biological problem at the root of many types of schizophrenia. As Table 15.3 shows, risk of schizophrenia increases with genetic similarity (Gottesman, 1991; Gottesman et al., 1982, 1987). Interestingly, the genetic factors appear to be sex-linked. That is, it is more likely that a relative of the *same sex* as the schizophrenic will get the disorder (DeLisi & Crow, 1989; Wolyniec et al., 1992).

Of course, schizophrenia is not entirely genetic. If it were, every identical twin of a schizophrenic would also develop schizophrenia. As you can see from Table 15.3, less than half of these twins do. The genetic influence in schizophrenia is, however, quite strong.

Just how the genes influence schizophrenia is not yet known. Researchers have found a variety of "possibly inherited" differences in schizophrenics' brains. For example, there is evidence that schizophrenics' brain are "less dense" (Golden et al., 1980, 1981); that their left hemispheres have less blood flow than their right hemispheres (Golden et al., 1985); that their cerebellums are defective (Filteau et al., 1991); that their ventricles (the fluid-filled cavities in the brain) are larger (Van Horn & McManus, 1992); and that their right hemispheres are damaged (Cutting, 1992).

Some or all of these differences might lead to schizophrenia. As we will see in a moment, however, the reverse is also possible. Disturbed behavior may produce disturbed brains.

We should also note that brain abnormalities are not necessarily inherited. They could result from injury, prenatal or postnatal illness, or birth complications (Lewis & Murray, 1987). For example, there is increasing evidence that influenza may place a pregnant mother's unborn child at risk for schizophrenia (Barr et al., 1990; Mednick et al., 1988; O'Callaghan et al., 1991; Sham et al., 1992).

In recent years a great deal of interest has centered on the neurotransmitter *dopamine* as a factor in schizophrenia. We know that drugs that are effective in *treating* schizophrenia also block the receptors for dopamine (Seeman & Lee, 1975). We know that heavy amphetamine use, which stimulates the brain's own dopamine system, also *produces* schizophrenia-like symptoms (Snyder, 1978). And we know that giving schizophrenics amphetamines makes their symptoms *worse* (Angrist et al., 1974). So it seems reasonable to conclude that dopamine may be responsible for some of the symptoms of schizophrenia (Meltzer & Stahl, 1976; Nicol & Gottesman, 1983). But rather than having an extra amount of dopamine in their brains, it now seems more likely that schizophrenics are *more sensitive* to dopamine (Lee & Seeman, 1980). How the sensitivity develops, however, is still a mystery.

The research with dopamine is promising, but it is only a beginning. As we've noted before, there are many different chemicals involved in the transmission of even a simple behavior. Dopamine is only one of many components in the complex behaviors of schizophrenia. Some researchers believe that dopamine may be more important for *positive* symptoms of schizophrenia while the type of structural deficits we noted earlier may be more important for *negative* symptoms (Andreason, 1987; Buchsbaum & Haier, 1987; Meltzer, 1987).

Naturally, the hope is that we could cure schizophrenia if we could somehow bring the person's brain chemistry back to normal. However, almost all of the neurochemical differences reported in schizophrenic patients so far can be caused in *normal* individuals—and in animals—by changes in diet, social stress, daily routine, and drug use. Furthermore, no one to date has been able to cure schizophrenia by altering the levels of neurotransmitters in a schizophrenic's brain.

In almost all the studies which report correlations between brain chemistry and schizophrenia, the researchers have compared subjects already diagnosed as being schizophrenic (many of whom have been hospitalized for years) with normal individuals. As British psychiatrist Steven Rose points out, this sort of comparison may be misleading. When researchers find structural or functional abnormalities in the brains of schizophrenic patients, Rose says, the scientists tend to assume these physical abnormalities *caused* the mental disorder. It is more likely, Rose contends, that the *mental disorder caused the structural changes*.

Rose also cites considerable evidence suggesting that subjects with genetic markers for schizophrenia only become mentally disordered in certain types of social environments. Therefore, schizophrenia should be considered a *bio-psycho-social* disorder, and not a medical disease (Rose, 1984). Gerald Davison and John Neale reach a similar conclusion. Their viewpoint is sometimes called the **diathesis-stress hypothesis.** This perspective affirms that both a genetic predisposition (diathesis) and a noxious environment (stress) are necessary to produce psychopathology (Davison and Neale, 1990).

Diathesis-stress hypothesis. The idea that a disorder is the result of the combination of an inherited tendency *and* stressful environment. "Diathesis" (di-ATH-ih-sis) is a technical term for predisposition or vulnerability.

NON-BIOLOGICAL FACTORS IN SCHIZOPHRENIA   Contemporary theories of schizophrenia generally assume that biological factors create a vulnerability to schizophrenia. They also assume that intra-psychic and social factors can increase this vulnerability and may eventually trigger the disorder.

In their search for non-biological causes, most researchers have concentrated on the schizophrenic's family. Some investigators suggest that vague and contradictory communication from the parents leads to schizophrenia by confusing and undermining a child's sense of reality (Bateson et al., 1956; Bateson, 1960; Goldstein, 1984; Singer et al., 1978). Other researchers believe that risk increases in families with a high level of conflict between parents or where one parent completely dominates the relationship (Arieti, 1974; Roff & Knight, 1981).

Much recent research focuses on "expressed emotion" (EE) in the families of schizophrenics. Excessive levels of criticism, emotional overinvolvement, or hostility characterize high EE families (Leff & Vaughn, 1980). Recovering schizophrenics in these families show relapse rates two to three times that of similar individuals in low EE families (Kavanagh, 1992). High EE may also be involved in the onset of schizophrenia, although the matter of causality is unresolved (Mavreas et al., 1992). That is, a vulnerable individual may respond negatively to high EE and become schizophrenic; but high EE could also *result* from the stress of living with a schizophrenic individual. Once again, we need to be careful not to assume a cause-effect relationship from a correlational observation.

SCHIZOPHRENIA: AN INTERACTIVE MODEL   Although some theorists still take a narrowly focused view of the causes of schizophrenia, most scientists now believe this mental disorder is "multi-determined." They suggest there is a genetic predisposition toward schizophrenia which is expressed only in certain stressful environments. Family environments have the potential to be particularly stressful, but cultural conditions can add destructive pressures as well. Thus, there is no single cause for this mental disorder. Rather, schizophrenia is a developmental problem determined by biological, intra-psychic, and social/behavioral factors. It is the combination of these factors which causes the disorder to surface.

Today, most theories of schizophrenia suggest that environmental stress contributes to the onset of the disorder in an individual who is biologically predisposed to the problem.

Personality Disorders

In Chapter 14 we said that your personality is the "pattern of psychological and physical processes which controls your characteristic behavior and thought." From time to time we all think or behave inappropriately or maladaptively. But if these behaviors and thoughts become *characteristic* of us we may suffer from a personality disorder. Personality disorders are continuing patterns of maladaptive thought and behavior that cause distress to the individual or to others.

Personality disorders usually appear by adolescence and continue through adulthood. Thus, the diagnosis of a personality disorder is made when the behavior in question is part of a person's typical long-term functioning, and not merely the result of a short period of disturbance.

Over the years there have been many different efforts to classify personality disorders (Widiger & Frances, 1985). Figure 15.2 describes and groups the traditional DSM subtypes into three major categories according to their characteristic way of relating to other people (Millon, 1981).

The four types in the first group are excessively anxious about their relationships with other people and fearful of rejection by them. In the second group, socially aloof and inappropriate behaviors predominate. In the third group, overly dramatic behavior characterizes the histrionic and narcissistic types, and impulsiveness distinguishes the borderline and antisocial disorders. Since this last type has received by far the greatest attention from researchers, let's examine it in greater detail.

ANTISOCIAL PERSONALITY

Whatever their causes or cures, most mental disorders typically give the most pain and unhappiness to the individual concerned. Someone with an antisocial personality disorder, however, is likely to cause more problems for others than for the per-

FIGURE 15.2

The traditional DSM subtypes of personality disorders grouped into three major categories according to type of dysfunction in their characteristic way of relating to other people. (Based on Millon, 1981, 1991). DSM-IV does not include a passive-aggressive category, but suggests this diagnosis belongs in a more general category called "personality disorders not otherwise specified."

INTERACTIONAL DYSFUNCTION	DSM LABEL	DESCRIPTION
Fearful and anxious	Avoidant personality disorder	Guarded; overly sensitive to possible rejection or humiliation; socially withdrawn despite the desire for acceptance by others
	Dependent personality disorder	Timid; overly lacking in self-esteem and self-reliance; passive; constantly subordinating own needs to the needs of others
	Passive-aggressive personality disorder	Stubborn; indirectly resistant to demands for adequate social and occupational performance; uncooperative
	Compulsive personality disorder	Perfectionistic; conventional; preoccupied with organization, rules, schedules, lists, trivial details; serious; unable to express warm emotions
Unusual or eccentric	Schizoid personality disorder	Aloof; complacent; defective in ability to form social relationships; lacking in warmth and tender feelings for others
	Schizotypal personality disorder	Detached and secretive; withdrawn; showing social deficits and oddities of thought, perception, and communication that resemble schizophrenia
	Paranoid personality disorder	Wary and defensive; showing pervasive and unwarranted suspiciousness and mistrust; overly sensitive; prone to jealousy; quarrelsome
Dramatic or impulsive	Histrionic personality disorder	Overly dramatic; tending to exaggerated expressions of emotion; egocentric; flirtatious; flighty
	Narcissistic personality disorder	Arrogant; self-important; expecting special treatment; preoccupied with success fantasies; exploitive; lacking empathy
	Borderline personality disorder	Temperamental; capricious and unpredictable; unstable in self-image, mood, and relationships; spontaneous; disorganized
	Antisocial personality disorder	Exploitive and reckless; failing to accept social norms; unable to form attachments to others; chronically violating the rights of others

The character played by Michael Douglas in the movie "Wall Street" was an anti-social personality who manipulated and "conned" other people for his own profit, apparently feeling no pity or remorse.

son with the deviant behaviors. This is because "antisocial" does not refer to a desire to avoid social interaction. Rather, antisocial means the person *rejects widely accepted social norms*. As a result, antisocial personalities seem to lack a "conscience," and experience little or no guilt about breaking social laws. They appear to be greedy, impulsive, egocentric men and women who cannot comprehend the social consequences of their actions (Elliott, 1992).

While many mass murderers and other criminals fall into this category, so do other more "legal" social predators. Unscrupulous politicians and businessmen, "Don Juans," and "manipulators" of all types may also be antisocial personalities.

According to the 1984 NIMH report, about 1.4 million Americans currently could be diagnosed as having an antisocial personality. More men than women receive this diagnosis—by a ratio of 4 to 1 (Reich, 1987).

There is no agreement among experts as to what causes a person to experience this problem. On the biological side, Robert Hare and others report unusual brainwaves and abnormal levels of serotonin and other neurotransmitters in the central nervous system of antisocial personalities (Hare, 1978, 1982; Hare & Jutai, 1983; Lewis, 1991). These differences may account for the difficulty that antisocial personalities have in learning to respond to punishment. Finnish researcher Matti Virkkunen reports that violent prisoners diagnosed as being antisocial personalities tend to secrete insulin more rapidly than do normals. This fact might account for the easily aroused emotions of some antisocial personalities (Virkkunen, 1986). In addition, there is some evidence for the genetic transmission of an antisocial predisposition (Cadoret et al., 1985; Crowe, 1983).

From a theoretical perspective it seems reasonable to expect that antisocial personalities might develop from poor socialization experiences in the family. Parents who do not train their children adequately might be expected to produce antisocial traits in their offspring. And there is some evidence to support this position (Meyer, 1980, Robins, 1966). However, many children from socially deficient backgrounds do not become antisocial adults, and many antisocial adults do not come from obviously deficient backgrounds.

Unfortunately, antisocial personalities do not normally seek help, unless they run afoul of the law, because they feel little guilt and see nothing wrong with their behavior. As a result, our knowledge of this disorder is severely limited. When they do seek help, antisocial personalities are notoriously difficult to treat. On the positive side, for unknown reasons, many antisocial personalities "settle down" by age 40 or so.

Many psychologists consider Adolf Hitler to be the "prototype" of someone with an antisocial personality disorder. What other political leaders also seem to fit the description of antisocial personalities? Why might their followers disagree with you?

CROSS-CULTURAL CONSIDERATIONS

Throughout this chapter we have said several times that culture influences abnormality. More specifically, we noted:

1. Cultures affect the definition of mental disorders.
2. Some mental disorders are more common in certain cultures.
3. Cultures influence the display of symptoms for mental disorders.
4. Cultures affect the onset and course of mental disorders.

Let's review each of these points briefly.

First, cultures influence abnormality by defining what is normal and what is abnormal. For example, in some Native American tribes, hearing the voice of one's dead husband or wife is considered a normal part of grieving (Kleinman, 1988). Among the Ik tribe of Uganda, cruelty even to one's family is acceptable for personal gain (Turnbull, 1972). Most contemporary North Americans, however, would consider both of these examples as illustrations of abnormal behavior.

In North America, the American Psychiatric Association officially dropped homosexuality from its list of mental disorders in 1973. So cultures define abnormality, and as cultures change so do the definitions.

Second, while mental disorders are a universal problem, some disorders are more common in certain cultures. For example, eating disorders and sexual problems are more common complaints in North America (Kendell, 1991). And phobias are more common in African-Americans than in those of European descent (Neal & Turner, 1991).

Schizophrenia also shows certain systematic differences in it occurrence. For example, it is more common among Irish Catholics in the Republic of Ireland (especially the western regions), among the very poor in North America, and among the wealthy in India (Murphy, 1968; Torrey, 1980; Torrey, et al., 1984). We do not know the reason for these differences, although they do suggest the influence of culture.

Third, cultures affect the way a disorder is expressed. We saw that African-Americans experiencing panic attacks are more likely to manifest "isolated sleep paralysis." Schizophrenics in cultures where witchcraft is common report voices from spirits. In North America, hallucinatory voices are more likely to come from inanimate objects. What's more, these voices tend to keep up-to-date with the times—coming from radios, televisions, satellites, and microwaves as technology advances!

Fourth, cultures may affect the onset of disorders by creating extra sources of stress, such as racism. On the other hand, cultures may *insulate* against stress by providing a network of support in the extended family and close-knit community. Schizophrenics in non-industrialized societies, for example, have a better recovery rate, presumably because of the broader basis of social support they receive (Lin & Kleinman, 1988).

Some cultures may include greater "insulation" against stress by providing a network of support in the extended family and close-knit community.

These are only a few of many cultural differences found in the definition, incidence, and symptomatology of mental disorders (Brislin, 1993; Dasen et al., 1988). What can we learn from them?

The most obvious lesson is that we need to be careful in generalizing beyond our own experience or beyond the findings of our research. Closely related to this lesson is the knowledge that culture *does* influence mental disorders. A complete understanding of these disorders must include analysis of the role that culture plays.

Beyond this, cross-cultural comparisons provide new leads in our search for understanding. For example, the observation that guilt is a common symptom among North American depressives but not among depressives in other cultures led to a correction in our analysis of depression (Draguns, 1990). We no longer see guilt as a necessary component of depressive disorders.

People suffer mental disorders in every culture around the world. Cross-cultural research can help to unravel the mysteries of this type of human suffering.

LABELING ABNORMALITY

As researchers continue to study abnormal behavior, the accuracy of our classification systems will no doubt increase. However, we need to remember the dangers of *any* system which leads us to label people.

For one thing, a label gives the illusion of an explanation. For example, "Why does John experience hallucinations?" "Because he has schizophrenia." "How do you know he has schizophrenia?" "Because he experiences hallucinations." The label "schizophrenia" merely *describes* a certain (somewhat arbitrary) group of symptoms. It *explains* nothing. Yet it is tempting to think we understand John's condition because we can call it "schizophrenia."

Labels can also lead to stereotypes. When we *expect* people to be "intelligent," or "friendly," or "disturbed"—that is, when we have labeled them—we tend to see what we expect to see. And furthermore, our behavior may actually *cause* the reaction we are looking for (Snyder, 1984).

The tendency has always been strong to believe that whatever received a name must be an entity or being, having an independent existence of its own. And if no real entity answering to the name could be found, men did not for that reason suppose that none existed, but imagined that it was something peculiarly abstruse and mysterious.

JOHN STUART MILL

Psychotic (sigh-KAH-tic). An older term for a person with a severe and usually incapacitating form of mental disorder that often requires hospitalization.

In a controversial study performed in 1973, psychologist David Rosenhan showed the power of psychological labels. Rosenhan asked several "normal" people to try to get into mental hospitals by pretending to be mentally ill. These pseudo-patients, as Rosenhan called them, asked for voluntary admission to several public and private mental hospitals. The pseudo-patients all stated that they "heard voices," and thus needed help. Other than on this one point, these quite normal people told the admitting psychiatrists the *absolute truth* about their lives and feelings. To Rosenhan's surprise, all of the pseudo-patients were admitted without question. They were all classed as being **psychotic.** About 95 percent of the time, they were diagnosed as being "schizophrenic."

After they were admitted, the pseudo-patients acted completely normal. What happened? Once they were labeled as mentally ill, many of their normal behaviors were considered *abnormal*. Taking notes on the ward was considered "pathological," lining up early for lunch (when there was nothing else to do) was a "characteristic of the oral-acquisitive nature of the syndrome," and even their normal backgrounds were interpreted as "disturbed."

On the average, it took the pseudo-patients more than two weeks to convince the authorities to release them. One man was detained (against his will) for almost two months. He finally escaped because, as he put it, the hospital was driving him crazy (Rosenhan, 1973).

What is perhaps more disturbing than the influence of labels on initial perceptions, is the power of labels to stick. When Rosenhan's pseudo-patients were released, were they "cured"? "Normal"? No. Their symptoms were considered to be "in remission"—but the individuals were presumably still schizophrenic.

A label such as "schizophrenic" can continue to influence not only the perceptions and expectations of other people, but the self-perceptions of the individual as well (Witztum et al., 1992). As Rosenhan says, "Eventually, the patient himself accepts the diagnosis, with all of its surplus meanings and expectations, and behaves accordingly" (Rosenhan, 1973).

If you observed an acquaintance of yours acting strangely, how would you be affected by learning that the person had just been discharged from a mental hospital?

If abnormality is so hard to define, and if classification systems have so many weaknesses, and if labels can be so harmful, why do we bother trying to diagnose abnormality at all? Actually, there are several good reasons for continuing to categorize mental disorders. First, as we said before, some system of diagnosis seems to be necessary for communication between mental health professionals. And second, as a diagnostic system is perfected it will help to specify treatment, predict the course of disorders, and direct research efforts.

Any diagnostic scheme that does not view people holistically, however, is bound to be limited. The DSM has been criticized for being narrowly sexist (Gaines, 1992b; Gert, 1992; Rosser, 1992), anti-religious (Lukoff et al., 1992; Post, 1992), culturally biased (Nikelly, 1992), and slanted towards a medical interpretation of disorders (Schacht & Nathan, 1977; Szasz, 1974). As it has evolved, however, the DSM has taken steps to overcome these difficulties and achieve a more holistic view of abnormality.

In the long run, a theory of mental illness—or a set of diagnostic categories—stands or falls on its ability to help people get better. Thus, we cannot make a final evaluation of the DSM, or any other similar scheme, until we discover what kind of "cure rate" it gives us.

As we have said many times, all behavior is multi-determined. Human problems, like human successes, are almost always due to interactions of biological, psychological, and sociological forces. As we will see in the next chapter, the holistic approach to treating mental illness apparently produces the best record of patient improvement. And perhaps that is the strongest evidence we can offer in favor of viewing human beings as highly complex living systems.

SUMMARY

1. The study of **abnormal psychology** is controversial because "mental abnormalities" have been defined in many different ways.

2. One useful definition of mental disorders is that they are **harmful dysfunctions** of mental processes.

3. Although abnormal behavior is **statistically unusual,** not all unusual behavior is abnormal in the sense of being undesirable.

4. All definitions of abnormal are based on some concept of what is "healthy" or "normal" for a given person **in a given culture.**

5. Psychologists and other mental health professionals are concerned with abnormalities that have a **mental** basis. The mental basis of psychological disorders may involve **biological** or **social/environmental** factors.

6. Psychiatrists and psychologists use many different diagnostic systems to describe and interpret thoughts or actions that are presumed to be abnormal. The most popular systems are the **Diagnostic and Statistical Manual of Mental Disorders (DSM)** and the **International Classification of Disease and Related Health Problems (ICD).**

7. The main feature of **anxiety disorders** is the anxiety or personal distress they cause the sufferer.

8. There are several kinds of anxiety disorders, including **generalized anxiety disorder, panic disorders, phobic disorders, obsessive-compulsive disorders, and posttraumatic stress disorders.**

9. The main characteristic of anxiety disorders is the **personal distress** of their sufferers.

10. The **conversion disorders** and **hypochondriasis** are examples of **somatoform disorders.** Somatoform disorders involve physical complaints without an organic basis.

11. In the **dissociative disorders,** certain memories become inaccessible to consciousness. In **dissociative amnesia** the individual loses memory for certain events, facts, or people. In **dissociative fugue** the person forgets who he or she is and takes on a new identity. In **multiple personality disorders** one or more additional personalities "split off" and seem to take on a life of their own.

12. The two major types of mood disorders are **depressive disorders** and **bipolar disorders.** These disorders seem to result from a combination of biological, intrapsychic, and social/behavioral factors.

13. **Schizophrenia** typically involves disordered thinking, perception, emotions, relationship to the external world, and psychomotor behavior.

14. Different **classification systems for schizophrenia** have been proposed based on groups of symptoms, **positive** and **negative symptoms,** or the age when the disorder first occurs.

15. There is some evidence that the tendency to suffer schizophrenia is biological and may be partially **inherited.** But it must be **triggered** by stressful situations, especially those involving family relationships.

16. The **personality disorders** are long-standing patterns of maladaptive behavior.

17. The **antisocial personality disorder** includes impulsive behavior and an apparent lack of conscience. It is found primarily in men.

18. **Cross-cultural research** indicates the influence of culture on psychological abnormality and it helps to refine our understanding of important variables.

19. **Labeling** mental disorders can be **harmful**. Labels can lead us to expect and even create what the label stands for. Labels give the illusion of explaining when they only describe. And labels tend to "stick" beyond their usefulness.

ANSWERS FOR THOUGHT

1. *You have . . . does your answer to that question tell you about your own "theory of abnormality"?*

   Perhaps their emotions were absent or inappropriate—they were unusually happy, sad, or anxious; perhaps they harmed themselves or others; perhaps they responded inappropriately to their environment and other people. Personal theories of abnormality tend to rely on comparison with an internal standard of what's "normal" or "appropriate."

2. *How might the personality theory . . . affect your judgment . . . wrong with the person?*

   Psychodynamic theories look for personal distress and excessive use of defense mechanisms to deal with repressed conflict and trauma. Humanistic theories look for failure to fulfill one's potential as the result of a restrictive environment. Social learning theories look for maladaptive behavior produced by inappropriate modeling and self-defeating cognitions. Trait theories look for statistically abnormal stable methods of response as a result of inherited and acquired characteristics.

3. *Can you think of some reasons that some phobias are more common than others?*

   Besides the fact that some objects are simply more dangerous, here are some other factors which might determine the types of objects that can develop phobias: objects that are difficult to control (e.g., snakes, mice, cockroaches), objects whose occurrence is hard to predict (e.g., tornadoes, death), objects whose ultimate harm to us is unknown (e.g., exams, airplanes).

4. *Highly traumatized veterans of World War I often suffered from what was called "shell shock" . . . ?*

   The reactions of veterans seems to be related to their society's perception of the war in which they fought. In WWI "shell shock" and participation in war were probably more socially acceptable—even admirable. Society seems to have forced Vietnam veterans to feel ashamed of their experience, perhaps because society was not willing to accept responsibility for Vietnam veterans' suffering. If the Gulf war continues to be evaluated as successful and worthwhile by American society, PTSD will probably be minimized.

5. *What similarities do you see between patients with "multiple personalities" and the . . . ?*

   Both involve dissociation, or a division in consciousness; in both cases one part of consciousness may be aware of another without the other being aware of the first. Both may be "suggested" and therefore brought about by the circumstances.

6. *How would you relate Seligman's view of depression to the fact that twice as many women . . . ?*

   Perhaps women have been socialized to be more submissive and "helpless" than men. Another (unrelated) possibility is that women internalize their frustration and become depressed, whereas men externalize and act out their frustration in aggressive acts, alcoholism, and other destructive behaviors.

7. *What reasons can you think of to explain the dramatic rise in the suicide rate?*

Some reasons for increases in suicide could be rapid social, economic, political, and technological change; shifting values and ideologies; increased drug use.

8. *Many psychologists consider Adolf Hitler to be the "prototype" of someone with an anti-social personality disorder. What other political leaders . . . ?*

Some leaders who might have been diagnosed as having an antisocial personality disorder are Stalin, Idi Amin, Pol Pot, Pinochet, Saddam Hussein. . . . Their followers might be persuaded to see their deeds as necessary to bring in a "better order." Their followers might be ignorant of their leaders' deeds.

9. *If you observed an acquaintance of yours acting strangely, how would you be affected . . . ?*

If you assumed the person was normal you might say that their behavior was unusual, excusable, an exception, the result of fatigue or drugs, or that he or she was "temporarily out of form." However, if you had a label in mind such as "mentally ill" (even formerly mentally ill) you might see the behavior in a completely different way, as a symptom of "illness." (We will discuss this process of attribution of causes for behavior in Chapter 17.)

CHAPTER 16

THERAPY

" . . . Do you wish for instruction in the building up of the personality?"

"Yes, please."

"Then be so kind as to place a few dozen of your pieces at my disposal."

"My pieces—?"

"Of the pieces into which you saw your so-called personality broken up. I can't play without pieces."

He held up a glass to me and again I saw the unity of my personality broken up into many selves whose number seemed even to have increased. The pieces were now . . . very small, about the size of chessmen. The player took a dozen or so of them in his sure and quiet fingers and placed them on the ground near the board.

" . . . The separation of the unity of the personality into these numerous pieces passes for madness. Science has invented the name Schizomania for it. . . . We demonstrate to anyone whose soul has fallen to pieces that he can rearrange these pieces of a previous self in what order he pleases, and so attain to an endless multiplicity of moves in the game of life. As the playwright shapes a drama from a handful of characters, so do we from the pieces of the disintegrated self build up ever new groups, with ever new interplay and suspense, and new situations that are eternally inexhaustible. Look!"

HERMANN HESSE
STEPPENWOLF

PUTTING THE PIECES BACK TOGETHER

In Chapter 14 we examined different perspectives on how the "pieces" of personality fit together. In Chapter 15 we considered how these perspectives would explain "broken personalities," and we looked at some different types of "broken personalities." In this chapter we will consider how different therapeutic perspectives try to fit the pieces back together again. We will see that the type of help therapists offer depends on how the therapists view the "pieces."

Older Views

The Cree Eskimos and Ojibwa Indians of Canada occasionally suffer from a psychosis known as *witigo,* or devil-caused cannibalism. The first symptoms are usually a loss of appetite, vomiting, and diarrhea—as well as the person's morbid fear that she or he has been possessed by a *witigo,* or witch, who consumes human flesh. The affected individual becomes withdrawn, brooding, and cannot eat or sleep. The person's family, fearing for their very lives, immediately calls in a "witch doctor" to cast out the *witigo* by saying magic words or casting spells. If the family can't find a witch doctor in time, however, the *witigo*'s powers may overwhelm the affected individual and the person may kill and eat one or more members of the family (Goldenson, 1970).

In Malaysia, in Southeast Asia, young males occasionally suffer from a different type of possession, called running amok (which means "to engage furiously in battle"). At first the man becomes more withdrawn, depressed, and brooding than usual. Then he will suddenly leap to his feet with a blood-curdling scream, pull out a dagger, and begin stabbing anyone or anything in his path.

In other cultures and times, mentally disturbed individuals visited witch doctors, or perhaps tied a list of their problems to a tree and "left them behind."

"Therapy" for running amok usually consists of either killing the "amoker" before he can kill you, or keeping everyone out of the amoker's way until he kills himself. The few men who have survived this type of "seizure" have often said the world suddenly "turned black," and they had to slash their way out of the darkness with a knife (Gaw & Bernstein, 1992; Goldenson, 1970).

In Spain and Morocco, the name given to this form of mental disorder is *juramentado*, the Spanish word for "cursed person." In the United States, we sometimes call it *homicidal mania*. The DSM calls it "an explosive disorder of impulse control." It surely won't shock you to learn that this disorder is also correlated with depression and alcoholism (Virkkunen, 1986).

Why would the therapy you suggested for "running amok" vary according to the label you put on the problem?

Many Chinese believe that mental and physical disorders result from an imbalance of Yang and Yin, the masculine and feminine "powers" that control the entire spiritual universe. Chinese males occasionally suffer from an odd phobia called *koro*—a dismal fear that their penis is about to be sucked up into their stomach and disappear, causing death and other disappointments.

Victims believe *koro* is the result of a sudden upsurge in the strength of their Yin, or femininity. Thus, they can be cured by taking a "masculine" medicine containing a strong Yang factor, such as powdered rhinoceros horn. If this therapy fails, the man may use a special clasp that holds his penis out from his body mechanically.

On the Pacific island of Borneo, a similar disorder affects women who fear that their breasts and genitalia are being pulled up into their bodies. Therapy in Borneo often consists of asking a witch doctor to remove the curse, which presumably was laid on the woman by a "witch" jealous of the woman's physical beauty (Goldenson, 1970).

Several recent reports indicate that although it is most common in Asians, Americans, and Western Europeans also may experience *koro* (Chowdhury, 1989; de Leo, et al., 1989; Fishbain et al., 1989). Western clinicians would call *koro* "an acute anxiety or panic disorder." It may be associated with sexual conflicts, or even a schizophrenic disorder.

The belief that people who behaved abnormally were "possessed" led to abusive "cures." This "tranquilizing chair" was invented in the 1700s.

Modern Methods

Modern (Western) views of psychological disorders tend to deny the influence of outside spirits or unknown forces on our thoughts and behavior. These views assume that there are known (or knowable) physical, psychological, and social causes for our responses. And they believe that once we know the causes we can control the responses.

Earlier we discussed several modern views of the person under the headings of "psychodynamic," "humanistic," "social learning," and "trait" theories of personality. Now we will look at some therapies which grew out of these personality theories. First, we will consider biological therapies. (We did not discuss a biological theory of personality; although trait theories emphasize stable inherited characteristics, they do not advocate any particular therapy.) Next, we will look at intra-psychic therapies. (Psychodynamic, humanistic, and cognitive theories all lead to intra-psychic therapies.) Finally, we will discuss social/behavioral therapies. (Skinner's learning theory, from Chapter 9, and Bandura's social learning theory underlie many social/behavioral therapies.)

Thus, we will see that even in North America—where most people don't believe in witches, demons, and evil spirits—our therapies still stem from our theories of what causes human behavior. If we see a mental disorder as being due primarily to

Psychotherapy. A general term for all attempts by trained professionals to help relieve mental distress through conversation between therapist and client (or patient).

physical causes, we tend to treat the patient with physical measures, such as drugs, electric shock, and surgery. If we see a disorder as being due primarily to a conflict between ego and superego, we use psychoanalysis to help bring some rational resolution to the conflict. If we assume that deviant behavior is primarily the consequence of inappropriate rewards and punishments, we might prescribe behavior therapy or somehow attempt to alter the person's social environment.

In *The Encyclopedia of Psychology*, Frank Auld defines **psychotherapy** as "a procedure for treating psychological problems through psychological methods—that is, by a trained therapist's talking with a patient" (Auld, 1981). Thus, strictly speaking, biological treatments are not psychotherapy. However, because they deal with psychological problems, and because they are often used along with more psychological methods, we will consider them with the other therapies.

Evaluating Therapy

In this chapter we will discuss several special forms of treatment, and the theories that gave rise to them. But before we can evaluate the various forms of therapy, we must raise several pertinent issues:

1. How successful is the therapy? That is, what is its "cure rate"? Would the patient have recovered anyhow, even if we hadn't done anything? Would a "witch doctor," or someone using a different form of treatment, have done as well? In short, does the therapy make a *significant difference* in helping the patient? Is it a *valid* form of treatment?

2. Assuming the therapy does make a significant difference, how *reliable* is it? Does it work all the time, or just occasionally? Is it effective with all sorts of patients, or does it succeed better with some than with others?

3. What are the *side effects?* What else happens to the patient when we apply the treatment? Is the "cure" sometimes worse than the "disease"?

4. And cutting across all these issues is the basic question: "What do we mean by *cure?*" How shall we define "improvement"? Just as important, how shall we measure it?

We will have much more to say about these issues as we discuss the three main types of psychotherapy. We will also find it all too customary for therapists of opposing views to call each other "witch doctors," and to accuse each other of using "black magic" rather than "scientific magic."

BIOLOGICAL THERAPY

Lunatic asylums. In Europe during the Middle Ages, many people believed that insanity was caused by some influence the moon had on human behavior. *Luna* is the Latin word for "moon," thus mental illness came to be called "lunacy," and mentally ill individuals were called "lunatics."

When the "demon theory" was the accepted explanation of most mental disorders, the therapy of choice was *punishment.* The belief was that if you whipped a patient vigorously enough, you could "beat the devil" out of the person. The fact that some patients did improve after whippings was evidence enough to support the validity of the theory. It was not until scientific investigations suggested that the "cure rate" for unbeaten patients was higher than for those who were beaten that we finally hung up the whip. But some of the alternatives were not much better. Patients in **lunatic asylums** have been given cold baths, hot baths, they have been placed in uncomfortable restraining devices, and been spun around in circles until they lost consciousness. Whether our present forms of psychotherapy are all that much more effective, however, is a point much debated today in psychology and psychiatry (Garfield, 1983b).

As we suggested in the last chapter, some disorders do seem directly related to abnormalities in the central nervous system or to neurological imbalances. Perhaps for that reason, many of the therapies used to treat "organic" disorders are explicitly *biological*—the three main types being artificially induced *seizures*, *psychosurgery*, and *drugs*.

Convulsive Therapy

In 1935 a Hungarian psychiatrist named Ladislaus J. Meduna noted an odd fact: very few of the schizophrenic patients he worked with also suffered from epilepsy. Meduna concluded that seizures somehow *prevented* schizophrenia. If he could induce epileptic-type seizures in his schizophrenic patients, he reasoned, he might be able to cure them of their problems.

As a test, Meduna injected schizophrenic patients with drugs that caused seizures. Many patients did show some improvement, but the treatment severely injured or killed an alarming number of them. Other patients showed intense apprehension about the unpleasantness of the experience. Meduna abandoned the treatment as "barbaric," but the idea lived on (Breggin, 1979).

If therapy is extremely painful—be it whippings or convulsions—why might some patients show immediate improvement?

ELECTRO-CONVULSIVE THERAPY

In 1938 two Italian psychiatrists, Ugo Cerletti and L. Bini, began using electrical current rather than drugs to induce seizures. Today, if you suffered from severe depression, you might be given electro-convulsive therapy (ECT). A psychiatrist would probably apply it in the following way. The psychiatrist would administer (1) a muscle relaxant, (2) a drug to prevent you from choking and perhaps a rubber device to put in your mouth to keep you from biting your tongue, and (3) a fast-acting anesthetic to put you to sleep. Then, attendants would strap you to a padded bed in order to reduce the possibility of your breaking an arm or leg during the seizure.

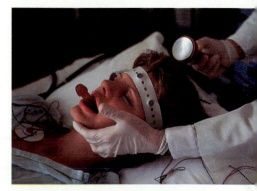

An anesthetized patient is given a short jolt of electric current from electrodes attached to the side of the skull. The patient will rest, and then probably go home, not remembering the treatment.

When you were unconscious (from the drug), the psychiatrist would apply electrodes to your head, and pass a brief but fairly strong electrical current directly through your brain. Your muscles would become rigid for about ten seconds. Then you would go into convulsions, but because of the muscle relaxant, these would be limited to twitching of your feet. The twitching would last for a minute or two, but you would remain unconscious for up to 30 minutes and would be drowsy or confused for many hours thereafter. Because seizures induce *retrograde amnesia*, you probably would not remember the shock or the events immediately preceding it. Typically, you would be given ECT three times a week for a period of a few weeks, or until you showed some recovery (Abrams & Essman, 1982).

Use of ECT reached a peak in the 1960s, then fell dramatically, only to rise again in recent years. In 1980, the National Institute of Mental Health reported that about 33,000 patients were given ECT. However, by 1985, the number had increased dramatically to more than 100,000. Most of these patients given ECT were in private, not public hospitals (Holden, 1985).

What social and financial factors might encourage the increased use of ECT?

EFFECTIVENESS OF ECT

There is considerable argument about the effectiveness of ECT. Many psychiatrists believe ECT can help with severely depressed patients. Evidence to support this view comes from many sources. In 1985, a panel assembled by the National Institutes of Health (NIH) gave "cautious endorsement" to the use of ECT—but only as short-term treatment with patients who suffer from *severe depression*. A few psychiatrists also believe ECT is effective with schizophrenic patients. According to the NIH report, however, the research data do not presently support use of electroshock treatment for any disorder other than depression (Holden, 1985). Perhaps this is not surprising, for Meduna based his original observations about schizophrenia and epilepsy on a mistaken idea. He apparently did not realize that hospital policy placed all patients with epilepsy *and* schizophrenia in a different ward from the one he was working on.

DANGERS OF ECT

There are many dangers associated with the use of ECT. To begin with, this type of treatment causes dramatic changes in the neurological and biochemical functioning of the brain. Thus, even when ECT *is* effective with depressed patients, we do not as yet know *why* the treatment works (Klerman, 1972, 1988).

There is also the question of side effects. A few patients do die as a result of treatment, but the death rate typically is well below 1 percent. As we mentioned, some patients given ECT report fairly severe memory problems. According to psychiatrist Larry Squire, most of this memory loss is temporary, and disappears after a few weeks (Squire, 1982). Other researchers, however, report a variety of cognitive deficits after ECT treatments (Figiel et al., 1992; Rosen et al., 1992; Steif et al., 1986).

Psychiatrist Peter Roger Breggin admits some depressed patients do show improvement after ECT. But he states that the effects of ECT on the brain are often "severe," "catastrophic," and "devastating." Breggin believes that most of the perceived benefits of ECT are due to the **placebo** effect. In fact, several studies show that patients who *thought* they were given convulsive therapy showed almost as much improvement as did patients who actually receive shock. Breggin notes as well that the "cure rate" for depression achieved by psychiatrists who refuse to administer ECT is as high as or higher than that among psychiatrists who use shock extensively (Breggin, 1979).

To summarize, ECT appears to be a fairly effective "treatment of last resort" with severely depressed patients for whom all other forms of therapy have failed. Since suicide is always a danger with severely depressed patients, many psychiatrists view ECT as a "lifesaver." However, there is at present no scientific evidence that ECT is of value with any other type of disorder.

Some patients request ECT, particularly after they have been performing badly for a period of time. How might Freud's notions about unconscious motivation explain the patients' request for ECT?

Psychosurgery

As you will remember from reading the early chapters of this book, the brain's *limbic system* controls many types of emotional responses. Emotional reactions also involve portions of the thalamus and the frontal lobes. In 1935, John Fulton and C. E. Jacobsen demonstrated that surgery on the prefrontal lobes had a calming effect on two chimpanzees they were working with. After learning of this research, a Portuguese psychiatrist named Egas Moniz decided that cutting the prefrontal lobes—an operation called a **lobotomy**—might help aggressive or hyper-emotional patients. In 1936 Moniz and his associates reported that lobotomy did seem to be effective with some of these patients (Valenstein, 1980). Moniz later received the Nobel Prize for his work.

Placebo. A harmless unmedicated treatment used for its psychological effect, often as a comparison with other treatments.

Lobotomy (loh-BOTT-toe-mee). A surgical technique involving cutting the nerve pathways that run to any one of the four cerebral lobes. Usually means "prefrontal lobotomy," or cutting the connections between the thalamus and the prefrontal lobes.

Walter Freeman and his colleagues introduced lobotomies to the United States in 1942. Before his retirement, Freeman performed more than 3,500 lobotomies. Other psychiatrists soon reported that cutting the *connections* between the lower brain centers and the prefrontal lobes seemed to work just as well as *removing* the prefrontal lobes.

The question is, of course, "Work as well as what?" Many lobotomy patients do show an improvement after the operation, but many do not. And the fatality rate from the operation may run as high as 4 percent. (We might note that the "fatality rate" must include Moniz himself, who was paralyzed after being shot by one of his lobotomy patients.)

Lobotomy is sometimes used as a treatment of last resort with patients suffering from severe attacks of *grand mal* epilepsy. There are, however, rather serious cognitive deficits associated with the operation. British psychiatrist Robin Jacobson found that, 10 years after psychosurgery, one patient had severe problems recognizing people's faces and had lost much of her "social self-control" (Jacobson, 1986). And Mayo Clinic researchers Robert Ivnik and his colleagues report that, while IQ tended to remain the same after lobotomy, patients whose left hemispheres were removed showed a significant decrease in language-dependent cognitive tasks (Ivnik et al., 1987). University of Michigan psychologist Elliot Valenstein points out well-controlled comparisons of patients given lobotomies and those given other forms of treatment suggest that the operation is neither effective nor reliable as a "cure" for any type of mental illness (Valenstein, 1986).

Today, psychosurgeons perform very limited operations in which they sever a few nerves in highly specific areas of the brain. Some types of psychosurgery can relieve symptoms of obsessive compulsive disorder, severe depression, or intractable pain (Poynton et al., 1988; Tippin & Henn, 1982). Side effects of these operations are rare, but since the operations are neither reversible nor 100 percent effective, psychosurgery is appropriate only as a last resort.

Why might many physicians be more interested in performing operations on patients with mental disorders than in giving the patients long-term psychotherapy?

Drug Therapy

There are a number of *psychoactive drugs*—that is, chemicals that have a psychological effect. We discussed many of them in Chapter 5. Among the most widely used psychoactive compounds are the major and minor tranquilizers and the antidepressants. The major tranquilizers are considered **antipsychotic drugs** because they relieve many psychotic symptoms. They are also sometimes called "neuroleptics" (a term derived from the Greek meaning "to clamp the neuron"). As we will see, many scientists today believe that the side effects of these drugs are worse than whatever benefits they may bring.

Antipsychotic drugs. Drugs which work to reduce the symptoms of severe psychological disorders (previously called "psychoses"). Most of these drugs reduce "positive" symptoms such as hallucinations, but they also have harmful side effects.

MAJOR TRANQUILIZERS AND SCHIZOPHRENIA

For many centuries medical practitioners in India have given tense or manic patients a drug made from the snake root plant because it seems to calm the patients down. We now call this drug *reserpine*. In 1953 the Indian physician R.A. Hakim reported that reserpine seemed to be effective with some schizophrenic patients. When Nathan Kline tried reserpine in the United States in 1954, he stated that it brought about marked improvement in 86 percent of the schizophrenic patients he tried it with (Breggin, 1983).

At about the same time, a French surgeon named Henri Laborit suggested that giving a powerful drug called *chlorpromazine* to schizophrenic patients might make

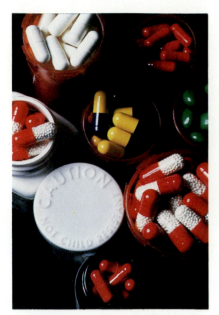

Many different kinds of drugs are prescribed in an effort to relieve psychological distress.

them more manageable. Research soon showed that the drug not only gradually calmed these patients down, but seemed to relieve some of their symptomatic behaviors as well.

Reserpine and chlorpromazine (tradename Thorazine) were the first of many tranquilizing *antipsychotic drugs* that became widely used with mental patients. Some others are haloperidol (Haldol) and the thioxanthenes (Mellaril and Taractan). As we saw in the last chapter, these drugs seem to work by reducing the potency of the neurotransmitter *dopamine* (Pickar et al., 1984). Patients with *positive* symptoms of schizophrenia, such as delusions, hallucinations, and hyperactivity, often find relief through these "dopamine inhibitors."

Recently, psychiatrists have been experimenting with a new type of antipsychotic drug called clozapine (tradename Clozaril). Clozapine can help to overcome some *negative* symptoms of schizophrenia (apathy, withdrawal, flattened emotions). Apparently clozapine does *not* work by inhibiting dopamine and thus it apparently does not produce the motor problems of some other antipsychotics (Coward, 1992). However, it can also make patients vulnerable to infection by impairing the immune system. Clozapine therapy is also very expensive.

MINOR TRANQUILIZERS AND ANXIETY

Drugs such as Valium and Librium are called "minor" tranquilizers because they have less dramatic effects on behavior and mental functioning than do the major tranquilizers. Psychiatrists often prescribe minor tranquilizers for the anxiety that accompanies the "anxiety disorders."

Valium and Librium may be among the most abused drugs in the United States today, in part because many patients seem to enjoy their effects. These drugs are obviously addictive. Recent studies suggest that they may cause birth defects if women take them during their pregnancy.

Some research suggests, however, that these dangers may be exaggerated. Robert Caplan and his colleagues report that long-term use of Valium apparently has little effect on the quality of life, on emotionality, job performance, stress, social support, coping, or physical health (Caplan et al., 1985). In a study of 600 patients, VA researcher J.C. Mason found that both the "addictive nature" and problems associated with withdrawal of the drug "have been previously overstated" (Mason, 1985).

ANTIDEPRESSANTS AND MOOD DISORDERS

Like the antipsychotic drugs, the antidepressants exert their effects *gradually*. Over a period of weeks they slowly lift the patient's mood and relieve the feelings of depression. Antidepressants affect the action of neurotransmitters (especially dopamine, norepinephrine, and serotonin) in the brain.

In the past, the most commonly prescribed antidepressant drugs were from the class known as tricyclics (e.g., Elavil and Tofranil) (Joyce & Paykel, 1989). Tricyclics are effective for 60 to 80 percent of depressed patients (Davis & Glassman, 1989). But tricyclics can produce disturbing side effects, including irregular heartbeat, blurred vision, and constipation.

Recently, psychiatrists report promising results from a newer drug called fluoxetine (tradename Prozac). Fluoxetine works quickly, with fewer and (for the most part) milder side effects than other antidepressants. For these reasons, fluoxetine is now the most widely prescribed antidepressant in the United States (Grilly, 1989). Fluoxetine has also been prescribed for eating disorders, obsessive compulsive disorders, and numerous other problems (Bulik et al., 1992; Burstein, 1992; Shay, 1992; Stein et al., 1992; Zetin & Kramer, 1992). But fluoxetine is not a "miracle drug"; possible side effects include seizures, bleeding, aggressive behavior, and suicidal thinking (Aranth & Lindberg, 1992; Hargrave & Bernstein, 1992; Jenike et al., 1990; Selzer, 1992).

Since the mid-1970s, patients displaying *bi-polar affective disorders* have used a drug called **lithium carbonate,** with varying degrees of success. Lithium carbonate can have a calming effect during manic episodes, although the biochemical basis for its effect is not known (Carlson, 1991). The drug does not help all manic patients though, and it has dangerous (even deadly) side effects (Breggin, 1983).

Besides its dangerous side effects, some people are reluctant to take lithium because it prevents them from feeling extremely *good* on occasion. However, for those people who are willing to take it under close medical supervision, lithium is often effective in controlling the extremes of bipolar affective disorders (Jefferson & Greist, 1989). There is also some evidence that lithium helps promote abstinence in some alcoholics (Fawcett et al., 1987).

Lithium carbonate. A drug which is very effective (for unknown reasons) in bringing under control the violent mood swings associated with bipolar disorders. Lithium takers must have their blood monitored, as excessive amounts of lithium can be fatal.

THE DRUG DILEMMA

The field of psychiatry faces rather a severe problem concerning the use of medication to treat mental disorders. On the one hand, antipsychotic drugs are apparently effective in helping more than 70 percent of those patients diagnosed as having schizophrenic disorders (Koob, 1984; Leff, 1992). On the other hand, some 60 percent of patients taking these drugs develop "motor side effects" or movement disorders (Ayd, 1983). These movement disorders often include loss of control of facial muscles, slow initiation of movements, and soft and monotonous speech—all of which can be confused with actual schizophrenic *symptoms* (Blanchard & Neale, 1992).

In addition, from 40 to 50 percent of those patients who take chlorpromazine and its related drugs on a chronic basis develop a Parkinson-like disorder called **tardive dyskinesia** (Coyle & Enna, 1983). *Tardive dyskinesia* typically involves uncontrollable movements of one kind or another, including eye blinks, shaky hands, and a peculiar way of walking. The disorder can sometimes involve breathing irregularities, particularly in elderly patients. Unfortunately, when it involves the respiratory tract, a small but significant number of the patients may die (Howell et al., 1986; Shah & Donald, 1986).

According to psychiatrist Ian Wilson, a significant number of patients who develop tardive dyskinesia suffer such severe brain damage that they lapse into a form of *senile dementia*. In this case, the "cure" for a mental disorder can *cause* a physical illness that is worse than the original problem (Wilson et al., 1983).

Tardive dyskinesia (TAR-dive dis-kin-KNEE-see-ah). A disfiguring disorder of motion control. Patients given psychoactive drugs often lose the ability to exercise normal voluntary control over certain muscles, especially facial muscles.

About 2 percent of the patients given antipsychotic drugs develop a condition called *neuroleptic malignancy syndrome*, or NMS, which can involve fever, elevated blood pressure, kidney failure, brain damage, and coma. About 20 percent of the patients who suffer from NMS die from the condition (Hermesh et al., 1992; Pope et al., 1986).

Drug therapy has serious risks. Psychiatrist Peter Breggin puts the matter this way: "Psychiatrists simply cannot admit that they have effectively 'lobotomized' millions of patients with chemicals that are toxic to the brain" (Breggin, 1983). Phil Brown and Steven Funk echo Breggin's sentiments. They believe that psychiatrists are "resisting the truth" about the dangers associated with psychoactive drugs. Brown and Funk state that the problem is due to "sociomedical" factors, not to a lack of understanding of the "biomedical" data (Brown & Funk, 1986).

Fortunately, as we will see, there is also a growing recognition that psychotherapy and behavioral treatment can often achieve the same results as do the psychoactive drugs—and with significantly smaller risks.

Abraham Maslow once said, "If the only tool you have is a hammer, you tend to see every problem as a nail." How might Maslow's words be applied to the use of psychoactive drugs?

DRUGS ALONE DON'T "CURE"

Scarcely a month goes by that the popular press doesn't serve up a juicy story about some new drug that seems to offer "miracle cures" for many types of psychological problems. Most of the reports need to be taken with a grain of salt, however.

First, chemicals *by themselves* seldom solve mental, social, or behavioral problems. They do not teach people to cope with their circumstances, they do not change cognitive habits, and they do not change environmental stressors. Even if the drug "cures" some underlying biological dysfunction, the patient will still need psychological and social help in adjusting to life. Thus, drug therapy is at best no more than the *first step* in treating mental disorders.

Second, not all of the drug research reported in the popular press has been as well planned and nicely controlled as we might wish. In particular, many drug studies have not been **double blind.** Thus the results reported may well be due to placebo effects.

Double blind. A method of testing a drug in which neither the person administering the drug nor the person receiving the drug knows whether the drug is a placebo or the real thing.

Consider the case of psychiatrist Werner Mendel. As part of his training, Mendel served a psychiatric residency at St. Elizabeth's Hospital in Washington, DC. At the time, this institution was the largest of all the U.S. government facilities dealing with psychiatric patients. When Mendel arrived at St. E's, he was put in charge of a ward of Spanish-speaking patients, most of whom came from Puerto Rico or the Virgin Islands. All of these patients were diagnosed as being hostile, aggressive individuals. Many were considered so dangerous to themselves and others that they were confined to "padded cells" or were kept in straight-jackets. Mendel says he usually took two attendants along with him whenever he visited the wards. And because the patients spoke little or no English, and Mendel spoke no Spanish, there was little he could do in the way of treatment.

Fortunately, it was just at this time that news of the apparent effectiveness of reserpine spread to the United States. The authorities at St. E's decided to test the drug. To make the test scientifically valid, they used the *double blind method*. That is, they selected certain wards whose patients would be given reserpine. But they also needed some *comparison groups* to make sure that the changes they noted in the patients given reserpine (the "experimental groups") were due to the drug and not just to the fact that the patients had been given pills. So the researchers selected an equal number of wards whose patients were given "sugar pills" rather than reserpine (the "control groups"). The pills looked the same no matter what was in them. The experiment was "double blind" because neither the patients nor the doctors in charge of the wards knew which drug the patients on any particular ward were actually receiving.

The experiment ran for several months, during which the researchers recorded, as carefully as possible, any improvement in the patients. Mendel's ward of Spanish-speaking patients was one of those chosen for the experiment. Mendel reports that, almost as soon as the study began, his patients calmed down dramatically. Within a short period of time they were so tranquil that many of them could be released from restraint. Mendel was convinced that a psychiatric revolution had begun.

Then the experiment ended and the results were announced. To Mendel's amazement, he learned his ward had been one of the "controls." All of his patients had received *placebos* instead of reserpine. Yet they had shown marked improvement! It occurred to Mendel that, when the experiment began, he unconsciously changed his attitude toward the patients. Convinced they were becoming more peaceful, he then treated them as if they were improving. And they did improve—not because of the drug but because of the way in which he responded to them (Mendel, 1966, 1969).

The St. Elizabeth's experiment points up one dramatic difficulty in evaluating any psychiatric research: The good results that an experimenter obtains may be due to *chance factors*, or to factors the scientist *failed to control*. Patients always take drugs in a social setting. The patient's attitude, and the doctor's, may be more influential than the chemical's effects on the patient's body. Likewise, if a surgeon communicates to the patient the belief that psychosurgery will surely solve the person's problems, the patient may very well get better after the operation—for all the "wrong" reasons (Kline & Angst, 1979).

Evaluating Biological Therapies

What goes on in your body surely affects what goes on in your mind, and vice versa. *Some* types of biological therapies will surely help *some* types of patients suffering from *some* kinds of mental disorders. Thus, we should use biotherapies when the data strongly suggest they are valid and reliable forms of treatment. Drug therapy can also calm hospitalized patients, and even allow their return to the community. However, unless we also deal with other problems in our patients' lives, we may be doing little more than using biotherapies as a modern "straight-jacket" to make our patients easier to handle. Research indicates that we have not yet discovered any "magic pill" that will *cure* most types of psychosocial abnormalities.

With that sobering thought in mind, let's look at other types of treatment, for most supporters of drug therapy recognize that it is more effective when combined with additional help.

We are not ourselves
When nature, being oppress'd, commands the mind
To suffer with the body.

SHAKESPEARE (*KING LEAR*)

INTRA-PSYCHIC THERAPY

Most personality theorists believe that abnormal thoughts and behaviors are mere symptoms of an underlying dysfunction in an individual's basic personality. To "cure" the symptom without handling the underlying problem would, therefore, be as senseless as giving aspirin to a patient suffering from yellow fever. The drug might decrease the fever symptom, it is true. But aspirin wouldn't kill the virus that is really responsible for the disease. Removing the fever with aspirin might delude patients into thinking they had been "cured" when, in fact, the patients might still be carrying the virus. A "deeper" form of therapy is necessary to kill the virus. In a similar fashion, using drugs to control psychological symptoms does not solve the problem. From the intra-psychic perspective, symptoms are only signs of an underlying

Be transformed by the renewing of your mind.

BIBLE (ROM. 12:2)

psychological disturbance. The personality, not behavior, needs treatment; the symptomatic behaviors will disappear naturally as the cure progresses.

If you ever have need for intra-psychic therapy, you would seem to have your choice between two major types: (1) those methods that are primarily designed to help you understand your present self by giving you *insight* into what has gone wrong in your past; and (2) those techniques that focus on future goals in order to help you change your present mode of existence. (In fact, the difference between the two types may be more a matter of emphasis than anything else. Highly successful therapists appear to treat their patients in similar ways despite the fact that their theories may be quite different.)

Most *psychodynamic* approaches, such as we saw in Chapter 14, follow the first method. That is, they concentrate on discovering traumas that occurred during psychosexual development in order to help patients set their "mental and emotional houses" in order. Psychoanalytic theory suggests that if you complete your analysis and gain insight into your problems, you should experience a full recovery. As we noted in Chapter 15, this type of treatment follows from what is called the *medical model of mental illness*.

The *humanistic* psychologists, on the other hand, mostly follow the second method. They hope to make you aware both of your present condition and of your ultimate goals, so you can shorten the distance between the two and hence move toward self-actualization.

The *cognitive* approaches also focus on goals. Their method, however, is to break long-term goals down into smaller steps along the way. They then work to change your habitual thought patterns which are preventing you from changing in the way you would like.

Psychoanalytic Therapy

There is no single accepted and approved method of psychoanalytic treatment—it varies widely according to the patient's needs and the analyst's skills and beliefs. Freud compared analysis to a chess game in which only the opening moves could be standardized. Thereafter, he said, endless variations may develop (Freud, 1913/1958). Furthermore, in addition to "classic" Freudian analysis, there are a number of newer, briefer types of analytic treatment. Since most of the more modern approaches are extensions of Freud's original techniques, however, we will focus on Freud's methods.

Imagine you are in therapy with Freud. You would spend much of your time "free associating," and talking about your dreams. In **free association** one thought leads to another, and Freud would ask you to say *whatever* came to mind, regardless of how foolish, embarassing, or insignificant it seemed. For his part, Freud would *interpret* everything you said. He would look for the *underlying* meaning of your dreams. He would *analyze* your free associations, looking for pauses, and links between your thoughts. Freud believed that his interpretations gave his patients *insight* into their unconscious drives, wishes, and fears. (If you did not agree with Freud's interpretation, you were showing *resistance*.)

But interpretation and insight are only the "cognitive" parts of psychoanalysis. For insight to be effective in changing personality it must also include the release of pent-up emotions. Your problems, Freud believed, were caused by repressing thoughts and feeling in your unconscious mind because you were afraid of them. You need to become *aware* of these threatening thoughts and emotions, and you need to *express* them—a process called **catharsis.**

Catharsis is made easier in psychoanalysis by the strong emotional relationship you would build up with Freud over the course of many months and years of treatment. During this period Freud would become the object of many of the strong emotions you originally felt toward your parents and other significant people in your life.

Traditionally, psychoanalytic patients reclined on a couch while the therapist sat behind them out of view. Today, most intra-psychic therapy takes the form of a face-to-face conversation.

Free association. A psychoanalytic technique whereby the patient says whatever comes to mind in a kind of "verbal stream of consciousness." It is intended to display thought processes so that the analyst can uncover underlying conflicts and other repressed material.

Catharsis (kath-AR-sis). The relieving of repressed emotions by bringing them to consciousness and giving them expression.

As therapy progressed you would begin to *transfer,* or redirect, these feelings to Freud. The process of **transference** would enable you to express the feelings you have and gain further insight into yourself.

Freud viewed psychoanalysis as a way to bring about a basic reconstruction of your personality. As you become aware of troublesome unconscious processes and give vent to them, you defuse their disruptive influence, and you can begin the process of integrating these experiences into your conscious ego. In this way you strengthen your ego and give it greater power over your id. In Freud's words, successful therapy means, "Where id was, there ego shall be."

But the task is not an easy one. Psychoanalysis typically takes from 2 to 5 years of 50-minute-long therapy sessions, 3 to 5 times a week. Costs for a complete analysis typically run from $30,000 to $50,000 (or more). Although psychoanalysts occasionally treat individuals with severe disturbances, most of their patients suffer from milder disorders. The most successful patients seem to be between 15 and 50 years of age. They are bright, verbal, self-motivated, and willing to cooperate with the therapist.

Psychoanalysis takes so long, and there are so few analysts available, that only a tiny fraction of the people who need help ever undergo this process. Most patients settle for briefer, less intensive (and less expensive) types of treatment.

Psychoanalytic theory has influenced almost all other forms of intra-psychic therapy. Any type of treatment that concentrates on explaining the present in terms of past experience and unconscious motivations owes a large debt to Sigmund Freud.

Humanistic Therapy

Freud grew up in Austria, a land of kings and emperors who possessed "divine rights" their subjects dared not question. Austrian fathers typically claimed the same privileges—when the man of the family spoke, the children listened and obeyed. Perhaps it is understandable, then, that in psychoanalysis the "parental" analyst often sets the goals of therapy and urges the patient onward.

Humanistic psychology developed in egalitarian American society. Modern humanistic psychologists reject the "divine right" of the therapist to determine what is mentally healthy for the patient. In humanistic therapy, the patient rather than the therapist is king.

Humanistic psychologists like Carl Rogers and Abraham Maslow emphasize the *conscious* determinants of behavior. They presume all human beings have a positive drive toward good mental health. The therapist's role is merely to establish the conditions—the environment—for growth. Given a healthful environment, the client will naturally grow into a "self-actualizing" or "fully functioning" person.

CLIENT-CENTERED THERAPY

According to Christopher Monte, "The client who faces Rogers in therapy finds himself confronted with a warm, evenhanded, non-evaluative person sincerely attempting to understand his client's meanings. Perhaps for the first time in his or her life, a Rogerian client discovers that in the presence of another human being, he or she is fully free to be" (Monte, 1991).

In 1942, Rogers listed four important principles of "client-centered therapy":

1. "Therapy is not a matter of doing something *to* the individual, or of inducing him to do something about himself. It is instead a matter of freeing him for normal growth and development."

2. In client-centered therapy there is a "greater stress upon the emotional elements, the feeling aspects of the situation, than upon the intellectual aspects."

Transference. In psychoanalysis, the process of directing towards the analyst the feelings one has towards other significant people in ones life—usually one's father or mother. Expressing these feelings helps to release pent-up emotional energy and also provides the analyst with insight into the patient's relationships.

"I am *not* criticizing you. *My* therapist has told me that my technique is perfectly acceptable."

The art of medicine consists of amusing the patient while nature cures the disease.

VOLTAIRE

Carl Rogers attempted to provide a warm, accepting atmosphere where his clients could truly be themselves. He believed this unconditional acceptance and positive regard would release natural processes of growth within the clients.

3. There is a "greater stress upon the immediate situation than upon the individual's past."

4. There is "great stress upon the therapeutic relationship itself as a growth experience" (Rogers, 1942).

In 1951, Rogers added a fifth principle: "The client . . . is one who comes actively and voluntarily to gain help on a problem, but without any notion of surrendering his own responsibility for the situation" (Rogers, 1951).

As we noted in Chapter 14, one of the major aspects of Rogerian non-directive therapy is that the therapist must give the client *unconditional positive regard*.

HALLMARKS OF SUCCESSFUL TREATMENT

According to Rogers, the client who undergoes successful therapy shows three major characteristics:

First, the client is now a *fully functioning individual,* by which Rogers meant that the person is "fully open to experience." The person no longer feels the need to distort reality or repress his or her feelings.

Second, the person now has the ability to *live in an existential fashion.* The person realizes that "What I will be in the next moment, and what I will do, grows out of that moment, and cannot be predicted in advance either by me or others" (Rogers, 1964).

Third, people who are fully functioning have an "increased trust in their own organisms." That is, they feel free to do whatever "feels right" at any point in time, because they know they are competent to meet any challenge (Monte, 1991).

WAS ROGERS A ROGERIAN?

Most of the people practicing intra-psychic therapy in the United States today are neither "pure" Freudians, "pure" humanistic psychologists, nor "pure" followers of any other theory. Rather, therapists tend to be *eclectic*—they make use of whatever psychological techniques seem to work best for them and their clients. And they may do so almost without realizing it.

As we noted in Chapter 14, Rogers apparently rejected any form of "therapist control" because he felt that his own parents were too manipulative. And, in particular, Rogers was dismayed by behavior therapy, in which the therapist deliberately "shapes" the thoughts and behaviors of the client. Rogers and B.F. Skinner debated this issue on many occasions. Oddly enough, during these famous debates, Skinner seldom bothered to reinforce Rogers in any fashion, and Rogers surely showed Skinner less than "unconditional positive regard" (McConnell, 1985).

As far as therapy goes, there is some question as to just how "non-directive" Rogers really was. For example, C.B. Truax studied tapes and movies made of Rogers and other Rogerians as they actually performed therapy. Far from providing his patients with "unconditional positive regard," Truax says, Rogers was unconsciously "shaping" his patients by rewarding "healthy self-statements" with head nods and smiles. Rogers also tended to ignore any "unhealthy statements" the patient made (Truax, 1968). And after analyzing several interview tapes, therapist James Carnevale concludes, "Even Carl Rogers, the epitome of client-centered counseling, trained his clients to be client-centered clients." He adds, "Dr. Rogers may have been an unobtrusive teacher, but he certainly taught his clients to be *his* clients" (Carnevale, 1989).

We will have more to say about unconscious "shaping" later in this chapter. For the moment, we need only note that even Carl Rogers was perhaps a bit more eclectic, and perhaps even a bit more directive, than he intended to be.

TRANSACTIONAL ANALYSIS AND GESTALT THERAPY

Both Gestalt therapy and transactional analysis were developed by former psychoanalysts with strong humanistic leanings. Since both types of treatment are somewhat more likely to be used with groups than with individuals, we will postpone discussing them until later in this chapter.

Cognitive Therapy

Cognitive therapists believe that cognitions are the major cause of behavior and emotions. If behaviors or emotions are abnormal, it is the result of "irrational," "distorted," or "dysfunctional" thoughts and beliefs (Bandura, 1984; Ellis, 1962; Mahoney, 1974; Meichenbaum, 1977).

If you went to a cognitive therapist, the therapist would first help you to become aware of the beliefs and "self-talk" which are disturbing your behavior and emotions. Next, the therapist would point out the irrational or unproductive nature of your beliefs, and help you to think about yourself more realistically and optimistically.

For example, some people tend to believe, "Unhappiness is a function of events outside the control of the individual." A cognitive therapist (using Albert Ellis's "Rational Emotive Therapy"), might point out that this is an irrational and self-limiting belief. The therapist might teach the client to think along the following lines:

> "Actually most outside events that we perceive as harmful are only psychologically harmful; we cannot be hurt unless we allow ourselves to be affected by our attitudes and reactions. A person disturbs himself by telling himself how horrible it is when someone is unkind, rejecting, or annoying. If he realized that disturbances consist of his own perceptions and internalized verbalizations, he could control or change these disturbances" (George & Cristiani, 1990).

One of the best-known applications of cognitive therapy is Aaron Beck's work with depressed individuals (Beck, 1976; Hollon & Beck, 1979). Beck's approach is less confrontative than Ellis's. Beck tries to get his patients to discover for themselves that their discouraging beliefs are not accurate. For example, he may ask a patient to record for one week every time something good happens to the patient. The patient will then discover for *himself* or *herself* that life is not all negative and

No object is mysterious. The mystery is your eye.

ELIZABETH BOWEN

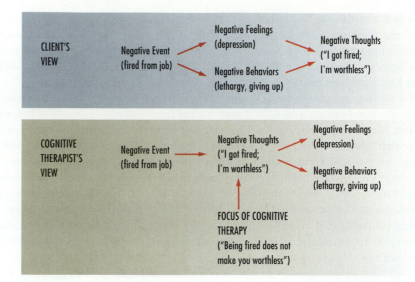

FIGURE 16.1

Cognitive therapy shows clients that their thoughts control their feelings and behaviors, and that they can gain control over their thoughts.

bleak. Beck may also help the patient to see that a negative conclusion ("I am worthless") does not logically follow from negative events ("I was fired") see Figure 16.1.

Cognitive therapy has been adapted to treat depression, anxiety, fears, stress, and many other problems (Brammer et al., 1989). By helping clients change the way they think about their experiences, cognitive therapy changes the way they feel and behave.

In Figure 16.1, illustrating cognitive therapy, which view best represents the biological therapists' perspective, and where do they focus their efforts for change?

Evaluating Intra-Psychic Therapy

Does intra-psychic therapy work? As you can imagine, personality theorist Hans Eysenck stirred up tremendous controversy when he said the answer to this question was "No."

As we noted in Chapter 14, immediately after World War II, Eysenck investigated several thousand cases of mental patients in a British hospital. Eysenck reported in 1952 that the overall improvement rate among those patients given psychoanalytic treatment was about 44 percent. The improvement rate for patients given any other form of psychotherapy was about 64 percent. Several hundred other patients received no psychotherapy at all. Their physical ailments were treated as necessary, but they were given no psychological therapy. The improvement rate among these untreated patients, Eysenck claimed, was about 72 percent. These data led some scientists to compare psychoanalysis with "witch doctoring," and to suggest that psychoanalysis might actually retard the patient's progress (Eysenck, 1952).

Eysenck's research provoked a storm of protest, and several weaknesses in his study were identified. It now seems that the rate of **spontaneous recovery** is closer to 40 or 50 percent than the 72 percent figure Eysenck reported (Garfield, 1983b). And the relative effectiveness of psychoanalysis is still hotly debated.

Eysenck's study, and the research it stimulated, helped us realize some of the problems involved in making a scientific assessment of psychotherapy. For one thing, science deals with objective events, things that can readily be measured. But by its very nature, therapy, especially intra-psychic therapy, concerns itself with personality changes (and other variables) that seldom can be viewed in detail or measured precisely. Thus, we must always consider the success rates of various forms of treatment in terms of *the results both clients and therapists hope to achieve*.

Spontaneous recovery. Any "cure" or improvement due to natural circumstances, and hence not due to therapeutic intervention. Research suggests that 40 to 50 percent of people who experience mental problems will recover "spontaneously" in a year or so, even if not given treatment.

Some psychiatrists see therapy as an "art form," thus something that *cannot* be measured objectively (Friedlander, 1992). One such person is Jerome Frank, who compares therapy to music. "To try to determine by scientific analysis how much better or worse . . . Gestalt therapy is than Transactional Analysis, is in many ways equivalent to attempting to determine by the same means the relative merits of the music of Cole Porter and Richard Rodgers. To ask the question is to reveal its absurdity" (Frank, 1973).

Although Frank's viewpoint has its merits, other psychiatrists are willing to use less subjective measures of improvement—such as modifications in the patient's overt behavior and the gradual disappearance of neurotic or psychotic symptoms. At least these changes can be observed and agreed upon by people other than the therapist.

Psychologist Sol Garfield has written extensively on the effectiveness of psychotherapy (Garfield, 1983a, 1983b, 1987). In one article, Garfield discusses one of the most widely publicized studies on *psychoanalytic* treatment, which was performed at the Menninger Foundation. The Menninger experiment involved 21 patients given psychoanalysis and 21 given analytically oriented "insight" therapy. Researchers followed both sets of patients for many years. Garfield concludes:

> "My understanding or interpretation of this material is that 6 patients were judged to be worse at the end of therapy, 11 were unchanged, 7 showed slight improvement, and 18 (or 43 percent) showed moderate or marked improvement. If one takes my interpretation as provisionally valid, the results cannot be viewed as a very convincing demonstration of the efficacy of psychotherapy—particularly when the therapy is so expensive and time-consuming" (Garfield, 1981).

In a "final summing up" of the Menninger project, psychiatrist Robert Wallerstein notes that giving patients "insight" into their problems probably was *less effective* than was "supporting their attempts to solve their own problems." Wallerstein suggests that psychoanalysis should primarily be used with "less disturbed" patients (Wallerstein, 1988).

In 1980, the National Institute of Mental Health (NIMH) began a long-term study of the effects of several types of psychotherapy on the treatment of depression. In 1985, Irene Elkin and her colleagues reported the first results, with more thorough analyses reported in 1989 (Elkin et al., 1985, 1989).

Elkin and her group studied 239 moderately to severely depressed patients at three noted medical centers: George Washington University, the University of Oklahoma, and the University of Pittsburgh. The researchers divided the patients into four groups. They arranged for therapists to give one group an antidepressant drug; a second group a "pill placebo"; a third group Beck's "cognitive behavior therapy"; and the fourth group "interpersonal therapy." Therapists administered treatment over a 16-week period.

As we noted earlier, cognitive therapy attempts to correct distorted thinking and the patients' negative views of themselves (Beck & Emery, 1985). Interpersonal therapy, Elkin says, tries to help patients develop better ways of relating to members of their families, friends, and co-workers in job-related situations.

Patients in the two drug-related groups were treated by psychiatrists. Patients in the two psychotherapy groups were treated by 18 psychotherapists, all of whom received special training in the type of treatment they were to use. Judgments of improvement were made by the patients themselves, by their therapists, and by independent clinicians (Elkin et al., 1985, 1989).

Elkin reports that about 29 percent of the patients given pill placebos "recovered with no serious symptoms after 16 weeks." In contrast, the "cure rate" in the three treatment groups was greater than 50 percent. Thus, "real" therapy was significantly better than was pill "placebo" treatment.

There were, however, other differences between the groups. Elkin notes that the least-depressed patients "did surprisingly well" in the pill placebo group. Severely depressed patients, however, did not respond at all well to the placebo, but did respond well both to the antidepressant and to interpersonal therapy. Married patients with lengthy histories of *moderate* depression did best when given cognitive behavioral treatment, but the antidepressant worked best with married patients with *severe* depression.

As you might imagine, some therapists seemed to have significantly higher "cure rates" than did others. Overall, however, *psychotherapy* was as effective in treating all but the most severe forms of depression as was *drug therapy* (Elkin et al., 1985, 1989).

Does intra-psychic therapy work? Apparently, yes. But we must always weigh its effectiveness, and the effectiveness of any therapy, against the rate of spontaneous recovery. And we must be aware of important differences which exist in the way effectiveness is defined.

In psychoanalysis, the *therapist* usually decides whether or not a "cure" has taken place. But in the humanistic therapies, the *client* usually determines whether the therapy was successful or not. Rogers does have objective tests that measure changes in the client's *perceptions* of his or her progress, and the tests do seem to be reliable. Whether or not "perceptual changes" should be the major goal of therapy, however, is an open question. Cognitive therapists also attempt to be objective in their measurement of change. But as long as the focus of attention is on intra-psychic events—whether insight, perceptions, or cognitions—problems in objectivity will remain.

We will have more to say about the effectiveness of psychotherapy later in this chapter. First, let's look at the third major type of treatment, *social/behavioral therapy*.

Why would it be more difficult to prove that therapy "works" using objective criteria than if you merely measured the subjective opinions of the clients and therapists?

SOCIAL/BEHAVIORAL THERAPY

Up until fairly recently, most of our laws, customs, and philosophies have been based on the assumption that psychological problems existed *within* an individual. When factors *outside* the individual contributed to "mental disorders," these factors were presumed to be primarily supernatural—gods, witches, and evil spirits. Most forms of biological and intra-psychic therapy can be seen as attempts to treat the patient by working *from the inside out*.

Within the last century, rather a different point of view has emerged—a belief that "mental illness" is as much a disruption of relationships *between* people as it is a disruption of one person's inner personality. Abnormal behavior is almost always expressed in social situations. We send "crazy people" to hospitals or to see a therapist usually because they disturb or upset *others*.

From a social/behavioral point of view, the goal of treatment is not merely altering the function of the patient's body or brain. Nor is the goal just to change the patient's personality. Rather, the purpose of treatment is that of helping the patient *get along better with others*. Indeed, in many instances, the group of people around the patient may actually be contributing to the "craziness" without realizing it. In such cases, the best form of therapy may be removing the person from that environment—or somehow getting other people to behave differently toward the patient. It also helps the patient get along better in interpersonal and job situations if he or she learns *social* and *job-related skills*. This type of treatment obviously works *from the outside in*.

The three major types of social/behavioral treatment are (1) group therapy, in which the patient learns better ways of responding and gains support from being with

From a social/behavioral point of view, mental disorders involve disturbed relationships with other people, and changing these relationships may be a necessary part of overcoming the problem.

a group of people who often have similar problems; (2) environmental therapy, in which the patient's social environment or **milieu** becomes the focus for treatment; and (3) behavioral therapy, including situations where patients are rewarded for getting better.

Milieu. The context or surroundings; the immediate environment.

Group Therapy

The therapeutic potential of groups first gained scientific notice in 1905, when a Boston physician named J. H. Pratt made a fortunate mistake. Pratt found that patients suffering from tuberculosis were often discouraged and depressed. He first believed their despondency was due to ignorance on their part—they simply didn't know enough about the disease they suffered from. So he brought them together in groups to give them lectures about "healthy living." The lectures soon turned into very intense discussions among the patients about their problems. It is to Pratt's credit that he recognized his patients gained more strength from learning they were not alone in their suffering than they did from his lectures (Scheidlinger, 1982).

Group therapy did not really catch on, however, until World War II produced more psychological casualties than the relatively expensive and time-consuming therapies of the day could handle. It wasn't long until groups developed around nearly every type of psychotherapy (Yalom, 1985). Today, new types of groups continue to form.

Some of the more familiar group therapies are:

1. *Gestalt therapy*. Gestalt therapy is based on the belief that people should "take responsibility for themselves," and should "focus attention primarily on the here and now" (Perls et al., 1951). Therapists encourage participants to express and act out their current feelings.

2. *Transactional analysis*. Transactional analysis (TA), is based on the idea that we tend to interact in certain stereotyped ways, depending on whether a "child," "adult," or "parent" ego-state is in control. Therapy involves using role-playing to learn to interact in a rational "adult" way (Berne, 1958, 1964).

3. *Encounter groups*. The general goal of encounter groups is to bring feelings out into the open, and to learn more honest ways of communicating with each other. Beyond this, encounter groups vary tremendously. As a vehicle for self-discovery,

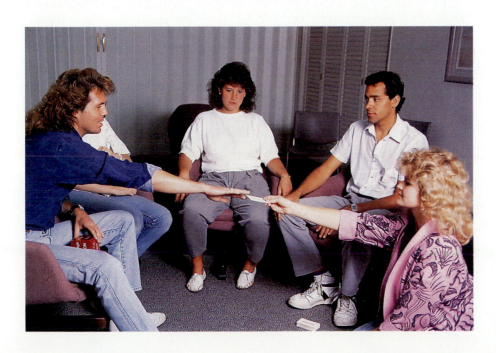

There are many different kinds of group therapy. Groups such as this one often provide opportunities for members to role play problem situations.

Psychodrama. A form of therapy in which some part of the patient's life is acted out on stage. The patient may play one of the roles, or may simply observe. The therapist usually serves as the director.

some groups use acting **(psychodrama),** some use childish games ("play therapy"), and some even meet in the nude (Yalom, 1983).

4. *Stress debriefing groups.* Recently, group processes have been found to be helpful in avoiding and overcoming post-traumatic stress disorders. Not only combat veterans, but also victims of mass disasters, rescue personnel, and victims of crime benefit from stress debriefing in a group setting (Hartsough & Myers, 1985; Makler et al., 1990).

5. *Self-help groups.* Many modern groups are simply specialized "self-help" meetings, organized by concerned lay-people with a common problem. They may follow a structured format, such as that used by Alcoholics Anonymous, or they may be more free-wheeling social interactions. Self-help groups provide support and advice in areas such as illnesses, substance abuse, and interpersonal problems, as well as psychological disturbances. Some examples are Alcoholics Anonymous (AA), Alateen, Weight Watchers, and Eaters Anonymous. There are over 500,000 self-help groups in the United States (Gartner & Riessman, 1984).

As you can see, these various forms of group treatment differ considerably among themselves. Rickey George and Therese Cristiani identify the following advantages *common* to different types of group therapy:

1. Group therapy is efficient. Counselors can provide services to many more clients.

2. Group counseling provides a social interpersonal context in which to work on interpersonal problems.

3. Clients have the opportunity to practice new behaviors.

4. It enables clients to put their problems in perspective and to understand how they are similar to and different from others.

5. Clients form a support system for each other.

6. Clients learn interpersonal communication skills.

7. Clients are given the opportunity to give as well as to receive (George & Christiani, 1990).

Group therapy obviously has some advantages. However, there are also certain disadvantages associated with this type of treatment. Beyond merely being ineffective, group processes can sometimes be so stressful as to be harmful, particularly for seriously disturbed individuals (Finkelstein et al., 1982).

We will evaluate group therapies more thoroughly in a moment. However, there is one type of group therapy which deserves further attention because of the special relationship the group members bear to one another. This type of group therapy is *family* therapy.

FAMILY THERAPY

In group psychotherapy, a number of people with no prior relationships get together to work out their individual difficulties in the presence (and with the support) of others. Unlike most other forms of group treatment, however, in *family therapy* the "group" has been in existence for some time. Rather than focusing on individuals, the family therapist strives to change the functioning or the structure of the *family itself* (Green & Framo, 1981).

Family therapy grew out of "systems theory," which views the family as a *social system*. Almost any difficulty an individual member of the family has is thought to result from a "faulty system" rather than from "individual deficits." For example, if the teenaged daughter in a family is bulimic, her eating disorder is viewed as a family problem, not a difficulty that somehow exists within the young woman's mind or personality. Perhaps the mother is "over controlling," or the father is "withdrawn and punitive," or other children are "too competitive" for the parents' attention and

In family therapy the problems of the individuals are seen as part of the social system of the family. The therapy's goal is to improve the functioning of that system so that the individuals can also function better. This therapist uses props, such as a stuffed bear and a magic wand, to represent problems and solutions.

affection. The "cure," therefore, must come in a change in the relationships between the girl and all other members of the family (Berger et al., 1984).

Family therapy can be helpful for many types of families, including those with retarded adolescents, married couples with sexual problems, and families where one or more members are physically abusive or even suicidal (Brammer et al., 1989; Deschner & McNeil, 1986; Douglas, 1986; Parker et al., 1987). Family therapy is often combined with other types of treatment, such as psychodrama, Gestalt therapy, transactional analysis, and even psychoanalysis (Bradley, 1987; Bredehoft, 1986; Collison & Miller, 1985; Lawe & Smith, 1986). In extreme cases, severely troubled families may benefit from "hospitalization" of the entire family in a hospital-apartment (Brendler, 1987).

There seems to be little difference between the "cure rates" claimed for family therapy and other types of group (or even individual) treatment. And family therapy appears to "fail" in precisely the same sorts of situations where other forms of treatment fail—with exceptionally difficult cases, including those where one or more family members have major mental disorders (Coleman, 1985).

EVALUATING GROUP THERAPY

There is still some argument as to how useful group therapy actually is. In a survey of 32 studies, Ronald Toseland and Max Siporin found that group therapy was more effective than several other methods of therapy. And they say that, "In no case was individual treatment . . . more effective than group treatment" (Toseland & Siporin, 1986). In a similar survey, VA psychiatrist Nick Kanas found that group treatment was effective with 67 percent of hospitalized schizophrenics and 80 percent of outpatient schizophrenics. Kanas notes, however, that "insight-oriented" group treatment was less effective than "interaction-oriented" group treatment, and that the insight-oriented approaches were harmful for some subjects (Kanas, 1986). We should note, however, that few of the studies cited by Toseland and Siporin—or by Kanas—included adequate control groups.

Perhaps the best evaluation of the effectiveness of different types of group therapy comes from a series of studies performed by psychiatrist Irvin Yalom and his colleagues. This research on group therapy began at Stanford in 1968 and is still going on. Over the years, Yalom and his associates have studied almost every type of group treatment offered to the public. Typically, these researchers investigate the group leader's perceptions of what went on, and ask the participants to evaluate the experience immediately after treatment and at some later time. The scientists also ask close friends or relatives of the participants to rate the participants' progress.

Yalom reports that his studies offer little scientific evidence that group therapy is of much *therapeutic* value. Indeed, it may often do real harm. Yalom states that about 8 percent of the participants are "casualties"—that is, people who show evidence of serious psychological damage that can be attributed to the group experience. Overall, however, *on a long-term basis,* about a third of the group members get better, about a third get worse, and the rest seem unchanged (Yalom, 1985). According to Yalom, there are few differences among the various types of group therapy as far as their effectiveness is concerned (Yalom, 1983).

Yalom concludes that none of the groups he and his colleagues studied were particularly effective as *change agents.* However, the groups can excel at creating instant, brief, and intense *interpersonal experiences.* Yalom believes this chance to learn something about yourself from the open reactions of others is important, and not often available in our society. In some situations—if, for example, you were a patient with terminal cancer, or were close to someone facing a similar problem—having the support of others with similar difficulties could give you social and psychological support. In most other situations, Yalom says, group therapy simply does not alter people permanently for the better (Yalom, 1985).

Environmental Therapy

One thing we have slowly come to realize in recent years is our sensitivity to our environments. The ecologists have made us aware of the disasters that can occur when we pollute the *physical* world around us. But polluted *psychological* environments can kill or corrupt the spirit as readily as dirty air and water can kill or corrupt the body. Thus, the job of the *environmental psychotherapist* is similar to that of the ecologist—to identify sources of pollution and remove them. If the therapist cannot easily find ways of removing the "psycho-pollution" from a patient's world, or of helping the person live more happily despite the pollution, then more radical treatment is usually needed. Typically this treatment takes the form of moving the individual to different surroundings, such as a mental hospital.

MILIEU THERAPY

Social/behavioral therapists tend to see unhealthy living conditions—not character defects or mental weakness—as the cause of mental illness. It is the failure of society to *teach* people healthy behaviors, not the failure of people to *learn,* that causes mental disorders or antisocial behaviors. The best form of treatment, these therapists claim, would be putting the person in a new context or *milieu.* Each aspect of this new milieu would be carefully designed to help the individual learn better habits of adjustment.

In 1953, British psychiatrist Maxwell Jones coined the term "therapeutic community" to refer to this type of *milieu therapy.* But according to psychiatrist Thomas Gutheil, in recent years "the therapeutic milieu has undergone significant alteration and corruption by the increased use of pharmacotherapy [drug therapy], high staff turnover, and a lack of trained staff. However, the hallmarks of milieu therapy (e.g., patients' participation in decision making, collective responsibility for ward events) remain a part of many modern inpatient settings" (Gutheil, 1985).

Therapeutic communities exist for treating schizophrenic patients, elderly people in nursing homes, drug addicts, retarded and emotionally disturbed children, and prisoners (Blotcky & Dimperio, 1987; Khan & Cohen, 1987; Simons, 1985; Van

Bilsen & Van Emst, 1986; Waters, 1984). Just how effective this type of treatment is remains a matter of debate.

Many people have definite opinions about therapeutic communities. Thomas Gutheil believes that "milieu therapy remains a viable treatment modality," particularly when it has a psychoanalytic focus (Gutheil, 1985). A different view comes from research by VA psychologists Morris Bell and Edward Ryan, however. Bell and Ryan studied three therapeutic communities: one with a biological orientation, one with a psychoanalytic orientation, and one with a "rehabilitative" (skills training) focus. Only the rehabilitative community seemed to be effective (Bell & Ryan, 1985).

TOKEN ECONOMIES

Behavior therapists favor rather specific and focussed type of environmental treatment. Their aim is to change individual habit patterns that are causing problems for the individual.

Patients in mental hospitals often develop what is called an **institutional neurosis.** That is, the patients lose interest in the world and the people around them, develop hallucinations and fantasies, and become quarrelsome, resentful, and hostile. Institutional neurosis appears to be caused in part by the fact that, in most hospitals, patients often are *given* everything they might need by the staff. Under these conditions, many of the patients develop a rather child-like dependency on the staff (Jha, 1972; Liberakis, 1981).

Behavioral psychologists believe the best cure for institutional neurosis is to make the patients take as much responsibility for their own improvement as possible. To help achieve this goal, the behaviorists use what they call a *token economy*. In the money economy that operates in the world outside the hospital, you typically must work to live. The better you work, generally speaking, the more money you make. If you perform poorly or refuse to work, you may very well starve. In contrast, mental hospitals typically operate on a "free economy." That is, the patients are given whatever they need merely by asking for it. In fact, the *worse* they behave, the *more* attention and help they usually receive (Paul & Lentz, 1978).

In a token economy, each patient must decide what rewards he or she wants to work for. The staff members then reinforce "socially approved" or "healthy" behaviors by giving the patients tokens. The patients can exchange the tokens for more

Institutional neurosis. An abnormally strong dependency on a hospital or its staff. The result of subtle (and not-so-subtle) characteristics of institutional settings.

In a token economy patients are given tokens for "socially approved" or "healthy" behaviors. They can then exchange these tokens for useful rewards.

Many patients display an "institutional neurosis" when they are hospitalized. These problems have been treated by giving the patients more responsibility for their own improvement.

valuable items or for privileges. Staff members ignore "inappropriate" or "abnormal" behaviors. The staff give the tokens as visible evidence that the patient is making progress (Kazdin, 1974, 1978). Token economies have been used effectively with schizophrenic patients, with mentally retarded young adults, with autistic children, and in a variety of school settings (Hikita, 1986; Sandford et al., 1987; Mangus et al., 1986; von Brock & Elliott, 1987).

One major difference between studies on the effectiveness of token economies and studies on other forms of treatment is this: Behaviorally oriented psychologists almost always measure outcome variables precisely, and almost always use experimental controls of one kind or another. Thus, evidence supporting the efficacy of token economies is much stronger (from a scientific point of view) than it is for other types of therapy (Paul & Lentz, 1978). Indeed, as VA psychologist Patrick Boudewyns and his colleagues point out, the surprising thing is that token economies aren't used more often. Boudewyns and his associates surveyed 152 VA medical centers and found that only 10 had token economy programs. Boudewyns and his colleagues believe that "staff shortages and staff resistance" account for the minimal use of this highly effective approach to treatment (Boudewyns et al., 1986).

The criticism most often raised against the token economy is that it is mechanistic and dehumanizing because it focuses on observable behaviors—on symptoms—rather than dealing with underlying, dynamic psychological problems. However, an extensive study by Temple University psychiatrists showed that (1) behavioral treatment of mental patients was at least as effective as was "insight-oriented" treatment for most problems; (2) behavioral therapy was significantly more effective at helping patients deal with social and work-related problems than was "insight-oriented" treatment; and (3) patients perceived behavioral therapists as being significantly warmer and more supportive than the "insight-oriented" therapists (Sloane et al., 1975).

Behavior Therapies

One interesting development in the field of therapy in recent years has been the increased use of the various types of *behavioral therapies*. Thirty years ago, there were two major types of behavioral treatment: (1) Wolpe's *systematic desensitization*, based on extinction of a conditioned emotional response and (2) therapy based on Skinner's "shaping" techniques. Now there are dozens of different types of treatment roughly based on a learning model. Many of these combine a cognitive perspective with a learning emphasis, including Beck's cognitive behavioral treatment, cognitive strategies for the control of stress and pain, family therapy, and Bandura's modeling therapy.

Most behaviorally oriented therapists perceive human problems as *failures to learn* the proper cognitive, behavioral, or social skills. The emphasis in treatment, therefore, is on training and rehabilitation, not on such things as "talking through your problems," "catharsis," "insight," or "explorations of human potential." Some eclectic behavioral therapists do, however, combine "skills learning" with some of the techniques used by psychoanalytic or humanistic therapists.

In most types of behavioral therapy, the focus is on achieving *measurable change*, either in the client's cognitions or in the person's observable behaviors or physiological reactions. While behavior therapists often employ "counter-conditioning" and "biofeedback" for dealing with phobias and headaches, their major emphasis is usually on helping the client acquire "self-control" and learn more effective skills for dating with the social environment. As we saw in Chapter 9, some researchers have found a skills-training approach to be more successful in the treatment of alcohol abuse than the approach of complete abstinence. Training in social skills can also help psychiatric patients deal more effectively with problems related to their social environment (Corrigan, 1991).

Generally speaking, behavioral treatment begins with goal setting. For example, this might mean a *limited* use of alcohol and only on *appropriate* occasions—say one drink with friends, once a week. The therapist then encourages the client to carefully monitor his or her own behavior and "take a baseline." (The baseline is the starting level of a behavior before change is attempted. It provides a comparison for improvement.) The self-observation necessary to obtain a baseline helps the client and the therapist identify the conditions under which the client drinks excessively. It may also help to determine those strengths the person can build on in order to reach the therapeutic goals. Together, the therapist and client identify some *healthful* ways the client reacts to the environment instead of drinking, and perhaps certain friends with whom the client drinks only in moderation. They will also identify other conditions which lead to problem drinking and then practice behaviors to avoid those situations.

Next, the therapist and the client work out a treatment plan in which the therapist encourages the client to move in small steps from the present situation toward the goal through the use of positive feedback and other forms of reinforcement. They might engage the support of family or friends to provide social rewards (praise and approval) or even material rewards, when the client succeeds at each step. Finally, therapists often teach clients ways of undertaking similar projects *on their own* in the future.

Behavior therapy for problem drinking would include identifying situations in which the client drinks excessively. The therapist would teach the client to avoid or change those situations.

Evaluating Social/Behavioral Therapies

Behavioral therapies seem particularly effective at increasing "desirable" responses and at decreasing "symptomatic" or "undesirable" behavior patterns. And, as we noted in Chapter 9, and earlier in this chapter, *cognitive* behavior modification is useful in altering both perceptions and attitudes (Ollendick et al., 1991; Valliant & Antonowicz, 1991).

As for milieu therapy, it does seem effective in teaching people to learn to live together better when the focus is on helping people acquire interpersonal skills. However, milieu therapy doesn't seem to work as well when the focus is on changing "feelings" or on "uncovering deep-seated emotional problems" (Bell & Ryan, 1985; Yalom, 1985).

Twenty years ago, many traditional psychotherapists rejected behavioral treatment out of hand as being "too mechanistic" and "too cold and impersonal." However, research by Bruce Sloane and his colleagues soon showed that most patients perceived behavior therapists as being significantly "warmer, more involved, more genuine, and as having greater and more accurate empathy" than traditional psychotherapists (Sloane et al., 1975). And most recent research suggests that behavioral treatment is even more effective than psychotherapy when treatment goals can be specified in measurable terms, or when the focus is on helping individuals learn interpersonal or job-related skills.

THERAPY: A SUMMARY

Is psychotherapy effective? As we noted, the answer to this question depends in large part on what you think the *goal* of psychotherapy should be. Not all types of treatment have the same goals, nor should we expect any one type of therapy to work with *all* types of psychological disorders. Indeed, as Laurence Grimm points out, "There simply is no universally accepted set of measures to define the effectiveness of treatment and little agreement on what aspects of the client's behavior are most critical to change" (Grimm, 1981).

Generally speaking, however, it does seem that, when properly used, psychotherapy can have a positive effect. Although several well-known studies of "cure rates" in psychotherapy have not yielded outstanding results, the *overall trend* is encouraging.

In 1977, M. L. Smith and G. V. Glass reported on the use of a new "trend analysis" technique called **meta-analysis.** This technique involves analyzing hundreds of studies at one time. Smith and Glass performed this "meta-analysis" on the effects of therapy, and then added up the number of studies with positive results and the number of studies with negative outcomes. Smith and Glass report that their "meta-analysis box score" supports the belief that psychotherapy is effective (Smith & Glass, 1977; Smith et al., 1980).

Several other authors have also reported favorable "box scores" using the meta-analysis technique (Bowers & Clum, 1988; Clum & Bowers, 1990; Michelson, 1985; Lambert et al., 1986). However, some researchers have obtained negative results when using meta-analysis. And behavioral psychologists (in particular) have been highly critical of the meta-analysis technique itself (Brody, 1990; Rachman & Wilson, 1980; Wilson & Rachman, 1983).

Taking all the data into account, however, we can tentatively draw the following conclusions:

1. The "spontaneous recovery" rate varies between 30 and 50 percent. That is, about 30 to 50 percent of the patients with mental disorders will show "spontaneous" improvement whether treated or not. The spontaneous cure rate appears to be lowest with severely disturbed patients, and is highest with mildly disturbed patients (Elkin et al., 1985).

2. The "treatment" cure rate for most types of therapy is about 70 percent. The actual figure varies with the type of treatment used and the type of problem addressed. Of the various forms of psychotherapy, psychoanalysis appears to have the lowest cure rate. It also is the most expensive and takes the longest (Garfield, 1983a, 1983b). Cognitive and insight-oriented therapies do best at achieving changes in cognitive processes, whether the method is applied to individuals or to groups. Behavior therapies do best when aimed at teaching people self-management or social skills. Under these conditions, the cure rate for behavioral treatment can reach 80 to 90 percent (Sloane et al., 1975).

3. There is actually little difference in the reported cure rates for the various forms of "talk therapies." As Smith and Glass put it, "Despite volumes devoted to the theoretical differences among different schools of psychotherapy, the results of research demonstrate negligible differences in the effects produced by different therapy types" (Smith & Glass, 1977).

4. Since *any* form of psychotherapy appears to be more effective than is no therapy at all, and since *all types* of treatment appear to yield similar cure rates, it would seem that improvement is the result of features which are common to all therapeutic settings. Common features would include the patient's belief in therapy as well as general characteristics of successful therapists (Berman, 1981). (We will discuss features which successful therapies have in common in a moment.)

5. Drug therapy seems to be more effective with severely disturbed patients *in the short run* than is psychological or behavioral treatment. However, 40 to 50 percent of the patients given psychoactive drugs on a chronic basis develop drug-related side effects, some of which can be fatal.

6. *Negative outcomes* are more likely with biologically oriented therapies, with psychoanalysis, and with intensive groups therapies, than with other forms of treatment (Bergin & Lambert, 1978; Finkelstein et al., 1982; Gunderson & Frank, 1985; Sloane et al., 1975). Negative results are also more common (as you might suspect) the more severely disturbed the patient was to begin with. Negative out-

Meta-analysis. A statistical technique for combining the results of several published studies to get a measure of the effect of a particular variable across all the studies. One problem with meta-analysis is that scientists tend to publish studies that yield positive results, but not to publish experiments that yield negative or insignificant results. Thus, a meta-analysis based only on published work may have a "positive bias."

comes may be less common with the behavioral treatment than with any other type (Mays & Franks, 1985).

7. *Research* on the effectiveness of psychotherapy appears to have little if any effect on *actual practice*. For example, Cheryl Morrow-Bradley and Robert Elliott report that 62 percent of the practicing clinicians they polled had not published even one research paper. When asked how much psychotherapy research influenced the way they practiced, only 17 percent said "quite a bit," only 10 percent said "a great deal," while not one person said "more than anything else" (Morrow-Bradley & Elliott, 1986). Indeed, as Lawrence Cohen, Meredith Sargent, and Lee Sechrest note, practicing therapists seldom read the research literature and tend to *repress* any research findings that contradict the therapists' views of "what works best" (Cohen et al., 1986).

8. There have been surprisingly few attempts to test the effects of using *different types of therapy* at different stages during treatment. Alan Marlatt found that aversive therapy worked best at the start of treatment of alcoholic patients, while behavioral treatment was more effective during later stages (Marlatt, 1983). But few other researchers have examined this variable.

Perhaps the future of psychotherapy lies in this direction: discovering *what types* of treatment are most effective with *what kinds* of patients during *which* of the various stages of the treatment process. Oddly enough, this approach is precisely that pioneered by one of the early giants in the mental health movement, Adolf Meyer.

Therapy and the Whole Individual

Adolf Meyer believed in the *holistic* approach to treating people, and recognized there were multiple causes for even the simplest of behaviors. Rather than passing verdicts on patients by labeling them as "schizophrenics" or "neurotics," Meyer preferred to discover both what was wrong and what was right with the patients at all levels of analysis—the biological, the psychological, and the sociological.

Meyer also attempted to determine those *normal* aspects of behavior that the patient might still have available. He then tried to build on these psychological assets to bring about change. Meyer believed that the patient should set both the goals and the pace of therapy, and that the therapist should work as hard at changing the patient's home (or hospital) environment as in changing the patient's psyche or behaviors. Meyer called his approach *critical common sense* (Meyer, 1951).

If we apply Adolf Meyer's "critical common sense" to an analysis of the strengths and weaknesses of all the various types of therapy, we would discover that most successful forms of treatment have several things in common:

1. Psychological change almost always occurs in a supportive, warm, rewarding environment. People usually "open up" and talk about things—and try new approaches to life—when they trust, admire, or want to please the therapist. Criticism seldom changes thoughts or behaviors, and it often kills all chance of improvement.

2. Most successful forms of treatment can be seen as feedback mechanisms. That is, appropriate feedback provides you with information about your past, puts you in touch with the functioning of your body, and makes you aware of how your behavior actually affects other people. Feedback also helps you realize the distance between your desired goals and your present achievements, and offers information on how the social environment influences your thoughts, feelings, and behaviors. Ideally, a complete form of therapy would do all these things, while helping you to make even better use of feedback in the future.

3. Only magic can "cure" mental illness overnight; psychotherapy takes longer. It takes many years of stressful experiences (and perhaps a particular genetic

All successful therapies, regardless of theoretical orientation, have in common a warm, supportive, rewarding environment, where therapist and client are both optimistic about the possibility of change.

predisposition) for a serious disorder to develop. It is not surprising then that the road to recovery is usually a fairly lengthy one.

4. The attitudes of both the patient and the therapist are of critical importance. Patients often see their therapists as being models of mentally healthy or socially approved behaviors. Effective therapists (witch doctors, psychoanalysts, humanists, or behaviorists) usually practice what they preach.

5. The best forms of therapy seem to build on strengths rather than on attacking weaknesses. By helping the patient work toward positive improvement—toward problem solving, good social behaviors, and self-actualization—the therapist motivates the patient to continue to grow and change. Therapies that focus entirely on uncovering or discussing psychological problems may merely confirm the patient's attitude that sickness is inevitable.

The Future of Therapy

It is likely that, in the coming years, we will take Adolf Meyer's ideas more seriously than we have in the past. That means we will treat the whole patient as a unique individual rather than treating just one aspect of the person's difficulties.

THE "TEAM APPROACH"

Already in some hospitals there is a *team of therapists* available to work with each patient. One member of the team looks at the person's physical or biological problems. Another deals with the person's intra-psychic dynamics. A third helps the patient change behavior patterns. A fourth team member is an expert in altering social environments. The patient can then get as much, or as little, of each type of therapy as his or her own particular case demands.

Ideally, the goals of therapy should be spelled out in a written contract agreed to by the patient and all members of the therapeutic team. And the patient's progress should be recorded regularly on a graph of some kind so all team members are aware of the patient's achievements. As this "team-contracting approach" increases in popularity, our success rate in curing mental illness is likely to show a significant increase.

CULTURAL DIVERSITY

We must also bear in mind what we said at the beginning of the chapter: therapy follows from theory. The therapies we have been discussing grew out of theories of the person which are based on a fairly restricted segment of Western culture. As we approach members from other cultures and ethnic groups, we must be prepared to expand our understanding of human nature and adapt our methods accordingly (Pedersen, 1987; Tharp, 1991).

For example, members of ethnic minorities are more likely to seek help from a caregiver who has "established credibility" in the minority culture—perhaps by "word of mouth" testimonials or by training *recognized* within the subculture (Brislin, 1993). Patients are also more likely to *return* to therapists who meet their cultural expectations for a caregiver. Stanley Sue and his colleagues found that African-, Asian-, Native-, and Hispanic-Americans were much more likely to drop out of treatment than were Anglo-Americans (Sue et al., 1978). Minority groups in the United States often expect direct advice (Sue & Zane, 1987; Sue, 1988). When a therapist fails to offer such advice, the clients simply don't come back (Brislin, 1993).

We must be prepared to modify our approach to meet the unique needs of each client. This means being sensitive to gender, religious, cultural, and any other bias in our theories and methods (Brown & Ballou, 1992; Noon & Lewis, 1992;

Worthington, 1989, 1990). But this does *not* mean, for example, that only an "African-American Muslim therapist" can help an "African-American Muslim client." We cannot learn about, much less experience, each client's unique background. But we can be *sensitive* to the effect of this background and its *importance to the client*.

CONCLUSION

Perhaps the single most important thing we have learned about mental health in the past 30 years is that neither problems nor cures occur in a vacuum. No matter how well a patient may respond in a hospital setting, and no matter what insights a client achieves in a therapist's office, the ultimate test of therapy comes when the person returns to her or his usual environment. If the patient can function successfully and happily in the real world, we can then conclude that a "cure" has indeed taken place.

It is thus to the complexities of the social environment that we now must turn our attention.

SUMMARY

1. The types of therapy that we prescribe for mentally ill persons usually stem from our **theoretical explanations** of what causes the people's problems.

2. In some societies, insanity is said to be caused by **possession.** That is, a **spirit** of some kind is thought to take over the sick person's mind.

3. Primitive forms of **psychotherapy** typically involve the use of magic to "cast out the witch," or painful whips to **beat the devil** out of the patient.

4. As our scientific explanations of the causes of human behavior have changed, so have our types of treatment. In evaluating any form of therapy, we must ask ourselves four questions:
   a. How successful or **valid** is the treatment?
   b. How **reliable** is the therapy?
   c. Are there unfortunate **side effects?**
   d. How shall we define "success" or **cure rate?**

5. Biological treatment typically involves the use of **electro-convulsive shock, psychosurgery,** or the use of **psychoactive drugs.**

6. **ECT** is most often used for severe **depression. Lobotomies** were once used with aggressive or highly emotional patients. Both types of treatment can have undesirable side effects.

7. The major tranquilizers or **antipsychotic** drugs, are widely used with hospitalized and severely disturbed patients. These drugs bring about improvement in some 70 percent of **schizophrenic** patients. Some patients taking antipsychotic drugs develop other problems including a movement disorder called **tardive dyskinesia.**

8. There are many forms of **intra-psychic treatment,** including psychoanalysis, humanistic therapy, and cognitive therapy.

9. In **psychoanalysis,** the client is encouraged to undergo a **transference** relationship in which the analyst represents other significant people. The therapist often **interprets** the client's free associations, feelings, and dreams in psychoanalytic terms in order to determine the client's unconscious psychodynamics and allow the patient to release **repressed feelings.**

10. In **humanistic therapy,** the client sets his or her own therapeutic goals and determines the pace at which treatment proceeds.

11. In Rogerian or **client-centered therapy,** the stress is on the emotional aspects of

the situation, upon the present rather than on the past, and on the therapeutic relationship itself as a growth experience.

12. In **cognitive therapy** the client is taught to substitute realistic, positive thoughts and beliefs for irrational and unproductive ones.

13. All therapy must be judged in relationship to the rate of **spontaneous recovery** patients show without treatment. In most recent studies, this rate has been between 30 and 50 percent.

14. Some psychiatrists consider therapy to be an **art form** which cannot be judged using the **scientific method.** Other therapists admit that the effects of treatment must be measured **objectively.**

15. In the Menninger study of psychoanalytic treatment, the "cure rate" was about 43 percent. **Psychoanalytic treatment** seems to work best with educated, highly verbal, mildly disturbed patients; it seems not to work well with severely disturbed psychotic patients.

16. A large study by NIMH suggests that **drug therapy** works best with severely depressed patients, but that **cognitive** and **behavioral treatment** is as effective as drug therapy with moderately or mildly depressed patients.

17. There are many types of **group therapy,** including Gestalt therapy, transactional analysis, encounter groups, stress debriefing groups, self-help groups, and family therapy.

18. Group therapies seem better as ways of encouraging people to **explore** and **express themselves** than as change agents, but some 8 percent of the clients end up as **psychological casualties** who are worse after treatment than before.

19. Environmental therapies attempt to change the patient by altering the patient's **milieu** and **social behaviors.**

20. Milieu therapy involves **changing the patient's environment** so that the person may grow in psychologically healthy ways.

21. Behavioral psychologists often use a **token economy** to help patients overcome institutional neuroses. Patients are **rewarded** for achievements with tokens, while inappropriate behaviors are ignored.

22. Behavioral treatment usually proceeds in five steps: (1) setting a **goal,** (2) taking a **baseline,** (3) making a **treatment plan** that involves moving toward the goal in small steps, (4) using **positive reinforcement,** and (5) teaching the client **self-change skills.**

23. Behavior therapy is particularly effective when the client has **measurable goals,** or needs to learn **interpersonal** or **job-related skills.**

24. Research suggests that there is little difference in the actual **cure rates** achieved by the various types of group therapy, but behavioral treatment is highly effective when the goal is that of changing **specific behaviors.**

25. Research studies using **meta-analysis** suggest that almost all forms of psychotherapy achieve a "cure rate" of about 70 percent, a figure that is significantly greater than the **spontaneous cure rate.**

26. **Negative outcomes** are more likely with drug therapy, psychoanalysis, and intensive group experiences, than with other form of treatment.

27. Research on the effectiveness of psychotherapy appears to have **little influence** on actual practice.

28. Most effective therapy takes place in a **warm, supportive environment** in which patients are given appropriate **feedback.** The **attitudes** of both patient and therapist are important, as is **building on strengths** rather than merely correcting weaknesses.

29. It is likely that, in the future, a **team approach** to treatment will prove to be highly effective, particularly if **patient-therapist contracts** are employed.

1. *Why would the therapy you suggested for "running amok" vary according to the label you put on the problem?*

   If you felt the disorder was caused by forces beyond your control, your "therapy" might be to kill the person (as the Malaysians do). If you believed you could influence the spirits causing the problem, you might try rituals recommended by your religious tradition. If you believed the problem was physical, you might give various "potions."

2. *If therapy is extremely painful—be it whippings or convulsions—why might some patients show immediate improvement?*

   They might decide the therapy is not worth the "benefits" of the disorder. Painful therapy might act as punishment for the disturbed behavior (symptoms), leading to a reduced rate of responding. In other words, therapy might *extinguish* the disturbed response.

3. *What social and financial factors might encourage the increased use of ECT?*

   ECT might become more attractive because it is inexpensive, fast, and "technological"—all desirable characteristics in the 1990s.

4. *Some patients request ECT, particularly after they have been performing badly for a period of time. . . ?*

   ECT might be seen as a form of self-punishment which patients request to reduce their feelings of guilt. It might also be related to "thanatos," the instinct to self-destruction.

5. *Why might many physicians be more interested in performing operations on patients with mental . . . ?*

   Physicians' training leads them to expect disorders to have a physiological cause. Denying a physical cause might be seen by some physicians as admitting their helplessness, and even failure. In addition, surgery is faster and cheaper than long-term psychotherapy.

6. *Abraham Maslow once said, "If the only tool you have is a hammer, you tend to see every problem . . . ?*

   In some cases drugs seem to be the best or only way to treat a problem. The success of drugs in some cases leads many people (physicians, patients, and their families) to expect drugs to be effective in all cases. Very few other means are available from a biological perspective.

7. *In Figure 16.1, illustrating cognitive therapy, which view best represents the biological . . . ?*

   Biological therapists are more likely to view thoughts as the consequence of behavior and feelings. They would try to change thought by changing feelings and behaviors first, biologically.

8. *Why would it be more difficult to prove that therapy "works" using objective criteria than if . . . ?*

   Subjective opinions of various clients and therapists may be based on entirely different criteria. Also, subjective opinions are influenced by many irrelevant factors, especially expectations. For example, clients and therapists tend to exaggerate symptoms at the beginning of therapy, and to minimize them at the end of therapy. (This is sometimes called the "hello-goodbye effect.")

CHAPTER 17

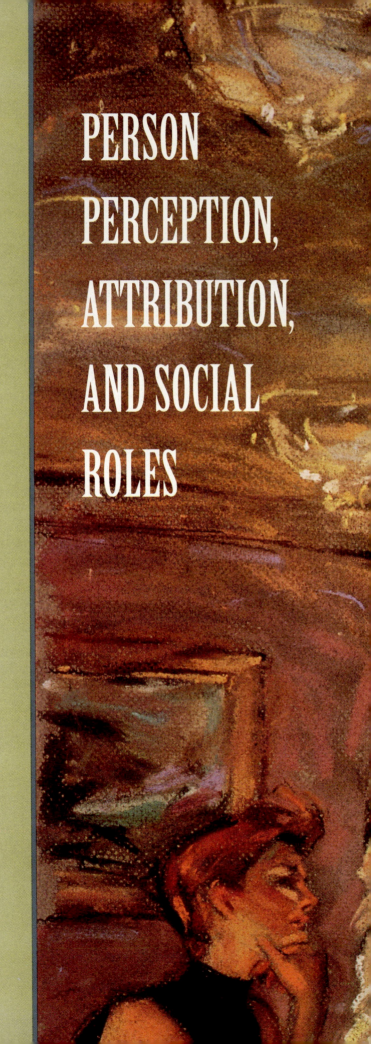

PERSON PERCEPTION, ATTRIBUTION, AND SOCIAL ROLES

When Janie had finished indoors she sat down in the barn with the potatoes. But springtime reached her in there so she moved everything to a place in the yard where she could see the road. The noon sun filtered through the leaves of the fine oak tree where she sat and made lacy patterns on the ground. She had been there a long time when she heard a whistling coming down the road.

It was a cityfied, stylish dressed man with his hat set at an angle that didn't belong in these parts. His coat was over his arm, but he didn't need it to represent his clothes. The shirt with the silk sleeveholders was dazzling enough for the world. He whistled, mopped his face and walked like he knew where he was going. He was a sealbrown color but he acted like Mr. Washburn or somebody like that to Janie. Where would such a man be coming from and where was he going? He didn't look her way nor no other way except straight ahead, so Janie ran to the pump and jerked the handle hard while she pumped. It made a loud noise and also made her heavy hair fall down. So he stopped and looked hard, and then he asked her for a cool drink of water.

Janie pumped it off until she got a good look at the man.

He talked friendly while he drank.

ZORA NEALE HURSTON
THEIR EYES WERE WATCHING GOD

SOCIAL PSYCHOLOGY

I n Chapter 14 we said personality theorists study "everything about you that is uniquely typical of you—that which distinguishes you from everyone else." In this chapter and the next we will look at some of the *similarities* between people. Social psychologists tend to focus on different social factors that lead people to respond in similar ways—for example, how people attract one another, play certain roles, or conform to group pressures. Consider Janie in the chapter opening selection. Social psychologists might ask, "How could Janie tell so much about the man without talking to him?" "How did she know that her social role did not permit her to approach the man directly?" And, "What social pressures led him to dress in such an impractical way?"

What, then, is *social psychology,* and how does it differ from all the other areas of psychology we have discussed? According to social psychologist Charles Kimble, the major difference is that social psychology pays attention chiefly to *interactions* between people, while most of the rest of the field focuses on the individual (Kimble, 1990). Social psychologist Richard Lippa says, "Social psychology studies how people influence people" (Lippa, 1990). Perhaps that is as good a place as any to begin. As you will see, social psychology contains some of the most interesting research findings in all of psychology. But before we can discuss these findings we need to look at four important issues.

Social psychologists are interested in the individual within a group.

Four Important Issues in Social Psychology

There are several major issues social psychologists typically deal with. Four of the most significant issues are as follows:

1. In describing social relationships, should we look at how the individual affects the group, or how the group influences the individual?
2. When we attempt to study social variables, should we look primarily at internal processes such as *attitudes,* or at objective events such as *behaviors?*
3. Are social responses mostly learned, or determined by the genes?
4. Is social psychology primarily a *theoretical* or an *applied* science?

Some of these questions may sound a bit familiar. But let's look at them briefly from a new perspective as we begin our discussion of social psychology.

THE INDIVIDUAL OR THE GROUP?

Should social psychologists study individuals, or groups? The answer, of course, is *both.* In this chapter, our focus will primarily be on the *individual.* How, for instance, do you perceive others, and how do they perceive you? How do you influence others, and how do they affect your thoughts and behaviors?

In Chapter 18, our focus will primarily be on *groups* and *organizations.*

ATTITUDES OR BEHAVIORS?

Traditionally, social psychologists have focused more on measuring and describing **attitudes** than on *behaviors.* Sixty years ago, Gordon Allport stated that *attitude* is "the single most distinctive and indispensable concept in contemporary American social psychology" (Allport, 1935). The traditional way of defining an attitude is, "It is a consistent way of thinking about, feeling toward, or responding to some environmental stimulus or input" (Newcomb, 1961). Thus, attitudes are composed of cognitive, emotional, and behavioral components. Some social psychologists emphasize the cognitive aspects of attitudes, some focus more on emotions, while a few try to deal with both cognition and affect (Hamilton, 1981).

Other social psychologists prefer to deal with measurable behaviors. For example, Peter Drucker says, "In a good many social matters, attitudes are secondary and attitude surveys are a snare and delusion. What matters is what people do, not what they say they will do" (Drucker, 1981).

Social learning theory offers a compromise between the two extreme positions. Social learning theorists believe that attitudes are "cognitive structures" that allow you to process environmental inputs in consistent ways. Thus, in many (but not all) situations, attitudes control behaviors. But the social learning theorists also believe that you acquire new cognitive structures as you learn new behavioral habits. So behaviors influence attitudes. And to explain social relationships completely you must deal with *both* attitudes and behaviors (Bandura, 1986a).

LEARNED OR INNATE?

The nature-nurture controversy gained prominence in social psychology with the publication of Edward Wilson's theory of **sociobiology.** Wilson believes that most of your social responses come from an inherited desire to *help your genes survive.* Wilson says that your genes control your own particular social attitudes in large part. You perceive your family in a favorable light, and perceive strangers in an unfriendly manner, because you realize that your relatives "carry your genes" (Wilson, 1975). To Wilson, social behaviors are innate.

Attitudes. Attitudes are "internal processes"; your presumed ways of thinking about, feeling toward, or responding to a person, thing, or concept.

Sociobiology. A theory by biologist Edward Wilson, based on Darwinian ideas, that states your major motive in life is passing along and protecting your genes. According to Wilson, almost all social behaviors can be seen as innately determined attempts to enhance the survival value of one's genes.

Very few social psychologists take Wilson's point of view. Rather, the strong tendency is to believe that we *learn* most social behaviors.

THEORIES OR APPLICATIONS?

In some ways there is a basic division in psychology. Some scientists spend most of their time generating knowledge—that is, in performing experiments and creating new theories. Other psychologists try to put knowledge to use—that is, they like to help people, groups, and organizations solve real-life problems.

Although there are a great many theories (and theorists) in social psychology, the field has always leaned ever so slightly toward applications. There are many reasons for this emphasis on the applied.

Action research. Kurt Lewin's term for research that involves solving problems in real-life social settings rather than in the laboratory. Lewin believed action research was "superior" in some ways to laboratory studies because it yielded both knowledge and "social good."

To begin with, social problems are often highly visible and of obvious importance. And the desire to *change society* in some positive fashion is what originally attracted many social psychologists to the field. For example, Kurt Lewin was a pioneer in the field of social psychology. James Alcock describes Lewin's approach in these words: "the researcher obtains data about a problem or organization, feeds these data into the relevant system in order to influence change, measures the changes, and then repeats the process." Lewin called his approach **action research.** In action research "the psychologist must become an agent of change, a skilled advocate of politics, as well as a theoretician and researcher" (Alcock et al., 1991). Social psychologists stress the importance of applications to "real life."

It is also true that a lot of social psychological research *of necessity* takes place in real-life settings. Social psychologists study *people*, and there are both ethical and practical constraints on the experimental study of human subjects. For instance, we can't bring two people who are friends into a laboratory and deliberately create hostility and conflict between them. We can, though, study hostility and conflict *as they already exist* in real life. We might try to find ways of reducing interracial tensions in an integrated school or housing project, for example. Discovering new methods of helping people "get along better" would not only solve a pressing social problem, but would create new knowledge as well. Little wonder, then, that many social psychologists adopt Kurt Lewin's motto, "The world is my laboratory."

The "Social Interaction Sequence"

Social psychologists study *people interacting with other people*. Suppose we want to study *your* interactions with another individual. What we would immediately discover is this important fact: How you behave toward another individual is determined, in large part, by how you perceive the other person. Thus, in part, social psychology is the study of *social perceptions*.

According to John Darley and Russell Fazio, "Perception is a constructive, interpretative process. Such interpretation is particularly critical in the perception of other people. The actions of another person do not automatically convey meanings, but are given meanings by the perceiver" (Darley & Fazio, 1980). With this thought in mind, Darley and Fazio state that the "social interaction sequence" typically has five distinct steps:

1. When you meet someone, you develop a *set of expectancies* about the other person.

2. You then *act* toward the person in a way that is consistent with your expectancies.

3. The other person *interprets* the meaning of your actions.

4. Based on this interpretation, the other person *responds*.

5. You then *interpret* the meaning of the other person's response (Darley & Fazio, 1980).

As we go through the chapter, we will touch on each of these five points in the social interaction sequence. And we will begin by trying to find out how you *generate a set of expectancies* about others.

When you meet someone new, what do you look for in that person? And what about that person is most likely to influence whether or not you like the individual?

PERSON PERCEPTION

One common social sequence is this: You meet someone new, you decide you like this person, and thus you see the individual more frequently in the future. Your relationship may become a warm friendship or even a companionate or *passionate* love affair. Social psychologists have spent a great amount of time studying, and theorizing about, this type of social interaction. You may perceive this sequence of events as "happening naturally." Social scientists, however, have discovered that factors you may be unaware of may strongly affect your perceptions, attitudes, and actions throughout this seemingly natural social sequence. But what *does* influence your perception of another individual? The many different answers to this question make up the fascinating field of *person perception*.

"Person perception" is the process of trying to understand what other people are like. It is the act of "sizing up" another person. As we will see, many factors influence your perceptions of other people, and their perceptions of you.

First Impressions

Suppose some good friends of yours talk you into going to a party with a "blind date." They paint a glowing picture of your date as a kind of super-person in order to get you to agree to the date. When the fateful moment comes and you meet the person, what sorts of things do you look for first? That is, what *immediate stimulus clues* influence your *judgment* of the individual?

You may remember from Chapter 4, that you see what you expect to see. Before you meet your date, your friends will have biased your perceptions by their descriptions of the individual. If they have told you the person is warm, affectionate, responsive, and outgoing, you will probably look for these attributes in your date as soon as the two of you meet. Certainly your attitude toward the person will be different than if your friends have told you your date is rather intellectual, cold, withdrawn, quiet, and self-possessed. And your attitude will continue to affect your perceptions of your date, even after you are no longer aware of where the attitude came from (Hill et al., 1989).

The question then becomes, how do attitudes affect perceptions?

ATTITUDES

As we noted earlier, an *attitude* is a consistent way of thinking about, feeling toward, or responding to some aspect of your environment (or toward yourself). Thus, an attitude is actually a sort of "cognitive structure" that allows you to process and respond to social inputs in an efficient manner (Jones, 1986).

But an attitude is also a "mental program" for *coding* experiences in order to store them in long-term memory. Therefore, your attitudes affect not only your present perceptions and responses, they also help determine your future memories of what

A couple on a blind date may be more likely to perceive each other in terms of what friends have told them than in terms of what can actually be observed.

you saw and did in the present. We can illustrate that point by looking at how you form "first impressions" of the people you meet.

REPUTATIONS

When your friends describe your blind date to you, they are telling you something about that person's *reputation*. That is, your friends are describing how most people perceive your date, or the attitude most people have toward the person.

Social psychologist Harold Kelley tested the importance of "reputations" in a study performed at MIT in the late 1940s. Kelley told a large class of undergraduates they would have a visiting lecturer for the day, and that the students would be asked to evaluate this man at the end of the class. Kelley then passed out a brief biographical note about the teacher, presumably to help the students with their evaluation. Although the students did not realize it, the description half the class received referred to the lecturer as being "rather a warm individual," while the description given the rest of the class called the man "rather a cold intellectual."

After the class had read the printed comments, the man arrived and led the class in a 20-minute discussion. Kelley watched the students and recorded how often each of them asked a question or made a comment. Afterward, Kelley asked the students to rate the man on a set of attitude scales and to write a brief description of him.

Although everyone in the class had witnessed *exactly* the same performance at *exactly* the same time, the descriptions each student had read measurably affected their responses. Those students who had been told the instructor was "warm" tended to rate him as much more informal, sociable, popular, good-natured, humorous, and humane than the students who had been told the same man was "cold."

More than this, the subjects *reacted* to the man quite differently. The students who were told he was warm spoke to him in class much more frequently than did the students who were told he was cold (Kelley, 1950).

More recently, Gerald Connors and Mark Sobell studied the responses of undergraduate males in a social drinking situation. The subjects drank either one or two doses of alcohol in the presence of another young male who actually was a confederate of the experimenters. Part of the time, the confederate pretended to drink, and then acted intoxicated. Part of the time, the confederate did *not* pretend to drink, but then acted in the same uninhibited way he did as when he pretended to drink (and be intoxicated). The undergraduates tended to rate the confederate as being "more friendly, admirable, responsive, warmer, and less reserved" when he *pretended* to drink than when he didn't, although his behavior was the same in both situations. Thus, Connors and Sobell say, it was the confederate's *reputation* as being "a drinker" that influenced the manner in which the subjects perceived him (Connors & Sobell, 1986).

How might Kelley's research help explain the difficulty that Rosenhan's "pseudo-patients" had in convincing mental hospital staffs that they (the "pseudo-patients") were really normal?

AUTISTIC HOSTILITY AND NEGATIVE REPUTATIONS

Judging from much of the research on "reputations," once you believe you *won't* like a person on the basis of his/her reputation, you tend to avoid him or her in the future. Theodore Newcomb called this avoidance response **autistic hostility,** and he suggests that it may apply to interactions among groups as well as among individuals (Newcomb, 1961).

However, you might well be able to *compensate* for a poor reputation if you try hard enough. In one study, James Hilton and John Darley told some students, called

Autistic hostility. Autism is the act of withdrawing into oneself, of shutting off external stimulation. Autistic hostility is the act of cutting off or denying favorable inputs about people or things we don't like. "My mind is made up—don't confuse me with facts. "

the "evaluators," that they would meet another student (the "target") who had a "cold" personality. Then they told some of the "target" students that the "evaluator" they would meet *believed them to be cold.* Other "targets" were not given this information. Hilton and Darley reports that the "evaluators" did, indeed, perceive the uninformed "targets" as being "cold." However, the "targets" who knew what their reputation was supposed to be apparently were able to overcome this negative evaluation. The prepared "targets" were perceived as significantly warmer than the unprepared "targets"—they overcame their "reputation" (Hilton & Darley, 1985). Research also indicates that "evaluators" who are warned about negative reputations and who are motivated to make *accurate* evaluations, can successfully avoid the effects of negative expectations (Neuberg, 1989).

STEREOTYPES

When you don't know a given person's "reputation," your initial impressions are likely to grow out of the **stereotypes,** or preconceived ideas, that you have about certain types or groups of people. If you assume all blacks are lazy, dull, ignorant but musical, you will tend to "see" these attributes, even in an energetic, bright black doctor who perhaps couldn't carry a tune in a handbag. If your attitude toward Arabs is that they are anti-American, war-like fanatics, you may react totally inappropriately to peaceful law-abiding American citizens of Arab descent.

Any time you react to an individual *primarily* in terms of that person's membership in some group, or in terms of that person's physical characteristics, race, or religion, you are guilty of *stereotyping.* That is, you have let the reputation of the group influence your perception of the individual who belongs to that group (Hamilton, 1981). If your stereotype of a group leads to negative attitudes and behaviors towards group members, you are guilty of **prejudice** and **discrimination.** (We will discuss efforts to reduce prejudice and discrimination in the next chapter.)

Are stereotypes, prejudices, and discrimination always harmful?

Mark Snyder points out that, once you form a *stereotype* of a given group, you tend to seek out information that *confirms* the stereotype, and *repress* information that doesn't. Furthermore, Snyder says, when you interact with people you've stereotyped, you tend to behave toward them in ways that will *elicit* responses that fit the stereotype (Snyder, 1983).

Put in more cognitive terms, when you stereotype people, you are using what Piaget called the process of "assimilation." That is, you are forcing your perception of the individual to fit your *schema* for remembering or classifying that type of person. When you change your perception to fit the facts, you are "accommodating" to the real world by altering your schema.

How would you explain Newcomb's concept of "autistic hostility" in terms of Piaget's "process of assimilation"?

SELF-FULFILLING PROPHECIES

Perceiving a person in a biased fashion often leads us to *behave* toward that individual in a stereotyped fashion. And, in response, the individual may *react* to us in a way that confirms our original perception. Evidence for this statement comes from work by psychologists Mark Sibicky and John Dovidio.

Sibicky and Dovidio studied the social behaviors of 136 undergraduates who were paired off in a "get-acquainted" situation. One of the students in each pair was "the

Stereotypes. A fixed attitude or perception; a way of responding to some person or object solely in terms of the person's (or object's) class membership. The failure to treat people as individuals, each different from the other, is the act of stereotyping.

Prejudice. A negative *attitude*, which is unjustified, towards a group of people and the individual persons in the group—often based on stereotypes.

Discrimination. Negative *behavior*, which is unjustified, towards a group of people and the individual persons in the group. Racism, sexism, and ageism are prejudicial attitudes *and* discriminatory behavior based on race, sex, and age, respectively.

Many interactions between people of different racial or ethnic groups are influenced by stereotyping.

evaluator," while the other student was "the target." The experimenters told the evaluators that the "target" he/she would meet was either (1) a "client" seeking psychological therapy, or (2) a student in an introductory psychology course. They did not tell the "targets" anything at all about the experiment.

During the "get-acquainted" meeting, those evaluators who thought their target-partners were "therapy clients" treated their partners more negatively than did evaluators who thought they were meeting "just another student." The evaluators also gave "therapy-client-targets" lower ratings than they gave to "student-targets."

More than this, Sibicky and Dovidio report, during the meeting itself, the "client-targets" responded to their evaluators in "less socially desirable ways" than did "student-targets." Sibicky and Dovidio believe that the evaluators *elicited* behaviors from their partners that would fulfill the evaluators' expectations (Sibicky & Dovidio, 1986).

Put in simple terms, when you perceive someone in a stereotyped fashion, you predict how the person will respond. You then may act toward that individual in a manner that almost *forces* the person to respond in ways that confirm your stereotyped expectations. Social psychologists call this sequence of behavior a *self-fulfilling prophecy* (Jones, 1986; Miller, 1982).

What kind of first impression do you think you give the people you meet? Why do you think they perceive you this way? Are strangers more influenced by what you are really like "deep down inside," or by how you look?

Non-Verbal Factors in Person Perception

The way you perceive someone you have just met is obviously affected by such *internal processes* as attitudes, reputations, and stereotypes. But your perceptions are also influenced by *present stimulus inputs*.

When you meet someone new, you transmit information about yourself to that person by way of *two main channels of communication*: what you do with your body and what you say with your tongue. The way you look and dress and move—these are part of your body language. What you say, the opinions you express, and the verbal responses you make—these are part of your verbal language. Surprisingly enough, when it comes to first impressions, your looks and physical movements often speak louder than what you actually say. Needless to say, your "first impressions" of others are also highly responsive to their physical attractiveness and body language.

Suppose you met two people, one with obvious good looks, the other with average looks. Which person do you think would be the happier? Why?

PHYSICAL APPEARANCE

Although it may be "undemocratic"—to use Elliot Aronson's term—the plain fact is that good looks tend to impress us (Aronson, 1984). Indeed, most of us tend to *attribute* highly positive characteristics to handsome individuals. And, far too often, we tend to attribute negative characteristics to individuals who are "below average" in terms of their physical appearances. This fact led psychologists Karen Dion, Ellen Berscheid, and Elaine Walster to conclude that, to most of the people they studied, "beautiful is good" (Dion, 1972; Dion et al., 1972).

Dion, Berscheid, and Walster are pioneers in the study of the effects of physical attractiveness on social behavior. In an early experiment on "computer dating," Elaine Walster discovered that "good looks" was the only factor that could predict how much both the male and female subjects liked their dates. Furthermore, the importance of "good looks" tended to increase from the first to the fifth date in both men and women (Walster et al., 1966). More recently, Paul Sergios and James Cody obtained similar results in a "computer dating" study of homosexual males (Sergios & Cody, 1985–1986).

According to Elaine Walster (now Hatfield) and Susan Sprecher, most of us consider attractive people to be more sensitive, strong, modest, sociable, outgoing, kind, interesting, and sexually warm than unattractive people. We also tend to believe that handsome individuals are more likely to have important jobs, happy marriages, and to "enjoy life to the fullest" (Hatfield & Sprecher, 1986).

Other research has shown that strangers are more likely to help someone who is good looking, that handsome criminal defendants are less likely to be convicted (and if convicted, to get shorter terms) than are ugly criminal defendants, that attractive mental patients are more likely to recover and to be accepted back in the community after release from a mental hospital, and that physically attractive individuals are more likely to be hired for jobs than are less good-looking people (Bardack & McAndrew, 1985; Benson et al., 1976; Burns & Farina, 1987; Miller, 1986).

We are also more likely to ascribe *negative* characteristics to people who are not beautiful. For example, Karen Dion found that most teachers believe that unattractive students are more likely to have "a chronic disposition to commit bad acts" than are attractive children (Dion, 1972). Teachers believe that attractive students, on the other hand, are generally more intelligent, academically, gifted, and socially skilled (Ritts et al., 1992).

Why this "beauty bias"? Ellen Berscheid believes that the less information you have about someone, the more likely it is that you will judge that person in terms of his or her looks. After you get to know the person, however, you may be more impressed by other factors. Berscheid believes, however, that, in terms of *sexual attraction*, beauty remains important over long periods of contact (cited in Leff, 1981). And a research meta-analysis by Alan Feingold confirms the popular view that being attractive is more important for women than for men (Feingold, 1990, 1991).

An additional explanation of our bias toward beauty comes from studies on the *visual complexity* of physical beauty. As we noted in Chapter 4, Judith Langlois and her colleagues found that infants spent more time looking at attractive than unattractive faces ("attractiveness" judged by adult standards). Langlois and her

Beauty is power; a smile is its sword.

CHARLES READE

Attractive faces are often more "juvenile" in their appearance.

associates note that "pretty" faces tend to be highly symmetrical, smooth, and almost "juvenile" in their features (Langlois et al., 1987). Such faces are also *less complex visual stimuli* (and hence are easier to process) than are irregular, marked, "unattractive" faces.

In another study, Langlois and her associates used a computer to "average" the facial features of several different photographs. They found that adult judges rated the "averaged" faces as more attractive than the originals—leading Langlois and Roggman to title their report "Attractive Faces are Only Average" (Langlois & Roggman, 1990). Other researchers report similar results using different methods (Cunningham et al., 1990; Symons, 1987). Thus, the phrase "easy on the eyes" may well offer a valid explanation of our preference for certain facial features.

Langlois and Roggman suggest that there may be universal features of faces that infants, older children, and adults in *different cultures* consider attractive. They point out that (1) very young infants are drawn to attractive faces, presumably before they have had opportunity to learn cultural standards, and (2) there is a high level of agreement among judges rating beauty in different cultures. These facts suggest that we inherit highly similar standards of beauty, or at least acquire them very early (Langlois & Roggman, 1990).

To summarize, beauty may be "in the eye of the beholder," but it obviously does shape our perceptions of others to a greater extent than many of us would like to believe is the case.

Why do you think beautiful children tend to score higher on individually administered intelligence tests than when they take a written test administered to a whole group of children?

PERSONAL SPACE

Invasions of *personal space* can also affect first (and subsequent) impressions. Anthropologist Edward Hall coined the term personal space to refer to the bubble of space we try to keep around ourselves when we interact (Hall, 1966). Psychologist Robert Sommer notes that in a number of studies, subjects have shown a dramatic increase in nervousness when an experimenter moved to within a foot or so of them. Most of the subjects "defended their territories" either by moving away from the intruder, or by becoming increasingly hostile.

Beauty—the adjustment of all parts proportionately so that one cannot add or subtract or change without impairing the harmony of the whole.

LEION BATTISTA ALBERTI (1404–1472).

In some cultures a comfortable distance for conversation is much smaller than Americans find comfortable.

Sommer states that the size of your own personal space bubble is influenced by such factors as your personality, status, and the present social situation. For middle-class Americans, this private area extends outward about two feet from any part of the body. For people in the Middle East and South America, the space is usually much smaller. For Scandinavians and Japanese, the bubble is typically larger. However, the size of each person's "space bubble" may expand or contract depending on the circumstances (Sommer, 1969).

According to John Lombardo, men respond more negatively to invasions of their personal space in face-to-face confrontations, while women respond more negatively to side-by-side invasions. In addition, Lombardo found that both men and women with "traditional sex-role stereotypes" found invasions of their space more threatening than did men and women with less traditional views (Lombardo, 1986).

Psychologists Nan Sussman and Howard Rosenfeld report that personal space varies with the language you're speaking. Sussman and Rosenfeld asked students from different cultures to "sit and converse" in their *native tongues*. The students from South America sat closer together than did students from the United States. But Japanese students sat several inches farther apart than did the Americans. However, when the researcher asked the students to converse in English, the Japanese students sat closer to each other, and the South Americans moved farther away. Apparently these students were quite aware that the size of the "space bubble" in North America is different from their own—and they tried to imitate our space requirements while speaking in our tongue (Sussman & Rosenfeld, 1982).

Would having clear-cut territories reduce or increase the stress most people feel when forced to live together in crowded conditions?

BODY POSTURE

Even when you respect other people's "personal space" or territories by standing at just the right distance from people to make them comfortable, the way that you *hold your body* influences the impressions that you give to others. In North American culture, most people assume that if you lean toward them, you like them (and perhaps are inviting intimacy). But if you lean away from them, they may assume you dislike or reject them.

In a study on body posture, Albert Mehrabian asked men and women to act out the way they would sit when speaking to someone they liked or disliked. Mehrabian reports that both men and women leaned *forward* to express liking, but that men (more than women) leaned back or became more tense when addressing someone they disliked (Mehrabian, 1981).

Once you establish a proper distance to stand from an individual, any further movement you may signal a *change* in your feelings. Donn Byrne and his associates set up an experiment in which a computer matched couples for blind dates. After the young man and woman had gotten to know each other briefly, they were called into Byrne's office and stood before his desk for further instructions. Byrne then separated the subjects and asked them to fill out a questionnaire indicating how much they liked their dates. Byrne and his colleagues report that couples who liked each other had stood closer together in front of the desk than did couples who didn't care much for each other (Byrne et al., 1970).

"Of course it's not easy to read the body language of someone who's basically inert."

If a woman stared at you intensely while talking to you, what motives would you attribute to her? If she averted her eyes while listening to you, would you think she was showing disinterest or respect?

The rules of eye contact are learned very early and are usually followed unconsciously.

EYE CONTACT

Movements of your face and eyes are often as critical to the first impression you give as are how close you stand and whether you lean toward or away from someone. The *eye contact* you make with people often controls both the flow of conversation and their initial opinion of your honesty and aggressiveness. Eye contact may well be the single most important feature of nonverbal communication (Brown & Keller, 1979).

The "rules of eye contact" vary considerably from one society to another, and thus seem to be primarily learned behaviors (Nadler & Nadler, 1987). However, the *reason* there are rules is probably grounded in innate emotional responses. Among both primates and people, prolonged "direct eye contact" is a mark of intense emotionality (Strom & Buck, 1979). Primates usually respond hostilely to prolonged stares. (Next time you're at a zoo, try staring directly at a monkey's eyes and watch how the animal responds.) Among humans, "mutual gazing" of any duration occurs primarily among (1) lovers, (2) two people locked in some kind of emotional confrontation, and (3) a mother and her infant (Patterson, 1983; Patterson et al., 1984).

Humans avoid the emotionality of direct "mutual gazing" by developing rules that govern who looks at whom, and when. For example, if you happen to be a middle-class adult, you probably gaze *at* people when they are talking or lecturing. Staring directly at a speaker is your way of encouraging that person to continue conversing, particularly if you also nod or smile in agreement. When you look *away* from whoever is talking, however, you signal that you are bored or that you want to take over the talking role yourself (Argyle & Cook, 1976).

When *you* are telling a story or making a point, though, chances are you will gaze *away* from your audience—particularly if you are trying to think through what you are talking about. While you speak, you may glance back at your audience from time to time to make sure they are still with you (that is, still looking at you), then look away again as you continue talking (Kleinke, 1986).

These "rules of eye contact" vary not only from culture to culture, but also *within* a particular culture. For example, individuals brought up in lower-class environments in the United States have eye signals that are almost the direct opposite of those found in middle-class society. People reared in lower-class homes tend to stare directly at others when talking, but avert their eyes when listening to show respect (particularly if listening to someone of higher status) (Brown & Keller, 1979).

In middle-class America, people who engage in prolonged direct gaze are often perceived as being more powerful and of higher social status. For example, psychologists Charles Brooks, Michael Church, and Lance Fraser had undergraduates view video tapes of a woman student who maintained direct eye contact with an interviewer for 5, 30, or 50 seconds. The students tended to rate the woman as being more socially "potent" (and as having a higher grade-point average) the *longer* she engaged in direct mutual gaze with the interviewer (Brooks et al., 1986).

You learn the "rules of eye contact" so early in life that you may not be aware of how strongly they influence your perceptions and behaviors. Unless you understand how these rules affect your first impressions, however, you are likely to *misinterpret* the eye signals that someone from another culture or socioeconomic class gives to you (Kleinke, 1986).

What sorts of "body language" cues do you look for when you try to determine whether someone is lying?

DECEITFUL BODY LANGUAGE

Studies by psychologist Robert Rosenthal and his colleagues suggest that the old belief that "people who look you straight in the eye are telling the truth" has little or no validity to it. Indeed, people who tell embarrassing *truths* are more likely to maintain poor eye contact than are people who are deliberately *lying* (Zuckerman et al., 1982). Nervous speech apparently is a better indication of lying (or emotionality) than is poor eye contact (Scherer et al., 1985).

While we can successfully lie with our words and our eyes, it is much harder to deceive with the limbs and torso of our body. Several studies report that subjects could detect false emotions better if they watched a person's body, than if they watched the person's face. One bodily cue strongly associated with lying is a gesture called a "self-adaptor" (touching one's own body with a hand) (DePaulo et al., 1985; Ekman & Friesen, 1969, 1974; Eckman, 1985; Stiff et al., 1989).

If you encountered a patient in a mental hospital who refused to look at you, what would be your "first impression" of the reason for avoiding eye contact?

THE ATTRIBUTION PROCESS

By now, you have learned some of the rules that influence the way you perceive people, particularly someone you've just met. But *why* do you think this way? For instance, why do you often "stereotype" people? According to Fritz Heider, you do so to *avoid stress*. Heider notes that most of us become alarmed whenever we cannot guess fairly accurately what will happen to us next. By using what Heider calls the **attribution process,** we assign to others various motives that make their actions more predictable (and hence less stressful) to us.

According to Heider, when you perceive a woman's actions as being an expression of her character, you are actually *attributing* certain personality traits to the woman. Probably most of these *attributed traits* are stereotypes, for she may not possess these characteristics at all. But once you stereotype her, you have a ready-made attitude or perception to fit her. Then you not only can predict her *actions* (or so you think), but you have a way of *responding* to her as well (Heider, 1958).

But we have seen enough examples of social/behavioral research in previous chapters to know that a person's actions are not always the result of internal dispositions or traits. More importantly, we know from our own experience that we do not react to every situation in the same way. Why? It depends on the *situation*. Our environment can exert a powerful influence over our behavior, and so we often attribute the causes for our actions to our *external* situation rather than our *internal* disposition.

Thus, one of the most important questions in the study of attribution is, "When do we attribute *internal* causes, and when do we attribute *external* causes for behavior?" For example: "Did he donate the money because he is generous (internal), or because he wanted to be *seen* as generous (external)?" "Did she go out with me because she likes me (internal), or because she wanted to see the movie (external)?" "Did the soldier kill children and babies because he is cruel and evil (internal), or because he was ordered to (external)?"

In several earlier chapters we have seen the effect of different types of attribution. How many can you recall?

Attributional Biases

By studying the way we make attributions, social psychologists are shedding light on our social motivation. In the process, they have identified several consistent biases in the way we think about the causes for behavior. (Remember that each of these is a bias, or tendency, and does not operate in every situation.)

Attribution process. The act of inferring personality traits or motives in others so you can explain their past or present behavior, hence predict what they may do in the future.

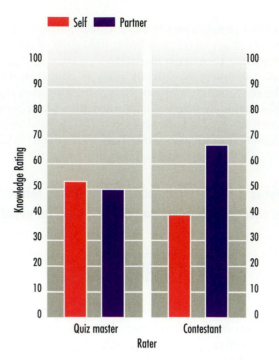

FIGURE 17.1

Ross and his colleagues found that "contestants" failed to take into account the influence of the situation when making attributions about the "knowledgeability" of the quiz masters and contestants. (Ross et al., 1977.)

Fundamental attribution error. The general tendency we have to see behavior (ours and others') as a product of internal dispositional motivation—a product of personality traits—rather than external situational factors.

THE FUNDAMENTAL ATTRIBUTION ERROR

Researchers find that we have a consistent tendency to attribute behavior to *internal* rather than external causes, even when we should know better. We might say that in our personal theories of personality we incline towards a "trait" perspective rather than a "social/behavioral" view.

Put yourself in this research example: Who would you say was more knowledgeable, quiz masters who made up the quiz questions, or contestants who got several of them wrong? Of course, objectively, we know that this situation does not permit a comparison of "knowledgeability"—it is stacked in favor of the quiz masters. They made up the questions so they should know the answers. (Subsequent testing revealed no differences in knowledge level between contestants and quiz masters.) However, Lee Ross and his colleagues found that both the contestants as well as observers rated the quiz masters as more knowledgeable. Only the quiz masters seemed to realize the situation was biased to make them look good, and rated themselves equal to the contestants (see Figure 17.1) (Ross et al., 1977).

This study, and others like it, reveal a general tendency we have to ignore external influences on behavior, and to emphasize internal causes. Ross has labelled this tendency the **fundamental attribution error** (Ross, 1977).

The tendency to ignore external situational causes helps to explain how we develop negative stereotypes about disadvantaged groups. We may tend to see their poverty, or low educational level, as a result of traits of "laziness," or "stupidity," rather than recognizing the external social forces controlling their behavior (Pettigrew, 1979).

Canadian researchers Serge Guimond and Douglas Palmer found that being aware of social forces helps to reduce this attributional bias. They had college students complete a questionnaire which assessed the students' tendency to blame either the *situation*, or the *person*, for suffering poverty, unemployment, and economic inferiority. The researchers compared the responses of social science students, engineering students, and commerce students, in their first, or third and fourth years. They found no difference in perception among students in their first year of study. However, among students in their third or fourth year, the social science students were much more likely to blame the "system," and commerce students were more likely to blame the individual (see Figure 17.2) (Guimon et al., 1989; Guimond & Palmer, 1990).

So, we are inclined to attribute *internal* rather than *external* motives for behavior. And we probably acquire this tendency through socialization processes, since learning about social influence apparently leads to more external attributions. As we will see next, however, we make fewer internal attributions when we are in the situation ourselves.

How might a trait personality theorist and a social/behavioral personality theorist disagree about the fundamental attribution "error"?

ACTOR-OBSERVER BIAS

There are many situations in which we are unsure of our own motivation. In these situations we often make attributions about our own motives just as we would about someone else's actions (Bem, 1972). However, we seem to be biased towards external causes in our self-attributions, but biased towards internal causes in our attributions of others. In short, we tend to blame the situation for our own acts, and internal dispositions for the acts of others.

You may be able to demonstrate this effect to yourself. Stop and ask yourself why you chose the major you are studying. When you have thought of the main reasons, ask yourself why a good friend of yours chose the major he or she is studying. Reasons such as "I'm good at physics," or "I like to work with numbers," are internal attributions; reasons such as "It's a high-paying field," or "My parents and friends expect me to," are external attributions. If you are like the college students studied by Richard Nisbett and his colleagues, you made more *internal* attributions for your friend than for yourself (Nisbett et al., 1973).

The tendency we have to "blame" our behavior on our situation, and other people's behavior on their personality, is called the **actor-observer bias.** In fact, the actor-observer bias is often found together with the fundamental attribution error. The result is that our tendency to over-emphasize internal causes (fundamental attribution error), is especially strong when we are evaluating other people's motives (actor-observer bias) (Watson, 1982).

Consider another study by Nisbett and his colleagues. They asked subjects to rate themselves, a friend, their father, and TV newscaster Walter Cronkite on a list of several traits. The subjects could choose one of three alternatives for each trait: (1) the person possessed the trait, (2) the person possessed the opposite trait, or (3) the person didn't have either trait, but rather "it depends on the situation." Results were as predicted by the actor-observer bias. Subjects chose "it depends on the situation" most for themselves, less for their friends and fathers, and least for Walter Cronkite. In other words, subjects were *most* willing to attribute traits to people they knew the *least* (Walter Cronkite), and *least* willing to attribute traits to people they knew the *best* (themselves) (Nisbett et al., 1973).

SELF-SERVING BIAS

The fundamental attribution error and the actor-observer effect suggest that we tend to give full credit to external causes for our own behavior. But is this always the case? Apparently not when it is to *our advantage* to attribute *internal* causes.

If you do well on an exam, do you say, "It was an easy exam," or "I lucked out" (external causes)? Perhaps. But more likely, you would like to receive at least some of the credit yourself (internal causes). You would like to believe, "I'm smart," or "I worked hard." In competitive, achievement situations, we tend to emphasize internal causes for our successes and external causes for our failures (Davis & Stephan,

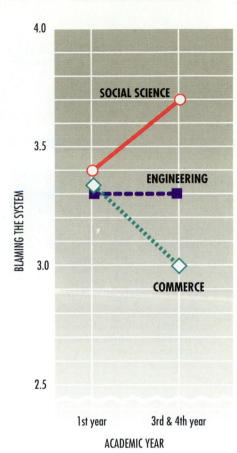

FIGURE 17.2

Guimond and Palmer found that as social science students progressed in their education, they became more likely to blame the system for social disadvantages; commerce students became less likely to blame the system. (Guimond & Palmer, 1990.)

Actor-observer bias. The tendency we have to see our own behavior as caused by external circumstances, and other people's behavior as caused by their internal dispositions.

Self-serving bias. The tendency we have to attribute our successes to internal characteristics, and our failures to external circumstances.

In competitive achievement situations, we tend to take personal credit for success, and attribute failure to circumstances beyond our control.

Self-handicapping strategy. Actions we go through which increase our chance of failure, but which also provide a more "acceptable" cause to which we can attribute our failure.

1980; Griffin et al., 1983). We call this pressure to attribute success to our ability and failure to circumstances beyond our control, the **self-serving bias** (Weiner et al., 1972).

Looking at this bias another way, when we use the attribution process to explain our own faults, we attribute these faults to the environment, not to our own personality. We see ourselves as merely reacting to whatever situation we find ourselves in. However, when we observe inconsistent behaviors in *others,* we tend to ignore the social background. Instead, we attribute their actions to some inner need, motive, or flaw of character. In general, we perceive ourselves as being *forced* to act in inappropriate ways from time to time. But when others misbehave, we perceive them as *wanting* to act that way.

Psychologists Richard Lau and Dan Russell call this the "I win because of me: I lose because of you" effect. Lau and Russell studied the explanations offered by professional players and coaches after important baseball and football games. More than 80 percent of the time, the athletes claimed that "wins" were due to their own superior performance. About half the time, however, they attributed "losses" to such factors as bad luck, bad officiating, or injuries to key players (Lau & Russell, 1980).

SELF-HANDICAPPING

Have you ever felt that you were going to fail at some important task, such as a big exam, and wished you had a good excuse? If you have, you may have consciously (or unconsciously) set-up a good excuse and *contributed to your own failure* at the same time!

For example, students who are unsure of their abilities might purposely not study, or even stay up all night partying, in order to be able to blame their failure on an *external* cause. They find it more acceptable to say, "I failed because I partied all night," than to have to say, "I failed because I'm not smart enough."

This strategy not only provides an excuse, but unfortunately, it also contributes to failure. Thus it is called a **self-handicapping strategy.** The self-handicapping strategy is a distortion or bias in our attribution of causes for our own behavior. It is brought on by fear of failure. Anticipated failure leads us to search for, and even create, *external* causes to replace the internal causes we would like to hide (Berglas & Jones, 1978).

How might an athlete use a self-handicapping strategy?

Culture and Attributions

A general theme among attributional biases is our tendency to attribute dispositional causes without sufficient justification—thus the term the *fundamental* attribution error. This tendency is particularly strong when we evaluate other people's motives (actor-observer bias), or when it is to our advantage (self-serving bias). On the other hand, we sometimes go to great pains to *avoid* a dispositional attribution for our own failures (self-handicapping strategy).

However, we must be careful not to assume that our general tendency to overemphasize dispositional attributions is universal. Some research suggests that internal attributions are associated with a North American emphasis on individualism. In non-individualistic Eastern cultures ("sociocentric" or "collectivistic" cultures), such as India and Japan, there is a much greater tendency to give *external*, social explanations for behavior (Cousins, 1989; Miller, 1984, Miller et al., 1990). In sociocentric cultures, people act, and recognize that others act, for the good of the group and to preserve group solidarity. As a result, other people don't necessarily see the actors' behaviors indicating their *personal* needs, motives, and traits.

Thus culture exerts an influence in emphasizing certain attributional biases. But culture also divides people into groups—who sometimes look at *each other* through distorted attributional lenses. This can lead to the **ultimate attribution error.**

The ultimate attribution error is our tendency to use *internal* attributions to explain socially desirable actions by members of our own group, and socially undesirable actions by members of an opposing group. The same bias leads us to use *external* attributions to explain socially undesirable actions of our own group, and socially desirable actions of our foes (Hewstone, 1988; Pettigrew, 1979; Taylor and Jaggi, 1974). In short, we are biased towards saying, "We do good because we *want* to; they do good because they *have* to," and "We were *forced* to do bad, but they *wanted* to do it." For example, we might say, "Our group supports charities out of love for humanity; others do it to look good." Or, "Our soldiers fight because they have to" (external attribution), but "Our enemies fight because they are war-like" (internal attribution).

Taylor and Jaggi found that Hindu subjects attributed socially desirable actions to the good character of Hindus, but attributed the same actions in Muslims to external circumstances. In addition, Hindu subjects blamed socially *undesirable* actions on Hindus' circumstances and Muslims' character (Taylor & Jaggi, 1974).

Like all attributional biases, the ultimate attribution error does not operate in every situation—it is a *tendency*. However, being aware of this tendency and of our cultural bias towards dispositional attributions generally may help us to avoid incorrect inferences about the motives of individuals from other cultures. As we will see in the next section, without this kind of understanding, it is very hard to change incorrect attributions.

Attributional Conflicts

One person who has advanced attribution theory significantly over the past several years is Harold Kelley. Kelley is interested more in long-term relationships between people than in first impressions.

Kelley points out that even loving couples occasionally have problems. Research shows that marriage partners tend to explain problems in their relationship in terms of *attributed traits* and not just *specific behaviors* or environmental circumstances (Baucom et al., 1989; Bradbury & Fincham, 1990). Thus, a wife who is upset with her husband typically won't speak of the actions that bother her: He leaves his dirty underwear on the floor for her to pick up, doesn't listen to her, or won't do his share of the housework. Rather, she will describe the problem in terms of his personality and his presumed attitude and feelings toward her: he is sloppy, lazy, and doesn't love her. In this *internal* attribution, the wife calls attention to what the husband is doing wrong and challenges him to prove that her attribution of the causes is incorrect.

The husband, on the other hand, will attribute his faults to *external* environmental stress, such as problems he is experiencing at work. He perceives himself as still being deeply in love with her, and believes she ought to forgive him for his minor misbehaviors because his intentions are good. When his wife fails to forgive him, he attributes her anger to such traits as "moodiness" and "bad temper."

If the husband changes his behaviors, it may not satisfy the wife if she thinks he is merely trying to appease her. Because she attributes his actions to underlying traits and attitudes, she wants an attitudinal change from him rather than a mere shift in the way he acts. At this point, Kelley notes, the husband is in something of a bind. Since his wife can never *see* his attitudes or intentions directly, the only thing he can do is to change his behaviors toward her. But she is always free to *interpret* these behavioral changes any way she wishes, and he cannot prove her wrong (Kelley, 1979, 1984; Kelley et al., 1983).

Kelley and his colleagues believe that attributional conflicts are usually not resolvable. Why? For three reasons. First, there are no objective (behavioral)

Ultimate attribution error. The combination of biases in attribution that leads us to praise our own group but not other groups for good behavior and blame other groups but not our own group for bad behavior.

standards by which one person can *prove* another's attributions are wrong, or his or her own attributions are correct. Second, most people *genuinely believe* they have an accurate understanding of why they act as they do, and that "the facts" justify their explanations of "why." Third, most people perceive explaining their actions as a "good behavior" designed to reduce social stress. Thus, when you use the attribution process, you may actually see yourself as "playing the peacemaker's role." And most of us are extremely reluctant to give up what we perceive as "socially approved roles" (Kelley et al., 1983).

How does the attribution process help explain the popularity of the "trait approach" to describing human personality?

SOCIAL ROLES

Attributions are *highly personal* explanations for behaviors. But you may also excuse your actions in terms of *social expectations*. That is, you may describe what you did as "merely playing the role that society has put you in."

As we shift our attention from attributions to social roles, we move away from the individual toward larger social systems. For "traits" are generally perceived as intrapsychic factors. Roles, however, are *systematic behavior patterns* that are embedded in the structure of groups, organizations, and societies rather than inside the individual's psyche. You *are* generous or stingy. But you *play the role* of doctor, lawyer, merchant, or thief in a social system.

Are social roles learned or innate?

A *social role* is a more-or-less stereotyped set of responses that you make to related or similar situations. Some roles (such as socially approved "masculine" and "feminine" behaviors) are a basic part of your personality throughout life and are influenced by your genetic blueprint. Other roles seem to be entirely learned, such as that of "leader" or "manager."

Learned, innate, or (more likely) a mixture thereof, two things seem to be true of roles: First, society's norms may well generate the *concept* of a role. However, both your genes and your unique personality determine the manner in which you play a role. Second, the *purpose* of most roles seems to be that of making "social interactions" go more smoothly by reducing uncertainty and providing guidelines for acceptable behavior (Newcomb, 1961).

There are many types of roles. And, as Shakespeare put it centuries ago, "One man in his time plays many parts." This much everyone admits, just as most psychologists agree that role-learning usually occurs through imitation. However, there is little agreement on how and why you switch from one role to another in certain situations. Also, there isn't a consensus on which social roles are the most important ones to study.

Social psychologists have researched the *leadership role* for many years, however. While theorists disagree on why certain individuals become leaders and others don't, some aspects of the leader's role are fairly well defined (at least for our culture). Given the amount of information we have on the subject of leadership, therefore, suppose we look at this topic first.

When cultures meet, culturally defined roles sometimes clash. This man's culture may have taught him that it is not appropriate for a woman to tell him what to do.

Assume you have a "social interaction sequence" with a physician. How would your knowledge about social roles affect the way you perceived and responded

to this individual? Would you have reacted differently had the other person been a "janitor" rather than a "doctor"? Why? And how does the presence of clearly understood roles help reduce stress in "social interaction sequences"?

Leadership Roles

Many years ago, sociologist Robert Bales and his colleagues performed a classic set of experiments on leadership. Their subjects were groups of male college students brought together in a laboratory and given certain intellectual problems to solve. The researchers measured each man's verbal behaviors as objectively as they could. And at the end of each problem-solving session, the experimenters asked the subjects to rate each member of the group in a number of ways, including how much the man liked the others and which men seemed to be leaders or have the best ideas (Bales, 1953).

TWO TYPES OF SPECIALISTS

Bales and his associates report that two types of people get high scores on leadership rating scales: the "idea generator" (or *task specialist*) and the "social facilitator" (or *social-emotional specialist*).

During group sessions, the task specialist gives opinions and makes suggestions more often than anyone else. He or she keeps reminding the group of its goals and brings the group back to the task at hand whenever the members stray from problem solving. These behaviors apparently cause other group members to rate the person as a good leader or idea-generator.

The social-emotional specialist, on the other hand, is much more likely to *ask* for suggestions than to give them. He or she is particularly sensitive to the needs of others. This person makes extensive use of praise and other forms of feedback, and he or she smooths over arguments in order to create what Bales calls *group solidarity*. In short, the "social-emotional specialist" shapes the group into moving further toward its goals.

According to Bales, the "task specialist" directs the cognitive or intellectual resources of the group, and the group respects the specialist's knowledge and expertise. The "social facilitator" directs the emotional resources of the group, and the group warmly likes this person for keeping the group functioning as a cohesive unit (Bales, 1953).

Fred Fiedler points out that one leadership style is not best for all situations. The best style depends on the demands of the situation. Fiedler encourages managers to: (1) examine the situation—the task, the people, and the organization; (2) be flexible in the use of different skills within their preferred style; and (3) consider modifying elements of their jobs to obtain a better match with their preferred style (Fiedler, 1967; Fiedler & Garcia, 1987).

The Chinese scholar Lao-Tzu once said, "When a great leader finishes a project, the people rejoice and say, 'We did this ourselves.'" Which of the two types of leaders did Lao-Tzu apparently have in mind?

LEADERSHIP "TRAITS" OR LEADERSHIP "BEHAVIORS"?

There have been hundreds, if not thousands, of studies attempting to determine the "traits of leadership." One of the "personality characteristics" of any great leader is supposed to be *charisma,* which Webster's defines as "a personal magic of leadership arousing special popular loyalty or enthusiasm." But according to management expert Peter Drucker, effective leadership "has little to do with 'leadership qualities' and even less to do with 'charisma.' It is mundane, unromantic and boring. Its essence is performance" (Drucker, 1988).

The most charismatic leaders of this century, Drucker says, were Hitler, Stalin, and Mao—"the misleaders who inflicted as much evil and suffering on humanity as have ever been recorded. . . . Dwight Eisenhower, George Marshall and Harry Truman were singularly effective leaders yet none possessed any more charisma than a dead mackerel" (Drucker, 1988).

Nor is there a "leadership personality," Drucker says. Rather, he claims, leadership is mostly *hard work*. Effective leaders set clear-cut goals, establish standards of conduct (and enforce them), listen attentively to their subordinates, and "praise and promote" those subordinates for actual achievement (Drucker, 1988).

What Drucker seems to be saying, of course, is that social roles must be defined in terms of *behaviors*, not in terms of "attitudes" or "personality traits."

SUCCESSFUL MANAGERS

Jay Hall and Susan Donnell report a study which seems to support Drucker's views. Hall and Donnell measured the attitudes and behaviors of more than 12,000 managers in 50 different American business and government organizations. By determining how rapidly each manager moved up through the corporate structure, Hall and Donnell were able to identify "successful," "average," and "unsuccessful" managers.

Hall and Donnell found that *successful* managers almost always sought the opinions and consent of the people who worked for them. *Average* and *unsuccessful* managers, however, did not encourage much participation at all from their subordinates.

Hall and Donnell believe that a manager's *goals* in large part determine how successful the manager will be. They report that successful managers showed both a strong interest in achieving organizational goals and in helping their subordinates satisfy their personal needs. "Average" managers also tried to "get the task done," but had considerably less concern about what happened to their employees in the process. The unsuccessful managers appeared to be protecting themselves. They had little commitment either to the goals of the organization or to satisfying the needs of those individuals whom they supervised (Hall & Donnell, 1979).

Jan Muczyk and Bernard Reimann add that successful managers don't just seek the opinions and consensus of those under them and assume that agreed-upon actions will be carried out. Rather, successful managers know that at times they will need to be quite directive. This is especially true when their subordinates do not see their roles requiring them to show initiative and follow through without close supervision (Muczyk & Reimann, 1989).

FEMALE MANAGERS

The first study by Hall and Donnell dealt exclusively with male managers. In their second study, they gave similar measures to female managers and to their subordinates in similar situations. Donnell and Hall conclude that "women, in general, do not differ from men, in general, in the ways in which they administer the management process" (Hall & Donnell, 1979).

Then why do women occupy only 5 percent of the top executive positions in American business and less than 3 percent in international management (Adler, 1984; Trafford et al., 1986)? Maybe because we are still using inaccurate stereotypes of both women and managers. As Marian Jelinek and Nancy Adler point out, "In study after study, undergraduates, MBAs, and managers (male and female) in the United States have tended to identify stereotypically 'masculine' (aggressive) characteristics as managerial and stereotypically 'feminine' (cooperative and communicative) characteristics as unmanagerial" (Jelinek & Adler, 1988; Powell & Butterfield, 1979).

Women may be underrepresented in management positions because of inaccurate stereotypes of both female characteristics and leadership roles.

It is impossible to say how many women have been excluded from managerial positions because of inaccurate stereotypes of women and managers. Even if the stereotype of "feminine" behaviors was generally accurate, there would be no reason to expect women to be inferior leaders. As we saw earlier, one very effective type of leader is the "social-emotive specialist," who is sensitive to the needs of others and promotes cooperation among the group. Unfortunately, most people's stereotype of a leader does not emphasize these characteristics.

On the other hand, Jelinek and Adler suggest that "feminine" stereotypes can be an advantage in certain international situations. They quote women managers from different countries:

(Korea) "Women are better at treating men sensitively, and they just like you."

(India and Pakistan) "I got in to see customers because they had never seen a female banker before. . . . Having a female banker adds value for the client."

(Thailand) "Being a woman is never a detriment. They remembered me better. Fantastic for a marketing position. It's better working with Asians than with the Dutch, British, or Americans."

(Japan) "Women are better at putting people at ease. It's easier for a woman to convince a man. . . . The traditional woman's role . . . inspires confidence and trust, there's less suspicion, and I'm not threatening" (Jelinek & Adler, 1988).

Given the fact that women appear to be as effective leaders as are men, why has the United States never elected a woman as president? Why not a black president? What do your answers tell you about the influence of environmental factors on social roles?

LEADERSHIP: PERSONAL QUALITIES OR SITUATION?

Many people, particularly those with a "disposition" toward explaining human behavior in terms of inner traits, continue to believe that you are either a "born leader," or that you become one because of the structure of your personality. At the most, these people say, the environment may *restrict* your opportunities for taking on a leadership role (Graumann & Moscovici, 1986).

Anyone can hold the helm when the sea is calm.

PUBLILIUS SYRUS (1ST CENTURY B.C.)

However, a growing number of people see social roles as resulting from an *interaction* between "person and situation" (Magnusson, 1981). Data to support this view come from research by Reuven Gal, who was, for many years, chief psychologist of the Israeli Defense Forces. Gal studied 77 soldiers who were decorated for bravery during the Yom Kippur war. He then compared these "heroic leaders" with 273 similar soldiers who had not received medals. All the soldiers had taken psychological tests *before* the war broke out. Gal found that the "heroes" were significantly higher on four traits: leadership, devotion to duty, decisiveness, and perseverance under stress.

Gal then asked three military psychologists to analyze the actual battle conditions under which the "heroes" had won their medals. He concluded that "In many of the given cases it was predominantly the specific . . . circumstances that evoked the exceptional behavior, while the determination of the particular individual who would accomplish this behavior was almost by chance" (cited in Horn, 1985; Gal, 1986).

Some soldiers win medals; others don't. Some military personnel are high-paid officers with special privileges; others are low-paid enlisted personnel. But almost all soldiers risk their lives during a war. Is this "inequity" fair?

Social Exchange Theory

All groups, organizations, and societies have certain *resources* available to them. Some of these "resources" may be material; others are psychological or social. Within any group, however, certain "roles" (such as those associated with leadership) have a stronger claim on available resources than do other more subordinate "roles." If there is to be *stability* in a group or organization, however, there must be some *equity* in the way the group shares, or exchanges, resources (Thibaut & Kelley, 1959).

Japanese psychologist Kazuko Inoue studied *equity relationships* in couples who were "going steady." Inoue found that both male and female "dating partners" tended to agree as to how *equitable* their relationships were. The more *inequitable* the relationships, the more distress both partners felt. Generally speaking, both partners strove to restore and maintain equity in the relationship. If they failed, they tended to break off the romance—and seek more equitable relationships with other people (Inoue, 1985).

But what is "equity in human interaction," and how do people achieve it? Harry Triandis views the process of human interaction from the perspective of *social exchange theory*. Triandis suggests the "exchange of resources" governs human relations. You want things from me, and I want things from you. The question then becomes, how do I discover what you want, and how do we negotiate an exchange of resources that satisfies both of us?

ROLES AS "BEHAVIORAL INTENTIONS"

Triandis believes that two things primarily determine your actions: habits and behavioral intentions. Habits are those stereotyped ways you have of responding to specific situations. Your *behavioral intentions* are, more or less, whatever set of goals you are trying to reach at any given moment. Many things affect these momentary goals—the roles you have learned, your emotional reactions, and your cognitive expectancies (Triandis, 1984).

Triandis believes the first thing you must do when you learn a new role is this: You have to discover what *behavioral intentions* are associated with that role. Thus, when you meet someone new, learning what role the person has assumed will tell you a great deal about that person's intentions. Therefore, you learn about other people's

Cultural differences often contribute to misunderstanding between individuals. Cultural sensitivity is necessary for successful communication at both a personal and business level.

roles in order to find what "social exchanges" interest them (Triandis & Lambert, 1980).

According to Triandis, if you know my intentions, you can guess at what I want—and what I am willing to pay for satisfying this goal. But *your own social expectations* strongly influence the intentions you attribute to me. And your expectations, of course, are strongly influenced by the society you grew up in (Triandis & Brislin, 1984). For example, imagine that you go to your psychology professor to dispute your mark on the last exam. Your expectations of the professor's response are strongly influenced by what society has taught you about the role of professors. Are professors obliged to be sympathetic to student opinion or must they be firm and unmoving? Does their role make them vulnerable to student complaints to the Dean, or is their position secure? The way you act (and the way your professor acts) will be affected by the social expectations society has given you (and your professor) for your respective roles.

CULTURAL INFLUENCE

In their research, Triandis and his colleagues examined what happens when two people from different cultures meet and interact. Most subjects Triandis and his associates have studied assume that someone from a different country *must have the same intentions as they do*. Thus, most Japanese will explain the behavior of Americans in terms of Japanese tradition and culture, while Americans find it difficult to believe that American intentions don't motivate the Japanese. These assumptions, although inaccurate, serve to reduce uncertainty and anxiety in cross-cultural contact (Gudykunst, 1988; Hui & Triandis, 1986; Kashima & Triandis, 1986).

Doubtless it is true, as Triandis and others claim, that behavior is determined by the *interaction* between situational and personal factors. However, to date no theory tells us which of these two influences will predominate in any given setting. If you are like most people, you probably assume that your own long-standing goals and values will assert themselves no matter what. However, as you are about to see, there are times when the situational factors are so powerful that almost anyone will behave in an unusual, or even shocking, fashion.

From your own experience, which "role" do you know the most about, that of "prison guard" or that of "prisoner"?

Zimbardo's research showed that social roles are a powerful influence on the way guards and prisoners act toward each other.

Zimbardo's "Jail"

As we noted, roles can be thought of as a set of behavioral expectancies. For example, you could play the role of a police officer if you were called upon to do so. You would know you were "just acting a part." However, someone watching you perform might well *attribute* your actions to some deep-seated character trait. The fact that most people in our culture tend to perceive behaviors as being caused more by attributed traits than role-play may explain why the public reacted so negatively to research performed by psychologist Philip Zimbardo (Haney et al., 1981; Zimbardo et al., 1973).

Several years ago, Zimbardo and his students studied the "roles" that people play in prison situations. Zimbardo and his group took over a basement corridor in the psychology building at Stanford University and converted it into a mock prison. Next, they put an ad in two local papers offering to hire students to play the roles of prisoners and guards for a two-week period. Zimbardo interviewed all the volunteers, screened them for physical and mental health problems, and then selected the 21 men who seemed most healthy, mature, and "normal." On a random basis, he chose 11 of them to be "guards," while the other 10 became "prisoners."

Zimbardo gave the guards special uniforms designed to look "official." He required the prisoners to wear muslin smocks, a light chain and lock around one ankle, and a cap made from a nylon stocking. Zimbardo gave each prisoner a toothbrush, towels, soap, and bed linen. He did not allow any personal belongings in the cells.

Zimbardo and the guards developed a set of "rules" that they expected the prisoners to memorize and follow while in jail. Zimbardo expected the prisoners to "work" in order to earn their $15 daily payment. Twice a week, Zimbardo allowed the prisoners to see visitors. The guards could also give them a variety of "rewards" for good behavior, including the right to exercise in the "yard" and to attend movies.

The first clue as to how the study would turn out came during the "count" of the prisoners that the guards took three times daily. The first day, the "count" took 10 minutes or less. But by the second day, the guards starting using "count time" to harass the prisoners, so the time increased. By the 5th day, some of the "counts" lasted for several hours as the guards berated the prisoners for minor infractions of the "rules."

DEINDIVIDUATION

Deindividuation. The process of becoming less like an individual—less like a person—and more of an impersonal component of a group. The result is that situational influences tend to override our internal dispositional influences. We sometimes use expressions like "becoming just a number," or "being a faceless member of the crowd, "to illustrate this experience.

Zimbardo had designed his experiment in an attempt to study some of the conditions that lead to **deindividuation,** or "depersonalization." Deindividuation is the term given by Leon Festinger, Albert Pepitone, and Theodore Newcomb to the experience of "losing our identity" when we become "submerged in a group" (Festinger et al., 1952). When we are anonymous members of a crowd we will often behave in ways that we *never* would when we are easily identified individuals: Crowds "*de*-individualize" us. As a result crowds become mobs and individuals become apathetic or even enthusiastic participants; as if individual *personalities* fade and *situations* take over. In his prison study, Zimbardo quickly discovered that the guards rapidly began treating the prisoners as "non-persons," beings who weren't really humans at all.

As far as "deindividuation" went, however, the *reactions* of the prisoners were probably just as important as the *actions* of the guards. Instead of protesting their treatment, some of the prisoners began to act in depressed, institutionalized, dependent ways—exactly the role behaviors shown by many real-life prisoners and mental patients. And, as you might guess, the more the prisoners acted like "non-persons," the more the guards mistreated them.

By the end of the 6th day, the situation had nearly gotten out of hand. The guards began modifying or changing the prison "rules" and routines to make them increasingly more punitive. Some of Zimbardo's students got so caught up in the spirit of things, they neglected to give the prisoners the privileges they had earned.

At this point, wisely, Zimbardo called a halt to the proceedings (Zimbardo, 1975).

How do the actions of the guards and the reactions of the prisoners fit Darley and Fazio's "five-step social interaction process"?

THE RESULTS

After stopping the experiment, Zimbardo and his students interviewed all of the subjects and analyzed the video tapes they had made during the 6 days. Perhaps their most important finding is that the subjects simply "became" the roles that they played. *All* of the 11 guards behaved in abusive, dehumanizing ways toward the prisoners. Some of them did so only occasionally. But *more than a third* of the guards were so consistently hostile and degrading that Zimbardo refers to their behavior as sadistic.

Many (but not all) of the prisoners, on the other hand, showed a reaction that in Chapter 8 we called *learned helplessness*. Day by day, these prisoners did less and less, initiated fewer conversations, and became more surly and depressed. Five of the prisoners were unable to cope with their own reactions and asked to leave. But the other five seemed to accept their fates and (in a few cases) didn't even bother to "request parole" when given a chance to do so.

The second important finding Zimbardo made is obvious but, to most people, simply unbelievable: There was absolutely *no prior evidence* that the subjects would react as they did. Before their random selection as guard or prisoner, the two groups did not differ from each other in any way that Zimbardo could discover. All 21 were healthy, normal, mature young men—and not one of them predicted he would act as he did. Furthermore, there is no reason to believe that the study would have turned out any different *had the roles of the two groups been reversed*.

One of the personality tests Zimbardo used to assess his subjects is the F-Scale, which measures **authoritarianism.** Surprisingly enough, the guards didn't differ from the prisoners on this scale, nor were the "sadistic" guards more authoritarian than were the more "humanitarian" guards. However, the prisoners who refused to leave were, generally speaking, the ones who scored as being the *most authoritarian*. Zimbardo believes these men were psychologically better prepared to cope with the highly structured and punitive environment of the prison.

The third finding is perhaps less surprising. At no time did any guard ever *reward* a prisoner for anything. The only "correctional" techniques the guards ever employed were criticism, punishment, and harassment.

Authoritarianism. An attitude of emphasis on lines of authority, strict discipline, and subservience to a clearly defined heirarchy of command.

Given the data, can you be sure that you wouldn't have played the guard or prisoner role exactly as Zimbardo's subjects did?

PUBLIC REACTION

The results of his experiment distressed Zimbardo so much that he made them available to the news media almost immediately. Public reaction was swift, and primarily punitive. Many critics found it inconceivable that a "noted Stanford professor" would undertake such a dehumanizing study. Most of these same critics also suggested Zimbardo must have picked a very abnormal bunch of young men for his subjects. Surely, ordinary citizens wouldn't behave in that fashion.

In fact, there is no better illustration of the *attribution process* at work than Zimbardo's study. At first, the prisoners tended to blame their behaviors on the

The authoritarian personality has been described by T.W. Adorno as the "bicycle personality" because people like this fit well into rigid hierarchies by "bowing" to those over them, and "kicking" those under them.

situation they were in. But, eventually, many of them became depressed and attributed their failure to cope to their own "innate trait of spinelessness" (the fundamental attribution error strikes again). The guards tended to justify their harassment in terms of "being paid to do the job," as well as the "criminal instincts" they perceived in the prisoners (actor-observer bias). The critics attributed both the brutality of the guards and the "helpless" behaviors of the prisoners to innate character flaws in *those* specific men (fundamental attribution error). No one caught up in the experiment—including, at times, Zimbardo and his students—perceived that the *environment* was almost entirely responsible for the behaviors of both guards and prisoners. No one saw that the men were just "playing roles."

One of the problems that psychologists often face is this: Their research findings occasionally contradict rather cherished notions other people have about human behavior. If you had been Zimbardo, how would you have gone about trying to convince people your results were valid?

Social Roles Versus Attributed Motives

Social roles are patterns of attitudes, emotions, perceptions, expectations, and behaviors that are "the norm" for a particular group, organization, or culture. They seem to be learned early in life, primarily through observation and imitation. Although some aspects may be innately determined, *roles are primarily determined by the social situation*.

Most of the things you do, think, and feel are at least partially the result of the conditions you grew up in and your present social milieu. But society still *attributes* the causes of human behavior to such internal processes as "personality" and "character." So if you find yourself attributing motives and intentions to other people, perhaps that is merely a role *you* have been taught to play.

Fortunately, however, there are ways to change both perceptions and roles.

Changing Perceptions, Changing Roles

At the beginning of this chapter, we listed five steps that John Darley and Russell Fazio believe define the social interaction sequence: First, you perceive someone else (usually in a stereotyped fashion) and generate expectancies about that individual. Next, you act in accord with your perception. Then, the other person interprets the "meaning" of your action, and responds accordingly. Finally, you interpret the other person's response, and then either break off the interaction or move on to another five-step sequence. Darley and Fazio note, however, that occasionally there is a sixth step to the sequence. That is, at some point you may pause and wonder *why* you responded the way you did.

Most of the time, of course, you may interpret your own actions as appropriate and as being "caused" by the other person. But, occasionally, you might well learn something new about yourself. And as a result of this gain in self-knowledge, you could change your perception both of yourself and of others (Darley & Fazio, 1980).

Now that you know something about person perception, stereotypes, attribution conflicts, and role theory, perhaps you might wish to add step six to more of your own social interaction sequences.

Social situations can have a strong influence on behavior. It is unlikely that any one of these young men would engage in this behavior if he were alone.

SUMMARY

1. **Social psychology** deals with **similarities** between people in the ways they **interact,** while personality theory tends to focus on the **uniqueness** of the **individual.**

2. Four important issues **social psychologists** deal with are
   a. Should the focus be on the **individual** or the **group?**
   b. Is social psychology the study of **attitudes** or **behaviors?**
   c. Are attitudes and behaviors **learned** or **innate?**
   d. Is social psychology primarily **theoretical** or **applied?**

3. **Attitudes** are consistent ways of thinking about, feeling toward, or responding to some environmental stimulus or input. Generally speaking, attitudes are **learned** by acquiring new **behaviors.**

4. Social psychology tends to be more **applied** than other areas, in part because of its use of human subjects. **Action research** involves experiments performed in real-life settings.

5. The **social interaction sequence** has five steps: (a) You meet someone and **generate expectancies,** (b) you **act** in accordance with your expectancies, (c) the other person **interprets** the meaning of your actions, (d) the other person then responds, and (e) you then **interpret** the meaning of the other person's response.

6. **Person perception** is the process by which you come to perceive, remember, and respond to people as you do.

7. **First impressions** of people are determined by such factors as **prior attitudes, reputations, stereotypes, self-fulfilling prophecies,** and by **autistic hostility,** or the tendency to reject favorable data about people (or things) you dislike.

8. First impressions of someone are also influenced by **present stimulus inputs,** including the person's **physical appearance, personal space, body posture,** and **eye contact.**

9. We tend to attribute **good traits** to good-looking people and **bad traits** to less attractive individuals.

10. Each of us seems to have a **personal space** around us that we defend as our psychological territory. The size of our territory is determined by the culture we grew up in and by our **status** in that culture. We tend to **approach** (or lean toward) people we like, and **retreat** (or lean away from) people we don't like.

11. Each culture has its own rules for **eye contact** that determine the ways in which people converse with each other—and sometimes make it hard for people from different cultures to communicate with one another.

12. We tend to perceive people with **inappropriate eye contact** as being of low status, or as being mentally or socially handicapped.

13. In order to predict and influence the actions of others, we use the **attribution process.** That is, we attribute motives and intentions to them that make their behaviors understandable to us.

14. In general we tend to attribute **internal** motives more often than we should (the **fundamental attribution error**). We also tend to blame other people for their actions, but our circumstances for our own behavior (**actor-observer bias**).

15. We are inclined to attribute our successes to our good character, and our failures to bad circumstances (**self-serving bias**).

16. At times our fear of failure might lead us to **handicap** ourselves in a way which increases our chances of failure but provides an external (and thus less disturbing) attribution for failure. This is called a **self-handicapping strategy.**

17. Like other people, marriage partners are inclined to explain problems in terms of **attributed traits** rather than **observed behaviors.** To resolve the problems, both partners may desire **attitudinal change** rather than mere **behavioral change.**

18. Both our genes and our early experiences affect our **social roles.**

19. Research on problem solving in small groups suggests that there are two types of **leadership roles,** the **task specialist** and the **social-emotional specialist.**

20. Studies of business managers suggest that successful supervisors tend to use **participatory management** techniques, while average or below-average supervisors tend to manage in an **authoritarian** way.

21. Overall, there is little difference between men and women managers in their degree of **task orientation** or their level of **social-emotional** facilitation.

22. **Leadership** appears to be a quality that emerges in certain **specific situations.**

23. Triandis views the process of human interaction as little more than an **exchange of resources.** In order to get what we want from others, we must therefore guess their **behavioral intentions.**

24. Zimbardo's **jail study** suggests that **authoritarianism, social aggression,** and **deindividuation** may be a product of **role behaviors** determined primarily by the **social milieu** in which they occur.

25. Critics of Zimbardo's research prefer to **attribute** his results to **innate traits,** but the critics themselves may be just playing a **learned social role.**

26. An occasional **sixth step** in the **social interaction sequence** is that of **changing** your attitudes, perceptions, and behaviors based on what you have *learned* from the sequence.

ANSWERS FOR THOUGHT

1. *When you meet someone new, what do you look for in that person? And what about that person is most . . . ?*

   If you are like most people, you notice sex, age, and physical attractiveness first. Some common factors in liking are attractiveness, similarity to you, whether or not the person meets your expectations for their stereotype and reputation, and their potential to give you some benefit.

2. *How might Kelley's research help explain the difficulty that Rosenhan's "pseudo-patients" had . . . ?*

   The "pseudo-patients" had presented themselves at the hospital as potential patients, leading the staff to *expect* them to be abnormal, just as Kelley's students had been led to expect the instructor to be either warm or cold. This reputation based on a stereotype was difficult to overcome.

3. *Are stereotypes, prejudices, and discrimination always harmful?*

   Stereotypes limit our perceptions of other people, but they may be positive as well as negative—and they are sometimes accurate. Prejudice and discrimination are *unjustified* negative attitudes and behavior. They are always harmful. However, although we probably all hold prejudices (and are the objects of other people's prejudice), we do not all have the power to discriminate against or oppress others.

4. *How would you explain Newcomb's concept of "autistic hostility" in terms of Piaget's "process of assimilation"?*

   Autistic hostility may be seen as the assimilation of new information to an existing negative reputation schema. The new information is "made to fit" the existing conceptual schema. Information which cannot be made to fit is ignored.

5. *What kind of first impression do you think you give the people you meet? Why do you think they perceive . . . ?*

What you think of your own first impression probably reflects your evaluation of your appearance as well as your self-esteem. This self-evaluation is largely a product of your past experiences in meeting people for the first time. It is also affected by how well you think you meet cultural standards of attractiveness. Strangers are most affected by how you look.

6. Suppose you met two people, one with obvious good looks, the other with average looks. Which person . . . ?

We generally expect the person with good looks to be happier, first, because we know that attractiveness is a valuable social commodity, and so the attractive person has an advantage, and second, we tend to see attractive people as having other desirable characteristics as well (which would presumably lead to success and happiness).

7. *Why do you think beautiful children tend to score higher on individually administered intelligence . . . ?*

Test administrators are more likely to give an attractive child the benefit of any doubt. For example, they may explain instructions more carefully, and they may act more pleasantly to the child. And they may subtly convey their positive expectations to the child, increasing the child's self-confidence, thus creating a self-fulfilling prophecy. Group tests are not as open to this kind of bias.

8. *Would having clear-cut territories reduce or increase the stress most people feel when forced to live together in crowded conditions?*

Clear-cut territories tend to reduce the stress of living in crowded conditions. For example, fences are more important in crowded urban neighborhoods than in open rural areas.

9. *If a woman stared at you intensely while talking to you, what motives would you attribute to her? If she . . . ?*

In middle-class North American culture, intense staring while talking indicates emotionality, perhaps anger, authority, or great interest. Averted eyes while listening indicates lack of interest and perhaps disrespect. However, in other cultures it is *normal* to look while talking, and look away while listening. Being unaware of these patterns can lead to misunderstanding and negative feelings when individuals from different cultures interact.

10. *What sorts of "body language" cues do you look for when you try to determine whether someone is lying?*

Most people watch a person's face to see if the person is lying. However, people are generally good at disguising their true feelings with their face. More effective cues (and ones that most people don't use) are pupil dilation and "adaptors" (self-directed gestures).

11. *If you encountered a patient in a mental hospital who refused to look at you, what would be your "first impression" . . . ?*

Our first impression would probably be that the person was guilty, embarrassed, or depressed (or all three).

12. *In several earlier chapters we have seen the effect of different types of attribution. How many can you recall?*

In Chapter 6: "Internals" attribute control over their circumstances to factors within themselves; "externals" blame factors outside of themselves and beyond their control. In Chapters 8, 9, 15, and later in this chapter: "Learned helplessness" is the result of attributing negative circumstances to external and unchangeable forces. In Chapters 15 and 16: Beck considers depression to be at least partly the result of faulty attributions. Therapy consists of changing these attributions and other cognitions. As these examples suggest, our attributions can affect not only our thoughts, but also our emotions, our self-esteem, and our general sense of well-being.

13. *How might a trait personality theorist and a social/behavioral personality theorist disagree about the fundamental attribution "error"?*

A trait theorist emphasizes the importance of internal dispositional causes of behavior. The trait theorist might question whether a tendency towards making internal attributions should be called an "error." The social/behavioral theorist would probably believe the trait theorist was particularly prone to the fundamental attribution error.

14. *How might an athlete use a self-handicapping strategy?*

If an athlete expected to lose a contest, he or she might be tempted to "manufacture" an excuse for losing. For example, the athlete might skip practices, or party late on the night before a big game or meet. These actions provide an excuse but they also contribute to failure.

One of your authors (RP) recently played a friendly game of racquetball with a colleague: I arrived early and ran 3 miles before our match. Later, I realized the run was probably a self-handicapping strategy. Being tired from running provided a good excuse if I happened to lose—which I did. (I used the excuse.)

15. *How does the attribution process help explain the popularity of the "trait approach" to describing human personality?*

We have a general tendency to attribute internal causes for behavior (leading to the fundamental attribution error). This means we are inclined to see people's behavior as an expression of enduring personal *traits*.

16. *Are social roles learned or innate?*

Like most behaviors, social roles are both learned and innate. Some roles appear to be more heavily influenced by heredity (for example, sex roles), others are entirely learned (your role in a play). Most roles are affected in varying degrees by both heredity and environment.

17. *Assume you have a "social interaction sequence" with a physician. How would your knowledge about social . . . ?*

A knowledge of social roles leads you to expect the physician to be confident, intelligent, and perhaps assertive. You would probably adopt a submissive and cooperative role in response. If the person was a janitor you might be less submissive and less willing to take his or her advice. Social roles help to establish status relationships and set the pattern for interaction, thus reducing confusion and stress.

18. *The Chinese scholar Lao-Tzu once said, "When a great leader finishes a project, the people rejoice and . . . ?*

Lao-Tzu apparently had the "social-emotional specialist" in mind. This type of leader encourages the group to come up with its own solutions, and stimulates them into enacting the solution themselves. The leader does not try to receive all the credit.

19. *Given the fact that women appear to be as effective leaders as are men, why has the United States never . . . ?*

Many people are still unable to see the roles of women and black as including the functions of leadership. This handicaps individuals who are capable of taking leadership roles at *all* levels. When women and blacks are prevented from taking even minor leadership roles they cannot ascend the social-political ladder to get in a position to seek the presidency. Social roles are firmly embedded in the cultural environment and they change very slowly.

20. *Some soldiers win medals; others don't. Some military personnel are high-paid officers with special privileges . . . ?*

    The "inequity" is based on the need for a clear heirarchy of command. It is efficient and stable. Whether or not it is "fair" probably depends on your assessment of the balance between merit and reward.

21. *From your own experience, which "role" do you know the most about, that of "prison guard" or that of "prisoner"?*

    Your response depends on your own experience. Assuming you have not actually been either a prisoner or a guard, which experiences have you had that are similar? Probably everyone has both given and taken orders. Have you worn a uniform and felt some authority? Have you been institutionalized and had some of your freedoms removed? How did you feel?

22. *How do the actions of the guards and the reactions of the prisoners fit Darley and Fazio's "five-step social interaction process"?*

    1. Guards and prisoners had clear *expectations* of each other. Guards expected to give orders and have prisoners obey. Prisoners expected to be told what to do.

    2. Guards gave orders and expected prisoners to obey their commands. Prisoners obeyed orders without questioning.

    3. Prisoners interpreted guards' orders and brutal treatment as evidence of their authority. Guards interpreted prisoners' submission as validation of their authority.

    4. Prisoners responded by submitting further and even gave up asking for privileges they had earned. Guards responded by becoming more domineering and arbitrary in their roles.

    5. Guards and prisoners continued to become entrenched in their roles. Guards became more brutal and arbitrary in their orders. Prisoners felt greater inferiority in their roles and, gradually, inferiority in themselves.

23. *Given the data, can you be sure that you wouldn't have played the guard or prisoner role exactly as Zimbardo's subjects did?*

    Without being in the situation we cannot say how we would react. There is no reason to expect that we would behave any differently.

24. *One of the problems that psychologists often face is this: Their research findings occasionally contradict . . . ?*

    The difficulty is part of a general tendency to ignore situational influence and to blame the person rather than the social situation—the fundamental attribution error. We could try to make people aware of this error by using examples from other situations. We could point out some situations in which people get carried along by social roles. For example we could show the effects on behavior of occupational roles (salesperson, teacher, policeperson), family roles (mother, daughter, etc.), leisure roles (athlete, referee, fan). In a more disturbing vein, we could point out that sometimes roles lead good people to do bad things, as we will see in the next chapter.

CHAPTER 18

A certain man went down from Jerusalem to Jericho, and fell among thieves, which stripped him of his raiment, and wounded him, and departed, leaving him half dead. And by chance there came down a certain priest that way: and when he saw him, he passed by on the other side. And likewise a Levite, when he was at the place, came and looked on him, and passed by on the other side. But a certain Samaritan, as he journeyed, came where he was: and when he saw him, he had compassion on him, and went to him, and bound up his wounds, pouring in oil and wine, and set him on his own beast, and brought him to an inn, and took care of him. And on the morrow when he departed, he took our two pence, and gave them to the host, and said unto him, 'Take care of him; and whatsoever thou spendest more, when I come again, I will repay thee.' Which now of these three, thinkest thou, was neighbour unto him that fell among the thieves?

LUKE 10:30–36

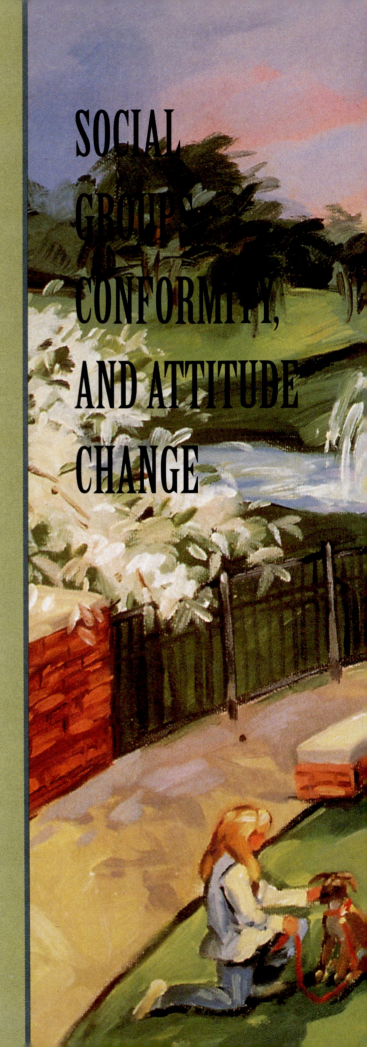

SOCIAL GROUPS, CONFORMITY, AND ATTITUDE CHANGE

Do these people constitute a group? The answer is yes: they all live in the same New York neighborhood. Despite their ethnic and cultural differences, they are likely to share concerns about community issues.

Social group. A set of persons considered as a single unit. Two or more individuals who are psychologically related to one another.

W hy did the "good" Samaritan help when the priest and Levite walked by? Why do *we* sometimes offer help and sometimes ignore need? And how do *other people* influence our willingness to help? These are the type of questions we will consider in this chapter.

We will be particularly concerned with groups and how they function. We will also look at pressures to conform to a group or authority—pressures that lead us to do what we otherwise wouldn't and pressures to be apathetic when we might otherwise act (and, for example, offer help).

As you will see, one important characteristic of groups is that their members tend to have *shared attitudes*. So we will also look at our attitudes—how we form them, maintain them, and change them. At that point, we will also investigate such interesting topics as persuasion, propaganda, and advertising. Finally, we will consider how we might change *conflicting attitudes* between groups as we look at conflict-resolution. In all these cases, you will see, some group (or organization) influences the attitudes and behaviors of some other group or set of individuals.

But the first question we must ask is, what *is* a group, and why would you want to belong to one?

How many groups do you think you belong to?

SOCIAL GROUPS

Whenever you set up a continuing relationship of some kind with one or more other people, you have in fact either started a new **social group** or joined one already in existence. In the strictest of terms, a group is a *social system* made up of two or more individuals who are psychologically related, or who are in some way dependent on one another. Generally speaking, people who are dependent on each other are, in fact, seeking a common goal. Thus, groups, like all other living and social systems, are *goal oriented*.

You belong to dozens, if not hundreds of groups. Some are *formal membership groups*. For instance, you apply for membership in most colleges, religious groups, and tennis clubs. But you are born into *family groups* and *ethnic groups*. Some groups, such as "all the people attending a party," are fairly temporary or very informal systems. Other groups, such as friends and lovers, are informally structured but may exist for months or years. The most important groups in your life are typically those that (1) last a long time, and (2) are made up of people with whom you have frequent, face-to-face interactions (Blumberg et al., 1983).

Forming Groups

Whenever you set up a new friendship, you have formed a group. You give up some part of your own personal *independence* to create a *state of interdependence* between you and the other person. Whenever you join or create a group, you lose the privilege of "just being yourself" and of ignoring the other group members. But you may gain many things that compensate for this loss (Newcomb, 1981).

As Theodore Newcomb noted many years ago, groups typically form when two or more people sense that the pleasure of each other's company would be more *rewarding* than remaining socially isolated (Newcomb, 1961). Most such groups are informal.

Generally speaking, an informal group does not have a *stated set of regulations* governing the behavior of its members (as does a formal group). But informal groups do have "informal rules," most of which are based on *cultural expectations* of how people should behave when they are together. If you misbehave at a party—if you are too noisy, if you spill drinks on people, or assault the host or hostess—you might well be asked to leave the group.

Group Structure

As Newcomb points out, one of the major characteristics of any group is the *shared acceptance of group rules by all the members*. This acceptance may be conscious or unconscious, but it is almost always present in one form or another (Newcomb, 1981).

Part of the fun of forming a two-person friendship group (becoming friends or lovers) often is trying to understand what the other person wants. That is, the early pleasures often come from determining what *rules of the game* the two of you believe ought to be followed. If the person is very much like you, perhaps little or no discussion of the rules may be necessary. If the person is very different from you, the dyad may not last for long (although it can be an exciting relationship at the very beginning).

In most cases where the members of a dyad are neither too similar nor too different, each person will compromise a little. No group can maintain itself unless there is **consensus,** or at least minimal agreement, as to what its members can and can't do.

Consensus. A coming together. Agreement on a particular point.

How would "social exchange theorists" probably define a group?

GROUP NORMS

Newcomb also noted that the ability to predict the behavior of people and objects in our world appears to be innately rewarding. One of the most reinforcing aspects of belonging to a group is that each member can to some extent predict what the other members are likely to think and do in most situations. Perhaps that is why we almost always state group rules in terms of behavioral or attitudinal *norms*. That is, the rules specify what the average or *norm-al* behavior of each member should be, or what role(s) each member should play (Levine & Moreland, 1990; Newcomb, 1981).

No group member will fit all the norms *exactly*. Most groups tolerate some deviation from the norm, so long as the group does not perceive the member as playing "*too* abnormal" a role. The more similar the group's members are to each other, and the more emphasis the group places on "following the rules," the less deviation the group will usually tolerate (Asch, 1987). Perhaps we can demonstrate this point with an example.

Suppose we measure the attitudes toward premarital sex of two different groups—a class of students taking introductory psychology (at a non-religious college), and a group of young adults at a campus church or religious center. We will ask the members of both groups to record their agreement or disagreement with a statement about sex by placing a check mark on the 9-point attitude scale shown in Figure 18.1.

After both groups respond, we measure the position each person has marked on the 9-point scale. We can then use the number closest to each check mark as a *scale score* that represents each member's attitude toward the statement on premarital sex. And, since we have a number, or score, for each person, we can calculate the **mean** or *average* attitude for both groups. This average would, presumably, be the group norm. We can also measure the *spread* of the scores by calculating the **range** and the

"Premarital sex is generally so damaging from both a psychological and moral point of view that it should be avoided at all cost."

1	Very strongly agree
2	Strongly agree
3	Agree
4	Agree somewhat
5	Neutral: neither agree nor disagree
6	Disagree somewhat
7	Disagree
8	Strongly disagree
9	Very strongly disagree

FIGURE 18.1

Possible scale for measuring agreement to a statement on premarital sex.

Mean. The "average" calculated by adding all the scores and dividing by the number of scores.

Range. The spread of the scores from highest to lowest.

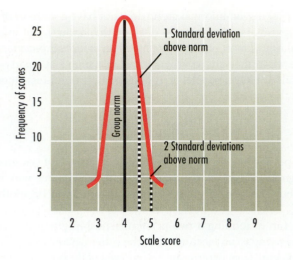

FIGURE 18.2

In Figure 18.2 the scores are grouped around the norm. This is a homogeneous distribution. It has a *low* standard deviation.

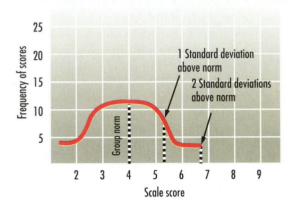

FIGURE 18.3

In Figure 18.3 the scores are spread further out from the norm than they are in Figure 18.2. This is a heterogeneous distribution of scores. It has a higher standard deviation. Both distributions have the same group norm as expressed by the mean, the median, and the mode.

Standard deviation. A statistical measure of the variability of scores in a distribution.

Homogeneous (ho-moh-GEE-knee-us). Being *similar*, or *alike* (from the Greek words meaning "same kind"). In more technical terms, the smaller the standard deviation of a distribution of test scores, the more homogeneous the scores are.

Heterogeneous (HETT-turr-oh-GEE-knee-us). Being *dissimilar* (from the Greek words meaning "different kinds"). The more dissimilar the members of a group are, the more heterogeneous the group is.

standard deviation of scores for both groups. (See the Statistical Appendix for further discussion of "range" and "standard deviation.")

For the sake of this discussion, let us assume that the mean or norm for both groups happened to be a scale score of 4: "Agree somewhat." This result might suggest to you that the church group and the psychology class were very similar, since the norm seems to be the same in both groups. But ask yourself this question: If your own position was a 6 ("Disagree somewhat"), would either group perceive you as being "too abnormal" to belong to that group?

The answer is: It depends on what each group's *standard deviation* is—on how spread out the scores are. Church groups, in general, are much more alike, or **homogeneous,** in their attitudes toward sexual behavior than are the more random collections of students who make up classroom groupings. The scores for the church group would probably be grouped closely together like those shown in the distribution in Figure 18.2. The scores for the classroom group, however, would probably be more spread out like those shown in the distribution in Figure 18.3.

As you can see, your score of 6 would be well over 2 standard deviations from the church group norm, but only about 1½ standard deviations from the psychology class norm. The church group would consider your attitude "significantly deviant," while the classroom group probably would not (Rouan & Thaon, 1985).

Generally speaking, the more *homogeneous* the group, the more "tightly grouped" will be its scores on most scales. (And the smaller the standard deviation of scores.) The more **heterogeneous** the group, the more "loosely grouped" will be its scores on most measures. (And the larger the standard deviation of scores.) The homogeneity (or heterogeneity) of a group is directly related to group cohesion.

GROUP COHESION

According to Theodore Newcomb, *cohesiveness* is the psychological glue that keeps group members sticking together. The more cohesive a group, the longer it will typically last and the more resistant it will be to external pressures (Levine & Moreland, 1990; Newcomb, 1981).

In ordinary situations, cohesion is often a function of the homogeneity of the group. The more homogeneous the attitudes or behaviors of the members, the more cohesive the structure of the group will be. However, even such heterogeneous groups as introductory psychology classes can be made cohesive if some outside force threatens the group (Rouan & Thaon, 1985), or if they remain together long enough (Hogg, 1987; Manning & Fullerton, 1988).

According to Stanford Gregory, members of an "established group" often adopt their own "group jargon," or unusual patterns of speech. The jargon not only is a "badge of group membership," but also tends to increase group cohesiveness, since outsiders often can't understand what members of the group are talking about (Gregory, 1986).

TEMPORARY VERSUS PERMANENT GROUPS

Some groups are permanent; others are temporary. People riding together in an elevator are not usually considered a group, for they have no real psychological interdependencies, and their attitudes are likely to be very dissimilar on most subjects. However, if the electric power fails, trapping the people together in the elevator for several hours, this very heterogeneous bunch of people may quickly form into a group. They will give each other psychological support and comfort, and work together on the goal of escaping.

Releasing the people from the stalled elevator, however, immediately removes the common threat to their survival. At this point, the heterogeneity of the members' attitudes and behaviors will probably overcome the temporary cohesion and the group will disband (Asch, 1987). (Individual members of the group may be similar enough to strike up friendships as a result of the experience, however.)

Do you join groups because they are made up of people like yourself? Or do you join groups and then become similar to the people who make up the group?

Group Functions

Group membership accomplishes many things for an individual. Some of the rewards for group membership are social. For example, you gain someone to talk to—someone to be with and to share things with. Other rewards are more practical or task oriented. For instance, pushing a car out of the mud, playing tennis, and rearing a family are activities that typically are more reinforcing if two or more individuals participate. And groups help us to establish who we are by offering us a social identity if we will join.

GROUPS AND SOCIAL IDENTITY

British psychologist Henri Tajfel believes one function of groups is to help define our social identity. He explains most group behaviors in terms of what he called "Social Identity Theory." According to Tajfel, you first define *who you are*, then you join groups of other people whom you *perceive* as being similar to you in one way or another (Tajfel, 1982a).

Tajfel believes that, at some point in your life, you "categorize" all the people around you into various groups. Then you deliberately affiliate with some of those

According to Tajfel's social identity theory, we define ourselves by the people we choose to associate with and the groups we choose to join. What kind of social identity is defined by this gathering on Earth Day?

groups, but not with others. The groups you join *define your social identity*. As Tajfel puts it, social identity is "the portion of an individual's self-concept that results from knowledge of his or her membership in some social groups together with the value and emotional significance attached to that membership" (Tajfel, 1982a).

Tajfel further presumes that you wish to "attain or maintain a positive social identity." Therefore, he says, you are strongly motivated to distinguish between *your* groups and *other* groups by assigning positive traits to your groups and negative traits to others. Tajfel suggests that one major reason people are prejudiced against others is their need to "maintain a positive social identity" (Tajfel, 1979, 1982b).

Many American social psychologists disagree with Tajfel. For instance, according to social learning theory, typically, your *environment* pushes you into various groups. Then you *learn* the group's norms and adhere to them (rather than picking groups in terms of norms you already have.) Thus, if your group happens to take a prejudiced view toward some other group, you are likely to acquire this prejudice as a consequence of group membership. But because the prejudice is *learned*, it can be *unlearned* through experience (Bandura, 1986a).

In fact, the truth seems to lie somewhere between these two extremes. As we noted earlier, you are "born into" family, religious, and other types of groups. You then take on the values of these groups through the *socialization* process during your early years. But, later on, you obviously pick some groups to join because the members share values you already have. And then you become even more like the members of the groups you've voluntarily joined.

GROUP COMMITMENT

The members of a group often are free to abandon the group whenever they wish. But a group can survive only if it can hold its members together. One of the functions of any group, then, seems to be that of inducing the highest-possible *commitment* among its members. For the more committed to the group's norms and goals the members become, the more cohesive the group typically will be and the more homogeneous the group members' attitudes will become.

There is some evidence that the more you have to pay for group membership, the more highly you value it. Elliot Aronson and Judson Mills offered college women a chance to participate in a discussion group—if they were willing to pay a price. The experimenters required half of the women to suffer a very embarrassing initiation in order to "buy" entrance to their discussion group. They put the other half of the women through a much milder form of initiation. The women who suffered less embarrassment liked their discussion group significantly *less* than did the women who had committed themselves to paying the much higher psychological price (Aronson & Mills, 1959).

Psychologist Larry Ingram notes that religious groups often use "public testimonies" to enhance group commitment. That is, during meetings, members testify as to why they belong to group and why their commitment to the group is so strong. According to Ingram, "testimony" can be seen as a "test of membership," and attempts by members to "enhance their status in the group." One major result of these "testimonies," however, appears to be that of strengthening group commitment by protecting members against "outside threats." Another result, of course, is that of encouraging members to *conform* to group norms (Ingram, 1986).

Which country club would seem more desirable to you, one that charged a $1,000 membership fee or one that charged but $100?

CONFORMITY

Most of us believe our attitudes toward such things as sexual behavior, politics, economics, and religion are primarily the result of our own objective decision making. In truth, what other people do, what they tell us to do, and what they do when we comply, greatly influences not only our attitudes, but our perceptions and behaviors as well. As Harold Kelley points out, we use other people and groups as reference points, or guides, for much of what we think and do (Kelley, 1952, 1983).

Conforming to a Group

According to Kelley, **reference groups** influence your behavior in at least two ways: First, reference groups provide comparison points which you use in evaluating yourself and others. And second, reference groups set standards and reward you when you conform and punish you when you do not conform to these norms. As Kelley has shown, group members typically pressure other members who express opinions, attitudes, or judgments too far from the reference group norm, forcing them to fall back into line (Kelley, 1952, 1983).

Reference groups. Those groups that set social norms you are expected to live up to. Reference groups typically determine the goals you and other members should attain, then reward you for moving toward those goals and punish you for moving away from the goals.

Your most important reference group is usually your family. How did members of your family set and enforce group norms when you were growing up?

THE SHERIF EXPERIMENT

The study of how groups induce their members to conform to group norms is one of the most fascinating areas of social psychology, and probably one of the most relevant to our everyday experience. Scientific experiments on this topic date back to 1935, when social psychologist Muzafer Sherif first demonstrated the effects of group pressures on visual perception. Sherif asked students to observe a pinpoint of light in a dark room and tell him how much the light moved. (The light in this situation did not move but only *appeared* to—a phenomenon called the *autokinetic effect*.)

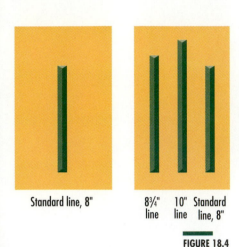

Standard line, 8"   8¾"   10"   Standard
                     line   line   line, 8"

FIGURE 18.4

Solomon Asch showed subjects the "standard line" (on the left) and asked them to choose the line that was the same length from the three on the right.

Conformity is the jailer of freedom and the enemy of growth.

JOHN F. KENNEDY

When the students made their judgments sitting alone in the room, each student gave responses as he or she saw them. But when Sherif tested the students in groups, the first members to give their judgments created a perceptual "group norm" that the others had trouble resisting (Sherif, 1935). Attitudes expressed verbally in groups almost always tend to be more homogeneous than those the group members express if questioned in private (Sherif, 1936).

THE ASCH EXPERIMENT

Several years after Sherif reported his findings, social psychologist Solomon Asch carried the matter a step further. Asch first tested the perceptual abilities of a group of students who served as "control subjects" for the latter part of his experiment. Asch showed these controls a white card that had a black line 8 inches long drawn on it, as shown in Figure 18.4. He referred to this as the "standard line" and asked the controls to remember it well.

Then Asch removed the first card and showed the subjects a second card that had three comparison lines drawn on it. The first of these lines was 8.75 inches long, the second was 10 inches, while the third was the same 8-inch length as the standard. Asch then asked the control subjects to report *privately* which comparison line matched the standard. To no one's surprise, the controls picked the correct answer some 99 percent of the time.

With his "experimental subjects," Asch played a much more subtle game. He asked these volunteers to appear at his laboratory at a certain time. But when each young man arrived, he found several other students waiting to participate in the experiment. What the experimental subject did not realize was that the others were "confederates"—that is, accomplices paid by Asch to give occasional false judgments. After the confederates and the experimental subject had chatted for a few moments, Asch ushered them into his laboratory and gave them several opportunities to judge line lengths for him. Everyone gave their judgments *out loud*, so that the others could hear, and much of the time the confederates reported *before* the experimental subject did.

During the first two trials, the confederates picked the *correct* comparison line, as did the experimental subject. But on the third trial, each of the confederates calmly announced that the 10-inch line matched the 8-inch line! These false judgments created an *incorrect group perceptual norm,* and apparently put the experimental subjects under tremendous pressure to conform. In this first study, the experimental subjects "yielded" to group pressures almost one-third of the time by reporting that the two lines matched. In later studies, when the judgments were more difficult to make, the experimental subjects yielded to the group of confederates about two-thirds of the time (Asch, 1951).

SIZE OF GROUP   In another experiment Asch varied the number of confederates who reported before the experimental subject did. While the presence of one, two, or three confederates did induce some conformity, subjects felt the maximum pressure to yield when four confederates gave false reports. Having 14 or even 40 confederates doesn't increase conformity much more than having four. However, if even one confederate out of 40 gives the "correct" answer, this breaks the homogeneity of the group and lifts much (but not all) of the "group pressure." Under these conditions, the experimental subject "yields" only about one-fourth as often as when the confederates give a unanimous report (Asch, 1956; Levine, 1989).

REASONS FOR CONFORMING   The importance of the Asch study lies not merely in its dramatic demonstration that people tend to conform to temporary reference groups, but in the reasons they gave for doing so. If you were to ask the subjects who "conformed" *why* they judged the 8-inch line as being as long as the 10-inch line, *most of them* would look at you sheepishly and confess that they couldn't stand the pressure. They might say they figured something was wrong, or they thought the confederates "saw through a trick" they hadn't recognized. Or they might say they simply didn't want to "rock the boat" by giving a judgment that went against the group norm. The few remaining "conformers" are far more interesting, however. They typically insist they *actually saw* the two lines as being identical. That is, they were seemingly unaware of "yielding" at all (Asch, 1956, 1987).

These studies suggest that group norms not only influence your attitudes toward complex social issues, but your perceptions of even the simplest objects as well.

Would you obey your government the way many Germans did in carrying out Hitler's fiendish orders?

Conforming to an Order: Obedience

One interesting sidelight to the conformity studies is this: in most of the experiments, no one told the subject that he or she *had to yield* to the group norm. Indeed, many of the subjects were quite unaware they had given in to group pressures. Some people even *denied* they had done so. So let us next ask a very important question: What might the results have been had the experimenter *ordered* the subjects to yield?

THE MILGRAM EXPERIMENTS

The answer to this question may well come from a fascinating set of experiments performed by psychologist Stanley Milgram in the 1960s at Yale. His subjects were men who ranged in age from young to old, and who came from many different walks of life. Milgram paid the men to participate in what they thought was a study on the effects of punishment on learning.

"TEACHERS" AND "LEARNERS"   In the first experiment, each man arrived at Milgram's laboratory to find another subject (actually a confederate) also present. The confederate was supposed to be the "learner" who would have to memorize a list of word pairs. The experimental subject was supposed to be the "teacher" who would punish the confederate if he made any mistakes. The subject watched the experimenter take the confederate into another room and strap him into a chair so he couldn't escape when the punishment became severe. The confederate was then out of sight for the rest of the experiment.

Sitting in front of the experimental subject was a very impressive piece of electrical equipment that *supposedly* was a powerful shock generator. In fact, the machine was a fake. *No shock was ever delivered during the experiment.* This "fake" generator had 30 switches on it to control the (apparent) strength of the electrical current. Labels on these switches ranged from "Slight Shock" (15 volts) to "Danger: Severe Shock" (405 volts) to "XXX" (450 volts).

The first time the confederate made a mistake, the subject was to give him 15 volts of shock. For each subsequent mistake, the subject was to increase the shock intensity by flipping on the next-highest switch. The apparatus was so ingeniously designed that none of the subjects guessed the confederates actually weren't receiving shocks from the machine.

At the beginning of the session, things were easy for the experimental subject. The confederate got most of the word pairs correct, and the "shocks" delivered for making errors were presumably very mild. As time wore on, however, the confederate made more "mistakes" and the "shocks" became more and more severe. When the shock level reached what seemed to be a fairly high point, the confederate suddenly pounded on the wall in protest. Then the confederate *stopped responding entirely*, as if he had fainted or had suffered an attack of some kind.

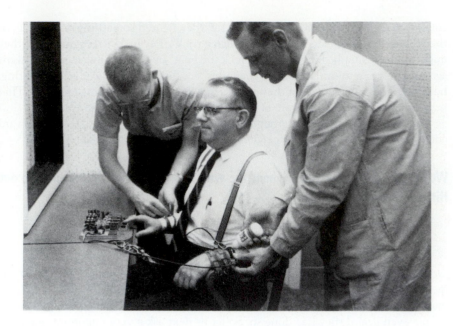

A "learner" in the Milgram study being wired to the console. The "learner" is a confederate of the experimenter. Although the learner never received any shocks, the experiment was designed so that the "teacher" (standing on left) thought he did.

At this point the experimenter told the "teacher" to continue anyway—no matter how dangerously high the shock might get. If at any time the subject wanted to stop, the experimenter told him in a very stern voice, "Whether the learner likes it or not, you *must go on* until he has learned all the word pairs correctly. So please go on." However, the experimenter never *forced* the "teacher" to continue (Milgram, 1963).

What would you do in this situation? Would you refuse to cooperate, or would you "obey" the experimenter and go on shocking the confederate right up to what you believed were the limits of the electrical generator?

And how do you think most other people would react if they faced this challenge?

SOME "SHOCKING" FACTS   After Milgram had completed his first study, he asked a great many college students how they thought most people would react when told to shock the "learner." If you are like Milgram's students, you will insist that you—and most other people—would refuse to continue the experiment when a dangerously high shock level was reached (and particularly when the "learner" apparently had fainted or died in the other room). But, in fact, your guess (at least about other people) would be wrong. For out of the first 40 subjects Milgram tried, almost 65 percent continued to "obey orders" right up to the bitter end. Most of these subjects were extremely distressed about doing so. They complained, they showed tension, and they said they wanted to stop again and again. But some 65 percent obeyed completely in spite of their inner conflict. Milgram found essentially the same outcomes with both college and non-college populations (Milgram, 1964).

FACTORS INDUCING OBEDIENCE   As you know, we don't always obey authorities. In subsequent experiments, Milgram uncovered a variety of ways in which he could increase or decrease obedience. For example, the more distant the authority, the fewer the number of people who obeyed. When the experimenter stood right over the experimental subjects, breathing down their necks and ordering them on, about 65 percent followed through to the end. But when the experimenter was out of the room and gave his orders by telephone, only some 22 percent of the subjects were completely obedient.

In the first experiment, the subjects could not see or hear the confederate in the other room. In subsequent studies, Milgram changed this. If the confederate began moaning, or complaining about his heart, fewer subjects obeyed orders. Having the confederate physically present in the same room so that the subject could see the supposed pain from each shock reduced obedience even more. And if the subject had

The results . . . are . . . disturbing. They raise the possibility that human nature, or—more specifically—the kind of character produced in American democratic society, cannot be counted on to insulate its citizens from brutality and inhumane treatment at the direction of malevolent authority. A substantial proportion of people do what they are told to do, irrespective of the content of the act and without limitations of conscience, so long as they perceive that the command comes from a legitimate authority.

STANLEY MILGRAM (1974)

to grab hold of the confederate's hand and force it down on a metal "shock plate" before each punishment, very few of the subjects followed instructions to the end. Put more simply, the subjects were more likely to deliver severe punishment if they couldn't see the *consequences* of their actions (Milgram, 1964).

GROUP PRESSURES AND OBEDIENCE   In a later experiment, Milgram added the group-pressures technique to his own method of studying obedience. In this experiment, Milgram used three confederates with each experimental subject. One of the confederates, as usual, was the "learner" seated in the next room. The other two were supposed to be "teachers" working in a team with the subject.

The experiment proceeded as before, except that one of the confederate-teachers backed out as soon as the "shock" reached a medium-low intensity. Saying that he refused to continue, this confederate simply took a seat as far from the shock machine as he could. When the "shock" reached a medium-high level, the other confederate-teacher also refused to continue. The subject then was faced with *conflicting social norms*. The experimenter kept pressuring him to continue, while the "group" of confederate-teachers was exerting pressure to stop. Under these conditions, group influence won out over the experimenter's orders. More than 90 percent of the subjects refused to complete the experiment (Milgram, 1965).

Society teaches us to obey, just as it trains us to conform. The possible effects are disturbing. Recent history contains several sad examples of what Herbert Kelman and Lee Hamilton call "crimes of obedience"—the My Lai massacre, Watergate, the Iran-contra affair (Kelman & Hamilton, 1989). If you consider the great rewards and massive punishments that groups can administer to their members, perhaps it is not so surprising that many of us obey and conform rather readily.

What do you think would have happened in Zimbardo's prison study had the "warden" ordered the guards to punish the prisoners severely for infractions of "the rules"?

ATTRIBUTION THEORY AND OBEDIENCE

Before we go any further with our discussion of obedience, let's ask a question. Suppose, in one of his studies, Milgram had allowed the "teacher" to *set the shock level himself*. That is, rather than insisting that the "teacher" blindly increase the amount of shock given the "learner" after each trial, suppose Milgram had told the "teacher" to decide how much punishment would be appropriate. The "teacher" could increase the shock to the maximum level, keep it in the "mildly painful" range, or decrease the shock to almost zero.

Under these circumstances, how much shock do *you* think the average "teacher" would eventually administer? And what percentage of the "teachers" do you think would give the maximum amount of electricity? Why not write your predictions down on a sheet of paper, and then see what actually happened.

In fact, Milgram actually performed this experiment and reported the results in 1974. He began by giving all the teachers themselves a mildly painful shock of 45 volts, so they would "understand how shock felt." Thereafter, he allowed the "teachers" to administer to the "learner" (false) shock that could vary from 15 up to 450 volts. Milgram found that almost all of the "teachers" maintained the shock in the "mildly painful" range (45 to 60 volts). Only one "teacher" out of 40 administered the maximum shock of 450 volts (Milgram, 1974). That finding itself is very interesting. However, an extension of this research by Martin Safer yielded even more intriguing results.

Safer began by showing a film of Milgram's original study to 132 students in an introductory psychology class. He then asked the students to *predict* what the "teachers" would do if allowed to set their own shock levels. Safer found that the students systematically *overestimated* the amount of shock they thought the "teachers" would administer. They guessed that about 12 percent of the "teachers" would give 450 volts, and that the average "teacher" would end up giving about 175 volts!

Safer believes that his students *attributed evilness* to the "teachers." That is, the students apparently assumed most people have a "cruel streak" in them, and that they will express this trait if given a chance. Safer points out the paradox of his findings. First, before learning about Milgram's research, most students presume that *almost nobody* would shock an innocent "learner." When they learn what actually happened in Milgram's laboratory, however, the students attributed the results to some character flaw inside the "teachers." For the students failed to perceive that the "teachers" actions were due to the *social environment,* not to some personality trait. Thus, when asked how the "teachers" would react when allowed to set their own shock levels, the students predicted on the basis of *attributed traits,* not on the basis of the actual situation the "teachers" were in (and responding to).

People may commit evil acts, not because they are abnormal, but because they act under authority and are carried along by their circumstances.

Safer concludes that *few people* "appear to have insight into the crucial situational factors affecting behavior in the obedience . . . experiments" (Safer, 1980). This, of course, is the fundamental attribution error once again. Did it affect your predictions?

THE ETHICS OF DECEPTION

The Milgram studies, the Zimbardo prison research, and many other experiments raise a number of complex but important questions about the *ethics* of using humans as subjects in scientific experiments. One of these questions involves the morality of *deceiving* the subjects as to the real purpose of the study, even if the experimenter believes such deception is necessary (because people seldom act naturally when they know they're being observed) (Schuler, 1982).

MILGRAM'S CRITICS   When Milgram published his research, sincerely concerned individuals raised a storm of protest. They urged authorities to ban or prohibit studies such as Milgram's. This same barrage of criticism, as we noted in the last chapter, occurred when Zimbardo released the results of his prison experiment. In consequence, a number of codes of ethics were proposed. However, workable guidelines for experimentation on humans are not easy to agree upon. Given a little time and motivation, we could all think of certain types of studies in which deception might be morally justified. And we could think of other experiments in which misleading the subjects would be both a legal and an ethical outrage.

WHEN IS DECEPTION ETHICAL?   Obviously we should always consider the actual results of experiments before drawing hasty conclusions about what is and isn't ethical, but we should not be trapped into thinking that the ends justify the means. Viewed in this perspective, Milgram comes off fairly well, for he did discover some fascinating facts. More important, there is no evidence reported in the scientific literature that any of his subjects suffered ill effects. In truth, Milgram seems to have employed little more deception in his work than is used regularly on TV programs such as "Candid Camera," or "Totally Hidden Video." Yet nagging question— "When is it ethical to use deception?"—remains for the most part unanswered.

Some of the emotional reaction to Milgram's experiments probably stemmed from the rather unflattering picture his results gave us of ourselves. Had most of Milgram's subjects *refused* to obey blindly, perhaps he would not have been so vigorously attacked. Despite the emotionality of some of Milgram's critics, however, the issue of experimenter responsibility remains a crucial one. In response, the American Psychological Association has taken a stand against the unwarranted use of deception in similar research. Comparable codes are now in force in several other countries, including Canada, Poland, Germany, France, and the Netherlands.

Under what circumstances do you personally think that deceiving subjects in a scientific experiment might be ethically warranted or justified?

HELPING IN A CRISIS

Milgram created problems for his subjects because he told them what to do. In real-life conflicts, there often isn't anyone around to give you directions, and you must act (or fail to act) on your own. In the story of the "Good Samaritan," each passerby had to decide alone how he would respond to the man who was beaten and left beside the road. If there are other people around when a crisis occurs, however, you

Does this person need help? Is he (she) sleeping? drunk? injured? If you decide the person needs help, your response may depend on how many other observers there are to "diffuse" your sense of responsibility, whether or not you have learned appropriate ways of helping, your assessment of the potential "costs" and "rewards," or your feelings of empathy for the victim.

The worst sin towards our fellow creatures is not to hate them, but to be indifferent to them; that's the essence of inhumanity.

GEORGE BERNARD SHAW

may look at them as "models" of what you ought to do. And you may assume that *they are as responsible as you are* for taking action (or not doing anything) in an emergency. Thus, if your "models" fail to react, you may feel strong group pressures to follow their lead. Keep that thought in mind as we describe a particularly gruesome murder.

What would you do if, late some dark night, you heard screams outside your home? Would you rush out at once, or would you first go to the window to see what was happening? If you saw a man with a knife attacking one of your neighbors, how would you react? Might you call the police, or go to the neighbor's aid? Or would you remain apathetic and unresponsive? And if you failed to assist the neighbor in any way, how would you respond if someone later on asked why you didn't help?

Before you answer, consider the following facts. Early one morning in 1964, a young New York woman named Kitty Genovese was returning home from work. As she neared her front door, a man jumped out of the shadows and attacked her. She screamed and attempted to defend herself. Because she screamed loudly, 38 of her neighbors came to their windows to see what was happening. And because she fought valiantly, it took the man almost 30 minutes to kill Kitty Genovese. During this period of time, not one of those 38 neighbors came to her aid. Not one of them even bothered to call the police (Cunningham, 1984; Darley & Latané, 1968).

The Darley-Latané Studies

Kitty Genovese's death so concerned scientists John Darley and Bibb Latané, they began a study of why people refuse to help others in similar situations.

In one experiment, Darley and Latané staged a disaster of sorts for their subjects. They paid people $2 to fill out a survey form that was given to them by an attractive young woman. While the people were in an office filling out the forms, the woman went into the next room. Shortly thereafter, the subjects heard a loud crash from the next room, and the woman began moaning loudly that she had fallen and was badly hurt and needed help.

Now, how many of the subjects do you think came to her rescue?

The answer is—it depends. Some of the subjects witnessed this little drama when they were all by themselves in the testing room. About 70 percent of the "alone" subjects offered help. Another 40 subjects faced this apparent emergency in pairs. Only

8 of these 40 people responded by going to the woman's aid. The other 32 subjects simply sat there listening to the moans and groans.

Were the subjects who failed to rush to the woman's assistance merely apathetic and uncaring? Apparently. Many of the unresponsive bystanders informed the experimenters they hadn't really thought the woman was seriously hurt and were afraid of embarrassing her if they intervened. But we should note that the presence or absence of someone else in the testing room strongly influenced the subject's *perception* of the emergency.

In another experiment, subjects heard a young man (presumably in the next room) discuss the fact that he frequently had seizures similar to *grand mal* epilepsy. Shortly thereafter, the confederate began crying for help, saying he was about to have an attack and would die if no one came to help him. About 85 percent of the subjects who were "alone" rushed to the confederate's assistance. However, only 62 percent of the subjects who were in pairs offered aid, while but 31 percent of those in 5-person groups overcame their apathy (Darley & Latané, 1968; Latané & Darley, 1975).

Who Intervenes and Why?

The concern over apathy in a crisis has generated not only a great deal of research, but also several attempts to explain helping behavior. As you will see, most of these explanations rely heavily on *external* attributions.

LATANÉ'S "THEORY OF SOCIAL IMPACT"

In 1981, Bibb Latané proposed a "theory of social impact." Latané states, "As social animals, we are drawn by the attractiveness of others and aroused by their mere presence. . . . We are influenced by the actions of others, stimulated by their activity and embarrassed by their attention. . . . I call all these effects, and others like them, 'social impact.'"

Latané believes the impact of your social environment can be determined by three factors: The *strength*, and the *immediacy* of the event, and the *number* of people around you. The more people involved in a given situation, the more diluted or diffused you will perceive your own responsibility as being. Thus, Latané says, each person who witnessed Kitty Genovese's murder felt but a fraction of the responsibility for helping the woman or reporting the crime. Therefore, while the murder itself had a strong and immediate impact on the neighbors, the number of people was so great that it diffused each person's sense of responsibility to the point where no one took action (Latané, 1981).

Consider those 38 neighbors as an Asch-type "conformity group." Why would each person be under strong pressures not to intervene if one of the other 37 did?

A "HELPING HABIT"

Psychologist Ted Huston and his colleagues offer an interesting comparison between people who have helped crime victims and those who have not. The state of California has long compensated "Good Samaritans" who are injured when they intervene to give assistance in holdups, assaults, burglaries, or other serious crimes. Huston and his colleagues interviewed 32 people who had received "Good Samaritan" awards and contrasted them with 32 "control subjects"—individuals from the same community who were identical in most other ways but hadn't intervened in a crime for at least the previous 10 years.

According to Huston and his group, the "interveners" and the "controls" had strikingly similar scores on standardized personality tests. The interveners were no more sympathetic or socially responsible, nor were they more likely to *state* they would be willing to help others. The one personality test difference was that the interveners *perceived* themselves to be stronger, more aggressive, and more emotional than did the controls.

In terms of *experience with crime*, however, there was a marked contrast between the two groups. The interveners had witnessed crimes at least nine times as often as had the control subjects (although the two groups lived in the same community). In addition, the "Good Samaritans" had themselves been crime *victims* more than twice as often as the controls. Just as important, the interveners had much higher levels of training in such *skills* as life-saving, first aid, and self-defense.

Huston's work suggest that people who have experience and *believe* that they can help are more likely to intervene in a crisis. Huston and his associates also note that helping out in crisis situations may be habit forming. Some 34 percent of those individuals who received "Good Samaritan" compensation reported they had intervened in at least one crime other than the one they got the award for (Huston et al., 1981).

SOCIAL EXCHANGE

As we saw in Chapter 17, social exchange theorists explain our interactions in terms of the exchange of benefits (Thibaut & Kelley, 1959; Triandis, 1984). We generally try to maximize our rewards and minimize our losses.

Social exchange theorists predict our behavior in a situation of need on the basis of anticipated "costs" and "benefits." In the Kitty Genovese case, for example, social exchange theory would say the *cost* of phoning the police, and possibly becoming involved in a lengthy court case, outweighed the possible *benefits* of the witnesses to Kitty Genovese's murder.

EMPATHY

Altruistic (all-troo-ISS-tic). Helping without thought of reward.

Daniel Batson has conducted many studies on helping behavior. His tentative conclusion is that we help because we feel *empathy* for the victim. At times, external factors may interfere, as in the Kitty Genovese case, and we fail to help. "Concern for others," he says, "is a fragile flower, easily crushed by self-concern." But feeling empathy, compassion, sympathy, or tenderness for someone in need, leads us to help. And this help is truly **altruistic,** or unselfish (Batson, 1990; Dovidio et al., 1990).

Should there be laws to require people to help, and punish them if they don't?

Perhaps you have noticed a certain similarity between the research on bystander apathy, the group-pressures experiments, and the obedience studies. These cases intrigue us because we often fail to recognize how immensely sensitive we are to group pressures, even though it is a *natural function of a group* to exert these pressures.

Given the fact that so few of us ever perceive what strong control our environments exercise over us, perhaps it is not surprising we invent all kinds of "rational explanations" that emphasize the importance of intra-psychic processes in determining how we think and behave. These "inventions" include most of our theories about "traits," "personality factors," and *"attitudes."*

ATTITUDES

At the start of Chapter 17, we listed four significant issues that concern social psychologists. One of these issues dealt with what the *content* of social psychology should be. Namely, should researchers and theorists pay attention to such internal processes as *attitudes?* Or should they focus almost entirely on measurable outputs, such as *behaviors?* More to the point, perhaps, can you predict what people will *do* if you know their attitudes? Perhaps it is time we tried to resolve this issue—as best we can. Let's look at why attitudes are important, why some of them remain fairly stable throughout our lives, why other attitudes appear to be so changeable, and finally, the relationship between attitudes and behaviors.

Advertising, Education, and Propaganda

What brand of toothpaste do you use? No matter what your answer, there's a much more interesting question to ask: How did you happen to pick that particular brand? Was it the flavor that attracted you to it, or the approval of a dentists' organization, or the low price? Or did you choose it because it's the same brand that the rest of your family uses?

Whatever reason you give, chances are that you probably won't list *advertising* as the factor behind your choice. And yet, if you think about it, how would you have known about this brand if it had never been advertised? Furthermore, if you were subjected to "blind" tests (where you couldn't tell which brand you were using), are you absolutely confident you could pick your favorite toothpaste—or cola, soup, or shampoo—from others on the market?

Most of us like to think our decisions to buy a particular product, to vote for a certain politician, or our opinions about war and sex and minority groups are *rational* decisions. However, while we do sometimes think through such matters logically, our viewpoints are often created *unconsciously*, without our being aware of how various forces in our social environments shape our thoughts and preferences. One such force is advertising (Cialdini, 1985).

North Americans spend more money each year on advertising than they do on education, or on pollution control, mental health, poverty relief, or scientific research (Mayer, 1958). If the advertisers didn't believe they could influence your attitudes toward their products—whether or not you were aware of their efforts—would they spend so much?

But advertising does more than just sell products—it also tends to *reinforce social stereotypes* (Krupka & Vener, 1992; Mosher, 1976). Canadian psychologists Diana Rak and Linda McMullen studied "sex-role stereotyping" in 60 daytime and 60

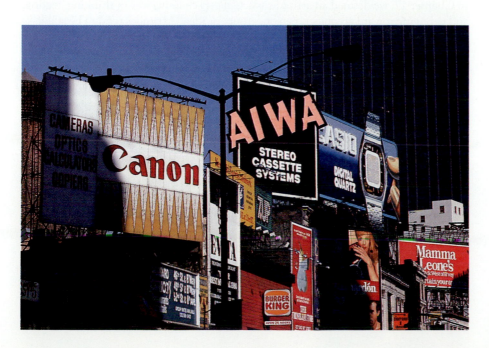

Although we are often skeptical about the effect of advertising on our behavior, advertisers would not spend millions of dollars on advertising each year if it did not affect us.

Propaganda. Ideas or doctrine (from the Latin word meaning "to create offspring"). You "propagate" plans when you plant seeds. You propagate ideas when you try to convince people to believe in them.

The purpose of public relations in its best sense is to inform and to keep minds open; the purpose of propaganda in the bad sense is to misinform and to keep minds closed.

JOHN W. HILL

prime time television commercials, in which a man and a women exchanged comments on some subject (chiefly on the product being sold). According to Rak and McMullen, traditional "male-female" role differences were present in almost all the ads, but were more apparent in daytime commercials (Rak & McMullen, 1987).

Advertisers aren't the only ones who wish to bend your opinions to their purposes. Almost every press release put out by the government, or by individual politicians, is aimed at getting you to think favorably of the person or agency involved. News stories about movie stars, rock musicians, professional athletes, and university professors are almost always "handouts" from publicity agents—**propaganda** designed to make you think more highly of their subjects. In fact, the majority of what passes for "news" on television and in many newspapers actually comes from public relations specialists and not from a reporter who has "dug up the facts" on his or her own time (Schwager, 1986).

Whenever a teacher criticizes or praises a certain theory, whenever a religious leader preaches, whenever a parent "lectures" or a friend offers advice—aren't these people trying to affect your attitudes? And whenever you "dress up to make a good impression," or compliment someone in authority, aren't you "advertising" too?

It is the job of public relations specialists to find ways to influence people's attitudes toward a given product, organization, idea, or individual. Most of these specialists consider their messages informative and educational. For instance, in a survey of attitudes toward *psychology*, Ludy Benjamin found that (generally speaking) Americans have a favorable impression of psychologists. However, Benjamin reports, most Americans have little idea of what psychologists actually do, nor what influence psychology has on their lives. And he concludes that "without some significant public policy campaigning, psychologists should expect to continue to encounter problems created by the public's [lack of] information" (Benjamin, 1986). Thus, even psychologists resort to "educational advertising" when such actions suit their needs.

Advertisers, governments, and other organizations consider their messages to be informative and educational. When is a message "education" and when is it "propaganda"?

Attitude Stability

In Chapter 17, we defined an attitude as a *relatively enduring* way of thinking, feeling, and behaving toward an object, person, group, or idea. Attitudes tend to be stable—probably more stable than you realized. Consider the following study by Theodore Newcomb.

In the mid-1930s, Newcomb studied the political attitudes of women attending Bennington College in Vermont. Most of the women attending Bennington came from wealthy and rather conservative homes. As Newcomb and others have noted, colleges and universities are populated by professors who often have very liberal political opinions (social science faculty are generally the most radical) (Newcomb, 1943, 1967; Ladd & Lipset, 1975, 1976). When a student from a politically conservative family arrives on such a campus, the student often comes under fairly intense social pressure to change her or his attitudes. If you were such a student, do you think you would change, or would you retain your old attitudes despite the pressure?

In the first part of his research, Newcomb found that the more prestige or status a woman had among her fellow students, the more likely it was that she was also very liberal in her views. Conservative students typically were looked down upon; liberal students were very much looked up to. Seniors were significantly less conservative than were freshmen.

Under these conditions, the entire college population acted rather like a *reference group* that rewarded liberal attitudes and punished political conservatism. Those

Leaders of the 1960s free speech movement remained politically active and liberal even when studied fifteen years later.

women who *identified* with the college community tended to become much more liberal during their four years at Bennington. However, those women who tended to identify more with their parents than with their classmates *resisted* the liberal college tradition (Newcomb, 1943).

To find out how their attitudes would change over time, Newcomb followed 150 of the most liberal of these women for the next 25 years of their lives. Although he originally had suspected the students might revert to a more conservative position, this turned out not to be the case with many of them. In fact, during the entire 25 years, most of the women remained liberal in their outlooks despite family pressures. But why?

Newcomb reports that most of these women *deliberately* set out to remain liberal in spite of their social backgrounds. They tended to select liberal (or non-conservative) husbands who would reinforce their political views. They found little pockets of liberalism in their environments and tried to stay entirely within these pockets. And they kept in close touch with their Bennington classmates who were also liberal. These students also tended to ignore those "old classmates" who weren't as liberal as they.

Newcomb believes that if maintaining a given attitude is important enough, you will consciously or unconsciously select environments that will continue to support that attitude. You may also shut out incoming sensory messages that tend to disrupt the attitudes you already hold (a form of *autistic hostility*) (Newcomb, 1967).

More recently, Alberta Nassi and her associates found that student activists from the 1960s found environments that would protect them from change and maintained their more radical political philosophy 15 years later (Hoge & Ankney, 1982; Nassi, 1981). Similarly, Rachel Ivie and her colleagues found that persons with military experience in their youth maintained stable "pro-military" attitudes over several decades through friendships and other social ties (Ivie et al., 1991).

How would Tajfel's "Social Identity Theory" explain this choice of environments?

These studies are among a very few aimed at measuring *stability* of attitudes. Attitude *change* is much easier to investigate, in no small part because the subjects need not be studied over such a long time span. Indeed, as you will see, it seems that much of what we know about attitude stability comes from experiments designed to change people's opinions.

Persuasion and Attitude Change

According to psychologist Icek Ajzen, "Social psychologists probably have expended more time, effort, and ingenuity on the study of persuasion than on the study of any other single issue." And until recently, Ajzen says, research on persuasion was primarily "guided by a conceptual framework developed in the 1950s by Carl Hovland and his associates at Yale University" (Ajzen, 1987).

Let's begin our survey of the literature on persuasion, then, by looking at what Hovland and his colleagues did, and at the theoretical model they created for describing the communication process.

THE "YALE MODEL"

In one of their first major publications the Yale group stated that persuasive communications have four main factors: the *communicator*, the *message*, the *audience*, and the *feedback loop* between the audience and the communicator (Hovland et al., 1953). This viewpoint is often called the "Yale model" of persuasion.

Over the years this model has stimulated a great deal of research—although some of the findings turned out to be more complex than originally expected. Let's look at some general conclusions concerning the communicator, the message, the audience, and the feedback loop.

THE COMMUNICATOR   Not surprisingly, popular and attractive communicators are more persuasive than unpopular or unattractive ones (Baker & Churchill, 1977; Chaiken, 1979). In addition, experts are more persuasive than nonexperts (Hovland & Weiss, 1951). You may be surprised to learn, however, that communicators who speak rapidly are more convincing than those who speak slowly (Miller et al., 1976). This may be because we assume that rapid speech indicates that the speaker is not only familiar with a topic but is also an expert in the area.

Another interesting twist is that when we first hear a message and don't believe it—perhaps because we don't trust the communicator—we may later change our attitude to go along with the message. Apparently, we remember the message and forget where we heard it (Hovland & Weiss, 1951). We would be most likely to experience this **sleeper effect** in the following way: Immediately after hearing a very persuasive message we discover the source is totally lacking in credibility; we are not persuaded. Several weeks later, however, we find our attitude has shifted in the direction of the persuasive communication (Gruder et al., 1978; Pratkanis et al., 1988).

Sleeper effect. The increased influence of an originally ineffective persuasive message after the passage of time—presumably because the original reason for not accepting the message has been forgotten.

Can you see a connection between the sleeper effect and the power of rumors?

THE MESSAGE   Would-be persuaders can either tell us just their side of an issue or they can present both sides. A one-sided message is most effective when the audience already generally agrees with the communicator (Hovland et al., 1957). When the audience does *not* initially agree with the communicator, or if the audience is likely to hear a message from the other side, a two-sided message is more effective. Presenting both sides gives the communicator opportunity to show that he or she can handle the *counterarguments* that the audience will produce—at least to themselves—when they hear the would-be persuader's message (DeBono, 1987; Leippe & Elkin, 1987).

Many messages, especially those dealing with health and safety, try to persuade us by describing in gory detail the dire consequences we face if we do not change. However, research suggests that these fear-arousing messages are not always effective.

For example, in 1953, Irving Janis and Seymour Feshback investigated the effects of fear-arousing communications on high school students. The researchers picked "dental hygiene" as their topic. They wrote three different 15-minute lectures on tooth decay. The first was a "high fear" lecture that contained 71 references to pain, cancer, paralysis, blindness, mouth infections, inflamed gums, ugly or discolored teeth, and dental drills. The second, or "moderate fear," lecture was somewhat less threatening. But the third, or "minimal fear," lecture was quite different. It made no mention at all of pain and disease. Instead, the "minimal fear" message suggested ways of *avoiding* cavities and decayed teeth through proper dental hygiene.

Janis and Feshback presented each of the three appeals to a different group of 50 high school students (a fourth group of students heard no lecture at all and thus served as a control group). Janis and Feshback found that *immediately afterwards*, the subjects exposed to the "high fear" lecture were highly impressed with what they heard. A week later, however, only 28 percent of the "high fear" group had brushed their teeth more often, and 20 percent of them were actually *doing worse*. In marked contrast, the "low fear" students were not particularly impressed with the lecture—but a week later 50 percent of them were "brushing better" and only 14 percent were doing a worse job (Janis & Feshback, 1953).

The high fear appeal apparently evoked strong emotional responses in the students, many of whom thought that being frightened was somehow "good for them." When it came to actually *changing behaviors*, though, the high-fear message simply didn't work as well as did the minimal-fear message.

Subsequent research indicates that fear-arousing messages *can* be effective in certain circumstances. First, the message must arouse *substantial fear*. Second, the audience must believe that the feared outcome is *very likely* if the message is not followed. Third, the audience must believe that following the message will *eliminate* the feared outcome. And fourth, the audience must believe that they are *capable of carrying out the avoidance behaviors* advocated in the message (Leventhal, 1970; Rogers, 1975, 1983; Seydel et al., 1990).

Yet hold it more humane, more heav'nly, first,
By winning words to conquer willing hearts,
And make persuasion do the work of fear.

JOHN MILTON (1671)

Fear-producing messages catch our attention and evoke an emotional reaction. However, they are not always as effective as we might believe.

THE AUDIENCE   The character traits and past experiences of the audience are factors that affect how the audience will perceive and respond to a message (Rhodes & Wood, 1992). A good communicator attempts to discover as much as possible about the audience, and then *shapes* the message to suit both the occasion and the people receiving the message. For example, complex arguments and philosophical justifications might be lost on one audience but be entirely appropriate for another.

In addition, research indicates that some people are simply more "influenceable" than other people (Abelson & Lesser, 1959; Janis & Field, 1959; King, 1959). However, researchers have had difficulty in relating "influenceability" to more specific individual differences. There is some evidence that more intelligent people are more difficult to influence (Rhodes & Wood, 1992), but this effect is unreliable and weak. There is stronger evidence that individuals with high self-esteem are more difficult to persuade, while those with low self-esteem are susceptible to persuasion from attractive or high-status sources (Janis 1954; Janis & Rife, 1959; Lesser & Abelson, 1959; Rhodes & Wood, 1992).

THE FEEDBACK LOOP   Knowing something about your audience doesn't always guarantee you will be able to get your message through to them. Several years ago, Shirley Star and Helen Hughes helped lead a monumental advertising campaign designed to inform the citizens of Cincinnati about the great value of the United Nations. Star and Hughes began by taking surveys to determine what people thought about the UN. The groups who knew the least about the UN (and who liked it the least) included the relatively uneducated, the elderly, and the poor.

Once Star and Hughes knew the characteristics of their target audience, they carried on a six-month "pro–United Nations" campaign. Unfortunately, the messages apparently reached or persuaded few of the target population. Instead, the propaganda was effective primarily with young people and with the better-educated and relatively well-to-do segment of the general public. These were, of course, the very people who were already favorably disposed toward the world organization (Star & Hughes, 1950).

How might you explain the response of the "target audience" in the Star and Hughes study in terms of autistic hostility?

Why did the Cincinnati campaign fail to affect its intended audience? There probably are many different reasons. To begin with, we have no guarantee that Star and Hughes knew what kinds of messages would be most likely to reach their target audience (the poor, the uneducated, the elderly). Nor can we be sure that those involved in creating the propaganda knew what sorts of appeals would convince the targets to change their attitudes (McConnell, 1966).

A more glaring omission, however, was the fact that Star and Hughes did nothing to establish feedback loops to monitor the *effects* of their propaganda campaign while it was going on. The Cincinnati communicators talked—and *assumed* the audience would listen and respond appropriately. Even the original work of the Yale group recognized that audience feedback was important.

Not all social scientists take the time to interview their subjects after an experiment to ask the subjects why they responded as they did. Why might this sort of interviewing be helpful?

THE YALE STUDIES: AN EVALUATION   As we noted earlier, the research by Carl Hovland and this colleagues at Yale had a tremendous impact on the study of persuasion and communication. The Yale group's approach seemed to promise that changing attitudes could be an effective method of combating prejudice, stereotypes, delinquency, and the negative effects of propaganda.

However, as Richard Petty, Thomas Ostrom, and Timothy Brock point out, in recent years the Yale group's work "has fallen on hard times." Many of their original generalizations have been qualified by subsequent research. Both the communication process and the social issues Hovland and his associates were studying turned out to be more complex than they had assumed (Petty et al., 1981). Weaknesses in the Yale group's approach led Richard Petty and John Cacioppo to propose their own analysis of persuasion, which they call the "elaboration likelihood model."

THE ELABORATION LIKELIHOOD MODEL

According to Petty and Cacioppo, factors such as the "communicator, message, and audience" are of secondary importance when it comes to attitude change. These "secondary factors" have an effect on your attitudes only when you aren't really involved in the situation. Do you really care about many of the products you see advertised? If not, then indeed the "attractiveness" of a communicator might sway you.

However, Petty and Cacioppo say, when it comes to the *primary* issues in your life, you "thoughtfully assess and elaborate on the central merits" of the persuasive messages you receive. If your *assessment* is positive, your attitudes will change in a positive direction. However, it is your *cognitive response* to the message that changes your attitudes. Petty and Cacioppo's **elaboration likelihood model** states that the more you think about ("elaborate on") persuasive messages, the greater the "likelihood" that they will affect you (Petty & Cacioppo, 1986).

According to the model, we process messages relating to unimportant issues by a "peripheral route." We invest little cognitive effort in this type of processing. And we make decisions using *heuristics* or "rules of thumb"—such as "I'll believe an attractive communicator more than an unattractive one." On the other hand, when an issue is important to us, it undergoes more intense processing via the "central route." Central route processing involves careful analysis of an issue and the arguments. In this case, we change our attitudes if we find the arguments cogent and strong, and if the communicator presents relevant facts for his or her position. These two processes are illustrated in Figure 18.5.

Many of the influences identified by the older Yale model are apparently heuristics that we rely on for relatively unimportant decisions—the peripheral route (Chaiken, 1987). When we have the ability and motivation to *analyze* an issue, rational cognitive variables become more important. As a result we *elaborate* on the matter *cognitively*—the central route. This does not necessarily mean the cognitive approach will always persuade us on important issues; we may develop strong counterarguments and remain unchanged. It does mean that the *basis* for change is quite different for peripheral and central attitudes.

Icek Ajzen believes the Petty and Cacioppo model is superior to that offered by Hovland and the Yale group. But it too has its flaws, Ajzen says. Petty and Cacioppo

Elaboration likelihood model. A view of the effect of communications which says that a message will have a greater effect on you if you think about it in various ways (elaborate on it). (Note the similarity with the "depth of processing" view of memory we discussed in Chapter 10.)

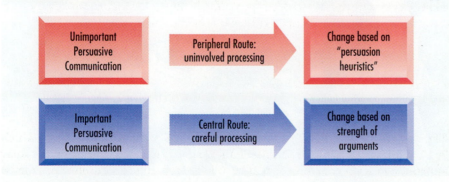

FIGURE 18.5

A cognitive analysis of two routes of persuasive messages according to the "elaboration likelihood model" (Petty & Cacioppo, 1986). Unimportant messages are processed superficially by "rules of thumb" or heuristics such as: "Attractive or expert communications are more believable." Messages of greater concern to us are processed in more depth by analyzing the facts they present and the strength of their arguments.

pay little attention to fear-arousing messages, or how "elaborated thoughts" get incorporated into "permanent belief systems" (Ajzen, 1987).

There is another important point that Petty and Cacioppo must address: the relationship between *attitudes* and *behaviors*. They note that attitudes changed by "elaborated thoughts" are more *predictive* of future behaviors than are attitudes changed via the Yale model. However, Petty and Cacioppo do not specify how attitudes get *translated* into behaviors.

It's time we addressed just that issue.

Attitudes Versus Behaviors

According to most social psychologists, whenever you state an attitude, you are making a prediction about your future thoughts, feelings, and behaviors. But what are we to think if your attitudinal statement doesn't predict what you actually do at some future time?

CHINESE AND BLACKS KEEP OUT!

The research study that first opened up this problem was reported many years ago by Richard LaPiere. Just prior to the Second World War, LaPiere spent considerable time driving through the United States with a Chinese couple as his companions. Despite the very strong "anti-Chinese" prejudice to be found among many Americans at that time, LaPiere and his friends were refused service only once during 10,000 miles of travel.

Later, when they were safely home, LaPiere sent questionnaires to all the hotels and cafes where they had stopped. One item on the questionnaire asked, "Will you accept members of the Chinese race as guests in your establishment?" More than 90 percent of the places responded with a very firm "no," and yet all but one of these hundreds of establishments actually had accepted the Chinese couple without question or comment. Obviously there was a very marked difference between "attitude" and "behavior" on the part of these establishments (LaPiere, 1934).

In a similar study by Bernard Kutner and his associates, three young women visited various restaurants in a fashionable suburban community in the northeastern part of the United States. Two of the women were white; the third was black. The two white women always arrived at the restaurant first, asked for a table for three,

Research indicates that prejudiced attitudes do not always lead to discriminatory behavior. Sometimes acting against our attitudes leads us to change our attitudes to be consistent with our behavior.

and were seated. Shortly thereafter, the black woman entered, informed the head waiter or hostess that she was with friends who were already seated, found the table, sat down with the two white women, and was served without question.

Two weeks after each visit, Kutner wrote a letter to each restaurant asking if they would serve blacks. Not one replied. The experimenters then called the manager of each establishment on the phone. The managers uniformly responded in a very cool and distant manner, suggesting that they held a highly prejudiced attitude toward serving blacks. Yet, as in the LaPiere study, this attitude was simply not translated into action when the restaurant personnel were faced with seating a black person (Kutner et al., 1952).

Since 1965, there have been dozens of similar experiments, all of which suggest that attitudes (as measured by questionnaires) are often poor indicators of what people actually do, think, and feel in real-life situations.

PSYCHOLOGICAL TRAPS

One explanation of the LaPiere study comes from an article by Jeffrey Rubin. Once you "invest too much" in a situation, Rubin says, you may continue in a given line of behavior simply because you can't find an easy way out. Rubin calls these situations "psychological traps."

For example, suppose you call someone on the phone and are put on hold. You wait a while and wonder if you shouldn't hang up. But if you do, you'll just have to call again. So you wait some more. Then you decide that, since you've waited so long already, you will "lose" the time you've already waited if you hang up. So you wait still longer.

Rubin gives another example of a psychological trap that seems unbelievable to many people—until they get caught up in it. Some years ago, Yale economist Martin Shubik auctioned off a dollar bill to friends at a cocktail party. The money went to the highest bidder. The "trap" came from the fact that the person who made the second-highest bid also had to pay whatever he or she had bid, but didn't get the dollar. In other words, both bidders paid what they bid, but only the highest bidder got the dollar. Thus, once you started to bid, you had to win—you were trapped. Rubin reports that "Several researchers have had people play the Dollar Auction game under controlled laboratory conditions and have found that the participants typically end up bidding far in excess of the $1 prize at stake, sometimes paying as much as $5 or $6 for a dollar bill" (Rubin, 1981).

The interesting question is, "Why do people engage in such a self-defeating course of action?" According to Allan Teger, participants in the Dollar Auction typically offer two reasons for their behavior. The first reason has to do with economics—they genuinely want the money (at first). Then a desire to regain their losses or to avoid losing more money motivates them. The second reason is intra-psychic—a desire to "save face," a desire to prove yourself as the "best player," or an urge to "punish the other person." However, these are all *after-the-fact* attitudes expressed by people to explain why they behaved in a self-defeating manner (cited in Rubin, 1981).

Rubin's work suggests that when, for example, two white women are seated in a restaurant, the manager *has an investment* in these customers. Thus, when a black woman arrives to join the two whites, the manager may feel "trapped." For to refuse service to the newcomer means "a messy scene" in which the white women may get up and leave. Thus, the *social situation* may determine which of two attitudes ("not wanting to serve blacks" versus "not wanting to make a scene and lose customers") actually prevails.

ATTITUDES FOLLOW BEHAVIORS

Daryl Bem presents a radically different approach to the subject, however. According to Bem, attitudes are simply *verbal statements* about your own behaviors.

In selling a product we may gradually come to believe we like the product—our attitudes may follow our behavior.

Bem points out that LaPiere really measured two quite different attitudinal responses that occurred in two very different environments. LaPiere's questionnaire seemed designed to elicit negative responses from the hotel and innkeepers who received it. But when LaPiere presented himself and a well-dressed Chinese couple at the desk of the hotel, the stimulus situation was so different from that evoked by the questionnaire that the behavioral response of the innkeeper was bound to be different as well (Bem, 1977; Bem & Allen, 1974).

Bem believes that there really are no such things as "attitudes," unless you wish to consider them as verbal explanations of why you do what you do. Attitudinal statements then don't predict behaviors well at all—they merely give a *rationalization* of what you've already done. We might summarize Bem's position as follows: "How do I know my attitude until I know where I am and see what I've done?"

A different view of the influence of behavior on attitudes comes from a classic series of experiments conducted by Leon Festinger and his colleagues. In perhaps the best known of his experiments, Festinger and J. M. Carlsmith asked college students to do about 30 minutes of very tedious and boring work. The subjects performed these repetitive and uninteresting tasks while alone in a laboratory room.

After the students had completed the chores, Festinger and Carlsmith offered some of them a dollar as a reward to tell the next subject what an exciting and thrilling task it had been. They paid other subjects $20 for doing exactly the same thing. Afterward, no matter how good a "selling job" the person had done, the experimenters asked each subject to express her or his actual attitude towards how pleasurable the work was.

Festinger and Carlsmith report that the students paid $20 rated the tasks as being dull, as did a group of subjects who were not asked to "sell" the experiment to another student. However, the subjects paid just $1 thought the chores were really pretty *interesting* and *enjoyable* (Festinger & Carlsmith, 1959)!

Why did the subjects who were paid $1 rate the work as being much more pleasant than one might have expected? Festinger believes they had a difficult job rationalizing their actions, for they had *lied* about how interesting the task was supposed to be. The subjects paid $20 for lying apparently were willing to face the fact they had "fudged" a bit for the money. The students who were paid but a single dollar couldn't admit that they'd "sell out" for so little money. Therefore, they changed their *attitude* towards the experiment (Festinger, 1957). Their attitudes then were *rationalizations* of what they had *already done*.

According to Festinger, whenever we are in conflict situations we experience **cognitive dissonance.** That is, whenever we do something we think we shouldn't, we face the problem of explaining our actions to ourselves and others. We are usually highly motivated to reduce cognitive dissonance when it occurs, and we do so chiefly by changing our *attitudes* to make them agree with our *actual behaviors* (Festinger, 1957).

A similar process seems to underly the experience of "brainwashing." Prisoners are persuaded, with minimal coercion, to cooperate with their captors in very insignificant ways at first—perhaps by accepting a cigarette or stick of gum. Then they might be asked to make a trivial statement about their country, such as admitting that it is not perfect. Very gradually the prisoners begin to cooperate in more significant ways. If the coercion of the enemy is so subtle that prisoners cannot justify their new behaviors by external pressures, the prisoners may change their attitudes to be consistent with their new behavior. Eventually they may denounce their country and even betray their fellow prisoners (Schein, 1956).

Cognitive dissonance. The feeling you get from incompatible thoughts, for example if you act contrary to your values. According to Festinger, you are strongly motivated to reduce this dissonance. You might do so either by changing your values or by changing your behaviors.

What similarities do you see between Festinger's theory of cognitive dissonance and Piaget's description of how "dis-equilibrium" drives us to change our perceptions of the world?

RECIPROCAL DETERMINISM

Are your actions regulated by internal processes such as attitudes? Or by environmental inputs that directly influence your visible behaviors? Do you "change your mind," and let your actions follow suit? Or do you first change the way you act, and then alter your attitudes to fit your behaviors?

According to Albert Bandura, you do both at the same time. Bandura believes that explanations of human behavior generally emphasize *either* environmental *or* internal determinants of behavior. "In social learning theory," Bandura says, "causal processes are conceptualized in terms of **reciprocal determinism**" (Bandura, 1978). Bandura goes on to say that, from his point of view, psychological functioning involves a *continuous* interaction between behavioral, cognitive, and environmental influences.

Bandura believes that you first build up "behavioral standards" by observing others and by noticing the consequences of their actions. You may then test these standards yourself, to determine if you will be rewarded or punished for thinking and acting in a similar way. Once your standards are set, though, you tend to *evaluate* future social information, or inputs, in terms of the possible consequences of acting or thinking in a given way. Thus, these factors are *reciprocal influences* on each other (Bandura, 1977b).

To give an example of what Bandura is talking about, consider the following: Other people obviously influence your internal standards. That's the external environment at work. However, as Newcomb has shown, you tend to avoid people who don't share your standards and seek out those who do. So, you *influence your environment* by seeking out those settings that will allow you to act in the way that your internal standards dictate. You may also try to influence the people around you, so that they reinforce you for what you consider appropriate behavior.

The notion of "self-regulating systems" lies at the heart of Bandura's position. He sees you not as the "passive audience" for persuasive messages from your environment, which was the position of Hovland and the Yale group. Nor does Bandura view your mind as a "behavior-producing machine," as do trait theorists. Nor does he assume that all of your responses are conditioned reactions triggered by external inputs, as does Skinner. Instead, Bandura believes that there is a reciprocal *interplay* between your social inputs, your perceptions, and your responses. You continually evaluate the consequences of perceiving a given stimulus in a particular way. And you change both your behaviors and your attitudes in order to achieve your own particular goals (Bandura, 1986a).

Reciprocal determinism. Bandura's belief that psychological processes are a joint function of behavioral, cognitive, and environmental influences. Each influences the other. For example, you choose your environment and your environment influences you.

We shape our buildings; thereafter they shape us.

WINSTON CHURCHILL

When most people diet, they tend to avoid banquets and bakery shops. How does this wise decision on the dieter's part tend to support Bandura's views?

The critical importance of the attitude-behavior interaction becomes particularly clear in studies on *conflict* between various social groups. For, as we will see, the most effective way of changing one is to change the other at the same time.

CONFLICT, WAR, AND PEACEMAKING

Social psychologist Ronald Fisher, of the Canadian Institute for International Peace and Security, says, "Destructive intergroup conflict is the most complex and costly enigma facing humankind. It is the preeminent social issue of our time in that it ruthlessly saps the resources required for human development and productivity, and in the extreme threatens our very survival" (Fisher, 1990). Thus, the understanding and resolution of conflicts is potentially one of the most valuable areas of "action research" (Pruitt & Rubin, 1986; Stroebe et al., 1987). If we can understand the forces which produce hostility between individuals, racial groups, or nations, perhaps we can prescribe steps to reduce *prejudice, discrimination,* and *war*. With this in mind, let's look at how social psychologists grapple with this important social problem.

Sherif and "Robber's Cave"

Muzafer Sherif was born in Smyrna, Turkey, in 1906. During the first world war, when Sherif was about 13, Greek soldiers invaded his village. Sherif and other townspeople rushed out to defend themselves, but were powerless against the better-equipped Greek forces. A Greek soldier came directly at Sherif, bayonet drawn, and actually killed the man standing next to Sherif. Then, for reasons Sherif says he still doesn't understand, the Greek soldier turned and walked away, sparing Sherif (Trotter, 1985). As you might expect, that early experience of bloody conflict between two warring nations left an indelible impression on Sherif. After coming to the United States and taking his doctorate in psychology at Harvard, Sherif devoted his life to the study of *conflict resolution.*

During the late 1950s, as part of a research project, Sherif and his colleagues helped run a summer camp for 11- and 12-year-old boys at Robber's Cave Park, Oklahoma. The boys were carefully selected to be happy, healthy individuals who had no difficulty getting along with other young men their age. None of the boys knew each other before being admitted to the camp. Nor did any of them realize that they were to be subjects in Sherif's experiments.

The camp itself had two rather separate housing units. The boys living in one unit were called the "Eagles," while the other group was called the "Rattlers." Since there were no pre-existing friendships among the boys, group commitment and cohesion in both units was very low on the first day of camp. In an attempt to increase group cohesion, Sherif gave both the Eagles and the Rattlers various problems that could be solved only if the boys in each separate unit worked together effectively. As each unit overcame the difficulties Sherif put to it, the boys came to like the other boys in the same unit more and more. The Eagles and the Rattlers each became a "natural group," and commitment to the specific group (and to its particular emerging norms) increased significantly.

After the Eagles and the Rattlers had shown considerable cohesion, Sherif introduced a series of contests designed to make the two groups hostile toward one another. As the groups competed for prizes, conflict developed, since one group could win only at the expense of the other. Very soon the Eagles were making nasty comments about the Rattlers, and vice versa. Most of this hostility consisted of one group's attributing selfish or hostile motives to the other group. Name calling, fights, and raids on the cabins belonging to the other group became commonplace. Sherif had created an experimental context for his study of conflict resolution.

Sources of Conflict

Conflict spiral view. A view of international conflicts which sees them escalating into war as the result of competition and fear.

Sherif's "Robber's Cave" research demonstrates a powerful source of conflict: competition. Competition for a limited resource, whether it is money, land, prestige, or any other desirable commodity, is a major factor in many disputes. Competition is the basis for the **conflict spiral view** of war. In this view, each side feels threatened by the actions of the other side. They believe their goals are incompatible and so they fear each other. Every success by one side draws renewed efforts from the other side to excel. This leads to a "spiral" in competition (for example, an arms race) and ultimately, armed conflict results. World War I was apparently caused by an unintended "conflict spiral."

Conflict often erupts as the result of competition for limited resources. It may then spiral into a dangerous confrontation.

But competition is not always the main factor in war. According to the **deterrence view** of war, one side may be happy with the "status quo" and the other side becomes the "aggressor." If the aggressor power doubts the will or the ability of the status quo power to resist its actions, it may make expansionary demands. These demands grow until the status quo power finally resists and war results. World War II resulted when the status quo powers (the Allies) finally resisted Hitler's expansion after allowing him some earlier gains (a result of the policy of appeasement). According to international conflict expert Ralph White, aggressor nations tend to overestimate the likelihood that fear will deter third countries (status quo powers) from coming to the aid of victims of aggression (White, 1987). In the deterrence view, war can only be prevented if the status quo power has the capacity and will to fight (Tetlock, 1983, 1987).

Deterrence view. A view of international conflict that sees one side as a "status quo" power whose role it is to deter "aggressor" powers. If the status quo power is unwilling or unable to deter the aggressor, the aggressor expands until the status quo power is forced into war.

Which view of international conflict best describes the relationship between the United States and the Soviet Union during the "cold war"? Or between the United States and Iraq leading up to the Gulf war?

In Chapter 17 we saw several other possible contributors to misunderstanding between groups. For example, stereotypes and autistic hostility distort our assessment of other groups. Self-fulfilling prophecies lead others to conform to our negative stereotypes. And whenever cultural differences exist, for example in nonverbal communication, there is the possibility for misunderstanding and strife.

We also saw how biases in our attributions often cause us to blame others for their failures and other negative events, while excusing the same things in ourselves. These processes seem to be equally potent in inter-group attributions. In fact, groups are often guilty of the *ultimate attribution error*—attributing good acts to their own character, and bad acts to their own circumstances and their enemies' character (Pettigrew, 1979; Taylor & Jaggi, 1974).

So social psychologists have identified several possible sources of conflict. But what have they discovered about *reducing* conflict? Muzafer Sherif made Eagles and Rattlers enemies, but could he make them friends? Let's see what he learned.

Reducing Inter-Group Conflict

Once the Eagles and Rattlers were at each other's throats, Sherif tried to bring them back together again. In his first experiment, Sherif attempted to unite the two groups by giving them a common enemy—a group of threatening outsiders. This technique worked fairly well, in that it brought the Eagles and the Rattlers closer together. But they still held hatred for their common enemy.

The next year Sherif and his colleagues repeated the group-conflict experiment with a different set of boys. Once inter-group hatred had reached its peak, Sherif brought the two units into very pleasant, non-competitive contact with each other. They sat together in the same dining hall while eating excellent food, and they watched movies together. However, this approach didn't succeed, for the groups merely used these occasions for fighting and shouting at each other.

Sherif then confronted the hostile groups with problem situations that could be solved only if the two units *cooperated* with each other. First, a water shortage "suddenly developed," and all the boys had to ration themselves. Next, Sherif offered to show the whole camp an exciting movie—but to see it, both units had to pool their resources. And one time when all the boys were particularly hungry, the transportation for their food "broke down." It could be fixed only if both groups worked together quickly and effectively.

Sherif reports that his technique succeeded beautifully. The two groups did indeed cooperate—reluctantly at first, but more and more willingly as their initial efforts were reinforced.

Before the "crises" occurred, almost none of the boys had friendships outside their units. Afterward, some 30 percent of the friendships were inter-group rather than in-group. During the hostile period, about one-third of the members of each group rated the members of the other group as being "stinkers," "smart alecks," or "sneaky." Afterward, less than 5 percent of the boys gave the members of the other group such highly unfavorable ratings (Sherif et al., 1961).

Sherif believes that the best way to reduce inter-group conflicts is by giving both parties "overriding, superordinate goals" that they can achieve only if the groups work together. However, he laments the fact that many group leaders typically see "striving toward common goals" as a sign of weakness and compromise, not a movement toward healthy conflict resolution (Trotter, 1985).

Peacemaking Strategies

Sherif's research demonstrates several facts about conflict reduction: First, we can see that bringing the boys together, even under pleasant, non-competitive circumstances, did not reduce conflict. Other examples also indicate that mere contact is not enough to reduce inter-group hostility. For example, when the contact between racial groups is on an *un*equal basis, group members tend to form attitudes which justify and *perpetuate* the inequality rather than reduce it. To be effective in lowering hostility, contact between groups must be in a non-competitive situation where both groups enjoy equal status (Ramirez, 1977, 1988; Soriano & Ramirez, 1991). And, as Sherif's work indicates, even this is not always adequate.

The second lesson we can learn from Sherif's research is that working together on a *joint problem* is an effective way of reducing conflict and promoting cooperation. Elliot Aronson and others also report positive effects on race relations with a similar strategy in desegregated schools (Aronson & Bridgeman 1979; Aronson & Gonzalez, 1988; Johnson & Johnson, 1989). Working together on a joint problem may reduce conflict because members of both groups come to see themselves as belonging to a single group (Gaertner et al., 1990). According to Ronald Fisher, joint problem solving is now "generally the preferred strategy in interpersonal relations and organizational settings" (Fisher, 1990).

A third feature of Sherif's, and many other successful efforts at conflict reduction, is the use of a third party. Warring groups are often unable or unwilling to settle their differences without outside help. In the "Robber's Cave" study Sherif merely introduced the problem which ultimately brought the groups together. In other situations, however, the third-party peacemaker has a more extensive role to play, consulting, mediating, and more actively arbitrating (Fisher, 1990; Fisher & Ury, 1983; Parker, 1989). It seems unlikely that Middle Eastern conflicts, such as with Iraq or between Israel and the Palestinians, will be resolved without extensive work by third-party peacemakers.

Finally, we should note that in addition to contact, joint problem-solving, and third-party intervention, peacemakers can make effective use of *conciliation*. Research shows that in *conflict spiral situations*, an unconditional gesture of goodwill by one group can sometimes lead an opposing group to reciprocate with a similar benevolent act. In this way a downward spiral of decreasing hostility begins, and other forms of cooperation increase (Lindskold, 1986; Osgood, 1962; Fisher, 1990).

Each of these strategies has advantages and disadvantages, and each is more appropriate in some conflict situations than in others. However, as Muzafer Sherif observed, we do not have a "cure" for inter-group hostility. The seriousness of national, racial, and other conflicts will continue to motivate social psychologists in this area.

Now that we have looked at the various areas ways in which psychologists study human behavior, from individual reflexes to international conflicts, it is time to put psychology in a global context. So let's turn to a consideration of psychology around the world.

Research shows that working together to solve a common problem is one of the best ways of reducing hostility between groups.

SUMMARY

1. **A group** is a set of persons considered as a social system—a collection of two or more individuals who are psychologically related to or dependent upon one another and who share common goals.

2. The more similar the members of a group, the more **cohesive** the group and the more **homogeneous** it becomes. The more cohesive a group, the more **commitment** the members are likely to have toward the group and its goals.

3. Our **reference groups** are those we look to as social **models** or **norms.** Reference groups give us **feedback** on our behavior by rewarding movements toward and punishing movements away from the **group norm.**

4. Whenever we make a judgment or give an opinion that is different from the perceived group norm, we typically find ourselves under strong psychological **pressure to conform** more closely to the group standard.

5. Group pressures to **conformity** become most effective when at least four group members have announced their judgments or opinions without being openly contradicted. If even one group member disagrees openly, **group cohesion** may be destroyed.

6. Some group members know when they are conforming (but do so anyway), but others **yield to pressures** because these pressures affect their **perceptions** of what has taken place.

7. Milgram's research suggests that, when given orders from a higher authority, most of us tend to show **obedience,** even if we sometimes end up hurting ourselves or others. We are particularly likely to obey orders if the people around us are doing so.

8. Latané's **theory of social impact** states that **bystander apathy** occurs in part because groups tend to **dilute** feelings of responsibility. Some bystanders may help because they have **learned** more relevant skills. **Social exchange** theory says

that helping behavior depends on the potential costs and benefits of helping. Batson believes true **altruism** is based on **empathy** for the victim.

9. We tend to adopt attitudes like those around us and then seek out friends and groups with **similar attitudes.** As a result many of our attitudes tend to remain **stable** over long periods of time.

10. According to the "Yale model," the **communication process** is influenced by four important factors: the **communicator,** the **message,** the **audience,** and the **feedback** from the audience to the communicator.

11. **Popular, attractive, expert,** and **fast talking** communicators tend to influence us the most.

12. Sometimes we reject a message from a **low credibility source** and then forget the source. As a result several weeks later we are more influenced by the actual content of the message than by its source. This phenomenon is called the **sleeper effect.**

13. If the audience initially agrees with the communicator, a **one-sided message** is most effective. If the audience does not agree, or if the audience is likely to hear persuasion from the other side, a **two-sided message** is more effective.

14. When we receive **fear-arousing messages,** our first impression may be that the stimulus is a very persuasive one. However, studies show that fear usually achieves little more than repression unless the audience is shown **how to avoid** the feared consequence and convinced that they are capable of carrying out the avoidance behavior.

15. It is important to fit a message to the audience. Some people are **more easily influenced** than other people. This may be partly related to intelligence and self-esteem.

16. If a communicator ignores **feedback from the audience,** the communicator may be ineffective in changing the attitudes of the audience.

17. According to the **elaboration likelihood model** of persuasion, the more that you **elaborate** or think about a message, the greater the **likelihood** that you will change your attitudes.

18. Messages that are *not* important to us are processed by the **peripheral route** and may be judged **heuristically.** Messages that we consider significant are processed by the **central route** and are more carefully analyzed for the strength of their arguments.

19. Some studies suggest that attitudes are poor predictors of what people actually do. One reason may be that attitudes are **verbal statements about your own behaviors.** Or, you may invest so much in a situation you are **psychologically trapped** into behavior in ways counter to your attitudes.

20. **Cognitive dissonance** develops when your attitudes differ from your behaviors. According to Festinger, all people act to **reduce dissonance,** often by changing their **attitudes** rather than by changing their actual behaviors.

21. Bandura believes psychological functions are determined by **reciprocal determinism**—a continuous interaction among behavioral, cognitive, and environmental influences. Thus, you change both your attitudes and behaviors **simultaneously** in order to achieve your goals.

22. **Social conflicts** can occur between groups that must compete for limited resources. Two descriptions of international conflict situations are the **conflict spiral view** and the **deterrence view.**

23. Sherif has shown **inter-group conflicts** can be reduced if the groups are either **threatened** by an outside danger or **rewarded** for working toward a common goal of overriding importance.

24. **Peacemaking** or **conflict resolution** may be enhanced by bringing groups into **equal-status contact, collaborating** on a common problem, consulting with a **third-party negotiator,** or taking steps of **reciprocal conciliation.**

ANSWERS FOR THOUGHT

1. *How many groups do you think you belong to?*

   Some possibilities: family, sports teams, fan clubs, hobby clubs, choir, student body, student government, labor union, church, ethnic group, racial group, national group (country) . . . .

2. *How would "social exchange theorists" probably define a group?*

   From a social exchange point of view, a group is two or more people who have agreed, implicitly or explicitly, to give up something which they have a right to (freedom, time, money, etc.), *in exchange for* something which the group has to offer.

3. *Do you join groups because they are made up of people like yourself? Or do you join groups . . . ?*

   Probably both processes take place. There must be some common interest in order for a group to attract us. However, if we continue to have similar interests, and so remain in a group, it is probably inevitable that group pressures will lead us to become more similar to the other members of the group.

4. *Which country club would seem more desirable to you, one that charged a $1,000 members fee or one that charged but $100?*

   Most research and personal experience indicates that we tend to value more highly the things which cost us more. (Some psychoanalysts feel this is an important part of their more expensive kind of therapy.) The club with the $1,000 fee would probably seem more desirable. On the other hand, perhaps you would agree with Groucho Marx: "I wouldn't want to join any club that would have me as a member."

5. *Your most important reference group is usually your family. How did members of your family set . . . ?*

   All of the processes of learning were probably involved: reward, punishment, modeling and imitation. You may have heard statements like, "We don't do that in our family," or, "In our family you are expected to. . . ." This kind of message, whether communicated openly or merely implied, is saying, "If you want to remain an accepted member of our family, you will conform to the family norms."

6. *Would you obey your government the way many Germans did in carrying out Hitler's fiendish orders?*

   We would like to think we wouldn't obey evil orders, and perhaps we wouldn't. But history contains many disturbing examples of "good people" in "bad situations." The important message we can learn from the study of obedience is to guard against the subtle yet powerful influence of social pressures which can sometimes obscure our personal moral and ethical standards.

7. *What do you think would have happened in Zimbardo's prison study had the "warden" ordered . . . ?*

   It seems likely that given the power of social roles combined with the influence of legitimate authority the guards would probably have carried out the warden's orders.

8. *Under what circumstances do you personally think that deceiving subjects in a scientific experiment . . . ?*

   Virtually all psychological research involving experimental manipulation is conducted under "informed consent." Subjects consent to participate only after they are informed about the study. Yet it is impossible to explain every possible aspect and implication of a study, so in a sense, information is always being withheld. The decision of what a subject needs to know and what is unnecessary, is not always easy. In some cases the research could not be conducted without significant (temporary) deception. In these cases researchers are obligated to insure that the "end justifies the means." This leads us back to our question and to a personal decision on *which ends* justify *which means*.

9. *Consider those 38 neighbors as an Asch-type "conformity group." Why would each person be under . . . ?*

   Each person could see at least some of the others looking out of their windows. They thus formed a group where "inaction" was the norm. In other words, each person, unsure of what to do in this situation, would look around at the others to see what was appropriate. What they saw was inaction, and they conformed.

10. *Should there be laws to require people to help, and punish them if they don't?*

    Such laws are notoriously difficult to enforce. The problem is in showing that someone had a responsibility to help. For example, out of all the people on a beach when someone drowns in the water nearby, *who* is responsible? Prosecuting thousands of people is not practical. Where there is a clear obligation of responsibility, we already have laws. An on-duty lifeguard who didn't try to help, or the parent of a young child who was left in the water alone, would be charged for their negligence. On the other hand, you may also be prosecuted if you have no special obligation to the victim, but you try to help and make matters worse, perhaps by preventing a successful rescue. (Some jurisdictions have instituted special laws to protect physicians and nurses from this kind of litigation.)

11. *Advertisers, governments, and other organizations consider their messages to be informative and . . . ?*

    Education and propaganda are both terms for messages that attempt to change the attitudes and behavior of their audience. For many people, "propaganda" has negative connotations of distortion and deception. Which messages are "education" and which are "propaganda" then, depends on the values of the person judging. We tend to consider a message as education when we believe it, and as propaganda when we don't. Thus, our own government's messages are *education* to us, but *propaganda* to our enemies—and vice versa for messages from our enemy's government. The term "propaganda" also suggests a more emotional, less rational, appeal. Your authors use the term "propaganda" in its original sense of "propagating, or spreading, an idea or message"—and are not necessarily implying truth or falsity.

12. *How would Tajfel's "Social Identity Theory" explain this choice of environments?*

    Social Identity Theory would say the young people defined who they were in their college years. Later, they continued to join groups (formal and informal) which they perceived as being similar to themselves. In this way they perpetuated their social identity. (Bandura would call this action "reciprocal determinism.")

13. *Can you see a connection between the sleeper effect and the power of rumors?*

    One reason rumors may be so dangerous is that we may remember the story but forget that we heard it as a "rumor" from a very unreliable source. Over time, the highly suspect story gains credibility as we forget the source.

14. *How might you explain the response of the "target audience" in the Star and Hughes study in terms of autistic hostility?*

    The target audience had negative attitudes towards the United Nations to start with. These negative attitudes created autistic hostility towards contrary viewpoints. This meant that they were intolerant of the Star and Hughes messages and rejected them without considering them first. (Festinger would say they wanted to avoid the dissonance which they knew the new message would produce.)

15. *Not all social scientists take the time to interview their subjects after an experiment to ask the subjects . . . ?*

    Subjects might have responded for reasons different from those the experimenters assumed. For example, subjects might have misunderstood the instructions, or there might be reasons for the subjects' responses which the experimenters hadn't thought of. Feedback is important here, too (as well as in attitude change).

16. *What similarities do you see between Festinger's theory of cognitive dissonance and Piaget's description . . . ?*

    Both views describe cognitions which don't fit with existing mental representations (schema or other cognitions). Both theories suggest that this situation is unstable and brings about a change. Festinger calls it "dissonance reduction"; Piaget calls it "accommodation." The result is that we are driven to change our perceptions to agree with existing cognitions or schema.

17. *When most people diet, they tend to avoid banquets and bakery shops. How does this wise decision . . . ?*

    These people are showing that they are aware (*cognitive*) of the effect of their *environment* on their *behavior*. They are choosing to avoid an environment which they know is likely to produce the kind of behavior they want to eliminate. Or conversely, they are selecting an environment which will encourage the desired type of behavior.

18. *Which view of international conflict best describes the relationship between the United States and . . . ?*

    The United States and the Soviet Union were engaged in a "conflict spiral" during the cold war. Competition and mutual fear escalated the conflict to dangerous levels. In the Gulf, the "deterrence" view seems to fit better. Iraq (the aggressor) seems to have believed that the United States would not intervene in Kuwait, and that the United Nations would not achieve the consensus necessary for joint action. Iraq may have overestimated the fear of war in the minds of the leaders of the status quo power (the United States and the coalition partners).

CHAPTER 19

PSYCHOLOGY IN A WORLD CONTEXT

Mariko was a recently arrived student from Japan at a large U.S. university. Although at first apprehensive, she was now accustomed to the different routines and lifestyle and was doing quite well in her courses. She had become quite good friends with one of her classmates, Linda, and they often had lunch together. One afternoon the professor in their class asked for two volunteers to come in early the next morning to help code some research data. Linda volunteered and suggested Mariko might also be willing. Mariko replied hesitantly that she did not think her English was good enough to do it and that it would be better to ask someone else. Linda said that she would be quite capable and told the professor they would do it. The next day Mariko failed to turn up and Linda was obliged to do all the work herself. The next time she saw Mariko she asked her rather coldly what had happened to her. Mariko apologized and said that she'd had to work for an exam that day and she didn't really feel capable of doing the work. Linda exasperatedly asked her why she had not said so clearly at the time. Mariko just looked down and said nothing.

BRISLIN, CUSHNER, CHERRIE, & YONG 1986
INTERCULTURAL INTERACTIONS

Culture. Another one of those "primitive terms" (like "mind") which we all understand, but cannot define to everyone's satisfaction. Generally, it is the objects, ideas, and institutions produced by human beings living in a certain place at a specific time; a particular part of civilization.

Richard Brislin and his colleagues use this example to illustrate a subtle difference in role expectations between Japanese and American **culture** (Brislin et al., 1986). In Mariko's culture it was wrong to give a direct refusal to the professor. Mariko thought that her remarks about her English *would be interpreted* as a message that she would not turn up to code the data. Linda did not understand this.

This type of "well-meaning clash" exemplifies the power of culture to influence and often disrupt interpersonal relationships. In this chapter we will consider how psychologists study such cultural influences. We will look at *cross-cultural psychology*, including its applications in a *multicultural* society. We will also examine efforts to develop a psychology that spans international borders. In other words, in this final chapter we will be fixing our sights on "the broader context" for understanding human behavior. Let's begin by setting a *global* perspective for modern psychology.

BEYOND THE BORDERS

Why study psychology in its global context? Australian Roger Russell gives one answer:

> One lesson of the 20th century has been that no one society in today's world can long exist in isolation—nor can its sciences or its professions. Expanding the focus of undergraduate and graduate education and training in psychology to include an understanding of the discipline in other parts of the world can make for better-educated graduates and for a better psychology at home (Russell, 1984).

Americans Virginia Staudt Sexton and Henryk Misiak agree:

> The value of knowing psychology in other countries and the need to maintain close relationships with psychologists abroad cannot be overemphasized (Sexton & Misiak, 1984).

Let's look more closely at what is behind this advice. First, at the end of the 20th century, it is virtually impossible to exist in isolation from the rest of the world. Advances in technology and communication bring the world into our homes nightly. International economic and political forces won't leave us alone. And environmental concerns reach far beyond any national boundaries. Whether we like it

We are an international community, and we must learn to live with a global perspective.

or not, we are an *international* community. An effective psychology, therefore, must be international.

Second, beyond being *forced* to interact globally, there is much to be *gained* from international communication. Psychologists in other Western countries (for example, Piaget, Freud, Binet) have contributed significantly to the field. There is much more we can learn by seeking even broader perspectives. Psychologists Robert and Barbara Sommer report that after teaching in the Soviet Union, they "are more sensitive to the needs of foreign scholars" and they "recognize how much our subject matter is culture bound" (Sommer & Sommer, 1991). In addition, many of the things that interest us in our own culture (including psychology) did not originate with us. We can understand them better if we examine their roots.

Finally, by interacting internationally with psychologists and their different cultures, we can learn more about ourselves. For example, if we study how arranged marriages work in other cultures we might be motivated to re-examine marriage in our own culture.

As we have said many times, our perceptions, thoughts, and personalities are the combined result of biological, intra-psychic, and *social* influences. And "culture" may exert the strongest social influence of all. As we look at the way other cultures have shaped psychology, we will become more aware of the influence of our own culture on our psychological perspective.

PSYCHOLOGY WORLDWIDE

You can find psychologists in almost any country of the world. They may speak Mandarin, Russian, English, or Swahili, but they identify themselves as psychologists (Ardila, 1982).

Although psychologists worldwide have a common interest in human thought and behavior, there are many differences among them. For example, psychologists from India, Black Africa, or America will probably have very different views of religious and philosophical issues, the relationships between people, or the role of science in studying human problems. We will look at some of these differences in a moment.

Many factors cause differences among psychologists in different countries. For example, economic factors limit the number of psychologists available, and may restrict them to studying only the most *practical* problems. Political factors may define the goals of psychological research. Historical, religious, and philosophical factors influence psychologists' views of the world and the person. And geographical factors may limit the amount and type of contact psychologists have with their colleagues in other countries.

Let's look at some of the differences between psychologists around the world, as well as some of the causes for these differences. We will focus on major regions of the world, with an occasional look at individual countries. After we consider psychology around the world, we will close our discussion with an examination of two major ways in which international understanding in psychology is developing—"cross-cultural psychology" and "international psychology."

We are citizens of the world; and the tragedy of our times is that we do not know this.

WOODROW WILSON

North America

The methods and practices of psychology in Canada and the United States are virtually indistinguishable. Many Canadian psychologists received part of their training in the United States and vice versa. Canadian and American professional psychological associations work together and reciprocate benefits to members.

Indigenous (in-DIJ-en-us). Belonging naturally to an area. An indigenous psychology is a psychology which is thoroughly integrated with a local culture.

Although some Canadian psychologists study uniquely Canadian problems and thus contribute to an **indigenous** Canadian psychology, most Canadian psychologists have been content to be assimilated to American traditions and practices (Berry, in press). The differences between psychology in Canada and the United States are small—especially when compared to differences between other countries. However, although they are similar in many ways, Canadian and American psychology are very different in the influence they exert.

It is no exaggeration to say that American psychology is the single biggest influence on psychology in the world today (Simonton, 1992). Consider some of the reasons: The majority of contemporary psychologists—more than 100,000—live in the United States. The membership of the American Psychological Association alone is almost equal to the total membership of the other 43 members of the International Union of Psychological Science (IUPsyS). Psychologists around the world read American English-language journals, making English the accepted international language of psychology. And the biggest contribution to these journals is from American psychologists (who also publish in journals from other countries) (Ardila, 1982; Gilgen & Gilgen, 1987; Russell, 1984; Segall et al., 1990; Triandis, 1980).

Although modern psychology began in 19th-century Germany, with the work of Wilhem Wundt, Hermann Ebbinghaus, and others, social, economic, and political forces shifted the balance to America in the 20th century (Ardila, 1982). Many of the best minds in psychology came to America seeking opportunity or fleeing Nazism. These included important Gestalt psychologists and many significant psychoanalysts (Sexton & Misiak, 1984).

Provincialism. Narrow distinctiveness; a restricted point of view associated with a particular area.

Unfortunately, the dominance of American psychology has led to a certain amount of **provincialism** and isolation. For example, there are fewer foreign students in American psychology than in all other major disciplines. Few North American psychologists read books or articles published in languages other than English. In fact, most American graduate programs no longer require their graduates to know a second language. And in contrast to other scientific disciplines, most research reports by American psychologists do not mention a single foreign source (Greeson, 1991; Rosenzweig, 1984; Segall et al., 1990).

In most of this book we have focussed on North American psychology. In looking at psychology in other countries you will see that North American psychology has several distinctive features which may not be obvious from your own perspective. For example, psychologists in North America enjoy a higher level of professional recognition than in most other countries. More of them are in academic and research positions, where they have the freedom to study problems that don't have an immediate practical application. North American psychologists also make more extensive use of modern technology and laboratory experimentation.

Philosophically, psychology in North America tends to operate from a secular humanist perspective, focusing on evolutionary adaptation. For example, when American David Buss and his collaborators in other countries studied mate selection around the world, they were looking for factors with an *evolutionary* basis. They note, "the study of mate preferences has received increasing attention as a central evolutionary force" (Buss, 1990). In many other countries, different religious and philosophical views are predominant, and as we will see, *color* psychological investigations in these countries.

In what ways does North American psychology reflect North American culture?

Europe

Modern Europe is very different from the Europe that gave birth to psychology—and it is changing rapidly. Commenting on the 1989 First European Congress of Psychology, American psychologist John Hall says, "Europe is, and will be for the foreseeable future, an exciting place to be. European psychology, as a result of significant political and economic changes, will become stronger and more dominant within the world context" (Hall, 1990). One important change is that the distinction between Eastern and Western Europe has lost some of its significance. However, we will examine these two areas separately because their divergent historical and political backgrounds have left distinctive imprints on psychology there.

WESTERN EUROPE

Although the origins of psychology could be traced back to humanity's earliest self-reflections, modern psychology, and certainly Western **scientific psychology,** developed most directly from 19th century Germany (as we saw in Chapter 1). Between 1858 and 1881 the German physiologist Wilhelm Wundt accomplished several remarkable "firsts" in psychology. Wundt published the first proposal for an independent science of psychology, he offered the first course in psychology, he founded the first laboratory of experimental psychology, and he founded the first journal of experimental psychology. Wundt used the **scientific method** of the established sciences to investigate the basic elements of consciousness in the areas of sensation, perception, reaction, attention, feeling, and association. Many individuals contributed to the development of the new psychology. British philosophers, for example, laid the groundwork for a scientific approach to knowledge by emphasizing **empiricism.** And British **associationism** became an important idea in Western psychology. Still, Wundt is generally recognized as the founder and the catalyst who shaped the influences into a new discipline (Donald & Canter, 1987; Schultz & Schultz, 1987).

As the fame of Wundt's Leipzig laboratory spread, people travelled from all over the world to study with Wundt. For example, Titchener, a student of Wundt's, brought his version of Wundt's psychology to the United States. Thus German psychology was not just the *first,* but also the *main* source of Western-style scientific psychology.

Today there are more psychologists per million of population in Western Europe than anywhere else, except North America (Russell, 1984). In fact, the ratio of psychologists to population may be higher in some Western European countries, such as Denmark, the Netherlands, and Sweden, than in North America, as suggested in Figure 19.1 (Rosenzweig, 1984).

What difficulties can you see in counting the number of psychologists around the world?

Although "cut from the same cloth" as North American psychology, modern Western European psychology does have several distinctive features. First, it is more international in scope, benefitting from not only American psychology, but also Soviet psychology, and the psychology of its own countries. This international awareness also makes Western European psychologists more sensitive to cultural influences on psychology. And several countries (for example, Germany and France) have made a conscious effort to "Europeanize" their psychology (Graumann & Metrauz, 1987; Trognon, 1987). A second feature of psychology in Western Europe is its broader view of psychology as a science. While North American psychology has tended to emphasize a rigid scientific method, using physics as a model, Western European psychology takes a broader view of its scientific role. Western European psychologists are more open to anecdotal evidence and the study of the humanities (Hall, 1990). Third, psychology in Western Europe (and most of the world beyond North America), is under greater pressure to be socially relevant. This means that to survive and gain respect, psychology in these countries must show *practical results—*

Scientific psychology. An approach to understanding human thought and behavior through the application of the scientific method. Other "psychologies" might attempt to understand the individual through intuition, revelation, or magic.

Scientific method. A systematic procedure for solving a problem. It usually involves the following steps: stating the problem, forming an hypothesis, testing the hypothesis, interpreting the results, and drawing conclusions. The solution to the problem is an *inference,* or "most likely" conclusion, from the data.

Empiricism. The philosophical position that all knowledge is derived from sensory experience. No knowledge is innate. This view was most clearly expounded by the British philosopher John Locke (1632–1704). One consequence of this view was that the understanding of human behavior was largely taken away from philosophical speculation and given to the *empirical* science of psychology.

Associationism. Associations develop when sensations or ideas occur in close temporal sequence. Later, when one occurs the other also occurs. *Associationism* is the view that *all* behaviors and mental processes are the result of simple associations. Although many other people have used this concept, it was given its clearest articulation by the British philosopher David Hartley (1705–1757).

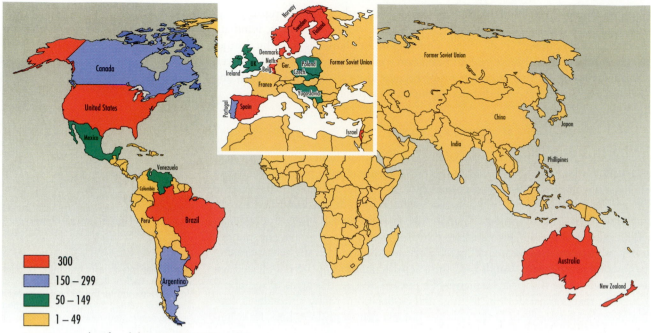

FIGURE 19.1

Distribution of psychologists in different areas of the world. (Based on Gelgen & Gelgen, 1987; Rosenzweig, 1984; Russell, 1984.)

Ideas move fast when their time comes.

CAROLYN HEILBRUN

it must "produce." This is at least partly the result of economic necessity and strong political control (for example in Norway, 90 percent of the psychologists receive their salary from the government) (Donald & Canter, 1987; Ursin, 1987).

EASTERN EUROPE

Scientific psychology in Eastern Europe emerged at much the same time as in Western Europe—although the two developments were relatively independent. This fact reflects the idea that new ideas and movements are as much a product of their times as they are the work of a single great leader, such as Wundt. The 19th century was a time of scientific growth throughout Europe, and it seemed a natural step to apply the methods of science to the understanding of human behavior. However, a few psychologists from Eastern Europe did travel to Wundt's laboratory and take back with them some of his experimental interests (Hall, 1990).

Today, the number of psychologists in Eastern Europe is not large. In fact, there are less than 20 psychologists per million of population.

According to psychologist Ruben Ardila, psychology in communist Eastern Europe displayed three major distinguishing characteristics. First, there was a heavy political emphasis—an emphasis on psychology's role in building a communist society. Second, there was a surprising tendency by psychologists to quote phrases by communist leaders, such as Marx and Engels, in their writing. And third, there was strong government control over psychologists' activities, education, and research. In research, for example, the government made it clear that acceptable topics had to have practical applications consistent with the goals of the state (Ardila, 1982). Beyond these differences, psychology in Eastern Europe has shared much in common with Western psychology—for example, an emphasis on the scientific method. And Western psychology has gained a great deal from Eastern European researchers like Pavlov, Bechterev, Vygotsky, and Luria.

The political changes now taking place in Eastern Europe may mean that Eastern and Western Europe will become more similar. For the immediate future, they certainly mean that Eastern European psychology will become more open and more diverse. Lloyd Strickland notes, for example, that psychology in the former Soviet

Union is exploring problems that were previously "off limits." These include the psychological roots of Stalinism, and "new" social problems such as suicide, drugs, prostitution, and family disintegration (Strickland, 1991). E. V. Subbotski admonishes his East European colleagues, "The need for practical psychology is obvious; the need for basic psychology must be insisted upon. But the most important thing, let me repeat, is to struggle for morality and freedom in science" (quoted in Strickland, 1991).

The changes in Eastern Europe also mean that psychologists, both Eastern and Western, have an unprecedented opportunity to study the psychological impact of dramatic social, economic, and political change (Lesse, 1990a, 1990b).

What kind of changes do you think might take place in Eastern Europe which could be of interest to psychologists?

Asia

Asian psychology, like Asian culture, has very different roots from those of Western psychology. While we can trace the distant roots of Western psychology to Greek and Roman ideas (revived in the last few centuries), we must go further back, and in a different direction, to find the origins of Asian psychology. In the East, figures such as Gautama Siddhartha (Buddha) or Confucius provided the most influential insights into human behavior and the human condition. These insights continue to influence Asian psychology today.

INDIA

Modern psychology in India began in 1915 with the establishment of the first psychological laboratory at Calcutta University. The laboratory, and Indian psychology at the time, was largely a "transplant" of Wundtian-style Western psychology. Over the years, the traditional wisdom from ancient religious and philosophical systems has exerted some influence. However, psychology in India is still very Western, especially American. As a result, Indian psychology is often not relevant to Indian problems (Sinha, 1987).

Indian psychologists are trying to help with India's many social and economic problems.

Indian psychologist Durganand Sinha estimates that there are over 4,000 psychologists in India. However, considering the size of India's population, and developments in other areas of science in India, this is a relatively low percentage (Rosenzweig, 1984). Most Indian psychologists work in teaching and research institutions. Sinha comments that there is "a feeling of general dissatisfaction with the professional development of psychology in India" (Sinha, 1987).

In spite of its low profile and apparent stagnation, Indian psychology has recently begun to show signs of becoming a vital influence, and truly "Indian." Psychologists are beginning to study the ancient wisdom and insights associated with Hinduism and Buddhism. For example, they are studying physiological and psychological processes in yogic states, relaxation, and healing, and they are integrating their findings with the ancient views (Jain, 1992; Kakar, 1982; Paranjpe, 1984; Sarma & Satyanarayana, 1992). They are also struggling to be relevant to India's many social and economic problems. As a result, new specialities are emerging, for example, to deal with "rural psychology," poverty, and child labor (Fernandes, 1992; Narayana, 1992; Sinha, 1987).

CHINA

Modern psychology did not begin in China until the 1920s (Sun, 1992). In 1921 the Chinese Psychological Society was formed, and in 1927 the first psychological laboratory was set up at Beijing University. Until 1949, psychology was largely imported from Western Europe and the United States. When the People's Republic of China was established in 1949, Western influence was cut off. Although at first the views of Pavlov and other Soviet psychologists were studied, today the dominant influence on psychology in the new Republic is government policy. The Chinese government expects psychologists to apply Marxist doctrine to social construction and achievement of the "four modernizations" (a plan for revitalizing China's economy) (Hou-can, 1987; Russell, 1984).

In 1984 there were approximately 2,000 members in the Chinese Psychological Association. This number is surprisingly low for the size of the population. The small number of psychologists is a reflection of government policy. In 1949 the government banned the practice of social psychology as being contrary to Marxist-Leninist doctrine. From 1956 to 1976 government policy was antagonistic to *all* psychology, and many psychologists were persecuted. Fortunately, recent government support of psychology has increased psychology's popularity. In fact, students in China are now *required* to take psychology as part of their basic college or university education (Hou-can, 1987).

Contemporary Chinese psychology has several distinctive features. The most obvious is its service to government objectives, such as the promotion of moral development and Marxist ideals. In recent years, Chinese psychologists have once again been introducing modern foreign perspectives to their field, albeit with a Chinese flavor. For example, they study cognitive processes in the learning of the Chinese pictographic written language. Chinese psychology continues to stress *group* processes—even the Chinese word for "psychology" implies more of a social trend or public opinion than a private psyche (Blowers, 1991; Sun, 1992).

Some Chinese psychologists find the roots of modern behavior in ancient Chinese wisdom. Confucius taught duty to the family, the state, and society. This teaching has been woven into Chinese culture for thousands of years. Today, Chinese researchers report that Chinese working in a group are less likely to "loaf" when they are not being observed than individuals in other cultures (Gabrenya et al., 1983, 1985). Even Confucius and Marx can find common ground!

Like other Asian psychologies, Chinese psychology differs from Western psychology in incorporating many religious and philosophical ideas into its view of the person (Corsini, 1977). In their clients and research subjects, Chinese psychologists may find moral and ethical standards from Confucism, as well as philosophical speculation and metaphysical striving from Buddhism and Taoism (Page & Cheng,

To learn, and not to think over [what one has learnt] is useless; to think without learning is dangerous.

CONFUCIUS

FIGURE 19.2

The Chinese symbols of Yin and Yang representing the ancient Chinese idea of complementarity and balance in all things. Such ancient ideas continue to influence Chinese views of the person.

1992). These ideas shape Chinese psychologists' views of what people are like, just as Western ideas shape North American psychologists' assumptions about human nature (Engler, 1991).

JAPAN

Scientific psychology entered Japan earlier than most other Asian countries. Before the end of the 19th century, Western-trained Japanese were teaching psychology in Japanese universities (Kaneko, 1987).

Hiroshi Azuma uses the development of Japanese psychology as an example of how Western psychology can be blended with the concepts and needs of a non-Western country. Azuma says that in Japan, psychology passed through five stages of development: a "pioneer period," an "introductory period," a "translation and modeling period," an "indigenization period," and an "integration period." The psychology of Japan today is "freed, to a certain extent, from the rigid but otherwise unnoticed mold of traditionally Western concepts and logic" (Azuma, 1984).

Although some Japanese psychology still follows the trends of Western psychology (for example, attention to **industrial and organizational psychology** and a current interest in cognitive processes), there is much that is unique. The distinctive features of Japanese psychology arise from the extensive blending of East and West which has taken place in Japan (Psathas, 1992).

The government exerts much less control over psychology in Japan than in some other countries. Often, large corporations provide significant support for psychological research. Some Japanese psychologists work to integrate ancient religious and cultural ideals with modern scientific psychology. They study Shintoism, Zen Buddhism, the value of family and other group memberships, leadership, and the need for social approval—all of special interest to Japanese society. These strong cultural influences add to the distinctiveness of Japanese psychology (Corsini, 1977; Hotta & Strickland, 1991; Kaneko, 1987).

Australia and New Zealand

Because of their relatively late emergence as nations, Australia and New Zealand also have short histories in psychology. Psychology's development was minimal prior to World War II. Since that time, however, it has flourished. Today there are more than 235 psychologists per million of population, the third highest concentration of psychologists in the world (after North America and Western Europe) (Nixon, 1987; Russell, 1984).

Unlike Japanese psychology, Australian research receives very little support from non-government sources. Western psychology exerts a strong influence in Australia. Most textbooks are from the United States, some are from Britain, and a few originate in Australia. Many Australian faculty receive at least part of their training in the United States or Britain. Many more take advantage of government exchange programs for sabbatical or research leaves in the United States or Britain. Australian psychologists conduct similar research studies to those in the United States, and often publish their results in American journals.

Australian psychology does differ from psychology in the United States in several ways, however. For example, there is a greater reliance on government finances and policies, a lower level of professional organization, and a lower percentage of women in psychology (Nixon, 1987).

Latin America

In Latin America, psychology appears to have developed more gradually than in many other parts of the world. Early Aztec, Mayan, and Inca cultures showed an interest in the same problems as modern psychology. Some Aztec priests, for example, restored the "spiritual balance" of their patients by means of a "long talk,"

Like their counterparts in North America, industrial and organizational psychologists in Japan study behavior in the workplace, and make suggestions in order to improve productivity, safety, and job satisfaction.

Industrial and organizational psychology. A branch of psychology that studies and attempts to improve work-related behavior.

Compared to psychology in North America, Latin American psychology has a higher percentage of women and focuses more on developmental problems.

apparently anticipating what Freud called the "talking cure"—psychotherapy (Diaz-Loving & Medina-Liberty, 1987). In the 16th century, Spanish colonists wrote about psychological matters and established a psychiatric hospital in Mexico City. The rapid development of German scientific psychology in the 19th century had relatively little influence in Latin America. To this day, Latin American psychology shows a greater allegiance to French, Swiss, Austrian, and Spanish viewpoints than to those from Germany or America. The followers of Freud and Piaget outnumber those of Skinner or other strict experimentalists.

In Latin American psychology, the most rapid growth occurred after World War II, from which time psychology could be called truly modern. In each country of Latin America, however, political and economic forces have played an important role in determining the fortunes of psychology. Latin American psychology appears to have reached its highest level of development in Brazil, Colombia, Mexico, and Venezuela. (Brazil has the largest number of psychologists at 37,580 [Biaggio, 1987]).

In most Latin American countries, psychologists enjoy a high level of professional development and corresponding social status. Unlike many other regions, Latin America has more women than men in psychology. There is a strong emphasis on the *applications* of psychological knowledge throughout Latin America. Theory and basic research are not emphasized. The focus of attention is on child development, education, and the problems associated with poverty. There is also a lively interest in clinical psychology, particularly in Mexico and Brazil. The dominant perspectives are primarily those of Piaget (in child development and education) and Freud (in clinical therapy).

Africa

The size and diversity of Africa makes it very difficult to summarize the characteristics of its psychology. We will focus on what African psychologist M.O.A. Durojaiye calls "Black Africa," covering the area south of the Sahara and north of the Limpopo River.

Psychology as a professional discipline is a recent development in Black Africa. Missionary educators first taught psychological principles as part of teacher training, although they did not usually identify the material as psychology. Psychology remains closely tied to education today. The University of Nigeria in Nskukka and Makerere University in Uganda developed the first separate departments of psychology in 1960 and 1973, respectively. Today, however, virtually every teacher's college offers psychology courses. The faculty teaching psychology is 80 percent black and 20 percent white.

For economic reasons, and because psychology is so new to Black Africa, many countries do not have professional associations of psychologists. Thus, statistics on the number of psychologists are scarce, and comparisons between countries are difficult. Black African psychology has attained its highest level of recognition and professional development in Zambia and Zimbabwe. Nigeria, however, has the largest number of psychologists (over 200) with degrees and at least three years experience (Durojaiye, 1987).

In addition to economic limitations, distrust and fear have held back the development of psychology in Africa. There is fear that this "white witchcraft" might replace the powers of traditional witch doctors, as well as the influence of some newer religious cults.

The dominant perspective of Black African psychology is humanistic. Originally derived from the Christian missionary emphasis on the importance of human beings, this orientation is now more secular. Like other less-affluent non-Western areas, psychology in Black Africa is very practical. There are very few psychology laboratories. Rather, the focus is on applying African psychologists' insights to African society's problems, and in this way developing an indigenous *African* psychology (Durojaiye, 1987).

The Middle East

The impact of psychology in Middle Eastern countries closely parallels the extent of the countries' acceptance of Western culture. Arab culture is very different from Western culture. By American standards, Arabs are religious, conservative, generous, and emotional (Nydell, 1987; Farag, 1990). As a result of perceived differences, the Arab oil-producing countries have viewed psychology with suspicion—as a tool of atheistic, materialistic, Western imperialism. Although the situation has improved in some areas, such as in Saudi Arabia, it has not changed entirely (Mehryar, 1984; Melikian, 1984; Prothro & Melikian, 1955). Suspicion and traditional prohibitions make research difficult on topics such as sexuality, attitude formation, and personality disorders (Farag, 1987).

Egypt, which is much more open than other Arab countries, does not support its psychologists well. Many have moved to the oil-producing Arab countries, or Canada and the United States. Those who remain often hold joint appointments in other countries. I. H. Melikan summarizes the status of Arab psychology as follows: ". . . psychology has not left a noticeable impact on industry or government. It has not been recognized as a potential contributor to developmental planning. Whatever consulting role psychologists have played has been primarily restricted to ministries of education and occasionally ministries of health" (Melikian, 1984). Overall, psychology in the Arab Middle East does not enjoy a high level of professional development or social impact (Farag, 1987).

In contrast, Israeli psychology is vital and strong. Israel has over 2,000 psychologists, placing it among the top five countries in psychologists per capita worldwide (Halpern, 1987).

Israeli psychology developed rapidly with the mass immigration following establishment of Israel as a state. The two main characteristics of Israeli psychology are its diversity and its unique social setting. The psychoanalytic orientation of European immigrants balances the experimental influence from North America. Research, which is mostly applied in nature, focuses on Israel's unique social phenomena. These include mass immigration, kibbutz living, ethnic integration, and the effects of stress caused by threats from surrounding countries. Psychologists work in a variety of settings, and are well accepted in Israeli society (Halpern, 1987).

In Israel, psychologists focus on problems of mass immigration, ethnic integration, and stress, or difficulties such as those these children might face living in a Kibbutz.

Psychology Worldwide: A Summary

In its broadest sense, psychology is the study of human thought and behavior in an effort to understand and influence people in positive ways. However, the *methods* and *work* of psychologists vary greatly around the world. Economic restrictions often limit the number of psychologists available and confine their attention to pressing practical problems. Political forces may direct the efforts of psychologists towards **ideological** goals. And religious, philosophical, and cultural ideals influence psychologists' views of the person and of the world. These forces also affect psychologists' choice of the scientific method versus more traditional explanations for human behavior.

Most psychologists, especially in North America, are not aware of the many faces of psychology around the world. Let's look at some ways of reducing this unfamiliarity.

Ideological. A system of thought (usually political) based on ideals or principles.

BRIDGING THE GAP

In our brief tour of world psychology we have seen that despite tremendous economic, social, political, religious and philosophical diversity, psychology around the world continues to show a strong Western, primarily American, influence. Not only were most of the first psychologists trained in the West, but Western English-language journals dominate the field. In many places, American psychological texts and tests are still being translated and used with little adaptation to the local culture.

Why is it easier to accept an American version of psychology than to develop a psychology suited to each country (an indigenous psychology)?

Western psychology has a lot to offer. But as long as a single culture dominates, psychology will not develop to its potential. Colombian psychologist Ruben Ardila says, ". . . contemporary psychology is still far from being an international psychology. Interest in psychology is worldwide, but as long as the discipline is influenced so much by one culture (and it does not matter which culture), there cannot be a truly international psychology" (Ardila, 1982).

There are two main ways in which psychology can build on international diversity. The first is through the study of "cross-cultural psychology"; the second is through the growth of "international psychology."

Cross-Cultural Psychology

In previous chapters we have often referred to the "social," or "social/behavioral" perspective on understanding our behavior. By this we meant all of the external or environmental influences on us, including physical, social, and *cultural* factors. In addition, at several points we noted the way *culture* influences behavior more specifically. Although we have seen several examples of cultural influence, to examine cross-culturally *all* of the topics we have considered would require many more volumes (see Berry et al., 1992; Segall et al., 1990; Triandis et al., 1980–1981).

At times, the comparisons we made were between cultures in different countries; at other times they were made between cultures or **ethnic** groups within the same country. These comparisons often raised the question of how broadly our conclusions applied to people in other cultures. It is time that we looked at this question more directly.

Ethnic group. A set of people having common ancestors derived from the same culture and with common feelings of identification as a traditionally distinct group. (Not to be confused with *racial* groups, which are collections of people distinguished by somewhat arbitrary and superficial physical differences.)

How many examples of cultural influences can you recall from earlier chapters?

Psychologists who study the influence of culture and compare results from different cultures work in the field of **cross-cultural psychology.** Cross-cultural psychologists Harry Triandis and Richard Brislin define their field as follows:

> Cross-cultural psychology refers to the collective efforts of researchers who work among people who speak various languages, live in societies ranging from technologically unsophisticated to highly complex and industrialized, and who live under different forms of political organization. Ideally, various aspects of people's culture are carefully identified and related to important theoretical issues in psychological theory, resulting in conclusions about the culture's influence on behavior. These in turn improve the theory (Triandis & Brislin, 1984).

More simply, Marshall Segall and his colleagues say cross-cultural psychology is "... the scientific study of the ways in which social and cultural forces shape human behavior" (Segall et al., 1990).

UNCOVERING PSYCHOLOGY'S ETHNOCENTRISM

Although Wundt proposed the development of a "folk" or cultural psychology almost a century ago, its progress has been slow (Schneider, 1990; Wundt, 1900–1920). With the rapid globalization of the last few decades, however, psychologists have become increasingly aware of the possibility of their own "culture blindness," or **ethnocentrism.** As a result, more and more psychologists are studying the role that culture plays in the production of human thought and behavior. Moreover, some psychologists are beginning to point out the limitations of North American psychology.

Hazel Markus and Shinobu Kitayama, for example, suggest that North American psychology assumes a view of the person which simply does not apply in many other parts of the world—including Asia, Africa, Latin America, and southern Europe (Kitayama & Markus, 1992; Markus & Kitayama, 1991). American, Canadian, and most Western European cultures are what cross-cultural psychologists call **individualistic.** Individualistic cultures emphasize the *individual person.* They give priority to personal goals over the goals of the group. Asian, African, Latin American, and Southern European cultures are **collectivist.** Collectivist cultures emphasize the "collective" or *group.* They give priority to in-group goals over personal goals (Hofstede, 1980; Triandis, 1989, 1994).

People may develop very differently in different cultures. For example, if you grew up in an individualistic culture, your culture would encourage you to develop an *independent* view of yourself. You would tend to assume that people have within them important dispositional attributes that continue to exist even when contexts change. You would possess an individualized and specific sense of identity: "I am a person like no one else; I have unique characteristics." In answer to the question "Who am I?" you would probably mention personal attributes and preferences. The type of personality theories we discussed in Chapter 14 are a product of this type of *individualistic* view of the person.

On the other hand, if you grew up in a collectivist culture, you would develop a more *interdependent* self-concept. You would define yourself *in relation to others.* For example, Japanese subjects refer to many more *social roles* than do North Americans in answering the question "Who am I?": "I am my father's son, a descendent of _____ , a Japanese, and a Buddhist" (Draguns, 1988). Your self would be complete, indeed you would feel most fully human, *only* as you see yourself in a social relationship with others (Lebra, 1976; Markus and Kitayama, 1991). Figure 19.3 illustrates the relationship between self and others for independent and interdependent selves.

Cross-cultural psychology. The scientific study of cultural influences on human thought and behavior, including the identification of both *culture-universal* and *culture-specific* factors.

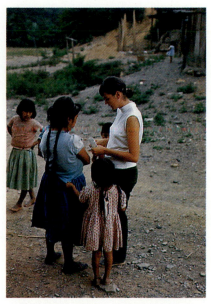

Cross-cultural psychologists study the way culture affects human behavior.

Ethnocentrism. The tendency to believe that one's own ethnic and cultural group is superior and that other groups are inferior.

Individualistic. An emphasis on the autonomy of the isolated person and a corresponding lack of emphasis on the interdependence between people.

Collectivist. An emphasis on the mutual interdependence of people and a corresponding de-emphasis on individual autonomy.

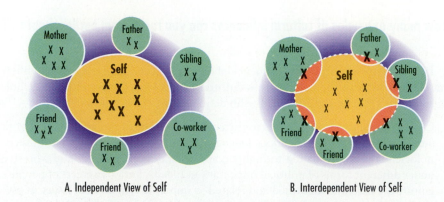

FIGURE 19.3

Two different representations of the self. The independent view (A) is typical of individualistic cultures, such as in the West; the interdependent view (B) is more typical of the universalist cultures of the East. (Based on Markus & Kitayama, 1991.)

In this context, we must take a different perspective on many of our Western self-related ideas. For example, Markus and Kitayama suggest that self-esteem, based on self-expression and the validation of internal attributes, may be primarily a Western phenomenon. In contrast, persons with an *interdependent* view of the self feel good when they fulfill the expectations of *others*, and when they maintain harmony with the social context. But this feeling, Markus and Kitayama suggest, is more akin to self-satisfaction than to self-esteem (Markus & Kitayama, 1991; Solomon et al., 1991).

In Chapter 17 we noted that individuals in collectivist cultures may not exhibit many of the "attributional biases" that North Americans do. For example, North Americans like to accept praise for their successes and blame others or circumstances for their failures—the "self-serving bias" (Gilovich, 1983; Lau, 1984; Whitely & Freeze, 1985). North Americans also like to believe they are better than their peers (Harter, 1990; Wylie, 1979). However, Japanese, Korean, Taiwanese, and Thai subjects do not show these tendencies (Markus & Kitayama, 1991; Kitayama & Markus, 1992; Shikanai, 1978, 1983, 1984). Instead they more readily accept blame for their failures and consider themselves to be average members of their groups. Kitiyama and Markus conclude that while North Americans reveal a general tendency towards self-*enhancement*, Asians are more likely to exhibit self-*effacement* (Kitayama & Markus, 1992).

Our self-concept is only one way in which our culture influences us—although it may be the most important way. Our thoughts, emotions, motivations, attitudes, and consequently our interpersonal behaviors, *all* flow from "*who* we are." Cross-cultural psychology helps us to remove our "cultural blinders" and realize the limitations of our particular "brand" of psychology.

APPRECIATING CULTURAL DIVERSITY

Perhaps the most obvious contribution of cross-cultural psychology is the appreciation for cultural diversity which it can give us. For example, David Buss shows how cross-cultural research clarifies our perspective on mate selection. Buss and 49 collaborators in 33 countries asked young men and women (average age 23 years) about the attributes they looked for in potential mates. The researchers found many differences among cultures. The most pervasive difference they found was the emphasis given to "traditional" versus "modern" attributes. Young people looking for a mate in China, India, Iran, and Nigeria place great value on the traditional attributes of chastity, home and children, domestic skills, and providing for the family. At the other extreme, in the Netherlands, Great Britain, Finland, and Sweden young people looking for mates did not consider these attributes very important. (Canadian and American values were in between these extremes.)

American young people differed from the international average by placing a higher value on a college degree, earning capacity, heredity, and "an exciting personality." They placed a relatively low value on housekeeping skills and intelligence

(Buss, 1990). Without this kind of information it would be easy for us to assume that people in other cultures look for the same qualities in their potential mates as we do. Cross-cultural research keeps us from this kind of narrowness.

Cross-cultural psychology also makes us aware of factors in our environment which we normally take for granted. David Ho's clinical experience in Hong Kong and the United States has convinced him that Americans are not aware of the degree to which their *individualist* culture affects their behavior. He suggests that this blindness prevents American psychologists from recognizing the role which *individualism* plays in creating psychological disturbances. His cross-cultural perspective also suggests to Ho some aspects of Hong Kong's *collectivism* which might contribute to unique patterns of disturbance there (Ho, 1985).

How might a cultural emphasis on individualism contribute to psychological stress and disturbance?

Cross-cultural psychology can also help us to "unconfound" experimental variables. Harry Triandis and Richard Brislin suggest, for example, that if we found that a certain ethnic group had a high rate of alcohol use, at least two explanations are possible. It could be that there is a *biological* factor associated with the ethnic group, or it may be that there are *cultural values* associated with the ethnic group. By comparing members of the ethnic group in their original culture with those who have adapted to a different culture, we can test the two explanations. If alcohol use changes, it is cultural; if alcohol use remains unchanged it is probably biological (Triandis & Brislin, 1984).

Stanley Sue and his colleagues made these comparisons for Japanese in America and in Japan. They found that the higher rate of alcohol use by American Japanese was related to their *new culture* and was *not* a biological predisposition (Sue et al., 1979).

To summarize, cross-cultural research helps us to avoid ethnocentrism, it sensitizes us to factors we were not aware of, it enables us to unconfound variables, and generally gives us an appreciation for cultural diversity. Sometimes this diversity exists very close to home. Let's look briefly at cross-cultural research in our own "back yard." We will see that cross-cultural research has an important contribution to make here as well.

MULTICULTURAL RESEARCH

Cross-cultural research is not just comparing primitive or exotic cultures in faraway places. Cross-cultural research studies the ways in which human behavior is shaped by culture—*any* culture. This means we are also doing cross-cultural research when we study *ethnic* groups within our own **multicultural** society.

Large-scale migration of cultural groups continues to be a prominent feature of the social landscape at the end of the 20th century. As a result, North American, and most other contemporary societies, are increasingly *culturally diverse*. Whether uprooted by wars and famines, freed by the collapse of repressive regimes, or simply drawn by the hope of a better life, people move and adapt to new cultures. And as they adapt, immigrants also *influence* their new "host" culture. Social scientists use the term **acculturation** to refer to the changes that occur as a result of ongoing contact between two distinct cultures (Berry et al., 1986).

Many factors affect the relationship between ethnic groups in a culturally diverse society—for example, the attitudes of the host society. The United States has historically taken a "melting pot" approach to subordinate groups, assuming they would assimilate into mainstream American culture. More recently, a "salad bowl" analogy has been proposed. The "salad bowl" analogy implies that minority groups can

Multicultural. Literally, "many cultures." A society is multicultural when it is made up of people with different ethnic identities. (Such a society may also be called "pluralistic.")

Acculturation. The mutual change or adaptation that takes place when two cultures are in contact over an extended period of time. Where one culture is clearly the dominant culture, the focus of attention is usually on adaptation in the minority culture.

Historically the United States has taken a "melting pot" approach to immigrants from other countries. They were expected to leave their original culture behind and adopt American culture.

Many immigrant ethnic groups retain their original culture while still contributing to and identifying with their new culture.

Multiculturalism. The ideological view that ethnic groups should maintain their distinctiveness within a larger pluralistic society; the view that ethnic groups are entitled to equal respect, that "life-styles should not limit life chances."

contribute to the larger culture by *maintaining* their cultural *distinctiveness*. In Canada, this approach, called **multiculturalism,** is explicit government policy (Berry, 1984). Many other factors affect acculturation. Some of these are prejudice and discrimination, the visibility of the minority group, the conditions of contact (e.g., forced versus voluntary), and the compatibility of cultural values (Berry & Kim, 1988).

PATTERNS OF ACCULTURATION   John Berry and his colleagues suggest that two main attitudes determine a minority person's pattern of acculturation. We might see these influences as the answer to two questions: (1) "Is it important for me to identify with and maintain the unique characteristics of my ethnic group?" and (2) "Is it important for me to establish good relationships with other ethnic groups and the larger society?" Combining positive and negative responses to these two questions yields four possible acculturation patterns.

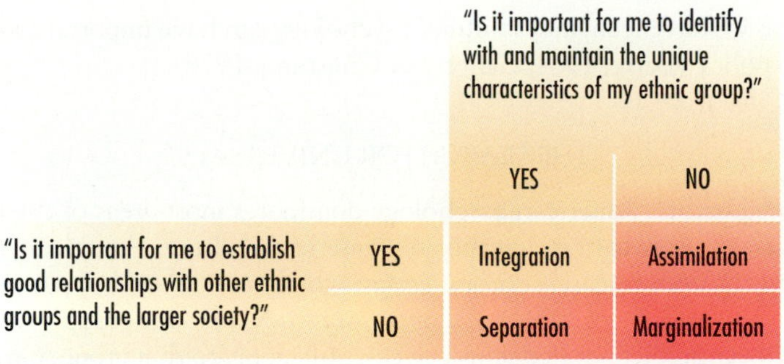

		"Is it important for me to identify with and maintain the unique characteristics of my ethnic group?"	
		YES	NO
"Is it important for me to establish good relationships with other ethnic groups and the larger society?"	YES	Integration	Assimilation
	NO	Separation	Marginalization

FIGURE 19.4

Four patterns of acculturation produced by positive and negative responses to two questions concerning relationships with one's ethnic group and the larger society. (Based on Berry & Kim, 1988).

When the answer to both questions is positive, the individual identifies strongly with both the dominant society *and* the traditional ethnic culture. This process is known as "integration." When the individual identifies only with the ethnic group and avoids the dominant society, this is called "separation." Conversely, when the individual identifies solely with the dominant society and gives up all ties to the ethnic culture, the individual experiences "assimilation." And finally, when the answer to both questions is negative—the individual has lost his or her original ethnic identity and has not become involved with the surrounding culture—the result is "marginality" (Berry et al., 1989). Figure 19.4 illustrates the combinations which yield these four patterns.

ACCULTURATION AND SELF-ESTEEM Recently, Jean Phinney, Victor Chavira, and Lisa Williamson examined these patterns of acculturation among a culturally diverse sample of high school and college students. The students included 205 Asians, 148 blacks, 164 Hispanics, 55 whites, and 68 persons classified as "mixed" or "other." The investigators were interested in two main questions: (1) "Which pattern of acculturation would the students endorse most strongly?" and (2) "Which pattern of acculturation would be most strongly associated with psychological adjustment as reflected in self-esteem?"

Overall, students showed a strong preference for the "integration" pattern. In effect, they said, "I believe that ethnic minority groups should maintain and practice their own cultural traditions, but also learn to get along in mainstream American society." "Assimilation" received the next most support. These students were saying, "I feel that the best way for members of ethnic minority groups to get along is to play down their own culture and to become part of American society by being as much like other Americans as possible." "Separation" received little support. ("Marginality" was not considered a viable option and was not included in the study.)

Students who more strongly supported "integration" tended to have the highest self-esteem. (The correlation between self-esteem and support for "integration" was positive in 12 out of 14 groups.) In contrast, students who more strongly supported "assimilation" tended to have lower self-esteem. (The correlation between self-esteem and support for assimilation was negative in 12 out of 14 groups.) In other words, high self-esteem went with strong ethnic *and* majority identification. Low self-esteem went with strong cultural identification *only* (Phinney et al., 1992).

What do Phinney et al.'s results suggest about "melting pot" and "salad bowl" approaches to acculturation?

We might think of multi-cultural research as a sub-set of cross-cultural psychology. As such it offers the same advantages we noted for cross-cultural psychology. In addition, as we have seen, multicultural psychology can have important implications for public policy (Berry, 1984; Cafferty & Chestang, 1976).

THE SEARCH FOR UNIVERSALS

As we noted earlier, American psychology dominates most areas of the contemporary field. And despite the diversity of American culture, American psychology derives largely from research on one group: white middle- and upper-middle-class college students (Graham, 1992). As long as we study only one group—cultural, ethnic, or socioeconomic—our conclusions can only apply to that group. Cross-cultural psychologists are working to get us out of this narrow bind. They are looking for concepts and principles, called "etics," that apply to *all* cultures. And they are trying to distinguish these from culturally *restricted* concepts and principles, called "emics."

For example, intelligence, as the ability to "think well" or to "solve unfamiliar problems," is apparently an *etic* concept because it is found in all cultures. However, the idea which many North Americans hold that intelligence is "quick thinking" is a cultural *emic*. In some cultures intelligence involves *slow* and *deliberate thought* (Berry & Bennett, 1992; Brislin, 1993).

Consider another example: We noted earlier that David Buss found several cultural differences (emics) in the attributes young people look for in a potential mate.

FIGURE 19.5

Cross-cultural psychologists study behavior in different cultures. They want to know which influences on behavior are culture-specific, and which are culture-universal. Their goal is the *understanding of human behavior* within societies and around the world.

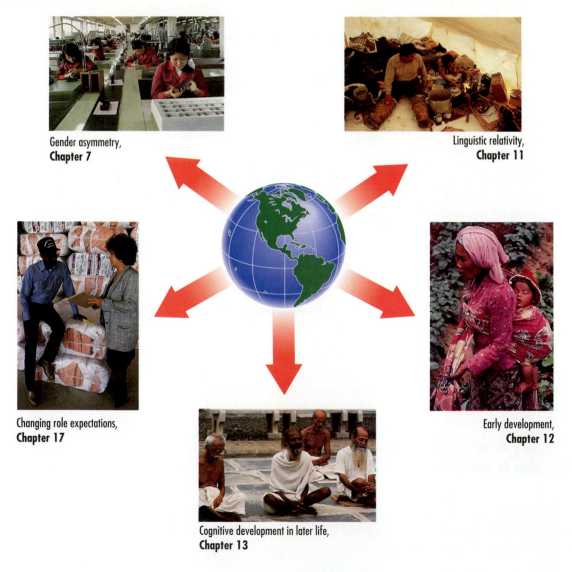

Gender asymmetry,
Chapter 7

Linguistic relativity,
Chapter 11

Changing role expectations,
Chapter 17

Cognitive development in later life,
Chapter 13

Early development,
Chapter 12

Subsequent research by Alan Feingold also found *cultural universals* (etics) in the same area. Feingold combined Buss's data with additional information from other research and then examined gender differences across *all* the studies (a "meta-analysis"). He found that across cultures men valued attractiveness more than women did, and that women valued socioeconomic status and ambitiousness more than men did (Feingold, 1992). Thus, mate preferences show both cultural emics and cultural etics.

The distinction we noted earlier between individualistic and collectivist cultures also appears to be a universal. When we rate *any* culture on this dimension we gain insight into many otherwise puzzling differences. Of course, cultures differ in many ways besides individualism-collectivism (Hofstede, 1980). But we must study this type of cross-cultural variable, and incorporate it into our theories. Otherwise, we will never overcome our psychological ethnocentrism, nor will we *understand human behavior* around the world.

PROBLEMS IN CROSS-CULTURAL PSYCHOLOGY

Cross-cultural research is indispensable for understanding human behavior. Cross-cultural research, however, is not easy.

It is difficult enough to study and compare ethnic groups in one's own *multicultural* society. But the problems multiply when investigators study cultures that are remote and "strange" (to the investigator). There are problems of language, acceptance within the culture, and understanding of unspoken traditions and subtle social norms. In these situations, the cross-cultural psychologist must also become something of a **cultural anthropologist.**

Cross-cultural psychologists attempt to see behavior through the eyes of people *in other cultures*, for only then can they investigate *culturally equivalent* phenomena. This is not an easy task, but if it leads to understanding as well as tolerance it is worth it. As Richard Brislin notes:

> [Cross-cultural psychologists] are not imposing their own viewpoints. . . . They are not imposing their own emics by assuming that they are etic, and they are not assuming that their own understanding of complex concepts are universally equivalent. This sensitivity to others, and the quest to understand the cultural background of seemingly strange behaviors, are good goals for all people who deal with cultural diversity (Brislin, 1993).

Cultural anthropologist. A person who studies cultural differences between people—often the ideas, customs, and social relationships of nonliterate societies. (Sometimes called social anthropology or ethnology.)

International Psychology

An appreciation of cultural diversity and the study of its effects are necessary steps toward a truly cross-cultural psychology. These steps, however, will not be taken without a truly international perspective. Summarizing his experience at the First European Congress of Psychology, John Hall asserts, "I believe, even more strongly than before, that we must strive to be more international in our approach to our discipline and must convey an international perspective to students of psychology" (Hall, 1990). This chapter is an attempt to do just that. Let's conclude our discussion with a look how international psychology is growing, and examine some ways in which psychologists and students of psychology might participate in this growth.

One way psychologists gain an international perspective is through professional exchanges—that is, through working and studying in another country. As we noted earlier, one reason for the dominance of Western scientific psychology, is the fact that early psychologists travelled from all over the world to study in Wundt's German laboratory. Today, international psychology continues to develop through faculty and student exchange programs in which participants live and study abroad for varying periods of time (Cole, 1984; Russell, 1984).

No culture can live, if it attempts to be exclusive.

MAHATMA GANDHI

Psychologists broaden their perspectives by attending international meetings of psychologists.

Another valuable mechanism for international communication is the publication of internationally circulated journals. Some of these are the *International Journal of Psychology*, the *Interamerican Journal of Psychology*, the *German Journal of Psychology*, and the *Journal of Cross-Cultural Psychology*. The *Journal of Cross-Cultural Psychology* is the only journal in the world devoted exclusively to the publication of cross-cultural research. The *American Psychologist*, and the *Annual Review of Psychology* also occasionally publish articles on international psychology. In addition, many journals publish cross-cultural studies in their area of specialization.

Psychologists and students can also broaden their perspective on psychology by attending, and even participating in, international meetings. They may also join some of the associations sponsoring these meetings. The foremost international association for psychologists is the International Union of Psychological Science (IUPsyS), which was elected to the prestigious International Council of Scientific Unions in 1982. National psychological associations, not individuals, make up the membership of IUPsyS.

Individuals may belong to the International Association for Cross-Cultural Psychology, which is the leading worldwide group promoting the aims of cross-cultural psychology. Individuals may also join the International Association of Applied Psychology, which is the oldest international psychological association, or they may join the International Council of Psychologists. Several other international societies exist to study psychology in specialized areas. In addition, foreign psychological associations usually invite members and student affiliates of associations in other areas (including North America) to attend their meetings.

These are some of the opportunities which exist for international communication in psychology. Psychology will continue to grow on a world level as more and more psychologists not only study cross-cultural influences but also take advantage of professional opportunities to look beyond their borders.

SUMMARY

1. Although it varies from region to region, psychology exists in almost every country around the world. Some factors that cause psychology to vary are: **economic, political, geographical,** and **religious** and **philosophical** differences.

2. **American** psychology continues to dominate world psychology. Some reasons for this dominance are: (1) there are more psychologists in America than in any other country, (2) English is the accepted language of psychology, (3) American research journals and American research in foreign journals dominate the research literature, and (4) America has attracted many prominent psychologists from other countries.

3. Psychology began in Western Europe in the middle of the 19th century. The German physiologist, **Wilhelm Wundt,** is usually considered to be the founder of psychology based on the scientific method. Many forces contributed to the development of psychology, including the empiricism and associationism of **British philosophers.**

4. The **highest ratio** of psychologists to population is in North America, Western Europe, Australia, and New Zealand.

5. In most countries outside North America, there is a greater emphasis on research and professional roles which have an **applied** function.

6. In **Eastern Europe** and **China,** psychology has been strongly influenced by authoritarian Marxist governments. Psychologists are expected to serve the ideological goals of the state.

7. Psychology in **Asia, Latin America,** and **Black Africa** is influenced by religious and philosophical ideas native to these areas.

8. Psychologists in **South America** enjoy a high level of professional development and social status. They work primarily in the areas of education, child development, and clinical psychology.

9. In **Black Africa,** psychology is still strongly associated with teacher education, where it was first introduced by missionary educators.

10. Psychology is **not highly developed** in Black Africa, because of fear and distrust as well as economic limitations. Black African psychology is forced to be very **practical.**

11. In the **Middle East,** only Israeli psychology is strong. Traditional beliefs and suspicion of Western ideas restricts psychology in Arab countries.

12. **Indigenous psychology** is developing around the world as Western materials, such as textbooks and tests, are adapted for the local culture or replaced entirely. Western emphases on technology, laboratory experimentation, secular humanism, and evolutionary adaptation are often modified with native beliefs and traditions.

13. **Cross-cultural research** helps us to avoid **ethnocentrism,** it sensitizes us to factors we were not aware of, it enables us to **unconfound** variables, and generally it gives us an appreciation for cultural diversity.

14. **Multicultural research** examines different **ethnic** groups within a larger society. A major topic of this research is the effects of **acculturation.**

15. A global understanding of human behavior depends on cross-cultural researchers distinguishing between **cultural universals** and **culturally restricted** concepts.

16. An international awareness within psychology will develop as more psychologists become aware of **cross-cultural** variables in their research, and as they engage in interaction at the **international** level.

---

1. *In what ways does North American psychology reflect North American culture?*

   Like North American culture, psychology tends to emphasize (in comparison with other cultures), technology, materialism, growth, pleasure, and individualism.

ANSWERS FOR THOUGHT

2. *What difficulties can you see in counting the number of psychologists around the world?*

Many countries do not keep statistics on the number of psychologists. Not all psychologists belong to national associations, and the percentage who do varies greatly from country to country. The definition of a "psychologist" is not the same everywhere. In North America a Ph.D. or Psy.D. is usually assumed. In many countries the standards are necessarily far lower.

3. *What kind of changes do you think might take place in Eastern Europe which could be of interest to psychologists?*

Rapid changes could lead to insecurity, stress, and psychological disturbance. High expectations might lead to frustration and possibly violence. These changes could in turn lead to a return to authoritarian rule as the "lesser evil."

4. *Why is it easier to accept an American version of psychology than to develop a psychology suited to each country (an indigenous psychology)?*

American materials (textbooks, psychological tests, research journals) are readily available. It requires considerable effort to adapt these thoroughly or to create new ones. American psychology (and America generally) is apparently successful. Why "reinvent the wheel"?—especially when resources in many countries are so limited.

5. *How many examples of cultural influences can you recall from earlier chapters?*

In virtually every chapter we noted the impact of culture on the topics we were discussing. We often pointed out that research results and theories do not apply in the same way to individuals in cultures that the researchers and theorists have not studied. We also noted many differences where cultures *have* been studied. For example, culture influences the perception of illusions; the expression of gender roles and sexual behavior; the definition and testing of intelligence; attitudes to children, adolescents, aging, and death; definitions and expressions of abnormality; and attributions for social behavior. For a more complete listing, you might want to consult the entries under "culture" in the Index at the back of this book.

6. *How might a cultural emphasis on individualism contribute to psychological stress and disturbance?*

Extreme individualism says the normal healthy person is autonomous, doesn't need other people, and can "make it" on his or her own. If you realize you need others, you may tend to feel inadequate and even unhealthy in a society which emphasizes this value. And if you need *extra* help, through no fault of your own, the individualistic society will show a more extreme *attributional bias*, and will blame you rather than the situation.

7. *What do Phinney et al.'s results suggest about "melting pot" and "salad bowl" approaches to acculturation?*

The researchers conclude, "These results support the idea that multiculturalism is a more appropriate model than assimilation for a diverse society that wishes to promote the optimal development for the members of all groups." In other words, a "salad bowl" appears to be preferable to a "melting pot."

A P P E N D I X   A

RESEARCH METHODS IN PSYCHOLOGY

This appendix is intended as an "aside" or "time out" to help you understand the various ways psychologists conduct research. It is a "time out" from content to look at the "how and why" of different psychological research methods. The broad array of procedures which we call "psychological research" can be quite confusing. In order to understand better why psychologists use these different methods, we recommend that you take a few moments and consider some of the advantages and disadvantages of each method.

In Chapter 1 we said that psychology is the scientific study of thought and behavior. We also said that psychologists adopt a logical process called the *scientific method* in order to unravel the mysteries of human thinking and acting. The core of the scientific method, and all research in psychology, is *careful observation*. But psychological research through careful observation can take place in many different ways.

Quite often it matters little what your guess is; but it always matters a lot how you test your guess.

GEORGE POLYA

As a psychological researcher you might study a single individual, or study a group; you might interview people to get their points of view, or observe them perform a task; you might change some of the conditions in a situation, or let events occur without your intervention; you might conduct your study in a laboratory, or in a "natural" setting. In every situation you would make careful observations, but the type of observations you make and the conclusions you could draw would be different.

Bryan Hendricks and his colleagues suggest that research methods in psychology vary along three separate dimensions (Hendricks et al., 1990). These three dimensions are (1) method of data collection, (2) type of research design, and (3) kind of research setting. You might think of these dimensions as answers to the following questions:

1. Should I ask the participants (usually called "subjects") for their personal thoughts about the problem? Or should I observe their performance on a relevant task?
2. Should I attempt to control and vary what I believe are important factors (independent variables) in the situation? Or should I stand back and let events occur on their own?
3. Should I make my observations in a controlled and perhaps artificial laboratory setting? Or should I study my subjects in their natural "real-life" surroundings?

Your answers to these questions will not only affect how you conduct your study, but will also determine the kinds of conclusions you can draw from the results. Each type of research has both strengths and weaknesses.

THREE DIMENSIONS OF RESEARCH: SINGLE SUBJECTS

For simplicity, we will consider research with individual (or few) subjects first. Later we will look at research with groups. Both situations involve the same three basic dimensions.

In order to illustrate each research method we will use examples—mostly fictional—based on the case of "Clever Hans," the horse who could "read minds." (See Chapter 1 if you would like to refresh your memory for the details of Hans's "horsesense.")

Data Collection

The first way in which psychological research varies is in the *source* of the data. The source may be either (1) observations by the experimenter or (2) self-reports from the subject. When Pfungst first began to study Clever Hans, he used the first method—*observation*. If Clever Hans could talk, Pfungst might have used the second method—self-report. In this case, Pfungst could have *asked* Clever Hans how he accomplished his "mind reading."

As a psychologist, if you wanted a self-report you might conduct an "open-ended" interview, almost like a casual conversation; you might conduct a "structured" interview which covered predetermined topics; or you might administer a carefully planned series of questions in a "questionnaire." Personality, aptitude, and attitude scales are familiar examples of questionnaires.

Self-reports allow subjects to express what is important to them—to explain the situation as well as their thoughts and feelings *from their point of view*. Self-reports are a valuable source of new information. However, self-reports are open to several *experimental biases*. For example, researchers may tend to see what they want to see. And subjects may say what they think the experimenter wants (or doesn't want) to hear. Also, subjects vary greatly in their ability to understand themselves and in their ability to express verbally what they are thinking or feeling.

In contrast to self-reports, objective measures are more reliable and they can be compared more easily. Objective measurement techniques range from simple observation to the use of sophisticated electronic and computerized recording apparatus.

In the case of Clever Hans, a self-report from Hans was not possible, and Pfungst's observations of Hans were inconclusive. Pfungst knew that Clever Hans performed remarkable feats under certain conditions. But he did not know if this ability was due to Hans's understanding of language and his "mind reading" or to some other cause. In order to obtain information on possible cause-effect relationships, Pfungst needed a different *research design*.

Research Design

The second way in which psychological research varies is in the *design* of the study. The "design" refers to the procedures that the experimenters use and the way in which the experimenters organize these procedures.

In order to draw conclusions about causes and effects (or the relationship between independent and dependent variables), researchers must design an experiment which isolates the possible causes. This means that the researcher must systematically *change*, or vary one condition (the independent variable) while holding others constant.

For example, after Pfungst had made his observations, he systematically varied the information that Clever Hans received. When Pfungst put blinders on Clever Hans so that he couldn't see his questioners, the horse's performance dropped significantly. Other similar changes soon made it clear that Hans's "mind reading" depended on the visual and auditory cues that his audience gave to him. When Pfungst varied these cues (the independent variable), Hans's performance (the dependent variable) also varied. When Pfungst saw that changing audience cues affected Hans's performance, Pfungst gained confidence in his hypothesis that audience cues *caused* variations in Hans's performance.

Some research, especially in the beginning stages, does not involve experimenter intervention and manipulation of variables. Sometimes a researcher does not know which variable to manipulate; sometimes she does not have the freedom to change the situation. In these cases, she may simply collect information.

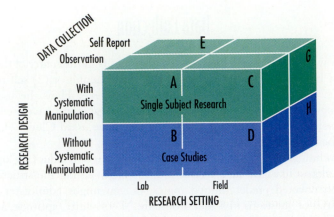

Methodological cube of single-subject research methods. (Adapted from Hendricks et al., 1990.) Table A.1 presents examples of each cell in the cube, using the Clever Hans story from Chapter 1.

Research without systematic manipulation is easier to conduct, and it provides us with valuable data. However, as long as we don't systematically vary relevant conditions, and observe the results, we cannot be sure which of the many circumstances surrounding a behavior *caused* the behavior. We observe and summarize, we may even note which behaviors and conditions occur together, but we can draw no conclusions about causes and effects.

Research Setting

The third way in which psychological research varies is in the setting in which it is conducted. Sometimes psychologists gather their data by observing or questioning people in their normal surroundings—that is, in the "field." And sometimes psychologists gather their data in a lab.

Laboratory research has several advantages: It provides better control of surrounding conditions, it permits the use of sophisticated measuring instruments, and it prevents unwanted intrusions. On the other hand, field research tends to provide greater realism. This makes it easier to disguise the research project and to reduce the tendency of subjects to react to the situation as an experiment.

Pfungst observed Clever Hans in his natural setting. We call this type of observation a **field study.** Later, Pfungst systematically varied conditions in Hans's environment. We call this type of study a **field experiment.**

You can see each of these three dimensions of psychological research and their various combinations in Figure A.1. Table A.1 presents examples of research studies to illustrate each combination. These examples are based on the case of Clever Hans, and as you will see, most of them are fictitious.

Field study. Research conducted by making observations in a natural setting.

Field experiment. Research conducted by systematically manipulating certain parts of a natural setting in order to observe the outcome.

THREE DIMENSIONS OF RESEARCH: GROUPS

Research with a single individual can tell as a great deal about one person. But psychologists are often interested in the "typical" person rather than any particular individual. Consequently, they frequently combine the results of data collected from *groups,* and they calculate an average or "typical" response.

If psychologists wish to draw conclusions about individuals outside of the group that they are testing, they must take steps to ensure that the sample of individuals in the group is *representative.* They accomplish this by using **random selection** in their choice of research participants. Random selection means that the psychologists choose their sample of participants in their study *randomly* (by chance) from among the total population about which they wish to draw their conclusions.

Random selection. The choosing of participants for an experiment on the basis of chance. In order to draw conclusions about a larger group, each person in the larger group must have an equal chance of being selected for the experiment.

Cell A:	Pfungst observes and records Clever Hans's performance in his laboratory while using blinders and earplugs to systematically vary the information Hans receives.
Cell B:	Mr. van Osten and Clever Hans are invited to perform in Pfungst's laboratory. Pfungst observes carefully, and then writes a detailed report.
Cell C:	Pfungst systematically varies the cues Clever Hans can receive, while he measures his performance in the horse's "home field."
Cell D:	Pfungst carefully observes Clever Hans perform in his own home field, and then summarizes his observations in a detailed report.
Cell E:	In his laboratory, Pfungst discusses with (very) Clever Hans his experience in trying to read minds while having available cues systematically varied.
Cell F:	In his laboratory, Pfungst records his discussion with Clever Hans on what it is like to read minds and how he does it.
Cell G:	Clever Hans tells Pfungst how he has tried reading minds with and without seeing his audience, and with and without hearing them.
Cell H:	Clever Hans retires from public life and writes his memoirs.

TABLE A.1

Examples of Each Cell in Figure A.1

We will continue to use Clever Hans as our example, assuming now that Pfungst is investigating whether or not *horses in general* can read minds. First Pfungst must decide on the nature of his sample (assuming he doesn't plan to test every horse in the world). If Pfungst wants to make a statement about *all* horses, he must draw his sample in such a way that every horse in the world, from the wild horses of the American plains to the trained horses in numerous circuses, has an equal chance of being selected. Clearly this is impractical, so Pfungst very wisely decides to limit his conclusions to horses in his part of Germany. From this group he selects a sample by assigning each horse a number, and then choosing 20 numbers from a table of random numbers. The horses with the chosen numbers became his sample. Pfungst then carries out his research with his sample of 20 horses. When he's finished he will draw conclusions about horses *in his part of Germany only*. (Note: The *representativeness* of a sample is much more dependent on the method used to select the sample than on the size of the sample.)

Data Collection

Once again, with groups as with individuals, psychologists can collect data through observations or through self-reports. A psychologist may observe subjects by listening or watching them directly, or the psychologist may use electronic apparatus or the reports of other people to "observe" them indirectly. Both direct and indirect methods are forms of observation.

Self-reports include all kinds of self-revelation—from an extensive autobiography, to an interview, to a simple debriefing at the end of an experiment. In order to handle the larger body of data from groups, self-reports are frequently structured in the form of surveys or questionnaires.

Returning to Pfungst, we find that having judiciously chosen his sample, he now begins to *observe* his horses for signs of mind reading. When this appears to be going nowhere, he turns to self-reports. Pfungst reasons that if horses can read minds they should be able to understand speech and communicate with an "answer board." So he constructs a survey and wanders around the pasture with his answer board seeking *self-reports*.

Research Design

When we study groups, we have a greater variety of research designs at our disposal. For example, not only can we compare the *same subjects* under different

Within subjects design. A test of experimental effects based on comparison of *the same individuals* under different research conditions.

Between subjects design. A test of experimental effects based on comparison of *different individuals* in different research conditions.

Random assignment. The distribution of participants to experimental groups on a chance basis.

Quasi-experimental research. Experimental procedures where groups are given different treatments (as in the true experiment), but where random assignment of subjects is not used.

Correlational design. The measurement of two (or more) variables in order to determine the strength of their relationship. The stronger the correlation, the more knowing one variable allows us to predict the other.

experimental conditions, but we can also compare *different subjects* under different experimental conditions.

Consider a study in which we want to compare the effects of two drugs. We could give a group of people *both* drugs (one at a time) and then compare their performance under drug A with their performance under drug B. When we use the same subjects for different experimental conditions, we are using a **within subjects design.** On the other hand, we could give the two drugs to two different groups, and compare the performance of the two groups. When we use different subjects for different experimental conditions, we are using a **between subjects design.**

In either case, true experimental research with groups involves not only systematic manipulation, as we discussed above, but also **random assignment** of subjects and conditions. In a *between subjects* design, we randomly assign subjects to different experimental conditions. In a *within subjects* design we randomly assign different orders of the experimental conditions to subjects.

For example, if Pfungst wanted to test his hypothesis that horses with blinders performed more poorly than horses without blinders, he might conduct a "between groups" experiment by first dividing his sample into two groups. He would then test one group with blinders and one group without. It is important that he divide the horses into groups on the basis of chance alone (for example, by tossing a coin). This is necessary so that factors that might influence the results unexpectedly are evenly distributed among the groups.

If Pfungst did not have enough horses to create two reasonably sized groups, he might conduct a "within subjects" experiment. In this case the order of assigning different *treatment conditions* must be random. Pfungst might toss a coin to decide whether to test first with blinders or without blinders, for each horse. He would test each horse under both conditions, but the *order* in which he tested the conditions would be random. Once again, this is done in order to evenly distribute the effects of unexpected or irrelevant factors between the conditions. For example, if Pfungst always tested without blinders first and then tested with blinders second, horses might do worse with blinders simply because they were getting tired of the experiment.

Sometimes it is not possible or convenient to assign subjects to conditions (or conditions to subjects) randomly. For example, if you wanted to compare two teaching procedures using two classrooms of students, it might be less disruptive if you assigned one complete class to each condition. This procedure illustrates a **quasi-experimental research** design. If you found differences between the classes, you could not be completely sure that they were the result of the different teaching procedures and not caused by some preexisting difference between the classes.

Imagine Pfungst decides that it is too much trouble to carry his apparatus (blinders, horse-size earplugs, and answer board) all over Germany. So he sets up the apparatus near his home and tests one group of horses—the one given the blinders and earplugs to restrict the cues they can receive. He then travels to other areas and tests the horses in the other condition—without the blinders and earplugs. If he finds that horses in the first group perform more poorly than those in the second, he would have greater confidence in his audience-cueing explanation. Strictly speaking, however, with this experimental design, at least one other explanation is always possible. For example, horses living near his home may not be as intelligent as horses living in other areas. Thus, the quasi-experimental design helps examine causality, but it does not establish it convincingly.

Even less convincing is the **correlational design.** Here we have neither random assignment nor systematic manipulation. The correlational design is an in-depth examination of which variables go together. (We will discuss correlation *statistics* in Appendix B.) In correlational research, a researcher measures several variables—for example, behaviors and environmental conditions—and observes which one(s) tend to go together.

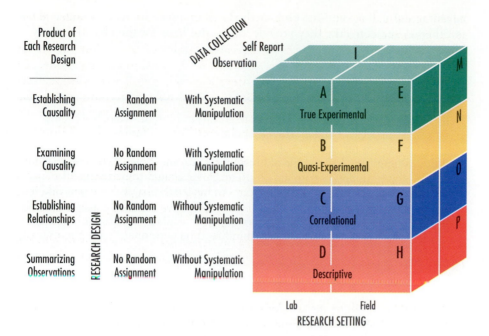

| Product of Each Research Design | | DATA COLLECTION | Self Report Observation | | | |

FIGURE A.2

Methodological cube of group research methods. (Adapted from Hendricks et al., 1990.) Table A.2 presents examples of each cell in the cube, using the Clever Hans story from Chapter 1.

Correlational research gives a researcher ideas about which factors *might* be influencing certain behaviors. The important point to note with correlational research, however, is that observing two variables occur together does *not* indicate that one caused the other. For example, smoking and lung cancer tend to occur together: We say they are "correlated." And there are good reasons to believe that smoking does *cause* lung cancer. But from the correlation *alone*, we are not justified in drawing this conclusion. Other explanations are always possible, at least theoretically. For example, Hans Eysenck argues that some people inherit a "disease-prone personality" that makes them both vulnerable to cancer *and* likely to smoke (Eysenck, 1981, 1991).

Suppose Pfungst observes that horses are much better at reading minds when someone in the audience *believes* that horses have this ability. Can Pfungst conclude that belief *causes* the phenomenon? No, he can't. For one thing, the reverse is probably true—success leads to belief. Or alternatively, a "believer" might be more likely to unwittingly provide the horse with the necessary cues. Correlational designs establish *relationships*; they do not establish *causality*.

Least definitive of all is the **descriptive study.** A descriptive study involves in-depth observation and objective description of something that interests the researcher. Case histories of psychiatric patients are examples of descriptive studies. Descriptive studies provide a broad base of factual information. They are often helpful in pointing to possible relationships and suggesting directions for further research. However, additional research is always necessary to test the ideas derived from descriptive studies.

Descriptive study. In-depth observation and description of a person or phenomenon as it is found to occur naturally. Gathering all relevant information about an individual for a "case history" is an example of a descriptive study.

Research Setting

The research setting dimension is the same for groups as for individual subjects. The research investigation may take place in either a laboratory or a field setting.

Figure A.2 presents each of the three dimensions of psychological research with groups. Table A.2 suggest fictitious examples for each of the research dimension combinations.

You can see that there are many different ways to carry out psychological research. We can summarize the primary differences between the methods in terms of "data collection," "research design," and "research setting." Each method has both

That is a question which has puzzled many an expert, and why? Because there is no reliable test. Now we have the Sherlock Holmes test, and there will no longer be any difficulty.

SIR ARTHUR CONAN DOYLE

advantages and disadvantages; each method is appropriate in some settings and not in others. Used correctly, they provide a powerful basis for the objective study of human behavior.

TABLE A.2

Examples of Each Cell in Figure A.2

Cell A:	Horses are randomly assigned to groups in Pfungst's laboratory. One group wears blinders, the other does not. Their mind-reading performance is recorded.
Cell B:	Pfungst finds that some of his subjects become violent when he tries to place blinders or earplugs on them. So he assigns these to the unrestricted group. He tests his groups in his laboratory and compares their performance.
Cell C:	In his laboratory, Pfungst measures and calculates the strength of the relationship between horses' mind-reading performance and their visual acuity.
Cell D:	Pfungst brings a number of horses into his laboratory, one by one, and carefully observes and records their performance on his mind-reading task.
Cell E:	Pfungst randomly assigns his horses to groups given blinders or not. He then observes their mind-reading ability in their home fields.
Cell F:	Pfungst uses blinders and earplugs with the horses he tests near his home. He then travels to another part of Germany and tests horses without blinders and earplugs. He compares their performance.
Cell G:	Pfungst observes his sample of horses perform in their home fields. He measures their performance and the level of background noise. He then calculates the strength of the relationship between these two variables.
Cell H:	Pfungst travels about, observing his sample of horses perform in their home fields.
Cell I:	Testing his subjects in his laboratory, Pfungst randomly assigns them to groups with blinders and without. They then complete a questionnaire assessing their awareness of the nature of their ability.
Cell J:	Having misplaced the blinders, Pfungst assigns the first horses to appear in his laboratory to the "no-blinder" group. He finds the blinders halfway through his study and assigns the second half of his subjects to the "blinder" group. He interviews them all about their mind-reading, including how it is affected by blinders.
Cell K:	In the laboratory, horses are given the mind-reading task and the new "Horses IQ" test (HIQ). Pfungst then calculates the strength of the relationship between mind-reading ability and HIQ score.
Cell L:	Pfungst interviews horses in his laboratory on their views of mind-reading. He records and summarizes his findings.
Cell M:	Horses are randomly assigned to three groups given blinders, earplugs, or nothing. They are then interviewed in their home fields to get their opinions on whether or not they feel their mind-reading ability has been affected.
Cell N:	Horses that voice their objections to blinders and earplugs are placed in the unrestricted group; horses that say nothing are given blinders or earplugs. They are interviewed in their home fields concerning their views of mind-reading with and without cue restriction.
Cell O:	Pfungst interviews horses in the field to determine the relationship between mind-reading ability and their political persuasion.
Cell P:	Horses are interviewed in their home fields after watching a demonstration by Clever Hans.

A P P E N D I X   B

STATISTICS AS A WAY OF THINKING

THE RED LADY

D r. McConnell was sitting in the student union talking with a friend of his named Gersh, when two young women came over to their table and challenged them to a game of bridge. The two women—Joan and Carol were their names—turned out to be undergraduates. They also turned out to be card sharks, for they beat Dr. McConnell and Gersh handily. Joan was particularly clever at figuring out how the cards were distributed among the four bridge hands—and hence good at figuring out how to play her own cards to win the most tricks.

Dr. McConnell was especially impressed with one hand and what Joan said afterwards. He relates his experience this way:

> "Joan had bid four spades, and making the contract depended on figuring out who had the Queen of Diamonds—Gersh or me. Joan thought about it for a while, then smiled sweetly at Gersh. 'I think you've got the Red Lady,' she said, and promptly captured Gersh's Queen of Diamonds with her King.
>
> Gersh, who hates to lose, muttered something about 'dumb luck.'
>
> 'No luck to it, really,' Joan replied. 'I knew you had 5 diamonds, Gersh, while Doc here had only 2. One of you had the Queen, but I didn't know which. But since you had 5 of the missing diamonds, Gersh, the odds were 5 to 2 that you had the Little Old Lady. Simple enough, when you stop to think about it.'
>
> While Gersh was dealing the next hand with noisy frustration, Joan turned to me. 'I know you're a professor, but I don't know what you teach.'
>
> 'Psychology,' I said, picking up my cards for the next hand. The cards were rotten, as usual.
>
> 'Oh, you're a psych teacher! That's great,' Joan said with a smile. 'I really wanted to study psych, but they told me I had to take statistics. I hate math. I'm just *no good at figuring out all those complicated equations*. So I majored in history instead.'"

Dr. McConnell shook his head in amazement at what Joan had said.

STATISTICS: A WAY OF THINKING

Students frequently say the same thing as Joan—they're rotten at mathematics, or they just can't figure out what statistics is all about. But these same students manage to play bridge superbly, or figure out the stock market, or they can tell you the batting averages of every major league baseball player, or how many miles per gallon their car gets on unleaded gasoline.

Statistics is not just a weird bunch of mathematics—it's a way of thinking. If you can think well enough to figure out how to play cards, or who is likely to win the next election, or what "grading on the curve" is all about, then you're probably already pretty good at statistics. In fact, you surely use statistics intuitively every minute of your life. If you didn't, you'd be dead or in some institution by now.

Sure, a few of the equations that statisticians throw around get pretty fancy. But don't let that fact discourage you. Even many psychology professors don't understand all the equations in the statistical and psychological journals. However, those "fancy formulas" are usually of interest only to specialists. Forget about them—unless you happen to be a nut about mathematics. The truth is that you *already know* most of the principles involved in basic statistics—if, like Joan, you're willing to stop and think about them. Yet, many psych students reject statistics with the same sort of emotionality that they show when somebody offers them fried worms and rattlesnake meat for dinner. Well, worms are rich in protein, and rattlesnake meat is safe to eat—if you don't have to catch the snake first. But you may have to overcome some pretty strong emotional prejudices before you're willing to dig in and see what snake meat (or stats) is all about.

Odds and Ends

Serious gamblers are comfortable with numbers and "odds." But whether you realize it or not, you're a gambler, too. And you (like Joan) are pretty good at figuring out all kinds of odds and *probabilities*. Every time you cross the street, you gamble that the odds are "safely" in your favor. Each time you drive your car through a green light without slowing down, you gamble that some "odd" driver won't run the red light and hit you broadside. Every time you study for a true-false exam, you're gambling that you can learn enough to do better than somebody who refuses to study and who just picks the answers randomly. And whenever you go out with somebody on a date, you're gambling that you can predict that person's future behavior (on the date) from observing the things that the person has done in the past.

So you're a gambler, too, even if you don't think of yourself as being one. But if you're going to gamble, wouldn't it be helpful to know something about odds and probabilities? Because if you know what the odds are, you can often do a much better job of achieving whatever goals you have in mind.

One way or another, almost everything in statistics is based on *probability theory*. And, as luck would have it, probability theory got its start some 300 years ago when some French gamblers got worried about what the pay-offs should be in a dice game. So the gamblers—who were no dummies—hired two brilliant French mathematicians to figure out the probabilities for them. From the work of these two French geniuses came the theory that allows the casinos in Las Vegas and Atlantic City to earn hundreds of millions of dollars every year, that lets the insurance companies earn even more by betting on how long people will live—and that lets psychologists and psychiatrists employ the mental tests that label some people as being "normal" and others as being "abnormal."

The Odds in Favor

If you want to see why Joan was so good at playing bridge, get a deck of cards and pull out the 2, 3, 4, 5, 6, 7, and Queen of Diamonds. Turn them face down on a table and shuffle them around so you won't know which card is which. Now try to pick out the Queen just by looking at the back of the cards.

If the deck is "honest" (unmarked), what are the odds that you will pick the Red Lady instead of the 2, 3, 4, 5, 6, or 7? As you can see, the odds are exactly 1 in 7. If you want to be fancy about all this, you can write an equation (which is what Joan did in her mind) as follows:
The probability (*p*) of picking the Queen is 1 out of 7, therefore

$$pQ = 1/7$$

Next, shuffle the cards again, place them face down on the table, and then randomly select two of the cards and put them on one side of the table, and the remaining five on the other side of the table. Now, what are the odds that the Queen is in the stack of five cards (Gersh's bridge hand), and what are the odds that the Queen is in the stack of two cards (Dr. McConnell's bridge hand)?

Well, you already know that the probability that any one card will be the Queen is 1/7. Dr. McConnell has two cards, therefore, he has two chances at getting the Queen, and the equation reads:

$$pQ \text{ (Dr. McC)} = 1/7 + 1/7 = 2/7$$

Gersh had five cards, so his probability equation is:

$$pQ \text{ (Gersh)} = 1/7 + 1/7 + 1/7 + 1/7 + 1/7 = 5/7$$

So, if you dealt out the seven cards randomly 70 times, Gersh would have the Queen about 50 times, and Dr. McConnell would have the Queen about 20 times. No wonder Joan wins at bridge! When she assumed that Gersh had the Queen, she didn't have a sure thing—but the odds were surely in her favor.

Outcomes and Incomes

Now let's look at something familiar to everyone, the true-false examination. Suppose that you go to a history class one day, knowing there will be a test, but the teacher throws you a curve, for the exam you get is written in Chinese, or Greek, or some other language you simply can't read a word of. The test has 20 questions, and it's obviously of the true-false variety. But since you can't read it, all you can do is guess. What exam score do you think you'd most likely get—0, 10, or 20?

Maybe you'd deserve a 0, since you couldn't read the exam. But you realize intuitively that you'd most likely get a score of about 10. Why?

Well, what are the *odds* of your guessing any single question right, if it's a true-false exam?

If you said, "Fifty percent chance of being right," you're thinking clearly. (See how statistics can be a way of thinking?)

The probability (p) of your getting the first question right (R_1) is 50 percent, or 1/2. So we write an equation that says:

$$pR_1 = 1/2$$

The probability of your getting the first question wrong (W_1) is also 50 percent, or 1/2. So we write another equation:

$$pW_1 = 1/2$$

Furthermore, we can now say that, on the first or any other equation, the

$$pR + pW = 1/2 + 1/2 = 1$$

Which is a fancy way of saying that whenever you guess the answer on a true–false exam, you have to be either right or wrong—because those are the only two *outcomes* possible.

Now, suppose we look at the first two questions on the test. What is the probability that you will get *both* of them right if you are just guessing at the answers?

Well, what outcomes are possible? You could miss both questions (W_1W_2), or you could get them both right (R_1R_2), or you could get the first answer right and the second answer wrong (R_1W_2), or you could get the first one wrong and the second right (W_1R_2).

Thus, there are four different outcomes, and since you would be guessing at the right answer on both questions, these four outcomes are *equally likely to occur*. Only one of the four outcomes (R_1R_2) is the one we're interested in, so the odds of your getting both questions right is 1/4.

$$pR_1R_2 = 1/4$$
$$pW_1W_2 = 1/4$$
$$pR_1W_2 = 1/4$$
$$pW_1R_2 = 1/4$$

and

$$pR_1R_2 + pW_1W_2 + pR_1W_2 + pW_1R_2 = 1/4 + 1/4 + 1/4 + 1/4 = 1$$

In a sense, getting both questions right is like selecting the Queen of Diamonds when it is one of four cards face down on the table in front of you. In both cases, you have four equally likely outcomes, so your chances of getting the Queen (or being right on both answers) is one out of four, or 1/4.

As you can see, if you're taking an exam, playing bridge, or trying to add to your income by buying a lottery ticket, it will surely pay you to consider all the possible outcomes.

Actually, we can figure the odds of your answering the first two questions correctly in a much simpler way. We simply multiply the odds of your getting the first question right (pR_1) by the odds of your getting the second question right (pR_2):

$$pR_1R_2 = pR_1 \times pR_2 = 1/2 \times 1/2 = 1/4 = 25\%$$

Maybe you can see, too, that the odds of your getting both answers *wrong* would be exactly the same:

$$pW_1W_2 = pW_1 \times pW_2 = 1/2 \times 1/2 = 1/4 = 25\%$$

If the exam had just three questions to it, the odds of your getting all the answers right by chance alone (that is, by guessing) would be:

$$pR_1R_2R_3 = pR_1 \times pR_2 \times pR_3 = 1/2 \times 1/2 \times 1/2 = 1/8 = 12.5\%$$

To put the matter another way, on a three-question exam, there are eight different outcomes:

$R_1R_2R_3$	$W_1R_2R_3$
$R_1R_2W_3$	$W_1R_2W_3$
$R_1W_2R_3$	$W_1W_2R_3$
$R_1W_2W_3$	$W_1W_2W_3$

Since only one of these eight possible outcomes is the one you want ($R_1R_2R_3$), the odds in your favor are only 1 in 8.

If the test had four true-false questions, there would be sixteen different outcomes—twice as many as if the test had but three questions. These outcomes would range from $R_1R_2R_3R_4$, $R_1R_2R_3W_4$ . . . all the way to $W_1W_2W_3R_4$ and $W_1W_2W_3W_4$. If there are 16 different outcomes, only one of which is "all answers right," or $R_1R_2R_3R_4$, what would be the odds of your guessing all the answers right on a four-question true-false test?

(If you said "1 in 16," congratulations!)

Now, let's take a giant leap.

If the exam had 10 questions, the odds of your getting all 10 answers right by guessing would be:

$$pR_1R_2R_3R_4R_5R_6R_7R_8R_9R_{10} = 1/2 \times 1/2 \times 1/2 \times 1/2 \times 1/2 \times 1/2 \times 1/2 \times 1/2 \times 1/2 \times 1/2 = 1/1,024$$

So if you took the exam 1,024 times and guessed randomly at the answers each time, just *once* in 1,024 times would you expect to get a score of 0, and just *once* in 1,024 times would you expect to get a score of 10.

Now, at last, we can answer the question we asked you a few paragraphs back: If you took a 20-question exam on which you had to guess at each answer, what exam score do you think you'd most likely get—0, 10, or 20?

Well, what are the odds that you'd get a score of flat 0? In fact, the odds are astronomically against you, just as they are astronomically against your getting a score of 20 right. In either case, the probability would be:

$$pW_{1-20} = pR_{1-20} = 1/2 \times 1/2 \times 1/2 \ldots (20 \text{ times!}) = 1,048,576 \text{ to } 1!$$

So the odds are more than a million to one that you won't get all the answers right or all the answers wrong on a 20-question true-false exam just by guessing. Which might give you good reason to study for the next exam you have to take!

Normal Curves

Next, let's throw in some pictures just to liven things up a bit. Statisticians have a way of plotting or graphing probabilities that may make more sense to you than equations do. Figure B.1 shows a diagram of the *distribution* of outcomes when you take a 10-question true-false exam.

As we mentioned earlier, the number of possible outcomes in a 10-question exam is 1,024. So the odds of getting all 10 questions right by just guessing ("by chance alone") would be 1 in 1,024. Not very good odds. But the probability of your getting 4, 5, or 6 questions right would be well above 60 percent! That makes sense, because just looking at the curve you can see that better than 60 percent of the possible outcomes are bunched up right in the middle of the curve.

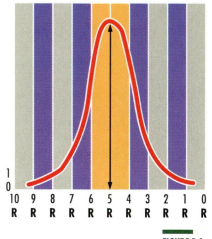

FIGURE B.1

A bell-shaped curve showing the distribution of "right answers" expected by chance alone when taking a 10-item true-false exam.

DESCRIPTIVE STATISTICS

The curve we've just drawn is the world-famous, ever-popular "bell-shaped curve." In fact, the curve describes a *random distribution of scores* or outcomes. That is, the curve describes the outcomes you'd expect when students are forced to guess—more or less at random—which answers on a true-false exam are correct. Naturally, if the exam were written in clear English, and if the students knew most of the material they were being examined on, the curve, or *distribution of scores*, would look quite different.

There are many sorts of "outcomes" that fit the bell-shaped curve rather nicely. For example, if you randomly selected 1,000 adult U.S. males and measured their heights, the results you'd get would come very close to matching the bell-shaped curve shown in Figure B.2. Which is to say that there would be a few very short men, a few very tall men, but most would have heights around 5' 10". The same bell-shaped curve would fit the distribution of heights of 1,000 adult women selected at random—except that the "middle" or peak of the bell-shaped curve would be about 5' 5".

Measures of Central Tendency

Intelligence tests are constructed so that the scores for any age group will approximate a bell-shaped curve. In this case, the peak, or "middle," of the distribution of IQs will be almost precisely at 100. A very few individuals would have IQs below 50,

FIGURE B.2

A bell-shaped curve showing the distribution of heights of a thousand men and a thousand women selected at random.

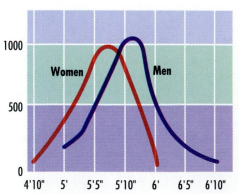

a very few would have scores above 150. But some two-thirds of the scores would fall between 84 and 116 (see Figure 15.1).

Why this bulge in the middle as far as IQs are concerned? Well, think back for a moment to the true-false test we were discussing earlier that had 10 questions on it. There are 1,024 possible outcomes. If you wanted to get all 10 questions right, there was only one way you could answer the 10 questions—all had to be correct. But there were 256 ways in which you could answer the questions to get a score of 5—right in the middle.

There is only one way you can earn a top score on an intelligence test—you've got to answer all the questions rapidly and precisely the way the people who constructed the test say is "right." But there are thousands of different ways you can answer the questions on the usual test to get a "middle score," namely, an IQ between 84 and 116.

In a similar vein, there are precious few ways in which you can earn a million dollars, but there are dozens and dozens of ways in which you can earn between $15,000 and $20,000 a year. So if we selected 1,000 adult North American citizens at random, asked them what their incomes were, and then "took an average," what kind of curve (distribution of incomes) do you think we'd get?

Whenever we measure people psychologically, biologically, socially, intellectually, or economically, we often generate a distribution of outcomes that looks very much like a bell-shaped curve. Each person in the world is unique, it's true. But it is equally true that, on any given *single* measuring scale (height, weight, grade-point average, income), most people's scores will be somewhere in the *middle* of the range of possible outcomes.

Psychologists have a variety of tools for measuring the "middle" of any curve, or distribution, of outcomes. These techniques are often called *measures of central tendency*, which is a fancy way of saying that these techniques allow us to measure the center, or midpoint, of any distribution of scores or outcomes.

Mean, Median, and Mode

1. *The Mean*. The *mean* is simply the statistical "average" of all the scores or outcomes involved. When you figure your grade-point average (GPA) for any semester, you usually multiply your grade in each course by the number of credit hours, add up the totals, and divide by the number of hours credit you are taking. Your GPA is actually the *mean*, or mathematical average, of all your grades (see Table B.1).

2. *The Median*. Since the mean is a mathematical average, it sometimes gives very funny results. For example, according to recent government figures, the "average" U.S. family was made up of about 4.47 people.

   Have you ever known a family that had 4.47 people in it? For another example, if you got two A's and two C's one semester, your average, or "mean," grade would be a B. Yet you didn't get a B in any of the courses you took.

   There are times when it makes more sense to figure the exact *midpoint score* or outcome, rather than figuring out the *average* score. At such times, psychologists often use the *median*, which is the score that's in the precise middle of the distribution—just as the "median" of an expressway is the area right down the middle of the highway.

   The median is often used as a "measure of central tendency" when a distribution has one or two extreme scores in it. For instance, if nine people earn $1 a year, and a tenth earns $100,000, what is the *mean* income of these 10 people? About $10,001 a year, which is a misleading statistic, to say the least. However, the *median* income is $1, which describes the actual income of the *majority* of the group somewhat better than does the mean of $10,001.

COURSE	HOURS CREDIT	GRADE	(POINTS)	HOURS × GRADE
History	3	A	(4)	3 × 4 = 12
Psychology	4	A	(4)	4 × 4 = 16
Mathematics	4	C	(2)	4 × 2 = 8
Spanish	4	B	(3)	4 × 3 = 12
Totals	15			48

GPA = 48/15 = 3.2

TABLE B.1

Table of Grade-Point Averages

3. *The Mode*. The word *mode* is defined in the dictionary as "the prevailing fashion or most popular custom or style." When we are talking about distributions of scores or outcomes, *mode* means the most popular score. That is, the mode is the highest point (or points) on the curve. If the distribution has two points that are equally high, then there are two scores that are *modal*, and we can call the curve *bi-modal* (having two modes).

Skewedness

If the distribution of scores is more or less bell-shaped, then the mean, median, and mode usually come out to be the same. But not all curves do us the favor of being so regular in shape. For example, suppose you were interested in whether a particular teacher—Dr. Johnson—started and ended her classes on time. To find out, you take a very accurate watch with you all semester long and make a scientific study of Dr. Johnson's behavior.

During the term, let's say, there are supposed to be 50 lectures by Dr. Johnson. So the number of possible start-time scores or outcomes will be 50. For the most part, Dr. Johnson begins on time, but occasionally she starts a minute or two early, and sometimes she's a minute or two late. Now and again, she is fairly tardy in getting to class, and once she didn't show up at all. But she *never* begins a class more than two minutes early. If you put all of her starting times on a graph, it would look something like the curve on the left side of Figure B.3. If you plotted all her closing time scores on a similar graph, it would look like the curve on the right in Figure B.3.

The term we use to describe these curves is *skewedness*, which means they are "slanted" or "pushed out of shape." In the starting-time example, the tail of the curve slants out far to the right-hand side, so we say that the curve is "skewed to the right." The other curve has a tail that slants out to the left, so the curve is "skewed to the left." As is the case in many distributions where the scores are measures of reaction times or beginning times, the mean, median, and mode are fairly different.

FIGURE B.3

A plot of Dr. Johnson's "starting times" and "closing times."

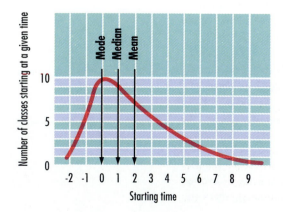

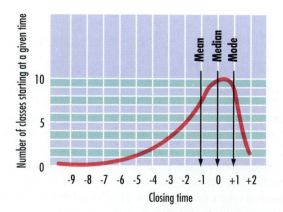

Range and Variation

There are two more important concepts we have to get out of the way before we can finish our discussion of *descriptive statistics*—which is to say, statistics that measure or describe something. The first concept is the *range* of possible scores or outcomes; the second is the *variability* of the scores. The first concept is easy to understand, but the second will take some careful thought on your part.

What is the *range* of possible scores on a 10-item "fill in the blanks" test? From 0 to 10, of course. And since you can't guess as easily on this type of test as on a true-false examination, you can't really tell ahead of time what the class average is likely to be. The range on a 100-item test would be from 0 to 100—and again, you have no way of knowing before you take the test what the "mean," or average, score is likely to be.

Let's suppose that you took a 10-item "fill in the blanks" exam and got a score of 8 right, which also turned out to be the mean, or average, score for the whole class. Then you took a 100-item "fill in the blanks" test and again you got a score of 8, which again turned out to be the class average. What does knowing the *range* of possible scores tell you about the level of difficulty of the two tests? Wouldn't you say that the 100-item test was considerably more difficult, even though the class average was the same on both tests?

Now, let's add one more dimension. Suppose that on the 10-item examination, *everybody in class* got a score of 8! There would be no *variation* at all in these scores, since none of the scores *deviated* (were different from) the mean. But suppose on the 100-item "fill in the blanks" exam, about 95 percent of the class got scores of flat 0, you got an 8, and a few "aces" got scores above 85. Your score of 8 would still be the *mean* (but not the median or mode). But the *deviation* of the rest of the scores would be tremendous. Even though you scored right at the mean on both tests, the fact that you were better than 95 percent of the class on the 100-item test might well be very pleasing to you.

The variation or variability of test scores is simply a measure of *how spread out across the range* the scores actually are. Thus, the variability of a distribution of scores is a very important item to know if you're going to evaluate how you perform in relation to anybody else who's taken the test.

The Standard Deviation

If you know the range of scores, plus the mean, median, and mode, you can usually get a fairly good notion of what shape the curve might take. Why? Because these two bits of information tell you something about how the scores are *distributed*. If the mean, median, and mode are almost the same, and they fall right at the center of the range, then the distribution curve must be "vaguely" bell-shaped, or regular in shape.

But why do we say "vaguely" bell-shaped? In Chapter 18, we discussed the distribution of scores on an attitude questionnaire in two different groups. In the homogeneous groups, as Figure B.4 shows, the range of scores was very small. But in the heterogeneous group, as Figure B.5 shows, the range was much larger. The means for the two distributions were the same, and if the groups had been large enough, we might even have found that the ranges of the two distributions were the same. However, in the homogeneous group, the scores were all bunched up close to the mean, while in the heterogeneous group, the scores were broadly *dispersed*, or spread out.

In Chapter 18 we also introduced a concept we called the *standard deviation* to describe the *dispersion of scores* across the range (or around the mean). The larger the standard deviation, the more widely the scores vary around the mean (and the more heterogeneous the group probably is). The smaller the standard deviation, the more

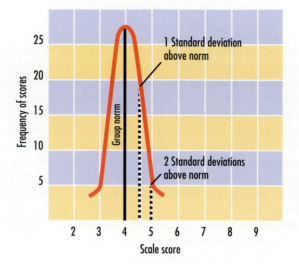

FIGURE B.4

A distribution of attitude scores for a homogenous group.

bunched up the scores are around the mean (and the more homogeneous the group probably is).

We can now define the *standard deviation* as a statistical term meaning the variability of scores in a distribution.

There are a variety of mathematical formulas for figuring out such statistics as the standard deviation. Once upon a time, students were required to memorize these formulas and grind out statistical analyses using nothing more than their brains (and perhaps their fingers and toes to count on). Nowadays, however, even cheap pocket calculators will figure out the standard deviation of a distribution of scores almost instantaneously (if you input the right data in the first place).

However, as we said earlier, statistics is more a way of thinking than it is a bunch of fancy formulas. *Descriptive statistics* are shorthand ways of describing large bunches of data. They are "thought tools" that let you think about the world in convenient symbols.

Let's now see how you can use "descriptive" statistics to help you *make inferences*, or draw conclusions, about the data you're mulling over in your mind.

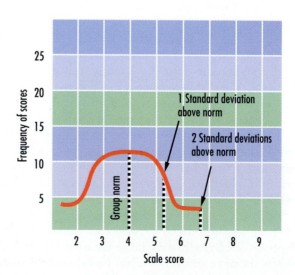

FIGURE B.5

A distribution of attitude scores for a heterogeneous group.

INFERENTIAL STATISTICS

When you test a hunch or a scientific hypothesis, you often are hunting for *reliable* differences between two groups of subjects or between two sets of data. Again, there are *many* different formulas for figuring out how reliable (or important) the group differences really are. But one of the simplest, and most often used, is the standard deviation. By convention, scientists accept differences as being "real" if the means of the two groups depart by 2 or more standard deviations from each other.

We pick 2 standard deviations for a very understandable reason. If on a bell-shaped curve we measure out from the mean a distance of 2 standard deviations, we will take into account about 95 percent of all the IQ scores described by the curve. Any score falling outside of this distance will be there *by chance alone* less than 5 percent of the time. So the odds of your getting an IQ of 132 are but 5 in 100, or 1 in 20. Since these odds are pretty impressive, we can assume that your score didn't occur "by chance alone," and thus the score suggests you are "brighter than average."

Differences between Groups

Now, suppose we compare the IQs of two people, Bill and Mary. Bill has a score of 84, which is exactly 1 standard deviation from the mean of 100. He might have "below average" intelligence, true. But he's so close to the mean that we might as well call him "average," since he might have been overly tired when he took the test. (In fact, even if his *true* IQ was 100, Bill would get a *measured* score of between 84 and 100 about one-third of the time that he took the test. Can you guess why this would be the case?)

Mary has an IQ of 116, which is exactly 1 standard deviation above the mean. But again, her score isn't all that different from the mean, so we could (technically speaking) say that she too has "average intelligence." (She too would be expected to get a *measured* score between 100 and 116 one-third of the time if her *true* IQ was 100. And, like Bill, she would also get a *measured* score between 84 and 100 a third of the time.)

Since both Bill and Mary have IQs that "vary" from the mean but 1 standard deviation, their scores of 84 and 116 don't differ reliably from each other, right?

Wrong! (As if you didn't know that intuitively, anyhow.)

Bill's score differs form Mary's by 2 standard deviations, thus the odds are at least 20 to 1 that Mary's *true* IQ score is significantly higher than Bill's. (And wouldn't you have been willing to make a small wager that was the case the moment you knew what their scores were?)

Significant Differences

Whenever you hear scientists say that their "findings are significant at the 5 percent level," you can translate this to mean that their groups differed by about 2 standard deviations. In general, if the odds are not at least 20 to 1 in support of the hunch you're trying to support, you probably shouldn't use the word "significant" in describing your results.

There are many different tests or formulas you could use for calculating whether the results of an experiment were significant or not. Among the best-known of such statistical devices are the *t-test* and the *critical ratio*. Should you ever need to employ one of these tests, you'd do well to read about them in a statistics text.

	ENTRANCE TEST IQ SCORE	GRADE-POINT AVERAGE (GPA)
Ann	152	3.91
Bill	145	3.46
Carol	133	2.77
Dick	128	2.35
Elmer	112	1.51
Σ(Sum of)	670	14.00
Mean	134	2.80
SD	15.54	0.94

TABLE B.2

Relationship Between IQ Score and GPA

Correlation Coefficients

In several chapters of this book, we have mentioned the term *correlation* to suggest that two events or traits were somehow connected or associated with each other. The mathematics underlying correlations are not too difficult to understand. However, as we saw in Chapter 1, the correlation concept itself has a "problem" buried deep within it that makes it one of the most misunderstood and misused ideas in all of human experience. We'll come back to this problem in just a moment. First, let's look at how one figures out if two sets of scores are correlated.

As we noted in Chapter 11, there is a strong relationship between IQs and grades in school, and for a very good reason. Intelligence tests are usually devised so that they will predict academic success, and the items on most such tests are juggled around until the final score does in fact yield the expected predictions. Thus, if we give intelligence tests to all incoming freshmen, and we know their grades at the end of their first collegiate year, we should expect to find the sort of relationship between these measures shown in Table B.2.

Just looking at the rank orderings of these scores, you can tell that a strong correlation exists between the two distributions. As Figure B.6 shows, if we plotted the data on what is called a *scatter diagram,* we'd get pretty much a straight line. (A scatter diagram shows how the scores for each subject are *scattered,* or distributed, across the graph or diagram.)

If we reversed the scores, so that Ann has an IQ of 152 but a GPA of 1.51, Bill got an IQ of 145 and a GPA of 2.35, and so forth, we'd get a scatter diagram that looked like the one in Figure B.7.

Generally speaking, the closer the scatter diagram comes to being a straight line tilted to the right or left as these are, the higher the correlation between the two variables (scores).

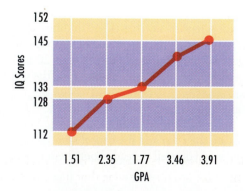

FIGURE B.6

A scatter diagram showing the positive correlation between IQs and grade-point averages.

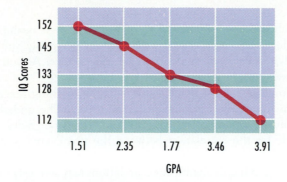

FIGURE B.7

A scatter diagram showing a negative correlation between IQs and grade-point averages.

There are several formulas for figuring out the *mathematical* correlation between two sets of scores that we needn't go into here. All of these formulas yield what is called a *correlation coefficient*, which is merely a "coefficient" or number between +1 and −1.

A correlation coefficient of +1 indicates that the two sets of scores are *perfectly correlated in a positive way*. Which is to say, the person who got the *highest* score on one test got the *highest* on the second test, the person who got the second *highest* score on one test got the second *highest* on the other test, and so forth.

A correlation coefficient of -1 indicates that the two sets of scores are *perfectly correlated in a negative way*. Which is to say that the person who got the *highest* score on the first test got the *lowest* score on the second, the person who got the second *highest* score on the first test got the second *lowest* score on the other test, and so forth.

A correlation coefficient of +.75 suggests there is a strong (but not perfect) association between the two sets of scores. A coefficient of −.75 would indicate the same strength of association, but in a negative direction.

A correlation coefficient of 0 (or close to it) tells you that there is little or no significant relationship between the two sets of scores.

Uses and Abuses of Correlation Coefficients

The ability to make quick correlations is just about the most useful trait that your mind has available to it. Whether you realize it or not, your brain is so built that it automatically makes connections between incoming stimuli. Think back to the discussion of Pavlovian conditioning you read about in Chapter 9. When you ring a bell, and then give food to a dog, the animal's brain soon comes to associate the sound of the bell with the appearance of the food. When the dog eventually salivates to the sound of the bell *before* food arrives, its nervous system has calculated a crude sort of "correlation coefficient" between the onset of the bell and the presentation of the food. Since (in the experiment) the two events *always* occur together, the correlation coefficient of the two events would be close to +1. Thus, the dog can anticipate (predict) the stimulus input "food" as soon as the stimulus input "bell" has occurred.

If dogs could talk, how might they explain their conditioned responses? Don't you imagine that Pavlov's beasts might explain matters in *causal* terms? That is, might not a well-conditioned canine remark that the bell has "magic powers" that cause the food to appear?

As peculiar as this notion may sound to you, evidence in its favor comes from some real-life experiments. In several studies, bell-food conditioned animals have later been trained to turn on the bell themselves by pressing a bar in their cages. What do you think the animals do when they become hungry? Of course, they turn on the bell.

As we mentioned earlier, the concept of correlation has a problem buried in it. The problem is this: We too often assume that if event A is *correlated* with event B, then A must somehow *cause* the appearance of B. This "causal assumption" gets us into a lot of trouble. For example, does the sound of the bell really *cause* the food to appear? Do high IQs really *cause* students to get good grades? As you can see, the answers in both cases must be a resounding *no*.

Scores on an intelligence test don't cause much of anything (except, perhaps, favorable reactions from college admissions committees). The underlying trait of intelligence presumably causes both the high IQ and the good grades. Thus, *intelligence* is responsible for the correlation between the two events, just as Pavlov's desires were responsible for the correlation between the bell and the food.

There are times when highly significant correlations may seriously mislead us. As we have mentioned several times, there is a high correlation between going to a psychotherapist and "getting better." But as many studies have shown, you are just about as likely to show improvement if you *don't* seek help as if you do. But the fact that you (1) went to a therapist and (2) solved some of your problems may incorrectly convince both you and your therapist that it was the *treatment* that primarily caused your improvement.

At their very best, correlations can help us predict future stimulus inputs and give us clues as to what the underlying causal connections among these inputs might be. However, in daily life, we too often misuse correlations. If you want to make your psychology teacher very happy indeed, say "Correlations don't determine causes" over and over again—until you're conditioned to believe it!

STATS AND EVERYDAY LIFE

Why statistics? Or, to phrase the question more precisely, is there any correlation between knowing something about stats and knowing something about yourself and the people around you?

As it happens, the difference between knowing stats and not knowing stats is highly significant. All of your future life you will be performing "little experiments" in which you try to understand the people around you. It's likely (at the 5 percent level) that you will probe your environment better if you know how to interpret the results of your informal experimentation. If you are introspective, an understanding of correlations and conditioning could help tell you some very important facts about how you have acquired many of your values and attitudes. And, if nothing else, understanding what a bell-shaped curve is all about could save you a lot of money should you ever happen to visit Las Vegas.

The second reason for imposing statistics on you, willy-nilly, is that you may wish to take further courses in psychology. If you do, you may be encouraged (or even required) to perform one or more controlled experiments, either in a laboratory or in a real-life setting. Therefore, you might as well learn the first law of statistics right now:

Your statistical inferences are never better than your experimental design will allow.

The topic of how to design a good experiment has filled many a thick textbook, and there's little sense in subjecting you to more grief than we've done already. What we can say is this—the secret of good experimentation lies in *controlling variables*. If you want to pick a random sample of people for a political poll, make sure your sample is *really random*. Just asking a few of your friends what they think won't do, because your method of choice was highly biased—and hence not random at all.

Several times in this book we've mentioned the concept of a "control group" that some scientist(s) used in an experiment. There probably is no more powerful way of making sure your results are reliable than by incorporating as many groups as possible in your study—one group to *control* for each factor (variable) that might influence the results of your study.

But, most important of all, if you must run a scientific study, think it through carefully *before you start*. Then you can design your study intelligently so that the data you gather will be easy to analyze, and so your expected results will be as truthful and as reliable as you can make them. Scientists are probably about as honest and as open in their work as any professional group can be. And yet, all of us may unconsciously bias our results if we feel passionately about the subject we're studying. So we should use control group after control group—just to make sure that we screen out our unconscious biases before they can affect our results. Anything that you love, or that is important enough to you, is worth working hard for—and worth being entirely honest about.

Animals show a lot of intelligent behaviors. They "sing," and monkeys even draw pictures of a sort. But only human beings run experiments, control for bias, select their subjects randomly, and perform statistical analyses. Being a scientist is thus one of the most *humane* occupations you can have, because we all need reliable and valid data about how things are so that we can truly "understand human behavior."

REFERENCES

Abel, E. L., & Sokol, R. J. (1987). Incidence of fetal alcohol syndrome and economic impact of FAS-related anomalies. *Drug and Alcohol Dependence, 19*, 51–70.

Abelson, R. P., & Lesser, G. S. (1959). The measurement of persuasibility in children. In I. L. Janis, C.I. Hovland, P. B. Field, H. Linton, E. Graham, A. R. Cohen, D. Rife, R. P. Abelson, G. S. Lesser, & B. T. King (Eds.), *Personality and persuasibility*. New Haven, CT: Yale University Press.

Abrams, R., & Essman, W. B. (Eds.). (1982). *Electroconvulsive therapy: Biological foundations and clinical applications*. New York: SP Medical & Scientific Books.

Abramson, L. Y., Metalsky, G. I., & Alloy, L. B. (1989). Hopelessness depression: A theory-based subtype of depression. *Psychological Review, 96(2)*, 358–372.

Adams, D. B., Gold, A. R., & Burt, A. D. (1978). Rise in female-initiated sexual activity at ovulation and its suppression by oral contraceptives. *New England Journal of Medicine, 299*, 1145–1150.

Adams, L. T., Kasserman, J. E., Yearwood, A. A., Perfetto, G. A., Bransford, J. D., & Franks, J. J. (1988). Memory access: The effects of fact-oriented versus problem-oriented acquisition. *Memory and Cognition, 16*, 167–175.

Adams, P. L., Milner, J. R., & Schrepf, N. A. (1984). *Fatherless children*. New York: Wiley.

Adan, A. (1990). Adaptation and standardization of a Spanish version of the morningness-eveningness questionnaire: Individual differences. *Personality and Individual Differences, 11*, 1123–1130.

Adan, A. (1991). Influence of morningness-eveningness preference in the relationship between body temperature and performance: A diurnal study. *Personality and Individual Differences, 12*, 1159–1169.

Adan, A. (1992). The influence of age, work schedule and personality on morningness dimension. *International Journal of Psychophysiology, 12*, 95–99.

Adesso, V. J. (1985). Cognitive factors in alcohol and drug use. In M. Galizio and S. A. Maisto (Eds.), *Determinants of substance abuse*. New York: Plenum Press.

Adler, A. (1931). *What life should mean to you*. New York: Putnam.

Adler, A. (1959). *The practice and theory of individual psychology*. Totowa, NJ: Littlefield-Adams.

Adler, N., Pfaff, D., & Goy, R. W. (Eds.). (1985). *Handbook of behavioral neurobiology Vol. 7: Reproduction*. New York: Plenum.

Adler, N. J. (1984). Women in international management: Where are they? *California Management Review, 26(4)*, 78–89.

Ainsworth, M. D. S., (1973). The development of infant-mother attachment. In B. Caldwell & H. Ricciuti (Eds.), *Review of child development research* (Vol. 3). Chicago: University of Chicago Press.

Ainsworth, M. D. S., Blehar, M., Waters, E., & Wall, S. (1978). *Strange-situation behavior of one-year-olds: Its relation to mother-infant interaction in the first year and to qualitative differences in the infant-mother attachment relationship*. Hillsdale, NJ: Erlbaum.

Ainyette, I. D. G. (1989). *Medical aspects of human sexuality*. New York: Reed.

Ajzen, I. (1987). A new paradigm in the psychology of persuasion. *Contemporary Psychology, 32*, 1009–1010.

Akerstedt, T. (1985). Shifted sleep hours. *Annals of Clinical Research, 17(5)*, 273–279.

Akerstedt, T., & Froberg, J. (1976). Interindividual differences in circadian patterns of catecholamine excretion, body temperature, performance, and subjective arousal. *Biological Psychology, 4*, 277–292.

Al-Issa, I. Gender role. (1987). In L. Diamant (Ed.), *Male and female homosexuality: Psychological approaches*. Washington: Hemisphere.

Alcock, J. E., Carment, D. W., & Sadava, S. W. (1991). *A textbook of social psychology* (2nd ed.). Scarborough, Ont: Prentice-Hall Canada Inc.

Allain, H., Moran, P., Bentue-Ferrer, D., Martinet, J. P., & Lieury, A. (1989). Pharmacology of the memory process. *Archives of Gerontology and Geriatrics, Suppl. 1*, 109–120.

Alloy, L. B., & Abramson, L. Y. (1988). Depressive realism: Four theoretical perspectives. In L. B. Alloy (Ed.), *Cognitive processes in depression*. New York: Guilford Press.

Alloy, L. B., Lipman, A. J., & Abramson, L. Y. (1992). Attributional style as a vulnerability factor for depression: Validation by past history of mood disorders. *Cognitive Therapy and Research, 16(4)*, 391–407.

Allport, G. (1935). Attitudes. In G. Murchison (Ed.), *Handbook of social psychology*. Worcester, MA: Clark University Press.

Allport, G. W. (1937). *Personality: A psychological interpretation*. New York: Henry Holt.

Allport, G. W. (1960). *Personality and social encounter: Selected essays*. Boston: Beacon Press.

Allport, G. W. (1961). Pattern and growth in personality. New York: Holt, Rinehart and Winston.

Allport, G. W. (1966). Traits revisited. *American Psychologist, 21*, 1–10.

Allport, G. W. (1967). Autobiography. In E. G. Boring & G. Lindzey (Eds.), *A history of psychology in autobiography* (Vol. 5). New York: Appleton.

Allport, G. W. (1968). *The person in psychology: Selected essays*. Boston: Beacon Press.

Allport, G. W,, & Odbert, H. S. (1936). Trait names: A psycho-lexical study. *Psychological Monographs, 47*, 1–171. Ansbacher, H. L., & Ansbacher, R. R. (1956). *The individual psychology of Alfred Adler: A systematic presentation in selections from his writings*. New York: Viking.

Altura, B. M., Altura, B. T., Carella, A., Chatterjee, M., Halevy, S., & Tejani, N. (1982). Alcohol produces spasms of human umbilical blood vessels: Relationship to fetal alcohol syndrome (FAS). *European Journal of Pharmacology, 86*, 311–312.

Ambelas, A. (1987). Life events and mania: A special relationship? *British Journal of Psychiatry, 150*, 235–240.

American Psychiatric Association. (1993). *Diagnostic and statistical manual of the mental disorders* (4th ed.). Washington, DC: Author.

Amoore, J. E. (1977). Specific anosmia and the concept of primary odors. *Chemical Senses and Flavor, 2,* 267–281.

Andersen, A. E. (1985) *Practical comprehensive treatment of anorexia nervosa and bulimia.* Baltimore, MD: Johns Hopkins University Press.

Anderson, J. R. (1976). *Language, memory, and thought.* Hillsdale, NJ: Erlbaum.

Anderson, J. R. (1985). *Cognitive psychology and its implications.* San Francisco: Freeman.

Andreason, N. C. (1987). Creativity and mental illness: Prevalence rates in writers and their first-degree relatives. *American Journal of Psychiatry, 144,* 1288–1292.

Andreason, N. C., & Olsen, S. A. (1982). Negative versus positive schizophrenia: Definition and validation. *Archives of General Psychiatry, 39,* 789–794.

Angrist, B., Lee, H. K., & Gershon, S. (1974). The antagonism of amphetamine-induced symptomatology by a neuroleptic. *American Journal of Psychiatry, 131,* 817–819.

Annett, M., & Kilshaw, D. (1982). Mathematical ability and lateral asymmetry. *Cortex, 18,* 547–568.

Ansbacher, H. L., & Ansbacher, R. R. (1956). *The individual psyhology of Alfred Adler: A systematic presentation in selections from his writings.* New York: Viking.

Ansbacher, H. L., & Ansbacher, R. R. (Eds.). (1973). *Superiority and social interest: A collection of Alfred Adler's later writings.* New York: Viking.

Antrobus, J. (1987). Cortical hemisphere asymmetry and sleep mentation. *Psychological Review, 94(3),* 359–368.

Arafat, I. S., & Cotton, W. L. (1974). Masturbation practices of males and females. *Journal of Sex Research, 10,* 293–307.

Aranth, J., & Lindberg, C. (1992). Bleeding, a side effect of fluoxetine. *American Journal of Psychiatry, 149(3),* 412.

Ardila, R. (1982). International psychology. *American Psychologist, 37(3),* 323–329.

Ardila, R. (1987). Colombia. In A. R. Gilgen and C. K. Gilgen (Eds.), *International handbook of psychology.* New York: Greenwood Press.

Argyle, M., & Cook, M. (1976). *Gaze and mutual gaze.* London: Cambridge University Press.

Argyris, C., Putnam, R., & Smith, D. McL. (1985). *Action science: Concepts, methods and skills for research and intervention.* San Francisco: Jossey-Bass.

Arieti, S. (1974). *Interpretation of schizophrenia.* New York: Basic Books.

Armstrong, P., & McDaniel, E. (1986). Relationships between learning styles and performance on problem-solving tasks. *Psychological Reports, 59,* 1135–1138.

Arnheim, R. (1986). The two faces of Gestalt psychology. *American Psychologist, 41,* 820–824.

Arnold, M. B. (1960). *Emotion and personality.* New York: Columbia University Press.

Arnold, M. B. (1981). Reinventing the wheel. *Contemporary Psychology, 26,* 535–536.

Aronson, E. (1984). *The social animal* (4th ed.). New York: W. W. Freeman.

Aronson, E., & Bridgeman, D. (1979). Jigsaw groups and the desegregated classroom: In pursuit of common goals. *Personality and Social Psychology Bulletin, 5,* 438–446.

Aronson, E., & Gonzalez, A. (1988). Desegregation, jigsaw, and the Mexican-American experience. In P. A. Katz & D. Taylor (Eds.), *Towards the elimination of racism: Profiles in controversy.* New York: Plenum.

Aronson, E., & Mills, J. (1959). The effect of severity of initiation on liking for a group. *Journal of Abnormal and Social Psychology, 59,* 177–181.

Asch, S. E. (1946). Forming impressions of personality. *Journal of Abnormal and Social Psychology, 41,* 258–290.

Asch, S. E. (1951). Effects of group pressure upon the modification and distortion of judgments. In H. Guetzkow (Ed.), *Groups, leadership, and men.* Pittsburgh: Carnegie Press.

Asch, S. E. (1956). Studies of independence and conformity: A minority of one against a unanimous majority. *Psychological Monographs, 70,* (Whole no. 416).

Asch, S. E. (1987). *Social psychology.* Oxford, England: Oxford University Press.

Atchley, R. C. (1992). What do social theories of aging offer counselors? *The Counseling Psychologist, 20(2),* 336–340.

Atwood, G. E., & Tomkins, S. (1976). On the subjectivity of personality theory. *Journal of the History of the Behavioral Sciences, 12,* 166–177.

Atwood, J. D., & Gagnon, J. (1987). Masturbatory behavior in college youth. *Journal of Sex Education and Therapy, 13,* 35–42.

Auld, F. (1981). Psychotherapy. In *The encyclopedia of psychology.* Guilford, CT: DPG Reference Publishing Inc.

Averill, J. R. (1982). *Anger and aggression: An essay on emotion.* New York: Springer-Verlag.

Avery, D., Bolte, M. A., & Millet, M. (1992a). Bright dawn simulation compared with bright morning light in the treatment of winter depression. *Acta Psychiatra Scandinavia, 85,* 430–434.

Avery, D., Bolte, M. A. P., Cohen, S., & Millet, M. S. (1992b). Gradual versus rapid dawn simulation treatment of winter depression. *Journal of Clinical Psychiatry, 53(10),* 359–363.

Ayd, J. F., Jr. (1983). Early-onset neuroleptic-induced extrapyramidal reactions: A second survey, 1961–1981. In J. T. Coyle & S. J. Enna (Eds.), *Neuroleptics: Neurochemical, behavioral and clinical perspectives.* New York: Raven.

Ayres, T. J., & Hughes, P. (1986). Visual acuity with noise and music at 107 dbA. *Journal of Auditory Research, 26(1),* 65–74.

Azmitia, M. (1987). Why the whole is not the sum of its parts. *Contemporary Psychology, 32,* 469.

Azuma, H. (1984). Psychology in a non-Western country. *International Journal of Psychology, 19,* 45–55.

Baars, B. J. (1988). *A cognitive theory of consciousness*. Cambridge, England: Cambridge University Press.

Bachetti, P., & Moss, A. R. Incubation period of AIDS in San Francisco. *Nature, 338,* 251–253.

Baddeley, A. (1982). *Your memory: A user's guide*. New York: MacMillan.

Baddeley, A. (1992). Working memory: The interface between memory and cognition. *Journal of Cognitive Neuroscience, 4(3),* 281–288.

Bailey, S. L., Flewelling, R. L., & Rachal, J. V. (1992). Predicting continued use of marijuana among adolescents: The relative influence of drug-specific and social context factors. *Journal of Health and Social Behavior, 33,* 51–66.

Baillargeon, R. (1987). Object permanence in $3\frac{1}{2}$ and $4\frac{1}{2}$-month-old infants. *Developmental Psychology, 23,* 655–664.

Baird, L. L. (1990). A 24-year longitudinal study of the development of religious ideas. *Psychological Reports, 66,* 479–482.

Baker, M. J., & Churchill, G. A., Jr. (1977). The impact of physically attractive models on advertising evaluations. *Journal of Marketing Research, 4,* 538–555.

Baldwin, J. D., Whiteley, S., & Baldwin, J. I. (1992). The effect of ethnic group on sexual activities related to contraception and STDs. *The Journal of Sex Research, 29,* 189–205.

Balentine, M., Stitt, K., Bonner, J., & Clark, L. (1991). Self-reported eating disorders of Black, low-income adolescents: Behavior, body weight perceptions, and methods of dieting. *Journal of School Health, 61,* 392–396.

Bales, R. F. (1953). The equilibrium problem in small groups. In T. Parsons, R. F. Bales, and E. A. Shils (Eds.), *Working papers in the theory of action*. Glencoe, IL: Free Press.

Baltes, P. D. (1982). *Life-span development and behavior*. New York: Academic Press.

Bandura, A. (1977a). Self-efficacy: Toward a unifying theory of behavioral change. *Psychological Review, 84,* 191–215.

Bandura, A. (1977b). *Social learning theory*. Englewood Cliffs, NJ: Prentice-Hall.

Bandura, A. (1978). The self system in reciprocal determinism. *American Psychologist, 33,* 344–358.

Bandura, A. (1983). Self-efficacy determinants of anticipated fears and calamities. *Journal of Personality & Social Psychology, 45,* 464–468.

Bandura, A. (1984). Representing personal determinants in causal structures. *Psychological Review, 91,* 508–511.

Bandura, A. (1986a). The explanatory and predictive scope of self-efficacy theory. *Journal of Social and Clinical Psychology, 4,* 359–373.

Bandura, A. (1986b). *The social foundations of thought and action: A social cognitive theory*. Englewood Cliffs, NJ: Prentice-Hall.

Bandura, A., & Cervone, D. (1983). Self-evaluative and self-efficacy mechanisms governing the motivational effects of goal systems. *Journal of Personality and Social Psychology, 45,* 1017–1028.

Bandura, A., & O'Leary, A. (1987). Perceived self-efficacy and pain control: Opioid and nonopioid mechanisms. *Journal of Personality and Social Psychology, 53,* 563–571.

Bandura, A., Ross, D., & Ross, S. A. (1963). Vicarious reinforcement and imitative learning. *Journal of Abnormal and Social Psychology, 67,* 601–607.

Barber, B. L., & Eccles, J. S. (1992). Long-term influence of divorce and single parenting on adolescent family- and work-related values, behaviors, and aspirations. *Psychological Bulletin, 111,* 108–126.

Barber, T. X. (1969). *Hypnosis: A scientific approach*. New York: Van Nostrand Reinhold.

Barber, T. X. (1970). *LSD, marihuana, yoga and hypnosis*. Chicago: Aldine-Atherton.

Barber, T. X. (1978). Hypnosis, suggestions, and psychosomatic phenomena: A new look from the standpoint of recent experimental studies. *American Journal of Clinical Hypnosis, 21(1),* 13–27.

Barber T. X., Wilson, S. C., & Scott, D. S. (1980). Effects of a traditional trance induction on response to "hypnotist-centered" versus "subject-centered" test suggestions. *Journal of Clinical & Experimental Hypnosis, 28(2),* 114–125.

Bardack, N. R., & McAndrew, F. T. (1985). The influence of physical attractiveness and manner of dress on success in a simulated personnel decision. *Journal of Social Psychology, 125,* 777–778.

Bardin, C. W., & Catterall, J. F. (1981). Testosterone: A major determinant of extragenital sexual dimorphism. *Science, 211,* 1285–1293.

Barglow, P., Vaughn, B. E., & Molitor, N. (1987). Effects of maternal absence due to employment on the quality of infant-mother attachment in a low-risk sample. *Child Development, 58,* 945–954.

Barlett, D. L., & Steele, J. B. (1979). *Empire: The life, legend and madness of Howard Hughes*. New York: Norton.

Barlow, D. H., & Waddell, M. T. (1985). Agoraphobia. In D. H. Barlow (Ed.), *Clinical handbook of psychological disorders*. New York: Guilford Press.

Barlow, H. B., & Mollon, J. D. (Eds.). (1982). *The Senses: Cambridge texts in the physiological sciences*, (Vol. 3). Cambridge, England: Cambridge University Press.

Barnes, J. A., (1982). *Who should know what?: Social science, privacy and ethics*. Cambridge, England: Cambridge University Press.

Barr, C. E., Mednick, S. A., & Munk-Jorgenson, P. (1990). Maternal influenza and schizophrenic births. *Archives of General Psychiatry, 47,* 869–874.

Barr, L. C., Goodman, W. K., Price, L. H., McDougle, C. J., & Charney, D. S. The serontonin hypothesis of obsessive compulsive disorder: Implication of pharmacologic challenge studies. *The Journal of Clinical Psychiatry, 53(4-suppl),* 17–28.

Barrett, G. V., & Depinet, R. L. (1991). A reconsideration of testing for competence rather than for intelligence. *American Psychologist, 46(10),* 1012–1024.

Barrios, B. A., & Pennebaker, J. W. (1983). A note on the early detection of bulimia nervosa. *Behavior Therapist, 6(2),* 18–19.

Barry, K. (1986). *Female sexual slavery*. New York: Avon.

Bartley, S. H. (1980). *Introduction to perception*. New York: Harper & Row.

Barton, C. *Howard Hughes and his flying boat*. (1982). Blue Ridge Summit, PA: Tab Books.

Baruch, G. K., Biener, L., & Barnett, R. C. (1987). Women and gender in research on work and family stress. *American Psychologist, 42*, 130–136.

Baruss, I. (1987). Metanalysis of definitions of consciousness. *Imagination, Cognition and Personality, 6(7)*, 321–329.

Bassoff, E. S., & Glass, G. V. (1982). The relationship between sex roles and mental health: A meta-analysis of twenty-six studies. *Counseling Psychologist, 10*, 105–110.

Bateson, G. (1960). Minimal requirements for a theory of schizophrenia. *Archives of General Psychiatry, 2*, 477–491.

Bateson, G., Jackson, D. D., Haley, J., & Weakland, J. H. (1956). Toward a theory of schizophrenia. *Behavioral Science, 1*, 251–264.

Batson, C. D. (1990). How social an animal? The human capacity for caring. *American Psychologist, 45(3)*, 336–346.

Battaglia, D., & Cavallero, C. (1987). Temporal reference of the mnemonic source of dreams. *Perceptual and Motor Skills, 64(3)*, 979–983.

Baucom, D. H., Sayers, S. L., & Duhe, A. (1989). Attributional style and attributional patterns among married couples. *Journal of Personality and Social Psychology, 56(4)*, 596–607.

Baum, S. K., & Stewart, R. B. (1990). Sources of meaning through the lifespan. *Psychological Reports, 67*, 3–14.

Bauman, K. E., & Wilson, R. R. (1976). Premarital sexual attitudes of unmarried university students: 1968 vs. 1972. *Archives of Sexual Behavior, 5*, 29–37.

Baumrind, D. (1991). Parenting styles and adolescent development. In J. Brooks-Gunn, R. Lerner, & A. C. Petersen (Eds.), *The encyclopedia of adolescence*. New York: Garland.

Bayer, R., & Spitzer, R. L. (1985). Neurosis, psychodynamics, and DSM-III: A history of the controversy. *Archives of General Psychiatry, 42*, 187–196.

Beach, F. A., Hebb, D. O., Morgan, C. T., & Nissen, H. W. (1960). *The neuropsychology of Lashley*. New York: McGraw-Hill.

Beauchamp, G. K. (1987). The human preference for excess salt. *American Scientist, 75(1)*, 27–33.

Beck, A. T. (1972). *Depression: Causes and treatment*. Philadelphia: University of Pennsylvania Press.

Beck, A. T. (1976). *Cognitive therapy and the emotional disorders*. New York: International Universities Press.

Beck, A. T., Brown, G., Eidelson, J. I., Steer, R. A., & Riskind, J. H. (1987). Differentiating anxiety and depression: A test of the cognitive content-specificity hypothesis. *Journal of Abnormal Psychology, 96(3)*, 179–183.

Beck, A. T., & Burns, D. (1978). Cognitive therapy for depressed suicidal outpatients. In J. O. Cole, A. F. Schatzberg, & S. H. Frazier (Eds.), *Depression: Biology, psychodynamics, and treatment*. New York: Plenum.

Beck, A. T., & Emery, G. (1985). *Anxiety disorders and phobias: A cognitive perspective*. New York: Basic Books.

Beck, J., & Morgan, P. A. (1986). Designer drug confusion: A focus on MDMA. *Journal of Drug Education, 16(3)*, 287–302.

Becker, H. S. (1953). Becoming a marijuana user. *American Journal of Sociology, 59*, 235–242.

Beecher, H. K. (1959). *Measurement of subjective responses: Quantitative effects of drugs*. New York: Oxford University Press.

Belcastro. P. A. (1985). Sexual behavior differences between black and white students. *Journal of Sex Research, 21*, 56–67.

Belicki, K. (1992). Nightmare frequency versus nightmare distress: Relations to psychopathology and cognitive style. *Journal of Abnormal Psychology, 101(3)*, 592–597.

Bell, A. P., Weinberg, M. W., & Hammersmith, S. K. (1981). *Sexual preference*. Bloomington, IN: Indiana University Press.

Bell, C., & Kirkpatrick, S. W. (1986). Body image of anorexic, obese, and normal females. *Journal of Clinical Psychology, 42(3)*, 431–439.

Bell, M. D., & Ryan, E. R. (1985). Where can therapeutic community ideals be realized? An examination of three treatment environments. *Hospital and Community Psychiatry, 26*, 1286–1291.

Bellodi, L., Bussoleni, C., Scorza-Semeraldi, R., Grassi, G., Zacchetti, L., & Smeraldi, E. (1986). Family study of schizophrenia: Exploratory analysis for relevant factors. *Schizophrenia Bulletin, 12(1)*, 120–128.

Belsky, J. (1986). Infant day care: A cause for concern. *Zero to Three, 7(1)*, 1–7.

Belsky, J., & Steinberg, L. D. (1978). The effects of day care: A critical review. *Child Development, 49*, 929–949.

Bem, D. J. (1972). Self-perception theory. In L. Berkowitz (Ed.), *Advances in experimental social psychology*. Vol. 6. New York: Academic Press.

Bem, D. J. (1977). Predicting more of the people more of the time: Some thoughts on the Allen-Potkay studies of intraindividual variability. *Journal of Personality, 45*, 327–333.

Bem, D. J. (1982). Toward a response style theory of persons in situations. *Nebraska Symposium on Motivation*, 201–231.

Bem, D. J. (1983). Constructing a theory of the triple typology: Some (second) thoughts on nomothritic and idiographic approaches to personality. *Journal of Personality, 51*, 566–577.

Bem, D. J., & Allen, A. (1974). On predicting some of the people some of the time: The search for cross-situational consistencies in behavior. *Psychological Review*, 81, 506–520.

Bem, S. L. (1975). Sex role adaptability: One consequence of psychological androgyny. *Journal of Personality and Social Psychology, 31*, 634–643.

Bem, S. L. (1981). Gender schema theory: A cognitive account of sex typing. *Psychological Review, 88*, 354–364.

Bem, S. L. (1983). Gender schema theory and its implications for child development: Raising gender-aschematic children in a gender-schematic society. *Signs: Journal of Women in Culture and Society, 8*, 598–616.

Ben-Porath, Y. S., & Butcher, J. N. (1989). Psychometric stability of rewritten MMPI items. *Journal of Personality Assessment, 53*, 645–653.

Benbow, C. P. (1987). Possible biological correlates of precocious mathematical reasoning ability. *Trends in Neurosciences, 10(1)*, 17–20.

Benca, R. M., Obermeyer, W. H., Thisted, R. A., & Gillin, C. Sleep and psychiatric disorders: A meta-analysis. *Archives of General Psychiatry, 49*, 651–668.

Bengtson, V. L., Cuellar, J. B., & Ragan, P. K. (1977). Stratum contrasts and similarities in attitudes toward death. *Journal of Gerontology, 32*, 76–88.

Benjamin, L. T. (1986). Why don't they understand us? A history of psychology's public image. *American Psychology, 41*, 941–946.

Bennett, W., & Gurin, J. (1982). *The dieter's dilemma*. New York: Basic Books.

Benson, P. L., Karabenick, S. A., & Lerner, R. M. (1976). Pretty pleases: The effects of physical attractiveness, race, and sex on receiving help. *Journal of Experimental Social Psychology, 12*, 409–415.

Berch, D. B., & Bender, B. G. (1987). Margins of sexuality. *Psychology Today, 21(12)*, 54–57.

Berg, C. A. & Sternberg, R. J. (1985). A triarchic theory of intellectual development during adulthood. *Developmental Review, 5*, 334–370.

Berger, K. S. (1988). *The developing person through the life span*. New York: Worth Publishers.

Berger, M., Jurkovic, J., and associates. (1984). *Practicing family therapy in diverse settings: New approaches to the connections among families, therapists, and treatment settings*. San Francisco: Jossey-Bass.

Bergin, A. E. (1991). Values and religious issues in psychotherapy and mental health. *American Psychologist, 46*, 394–403.

Bergin, A. E., & Lambert, M. J. (1978). The evaluation of therapeutic outcomes. In S. L. Garfield & A. E. Bergin (Eds.), *Handbook of psychotherapy and behavior change* (2nd ed.). New York: Wiley.

Berglas, S., & Jones, E. E. (1978). Drug choice as a self-handicapping strategy in response to noncontingent success. *Journal of Personality and Social Psychology, 36*, 405–417.

Bergum, J. E., Bergum, B. O. (1980). Reliability of reversal rates as a measure of perceptual stability. *Perceptual & Motor Skills 50(3)*, 1038.

Berlin, F. S., & Meinecke, C. F. (1981). Treatment of sex offenders with antiandrogenic medication: Conceptualization, review of treatment modalities, and preliminary findings. *American Journal of Psychiatry, 138*, 601–607.

Berman, J. S. (1981). Will wise words fall on deaf ears? *Contemporary Psychology, 26*, 665–666.

Berne, E. (1958). Transactional analysis: A new and effective method of group therapy. *American Journal of Psychotherapy, 12*, 735–743.

Berne, E. (1964). *Games people play*. New York: Grove, 1964.

Berne, R. M., & Levy, M. N. (1990). *Principles of physiology*. St. Louis, MO: Mosby.

Bernsen, N. O. (1991). General introduction: A European perspective on cognitive science. In J. Rasmussen and H. B. Andersen (Eds.), *Human-computer interaction: Research direction in cognitive science European perspectives*, Vol. 3. Hillsdale, NJ: Lawrence Erlbaum Associates.

Bernstein, B. (1970). A sociolinguistic approach to socialization: With some reference to educability. In F. Williams (Ed.), *Language and poverty: Perspectives on a theme*. Chicago: Markham.

Berry, J. (1983). The sociogenesis of social sciences: An analysis of the cultural relativity of social psychology. In B. Bain (Ed.), *The sociogenesis of language and human conduct*. New York: Plenum.

Berry, J. (1984). Multicultural policy in Canada: A social psychological analysis. *Canadian Journal of Behavioural Science, 16*, 353–370.

Berry, J. W., & Bennett, J. A. (1992). Cree conceptions of cognitive competence. *International Journal of Psychology, 27(1)*, 73–88.

Berry, J., & Kim, U. (1988). Acculturation and mental health. In P. R. Dasen, J. W. Berry, & N. Sartorius (Eds.), *Health and cross-cultural psychology: Towards applications*. Newbury Park, CA: Sage.

Berry, J., Kim, U., Power, S., Young, M., & Bujaki, M. (1989). Acculturation attitudes in plural societies. *Applied Psychology: An International Review, 38*, 185–206.

Berry, J. W., Poortinga, Y. H., Segall, M. H., & Dasen, P. R. (1992). *Cross-cultural psychology: Research and applications*. Cambridge and New York: Cambridge University Press.

Berry, J., Trimble, J., & Olmedo, E. (1986). The assessment of acculturation. In W. Lonner & J. Berry (Eds.), *Field methods in cross-cultural research*. Beverly Hills, CA: Sage.

Bertelsen, A. (1979). A Danish twin study of manic-depressive disorders. In M. Schou & E. Strömgren (Eds.), *Origin, prevention, and treatment of affective disorders*. Orlando, FL: Academic Press.

Best, J. B. (1989). *Cognitive psychology* (2nd ed.). St. Paul, MN: West.

Best, J. B. (1992). *Cognitive psychology* (3rd ed.). St. Paul, MN: West.

Bexton, W. H., Heron, W., & Scott, T. H. (1954). Effects of decreased variation in the sensory environment. *Canadian Journal of Psychology, 8*, 70.

Biaggio, A. M. B. (1987). In A. R. Gilgen and C. K. Gilgen (Eds.), *International handbook of psychology*. New York: Greenwood Press.

Bickhard, M. H., & Richie, D. M. (1983). *On the nature of representation: A case study of James Gibson's theory of perception*. New York: Praeger.

Bierman, K. L., & Miller, C. L. (1987). Improving the social behavior and peer acceptance of rejected boys: Effects of social skill training with instructions and prohibitions. *Journal of Consulting and Clinical Psychology, 55(2)*, 194–200.

Biron, M., Risch, N., Hamburger, R., Mandel, B., Kushner, S., Newman, M., Drumer, D., & Belmaker, R. H. (1987). Genetic linkage between X-chromosome markers and bipolar affective illness. *Nature*, *326*, 289–292.

Birren, J. E., Butler, R. N., Greenhouse, S. W., Sokoloff, L., & Yarrow, M. R. (Eds.). (1963). *Human aging: A biological and behavioral study*. Publication No. (HSM) 71–9051. Washington, DC: U.S. Government Printing Office.

Bjorklund, D. F. (1989). *Children's thinking: Developmental function and individual differences*. Pacific Grove, CA: Brooks/Cole Publishing.

Björkqvist, K., Lagerspetz, K. M. J., & Kaukiainen, A. (1992). Do girls manipulate and boys fight? *Aggressive Behavior*, *18*, 117–127.

Björkqvist, K., & Niemelä, P. (Eds.). (1992). *Of mice and women: Aspects of female aggression*. New York: Academic Press.

Black, J. E., Sirevaag, A. M., Wallace, C. S., Savin, M. H., and Greenough, W. T. (1989). Effects of complex experience on somatic growth and organ development in rats. *Developmental Psychology*, *22*, 727–752.

Blackmore, S. (1985). The adventures of a psi-inhibitory experimenter. In P. Kurtz (Ed.), *A skeptic's handbook of parapsychology*. Buffalo, NY: Prometheus Books.

Blackmore, S. (1986). A critical guide to parapsychology. *Skeptical Inquirer*, *11(1)*, 97–102.

Blackmore, S. (1990). Consciousness: Science tackles the self. In M. Walraven & H. Fitzgerald (Eds.), *Psychology 90/91*. Guilford, CT: Dushkin.

Blair, S. N., Goodyear, N. N., Gibbons, L. W., & Cooper, K. H. (1984). Physical fitness and incidence of hypertension in healthy normotensive men and women. *Journal of the American Medical Association*, *252*, 487–490.

Blanchard, R., & Sheridan, P. M. (1992). Sibship size, sibling sex ratio, birth order, and parental age in homosexual and nonhomosexual gender dysphorics. *The Journal of Nervous and Mental Diseases*, *180*, 40–47.

Blanchard, J. J., & Neale, J. M. (1992). Medication effects: Conceptual and methodological issues in schizophrenia. *Clinical Psychology Review*, *12*, 345–361.

Blass, E. M., & Teicher, M. H. (1980). Suckling. *Science*, *210*, 15–20.

Blau, Z. S. (1981). *Black children/white children: Competence, socialization, and social structure*. New York: Free Press.

Blazer, D. G., Hughes, D., George, L. K., Swartz, M., & Boyer, R. (1991). Generalized anxiety disorder. In L. N. Robins & D. A. Regier (Eds.), *Psychiatric disorders in America: The epidemiologic catchment area study*. New York: Free Press.

Blechman, E. A., McEnroe, M. J., Carella, E. T., & Audette, D. P. (1986). Childhood competence and depression. *Journal of Abnormal Psychology*, *95(3)*, 223–227.

Bleier, S. N., Houston, L., & Byne, W. (1986). Can the corpus callosum predict gender, age, handedness, or cognitive differences? *Trends-in-Neurosciences*, *9(9)*, 391–394.

Bloch, G. (1980). *Mersmerism: A translation of the original scientific and medical writings of F.A. Mesmer*. Los Altos, CA: William Kaufman.

Block, J. (1982). Assimilation, accommodation, and the dynamics of personality development. *Child Development*, *53*, 281–295.

Bloom, A. H. (1986). Psychological ingredients of high-level moral thinking: A critique of the Kohlberg-Gilligan paradigm. *Journal for the Theory of Social Behaviour*, *16(1)*, 89–103.

Bloom, B. S. (1982). *Human Characteristics & School Learning*. New York: McGraw-Hill.

Bloom, B. S. (Ed.). (1985). *Developing talent in young people*. New York: Ballantine.

Bloom, F. E., & Lazerson, A. (1988). *Brain, mind, and behavior*. New York: Freeman.

Blotcky, M. J., & Dimperio, T. L. (1987). A systems model for residential treatment of children. *Residential Treatment for Children and Youth*, *5(1)*, 55–66.

Blowers, G. H. (1991). Assessing the impact of Western Psychology in Hong Kong. *International Journal of Psychology*, *26(2)*, 254–268.

Blumberg, H. H., Hare, A. P., Kent, V., & Davies, M. F. (Eds.). (1983). *Small groups and social interaction*, Vol. 1. Chichester, England: Wiley.

Blumer, D. (1970). Hypersexual episodes in temporal lobe epilepsy. *American Journal of Psychiatry*, *126*, 1099–1106.

Boas, G. (1990). *The cult of childhood*. Dallas, TX: Spring Publications.

Bock, R. D., & Moore, E. G. J. (1986). *Advantage and disadvantage: A profile of American youth*. Hillsdale, NJ: Erlbaum.

Boden, M. A. (1979). *Jean Piaget*. New York: Viking Press.

Boles, D. B. (1989). Do visual asymmetries intercorrelate? *Neuropsychologia*, *27(5)*, 697–704.

Bolles, R. C. (1975). *Theory of motivation*. New York: Harper & Row.

Bolles, R. C. (1978). What happened to motivation? *Educational Psychologist*, *13*, 1–13.

Bolles, R. C. (1979). *Learning theory*. New York: Holt, Rinehart and Winston.

Bond, M. H. (1988). Finding universal dimensions of individual variation in multicultural studies of values: The Rokeach and Chinese values surveys. *Journal of Personality and Social Psychology*, *55*, 1009–1015.

Booth-Kewley, S., & Friedman, H. S. (1987). Psychological predictors of heart disease: A quantitative review. *Psychological Bulletin*, *101*, 343–362.

Boring, E. G. (1950). *A history of experimental psychology*. New York: Appleton-Century-Crofts.

Bostwick, T. D., & DeLucia, J. L. (1992). Effects of gender and specific dating behaviors on perceptions of sex willingness and date rape. *Journal of Social and Clinical Psychology*, *11*, 14–25.

Botstein, D. (1986). The molecular biology of color vision. *Science*, *232*, 142–143.

Bouchard, C., Tremblay, A., Despres, J. P., Nadeau, A., Lupien, P. J., Theriault, G., Dussault, J., Moorjani, S., Pinault, S., & Fournier, G. (1990). The response to long-term overfeeding in identical twins. *The New England Journal of Medicine, 322,* 1477–1482.

Bouchard, T. J. (1983). Do environmental similarities explain the similarity in intelligence of identical twins reared apart? *Intelligence, 7,* 175–184.

Boudewyns, P. A., Fry, T. J., & Nightingale, E. J. (1986). Token economy programs in VA medical centers: Where are they today? *Behavior Therapist, 9(6),* 126–127.

Bourdon, K. H., Rae, D. S., Locke, B. Z., Narrow, W. E., & Regier, D. A. (1992). Estimating the prevalence of mental disorders in U.S. adults from the epidemiologic catchment area survey. *Public Health Reports, 107(6),* 663–668.

Bourne, L. E., Young, S. R., & Angell, L. S. (1986). Resource allocation in reading: An interactive approach. *Zeitschrift fur Psychologie, 194(2),* 155–176.

Bower, B. (1985). Taking food from thought: Fruitful entry to the brain's word index. *Science News, 128,* 85.

Bower, B. (1986a). Recurrent dreams: Clues to conflict. *Science News, 129,* 197.

Bower, B. (1986b). Babies sound off: The power of babble. *Science News, 129,* 390.

Bower, B. (1986c). Steady cocaine use linked to seizures. *Science News, 130,* 214.

Bower, B. (1986d). Winter depression: Rise and shine? *Science News, 130,* 390.

Bowers, K. S. (1989). Unconscious influences and hypnosis, In J. E. Singer (Ed.), *Repression: Defense mechanisms and personality style.* Chicago: University of Chicago Press.

Bowers, T., & Clum, G. (1988). Relative contributions of specific and nonspecific treatment effects: Meta-analysis of placebo-controlled behavior therapy research. *Psychological Bulletin, 103,* 315–323.

Bowlby, J. (1973). *Attachment and loss: Separation,* (Vol. 2). New York: Basic Books.

Bowlby, J. (1989). *Secure attachment.* New York: Basic Books.

Boxer, A. M., & Petersen, A. C. (1986). Pubertal change in a family context. In G. K. Leigh & G. W. Petersen, (Eds.), *Adolescents in families.* Cincinnati: South-Western Publishing Company.

Boynton, R. (1980). Vision. In D. McFadden (Ed.), *Neural mechanisms in behavior.* New York: Springer-Verlag.

Bracey, D. (1983). The juvenile prostitute: Victim *and* offender. *Victimology, 8,* 151.

Bradbury, T. N., & Fincham, F. D. (1990). Attributions in marriage: Review and critique. *Psychological Bulletin, 107(1),* 3–33.

Bradley, S. S. (1987). Family therapy within a psychodynamic treatment milieu. *Psychiatric Clinics of North America, 10(2),* 289–308.

Braginsky, D. D., & Braginsky, B. J. (1971). *Hansels and Gretels: Study of children in institutions for the mentally retarded.* New York: Holt, Rinehart and Winston.

Brammer, L. M., Shostrom, E. L., & Abrego, P. J. (1989). *Therapeutic psychology: Fundamentals of counseling and psychotherapy,* 5th ed. Englewood Cliffs, NJ: Prentice Hall.

Bransford, J., Sherwood, R., Vye, N., & Rieser, J. (1986). Teaching thinking and problem solving. *American Psychologist, 41(10),* 1078–1089.

Brazelton, T. B. (1986). Issues for working parents. *American Journal of Orthopsychiatry, 56(1),* 14–25.

Brazelton, T. B. (1987). "On infant day care" Dr. Brazelton replies. *American Journal of Orthopsychiatry, 57(1),* 140–141.

Brazelton, T. B., & Als, H. (1979). Four early stages in the development of mother-infant interaction. *Psychoanalytic Study of the Child, 34,* 349–369.

Brecher, E. M. (1984). *Love, sex, and aging: A Consumer's Union report.* Boston: Little, Brown.

Bredehoft, D. J. (1986). An evaluation of self-esteem: A family affair. *Transactional Analysis Journal, 16,* 175–181.

Breggin, P. R. (1979). *Electroshock: Its brain-disabling effects.* New York: Springer.

Breggin, P. R. (1983). *Psychiatric drugs: Hazards in the brain.* New York: Springfield.

Brehm, J. W., & Mann, M. (1975). Effect of importance of freedom and attraction to group members on influence produced by group pressure. *Journal of Personality and Social Psychology, 31,* 816–824.

Breland, K., & Breland, M. (1961). The misbehavior of organisms. *American Psychologist, 16,* 661–664.

Bremmer, J. D., Southwick, S., Brett, E., Fontana, A., Rosenheck, R., & Charney, D. S. (1992). Dissociation and posttraumatic stress disorder in Vietnam combat veterans. *American Journal of Psychiatry, 149(3),* 328–332.

Brendler, J. (1987). A perspective on the brief hospitalization of whole families. *Journal of Family Therapy, 9(2),* 113–130.

Brennan, J. F. (1991). *History and systems of psychology,* 3rd ed. Englewood Cliffs, NJ: Prentice-Hall.

Breslau, N., & Davis, G. C. (1987). Posttraumatic stress disorder: The stressor criterion. *Journal of Nervous and Mental Disease, 175(5),* 255–264.

Bridgeman, B., & Fisher, B. (1990). Saccadic suppression of displacement is strongest in central vision. *Perception, 19,* 103–111.

Briggs, S. R. (1987). Hawking a good theory. *Contemporary Psychology, 32,* 854–865.

Briggs, S. R. (1992). Assessing the five-factor model of personality description. *Journal of Personality, 60(2),* 253–293.

Brislin, R. (1993). *Understanding culture's influence on behavior.* Fort Worth, TX: Harcourt Brace Jovanovich.

Brislin, R. W., Cushner, K., Cherrie, K., & Yong, M. (1986). *Intercultural interactions: A practical guide.* Newbury Park, CA: Sage.

Brockway, S. S. (1987). Group treatment of combat nightmares in post-traumatic stress disorder. *Journal of Contemporary Psychotherapy, 17(4),* 270–284.

Brody, N. (1990). Behavior therapy versus placebo: Comment on Bowers and Clum's meta-analysis. *Psychological Bulletin, 107(1),* 106–109.

Brone, R. J., & Fisher, C. B. (1988). Determinants of adolescent obesity: A comparison with anorexia nervosa. *Adolescence, 23(89),* 155–169.

Bronfenbrenner, U., Kessel, F., Kessen, W., & White, S. (1986). Toward a critical social history of developmental psychology: A propaedeutic discussion. *American Psychologist, 41,* 1218–1230.

Brooks, C. I., Church, M. A., & Fraser, L. (1986). Effects of duration of eye contact on judgments of personality characteristics. *Journal of Social Psychology, 126(1),* 71–78.

Brooks-Gunn, J., & Ruble, D. N. (1983). The development of menstrual-related beliefs and behaviors during early adolescence. *Child Development, 53,* 1567–1577.

Brooks-Gunn, J., & Ruble, D. N. (1984). The experience of menarche from a developmental perspective. In J. Brooks-Gunn & A. C. Petersen (Eds.), *Girls at puberty: Biological, psychological, and social perspectives.* New York: Plenum.

Brown, A. S. (1991). A review of the tip-of-the-tongue experience. *Psychological Bulletin, 109(2),* 204–223.

Brown, C. T., & Keller, P. W. (1979). *Monologue to dialogue.* Englewood Cliffs, NJ: Prentice-Hall.

Brown, H. P., Peterson, J. H., & Cunningham, O. (1988). A behavioral/cognitive spiritual model for a chemical dependency aftercare program. *Alcohol Treatment Quarterly, 5(1–2),* 153–175.

Brown, J. A. (1958). Some tests of the decay theory of immediate memory. *Quarterly Journal of Experimental Psychology, 10,* 12–21.

Brown, L., & Ballou, M. (Eds.). (1992). *Personality and psychopathology: Feminist reappraisals.* New York: Guilford Press.

Brown, P., & Funk, S. C. (1986). Tardive dyskinesia: Barriers to the professional recognition of an iatrogenic disease. *Journal of Health and Social Behavior, 27(2),* 116–132.

Brown, R. (1986). *Social psychology* (2nd ed.). New York: Free Press.

Brown, R., & McNeill, D. (1966). The "tip of the tongue" phenomenon. *Journal of Verbal Learning and Verbal Behavior, 5,* 325–337.

Brown, T. S., & Wallace, P. M. (1980). *Physiological psychology.* New York: Academic Press.

Brownell, H. H., Michel, D., Powelson, J., & Gardner, H. (1983). Surprise but not coherence: Sensitivity to verbal humor in right-hemisphere patients. *Brain and Language, 18,* 20–27.

Brownell, K. (1989, June). When and how to diet. *Psychology Today,* pp. 40–46.

Bruch, H. (1973). *Eating disorders.* New York: Basic Books.

Bruch, H. (1978). *The golden cage.* Cambridge, MA: Harvard University Press.

Bruner, J. (1984). Interaction, communication, and self. *Journal of the American Academy of Child Psychiatry, 23(1),* 1–7.

Buchanan, C. M., Eccles, J. S., & Becker, J. B. (1992). Are adolescents the victims of raging hormones: Evidence for activational effects of hormones on moods and behavior at adolescence. *Psychological Bulletin, 111(1),* 62–107.

Buchner, D. M., Beresford, S. A. A., Larson, E. B., LaCroix, A. Z., & Wagner, E. H. (1992). Effects of physical activity on health status in older adults II: Intervention studies. *Annual Review of Public Health, 13,* 469–488.

Buchsbaum, M. S., & Haier, R. J. (1987). Functional and anatomical brain imaging: Impact on schizophrenia research. *Schizophrenia Bulletin, 13(1),* 115–132.

Budman, S. H. (1987). Discussion of "peer relationships, self-esteem, and the self,": Implications for the group therapist. *International Journal of Group Psychotherapy, 37(4),* 515–518.

Buell, S. J., & Coleman, P. D. (1981). Quantitative evidence for selective growth in normal human aging but not in senile dementia. *Brain Research, 214,* 23–41.

Buhler, C. (1968). The developmental structure of goal setting in group and individual studies. In C. Buhler & F. Massarik (Eds.), *The course of human life.* New York: Springer.

Bulik, C. M., Beidel, D. C., Duchmann, E., Weltzin, T. E., & Kaye, W. H. (1992). Comparative psychopathology of women with bulimia nervosa and obsessive-compulsive disorder. *Comprehensive Psychiatry, 33(4),* 262–268.

Burns, G. L., & Farina, A. (1987). Physical attractiveness and self-perception of mental disorder. *Journal of Abnormal Psychology, 96(2),* 161–163.

Burstein, A. (1992). Fluoxetine-lithium treatment for kleptomania. *Journal of Clinical Psychiatry, 53(1),* 28–29.

Burt, C. (1962). The concept of consciousness. *British Journal of Psychology, 53,* 229–242.

Buss, A. H. (1989). Personality as traits. *American Psychologist, 44(11),* 1378–1388.

Buss, A. H. (1990). Toward a biologically informed psychology of personality. *Journal of Personality, 58(1),* 1–16.

Buss, D. M., Abbott, M., Angleitner, A., Asherian, A., Biaggio, A., Blanco-Villasenor, A., Bruchon-Schweitzer, M., Hai-Yuan Ch'U, Czapinski, J., Deraad, B., Ekehammar, B., Lohamy, N. E., Fioravanti, M., Georgas, J., Gjerde, P., Guttman, R., Hazan, F., Iwawaki, S., Janakiramaiah, N., Khosroshani, F., Kreitler, S., Lachenicht, L., Lee, M., Liik, K., Little, B., Mika, S., Moadel-Shahid, M., Moane, G., Montero, M., Mundy-Castle, A. C., Niit, T., Nsenduluka, E., Pienkowski, R., Pirttila-Backman, A., Ponce De Leon, J., Rousseau, J., Runco, M. A., Safir, M. P., Samuels, C., Sanitioso, R., Serpell, R., Smid, N., Spencer, C., Tadinac, M., Todorova, E. N., Troland, K., Van Den Brande, L., Van Heck, G., Van Langenhove, L., & Yang, K. (1990). International preferences in selecting mates: A study of 37 cultures. *Journal of Cross-Cultural Psychology, 21(1),* 5–47.

Bussey, K., & Bandura, A. (1984). Influence of gender constancy and social power on sex-linked modeling. *Journal of Personality and Social Psychology, 47,* 1292–1302.

Butcher, J. N. (1989). *User's guide for the MMPI-2 Minnesota Report: Adult Clinical System.* Minneapolis: National Computer Systems.

Butcher, J. N., Dahlstrom, W. G., Graham, J. R., Tellegen, A., & Kraemmer, B. (1989). *Minnesota Multiphasic Personality Inventory-2 (MMPI-2): Manual for administration and scoring.* Minneapolis: University of Minnesota Press.

Butcher, J. N., Graham, J. R., Williams, C. L., & Ben-Porath, Y. S. (1990). *Development and use of the MMPI-2 Content Scales*. Minneapolis: University of Minnesota Press.

Butcher, J. N., & Pope, K. S. (1992). The research base, psychometric properties, and clinical uses of the MMPI-2 and MMPI-A. *Canadian Journal of Psychology, 33(1)*, 61–78.

Butler, R. (1974). Successful aging and the role of life review. *Journal of the American Geriatrics Society, 22*, 529–535.

Butler, R. W., Braff, D. L., Rausch, J. L., Jenkins, M. A., Sprock, J., & Geyer, M. A. (1990). Physiological evidence of exaggerated startle response in a subgroup of Vietnam veterans with combat-related PTSD. *American Journal of Psychiatry, 147(10)*, 1308–1312.

Butterfield, F. (1990, January). Why they excel. *Parade*, pp. 4–5.

Butters, R. R. (1989). *The death of Black English: Divergence and convergence in black and white vernaculars*. New York: Peter Long.

Butterword, G. (1983). Structure of the mind in human infancy. *Advances in Infancy Research, 2*, 1–29.

Buunk, A. P., & Janssen, P. (1987). Social support at home and psychosocial stress at work. *Gedrag and Gezondheid Tijdschrift voor Psychologie and Gezondheid, 15(4)*, 147–154.

Buzzanga, V. L., Miller, H. R., Perne, S. E., Sander, J. A., & Davis, S. F. (1989). The relationship between death anxiety and level of self-esteem: A reassessment. *Bulletin of the Psychonomic Society, 27*, 570–572.

Byer, C. O., & Shainberg, L. W. (1991). *Dimensions of human sexuality* (3rd ed.). Dubuque, IA: Wm. C. Brown.

Byerley, W. F., Risch, S. C., Gillin, J. C., Janowsky, D. S., Parker, D., Rossman, L. G., & Kripke, D. F. (1989). Biological effect of bright light. *Progress in Neuro Psychopharmacology and Biological Psychiatry, 13(5)*, 683–686.

Byrne, D., Ervin, C. R., & Lamberth, J. (1970). Continuity between the experimental study of attraction and real-life computer dating. *Journal of Personality and Social Psychology, 16*, 157–165.

Cacioppo, J. T., Uchino, B. N., Crites, S. L., Snydersmith, M. A., Smith, G., & Berntson, G. G. (1992). Relationship between facial expressiveness and sympathetic activation in emotion: A critical review, with emphasis on modeling underlying mechanisms and individual differences. *Journal of Personality and Social Psychology, 62*, 110–128.

Cadoret, R. J., O'Gorman, T. W., Troughton, E., & Heywood, E. (1985). Alcoholism and antisocial personality: Interrelationships and environmental factors. *Archives of General Psychiatry, 42*, 161–167.

Cafferty, P., & Chestang, L. (Eds.). (1976). *The diverse society: Implications for social policy*. Washington, DC: National Association of Social Workers.

Cain, W. S. (1982). Odor identification by males and females: Predictions vs. performance. *Chemical Senses, 7*, 129–142.

Callahan, P. M., & Appel, J. B. (1988). Differences in the stimulus properties of 3,4-methylenedioxyamphetamine and 3,4-methelenedioxymethamphetamine in animals trained to discriminate hallucinogens from saline. *Journal of Pharmacology and Experimental Therapeutics, 246(3)*, 866–870.

Camel, J. E., Withers, G. S., & Greenough, W. T. (1986). Persistence of visual cortex dendritic alterations induced by postweaning exposure to a "superenriched" environment in rats. *Behavioral Neuroscience, 100*, 810–813.

Cameron, D. E. (1967). Magnesium pemoline and human performance. *Science, 157*, 958–959.

Caminada, H., & De Bruijn, F. (1992). Diurnal variation, morningness-eveningness, and momentary affect. *European Journal of Personality, 6*, 43–69.

Cannon, W. B. (1927). The James-Lange theory of emotions: A critical examination and an alternative. *American Journal of Psychology, 39*, 106–124.

Cannon, W. B. (1929). *Bodily changes in pain, hunger, fear and rage* (2nd ed.). New York: Appleton.

Canon, W. B. (1939). *The wisdom of the body*. New York: Norton.

Cantor, N. (1990). From thought to behavior: "Having" and "doing" in the study of personality and cognition. *American Psychologist, 45(6)*, 735–750.

Cantor, N., & Genero, N. (1986). Psychiatric diagnosis and natural categorization: A close analogy. In T. Millon & G. Klerman (Eds.), *Contemporary issues in psychopathology: Toward the DSM-IV*. New York: Guilford Press.

Caplan, A. L. (Ed.). (1978). *The sociobiology debate: Readings and ethical and scientific issues*. New York: Harper & Row.

Caplan, L. R., & Ahmed, I. (1992). Depression and neurological disease. *General Hospital Psychiatry, 14*, 177–185.

Caplan, P. U. (1985). *The myth of women's masochism*. New York: Dutton.

Caplan, R. D., Andrews, F. M., Conway, T. L., Abbey, A., Abramis, D. J., & French, R. P., Jr. (1985). Social effects of diazepam use: A longitudinal field study. *Social Science and Medicine, 21(8)*, 887–898.

Carballo, M., Cleland, J., Carael, M., & Albrecht, G. (1989). A cross-national study of patterns of sexual behavior. *Journal of Sex Research, 26*, 287–299.

Carey, S. (1978). The child as word learner. In M. Halle, J. Bresnan, & G. A. Miller (Eds.), *Linguistic theory and psychological reality*. Cambridge, MA: MIT Press.

Carlin, A. S., Bakker, C. B., Halpern, L., & Post, R. D. (1972). Social facilitation of marihuana intoxication: Impact of social set and pharmacological activity. *Journal of Abnormal Psychology, 80*, 132–140.

Carlson, C. R., & White, D. K. (1982). Night terrors: A clinical and empirical review. *Clinical Psychology Review, 2*, 455–468.

Carlson, J. C., & Forbes, W. F. (1992). The free radical theory of aging: A critique and unresolved questions. *Canadian Journal on Aging, 11(3)*, 262–268.

Carlson, J. G., & Hatfield, E. (1992). *Psychology of emotion*. Fort Worth, TX: Harcourt Brace Jovanovich.

Carlson, N. R. (1988). *Foundations of physiological psychology*. Boston: Allyn and Bacon, Inc.

Carlson, N. R. (1991). *Physiology of behavior* (4th ed.). Boston: Allyn & Bacon.

Carlson, R. (1980). Studies of Jungian typology: II. Representations of the personal world. *Journal of Personality and Social Psychology, 38,* 801–810.

Carnevale, J. P. (1989). *Counseling gems: Thoughts for the practitioner.* Muncie, IN: Accelerated Development Inc.

Caron, S. L., Davis, C. M., Wynn, R. L., & Roberts, L. W. (1992). "America responds to AIDS," but did college students? Differences between March, 1987, and September, 1988. *AIDS Education and Prevention, 4,* 18–28.

Carreiras, M., & Codina, B. (1992). Spatial cognition of the blind and sighted: Visual and amodal hypotheses. *European Bulletin of Cognitive Psychology, 12(1),* 51–78.

Carroll, W. R., & Bandura, A. (1985). Role of timing of visual monitoring and motor rehearsal in obser-vational learning of action patterns. *Journal of Motor Behavior, 17,* 269–281.

Carson, R. C. (1989). Personality. *Annual Review of Psychology, 40,* 227–248.

Carson, R. C. (1991). Dilemmas in the pathway of the DSM-IV. *Journal of Abnormal Psychology, 100(3),* 302–307.

Carson, R. C., Butcher, J. N., & Coleman, J. C. (1988). *Abnormal psychology and modern life,* (8th ed.). Glenview, IL: Scott, Foresman and Company.

Caspi, A., Elder, G. H., & Bem, D. J. (1987). Moving against the world: Life-course patterns of explosive children. *Developmental Psychology, 23,* 308–313.

Castle, D. J., & Murray, R. M. (in press). Aetiology and genetics. In J. R. M. Copeland, M. T. Abou-Saleh, & D. G. Blazer (Eds.), *The psychiatry of old age: An international textbook.* Chichester, England: John Wiley & Sons.

Catania, A. C. (1984). *Learning,* 2nd ed. Englewood Cliffs, NJ: Prentice-Hall.

Cattell, R. B. (1950). *Personality: A systematic theoretical and factual study.* New York: McGraw-Hill.

Cattell, R. B. (1957). *Personality and motivation structure and measurement.* Yonkers-on-Hudson, NY: World Book.

Cattell, R. B. (1965). *The scientific analysis of personality.* Baltimore: Penguin Books.

Cattell, R. B. (1971). *Abilities: Their structure, growth, and action.* Boston: Houghton Mifflin.

Cattell, R. B. (1982). *The inheritance of personality and ability: Research methods and findings.* New York: Academic Press.

Centers for Disease Control and Prevention. (1989) *Morbidity and Mortality Weekly Report, 38,* S-4.

Centers for Disease Control and Prevention. (1993). *HIV/AIDS surveillance: U.S. AIDS cases reported through December 1992.*

Cermak, L. (1978). *Improving your memory.* New York: McGraw-Hill.

Chaiken, S. (1979). Communicator physical attractiveness and persuasion. *Journal of Personality and Social Psychology, 37(8),* 1387–1397.

Chaiken, S. (1987). The heuristic model of persuasion. In M. P. Zanna, J. M. Olson, & C. P. Herman (Eds.), *Social Influence: The Ontario symposium* (Vol. 5). Hillsdale, NJ: Erlbaum.

Chamber, M. J., & Alexander, S. (1991). Insomnia treatment outcome: Factor analysis of a follow-up questionnaire. *Sleep Research, 20,* 223.

Chambers, M. J. (1992). Therapeutic issues in the behavioral treatment of insomnia. *Professional Psychology: Research and Practice, 23,* 131–138.

Chan, C. H., Janicak, P. G., Davis, J. M., Altman, E., Andriukaitis, S., & Hedeker, D. (1987). Response of psychotic and nonpsychotic depressed patients to tricyclic antidepressants. *Journal of Clinical Psychiatry, 48(5),* 197–200.

Chance, P. (1984). Food madness. *Psychology Today, 18(6),* 14.

Chance, P. (1989, February). Kids without friends. *Psychology Today,* 28–31.

Chapouthier, G. (1989). The search for a biochemistry of memory. *Archives of Gerontology and Geriatrics, Suppl. 1,* 7–19.

Chase, M., & Weitzman, E. D. (Eds.). (1983). *Sleep disorders: Basic and clinical research. Advances in sleep research,* (Vol. 8). New York: SP Medical & Scientific Books.

Cheek, J. M., & Melchoir, L. A. (1990). Shyness, self-esteem, and self-consciousness. In H. Leitenberg (Ed.). *Handbook of social and evaluation anxiety.* New York: Plenum.

Chi, M. T. H. (1978). Knowledge structure and memory development. In R. Siegler (Ed.), *Children's thinking: What develops?* Hillsdale, NJ: Lawrence Erlbaum.

Chick, D., & Gold, S. R. (1987–88). A review of influences on sexual fantasy: Attitudes, experience, guilt, and gender. *Imagination, Cognition and Personality, 7,* 61–76.

Child, I. L. (1985). Psychology and anomalous observations: the question of ESP in dreams. *American Psychologist, 40,* 1219–1239.

Chilman, C. S. (1983). *Adolescent sexuality in a changing American society,* 2nd ed. New York: Wiley.

Chisholm, J. S. (1983). *Navajo infancy: An ethological study of child development.* New York: Aldine.

Chollar, S. (1989). Conversations with the dolphins. *Psychology Today,* pp. 52–57.

Chomsky, N. (1986). *Knowledge of language: Its nature, origin, and use.* New York: Praeger.

Chowdhury, A. N. (1989). Penile perception of koro patients. *Acta Psychiatrica Scandinavica, 80(2),* 183–186.

Church, A. T., & Katigbak, M. S. (1988). Imposed-etic and emic measures of intelligence as predictors of early school performance of rural Philippine children. *Journal of Cross-Cultural Psychology, 19(2),* 164–177.

Church, A. T., & Katigbak, M. S. (1989). Internal, external, and self-report structure of personality in a non-Western culture: An investigation of cross-language and cross-cultural generalizability. *Journal of Personality and Social Psychology, 57(5),* 857–872.

Church, A. T., & Katigbak, M. S. (1992). The cultural context of academic motives: A comparison of Filipino and American college students. *Journal of Cross-Cultural Psychology, 23(1),* 40–58.

Cialdini, R. B. (1985). *Influence: Science and practice*. Glenview, IL: Scott, Foresman.

Clark, J. (1985). *The cell*. New York: Torstar Books.

Clarke, A. D., & Clarke, A. M. (1982). "Sleeper effects" in development: Fact or artifact? *Annual Progress in Child Psychiatry and Child Development*, 94–112.

Clausen, J. A. (1975). The social meaning of differential physical and sexual maturation. In S. E. Dragastin & G. H. Elder, Jr. (Eds.), *Adolescence in the life cycle: Psychological change and social context*. New York: Wiley.

Clayton, V. (1982). Wisdom and intelligence: The nature and function of knowledge in the later years. *International Journal of Aging and Human Development*, *15*, 315–321.

Clayton, V., & Birren, J. E. (1980). The development of wisdom across the life span: A reexamination of an ancient logic. In P. B. Baltes & O. G. Brim (Eds.), *Life-span development and behavior* (Vol. 3). New York: Academic Press.

Climko, R. P., Roehrich, H., Sweeney, D. R., & Al-Razi, J. (1986–7). Ecstasy: A review of MDMA and MDA. *International Journal of Psychiatry in Medicine*, *16(4)*, 359–372.

Cloninger, C. R., & Gilligan, S. B. (1987). Neurogenetic mechanisms of learning: A phylogenetic perspective. *Journal of Psychiatric Research*, *21(4)*, 457–472.

Clum, G. A., & Bowers, T. G. (1990). Behavior therapy better than placebo treatments: Fact or artifact? *Psychological Bulletin*, *107(1)*, 110–113.

Cohen, A. S., Rosen, R. C., & Goldstein, L. (1985). EEG hemispheric asymmetry during sexual arousal: Psychophysiological patterns in responsive, unresponsive, and dysfunctional men. *Journal of Abnormal Psychology*, *94*, 580–590.

Cohen, L. H., Sargent, M. D., & Sechrest, L. B. (1986). Use of psychotherapy research by professional psychologist. *American Psychologist*, *41*, 198–206.

Cohen, N. J., & Squire, L. R. (1980). Preserved learning and retention of pattern-analyzing skill in amnesia: Dissociation of knowing how and knowing that. *Science*, *210*, 207–210.

Cohen, P. T., Sande, M. A., & Volberding, P. A. (Eds.). (1990). *The AIDS knowledge base*. Waltham, MA: The Medical Publishing Group.

Cohler, B. J. (1987). Competence and the chronic psychiatric patient. *Contemporary Psychology*, *32*, 459–460.

Cole, M. (1984). The world beyond our borders: What might students need to know about it? *American Psychologist*, *39(9)*, 998–1005.

Coleman, R. M. (1986). *Wide awake at 3:00 a.m.: By choice or by chance?* New York: W. H. Freeman.

Coleman, S. B. (Ed.). (1985). *Failures in family therapy*. New York: Guilford Press.

Colligan, R. C. (1983). *The MMPI: A contemporary normative study*. New York: Praeger.

Collison, C. R., & Miller, S. L. (1985). The role of family re-enactment in group psychotherapy. *Perspectives in Psychiatric Care*, *23*, 74–78.

Conners, G. J., & Sobell, M. B. (1986). Alcohol and drinking environment: Effects on affect and sensations, person perception, and perceived intoxication. *Cognitive Therapy and Research*, *10*, 389–402.

Conway, J. B. (1992). Presidential address: "A world of differences among psychologists." *Canadian Psychology*, *33*, 1–24.

Cook, E. P. (1985). *Psychological androgeny*. New York: Pergamon Press.

Cook, M. (Ed.). (1984). *Issues in person perception: Psychology in progress*. London: Methuen.

Cook, T. D., Gruder, D. L., Hennigan, K. M., & Flay, B. R. (1979). History of the sleeper effect: Some logical pitfalls in accepting the null hypothesis. *Psychological Bulletin*, *86*, 662–679.

Coolfront Report. (1986). A PHS plan for prevention and control of AIDS and the AIDS virus. *Public Health Reports*, *101*, 341–348.

Coons, P. M., Bowman, E. S., & Milstein, V. (1988). Multiple personality disorder: A clinical investigation of 50 cases. *Journal of Nervous and Mental Disease*, *176*, 519–527.

Cooper, C. L. (Ed.). (1983). *Stress research: Issues for the eighties*. Chichester, England: Wiley.

Cooper, G. D., Adams, H. B., & Scott, J. C. (1988). Studies in REST: I. Reduced Environmental Stimulation Therapy (REST) and reduced alcohol consumption. *Journal of Substance Abuse Treatment*, *5*, 61–68.

Cooper, J., & Fazio, R. H. (1984). A new look at dissonance theory. In L. Berkowitz (Ed.), *Advances in experimental social psychology*, (Vol. 17). New York: Academic Press.

Cooper, K. H. (1982). *The aerobics program for total well-being: Exercise, diet, emotional balance*. New York: Bantam Books.

Copolov, D. L., Rubin, R. T., Mander, A. J., Sashidharan, S. P., Whitehouse, A. M., Blackburn, I. M., Freeman, C. P., & Blackwood, D. H. R. (1987). DSM-III melancholia: Do the criteria accurately and reliably distinguish endogenous pattern depression? *Journal of Affective Disorders*, *10(3)*, 191–202.

Coren, S., & Ward, L. M. (1989). *Sensation & perception* (3rd ed.). New York: Harcourt Brace Jovanovich.

Corning, W. C., Dyan, J. A., & Willows, A. O. (1973). *Invertebrate learning: 1. Protozoans through annelids*. New York: Plenum Press.

Corning, W. C., & John, E. R. (1961). Effects of ribonuclease on retention of conditioned response in regenerated planarians. *Science*, *134*, 1363–1365.

Corrigan, P. W. (1991). Social skills training in adult psychiatric populations: A meta-analysis. *Journal of Behavior Therapy and Experimental Psychiatry*, *22(3)*, 203–210.

Corsi-Cabrera, M., & Becker, J. (1986). Dream content after using visual inverting prisms. *Perceptual and Motor Skills*, *63*, 415–423.

Corsini, R. J. (Ed.). (1977). *Current personality theories*. Itasca, IL: F. E. Peacock Publishers.

Cosby, B. (1988). *Time flies*. New York: Bantam.

Costa, P. T., Jr., & McCrae, R. R. (1978). Objective personality assessment. In M. Storandt, I. C. Siegler, & M. F. Elias (Eds.), *The clinical psychology of aging*. New York: Plenum.

Costa, P. T., Jr., & McCrae, R. R. (1980). Still stable after all these years: Personality as a key to some issues in adulthood and old age. In P. B. Baltes & O. G. Brim, Jr. (Eds.), *Life-span development and behavior* (Vol. 3). New York: Academic Press.

Costa, P. T., Jr., & McCrae, R. R. (1992). Four ways five factors are basic. *Personality and Individual Differences, 13(6)*, 653–665.

Cousins, S. D. (1989). Culture and self-perception in Japan and the United States. *Journal of Personality and Social Psychology, 56(1)*, 124–131.

Coward, D. M. (1992). General pharmacology of clozapine. *British Journal of Psychiatry, 160 (suppl. 17)*, 5–11.

Cox, M. V. (Ed.). (1985). *Are young children egocentric?* New York: St. Martin.

Coyle, J. T., & Enna, S. J. (Eds.). (1983). *Neuroleptics: Neurochemical, behavioral, and clinical perspectives.* New York: Raven Press.

Craft, S., Willerman, L., & Bigler, E. D. (1987). Callosal dysfunction in schizophrenia and schizoaffective disorder. *Journal of Abnormal Psychology, 96*, 205–213.

Craik, F. I. M., & Lockhart, R. S. (1972). Levels of processing: A framework for memory research. *Journal of Verbal Learning and Verbal Behavior, 11*, 671–684.

Craik, F. I. M., & Tulving, E. (1975). Depth of processing and the retention of words in episodic memory. *Journal of Experimental Psychology, 104*, 268–294.

Crain, S. (1991). Language acquisition in the abscence of experience. *Behavioral and Brain Sciences, 14(4)*, 597–650.

Crandall, C. S., Preisler, J. J., & Aussprung, J. (1992). Measuring life event stress in the lives of college students: The Undergraduate Stress Questionnaire (USQ). *Journal of Behavioral Medicine, 15(6)*, 627–662.

Crano, W. D. (1983). The second time around. *Contemporary Psychology, 28*, 913–915.

Crocker, J. (1988). Self-monitering: Fifteen years of research. *Contemporary Psychology, 33*, 16–17.

Crowe, R. (1983). Antisocial personality disorder. In R. Tarter (Ed.), *The child at psychiatric risk.* New York: Oxford University Press.

Crowe, R. A. (1990). Astrology and the scientific method. *Psychological Reports, 67*, 163–191.

Cumming, E., & Henry, W. H. (1961). *Growing old: The process of disengagement.* New York: Basic Books.

Cunningham, M. R., Barbee, A. P., & Pike, C. L. (1990). What do women want? Facialmetric assessment of multiple motives in the perception of male facial physical attractiveness. *Journal of Personality and Social Psychology, 59(1)*, 61–72.

Cunningham, S. (1984). Genovese: 20 years later, few heed a stranger's cries. *Social Action and the Law, 10(1)*, 24–25.

Cutting, J. (1992). The role of right hemisphere dysfunction in psychiatric disorders. *British Journal of Psychiatry, 160*, 583–588.

D'Agostino, F. (1986) *Chomsky's system of ideas.* Oxford, England: Oxford University Press.

d'Ailly, H. H. (1992). Asian mathematics superiority: A search for explanations. *Educational Psychologist, 27(2)*, 243–261.

D'Attilio, J. P., Campbell, B. M., Lubold, P., Jacobson, T., & Richard, J. A. (1991). Social support and suicide potential: Preliminary findings for adolescent populations. *Psychological Reports, 69*, 1–2.

Daley, D. C. (1989). A psychoeducational approach to relapse prevention. *Journal of Chemical Dependency treatment, 2(2)*, 105–124.

Dallenbach, K. M. (1959). Twitmyer and the conditioned response. *American Journal of Psychology, 72*, 255–262.

Damasio, A. R., & Bellugi, U. (1986). Sign language aphasia during left-hemisphere amytal injection. *Nature, 322*, 363–365.

Darian-Smith, I., Sugitani, M., & Heywood, J. (1982). Touching textured surfaces: Cells in somatosensory cortex respond to finger movement and to surface features. *Science, 218*, 906–909.

Darley, J. M., & Fazio, R. H. (1980). Expectancy confirmation processes arising in the social interaction sequence. *American Psychologist, 35*, 867–881.

Darley, J. M., & Latané, B. (1968). Bystander intervention in emergencies: Diffusion of responsibility. *Journal of Personality and Social Psychology, 8*, 377–383.

Darwin, C. (1872). *The expression of emotions in man and animals.* London: J. Murray.

Dasen, P. R. (Ed.). (1977). *Piagetian psychology: Cross-cultural contributions.* New York: Gardner Press.

Dasen, P. R., Berry, J. W., & Sartorius, N. (Eds.). (1988). *Health and cross-cultural psychology: Toward applications.* Newbury Park, CA: Sage.

Davey, G. C. L. (1992). Classical conditioning and the acquisition of human fears and phobias: A review and synthesis of the literature. *Advances in Behavioral Research and Therapy, 14*, 29–66.

Davidson, J., Kudler, H., Smith, R., Mahorney, S. L., Lipper, S., Hammett, E., Saunders, W. B., & Cavenar, J. O., Jr. (1990). Treatment of Posttraumatic stress disorder with amitriptyline and placebo. *Archives of General Psychiatry, 47*, 259–264.

Davidson, J. K., & Hoffman, L. E. (1986). Sexual fantasies and sexual satisfaction: An empirical analysis of erotic thought. *Journal of Sex Research, 22*, 184–205.

Davidson, R. J. (1992). Emotion and affective style: Hemispheric substrates. *Psychological Science, 3(1)*, 39–43.

Davidson, R. J., Chapman, J. P., & Chapman, L. J. (1987). Task-dependent EEG asymmetry discriminates between depressed and non-depressed subjects. *Psychophysiology, 24*, 585.

Davies, D. L. (1962). Normal drinking in recovered addicts. *Quarterly Journal of Studies in Alcohol, 23*, 94–104.

Davis, J. M., & Glassman, A. H. (1989). Antidepressant drugs. In H. I. Kaplan & B. J. Sadock (Eds.), *Comprehensive textbook of psychiatry/V.* Baltimore: Williams & Wilkins.

Davis, L. B., & Porter, R. H. (1991). Persistent effects of early odor exposure on human neonates. *Chemical Senses, 16(2)*, 169–174.

Davis, M. H., & Stephan, W. G. (1980). Attributions for exam performance. *Journal of Applied Social Psychology, 10*, 235–248.

Davis, S. F., Miller, K. M., Johnson, D., McAuley, K., & Dinges, D. (1992). The relationship between optimism-pessimism, loneliness, and death anxiety. *Bulletin of the Psychonomic Society, 30(2)*, 135–136.

Davison, G. C., & Neale, J. M. (1990). *Abnormal psychology: An experimental clinical approach* (5th ed.). New York: Wiley.

DeBono, K. G. (1987). Investigating the social-adjustive and value-expressive functions of attitudes: Implications for persuasion processes. *Journal of Personality and Social Psychology, 52*, 279–287.

DeCasper, A. J., & Prescott, P. A. (1984). Human newborns' perception of male voices: Preference, discrimination, and reinforcing value. *Developmental Psychobiology, 17(5)*, 481–491.

DeCasper, A. J., & Spence, M. J. (1986). Prenatal maternal speech influences newborns' perception of speech sounds. *Infant Behavior and Development, 9(2)*, 133–150.

Degreef, G., Ashtari, M., Bogerts, B., Bilder, R. M., Jody, D. N., Alvir, J. M. J., Lieberman, J. A. (1992). Volumes of ventricular system subdivisions measured from magnetic resonance images in first-episode schizophrenic patients. *Archives of General Psychiatry, 49*, 531–537.

de la Haye, A. M., & Askevis, M. (1988). Heterogeneite des schemas de genre chez des adolescents des deux sexes. *Enfrance, 41(1)*, 39–51.

de Leo, D., Mauro, P., & Pellegrini, C. (1989). An organic triggering factor in koro syndrome? A case report. *European Journal of Psychiatry, 3(2)*, 77–81.

De Raad, B. (1992). The replicability of the Big Five personality dimensions in three word-classes of the Dutch language. *European Journal of Personality, 6*, 15–29.

Deaux, K., & Lewis, L. L. (1984). Structure of gender stereotypes: Interrelationships among components and gender label. *Journal of Personality and Social Psychology, 46*, 991–1004.

deLeon, M. J., George, A. E., Tomanelli, J., Christman, D., Kluger, A., Miller, J., Ferris, S. H., Fowler, J., Brodie, J. D., Van Gelder, P., Klinger, A., & Wolf, A. P. (1987). Positron emission tomography studies of normal aging: A replication of PET III and 18-FDG using PET VI and 11-CDG. *Neurobiological Aging, 8*, 319–323.

Dellinger, R. W. (1978). Investigative hypnosis. Tapping our cerebral memory banks. *Human Behavior, 1(1)*, 36–37.

DeLisi, L. E., & Crow, T. J. (1989). Evidence for a sex chromosome locus for schizophrenia. *Schizophrenia Bulletin, 15(3)*, 431–440.

DeMartino, M. F. (1979). *Human autoerotic practices*. New York: Human Sciences Press.

Demo, D. H. (1992). Parent-child relations: Assessing recent changes. *Journal of Marriage and the Family, 54*, 104–117.

DePaulo, B. M., Stone, J. I., & Lassiter, D. G. (1985). Telling ingratiating lies: Effects of target sex and target attractiveness on verbal and nonverbal deceptive success. *Journal of Personality and Social Psychology, 48*, 1191–1203.

Deschner, J. P., & McNeil, J. S. (1986). Results of anger control training for battering couples. *Journal of Family Violence, 1(2)*, 111–120.

DeSouza, E. R., Pierce, T., Zanelli, J. C., & Hutz, C. (1992). Perceived sexual intent in the U.S. and Brazil as a function of nature of encounter, subjects' nationality, and gender. *The Journal of Sex Research, 29*, 251–260.

Deutsch, J. A. (Ed.). (1983). *The physiological basis of memory* (2nd ed.). New York: Academic Press.

DeVos, G. A. (1968). Achievement and innovation in culture and personality. In E. Norbeck, D. Price-Williams, & W. M. McCord (Eds.), *Personality: An interdisciplinary approach*. New York: Holt, Rinehart and Winston.

Dewsbury, D. A. (Ed.). (1981). Mammalian sexual behavior: Foundations for contemporary research. *Benchmark Papers in Behavior*, (Vol. 15). Stroudsburg, PA: Hutchinson Ross.

Dhooper, S. S. (1992). Caregivers of Alzheimer's disease patients: A review of the literature. *Journal of Gerontological Social Work, 18(1/2)*, 19–37.

Diamond, M. C. (1978). Aging and cell loss: Calling for an honest count. *Psychology Today, 12(9)*, 126.

Diamond, M. C., Johnson, R. E., & Ehlert, J. (1979). A comparison of cortical thickness in male and female rats—normal and gonadectomized, young and adult. *Behavioral and Neural Biology, 25*, 485–491.

Diaz-Loving, R., & Medina-Liberty, A. (1987). Mexico. In A. R. Gilgen and C. K. Gilgen (Eds.), *International handbook of psychology*. New York: Greenwood Press.

Dick, A. O. (1974). Iconic memory and its relation to perceptual processing and other memory mechanisms. *Perception & Psychophysics, 16*, 575–596.

Dietz, W. H., Jr., & Gortmaker, S. L. (1984). Factors within the physical environment associated with childhood obesity. *American Journal of Clinical Nutrition, 39*, 619–624.

Digman, J. M., & Inouye, J. (1986). Further specifications of the five robust factors of personality. *Journal of Personality and Social Psychology, 50*, 116–123.

Dintiman, G. B., Davis, R. G., Pennington, J. C., & Stone, S. F. (1989). *Discovering lifetime fitness: Concepts of exercise and weight control*. St. Paul, MN: West.

Dion, K. K. (1972). Physical attractiveness and evaluation of children's transgressions. *Journal of Personality and Social Psychology, 24*, 207–213.

Dion, K. K., Berscheid, E., & Walster, E. (1972). What is beautiful is good. *Journal of Personality and Social Psychology, 24*, 285–290.

Dixon, B. (1986). Dangerous thoughts: How we think and feel can make us sick. *Science, 7(3)*, 63–66.

Dobson, J. (1989). *Preparing for adolescence*. Ventura, CA: Regal.

Dodwell, P. C., & Caelli, T. (Eds.). (1984). *Figural synthesis*. Hillsdale, NJ: Erlbaum.

Doell, R. G., & Longino, H. E. (1988). Sex hormones and human behavior: A critique of the linear model. *Journal of Homosexuality, 15(3/4)*, 55–78.

Donald, I. J., & Canter, D. (1987). United Kingdom. In A. R. Gilgen and C. K. Gilgen (Eds.), *International handbook of psychology*. New York: Greenwood Press.

Dormen, L., & Edidin, P. (1989, July/August). Original spin. *Psychology Today*, 46–52.

Dörner, G. (1976). *Hormones and brain differentiation*. Amsterdam: Elsevier Scientific Publishing.

Dörner, G. (1988). Neuroendocrine response to estrogen and brain differentiation in heterosexuals, homosexuals, and transsexuals. *Archives of Sexual Behavior, 17*, 57–75.

Doty, R. W., Megrao, N., & Yamaga, K. (1973). The unilateral engram. *Acta Neurobiologiae Experimentalis, 33*, 711–728.

Doty, R. L., Shaman, P., Applebaum, S. L., Gilberson, R., Sikorski, L., & Rosenberg, L. (1984). Smell identification ability: Changes with age. *Science, 226*, 1441–1442.

Douglas, C. J., Kalman, C. M., & Kalman, T. P. (1985). Homophobia among physicians and nurses: An empirical study. *Hospital and Community Psychiatry, 36(12)*, 1309–1311.

Douglas, L. (1986). Is adolescent suicide a third-degree game, and who is the real victim? *Transactional Analysis Journal, 16*, 165–169.

Dovidio, J. F., Allen, J. L., & Schroeder, D. A. (1990). Specificity of empathy-induced helping: Evidence for altruistic motivation. *Journal of Personality and Social Psychology, 59(2)*, 249–260.

Doyle, J. A. (1983). *The male experience*. Dubuque, IA: Wm. C. Brown.

Draguns, J. G. (1987). Psychological disorders across cultures. In P. Pedersen (Ed.), *Handbook of cross-cultural counseling and therapy*. New York: Praeger.

Draguns, J. G. (1988). Personality and Culture: Are they relevant for the enhancement of quality of mental life? In P. R. Dasen, J. W. Berry, and N. Sartorius (Eds.), *Health and cross-cultural psychology: Toward applications*. Newbury Park, CA: Sage.

Drucker, P. F. (1981). Working women: Unmaking the 19th century. *Wall Street Journal*, 6 July.

Drucker, P. F. (1988). Leadership: More doing than dash. *Wall Street Journal*, 6 January.

Duda, J. L., & Allison, M. T. (1989). The attributional theory of achievement motivation: Cross-cultural considerations. *International Journal of Intercultural Relations, 13(1)*, 37–55.

Duncker, K. (1945). On problem solving. *Psychological Monographs, 58* (5, whole no. 270).

Dunn, G. E. (1992). Multiple personality disorder: A new challenge for psychology. *Professional Psychology: Research and Practice, 23(1)*, 1–6.

Dunn, J., & McGuire, S. (1992). Sibling and peer relationships in childhood. *Journal of Child Psychology and Psychiatry, 33(1)*, 67–105.

Dunnett, B. (1986). Drugs that suppress immunity. *American Health, 5(9)*, 43–45.

Durojaiye, M. O. A. (1987). Black Africa. In A. R. Gilgen and C. K. Gilgen (Eds.), *International handbook of psychology*. New York: Greenwood Press.

Dusek, D. E., & Girdano, D. A. (1987). *Drugs: A factual account* (4th ed.). New York: Random House.

Dustman, R. E., Emmerson, R. Y., Stainhaus, L. A., Shearer, D. E., & Dustman, T. J. (1992). The effects of videogame playing on neuropsychological performance of elderly individuals. *Journal of Gerontology: Psychological Sciences, 47(3)*, 168–171.

Dutton, D. G., & Aron, A. P. (1974). Some evidence for heightened sexual attraction under conditions of high anxiety. *Journal of Personality and Social Psychology, 30*, 510–517.

Dutton, D. G., & Aron, A. (1989). Romantic attraction and generalized liking for others who are sources of conflict-based arousal. *Canadian Journal of Behavioral Science, 21*, 246–257.

Dworetzky, J. P. (1990). *Introduction to child development* (4th ed.). St. Paul, MN: West Publishing.

Eastman, C. (1990). Natural summer and winter sunlight exposure patterns in seasonal affective disorder. *Physiology and Behavior, 48*, 611–616.

Eaton, W. O., & Saudino, K. J. (1992). Prenatal activity level as a temperamental dimension? Individual differences and developmental functions in fetal movement. *Infant Behavior and Development, 15*, 57–70.

Eaton, W. W., Dryman, A., & Weissman, M. M. (1991). Panic and phobia. In L. N. Robins & D. A. Regier (Eds.), *Psychiatric disorders in America: The epidemiologic catchment area study*. New York: Free Press.

Eaves, L. J., Eysenck, H. J., & Martin, N. G. (1989). *Genes, culture and personality*. New York: Academic Press.

Ebbinghaus, H. (1885/1964). *Memory: A contribution to experimental psychology*. New York: Dover.

Ebersole, P., & Hess, P. (1985). *Toward healthy aging: Human needs and nursing responses* (2nd ed.). St. Louis: C. V. Mosby.

Edens, J. L., Larkin, K. T., & Abel, J. L. (1992). The effect of social support and physical touch on cardiovascular reactions to mental stress. *Journal of Psychosomatic Research, 36(4)*, 371–382.

Edge, H. L., Morriss, R. L., Rush, J. H., & Palmer, J. (1986). *Foundations of parapsychology: Exploring the boundaries of human capability*. Boston: Routledge & Kegan Paul.

Edwards, D. D. (1988). New gene may solve the Y (and X) of sex. *Science News. 133*, 4.

Edwards, D. L. (1972). *General Psychology* (2nd ed.). New York: Macmillan.

Egan, V. (1992). Neuropsychological aspects of HIV infection. *AIDS Care, 4*, 3–10.

Egan, V., & Goodwin, G. M. (1992). HIV and AIDS. In A. Smith & D. Jones (Eds.) *Factors affecting human performance: Vol. II: Health and Illness*. London: Academic Press.

Egeland, J. A., Gerhard, D. S., Pauls, D. L., Sussex, T. N., Kidd, K. K., Allen, C. R., Hostetter, A. M., & Housman, D. E. (1987). Bipolar affective disorders linked to DNA markers on chromosome 11. *Nature, 325*, 783–787.

Ehrhardt, A. A., & Meyer-Bahlburg, H. F. L. (1981). Effects of prenatal sex hormones on gender-related behavior. *Science, 211*, 1312–1317.

Eichorn, D. H., Hunt, J. V., & Honzik, M. P. (1981). Experience, personality, and IQ: Adolescence to middle age. In D. H. Eichorn, J. A. Clausen, M. P. Honzik, & P. H. Mussen (Eds.), *Present and past in middle life*. New York: Academic Press.

Eilers, R. E., & Oller, D. K. (1985). Developmental aspects of infant speech discrimination: The role of linguistic experience. *Trends in Neurosciences, 8(10)*, 453–456.

Eiser, J. R. (1986). *Social psychology: Attitudes, cognition and social behavior*. New York: Cambridge University Press.

Ekman, P. (1972). Universal and cultural differences in facial expressions of emotion, In J. Cole (Ed.), *Nebraska Symposium on Motivation*. Lincoln: University of Nebraska Press.

Ekman, P. (Ed.). (1982). *Emotion in the human face* (2nd ed.). Cambridge, England: Cambridge University Press.

Ekman, P. (1985). *Telling Lies*. New York: Berkley Books.

Ekman, P. (1992a). An argument for basic emotions. *Cognition and Emotion, 6(3/4)*, 169–200.

Ekman, P. (1992b). Facial expressions of emotion: An old controversy and new findings. *Philosophical Transactions of the Research Society of London, 335*, 63–69.

Ekman, P., & Friesen, W. V. (1969). Nonverbal leakage and clues to deception. *Psychiatry, 32*, 88–106.

Ekman, P., & Friesen, W. V. (1971). Constants across cultures in the face and emotion. *Journal of Personality and Social Psychology, 17*, 124–129.

Ekman, P., & Friesen, W. V. (1974). Detecting deception from the body or face. *Journal of Personality and Social Psychology, 29*, 288–298.

Ekman, P., & Friesen, W. V. (1986). A new pan-cultural facial expression of emotion. *Emotion and Motivation, 10*, 159–168.

Ekman, P., Sorenson, E. R., & Friesen, W. V. (1969). Pan-cultural elements in facial displays in emotion. *Science, 764*, 86–88.

Elkin, I., Parloff, M. B., Hadley, S. W., & Autry, J. H. (1985). The NIMH treatment of depression collaborative research program: Background and research plan. *Archives of General Psychiatry, 42*, 305–316.

Elkin, I., Shea, M. T., Watkins, J. T., Imber, S. D., Sotsky, S. M., Collins, J. F., Glass, D. R., Pilkonis, P. A., Leber, W. R., Docherty, J. P., Fiester, S. J., & Parloff, M. B. (1989). National Institute of Mental Health treatment of depression collaborative research program. *Archives of General Psychiatry, 46*, 971–982.

Elliott, C. (1992). Diagnosing blame: Responsibility and the psychopath. *The Journal of Medicine and Philosophy, 17*, 199–214.

Ellis, A. (1962). *Reason and emotion in psychotherapy*. New York: Lyle Stewart.

Ellis, L., & Ames, M. A. (1987). Neurohormonal functioning and sexual orientation. *Psychological Bulletin, 1012*, 233–258.

Ellis, P., & Mellsop, G. (1990). The development of DSM-IV. *Archives of General Psychiatry, 47*, 92.

Ely, J. W., Peters, P. G., Zweig, S., Elder, N., & Schneider, F. D. (1992). The physician's decision to use tube feedings—the role of the family, the living will, and the Cruzan decision. *Journal of the American Geriatrics Society, 40(5)*, 471–475.

Emde, R. N. (1983). The prerepresentational self and its affective core. *Psychoanalytic Study of the Child, 38*, 165–192.

Emery, C. F., & Blumenthal, J. A. (1990). Perceived changes among participants in an exercise program for older adults. *The Gerontologist, 30*, 516–521.

Engel, J. M. (1992). Relaxation training: A self-help approach for children with headaches. *American Journal of Occupational Therapy, 46(7)*, 591–596.

Engen, T. (1982). *The perception of odors*. New York: Academic Press.

Engen, T. (1987). Remembering odors and their names. *American Scientist, 75*, 497–503.

Engler, B. (1991). *Personality theories* (3rd ed.). Boston: Houghton Mifflin.

Erikson, E. (1950). *Childhood and society*. New York: W. W. Norton.

Erikson, E. (1978). *Adulthood*. New York: W. W. Norton.

Erikson, E. H. (1974). *Dimensions of a new identity: Jefferson Lectures, 1973*. New York: W. W. Norton.

Erikson, E. H. (1982). *The life cycle completed: A review*. New York: Simon.

Escobar, J. I. (1987). Posttraumatic stress disorder and the perennial stress-diathesis controversy. *Journal of Nervous and Mental Disease, 175(5)*, 265–266.

Estioko-Griffin, A. (1985). Women as hunters: The case of an Eastern Cagayan Agta group. In P. B. Griffin, & A. Estioko-Griffin, (Eds.), *The Agta of Northeastern Luzon: Recent Studies*. Cebu City, Philippines: San Carlos Publishing.

Etaugh, C., & Liss, M. B. (1992). Home, school, and playroom: Training grounds for adult gender roles. *Sex Roles, 26*, 129–147.

Everstine, D. S., & Everstine, L. (1989). *Sexual trauma in children and adolescents*. New York: Brunner/Mazel.

Exner, J. (1986). *The Rorschach: A comprehensive system. Volume 1: Foundations* (2nd ed.). New York: Wiley.

Exner, J. (1990). *Rorschach interpretation assistance program, Version 2*. Asheville, NC: Rorschach Workshops.

Eysenck, H. (1981). *The causes and effects of smoking*. London: Sage.

Eysenck, H. J. (1947). *Dimensions of personality*. London: Routledge & Kegan Paul.

Eysenck, H. J. (1952). *The scientific study of personality*. London: Routledge & Kegan Paul.

Eysenck, H. J. (1957). *The dynamics of anxiety and hysteria: An experimental application of modern learning theory to psychiatry.* London: Routledge & Kegan Paul.

Eysenck, H. J. (1972). *Psychology is about people.* New York: Library Press.

Eysenck, H. J. (1975). A genetic model of anxiety. In L. G. Sarason & C. D. Speilberger (Eds.), *Stress and anxiety:* (Vol. 2). New York: Wiley.

Eysenck, H. J. (1986). A critique of contemporary classification and diagnosis. In T. Millon & G. L. Klerman (Eds.), *Contemporary directions in psychopathology: Toward the DSM-IV.* New York: Guilford.

Eysenck, H. J. (1991). *Smoking, personality, and stress.* New York: Springer-Verlag.

Eysenck, H. J. (1992). The definition and measurement of psychoticism. *Personality and Individual Differences, 13(7),* 757–785.

Eysenck, H. J., & Eysenck, M. W. (1985). *Personality and individual differences: A natural science approach.* New York: Plenum Press.

Fagot, B. I., Leinbach, M. D., & O'Boyle, C. (1992). Gender labeling, gender stereotyping, and parenting behaviors. *Developmental Psychology, 28,* 225–230.

Falbo, T., & Shepperd, J. A. (1986). Self-righteousness: Cognitive, power, and religious characteristics. *Journal of Research in Personality, 20,* 145–157.

Fancher, R. E. (1985). *The intelligence men.* New York: W. W. Norton.

Fantuzzo, J. W., & Jurecic, L. (1988). Effects of adult and peer social initiations on the social behavior of withdrawn, maltreated preschool children. *Journal of Consulting and Clinical Psychology, 56(1),* 34–39.

Fantz, R. L. (1963). Pattern vision in newborn infants. *Science, 140,* 296–297.

Fantz, R. L., Fagan, J. F., & Miranda, S. (1975). Early visual selectivity. In L. Cohen & P. Salapatek (Eds.), *Infant perception: From sensation to cognition.* New York: Academic Press.

Farag, S. E. (1987). Egypt. In A. R. Gilgen and C. K. Gilgen (Eds.), *International handbook of psychology.* New York: Greenwood Press.

Farag, S. E. (1990). Review of: "Understanding Arabs" by M. K. Nydell. *Journal of Cross-Cultural Psychology, 21(1),* 125–126.

Farley, F. (1986). The big T in personality. *Psychology Today, 20(5),* pp. 44–52.

Farran, D. C., & Ramay, C. T. (1977). Infant day care and attachment behaviors toward mothers and teachers. *Child Development, 48,* 1112–1116.

Farrell, M. P., & Rosenberg, S. D. (1981). *Men at midlife.* Boston: Auburn House.

Faust, D., & Ziskin, J. (1988). The expert witness in psychology and psychiatry. *Science, 241,* 31–35.

Fawcett, J., Clark, D. C., Aagesen, C. A., Pisani, V. D., Tilkin, J. M., Sellers, D., McGuire, M., & Gibbons, R. D. (1987). A double-blind, placebo-controlled trial of lithium carbonate therapy for alcoholism. *Archives of General Psychiatry, 44,* 248–256.

Fay, R. E., Turner, C. F., Klassen, A. D., & Gagnon, J. H. (1989). Prevalence and patterns of same-gender sexual contact among men. *Science, 243,* 338–348.

Feifel, H. (1990). Psychology and death: Meaningful rediscovery. *American Psychologist, 45(4),* 537–543.

Feingold, A. (1990). Gender differences in effects of physical attractiveness on romantic attraction: A comparison across five research paradigms. *Journal of Personality and Social Psychology, 59(5),* 981–993.

Feingold, A. (1991). Sex differences in the effects of similarity and physical attractiveness on opposite-sex attraction. *Basic and Applied Social Psychology, 12(3),* 357–367.

Feingold, A. (1992). Sex differences in variability in intellectual abilities: A new look at an old controversy. *Review of Educational Research, 62,* 61–84.

Feingold, A. (1992). Gender differences in mate selection preferences: A test of the parental investment model. *Psychological Bulletin, 112(1),* 125–139.

Feist, J. (1990). *Theories of personality* (2nd ed.). Fort Worth, TX: Holt, Rinehart and Winston.

Feldman, S. S., & Quatman, T. (1988). Factors influencing age expectation for adolescent autonomy: A study of early adolescents and parents. *Journal of Early Adolescence, 8(4),* 325–343.

Feldman, S. S., & Rosenthal, D. A. (1990). The acculturation of autonomy expectations in Chinese high schoolers in two Western nations. *International Journal of Psychology, 25(3),* 259–281.

Feldman, S. S., & Rosenthal, D. A. (1991). Age expectations of behavioral autonomy in Hong Kong, Australian and American youth: The influence of family variables and adolescents' values. *International Journal of Psychology, 26(1),* 1–23.

Fellman, B. (1985). Clockwork gland. *Science 85, 6(4),* 77–81.

Ferber, R. (1989). Sleepwalking, confusional arousals, and sleep terrors in the child. In M. H. Kryger, T. Roth, & W. C. Dement (Eds.), *Principles and practice of sleep medicine.* Philadelphia: W. B. Saunders.

Fernald, D. (1984). *The Hans legacy.* Hillsdale, NJ: Lawrence Erlbaum Associates.

Fernandes, W. (1992). Child labour and the processes of exploitation. *Indian Journal of Social Work, 53(2),* 171–190.

Fernando, T., Mellsop, G., Nelson, K., Peace, K., & Wilson, J. (1986). The reliability of axis V of DSM-III. *American Journal of Psychiatry, 143,* 752–755.

Ferster, C. B., & Skinner, B. F. (1957). *Schedules of reinforcement.* New York: Appleton-Century-Crofts.

Festinger, L. (1957). *A theory of cognitive dissonance.* Stanford, CA: Stanford University Press.

Festinger, L. (1980). *Retrospections on social psychology.* New York: Oxford Press.

Festinger, L., & Carlsmith, J. M. (1959). Cognitive consequences of forced compliance. *Journal of Abnormal and Social Psychology, 58,* 203–210.

Festinger, L., Pepitone, A., & Newcomb, T. (1952). Some consequences of deindividuation in a group. *Journal of Abnormal and Social Psychology, 47,* 382–389.

Festinger, L., Riecken, H., & Schachter, S. (1956). *When prophecy fails.* Minneapolis: University of Minnesota Press.

Fiedler, F. E. (1967). *A theory of leadership effectiveness*. New York: McGraw-Hill.

Fiedler, F. E., & Chemers, M. M. (1974). *Leadership and effective management*. Glenview, IL: Scott, Foresman & Company.

Fiedler, F. E., & Garcia, J. E. (1987). *Leadership: Cognitive resources and performance*. New York: Wiley.

Fiegel, G. S., Botteron, K., Zorumski, C. F., Jarvis, M. R., Doraiswamy, M., & Krishnan, R. (1992). The treatment of late age onset psychoses with electroconvulsive therapy. *International Journal of Geriatric Psychiatry, 7*, 183–189.

Field, T., Goldstein, S., Vega-Lahr, N., & Porter, K. (1986). Changes in imitative behavior during early infancy. *Infant Behavior and Development, 9*, 415–421.

Field, T., Sandberg, D., Garcia, R., Vega-Lahr, N., Goldstein, S., & Guy, L. (1985). Pregnancy problems, postpartum depression, and early mother-infant interactions. *Developmental Psychology, 21*, 1152–1156.

Fieve, R. R., Go, R., Dunner, D. L., & Elston, R. (1984). Search for biological/genetic markers in a long-term epidemiological and morbid risk study of affective disorders. *Journal of Psychiatric Research, 18*, 425–445.

Filteau, M., Pourcher, E., Bouchard, R. H., Baruch, P., Mathieu, J., Bédard, F., Simard, N., & Vincent, P. (1991). Corpus callosum agenesis and psychosis in Andermann syndrome. *Archives of Neurology, 48*, 1275–1280.

Finch, C. E. (1985). *Research on the biochemistry of Alzheimer's disease*. Invited symposium presented at the 93rd Annual Meeting of the American Psychological Association, Los Angeles.

Fingarette, H. (1988). *Heavy drinking: The myth of alcoholism as a disease*. Berkeley, CA: University of California Press.

Fingarette, H. (1990, February). We should reject the disease concept of alcoholism. *Harvard Medical School Mental Health Letter, 6(8)*, 4–6.

Fink, D. (1991). The comorbidity of multiple personality disorder and DSM-III-R axis II disorders. *Psychiatric Clinics of North America, 14(3)*, 547–566.

Fink, D. (1992). The psychotherapy of multiple personality disorder: A case study. *Psychoanalytic Inquiry, 12(1)*, 49–70.

Finkelhor, D. (1979). *Sexually victimized children*. New York: Free Press.

Finkelhor, D. (1980). Sex among siblings. *Archives of Sexual Behavior, 9*, 171–194.

Finkelhor, D. (1984). *Child sexual abuse*. New York: Free Press.

Finkelstein, P., Wenegrat, B., & Yalom, I. (1982). Large group awareness training. *Annual Review of Psychology, 33*, 515–539.

Fischer, G. J. (1986a). College student attitudes toward forcible date rape: I. Cognitive predictors. *Archives of Sexual Behavior, 15(6)*, 457–466.

Fischer, G. J. (1986b). College student attitudes toward forcible date rape: Changes after taking a human sexuality course. *Journal of Sex Education and Therapy, 121*, 42–46.

Fischhoff, B. (1992). Giving Advice: Decision theory perspectives on sexual assault. *American Psychologist, 47*, 577–588.

Fischhoff, B., Furby, L., & Morgan, M. (1987). Rape prevention: A typology of strategies. *Journal of Interpersonal Violence, 2*, 303–305.

Fischman, J. (1986). Golden years and restless nights. *Psychology Today, 20(2)*, 70.

Fishbain, D. A., Barsky, S., & Goldberg, M. (1989). "Koro" (genital retraction syndrome): Psychotherapeutic interventions. *American Journal of Psychotherapy, 43(1)*, 87–91.

Fisher, R. J. (1990). *The social psychology of intergroup and international conflict resolution*. New York: Springer-Verlag.

Fisher, R., & Ury, W. (1983). *Getting to yes: Negotiating agreement without giving in*. New York: Penguin.

Fishman, S. M., & Sheehan, D. V. (1985). Anxiety and panic: Their cause and treatment. *Psychology Today, 19(4)*, 26–32.

Fixx, J. F. (1977). *The complete book of running*. New York: Random House.

Flavell, J. H. (1985). *Cognitive Development* (2nd ed.). Englewood Cliffs, NJ: Prentice-Hall.

Flavell, J. H., Shipstead, S. G., & Croft, K. (1980). What young children think you see when their eyes are closed. *Cognition, 8(4)*, 369–387.

Fling, S., Thomas, A., & Gallaher, M. (1981). Participant characteristics and the effects of two types of meditation vs. quiet sitting. *Journal of Clinical Psychology, 37*, 784–790.

Flora, S. R., & Pavlik, W. B. (1990). An objective and functional matrix for introducing concepts of reinforcement and punishment. *Teaching of Psychology, 17(2)*, 121–122.

Foley, J. P., Jr. (1935). The criterion of abnormality. *Journal of Abnormal and Social Psychology, 30*, 279–291.

Fonow, M. M., Richardson, L., & Wemmerus, V. A. (1992). Feminist rape education: Does it work? *Gender and Society, 6*, 108–121.

Forehand, R. (1992). Parental divorce and adolescent maladjustment: Scientific inquiry vs. public information. *Behavior Research and Therapy, 30(4)*, 319–327.

Foster, S. (1988, March). Counseling survivors of incest. *Medical Aspects of Human Sexuality*, pp. 114–123.

Fowler, R. D. (1986, May). Howard Hughes: A psychological autopsy. *Psychology Today*, 22–33.

Fox, M. F., & Firebaugh, G. (1992). Confidence in science: The gender gap. *Social Science Quarterly, 73*, 101–114.

Fraiberg, S. (1977). *Insights from the blind: Comparative studies of blind and sighted infants*. New York: Basic Books.

Francis, A., Pincus, H. A., Widiger, T. A., Davis, W. W., & First, M. B. (1990). DSM-IV: Work in progress. *American Journal of Psychiatry, 147(11)*, 1439–1448.

Frank, J. D. (1973). *Persuasion and healing: A comparative study of psychotherapy*. Baltimore: Johns Hopkins Press.

Franklin, D. (1987). The politics of masochism. *Psychology Today, 21(1)*, 53–57.

Freedman, D. G., & DeBoer, M. (1979). Biological and cultural differences in child development. *Annual Review of Anthropology, 8*, 579–600.

Freud, S. (1887-1902/1954). *The origins of psycho-analysis, letters to Wilhelm Fliess, drafts and notes: 1887-1902*. New York: Basic Books.

Freud, S. (1893/1963). Some points in a comparitive study of organic hysterical paralyses. In M. Meyer (Ed.), *Freud: Early psycholanalytic writings*. New York: Collier Books.

Freud, S. (1900/1953). *The interpretation of dreams*. In J. Strachey (Ed. and Trans.), *The standard edition of the complete psychological works of Sigmund Freud* (Vols. 4 & 5). London: Hogarth Press and the Institute of Psycho-Analysis.

Freud, S. (1901/1960). *Psychopathology of everyday life*. In J. Strachey (Ed. and Trans.), *The standard edition of the complete psychological works of Sigmund Freud* (Vol. 6). London: Hogarth Press and the Institute of Psycho-Analysis.

Freud, S. (1905/1953). Three essays on the theory of sexuality. In J. Strachey (Ed. and Trans.), *The standard edition of the complete psychological works of Sigmund Freud* (Vol. 7). London: Hogarth Press and the Institute of Psycho-Analysis.

Freud, S. (1908/1959). On the sexual theories of children. In J. Strachey (Ed. and Trans.), *The standard edition of the complete psychological works of Sigmund Freud* (Vol. 9). London: Hogarth Press and the Institute of Psycho-Analysis.

Freud, S. (1911/1958). Formulations of the two principles of mental functioning. In J. Strachey (Ed. and Trans.), *The standard edition of the complete psychological works of Sigmund Freud* (Vol. 12). London: Hogarth Press and the Institute of Psycho-Analysis.

Freud, S. (1912/1958). A note on the unconscious in psychoanalysis. In J. Strachey (Ed. and Trans.), *The standard edition of the complete psychological works of Sigmund Freud* (Vol. 12). London: Hogarth Press and the Institute of Psycho-Analysis.

Freud, S. (1913/1958). On the beginning of treatment. In J. Strachey (Ed. and Trans.), *The standard edition of the complete psychological works of Sigmund Freud* (Vol. 12). London: Hogarth Press and the Institute of Psycho-Analysis.

Freud, S. (1916/1963). Introductory lectures on psychoanalysis. In J. Strachey (Ed. and Trans.), *The standard edition of the complete psychological works of Sigmund Freud* (Vols. 15 & 16). London: Hogarth Press and the Institute of Psycho-Analysis.

Freud, S. (1920/1955). Beyond the pleasure principle. In J. Strachey (Ed. and Trans.), *The standard edition of the complete psychological works of Sigmund Freud* (Vol. 18). London: Hogarth Press and the Institute of Psycho-Analysis.

Freud, S. (1923/1961). The ego and the id. In J. Strachey (Ed. and Trans.), *The standard edition of the complete psychological works of Sigmund Freud* (Vol. 21). London: Hogarth Press and the Institute of Psycho-Analysis.

Freud, S. (1924/1961). The dissolution of the Oedipus complex. In J. Strachey (Ed. and Trans.), *The standard edition of the complete psychological works of Sigmund Freud* (Vol. 19). London: Hogarth Press.

Freud, S. (1925). Some psychical consequences of the anatomical distinction between the sexes. In J. Strachey (Ed. and Trans.), *The standard edition of the complete psychological works of Sigmund Freud* (Vol. 19). London: Hogarth Press and the Institute of Psycho-Analysis.

Freud, S. (1933/1964). New introductory lectures. In J. Strachey (Ed. and Trans.), *The standard edition of the complete psychological works of Sigmund Freud* (Vol. 22). London: Hogarth Press and the Institute of Psycho-Analysis.

Freud, S. (1935/1960). *A general introduction to psychoanalysis*. New York: Washington Square Press.

Freud, S. (1940/1964). An outline of psychoanalysis. In J. Strachey (Ed. and Trans.), *The standard edition of the complete psychological works of Sigmund Freud* (Vol. 23). London: Hogarth Press and the Institute of Psycho-Analysis.

Friday, N. (1973). *My secret garden*. New York: Trident.

Friedlander, M. L. (1992). Psychotherapeutic processes: About the art, about the science. *Journal of Counseling and Development, 70*, 740–741.

Friedman, H. W., & Booth-Kewley, S. (1987). The "disease-prone personality": A meta-analytic view of the construct. *American Psychologist, 42*, 539–555.

Friedman, L. (1989). Mathematics and the gender gap: A meta-analysis of recent studies of sex differences in mathematical tasks. *Review of Educational Research, 69*, 185–213.

Friedman, M. J. (1988). Toward rational pharmacotherapy for posttraumatic stress disorder: An interim report. *American Journal of Psychiatry, 145(3)*, 281–285.

Friedman, M., & Rosenman, R. (1974). *Type A behavior and your heart*. New York: Knopf.

Friedman, R. C. (1988). *Male homosexuality: A contemporary psychoanalytic perspective*. New Haven: Yale University Press.

Friesen, W. V. (1972). Cultural differences in facial expression in a social situation: An experimental test of the concept of display rules. Unpublished doctoral dissertation. University of California, San Francisco.

Fromme, K., & Dunn, M. E. (1992). Alcohol expectancies, social and environmental cues as determinants of drinking and perceived reinforcement. *Addictive Behaviors, 17*, 167–177.

Fry, P. S. (1992). Major social theories of aging and their implications for counseling concepts and practice: A critical review. *The Counseling Psychologist, 20*, 246–329.

Fuenning, S. I. (1981). *Physical fitness and mental health*. Lincoln, NE: University of Nebraska Foundation.

Fukoda, H., & Blake, R. (1992). Spatial interactions in binocular rivalry. *Journal of Experimental Psychology: Human Perception and Performance, 18*, 362–370.

Furman, W., & Buhrmester, D. (1992). Age differences in perceptions of networks of personal relationships. *Child Development, 63(1),* 103–115.

Furnham, A. (1992). Prospective psychology students' knowledge of psychology. *Psychological Reports, 70,* 375–382.

Furomoto, L., & Scarborough, E. (1986). Placing women in the history of psychology: The first American women psychologists. *American Psychologist, 41,* 35–42.

Furstenberg, F. F., Morgan, S. P., Moore, K. A., & Peterson, J. L. (1987). Race differences in the timing of adolescent intercourse. *American Sociological Review, 52,* 511–518.

Furth, H. G. (1966). *Thinking without language: Psychological implications of deafness.* New York: The Free Press.

Gabrenya, W. K., Jr., Latane, B., & Wang, Y. E. (1983). Social loafing in cross-cultural perspective: Chinese on Taiwan. *Journal of Cross-Cultural Psychology, 14,* 368–384.

Gabrenya, W. K., Jr., Wang, Y. E., & Latane, B. (1985). Social loafing on an optimizing task: Cross-cultural differences among Chinese and Americans. *Journal of Cross-Cultural Psychology, 16,* 223–242.

Gabuza, D. H., & Hirsch, M. H. (1987). Neurologic manifestations of infection with human immunodeficiency virus. *Annals of Internal Medicine, 107,* 383–391.

Gackenbach, J. (1989). *Control your dreams.* New York: Harper & Row.

Gackenbach, J., Heilman, N., Boyt, S., & LaBerge, S. (1985). The relationship between field independence and lucid dreaming ability. *Journal of Mental Imagery, 9(1),* 9–20.

Gaertner, S. L., Mann, J. A., Dovidio, J. F., Murrell, A. J., & Pomare, M. (1990). How does cooperation reduce intergroup conflict? *Journal of Personality and Social Psychology, 59(4),* 692–704.

Gaines, A. D. (1992a). Ethnopsychiatry: The cultural construction of psychiatries. In A. D. Gaines (Ed.), *The cultural construction of professional and folk psychiatries.* New York: State University of New York Press.

Gaines, A. D. (1992b). From DSM-I to III-R; voices of self, mastery and the other: A cultural constructivist reading of U.S. psychiatric classification. *Social Science and Medicine, 35(1),* 3–24.

Gal, R. (1986). Unit morale: From a theoretical puzzle to an empirical illustration: An Israeli example. *Journal of Applied Social Psychology, 16,* 549–564.

Galambos, N. L. (1992). Parent-adolescent relations. *Current Directions in Psychological Science, 1,* 146–149.

Galanter, E. (1962). Contemporary psychophysics. In *New directions in psychology,* (Vol. 1). New York: Holt, Rinehart and Winston.

Galassi, J. P., & Perot, A. R. (1992). What you should know about behavioral assessment. *Journal of Counseling and Development, 70,* 624–631.

Galin, D., Johnstone, J., & Herron, J. (1978). Effects of task difficulty on EEG measures of cerebral engagement. *Neuropsychologia, 16,* 461–472.

Gallagher, W. (1986). The etiology of orgasm. *Discover, 7(2),* 51–59.

Gallimore, R. (1974). Affiliation motivation and Hawaiian-American achievement. *Journal of Cross-Cultural Psychology, 5,* 481–491.

Gallup, A. (1985). Premarital sex. *The Gallup Report,* No. 237, 28.

Galvin, R. M. (1982). Control of dreams may be possible for a resolute few. *Smithsonian, 13(5),* 100–106.

Gardner, H. (1981). How the split brain gets a joke. *Psychology Today, 15(2),* 74–84.

Garfield, S. L. (1981). Psychotherapy: A 40-year appraisal. *American Psychologist, 36,* 174–183.

Garfield, S. L. (1983a). *Clinical psychology: The study of personality and behavior* (2nd ed.). New York: Aldine.

Garfield, S. L. (1983b). Effectiveness of psychotherapy: The perennial controversy. *Professional Psychology, 14(1),* 35–43.

Garfield, S. L. (1987). Ethical issues in research on psychotherapy. *Counseling and Values, 31(2),* 115–125.

Garmon, L. (1985). Of hemispheres, handedness, and more. *Psychology Today, 19(11),* 40–48.

Gartner, A., & Riessman, F. (Eds.). (1984). *The self-help revolution.* New York: Human Sciences Press.

Gaw, A. C., & Bernstein, R. L. (1992). Classification of amok in DSM-IV. *Hospital and Community Psychiatry, 43(8),* 789–793.

Gazzaniga, M. S. (1985). The social brain. *Psychology Today, 19(11),* pp. 29–38.

Gazzaniga, M. S., & LeDoux, J. E. (1978). *The integrated mind.* New York: Plenum Press.

Geary, D. C., Fan, L., & Bow-Thomas, C. C. (1992). Numerical cognition: Loci of ability differences comparing children from China and the United States. *Psychological Science, 3(3),* 180–185.

Geldard, F. A., & Sherrick, C. E. (1986). Space, time and touch. *Scientific American, 255(1),* 91–95.

Geller, E. S. (1989). The airline lifesaver: In pursuit of small wins. *Journal of Applied Behavior Analysis, 22,* 333–335.

Geller, E. S. (1990a). Behavior analysis and environmental protection: Where have all the flowers gone? *Journal of Applied Behavior Analysis, 23(3),* 269–273.

Geller, E. S. (1990b). Environmental determinants of party drinking. *Environment and Behavior, 22(1),* 74–90.

Geller, E. S. (1990c). Preventing injuries and deaths from vehicle crashes: Encouraging belts and discouraging booze. In J. Edwards, R. S. Tindale, L. Heath, & E. J. Posavac (Eds.), *Social influence processes and prevention.* New York: Plenum Press.

Geller, E. S. (1991). Beer versus mixed-drink consumption at fraternity parties. *Journal of Studies on Alcohol, 52(3),* 197–204.

Geller, E. S. (1991). The buckle-up promise card: A versatile intervention for large-scale behavior change. *Journal of Applied Behavior Analysis, 24,* 91–94.

Geller, E. S. (1991). War on the highways: An international tragedy. *Journal of Applied Behavior Analysis, 24*, 3–7.

Gelman, B. P. (1985). Cognitive development of women. *New Directions for Student Services*, No. 29, 29–44.

George, M. S., & Ballenger, J. C. (1992). The neuroanatomy of panic disorder: The emerging role of the right parahippocampal region. *Journal of Anxiety Disorders, 6*, 181–188.

George, R. L., & Cristiani, T. S. (1990). *Counseling: Theory and practice* (3rd ed.). Englewood Cliffs, NJ: Prentice Hall.

Gerard, R. W. (1953). What is memory? *Scientific American, 189(3)*, 118.

Gerler, E. R., Jr., & Moorhead, S. (1988). Drug information: The facts about drugs and where to go for help. *Elementary School Guidance & Counselling, 23*, 139–145.

Gert, B. (1992). A sex-caused inconsistency in DSM-III-R: The definition of mental disorders and the definition of paraphilias. *The Journal of Medicine and Philosophy, 17*, 155–171.

Geschwind, N., & Galaburda, A. M. (1987). *Cerebral lateralization: Biological mechanisms, associations, and pathology*. Cambridge, MA: MIT Press.

Gibson, E. J. (1981). The ecological approach to perception and its significance for developmental psychology. *International Journal of Behavioral Development, 4*, 477–480.

Gibson, E. J., & Rader, N. (1979). Attention: The perceiver as performer. In G. Hale & M. Lewis (Eds.), *Attention and cognitive development*. New York: Plenum.

Gibson, E. J., & Walk, R. (1960). The "visual cliff." *Scientific American, 202*, 64–71.

Gibson, E. J., & Walker, A. S. (1984). Development of knowledge of visual-tactual affordances of substance. *Child Development, 55*, 453–560.

Gibson, J. J. (1950). *Perception of the visual world*. Boston: Houghton.

Gibson, J. J. (1983). Notes on affordances. In E. Reed & R. Jones (Eds.), *Reasons for realism*. Hillsdale, NJ: Lawrence Erlbaum.

Gilbert, A. N., & Wysocki, C. J. (1987). The smell survey. *National Geographic, 172*, 514–525.

Gilgen, A. R., & Gilgen, C. K. (Eds.). (1987). *International handbook of psychology*. London: Aldwych Press.

Gilligan, C. (1983). *In a different voice: Psychological theory and women's development*. Cambridge, MA: Harvard University Press.

Gilligan, C. (1986). On "In a different voice" An interdisciplinary forum: Reply. *Signs, 11*, 324–333.

Gilovich, T. (1983). Biased evaluation and persistence in gambling. *Journal of Personality and Social Psychology, 40*, 797–808.

Gilson, M., Brown, E. C., & Daves, W. F. (1982). Sexual orientation as measured by perceptual dominance in binocular rivalry. *Personality and Social Psychology Bulletin, 8*, 494–500.

Glaser, R. (1984). Education and thinking. *American Psychologist, 39*, 93–104.

Gleason, J. B. (1987). The contents of children's minds. *Contemporary Psychology, 32*, 147.

Glenn, N. D., & Weaver, C. N. (1979). Attitudes toward premarital, extramarital, and homosexual relations in the United States in the 1970s. *Journal of Sex Research, 15*, 108–118.

Glick, P., & Gottesman, D. (1989). The fault is not in the stars: Susceptibility of skeptics and believers in astrology to the Barnum effect. *Personality and Social Psychology Bulletin, 15(4)*, 572–583.

Glotzbach, P. A. (1992). Determining the primary problem of visual perception: A Gibsonian response to the "correlation" objection. *Philosophical Psychology, 5*, 69–94.

Goldberger, L., & Breznitz, S. (Eds.). *Handbook of stress: Theoretical and clinical aspects*. New York: Free Press.

Golden, C. J., Graber, B., Blose, I., Berg, R., Coffman, J., & Bloch, S. (1981). Differences in brain densities between chronic alcoholic and normal control patients. *Science, 211*, 508–510.

Golden, C. J., Graber, B., Coffman, J., Berg, R., Bloch, S., & Brogan, D. (1980). Brain density deficits in chronic schizophrenia. *Psychiatry Research, 3*, 179–184.

Golden, C. J., Graber, B., Coffman, J., Berg, R. A., Newlin, D. B., & Bloch, S. (1981). Structural brain deficits in schizophrenia. Identification by computed tomographic scan density measurements. *Archives of General Psychiatry, 38*, 1014–1017.

Golden, C. J., Scott, M., Strider, M. A., Chou-Chu, C., Ruedrich, S., & Graber, B. (1985). Neuropsychological deficit and regional cerebral blood flow in schizophrenic patients. *Hillside Journal of Clinical Psychiatry, 7*, 3–15.

Goldenson, R. M. (1970). *The encyclopedia of human behavior*. New York: Doubleday.

Goldstein, E. B. (1989). *Sensation and perception* (3rd. ed.). Belmont, CA: Wadsworth.

Goleman, D. (1983). A conversation with Ulric Neisser. *Psychology Today, 17(5)*, 54–62.

Golombok, S., (1986). The role of anxiolytic and antidepressant drugs in the development and treatment of sexual dysfunction. *Sexual and Marital Therapy, 1(1)*, 43–47.

Goodglass, H. (1980). Disorders of naming following brain injury. *American Scientist, 68*, 647–655.

Goodheart, C. D., & Markham, B. (1992). The feminization of psychology: Implications for psychotherapy. *Psychotherapy, 29*, 130–138.

Goodman, M. J., Griffin, P. B., Estioko-Griffin, A. A., & Grove, J. S. (1985). The compatibility of hunting and mothering among the Agta hunter-gatherers of the Philippines. *Sex Roles, 12*, 1199–1209.

Gopnik, M. (1990). Feature-blind grammar and dysphasia. *Nature, 344(6268)*, 715.

Gottesman, I. I. (1991). *Schizophrenic genesis: The origins of madness*. New York: W. H. Freeman.

Gottesman, I. I., McGuffin, P., & Farmer, A. E. (1987). Clinical genetics as clues to the "real" genetics of schizophrenia. *Schizophrenia Bulletin, 13*, 23–47.

Gottesman, I. I., & Shields, J. (1982). *Schizophrenia: The epigenetic puzzle*. Cambridge, MA: Cambridge University Press.

Gottesman, I. I., & Shields, J. (with Hanson, D. R.). (1982). *Schizophrenia*. Cambridge, England: Cambridge University Press.

Gould, J. L., & Gould, C. G. (1981). The instinct to learn. *Science 81, 2(5)*, 44–50.

Gould, R. L. (1972). The phases of adult life: A study in developmental psychology. *American Journal of Psychiatry, 129*, 521–531.

Gould, S. J. (1981). *The mismeasure of man.* New York: W. W. Norton.

Gould, S. J. (1982). Of wasps and WASPS. *Natural History, 91(12)*, 8–15.

Graf, P., Mandler, G., & Haden, P. (1982). Simulating amnesic symptoms in normal subjects. *Science, 218(4578)*, 1243–1244.

Grafman, J. (1985). Effects of left-hand preference on post-injury measures of distal motor ability. *Perceptual & Motor Skills, 61*, 615–624.

Graham, S. (1992). Most of the subjects were white and middle class: Trends in published research on African Americans in selected APA journals, 1970–1989. *American Psychologist, 47(5)*, 629–639.

Graumann, C. F., & Metraux, A. (1987). Federal Republic of Germany. In A. R. Gilgen and C. K. Gilgen (Eds.), *International handbook of psychology.* New York: Greenwood Press.

Graumann, C. F., & Moscovici, S. (Eds.). (1986). *Changing conceptions of leadership.* New York: Springer-Verlag.

Gray, T. (1990). Questionnaire format and item context affect level of belief in both scientifically unsubstantiated and substantiated phenomena. *Canadian Journal of Behavioral Science, 22(2)*, 173–180.

Gray, T. & Mill, D. (1990). Critical abilities, graduate education (Biology versus English), and belief in scientifically unsubstantiated and substantiated phenomena. *Canadian Journal of Behavioral Science, 22(2)*, 162–172.

Green, R. (1987). *The "Sissy Boy Syndrome" and the development of homosexuality.* New Haven, CT: Yale University Press.

Green, R. J., & Framo, J. L. (Eds.). (1981). *Family therapy: Major contributions.* New York: International Universities Press.

Greenberg, M. S., & Farah, M. J. (1986). The laterality of dreaming. *Brain and Cognition, 5(3)*, 307–321.

Greenhill, M. H., & Gralnick, A. (Eds.). (1983). *Psychopharmacology and psychotherapy.* New York: Free Press.

Greenough, W. T., & Bailey, C. H. (1988). The anatomy of a memory: Convergence of results across a diversity of tests. *Trends in Neuroscience, 11*, 142–146.

Greenough, W. T., Black, J. E., & Wallace, C. S. (1987). Experience and brain development. *Child Development, 58*, 539–559.

Greenspoon, J., & Lamal, P. A. (1987). A behavioristic approach. In L. Diamant (Ed.), *Male and female homosexuality: Psychological approaches.* Washington: Hemisphere.

Greenwald, A. G., Pratkanis, A. R., Leippe, M. R., & Baumgardner, M. H. (1986). Under what conditions does theory obstruct research progress? *Psychological Review, 93*, 216–229.

Greenwald, E., & Leitenberg, H. (1989). Long-term effects of sexual experiences with siblings and non-siblings during childhood. *Archives of Sexual Behavior, 18*, 389–399.

Greer, G. (1984, April). The uses of chastity and other paths to sexual pleasure. *Ms*, 53–96.

Greer, M., & Levine, E. (1991). Enhancing creative performance in college students. *The Journal of Creative Behavior, 25(3)*, 250–255.

Greeson, L. E. (1991). Cultural ethnocentrism and imperialism in citations of American and Scandinavian psychological research. *International Journal of Psychology, 26(2)*, 262–267.

Gregory, R. L. (1978). *Eye and brain: The psychology of seeing* (3rd ed.). New York: World University Library.

Gregory, R. L. (1988). *Odd perceptions.* London: Methuen.

Gregory, S. W. (1986). A sociolinguistic indicator of group membership. *Journal of Psycholinguistic Research, 15(3)*, 189–207.

Greif, E. B., & Ullman, K. J. (1982). The psychological impact of menarche on early adolescent females: A review of the literature. *Child Development, 53*, 1413–1430.

Gremillion, H. (1992). Psychiatry as social ordering: Anorexia nervosa, a paradigm. *Social Science and Medicine, 35(1)*, 57–71.

Griest, J. H. Jefferson, J. W., & Spitzer, R. L. (Eds.). *Treatment of mental disorders.* New York: Oxford University Press.

Griffin, B. Q., Combs, A. L., Land, M. L., & Combs, N. N. (1983). Attribution of success and failure in college performance. *Journal of Psychology, 114*, 259–266.

Griffith, R. M., Miyagi, O., & Tago, A. (1958). The universality of typical dreams: Japanese vs. Americans. *American Anthropologist, 60*, 1172–1179.

Griffiths, R. R., Bigelow, & Liebson, I. A. (1989). Reinforcing effects of caffeine in coffee and capsules. *Journal of the Experimental Analysis of Behavior, 52*, 127–140.

Griffiths, R. R., Evans, S. M., Heishman, S. J., Preston, K. L., Sannerud, C. A., Wolf, B., & Woodson, P. P. (1990a). Low-dose caffeine discrimination in humans. *The Journal of Pharmacology and Experimental Therapeutics, 252*, 970–978.

Griffiths, R. R., Evans, S. M., Heishman, S. J., Preston, K. L., Sannerud, C. A., Wolf, B., & Woodson, P. P. (1990b). Low-dose caffeine physical dependence in humans. *The Journal of Pharmacology and Experimental Therapeutics, 255*, 1123–1132.

Griffiths, R. R., & Woodson, P. P. (1988). Reinforcing effects of caffeine in humans. *The Journal of Pharmacology and Experimental Therapeutics, 246*, 21–29.

Grilly, D. M. (1989). *Drugs and human behavior.* Boston: Allyn and Bacon.

Grimm, L. G. (1981). Catholic views on the long-term effects of psychotherapy. *Contemporary Psychology, 26*, 750–752.

Gropen, J., Pinker, S., Hollander, M., & Goldberg, R. (1991). Syntax and semantics in the acquisition of locative verbs. *Journal of Child Language, 18(1)*, 115–151.

Groves, P. M., & Rebec, G. V. (1992). *Introduction to biological psychology* (4th ed.). Dubuque, IA: Wm. C. Brown.

Gruder, C. L., Cook, T. D., Hennigan, K. M., Flay, B. R., Alessis, C., & Halamaj, J. (1978). Empirical tests of the absolute sleeper effect predicted from the discounting cue hypothesis. *Journal of Personality and Social Psychology, 36*, 1061–1074.

Grunberg, N. E., & Bowen, D. J. (1985). The role of physical activity in nicotine's effects on body weight. *Pharmacology, Biochemistry and Behavior, 23*, 851–854.

Grunberg, N. E., Bowen, D. J., Maycock, V. A., & Nespor, S. M. (1985). The importance of sweet taste and caloric content in the effects of nicotine on specific food consumption. *Psychopharmacology, 87*, 198–203.

Grunberg, N. E., & Straub, R. O. (1992). The role of gender and taste class in the effects of stress on eating. *Health Psychology, 11*, 97–100.

Grunebaum, H., & Solomon, L. (1987). Peer relationships, self-esteem, and the self. *International Journal of Group Psychotherapy, 37(4)*, 475–513.

Grzesiuk, L. (1987). Poland. In A. R. Gilgen & C. K. Gilgen (Eds.), *International handbook of psychology*. New York: Greenwood Press.

Gudykunst, W. B. (1988). Uncertainty and anxiety. In Y. Y. Kim and W. B. Gudykunst (Eds.), *Theories in intercultural communication*. Newbury Park, CA: Sage Publications.

Guenther, K. (1988). Mood and memory. In G. M. Davies & D. M. Thomson (Eds.), *Memory in context: Context in memory*. New York: Wiley.

Guilford, J. P. (1959). *Personality*. New York: McGraw-Hill.

Guilford, J. P. (1967). *The nature of human intelligence*. New York: McGraw-Hill.

Guilford, J. P. (1984). Varieties of divergent production. *Journal of Creative Behavior, 18(1)*, 1–10.

Guilleminault, C. (1989). Sleepwalking and night terrors. In M. H. Kryger, T. Roth, & W. C. Dement (Eds.), *Principles and practice of sleep medicine*. Philadelphia: W. B. Saunders.

Guimond, S., Begin, G., & Palmer, D. L. (1989). Education and causal attributions: The development of "person-blame" and "system-blame" ideology. *Social Psychology Quarterly, 52*, 126–140.

Guimond, S., & Palmer, D. L. (1990). Type of academic training and causal attributions for social problems. In B. Earn and S. Towson *Social Psychology: Readings for the Canadian context*. Peterborough, Ont: Broadview Press.

Gulevich, G., Dement, W. C., and Johnson, L. (1966). Psychiatric and EEG observations on a case of prolonged (264 hours) wakefulness. *Archives of General Psychiatry, 15*, 29–35.

Gunderson, J. G., & Frank, A. F. (1985). Effects of psychotherapy in schizophrenia. *Yale Journal of Biological Medicine, 58*, 373–381.

Guralnick, M. J., & Groom, J. M. (1987). Dyadic peer interactions of mildly delayed and nonhandicapped preschool children. *American Journal of Mental Deficiency, 92(2)*, 178–193.

Gurin, J. (1989, June). The new diet mindset. *Psychology Today*, pp. 32–36.

Gutheil, T. G. (1985). The therapeutic milieu: Changing themes and theories. *Hospital and Community Psychiatry, 36*, 1279–1285.

Guthrie, R. V. (1976). *Even the rat was white: A historical view of psychology*. New York: Harper & Row.

Haaland, K. Y. (1992). Introduction to the special section on the emotional concomitants of brain damage. *Journal of Consulting and Clinical Psychology, 60(3)*, 327–328.

Haber, R. N., & Hershenson, M. (1973). *The psychology of visual perception*. New York: Holt, Rinehart and Winston.

Hage, P., & Miller, W. (1976). "Eagle"="bird": A note on the structure and evolution of Shoshoni ethnoornithological nomenclature. *American Ethnology, 3*, 481–488.

Hains, A. A. (1992). Comparison of cognitive-behavioral stress management techniques with adolescent boys. *Journal of Counseling and Development, 70*, 600–605.

Haith, M. M. (1980). *Rules that babies look by: The organization of newborn visual activity*. Hillsdale, NJ: Erlbaum.

Halgren, E., Babb, T. L., & Crandall, P. H. (1978). Activity of human hippocampal formation and amygdala neurons during memory tests. *Electroencephalography and Clinical Neurophysiology, 45*, 585–601.

Hall, E. T. (1966). *The hidden dimension*. New York: Doubleday.

Hall, E. (1983). A conversation with Erik Erikson. *Psychology Today, 17(6)*, pp. 22–30.

Hall, H. (1987). Beauty is in the eye of the baby. *Psychology Today, 21(8)*, 12.

Hall, M. H. (1968). A conversation with Abraham Maslow. In R. E. Schell (Ed.), *Readings in developmental psychology today*. New York: CRM Books.

Hall, J. P. (1990). Lessons from the First European Congress of Psychology. *American Psychologist*, 978–980.

Hall, J., & Donnell, S. M. (1979). Managerial achievement: The personal side of behavioral theory. *Human Relations, 32*, 77–101.

Halpern, D. F. (1986). *Sex differences in cognitive abilities*. Hillsdale, NJ: Erlbaum.

Halpern, D. F. (1989). The disappearance of cognitive gender differences: What you see depends on where you look. *American Psychologist, 44(8)*, 1156–1158.

Halpern, E. (1987). Israel. In A. R. Gilgen and C. K. Gilgen (Eds.), *International handbook of psychology*. New York: Greenwood Press.

Hambert, O. (1984). Narcolepsy. *Nordisk Psykiatrisk Tidsskrift, 38*, 481–491.

Hamilton, D. L. (Ed.). (1981). *Cognitive processes in stereotyping and intergroup behavior*. Hillsdale, NJ: Erlbaum.

Hampson, E., & Kimura, D. (1988). Reciprocal effects of hormonal fluctuations on human motor and perceptual-spatial skills. *Behavioral Neuroscience, 102(3)*, 456–459.

Hampson, S. E. (1985). The focus of semantic categorization of personality: A revision. *Boletin de Psicologia, 9*, 7–27.

Haney, C., Banks, C., & Zimbardo, P. G. (1981). A study of prisoners and guards in a simulated prison. In E. Aronson (Ed.), *Readings about the social animal* (3rd ed.). San Francisco: W. H. Freeman.

Harcum, E. R. (1988). Defensive reactance of psychologists to a metaphysical foundation for integrating different psychologies. *The Journal of Psychology, 122,* 217–235.

Hare, R. D. (1978). Electrodermal and cardiovascular correlates of sociopathy. In R. D. Hare and D. Schalling (Eds.), *Psychopathic behavior: Approaches to research.* New York: Wiley.

Hare, R. D. (1982). Psychopathy and physiological activity during anticipation of an aversive stimulus in a distraction paradigm. *Psychophysiology, 19,* 266–271.

Hare, R. D., & Jutai, J. W. (1983). Psychopathy and electrocortical indices of perceptual processing during selective attention. *Psychophysiology, 20,* 146–151.

Hargrave, R., & Bernstein, A. J. (1992). Fluoxetine-induced seizures. *Psychosomatics, 33(2),* 236–237.

Hariton, E. B., & Singer, J. L. (1974). Women's fantasies during marital intercourse: Normative and theoretical implications. *Journal of Consulting and Clinical Psychology, 42,* 313–322.

Harlow, H. F. (1973). *Learning to love.* New York: Ballantine.

Harlow, H. F., Harlow, M. K., & Suomi, S. J. (1971). From thought to therapy: Lessons from a primate laboratory. *American Scientist, 59,* 539–549.

Harmon, D. (1987). The free-radical theory of aging. In H. R. Warner, R. N. Butler, R. L. Sprott & E. L. Schneider (Eds.), *Modern biological theories of aging.* New York: Raven Press.

Harrell, R. L., & Strauss, F. A. (1986). Approaches to increasing assertive behavior and communication skills in blind and visually impaired persons. *Journal of Visual Impairment and Blindness, 80,* 794–798.

Harris, M. B., Walters, L. C., & Waschull, S. (1991). Altering attitudes and knowledge about obesity. *The Journal of Social Psychology, 131,* 881–884.

Harris, R. J., Schoen, L. M., & Hensley, D. L. (1992). A cross-cultural study of story memory. *Journal of Cross-Cultural Psychology, 23(2),* 133–147.

Harrison, D. E. (1985). Cell and tissue transplantation: A means of studying the aging process. In C. E. Finch & E. L. Schneider (Eds.), *Handbook of the biology of aging* (2nd ed.). New York: Van Nostrand Reinhold.

Hart, J., Berndt, Rita S., & Cramazza, A. (1985). Category-specific naming deficit following cerebral infarction. *Nature, 31(6),* 439–440.

Harter, S. (1990). Causes, correlates and the functional role of global self-worth: A life span perspective. In R. J. Sternberg & J. Kolligian Jr. (Eds.), *Competence considered.* New Haven, CT: Yale University Press.

Hartman, E. (1978). *The sleeping pill.* New Haven, CT: Yale University Press.

Hartman, E. (1983). Two case reports: Night terrors with sleepwalking—a potentially lethal disorder. *Journal of Nervous & Mental Disease, 171,* 503–505.

Hartmann, E. (1984). *The nightmare: The psychology and biology of terrifying dreams.* New York: Basic Books.

Hartry, A. L., Keith-Lee, P., & Morton, W. D. (1964). Planaria: Memory transfer through cannibalism reexamined. *Science, 146,* 274–275.

Hartsough, D. M., & Meyers, D. G. (1985). *Disaster work and mental health: Prevention and control of stress among workers.* Washington, DC: NIMH, Center for Mental Health Studies of Emergencies.

Hartup, W. W. (1983). The peer system. In P. H. Mussen (Ed.), *Handbook of child psychology: Vol. 4. Socialization, personality, and social development.* New York: Wiley.

Hartup, W. W. (1989). Social relationships and their developmental significance. *American Psychologist, 44,* 120–126.

Hatcher, R. A., Stewart, F., Trussell, J., Kowal, D., Guest, F., Sterart, G. K., & Cates, W. (1990). *Contraceptive technology, 1990–1992, with special section on AIDS and condoms* (15th ed.). New York: Irvington.

Hatfield, E., & Rapson, R. L. (1987). Passionate love/sexual desire: Can the same paradigm explain both? *Archives of Sexual Behavior, 16,* 259–278.

Hatfield, E., & Sprecher, S. (1986). *Mirror, mirror: The importance of looks in everyday life.* Albany: University of New York Press.

Hatfield, E., & Walster, G. W. (1985). *A new look at love.* Lanham, MD: University Press of America.

Haugeland, J. (1985). *Artificial intelligence: The very idea.* Cambridge, MA: MIT Press.

Havighurst, R. J. (1972). *Developmental tasks and education* (2nd ed.). New York: McKay.

Hawkins, S. A., & Hastie, R. (1990). Hindsight: Biased judgments of past events after the outcomes are known. *Psychological Review, 107,* 311–327.

Hayflick, L. (1965). The limited in-vitro lifetime of human diploid cell strains. *Experimental Cell Research, 37,* 614–636.

Hayflick, L. (1970). Aging under glass. *Experimental Gerontology, 5,* 291–303.

Healy, D., & Williams, J. M. G. (1988). Dysrhythmia, dysphoria, and depression: The interaction of learned helplessness and circadian dysrhythmia in the pathogenesis of depression. *Psychological Bulletin, 103(2),* 163–178.

Hebb, D. O. (1955). Drives and the C.N.S. (Conceptual nervous system). *Psychological Review, 62,* 243–254.

Hebb, D. (1958). *A textbook of psychology.* Philadelphia: Saunders.

Heckhausen, H., & Beckmann, J. (1990). Intentional action and action slips. *Psychological Review, 97(1),* 36–48.

Heeren, J., & Shichor, D. (1984). Mass media and delinquency prevention: The case of "scared straight": *Deviant Behavior, 5,* 375–386.

Heider, F. (1958). *The psychology of interpersonal relations.* New York: Wiley.

Heil, J. (1983). *Perception and cognition.* Berkley, CA: University of California Press.

Heiman, J. R. (1977). A psychophysiological exploration of sexual arousal patterns in females and males. *Psychophysiology, 14,* 266–274.

Helzer, J. E., & Robins, L. N. (1987). Post-traumatic stress disorder in the general population: Findings of the epidemiological catchment area survey. *New England Journal of Medicine, 317(26)*, 1630–1634.

Hendricks, B., Marvel, M. K., & Barrington, B. L. (1990). The dimensions of psychological research. *Teaching of Psychology, 17(2)*, 76–82.

Henning, H. (1916). Die Qualitatsreibe des Geschmacks. *Zeitschrift fur Psychologie, 74*, 203–219.

Henning-Stout, M., & Conoley, J. C. (1992). Gender: A subtle influence in the culture of the school. In F. C. Medway and T. P. Cafferty (Eds.) *School psychology: A social psychological perspective*. Hillsdale, NJ: Lawrence Erlbaum Associates.

Henriques, J. B., & Davidson, R. J. (1990). Regional brain electrical asymmetries discriminate between previously depressed and healthy control subjects. *Journal of Abnormal Psychology, 99(1)*, 22–31.

Hensel, H. (1981). *Thermoreception and temperature regulation*. London: Academic Press.

Hensel, H. (1982). *Thermal sensations and thermoreceptors in man*. Springfield, IL: Charles C. Thomas.

Herbert, H. (1983). Depression: Too much vigilance? *Science News, 124*, 13.

Herbert, W. (1983a). Canine clues to narcolepsy. *Science News, 1123*, 292–293.

Herbert, W. (1983b). Memory in the rough. *Psychology Today, 17(9)*, 18.

Herbert, W. (1983c). Modeling bulimia. *Science News, 123*, 316.

Herbert, W. (1986). Sweet treatment. *Psychology Today, 20(12)*, 6–7.

Hergenhahn, B. R. (1984). *An introduction to theories of personality* (2nd ed.). Englewood Cliffs, NJ: Prentice-Hall.

Hermesh, H., Aizenberg, D., Weizman, A., Lapidot, M., Mayor, C., & Munitz, H. (1992). Risk for indefinite neuroleptic malignant syndrome. *British Journal of Psychiatry, 161*, 254–257.

Heron, W., Doane, B. K., & Scott, T. H. (1956). Visual disturbances after prolonged perceptual isolation. *Canadian Journal of Psychology, 10*, 13.

Hersey, W. D. (1989). *Blueprints for memory*. New York: American Management Association.

Hershberger, S. L., & S'Augelli, A. R. (1992). The relationship of academic performance and social support to graduation among African-American and white university students: A path-analytic model. *Journal of Community Psychology, 20, 188–199*.

Herzog, A. R., & Dielman, L. (1985). *Age differences in response accuracy for factual survey questions. Journal of Gerontology, 40*, 350–357.

Herzog, D. B., & Keller, M. B. (1988). Outcome in anorexia nervosa and bulimia nervosa: A review of the literature. *Journal of Nervous and Mental Disease, 176(3)*, 131–143.

Herzog, E., & Sudia, C. E. (1968). Fatherless homes: A review of research. *Children, 15*, 177–182.

Hess, E. H. (1965). Attitude and pupil size. *Scientific American, 212*, 46–54.

Hess, E. H. (1975a). The role of pupil size in communication. *Scientific American, 233*, 110–119.

Hess, E. H. (1975b). *The tell-tale eye*. New York: Van Nostrand.

Hetherington, E. M. (1981). Tracing children through the changing family. *APA Monitor, 12*, 14–22.

Hetherington, E. M., Cox, M., & Cox, R. (1975). Beyond father absence: Conceptualization of effects of divorce. Paper presented at the annual meeting of the Society for Research in Child Development. Denver, 1975.

Hetherington, E. M., Cox, M., & Cox, R. (1985). Long-term effects of divorce and remarriage on the adjustment of children. *Journal of the American Academy of Child Psychiatry, 24(5)*, 518–530.

Hettlinger, R. (1974). *Human sexuality, a psychosocial perspective*. Belmont, CA: Wadsworth.

Hewstone, M. (1988). Causal attributions: From cognitive processes to collective beliefs. *The Psychologist, 8*, 323–327.

Hierholzer, R. W., & Liberman, R. P. (1986). Successful living: A social skills and problem-solving group for the chronic mentally ill. *Hospital and Community Psychiatry, 37(9)*, 913–918.

Hikita, K. (1986). The effects of token economy procedures with chronic schizophrenia patients. *Japanese Journal of Behavior Therapy, 11(2)*, 55–76.

Hilgard, E. R. (1965). *Hypnotic susceptibility*. New York: Harcourt, Brace and World.

Hilgard, E. R. (1986). A study in hypnosis. *Psychology Today, 20(1)*, 23–27.

Hilgard, E. R. (1987). *Psychology in America: A historical survey*. New York: Harcourt Brace Jovanovich.

Hilgard, E. R. (1992). Theoretical focus: Divided consciousness and dissociation. *Consciousness and Cognition, 1*, 16–31.

Hilgard, J. R., & LeBaron, S. (1984). *Hypnotherapy of pain in children with cancer*. Los Altos, CA: William Kaufmann.

Hill, T., Lewicki, P., Czyzewska, M., & Boss, A. (1989). Self-perpetuating development of encoding biases in person perception. *Journal of Personality and Social Psychology, 57(3)*, 373–387.

Hiller, W., Zaudig, M., & Mombour, W. (1990). Development of diagnostic checklists for use in routine clinical care. *Archives of General Psychiatry, 47*, 782–784.

Hilton, J. L., & Darley, J. M. (1985). Constructing other persons: A limit on the effect. *Journal of Experimental Social Psychology, 21(1)*, 1–18.

Hirschfield, R. M. A., & Goodwin, F. K. (1988). Mood disorders. In J. A. Talbott, R. E. Hales, & S. C. Yudofsky (Eds.), *The American Psychiatric Press textbook of psychiatry*. Washington, DC: American Psychiatric Press.

Hite, S. (1977). *The Hite report*. New York: Dell, 1977.

Ho, D. Y. F. (1985). Cultural values and professional issues in clinical psychology: Implications from the Hong Kong experience. *American Psychologist, 40(11)*, 1212–1218.

Hochberg, J. (1984). Visual perception. In P.C. Dodwell & T. Caelli (Eds.), *Figural Synthesis*. Hillsdale, NJ: Erlbaum.

Hodgkinson, S., Sherrington, R., Gurling, H., Marchbanks, R., Reeders, S., Mallet, J., MacInnis, M., Petursson, H., & Brynjolfsson, J. (1987). Molecular genetic evidence for heterogeneity in manic depression. *Nature, 325*, 805–806.

Hoffman, D. D. (1983). The interpretation of visual illusions. *Scientific American, 249(6)*, 154–162.

Hoffman, J. W., Benson, H., Arns, P. A., Stainbrook, G. L., Landsberg, L., Young, J. B., & Gill, A. (1982). Reduced sympathetic nervous system responsivity associated with the relaxation response. *Science, 215*, 190–192.

Hoffman, M. L. (1984). Empathy, its limitations, and its role in a comprehensive moral theory. In J. Gerwitz & W. Kurtines (Eds.), *Morality, moral development and moral behavior*. New York: Wiley.

Hoffman, M. L. (1987). The contribution of empathy to justice and moral development. In N. Eisenberg & J. Strayer (Eds.), *Empathy and its development*. New York: Cambridge University Press.

Hoffman, R. S., & Koran, L. M. (1984). Detecting physical illness in patients with mental disorders. *Psychosomatics, 25*, 654–660.

Hofstede, G. (1980). *Culture's consequences: International differences in work-related values*. London: Sage.

Hoge, D. R., & Ankney, T. L. (1982). Occupations and attitudes of former student activists 10 years later. *Journal of Youth and Adolescence, 11*, 355–371.

Hogg, M. (1987). Social identity and group cohesiveness. In J. C. Turner (Ed.), *Rediscovering the social group: A self-categorization theory*. Oxford: Basil Blackwell.

Holden, C. (1985). A guarded endorsement for shock therapy. *Science, 228*, 1510–1511.

Holden, C. (1986). Giving mental illness its research due. *Science, 232*, 1084–1085.

Holden, C. (1987). A top priority at NIMH. *Science, 235*, 431.

Hole, J. W., Jr. (1990). *Human anatomy and physiology* (5th ed.). Dubuque, IA: Wm. C. Brown Publishers.

Hollon, S. D., & Beck, A. T. (1979). Cognitive therapy of depression. In P. C. Kendall & S. D. Hollon (Eds.), *Cognitive-behavioral interventions*. New York: Academic Press.

Holmes, T. H., & Rahe, R. H. (1967). The social readjustment rating scale. *Journal of Psychosomatic Research, 11*, 213–218.

Holmstrom, R. W., Karp, S. A., & Silber, D. F. (1992). Factor structure of the apperceptive personality test (APT). *Journal of Clinical Psychology, 48(2)*, 207–210.

Holzman, A. D., & Turk, D. C. (Eds.). (1986). *Pain management: A handbook of psychological treatment approaches*. New York: Pergamon Press.

Homant, R. J., & Osowski, G. (1981). Evaluation of the "scared straight" model: Some methodological and political considerations. *Corrective and Social Psychiatry and Journal of Behavior Technology, Methods, and Therapy, 27(3)*, 130–134.

Hoppe, R. B. (1988). In search of a phenomenon: Research in parapsychology. *Contemporary Psychology, 33*, 129–130.

Hopson, J. L. (1986, June). The unraveling of insomnia. *Psychology Today*, pp. 42–49.

Hopson, J. L. (1990). A pleasurable chemistry. In M. Walraven & H. Fitzgerald (Eds.), *Psychology 90/91*. Guilford, CT: Dushkin.

Horn, J. C. (1985). A call to glory. *Psychology Today, 19(12)*, p. 20.

Horn, J. L. (1982). The theory of fluid and crystallized intelligence in relation to concepts of cognitive psychology and aging in adulthood. In F. I. M. Craik & S. Trehub (Eds.), *Aging and cognitive processes*. New York: Plenum Press.

Horn, J. (1989, July/August). The mid-life fitness peak. *Psychology Today*, pp. 32–34.

Horn, J. L., & Cattell, R. (1967). Age differences in fluid and crystallized intelligence. *Acta Psychologica, 26*, 107–129.

Horne, J. A., & Östberg, O. (1976). A self-assessment questionnaire to determine morningness-eveningness in human circadian rhythms. *International Journal of Chronobiology, 4*, 97–110.

Horney, K. (1945). *Our inner conflicts*. New York: Norton.

Horney, K. (1950). *Neurosis and human growth*. New York: Norton.

Hothersall, D. (1990). *History of psychology* (2nd ed.). New York: McGraw-Hill.

Hotta, M., & Strickland, L. H. (1991). Social psychology in Japan. *Canadian Psychology, 32(4)*, 596–607.

Hou-can, Z. (1987). People's Republic of China. In A. R. Gilgen and C. K. Gilgen (Eds.), *International handbook of psychology*. New York: Greenwood Press.

Hoult, T. F. (1984). Human sexuality in biological perspective: Theoretical and methodological considerations. *Journal of Homosexuality, 9(2/3)*, 137–155.

Hovland, C. I., Harvey, O., & Sherif, M. (1957). Assimilation and contrast effects in reactions to communication and attitude change. *Journal of Abnormal and Social Psychology, 55*, 244–252.

Hovland, C. I., Janis, I. L., & Kelley, H. H. (1953). *Communication and persuasion*. New Haven, CT: Yale University Press.

Hovland, C. I., & Weiss, W. (1951). The influence of source credibility on communication effectiveness. *Public Opinion Quarterly, 15*, 635–650.

Howard, A., Pion, G. M., Gottfredson, G. D., Flattau, P. E., Oskamp, S., Pfafflin, S. M., Bray, D. W., & Burstein, A. G. (1986). The changing face of American psychology: A report from the committee on employment and human resources. *American Psychologist, 41*, 1311–1327.

Howell, T., Bauwens, S. F., & Thurrell, R. J. (1986). Neuroleptic-induced respiratory dyskinesia in the elderly: Two case reports and a brief review. *Clinical Gerontologist, 4(3)*, 17–22.

Howes, C., Phillips, D. A., & Whitebook, M. (1992). Thresholds of quality: Implications for the social development of children in center-based child care. *Child Development, 63*, 449–460.

Howes, J. L., & Katz, A. N. (1992). Remote memory: Recalling autobiographical and public events from across the lifespan. *Canadian Journal of Psychology, 46(1)*, 92–116.

Hudiburg, R. (1989). Psychology of computer use: XVII. The Computer Technology Hassles Scale: Revision, reliability, and some correlates. *Psychological Reports, 65(3, Pt 2)*, 1387–1394.

Huertas-Rodriguez, E. (1985). The role of awareness in the classical conditioning of autonomic responses in humans. *Revista de Psicologia General y Aplicada, 40(3)*, 473–484.

Huessy, H. R. (1982). Letters: Schizophrenia and kibbutzim. *Science News, 122*, 207.

Huey, C. J., Kline-Graber, G., & Graber, B. (1981). Time factors and orgasmic response. *Archives of Sexual Behavior, 10*, 111–118.

Hui, C. H., & Triandis, H. C. (1986). Individualism-collectivism: A study of cross-cultural researchers. *Journal of Cross-Cultural Psychology, 17*, 225–248.

Humphrey, D., & Wickett, A. (1986). *The right to die.* New York: Harper & Row.

Hunt, E. (1989). Cognitive science: Definition, status, and questions. *Annual Review of Psychology, 40*, 603–629.

Hunt, M. (1975). *Sexual behavior in the 1970s.* New York: Dell.

Hunter, J. E. (1983). A causal analysis of cognitive ability, job, knowledge, job performance, and supervisor ratings. In F. Landy, S. Zedeck, & J. Cleveland (Eds.), *Performance measurement and theory.* Hillsdale, NJ: Lawrence Erlbaum Associates.

Hunter, J. E. (1986). Cognitive ability, cognitive aptitudes, job knowledge, and job performance. *Journal of Vocational Behavior, 29*, 340–362.

Huston, T. L., Ruggiero, M., Conner, R., & Geis, G. (1981). Bystander intervention into crime: A study based on naturally occurring episodes. *Social Psychology Quarterly, 44(1)*, 14–23.

Hyde, J. S. (1990). *Understanding human sexuality* (4th ed.). New York: McGraw-Hill.

Hyden, H., & Egyhazi, E. (1962). Nuclear RNA changes in nerve cells during a learning experiment in rats. *Proceedings of the National Academy of Sciences, 48*, 1366–1373.

Hyman, B. T., Damasio, H., Damasio, A. R., & Van Hoesen, G. W. (1989). Alzheimer's disease. *Annual Review of Public Health, 10*, 115–140.

Hyman, R., & Honorton, C. (1986). A joint communique: The psi ganzfield controversy. *Journal of Parapsychology, 50*, 351–364.

Iacono, W. G., & Beiser, M. (1992a). Where are the women in first-episode studies of schizophrenia? *Schizophrenia Bulletin, 18(3)*, 471–480.

Iacono, W. G., & Beiser, M. (1992b). Are males more likely than females to develop schizophrenia? *American Journal of Psychiatry, 149(8)*, 1070–1074.

Imperato-McGinley, J., Peterson, R. E., Gautier, T., & Sturla, E. (1979). Androgens and the evolution of male-gender identity among male pseudohermaphrodites with 5 alpha-reductase defeciency. *New England Journal of Medicine, 300*, 1233–1237.

Imperato-McGinley, J., Peterson, R. E., Leshin, M., Griffin, J. E., Cooper, G., Draghi, S., Berenyi, M., Imperato-McGinley, J., Gautier, T., Peterson, R. E., & Schackleton, C. (1986). The prevalence of 5 alpha-reductase deficiency in children with ambiguous genitalia in the Dominican Republic. *Journal of Urology, 134*, 867–873.

Ingram, L. C. (1986). Testimony and religious cohesion. *Religious Education, 81(2)*, 295–309.

Inoue, K. (1985). An examination of equity theory in dating couples' intimate romantic relationships. *Japanese Journal of Experimental Social Psychology, 24(2)*, 127–134.

Isaacson, R. L. (1974). *The limbic system.* New York: Plenum Press.

Ivie, R. L., Gimbel, C., & Elder, G. H. (1991). Military experience and attitudes in later life: Contextual influences across forty years. *Journal of Political and Military Sociology, 19*, 101–117.

Ivnik, R. J., Sharbrough, F. W., & Laws, E. R. (1987). Effects of anterior temporal lobectomy on cognitive function. *Journal of Clinical Psychology, 43(1)*, 128–137.

Izard, C. E. (1971). *The face of emotion.* New York: Appleton-Century-Crofts.

Izard, C. E., Kagan, J., & Zajonc, R. B. (Eds.). (1984). *Emotions, cognition, and behavior.* Cambridge, England: Cambridge University Press.

Jackson, L. A., Ialongo, N., & Stollak, G. E. (1986). Parental correlates of gender role: The relations between parents' masculinity, feminity, and child-rearing behaviors and of their children's gender roles. *Journal of Social and Clinical Psychology, 4*, 202–224.

Jacobs, B., & Scheibel, A. B. (1993). A quantitative dendritic analysis of Wernicke's area in humans. I. Lifespan changes. *Journal of Comparative Neurology* (in press).

Jacobs, B., Schall, M., & Scheibel, A. B. (1993). A quantitative dendritic analysis of Wernicke's area in humans. II. Gender, hemispheric, and environmental factors. *Journal of Comparative Neurology* (in press).

Jacobs, M. R., & Fehr, K. O'B. (1987). *Drugs and drug abuse: A reference text.* Toronto: Alcoholism and Drug Addiction Research Foundation.

Jacobson, R. R. (1986). Disorders of facial recognition, social behaviour and affect after combined bilateral amygdalotomy and subcaudate tractotomy: A clinical and experimental study. *Psychological Medicine, 16*, 439–450.

Jain, U. (1992). The subjective construction of morality: The Indian experience. *Indian Journal of Social Work, 52(3)*, 379–388.

James, W. (1884, January). On some omissions of introspective psychology. *Mind, 9*, 1–2b.

James, W. (1890). *Principles of psychology.* New York: Henry Holt.

James, W. (1909/1947). A pluralistic universe. In R. B. Perry (Ed.), *Essays in radical empiricism and a pluralistic universe.* New York: Longmans, Green.

Jampala, V. C., Sierles, F. S., & Taylor, M. A. (1988). The use of the DSM-III in the United States: A case of not going by the book. *Comprehensive Psychiatry, 29(1)*, 39–47.

Janis, I. L. (1954). Personality correlates of susceptibility to persuasion. *Journal of Personality, 22*, 504–518.

Janis, I. L., & Feshbach, S. (1953). Effects of fear-arousing communications. *Journal of Abnormal and Social Psychology, 48*, 78–92.

Janis, I. L., & Field, P. B. (1959). A behavioral assessment of persuasibility: Consistency of individual differences. In I. L. Janis, C. I. Hovland, P. B. Field, H. Linton, E. Graham, A. R. Cohen, D. Rife, R. P. Abelson, G. S. Lesser, & B. T. King (Eds.), *Personality and persuasibility.* New Haven, CT: Yale University Press.

Janis, I. L., & Rife, D. (1959). Persuasibility and emotional disorder. In I. L. Janis, C. I. Hovland, P. B. Field, H. Linton, E. Graham, A. R. Cohen, D. Rife, R. P. Abelson, G. S. Lesser, & B. T. King (Eds.), *Personality and persuasibility.* New Haven, CT: Yale University Press.

Jeffers, F. C., Nichols, C. R., & Eisdorfer, C. (1961). Attitudes of older persons to death. *Journal of Gerontology, 16*, 53–56.

Jefferson, J. W., & Greist, J. H. (1989). Lithium therapy. In H. I. Kaplan & B. J. Sadock (Eds.), *Comprehensive textbook of psychiatry/V.* Baltimore: Williams & Wilkins.

Jelinek, M., & Adler, N. J. (1989). In J. W. Newstrom & K. Davis (Eds.), *Organizational behavior: Readings and exercises* (8th ed.). New York: McGraw-Hill.

Jellinek, E. M. (1952). Phases of alcohol addiction. *Quarterly Journal of the Study of Alcohol, 13*, 673–678.

Jenike, M. A., Baer, L., & Greist, J. H. (1990). Clomipramine versus fluoxetine in obsessive-compulsive disorder: A retrospective comparison of side effects and efficacy. *Journal of Clinical Psychopharmacology, 10(2)*, 122–124.

Jensen, A. R. (1969). How much can we boost IQ and scholastic achievement? *Harvard Educational Review, 39(1)*, 1–123.

Jensen, A. R. (1979). *Bias in mental testing.* New York: Free Press.

Jha, B. K. (1972). Institutional neurosis: Its causes and remedy. *Indian Journal of Psychiatric Social Work, 1(1)*, 5–19.

Johnson, D. W., & Johnson, R. T. (1989). *A meta-analysis of cooperative, competitive, and individualistic goal structures.* Hillsdale, NJ: Erlbaum.

Johnson, R. T., Johnson, D. W., & Stanne, M. B. (1986). Comparison of computer-assisted cooperative, competitive, and individualistic learning. *American Educational Research Journal, 23*, 382–392.

Jones, E. E. (1986). Interpreting interpersonal behavior: The effects of expectancies. *Science, 234*, 41–46.

Jones, M. C. (1924). Elimination of children's fears. *Journal of Experimental Psychology, 7*, 382.

Joseph, R. (1988). Dual mental functioning in a split-brain patient. *Journal of Clinical Psychology, 44(5)*, 770–779.

Joseph, R. (1992). The limbic system: Emotion, laterality, and unconscious mind. *Psychoanalytic Review, 79*, 405–456.

Jouvet, M., Mouret, J., Chouvet, G., & Siffre, M. (1974). Toward a 48-hour day: Experimental bicircadian rhythm in man. In F. Schmidtt & F. Worden (Eds.), *The neurosciences third study program.* Cambridge, MA: MIT Press.

Joyce, P. R., & Paykel, E. S. (1989). Predictors of drug response in depression. *Archives of General Psychiatry, 46*, 89–99.

Jung, C. G. (1917/1966). Two essays on analytical psychology. In H. Read, M. Fordham, & G. Adler (Eds.), *The collected works of C. G. Jung* (Vol. 7). Princeton, NJ: Princeton University Press.

Jung, C. G. (1933/1971). The stages of life. (Translated by R. F. C. Hull) In J. Campbell (Ed.), *The portable Jung.* New York: Viking.

Jung, C. G. (1936/53). The archetypes and the collective unconscious. In H. Read, M. Fordham, & G. Adler (Eds.), *The collected works of C. G. Jung* (Vol. 9). Princeton, NJ: Princeton University Press.

Jung, C. G. (1964). *Man and his symbols.* New York: Doubleday.

Kabat-Zinn, J. (1990). *Full catastrophe living.* New York: Delacorte Press.

Kagan, J. (1986). Rates of change in psychological processes. *Journal of Applied Developmental Psychology, 7(2)*, 125–130.

Kagan, J. (1987). Essay. *Psychology Today, 21(5)*, 47.

Kagan, J. (1989). *Unstable ideas.* Cambridge, MA: Harvard University Press.

Kaitz, M., Good, A., Roken, A. M., & Eidelman, A. I. (1987). Mothers' recognition of their newborns by olfactory cues. *Developmental Psychobiology, 20*, 587–591.

Kaitz, M., Meschulach-Sarfaty, O., Auerbach, J., & Eidelman, A. (1988). A reexamination of newborn's ability to imitate facial expressions. *Developmental Psychology, 24*, 3–7.

Kakar, S. (1982). *Shamans, mystics and doctors: A psychological enquiry into India and its healing traditions.* Delhi: Oxford University Press.

Kalat, J. W. (1992). *Biological psychology* (4th ed.). Belmont, CA: Wadsworth.

Kales, A., Soldatos, C. R., Bixler, E. O., & Kales, J. D. (1982). Biopsychobehavioral correlates of insomnia: I. Role of sleep apnea and nocturnal myoclonus. *Psychosomatics, 23*, 589–600.

Kales, S., & Kales, J. D. (1984). *Evaluation and treatment of insomnia.* New York: Oxford University Press.

Kalin, R. (1972). Social drinking in different settings. In D.C. McClelland, W. Davies, R. Kalin, & E. Wanner (Eds.), *The drinking man.* New York: The Free Press.

Kalish, R. A., & Reynolds, D. K. (1981). *Death and ethnicity: A psychocultural study.* Farmingdale, NY: Baywood Publishing Company.

Kanas, N. (1986). Group therapy with schizophrenics: A review of controlled studies. *International Journal of Group Psychotherapy, 36*, 339–351.

Kaneko, T. (1987). Japan. In A. R. Gilgen and C. K. Gilgen (Eds.), *International handbook of psychology.* New York: Greenwood Press.

Kaniza, G. (1979). *Organization in vision: Essays on Gestalt perception.* New York: Praeger.

Kann, L., Anderson, J. E., Holtzman, D., Ross, J., Truman, B. I., Collins, J., & Kolbe, L. J. (1991). HIV-related knowledge, beliefs, and behaviors among high school students in the United States: Results from a national survey. *Journal of School Health, 61*, 397–401.

Kanner, A. D., Coyne, J. C., Schaefer, C., & Lazarus, R. S. (1981). Comparison of two modes of stress measurement: Daily hassles and uplifts versus major life events. *Journal of Behavioral Medicine, 4*, 1–39.

Kaplan, A., & Sedney, M. A. (1980). *Psychology and sex roles: An androgynous perspective.* Boston: Little, Brown.

Kaplan, B. H. (1992). Social health and the forgiving heart: The Type B story. *Journal of Behavioral Medicine, 15*, 3–14.

Kaplan, M. (1983). A woman's view of DSM-III. *American Psychologist, 38*, 786–792.

Karno, M., & Golding, J. M. (1991). Obsessive compulsive disorder. In L. N. Robins & D. A. Regier (Eds.), *Psychiatric disorders in America: The epidemiologic catchment area study*. New York: Free Press.

Karp, S. A., Holmstrom, R. W., & Silber, D. E. (1989). *Apperceptive Test manual (APT)*. Worthington, OH: International Diagnosis Systems, Inc.

Karp, S. A., Silber, D. E., Holmstrom, R. W., Banks, V., & Karp, J. (1992). Outcomes of thematic apperception test and apperceptive personality test stories. *Perceptual and Motor Skills, 74*, 479–482.

Kashima, Y., & Triandis, H. C. (1986). The self-serving bias in attributions as a coping strategy: A cross-cultural study. *Journal of Cross-Cultural Psychology, 17*, 83–97.

Kass, F., Spitzer, R. L., & Williams, J. B. (1983). An empirical study of the issue of sex bias in the diagnostic criteria of DSM-III axis II personality disorders. *American Psychologist, 38*, 799–801.

Kastenbaum, R. J. (1986). *Death, society, and the human experience*. Columbus, OH: Merrill.

Katz, A. N. (1986). The relationship between creativity and cerebral hemisphericity for creative architects, scientists, and mathematicians. *Empirical Studies of the Arts, 4(2)*, 97–108.

Katz, J. J., & Halstead, W. C. (1950). Protein organization and mental function. *Comparative Psychological Monographs, 20(1)*, 1–38.

Katz, S., & Kravetz, S. (1989). Facial plastic surgery for persons with Down syndrome: Research findings and their professional and social implications. *American Journal on Mental Retardation, 94(2)*, 101–110.

Katzell, R. A., & Austin, J. T. (1992). From then to now: The development of industrial-organizational psychology in the United States. *Journal of Applied Psychology, 77(6)*, 803–835.

Katzell, R. A., & Thompson, D. E. (1990). Work motivation: Theory and practice. *American Psychologist, 45(2)*, 144–153.

Katzman, R. (1984). *Clinical and pathologic aspects of Alzheimer's disease*. Invited paper presented at the 14th Annual Meeting of the Society for Neuroscience, Anaheim, CA.

Kavanagh, D. J. (1992). Recent developments in expressed emotion and schizophrenia. *British Journal of Psychiatry, 160*, 601–620.

Kay, D. W. K., & Bermann, K. (1982). Epidemiology of mental disorders among the aged in the community. In J. E. Birren & R. B. Sloane (Eds.), *Handbook of mental health and aging*. Englewood Cliffs, NJ: Prentice-Hall.

Kay, P., Berlin, B., & Merrifield, W. R. (1991). Bicultural implications of systems of color naming. *Linguistic Anthropology, 1*, 12–25.

Kazdin, A. (1974). A review of token economy treatment modalities. In D. Harshbarger & R. F. Maley (Eds.), *Behavior analysis and systems analysis: An integrative approach to mental health programs*. Kalamazoo, MI: Behaviordelia.

Kazdin, A. (1978). *History of behavior modification*. University Park: University of Maryland Press.

Keefe, F. J., Dunsmoore, J., & Burnett, R. (1992). Behavioral and cognitive-behavioral approaches to chronic pain: recent advances and future directions. *Journal of Consulting and Clinical Psychology, 60(4)*, 528–536.

Kelley, H. H. (1950). The warm-cold variable in first impressions of persons. *Journal of Personality, 18*, 431–439.

Kelley, H. H. (1952). Two functions of reference groups. In G. E. Swanson, T. M. Newcomb, & E. L. Hartley (Eds.), *Readings in social psychology*. New York: Holt.

Kelley, H. H. (1979). *Personal relationships: Their structures and processes*. Hillsdale, NJ: Erlbaum.

Kelley, H. H. (1983). The situational origins of human tendencies: A further reason for the formal analysis of structures. *Personality and Social Psychology Bulletin, 9(1)*, 8–36.

Kelley, H. H. (1984). Affect in interpersonal relations. *Review of Personality and Social Psychology, No. 5*, 89–115.

Kelley, H. H., Berscheid, E., Christensen, A. Harvey, J., Huston, T., Levinger, G., McClintock, E., Peplau, A., & Peterson, D. R. (1983). *Close relationships*. San Francisco: W. H. Freeman.

Kelley, K., & Byrne, D. (1992). *Exploring human sexuality*. Englewood Cliffs, NJ: Prentice-Hall.

Kelman, H. C., & Hamilton, V. L. (1989). *Crimes of obedience*. New Haven, MA: Yale University Press.

Kemp, S. (1987). Gestalt grouping effects in locating past events in timelines. *Acta Psychologica, 64(2)*, 139–149.

Kendall, P. C., & Hollon, S. D. (Eds.). (1979). *Cognitive-behavioral interventions*. New York: Academic Press.

Kendall, P. C., & Hollon, S. D. (Eds.). (1981). *Assessment strategies for cognitive-behavioral interventions*. New York: Academic Press.

Kendell, R. E. (1986). What are mental disorders? In A. M. Freedman, R. Brotman, I. Silverman, & D. Hutson (Eds.), *Issues in psychiatric classification: Science, practice and social policy*. New York: Human Sciences Press.

Kendell, R. E. (1991). Relationship between the *DSM-IV* and the *ICD-10*. *Journal of Abnormal Psychology, 100(3)*, 297–301.

Kendler, K. S. (1990). Toward a scientific psychiatric nosology. *Archives of General Psychiatry, 47*, 969–973.

Kendler, K. S., Neale, M. C., Kessler, R. C., Heath, A. C., and Eaves, L. J. (1992). The genetic epidemiology of phobias in women. *Archives of General Psychiatry, 49*, 273–281.

Kennell, J. N., & Klaus, M. (1979). *Maternal-infant bonding*. St. Louis: C. V. Mosby.

Kertesz, A., Polk, M., Howell, J., & Black, S. E. (1987). Cerebral dominance, sex, and callosal size in MRI. *Neurology, 37(8)*, 1385–1388.

Kesner, R. P. (1982). Brain stimulation: Effects on memory. *Behavioral and Neural Biology, 36*, 315–367.

Kessen, W. (1983). The child and other cultural inventions. In F. S. Kessel & A. W. Siegel (Eds.), *The child and other cultural inventions*, pp. 224–259. New York: Praeger.

Kestenberg, J. (1979). Orgasm in prepubertal children. *Medical Aspects of Human Sexuality, 13(7)*, 92–93.

Khan, A., & Cohen, S. (1987). Therapeutic role of a psychiatric intensive care unit in acute psychosis. *Comprehensive Psychiatry*, 28(3), 264–269.

Kiefer, C. W. (1988). *The mantle of maturity: A history of ideas about character development*. New York: State University of New York Press.

Kihlstrom, J. F. (1985). Hypnosis. *Annual Review of Psychology*, 36, 385–418.

Kihlstrom, J. F. (1987a). The cognitive unconscious. *Science*, 237, 1445–1452.

Kihlstrom, J. F. (1987b). Strong inferences about hypnosis. *Brain and Behavioral Sciences*, 9, 474–475.

Kilshaw, D., & Annette, M. (1983). Right- and left-hand skill: I. Effects of age, sex and hand preference showing superior skill in left-handers. *British Journal of Psychology*, 74, 253–268.

Kimble, C. E. (1990). *Social psychology: Studying human interaction*. Dubuque, IA: Wm. C. Brown Publishers.

Kimble, D. P. (1992). *Biological psychology* (2nd ed.). Fort Worth, TX: Harcourt Brace Jovanovich.

Kimble, G. A. (1984). Psychology's two cultures. *American Psychologist*, 39, 833–839.

Kimmel, D. C. (1990). *Adulthood and aging: An interdisciplinary, developmental view*. New York: Wiley.

Kimura, D. (1985). Male brain, female brain: The hidden difference. *Psychology Today*, 19(1), 52–58

Kimura, D. (1987). Are men's and women's brains really different? *Canadian Psychology*, 28, 133–147.

Kimura, D. (1988). Biological influences on cognitive function. *Behavioral and Brain Sciences*, 11(2), 200.

Kimura, D. (1989, November). Monthly fluctuations in sex hormones affect women's cognitive skills. *Psychology Today*, pp. 63–66.

King, A. (1991). Effects of training in strategic questioning on children's problem-solving performance. *Journal of Educational Psychology*, 83(3), 307–317.

King, A. (1992). Comparison of self-questioning, summarizing, and notetaking-review as strategies for learning from lectures. *American Educational Research Journal*, 29(2), 303–323.

King, B. T. (1959). Relationships between susceptibility to opinion change and child-rearing practices. In I. L. Janis, C. I. Hovland, P. B. Field, H. Linton, E. Graham, A. R. Cohen, D. Rife, R. P. Abelson, G. S. Lesser, & B. T. King (Eds.), *Personality and persuasibility*. New Haven, CT: Yale University Press.

Kinsey, A. C., Pomeroy, W. B., & Martin, C. E. (1948). *Sexual behavior in the human male*. Philadelphia: W. B. Saunders.

Kinsey, A. C., Pomeroy, W. B. Martin, C. E., & Gebhard, P. H. (1953). *Sexual behavior in the human female*. Philadelphia: W. B. Saunders.

Kitayama, S., & Markus, H. R. (1992, May). *Construal of the self as cultural frame: Implications for internationalizing psychology*. Paper presented at the Symposium on Internationalization and Higher Education, University of Michigan.

Klauer, K. J. (1992). In Mathematik mehr leistungsschwache Mädchen, im Lesen und Rechtschreiben mehr leistungsschwache Jungen? (More girls with poor math skills and more boys with poor reading and writing skills). *Zeitschrift Fur Entwicklungspsychologie und Pädagogische Psychologie*, 24, 48–65.

Klaus, M. H., & Kennell, J. H. (1983). *Bonding: The beginnings of parent to infant attachment*. St. Louis, MO: Mosby.

Kleinke, L. C. (1986). Gaze and eye contact: A research review. *Psychological Bulletin*, 100(1), 78–100.

Kleinman, A. (1988). *Rethinking psychiatry: From cultural category to personal experience*. New York: Free Press.

Kleitman, N. (1987). *Sleep and wakefulness*. Chicago: University of Chicago Press.

Klerman, G. L. (1972). Drug therapy of clinical depressions. *Journal of Psychiatric Research*, 9, 253–270.

Klerman, G. L. (1988). Depression and related disorders of mood (affective disorders). In A. M. Nicholi, Jr. (Ed.), *The new Harvard guide to psychiatry*. Cambridge, MA: Harvard University Press.

Klerman, G. L., & Weissman, M. M. (1986). The interpersonal approach to understanding depression. In T. Millon & G. L. Klerman (Eds.), *Contemporary directions in psychopathology: Toward the DSM-IV*. New York: Guilford Press.

Kline, N., & Angst, J. (1979). *Psychiatric syndromes and drug treatment*. New York: Aronson.

Klinnert, M. D., Emde, R. N., Butterfield, P., & Campos, J. J. (1986). Social referencing: The infant's use of emotional signals from a friendly adult with mother present. *Developmental Psychology*, 22(4), 427–432.

Kluever, H., & Bucy, P. C. (1937). "Psychic blindness" and other symptoms following bilateral temporal lobectomy in rhesus monkeys. *American Journal of Physiology*, 119, 352–353.

Kluft, R. P. (1987). Making the diagnosis of multiple personality disorder. In F. Flach (Ed.), *Diagnostics and psychopathology*. New York: Norton.

Koehler, W. (1929). *Dynamics in psychology*. New York: Liveright.

Kohen, D. P., Mahowald, M. W., & Rosen, G. M. (1992). Sleep-terror disorder in children: The role of self-hypnosis in management. *American Journal of Clinical Hypnosis*, 34, 233–244.

Kohlber, L. (1966). A cognitive-developmental analysis of children's sex-role concepts and attitudes. In E. E. Maccoby (Ed.), *The development of sex differences*. Stanford, CA: Stanford University Press.

Kohlberg, L. (1976). Moral stages and moralization: The cognitive-developmental approach. In T. Likona (Ed.), *Moral development and behavior: Theory, research, and social issues*. New York: Holt, Rinehart and Winston.

Kohn, J. P., & Frazer, G. H. (1986). An academic stress scale: Identification and rated importance of academic stressors. *Psychological Reports*, 59, 415–426.

Kolata, G. (1984). Studying learning in the womb. *Science*, 225, pp. 302–303.

Kolata, G. (1986a). Maleness pinpointed on Y chromosone. *Science*, 234, 234–235.

Kolata, G. (1986b). Weight regulation may start in our cells, not psyches, *Smithsonian*, 16(10), 91–97.

Kolata, G. (1987a). Associations or rules in learning language? *Science*, 237, pp. 113–114.

Kolata, G. (1987b). The metabolic catch-22 of exercise regimens. *Science*, 236, pp. 146–147.

Kolb, B., & Wishaw, I. Q. (1990). *Fundamentals of Human Neuropsychology* (3rd ed.). New York: Freeman.

Koob, G. F. (1984). Neuroleptics: Breaking the dopamine circle. *Contemporary Psychology, 29*, 733–734.

Kosslyn, S. M. (1983). *Ghosts in the mind's machine: Creating and using images in the brain.* New York: Norton.

Kosslyn, S. M. (1985). Stalking the mental image. *Psychology Today, 19(5)*, pp. 23–28.

Kozel, N. J., & Adams, E. H. (1986). Epidemiology of drug abuse: An overview. *Science, 234*, 970–974.

Kramer, D. A. (1983). Post-formal operations? A need for further conceptualization. *Human Development, 26*, 91–105.

Kramer, D. A. (1986). Practical intelligence and adult development: A world views perspective. *International Society for the study of Behavioral Development Newsletter, 1*, 1–3.

Krantz, D. S. (1986). An overview of the stress field. *Contemporary Psychology, 31*, 493–494.

Krasner, L. (1990). Abnormal psychology: Continuous expansion. *Contemporary Psychology, 35(3)*, 257–258.

Kroll, N. E. A., Schepeler, E. M., & Angin, K. T. (1986). Bizarre imagery: The misremembered mnemonic. *Journal of Experimental Psychology: Learning, Memory, and Cognition, 12(1)*, 42–53.

Krosnick, J. A., & Alwin, D. F. (1989). Aging and susceptibility to attitude change. *Journal of Personality and Social Psychology, 57(3)*, 416–425.

Krupinski, J. (1992). Social psychiatry and sociology of mental health: A view on their past and future relevance. *Australian and New Zealand Journal of Psychiatry, 26*, 91–97.

Krupka, L. R., & Vener, A. M. (1992). Gender differences in drug (prescription, nonprescription, alcohol and tobacco) advertising: Trends and implications. *The Journal of Drug Issues, 22(2)*, 339–361.

Kryger, M. H., Roth, T., & Dement, W. C. (Eds.). (1989). *Principles of sleep medicine.* Philadelphia: W. B. Saunders.

Kubler-Ross, E. (1969). *On death and dying.* New York: Macmillan Company.

Kubler-Ross, E. (1970). The dying patient's point of view. In O. G. Brim, Jr., H. E. Freeman, S. Levine, & N. A. Scotch (Eds.), *The dying patient.* New York: Russell Sage Foundation.

Kuhl, P. K., & Meltzoff, A. N. (1984). The intermodal representation of speech in infants. *Infant Behavior and Development, 7(3)*, 361–381.

Kuroda, Y. (1989). "Tracing circuit" model for the memory process in human brain: Roles of ATP and adenosine derivatives for dynamic change of synaptic connections. *Neurochemistry International, 14(3)*, 309–319.

Kurtines, W., & Grief, E. B. (1974). The development of moral thought: Review and evaluation of Kohlberg's approach. *Psychological Bulletin, 81*, 453–470.

Kurtines, W. M., Alvarez, M., & Azmitia, M. (1990). Science and morality: The role of values in science and the scientific study of moral phenomena. *Psychological Bulletin, 107*, 283–295.

Kutner, B. C., Wilkins, C., & Yarrow, P. R. (1952). Verbal attitudes and overt behavior involving racial prejudice. *Journal of Abnormal and Social Psychology, 47*, 649–652.

La Rue, A., Dessonville, C., & Jarvik, L. F. (1985). Aging and mental disorders. In J. E. Birren & K. W. Schaie (Eds.), *Handbook of the psychology of aging* (2nd ed.). New York: Van Nostrand Reinhold.

Labelle, L., Laurence, J. R., Nadon, R., & Perry, C. (1990). Hypnotizability, preference for an imagic cognitive style, and memory creation in hypnosis. *Journal of Abnormal Psychology, 99*, 222–228.

Laberge, S. (1986). *Lucid dreaming.* New York: Ballantine Books.

Laberge, S., & Rheingold, H. (1990). *Exploring the world of lucid dreaming.* New York: Ballantine Books.

Laberg, J. C., Fauske, S., & Loberg, T. (1989). Alcohol research at the Hjellestad Clinic. *British Journal of Addiction, 84(9)*, 999–1009.

Labich, K. (1986). The hunt is on for an antifat pill. *Fortune, 114(4)*, pp. 37–42.

Labouvie-Vief, G. (1982). Dynamic development and mature autonomy: A theoretical prologue. *Human Development, 25*, 161–191.

Labouvie-Vief, G. (1986, August). *Modes of knowing and life-span cognition.* Paper presented at the annual meeting of the American Psychological Association, Washington, DC.

Labov, W. (1970). The logic of nonstandard English. In F. Williams (Ed.), *Language and poverty: Perspectives on a theme.* Chicago: Markham.

Lacks, P., & Morin, C. M. (1992). Recent advances in the assessment and treatment of insomnia. *Journal of Consulting and Clinical Psychology, 60(4)*, 586–594.

Ladd, E. C., Jr., & Lipset, S. M. (1975). *The divided academy: Professors and politics.* Berkeley, CA: Carnegie Commission on Higher Education. (ERIC Microform NO. ED 109 957).

Ladd, E. C., Jr., & Lipset, S. M. (1976). *Survey of the social, political, and educational perspectives of American college and university faculty.* Final Report. Connecticut University. (ERIC Microform NO. ED 135 278).

Lahey, B. B. (1973). Minority group languages. In B. B. Lahey (Ed.), *The modification of language behavior.* Springfield, MO: Charles C. Thomas.

Laird, J. D. (1984). The real role of facial response in the experience of emotion: A reply to Torangeau and Ellsworth, and others. *Journal of Personality and Social Psychology, 47*, 909–917.

Lamb, M. E. (1981). The role of the father: An overview. In M. Lamb (Ed.), *The role of the father in child development* (2nd ed.). New York: Wiley.

Lamb, M. E. (1982). Second thoughts on first touch. *Psychology Today, 16(4)*, 9–11.

Lamb, M. E., & Brown, A. L. (Eds.). (1982). *Advances in developmental psychology.* Hillsdale, NJ: Erlbaum.

Lamb, M. E., Thompson, R. A., Gardner, W. P., Charnov, E. L., & Estes, D. (1984). Security of infantile attachment as assessed by the "strange situation": Its study and biological interpretation. *The Behavioral and Brain Sciences, 7*, 127–171.

Lambert, M. J., Shapiro, D. A., & Bergin, A. E. (1986). The effectiveness of psychotherapy. In S. L. Garfield & A. E. Bergin (Eds.), *Handbook of psychotherapy and behavior change* (3rd ed.). New York: Wiley.

Lamborn, S. D., Mounts, N. S., Steinberg, L., & Dornbusch, S. M. (1991). Patterns of competence and adjustment among adolescents from authoritative, authoritarian, indulgent, and neglectful families. *Child Development, 62*, 1049–1065.

Landau, B., Gleitman, H., & Spelke, E. (1981). Spatial knowledge and geometric representation in a child blind from birth. *Science, 213*, 1275–1278.

Langevin, R. (1983). *Sexual strands: Understanding and treating sexual anomalies in men.* Hillsdale, NJ: Erlbaum.

Langlois, J. H., & Roggman, L. A. (1990). Attractive faces are only average. *Psychological Science, 1(2)*, 115–121.

Langlois, J. H., Roggman, L. A., Casey, R. J., Ritter, J. M., Reiser-Danner, L. A., & Jenkin, V. Y. (1987). Infant preferences for attractive faces: Rudiments of a stereotype? *Development Psychology, 23*, 363–369.

Langlois, J. H., & Roggman, L. A. (1990). Attractive faces are only average. *Psychological Science, 1(2)*, 115–121.

Langlois, J. H., Roggman, L. A., Casey, R. J., Ritter, J. M., Reiser-Danner, L. A., & Jenkin, V. Y. (1987). Infant preferences for attractive faces: Rudiments of a stereotype? *Developmental Psychology, 23*, 363–369.

Lanyon, R. I., & Goodstein, L. D. (1982). *Personality assessment* (2nd ed.). New York: Wiley.

LaPiere, R. T. (1934). Attitudes versus actions. *Social Forces, 13*, 230–237.

Larsen, R. J., Kasimatis, M., & Frey, K. (1992). Facilitating the furrowed brow: An unobtrusive test of the facial feedback hypothesis applied to unpleasant affect. *Cognition and Emotion, 6(5)*, 321–338.

Latané, B. (1981). The psychology of social impact. *American Psychologist, 36*, 343–355.

Latané, B., & Darley, J. M. (1975). *Help in a crisis: Bystander response to an emergency.* Morristown, NJ: General Learning Press.

Lau, R. R. (1984). Dynamics of the attribution process. *Journal of Personality and Social Psychology, 46*, 1017–1028.

Lau, R. R., & Russell, D. (1980). Attributions in the sports pages. *Journal of Personality and Social Psychology, 39(1)*, 29–38.

Laughlin, H. T. (1967). *The neuroses.* Washington, DC: Butterworth.

Lawe, C. F., & Smith, E. W. (1986). Gestalt processes and family therapy. *Individual Psychology, 42*, 537–544.

Lawrence, J., & Adler, R. (1992). Childhood through the eyes of child psychiatrists and paediatricians. *Australian and New Zealand Journal of Psychiatry, 26(1)*, 82–90.

Lazarus, A. (1988). A multimodal perspective on problems of sexual desire. In S. R. Leiblum & R. C. Rosen (Eds.), *Sexual desire disorders.* New York: Guilford.

Lazarus, R. S. (1981, July). Little hassles can be hazardous to your health. *Psychology Today*, pp. 58–62.

Lazarus, R. S. (1982). Thoughts on the relations between emotion and cognition. *American Psychologist, 37*, 1019–1024.

Lazarus, R. S. (1984). On the primacy of cognition. *American Psychologist, 39*, 123–129.

Lazarus, R. S. (1991). Progress on a cognitive-motivational-relational theory of emotion. *American Psychologist, 46*, 819–834.

Lazarus, R. S., DeLongis, A., Folkman, S., & Gruen, R. (1985). Stress and adaptational outcomes: The problem of confounded measures. *American Psychologist, 40*, 770–779.

Lazarus, R. S., & Folkman, S. (1984). *Stress, appraisal, and coping.* New York: Springer Publishing.

Leahey, T. H. (1992). *A history of psychology: Main currents in psychological thought* (3rd ed.). Englewood Cliffs, NJ: Prentice-Hall.

Leak, G. K., & Christopher, S. B. (1982). Freudian psychoanalysis and sociobiology: A synthesis. *American Psychologist, 37(3)*, 313–322.

Leary, W. E. (1989, May 23). Campus AIDS survey finds threat is real but not yet rampant. *New York Times*, p. C12.

LeBow, M. D. (1981). *Weight control: The behavioural strategies.* Chichester, England: Wiley.

Lebra, T. S. (1976). *Japanese patterns of behavior.* Honolulu: University of Hawaii Press.

Lecanuet, J. P., Graner-Deferre, C., & Busnel, M. C. (1991). Prenatal familiarization. In G. Piéraut-Le Bonniec & M. Dolitsky (Eds.), *Language bases . . . Discourse bases.* Philadelphia, PA: John Benjamins Publishing.

Lecanuet, J. P., Graner-Deferre, C., Jacquet, A. Y., & Busnel, M. C. (1992). Decelerative cardiac responsiveness to acoustical stimulation in the near term fetus. *Quarterly Journal of Experimental Psychology, 44B*, 279–303.

Lederman, S. J. (1983). Tactual roughness perception: Spatial and temporal determinants. *Canadian Journal of Psychology, 37*, 498–511.

Lee, A. L., & Scheurer, V. L. (1983). Psychological androgeny and aspects of self-image in women and men. *Sex Roles, 9*, 289–306.

Lee, T., & Seeman, P. (1980). Elevation of brain neuroleptic/dopamine receptors in schizophrenia. *American Journal of Psychiatry, 137*, 191–197.

Leehey, K., Yates, A., & Shisslak, C. M. (1984). Alteration of case reports in "running-an analogue of anorexia?" *New England Journal of Medicine, 310*, 600.

Leff, J. (1992). World Health Organization evaluation of treatment outcomes in psychiatry: Schizophrenia and similar conditions. *International Journal of Mental Health, 21(2)*, 25–40.

Leff, J., & Vaughn, C. (1980). The interaction of life events and relatives' expressed emotion in schizophrenia and depressive neurosis. *British Journal of Psychiatry, 136*, 146–153.

Leff, W. F. (1981). Beautiful people. *OMNI, 4(2)*, 26.

Lehman, A. K., & Rodin, J. (1989). Styles of self-nurturance and disordered eating. *Journal of Consulting and Clinical Psychology, 57*, 117–122.

Lehne, G. K. (1976). Homophobia among men. In D.S. David & R. Brannon (Eds.), *The forty-nine percent majority*. Reading, MA: Addison-Wesley.

Leippe, M. R., & Elkin, R. A. (1987). When motives clash: Issue involvement and response involvement as determinants of persuasion. *Journal of Personality and Social Psychology, 52,* 269–278.

Lemon, B. W., Bengtson, V. L., & Peterson, J. A. (1972). An exploration of the activity theory of aging: Activity and life satisfaction among inmovers to a retirement community. *Journal of Gerontology, 27,* 511–523.

Lerner, R. M., & Shea, J. A. (1982). Social behavior in adolescence. In B. B. Wolman, G. Stricker, S. J. Ellman, P. Keith-spriegel, & D. S. Palermo (Eds.), *Handbook of developmental psychology*. Englewood Cliffs, NJ: Prentice-Hall.

Lesse, S. (1990a). The political and economic changes in Central and Eastern Europe: Possible macropsychosociologic implications. *American Journal of Psychotherapy, 44(2),* 157–159.

Lesse, S. (1990b). The relationship between socioeconomic and sociopolitical forces and individual psychologic behavior in Central and Eastern Europe. *American Journal of Psychotherapy, 44(3),* 317–320.

Lesser, G. S., & Abelson, R. P. (1959). Personality correlates of persuasibility in children. In I. L. Janis, C. I. Hovland, P. B. Field, H. Linton, E. Graham, A. R. Cohen, D. Rife, R. P. Abelson, G. S. Lesser, & B. T. King (Eds.), *Personality and persuasibility*. New Haven, CT: Yale University Press.

Leventhal, H. (1970). Findings and theory in the study of fear communication. In L. Berkowitz (Ed.), *Advances in experimental social psychology* (Vol. 5). New York: Academic Press.

Levin, R. J., & Levin, A. (1975, September). Sexual pleasure: The surprising preferences of 100,000 women. *Redbook, 51.*

Levin, I. (Ed.). (1986). *Stage and structure: Reopening the debate*. Norwood, NJ: Ablex.

Levine, J. M. (1989). Reaction to opinion deviance in small groups. In P. B. Paulus (Ed.), *Psychology of group influence*. Hillsdale, NJ: Erlbaum.

Levine, J. M., & Moreland, R. L. (1990). Progress in small group research. *Annual Review of Psychology, 41,* 585–634.

Levine, S. B. (1988). Intrapsychic and individual aspects of sexual desire. In S. R. Leiblum & R. C. Rosen (Eds.), *Sexual desire disorders*. New York: Guilford.

Levinson, D. J. (1978). *The seasons of a man's life*. New York: Knopf.

Levinson, D. J. (1986). A conception of adult development. *American Psychologist, 41,* 3–13.

Levy, J. A. (1989). Human immunodeficiency viruses and the pathogenesis of AIDS. *Journal of the American Medical Association, 261,* 2997–3006.

Levy, M. S. (1992). The disease controversy and psychotherapy with alcoholics. *Journal of Psychoactive Drugs, 24(3),* 251–256.

Lewine, R. J., Fogg, L., & Meltzer, H. Y. (1983). Assessment of negative and positive symptoms in schizophrenia. *Schizophrenia Bulletin, 9,* 968–976.

Lewinsohn, P. M. (1974). A behavioral approach to depression. In R. J. Friedman & M. M. Katz (Eds.), *The psychology of depression: Contemporary theory and research*. New York: Halsted.

Lewis, C. D., & Houtz, J. C. (1986). Sex-role stereotyping and young children's divergent thinking. *Psychological Reports, 58,* 113–122.

Lewis, C. E. (1991). Neurochemical mechanisms of chronic antisocial behavior (psychopathy): A literature review. *The Journal of Nervous and Mental Disease, 179(12),* 720–726.

Lewis, R. V. (1983). Scared straight—California style: Evaluation of the San Quentin Squires Program. *Criminal Justice and Behavior, 10,* 209–226.

Lewis, S. W., & Murray, R. M. (1987). Obstetric complications, neurodevelopmental deviance, and risk of schizophrenia. *Journal of Psychiatric Research, 21,* 413–421.

Lewy, A. J., Sack, R. L., Miller, L. S., & Hoban, T. M. (1987). Antidepressant and circadian phase-shifting effects of light. *Science, 235,* 352–354.

Liberakis, E. A. (1981). Factors predisposing to institutionalism. *Acta Psychiatrica Scandinavica, 63,* 356–366.

Lichtenberg, J. D. (1989). *Psychoanalysis and motivation*. Hillsdale, NJ: Analytic Press.

Lidz, T., Fleck, S., & Cornelison, A. R. (1965). *Schizophrenia and the family*. New York: International Universities Press.

Lieberman, H. R., Garfield, G., Waldhauser, F., Lynch, H. J., & Wurtman, R. J. (1985). Possible behavioral consequences of light-induced changes in melatonin availability. *Annals of the New York Academy of Sciences, 453,* 242–252.

Lieberman, J., Bogerts, B., Degreef, G., Ashtari, M., Lantos, G., & Alvir, J. (1992). Qualitative assessment of brain morphology in acute and chronic schizophrenia. *American Journal of Psychiatry, 149(6),* 784–794.

Lin, K., & Kleinman, A. M. (1988). Psychopathology and clinical course of schizophrenia: A cross-cultural perspective. *Schizophrenia Bulletin, 14,* 555–567.

Lindsay, P., & Norman, D. (1977). *Human information processing: An introduction to psychology*. New York: Academic Press.

Lindskold, S. (1986). GRIT: Reducing distrust through carefully introduced conciliation. In S. Worchel and W. G. Austin (Eds.), *Psychology of intergroup relations* (2nd ed.). Chicago: Nelson-Hall.

Linhart, J., & Kodym, M. (1987). Czechoslovakia. In A. R. Gilgen and C. K. Gilgen (Eds.), *International handbook of psychology*. New York: Greenwood Press.

Linn, M. C., & Petersen, A. (1986). A meta-analysis of gender differences in spatial ability: Implications for mathematics and science achievement. In J. S. Hyde & M. C. Linn (Eds.), *The psychology of gender: Advances through meta-analysis*. Baltimore, MD: Johns Hopkins University Press.

Linssen, A. C. G., & Spinhoven, P. (1992). Multimodal treatment programmes for chronic pain: A quantitative analysis of existing research data. *Journal of Psychosomatic Research, 36(3),* 275–286.

Linz, D., Wilson, B. J., & Donnerstein, E. (1992). Sexual violence in the mass media: Legal solutions, warnings, and mitigation through education. *Journal of Social Issues, 48*, 145–171.

Lippa, R. A. (1990). *Introduction to social psychology.* Belmont, CA: Wadsworth Publishing Company.

Lips, H. M. (1988). *Sex and gender: An introduction.* Mountain View, CA: Mayfield.

Lips, H. M. (1992). Gender- and science-related attitudes as predictors of college students' academic choices. *Journal of Vocational Behavior, 40*, 62–81.

Lipsitt, L. P. (1982). Infancy and life-span development. *Human Development, 25(1)*, 41–48.

Lipsitt, L. P. (1990). Learning processes in the human newborn: Sensitization, habituation, and classical conditioning. *Annals of the New York Academy of Sciences, 608*, 113–127.

Liskin, L., & Blackburn, R. (1986, July-August). AIDS: A public health crisis. *Population Reports,* Ser. L. no. 6.

Livsen, N., & Peskin, H. (1980). Perspectives on adolescence from longitudinal research. In J. Adelson (Ed.), *Handbook of adolescent psychology.* New York: Wiley.

Lloyd, B. B. (1986). Sex differences in development. In R. Harre & R. Lamb (Eds.), *The dictionary of developmental and educational psychology.* Cambridge, MA: The MIT Press.

Loftus, E. F. (1979). The malleability of human memory. *American Scientist, 67*, 312–320.

Loftus, E. F. (1984). Eyewitness: Essential but unreliable. *Psychology Today, 18(2)*, pp. 22–27.

Loftus, E. F. (1991). Made in memory: Distortions in recollection after misleading information. *The Psychology of Learning and Motivation, 27*, 187–215.

Loftus, E. F., & Hoffman, H. G. (1989). Misinformation and memory: The creation of new memories. *Journal of Experimental Psychology: General, 118*, 100–104.

Loftus, E. F., & Loftus, G. R. (1980). On the permanence of stored information in the human brain. *American Psychologist, 35*, 409–420.

Loftus, E. F., & Palmer, J. C. (1974). Reconstruction of automobile destruction: An example of the interaction between language and memory. *Journal of Verbal Learning and Verbal Behavior, 13*, 585–589.

Lohaus, A. (1992). Verbale und nonverbale Kommunikation im Kindesalter: Ergebnisse einer entwicklungspsychologischen Studie. *Zeitschrift für Entwicklungspsychologie und Pädagogische Psychologie, 24(1)*, 22–38.

Lombardo, J. P. (1986). Interaction of sex and sex role in response to violations of preferred seating arrangements. *Sex Roles, 15(3–4)*, 173–183.

Lomov, B. F. (1987). Soviet Union. In A. R. Gilgen and C. K. Gilgen (Eds.), *International handbook of psychology.* New York: Greenwood Press.

London, W. P. (1986). Handedness and alcoholism: A family history of lefthandedness. *Alcoholism Clinical and Experimental Research, 10(3)*, 357.

Loomis, L. L., & Napoli, A. M. (1975). Transfer of training through two cannibalisms of planaria. *Journal of Biological Psychology, 17(1)*, 37–40.

Lopez, F. G. (1987). The impact of parental divorce on college student development. *Journal of Counselling and Development, 65(9)*, 484–486.

Lopez, S., & Hernandez, P. (1986). How culture is considered in evaluations of psychopathology. *Journal of Nervous and Mental Disease, 174(10)*, 598–606.

LoPiccolo, J., & Friedman, J. M. (1988). In S.R. Leiblulm & R.C. Rosen (Eds.), *Sexual desire disorders.* New York: Guilford.

Loranger, A. W. (1990). The impact of DSM-III on diagnostic practice in a university hospital. *Archives of General Psychology, 47*, 672–765.

Lorayne, H. (1990). *Super memory super student: How to raise your grades in 30 days.* Boston: Little, Brown.

Lorayne, H., & Lucas, J. (1974). *The memory book.* New York: Ballantine Books.

Lorenz, K. (1957). Comparative study of behavior. In C. H. Schiller (Ed.), *Instinctive behavior.* New York: International Press.

Lortie-Lussier, M., Fellers, G. L., & Kleinplatz, P. J. (1986). Value orientations of English, French, and Italian Canadian children: Continuity of the ethnic mosaic? *Journal of Cross-Cultural Psychology, 17*, 283–299.

Lortie-Lussier, M., Simond, S., Rinfret, N., & De Kininck, J. (1992). Beyond sex differences: Family and occupational roles' impact on women's and men's dreams. *Sex Roles, 26(3/4)*, 79–96.

Lovibond, P. F. (1988). Animal learning theory and the future of human Pavlovian conditioning. *Biological Psychology, 27(2)*, 199–202.

Luchins, A. S. (1942). Mechanization in problem solving. *Psychological Monographs, 54* (Whole no. 248).

Lugaresi, E., & Medori, R. (1986). Fatal familial insomnia and dysautonoia with selective degeneration of thalamic nuclei. *New England Journal of Medicine, 315(16)*, 997–1003.

Lukoff, D., Lu, F., & Turner, R. (1992). Toward a more culturally sensitive DSM-IV: Psychoreligious and psychospiritual problems. *The Journal of Nervous and Mental Disease, 180(11)*, 673–682.

Luria, Z., & Meade, R. G. (1984). Sexuality and the middle-aged woman. In G. Baruch & J. Brooks-Gunn (Eds.), *Women in midlife.* New York: Plenum.

Luttges, J., Johnson, T., Buck, C., Holland, J., & McGaugh, J. M. (1966). An examination of "transfer of learning" by nucleic acid. *Science, 151*, 834–837.

Lyerly, S. B., Ross, S., Krugman, A. D., & Clyde, D. J. (1964). Drugs and placebos: The effects of instructions upon performance and mood under amphetamine sulphate and chloral hydate. *Journal of Abnormal and Social Psychology, 68*, 321–327.

Lykken, D. T. (1985). "Emergenic traits": Lykken replies. *Psychophysiology, 22(1)*, 122–123.

Lynn, S. J., & Rhue, J. W. (1988). Fantasy proneness: Hypnosis, developmental antecedents, and psychopathology. *American Psychologist, 43*, 35–44.

Lynn, S. J., Rhue, J. W., & Weekes, J. R. (1990). Hypnotic involuntariness: A social cognitive analysis. *Psychological Review, 97(2)*, 169–184.

Lyon, K. A. (1992). Shattered mirror: A fragment of the treatment of a patient with multiple personality disorder. *Psychoanalytic Inquiry, 12(1)*, 71–94.

Maccoby, E. E. (1990). Gender and relationships. *American Psychologist, 45(4)*, 513–520.

Maccoby, E. E., & Jacklin, C. N. (1974). *The psychology of sex differences.* Stanford, CA: Stanford University Press.

Maccoby, E., & Martin, J. (1983). Socialization in the context of the family: Parent-child interaction. In E. M. Hetherington (Ed.), P. H. Mussen (Series Ed.), *Handbook of child psychology: Vol. 4. Socialization, personality, and social development* (pp. 1–101). New York: Wiley.

MacLaury, R. E. (1991). Exotic color categories: Linguistic relativity to what extent? *Journal of Linguistic Anthropology, 1*, 26–51.

MacLaury, R. E. (1991). Prototypes revisited. *Annual Review of Anthropology, 20*, 55–74.

MacLaury, R. E. (1992). From brightness to hue: An explanatory model of color-category evolution. *Current Anthropology, 33*, 137–186.

MacLusky, N. J., & Naftolin, F. (1981). Sexual differentiation of the central nervous system. *Science, 211*, 1294–1302.

Mactutus, C. F., & Fechter, L. D. (1984). Prenatal exposure to carbon monoxide: Learning and memory deficits. *Science, 223*, 409–411.

Madaus, G. (1990). *From gatekeeper to Gateway: Transforming testing in America.* Washington, DC: National Commission on Testing and Public Policy.

Maddox, G. L. (1974). Disengagement theory: A critical evaluation. *Gerontologist, 4*, 80.

Maehr, M. L. (1987). Managing organizational culture to enhance motivation. *Advances in Motivation and Achievement, 5*, 287–320.

Magee, J. J. (1988). *A professional's guide to older adult's life review.* Lexington, MA: Lexington Books.

Magnusson, D. (Ed.). (1981). *Toward a psychology of situations: An interactional perspective.* Hillsdale, NJ: Erlbaum.

Magoun, H. W. (1981). John B. Watson and the study of human sexual behavior. *Journal of Sex Research, 17*, 368–378.

Mahoney, M. (1974). *Cognition and behavior modification.* Cambridge, MA: Ballinger.

Mahowald, M. B. (1992). To be or not to be a woman: Anorexia nervosa, normative gender roles, and feminism. *The Journal of Medicine and Philosophy, 17*, 233–251.

Maier, N. R. F. (1931). Reasoning in human beings: II. The solution of a problem and its appearance in consciousness. *Journal of Comparative Psychology, 12*, 181–194.

Maier, S. F., Seligman, M. E. P., & Solomon, R. L. (1969). Pavlovian fear conditioning and learned helplessness. In R. Church & B. Campbell (Eds.), *Aversive conditioning and learning.* New York: Appleton-Century-Crofts.

Malsbury, C., & Pfaff, D. W. (1974). Neural and hormonal determinants of mating behavior in adult male rats. In L. DiCara (Ed.), *Limbic and autonomic nervous system research.* New York: Plenum.

Makler, S., Sigal, M., Gelkopf, M., Kochba, B. B., & Horeb, E. (1990). Combat-related, chronic post-traumatic stress disorder: Implications for group-therapy intervention. *American Journal of Psychotherapy, 44(3)*, 381–386.

Mangus, B., Henderson, H., & French, R. (1986). Implementation of a token economy by peer tutors to increase on-task physical activity time of autistic children. *Perceptual and Motor Skills, 63(1)*, 97–98.

Manning, F. J., & Fullerton, T. D. (1988). Health and well-being in highly cohesive units of the U.S. Army. *Journal of Applied Social Psychology, 18*, 503–519.

Marcia, J. E. (1966). Development and validation of ego-identity status. *Journal of Personality and Social Psychology, 3*, 551–558.

Marcia, J. E. (1980). Identity in adolescence. In J. Adelson (Ed.), *Handbook of adolescent psychology.* New York: Wiley.

Mark, V. H., & Ervin, F. R. (1970). *Violence and the brain.* New York: Harper & Row.

Markus, H., & Kitayama, S. (1991). Culture and the self: Implications for cognition, emotion, and motivation. *Psychological Review, 98(2)*, 224–253.

Marlatt, G. A. (1983). The controlled-drinking controversy: A commentary. *American Psychologist, 38*, 1097–1110.

Marlatt, G. A. (1984). Innovative approaches to the treatment of alcoholism. *Contemporary Psychology, 29*, 103–105.

Marlatt, G. A., & Rohsenow, D. J. (1981). The think-drink effect. *Psychology Today, 15(12)*, 60–69.

Marlow, H. A., Jr., & Weinberg, R. B. (Eds.). (1985). *Competence development: Theory and practice in special populations.* Springfield, IL: Charles C. Thomas.

Marshall, D. (1971). Sexual behavior on Mangaia. In D. Marshall and R. Suggs (Eds.) *Human sexual behavior.* New York: Basic Books.

Martin, R. A., & Lefcourt, H. M. (1983). Sense of humor as a moderator of the relationship between stressors and moods. *Journal of Personality and Social Psychology, 45*, 1313–1324.

Martin, I., & Levey, A. B. (1989). Propositional knowledge and mere responding. *Biological Psychology, 28(2)*, 149–155.

Marx, J. L. (1982). Autoimmunity in left-handers. *Science, 219*, 141–142.

Marx, J. L. (1987). Antibody research garners Nobel Prize. *Science, 238*, 484–485.

Maslow, A. H. (1954/1970). *Motivation and personality* (2nd ed.). New York: Harper & Row.

Maslow, A. H. (1970). *Motivation and personality* (2nd ed.). New York: Viking.

Maslow, A. H. (1971). *The farther reaches of human nature.* New York: Viking.

Mason, J. C. (1985). The interdiction of diazepam provision. *Military Medicine, 150(7)*, 376–377.

Massaro, D. W. (1990). A review of "The pseudo-science of B. F. Skinner." *American Journal of Psychology, 103(2)*, 265–297.

Masters, W. H., & Johnson, V. E. (1966). *The human sexual response.* Boston: Little, Brown.

Masters, W. H., Johnson, V. E., & Kolodny, R. C. (1992). *Human sexuality* (4th ed.). New York: HarperCollins.

Matarrazo, J. D. (1983). The reliability of psychiatric and psychological diagnosis. *Clinical Psychology Review, 3*, 103–145.

Matarrazzo, J. D. (1984). Behavioral immunogens and pathogens in health and illness. In B. L. Hammonds & C. J. Scheirer (Eds.), *Psychology and health*. Washington, DC: American Psychological Association.

Matarrazzo, J. D. (1990). Psychological assessment versus psychological testing. *American Psychologist, 45(9)*, 999–1017.

Matlin, M. W. (1982). *Perception*. Boston: Allyn and Bacon.

Matlin, M. W. (1988). *Sensation and perception*. Boston: Allyn and Bacon.

Matlin, M. W. (1989). *Cognition* (2nd ed.). New York: Holt, Rinehart and Winston.

Matsumoto, D. (1990). Cultural similarities and differences in display rules. *Motivation and Emotion, 14*, 195–214.

Matsumoto, D. (1992). American-Japanese cultural differences in the recognition of universal facial expressions. *Journal of Cross-Cultural Psychology, 23*, 72–84.

Matsumoto, D., & Ekman, P. (1989). American-Japanese cultural differences in intensity of ratings of facial expressions of emotion. *Motivation and Emotion, 13*, 143–157.

Matteson, D. R. (1984). Identity: Is that all there is to adolescence? *Contemporary Psychology, 29*, 140–142.

Matthews, K. A. (1988). CHD and Type A behaviors: Update on and alternative to Booth-Kewley and Friedman quantitive review. *Psychological Bulletin, 104*, 373–380.

Maurer, D., & Maurer, C. (1988). *The world of the newborn*. New York: Basic Books.

Mavreas, V. G., Tomaras, V., Karydi, V., Economou, M., & Stefanis, C. N. (1992). Expressed emotion in families of chronic schizophrenics and its association with clinical measures. *Social Psychiatry and Psychiatric Epidemiology, 27*, 4–9.

Mayer, M. (1958). *Madison Avenue, USA*. New York: Harper & Row.

Mays, D. T., & Franks, C. M. (1985). *Negative outcome in psychotherapy and what to do about it*. New York: Springer.

McAuley, E., Courneya, K. S., & Lettunich, J. (1991). Effects of acute and long-term exercise on self-efficacy responses in sedentary, middle-aged males and females. *The Gerontologist, 31*, 534–542.

McCarthy, P. (1987). A quicker response. *Psychology Today, 21(10)*, 12.

McCauley, D., & Swann, C. (1980). Sex differences in the frequency and functions of fantasies during sexual activity. *Journal of Research in Personality, 14*, 400–411.

McClelland, D. C. (1961). *The achieving society*. New York: Van Nostrand.

McClelland, D. C., & Winter, D. G. (1971). *Motivating economic achievement*. New York: Free Press.

McClelland, J. L., & Rumelhart, D. E. (1986). A distributed model of human learning and memory. In J. L. McClelland & D. E. Rumelhart (Eds.), *Parallel distributed processing* (Vol. 2). Cambridge, MA: MIT Press.

McConnell, J. V. (1966). Persuasion and behavioral change. In *The art of persuasion in litigation handbook*. West Palm Beach, FL: American Trial Lawyers Association.

McConnell, J. V. (1968). The biochemistry of memory. *Medizinisches Prisma*, No. 3. Ingelheim am Rhein, Germany: Boehringer Sohn.

McConnell, J. V. (1985). Practicing what we preach. *Behavior Therapist, 8*, 176–177.

McConnell, J. V. (1985). Psychology of the scientist: LII. John B. Watson: Man and myth. *Psychological Reports, 56*, 683–705.

McConnell, J. V. (1990). Negative reinforcement and positive punishment. *Teaching of Psychology, 17(4)*, 247–249.

McConnell, J. V., Jacobson, A. L., & Kimble, D. P. (1959). The effects of regeneration upon retention of a conditioned response in the planarian. *Journal of Comparative and Physiological Psychology, 52*, 1–5.

McConnell, J. V., Jacobson, R., & Humphries, B. M. (1961). The effects of ingestion of conditioned planarians on the response level of naive planarians: A pilot study. *Worm Runner's Digest, 3(1)*, pp. 41–47.

McCrady, B. S. (1985). Comments on the controlled drinking controversy. *American Psychologist, 40*, 370–371.

McFarland, C., Ross, M., & Giltrow, M. (1992). Biased recollections in older adults: The role of implicit theories of aging. *Journal of Personality and Social Psychology, 62(5)*, 837–850.

McGaugh, J. L. (1973). Drug facilitation of learning and memory. *Annual Review of Pharmacology, 13*, 229–241.

McGaugh, J. L. (1990). Significance and remembrance: The role of neuromodulatory systems. *Psychological Science, 1(1)*, 15–25.

McGaugh, J. L. (1992). Affect, neuromodulatory systems and memory storage. In S.-Å. Christianson (Ed.), *The handbook of emotion and memory: Research and theory*. Hillsdale, NJ: Erlbaum.

McGaugh, J. L., & Gold, P. E. (1976). Modulation of memory by electrical stimulation of the brain. In M. R. Rosenzweig & E. L. Bennett (Ed.), *Neural mechanisms of learning and memory*. Cambridge, MA: MIT Press.

McGlashan, T. H. (1986). Predictors of shorter-, medium-, and longer-term outcome in schizophrenia. *American Journal of Psychiatry, 142*, 50–55.

McGue, M., Bouchard, T. J., Lykken, D. T., & Feuer, D. (1984). Information processing abilities in twins reared apart. *Intelligence, 8*, 239–258.

McGuigan, F. J. (1987). The current status of hypnosis. *Contemporary Psychology, 32*, 177–178.

McIntyre, A., & Lounsbury, K. R. (1988). Psychosocial characteristics of foster children. *Journal of Applied Developmental Psychology, 9(2)*, 125–137.

McKean, K. (1985). Intelligence: New ways to measure the wisdom of man. *Discover, 6(10)*, pp. 25–31.

McKean, K. (1986, October). Pain. *Discover*, 82–92.

McTear, M. (1985). *Children's conversation*. Oxford, England: Basil Blackwell.

Mednick, S. A., Machon, R., Huttunen, M. O., & Bonett, D. (1988). Fetal viral infection and adult schizophrenia. *Archives of General Psychiatry, 45*, 189–192.

Meer, J. (1985). Quiet: I'm driving. *Psychology Today, 19(1)*, p. 20.

Mehrabian, A. (1981). *Silent messages: Implicit communication of emotions and attitudes* (2nd ed.). Belmont, CA: Wadsworth.

Mehryar, A. H. (1984). The role of psychology in national development: Wishful thinking and reality. *International Journal of Psychology, 19*, 159–167.

Meichenbaum, D. H. (1977). *Cognitive-behavior modification: An integrative approach*. New York: Plenum.

Meichenbaum, D. H. (1985). *Stress inoculation training*. Oxford, England: Pergamon Press.

Meier, M. J. (1992). Modern clinical neuropsychology in historical perspective. *American Psychologist, 47(4)*, 550–558.

Meister, K. A. (1984). The 80s search for the fountain of youth comes up very dry. *American Council on Science and Health News & Views, 9/10*, 8–11.

Melikian, L. H. (1984). The transfer of psychological knowledge to the Third World countries and its impact on development: The case of five Arab Gulf oil-producing states. *International Journal of Psychology, 19*, 65–77.

Meltzer, H. Y. (1987). Biological studies in schizophrenia. *Schizophrenia Bulletin, 13(1)*, 77–111.

Meltzer, H. Y. (1990). Role of serotonin in depression. *Annals of the New York Academy of Sciences, 600*, 486–500.

Meltzer, H. Y., & Stahl, S. M. (1976). The dopamine hypothesis of schizophrenia: A review. *Schizophrenia Bulletin, 2*, 19–76.

Meltzoff, A. N. (1981). Imitation, intermodal co-ordination and representation in early infancy. In G. Butterworth (Ed.), *Infancy and epistemology*. Brighton, England: Harvester Press.

Meltzoff, A. N., & Moore, M. K. (1977). Imitation of facial gestures by human neonates. *Science, 198*, pp. 75–78.

Meltzoff, A. N., & Moore, M. K. (1983). The origins of imitation in infancy: Paradigm, phenomena, and theories. *Advances in Infancy Research, 2*, 265–301.

Meltzoff, A. N., & Moore, M. K. (1992). Early imitation within a functional framework: The importance of person identity, movement, and development. *Infant Behavior and Development, 15*, 479–505.

Melzack, R. (Ed.). (1983). *Pain measurement and assessment*. New York: Raven Press.

Melzack, R. (1989). Phantom limbs, the self and the brain (The D. O. Hebb memorial lecture). *Canadian Psychology, 30*, 1–16.

Melzack, R., & Wall, P. D. (1965). Pain mechanisms: A new theory. *Science, 150*, 971–979.

Mendel, W. M. (1966). Effect of length of hospitalization on rate and quality of remission from acute psychotic episodes. *Journal of Nervous and Mental Disease, 143(3)*, 226–233.

Mendel, W. M. (1969). Tranquilizer prescribing as a function of the experience and availability of the therapist. *American Journal of Psychiatry, 124(1)*, 16–22.

Mendez, M. F., Martin, R. J., Smyth, K. A., & Whitehouse, P. J. (1992). Disturbances of person identification in Alzheimer's disease. *The Journal of Nervous and Mental Disease, 180(2)*, 94–96.

Mendonsa, E. L. (1981). The status of women in Sisala society. *Sex Roles, 7*, 607–625.

Mendoza, R., & Miller, B. L. Neuropsychiatric disorders associated with cocaine use. *Hospital and Community Psychiatry, 43(7)*, 677–679.

Mendoza, R., Miller, B. L., & Mena, I. (1992). Emergency room evaluation of cocaine-associated neuropsychiatric disorders. In Marc Galanter (Ed.), *Recent developments in alcoholism. Vol 10: Alcohol and cocaine*. New York: Plenum Press.

Merskey, H. (1992). The manufacture of personalities: The production of multiple personality disorder. *British Journal of Psychiatry, 160*, 327–340.

Mervis, C. B., & Rosch, E. (1981). Categorization of natural objects. *Annual Review of Psychology, 32*, 89–115.

Metalsky, G. I., Haberstadt, L. J., & Abramson, L. Y. (1987). Vulnerability and invulnerability to depressive mood reactions: Toward a more powerful test of the diathesis-stress and causal mediation theory of depression. *Journal of Personality and Social Psychology, 52*, 386–393.

Metcalfe, J. (1990). Composite Holographic Associative Recall Model (CHARM) and blended memories in eyewitness testimony. *Journal of Experimental Psychology: General, 119*, 145–160.

Meyer, A. (1951). The psychobiological point of view. In E. E. Winters (Ed.), *Collected works of Adolph Meyer*. Baltimore: Johns Hopkins Press.

Meyer, R. (1980). The antisocial personality. In R. Woody (Ed.), *The encyclopedia of mental assessment*. San Francisco: Jossey-Bass.

Meyer-Bahlburg, H. F. L. (1977). Sex hormones and male homosexuality in comparative perspective. *Archives of Sexual Behavior, 6(4)*, 297–325.

Meyer-Bahlburg, H. F. L. (1979). Sex hormones and female homosexuality: A critical examination. *Archives of Sexual Behavior, 8(2)*, 101–119.

Michael, R. P. (1980). Hormones and sexual behavior in the female. In D. T. Krieger and J. C. Hughes (Eds.), *Neuroendocrinology*. Sunderland, MA: Sinauer.

Michelson, L. (Ed.). (1985). Meta-analysis and clinical psychology. [Special issue]. *Clinical Psychology Review, 5(1)*.

Michener, H. A., DeLamater, J. D., & Schwartz, S. H. (1986). *Social psychology*. New York: Harcourt Brace Jovanovich.

Mika, S. (1981). Some determinants of source credibility. *Polish Psychological Bulletin, 12(2)*, 79–86.

Mikulas, W. L. (1986). Self-control: Essence and development. *Psychological Record, 36*, 297–308.

Milgram, S. (1963). Behavioral study of obedience. *Journal of Abnormal Psychology, 67*, 371–378.

Milgram, S. (1964). Group pressure and action against a person. *Journal of Abnormal Social Psychology, 69*, 137–143.

Milgram, S. (1965). Liberating effects of group pressure. *Journal of Personality and Social Psychology, 1,* 127–134.

Milgram, S. (1974). *Obedience to authority.* New York: Harper & Row.

Millar, S. (1968). *The psychology of play.* Baltimore: Penguin Books.

Miller, A. G. (Ed.). (1982). *In the eye of the beholder: Contemporary issues in stereotyping.* New York: Praeger.

Miller, A. R. (1986). The physical attractiveness of physiques in determining certainty of guilt, recommended punishment, and rehabilitative potential of defendants. *Dissertation Abstracts International, 47(5–B).*

Miller, B. (1988). Date rape: Time for a new look at prevention. *Journal of College Student Development, 29(6),* 553–555.

Miller, B., & Marshall, J. C. (1987). Coercive sex on the university campus. *Journal of College Student Personnel, 28(1),* 38–47.

Miller, G. A. (1956). The magical number seven, plus or minus two: Some limits on our capacity for processing information. *Psychological Review, 63,* 81–97.

Miller, G. A. (1969). Psychology as a means of promoting human welfare. *American Psychologist, 24,* 1063–1075.

Miller, G. A. (1987). *Psychology: The science of mental life.* Penguin.

Miller, G. A. (1990). The place of language in a scientific psychology. *Psychological Science, 1(1)* 7–14.

Miller, G. A., & Gildea, P. M. (1987, September). How children learn words. *Scientific American,* pp. 94–99.

Miller, J. A. (1986). X chromosomes: Too few and too many. *Science News, 129,* p. 358.

Miller, J. G. (1978). *Living systems.* New York: McGraw–Hill.

Miller, J. G. (1984). Culture and the developments of everyday social explanation. *Journal of Personality and Social Psychology, 46,* 961–978.

Miller, J. G., Bersoff, D. M., & Harwood, R. L. (1990). Perceptions of social responsibilities in India and in the United States: Moral imperatives or personal decisions? *Journal of Personality and Social Psychology, 58,* 33–47.

Miller, K., Downer, A., & Kreuger, L. (1988). Reported sexual behavior differences between heterosexual and gay/lesbian populations. Presented at the IV International Conference on AIDS, Stockholm, June 12–16.

Miller, L. (1989). On the neuropsychology of dreams. *Psycholanalytic Review, 76(3),* 375–401.

Miller, N., Maruyama, G., Beaber, R. J., & Valone, K. (1976). Speed of speech and persuasion. *Journal of Personality and Social Psychology, 34,* 615–624.

Miller, N. E. (1974). Biofeedback: Evaluation of a new technique. *New England Journal of Medicine, 290,* 684–685.

Miller, N. E. (1985). Rx: Biofeedback. *Psychology Today, 19,* 54–59.

Miller, N. E., & Brucker, B. S. (1979). A learned visceral response apparently independent of skeletal ones in patients paralyzed by spinal lesions. In N. Birbaumer & H. D. Kimmel (Eds.), *Biofeedback and self-regulation.* Hillsdale, NJ: Erlbaum.

Miller, N. S., & Francis, R. J. (1989). New York Hospital Westchester Division Cornell University Medical College: A tradition in the treatment of alcoholism. *Journal of Substance Abuse Treatment, 6(3),* 201–204.

Miller, S. (1989). Optical differences in cases of multiple personality disorder. *Journal of Mental Disease, 177,* 480–486.

Miller, W. R., & Hester, R. K. (1980). Treating the problem drinker: Modern approaches. In W. R. Miller (Ed.), *The addictive behaviors: Treatment of alcoholism, drug abuse, smoking and obesity.* Oxford, England: Pergamon Press.

Miller, W. R. & Hester, R. K. (1986). The effectiveness of treatment techniques: What the research reveals. In W. R. Miller & N. Heather (Eds.), *Treating addicitive behaviors: Processes of change.* New York: Plenum Press.

Miller, W. R., & Lief, H. I. Masturbatory attitudes, knowledge and experience: Data from the sex knowledge and attitude test (SKAT). *Archives of Sexual Behavior, 5,* 447–467.

Millon, T. (1981). *Disorders of personality. DSM-III: Axis II.* New York: Wiley.

Millon, T. (1991). Classification in psychopathology: Rationale, alternatives, and standards. *Journal of Abnormal Psychology, 100,* 245–261.

Mills, C., & Walter, T. (1979). Reducing juvenile delinquency: A behavioral employment intervention program. In J. S. Stumphauzer (Ed.), *Progress in behavior therapy with delinquents.* Springfield, IL: Charles C. Thomas.

Mineka, S., & Sutton, S. K. (1992). Cognitive biases and the emotional disorders. *Psychological Science, 3(1),* 65–69.

Mingay, D. J. (1987). The effect of hypnosis on eyewitness memory: Reconciling forensic claims and research findings. *Applied Psychology: An International Review, 36,* 163–183.

Miró, J., & Raich, R. M. (1992). Personality traits and pain experience. *Personality and Individual Differences, 13,* 309–313.

Mischel, W. (1977). On the future of personality measurement. *American Psychologist, 32,* 246–254.

Mishkin, M., & Appenzeller, T. (1987, June). The anatomy of memory. *Scientific American,* pp. 80–89.

Money, J. (1987). Sin, sickness, or status? Homosexual gender identity and psychoneuroendcrinology. *American Psychologist, 42(4),* 384–399.

Money, J., Wiedeking, C., Walker, P. A., & Gain, D. (1976). Combined antiandrogenic and counseling program for treatment of 46, XY and 47, XYY sex offenders. In E. J. Sachar (Ed.), *Hormones, behavior, and psychopathology.* New York: Raven.

Monte, C. F. (1991). *Beneath the mask: An introduction to theories of personality* (4th ed.). New York: Holt, Rinehart and Winston.

Montplaisir, J., & Poirer, G. (1987). Narcolepsy in monozygotic twins. *Neurology, 37,* 1089.

Mook, D. G. (1987). *Motivation: The organization of action.* New York: Norton.

Moon, Y. (1986). A review of cross-cultural studies on moral judgment development using the Defining Issues Test. *Behavior Science Research, 20(1–4),* 147–177.

Mooney, D. K., Fromme, K., Kivlahan, D. R., & Marlatt, G. A. (1987). Correlates of alcohol consumption: Sex, age, and expectancies relate differentially to quantity and frequency. *Addictive Behavior, 12,* 234–240.

Moore, B. C. J. (1989). *An introduction to the psychology of hearing* (3rd ed.). London: Academic Press.

Moore-Ede, M. C. (1982). What hath night to do with sleep? *Natural History, 91(9),* 22–24.

Moore-Ede, M. C., Sulzman, F. M., & Fuller, C. A. (1982). *The clocks that time us: Physiology of the circadian timing system.* Cambridge, MA: Harvard University Press.

Morawski, J. G. (1992). There is more to our history of giving: The place of introductory textbooks in American psychology. *American Psychologist, 47,* 161–169.

Morbidity and Mortality Weekly Report. (1987). Premature mortality in the United States. *MMWR (Suppl.), 35,* 1–11. United States Centers for Disease Control.

More, V. (1987). *Hospice care systems.* New York: Springer.

Morehouse, R. E., Farley, F., & Youngquist, J. V. (1990). Type T personality and the Jungian classification system. *Journal of Personality Assessment, 54(1–2),* 231–235.

Moritz, E., & Motta, R. W. (1992). Predictors of self-esteem: The roles of parent-child perceptions, achievement, and class placement. *Journal of Learning Disabilities, 25(1),* 72–80.

Morley, J. E., & Levine, A. S. (1980). Stress-induced eating is mediated through endogenous opiates. *Science, 209(4462),* 1259–1261.

Morokoff, P. J. (1986). Volunteer bias in the psychophysiological study of female sexuality. *Journal of Sex Research, 22,* 35–51.

Morris, C. D., Bransford, J. D., & Franks, J. J. (1977). Levels of processing versus transfer of appropriate processing. *Journal of Verbal Learning and Verbal Behavior, 16,* 519–533.

Morris, D. (1979). *Animal days.* London: Cape.

Morrison, A. (1983). A window on the sleeping brain. *Scientific American, 248(4),* 94–102.

Morrow-Bradley, C., & Elliott, R. (1986). Utilization of psychotherapy research by practicing psychotherapists. *American Psychologist, 41,* 188–205.

Mortimer, J. A., & Schuman, L. M. (1981). *The epidemiology of dementia.* New York: Oxford University Press.

Moscovici, S., Mugny, G., & Papastamou, S. (1981). Sleeper effect and/or minority effect? *Cahiers de Psychologice Cognitive, 1(2),* 199–221.

Moscovitch, M. (1979). Information processing and the cerebral hemispheres. In M. Gazzaniga (Ed.), *Handbook of behavioral neurology,* (Vol. 2). New York: Plenum Press.

Mosher, E. H. (1976). Portrayal of women in drug advertising: A medical betrayal. *Journal of Drug Issues, 6,* 72–78.

Muczyk, J. P., & Reimann, B. C. (1989). The case for directive leadership. In J. W. Newstrom and K. Davis (Eds.), *Organizational behavior: Readings and exercises* (8th ed.). New York: McGraw-Hill.

Muehlenhard, C. L. (1988). Misinterpreted dating behaviors and the risk of date rape. *Journal of Social and Clinical Psychology, 6(1),* 20–37.

Muehlenhard, C. L., & Linton, M. A. (1987). Date rape and sexual aggression in dating situations: Incidence and risk factors. *Journal of Counseling Psychology, 34(2),* 186–196.

Mukhopadhyay, C. C., & Higgins, P. J. (1988). Anthropological studies of women's status revisited: 1977–1987. *Annual Review of Anthropology, 17,* 461–495.

Murdock, B. B., Jr. (1961). The retention of individual items. *Journal of Experimental Psychology, 62,* 618–625.

Murdock, B. B., Jr. (1962). The serial position effect of free recall. *Journal of Experimental Psychology, 64* 482–488.

Murphy, C., Cain, W. S., Gilmore, M. M., and Skinner, R. B. (1991). Sensory and semantic factors in recognition memory for odors and graphic stimuli: Elderly versus young persons. *American Journal of Psychology, 104,* 161–192.

Murphy, H. B. (1968). Cultural factors in the genesis of schizophrenia. In D. Rosenthal & S. S. Kety (Eds.), *The transmission of schizophrenia.* Elmsford, NY: Pergamon Press.

Murphy, K. R., & Davidshofer, C. O. (1988). *Psychological testing: Principles & applications.* Englewood Cliffs, NJ: Prentice-Hall.

Murphy, M. R., & Gilmore, M. M. (1989). Quality-specific effects of aging on the human taste system. *Perception and Psychophysics, 45,* 121–128.

Murray, D. J. (1988). *A history of Western psychology* (2nd ed.). Englewood Cliffs, NJ: Prentice-Hall.

Murray, H. A. (1943). *Thematic Apperception Test manual.* Cambridge, MA: Harvard University Press.

Murray, J. B. (1989). Geophysical variables and behavior: Seasonal affective disorder and phototherapy. *Psychological Reports, 64(3),* 787–801.

Murray, J. B. (1992). Posttraumatic stress disorder: A review. *Genetic, Social, and General Psychology Monographs, 118(3),* 315–338.

Murray, R. M., O'Callaghan, E., Castle, D. J., & Lewis, S. W. (1992). A neurodevelopmental approach to the classification of schizophrenia. *Schizophrenia Bulletin, 18(2),* 319–322.

Mussen, P. H. (Ed.). (1983). *Handbook of child psychology,* (Vols. 1–4). New York: Wiley.

Mussen, P. H., Conger, J. J., Kagan, J., & Huston, A. C. (1990). *Child development & Personality* (7th ed.). New York: Harper & Row.

Musser, L. M., & Graziano, W. G. (1991). Behavioral confirmation in children's interactions with peers. *Basic and Applied Social Psychology, 12(4),* 441–456.

Mwamwenda, T. S. (1991). Psychological aspects of sex differences in moral reasoning. *Psychological Reports, 68,* 1239–1242.

Mwamwenda, T. S. (1992). Culture, environment: Value judgments about cognitive development. *Psychological Reports, 70,* 721–722.

Mwamwenda, T. S., & Mwamwenda, B. B. (1991). Africans' cognitive development and schooling. *International Journal of Educational Development, 11,* 129–134.

Myers, D. G. (1990). *Social psychology* (3rd ed.). New York: McGraw-Hill.

Myers, J. K., Weissman, M. M., Tischler, G. L., Holzer, C. E., Leaf, P. J., Orvaschel, H., Anthony, J. C., Boyd, J. H., Burke, J. D. Kramer, M., & Stolzman, R. (1984). Six-month prevalence of psychiatric disorders in three communities: 1980 to 1982. *Archives of General Psychiatry, 41,* 959–967.

Myers, R. E., & Sperry, R. W. (1958). Interhemispheric communication through the corpus callosum. *Archives of Neurological Psychiatry, 80,* 298–303.

Myers, R. D., & McCaleb, M. L. (1980). Feeding: Satiety signal from intestine triggers brain's noradrenergic mechanism. *Science, 209,* 1035–1037.

Myrtek, M. (1984). *Constitutional psychophysiology: Research in review.* Orlando, FL: Academic Press.

Nadler, L., & Nadler, Z. (1987). Overcoming the language barrier. *Training & Development Journal, 41(6),* 108–11.

Naftolin, F. (1981). Understanding the bases of sex differences. *Science, 211,* 1263–1264.

Nankano, K. (1991). The role of coping strategies on psychological and physical well-being. *Japanese Psychological Research, 33(4),* 160–167.

Narayana, E. A. (1992). Managing voluntary organizations with limited finances and unskilled personnel. *Indian Journal of Social Work, 53(3),* 361–368.

Narikiyo, T. A., & Kameoka, V. A. (1992). Attributions of mental illness and judgments about seeking help among Japanese-Americans and White American students. *Journal of Counseling Psychology, 39(3),* 363–369.

Nash, M. (1987). What, if anything is regressed about hypnotic age regression? A review of the empirical literature. *Psychological Bulletin, 102(1),* 42–52.

Nassi, A. J. (1981). Survivors of the sixties: Comparative psychosocial and political development of former Berkeley student activists. *American Psychologist, 36,* 753–761.

Nathans, J., Piantanida, T. P., Eddy, R. L., Shows, T. B., & Hogness, D. S. (1986). Molecular genetics of inherited variation in human color vision. *Science, 232,* 203–210.

Nathans, J., Thomas, D., & Hogness, D. S. (1986). Molecular genetics of human color vision: The genes encoding blue, green, and red pigments. *Science, 232,* 193–202.

National Institute of Mental Health (NIMH). (1984). *Depression: What we know.* (DHHS Pub. No. ADM 85–1318). Washington, DC: U.S. Government Printing Office.

Natsoulas, T. (1981). Basic problems of consciousness. *Journal of Personality and Social Psychology, 41,* 132–178.

Natsoulas, T. (1986–1987). The six basic concepts of consciousness and William James's stream of thought. *Imagination, Cognition and Personality, 6,* 289–319.

Natsoulas, T. (1991). The concept of consciousness: The interpersonal meaning. *Journal for the Theory of Social Behavior, 21,* 63–89.

Neal, A. M., & Turner, S. M. (1991). Anxiety disorders research with African Americans: Current status. *Psychological Bulletin, 109(3),* 400–410.

Neimark, E. D. (1982). Adolescent thought: Transition to formal operations. In B. B. Wolman (Ed.), *Handbook of developmental psychology.* Englewood Cliffs, NJ: Prentice-Hall.

Neiss, R. (1988). Reconceptualizing arousal: Psychobiological states in motor performance. *Psychological Bulletin, 103,* 345–366.

Neiss, R. (1990). Ending arousal's reign of error: A reply to Anderson. *Psychological Bulletin, 107,* 101–105.

Neisser, U. (1967). *Cognitive psychology.* New York: Appleton-Century-Crofts.

Nettelbeck, T., & Rabbitt, P. M. A. (1992). Aging, cognitive performance, and mental speed. *Intelligence, 16,* 189–205.

Neuberg, S. L. (1989). The goal of forming accurate impressions during social interactions: Attenuating the impact of negative expectancies. *Journal of Personality and Social Psychology, 56(3),* 374–386.

Neugarten, B. L. (1977). Personality and aging. In J. E. Birren & K. W. Schaie (Eds.), *Handbook of the psychology of aging.* New York: Van Nostrand Reinhold.

Newcomb, T. M. (1943). *Personality and social change: Attitude formation in a student community.* New York: Dryden Press.

Newcomb, T. M. (1961). *The acquaintance process.* New York: Irvington.

Newcomb, T. M. (1967). *Persistence and change: Bennington College and its students after 25 years.* New York: Wiley.

Newcomb, T. M. (1981). Heiderian balance as a group phenomenon. *Journal of Personality and Social Psychology, 40,* 862–867.

Newcombe, N., & Dubas, J. S. (1992). A longitudinal study of predictors of spatial ability in adolescent females. *Child Development, 63,* 37–46.

Newell, A., & Simon, H. A. (1972). *Human problem solving.* Englewood Cliffs, NJ: Prentice-Hall.

Nezu, A. M., Nezu, C. M., & Blisses, S. E. (1988). Sense of humor as a moderator of the relation between stressful events and psychological distress: A prospective analysis. *Journal of Personality and Social Psychology, 54,* 520–525.

Nicol, S. E., & Gottesman, I. I. (1983). Clues to the genetics and neurobiology of schizophrenia. *American Scientist, 71,* 398–404.

Niemark, J. (1986). Her nose knows best. *American Health, 5(5),* 36–40.

Nikelly, A. G. (1992). Can DSM-III-R be used in the diagnosis of non-Western patients? *International Journal of Mental Health, 21(1),* 3–22.

Nino, M. G., & Keenan, S. (1988). A multicomponent approach to the management of insomnia. *Annals of Behavioral Medicine, 10(3),* 101–106.

Nisbett, R. E., Caputo, C., Legant, P., & Marceek, J. (1973). Behavior as seen by the actor and as seen by the observer. *Journal of Personality and Social Psychology, 27*, 154–164.

Nissan, M., & Kohlberg, L. (1982). Universality and variation in moral judgment: A longitudinal and cross-sectional study in Turkey. *Child Development, 53*, 865–876.

Nixon, M. C. (1987). Australia. In A. R. Gilgen and C. K. Gilgen (Eds.), *International handbook of psychology*. New York: Greenwood Press.

Noller, P., Law, H., & Comrey, A. L. (1987). Cattell, Comrey, and Eysenck personality factors compared: More evidence for the five robust factors? *Journal of Personality and Social Psychology, 53*, 775–782.

Noon, J. M., & Lewis, J. R. (1992). Therapeutic strategies and outcomes: Perspectives from different cultures. *British Journal of Medical Psychology, 65*, 107–117.

Norman, W. T. (1961). Development of self-report tests to measure personality factors identified from peer nominations. *USAF ASK Technical Note*, No. 61–44.

Norman, W. T. (1963). Toward an adequate taxonomy of personality attributes: Replicated factor structure in peer nomination personality ratings. *Journal of Abnormal and Social Psychology, 66*, 574–583.

Norris, J., & Cubbins, L. A. (1992). Dating, drinking, and rape. *Psychology of Women Quarterly, 16*, 179–191.

Norris, R., Carroll, D., & Cochrane, R. (1992). The effects of physical activity and exercise training on psychological stress and well-being in an adolescent population. *Journal of Psychosomatic Research, 36*, 55–65.

Norton, G. R., Cox, B. J., & Schwartz, M. A. J. (1992). Critical analysis of the DSM III-R classification of panic disorder: A survey of current opinions. *Journal of Anxiety Disorders, 6*, 159–167.

Nydell, M. K. (1987). *Understanding Arabs*. Yarmouth, MN: International Press.

Nyquist, L., & Spence, J. (1986). Effects of dispositional dominance and sex role expectations on leadership behaviors. *Journal of Personality and Social Psychology, 50(1)*, 377–382.

O'Callaghan, E., Sham, P., Takei, N., Glover, G., & Murray, R. M. (1991). Schizophrenia after prenatal exposure to 1957 A2 influenza epidemic. *Lancet, 1*, 1248–1250.

Offer, D., Ostrov, E., & Howard, K. I. (1981). *The adolescent: A psychological self-portrait*. New York: Basic Books.

Offer, D., & Schonert-Reichl, K. A. (1992). Debunking the myths of adolescence: Findings from recent research. *Journal of the American Academy of Childhood and Adolescent Psychiatry, 31(6)*, 1003–1014.

Ohman, A. (1988). Nonconscious control of autonomic responses: A role for Pavlovian conditioning? *Biological Psychology, 27(2)*, 113–135.

Ollendick, T. H., Hagopian, L. P., & Huntzinger, R. M. (1991). Cognitive-behavior therapy and night-time fearful children. *Journal of Behavior Therapy and Experimental Psychiatry, 22(2)*, 113–121.

Oller, D. K., Eilers, R. E., Bull, D. H., & Carney, A. E. (1985). Prespeech vocalizations of a deaf infant: A comparison with normal metaphonological development. *Journal of Speech and Hearing Research, 28(1)*, 47–63.

Olney, R. L., & Scholnick, E. K. (1976). Adult judgments of age and linguistic differences in infant vocalization. *Journal of Child Language, 3(2)*, 145–155.

Olton, D. S., & Noonberg, A. R. (1980). *Biofeedback: Clinical applications in behavioral medicine*. Englewood Cliffs, NJ: Prentice-Hall.

Orbach, I., & Florian, V. (1992). Attitudes toward life and death, religiosity, and gender in Israeli children. *Omega, 24(2)*, 139–149.

Osarchuk, M., & Tatz, S. (1973). Effect of induced fear of death on belief in afterlife. *Journal of Personality and Social Psychology, 27*, 256–260.

Osgood, C. E. (1962). *An alternative to war of surrender*. Urbana: University of Illinois Press.

Otto, L. B. (1988). America's youth: A changing profile. *Family Relations, 37*, 385–391.

Overmier, J. B. (1986). Reassessing learned helplessness. *Social Science, 71(1)*, 27–31.

Overton, W. (1990). *Reasoning, necessity and logic*. Hillsdale, NJ: Lawrence Erlbaum.

Padilla, E. R., & O'Grady, K. E. (1983). *Sexuality among Mexican-Americans: An empirical approach*. Unpublished manuscript, University of New Mexico.

Page, J. (1984). Rural stress. *Science, 5(2)*, 104–105.

Page, R. C., & Cheng, H-P. (1992). A preliminary investigation of Chinese and American perceptions of the self. *Psychologia, 35*, 12–20.

Paivio, A. (1971). *Imagery and verbal processes*. New York: Holt, Rinehart and Winston.

Paivio, A. (1990). *Mental representations: A dual coding approach*. New York: Oxford University Press.

Paivio, A., Smythe, P. C., & Yuille, J. C. (1968). Imagery versus meaningfulness in paired-associate learning. *Canadian Journal of Psychology, 22*, 427–441.

Palka, J. (1990). Insights from broken brains. *Science, 248*, 812–814.

Panic disorder. (1990). *Clinician's Digest, 8(2)*, 5.

Papalia, D. E., & Olds, S. W. (1990). *A child's world: Infancy through adolescence* (5th ed.). New York: McGraw-Hill.

Paranjpe, A. C. (1984). *Theoretical psychology: The meeting of East and West*. New York: Plenum.

Paris, S. G., Saarnio, D. A., & Cross, D. R. (1986). A metacognitive curriculum to promote children's reading and learning. *Australian Journal of Psychology, 38(2)*, 107–123.

Parisi, T. (1987). Why Freud failed: Some implications for neurophysiology and sociobiology. *American Psychologist, 42*, 235–245.

Parker, T. (1989). *The road to Camp David: U.S. negotiating strategy towards the Arab-Israeli conflict*. New York: Peter Lang Publishing.

Parker, T., Hill, J. W., & Miller, G. (1987). Multiple family therapy: Evaluating a group experience for mentally retarded adolescents and their families. *Family Therapy, 14*, 43–51.

Parkes, J. D., & Lock, C. B. (1989). Genetic factors in sleep disorders. *Journal of Neurology, Neurosurgery and Psychiatry*, (June Special Supplement). 101–108.

Pascual-Leone, J. (1976). A view of cognition from a formalist's perspective. In K. F. Riegel, & J. Meacham (Eds.), *The developing individual in a changing world*. The Hague: Mouton.

Pascual-Leone, J. (1984). Attentional, dialectic, and mental effort. In M. L. Commons, F. A. Richards, & C. Armon (Eds.), *Beyond formal operations*. New York: Plenum.

Pascual-Leone, J., & Smith, J. (1969). The encoding and decoding of symbols by children: A new experimental paradigm and a neo-Piagetian model. *Journal of Experimental Child Psychology, 8*, 328–355.

Patterson, D. (1987). The causes of Down Syndrome. *Scientific American, 257(2)*, 52–60.

Patterson, M. L. (1983). *Nonverbal behavior: A functional perspective*. New York: Springer-Verlag.

Patterson, M. L., & Reidhead, S. M. (1984). A content-classified bibliography of research on the immediacy behaviors: 1965–1982. *Journal of Nonverbal Behavior, 8*, 360–393.

Pattison, E. M. (1987). Whither goals in the treatment of alcoholism? *Drugs and Society, 1(2–3)*, 153–171.

Paul, G. L., & Lentz, R. J. (1978). *Psychosocial treatment of chronic mental patients: Milieu versus social-learning programs*. Cambridge, MA: Harvard University Press.

Paunonen, S. V., Jackson, D. N., Trzebinski, J., & Forsterling, F. (1992). Personality structure across cultures: A multimethod evaluation. *Journal of Personality and Social Psychology, 62(3)*, 447–456.

Pavlov, I. (1927). *Conditioned reflexes*. Oxford, England: Clarendon Press.

Pearl, R. (1924). *Studies in human biology*. Baltimore: Williams & Wilkins.

Pearlson, G. D., Harris, G. J., Powers, R. E., Barta, P. E., Camargo, E. E., Chase, G. A., Noga, J. T., & Tune, L. E. (1992). Quantitative changes in mesial temporal volume, regional cerebral blood flow, and cognition in Alzheimer's disease. *Archives of General Psychiatry, 49*, 402–408.

Pearson, B. A., & Lee, K. S. (1992). Discourse structure of direction giving: Effects of native/nonnative speaker status and gender. *TESOL Quarterly, 26(1)*, 113–127.

Pecjak, V. (1987). Yugoslavia. In A. R. Gilgen and C. K. Gilgen (Eds.), *International handbook of psychology*. New York: Greenwood Press.

Pedersen, P. (Ed.). (1987). *Handbook of cross-cultural counseling and therapy*. New York: Praeger.

Pekala, R. J., Kumar, V. K., Cummings, J. (1992). Types of high hypnotically susceptible individuals and reported attitudes and experiences of the paranormal and the anomalous. *Journal of the American Society for Psychical Research, 86*, 135–150.

Pellegrini, A. D. (1987). Rough-and-tumble play: Developmental and educational significance. *Educational Psychologist, 22(1)*, 22–43.

Pendery, M., Maltzman, I., & West, L. J. (1982). Controlled drinking by alcoholics? New findings and a reevaluation of a major affirmative study. *Science, 217*, 169–174.

Perlmutter, R. A., & Jones, J. E. (1985). Problem solving with families in psychiatric emergencies. *Psychiatric Quarterly, 57(1)*, 23–32.

Perls, F., Hefferline, R., & Goodman, P. (1951). *Gestalt Therapy*. New York: Julian Press.

Pescosolido, B. A. (1992). Beyond rational choice: The social dynamics of how people seek help. *American Journal of Sociology, 97*, 1096–1138.

Petersen, S. E., Fox, P. T., Posner, M. I., Mintun, M., & Raichle M. E. (1988). *Nature, 331*, 585–589.

Peterson, C., & Seligman, M. E. P. (1984). Casual explanations as a risk factor for depression: Theory and evidence. *Psychological Review, 91*, 347–374.

Peterson, L. H. (1991). Gender and the autobiographical essay. *College Composition and Communication, 42*, 170–183.

Peterson, L. R. (1966). Short-term memory. *Scientific American, 215*, 90–95.

Peterson, L. R., & Peterson, M. J. (1959). Short-term retention of individual verbal items. *Journal of Experimental Psychology, 58*, 193–198.

Peterson, P. L., & Lowe, J. B. (1992). Preventing fetal alcohol exposure: A cognitive behavioral approach. *The International Journal of the Addictions, 27(5)*, 613–626.

Petri, H. L. (1986). *Motivation: Theory and Research* (2nd ed.). Belmont, CA: Wadsworth.

Pettigrew, T. F. (1979). The ultimate attribution error: Extending Allport's cognitive analysis of prejudice. *Personality and Social Psychology Bulletin, 5*, 461–476.

Petty, R. E., & Cacioppo, J. T. (1986). *Communication and persuasion: Central and peripheral routes to attitude change*. New York: Springer-Verlag.

Petty, R. E., Ostrom, T. M., & Brock, T. C. (Eds.). (1981). *Cognitive responses in persuasion*. Hillsdale, NJ: Erlbaum.

Philipchalk, R. P. (1972). Thematicity, abstractness, and the long-term recall of connected discourse. *Psychonomic Science, 27*, 361–362.

Philipchalk, R. P., & Sifft, C. R. (1985). Role of religious commitment in occupational and overall identity formation in college students. *Journal of Psychology and Christianity, 4*, 44–47.

Phillips, D., McCartney, K., & Scarr, S. (1987). Child-care quality and children's social development. *Developmental Psychology, 23*, 537–543.

Phillips, R. (1981, November 1). Incest. *Albany Times Union*, E-1, E-7.

Phinney, J. S., Chavira, V., & Williamson, L. (1992). Acculturation attitudes and self-esteem among high school and college students. *Youth and Society, 23(3)*, 299–312.

Piaget, J. (1965). *The moral judgment of the child*. New York: Free Press.

Piaget, J. (1972). Intellectual evolution from adolescence to adulthood. *Human Development, 15*, 1–12.

Piaget, J. (1976). *The child and reality*. Baltimore: Penguin.

Piaget, J. (1977). *The development of thought: Equilibration of cognitive structures*. New York: Viking.

Piaget, J. (1980). My position. In M. Piattelli-Palmarini (Ed.), *Language and learning: The debate between Jean Piaget and Noam Chomsky*. Cambridge, MA: Harvard University Press.

Piccione, C., Hilgard, E. J., & Zimbardo, P. G. (1987). *On the consistence of measured hypnotizability over a 25-year period*. Unpublished manuscript, Stanford University.

Piccirilli, M., Finali, G., & Sciarma, T. (1989). Negative evidence of difference between right- and left-handers in interhemispheric transfer of information. *Neuropsychologia, 27(7)*, 1023–1026.

Pickar, D., Labarca, R., Linnoila, M., Roy, A., Hommer, D., Everett, D., & Payl, S. M. (1984). Neuroleptic-induced decrease in plasma homovanillic acid and antipsychotic activity in schizophrenic patients. *Science, 225*, 954–957.

Pickles, J. O. (1982). *An introduction to the physiology of hearing*. London: Academic Press.

Pillon, A., Degauquier, C., & Duquesne, F. (1992). Males' and females' conversational behavior in cross-sex dyads: From gender differences to gender similarities. *Journal of Psycholinguistic Research, 21(3)*, 147–172.

Pinard, A. (1992). Métaconscience et métacognition. *Canadian Psychology, 33(1)*, 27–41.

Pinault, S., & Fournier, G. (1990). The response to long-term overfeeding in identical twins. *The New England Journal of Medicine, 322*, 1477–1482.

Pines, M. (1982). Infant-stim. *Psychology Today, 16(6)*, 48–53.

Pinizzotto, A. J. (1989). Memory and hypnosis: Implications for the use of forensic hypnosis. *Professional Psychology: Research and Practice, 20*, 322–328.

Pinker, S. (1984). *Language learnability and language development*. Cambridge, MA: MIT Press.

Pinker, S. (1991). Rules of language. *Science, 253(5019)*, 530–535.

Pinker, S., & Prince, A. (1987). On language and connectionism: Analysis of a parallel distributed processing model of language acquisition. *Occasional paper #33*. Cambridge, MA: MIT Press.

Pion, G. M., Bramblett, J. P., Jr., & Wicherski, M. (1987). *Preliminary report: 1985 doctorate employment survey*. Washington, DC: American Psychological Association.

Piotrowski, C. (1984). The status of projective techniques: Or, "Wishing won't make it go away." *Journal of Clinical Psychology, 40*, 1495–1502.

Piotrowski, C., & Keller, J. W. (1984a). Psychological testing: Trends in masters-level counseling psychology programs. *Teaching of Psychology, 11(4)*, 244–245.

Piotrowski, C., & Keller, J. W. (1984b). Attitudes toward clinical assessment by members of the AABT. *Psychological Reports, 55*, 831–838.

Piotrowski, C., Sherry, D., & Keller, J. W. (1985). Psychodiagnostic test usage: A survey of the Society for Personality Assessment. *Journal of Personality Assessment, 49*, 115–119.

Pitman, R. K., & Orr, S. P. (1987). *Psychophysiologic assessment of posttraumatic stress disorder imagery in Vietnam combat veterans*. Paper presented at the Second Annual Meeting of the Society for Traumatic Stress Studies, Chicago, IL.

Pittman, T. S., & Heller, J. F. (1987). Social motivation. *Annual Review of Psychology, 38*, 461–489.

Platt, J. J. (1986). *Heroin addiction: Theory, research, and treatment* (2nd ed.). Malabar, FL: Krieger.

Pleck, J. H., Lamb, M. E., & Levine, J. A. (1985–1986). Epilog: Facilitating future change in men's family roles. *Marriage and Family Review, 9(3–4)*, 11–16.

Plimpton, C. E., & Regimbal, C. (1992). Differences in motor proficiency according to gender and race. *Perceptual and Motor Skills, 74*, 399–402.

Pliner, P., & Cappell, H. (1974). Modification of affective consequences of alcohol: A comparison of social and solitary drinking. *Journal of Abnormal Psychology, 83(4)*, 418–425.

Plomin, R. (1990). The role of inheritance in behavior. *Science, 248*, 183–188.

Plomin, R., Defires, J. C., & McCleam, G. E. (1980). *Behavioral genetics*. New York: W. H. Freeman.

Plutchik, R. (1980). *Emotion: A psychoevolutionary synthesis*. New York: Harper & Row.

Plutchik, R., & Kellerman, H. (Eds.). (1980). *Emotion: Theory, research, and experience. Theories of Emotion, (Vol. 1)*. New York: Academic Press.

Polivy, J., & Herman, C. P. (1985). Dieting and binging: A causal analysis. American Psychologist, 40, 193–201.

Pomeroy, W. B., Flax, C. C., & Wheeler, C. C. (1982). *Taking a sex history: Interviewing and recording*. New York: Free Press.

Pope, H. G., Jr., & Hudson, J. I. (1984). *New hope for binge eaters: Advances in the understanding and treatment of bulimia*. New York: Harper & Row.

Pope, H. G., Keck, P. E., & McElvoy, S. L. (1986). Frequency and presentation of neuroleptic malignant syndrome in a large psychiatric hospital. *American Journal of Psychiatry, 143*, 1227–1233.

Porter, R. H., Balogh, R. D., Cernoch, J. M., & Franchi, C. (1986). Recognition of kin through characteristic body odors. *Chemical Senses, 11*, 389–395.

Porter, R. H., Cernack, J. M., & Balogh, R. D. (1985). Odor signatures and kin recognition. *Physiology and Behavior, 34*, 445–448.

Porter, R. H., Makin, J. W., Davis, L. B., & Christensen, K. M. (1991). An assessment of the salient olfactory environment of formula-fed infants. *Physiology and Behavior, 50*, 907–911.

Post, S. G. (1992). DSM-III-R and religion. *Social Science and Medicine, 35(1)*, 81–90.

Potter, P. A., & Perry, A. G. (1989). *Fundamentals of nursing: Concepts, process, and practice* (2nd ed.). St. Louis: C. V. Mosby.

Potter, S. M., & Graves, R. E. (1988). Is interhemisphere transfer related to handedness and gender? *Neuropsychologia, 26(2)*, 319–325.

Powell, G. N., & Butterfield, D. A. (1979). "The good manager": Masculine or androgenous? *Academy of Management Journal, 22(2)*, 395–403.

Powell, L. H. (1992). The cognitive underpinnings of coronary-prone behaviors. *Cognitive Therapy and Research, 16*, 123–142.

Powell, G. N., & Butterfield, D. A. (1979). "The good manager": Masculine or androgenous? *Academy of Management Journal, 22(2)*, 395–403.

Power, T. G., & Chapieski, M. L. (1986). Childrearing and impulse control in toddlers: A naturalistic investigation. *Developmental Psychology, 22*, 271–275.

Poynton, A., Bridges, P. K., & Bartlett, J. R. (1988). Psychosurgery in Britain now. *British Journal of Neurosurgery, 2,* 297–306.

Prager, K. (1986). Identity development, age, and college experience in women. *Journal of Genetic Psychology, 147,* 31–36.

Pratkanis, A. R., Greenwald, A. G., Leippe, M. R., & Baumgardner, M. H. (1988). In search of reliable persuasion effects: III. The sleeper effect is dead. Long live the sleeper effect. *Journal of Personality and Social Psychology, 54,* 203–218.

Pratt, W. F. (1990). Premarital sexual behavior, multiple partners, and marital experience. Paper presented at the annual meeting of the Population Association of America, May 2–4, Toronto, Canada.

Premack, D. (1986). *Gavagai! Or the future history of the animal language controversy.* Cambridge, MA: MIT Press.

Presti, D. E. (1987). What goes around comes around. . . . *Contemporary Psychology, 32,* 556–557.

Previc, F. H. (1991). A general theory concerning the prenatal origins of cerebral lateralization in humans. *Psychological Review, 98,* 299–334.

Price, R. A., Cadoret, R. J., Stunkard, A. J., & Troughton, E. (1987). Genetic contribution to human obesity: An adoption study. *American Journal of Psychiatry, 144,* 1003–1008.

Price, R. A., Kidd, K. K., & Weissman, M. M. (1987). Early onset (under age 30 years) and panic disorders as markers for etiologic homogeneity in major depression. *Archives of General Psychiatry, 44(5),* 434–440.

Progoff, I. (1953). *Jung's psychology and its social meaning.* London: Routledge and Kegan, Paul.

Prothro, E. T., & Melikian, L. (1955). Psychology in the Arab Near East. *Psychological Bulletin, 52,* 303–310.

Pruitt, D. G., & Rubin, J. Z. (1986). *Social conflict: Escalation, stalemate, and settlement.* New York: Random House.

Pryor, W. A. (1987). The free-radical theory of aging re-visited: A critique and a suggested disease-specific theory. In H. R. Warner, R. N. Butler, R. L. Sprott, & E. L. Schneider (Eds.), *Modern biological theories of aging.* New York: Raven Press.

Psathas, G. (1992). Phenomenology and the human sciences in Japan: A personal Odyssey. *Human Studies, 15(1),* 1–15.

Puente, A. E. (1992). The status of clinical neuropsychology. *Archives of Clinical Neuropsychology, 7,* 297–312.

Pumariega, A. J. (1986). Acculturation and eating disorders in adolescent girls: A comparative and correlational study. *Journal of the American Academy of Child Psychiatry, 25,* 276–279.

Pumariega, A. J., Palmer, E., & Mitchell, C. B. (1984). Anorexia nervosa in Black adolescents. *Journal of the American Academy of Child Psychiatry, 23,* 111–114.

Purves, D., & Hadley, R. D. (1985). Changes in the dendritic branching of adult mammalian neurons revealed by repeated imaging *in situ. Nature, 315,* 404–406.

Putnam, F. W. (1991). Recent research on multiple personality disorder. *Psychiatric Clinics of North America, 14(3),* 489–502.

Putnam, F. W., Guroff, J. J., & Silberman, E. K., Barban, L., & Post, R. M. (1986). The clinical phenomenology of multiple personality disorder: Review of 100 recent cases. *Journal of Clinical Psychiatry, 47(6),* 285–293.

Putnam, F., Zahn, T., & Post, R. (1990). Differential autonomic nervous system activity in multiple personality disorder. *Psychiatry Research, 31,* 251–260.

Quereshi, M. Y. (1992). Gender differences in surveys of psychology baccalaureates: An update. *Psychological Reports, 70,* 383–386.

Quinton, D., Rutter, M., & Liddle, C. (1984). Institutional rearing, parenting difficulties and marital support. *Psychological Medicine, 14,* 107–124.

Rachman, S. J., & Wilson, G. T. (1980). *The effects of psychotherapy* (2nd ed.). Elmsford, NY: Pergamon.

Radecki, T. (1990). *National Coalition against Television Violence Newsletter, 11.*

Rak, D. S., & McMullen, L. M. (1987). Sex-role stereotyping in television commercials: A verbal response mode and content analysis. *Canadian Journal of Behavioural Science, 19(1),* 25–39.

Ramachandran, V. S., & Anstis, S. M. (1986). The perception of apparent motion. *Scientific American, 254(6),* pp. 102–109.

Ramirez, A. (1977). Chicano power and interracial group relations. In J. L. Martinex (Ed.), *Chicano psychology.* New York: Academic Press.

Ramirez, A. (1988). Racism toward Hispanics: The culturally monolithic society. In P. A. Katz & D. A. Taylor (Eds.), *Eliminating racism: Profiles in controversy.* New York: Plenum.

Rao, K. R., & Palmer, J. (1987). The anomaly called psi: Recent research and criticism. *Behavioral and Brain Sciences, 10,* 539–551.

Rapoport, J. L. (1989). *The boy who couldn't stop washing his hands.* New York: Signet.

Raskin, A., Chien, C., & Lin, K. (1992). Elderly Chinese- and caucasian-Americans compared on measures of psychic distress, somatic complaints and social competence. *International Journal of Geriatric Psychiatry, 7,* 191–198.

Raths, L., Harmin, M., & Simon, S. B. (1978). *Values and teaching* (2nd ed.). Columbus, OH: Charles E. Merrill.

Ratner, H. H., Schell, D. A., Crimmins, A., Mittelman, D., & Baldinelli, L. (1987). Changes in adults' prose recall: Aging or cognitive demands? *Developmental Psychology, 23,* 521–525.

Ray, O. (1983). *Drugs, society, and human behavior.* St. Louis: Mosby.

Ray, W. A., Griffin, M. R. Schaffner, W., Baugh, D. K., & Melton, L. J. (1987). Psychotropic drug use and the risk of hip fracture. *New England Journal of Medicine, 316,* 363–369.

Ray, W. A., Blazer, D. G., Schaffner, W., & Federspiel, C. F. (1987). Reducing antipsychotic drug prescribing for nursing home patients: A controlled trial of the effect of an educational visit. *American Journal of Public Health, 77*, 1448–1450.

Ray, W. J., & Cole, H. W. (1985). EEG alpha activity reflects attentional demands, and beta activity reflects emotional and cognitive processes. *Science, 228*, 750–752.

Redfern, P. H. (1989). "Jet-lag": Strategies for prevention and cure. *Human Psychopharmacology Clinical and Experimental, 4(3)*, 159–168.

Redman, J., Armstrong, S., & Ng, K. T. (1983). Free-running activity rhythms in the rat: Entrainment by melatonin. *Science, 219*, 1089–1091.

Reed, E. S. (1988). *James J. Gibson and the psychology of perception*. New Haven: Yale University Press.

Reed, L. A., & Meyers, L. S. (1991). A structural analysis of religious orientation and its relation to sexual attitudes. *Educational and Psychological Measurement, 51*, 943–952.

Reeve, J. M. (1992). *Understanding motivation and emotion*. Fort Worth: Harcourt Brace Jovanovich.

Reich, J. (1987). Sex distribution of DSM-III personality disorders in psychiatric outpatients. *American Journal of Psychiatry, 144*, 485–488.

Reigle, T. G. (1985). Increased brain norepinephrine metabolism correlated with analgesia produced by the periaqueductal gray injection of opiates. *Brain Research, 338*, 155–159.

Reiman, E. M., Raichle, M. E., Butler, F. K., Herscovitch, P., & Robins, E. (1984). A focal brain abnormality in panic disorder, a severe form of anxiety. *Nature, 310*, 683–685.

Reinitz, M. T., Lammers, W. J., & Cochran, B. P. (1992). Memory-conjunction errors: Miscombination of stored stimulus features can produce illusions of memory. *Memory and Cognition, 20(1)*, 1–11.

Reisberg, B. (1983). Clinical presentation, diagnosis, and symptomatology of age-associated cognitive decline and Alzheimer's disease. In B. Reisberg (Ed.), *Alzheimers disease*. New York: Free Press.

Reisenzein, R., & Schönpflug, W. (1992). Stumpf's cognitive-evaluative theory of emotion. *American Psychologist, 47*, 34–45.

Renshaw, D. (1983). *Incest understanding and treatment*. Boston: Little, Brown.

Reppert, S. M. (1985). Maternal entrainment of the developing circadian system, *Annals of the New York Academy of Sciences, 453*, 162–169.

Reppert, S. M., Weaver, D. R., Rivkees, S. A., & Stopa, E. G. (1988). Putative melatonin receptors in a human biological clock. *Science, 242*, 78–81.

Rescorla, R. A. (1987). A Pavlovian analysis of goal-directed behavior. *American Psychologist, 42*, 119–129.

Rescorla, R. A. (1988a). Pavlovian conditioning: It's not what you think it is. *American Psychologist, 43(3)*, 151–160.

Rescorla, R. A. (1988b). Behavioral studies of Pavlovian conditioning. *Annual Review of Neuroscience, 11*, 329–352.

Retsinas, J. (1988). A theoretical reassesment of the applicability of Kübler-Ross's stages of dying. *Death Studies, 12(3)*, 207–216.

Retterstol, N. (1986). Classification of functional psychoses with special reference to follow-up studies. *Psychopathology, 19(1-2)*, 5–15.

Reynolds, A. G., & Flagg, P. W. (1983). *Cognitive psychology* (2nd ed.). Boston: Little, Brown.

Reynolds, D. K., & Farberow, N. L. (1981). *The family shadow: Sources of suicide and schizophrenia*. Berkeley, CA: University of California Press.

Rhodes, N., & Wood, W. (1992). Self-esteem and intelligence affect influenceability: The mediating role of message reception. *Psychological Bulletin, 111(1)*, 156–171.

Rice, M. L. (1989). Children's language acquisition. *American Psychologist, 44(2)*, 149–156.

Richardson, A. G. (1986). Two factors of creativity. *Perceptual and Motor Skills, 63*, 379–384.

Richardson, J. T. E., & Zucco, G. M. (1989). Cognition and olfaction: A review. *Psychological Bulletin, 105(3)*, 352–360.

Ridley, D. S. (1991). Reflective self-awareness: A basic motivational process. *Journal of Experimental Education, 60*, 31–48.

Riefer, D. M., & Rouder, J. N. (1992). A multinomial modeling analysis of the mnemonic benefits of bizarre imagery. *Memory and Cognition, 20(6)*, 601–611.

Rinfret, N., Lortie-Lussier, M., & De Koninck, J. (1992). The dreams of professional mothers and female students: An exploration of social roles and age impact. *Dreaming, 1(3)*, 179–191.

Risman, B., & Schwartz, P. (1988). Sociological research on male and female homosexuality. *Annual Review of Sociology, 14*, 125–147.

Risse, S. C., Raskind, M. A., Nochlin, D., Sumi, S. M., Lampe, T. H., Bird, T. D., Cubberley, L., & Peskind, E. R. (1990). Neuropathological findings in patients with clinical diagnoses of probable Alzheimer's disease. *American Journal of Psychiatry, 147*, 168–172.

Ritts, V., Patterson, M. L., & Tubbs, M. E. (1992). Expectations, impressions, and judgments of physically attractive students: A review. *Review of Educational Research, 62(4)*, 413–426.

Roberts, P., & Newton, P. M. (1987). Levinsonian studies of women's adult development. *Psychology and Aging, 2*, 154–163.

Robertson, I. (1989). Models of problem drinking and the place for causality: A reply to Gorman. *British Journal of Addiction, 84(8)*, 848–849.

Robins, L. N. (1966). *Deviant children grow up*. Baltimore: Williams & Wilkins.

Robinson, B. E., & Barret, R. L. (1986). *The developing father: Emerging roles in contemporary society*. New York: Guilford Press.

Robinson, V. M., (1983). Humor and health. In P. E. McGhee & J. H. Goldstein (Eds.), *Handbook of humor research: Vol. 2. Applied studies*. New York: Springer/Verlag.

Robinson, W. L. V., & Calhoun, K. S. (1983). Sexual fantasies, attitudes, and behavior as a function of race, gender, and religiosity. *Imagination, Cognition, and Personality, 2*, 281–290.

Roder, B. J., Bates, C., Crowell, S., Schilling, T., & Bushnell, E. W. (1992). The perception of identity by 6½-month-old infants. *Journal of Experimental Child Psychology, 54,* 57–73.

Rodgers, J. E. (1982). The malleable memory of eyewitnesses. *Science 82, 3(5),* 32–35.

Rodgers, W. L., & Herzog, A. R. (1987). Interviewing older adults: The accuracy of factual information. *Journal of Gerontology, 42,* 387–394.

Rodin, J. (1984, December). A sense of control. *Psychology Today,* pp. 38–45.

Rodin, J. (1984). Taming the hunger hormone. *American Health, 3(1),* 32–35.

Rodin, J. (1986). Health, control, and aging. In M. M. Baltes & P. B. Baltes (Eds.), *The psychology of control and aging.* Hillsdale, NJ: Erlbaum.

Rodin, J. (1991). Effects of pure sugar vs. mixed starch fructose loads on food intake. *Appetite, 17,* 213–219.

Rodin, J., & Salovey, P. (1989). Health psychology. *Annual Review of Psychology, 40,* 533–379.

Roff, J. D., & Knight, R. (1981). Family characteristics, childhood symptoms, and adult outcomes in schizophrenia. *Journal of Abnormal Psychology, 90,* 510–520.

Rogers, C. R. (1942). *Counseling and psychotherapy.* Boston: Houghton Mifflin.

Rogers, C. R. (1951). *Client-centered therapy.* Boston: Houghton Mifflin.

Rogers, C. R. (1959). A theory of therapy, personality and interpersonal relationships as developed in the client-centered framework. In S. Hoch (Ed.), *Psychology: A study of a science* (Vol. 3). New York: McGraw-Hill.

Rogers, C. R. (1961). *On becoming a person.* Boston: Houghton Mifflin.

Rogers, C. R. (1964). The concept of the fully functioning person. *Psychotherapy: Theory, research and practice, 1(1),* 17–26.

Rogers, C. R. (1967). Autobiography. In E. G. Boring & G. Lindzey (Eds.), *A history of psychology in autobiography* (Vol. 5). New York: Appleton.

Rogers, R. W. (1975). A protection motivation theory of fear appeals and attitude change. *Journal of Psychology, 91,* 93–114.

Rogers, R. W. (1983). Cognitive and physiological processes in fear appeals and attitude change: A revised theory of protection motivation. In J. Cacioppo & R. Petty (Eds.), *Social psychophysiology.* New York: Guilford.

Root, M. P. P., Fallon, P., & Friedrich, W. N. (1986). *Bulimia: A systems approach to treatment.* New York: Norton.

Rosch, E. H. (1973). Natural categories. *Cognitive Psychology, 4,* 328–350.

Rosch, E. H. (1977). Human categorization. In N. Warren (Ed.), *Advances in cross-cultural psychology,* (Vol. 1). London: Academic Press.

Rosch, E. H. (1978). Principles of categorization. In E. Rosch & B. Lloyd (Eds.), *Cognition and categorization.* Hillsdale, NJ: Erlbaum.

Rosch, E. H., Mervis, C. B., Gray, W. D., Johnson, D. M., & Boyes-Braem, P. (1976). Basic objects in natural categories. *Cognitive Psychology, 7,* 573–605.

Rose, S. P. (1984). Disordered molecules and diseased minds: Biological markers in mental disorders. *Journal of Psychiatric Research, 18,* 351–360.

Rose, S. P. R. (1989). Glycoprotein synthesis and postsynaptic remodelling in long-term memory. *Neurochemistry International, 14(3),* 299–307.

Rosen, C. M. (1987). The eerie world of reunited twins. *Discover, 8(9),* pp. 36–46.

Rosen, J., Mulsant, B. H., & Nebes, R. D. (1992). A pilot study of interictal cognitive changes in elderly patients during ECT. *International Journal of Geriatric Psychiatry, 7,* 407–410.

Rosenblatt, J. S. (1983). Olfaction mediates developmental transition in the altricial newborn of selected species of mammals. *Developmental Psychobiology, 16(5),* 347–374.

Rosenfeld, A. H. (1987). Fat, schmat, so long as you feel OK. *Psychology Today, 21(7),* 18.

Rosenhan, D. L. (1973). On being sane in insane places. *Science, 179,* 250–258.

Rosenhan, D. L. (1975). The contextual nature of psychiatric diagnosis. *Journal of Abnormal Psychology, 84,* 462–474.

Rosenhan, D. L., & Seligman, M. E. P. (1989). *Abnormal psychology* (2nd ed.). New York: Norton.

Rosenheimer, J. L. (1985). Effects of chronic stress and exercise on age-related changes in endplate architecture. *Journal of Neurophysiology, 53,* 1582–1589.

Rosenthal, R. R. (1965). *Clever Hans.* New York: Holt, Rinehart and Winston.

Rosenzweig, M. R. (1982). Trends in development and status of psychology: An international perspective. *International Journal of Psychology, 17,* 117–140.

Rosenzweig, M. R. (1984). Experience, memory, and the brain. *American Psychologist, 39,* 365–376.

Rosenzweig, M. R. (1984). U.S. psychology and world psychology. *American Psychologist, 39(8),* 877–884.

Ross, A. O. (1987). *Personality: The scientific study of complex human behavior.* New York: Holt, Rinehart and Winston.

Ross, C. A. (1989). *Multiple personality disorder.* New York: John Wiley & Sons.

Ross, C. A., & Joshi, S. (1992). Paranormal experiences in the general population. *Journal of Nervous and Mental Disease, 180(6),* 356–360.

Ross, D. R. (1992). Discussion: An agnostic viewpoint on multiple personality disorder. *Psychoanalytic Inquiry, 12(1),* 124–138.

Ross, E. D., & Mesulam, M. M. (1979). Dominant language functions of the right hemisphere? *Archives of Neurology, 36,* 241–248.

Ross, H. S., & Lollis, S. P. (1987). Communication within infant social games. *Developmental Psychology, 23,* 241–248.

Ross, L. (1977). The intuitive psychologist and his shortcomings: Distortions in the attribution process. In L. Berkowitz (Ed.), *Advances in experimental social psychology* (Vol. 10). New York: Academic Press.

Ross, L., Amabile, T. M., & Steinmetz, J. L. (1977). Social roles, social control, and biases in social perception processes. *Journal of Personality and Social Psychology, 35,* 485–494.

Ross, R. J., Ball, W. A., Sullivan, K. A., & Caroff, S. N. (1989). Sleep disturbances as the hallmark of post-traumatic stress disorder. *American Journal of Psychiatry, 146,* 697–707.

Ross, R. T. (1985). *Lives of the mentally retarded: A forty year follow-up study.* Stanford, CA: Stanford University Press.

Rosser, S. V. (1992). Is there androcentric bias in psychiatric diagnoses? *The Journal of Medicine and Philosophy, 17(2),* 215–231.

Rossi, A. S. (1980). Life-span theories in women's lives. *Signs, 6,* 4–32.

Rossi, A. S. (Ed.). (1985). *Gender and the life course.* New York: Aldine.

Roth, S., & Cohen, L. J. (1986). Approach, avoidance, and coping with stress. *American Psychologist, 41,* 813–819.

Rotheram, M. J., & Weiner, N. (1983). Androgeny, stress, and satisfaction. *Sex roles, 9,* 151–158.

Rotter, J. B. (1971). External control and internal control. *Psychology Today, 5(1),* 37–42.

Rotter, J. B. (1972). Beliefs, social attitudes, and behavior: A social learning analysis. In J. B. Rotter, J. E. Chance, & E. J. Phares (Eds.), *Applications of a social learning theory of personality.* New York: Holt, Rinehart and Winston.

Rotter, J. B. (1982). *The development and applications of social learning theory: Selected papers.* New York: Praeger.

Rouan, G., & Thaon, M. (1985). Rites of consensus in cultural life. *Connexions, No. 45,* 233–242.

Rowe, J. W., & Kahn, R. L. (1987). Human aging: Usual and successful. *Science, 237,* pp. 143–149.

Rownand, A. (1984). Hormone peaks level off with age. *Science News, 125,* 410.

Roy, A. (Ed.). (1986). *Suicide.* Baltimore: Williams and Wilkins.

Royeen, C. B., & Kannegieter, R. B. (1984). Factors affecting textural discrimination in normal children. *Occupational Therapy Journal of Research, 4,* 261–270.

Rubin, D. L., & Greene, K. (1992). Gender-typical style in written language. *Research in the Teaching of English, 26(1),* 7–40.

Rubin, J. Z., Provenzano, F. J., & Luria, Z. (1974). The eye of the beholder: Parents' views on sex of newborns. *American Journal of Orthopsychiatry, 43,* 720–731.

Rubin, J. Z. (1981). Psychological traps. *Psychology Today, 15(3),* pp. 52–63.

Rubin, K. H., Fein, G. G., & Vandenberg, B. (1983). Play. In E. M. Hetherington (Ed.), *Handbook of child psychology* (4th ed.). Vol. IV. New York: Wiley.

Rubin, R. T., Reinisch, J. M., & Haskett, R. F. (1981). Postnatal gonadal steroid effects on human behavior. *Science, 211,* 1318–1324.

Ruble, D. N., & Brooks-Gunn, J. (1982). The experience of menarche. *Child Development, 53,* 1557–1566.

Ruble, T. L. (1983). Sex stereotypes: Issues of change in the 1970s. *Sex Roles, 9,* 397–402.

Rumelhart, D. E., & McClelland, J. L. (1986). *Parallel distributed processing: Explorations in the microstructure of cognition.* Cambridge, MA: MIT Press.

Rumelhart, D. E., & McClelland, J. L. (1987). Learning the past tenses of English verbs: Implicit rules or parallel distributed processing? In B. MacWhinney (Ed.), *Mechanisms of language acquisition.* Hillsdale, NJ: Erlbaum.

Runco, M. A. (1986). Predicting children's creative performance. *Psychological Reports, 59,* 1247–1254.

Rusbult, C. E., Zembrodt, I. M., & Iwaniszek, J. (1986). The impact of gender and sex-role orientation on responses to dissatisfaction in close relationships. *Sex Roles, 15(1–2),* 1–20.

Rushton, W. A. H. (1975). Visual pigments and color blindness. *Scientific American, 232(3),* 64–74.

Russell, J. A. (1991). The contempt expression and the relativity thesis. *Motivation and Emotion, 15,* 1991.

Russell, R. W. (1984). Psychology in its world context. *American Psychologist, 39(9),* 1017–1025.

Ryan, E. B. (1992). Beliefs about memory changes across the adult life span. *Journal of Gerontology: Psychological Sciences, 47(1),* 41–46.

Rybash, J. M., Hoyer, W. J., & Roodin, P. A. (1986). *Adult cognition and aging.* New York: Pergamon.

Sacco, W. P., Beck, A. T. (1985). Cognitive therapy of depression. In E. E. Beckham & W. R. Leber (Eds.), *Handbook of depression.* Homewood, IL: Dorsey.

Sack, R. L., Lewy, A. J., White, D. M., Singer, C. M., Fireman, M. J., & Vandiver, R. (1990). Morning vs. evening light treatment for winter depression. *Archives of General Psychiatry, 47,* 343–351.

Sacks, O., & Wasserman, R. (1987). The case of the color-blind painter. *New York Review of Books,* (Nov. 19), pp. 25–34.

Safer, M. A. (1980). Attributing evil to the subject, not the situation: Student reaction to Milgram's film on obedience. *Personality and Social Psychology Bulletin, 6(2),* 205–209.

Saito, K., Takei, S., Ogino, M., Ohama, K., & Tatsuno, T. (1981). The development of communicative behaviour in the first two years of life: Analysis of child vocalization as related to child-mother interaction. *Japanese Journal of Educational Psychology, 29(1),* 20–29.

Salazar, J. M., & Sanchez, L. M. (1987). Venezuela. In A. R. Gilgen and C. K. Gilgen (Eds.), *International handbook of psychology.* New York: Greenwood Press.

Salkind, N. J., & Ambrom, S. R. (1987). *Child development* (5th ed.). New York: Holt, Rinehart and Winston.

Salthouse, T. A. (1984). Effects of age and skill in typing. *Journal of Experimental Psychology: General, 113,* 345–371.

Salthouse, T. A. (1987). Age, experience, and compensation. In C. Schooler & K. W. Schaie (Eds.), *Cognitive functioning and social structure over the life course.* Norwood, NJ: Ablex.

Sandford, D. A., Elizinga, R. H., & Grainger, W. (1987). Evaluation of a residential behavioral program for behaviorally disturbed, mentally retarded young adults. *American Journal of Mental Deficiency, 91,* 431–434.

Santrock, J. W. (1990). *Children* (2nd ed.). Dubuque, IA: Wm. C. Brown.

Sarason, I. G., Johnson, J. H., & Siegel, J. M. (1978). Assessing the impact of life changes: Development of the Life Experiences Survey. *Journal of Consulting and Clinical Psychology, 46,* 932–946.

Sarbin, T. (1969). The scientific status of the mental illness metaphor. In S. C. Pong & R. B. Edgerton (Eds.), *Changing perspectives in mental illness.* New York: Holt, Rinehart and Winston.

Sarbin, T. R. (1992). Accounting for "dissociative" actions without invoking mentalistic constructs. *Consciousness and Cognition, 1,* 54–58.

Sarma, P. G., & Satyanarayana, G. (1992). Temple-visiting psychiatry patients. *Indian Journal of Social Work, 53(2),* 250–266.

Saul, R. L., Gee, P., & Ames, B. N. (1987). Free-radicals, DNA damage, and aging. In H. R. Warner, R. N. Butler, R. L. Sprott & E. L. Schneider (Eds.), *Modern biological theories of aging.* New York: Raven Press.

Savage-Rumbaugh, E. S., Rumbaugh, D. M., & Boysen, S. (1980). Do apes use language? *American Scientist, 68(1),* 49–61.

Scarr, S. (1985). Constructing psychology: Making facts and fables for our times. *American Psychologist, 40,* 499–512.

Scarr, S. (1992). Developmental theories for the 1990s: Development and individual differences. *Child Development, 63,* 1–19.

Scarr, S., & Weinberg, R. A. (1983). The Minnesota adoption studies: Genetic differences and malleability. *Child Development, 54,* 260–267.

Scarr, S., & Weinberg, R. A. (1986). The early childhood enterprise: Care and education of the young. *American Psychologist, 41,* 1140–1146.

Schacht, T., & Nathan, P. E. (1977). But is it good for psychologists? Appraisal and status of DSM III. *American Psychologist, 32,* 1017–1025.

Schacter, D. L. (1983). Amnesia observed: Remembering and forgetting in a natural environment. *Journal of Abnormal Psychology, 92,* 236–242.

Schacter, D. L. (1992). Understanding implicit memory: A cognitive neuroscience approach. *American Psychologist, 47(4),* 559–569.

Schacter, D. L., & Graf, P. (1986). Preserved learning in amnesic patients: Perspectives from research on direct priming. *Journal of Clinical and Experimental Neuropsychology, 8,* 727–743.

Schacter, D. L., & Worling, J. R. (1985). Attribute information and the feeling-of-knowing. *Canadian Journal of Psychology, 39,* 467–4.

Schachter, S. (1971). *Emotion, obesity and crime.* New York: Academic Press.

Schachter, S. (1982). Don't sell habit-breakers short. *Psychology Today, 16(8),* p. 18.

Schachter, S., & Singer, J. S. (1962). Cognitive, social, and physiological determinants of emotional state. *Psychological Review, 69,* 379–399.

Schaie, K. W., Labouvie-Vief, G. (1974). Generational versus ontogenetic components of change in adult cognitive behavior: A fourteen-year cross-sequential study. *Developmental Psychology, 10,* 305–320.

Schaie, K. W., Labouvie, G. V., & Buech, B. U. (1973). Generational and cohort-specific differences in adult cognitive functioning. *Developmental Psychology, 9,* 151–166.

Schaie, K. W., & Willis, S. L. (1986). Can decline in adult intellectual functioning be reversed? *Developmental Psychology, 22,* 223–232.

Scheidlinger, S. (1982). *Focus on group psychotherapy: Clinical essays.* New York: International Universities Press.

Schein, E. H. (1956). The Chinese indoctrination program for prisoners of war: A study of attempted brainwashing. *Psychiatry, 19,* 149–172.

Scher, S. J., & Cooper, J. (1990). Motivational basis of dissonance: The singular role of behavioral consequences. *Journal of Personality and Social Psychology, 56(6),* 899–906.

Scherer, K. R., Feldstein, St., Bond, R. N., & Rosenthal, R. R. (1985). Vocal cues to deception: A comparative channel approach. *Journal of Psycholinguistic Research, 14,* 409–425.

Schiff, W. (1980). *Perception: An applied approach.* New York: Houghton Mifflin.

Schiffman, H. R. (1990). *Sensation and perception* (3rd ed.). New York: Wiley.

Schiffman, S. S. (1986). The use of flavor to enhance efficacy of reducing diets. *Hospital Practice, 21,* 44H-44R.

Schmidt, G., & Sigusch, V. (1970). Sex differences in response to psychosexual stimulation by films and slides. *Journal of Sex Research, 6,* 268–283.

Schmidt, H. (1976). PK effect on pre-recorded targets. *Journal of the American Society for Psychical Research, 70(3),* 267–291.

Schmidt, H. (1981). PK tests with pre-recorded and pre-inspected seed numbers. *Journal of Parapsychology, 45,* 87–98.

Schmidt, H. (1985). Addition effect for PK on prerecorded targets. *Journal of Parapsychology, 49,* 229–244.

Schmidt, H. D. (1981). PK tests with pre-recorded and pre-inspected seed numbers. *Journal of Parapsychology, 45,* 87–98.

Schmidt, H. D. (1985). Addition effect for PK on prerecorded targets. *Journal of Parapsychology, 49,* 229–244.

Schmidt, H. D. (1987). German Democratic Republic. In A. R. Gilgen & C. K. Gilgen (Eds.), *International handbook of psychology.* New York: Greenwood Press.

Schnarch, D. M. (1984). Save us from our sexual saviors. *Contemporary Psychology, 29,* 416–417.

Schneider, B. H. (1992). Didactic methods for enhancing children's peer relations: A quantitative review. *Clinical Psychology Review, 12(3),* 363–382.

Schneider, C. M. (1990). *Wilhelm Wundt's Völkerpsychologie.* Bonn: Bouvier.

Schneider, E. L., & Guralnik, J. M. (1990). The aging of America: Impact on health care costs. *Journal of the American Medical Association, 263,* 2335–2340.

Schuler, H. (1982). *Ethical problems in psychological research.* New York: Academic Press.

Schultz, D. P., & Schultz, S. E. (1992). *A history of modern psychology* (5th ed.). New York: Harcourt Brace Jovanovich.

Schulz, R., & Ewen, R. B. (1988). *Adult development and aging: Myths and emerging realities.* New York: Macmillan Publishing.

Schultze, A., Knussmann, R., & Christiansen, K. (1991). Male sex role identification and body build. *HOMO, 42,* 203–215.

Schwager, M. (1986). Training for television. Special Issue: Communications. *Training and Development Journal, 40(10),* 62–65.

Sedgwick, P. (1982). *Psycho politics.* New York: Harper & Row.

Seeley, R. R., Stephens, T. D., & Tate, P. (1989). *Anatomy & physiology.* St. Louis, MO: Times Mirror/Mosby.

Seeman, P., & Lee, T. (1975). Antipsychotic drugs: Direct correlation between clinical potency and presynaptic action on dopamine neurons. *Science, 188,* 1217–1219.

Segall, M. (1988). Psychocultural antecedents of male aggression: Some implications involving gender, parenting, and adolescence. In P. R. Dasen, J. W. Berry, and N. Sartorius (Eds.), *Health and cross-cultural psychology: Toward applications.* Newbury Park, CA: Sage.

Segall, M. H., Dasen, P. R., Berry, J. W., & Poortinga, Y. H. (1990). *Human behavior in global perspective: An introduction to cross-cultural psychology.* Elmsford, NY: Pergamon Press.

Segalowitz, S. J. (Ed.). (1983). *Language functions and brain organization.* New York: Academic Press.

Segraves, R. T. (1988). Hormones and libido. In S. R. Leiblum & R. C. Rosen (Eds.), *Sexual desire disorders.* New York: Guilford.

Segrin, C. (1990). A meta-analytic review of social skills deficits in depression. *Communication Monographs, 57,* 292–308.

Segrin, C. (1992). Specifying the nature of social skill deficits associated with depression. *Human Communication Research, 19(1),* 89–123.

Segrin, C., & Dillard, J. P. (1992). The interactional theory of depression: A meta-analysis of the research literature. *Journal of Social and Clinical Psychology, 11(1),* 43–70.

Seidenberg, M., & Berent, S. (1992). Childhood epilepsy and the role of psychology. *American Psychologist, 47(9),* 1130–1133.

Sekuler, R., & Blake, R. (1985). *Perception.* New York: Knopf.

Sekuler, R., & Mulvanny, P. (1982). 20/20 is not enough. *American Health, 1(5),* 50–56.

Seligman, M. E. P. (1975). *Helplessness.* San Francisco: W.H. Freeman.

Seligman, M. E. P. (1976). *Learned helplessness and depression in animals and humans.* Morristown, NJ: General Learning Press.

Selye, H. (1976). *The stress of life* (rev. ed.). New York: McGraw-Hill.

Selye, H. (1978). On the real benefits of eustress. *Psychology Today, 12(3),* pp. 60–70.

Selye, H. (Ed.). (1981–1983). *Selye's guide to stress research* [Series]. New York: Van Nostrand Reinhold.

Selzer, J. A. (1992). Fluoxetine, suicidal ideation, and aggressive behavior. *American Journal of Psychiatry, 149(5),* 708–709.

Senchak, M., & Leonard, K. E. (1992). Attachment styles and marital adjustment among newlywed couples. *Journal of Social and Personal Relationships, 9,* 51–64.

Sergent, J. (1983). Role of the input in visual hemispheric asymmetries. *Psychological Bulletin, 93,* 481–512.

Sergios, P., & Cody, J. (1985–1986). Importance of physical attractiveness and social assertiveness skills in male homosexual dating behavior and partner selection. *Journal of Homosexuality, 12(2),* 71–84.

Sexton, V. S., & Misiak, H. (1984). American psychologists and psychology abroad. *American Psychologist, 39(9),* 1026–1031.

Seydel, E., Taal, E., & Wiegman, O. (1990). Risk-appraisal, outcome and self-efficacy expectancies: Cognitive factors in preventive behaviour related to cancer. *Psychology and Health, 4,* 99–109.

Shafii, M., & Shafii, S. L. (Eds.). (1990). *Biological rhythms, mood disorders, light therapy, and the pineal gland.* Washington, DC: American Psychiatric Press.

Shah, N. S., & Donald, A. G. (Eds.). (1986). *Movement disorders.* New York: Plenum Medical.

Sham, P., O'Callaghan, E., Takei, N., Murray, G., Hare, E., & Murray, R. (1992). Schizophrenia following pre-natal exposure to influenza epidemics between 1939 and 1960. *British Journal of Psychiatry, 160,* 461–466.

Shaw, K. J., & Paul, R. H. (1990). Fetal responses to external stimuli. *Obstetrics and Gynecology Clinics of North America, 17,* 235–248.

Shay, J. (1992). Fluoxetine reduces explosiveness and elevates mood of Vietnam combat vets with PTSD. *Journal of Traumatic Stress, 5(1),* 97–101.

Sheehan, P. W. (1988). Memory distortions in hypnosis. *International Journal of Clinical and Experimental Hypnosis, 36,* 296–311.

Shell, E. R. (1986). Chemists whip up a tasty mess of artificial flavors. *Smithsonian, 17(2),* pp. 79–88.

Shepardson, D. P., & Pizzini, E. L. (1992). Gender bias in female elementary teachers' perception of the scientific ability of students. *Science Education, 76,* 147–153.

Shepherd-Look, D. L. (1982). Sex differentiation and the development of sex roles. In B. B. Wolman, (Ed.), *Handbook of developmental psychology.* Englewood Cliffs, NJ: Prentice-Hall.

Sherif, M. (1935). A study of some social factors in perception. *Archives of Psychology, 27, (187),* 1–60.

Sherif, M. (1936). *The psychology of social norms.* New York: Harper.

Sherif, M., Harvey, O., White, B., Hood, W., & Sherif, C. (1961). *Intergroup conflict and cooperation: The Robber's Cave experiment.* Norman: Institute of Group Relations, University of Oklahoma. Sherkat,

D. E., & Reed, M. D. (1992). The effects of religion and social support on self-esteem and depression among the suddenly bereaved. *Social Indicators Research, 26,* 259–275.

Sherwin, R., & Corbett, S. (1985). Campus sexual norms and dating relationships: A trend analysis. *Journal of Sex Research, 21,* 258–274.

Shikanai, K. (1978). Effects of self-esteem on attribution of success-failure. *Japanese Journal of Experimental Social Psychology, 18,* 47–55.

Shikanai, K. (1983). Effects of self-esteem on attributions of others' success or failure. *Japanese Journal of Experimental Social Psychology, 23,* 27–37.

Shikanai, K. (1984). Effects of self-esteem and one's own performance on attribution of others' success and failure. *Japanese Journal of Experimental Social Psychology, 24,* 37–46.

Shoben, E. J., Jr. (1957). Toward a concept of the normal personality. *American Psychologist, 12,* 183–189.

Shotland, R. L. (1985). When bystanders just stand by. *Psychology Today, 19(6),* pp. 50–55.

Shuman, R. B. (1992). Gender differences. *Educational Leadership, 49(7),* 86.

Sibicky, M., & Dovidio, J. F. (1986). Stigma of psychological therapy: Stereotypes, interpersonal reactions, and the self-fulfilling prophecy. *Journal of Counseling Psychology, 33(2),* 148–154.

Siddle, D. A., & Bond, N. W. (1988). Avoidance learning, Pavlovian conditioning, and the development of phobias. *Biological Psychology, 27(2),* 167–183.

Sieber, J. E. (Ed.). (1982). *The ethics of social research: Surveys and experiments.* New York: Springer-Verlag.

Siegel, R. K. (1982). Cocaine smoking. *Journal of Psychoactive Drugs, 14,* 271–359.

Siegel, R. K. (1992). A crack book. *Contemporary Psychology, 37,* 335.

Siegman, A. W., & Dembroski, T. M. (Eds.). (1989). *In search of coronary behavior: Beyond Type A.* Hillsdale, NJ: Lawrence Erlbaum Associates.

Sikdar, A. K. (1974). Identity crisis of adolescents across cultures. *Bulletin of Educational & Psychological Research,* Calcutta, 5, 43–45.

Silber, T. J. (1984). Anorexia nervosa in black adolescents. *Journal of the National Medical Association, 76,* 29–32.

Silber, T. J. (1986). Anorexia nervosa in blacks and Hispanics. *International Journal of Eating Disorders, 5,* 121–128.

Sill, J. S. (1980). Disengagement reconsidered: Awareness of finitude. *Gerontologist, 20,* 457–462.

Silverman, K., & Griffiths, R. R. (1992). Low-dose caffeine discrimination and self-reported mood effects in normal volunteers. *Journal of the Experimental Analysis of Behavior, 57,* 91–107.

Simon, C. (1989, June). The triumphant dieter. *Psychology Today,* pp. 48–52.

Simon, H. A. (1981). Studying human intelligence by creating artificial intelligence. *American Scientist, 69,* 300–308.

Simons, D. J. (1985). The relationship of sequential-simultaneous processing to emotionally disturbed children's behavior problems and to their improvement in milieu therapy. *Dissertation Abstracts International, 46(3–B),* 971.

Simonton, D. (1988). Age and outstanding achievement: What do we know after a century of research? *Psychological Bulletin, 104(2),* 251–267.

Simonton, D. (1990). Creativity in later years: Optimistic prospects for achievement. *The Gerontologist, 30(5),* 626–631.

Simonton, D. (1991). Creative productivity through the adult years. *Generations, 15(2),* 13–16.

Simonton, D. K. (1992). Leaders of American psychology, 1879–1967: Career development, creative output, and professional achievement. *Journal of Personality and Social Psychology, 62(1),* 5–17.

Sinclair, J. D. (1983). The hardware of the brain. *Psychology Today, 17(12),* pp. 8–12.

Singer, B., & Benassi, V. A. (1981). Occult beliefs. *American Scientist, 69(1),* 49–55.

Singer, E. (1991). Public attitudes toward genetic testing. *Population Research and Policy Review, 10,* 235–255.

Singh, A. K. (1989). Attribution research on poverty: A review. *Psychologia: An International Journal of Psychology in the Orient, 32(3),* 143–148.

Sinha, D. (1987). India. In A. R. Gilgen and C. K. Gilgen (Eds.), *International handbook of psychology.* New York: Greenwood Press.

Sinnott, J. D. (1981). The theory of relativity: A metatheory for development? *Human Development, 24,* 293–311.

Sinyagin, Y. V. (1985). A method of establishing valuation statements of group members. *Voprosy Psikhologii, 6,* 139–145.

Sizer, F. S. & Whitney, E. N. (1988). *Life choices: Health concepts and strategies.* St. Paul, MN: West.

Skeels, H. M. (1966). Adult status of children with contrasting early life experiences. *Monographs of the Society for Research in Child Development, 31,* (Serial No. 105).

Skeels, H. M., & Dye, H. B. (1939). A study of the effects of differential stimulation on mentally retarded children. *Program of the American Association of Mental Deficiency, 44,* 114–146.

Skinner, B. F. (1938). *The behavior of organisms: An experimental approach.* New York: Appleton-Century.

Skinner, B. F. (1950). Are learning theories necessary? *Psychological Review, 57,* 193–216.

Skinner, B. F. (1954). The science of learning and the art of teaching. *Harvard Educational Review, 24,* 86–97.

Skinner, B. F. (1960). Pigeons in a pelican. *American Psychologist, 15,* 28–37.

Skinner, B. F. (1971). *Beyond freedom and dignity.* New York: Bantam.

Skinner, B. F. (1978). *Reflections on behaviorism and society.* Englewood Cliffs, NJ: Prentice-Hall.

Skinner, B. F. (1987). *Upon further reflection.* Englewood Cliffs, NJ: Prentice-Hall.

Sloane, R. B., Staples, F. R., Cristol, A. H., Yorkston, N. J., & Whipple, K. (1975). *Psychotherapy versus behavior therapy.* Cambridge, MA: Harvard University Press.

Smilansky, J., & Halberstadt, N. (1986). Inventors versus problem solvers: An empirical investigation. *Journal of Creative Behavior, 20(3),* 183–201.

Smith, B. L., & Oller, D. K. (1981). A comparative study of pre-meaningful vocalizations produced by normally developing and Down's syndrome infants. *Journal of Speech and Hearing Disorders, 46(1)*, 46–51.

Smith, D., & Over, R. (1990). Enhancement of fantasy-induced sexual arousal in men through training in sexual imagery. *Archives of Sexual Behavior, 19*, 477–489.

Smith, D. D. (1993). Brain, environment, heredity, and personality. *Psychological Reports, 72*, 3–13.

Smith, D. E. P., Walter, T. L., Miller, S. D., & McConnell, J. V. (1985). Effect of using an auditory trainer on the attentional, language, and social behaviors of autistic children. *Journal of Autism and Developmental Disorders, 15*, 285–302.

Smith, E. M., Brown, H. O., Toman, J. E. P., & Goodman, L. S. (1947). The lack of cerebral effects of d-tubocurarine. *Anesthesiology, 8*, 1–14.

Smith, J. L., Glass, G. V., & Miller, T. I. (1980). *The benefits of psychotherapy*. Baltimore: Johns Hopkins Press.

Smith, L. (1991a). Primary teachers' beliefs about children's development. *Educational Psychology, 11(2)*, 111–128.

Smith, L. (1991b). Age, ability, and intellectual development in Piagetian theory. In M. Chandler & M. Chapman (Eds.), *Criteria for competence*. Hillsdale, NJ: Lawrence Erlbaum.

Smith, M. B., Bruner, J. S., & White, R. B. (1956). *Opinions and personality*. New York: Wiley.

Smith, M. L., & Glass, G. V. (1977). Meta-analysis of psychotherapy outcome studies. *American Psychologist, 32*, 752–760.

Smith, M. L., Glass, G. V., & Millter, T. I. (1980). *The benefits of psychotherapy*. Baltimore: Johns Hopkins Press.

Smith, P. K. (Ed.). (1984). *Play in animals and humans*. Oxford, England: Basil Blackwell.

Smith, T. W. (1990). *Adult sexual behavior in 1989: Number of partners, frequency, and risk*. Paper presented at the meeting of the American Association for the Advancement of Science, New Orleans, L. A.

Smotherman, W. P. (1982). Odor aversion learning by the rat fetus. *Physiology and Behavior, 29(5)*, 769–771.

Smotherman, W. P., & Robinson, S. R. (1985). The rat fetus in its environment: Behavioral adjustments to novel, familiar, aversive, and conditioned stimuli presented in utero. *Behavioral Neuroscience, 99(3)*, 521–530.

Snarey, J. R., Reimer, J., & Kohlberg, L. (1985a). The kibbutz as a model for moral education: A longitudinal cross-cultural study. *Journal of Applied Developmental Psychology, 6(2–3)*, 151–172.

Snarey, J. R., Reimer, J., & Kohlberg, L. (1985b). Development of social-moral reasoning among Kibbutz adolescents: A longitudinal cross-cultural study. *Developmental Psychology, 21(1)*, 3–17.

Snyder, M. (1983). The influence of individuals on situations: Understanding the links between personality and social behavior. *Journal of Personality, 51*, 497–516.

Snyder, M. (1984). When belief creates reality. In L. Berkowitz (Ed.), *Advances in experimental social psychology* (Vol. 18). New York: Academic Press.

Snyder, S. H. (1972). *Uses of marijuana*. New York: Oxford University Press.

Snyder, S. H. (1978). Dopamine and schizophrenia. In L. C. Wynne, R. L. Cromwell, & S. Matthysse (Eds.), *The nature of schizophrenia: New approaches to research and treatment*. New York: Wiley.

Snyder, S. H. (1984a). Drug and neurotransmitter receptors in the brain. *Science, 224*, 22–30.

Snyder, S. H. (1984b). Neurosciences: An integrative discipline. *Science, 225*, 1255–1257.

Snyder, S. H. (1987). *Drugs and the brain*. New York: W. H. Freeman.

Solomon, E. P., & Davis, P. W. (1983). *Human anatomy and physiology*. Philadelphia: Saunders.

Solomon, L. J., & Rothblum, E. D. (1986). Stress, coping, and social support in women. *Behavior Therapist, 9*, 199–204.

Solomon, S., Greenberg, J., & Pyszczynski, T. (1991). A terror management theory of social behavior: The psychological functions of self-esteem and cultural worldviews. In M. Zanna (Ed.), *Advances in experimental social psychology*. San Diego: Academic Press.

Solso, R. L. (1991). *Cognitive psychology*. Boston: Allyn and Bacon.

Sommer, R. (1969). *Personal space: The behavioral basis of design*. Englewood Cliffs, NJ: Prentice-Hall.

Sommer, R., & Sommer, B. A. (1991). Teaching psychology in Estonia, USSR. *Teaching of Psychology, 18(2)*, 105–107.

Sonderegger, T. B. (Ed.). (1984). *Psychology and gender. Nebraska symposium on motivation*, (Vol. 32). Lincoln: University of Nebraska Press.

Sorensen, T. I. A., Price, R. A., Stunkard, A. J., & Schulsinger, F. (1989). Genetics of obesity in adult adoptees and their biological siblings. *British Medical Journal, 298*, 87–90.

Sorenson, R. C. (1973). *Adolescent sexuality in contemporary America*. New York: World Publishing.

Soriano, F. I., & Ramirez, A. (1991). Unequal employment status and ethnicity: Further analysis of the USPI-ESPI model. *Hispanic Journal of Behavioral Sciences, 13(4)*, 391–400.

Sorrentino, R. M., Bobocel, D. R., Gitta, M. Z., Olson, J. M., & Hewitt, E. C. (1988). Uncertainty orientation and persuasion: Individual differences in the effects of personal relevance on social judgments. *Journal of Personality and Social Psychology, 55*, 371–375.

Soules, M. R., & Bremner, W. J. (1982). The menopause and climacteric: Endocrinologic basis and associated symptomatology. *Journal of the American Geriatrics Society, 30*, 547–561.

Spearman, C. (1904). General intelligence objectively determined and measured. *American Journal of Psychology, 15*, 201–293.

Spearman, G. (1904). General intelligence objectively determined and measured. *American Journal of Psychology, 15*, 201–293.

Spence, J. T. (1985). Achievement American style. *American Psychologist, 40*, 1285–1295.

Spence, J. T., & Robbins, A. S. (1992). Workaholism: Definition, measurement, and preliminary results. *Journal of Personality Assessment, 58,* 160–178.

Sperling, G. (1960). The information available in a brief visual presentation. *Psychological Monographs, 74,* (Whole no. 498).

Sperling, G. (1963). A model for visual memory tasks. *Human Factors, 5,* 19–30.

Sperry, R. W. (1968). Hemisphere deconnection and unity in conscious awareness. *American Psychologist, 23,* 723–733.

Sperry, R. W. (1982). Some effects of disconnecting the cerebral hemispheres. *Science, 217,* pp. 1223–1226.

Spiegel, D., & Hunt, T. (1988). Dissociation and hypnotizability in posttraumatic stress disorder. *American Journal of Psychiatry, 145(3),* 301–305.

Spitz, R. A. (1945). Hospitalization: An inquiry into the genesis of psychiatric conditions of early childhood. In A. Freud, A. H. Nagera, & W. E. Freud, (Eds.), *The psychoanalytic study of the child.* New York: International Universities Press.

Spitzer, M. E. (1988). Taste acuity in institutionalized and noninstitutionalized elderly men. *Journal of Gerontology: Psychological Sciences, 43,* P71–P74.

Spitzer, R. L. (1984a). A debate on DSM-III: First rebuttal. *American Journal of Psychiatry, 141,* 546–547.

Spitzer, R. L. (1984b). A debate on DSM-III: Second rebuttal. *American Journal of Psychiatry, 141,* 551–553.

Springer, J. F., & Gable, R. W. (1981). Modernization and sex roles: The status of women in Thai bureaucracy. *Sex Roles, 7,* 723–737.

Squire, L. (1982). Neuropsychological effects of ECT. In R. Abrams & W. B. Essman (Eds.), *Electroconvulsive therapy. Biological foundations and clinical applications.* New York: SP Medical & Scientific Books.

Squire, L. R. (1986). Mechanisms of memory. *Science, 232,* pp. 1612–1619.

Squire, L. R. (1987). *Memory and brain.* New York: Oxford University Press.

Squire, S. (1983). *The slender balance.* New York: G. P. Putnam's Sons.

St. George-Hyslop, P. H., Tanzi, R. E., Polinsky, R. J., Neve, R. L., Pollen, D., Drachman, D., Growdon, J., Cupples, L. A., Nee, L., Myers, R. H., O'Sullivan, D., Watkins, P. C., Amos, J. A., Deutsch, C. K., Bodfish, J. W., Kinsbourne, M., Feldman, R. G., Bruni, A., Amaducci, L., Foncin, J., & Gusella, J. F. (1987). Absence of duplication of chromosome 21 genes in familial and sporadic Alzheimer's disease. *Science, 238,* pp. 664–671.

Stack, C. B. (1986). The culture of gender: Women and men of color. *Signs, 11(2),* 321–324.

Stanton, T. L., Craft, C. M., & Reiter, R. J. (1984). Decreases in pineal melatonin content during the hibernation bout in the golden-mantled squirrel. Spermophilis lateralis. *Life Sciences, 35,* 1461–1467.

Star, S. A., & Hughes, H. McG. (1950). Report on an educational campaign: The Cincinnati plan for the United Nations. *American Journal of Sociology, 55,* 389–400.

Stark, E. (1984, May). The unspeakable family secret. *Psychology Today,* pp. 42–46.

Starr, B. D. (1987). Sexuality. In G. L. Maddox (Ed.), *The encyclopedia of aging.* New York: Springer.

Stebbins, W. C. (1983). *The acoustic sense of animals.* Cambridge, MA: Harvard University Press.

Steer, R. A., Beck, A. T., Riskind, J. H., & Brown, G. (1986). Differentiation of depressive disorders from generalized anxiety by the Beck Depression Inventory. *Journal of Clinical Psychology, 43,* 475–478.

Steif, B. L., Sackeim, H. A., Portnay, S., Decima, P., & Malitz, S. (1986). Effects of depression and ECT on anterograde memory. *Biological Psychiatry, 21,* 921–930.

Stein, D. J., Hollander, E., Anthony, D. T., Schneier, F. R., Fallon, B. A., Liebowitz, M. R., & Klein, D. F. (1992). Serotonergic medications for sexual obsessions, sexual addictions, and paraphilias. *Journal of Clinical Psychiatry, 53(8),* 267–271.

Stellar, J. R., & Stellar, E. (1985). *The neurobiology of motivation and reward.* New York: Springer-Verlag.

Stelmack, R. M. (1990). Biological bases of extraversion: Psychophysiological evidence. *Journal of Personality, 58(1),* 293–311.

Stephen, J., Fraser, E., & Marcia, J. E. (1992). Moratorium-achievement (MAMA) cycles in lifespan identity development: Value orientations and reasoning correlates. *Journal of Adolescence, 15(3),* 283–300.

Stern, D. N. (1983). Le but et la structure du jeu mere-nourrison. (The goal and structure of mother-infant play.) *Psychiatrie de l'Enfant, 26(1),* 193–216.

Stern, M., & Karraker, K. (1989). Sex stereotyping of infants: A review of gender labeling studies. *Sex Roles, 20(9/10),* 501–522.

Sternberg, R. J. (Ed.). (1982). *Handbook of human intelligence.* New York: Cambridge University Press.

Sternberg, R. J. (Ed.). (1984). *Human abilities: An information-processing approach.* New York: W. H. Freeman.

Sternberg, R. J. (1985). *Beyond IQ: A triarchic theory of human intelligence.* New York: Cambridge University Press.

Sternberg, R. J. (1986). *Intelligence applied.* New York: Harcourt Brace Jovanovich.

Stevens, J. C. (1990). Perceived roughness as a function of body locus. *Perception and Psychophysics, 47,* 298–304.

Stevenson, H., Azuma, H., & Hakuta, K. (1986). *Child development and education in Japan.* New York: Freeman.

Stewart, J. (1988). Current themes, theoretical issues, and preoccupations in the study of sexual differentiation and gender-related behaviors. *Psychobiology, 16,* 315–320.

Stiff, J. B., Miller, G. R., Sleight, C., Mongeau, P., Rogan, R., & Garlick, R. (1989). Explanations for visual cue primacy in judgments of honesty and deceit. *Journal of Personality and Social Psychology, 56(4),* 555–564.

Stillion, J. M. (1985). *Death and the sexes: An examination of differential longevity, attitudes, behaviors, and coping skills*. Washington, DC: Hemisphere Publishing Corporation.

Stratton, P. (Ed.). (1982). *Psychobiology of the human newborn*. Chichester, England: Wiley.

Strauss, R. P., Feuerstwin, R., Mintzker, Y., Rand, Y., & Wexler, M. (1989). Ordinary faces? Down syndrome, facial surgery, active modification, and social perceptions. *American Journal on Mental Retardation, 94(2)*, 115–118.

Stricker, L. J., & Ross, J. (1962). *A description and evaluation of the Myers-Briggs type indicator* (Research Bulletin). Princeton: Educational Testing Service.

Strickland, L. H. (1991). Russian and Soviet social psychology. *Canadian Psychology, 32(4)*, 580–593.

Striegel-Moore, R. H., Silberstein, L. R., and Rodin, J. (1986). Toward an understanding of risk factors for bulimia. *American Psychologist, 41*, 246–263.

Stroebe, W., Kruglanski, A., & Bar-Ral, D. (Eds.). (1987). *The social psychology of intergroup conflict*. New York: Springer-Verlag.

Strom, J. C., & Buck, R. W. (1970). Staring and participants' sex: Physiological and subjective reactions. *Personality and Social Psychology Bulletin, 5(1)*, 114–117.

Stryer, L. (1987). The molecules of visual excitation. *Scientific American, 257(1)*, pp. 42–50.

Stuart, R. B., & Jacobson, B. (1987). *Weight, sex, and marriage: A delicate balance*. New York: W. W. Norton.

Stunkard, A. J., Harris, J. R., Pedersen, N. L., & McClearn, G. E. (1990). The body-mass index of twins who have been reared apart. *New England Journal of Medicine, 322*, 1483–1487.

Stunkard, A. J., Sorensen, T. I. A., Hanis, C., Teasdale, T. W., Chakraborty, R., Schull, W. J., & Schulsinger, F. (1986). An adoption study of human obesity. *New England Journal of Medicine, 314*, 193–198.

Sue, S. (1988). Psychotherapeutic services for ethnic minorities: Two decades of research findings. *American Psychologist, 43*, 301–308.

Sue, S., Allen, D. B., & Conway, L. (1978). The responsiveness and equality of mental health care to Chicanos and Native Americans. *American Journal of Community Psychology, 6*, 137–146.

Sue, S., & Okazaki, S. (1990). Asian-American educational achievements: A phenomenon in search of an explanation. *American Psychologist, 45(8)*, 913–920.

Sue, S., & Okazaki, S. (1991). Explanations for Asian-Americans achievements: A reply. *American Psychologist, 46(8)*, 878–880.

Sue, S., & Zane, N. (1987). The role of culture and cultural techniques in psychotherapy: A critique and reformulation. *American Psychologist, 42*, 37–45.

Sue, S., Zane, N., & Ito, J. (1979). Alcohol drinking patterns among Asian and Caucasian Americans. *Journal of Cross-Cultural Psychology, 10*, 41–56.

Suedfeld, P. (1980). *Restricted environmental stimulation: Research and clinical applications*. New York: Wiley.

Suedfeld, P. (1990). *Restricted environmental stimulation and smoking cessation: A 15-year progress report*. *International Journal of the Addictions, 25*, 861–888.

Suedfeld, P., & Baker-Brown, G. (1987). Restricted environmental stimulation therapy of smoking: A parametric study. *Addictive Behaviors, 12*, 263–267.

Suedfeld, P., & Bruno, T. (1990). Flotation REST and imagery in the improvement of athletic performance. *Journal of Sport and Exercise Psychology, 12*, 82–85.

Suedfeld, P., & Coran, S. (1989). Perceptual isolation, sensory deprivation, and rest: Moving introductory psychology texts out of the 1950s. *Canadian Psychology, 30*, 17–29.

Suedfeld, P., & Kristeller, J. L. (1982). Stimulus reduction as a technique in health psychology. *Health Psychology, 1*, 337–357.

Suedfeld, P., & Metcalfe, J. (1987). Enhancement of scientific creativity by flotation REST (restricted environmental stimulation technique). *Journal of Environmental Psychology, 7*, 219–231.

Sun, L-K. (1992). Social psychology in the late Qing period. *Modern China, 18(3)*, 235–262.

Sussman, N. M., & Rosenfeld, H. M. (1982). Influence of culture, language, and sex on conversational distance. *Journal of Personality and Social Psychology, 42*, 66–74.

Symons, D. (1987). An evolutionary approach: Can Darwin's view of life shed light on human sexuality? In J. H. Geer & W. T. O'Donohue (Eds.), *Theories of human sexuality*. New York: Plenum Press.

Szabo, C. (1985). Effect of role-play on attitude change. *Magyar Pszichologiai Szemle, 42*, 495–507.

Szasz, T. (1974). *The myth of mental illness* (rev. ed.). New York: Harper & Row.

Tajfel, H. (1979). Individuals and groups in social psychology. *British Journal of Social and Clinical Psychology, 18(2)*, 183–190.

Tajfel, H. (1982a). Social psychology of intergroup relations. *Annual Review of Psychology, 33*, 1–39.

Tajfel, H. (Ed.). (1982b). *Social identity and intergroup relations*. Cambridge, England: Cambridge University Press.

Takooshian, H., & O'Connor, P. J. (1984). When apathy leads to tragedy: Two Fordham professors examine "Bad Samaritanism." *Social Action and the Law, 10(1)*, 26–27.

Tanfer, K., & Cubbins, L. A. (1992). Coital frequency among single women: Normative constraints and situational opportunities. *The Journal of Sex Research, 29*, 221–250.

Tanfer, K., & Schoorl, J. J. (1992). Premarital sexual careers and partner change. *Archives of Sexual Behavior, 21*, 45–68.

Tanner, J. M. (1970). Physical growth. In P. H. Mussen (Ed.), *Carmichaels's manual of child psychology* (Vol. 1). New York: Wiley.

Tanner, J. M. (1978). *Foetus into man*. London: Open Books.

Tanner, J. M. (1990). Sequence, tempo, and individual variation in growth and development of boys and girls aged twelve to sixteen. In R. E. Muuss (Ed.), *Adolescent behavior and society* (4th ed.). New York: McGraw-Hill.

Tanner, J. M., Whitehouse, R. H., & Takaishi, M. (1966). Standards from birth to maturity for height, weight, height velocity and weight velocity; British children, 1965. *Archives of the Diseases of Childhood, 41*, 455–471.

Tavris, C., & Wade, C. (1984). *The longest war: Sex differences in perspective* (2nd ed.). San Diego: Harcourt Brace Jovanovich.

Taylor, D. M., & Jaggi, V. (1974). Ethnocentrism and causal attribution in a South Indian context. *Journal of Cross-Cultural Psychology, 5*, 162–172.

Taylor, F. K. (1971). A logical analysis of the medico-psychological concept of disease. *Psychological Medicine, 1*, 356–364.

Taylor, S. E. (1990). Health psychology. *American Psychologist, 45(1)*, 40–50.

Tellegen, A., & Lykken, D. T. (1988). Personality similarity in twins reared apart and together. *Journal of Personality and Social Psychology, 54(6)*, 1031–1039.

Templer, D. I. (1991). Comment on large gender difference on death anxiety in Arab countries. *Psychological Reports, 69*, 1186.

TenHouten, W. D. (1991). Into the wild blue yonder: On the emergence of the ethnoneurologies—the social science-based neurologies and the philosophy-based neurologies. *Journal of Social and Biological Structures, 14(4)*, 381–408.

Teri, L., & Wagner, A. (1992). Alzheimer's disease and depression. *Journal of Consulting and Clinical Psychology, 60(3)*, 379–391.

Terrace, H. S. (1980). *Nim*. New York: Knopf.

Tetlock, P. E. (1983). Policymakers' images of international conflict. *Journal of Social Issues, 39*, 67–86.

Tetlock, P. E. (1987). Testing deterrence theory: Some conceptual and methodological issues. *Journal of Social Issues, 43*, 85–91.

Tharp, R. G. (1991). Cultural diversity and treatment of children. *Journal of Consulting and Clinical Psychology, 59(6)*, 799–812.

Thatcher, R. W., Walker, R. A., & Guidice, S. (1987). Human cerebral hemispheres develop at different rates and ages. *Science, 236*, 1110–1113.

Thibaut, J. W., & Kelley, H. H. (1959). *The social psychology of groups*. New York: Wiley.

Thigpen, C. H., & Cleckley, H. (1954). *The three faces of Eve*. Kingsport, TN: Kingsport Press.

Thompson, P. (1980). Margaret Thatcher: A new illusion. *Perception, 9*, 483–484.

Thompson, R. F. (1985). *The brain*. New York: W. H. Freeman.

Thompson, R. F. (1986). The neurobiology of learning and memory. *Science, 233*, pp. 941–947.

Thompson, R., & McConnell, J. V. (1955). Classical Conditioning in the planarian dugesia dorotocephala. *Journal of Comparative and Physiological Psychology, 48*, 65–68.

Thorndike, E. L. (1935). *The psychology of wants, interests and attitudes*. New York: Appleton-Century-Crofts.

Tierney, J. (1990, October 19). AIDS in Africa: Experts study role of promiscuous sex in the epidemic. *New York Times*, p. A10.

Tippin, J., & Henn, F. A. (1982). Modified leucotomy in the treatment of intractable obsessional neurosis. *American Journal of Psychiatry, 139*, 1601–1603.

Titchener, E. B. (1898). Postulates of a structural psychology. *Philosophical Review, 7*, 449–465.

Toates, F. (1985). Psychobiology. *Contemporary Psychology, 229*, 962–963.

Tobias, S. (1989, September). Tracked to fail. *Psychology Today*, pp. 54–60.

Tolchin, M. (1989, July, 19). When long life is too much: Suicide rises among elderly. *New York Times*, pp. A1, A15.

Tolman, E. C. (1938). The determiners of behavior at a choice point. *Psychological Review, 45*, 1–41.

Tomecek, O. (1990). A personal commentary on "Schizophrenia as a brain disease." *American Psychologist, 45(4)*, 550–551.

Torgersen, S. (1983). Genetic factors in anxiety disorder. *Archives of General Psychiatry, 40*, 1085–1089.

Torrey, E. F. (1980). Epidemiology. In L. Bellak (Ed.), *Disorders of the schizophrenic syndrome*. New York: Basic Books.

Torrey, E. F., McGuire, M., O'Hare, A., Walsh, D., & Spellman, M. P. (1984). Endemic psychosis in western Ireland. *American Journal of Psychiatry, 141*, 966–970.

Torsvall, L., & Akerstedt, T., & Froberg, J. (1983). On-call duty, sleep and wakefulness: An EEG study of engineers on ships in the Swedish merchant marine. *Stressforskningrapporter, no. 184*, 22.

Toseland, R. W., & Siporin, M. (1986). When to recommend group treatment: A review of the clinical and the research literature. *International Journal of Group Psychotherapy, 36*, 171–201.

Toth, N. (1985). Archeological evidence for preferential right-handedness in the lower and middle Pleistocene, and its possible implications. *Journal of Human Evolution, 14*, 607.

Trafford, A., Avery, R., Thornton, J., Carey, J., Galloway, J., & Sanoff, A. (1986, August). She's come a long way—Or has she? *U.S. News & World Report*, 44–51.

Triandis, H. C. (Ed.). (1972). *The analysis of subjective culture*. New York: Wiley.

Triandis, H. C. (1980). Preface. In H. C. Triandis & W. W. Lambert (Eds.), *Handbook of cross-cultural psychology* (Vol. 1). Boston: Allyn & Bacon.

Triandis, H. C. (1984). Toward a psychological theory of economic growth. *International Journal of Psychology, 19(1–2)*, 79–95.

Triandis, H. C. (1989). The self and social behavior in differing cultural contexts. *Psychological Review, 96*, 506–520.

Triandis, H. C. (1989, March). *Cross-cultural studies of individualism and collectivisim*. Paper presented at the Nebraska Symposium on Motivation, Lincoln, NE.

Triandis, H. C. (1994). *Culture and social behavior*. New York: McGraw-Hill.

Triandis, H. C., Bontempo, R., Villareal, M. J., Asai, M., & Lucca, N. (1988). Individualism and collectivism: Cross-cultural perspectives on self-ingroup relationships. *Journal of Personality and Social Psychology, 54*, 323–328.

Triandis, H. C., & Brislin, R. W. (1984). Cross-cultural psychology. *American Psychologist, 39(9)*, 1006–1016.

Triandis, H. C., & Lambert, W. W. (Eds.). (1980). *Handbook of cross-cultural psychology* (Vol. 1). Boston: Allyn & Bacon.

Triandis, H. C., Lambert, W., Berry, J., Lonner, W., Heron, A., Brislin, R., & Draguns, J. (Eds.). (1980–1981). *Handbook of cross-cultural psychology* (Vols. 1–6). Boston: Allyn & Bacon.

Trognon, A. (1987). France. In A. R. Gilgen and C. K. Gilgen (Eds.), *International handbook of psychology*. New York: Greenwood Press.

Tröster, H., & Brambring, M. (1992). Early social-emotional development in blind infants. *Child: Care, Health and Development, 18*, 207–227.

Trotter, R. J. (1985). A life of conflict and goals. *Psychology Today, 19(9)*, 54–59.

Trotter, R. J. (1986). The mystery of mastery. *Psychology Today, 20(1)*, 32–38.

Trotter, R. (1987). You've come a long way, baby. *Psychology Today, 21(5)*, 35–45.

Truax, C. B. (1968). Therapist interpersonal reinforcement of client self-exploration and therapeutic outcome in group psychotherapy. *Journal of Counseling Psychology, 15*, 225–231.

Truzzi, M. (1981). Reflections on paranormal communications: A zetetic's perspective. *Annals of the New York Academy of Sciences, 364*.

Tucker, L. A., Cole, G. E., & Friedman, G. M. (1986). Physical fitness: A buffer against stress. *Perceptual and Motor Skills, 63*, 955–961.

Tulving, E. (1972). Episodic and semantic memory. In E. Tulving & W. Donaldson (Eds.), *Organization of memory*. New York: Academic Press.

Tulving, E. (1978). Relation between encoding specificity and levels of processing. In L. S. Cermak & F. I. M. Craik (Eds.), *Levels of processing and human memory*. Hillsdale, NJ: Erlbaum.

Tulving, E. (1985). How many memory systems are there? *American Psychologist, 40*, 385–398.

Tulving, E., & Thomson, D. M. (1973). Encoding specificity and retrieval processes in episodic memory. *Psychological Review, 80*, 352–373.

Turkington, C. (1982). Hypnotic memory is not always accurate. *APA Monitor, 13(3)*, 46–47.

Turnbull, C. (1972). *The mountain people*. New York: Simon and Schuster.

Turner, R. J., & Avison, W. R. (1992). Innovations in the measurement of life stress: Crisis theory and the significance of event resolution. *Journal of Health and Social Behavior, 33*, 36–50.

Turner, S. M., Beidel, D. C., & Epstein, L. H. (1991). Vulnerability and risk for anxiety disorders. *Journal of Anxiety Disorders, 5(2)*, 151–166.

Turner, S. M., Beidel, D. C., & Nathan, R. S. (1985). Biological factors in obsessive-compulsive disorder. *Psychological Bulletin, 97(3)*, 430–450.

Turner, S. M., Beidel, D. C., & Stanley, M. A. (1992). Are obsessional thoughts and worry different cognitive phenomena? *Clinical Psychology Review, 12(2)*, 257–270.

Turner, S. M., Williams, S. L., Beidel, D. C., & Mezzich, J. E. (1986). Panic disorder and agoraphobia with panic attacks: Covariation along the dimensions of panic and agoraphobic fear. *Journal of Abnormal Psychology, 95*, 384–388.

Twitmyer, E. B. (1905). Knee-jerks without stimulation of the patellar tendon. *Psychological Bulletin, 2*, 43–44.

Tyler, L. E. (1973). A significant change in direction: Implications for measurement. *Proceedings of the Invitational Conference on Testing Problems, 1973*, 70–78.

Tyler, L. E. (1984). What tests don't measure. *Journal of Counseling & Development, 63(1)*, 48–50.

Tyler, L. E., & Walsh, W. B. (1979). *Tests and measurements* (3rd ed.). Englewood Cliffs, NJ: Prentice-Hall.

Tyndall, K. (1986). Down's syndrome. *Insight, 2(8)*, 60.

U.S. Bureau of the Census. (1988, 1989). *Marital status and living arrangements*. Current Population Reports, Series P-20. March, 1988; March, 1989.

U.S. Bureau of the Census. (1989).

U.S. Centers for Disease Control and Prevention. (1993, February). HIV/AIDS Surveillance Report.

U. S. Department of Health and Human Services (USDHHS). (1987). *Alcohol and health*. Rockville, MD: Author.

U.S. Department of Health and Human Services. (1987). Vital Statistics of the United States, 1984. Volume II-Mortality. National Center for Health Statistics, Hyattsville, MD.

Udry, J. R., & Morris, N. M. (1968). Distribution of coitus in the menstrual cycle. *Nature, 220*, 593–596.

Uhlenberg, P., & Eggebeen, D. (1986). The declining well-being of American adolescents. *The Public Interest, 82*, 25–38.

Ursin, H. (1987). Norway. In A. R. Gilgen and C. K. Gilgen (Eds.), *International handbook of psychology*. New York: Greenwood Press.

Uttal, W. R. (1981). *A taxonomy of visual processes*. New York: LEA.

Valenstein, E. S. (1980). *The psychosurgery debate: Scientific, legal, and clinical perspectives*. San Francisco: W. H. Freeman.

Valenstein, E. S. (1986). *Great and desperate cures: The rise and decline of psychosurgery and other radical treatments for mental illness*. New York: Basic Books.

Valliant, P. M., & Antonowicz, D. H. (1991). Cognitive behavior therapy and social skills training improves personality and cognition in incarcerated offenders. *Psychological Reports, 68*, 27–33.

Van Bilsen, H. P., & Van Emst, A. J. (1986). Heroin addiction and motivational milieu therapy. *International Journal of the Addictions, 21*, 707–713.

Van De Graaff, K. M., & Fox, S. I. (1989). *Concepts of human anatomy and physiology* (2nd ed.). Dubuque, IA: W. C. Brown.

Van Der Kolk, B. A. (1987). The drug treatment of post-traumatic stress disorder. *Journal of Affective Disorders, 13(2)*, 203–213.

Van Horn, J. D., & McManus, I. C. (1992). Ventricular enlargement in schizophrenia: A meta-analysis of studies of the ventricle: brain ratio (VBR). *British Journal of Psychiatry, 160*, 687–697.

Van Strien, J. W., Bouma, A., & Bakker, D. J. (1987). Birth stress, autoimmune diseases, and handedness. *Journal of Clinical and Experimental Neuropsychology, 9(6)*, 775–780.

van Toller, C., Dodd, G. H., & Billing, A. (1985). *Ageing and the sense of smell.* Springfield, IL: Charles C. Thomas.

Vandell, D. L., & Owen, M. T. (1988). Social development in infant twins: Peer and mother-child relationships. *Child Development, 59(1)*, 168–177.

Vandenberg, S. G., & Vogler, G. P. (1985). Genetic determinants of intelligence. In B. B. Wolman (Ed.), *Handbook of intelligence: Theories, measurements, and applications.* New York: Wiley.

Vassaf, G. Y. H. (1987). Turkey. In A. R. Gilgen & C. K. Gilgen (Eds.), *International handbook of psychology.* New York: Greenwood Press.

Vaughn, B. E., Lefever, G. B., Seifer, R., & Barglow, P. (1989). Attachment behavior, attachment security, and temperament during infancy. *Child Development, 60(3)*, 728–737.

Vinokur, A., & Ajzen, I. (1982). Relative importance of prior and immediate events: A casual primary effect. *Journal of Personality and Social Psychology, 42*, 820–829.

Virkkunen, M. E. (1986). Insulin secretion during the glucose tolerance test among habitually violent and impulsive offenders. *Aggressive Behavior, 12(4)*, 303–319.

Vitkus, J. (1988). *Casebook in abnormal psychology.* New York: Random House.

Vitz, P. C. (1990). The use of stories in moral development: New psychological reasons for an old education method. *American Psychologist, 45(6)*, 709–720.

Voelkl, J. E. (1986). Therapeutic activities with the impaired elderly. *Activities, Adaptation and Aging, 8(3-4)*, 37–45.

Volkmann, F. C. (1986). Human visual suppression. Special Issue: Twenty-fifth anniversary issue of Vision Research. *Vision Research, 26*, 1401–1416.

von Brock, M. B., & Elliott, S. N. (1987). Influence of treatment effectiveness information on the acceptability of classroom interventions. *Journal of School Psychology, 25*, 131–144.

von Sydow, K. (1992a). Eine Untersuchung zur weiblichen Sexualität im mittleren und höheren Erwachsenenalter. *Zeitschrift für Gerontologie, 25*, 105–112.

von Sydow, K. (1992b). Weibliche Sexualität im mittleren und höheren Erwachsenenalter: Übersicht über vorliegende Forschungsarbeiten. *Zeitschrift für Gerontologie, 25*, 113–127.

Wachs, T. D., & Gruen, G. E. (1982). *Early experience and human development.* New York: Plenum Press.

Wadden, T. A., Stunkard, A. J., Rich, L., Rubin, C. J., Sweidel, G., & McKinney, S. (1990). Obesity in black adolescent girls: A controlled clinical trial of treatment by diet, behavior modification, and parental support. *Pediatrics, 85*, 345–352.

Wagner, E. H., LaCroix, A. Z., Buchner, D. M., & Larson, E. B. (1992). Activity and Health I: Effects of habitual activity in older adults. *Annual Review of Public Health, 13*, 451–468.

Wakefield, J. C. (1989). Levels of explanation in personality theory. In D. M. Buss & N. Cantor (Eds.), *Personality psychology: Recent trends and emerging directions.* New York: Springer.

Wakefield, J. C. (1992a). The concept of mental disorder: On the boundary between biological facts and social values. *American Psychologist, 47(3)*, 373–388.

Wakefield, J. C. (1992b). Disorder as harmful dysfunction: A conceptual critique of DSM-III-R's definition of mental disorder. *Psychological Review, 99(2)*, 232–247.

Wall, P. D. (1979). On the relation of injury to pain. *Pain, 6*, 253–264.

Wallace, B. (1986). Latency and frequency reports to the Necker cube illusion: Effects of hypnotic susceptibility and mental arithmetic. *Journal of General Psychology, 113(2)*, 187–194.

Wallace, B. C. (1991). Crack cocaine: A practical treatment approach for the chemically dependent. New York: Brunner/Mazel.

Wallace, J. (1989). A biopsychosocial model of alcoholism. *Social Casework, 70(6)*, 325–332.

Wallbott, H. G. (1988). Big girls don't frown, big boys don't cry—Gender differences of professional actors in communicating emotion via facial expression. *Journal of Nonverbal Behavior, 12*, 98–106.

Wallerstein, R. S. (1988). Psychoanalysis, psychoanalytic science, and psychoanalytic research: 1986. *Journal of the American Psychoanalytic Association, 36(1)*, 3–30.

Wallston, B. S., & Wallston, K. A. (1981). Health locus of control. In H. Lefcourt (Ed.), *Research with the locus of control construct: Vol. 1. Assessment methods.* New York: Academic Press.

Wallston, K. A. (1989). Assessment of control in health-care settings. In A. Steptoe & A. Appels (Eds.), *Stress, personal control, and health.* Chichester, England: Wiley.

Wallston, K. A. (1992). Hocus-pocus, the focus isn't strictly on locus: Rotter's social learning theory modified for health. *Cognitive Therapy and Research, 16*, 183–199.

Walsh, B. T. (1992). Diagnostic criteria for eating disorders in DSM-IV: Work in progress. *International Journal of Eating Disorders, 11(4)*, 301–304.

Walsh, W. B. (1989). *Tests and measurements* (4th ed.). Englewood Cliffs, NJ: Prentice Hall.

Walster, E., Aronson, V., Abrahams, D., & Rottman, L. (1966). Importance of physical attractiveness in dating behavior. *Journal of Personality and Social Psychology, 4*, 508–516.

Warren, J. M., Zerweck, C., & Anthony, A. (1982). Effects of environmental enrichment on old mice. *Developmental Psychobiology, 15(1)*, 13–18.

Warren, K. R., & Bast, R. J. (1988). Alcohol-related birth defects: An update. *Public Health Reports, 103*, 638–643.

Warrington, E. K., & Weiskrantz, L. (1970). Amnesic syndrome: Consolidation or retrieval? *Nature, 228*, 629–630.

Waterman, A. S. (1982). Identity development from adolescence to adulthood: An extension of theory and a review of the research. *Developmental Psychology, 18,* 341–358.

Waters, E. R. (1984). Building on what you know: Techniques for individual and group counseling with older people. *Counseling Psychologist, 12(2),* 63–74.

Waters, H. S. (1987). Art through egocentric? Let me count the ways. *Contemporary Psychology, 32,* 573–574.

Watkins, C. E., Jr., Lopez, F. G., Campbell, V. L., & Himmell, C. D. (1986). Counseling psychology and clinical psychology: Some preliminary comparative data. *American Psychologist. 41,* 581–582.

Watkins, P. L., Fisher, E. B., Southard, D. R., Ward, C. H., & Schechtman, K. B. (1989). Assessing the relationship of Type A beliefs to cardiovascular disease risk and psychosocial distress. *Journal of Psychopathology and Behavioral Assessment, 11,* 113–125.

Watkins, P. L., Ward, C. H., & Southard, D. R. (1987). Empirical support for a Type A belief system. *Journal of Psychopathology and Behavioral Assessment, 9,* 119–134.

Watkins, P. L., Ward, C. H., Southard, D. R., & Fisher, E. B. (1992). The Type A belief system: Relationships to hostility, social support, and life stress. *Behavioral Medicine, 18,* 27–32.

Watson, D. (1982). The actor and the observer: How are their perceptions of causality divergent? *Psychological Bulletin, 92,* 682–700.

Watson, D. L. (1988). *Self-directed behavior: Self-modification for personal adjustment* (5th ed.). Monterey, CA: Brooks/Cole.

Watson, J. B. (1913). Psychology as the behaviorist views it. *Psychological Review, 20,* 158–177.

Watson, J. B. (1919). *Psychology from the standpoint of a behaviorist.* Philadelphia: Lippincott.

Watson, J. B. (1924). *Behaviorism.* New York: Norton.

Watson, J. B. (1929). Introduction. In G. B. Hamilton, *A research in marriage.* New York: A & C Boni.

Watson, J. B. (1936). Autobiography. In C. Murchison (Ed.), *A history of psychology in autobiography* (vol. 3, pp. 271–281). Worcester, MA: Clark University Press.

Watson, J. B., & Rayner, R. (1920). Conditioned emotional reactions. *Journal of Experimental Psychology, 3,* 1–14.

Watts, D. T. (1992). The family's will or the living will: Patient self-determination in doubt. *Journal of the American Geriatrics Society, 40(5),* 533–534.

Waxman, D., Misra, P. C., Gibson, M., & Basker, M. A. (Eds.). (1985). *Modern trends in hypnosis.* New York: Plenum Press.

Waynbaum, I. (1907). *La physionomie humaine: Son mecanisme et son role social* [The human face: Its mechanism and social function]. Paris: Alcan.

Weale, R. A. (1982). *Focus on vision.* Cambridge, MA: Harvard University Press.

Webb, W. B. (1975). *Sleep: The gentle tyrant.* Englewood Cliffs, NJ: Prentice-Hall.

Webb, W. B. (Ed.). (1982). *Biological rhythms, sleep, and performance.* Chichester, England: Wiley.

Webb, W. B. (1983). Theories in modern sleep research. In A. Mayes (Ed.), *Sleep mechanisms and functions in humans and animals: An evolutionary perspective.* London: Van Nostrand Reinhold.

Webb, W. B. (1988). An objective behavioral model of sleep. *Sleep, 11 (5),* 488–496.

Webster, J. D., & Cappeliez, P. (1993). Reminiscence and autobiographical memory: Complementary contexts for cognitive aging research. *Developmental Review, 13(1),* 54–91.

Wegrocki, H. J. (1939). A critique of cultural and statistical concepts of abnormality. *Journal of Abnormal and Social Psychology, 34,* 166–178.

Wehr, T. A., & Rosenthal, N. E. (1989). Seasonality and affective illness. *American Journal of Psychiatry, 146(7),* 829–839.

Wehr, T. A., Sack, D. A., & Rosenthal, N. E. (1987). Sleep reduction as a final common pathway in the genesis of mania. *American Journal of Psychiatry, 144,* 201–204.

Wehrung-Schaffner, L., & Sapona, R. H. (1990). May the FORCE be with you: A test preparation strategy for learning disabled adolescents. I. Academic Therapy, 25(3), 291–300.

Weinberg, M. S., & Williams, C. J. (1988). Black sexuality: A test of two theories. *Journal of Sex Research, 25,* 197–218.

Weinberg, S. K. (1955). *Incest behavior.* New York: Citadel.

Weiner, B. (1980). *Human motivation.* New York: Holt, Rinehart and Winston.

Weiner, B., Frieze, I., Kukla, A., Reed, L., Rest, S., & Rosenbaum, R. M. (1972). Perceiving the causes of success and failure. In E. Jones, D. Kanouse, H. Kelley, R. Nisbett, S. Valins, & B. Weiner (Eds.), *Attribution: Perceiving the causes of behavior.* Morristown, NJ: General Learning Press.

Weis, D. L., Rabinowitz, B., & Ruckstuhl, M. F. (1992). Individual changes in sexual attitudes and behavior within college-level human sexuality courses. *The Journal of Sex Research, 29,* 43–59.

Weisburd, S. (1988). Computer scents. *Science News, 133,* 27–29.

Weiss, J. M., Glazer, H. I., & Pohoresky, L. A. (1976). Coping behavior and neurochemical change in rats: An alternative explanation for the "learned helplessness" experiments. In G. Serban & A. King (Eds.), *Animal models in human psychobiology.* New York: Plenum.

Weitzman, N., Birns, B., & Friend, R. (1985). Traditional and nontraditional mothers' communication with their daughters and sons. *Child Development, 56,* 894–898.

Wellman, H. M., & Gelman, S. A. (1992). Cognitive development: Foundational theories of core domains. *Annual Review of Psychology, 43,* 337–375.

Wells, B. L. (1986). Predictors of female nocturnal orgasm. *Journal of Sex Research, 22,* 421–437.

Wells, G. L., & Lindsay, R. C. L. (1983). In S. M. A. Lloyd-Bostock & B. R. Clifford (Eds.), *Evaluating witness evidence: Recent psychological research and new perspectives.* Chichester, England: Wiley.

Wertheimer, M. (1987). *A brief history of psychology* (3rd ed.). New York: Holt, Rinehart and Winston.

Westman, A. S., & Lewandowski, L. M. (1991). How empathy, egocentrism, Kohlberg's moral development, and Erikson's psychosocial development are related to attitudes toward war. *Psychological Reports, 69,* 1123–1127.

Westra, H. A., & Kuiper, N. A. (1992). Type A, irrational cognitions, and situational factors relating to stress. *Journal of Research in Personality, 26,* 1–20.

Whitam, F. L., & Zent, M. (1984). A cross-cultural assessment of early cross gender behavioral and familial factors in male homosexuality. *Archives of Sexual Behavior, 13(5),* 427–441.

White, R. K. (1987). Underestimating and overestimating others' fear. *Journal of Social Issues, 43(4),* 105–109.

White, R. W. (1963). *Ego and reality in psychoanalytic theory: A proposal regarding independent ego energies* (Psychological Issues Monograph 11). New York: International Universities Press.

Whitley, B. E., Jr., & Frieze, I. H. (1985). Children's causal attributions for success and failure in achievement settings: A meta-analysis. *Journal of Educational Psychology, 77,* 608–616.

Whorf, B. L. (1956). Science and linguistics. In J. B. Carroll (Ed.) *Language, thought, and reality: Selected writings of Benjamin Lee Whorf.* Cambridge, MA: MIT Press.

Widiger, T. A., & Frances, A. (1985). The DSM-III personality disorders. *Archives of General Psychiatry, 42,* 615–623.

Wiggins, J. S., & Pincus, A. L. (1992). Personality: Structure and assessment. *Annual Review of Psychology, 43,* 473–504.

Will, J. A., Self, P. A., & Datan, N. (1976). Maternal behavior and perceived sex of infant. *American Journal of Orthopsychiatry, 46,* 135–139.

Williams, J. B., & Spitzer, R. L. (1983). The issue of sex bias in DSM-III: A critique of "A woman's view of DSM-III" by Marcie Kaplan. *American Psychologist, 38,* 793–798.

Williams, J. B., Spitzer, R. L., & Skodol, A. E. (1985). DSM-III in residency training: Results of a national survey. *American Journal of Psychiatry, 142,* 755–758.

Williams, M. E., Davison, G. C., Nezami, E., & DeQuattro, V. L. (1992). Articulated thoughts of Type A and B individuals in response to social criticism. *Cognitive Therapy and Research, 16,* 19–30.

Williams, R. (1989). *The Trusting Heart.* New York: Times Books.

Williams, R. W., & Herrup, K. (1988). The control of neuron number. *Annual Review of Neuroscience, 11,* 423–453.

Williams, R., Zyzanski, S. J., & Wright, A. L. (1992). Life events and daily hassles and uplifts as predictors of hospitalization and outpatient visitation. *Social Science Medicine, 34,* 763–768.

Willis, S. L., & Schaie, K. W. (1986). Training the elderly on the ability factors of spatial orientation and inductive reasoning. *Psychology and Aging, 1,* 239–247.

Wilson, C. (1972). *New pathways in psychology.* New York: Taplinger Publishing Co.

Wilson, E. O. (1975). *Sociobiology: The new synthesis.* Cambridge, MA: Harvard University Press.

Wilson, G. T., & Rachman, S. (1983). Meta-analysis and the evaluations of psychotherapy outcome: Limitations and liabilities. *Journal of Consulting and Clinical Psychology, 51,* 54–64.

Wilson, I., Garbutt, J. C., Lanier, C. F., Moylan, J., Nelson, W., & Prange, A. J., Jr. (1983). Is there a tardive dysmentia? *Schizophrenia Bulletin, 9(2),* 187–192.

Wilson, J.D., George, F. W., & Griffin, J. E. (1981). The hormonal control of sexual development. *Science, 211,* 1278–1284.

Windholz, G. (1986). A comparative analysis of the conditional reflex discoveries of Pavlov and Twitmyer, and the birth of a paradigm. *Pavlovian Journal of Biological Science, 21,* 141–147.

Winfree, A. T. (1986). Benzodiazepines set the clock. *Nature, 321,* 114–115.

Winfree, A. T. (1987). *The timing of biological clocks.* New York: Scientific American Books.

Winick, M., Meyer, K. K., & Harris, R. C. (1975). Malnutrition and environmental enrichment by early adoption. *Science, 190,* pp. 1173–1175.

Witelson, S. F. (1985). The brain connection: The corpus callosum is larger in left-handers. *Science, 229,* 665–667.

Witztum, E., Margolin, J., Bar-On, R., & Levy, A. (1992). Labeling and stigma in psychiatric misdiagnosis. *Israeli Journal of Psychiatry and Related Sciences, 29(2),* 77–88.

Wolyniec, P. S., Pulver, A. E., McGrath, J. A., & Tam, D. (1992). Schizophrenia: Gender and familial risk. *Journal of Psychiatric Research, 26(1),* 17–27.

Wong, P. T. P. (1992). Control is a double-edged sword. *Canadian Journal of Behavioral Science, 24(2),* 143–146.

Wood, A. V. (1987). Relaxation training and psychosomatic disorders. *Australian Journal of Hypnotherapy and Hypnosis, 8(1),* 51–54.

Wood, C. (1986). The hostile heart. *Psychology Today, 20(9),* 10–11.

Woodruff, D. S. (1983). A review of aging and cognitive processes. *Research on Aging, 5,* 139–153.

Woodruff-Pak, D. S. (1988). *Psychology and aging.* Englewood Cliffs, NJ: Prentice-Hall.

World Health Organization. (1990). *International classification of diseases and related health problems* (10th rev.). Geneva: Author.

Worthington, E. L., Jr. (1989). Religious faith across the life span: Implications for counseling and research. *The Counseling Psychologist, 17,* 555–612.

Worthington, E. L., Jr. (1990). Religious faith across the life span and counseling: A response to commentaries. *The Counseling Psychologist, 18,* 141–143.

Wright, A. A., Santiago, H. C., Sands, S. F., Kendrick, D. F., & Cook, R. G. (1985). Memory processing of serial lists by pigeons, monkeys, and people. *Science, 229,* 287–289.

Wundt, W. (1900–1920). *Völkerpsychologie: Eine Untersuchung der Entwicklungsgesetze von Sprache, Mythos und Sitte* (Vols. 1–10). Leipzig, Federal Republic of Germany: Engelmann und Kröner.

Wundt, W. (1908). Kritiche Nachlese zur Ausfrage Methode. *Archiv für die gesamte Psychologie, 11,* 445–459.

Wundt, W. (1912). *An introduction to psychology* (2nd ed.). New York: Macmillan.

Wyatt, G. E. (1989). Reexamining factors predicting Afro-American and white American women's age at first coitus. *Archives of Sexual Behavior, 18*, 271–298.

Wyatt, G. E., Peters, S. D., & Guthrie, D. (1988). Kinsey revisited, part II: Comparisons of the sexual socialization and sexual behavior of black women over 33 years. *Archive of Sexual Behavior, 17*, 289–332.

Wylie, R. C. (1979). *The self-concept: Vol. 2. Theory and research on selected topics.* Lincoln: University of Nebraska Press.

Yalom, I. D. (1983). *Inpatient group therapy.* New York: Basic Books.

Yalom, I. D. (1985). *Theory and practice of group psychotherapy* (2nd ed.). New York: Basic Books.

Yando, R., Setiz, V., & Zigler, E. (1979). *Intellectual and personality characteristics of children: Social-class and ethnic-group differences.* Hillsdale, NJ: Erlbaum.

Yang, N., & Linz, D. (1990). Movie ratings and the content of adult videos: The sex violence ratio. *Journal of Communication, 40*, 28–42.

Yarbrough, C. (1986). Language and communication. *Comparative Psychology Newsletter, 3(August),* 23–27.

Yates, A., Leehey, K., & Shisslak, C. M. (1983). Running—an analogue of anorexia? *New England Journal of Medicine, 308*, 251–255.

Yonas, A. (1979). Studies of spatial perception in infants. In A. D. Pick (Ed.), *Perception and its development: A tribute to Eleanor J. Gibson.* Hillsdale, NJ: Lawrence Erlbaum Associates.

Young, L. (1992). Sexual abuse and the problem of embodiment. *Child Abuse and Neglect, 16*, 89–100.

Youniss, J., & Smoller, J. (1985). *Adolescent relations with mothers, fathers, and friends.* Chicago: University of Chicago Press.

Yuen, S. A., & Kuiper, N. A. (1992). Type A and self-evaluations: A social comparison perspective. *Personality and Individual Differences, 13*, 549–562.

Yulsman, T. (1985). Down's syndrome: Postponing pregnancy. *American Health, 5(5)*, 8–9.

Yussen, S. R. (1977). Characteristics of moral dilemmas written by adolescents. *Developmental Psychology, 13*, 162–163.

Zachar, P., & Leong, F. T. L. (1992). A problem of personality: Scientist and practitioner differences in psychology. *Journal of Personality, 60(3)*, 665–677.

Zajonc, R. B. (1980). Feeling and thinking: Preferences need no inferences. *American Psychologist, 35*, 151–175.

Zajonc, R. B. (1984). On the primacy of affect. *American Psychologist, 39*, 117–123.

Zajonc, R. B. (1985). Emotion and facial efference: A theory reclaimed. *Science, 228*, pp. 15–21.

Zajonc, R. B., Murphy, S. T., & Inglehart, M. (1989). Feeling and facial efference: Implications of the vascular theory of emotion. *Psychological Review, 96*, 395–416.

Zax, M., & Cowen, E. L. (1976). *Abnormal psychology: Changing concepts* (2nd ed.). New York: Holt, Rinehart, and Winston.

Zax, M., & Stricker, G. (1963). *Patterns of psychopathology.* New York: Macmillan.

Zetin, M., & Kramer, M. A. (1992). Obsessive-compulsive disorder. *Hospital and Community Psychiatry, 43(7)*, 689–699.

Zimbardo, P. G. (1975). On transforming experimental research into advocacy for social change. In M. Deutsch & H. Hornstein (Eds.), *Applying social psychology.* Hillsdale, NJ: Erlbaum.

Zimbardo, P. G., Andersen, S. M., & Kabat, L. G. (1981). Induced hearing deficit generates experimental paranoia. *Science, 212*, 1529–1531.

Zimbardo, P. G., Haney, C., & Banks, W. C. (1973, April 8). Pirandellian prison: The mind is a formidable jailer. *New York Times Magazine*, pp. 38–60.

Zimmerman, M. (1990). Is DSM-IV needed at all? *Archives of General Psychiatry, 47*, 974–976.

Zimmerman, M., Coryell, W., Pfohl, B., & Stangel, D. (1987). Validation of definitions of endogenous depression: Reply. *Archives of General Psychiatry, 44*, 390–391.

Zinberg, N. E. (1984). *Drug, set, and setting: The basis for controlled intoxicant use.* New Haven, CT: Yale University Press.

Zucker, K. J. (1990). Gender identity disorders in children: Clinical descriptions and natural history. In R. Blanchard, B. W. Steiner (Eds.), *Clinical management of gender identity disorders in children and adults.* Washington, DC: American Psychiatric Press.

Zuckerman, M. (1990). The psychophysiology of sensation seeking. *Journal of Personality, 58(1)*, 313–345.

Zuckerman, M. (1992). What is a basic factor and which factors are basic? Turtles all the way down. *Personality and Individual Differences, 13(6)*, 675–681.

Zuckerman, M., Spiegel, N. H., DePaulo, B. M., & Rosenthal, R. R. (1982). Nonverbal strategies for decoding deception. *Journal of Nonverbal Behavior, 6(3)*, 171–187.

Zussman, L., Zussman, S., Sunley, R., & Bjornson, E. (1981). Sexual response for hysterectomy-oophorectomy. *American Journal of Obstetrics and Gynecology, 140*, 725–729.

COPYRIGHT ACKNOWLEDGMENTS

NAME INDEX

Aagesen, C.A., R-16
Abbey, A., R-9
Abel, E.L., 376
Abel, J.L., R-14
Abelson, R.P., 594, R-26, R-29
Abou-Saleh, M.T., R-10
Abrahams, D., R-55
Abramis, D.J., R-10
Abrams, R., 513, R-51
Abramson, L.Y., 493, 494, R-1, R-36
Abrego, P.J., R-7
Ackerman, D., 240
Adams, E.H., 166
Adams, H.B., R-11
Adams, L.T., 314
Adams, P.L., 217, 395
Adan, A., 149
Adelson, J., R-33
Adeso, V.J., 171
Adler, A., 449, 450–451, 458, 476
Adler, G., R-27
Adler, M., 416
Adler, N.J., 560, 561
Adler, R., 372
Adorno, T.W., 565
Ahmed, I., 494
Ainsworth, M.D.S., 389
Ainyette, I.D.G., 230
Aizenberg, D., R-24
Ajzen, I., 592, 595, 596
Akerstedt, T., 149, 150
Albrecht, G., R-9
Alcock, J.E., 544
Alessis, C., R-22
Alexander, S., 155
Al-Issa, I., 226
Allain, H., 323, 324, 325
Allen, A., 598
Allen, C.R., R-14
Allen, D.B., R-52
Allen, J.L., R-14
Allen, W., 225
Allison, M.T., 204
Alloy, L.B., 493, 494, R-1
Allport, F., 464, 466
Allport, G.W., 440, 464–465, 543
Al-Razi, J., R-11
Als, H., 390

Altura, B.M., 376
Altura, B.T., R-1
Alvarez, M., R-30
Alvir, J.M.J., R-13, R-32
Alwin, D.F., 426
Amabile, T.M., R-46
Amaducci, L., R-51
Ambelas, A., 494
Ambron, S.R., 345, 346
Ames, A., 119
Ames, B.N., R-47
Ames, M.A., 225
Anderson, A.E., 199–200
Andersen, H.B., R-5
Andersen, S.M., R-58
Anderson, J.R., 314, 315, 316
Andreason, N.C., 496, 497, 499
Andrews, F.M., R-9
Angell, J., 3, 7
Angell, L.S., R-7
Angin, K.T., R-30
Angrist, B., 498
Angst, J., 519
Ankney, T.L., 591
Ansbacher, H.L., 450, 451
Ansbacher, R.R., 450, 451
Anstis, S.M., 118
Anthony, A., R-55
Anthony, D.T., R-51
Antonowicz, D.H., 533
Antrobus, J., 148
Appel, J.B., 163n, 170
Appenzeller, T., 318
Applebaum, S.L., R-14
Aquinas, T., 334, 353
Arafat, I.S., 226
Aranth, J., 516
Ardila, R., 611, 612, 614, 620
Argyle, M., 552
Arieti, S., 499
Aristotle, 270, 337, 430
Armon, C., R-41
Armstrong, P., 342
Arnheim, R., 102, 110
Arnold, M.B., 249
Arns, P.A., R-25
Aron, A.P., 248, 267

Aronson, E., 548, 578, 579, 602, R-23
Aronson, V., R-55
Asai, M., R-53
Asch, S.E., 575, 577, 580–581
Ashtari, M., R-13, R-32
Asimov, I., 26
Askevis, M., 220
Atchley, R.C., 430
Atwood, G.E., 455
Atwood, J.D., 226
Audette, D.P., R-6
Auerbach, J., R-27
Augustine, St., 292
Auld, F., 512
Aurel, J.M., 332
Aussprung, J., R-12
Austin, J.T., 203
Austin, W.G., R-32
Autry, J.H., R-15
Averill, J.R., 255
Avery, D., 144
Avery, R., R-53
Avison, W.R., 261
Ayd, J.F., Jr., 517
Ayres, T.J., 77, 78
Azmitia, M., 370, R-30
Azuma, H., 362, 617

Baars, B.J., 141
Babb, T.L., R-22
Bachetti, P., 233
Baddeley, A., 303, 327
Baer, L., R-27
Bailey, C.H., 29
Bailey, S.L., 170
Baillargeon, R., 385
Baird, L.L., 426
Baker, M.J., 592
Baker-Brown, G., 95
Bakker, C.B., R-9
Baldinelli, L., R-43
Baldwin, J.D., 231
Baldwin, J.I., R-3
Baldwin, J.M., 4
Balentine, M., 198, 199
Bales, R.F., 559
Ball, W.A., R-46
Ballenger, J.C., 487
Ballou, M., 536

Balogh, R.D., R-42
Baltes, M.M., R-45
Baltes, P.B., R-11, R-12, R-45
Bandura, A., 5, 9, 289–290, 297, 402, 458, 459, 460, 487, 511, 523, 532, 543, 578, 599, 606
Banks, C., R-23, R-58
Barban, L., R-43
Barbee, A.P., R-12
Barber, B.L., 397
Barber, T.X., 158, 161
Bard, P., 247, 266
Bardack, N.R., 549
Barglow, P., 391, R-55
Barlett, D.L., 486
Barlow, D.H., 485
Barnett, R.C., R-4
Bar-On, R., R-57
Barr, C.E., 498
Barr, L.C., 487
Bar-Ral, D., R-52
Barret, R.L., 394
Barrett, G.V., 360
Barrington, B.L., R-24
Barry, K., 228
Barsky, S., R-17
Barta, P.E., R-41
Bartlett, J.R., R-43
Barton, C., 486
Baruch, G.K., 260, R-33
Baruch, P., R-17
Baruss, I., 141
Basker, M.A., R-56
Bassoff, E.S., 223
Bast, R.J., 376
Bates, C., R-45
Bateson, G., 499
Batson, C.D., 588
Battaglia, D., 151
Baucom, D.H., 557
Baum, S.K., 427
Bauman, K.E., 231
Baumgardner, M.H., R-43
Baumrind, D., 396
Bauwens, S.F., R-25
Beaber, R.J., R-37
Beauchamp, G.K., 69
Beck, A.T., 10, 494, 523, 524, 532, 569
Beck, J., 163n, 170
Beck, R.W., 552

SUBJECT INDEX